HAMLYN
GERMAN
DICTIONARY

GERMAN-ENGLISH   ENGLISH-GERMAN

Published by
The Hamlyn Publishing Group Limited
London · New York · Sydney · Toronto
Astronaut House, Feltham, Middlesex, England
© The Hamlyn Publishing Group Limited 1976
Reprinted 1977

ISBN 0 600 36564 6

Compiled by
Laurence Urdang Associates Ltd,
Aylesbury

Printed in Great Britain by
Butler and Tanner Ltd, Frome, Somerset

Foreword

This dictionary aims to give concise and accurate definitions of 24,000 of the most important words in use in the English and German languages today.

A pronunciation system based on the International Phonetic Alphabet is used (see *Key to symbols used in pronunciation*). Pronunciation is given for all headwords in both sections of the dictionary, and also for selected subentries in the German-English section.

Modern technical, commercial, and informal usage is given particular attention, in preference to outmoded terms or other expressions not in common contemporary use. Definitions are numbered in order to distinguish senses, and abbreviations are used to indicate use in specific technical, scientific, or commercial fields (see *Abbreviations used in the Dictionary*). An additional feature is the inclusion of idiomatic expressions and phrases, so necessary for the understanding and use of the foreign language.

This dictionary, with its emphasis on modernity, together with its compact form and clear typeface, should prove indispensable in the home, at school, in the office, and abroad.

Abbreviations used in the Dictionary

adj	adjective	*indef art*	indefinite article	*pol*	politics
adv	adverb	*inf*	informal	*poss*	possessive
anat	anatomy	*infin*	infinitive	*pref*	prefix
arch	architecture	*interj*	interjection	*prep*	preposition
aux	auxiliary	*invar*	invariable	*pron*	pronoun
aviat	aviation	*lit*	literature	*rel*	religion
bot	botany	*m*	masculine	*s*	singular
cap	capital	*math*	mathematics	*sci*	science
comm	commerce	*med*	medical	*sl*	slang
conj	conjunction	*mil*	military	*suff*	suffix
cul	culinary	*min*	minerals	*tab*	taboo
def art	definite article	*mod*	modal	*Tdmk*	trademark
derog	derogatory	*mot*	motoring	*tech*	technical
dom	domestic	*mus*	music	*Th*	theatre
educ	education	*n*	noun	*US*	United States
fam	familiar	*naut*	nautical	*v*	verb
fml	formal	*neg*	negative	*vi*	intransitive verb
game	cards, chess, etc.	*neu*	neuter	*v imp*	impersonal verb
gram	grammar	*pers*	person	*vr*	reflexive verb
geog	geography	*phot*	photography	*vt*	transitive verb
				zool	zoology

Key to symbols used in pronunciation

English

Vowels

iː	m*ee*t	u	p*u*t	ai	fl*y*	θ	*th*in	
i	b*i*t	uː	sh*oo*t	au	h*ow*	ð	*th*en	
e	g*e*t	ʌ	c*u*t	ɔi	b*oy*	ŋ	si*ng*	
æ	h*a*t	ə	*a*go	iə	h*ere*	j	*y*es	
ɑː	h*ear*t	əː	s*ir*	ɛə	*air*	ʃ	*sh*ip	
ɔ	h*o*t	ei	l*a*te	uə	p*oor*	ʒ	mea*s*ure	
ɔː	*ough*t	ou	g*o*			ʒ	*ch*in	
						tʃ	*ch*in	
						dʒ	*g*in	

Consonants

ˈ indicates that the following syllable is stressed, as in *ago* (əˈgou).

, placed under an *n* or *l* indicates that the *n* or *l* is pronounced as a syllable, as in *button* (ˈbʌtn̩) and *flannel* (ˈflænl̩).

German

Vowels

i	*ist*	a:	*Wagen*	y:	*fühlen*
i:	*wieder*	ɔ	*Holz*	œ	*Hölle*
e	*General*	o	*Forelle*	œ:	*lösen*
e:	*gegen*	o:	*ohne*	ə	*besser*
ɛ	*setzen*	u	*rund*	ai	*frei*
ɛ:	*Fähre*	u:	*Kugel*	au	*Haus*
a	*hat*	y	*Hütte*	ɔy	*treu*

Consonants

ç	*ich*
ʒ	*Garage*
ŋ	*lang*
ʃ	*Tisch*
j	*ja*
x	*lachen*

' indicates that the following syllable is stressed, as in *gegen* ('geːgən).
In pronunciations of certain words borrowed from French, nasalization is indicated by a tilde (~) over the appropriate vowel, as in *Pension* (paˈsjoːn).

Notes on the use of the Dictionary

An oblique stroke in a headword in the German-English section indicates that the part of the word before the oblique may be combined with other words or word endings shown in the text of the entry in heavy type after a dash, thus:-

  einwillig/en . . . *vi* agree, consent. **—ung** *nf* . . . agreement, consent.

In headwords with no oblique, the ending combines with the whole word. Since all German nouns are spelt with a capital initial letter, the subentry above should be spelt *Einwilligung*. Verbs, adjectives, or adverbs entered under a noun headword with an initial capital should be written with a lower-case letter. Where a reflexive verb is the headword, subentries do not take the pronoun *sich*.

A swung dash (~) before a change of part of speech indicates that the part of speech refers to the headword, not the preceding subentry shown in heavy type.

Irregular verbs in the headword lists of both sections are marked with an asterisk. The principal parts of these verbs are shown in the verb tables. For compounds with either separable or inseparable prefixes, see the base form shown in the table, e.g. for *verstehen*, see *stehen*.

Plurals of German nouns are shown after a hyphen immediately after the part of speech, as follows:-

  Feind . . . *nm* **-e** (plural is *die Feinde*)
  Empfang . . . *nm* **ᵕe** (plural is *die Empfänge*)
  Ablaß . . . *nm* **-lässe** (plural is *die Ablässe*)

Notes on the use of the Dictionary

However, a dash is used to indicate that a plural does not vary, or only takes an umlaut, as in the following examples:—

Kanzler . . . *nm* — (plural is *die Kanzler*)
Apfel . . . *nm* -̈ (plural is *die Äpfel*)

Exceptions are nouns that cannot form a plural, such as *Kost* or *Unterrichtung*. To form the plural of compounds, the user should refer to the headword of the principal (final) component, which is always the part that takes the plural, e.g. for *Armbanduhr*, see *Uhr*.

Parentheses are used to show optional forms, particularly in the English-German section, thus:—

deliver . . . *vt* . . . (ab-, aus-)liefern . . . (indicates that *liefern* may be used alone or with the prefixes shown, as *abliefern* or *ausliefern*)
inoculation . . . *n* (Ein)Impfung *f* . . . (indicates that *Impfung* or *Einimpfung* may be used)
wash . . . (*vi*),*vt* . . . (sich) waschen . . . (indicates that *waschen* is transitive, but that the intransitive sense of *to wash* may be translated by *sich waschen*)

Adverbs: German adjectives can function as adverbs without modification. Therefore, in the German-English section, no translation of such adverbs is given where the adverbial form of the English adjective shown in the definition would be appropriate. In the English-German section, regular adverbial forms of English adjectives (i.e. those ending in -*ly*) are not shown where the given German translation could be used as an adverb, or where the English adverb has no special meaning requiring a separate translation.

English attributive adjectives can often be translated in German by using nouns to form compounds. This is shown by a dash as follows:—

manual . . . *adj* Hand—.

Thus, *manual worker* may be translated as *Handarbeiter*.

Feminine forms: Only the most common feminine forms of nouns have been selected for inclusion. However the feminine of agent nouns or nationalities ending in -*er* is formed by adding the suffix -*in* to the masculine; for example, *Arbeiterin* – female worker; *Dichterin* – poetess; *Italienerin* – Italian woman, etc. Weak nouns drop the final -*e* and add -*in*; thus *Chinese* becomes *Chinesin*. Adjectival nouns, shown with a final *r* in parentheses, behave as a masculine or feminine adjective. Thus the feminine nominative singular of *Abgeordnete(r)* is *die Abgeordnete*.

Ausfall ('ausfal) *nm* ⁼e **1** loss. **2** falling out. **3** result. **4** attack, sortie.

ausfertigen ('ausfɛrtigən) *vt* **1** complete. **2** draw up. **3** issue. **4** execute.

ausfind/en* ('ausfindən) *vt* find out. **ausfindig machen 1** trace. **2** find out.

Ausflug ('ausflu:k) *nm* ⁼e excursion.

Ausfluß ('ausflus) *nm* **1** outflow, discharge. **2** outlet. **3** result.

ausfragen ('ausfra:gən) *vt* interrogate, question.

Ausfuhr ('ausfu:r) *nf* **-en** export(ing). **—handel** *nm* export trade.

ausführ/bar ('ausfy:rba:r) *adj* **1** practicable. **2** exportable. **—en** *vt* **1** lead out. **2** carry out, perform. **3** export. **—lich** *adj* detailed, full.

ausfüllen ('ausfylən) *vt* fill up or in.

Ausgabe ('ausga:bə) *nf* **-n 1** delivery. **2** issue. **3** edition. **4** expense, expenditure.

Ausgang ('ausgaŋ) *nm* ⁼e **1** door, exit. **2** result, end. **3** going out.

ausgeben* ('ausge:bən) *vt* **1** give out. **2** spend. **sich ausgeben für** pose as.

ausgeglichen ('ausgəgliçən) *adj* balanced.

ausgeh/en* ('ausge:ən) *vi* **1** go out, depart. **2** proceed. **3** end, run out. **4** fade. **—verbot** *n neu* curfew.

ausgelassen ('ausgəlasən) *adj* boisterous, unrestrained.

ausgemacht ('ausgəmaxt) *adj* settled, agreed.

ausgenommen ('ausgənɔmən) *prep* except.

ausgeprägt ('ausgəprɛ:kt) *adj* distinct, marked.

ausgerechnet ('ausgəreçnət) *adv* just, precisely. **ausgerechnet ich** I of all people.

ausgeschlossen ('ausgəʃlɔsən) *adj* impossible, out of the question.

ausgesprochen ('ausgəʃprɔçən) *adj* marked, pronounced.

ausgezeichnet ('ausgətsaiçnət) *adj* excellent.

ausgießen ('ausgi:sən) *vt* pour out.

Ausgleich ('ausglaiç) *nm* **-e 1** balance. **2** agreement, settlement. **3** compromise. **4** compensation. **5** adjustment. **—en*** *vt* **1** equalize, balance. **2** settle. **3** adjust.

Ausguß ('ausgus) *nm* **-güsse 1** pouring out. **2** spout. **3** gutter. **4** sink.

aushalten* ('aushaltən) *vi* **1** hold out. **2** persevere. *vt* endure, bear.

Aushang ('aushaŋ) *nm* ⁼e poster, notice. **—en*** ('aushɛŋən) *vt,vi* hang out.

ausharren ('ausharən) *vi* persevere.

ausheben* ('aushe:bən) *vt* **1** lift out. **2** enlist, recruit. **3** raid.

aushelfen* ('aushɛlfən) *vi* help out.

Aushilfe ('aushilfə) *nf* **-n** assistance, help, (temporary) aid.

sich auskennen* ('auskɛnən) *vr* know thoroughly.

auskleiden ('ausklaidən) *vt* **1** undress. **2** *tech* coat, line. **sich auskleiden** *vr* undress.

auskommen* ('auskɔmən) *vi* **1** come out. **2** escape. **3** manage, make do. **mit jemandem gut auskommen** get on well with someone. *n neu* — livelihood.

Auskunft ('auskunft) *nf* **-künfte** information. **—sbüro** *n neu* information bureau. **—smittel** *n neu* **1** escape. **2** expedient.

auslachen ('auslaxən) *vt* laugh at.

ausladen* ('ausla:dən) *vt* unload.

Auslage ('ausla:gə) *nf* **-n 1** outlay. **2** expense. **3** display.

Ausland ('auslant) *n neu* foreign countries. **im/ins Ausland** abroad. **—er** ('auslɛndər) *nm* — foreigner, alien. **—isch** ('auslɛndiʃ) *adj* foreign.

auslass/en* ('auslasən) *vt* **1** let out. **2** leave out, omit. **sich auslassen** *vr* express one's opinion. **—ung** *nf* **-en 1** omission. **2** remark. **—ungszeichen** *n neu* apostrophe.

Auslauf ('auslauf) *nm* ⁼e **1** flowing out. **2** outlet. **3** departure (of a ship). **4** *aviat* landing run. **5** (gradual) finish, run-out. **—en*** *vi* **1** run out. **2** leak. **3** come to an end.

ausleg/en ('ausle:gən) *vt* **1** lay out. **2** spend. **3** explain, interpret. **—ung** *nf* **-en** interpretation, explanation.

Auslese ('ausle:zə) *nf* **-n 1** selection. **2** choice wine.

ausliefer/n ('ausli:fərn) *vt* hand over, deliver (up). **—ung** *nf* **1** delivery. **2** extradition.

auslöschen ('ausløʃən) *vt* **1** extinguish. **2** erase. **3** switch off.

auslös/en ('auslø:zən) *vt* **1** release. **2** loosen. **3** ransom, redeem. **4** cause. **5** arouse. **—er** *nm* — **1** trigger. **2** release.

ausmachen ('ausmaxən) *vt* **1** put out (fire, lights). **2** constitute, make up. **3** make out, discern. **4** arrange. **5** agree. **es macht nichts aus** it doesn't matter.

Ausnahm/e ('ausna:mə) *nf* **-n** exception. **—efall** *nm* exceptional case. **—ezustand** *nm* state of emergency. **—slos** *adj* without exception. **—sweise** *adv* exceptionally, for once.

ausnehmen* ('ausne:mən) *vt* **1** take out. **2** except, exempt.

ausnutzen (ˈausnytsən) *vt also* **ausnützen** exploit, utilize.

auspacken (ˈauspakən) *vt* unpack.

auspräg/en (ˈausprɛːgən) *vt* 1 stamp, mark. 2 coin. —**ung** *nf* 1 coinage. 2 stamp(ing).

ausprobieren (ˈausprobiːrən) *vt* try, sample.

Auspuff (ˈauspuf) *nm* -e exhaust. —**rohr** *n neu* exhaust pipe. —**topf** *nm* silencer.

ausradieren (ˈausradiːrən) *vt* erase.

ausräumen (ˈausrɔymən) *vt* 1 clear (out). 2 empty.

ausrechnen (ˈausrɛçnən) *vt* calculate.

Ausrede (ˈausreːdə) *nf* -n (false) excuse.

ausreichen (ˈausraiçən) *vi* suffice. —**d** *adj* sufficient.

Ausreise (ˈausraizə) *nf* -n departure.

ausrichten (ˈausriçtən) *vt* 1 carry out, accomplish. 2 deliver. 3 adjust. 4 straighten.

ausrotten (ˈausrɔtən) *vt* 1 root out. 2 destroy (utterly), eradicate.

Ausruf (ˈausruːf) *nm* -e 1 cry. 2 proclamation. —**en*** *vt, vi* cry out, exclaim. —**ewort** *n neu* interjection. —**ung** *nf* -en 1 exclamation. 2 proclamation. —**ungszeichen** *n neu* exclamation mark.

ausruhen (ˈausruːən) *vi* rest.

ausrüst/en (ˈausrystən) *vt* 1 provide with, equip. 2 arm. —**ung** *nf* -en 1 equipment. 2 armament.

aussäen (ˈausːɛːən) *vt* sow.

Aussag/e (ˈausːaːgə) *nf* -n 1 declaration, deposition. 2 evidence. —**en** *vt* 1 declare, state. 2 give evidence.

Aussatz (ˈausːats) *nm* leprosy. —**ig** (ˈausːɛtsiç) *adj* leprous.

ausschalten (ˈausʃaltən) *vt* 1 switch off, disconnect, break. 2 eliminate, exclude.

ausscheid/en* (ˈausʃaidən) *vt* 1 eliminate. 2 separate. *vi* withdraw, retire.

ausschicken (ˈausʃikən) *vt* send out, dispatch.

ausschießen* (ˈausʃiːsən) *vt* shoot or cast out.

ausschiffen (ˈausʃifən) *vt* 1 disembark. 2 set sail.

ausschimpfen (ˈausʃimpfən) *vt* scold.

ausschlafen* (ˈausʃlaːfən) *vi* sleep late, lie in.

Ausschlag (ˈausʃlaːk) *nm* ⁻e 1 deflection. 2 rash, eruption. **den Ausschlag geben** tip the scales. —**en*** (ˈausʃlaːgən) *vt* 1 beat or knock out. 2 refuse, reject. 3 line or trim with. *vi* 1 lash out. 2 sprout, break into leaf. 3 turn out, develop. —**gebend** *adj* decisive.

ausschließ/en* (ˈausʃliːsən) *vt* shut out, exclude, bar. —**lich** *adj* exclusive. *prep* ex-

cluding, exclusive of. **Ausschluß** (ˈausʃlus) *nm* exclusion.

ausschneiden* (ˈausʃnaidən) *vt* cut out.

ausschöpfen (ˈausʃœpfən) *vt* 1 scoop out. 2 drain (off). 3 exhaust.

ausschreiben* (ˈausʃraibən) *vt* 1 write out, copy. 2 announce, advertise.

Ausschreitung (ˈausʃraituŋ) *nf* -en 1 excess. 2 transgression.

Ausschuß (ˈausʃus) *nm* 1 committee, commission. 2 scrap. 3 rejects.

ausschweif/en (ˈausʃvaifən) *vi* lead an immoral or dissolute life. —**ung** *nf* debauchery.

aussehen* (ˈausːzeːən) *vi* appear, look. **gut aussehend** good looking. *n neu* — 1 appearance. 2 exterior.

außen (ˈausən) *adv* 1 out(side), out of doors. 2 outwards. —**bordmotor** *nm* outboard motor. —**handel** *nm* foreign trade. —**minister** *nm* foreign minister. —**politik** *nf* foreign policy, foreign affairs. —**seite** *nf* outside. —**stände** *nm pl* arrears, outstanding debts or accounts. —**welt** *nf* 1 external world. 2 visible world.

aussenden* (ˈausːzɛndən) *vt* 1 send out. 2 emit, transmit.

außer (ˈausər) *prep* 1 outside. 2 out of. 3 besides. 4 except for. **außer Betrieb** out of order. **außer Dienst** off duty. **außer Fassung** disconcerted. **außer Kraft setzen** annul, cancel. ~*conj* except, but. **außer daß** except that. —**dem** *adv, conj* besides, moreover. —**gewöhnlich** *adj* extraordinary. —**halb** *prep* outside, beyond. —**ordentlich** (ausərˈɔrdəntliç) *adj* extraordinary, uncommon.

äußer/e (ˈɔysərə) *adj* external. *n neu* -n exterior, appearance. —**st** (ˈɔysərst) *adj* 1 outermost. 2 utmost. 3 extreme.

äußerlich (ˈɔysərliç) *adj* 1 external. 2 superficial.

äußer/n (ˈɔysərn) *vt* utter, express. —**ung** *nf* -en remark.

aussetzen (ˈausːzɛtsən) *vt* 1 set or put out. 2 suspend. 3 expose. 4 offer (money). 5 lower (a boat). *vi* stop, stall.

Aussicht (ˈausːziçt) *nf* -en outlook, prospect. —**slos** *adj* hopeless. —**spunkt** *nm* viewpoint.

aussondern (ˈausːzɔndərn) *vt* single out, separate.

ausspannen (ˈausʃpanən) *vt* stretch, extend. *vi* rest, relax.

ausspeien (ˈausʃpaijən) *vt* spit out.

Infinitive	Past Tense	Past Participle	Infinitive	Past Tense	Past Participle
abide	abode or abided	abode or abided	flee	fled	fled
			fling	flung	flung
arise	arose	arisen	fly	flew	flown
awake	awoke or awaked	awoke or awaked	forbid	forbade or forbad	forbidden or forbid
be	was	been	forget	forgot	forgotten or forgot
bear[1]	bore	borne or born			
beat	beat	beaten	forgive	forgave	forgiven
become	became	become	forsake	forsook	forsaken
begin	began	begun	freeze	froze	frozen
bend	bent	bent	get	got	got
bet	bet	bet	give	gave	given
beware[2]			go	went	gone
bid	hid	bidden or bid	grind	ground	ground
bind	bound	bound	grow	grew	grown
bite	bit	bitten or bit	hang[3]	hung or hanged	hung or hanged
bleed	bled	bled	have	had	had
blow	blew	blown	hear	heard	heard
break	broke	broken	hide	hid	hidden or hid
breed	bred	bred	hit	hit	hit
bring	brought	brought	hold	held	held
build	built	built	hurt	hurt	hurt
burn	burnt or burned	burnt or burned	keep	kept	kept
burst	burst	burst	kneel	knelt	knelt
buy	bought	bought	knit	knitted or knit	knitted or knit
can	could		know	knew	known
cast	cast	cast	lay	laid	laid
catch	caught	caught	lead	led	led
choose	chose	chose	lean	leant or leaned	leant or leaned
cling	clung	clung	leap	leapt or leaped	leapt or leaped
come	came	come	learn	learnt or learned	learnt or learned
cost	cost	cost	leave	left	left
creep	crept	crept	lend	lent	lent
crow	crowed or crew	crowed	let	let	let
cut	cut	cut	lie	lay	lain
deal	dealt	dealt	light	lit or lighted	lit or lighted
dig	dug or digged	dug or digged	lose	lost	lost
do	did	done	make	made	made
draw	drew	drawn	may	might	
dream	dreamed or dreamt	dreamed or dreamt	mean	meant	meant
			meet	met	met
drink	drank	drunk	mow	mowed	mown
drive	drove	driven	must		
dwell	dwelt	dwelt	ought		
eat	ate	eaten	panic	panicked	panicked
fall	fell	fallen	pay	paid	paid
feed	fed	fed	picnic	picnicked	picnicked
feel	felt	felt	put	put	put
fight	fought	fought	quit	quitted or quit	quitted or quit
find	found	found	read	read	read

English irregular verbs

Infinitive	Past Tense	Past Participle	Infinitive	Past Tense	Past Participle
rid	rid *or* ridded	rid *or* ridded	spill	spilt *or* spilled	spilt *or* spilled
ride	rode	ridden	spin	spun	spun
ring	rang	rung	spit	spat *or* spit	spat *or* spit
rise	rose	risen	split	split	split
run	ran	run	spread	spread	spread
saw	sawed	sawn *or* sawed	spring	sprang	sprung
say	said	said	stand	stood	stood
see	saw	seen	steal	stole	stolen
seek	sought	sought	stick	stuck	stuck
sell	sold	sold	sting	stung	stung
send	sent	sent	stink	stank *or* stunk	stunk
set	set	set	stride	strode	stridden
sew	sewed	sewn *or* sewed	strike	struck	struck
shake	shook	shaken	string	strung	strung
shall	should		strive	strove	striven
shear	sheared	sheared *or* shorn	swear	swore	sworn
			sweep	swept	swept
shed	shed	shed	swell	swelled	swollen *or* swelled
shine	shone	shone			
shoe	shod	shod	swim	swam	swum
shoot	shot	shot	swing	swung	swung
show	showed	shown	take	took	taken
shrink	shrank *or* shrunk	shrunk *or* shrunken	teach	taught	taught
			tear	tore	torn
shut	shut	shut	tell	told	told
sing	sang	sung	think	thought	thought
sink	sank	sunk	throw	threw	thrown
sit	sat	sat	thrust	thrust	thrust
sleep	slept	slept	traffic	trafficked	trafficked
slide	slid	slid	tread	trod	trodden *or* trod
sling	slung	slung			
slink	slunk	slunk	wake	woke	woken
slit	slit	slit	wear	wore	worn
smell	smelt *or* smelled	smelt *or* smelled	weave	wove	woven *or* wove
			weep	wept	wept
sow	sowed	sown *or* sowed	will	would	
speak	spoke	spoken	win	won	won
speed	sped *or* speeded	sped *or* speeded	wind	wound	wound
			wring	wrung	wrung
spell	spelt *or* spelled	spelt *or* spelled	write	wrote	written
spend	spent	spent			

[1] when *bear* means *give birth to*, the past participle is always *born*.

[2] used only in the infinitive or as an imperative.

[3] the preferred form of the past tense and past participle when referring to death by hanging is *hanged*.

Infinitive	Present Indicative	Imperfect Indicative	Past Participle	Infinitive	Present Indicative	Imperfect Indicative	Past Participle
backen	bäckt	backte	gebacken	**halten**	hält	hielt	gehalten
befehlen	befiehlt	befahl	befohlen	**hangen**	hängt	hing	gehangen
beginnen	beginnt	begann	begonnen	**hauen**	haut	haute or hieb	gehauen
beißen	beißt	biß	gebissen	**heben**	hebt	hob	gehoben
bergen	birgt	barg	geborgen	**heißen**	heißt	hieß	geheißen
bewegen[1]	bewegt	bewog	bewogen	**helfen**	hilft	half	geholfen
biegen	biegt	bog	gebogen	**kennen**	kennt	kannte	gekannt
bieten	bietet	bot	geboten	**klingen**	klingt	klang	geklungen
binden	bindet	band	gebunden	**kneifen**	kneift	kniff	gekniffen
bitten	bittet	bat	gebeten	**kommen**	kommt	kam	gekommen
blasen	bläst	blies	geblasen	**können**	kann	konnte	gekonnt[3]
bleiben	bleibt	blieb	geblieben	**kriechen**	kriecht	kroch	gekrochen
bleichen[2]	bleicht	blich	geblichen	**laden**	lädt	lud	geladen
braten	brät	briet	gebraten	**lassen**	läßt	ließ	gelassen
brechen	bricht	brach	gebrochen	**laufen**	läuft	lief	gelaufen
brennen	brennt	brannte	gebrannt	**leiden**	leidet	litt	gelitten
bringen	bringt	brachte	gebracht	**leihen**	leiht	lieh	geliehen
dreschen	drischt	drosch	gedroschen	**liegen**	liegt	lag	gelegen
dringen	dringt	drang	gedrungen	**lügen**	lügt	log	gelogen
dürfen	darf	durfte	gedurft[3]	**mahlen**	mahlt	mahlte	gemahlen
empfehlen	empfiehlt	empfahl	empfohlen	**meiden**	meidet	mied	gemieden
erschrecken[2]	erschrickt	erschrak	erschrocken	**melken**	melkt	melkte or molk	gemelkt or gemolken
essen	ißt	aß	gegessen	**messen**	mißt	maß	gemessen
fahren	fährt	fuhr	gefahren	**mißlingen**	mißlingt	mißlang	mißlungen
fallen	fällt	fiel	gefallen	**mögen**	mag	mochte	gemocht[3]
fangen	fängt	fing	gefangen	**müssen**	muß	mußte	gemußt[3]
fechten	ficht	focht	gefochten	**nehmen**	nimmt	nahm	genommen
finden	findet	fand	gefunden	**nennen**	nennt	nannte	genannt
flechten	flicht	flocht	geflochten	**pfeifen**	pfeift	pfiff	gepfiffen
fliegen	fliegt	flog	geflogen	**preisen**	preist	pries	gepriesen
fliehen	flieht	floh	geflohen	**quellen**[2]	quillt	quoll	gequollen
fließen	fließt	floß	geflossen	**raten**	rät	riet	geraten
fressen	frißt	fraß	gefressen	**reiben**	reibt	rieb	gerieben
frieren	friert	fror	gefroren	**reißen**	reißt	riß	gerissen
gären[4]	gärt	gor	gegoren	**reiten**	reitet	ritt	geritten
gebären	gebiert	gebar	geboren	**rennen**	rennt	rannte	gerannt
geben	gibt	gab	gegeben	**riechen**	riecht	roch	gerochen
gedeihen	gedeiht	gedieh	gediehen	**ringen**	ringt	rang	gerungen
gehen	geht	ging	gegangen	**rufen**	ruft	rief	gerufen
gelingen	gelingt	gelang	gelungen	**saufen**	säuft	soff	gesoffen
gelten	gilt	galt	gegolten	**saugen**	saugt	sog	gesogen
genesen	genest	genas	genesen	**schaffen**	schafft	schuf	geschaffen
genießen	genießt	genoß	genossen	**scheiden**	scheidet	schied	geschieden
gerinnen	gerinnt	gerann	geronnen	**scheinen**	scheint	schien	geschienen
geschehen	geschieht	geschah	geschehen	**schieben**	schiebt	schob	geschoben
gewinnen	gewinnt	gewann	gewonnen	**schießen**	schießt	schoß	geschossen
gießen	gießt	goß	gegossen	**schinden**	schindet	schund	geschunden
gleichen	gleicht	glich	geglichen	**schlafen**	schläft	schlief	geschlafen
gleiten	gleitet	glitt	geglitten	**schleichen**	schleicht	schlich	geschlichen
graben	gräbt	grub	gegraben	**schleifen**[5]	schleift	schliff	geschliffen
greifen	greift	griff	gegriffen	**schleißen**	schleißt	schliß	geschlissen
haben	hat	hatte	gehabt				

German irregular verbs

Infinitive	Present Indicative	Imperfect Indicative	Past Participle	Infinitive	Present Indicative	Imperfect Indicative	Past Participle
schließen	schließt	schloß	geschlossen	**stoßen**	stößt	stieß	gestoßen
schlingen	schlingt	schlang	geschlungen	**streichen**	streicht	strich	gestrichen
schmeißen	schmeißt	schmiß	geschmissen	**streiten**	streitet	stritt	gestritten
schmelzen	schmelzt	schmolz	geschmolzen	**tragen**	trägt	trug	getragen
schneiden	schneidet	schnitt	geschnitten	**treffen**	trifft	traf	getroffen
schreiben	schreibt	schrieb	geschrieben	**treiben**	treibt	trieb	getrieben
schreien	schreit	schrie	geschrie(e)n	**treten**	tritt	trat	getreten
schreiten	schreitet	schritt	geschritten	**triefen**	trieft	troff	getrieft
schweigen	schweigt	schwieg	geschwiegen	**trinken**	trinkt	trank	getrunken
schwellen	schwillt	schwoll	geschwollen	**trügen**	trügt	trog	getrogen
schwimmen	schwimmt	schwamm	geschwommen	**tun**	tut	tat	getan
schwingen	schwingt	schwang	geschwungen	**verderben**	verdirbt	verdarb	verdorben
schwören	schwört	schwur	geschworen	**verdrießen**	verdrießt	verdroß	verdrossen
sehen	sieht	sah	gesehen	**vergessen**	vergißt	vergaß	vergessen
sein	ist	war	gewesen	**verlieren**	verliert	verlor	verloren
senden	sendet	sandte	gesandt	**verzeihen**	verzeiht	verzieh	verziehen
singen	singt	sang	gesungen	**wachsen**	wächst	wuchs	gewachsen
sinken	sinkt	sank	gesunken	**weben**	webt	wob	gewoben
sinnen	sinnt	sann	gesonnen	**weichen**	weicht	wich	gewichen
sitzen	sitzt	saß	gesessen	**weisen**	weist	wies	gewiesen
sollen	soll	sollte	gesollt[3]	**wenden**	wendet	wandte or wendete	gewandt or gewendet
spinnen	spinnt	spann	gesponnen				
sprechen	spricht	sprach	gesprochen	**werben**	wirbt	warb	geworben
sprießen	sprießt	sproß	gesprossen	**werden**	wird	wurde	geworden[3]
springen	springt	sprang	gesprungen	**werfen**	wirft	warf	geworfen
stechen	sticht	stoch	gestochen	**wiegen**	wiegt	wog	gewogen
stehen	steht	stand	gestanden	**winden**	windet	wand	gewunden
stehlen	stiehlt	stahl	gestohlen	**wissen**	weiß	wußte	gewußt
steigen	steigt	stieg	gestiegen	**wollen**	will	wollte	gewollt[3]
sterben	stirbt	starb	gestorben	**ziehen**	zieht	zog	gezogen
stinken	stinkt	stank	gestunken	**zwingen**	zwingt	zwang	gezwungen

[1] strong conjugation in the meaning *induce, persuade*, but weak in the meaning *move*.
[2] strong conjugation when intransitive, but weak when transitive.
[3] when used as an auxiliary verb, the past participle has the same form as the infinitive.
[4] weak conjugation when figurative.
[5] strong conjugation in the meaning *polish, sharpen*, but weak in the meaning *drag*.

A

Aal (a:l) *nm* **-e** eel.

ab (ap) *adv* **1** off. **2** away. **3** down. **4** from. **ab und zu** sometimes, now and then. **weit ab** far off. *prep* from.

abänder/lich ('apɛndərliç) *adj* **1** alterable. **2** variable. **—n** *vt* **1** alter, change. **2** *pol* amend. **—ung** *nf* **-en** alteration.

abarbeiten ('aparbaitən) *vt* work off. **sich abarbeiten** *vr* overwork oneself.

Abbau ('apbau) *nm* reduction, dismantling, cutting down. **—en** *vt* **1** demolish. **2** reduce.

abberufen* ('apbəru:fən) *vt* recall.

abbestellen ('apbəʃtɛlən) *vt* cancel.

abbiegen* ('apbi:gən) *vi* turn off. *vt* turn aside.

Abbild ('apbilt) *n neu* **-er 1** image, copy. **2** likeness. **—en** *vt* **1** copy. **2** illustrate. **3** model. **—ung** ('apbilduŋ) *nf* **-en 1** copy(ing). **2** illustration. **3** picture.

abblenden ('apblɛndən) *vt* dim (one's headlights).

abbrechen* ('apbrɛçən) *vt,vi* **1** break off. **2** stop. *vt* tear down (houses).

abbremsen ('apbrɛmzən) *vi,vt* brake, slow down.

abbringen* ('apbriŋən) *vt* **1** divert. **2** dissuade.

Abbruch ('apbrux) *nm* **ⁱe 1** sudden end. **2** damage. **3** demolition.

abdank/en ('apdaŋkən) *vi* resign, abdicate. **—ung** *nf* **-en** abdication, resignation.

abdecken ('apdɛkən) *vt* **1** uncover. **2** *sport* protect or cover. **3** clear, strip.

abdichten ('apdiçtən) *vt* seal.

abdrehen ('apdre:ən) *vt* turn off.

Abdruck ('apdruk) *nm* **1** *pl* **-e** copy, print. **2** *pl* **ⁱe** cast, impression. **—en** ('apdrykən) *vt* squeeze. *vt,vi* shoot, fire (gun).

Abend ('a:bənt) *nm* **-e** evening, night. **gestern abond** last night. **heute abend** this evening. **abends** in the evening **—brot** *n neu* supper. **—essen** *n neu* evening meal, supper.

—dämmerung *nf* dusk. **—kleid** *n neu* evening dress or gown. **—land** *n neu* Occident, West. **—mahl** *n neu* (Holy) Communion.

Abenteuer ('a:bəntɔyər) *n neu* adventure. **—er** *nm* — **1** adventurer. **2** crook. **—lich** *adj* **1** adventurous. **2** fantastic.

aber ('a:bər) *conj* **1** but. **2** however. *adv* **1** however. **2** again. **aber ja** yes indeed.

Aberglaub/e ('a:bərglaubə) *nm* superstition. **ⁱisch** ('a:bərglɔybiʃ) *adj* superstitious.

Aberkennung ('apɛrkɛnuŋ) *nf* **-en** deprivation.

abermals ('a:bərma:ls) *adv* (once) again.

Abessin/ien (abɛ'si:niən) *n neu* Abyssinia. **—ier** *nm* — Abyssinian. **—isch** *adj* Abyssinian.

abfahr/en* ('apfa:rən) *vi* depart, start. *vt* drive off. **—t** *nf* **-en** departure.

Abfall ('apfal) *nm* **ⁱe 1** waste, rubbish. **2** slope. **3** decrease. **4** defection. **—eimer** *nm* dustbin. **—en*** *vi* **1** fall down or off. **2** desert. **3** decrease. **abfällig** ('apfɛliç) *adj* **1** disapproving, disparaging. **2** sloping.

abfassen ('apfasən) *vt* word, formulate.

abfertigen ('apfɛrtigən) *vt* **1** dispatch. **2** deal with.

Abfindung ('apfinduŋ) *nf* **-en** settlement, compensation.

abfliegen* ('apfli:gən) *vi* fly away, take off.

abfließen* ('apfli:sən) *vi* flow or drain away.

Abflug ('apfluk) *nm* **ⁱe** take-off, departure.

Abfluß ('apflus) *nm* **-flüsse 1** drain(ing). **2** discharge.

Abfuhr ('apfu:r) *nf* **-en 1** removal. **2** *inf* rebuff. **ⁱen** ('apfy:rən) *vt* lead off, take away. **ⁱmittel** ('apfy:rmitəl) *nu* laxative.

abfüllen ('apfylən) *vt* **1** fill. **2** bottle.

Abgabe ('apga:bə) *nf* **-n 1** delivery. **2** duty, tax, levy. **—nfrei** *adj* duty-free. **—npflichtig** *adj* taxable, liable to duty.

Abgang ('apgaŋ) *nm* **ⁱe 1** departure, exit. **2** loss.

Abgas ('apgas) *n neu* **-e** exhaust (gas).

abgeben* ('apge:bən) *vt* hand over, give up.

sich abgeben vr associate with, occupy one-self with.

abgegriffen ('apgəgrifən) adj 1 worn. 2 (of a book) well-thumbed.

abgehen* ('apge:ən) vi 1 go away or off, leave. 2 come or fall off. 3 branch off. **es ist alles gut abgegangen** everything went well.

Abgeordnete(r) ('apgəɔrdnətə) nm -n deputy, representative, Member of Parliament. **Abgeordnetenhaus** n neu Chamber of Deputies.

abgestanden ('apgəʃtandən) adj stale, flat.

abgestorben ('apgəʃtɔrbən) adj dead, numb.

abgezehrt ('apgətse:rt) adj emaciated.

Abgott ('apgɔt) nm -̈er idol.

abgrenz/en ('apgrɛntsən) vt mark off, delimit. **—ung** nf -en demarcation, delimitation.

Abgrund ('apgrunt) nm -̈e 1 precipice. 2 abyss.

abhalten ('aphaltən) vt 1 keep or hold off. 2 prevent.

Abhandlung ('aphandluŋ) nf -en essay, treatise.

Abhang nm -̈e slope, incline. **—en** ('aphɛŋən) vt 1 take down or off. 2 unhook. 3 disconnect. vi 1 depend on. 2 slope. **—ig** ('aphɛŋiç) adj 1 dependent. 2 sloping. 3 subject (to). **—igkeit** nf dependence.

abhauen ('aphauən) vt cut down or off. vi sl leave, go away.

Abhilfe ('aphilfə) nf -n remedy, relief.

abholen ('apho:lən) vt fetch (away), call for.

abhören ('aphœ:rən) vt overhear, listen to.

Abitur (abi'tu:r) n neu -e school leaving examination or certificate.

abkanzeln ('apkantsəln) vt scold, rebuke.

abkehren ('apke:rən) vt turn away.

abklingen ('apkliŋən) vi (of sound) die out, fade away.

Abkommen ('apkɔmən) n neu — agreement, treaty. vi 1 deviate. 2 lose one's way.

abkühl/en ('apky:lən) vt chill, cool. **—ung** nf cooling.

abkürz/en ('apkyrtsən) vt shorten, abbreviate. **—ung** nf -en abbreviation.

abladen* ('apla:dən) vt unload, dump.

Ablauf ('aplauf) nm -̈e 1 course of events. 2 end, expiry. 3 drain. **—en*** vi 1 run off or down. 2 expire. **gut ablaufen** pass off well, be a success.

Ablaut ('aplaut) nm -e gradation of vowels.

ablegen ('aple:gən) vt 1 take off (clothes). 2 lay down. 3 give up.

ablehn/en ('aple:nən) vt refuse, decline. **—ung** nf -en refusal, rejection.

ableit/en ('aplaitən) vt 1 divert. 2 derive. 3 draw off. **—ung** nf -en 1 diversion. 2 derivation.

ablenk/en ('aplɛŋkən) vt turn aside, divert. . **—ung** nf -en diversion, distraction.

abliefer/n ('apli:fərn) vt deliver. **—ung** nf -en delivery.

ablös/en ('aplœzən) vt 1 loosen, detach. 2 relieve (someone). **—ung** nf -en 1 loosening, detachment. 2 relief.

abmach/en ('apmaxən) vt settle, arrange. **abgemacht!** agreed! **—ung** nf -en agreement, arrangement.

sich abmeld/en ('apmɛldən) vr announce one's departure. **—ung** nf -en 1 notice of departure. 2 cancellation.

abmessen* ('apmɛsən) vt 1 measure off. 2 survey. 3 weigh (words).

Abnahme ('apna:mə) nf -n 1 removal, collection. 2 lessening, decrease. 3 acceptance.

abnehmen* ('apne:mən) vt take from or off. vi decrease.

Abneigung ('apnaiguŋ) nf -en dislike, aversion.

abnutzen ('apnutsən) vt also **abnützen** wear out.

Abonn/ement (abɔn'mã) n neu -s subscription. **—ent** (abɔ'nɛnt) nm -en subscriber. **—ieren** vi subscribe.

Abort (a'bɔrt) nm -e lavatory.

abräumen ('aprɔymən) vt clear away.

abrechn/en ('aprɛçnən) vt 1 deduct. 2 reckon up. 3 settle (with someone). **—ung** nf -en deduction, settlement.

Abrede ('apre:də) nf -n agreement. **in Abrede stellen** deny, dispute.

Abreise ('apraizə) nf -n departure. **—n** vi depart, set out.

abreißen* ('apraisən) vt 1 pull down. 2 tear off.

abrufen* ('apru:fən) vt 1 call back, recall. 2 cancel, call off.

Abrüstung ('aprystuŋ) nf -en disarmament.

Absage ('apza:gə) nf -n 1 refusal. 2 cancellation. **—n** vt 1 refuse. 2 cancel. 3 renounce.

Absatz ('apzats) nm -̈e 1 sale. 2 heel (of a shoe). 3 paragraph. 4 pause, intermission.

abschaff/en* ('apʃafən) vt abolish. **—ung** nf abolition.

abschalten ('apʃaltən) vt switch off.

abschätz/en ('apʃɛtsən) vt estimate, assess. **—ung** nf -en assessment, valuation.

Abscheu ('apʃɔy) nm,f horror, loathing. **—lich** (ap'ʃɔyliç) adj loathsome, repugnant.

abschicken (ˈapʃikən) vt send off, dispatch.

Abschied (ˈapʃiːt) nm -e parting, departure. **Abschied nehmen** take one's leave.

abschießen* (ˈapʃiːsən) vt 1 fire (a gun), shoot (off). 2 launch (a rocket).

Abschlag (ˈapʃlaːk) nm ⸚e reduction. **auf Abschlag** on account.

abschließen* (ˈapʃliːsən) vt 1 lock up, close (up). 2 settle, conclude.

Abschluß (ˈapʃlus) nm -schlüsse 1 conclusion, end. 2 settlement, deal.

abschnallen (ˈapʃnalən) vt unbuckle.

abschneiden* (ˈapʃnaidən) vt cut off or out. **gut/schlecht abschneiden** do well/badly.

Abschnitt (ˈapʃnit) nm -e section, portion.

abschrauben (ˈapʃraubən) vt unscrew.

abschrecken (ˈapʃrɛkən) vt frighten (off).

abschreiben* (ˈapʃraibən) vt 1 copy, write out. 2 write off.

Abschrift (ˈapʃrift) nf -en copy.

Abschuß (ˈapʃus) nm -schüsse 1 discharge, firing. 2 launching. **—rampe** nf launching pad.

abschwächen (ˈapʃvɛçən) vt weaken.

abseh/bar (ˈapzeːbaːr) adj 1 within sight. 2 foreseeable. **—en*** vt 1 foresee. 2 perceive. 3 aim at. 4 copy. **abgesehen von** apart from.

absend/en (ˈapzɛndən) vt send, dispatch. **—er** nm — sender. **—ung** nf -en dispatch(ing).

absetzen (ˈapzɛtsən) vt 1 put down. 2 remove, dismiss (someone). 3 sell.

Absicht (ˈapzɪçt) nf -en intention, purpose. **—lich** adj intentional.

absolut (apzoˈluːt) adj absolute.

absonder/n (ˈapzɔndərn) vt separate, isolate. **—ung** nf -en separation.

Absorption (apzɔrptsiˈoːn) nf -en absorption.

absperren (ˈapʃpɛrən) vt 1 cordon off, barricade. 2 shut off or away.

abspielen (ˈapʃpiːlən) vt perform (music). **sich abspielen** vr take place.

abspringen* (ˈapʃprɪŋən) vi 1 jump off. 2 break off, shatter. 3 desert.

abspülen (ˈapʃpyːlən) vt 1 wash up. 2 rinse.

Abstammung (ˈapʃtamuŋ) nf -en descent, ancestry.

Abstand (ˈapʃtant) nm ⸚e distance. **Abstand halten** keep one's distance.

abstatten (ˈapʃtatən) vt 1 give, render. 2 pay (a visit). 3 extend (thanks). 4 discharge (an obligation).

absteigen* (ˈapʃtaigən) vi 1 descend. 2 dismount, alight. 3 sport be relegated.

Abstieg (ˈapʃtiːk) nm -e 1 descent. 2 sport relegation.

Abstimmung (ˈapʃtimuŋ) nf -en vote, poll.

Abstinenz (apstiˈnɛnts) nf 1 abstinence. 2 teetotalism. **—ler** nm — 1 abstainer. 2 teetotaller.

abstoßen* (ˈapʃtoːsən) vt push away, repel.

abstrakt (apˈstrakt) adj abstract.

Abstufung (ˈapʃtuːfuŋ) nf -en graduation.

Absturz (ˈapʃturts) nm ⸚e 1 fall. 2 aviat crash. **—en** (ˈapʃtyrtsən) vi 1 fall (down). 2 aviat crash.

absurd (apˈzurt) adj absurd.

Abszeß (apsˈtsɛs) nm -zesse abcess.

Abt (apt) nm ⸚e abbott. **Äbtissin** (ɛpˈtisin) nf -nen abbess. **Abtei** (apˈtai) nf -en abbey.

Abteil (apˈtail) n neu -e compartment. **—en** (ˈaptailən) vt divide. **—ung** (apˈtailuŋ) nf -en division, department, group, section.

abtreib/en* (ˈaptraibən) vt 1 drive off. 2 abort. vi drift off. **—ung** nf -en abortion.

abtreten* (ˈaptreːtən) vt 1 cede. 2 wear out (shoes, etc). vi resign.

Abtritt (ˈaptrit) nm -e 1 withdrawal. 2 lavatory.

abtrocknen (ˈaptrɔknən) vt dry (up).

abtrünnig (ˈaptrynɪç) adj disloyal, rebellious.

abtun* (ˈaptuːn) vt 1 abolish. 2 settle. 3 put aside. 4 take off (clothes).

abwägen* (ˈapvɛːgən) vt consider, weigh.

abwand/eln (ˈapvandəln) vt 1 gram conjugate. 2 vary. **—lung** nf -en 1 gram inflection. 2 variation.

abwarten (ˈapvartən) vt wait for.

abwärts (ˈapvɛrts) adv 1 downwards. 2 aside.

abwaschen* (ˈapvaʃən) vt 1 wash off or away. 2 wash up.

abwechsel/n (ˈapvɛksəln) vi alternate. vt change. **—nd** adj alternating. **—ung** nf -en change, alternation.

Abwehr (ˈapveːr) nf -en defence, guard. **—en** vt ward off. **—stoff** nm antibody.

abweichen* (ˈapvaiçən) vi deviate, differ from. **—d** adj irregular, different.

abweisen* (ˈapvaizən) vt 1 turn away, dismiss. 2 reject.

abwenden* (ˈapvɛndən) vt 1 turn away. 2 prevent. **sich abwenden von** turn away from.

abwerfen* (ˈapvɛrfən) vt 1 throw off or away. 2 knock down. 3 yield. 4 drop (bombs).

abwert/en (ˈapvɛrtən) vt, vi devalue, devaluate. **—ung** nf -en devaluation.

abwesen/d (ˈapveːzənt) adj **1** absent. **2** absent-minded. **—heit** nf -en absence.

abwischen (ˈapviʃən) vt wipe off.

abzahlen (ˈaptsaːlən) vt pay off.

abzäunen (ˈaptsɔynən) vt fence off or in.

Abzeichen (ˈaptsaiçən) n neu badge, mark.

abziehen (ˈaptsiːən) vt **1** draw off, remove. **2** subtract. **3** distract. vi go away.

Abzug (ˈaptsuːk) nm ⁼e **1** deduction. **2** copy. **3** departure. **4** trigger. **5** outlet, vent. **6** (printing) proof. **⁼lich** (ˈaptsyːkliç) adv minus, less.

Abzweigung (ˈaptsvaiɡuŋ) nf -en branch.

ach (ax) interj oh!

Achse (ˈaksə) nf -n **1** axle. **2** axis.

Achsel (ˈaksəl) nf -n shoulder.

acht (axt) adj,nf eight. **—e** adj eighth. **heute in acht Tagen** today week.

Acht (axt) nf attention. **sich in Acht nehmen** look out, be on one's guard.

acht/en (ˈaxtən) vt respect. **achten auf** pay attention to. **—sam** adj attentive. **—geben** vi pay attention. **—ung** nf respect. interj attention, look out! **—ungsvoll** adj respectful.

achtzehn (ˈaxtseːn) adj,nf eighteen. **achtzehnte** adj eighteenth.

achtzig (ˈaxtsiç) adj,nf eighty. **achtzigste** adj eightieth.

ächzen (ˈɛçtsən) vi groan.

Acker (ˈakər) nm ⁼ **1** field, arable land. **2** (German) acre. **—bau** nm agriculture.

addier/en (aˈdiːrən) vt add. **—maschine** nf adding machine.

ade, adieu (aˈdeː; aˈdjøː) interj farewell.

Adel (ˈaːdəl) nm nobility, aristocracy. **adelig** adj also **adlig** noble. **Adlige(r)** (ˈaːdliɡə) nm -n nobleman, aristocrat. **Adelsstand** (ˈaːdəlsʃtant) nm **1** nobility. **2** peerage.

Ader (ˈaːdər) nf -n **1** vein. **2** artery.

Adjektiv (ˈatjɛktiːf) n neu -e adjective.

Adjutant (atjuˈtant) nm -en adjutant, aide.

Adler (ˈaːdlər) nm — eagle.

Admiral (atmiˈraːl) nm -e admiral.

adoptieren (adɔpˈtiːrən) vt adopt. **Adoptivkind** (adɔpˈtiːfkint) n neu adopted child.

Adrenalin (adreˈnaliːn) n neu adrenaline.

Adress/e (aˈdrɛsə) nf -n address. **—ieren** (adrɛˈsiːrən) vt address.

Adriatisches Meer (adriˈaːtiʃəs) n neu Adriatic (Sea).

Advokat (atvoˈkaːt) nm -en lawyer, advocate.

Affäre (aˈfɛːrə) nf -n **1** affair. **2** love affair.

Affe (ˈafə) nm -n **1** ape, monkey. **2** inf silly ass. **⁼n** (ˈɛfən) vt **1** deceive. **2** ape.

Afrika (ˈaːfrika) n neu Africa. **—ner** nm — African. **—nisch** adj African.

Ägäisches Meer (aˈɡɛiʃəs) n neu Aegean (Sea).

Agent (aˈɡɛnt) nm -en agent. **—ur** (aɡɛnˈtuːr) nf -en agency.

Agitation (aɡitatsiˈoːn) nf -en agitation.

Agnost/iker (aˈɡnɔstikər) nm — agnostic. **—isch** adj agnostic. **—izismus** (aɡnɔstiˈtsismus) nm agnosticism.

Ägypt/en (ɛˈɡyptən) n neu Egypt. **—isch** adj Egyptian.

Ahn (aːn) nm -en ancestor.

ähneln (ˈɛːnəln) vi resemble.

ahn/en (ˈaːnən) vt **1** suspect, guess. **2** foresee. **—ung** nf -en **1** idea, suspicion. **2** presentiment.

ähnlich (ˈɛːnliç) adj similar, like. **—keit** nf -en similarity, likeness.

Ahorn (ˈaːhɔrn) nm -e maple.

Akademie (akadeˈmiː) nf -n academy, college. **Akademiker** (akaˈdeːmikər) nm — academic. **akademisch** (akaˈdeːmiʃ) adj academic.

Akkord (aˈkɔrt) nm -e **1** arrangement, settlement. **2** mus chord. **im Akkord arbeiten** do piecework. **—arbeit** nf piecework.

Akrobat (akroˈbaːt) nm -en acrobat.

Akt (akt) nm -e **1** act, action. **2** nude study. **3** document.

Akte (ˈaktə) nf -n **1** document. **2** report. **3** file. **—nmappe** nf **1** folder. **2** portfolio. **3** briefcase. **—nschrank** nm filing-cabinet. **—ntasche** nf briefcase.

Aktie (ˈaktsiə) nf -n comm share. **—ngesellschaft** nf limited company.

Aktionär (aktsioˈnɛːr) nm -e shareholder.

aktiv (akˈtiːf) adj **1** active. **2** effective.

aktuell (aktuˈɛl) adj **1** topical. **2** present-day.

Akzent (akˈtsɛnt) nm -e accent, stress.

akzeptieren (aktsɛpˈtiːrən) vt accept.

Alabaster (alaˈbastər) nm alabaster.

Alarm (aˈlarm) nm -e alarm. **—ieren** vt alarm.

Alaun (aˈlaun) nm -e alum.

Alban/ien (alˈbaːniən) n neu Albania. **—ier** nm — Albanian. **—isch** adj Albanian.

Albatros (ˈalbatrɔs) nm -se albatross.

albern (ˈalbərn) adj silly, foolish.

Alge (ˈalɡə) nf -n seaweed.

Alger/ien (alˈɡeːriən) n neu Algeria. **—ier** nm — Algerian. **—isch** adj Algerian.

Alimente (aliˈmɛntə) n pl alimony.

Alkohol ('alkohol) nm -e alcohol. —**frei** adj
non-alcoholic. —**verbot** n neu prohibition.
—**isch** (alko'ho:liʃ) adj alcoholic. —**iker**
(alko'ho:likər) nm alcoholic.

all (al) pron all everything. adj all, every. **alles
in allem** on the whole. —**e** adv inf finished,
all gone. **alledem** ('aladе:m) pron **bei** or
trotz alledem in spite of all that.

All (al) n neu universe.

Allee (a'le:) nf -n avenue.

Allegorie (alego'ri:) nf -n allegory.

allein (a'lain) adv, adj alone, single. conj
but. —**ig** adj 1 sole. 2 exclusive.

allemal ('aloma:l) adv always. **ein für allemal**
once and for all.

allenfalls ('alənfals) adv if need be.

allerbest ('alərbɛst) adj best of all.

allerdings ('alərdiŋs) adv indeed, certainly.

allererst ('alərɛ:rst) adj,adv first of all.

allerhand ('alərhant) adj of all kinds, various.

allerhöchst ('alərhœçst) adj supreme.

allerlei ('alərlai) adj of all kinds, various.

allerliebst ('alərli:pst) adj 1 dearest (of all). 2
most lovely.

allerwenigst ('alərvе:niçst) adj the very least.

allezeit ('alatsait) adv always.

allgemein ('algəmain) adj general, common.

Alliierte(r) (a'li:rtə) nm -n ally.

alljährlich ('aljɛ:rliç) adj annual, yearly.

Allmacht ('almaxt) nf omnipotence. —**ig**
('almɛçtiç) adj almighty.

allmählich ('almɛ:liç) adj gradual.

allseitig ('alzaitiç) adj universal.

alltäglich ('altɛ:kliç) adj daily, common(place).

allzu ('altsu:) adv much too, far too.

Almanach ('almanax) nm -e almanac.

Almosen ('almo:zən) n neu alms.

Alpen ('alpən) n pl Alps.

Alphabet (alfa'be:t) n neu -e alphabet.

Alptraum ('alptraum) nm -e also **Alpdrücken** n
neu —nightmare.

als (als) conj 1 when. 2 as. 3 than. **als ob** also
als wenn as if. ~prep as. **nichts als** nothing
but.

alsbald (als'balt) adv at once.

alsdann (als'dan) adv 1 then. 2 after.

also ('alzo:) conj therefore. adv so.

alt (alt) adj old, ancient. —**e(r)** ('altə) nm old
one or man. —**klug** adj precocious. —**mod-
isch** adj old-fashioned. —**papier** n neu
wastepaper. —**stadt** nf old part of a town.
—**warenhändler** nm second-hand dealer.

Alt (alt) nm -e also **Altstimme** nf alto (voice).

Alter ('altər) n neu — (old) age. **im Alter von**
at the age of. —**sheim** n neu old people's
home. —**sversicherung** nf life insurance.

Altertum ('altərtu:m) n neu antiquity.

Aluminium (alu'mi:nium) n neu aluminium.

am (am) contraction of **an dem**

Amboß ('ambɔs) nm -bosse anvil.

Ameise ('a:maizə) nf -n ant.

Amerika (a'me:rika) n neu America. —**ner**
(ameri'ka:nər) nm — American. **amerikanisch** (ameri'ka:niʃ) adj American.

Ampel ('ampəl) nf -n 1 (hanging) lamp. 2 traffic
light.

Amsel ('amzəl) nf -n blackbird.

Amt (amt) n neu -̈er 1 office, (official) position.
2 charge, responsibility. **von Amts wegen**
officially, ex officio. —**lich** adj official.
—**mann** nm 1 official. 2 bailiff. —**sgeheim-
nis** n neu official secret. —**sgericht** n neu
district court.

amüs/ant (amy'zant) adj amusing. —**ieren**
(amy'zi:rən) vt amuse. **sich amusieren** vr
enjoy oneself.

an (an) prep 1 at. 2 on. 3 to. 4 against. 5 in. 6
by. **an (und für) sich** in itself. **von jetzt an**
from now on.

analog (ana'lo:k) adj analogous. —**ie** (analo-
'gi:) nf -n analogy.

Analphabet (analfa'be:t) nm -en illiterate.

Analys/e (ana'ly:zə) nf -n analysis. —**ieren**
(analy'zi:rən) vt analyse.

Ananas ('ananas) nf -se pineapple.

Anarchie (anar'çi:) nf -n anarchy.

Anatomie (anato'mi:) nf -n anatomy.

Anbau ('anbau) nm 1 pl -e cultivation. 2 pl -ten
annexe, outbuilding. —**en** vt 1 cultivate. 2
build (an extension).

anbeißen* ('anbaisən) vt bite into. vi swallow
the bait.

anbelangen ('anbəlaŋən) vt **was mich anbe-
langt** as for me.

anbet/en ('anbe:tən) vt worship, adore. —**ung**
nf worship.

Anbetracht ('anbətraxt) nf **in Anbetracht** in
view of.

anbetreffen* ('anbətrɛfən) vt concern.

anbieten* ('anbi:tən) vt offer.

Anblick ('anblik) nm -e view, sight. —**en** vt
look at.

anbrechen* ('anbrεçən) vt break into, open. vi
dawn.

anbringen* ('anbriŋən) vt 1 attach. 2 place. 3
install. 4 bring (a complaint).

Anbruch (ˈanbrux) *nm* ¨e beginning, opening.
Anbruch des Tages daybreak.

Andacht (ˈandaxt) *nf* -en devotion, prayers.
—**ig** (ˈandɛçtiç) *adj* 1 devout. 2 attentive.

andauern (ˈandauərn) *vi* continue, last.

Anden (ˈandən) *n pl* Andes.

Andenken (ˈandɛŋkən) *n neu* — 1 remembrance, memory. 2 souvenir, keepsake.

ander (ˈandər) *adj* other, different. **am anderen Tag** the next day. **einmal über das andere** again and again. **ein andermal** (ˈandərmaːl) *adv* another time. **andernfalls** (ˈandərnfals) *adv* otherwise. **anderntags** (ˈandərntaːks) *adv* the next day. **anderseits** (ˈandərzaits) *adv* or **andrerseits** on the other hand. **anders** (ˈandərs) *adv* differently, otherwise. **anderswo** (ˈandərsvoː) *adv* also **anderwärts** elsewhere, in another place. **anderweit** (ˈandərvait) *adv* 1 in another place. 2 in another way.

änder/n (ˈɛndərn) *vt* **sich ändern** *vr* change, alter. —**ung** *nf* -en change, alteration.

anderthalb (ˈandərthalp) *adj* one and a half.

andeut/en (ˈandɔytən) *vt* indicate, suggest. —**ung** *nf* -en indication, hint, suggestion.

Andrang (ˈandraŋ) *nm* press, rush, crowd.

andrehen (ˈandreːən) *vt* turn or switch on.

aneignen (ˈanaignən) *vt* appropriate, acquire.

aneinander (anainˈandər) *adv* 1 together. 2 to one another.

Anerbieten (ˈanɛrbiːtən) *n neu* — also **Anerbietung** *nf* -en offer, proposal.

anerkannt (ˈanɛrkant) *adj* recognized, acknowledged.

anerkenn/en* (ˈanɛrkɛnən) *vt* recognize, acknowledge. —**ung** *nf* -en recognition, acknowledgment.

anfahr/en* (ˈanfaːrən) *vt* 1 carry. 2 collide with. *vi* 1 approach. 2 (of a vehicle) begin to move. —**t** *nf* -en 1 arrival. 2 drive(way).

Anfall (ˈanfal) *nm* ¨e 1 attack. 2 fit.

Anfang (ˈanfaŋ) *nm* ¨e 1 beginning, introduction. 2 basis. **am Anfang** at the beginning. **von Anfang an** from the outset. —**en*** *vt,vi* begin, start. —**er** (ˈanfɛŋər) *nm* — beginner, novice. —**lich** (ˈanfɛŋliç) *adj* initial. —**s** *adv* at first, at the beginning.

anfassen (ˈanfasən) *vt* 1 seize. 2 touch, handle.

anfecht/en (ˈanfɛçtən) *vt* 1 contest, oppose. 2 trouble, bother. —**ung** *nf* -en 1 opposition. 2 temptation.

anfertig/en (ˈanfɛrtigən) *vt* manufacture, produce. —**ung** *nf* -en manufacture, fabrication.

Anforderung (ˈanfɔrdəruŋ) *nf* -en 1 claim, demand. 2 requirement.

Anfrage (ˈanfraːgə) *nf* -n enquiry. **anfragen** (ˈanfraːgən) *vi,vt* enquire, ask.

anführ/en (ˈanfyːrən) *vt* 1 lead. 2 quote, state. 3 deceive. —**er** *nm* — 1 commander, leader. 2 agitator. —**ung** *nf* -en 1 lead(ership). 2 quotation. —**ungszeichen** *n pl* quotation marks, inverted commas.

anfüllen (ˈanfylən) *vt* fill up.

Angabe (ˈangaːbə) *nf* -n 1 announcement, declaration. 2 information, details.

angeb/en* (ˈangeːbən) *vt* announce, state, give (reasons). *vi* 1 boast, pretend. 2 *game* deal first, serve. —**er** *nm* — 1 informer. 2 showoff, poseur. —**lich** (ˈangeːpliç) *adj* supposed, alleged.

angeboren (ˈangəboːrən) *adj* inborn.

Angebot (ˈangəboːt) *n neu* -e 1 bid, offer. 2 supply.

angehen* (ˈangeːən) *vi* begin. **das geht nicht an** that won't do. *vt* 1 approach (a person). 2 concern (a person). 3 tackle, attack. **das geht dich nichts an** that's none of your business.

angehör/en (ˈangəhøːrən) *vi* belong. —**ige(r)** *nm* -n 1 member. 2 relative.

Angeklagte(r) (ˈangəklaːktə) *nm* -n accused, defendant.

Angelegenheit (ˈangəleːgənhait) *nf* -en matter, affair, business.

angeln (ˈangəln) *vt,vi* angle, fish (for). *n neu* fishing, angling.

Angelsachs/e (ˈangəlzaksə) *nm* -n Anglo-Saxon. —**isch** (ˈangəlzɛksiʃ) *adj* Anglo-Saxon.

angemessen (ˈangəmɛsən) *adj* suitable.

angenehm (ˈangəneːm) *adj* pleasant, agreeable.

angenommen (ˈangənɔmən) *adj* 1 supposing, assuming. 2 approved.

angesehen (ˈangəzeːən) *adj* respected, distinguished.

Angesicht (ˈangəziçt) *n neu* -er face. —**s** *prep* in view of, considering.

Angestellte(r) (ˈangəʃtɛltə) *nm* -n 1 employee. 2 office worker.

angetan (ˈangətaːn) *adj* 1 dressed up. 2 likely.

angewandt (ˈangəvant) *adj* applied.

angewöhnen (ˈangəvøːnən) *vt* accustom. **sich angewöhnen** *vr* grow accustomed to.

Angewohnheit (ˈangəvoːnhait) *nf* -en habit, custom.

Angler (ˈanglər) *nm* — angler.

anglikanisch (angliˈkaːniʃ) *adj* Anglican.

angreif/en* (ˈangraifən) *vt* 1 attack, assault. 2

touch, grasp. **3** undertake. **—er** *nm* — aggressor, assailant.

angrenzen (ˈaŋgrɛntsən) *vi* border on.

Angriff (ˈangrif) *nm* **-e 1** attack. **2** undertaking. **—slustig** *adj* aggressive.

Angst (aŋst) *nf* ⁼e fear, fright, anxiety. **Angst haben** be afraid. **jemandem Angst machen** frighten someone. **⁼igen** (ˈɛŋstigən) *vt* frighten. **sich ⁼igen** *vr* worry, be anxious. **⁼lich** (ˈɛŋstliç) *adj* timid, anxious, cautious.

anhaben (ˈanha:bən) *vt* wear, have on.

Anhalt (ˈanhalt) *nm* **-e 1** support, hold. **2** clue, essential fact. **3** halt, stop. **—en*** *vt* check, stop. *vi* **1** stop. **2** continue, persist. **per Anhalter fahren** hitch-hike. **—spunkt** *nm* clue, lead.

Anhang (ˈanhaŋ) *nm* ⁼e **1** appendix. **2** following. **⁼en** (ˈanhɛŋən) *vt* hang on, attach. **⁼er** (ˈanhɛŋər) *nm* — **1** follower, disciple. **2** (baggage) tag, label. **3** *mot* trailer.

anhelmfallen* (ˈanhaimfalən) *vi* fall or come to (someone).

Anhöhe (ˈanhœ:ə) *nf* **-n** hill, rise.

anhören (ˈanhœ:rən) *vt* listen to.

Ankauf (ˈankauf) *nm* ⁼e purchase. **—en** *vt* purchase.

Anker (ˈaŋkər) *nm* — anchor. **—n** *vi* anchor.

Anklage (ˈankla:gə) *nf* **-n 1** accusation. **2** prosecution. **—n** *vt* accuse, charge.

Anklang (ˈanklaŋ) *nm* ⁼e **1** approval. **2** reminiscence.

anknüpf/en (ˈanknypfən) *vt* **1** fasten. **2** begin.

ankommen* (ˈankɔmən) *vi* arrive. **es kommt darauf an 1** it depends (on) . **2** it is important (to).

ankündigen (ˈankyndigən) *vt* announce.

Ankunft (ˈankunft) *nf* ⁼e arrival.

Anlage (ˈanla:gə) *nf* **-n 1** plan, lay-out. **2** park, gardens. **3** tendency. **4** talent, gift. **5** investment. **6** equipment, apparatus.

anlangen (ˈanlaŋən) *vi* arrive. *vt* concern (someone).

Anlaß (ˈanlas) *nm* **—lässe 1** cause. **2** occasion. **anlassen*** *vt* **1** leave on (a machine, etc.). **2** start, begin. **3** *mot* start (engine). **4** scold. **anläßlich** (ˈanlɛsliç) *prep* on the occasion of.

Anlauf (ˈanlauf) *nm* ⁼e start, take-off, run-up.

anlegen (ˈanle:gən) *vt* **1** lay or put on or against. **2** found. **3** invest. *vi* naut **1** berth. **2** land. **Feuer anlegen** start a fire.

Anleihe (ˈanlaiə) *nf* **-n** loan.

Anleitung (ˈanlaituŋ) *nf* **-en** instruction.

anlieg/en* (ˈanli:gən) *vi* **1** lie near. **2** fit well. *n neu* — request. **—end** *adj* adjacent.

anlocken (ˈanlɔkən) *vt* entice, attract.

Anmarsch (ˈanmarʃ) *nm* ⁼e *mil* approach, advance.

Anmaßung (ˈanmasuŋ) *nf* **-en 1** presumption. **2** insolence.

anmeld/en (ˈanmɛldən) *vt* **1** report. **2** declare, announce. **—ung** *nf* **-en 1** registration (with the police). **2** application. **3** announcement.

Anmerk/en (ˈanmɛrkən) *vt* note, observe. **—ung** *nf* **-en 1** remark, observation. **2** footnote.

Anmut (ˈanmu:t) *nf* grace, charm. **—ig** *adj* graceful, charming.

annähernd (ˈannɛ:ornt) *adj* **1** approaching. **2** approximate.

Annahme (ˈanna:mə) *nf* **-n 1** supposition. **2** acceptance.

annehmen* (ˈanne:mən) *vt* **1** accept, receive. **2** assume, suppose.

anonym (anoˈny:m) *adj* anonymous.

anordn/en (ˈanɔrdnən) *vt* arrange, order. **—ung** *nf* **-en 1** regulation. **2** direction, order.

anpacken (ˈanpakən) *vt* grasp, seize.

anpassen (ˈanpasən) *vt* **1** fit. **2** adapt, adjust. **sich anpassen** *vr* adapt, conform.

anrechn/en (ˈanrɛçnən) *vt* **1** think well of, value. **2** charge. **3** credit. **—ung** *nf* **-en** charge.

Anrede (ˈanre:də) *nf* **-n** address, speech. **—n** *vt* address, speak to.

anreg/en (ˈanre:gən) *vt* stimulate, excite, stir up. **—end** *adj* stimulating, exciting. **—ung** *nf* **-en 1** excitement. **2** inspiration. **3** suggestion.

anrichten (ˈanriçtən) *vt* **1** serve. **2** prepare. **3** cause.

Anruf (ˈanru:f) *nm* **-e 1** shout, call. **2** (telephone) call. **—en*** *vt* **1** ring up. **2** call, hail.

anrühren (ˈanry:rən) *vt* **1** touch. **2** mix.

ans (ans) contraction of **an das.**

Ansag/e (ˈanza:gə) *nf* **-n** announcement. **—er** *nm* — (radio) announcer.

ansammeln (ˈanzaməln) *vt* collect, amass. **sich ansammeln** *vr* gather, assemble.

ansässig (ˈanzɛsiç) *adj* resident, settled.

Ansatz (ˈanzats) *nm* ⁼e start, onset.

anschaffen* (ˈanʃafən) *vt* procure, buy.

anschalten (ˈanʃaltən) *vt* switch on, plug in.

anschau/en (ˈanʃauən) *vt* look at, view. **—lich** *adj* **1** vivid. **2** evident. **—ung** *nf* **-en 1** opinion, view. **2** conception, idea.

7

Anschein ('anʃain) nm **-e** appearance. **allem Anschein nach** to all appearances. **—end** adj apparent.

Anschlag ('anʃlaːk) nm **¨e** 1 striking, stroke. 2 poster. 3 plan, plot. 4 estimate. 5 (bomb) attack. **—en*** ('anʃlaːgən) vt 1 strike at. 2 affix. 3 value. vi 1 take effect. 2 attack, strike.

anschließen* ('anʃliːsən) vt connect, add, chain (up). **sich anschließen** vr join.

Anschluß ('anʃlus) nm **-schlüsse** connection, addition. **im Anschluß an** following.

anschnallen ('anʃnalən) vt fasten, buckle (on).

Anschovis (an'ʃoːvis) nf — anchovy.

Anschrift ('anʃrift) nf **-en** address.

anschuldigen ('anʃuldigən) vt accuse, charge.

anseh/en* ('anzeːən) vt 1 look at or upon. 2 consider. **ansehen für** take for. **—nlich** ('anzeːnliç) adj 1 good-looking. 2 considerable, important.

ansetzen ('anzɛtsən) vt 1 set or put on. 2 fasten. 3 add. 4 apply. vi begin.

Ansicht ('anziçt) nf **-en** 1 view, sight. 2 opinion. **meiner Ansicht nach** in my opinion. **zur Ansicht** on approval. **—s(post)karte** nf picture postcard.

ansiedeln ('anziːdəln) vt settle, colonize.

anspiel/en ('anʃpiːlən) vt allude, insinuate. **—ung** nf **-en** reference, allusion.

Anspruch ('anʃprux) nm **¨e** 1 claim, demand. 2 right, entitlement. **—slos** adj unassuming. **—svoll** adj 1 demanding. 2 sophisticated. 3 fastidious.

Anstalt ('anʃtalt) nf **-en** 1 institution. 2 pl arrangements.

Anstand ('anʃtant) nm **¨e** 1 decency, decorum. 2 hesitation. **¨ig** ('anʃtɛndiç) adj decent, respectable. **¨igkeit** nf decency, respectability.

anstatt (an'ʃtat) prep instead of.

ansteck/en ('anʃtɛkən) vt 1 fasten or pin on. 2 set fire to, light. 3 infect. **—end** adj infectious, contagious.

anstell/en ('anʃtɛlən) vt 1 employ, appoint. 2 turn on, start. 3 place near. 4 carry out, implement. vi 1 queue up. 2 behave, act. **—ung** nf **-en** appointment, post.

anstiften ('anʃtiftən) vt 1 cause. 2 instigate, incite.

Anstoß ('anʃtoːs) nm **-stösse** 1 impulse, stimulus. 2 knock, collision. 3 offence. 4 kickoff. **Anstoß nehmen** take offence. **—en*** vt 1 push (on or against). 2 knock. vi offend.

anstreng/en ('anʃtrɛŋən) vt 1 exert. 2 strain. 3 tire. **—ung** nf **-en** 1 exertion. 2 strain.

Antarktis (ant'arktis) nf Antarctic. **antarktisch** (ant'arktiʃ) adj Antarctic.

antasten ('antastən) vt 1 touch. 2 damage.

Anteil ('antail) nm **-e** 1 share. 2 interest. 3 sympathy.

Antenne (an'tɛnə) nf **-n** antenna, aerial.

Anthropologie (antropolo'giː) nf anthropology.

Antibiotikum (antibi'oːtikum) n neu **-ka** antibiotic.

antik (an'tiːk) adj 1 classical, ancient. 2 antique. **Antike** (an'tiːkə) nf antiquity.

Antiquar (anti'kvaːr) nm **-e** 1 second-hand bookseller. 2 antique dealer. **Antiquariat** (antikvari'aːt) n neu **-e** second-hand bookshop. **Antiquität** (antikvi'tɛːt) nf **-en** antique.

antisemitisch (antize'miːtiʃ) adj anti-Semitic.

antiseptisch (anti'zɛptiʃ) adj antiseptic.

Antonym (anto'nyːm) n neu **-e** antonym.

Antrag ('antraːk) nm **¨e** 1 application. 2 proposal. **—steller** nm — 1 applicant. 2 mover (of a proposal).

antreffen* ('antrɛfən) vt meet (with).

antreiben* ('antraibən) vt push or drive on. vi drift ashore.

antreten* ('antreːtən) vt 1 begin. 2 take up. 3 enter into. 4 approach.

Antrieb ('antriːp) nm **-e** 1 impulse. 2 power. 3 motive force.

Antritt ('antrit) nm **-e** 1 beginning. 2 taking up, assumption.

antun* ('antuːn) vt 1 put on. 2 do to.

Antwerpen (ant'vɛrpən) n neu Antwerp.

Antwort ('antvɔrt) nf **-en** answer, reply. **in Antwort auf** in reply to. **—en** vi answer, reply.

anvertrauen ('anfɛrtrauən) vt entrust.

Anwalt ('anvalt) nm **¨e** lawyer, advocate.

anwärmen ('anvɛrmən) vt warm (gently).

anweis/en* ('anvaizən) vt 1 assign. 2 instruct. 3 comm remit. **—ung** nf **-en** 1 money order, remittance. 2 instruction.

anwend/bar ('anvɛntbaːr) adj 1 applicable. 2 practicable. **—en*** ('anvɛndən) vt use, apply. **—ung** ('anvɛnduŋ) nf **-en** application, use.

anwesen/d ('anveːzənt) adj present. **—heit** nf in presence.

Anzahl ('antsaːl) nf 1 number. 2 quantity.

Anzeichen ('antsaiçən) n neu sign, sympton.

Anzeige/e ('antsaigə) nf **-n** 1 advertisement, notice, announcement. 2 denunciation. 3 notification, indication. **—en** vt 1 announce, advertise. 2 denounce. **—er** nm 1 indicator. 2 informer. 3 advertiser. 4 newspaper.

anzieh/en (ˈantsiːən) vt 1 put on (clothes). 2 attract. 3 pull or draw on. 4 tighten. **sich anziehen** vr dress. **—ungskraft** nf 1 attractive force, gravitation. 2 attractiveness.

Anzug (ˈantsuːk) nm ⁼e 1 suit. 2 clothing, dress. 3 approach.

anzünden (ˈantsyndən) vt light, set fire to.

Apennin (apeˈniːn) nm also **Appenninen** n pl Apennines.

Apfel (ˈapfəl) nm ⁼ apple.

Apfelsine (ˈapfəlziːnə) nf **-n** orange.

Apostel (aˈpɔstəl) nm — apostle.

Apotheke (apoˈteːkə) nf **-n** chemist's shop, pharmacy. **—r** nm — chemist, pharmacist.

Apparat (apaˈraːt) nm **-e** 1 apparatus, equipment. 2 device. 3 telephone. **am Apparat bleiben** hold the line.

appellieren (apeˈliːrən) vi appeal.

Appetit (apeˈtiːt) nm **-e** appetite. **—lich** adj appetizing.

Aprikose (apriˈkoːzə) nf **-n** apricot.

April (aˈpril) nm **-e** April.

Aquarell (akvaˈrɛl) n neu **-e** watercolour.

Aquarium (aˈkvaːrium) n neu **-rien** aquarium.

Äquator (ɛˈkvaːtɔr) nm Equator.

Äquivalent (ɛkvivaˈlɛnt) n neu **-e** equivalent.

Arab/er (ˈaraber) nm — Arab. **—ien** (aˈraːbiən) n neu Arabia. **—isch** (aˈraːbiʃ) adj Arabian, Arabic. n neu Arabic (language).

Arbeit (ˈarbait) nf **-en** 1 work, labour. 2 job. 3 effort. **—en** vi,vt work, labour. **—er** nm — worker, workman, labourer. **—erklasse** nf also **—erschaft** nf **-en** working class(es). **—geber** nm — employer. **—nehmer** nm — employee. **—sgemeinschaft** nf 1 syndicate. 2 partnership (employers and employees). 3 working party, study group. **—skräfte** nf pl personnel, staff, workforce. **—slos** adj unemployed. **—slosigkeit** nf unemployment.

Archäologie (arçɛoloˈgiː) nf archaeology.

Architekt (arçiˈtɛkt) nm **-en** architect. **—ur** (arçitɛkˈtuːr) nf **-en** architecture.

Archiv (arˈçiːf) n neu **-e** archives, records.

arg (ark) adj 1 bad, evil. 2 serious. n neu evil, malice. **—los** adj unsuspecting, innocent. **—wohn** (ˈarkvoːn) nm suspicion, distrust.

Argentin/ien (argɛnˈtiːniən) n neu Argentina. **—ier** nm — Argentine. **—isch** adj Argentinian.

Ärger (ˈɛrgər) nm 1 anger. 2 irritation, annoyance. **—lich** adj 1 angry. 2 annoying,

troublesome. **—n** vt annoy, irritate, bother. **—nis** n neu **-se** 1 nuisance. 2 offence.

Argument (arguˈmɛnt) n neu **-e** argument, case.

Aristokrat (aristoˈkraːt) nm **-en** aristocrat. **—ie** nf **-n** aristocracy. **—isch** adj aristocratic.

Arithmetik (aritˈmeːtik) nf arithmetic.

Arktis (ˈarktis) nf Arctic. **arktisch** (ˈarktiʃ) adj arctic.

arm (arm) adj poor. **—e(r)** nm **-n** poor man. **⁼lich** (ˈɛrmliç) adj poor, lowly (of clothes, a house, etc.). **—selig** adj miserable, wretched (of persons). **—ut** (ˈarmuːt) nf poverty.

Arm (arm) nm **-e** 1 arm. 2 (of rivers, etc.) branch. **—band** n neu bracelet. **—banduhr** nf wrist-watch. **—stuhl** nm arm-chair.

Armee (arˈmeː) nf **-n** army. **—korps** n neu army corps.

Ärmel (ˈɛrməl) nm — sleeve. **—kanal** nm (English) Channel.

Arrest (aˈrɛst) nm **-e** 1 arrest, seizure. 2 detention, imprisonment.

Art (aːrt) nf **-en** 1 sort, type, kind. 2 way, manner. 3 nature. 4 species. **—en nach** vi take after. **—ig** adj 1 well-behaved, polite. 2 kind. 3 good. **—igkeit** nf **-en** 1 politeness, good behaviour. 2 compliment. **—artig** (ˈaːrtiç) suff -like.

Artikel (arˈtiːkəl) nm — article.

Artillerie (artiləˈriː) nf **-n** artillery.

Artischocke (aːtiˈʃɔkə) nf **-n** artichoke.

Arznei (artsˈnai) nf **-en**, also **Arzneimittel** n neu medicine, drug.

Arzt (aːrtst) nm **-e** doctor, physician. **⁼in** (ˈɛːrtstin) nf **-nen** (woman) doctor. **⁼lich** (ˈɛːrtstliç) adj medical.

As (as) n neu **-se** ace.

Asbest (asˈbɛst) n neu **-e** asbestos.

Asche (ˈaʃə) nf **-n** ash, ashes, cinders. **—nbahn** nf cinder-track, dirt-track. **—nbecher** nm ashtray. **—rmittwoch** (aʃərˈmitvɔx) nm Ash Wednesday.

aß (aːs) v see **essen**.

Assistent (asisˈtɛnt) nm **-en** assistant.

Ast (ast) nm **⁼e** 1 bough, branch. 2 knot (in wood).

ästhetisch (esˈteːtiʃ) adj aesthetic.

Astronaut (astroˈnaut) nm **-en** astronaut.

Astronom (astroˈnoːm) nm **-en** astronomer. **—ie** (astronoˈmiː) nf astronomy.

Asyl (aˈzyːl) n neu **-e** asylum, sanctuary.

Atelier (ateˈljeː) n neu **-s** studio.

Atem (ˈaːtəm) nm breath. **außer Atem**

9

breathless. **—raubend** adj 1 breath-taking, terrifying. 2 fascinating. **—los** adj breathless.

Athe/ismus (ateˈismus) nm atheism. **—ist** (ateˈist) nm **-en** atheist.

Athen (aˈteːn) n neu Athens.

Äther (ˈɛːtər) nm ether. **—isch** (ɛˈteːriʃ) adj ethereal.

Äthiop/ien (ɛtiˈoːpiən) n neu Ethiopia. **—ier** nm — Ethiopian. **—isch** adj Ethiopian.

Athletik (atˈleːtik) nf athletics.

Atlantik (atˈlantik) nm also **Atlantischer Ozean** (atˈlantiʃər) Atlantic.

Atlas[1] (ˈatlas) nm **-lasse** satin.

Atlas[2] (ˈatlas) nm **-lanten** atlas.

atmen (ˈaːtmən) vi,vt breathe, respire.

Atmosphäre (atmosˈfɛːrə) nf **-n** atmosphere. **atmosphärisch** (atmosˈfɛːriʃ) adj atmospheric.

Atom (aˈtoːm) n neu **-e** atom. **—bombe** nf atom(ic) bomb. **—energie** nf atomic energy. **—kern** nm atomic nucleus. **—kraftanlage** nf nuclear power station. **—waffen** nf pl nuclear weapons.

Atten/tat (atɛnˈtaːt) n neu **-e** murderous attack, assault, (attempted) assassination. **—täter** (atɛnˈtɛːtər) nm — assassin, assailant.

ätzen (ˈɛtsən) vt corrode, etch.

Aubergine (oberˈʒiːnə) nf **-n** aubergine.

auch (aux) adv, conj 1 also, as well, too. 2 even. 3 indeed. **auch wenn** also **wenn auch** even if. **nicht nur...sondern auch** not only...but also. **wer auch** whoever.

Audienz (audiˈɛnts) nf **-en** audience, hearing.

auf (auf) prep 1 (up)on. 2 in. 3 to. 4 up. 5 against. **auf einmal** all at once. ~adv open, up(wards). interj (get) up!

Aufbau (ˈaufbau) nm **-e** or **-ten** 1 construction, erection. 2 composition, organization. 3 superstructure. **—en** vt construct, build up.

Aufbesserung (ˈaufbɛsəruŋ) nf **-en** 1 improvement. 2 increase (of salary etc.).

aufbewahren (ˈaufbəvaːrən) vt store, keep.

aufbleiben* (ˈaufblaibən) vi 1 stay up. 2 remain open.

aufblicken (ˈaufblikən) vi look up.

aufbrauchen (ˈaufbrauxən) vt use up, consume.

aufbrechen* (ˈaufbrɛçən) vt break open. vi 1 burst, open. 2 set off.

aufbringen* (ˈaufbriŋən) vt 1 bring up, raise. 2 irritate, anger.

aufdrehen* (ˈaufdreːən) vt 1 unscrew. 2 turn on.

aufdring/en* (ˈaufdriŋən) vt force on (someone). **—lich** adj intrusive, importunate.

aufeinander (aufainˈandər) adv 1 successively. 2 one on or against the other.

Aufenthalt (ˈaufɛnthalt) nm **-e** 1 stop, halt, delay. 2 stay, period (of residence).

auferlegen (ˈaufɛrleːgən) vt impose.

aufersteh/en* (ˈaufɛrˈʃteːən) vi rise from the dead. **—ung** nf **-en** resurrection.

auffahren* (ˈauffaːrən) vi 1 rise (up). 2 drive up. 3 start, jump. 4 become angry.

auffallen* (ˈauffalən) vi 1 fall upon. 2 be noticeable, evident. **es fiel mir auf, daß** it struck me that. **auffallend** (ˈauffalənt) adj also **auffällig** (ˈauffɛliç) striking, remarkable.

auffangen* (ˈauffaŋən) vt catch up, intercept.

auffass/en (ˈauffasən) vt 1 understand, interpret. 2 pick up. **—ung** nf **-en** 1 comprehension. 2 opinion. 3 conception.

auffinden* (ˈauffindən) vt find (out), discover.

auffliegen* (ˈauffliːgən) vi 1 fly up. 2 explode. 3 (of a door) fly open.

aufforder/n (ˈauffordərn) vt 1 challenge, invite. 2 summon. **—ung** nf **-en** 1 challenge, invitation. 2 summons.

auffressen* (ˈauffrɛsən) vt devour.

aufführ/en (ˈauffyːrən) vt 1 build. 2 perform. 3 specify. 4 list. 5 bring forward, introduce. **—ung** nf performance, presentation.

Aufgabe (ˈaufgaːbə) nf **-n** 1 task, duty. 2 problem. 3 giving up. 4 delivery.

Aufgang (ˈaufgaŋ) nm **-e** 1 ascent, rise. 2 staircase.

aufgeben* (ˈaufgeːbən) vt 1 give up or in. 2 deliver, surrender. 3 post (mail, etc.).

Aufgebot (ˈaufgəboːt) n neu **-e** public notice.

aufgehen* (ˈaufgeːən) vi 1 rise. 2 open. 3 math divide exactly, work out correctly.

aufgeklärt (ˈaufgəklɛːrt) adj enlightened.

aufgelegt (ˈaufgəleːkt) adj disposed, inclined. **gut/schlecht aufgelegt** in a good/bad mood.

aufhalten* (ˈaufhaltən) vt 1 hold open. 2 delay. **sich aufhalten** vr stay.

aufhängen* (ˈaufhɛŋən) vt hang (up).

aufheb/en* (ˈaufheːbən) vt 1 pick up, raise. 2 keep, store. 3 annul, cancel. 4 suspend. 5 reverse. n neu **——** 1 lifting up. 2 fuss, ado. **—ung** nf **-en** 1 abolition, repeal. 2 suspension.

aufhören (ˈaufhœːrən) vi cease, stop, discontinue.

aufklappen (ˈaufklapən) vt open.

aufklär/en (ˈaufklɛːrən) vt,vi 1 clear up. 2

enlighten. 3 correct. **—ung** nf **-en** 1 clearing up. 2 enlightenment. 3 explanation.

aufkleben ('aufkle:bən) vt paste on, affix.

aufknüpfen ('aufknʏpfən) vt 1 tie or hang up. 2 untie.

aufkommen* ('aufkɔmən) vi 1 rise. 2 recover. 3 make good. n neu **— 1** yield (of taxes). 2 recovery, rise.

aufladen* ('aufla:dən) vt load.

Auflage ('aufla:gə) nf **-n** 1 edition, impression. 2 circulation. 3 tax, duty.

auflassen* ('auflasən) vt leave open.

Auflauf ('auflauf) nm ⁼e 1 riot. 2 soufflé.

auflös/en ('auflø:zən) vt 1 untie, loosen. 2 dissolve. 3 break up. **—ung** nf **-en** 1 dissolution. 2 decomposition.

aufmachen ('aufmaxən) vt 1 open, undo. 2 put up (an umbrella). **sich aufmachen** vr set out.

Aufmarsch ('aufmarʃ) nm ⁼e mil 1 approach, marching up (of troops). 2 deployment. 3 parade.

aufmerk/sam ('aufmɛrkza:m) adj attentive. **—samkeit** nf attentiveness.

aufmuntern ('aufmuntərn) vt 1 rouse, encourage. 2 cheer up.

Aufnahme ('aufna:mə) nf **-n** 1 acceptance, reception, admission. 2 recording. 3 photograph.

aufnehmen* ('aufne:mən) vt 1 take or pick up. 2 receive, admit. 3 record. 4 photograph.

aufopfer/n* ('aufɔpfərn) vt sacrifice. **—ung** nf **-en** 1 sacrifice. 2 devotion.

aufpassen ('aufpasən) vi 1 watch. 2 pay attention.

Aufputz ('aufputs) nm finery, ornament.

aufräumen ('aufrɔymən) vt 1 tidy up. 2 clear away or out.

aufrecht ('aufrɛçt) adj 1 upright, erect. 2 honourable. **—erhalten*** vt maintain, support. **—erhaltung** nf maintenance.

aufreg/en ('aufre:gən) vt 1 excite. 2 irritate. 3 alarm. **sich aufregen** vr get excited. **—ung** nf **-en** excitement, agitation.

aufreiben* ('aufraibən) vt 1 chafe. 2 exhaust. 3 harass. 4 destroy, wipe out (an enemy).

aufricht/en ('aufrɪçtən) vt 1 erect, set up. 2 establish. **sich aufrichten** vr get or sit up. **—ig** adj honest, sincere. **—igkeit** nf sincerity.

Aufriß ('aufris) nm 1 sketch. 2 section. 3 plan.

aufrücken ('aufrʏkən) vi move up(wards).

Aufruf ('aufru:f) nm **-e** 1 call. 2 summons. 3 appeal.

Aufruhr ('aufru:r) nm **-e** 1 riot, uproar. 2 revolt. **—erisch** ('aufry:rəriʃ) adj mutinous.

aufrüsten ('aufrʏstən) vt (re)arm.

aufs (aufs) contraction of **auf das.**

aufsagen ('aufza:gən) vt recite.

Aufsatz ('aufzats) nm ⁼e 1 essay, article. 2 top piece. 3 centrepiece.

aufschieben* ('aufʃi:bən) vt 1 push open. 2 delay, postpone.

Aufschlag ('aufʃla:k) nm ⁼e 1 hit, impact. 2 rise (of prices). 3 cuff, lapel, facing (of clothes). 4 sport service. **—en*** ('aufʃla:gən) vt 1 break open, open. 2 put up, erect. 3 look or glance up.

aufschließen* ('aufʃli:sən) vt 1 unlock. 2 open up.

Aufschluß ('aufʃlus) nm 1 information. 2 explanation. **—reich** adj informative.

aufschneiden* ('aufʃnaidən) vt cut open or up vi brag, exaggerate.

Aufschnitt ('aufʃnit) nm **-e** slices of cold meats.

Aufschrei ('aufʃrai) nm **-e** 1 scream. 2 outcry.

aufschreiben* ('aufʃraibən) vt write down.

Aufschrift ('aufʃrift) nf **-en** 1 inscription. 2 address.

Aufschub ('aufʃup) nm ⁼e delay, postponement.

Aufschwung ('aufʃvuŋ) nm ⁼e 1 rise, upward impetus. 2 comm boom. 3 enthusiasm. **einen neuen Aufschwung nehmen** revive.

aufseh/en* ('aufze:ən) vi look up. n neu **—** sensation, stir. **—er** nm. **—** inspector, overseer, superintendant.

aufsetzen ('aufzɛtsən) vt 1 set up. 2 put on. **sich aufsetzen** vr sit up.

Aufsicht ('aufzɪçt) nf **-en** 1 supervision. 2 charge, care. **—sbehörde** nf controlling authority. **—srat** nm board of directors.

aufspringen* ('aufʃpriŋən) vi 1 jump up. 2 fly open. 3 crack.

Aufstand ('aufʃtant) nm ⁼e revolt, riot. **—isch** ('aufʃtɛndiʃ) adj rebellious.

aufstapeln ('aufʃta:pəln) vt 1 heap up. 2 store.

aufstehen* ('aufʃte:ən) vi 1 get or stand up. 2 rebel. 3 stand open.

aufsteigen* ('aufʃtaigən) vi 1 climb (up), mount. 2 rise.

aufstell/en ('aufʃtɛlən) vt 1 put or set up. 2 draw up. 3 nominate. 4 display. 5 state. **—ung** nf **-en** 1 erection. 2 position. 3 arrangement. 4 list, table. 5 nomination.

Aufstieg ('aufʃti:k) nm **-e** 1 ascent. 2 rise.

aufstützen (ˈaufʃtytsən) vt prop up.
aufsuchen (ˈaufzuːxən) vt seek (out). **jemanden aufsuchen** look up or visit someone.
auftanken (ˈauftaŋkən) vt fuel, fill up (with fuel).
auftauchen (ˈauftauxən) vi 1 emerge. 2 surface. 3 appear, crop up.
aufteilen (ˈauftailən) vt distribute, divide up.
Auftrag (ˈauftraːk) nm ⁼e 1 instructions, order. 2 task. 3 contract. 4 mandate. **im Auftrag von** by order of. —**geber** nm — comm customer.
auftreiben* (ˈauftraibən) vt 1 procure, obtain. 2 startle, rouse. 3 swell.
auftreten* (ˈauftreːtən) vi 1 come forward. 2 occur, appear. vt kick open. n neu — 1 appearance. 2 behaviour, manner.
Auftritt (ˈauftrit) nm -e 1 appearance. 2 Th scene.
auftun* (ˈauftuːn) vt 1 open. 2 start (up).
aufwachen (ˈaufvaxən) vi wake up.
aufwachsen* (ˈaufvaksən) vi grow up.
Aufwand (ˈaufvant) nm ⁼e 1 expenditure. 2 extravagance.
aufwärmen (ˈaufvɛrmən) vt 1 warm up. 2 rake up, revive (a dispute, story, etc.).
aufwärts (ˈaufvɛrts) adv upward(s).
aufwecken (ˈaufvɛkən) vt wake, rouse.
aufweisen* (ˈaufvaizən) vt present, show.
aufwend/en* (aufvendən) vt spend, expend. —**ung** nf -en expenditure.
aufwerfen* (ˈaufvɛrfən) vt 1 cast up. 2 throw open. 3 raise (a question).
aufwert/en* (ˈaufvɛrtən) vt revalue (upwards). —**ung** nf -en revaluation.
aufwischen (ˈaufviʃən) vt wipe up.
aufwühlen (ˈaufvyːlən) vt 1 dig up, turn up. 2 stir up.
aufzählen (ˈauftsɛːlən) vt count (up), enumerate.
aufzeichn/en (ˈauftsaiçnən) vt 1 draw, sketch. 2 note, record. —**ung** nf -en note, record.
aufziehen* (ˈauftsiːən) vt 1 pull or draw up, raise. 2 open. 3 bring up, rear.
Aufzug (ˈauftsuːk) nm ⁼e 1 lift, elevator, hoist. 2 parade. 3 act (of a play). 4 attire.
Augapfel (ˈaukapfəl) nm eyeball.
Auge (ˈaugə) n neu -n 1 eye. 2 bud. **blaues Auge** black eye. **ein Auge zudrücken** 1 wink at. 2 shut one's eyes to. **unter vier Augen** face to face (in private). —**nblick** nm instant, moment. —**nfällig** adj conspicuous, obvious.
August (auˈgust) nm August.

Aula (ˈaula) nf -len (great) hall.
au pair (oˈpɛːr) adj au pair.
aus (aus) prep 1 out (of). 2 from. 3 of. 4 by. adv 1 out. 2 over, finished.
ausarbeiten (ˈausarbaitən) vt 1 work out. 2 prepare.
Ausbau (ˈausbau) nm -e 1 completion. 2 extension (of a building).
ausbessern (ˈausbɛsərn) vt 1 repair, refit. 2 rectify.
Ausbeut/e (ˈausbɔytə) nf -n 1 profit, gain. 2 output. —en vt exploit, profit from. —**ung** nf -en exploitation.
ausbild/en (ˈausbildən) vt 1 educate, train. 2 form, develop. —**ung** nf 1 education, training. 2 development.
ausbleiben* (ˈausblaibən) vi stay away or out, be absent. n neu — absence, default.
Ausblick (ˈausblik) nm -e view, outlook.
ausbrechen* (ˈausbrɛçən) vi break out. vt vomit.
ausbreit/en (ˈausbraitən) vt 1 spread (out). 2 stretch, extend. 3 spread. —**ung** nf -en spread, increase.
ausbringen* (ˈausbriŋən) vt bring out. **eine Gesundheit ausbringen** propose a toast.
Ausbruch (ˈausbrux) nm ⁼e 1 burst. 2 outbreak. 3 eruption. 4 escape.
ausbrüten (ˈausbryːtən) vt 1 hatch. 2 plot.
Ausdauer (ˈausdauər) nf 1 endurance. 2 perseverance.
ausdehn/en (ˈausdeːnən) vt extend, stretch, expand. —**ung** nf 1 expansion. 2 range, extent.
ausdenken* (ˈausdɛŋkən) vt think out, work out. **sich ausdenken** vr think up, invent.
ausdrehen (ˈausdreːən) vt turn or switch off.
Ausdruck (ˈausdruk) nm ⁼e 1 expression, look. 2 expression, term. ⁼⁼en (ˈausdrykən) vt 1 express. 2 press or squeeze out. ⁼⁼lich (ˈausdrykliç) adj explicit.
auseinander (ausainˈandər) adv separately, apart (from one another). —**gehen*** 1 disperse. 2 separate. 3 differ. —**setzen** vt explain, expound. —**setzung** nf -en 1 discussion. 2 conflict. 3 arrangement. —**treiben*** vt disperse.
ausersehen* (ˈausɛrzeːən) vt 1 select, choose. 2 destine. adj (pre)destined.
auserwählen (ˈausɛrvɛːlən) vt choose, select.
ausfahr/en* (ˈausfaːrən) vi go for a drive. vt take (someone) for a drive. —**t** nf 1 drive, excursion. 2 way out, gateway. 3 departure.

Aussprache ('ausʃpraːxə) nf **-n 1** pronunciation. **2** discussion.

aussprechen* ('ausʃprɛçən) vt **1** pronounce. **2** express, say.

Ausspruch ('ausʃprux) nm saying, utterance.

ausspülen ('ausʃpyːlən) vt **1** wash or rinse out. **2** clean.

Ausstand ('ausʃtant) nm strike.

ausstatt/en ('ausʃtatən) vt **1** equip. **2** furnish. **—ung** nf **-en 1** equipment. **2** fittings.

ausstehen* ('ausʃteːən) vt endure, bear.

ausstell/en ('ausʃtɛlən) vt **1** exhibit. **2** issue. **—ung** nf exhibition.

aussterben* ('ausʃtɛrbən) vi die out.

Aussteuer ('ausʃtɔyər) nf **-n 1** dowry. **2** trousseau.

ausstoßen* ('ausʃtoːsən) vt **1** push or drive out, expel. **2** utter.

ausstrahlen ('ausʃtraːlən) vt,vi radiate.

ausstrecken ('ausʃtrɛkən) vt extend.

ausstreichen* ('ausʃtraiçən) vt cross out.

ausströmen ('ausʃtrœːmən) vi **1** stream out. **2** escape.

aussuchen ('auszuːxən) vt select, pick.

Austausch ('austauʃ) nm **-e** exchange, barter. **—en** vt exchange.

austeilen ('austailən) vt distribute, hand out.

Auster ('austər) nf **-n** oyster.

austragen* ('austraːgən) vt **1** distribute. **2** deliver. **3** decide (a contest).

Austral/ien (au'straːliən) n neu Australia. **—ier** nm Australian. **—isch** adj Australian.

austreiben* ('austraibən) vt **1** drive out, expel. **2** exorcize.

austreten* ('austreːtən) vi **1** go or step out. **2** withdraw. **3** resign from. vt tread out, stamp out. **Austritt** ('austrit) nm **-e 1** departure, exit. **2** resignation. **3** withdrawal.

ausüb/en ('ausyːbən) vt **1** practise. **2** carry out. **—ung** nf practice, execution.

Ausverkauf ('ausfɛrkauf) nm (clearance) sale.

Auswahl ('ausvaːl) nf **-en 1** selection. **2** variety. **—en** ('ausvɛːlən) vt choose, select.

Auswander/er ('ausvandərər) nm — emigrant. **—n** vi emigrate. **—ung** nf **-en** emigration.

auswärtig ('ausvɛrtiç) adj foreign. **das auswärtige Amt** foreign office.

auswärts ('ausvɛrts) adv **1** outward(s). **2** abroad. **3** outside.

Ausweg ('ausveːk) nm way out, expedient.

ausweichen* ('ausvaiçən) vi **1** make way for. **2** avoid.

ausweiden ('ausvaidən) vt gut, disembowel.

Ausweis ('ausvais) nm **-e 1** ticket. **2** identity card. **3** passport. **4** statement. **—en*** ('ausvaizən) vt turn out, expel, banish. **sich —en** vr prove one's identity. **—karte** nf identity card. **—papiere** n neu pl identification papers. **—ung** ('ausvaizuŋ) nf expulsion, deportation.

auswendig ('ausvɛndiç) adj external. **auswendig lernen** learn by heart, memorize.

auswerfen* ('ausvɛrfən) vt throw out, cast out.

auswerten ('ausvɛrtən) vt evaluate, analyse.

auswirken ('ausvirkən) vt **1** work out. **2** effect, bring about.

auswischen ('ausviʃən) vt wipe out, obliterate.

Auswuchs ('ausvuks) nm growth, deformity.

auszahlen ('austsaːlən) vt pay out or off.

auszeichn/en ('austsaiçnən) vt **1** mark out. **2** honour. **3** label. **—ung** nf **1** distinction, honour. **2** mark.

ausziehen* ('austsiːən) vt **1** draw or pull out. **2** make out (a bill). **3** take off (clothes). vi **1** move (out). **2** set forth. **sich ausziehen** vr undress.

Auszug ('austsuːk) nm **1** departure. **2** extract, abstract. **3** move, removal. **4** statement of account.

Auto ('auto) n neu **-s** (motor) car, automobile. **—bahn** nf motorway. **—bus** nm **-se** bus. **—fahrer** nm motorist, driver. **—heber** nm jack. **—rennen** n neu motor racing. **—stop** nm hitchhiking. **per Autostop fahren** hitchhike. **—unfall** nm motoring accident.

Autogramm (auto'gram) n neu **-e** autograph.

Auto/mat (auto'maːt) nm **-en** automat, vending machine. **—matisch** adj automatic. **—nom** (auto'noːm) adj autonomous.

Autor ('autɔr) nm writer, author.

Autorität (autori'tɛːt) nf **-en** authority.

Axt (akst) nf **ːe** axe.

Azoren (a'tsoːrən) n pl Azores.

B

Baby ('beːbi) n neu **-s** baby.

Bach (bax) nm **ːe** stream, brook.

Backbord ('bakbɔrt) n neu naut port (side).

Backe ('bakə) nf **-n** also **Backen** ('bakən) nm — cheek.

back/en* ('bakən) vt **1** bake. **2** fry. **ːer** ('bɛkər) nm — baker. **ːerei** (bɛkə'rai) nf **-en** bakery. **—pulver** n neu baking powder.

Bad (baːt) n neu **ːer 1** bath. **2** spa. **—ehose**

('ba:dəho:zə) *nf* bathing trunks. **—ekappe** ('ba:dəkapə) *nf* bathing cap. **—en** ('ba:dən) *vi,vt* bathe. **—etuch** ('ba:dətu:x) *n neu* bath towel. **—ewanne** ('ba:dəvanə) *nf* bath tub. **—ezimmer** ('ba:dətsimər) *n neu* bathroom.

Bagger ('bagə) *nm* — excavator.

Bahn (ba:n) *nf* **-en 1** way, path, track. **2** railway. **—hof** *nm* (railway) station. **—steig** *nm* **-e** platform. **—übergang** *nm* level crossing.

Bahre ('ba:rə) *nf* **-n** stretcher, bier.

Bai (bai) *nf* **-en** bay.

Bajonett (bajo'nɛt) *n neu* **-e** bayonet.

Bakterium (bak'te:rium) *n neu* **-rien** also **Bakterie** (bak'te:riə) *nf* **-n** bacterium.

balancieren (balā'si:rən) *vt* balance.

bald (balt) *adv* **1** soon, shortly. **2** almost. **bald...bald** now...now. **—ig** ('baldiç) *adj* **1** early. **2** quick, speedy. **—möglichst** *adv* as soon as possible.

Balken ('balkən) *nm* — beam, rafter, girder.

Balkon (bal'kõ:) *nm* **-s** balcony.

Ball[1] (bal) *nm* **˜e 1** ball. **2** globe.

Ball[2] (bal) *nm* **˜e** dance, ball.

Ballade (ba'la:də) *nf* **-n** ballad.

Ballast ('balast) *nm* **-e** ballast.

Ballen ('balən) *nm* **— 1** bale. **2** package.

Ballet (ba'lɛt) *n neu* **-e** ballet.

Ballon (ba'lõ:) *nm* **-e** balloon.

Balsam ('balza:m) *nm* **-e** balsam, balm.

baltisch ('baltiʃ) *adj* baltic. **baltisches Meer** *n neu* Baltic (sea).

Bambus ('bambus) *nm* **-se** bamboo.

Banane (ba'na:nə) *nf* **-n** banana.

Band[1] (bant) *n neu* **1** *pl* **-˜er** band, tape, ribbon. **2** *pl* **-˜er** ligament. **3** *pl* **-e** bond, tie. **—aufnahme** *nf* tape-recording.

Band[2] (bant) *nm* **˜e** volume, tome.

Bandage (ban'da:ʒə) *nf* **-n** bandage.

Bande ('bandə) *nf* **-n** band, gang.

bändigen ('bɛndigən) *vt* tame, subdue.

Bandit (ban'di:t) *nm* **-en** bandit.

bang(e) (baŋ) *adj* afraid, anxious.

Bank[1] (baŋk) *nf* **˜e** bench, seat.

Bank[2] (baŋk) *nf* **-en** *comm* bank. **—ier** (baŋk-'je:) *nm* **-s** banker. **—konto** *n neu* bank account. **—note** *nf* bank note. **—wesen** *n neu* banking.

Bankett (baŋ'kɛt) *n neu* **-e** banquet.

bankrott (baŋ'krɔt) *adj* bankrupt. *nm* **-e** bankruptcy.

Bann (ban) *nm* **-e 1** ban, proscription. **2** excom-

munication. **3** spell. **—en** *vt* **1** banish. **2** excommunicate. **3** enchant.

bar (ba:r) *adj* (of money) ready, in cash. **—fuß** *adj* barefoot. **—geld** *n neu* cash, ready money.

Bar (ba:r) *nf* **-s** tavern, bar.

Bär (bɛ:r) *nm* **-en** bear.

Barbar (bar'ba:r) *nm* **-en** barbarian. **—ei** (bar-ba'rai) *nf* **-en** barbarism. **—isch** *adj* barbarous.

Barbiturat (bar'bitura:t) *n neu* barbiturate.

Bariton ('bariton) *nm* **-e** baritone.

Barmädchen ('barmɛ:dçən) *n neu* — barmaid.

barmherzig (barm'hɛrtsiç) *adj* merciful.

Barock (ba'rɔk) *nm,neu* baroque.

Barometer (ba'rome:tər) *n neu* — barometer.

Baron (ba'ro:n) *nm* **-e** baron. **—in** *nf* **-nen** baroness.

Barre ('barə) *nf* **-n** bar.

Barriere (bari'ɛ:rə) *nf* **-n** barrier, bar.

barsch (barʃ) *adj* **1** harsh, rough. **2** rude.

Bart (ba:rt) *nm* **˜e** beard.

Base[1] ('ba:zə) *nf* **-n** female relative (especially a cousin).

Base[2] (be:s) *nf* **-n** base.

Basel ('ba:zəl) *n neu* Basle.

bas/ieren (ba'zi:rən) *vi* be based. **—is** ('ba:zis) *nf* **-sen** base, basis.

Baß (bas) *nm* **Bässe** bass. **—geige** *nf* double bass.

Bassist (ba'sist) *nm* **-en** bass singer, bass player.

Bastard ('bastart) *nm* **-e 1** bastard. **2** hybrid.

bas/teln ('bastəln) *vt* tinker with, potter around with. **—tler** ('bastlər) *nm* — **1** dabbler. **2** handyman.

bat (ba:t) *v* see **bitten.**

Bataillon (batai'ljo:n) *n neu* **-e** battalion.

Batterie (batə'ri:) *nf* **-n** battery.

Bau (bau) *nm* **-e, -ten 1** construction, building. **2** burrow. **3** mine. **4** cultivation. **—en** *vt* **1** build. **2** grow. **—fällig** *adj* in disrepair, dilapidated. **—herr** *nm* **1** builder. **2** person for whom a building is being constructed. **—kunst** *nf* architecture. **—meister** *nm* **1** builder. **2** architect. **—platz** *nm* also **-stelle** *nf* building site. **—sparkasse** *nf* building society. **—stein** *nm* building stone. **—werk** *n neu* building, structure.

Bauch (baux) *nm* **˜e** belly, stomach. **—schmerzen** *nm pl* stomach-ache. **—tanz** *nm* belly dance.

Bauer ('bauər) *nm* **-n 1** farmer. **2** peasant.

Bäuerin ('bɔyərin) nf **-nen** farmer's wife, peasant woman. **Bauernhaus** ('bauərnhaus) n neu farmhouse. **Bauernhof** ('bauərnho:f) nm farm(yard).

Baum (baum) nm **-e** 1 tree. 2 naut boom, mast. **—garten** nm orchard. **—wolle** nf cotton.

Bay/er ('baiər) nm **-n** Bavarian. **—ern** ('baiərn) n neu Bavaria. **—risch** ('bairiʃ) adj Bavarian.

Bazillus (ba'tsilus) nm **-illen** bacillus.

beabsichtigen (bə'apziçtigən) vt intend.

beacht/en (bə'axtən) vt pay attention to. **—enswert** adj noteworthy, notable. **—ung** nf considération.

Beamte(r) (bə'amtə) nm **-n, Beamtin** (bə'amtin) nf **-nen** 1 official. 2 civil servant.

beängstigen (bə'ɛŋstigən) vt frighten.

beanspruchen (bə'anʃpruxən) vt claim, require.

beanstand/en (bə'anʃtandən) vt object to. **—ung** nf objection.

beantragen (bə'antra:gən) vt 1 apply for. 2 propose.

beantwort/en (bə'antvɔrtən) vt answer. **—ung** nf reply, answer.

bearbeit/en (bə'arbaitən) vt 1 work. 2 revise, adapt. 3 cultivate. **—ung** nf 1 working. 2 treatment. 3 revision, adaptation.

beaufsichtig/en (bə'aufziçtigən) vt 1 supervise. 2 inspect. **—ung** nf supervision, control.

beauftragen (bə'auftra:gən) vt commission.

bebauen (bə'bauən) vt 1 build on. 2 cultivate.

beben ('be:bən) vi shake, tremble, shiver.

Becher ('bɛçər) nm — 1 cup. 2 beaker.

Becken ('bɛkən) n neu — 1 basin. 2 cymbal. 3 pelvis.

bedacht (bə'daxt) adj thoughtful. **bedacht auf** intent on. ~nm 1 caution. 2 consideration. **mit Bedacht** deliberately. **—ig** (bə'dɛçtiç) adj 1 deliberate. 2 cautious.

Bedarf (bə'darf) nm 1 need, want. 2 demand.

bedauer/lich (bə'dauərliç) adj unfortunate, regrettable. **—n** vt 1 regret. 2 deplore. 3 pity. n neu — 1 regret. 2 pity.

bedeck/en (bə'dɛkən) vt 1 cover. 2 protect. **—t** adj 1 covered. 2 (of the sky) overcast. **—ung** nf 1 covering. 2 protection. 3 escort.

bedenk/en (bə'dɛŋkən) vt consider, think about. **sich bedenken** vr deliberate. ~n neu — 1 doubt, reservation. 2 consideration. **—lich** adj 1 doubtful. 2 risky.

bedeut/en (bə'dɔytən) vt 1 mean. 2 signify. **—end** adj also **—sam** (bə'dɔytza:m) sig-

nificant, important. **—ung** nf **-en** 1 meaning. 2 importance. **—ungslos** adj 1 meaningless. 2 insignificant. **—ungsvoll** adj significant.

bedien/en (bə'di:nən) vt 1 wait on, serve. 2 operate (a machine). **sich bedien/en** vr make use of. **bedienen Sie sich!** help yourself! **—te(r)** (bə'di:ntə) nm **-n** servant. **—ung** nf **-en** service, attendance.

beding/t (bə'diŋkt) adj 1 conditional. 2 determined (by something). **—ung** nf **-en** condition, term. **—ungslos** adj unconditional.

Bedrängnis (bə'drɛŋnis) nf **-se** 1 distress. 2 oppression.

bedrohen (bə'dro:ən) vt threaten.

bedürf/en* (bə'dyrfən) vi need, require. **—nis** n neu **-se** need, want, requirement.

sich beeilen (bə'ailən) vr hurry, hasten.

beeinflussen (bə'ainflusən) vt influence.

beeinträchtigen (bə'aintrɛçtigən) vt 1 injure. 2 wrong. 3 interfere with. 4 impair.

beenden (bə'ɛndən) vt conclude, end, finish

Beerdigung (bə'e:rdiguŋ) nf **-en** burial.

Beere ('be:rə) nf **-n** berry.

Beet (be:t) n neu **-e** flower bed.

befähig/en (bə'fɛ:igən) vt enable. **—ung** nf **-en** 1 ability. 2 qualification.

befahl (bə'fa:l) v see **befehlen.**

befahr/bar (bə'fa:rba:r) adj 1 passable, navigable. 2 practicable. **—en*** vt 1 drive over. 2 navigate.

befallen* (bə'falən) vt 1 befall. 2 strike.

befangen (bə'faŋən) adj 1 embarrassed. 2 confused. 3 biased.

befassen (bə'fasən) vt touch. **sich befassen mit** be occupied with.

Befehl (bə'fe:l) nm **-e** command, order. **—en*** vt command, order. **—shaber** (bə'fe:lsha:bər) nm — commander, commanding officer.

befestig/en (bə'fɛstigən) vt 1 fasten. 2 fortify, strengthen. **—ung** nf **-en** 1 fortification. 2 strengthening. 3 fastening.

Befind/en (bə'findən) n neu — 1 health. 2 opinion. **sich befinden*** vr 1 be, be present. 2 feel. **—lich** (bə'fintliç) adj situated, present, existing.

beflecken (bə'flɛkən) vt stain, soil, dishonour.

beflissen (bə'flisən) adj 1 studious. 2 assiduous.

befohlen (bə'fo:lən) v see **befehlen.**

befolgen (bə'fɔlgən) vt 1 follow. 2 obey.

beförder/n (bə'fœrdərn) vt 1 transport, convey. 2 promote. 3 support. **—ung** nf **-en** 1 for-

befragen

warding. **2** transport. **3** advancement, promotion.

befragen (bə'fra:gən) *vt* question.

befrei/en (bə'fraiən) *vt* free, liberate. **—ung** *nf* **-en 1** liberation. **2** exemption.

sich befreunden (bə'frɔyndən) *vr* **sich mit jemandem befreunden** befriend someone.

befriedig/en (bə'fri:digən) *vt* **1** satisfy. **2** pacify. **—end** *adj* satisfactory. **—ung** *nf* **1** satisfaction. **2** pacification.

befruchten (bə'fruxtən) *vt* **1** fertilize. **2** impregnate. **3** stimulate.

befug/en (bə'fu:gən) *vt* empower, authorize. **—nis** (bə'fu:knis) *nf* **-se** authority, right.

befürcht/en (bə'fyrçtən) *vt* fear. **—ung** *nf* **-en** anxiety, fear.

befürworten (bə'fy:rvɔrtən) *vt* advocate.

begab/t (bə'ga:pt) *adj* talented, gifted. **—ung** (bə'ga:buŋ) *nf* **-en** talent, ability.

begann (bə'gan) *v* see **beginnen**.

begeben (bə'ge:bən) *vt comm* **1** endorse. **2** negotiate. **sich begeben** *vr* **1** go, proceed. **2** surrender, give up. **—heit** *nf* **-en** occurrence, event.

begegn/en (bə'ge:gnən) *vi* meet, encounter. **—ung** *nf* **-en** meeting, encounter.

begehen (bə'ge:ən) *vt* **1** walk (on), go (along). **2** commit (a crime, error, etc.).

begehr/en (bə'ge:rən) *vt* desire, long for. *n neu* **—** desire, longing. **—enswert** *adj* desirable.

begeister/n (bə'gaistərn) *vt* inspire. **—t** *adj* enthusiastic. **—ung** *nf* enthusiasm.

Begier (bə'gi:r) *nf* — *also* **Begierde** (bə'gi:rdə) *nf* **-n 1** desire, longing. **2** lust. **—ig** *adj* **1** covetous. **2** eager.

Beginn (bə'gin) *nm* **-e** beginning. **—en** *vt,vi* begin, start.

beglaubigen (bə'glaubigən) *vt* certify, authenticate.

begleit/en (bə'glaitən) *vt* accompany. **—er** *nm* **1** companion, attendant. **2** accompanist. **—ung** *nf* **-en 1** escort, retinue. **2** accompaniment.

beglück/en (bə'glykən) *vt* make happy. **—wünschen** *vt* congratulate.

begnadig/en (bə'gna:digən) *vt* pardon, reprieve. **—ung** *nf* **-en** pardon, reprieve, amnesty.

sich begnügen (bə'gny:gən) *vr* be satisfied.

begonnen (bə'gɔnən) *v* see **beginnen**.

begrab/en (bə'gra:bən) *vt* bury. *inter.* **—nis** (bə'grɛ:pnis) *n neu* **-se 1** burial, funeral. **2** tomb.

begreif/en (bə'graifən) *vt* understand, grasp. **—lich** *adj* understandable.

begrenzt (bə'grɛntst) *adj* limited, restricted.

Begriff (bə'grif) *nm* **-e 1** idea, concept. **2** understanding. **—en** *adj* engaged or occupied (in).

begründ/en (bə'gryndən) *vt* **1** found, establish. **2** base. **3** substantiate. **—er** *nm* **—** founder. **—et** (bə'gryndət) *adj* established. **—ung** *nf* **-en 1** foundation. **2** reason, substantiation.

begrüßen (bə'gry:sən) *vt* greet, welcome.

begünstig/en (bə'gynstigən) *vt* **1** favour. **2** further, promote. **—ung** *nf* **-en 1** favour. **2** encouragement.

begütert (bə'gy:tərt) *adj* wealthy, well-off.

behäbig (bə'hɛ:biç) *adj* **1** comfortable. **2** stout.

behaftet (bə'haftət) *adj* **1** burdened. **2** afflicted.

behag/en (bə'ha:gən) *vi* please, suit. *n neu* **—1** pleasure. **2** comfort. **—lich** (bə'ha:kliç) *adj* comfortable, snug.

behalt/en (bə'haltən) *vt* **1** keep. **2** remember. **3** retain. **—er** (bə'hɛltər) *nm* — *also* **—nis** (bə'hɛltnis) *n neu* **-se 1** container, holder. **2** case. **3** tank.

behand/eln (bə'handəln) *vt* treat, handle, manage. **—lung** *nf* treatment, handling, management.

beharr/en (bə'harən) *vi* **1** insist, remain firm. **2** endure. **—lich** *adj* persistent, stubborn. **—lichkeit** *nf* perseverance, determination.

behaupt/en (bə'hauptən) *vt* maintain, affirm, assert. **sich behaupten** *vr* be firm, hold one's own. **—ung** *nf* **-en** statement, assertion.

behend/(e) (bə'hɛnt) *adj* **1** agile. **2** dexterous. **—igkeit** (bə'hɛndiçkait) *nf* **1** agility. **2** dexterity.

beherbergen (bə'hɛrbergən) *vt* lodge, put up, house, shelter.

beherrschen (bə'hɛrʃən) *vt* **1** rule, govern, reign over. **2** master (a language). **3** control.

beherzigen (bə'hɛrtsigən) *vt* take to heart.

behilflich (bə'hilfliç) *adj* helpful.

behinder/n (bə'hindərn) *vt* hinder, obstruct. **—ung** *nf* **-en** hindrance, obstruction.

Behörd/e (bə'hœ:rdə) *nf* **-n 1** authority. **2** administrative or governing body. **3** *comm* board. **—lich** *adj* official.

behüten (bə'hy:tən) *vt* **1** preserve. **2** guard. **behutsam** (bə'hu:tza:m) *adj* careful, cautious.

bei (bai) *prep* **1** by. **2** at. **3** near. **4** beside. **5** with. **bei mir 1** at my house or home. **2** with or on me.

beibehalt/en* ('baibəhaltən) vt retain, maintain. **—ung** nf -en retention.

beibringen* ('baibriŋən) vt 1 bring forward, produce. 2 teach, impart.

Beicht/e ('baiçtə) nf -n confession. **—en** vi,vt confess. **—stuhl** nm confessional.

beide ('baidə) adj,pron both. **—rseitig** ('baidərzaitiç) adj joint, mutual, on both sides. **—rseits** ('baidərzaits) adv on both sides, mutually.

Beifahrer ('baifa:rər) nm 1 passenger. 2 co-driver.

Beifall ('baifal) nm 1 applause. 2 approval.

beifügen ('baify:gən) vt 1 add. 2 enclose.

beigeben* ('baige:bən) vt add. **klein beigeben** give in, knuckle under.

Beigeschmack ('baigəʃmak) nm 1 flavour, (after)taste. 2 tang, savour. 3 tinge, hint.

Beiheft ('baiheft) n neu supplement.

Beihilfe ('baihilfə) nf 1 aid, subsidy. 2 assistance, abetting.

Beil (bail) n neu -e hatchet, axe.

Beilage ('baila:gə) nf 1 supplement, insert, enclosure. 2 garnish.

beiläufig ('bailɔyfiç) adj 1 incidental. 2 casual. adv by the way.

Beileid ('bailait) n neu condolence.

beiliegend ('baili:gənt) adj enclosed.

beim (baim) contraction of **bei dem.**

Bein (bain) n neu -e 1 leg. 2 bone. **—bruch** nm fractured leg.

beinah(e) ('baina:) adv almost, nearly.

Beiname ('baina:mə) nm 1 nickname. 2 surname.

beirren (bə'irən) vt 1 mislead. 2 dissuade.

beisammen (bai'zamən) adv together.

beiseite (bai'zaitə) adv aside, apart.

beisetz/en ('baizetsən) vt 1 add. 2 put on or beside. 3 bury. **—ung** nf -en burial.

Beispiel ('baiʃpi:l) n neu example. **zum/als Beispiel** for example. **—haft** adj exemplary, model. **—los** adj unprecedented. **—sweise** adv for example, for instance.

beiß/en* ('baisən) vt,vi 1 bite. 2 burn. 3 itch.

Beistand ('baiʃtant) nm help, assistance.

beistehen* ('baiʃte:ən) vi aid, assist.

beistimmen ('baiʃtimən) vi agree (with).

Beitrag ('baitra:k) nm ⁻e 1 contribution. 2 fee. **—en*** ('baitra:gən) vt contribute. vi help.

beitreten* ('baitre:tən) vi 1 join. 2 assent (to).

Beiwagen ('baiva:gən) nm 1 side-car. 2 extra carriage.

beiwohnen ('baivo:nən) vi be present, attend.

beizeiten (bai'tsaitən) adv early, on time.

beizen ('baitsən) vt 1 corrode. 2 cauterize. 3 tan. 4 marinate. 5 stain (wood).

bejahen (bə'ja:ən) vt 1 affirm. 2 accept.

bekämpf/en (bə'kempfən) vt 1 fight, combat. 2 oppose. **—ung** nf -en 1 fight, struggle. 2 opposition.

bekannt (bə'kant) adj (well-)known. **—e(r)** nm acquaintance, friend. **—lich** adv as is well known. **—machen** vt announce, make known. **—machung** nf -en 1 publication. 2 announcement. **—schaft** nf -en acquaintance.

bekehr/en (bə'ke:rən) vt convert (to a religion, etc.). **—ung** nf -en (religious) conversion.

bekenn/en* (bə'kenən) vt confess, acknowledge. **Farbe bekennen** 1 be frank. 2 game follow suit. **—tnis** (bə'kentnis) n neu -se 1 confession. 2 denomination.

beklag/en (bə'kla:gən) vt 1 mourn. 2 deplore. **sich beklag/en** vr complain. **—te(r)** (bə'kla:ktə) nm -n accused, defendant.

bekleid/en (bə'klaidən) vt 1 clothe, dress. 2 cover. 3 occupy (a position, office). **—ung** nf clothing.

beklemmen (bə'klemən) vt stifle, oppress.

bekommen* (bə'kɔmən) vt 1 get, obtain. 2 receive. vi agree with (one's health).

bekräftigen (bə'kreftigən) vt 1 confirm. 2 strengthen.

bekreuz(ig)en (bə'krɔytsigən) vt make the sign of the cross over.

bekümmern (bə'kymərn) vt trouble, distress. **sich bekümmern um** 1 care for. 2 worry about.

bekunden (bə'kundən) vt 1 state. 2 show.

beladen* (bə'la:dən) vt load, burden.

Belag (bə'la:k) nm -e coat(ing), cover(ing).

belager/n (bə'la:gərn) vt besiege. **—ung** nf -en siege.

Belang (bə'laŋ) nm -e 1 importance. 2 interest. **—los** adj unimportant, insignificant.

belast/en (bə'lastən) vt 1 load. 2 weigh down (on), burden. 3 accuse. **—ung** nf -en 1 burden, load. 2 charge.

belästig/en (bə'lestigən) vt molest, bother. **—ung** nf -en 1 molestation. 2 inconvenience.

sich belaufen* (bə'laufən) vr **sich belaufen auf** total, amount to.

belauschen (bə'lauʃən) vt eavesdrop on.

beleb/en (bə'le:bən) vt 1 enliven, animate. 2 revive. **—t** adj 1 lively. 2 alive. 3 (of streets) crowded.

19

Beleg (bə'le:k) *n* -e 1 proof. 2 record. 3 evidence. 4 document. **—en** (bə'le:gən) *vt* 1 cover, lay (on). 2 reserve. **—schaft** *nf* -en 1 personnel, staff. 2 shift.

belehr/en (bə'le:rən) *vt* teach, instruct. **—ung** *nf* -en instruction.

beleidig/en (bə'laidigən) *vt* 1 insult. 2 offend. **—ung** *nf* -en 1 insult. 2 offence.

beleucht/en (bə'lɔyçtən) *vt* 1 light (up), illuminate. 2 elucidate. **—ung** *nf* -en 1 lighting. 2 elucidation.

Belg/ien ('bɛlgiən) *n neu* Belgium. **—ier** *nm* — Belgian. **—isch** *adj* Belgian.

Belgrad ('bɛlgra:t) *n neu* Belgrade.

belicht/en (bə'liçtən) *vt phot* expose. **—ung** *nf* -en exposure. **—ungsmesser** *nm* exposure or light meter.

belieb/en (bə'li:bən) *vt* like. *vi* please. *n neu* — 1 liking. 2 pleasure. 3 wish. **nach Belieben** according to one's liking or taste. **—ig** *adj* any, whatever. **—t** (bə'li:pt) *adj* 1 beloved. 2 favourite. **—theit** (bə'li:pthait) *nf* -en popularity.

bellen ('bɛlən) *vi* bark, bay.

belohn/en (bə'lo:nən) *vt* reward, remunerate. **—ung** *nf* -en reward, remuneration.

sich bemächtigen (bə'mɛçtigən) *vr* seize, take possession of.

bemerk/bar (bə'mɛrkba:r) *adj* noticeable, perceptible. **—en** *vt* perceive, notice, observe. **—enswert** *adj* remarkable, notable. **—ung** *nf* -en remark.

bemessen* (bə'mɛsən) *vt* 1 measure, judge. 2 adjust. 3 regulate.

bemitleiden (bə'mitlaidən) *vt* pity, sympathize with.

sich bemüh/en (bə'my:ən) *vr* 1 strive, endeavour. 2 take pains. **—ung** *nf* -en effort, trouble, pains.

benachbart (bə'naxba:rt) *adj* neighbouring.

benachrichtig/en (bə'naxriçtigən) *vt* 1 inform. 2 report. **—ung** *nf* -en 1 notification. 2 information.

Benehmen (bə'ne:mən) *n neu* — behaviour. **sich benehmen** *vr* act, behave.

beneiden (bə'naidən) *vt* envy. **—swert** *adj* enviable.

Benennung (bə'nɛnuŋ) *nf* -en name, term.

Bengel ('bɛŋəl) *nm* — 1 club, cudgel. 2 brat, urchin. 3 rascal. 4 lout.

benutz/en (bə'nutsən) *vt* use, make use of. **—ung** *nf* utilization.

Benzin (bɛn'tsi:n) *n neu* -e *mot* petrol. **—motor** *nm* petrol engine.

beobacht/en (bə'o:baxtən) *vt* 1 observe, watch. 2 keep (silence, etc.). **—er** *nm* — observer. **—ung** *nf* -en observation.

bepflanzen (bə'pflantsən) *vt* plant.

bequem (bə'kve:m) *adj* 1 comfortable. 2 convenient. **—lichkeit** *nf* -en 1 comfort. 2 convenience.

berat/en* (bə'ra:tən) *vt* advise, counsel. **—er** *nm* — adviser. **—ung** *nf* -en 1 consultation. 2 deliberation. **—ungsstelle** *nf* advisory board or office.

berauben (bə'raubən) *vt* 1 rob. 2 deprive.

berauschen (bə'rauʃən) *vt* intoxicate. **sich berauschen** *vr* become enchanted (with).

berechn/en (bə'rɛçnən) *vt* calculate, reckon. **—ung** *nf* calculation, estimate.

berechtig/en (bə'rɛçtigən) *vt* empower, authorize. **—ung** *nf* -en authorization, right, title.

bered/en (bə're:dən) *vt* 1 talk over. 2 persuade. **—sam** (bə're:tza:m) *adj also* **—t** (bə're:t) eloquent. **—samkeit** *nf* eloquence.

Bereich (bə'raiç) *nm* -e 1 region, area, district. 2 range, scope.

bereichern (bə'raiçərn) *vt* enrich.

bereit (bə'rait) *adj* ready, prepared. **—en** *vt* prepare, make (ready). **—halten*** *vt* keep or hold in readiness. **—s** *adv* already. **—schaft** *nf* -en 1 readiness. 2 (police) squad. **—stehen*** *vi* be prepared, stand by. **—ung** *nf* -en preparation. **—willig** *adj* willing, ready.

bereuen (bə'rɔyən) *vt* regret, repent of.

Berg (bɛrk) *nm* -e mountain, hill. **über Berg und Tal** over hill and dale. **—ab** ('bɛrk'ap) *adv* downhill. **—auf** (bɛrk'auf) *adv also* **—an** uphill, upwards. **—arbeiter** *nm* miner. **—bau** *nm* mining. **—kette** *nf* mountain range. **—mann** *nm* -leute miner. **—rutsch** *nm also* **—sturz** landslide. **—steiger** *nm* mountaineer, climber. **—werk** *n neu* mine.

bergen* ('bɛrgən) *vt* 1 save. 2 protect. 3 rescue. 4 conceal.

Bericht (bə'riçt) *nm* -e report, account. **—en** *vt, vi* report. **—erstatter** *nm* — reporter, informant.

berichtig/en (bə'riçtigən) *vt* correct, rectify. **—ung** *nf* -en correction, adjustment.

beritten (bə'ritən) *adj* mounted.

Bernstein ('bɛrnʃtain) *nm* amber.

berüchtigt (bə'ryçtiçt) *adj* notorious.

betreiben° (bə'traibən) vt operate, carry on (a business, etc.).

betreten° (bə'tre:tən) vt **1** step on. **2** enter, set foot in. adj **1** embarrassed. **2** disconcerted.

Betrieb (bə'tri:p) nm **-e 1** works, factory. **2** business. **3** working, operation, running. **4** bustle. **5** traffic. **außer Betrieb** out of order. **in Betrieb** in operation, working. **—sfähig** adj in working order. **—skapital** n neu working capital. **—skosten** nf pl working costs or expenses. **—sleiter** nm (works) manager. **—sordnung** nf company rules. **—sstoff** nm mot fuel. **—sunfall** nm industrial accident, accident at work.

betroffen (bə'trɔfən) adj **1** affected. **2** perplexed.

betrüb/en (bə'try:bən) vt grieve, sadden. **—nis** nf **-se** sorrow, grief.

Betrug (bə'tru:k) nm deceit, fraud. **—en** (bə'try:gən) vt defraud, deceive, cheat. **—er** (bə'try:gər) nm — swindler, cheat, deceiver.

betrunken (bə'truŋkən) adj drunk. **—heit** nf drunkenness.

Bett (bɛt) n neu **-en** bed. **—decke** nf **1** bedspread. **2** blanket. **—en** vt put to bed. **—tuch** n neu sheet. **—wäsche** nf also **—zeug** n neu bedding.

betteln ('bɛtəln) vi beg. **Bettler** ('bɛtlər) nm — beggar.

beugen ('bɔygən) vt **1** bend. **2** gram inflect. **sich beugen** vr **1** bend down or over. **2** bow. **3** humble oneself.

Beule ('bɔylə) nf **-n 1** swelling, boil. **2** dent.

beunruhigen (bə'unru:igən) vt disturb, upset.

beurkunden (bə'u:rkundən) vt prove, authenticate (by means of documents).

beurlauben (bə'u:rlaubən) vt give leave (of absence) to.

beurteil/en (bə'u:rtailən) vt judge, pass judgment on. **—ung** nf **-en** judgment.

Beute ('bɔytə) nf booty, spoil(s).

Beutel ('bɔytəl) nm — **1** bag. **2** purse.

bevölker/n (bə'fœlkərn) vt populate. **—ung** nf **-en** population. **—ungsdichte** nf population density.

bevollmächtig/en (bə'fɔlmɛçtigən) vt empower, authorize. **—te(r)** (bə'fɔlmɛçtiçtə) nm **1** (authorized) representative. **2** proxy. **3** deputy.

bevor (bə'fo:r) conj before. **bevor...nicht** until.

bevorstehen° (bə'fo:rʃte:ən) vi be near, be imminent.

bevorzugen (bə'fo:rtsu:gən) vt prefer.

bewachen (bə'vaxən) vt guard.

bewaffnen (bə'vafnən) vt arm.

bewahr/en (bə'va:rən) vt preserve, keep. **sich —en** vr prove oneself (efficient, successful, etc.). **—ung** nf test, trial. **—ungsfrist** nf probation.

bewältigen (bə'vɛltigən) vt **1** overcome. **2** finish.

bewandert (bə'vandərt) adj knowledgeable, expert.

Bewandtnis (bə'vantnis) nf **-se** condition, circumstance.

bewässer/n (bə'vɛsərn) vt water, irrigate. **—ung** nf watering, irrigation.

beweg/en° (bə've:gən) vt **1** move. **2** induce, persuade. **sich —en** vr move. **—grund** nm motive. **—lich** (bə've:kliç) adj **1** movable, mobile, moving. **2** versatile. **—lichkeit** nf mobility. **—ung** nf en motion, movement.

Beweis (bə'vais) nm **-e** proof. **—aufnahme** nf hearing of evidence. **—en°** (bə'vaizən) vt prove, demonstrate, show. **—grund** nm argument. **—kraft** nf conclusiveness. **—mittel** n neu evidence. **—stück** n neu **1** exhibit. **2** evidence.

bewenden (bə'vɛndən) vi **es dabei bewenden lassen** let the matter rest (at that).

sich bewerb/en° (bə'vɛrbən) vr **sich bewerben um 1** apply for. **2** seek. **—er** nm — **1** applicant. **2** competitor. **3** suitor.

bewerkstelligen (bə'vɛrkʃtɛligən) vt manage, accomplish.

bewillig/en (bə'viligən) vt **1** allow, grant. **2** approve. **—ung** nf **-en 1** consent, approval. **2** grant, allowance.

bewirken (bə'virkən) vt cause, effect.

bewirten (bə'virtən) vt **1** entertain. **2** receive.

bewohn/en (bə'vo:nən) vt inhabit. **—er** nm — inhabitant.

bewölkt (bə'vœlkt) adj cloudy, overcast.

Bewunder/er (bə'vundərər) nm — admirer. **—n** vt admire. **—nswert** adj admirable. **—ung** nf admiration.

bewußt (bə'vust) adj **1** conscious, aware. **2** deliberate. adv knowingly. **die bewußten Personen** the people in question. **—heit** nf awareness, consciousness. **—los** adj unconscious. **—sein** n neu consciousness.

bezahl/en (bə'tsa:lən) vt pay (for). **—ung** nf **-en** payment.

bezaubern (bə'tsaubərn) vt bewitch, enchant, charm.

bezeichn/en (bə'tsaiçnən) vt **1** mark. **2** designate, indicate. **—end** adj characteristic.

—ung nf -en 1 mark, sign. 2 marking. 3 designation.

bezeugen (bəˈtsɔygən) vt bear witness to, certify.

bezieh/en* (bəˈtsiːən) vt 1 cover. 2 move into. 3 receive. 4 obtain. **sich beziehen auf** vr relate to, refer to. **—ung** nf -en 1 reference. 2 relation(ship), connection. **—ungsweise** adv 1 or. 2 that is to say.

Bezirk (bəˈtsirk) nm -e district, area.

Bezug (bəˈtsuːk) nm 1 cover(ing). 2 comm supply, purchase. 3 pl income. **bezüglich (auf)** also **in Bezug auf** with regard to, concerning.

bezwecken (bəˈtsvɛkən) vt aim at.

bezweifeln (bəˈtsvaifəln) vt doubt, question.

bezwingen* (bəˈtsviŋən) vt 1 overcome. 2 master.

Bibel (ˈbiːbəl) nf -n Bible.

Biber (ˈbiːbər) nm — beaver.

Bibliographie (bibliograˈfiː) nf -n bibliography.

Bibliothek (biblioˈteːk) nf -en library. **—ar** (biblioteˈkaːr) nm -e librarian.

biblisch (ˈbiːbliʃ) adj biblical.

bieder (ˈbiːdər) adj 1 upright, honest. 2 simple-minded. **—mann** nm honest fellow.

biegen* (ˈbiːgən) vt bend.

Biene (ˈbiːnə) nf -n bee. **—nkorb** nm beehive.

Bier (biːr) n neu -e beer. **—garten** nm beer garden, (open air) cafe. **—krug** nm beermug.

bieten* (ˈbiːtən) vt offer.

Bigamie (bigaˈmiː) nf -n bigamy.

bigott (biˈgɔt) adj bigoted.

Bikini (biˈkiːniː) -s bikini.

Bilanz (biˈlants) nf -en balance (sheet).

Bild (bilt) n neu -er picture, image. **—erbuch** (ˈbildərbuːx) n neu picture book. **—fläche** nf 1 field of vision. 2 television or cinema screen. **—hauer** nm — sculptor. **—nis** n neu -se likeness, portrait. **—säule** nf statue. **—schön** adj lovely, (most) beautiful.

bild/en* (ˈbildən) vt 1 form. 2 educate. **—ung** nf -en 1 education. 2 culture. 3 formation, creation.

Billard (ˈbiljart) n neu -s billiards.

Billett (bilˈjɛt) n neu -e 1 note. 2 ticket.

billig (ˈbiliç) adj 1 cheap. 2 reasonable, just. **—en** (ˈbiligən) vt approve (of), sanction. **—keit** nf -en 1 cheapness. 2 fairness. **—ung** (ˈbiliguŋ) nf approval.

Bimsstein (ˈbimsʃtain) nm pumice-stone.

bin (bin) v see **sein²**.

Bind/e (ˈbində) nf -n 1 band. 2 bandage, sling. 3 sanitary towel. **—eglied** n neu connecting link. **—ostrich** nm hyphon. **—owort** n nou conjunction. **—faden** (ˈbintfaːdən) nm string, twine. **—ung** nf -en 1 bond. 2 binding.

binden* (ˈbindən) vt bind, tie.

binnen (ˈbinən) prep within. **—handel** nm domestic trade. **—land** n neu interior, inland.

Biographie (biograˈfiː) nf -n biography.

Biolog/e (bioˈloːgə) nm -n biologist. **—ie** (bioloˈgiː) nf biology. **—isch** (bioˈloːgiʃ) adj biological.

Birne (ˈbirnə) nf -n 1 pear. 2 (light) bulb.

bis (bis) prep 1 to. 2 up to. 3 until. conj 1 until. 2 by. **er wird bis morgen ankommen** he will arrive by tomorrow.

Bisam (ˈbiːzam) nm -e musk.

Bischof (ˈbiʃɔf) nm -̈e bishop.

bisexuell (bizɛksuˈɛl) adj hermaphroditic, bisexual.

bisher (bisˈheːr) adv until now, so far. **—ig** adj previous, until now.

biß (bis) v see **beißen**.

Biß (bis) nm **Bisse** bite. **—chen** (ˈbisçən) n neu,adj a little, a bit. **Bissen** (ˈbisən) nm — morsel, bite. **bissig** (ˈbisiç) adj 1 (of dogs) snappish. 2 cutting, biting.

bist (bist) v see **sein²**.

Bistum (ˈbistuːm) n neu -̈er bishopric.

bisweilen (bisˈvailən) adv sometimes.

bitt/e (ˈbitə) interj please! nf -n request. **—en*** (ˈbitən) vt ask, beg, request. **—schreiben** n neu also **—schrift** nf petition.

bitter (ˈbitər) adj 1 bitter. 2 severe. **—keit** nf bitterness.

Biwak (ˈbiːvak) n neu -s bivouac.

Bizeps (ˈbiːtsɛps) nm -e biceps.

Blam/age (blaˈmaːʒə) nf -n disgrace, scandal. **—ieren** (blaˈmiːrən) vt disgrace, compromise (someone). **sich —ieren** vr make a fool of oneself.

blank (blaŋk) adj 1 shiny, bright. 2 bare, naked.

blanko (ˈblaŋko) adj blank. **—scheck** nm blank cheque. **—vollmacht** nf full power of attorney.

Blas/e (ˈblaːzə) nf -n 1 blister. 2 bubble. 3 bladder. **—en*** vi,vt blow. **—instrument** n neu wind instrument. **—kapelle** nf brass band.

blaß (blas) adj pale. **Blässe** (ˈblɛsə) nf pallor, paleness.

Blatt (blat) n neu -̈er 1 leaf, blade. 2 page, sheet (of paper). 3 newspaper. **—̈ern**

('blɛtərn) vi **1** turn over the pages. **2** skim through a book. **˝-erteig** ('blɛtərtaik) nm puff-pastry.

blau (blau) adj **1** blue. **2** inf tipsy. n neu blue. **—beere** nf bilberry. **˝-e** ('bloyə) nf **1** blueness, azure. **—papier** n neu carbon paper.

Blech (blɛç) n neu **-e 1** sheet metal. **2** tin.

Blei (blai) n neu **-e** lead.

bleiben* ('blaibən) vi remain, stay.

bleich (blaiç) adj pale, pallid. **—e** nf **-n** paleness, pallor. **—en*** vt bleach. vi turn white or pale. **—sucht** nf anaemia.

Bleistift ('blaiʃtift) nm **-e** pencil. **—spitzer** nm — pencil-sharpener.

Blend/e ('blɛndə) nf **-n 1** blind, shutter. **2** phot diaphragm. **—en** vt **1** blind, dazzle. **2** deceive.

Blick (blik) nm **-e 1** look, glance. **2** gaze. **—en** vi look, glance.

blieb (bli:p) v see **bleiben.**

blind (blint) adj **1** blind. **2** false. **3** hidden. **4** tarnished. **blinder Passagier** nm stowaway. **—darm** nm anat appendix. **—darmentzündung** nf appendicitis. **—heit** nf blindness.

blinzeln ('blintsəln) vi **1** twinkle. **2** blink. **3** wink.

Blitz (blits) nm **-e** lightning. **—ableiter** nm — lightning-conductor. **—en** vi flash, lighten. **—krieg** nm lightning war, blitzkrieg. **—licht** n neu (photographic) flash. **—schnell** adj as quick as lightning.

Block/ade (blɔ'ka:də) nf **-n** blockade. **—flöte** ('blɔkfløːtə) nf music recorder. **—ieren** (blɔ'kiːrən) vt **1** obstruct, block. **2** blockade. jam.

blöd (bløːt) adj **1** silly, stupid. **2** imbecile. **3** shy, timid. **—heit** ('bløːthait) nf **-en** stupidity. **—sinn** ('bløːtsin) nm **1** nonsense. **2** idiocy. **—sinnig** ('bløːtsiniç) adj idiotic, silly.

blond (blɔnt) adj blond, light-coloured, fair.

bloß (bloːs) adj **1** bare. **2** mere. adv only, simply. **—stellen** vt expose.

blühen ('blyːən) vi **1** bloom, blossom. **2** flourish.

Blume ('bluːmə) nf **-n 1** flower. **2** aroma. **3** (of wine) bouquet. **—nkohl** nm cauliflower. **—nstrauß** nm bouquet. **—nzwiebel** n bulb.

Bluse ('bluːzə) nf **-n** blouse.

Blut (bluːt) n neu blood. **—arm** adj **1** anaemic. **2** extremely poor. **—egel** nm — leech. **—en** vi bleed. **—ig** adj **1** bloody. **2** complete, total. **—rünstig** adj bloody, blood-thirsty. **—schande** nf incest. **—spender** nm med blood-

donor. **—sturz** nm bleeding, haemorrhage. **—übertragung** nf blood transfusion. **—wurst** nf black pudding.

Blüte ('blyːtə) nf **-n 1** blossom, flower. **2** prime. **—zeit** nf **1** blossom-time. **2** prosperity, heyday.

Bö (bœ:) nf **-en** squall, gust.

Bock (bɔk) nm **˝-e 1** ram, he-goat. **2** buck. **3** sport buck (for vaulting). **4** trestle. **5** strut. **—bier** n neu strong dark beer. **—wurst** nf (thick) frankfurter sausage.

Boden ('boːdən) nm **˝- 1** ground, soil. **2** bottom, bed. **reform** nf land reform. **—schätze** nm pl mineral resources. **—tür** nf trap-door.

Bodensee ('boːdɑnze:) nm Lake Constance.

Bogen ('boːgən) nm **— 1** curve, arch. **2** mus, sport bow. **3** sheet (of paper). **—gang** nm arcade, colonnade. **—linie** nf curve. **—schütze** nm archer.

Böhm/e ('bœːmə) nm **-n** Bohemian. **—en** n neu Bohemia. **—isch** adj Bohemian.

Bohne ('boːnə) nf **-n** bean.

Bohnenkaffee ('boːnənkafe:) nm pure coffee.

bohr/en ('boːrən) vt, vi bore, drill. **—er** nm — borer, drill, gimlet.

Boje ('boːjə) nf **-n** buoy.

Bollwerk ('bɔlvɛrk) n neu bulwark.

Bolzen ('bɔltsən) nm **— 1** bolt, peg. **2** bolt, arrow.

Bombe ('bɔmbə) nf **-n** bomb. **—nerfolg** nm huge success. **—r** nm — bomber.

Bonbon (bõ'bõ) nm, neu **-s** sweet.

Bonze ('bɔntsə) nm **-n** sl boss, bigwig.

Boot (boːt) n neu **-e** boat.

Bord (bɔrt) nm **-e** border, rim. **an Bord** on board.

Bordell (bɔr'dɛl) n neu **-e** brothel.

borgen ('bɔrgən) vt borrow.

Borke ('bɔrkə) nf **-n** bark, rind.

Börse ('bœːrzə) nf **-n 1** purse. **2** stock exchange. **—nkurs** nm market rate.

Borste ('bɔrstə) nf **-n** bristle.

bös/artig ('bœːzartiç) adj **1** evil, malicious. **2** (illness) malignant. **—e** ('bœːzə) adj **1** evil, bad. **2** angry. **3** (of disease) malignant. **—ewicht** ('bœːzəviçt) nm **-e** villain, evil person.

bos/haft ('boːshaft) adj spiteful, malicious. **—heit** ('boːshait) nf **-en 1** spite, malice. **2** wickedness.

Boß (bɔs) nm **-e** inf boss, manager.

bot (boːt) v see **bieten.**

Botan/ik (bo'ta:nik) *nf* botany. **—iker** *nm* — botanist. **—isch** *adj* botanic(al).

Bot/e ('bo:tə) *nm* -n messenger. **—schaft** *nf* -en 1 embassy. 2 message. **—schafter** *nm* — ambassador.

Bottich ('bɔtiç) *nm* -e vat, tub.

Bowle (bo:lə) *nf* -n 1 bowl. 2 fruit cup, punch.

box/en ('bɔksən) *vi* box. **—er** *nm* — boxer.

brach[1] (brax) *v* see **brechen.**

brach[2] (brax) *adj* fallow, uncultivated.

brachte ('braxtə) *v* see **bringen.**

Branche ('brã:ʃə) *nf* -n 1 trade, line (of business). 2 department, branch.

Brand (brant) *nm* ̈-e 1 fire, burning. 2 gangrene. 3 mildew. **in Brand setzen** or **stecken** set on fire. **—bombe** *nf* incendiary bomb. **—sohle** *nf* inner sole, welt. **—stifter** *nm* incendiary, fire-raiser. **—stiftung** *nf* arson.

Brandung ('branduŋ) *nf* -en surf, breakers.

Branntwein ('brantvain) *nm* -e brandy.

Brasil/ianer (brazili'a:nər) *nm* — Brazilian. **—ianisch** *adj* Brazilian. **—ien** (bra'zi:liən) *n neu* Brazil.

brat/en° ('bra:tən) *vt,vi* 1 roast. 2 fry. 3 grill, broil. *n neu* — roast, joint. **—kartoffel** *nf* fried or roast potato. **—pfanne** *nf* frying pan. **—wurst** *nf* fried sausage.

Brauch (braux) *nm* ̈-e 1 custom. 2 usage. **—bar** *adj* 1 useful. 2 serviceable. **—en** *vt* 1 need, want. 2 use.

Braue ('brauə) *nf* -n brow.

brau/en ('brauən) *vt* brew. **—er** *nm* — brewer. **—erei** (brauə'rai) *nf* -en brewery.

braun (braun) *adj* brown. ̈-en ('brɔynən) *vi,vt* brown, tan.

Braunschweig ('braunʃvaik) *n neu* Brunswick.

Brause ('brauzə) *nf* -n 1 shower. 2 nozzle, spray. 3 mineral water. 4 lemonade. **—n** *vi* 1 effervesce. 2 spray, shower. 3 roar, rage.

Braut (braut) *nf* ̈-e 1 bride. 2 fiancée. ̈-igam ('brɔytigam) *nm* -e 1 bridegroom. 2 fiancé. **—jungfer** *nf* bridesmaid. **—kleid** *n neu* wedding dress. **—paar** *n neu* 1 bridal pair. 2 engaged couple.

brav (bra:f) *adj* 1 good. 2 honest. 3 brave.

brech/en° ('brɛçən) *vt* 1 break, crush. 2 refract. **—bohne** *nf* French bean.

Brei (brai) *nm* -e 1 pap, pulp 2 porridge.

breit (brait) *adj* broad, wide. **—e** *nf* -n 1 breadth, width. 2 latitude. 3 verbosity. **—en** *vt* spread (out), broaden. **—engrad** *nm* degree of latitude.

Brems/e[1] ('brɛmzə) *nf* -n brake. **—en** *vt,vi*

---

brake, apply the brakes. **—schuh** *nm* brake shoe.

Bremse[2] ('brɛmzə) *nf* -n gadfly, horse-fly.

brenn/bar ('brɛnba:r) *adj* inflammable. **—en**° *vi* burn, sting. *vt* 1 burn. 2 roast. 3 distil. **—er** *nm* — 1 (gas) burner. 2 distiller. 3 fire-raiser. **—erei** (brɛnə'rai) *nf* -en distillery, still. **—essel** ('brɛnnɛsəl) *nf* -n stinging-nettle. **—holz** *n neu* firewood. **—material** *n neu* fuel. **—punkt** *nm* focus, focal point. **—stoff** *nm* fuel.

Brett (brɛt) *n neu* -er 1 board, plank. 2 shelf.

Brezel ('bre:tsəl) *nf* -n pretzel.

bricht (briçt) *v* see **brechen.**

Brief (bri:f) *nm* -e letter. **—fach** *n neu* 1 pigeon-hole. 2 post-office box. **—kasten** *nm* letter box. **-lich** *adj* by letter. **—marke** *nf* (postage) stamp. **—tasche** *nf* wallet, pocketbook. **—träger** *nm* postman. **—umschlag** *nm* envelope. **—wechsel** *nm* correspondence.

Brigade (bri'ga:də) *nf* -n brigade.

Brikett (bri'kɛt) *n neu* -s briquette.

brillant (bril'jant) *adj* brilliant.

Brille ('brilə) *nf* -n 1 spectacles. 2 goggles.

bringen° ('briŋən) *vt* 1 bring. 2 take. 3 fetch. 4 lead. 5 carry. **jemanden um etwas bringen** deprive someone of something. **jemanden dazu bringen** induce someone to.

Brit/annien (bri'taniən) *n neu* Britain. **—e** ('britə) *nm* **—n** Briton. **—isch** ('britiʃ) *adj* British.

bröckel/ig ('brœkəliç) *adj* crumbly. **—n** *vt,vi* crumble.

Brokkoli ('brɔkoli) *n pl* broccoli.

Brom (bro:m) *n neu* bromine.

Brombeere ('brɔmbe:rə) *nf* -n blackberry.

Bronze ('brõ:sə) *nf* -n bronze.

Brosche ('brɔʃə) *nf* -n brooch.

Broschüre (brɔ'ʃy:rə) *nf* -n pamphlet, booklet, brochure.

Brot (bro:t) *n neu* -e 1 bread. 2 loaf. ̈-chen ('brøe:tçən) *n neu* — roll, bun.

Bruch (brux) *nm* ̈-e 1 break(ing), breach. 2 fracture. 3 rupture. 4 fraction. 5 crease, fold. **—ig** ('bryçiç) *adj* 1 fragile, brittle. 2 cracked. **—stück** *n neu* fragment. **—teil** *nm* fraction.

Brücke ('brykə) *nf* -n bridge.

Bruder ('bru:dər) *nm* ̈- brother. ̈-lich ('bry:-dərliç) *adj* fraternal. **—schaft** *nf* -en fraternity, brotherhood. ̈-schaft ('bry:dərʃaft) *nf* -en friendship.

Brühe (ˈbryːə) nf -n broth, stock, soup.
brüllen (ˈbrylən) vi 1 bellow. 2 roar.
Brumm/bär (ˈbrumbɛːr) nm,inf grumbler. **—en** vi 1 hum, buzz. 2 growl, grumble.
brünett (bryˈnɛt) adj brunette.
Brunnen (ˈbrunən) nm — 1 well. 2 fountain. 3 spring. **—kresse** nf watercress.
Brunst (brunst) nf ̶e 1 zool rut, heat. 2 (sexual) lust. **—ig** (ˈbrynstiç) adj 1 in heat. 2 lustful.
Brüssel (ˈbrysəl) n neu Brussels.
Brust (brust) nf ̶e breast, chest. **—bild** n neu half-length portrait. **—kasten** nm chest, thorax.
brutal (bruˈtaːl) adj brutal.
brüten (ˈbrytən) vi,vt 1 brood. 2 incubate.
brutto (ˈbruto) adj gross.
Bub(e) (ˈbuːbə) nm -(e)n 1 boy. 2 rogue. 3 game knave.
Buch (buːx) n neu ̶er book. **—erei** (byːçaˈrai) nf -en library. **—erschrank** (ˈbyːçərʃraŋk) nm bookcase. **—fink** nm chaffinch. **—halter** nm comm bookkeeper. **—handel** nm 1 book trade. 2 bookselling. **händler** nm bookseller. **—handlung** nf bookshop. **—lein** (ˈbyːçlain) n neu — booklet.
Buche (ˈbuːxə) nf -n beech.
Büchse (ˈbyksə) nf -n 1 box. 2 tin, can.
Buchstab/e (ˈbuːxʃtaːbə) nm -n letter, character. **großer Buchstabe** capital letter. **—ieren** (buːxʃtaˈbiːrən) vt spell. **—ierung** (buːxʃtaˈbiːruŋ) nf -en spelling. **—lich** (ˈbuːxʃtaˈpliç) adj literal.
Bucht (buxt) nf -en 1 bay, inlet. 2 bight.
Buck/el (ˈbukəl) nm — 1 bulge, hump. 2 humpback. 3 stud, boss.
sich bücken (ˈbykən) vr 1 bow. 2 stoop.
Bude (ˈbuːdə) nf -n 1 stall, booth. 2 inf digs, rooms.
Büfett (byˈfɛt) n neu -s buffet.
Büffel (ˈbyfəl) nm — buffalo, bison.
Bug (buːk) nm -e 1 naut bow. 2 aviat nose. 3 (of animals) shoulder.
Bügel (ˈbyːgəl) nm — 1 hanger. 2 grip. 3 stirrup. **—eisen** n neu (clothes) iron. **—n** vt iron, press.
Bühne (ˈbyːnə) nf -n 1 stage. 2 theatre.
Bulgar/ien (bulˈgaːriən) n neu Bulgaria. **—ier** nm — Bulgarian. **—isch** adj Bulgarian.
Bulle (ˈbulə) nm -n 1 bull. 2 sl policeman, copper.
Bumm/el (ˈbuməl) nm — stroll. **—eln** vi 1 stroll. 2 loiter. **—ler** nm — idler, loafer.

bumsen (ˈbumzən) vi bump. vi,vt tab copulate, have sexual intercourse.
Bund (bunt) nm ̶e 1 band. 2 league, (con)federation. n neu -e bundle, bunch. **—esgenosse** nm ally, confederate. **—eskanzler** nm Federal Chancellor. **—espräsident** nm president (of a federal state). **—esrat** nm 1 Upper House of Parliament (in Austria and West Germany). 2 Executive Federal Council (in Switzerland). **—esrepublik** nf Federal Republic. **Bundesrepublik Deutschland, B.R.D.** nf Federal Republic of Germany, F.R.G. **—esstaat** nm 1 federal state. 2 member state of a federation. **—estag** nm 1 (Lower House of) West German Parliament. **—eswehr** nf West German armed forces. **—nis** (ˈbyntnis) n neu -se alliance.
Bündel (ˈbyndəl) n neu — bundle, bunch.
bunt (bunt) adj colourful, bright.
Bürde (ˈbyrdə) nf -n burden.
Burg (burk) nf -en 1 castle. 2 fortress.
Bürg/e (ˈbyrgə) nm -n surety, guarantor, bail. **—en** vi 1 vouch (for). 2 stand bail (for). **—schaft** (ˈbyrkʃaft) nf surety, bond.
Bürger (ˈbyrgər) nm —, **Bürger/in** nf -nen 1 citizen. 2 townsman or townswoman. 3 bourgeois. **—krieg** nm civil war. **—lich** adj 1 middle-class. 2 civil(ian). 3 unpretentious, simple. **—meister** nm mayor. **—recht** n neu 1 civic rights. 2 citizenship. **—schaft** nf -en citizens. **—stand** nm middle class(es). **—steig** nm pavement.
Büro (byˈroː) n neu -s office. **—krat** (byroˈkraːt) nm -en bureaucrat. **—kratie** (byrokraˈtiː) nf bureaucracy.
Bursche (ˈburʃə) nm -n 1 youth, lad. 2 student. 3 orderly. 4 servant. 5 apprentice.
Bürst/e (ˈbyrstə) nf -n brush. **—en** vt brush.
Busch (buʃ) nm ̶e 1 bush(land). 2 shrub(s). 3 thicket. 4 tuft. **—ig** adj bushy.
Busen (ˈbuːzən) nm — 1 breast, bosom. 2 gulf, bay.
Buß/e (ˈbuːsə) nf -n 1 penance. 2 fine. **—en** (ˈbyːsən) vt,vi atone for, pay (for), do penance (for). **—er** (ˈbyːsər) nm penitent.
Büste (ˈbystə) nf -n bust. **—nhalter** nm bra, brassiere.
Butter (ˈbutər) nf butter. **—brot** n neu (slice of) bread and butter.

C

Café (ka'fe:) n neu **-s** cafe, coffee-house.

Camping ('kɛmpiŋ) n neu camping.

Cape (ke:p) n neu **-s** cape.

Cell/ist (tʃɛ'list) nm **-en** cellist. **—o** ('tʃɛlo) n neu **-s** cello.

Champagner (ʃam'panjər) nm — champagne.

Champignon ('ʃampinjɔ̃) nm **-s** mushroom.

Chance ('ʃā:sə) nf **-n** chance.

Chao/s ('ka:ɔs) n neu chaos. **—tisch** (ka'o:tiʃ) adj chaotic.

Charakter ('karaktər) nm **-e 1** character, nature. **2** letter, character. **—isieren** (karaktəri'zi:rən) vt characterize. **—istik** (karakta'ristik) nf **-en** characterization. **—istisch** (karakta'ristiʃ) adj characteristic.

charmant (ʃar'mant) adj charming.

Chauffeur (ʃo'fœ:r) nm **—** e driver, chauffeur.

Chaussee (ʃo'se:) nf **-n** main or high road.

Chef (ʃɛf) nm **-s** head, boss.

Chemi/e (çe'mi:) nf chemistry. **—kalien** (çemi'ka:liən) nf pl chemicals. **—ker** ('çe:mikər) nm — chemist (in science or industry). **—sch** ('çe:miʃ) adj chemical. **chemische Reinigung** dry cleaning.

Chil/e ('tʃi:lə) n neu Chile. **—ene** (tʃi'le:nə) nm **-n** Chilean. **—enisch** (tʃi'le:niʃ) adj Chilean.

Chin/a ('çi:na) n neu China. **—ese** (çi'ne:zə) nm **-n** Chinaman, Chinese. **—esisch** (çi'ne:ziʃ) adj Chinese.

Chirurg (çi'rurk) nm **-en** surgeon. **—ie** (çirur'gi:) nf surgery.

Chlor (klo:r) n neu chlorine.

Chloroform (kloro'fɔrm) n neu **-e** chloroform.

Chor (ko:r) nm **⸚e** choir, chorus.

Christ (krist) nm **-en** Christian. **—baum** nm Christmas tree. **—enheit** nf Christendom. **—entum** n neu Christianity. **—kind** n neu Christ-child. **—lich** adj Christian. **—us** ('kristus) nm Christ.

Chrom (kro:m) n neu chromium, chrome.

Chronik ('kro:nik) nf **-en** chronicle.

Computer (kɔm'pju:tər) nm — computer.

Creme (kre:m) nf **-s 1** cream. **2** cream pudding.

D

da (da) adv **1** there. **2** here. **3** then. conj **1** as. **2** when. **3** since.

dabei (da'bai) adv **1** by it. **2** nearby. **3** present. **4** at the same time. **5** thereby.

Dach (dax) n neu **⸚er** roof. **—boden** nm attic. **—fenster** n neu **—** skylight. **—luke** nf **-n** skylight. **—rinne** also **—traufe** nf **-n 1** eaves. **2** gutter.

Dachs (daks) nm **-e** badger.

Dachshund ('dakshunt) nm dachshund.

dachte ('daxtə) v see **denken.**

dadurch (da'durç) adv **1** through there. **2** thus, in that way.

dafür (da'fy:r) adv for that, in return.

dagegen (da'ge:gən) adv **1** against it. **2** in comparison. conj on the other hand, but.

daher (da'he:r) adv **1** from there. **2** therefore.

dahin (da'hin) adv there, to that place. **bis dahin** until then. **dahin sein** be lost or gone.

dahinten (da'hintən) adv behind (there).

dahinter (da'hintər) adv behind it or that. **—kommen*** vi find out (about it).

damals ('da:ma:ls) adv then, at that time.

Dame ('da:mə) nf **-n 1** lady. **2** game queen. **—spiel** n neu draughts.

damit (da'mit) adv **1** with or by it. **2** thereby. conj in order to, so (that).

Damm (dam) nm **⸚e 1** dam, dyke, embankment. **2** roadway. **⸚en** ('dɛman) vt dam, restrain.

Dämmerung ('dɛməruŋ) nf **-en 1** dawn. **2** dusk, twilight.

Dampf (dampf) nm **⸚e** steam, vapour. **—en** vi **1** steam. **2** inf smoke. **—maschine** nf steam engine. **—schiff** n neu steamship.

dämpf/en ('dɛmpfən) vt **1** quieten, muffle. **2** steam. **—er** nm — **1** damper, silencer **2** extinguisher.

danach (da'na:x) adv **1** after(wards). **2** accordingly.

Dän/e ('dɛ:nə) nm **-n** Dane. **—emark** ('dɛ:nəmark) n neu Denmark. **—isch** ('dɛ:niʃ) adj Danish. n neu Danish (language).

daneben (da'ne:bən) adv **1** near it. **2** nearby. **3** beside. conj. moreover, as well.

Dank (daŋk) nm. thanks. **vielen** or **schönen Dank!** many thanks! **—bar** adj thankful, grateful. **—barkeit** nf gratitude. **—e** interj thanks! thank you! **—en** vi thank.

dann (dan) adv then.

daran (da'ran) *adv also* **dran** at, on or by it or that. **daran gehen** set to work.

darauf (da'rauf) *adv also* **drauf 1** on it or that, thereupon. **2** later.

daraus (da'raus) *adv also* **draus 1** from or out of it or that. **2** from there.

darbieten* ('da:rbi:tən) *vt* offer, tender.

dareln (da'rain) *adv also* **drein** into it or that, therein.

darf (da:rf) *v see* **dürfen.**

darin (da'rin) *adv also* **drin** in it, that or there, within.

Darlegung ('da:rle:guŋ) *nf* -en statement, exposition.

Darlehen ('da:rle:ən) *n neu* — loan.

Darm (darm) *nm* -̈e intestine, bowel, gut.

darstell/en ('da:rʃtɛlən) *vt* **1** present, show. **2** represent, depict. —**ung** *nf* -en **1** presentation. **2** description, statement.

darüber (da'ry:bər) *adv* **1** about it or that. **2** over, above or beyond it or that. **darüber hinaus 1** moreover. **2** over and above that, beyond that.

darum (da'rum) *adv* **1** about or around it or that. **2** therefore.

darunter (da'runtər) *adv* **1** under it or that, underneath. **2** among them.

das (das) *def art* the. *pron* that, which.

dasein* ('da:zain) *vi* exist, be present. *n neu* existence, being, presence.

daß (das) *conj* that. **daß nicht** lest. **so daß** so that.

datieren (da'ti:rən) *vt* date.

Datum ('da:tum) *n neu* -ten date.

Dauer ('dauər) *nf* duration, period. **auf die Dauer** in the long run. —**haft** *adj* durable, lasting. —**lauf** *nm* endurance run. —**n** *vi* last, continue, take (time). **lange dauern** take a long time. —**nd** *adj* lasting, constant, permanent.

Daumen ('daumən) *nm* — thumb.

Daunendecke ('daunəndɛkə) *nf* (continental) quilt, duvet, eiderdown.

davon (da'fɔn) *adv* of, from or about it or that. —**kommen*** *vi* get away. —**tragen*** *vt* carry off.

davor (da'fo:r) *adv* **1** before or in front of it or that. **2** of or from it or that.

dawider (da'vi:dər) *adv* against it or that.

dazu (da'tsu:) *adv* **1** to or for it or that. **2** for that purpose. **3** in addition. —**kommen*** *vi* arrive, happen. —**tun*** *vt* add.

dazwischen (da'tsviʃən) *adv* **1** between or

among (them). **2** meanwhile. —**kommen*** *vi* **1** intervene, prevent. **2** come between. —**treten*** *vi* intervene.

Debatt/e (de'batə) *nf* -n debate, discussion.

Debet ('de:bɛt) *n neu* -s debit.

Deck (dɛk) *n neu* -e *naut* deck.

Deck/e ('dɛkə) *nf* -n **1** cover, blanket. **2** ceiling. —**el** *nm* — lid, cover. —**on** *vt* cover. **den Tisch decken** set or lay the table. —**mantel** *nm* **1** pretext. **2** cloak. **3** cover. —**name** *nm* assumed name. —**ung** *nf* -en **1** cover(ing), protection. **2** *mil* cover. **3** *comm* security.

defensiv (defɛn'zi:f) *adj* defensive. —**e** (defɛn'zi:və) *nf* -n **1** defensive. **2** defence.

defin/ieren (defi'ni:rən) *vt* define. —**ition** (definitsi'o:n) *nf* -en definition.

Defizit ('de:fitsit) *n neu* -e deficit.

Degen ('de:gən) *nm* — sword.

degenerieren (degene'ri:rən) *vi* degenerate.

dehnen ('de:nən) *vt* stretch, lengthen, expand.

Deich (daiç) *nm* -e dyke, embankment.

dein (dain) *poss adj,pron 2nd pers s fam* your, yours. —**er** *poss pron 2nd pers s fam* also **der** —**e** *or* **der** —**ige** yours. —**erseits** ('dainərzaits) *adv* on your part. —**esgleichen** *pron* people like you. —**ethalben** *adv* also —**etwegen** *or* —**etwillen** for your sake, on your account.

dekaden/t (deka'dɛnt) *adj* decadent. —**z** (deka'dɛnts) *nf* decadence.

Dekan (de'ka:n) *nm* -e dean.

Deklination (deklinatsi'o:n) *nf* -en *gram* declension.

Dekret (de'kre:t) *n neu* -e decree.

delikat (deli'ka:t) *adj* **1** delicate. **2** delicious.

Delikt (de'likt) *n neu* -e offence, crime.

Delphin (dɛl'fi:n) *nm* -e dolphin.

dem (de:m) *def art* to it. *pron* to it, that or whom.

dementieren (demɛn'ti:rən) *vt* deny.

demgemäß ('de:mgəmɛ:s) *adv* accordingly.

Demission (demisi'o:n) *nf* -en resignation.

demnach ('de:mna:x) *adv* accordingly.

demnächst ('de:mnɛçst) *adv* soon.

Demokrat (demo'kra:t) *nm* -en democrat. —**isch** *adj* democratic. —**ie** (demokra'ti:) *nf* -n democracy.

Demonstr/ation (demɔnstratsi'o:n) *nf* -en demonstration. —**ieren** (demɔn'stri:rən) *vt,vi* demonstrate.

Demut ('de:mu:t) *nf* humility. —**ig** ('de:my:tiç)

adj humble. **-igen** (ˈdeːmyːtigən) *vt* humble, humiliate.

demzufolge (ˈdeːmtsufɔlgə) *adv* accordingly.

den (deːn) *def art* 1 the. 2 *pl* (to) the. *pron* 1 that, which, whom. 2 *pl* to these or those. **denen** *pron* to these or those.

denk/en* (ˈdɛŋkən) *vt,vi* think. **denken an** or **über** think of or about. **—bar** *adj* conceivable. **—er** *nm* — thinker. **-mal** *n neu* **-er** monument, memorial. **—schrift** *nf* **-en** inscription, memorial. 2 report. 3 memorandum. **—(ungs)art** *nf* — way of thinking, mentality. **—würdig** *adj* notable, memorable.

denn (dɛn) *conj* for. *adv* then. **es sei denn, (daß)** unless.

dennoch (ˈdɛnɔx) *adv* yet, however.

Departement (departˈmãː) *n neu* **-s** department.

Depesche (deˈpɛʃə) *nf* **-n** 1 dispatch. 2 telegram.

deponieren (depoˈniːrən) *vt* deposit.

Depression (depresiˈoːn) *nf* **-en** depression.

deprimieren (depriˈmiːrən) *vt* depress.

der (deːr) *def art* 1 the. 2 of the. *pron* that, which, who.

derart (ˈdeːraːrt) *adv* in such a way. **—ig** *adj* such, of that kind.

derb (dɛrp) *adj* 1 sturdy, sound. 2 rough, coarse, crude.

deren (ˈdeːrən) *pron* whose, of which.

dergestalt (ˈdeːrgəʃtalt) *adv* in such a way.

dergleichen (deːrˈglaiçən) *pron* such (a thing), the like, of the kind.

derjenige, diejenige, dasjenige (ˈdeːrjeːnigə, ˈdiːjeːnigə, ˈdasjeːnigə) *pron m,f,neu* he or she who, that which, the one which.

dermaßen (ˈdeːrmaːsən) *adv* to such a degree.

derselbe, dieselbe, dasselbe (deːrˈzɛlbə, diːˈzɛlbə, dasˈzɛlbə) *pron m,f,neu* the same.

derzeitig (ˈdeːrtsaitiç) *adj* 1 present. 2 of or at that time.

des (dɛs) *def art* of the.

desgleichen (dɛsˈglaiçən) *pron* such (a thing). *adv* likewise.

deshalb (dɛsˈhalp) *adv* therefore.

Desin/fektionsmittel (dezinfɛktsiˈoːnzmitəl) *n neu* — disinfectant. **—fizieren** (dezinfiˈtsiːrən) *vt* disinfect.

dessen (ˈdɛsən) *pron* whose, of which. **—ungeachtet** (dɛsənungeˈaxtət) *adv* nevertheless.

desto (ˈdɛsto) *adv* so much, the. **je...desto**

the...the. **je mehr, desto besser** the more the better.

deswegen (dɛsveːgən) *adv* therefore.

Detail (deˈtai) *n neu* **-s** detail, item. **—handel** *nf* retail trade. **en detail** *adv* retail.

deut/en (ˈdɔytən) *vi* point (to). *vt* 1 explain. 2 show. **—lich** *adj* clear, distinct. **—lichkeit** *nf* distinctness. **—ung** *nf* **-en** explanation, interpretation.

deutsch (dɔytʃ) *adj* German. *n neu* German (language). **auf Deutsch** in German. **—e(r)** *nm* German. **—e Demokratische Republik, D.D.R.** *nf* German Democratic Republic, G.D.R. **—kunde** *nf* German studies. **—land** *n neu* Germany. **—sprachig** *adj* German-speaking. **—tum** *n neu* German nature or culture.

Devise (deˈviːzə) *nf* **-n** 1 *pl* foreign exchange. 2 motto, slogan.

Dezember (deˈtsɛmbər) *nm* December.

Dialekt (diaˈlɛkt) *nm* **-e** dialect.

Diamant (diaˈmant) *nm* **-en** diamond.

Diapositiv (diːapoziˈtiːf) *n neu* slide, transparency.

Diät (diˈɛːt) *nf* — diet.

Diäten (diˈɛːtən) *nf pl* allowance(s).

dich (diç) *pron* 2nd pers *s fam* you, yourself.

dicht (diçt) *adj* 1 dense, thick. 2 tight. 3 close (to). **—igkeit** *nf* **-en** *also* **—heit** 1 density, thickness. 2 imperviousness.

dicht/en (ˈdiçtən) *vt* compose (poetry). **—er** *nm* — poet. **—ung** *nf* **-en** 1 poetry, poem. 2 fiction.

dick (dik) *adj* thick, fat, large. **-e** *nf* **-n** 1 thickness, fatness. 2 size. **-kopf** *nm* thickhead. **—icht** *n neu* **-e** thicket.

die *def art* the. *pron* that, which, who, whom.

Dieb (diːp) *nm* **-e** thief, robber. **—isch** (ˈdiːbiʃ) *adj* thieving, dishonest. **—stahl** *nm* **-e** theft.

Diele (ˈdiːlə) *nf* **-n** 1 board, plank. 2 hall(way).

dien/en (ˈdiːnən) *vi* serve. **—er** *nm* — man-servant. **—erin** *nf* **-nen** maid-servant. **—erschaft** *nf* **-en** servants. **—st** (diːnst) *nm* **-e** 1 service. 2 duty. **außer Dienst** off duty. **—stbereit** *adj* ready for service. **—ststelle** *nf* place of work or service.

Dienstag (ˈdiːnstaːk) *nm* Tuesday.

dieser, diese, dieses (ˈdiːzər, ˈdiːzə, ˈdiːzəs) *pron,adj m,f,neu* this.

diesmal (ˈdiːsmaːl) *adv* this time.

diesseits (ˈdiːszaits) *adv* on this side.

Dietrich (ˈdiːtriç) *nm* **-e** skeleton key.

Diktat (dikˈtaːt) *n neu* **-e** 1 dictation. 2

command, decree. **—or** (dik'ta:tɔr) nm **-en** dictator. **—ur** (dikta'tu:r) nf **-en** dictatorship.

diktieren (dik'ti:rən) vt dictate.

Diner (di'ne:) n neu **-s** dinner.

Ding (dıŋ) n neu **-e** thing, object.

Diplom (di'plo:m) n neu **-e** diploma, certificate.

dir (di:r) pron 2nd pers s fam (to) you, yourself.

Dirig/ent (diri'gɛnt) nm **-en** mus conductor. **—ieren** (diri'gi:rən) vt **1** direct. **2** mus conduct.

Dirne ('dırnə) nf **-n 1** prostitute. **2** girl.

diskont/ieren (diskɔn'ti:rən) vt comm discount. **—satz** nm bank rate.

Diskothek (diskο'te:k) nf **-en** discotheque.

Disku/ssion (diskusi'o:n) nf **-en** discussion. **—tieren** (disku'ti:rən) vt,vi discuss, debate.

disponieren (dispο'ni:rən) vt,vi arrange, dispose.

Distel ('dıstəl) nf **-n** thistle.

Disziplin (distsi'pli:n) nf **-en** discipline.

doch (dɔx) adv **1** nevertheless. **2** indeed, really. conj but, however, yet.

Docht (dɔxt) nm **-e** wick.

Dock (dɔk) n neu **-s** dock(yard). **—arbeiter** nm docker.

Dogge ('dɔgə) nf **-n** bulldog.

Dogma ('dɔgma) n neu **-s** dogma. **—tisch** (dɔg'ma:tiʃ) adj dogmatic.

Doktor ('dɔktɔr) nm **-en** doctor.

Dolch (dɔlç) nm **-e** dagger.

dolmetsch/en ('dɔlmɛtʃən) vt,vi interpret. **—er** nm — interpreter.

Dom (do:m) nm **-e** cathedral. **—herr** nm rel canon.

dominieren (domi'ni:rən) vi,vt dominate, domineer.

Donau ('do:nau) nf Danube.

Donner ('dɔnər) nm thunder. **—n** vi thunder, roar.

Donnerstag ('dɔnərsta:k) nm Thursday.

Doppel ('dɔpəl) n neu — **1** duplicate. **2** double. **—bett** n neu double bed. **—decker-bus** nm double-decker bus. **—ehe** nf bigamy. **—n** vt double. **—punkt** nm colon. **—sinn** nm ambiguity. **—t** adj double.

Dorf (dɔrf) n neu **-er** village, hamlet. **—be-wohner** also **—ler** ('dɔrfbəvo:nər, 'doerflər) nm — villager.

Dorn (dɔrn) nm **-en** thorn. **—ig** adj thorny.

Dorsch (dɔrʃ) nm **-e** cod.

dort (dɔrt) adv there. **—her** adv from there. **—hin** adv to there or that place. **—ig** adj of that place or there.

Dose ('do:zə) nf **-n 1** box. **2** tin, can.

dösen ('dœzən) vi inf doze.

Dosis ('do:zis) nf **-sen** dose (of medicine etc.). **zu starke Dosis** overdose.

Dotter ('dɔtə) nm — yolk.

Dozent (do'tsɛnt) nm **-en** university or college lecturer.

Drache ('draxə) nm **-n** dragon.

Draht (dra:t) nm **-e** wire, cable. **—los** adj wireless. **—seilbahn** nf funicular, cable railway.

Drama ('dra:ma) n neu **-men** drama. **—tiker** (dra'ma:tikər) nm — playwright. **—tisch** (dra'ma:tiʃ) adj dramatic.

dran (dran) adv see **daran**.

Drang (draŋ) nm **-e 1** drive, urge, stress. **2** pressure. **—en** ('drɛŋən) vi,vt **1** press, hurry, urge. **2** crowd.

drapieren (dra'pi:rən) vt drape.

drauf (drauf) adv see **darauf**.

draußen ('drausən) adv outside, out of doors.

Dreck (drɛk) nm **1** filth, dirt. **2** excrement. **—ig** adj filthy, dirty, muddy.

dreh/en ('dre:ən) vt,vi **1** turn, twist, wind. **2** shoot (a film). **—bank** nf **-e** lathe. **—buch** n neu (film) script. **—punkt** nm pivot. **—scheibe** nf turntable. **—ung** nf **-en** turn, rotation, revolution.

drei (drai) adj,nf three. **—bein** n neu tripod. **—eck** n neu triangle. **—eckig** adj triangular. **—einigkeit** nf **-sen** Trinity. **—faltigkeit** nf — Trinity. **—erlei** ('draiərlai) adj of three kinds. **—fach** adj triple, threefold. **—mal** adv three times. **—rad** n neu tricycle.

dreißig ('draisiç) adj,nf thirty. **dreißigste** adj thirtieth.

dreist (draist) adj **1** impudent. **2** bold.

dreizehn ('draitse:n) adj,nf thirteen. **dreizehnte** adj thirteenth.

dresch/en* ('drɛʃən) vt thresh. **—flegel** nm flail.

dressieren (drɛ'si:rən) vt train (an animal).

drin (drin) adv see **darin**. **—nen** adv inside, indoors.

dring/en* ('driŋən) vi **1** urge, force, press. **2** penetrate. **—end** adj also **—lich** urgent.

dritt(e) (drit) adj third. **—el** n neu — one third, third part. **—ens** adv thirdly.

Drog/e ('dro:gə) nf **-n** drug. **—erie** (drogə'ri:) nf **-n** chemist's shop.

droh/en ('dro:ən) vi threaten. **—ung** nf **-en** threat.

Drohne ('dro:nə) nf **-n** drone.

drollig (ˈdrɔliç) adj droll, funny.

Drossel (ˈdrɔsəl) nf -n 1 thrush. 2 tech throttle.

drüben (ˈdryːbən) adv on the other side, over there.

drüber (ˈdryːbər) adv see **darüber.**

Druck (druk) nm 1 -e print, printing. 2 ⁼e pressure. **—en** vt print. **—er** nm — printer. **—erei** (drukəˈrai) nf -en printing works. **—fehler** nm misprint. **—knopf** nm 1 snap fastener. 2 push-button.

drück/en (ˈdrykən) vt,vi 1 press (on), squeeze. 2 oppress. **sich drücken** vr dodge work, shirk.

drunten (ˈdruntən) adv (there) below, down there.

drunter (ˈdruntər) adv see **darunter.**

Drüse (ˈdryːzə) nf -n gland.

Dschungel (ˈdʒuŋəl) nm,f,neu -n jungle.

du (duː) pron 2nd pers s fam you.

ducken (ˈdukən) vt duck.

Dudelsack (ˈduːdəlzak) nm ⁼e bagpipes.

Duell (duˈɛl) n neu -e duel. **sich —ieren** (duɛˈliːrən) vr duel.

Duett (duˈɛt) n neu -e duet.

Duft (duft) nm ⁼e aroma, scent. **—en** vi smell (sweet), be fragrant.

dulden (ˈduldən) vt suffer, bear, tolerate.

dumm (dum) adj stupid, silly. **—heit** nf -en 1 stupidity. 2 foolish action. **—kopf** nm blockhead, fool.

dumpf (dumpf) adj 1 musty, close (atmosphere). 2 dull, hollow (sound).

Düne (ˈdyːnə) nf -n dune.

Dünger (ˈdyŋər) nm dung, manure.

dunkel (ˈduŋkəl) adj 1 dark, dim, gloomy. 2 obscure. **—kammer** nf darkroom.

dünn (dyn) adj 1 thin. 2 sparse.

Dunst (dunst) nm ⁼e vapour, haze, smoke. **⁼en** (ˈdynstən) vt cul 1 steam. 2 stew.

Dur (duːr) n neu mus major.

durch (durç) prep through, during, by. adv completely, thoroughly.

durchaus (durçˈaus) adv absolutely, completely.

durchblicken (ˈdurçblikən) vt,vi look through, see through. **durchblicken lassen** give to understand.

durchbohren (ˈdurçboːrən) vt bore through, pierce.

durchbrechen* (ˈdurçbrɛçən) vt,vi break through or out. (durçˈbrɛçən) vt break through.

durchdringen* (vi ˈdurçdriŋən; vt durçˈdriŋən)

vi press or get through. vt 1 permeate. 2 penetrate.

durcheinander (durçainˈandər) adv 1 in confusion. 2 upset. n neu — disorder.

Durchfahrt (ˈdurçfaːrt) nf -en 1 passage or journey through. 2 passageway. 3 gateway.

Durchfall (ˈdurçfal) nm ⁼e 1 failure. 2 diarrhoea.

durchforschen (durçˈfɔrʃən) vt investigate.

durchführen (ˈdurçfyːrən) vt 1 lead through. 2 carry out.

Durchgang (ˈdurçgaŋ) nm ⁼e passage. **durchgehen*** (ˈdurçgeːən) vi 1 go or walk through. 2 run away. vt 1 examine. 2 wear out.

durch/lassen* (ˈdurçlasən) vt let through, pass. **—lässig** (ˈdurçlɛsiç) adj permeable.

durchlaufen* (ˈdurçlaufən) vi run through. vt wear out. (durçˈlaufən) vt run through.

durchleuchten (vi ˈdurçlɔyçtən; vt durçˈlɔyçtən) vi shine through. vt 1 X-ray. 2 investigate. 3 search.

durchlöchern (durçˈlœçərn) vt perforate, pierce.

durchmachen (ˈdurçmaxən) vt go through, experience, endure.

Durchmesser (ˈdurçmɛsər) nm — diameter.

durchqueren (durçˈkveːrən) vt cross, traverse.

Durchreise (ˈdurçraizə) nf -n passage, transit, journey through.

durchs (durçs) contraction of **durch das.**

durchschauen (vi ˈdurçʃauən; vt durçˈʃauən) vi look through. vt 1 see through. 2 examine.

Durchschlag (ˈdurçʃlaːk) nm ⁼e 1 carbon (copy). 2 strainer. 3 tech punch. **—papier** n neu carbon paper.

Durchschnitt (ˈdurçʃnit) nm -e 1 average. 2 cutting through. 3 (cross-)section. **—lich** adj average. **—smensch** nm man in the street.

durchsehen* (ˈdurçzeːən) vt 1 look through. 2 examine.

durchsichtig (ˈdurçziçtiç) adj transparent.

durchsuchen (ˈdurçzuːxən) vt examine (closely).

durchtrieben (durçˈtriːbən) adj cunning.

durchweg (ˈdurçvɛk) adv throughout.

sich durchwinden* (ˈdurçvindən) vr struggle through.

durchziehen* (ˈdurçtsiːən) vi march through. vt interlace. (durçˈtsiːən) vt draw or pass through.

dürfen* (ˈdyrfən) v mod aux be allowed, may.

dürftig (ˈdyrftiç) adj needy, poor.

dürr (dyr) adj 1 dry, arid. 2 thin. 3 barren.

Durst (durst) nm thirst. **—ig** adj thirsty.
Dusche ('duʃə) nf **-n** shower. **—n** vt shower.
Düse ('dy:zə) nf **-n** jet, nozzle. **—nflugzeug** n neu jet (plane).
düster ('dy:stər) adj dark, dusky, gloomy.
Dutzend ('dutsənt) n neu **-e** dozen.
duzen ('du:tsən) vt address (someone) familiarly with **du.**
Dynam/ik (dy'na:mik) nf dynamics. **—isch** adj dynamic.
Dynamit (dyna'mi:t) n neu **-e** dynamite.
Dynast/ie (dynas'ti:) nf dynasty.
D-Zug ('de:tsu:k) nm **-̈e** express train.

E

Ebbe ('ɛbə) nf **-n** ebb, low-tide. **—n** vi ebb.
eben ('e:bən) adj 1 level, even. 2 smooth. adv just, precisely. **—bild** n neu image. **—bürtig** ('e:bənbyrtiç) adj equal, of equal rank. **—e** nf **-n** 1 plain. 2 math plane. **—falls** adv likewise. **—heit** nf **-en** evenness, smoothness. **—holz** n neu ebony. **—so** adv just as. **der eine ist ebenso gut wie der andere** the one is just as good as the other. **—soviel** adv just as much.
Eber ('e:bər) nm **—** boar.
ebnen ('e:bnən) vt level, make smooth.
Echo ('ɛço) n neu **-s** echo.
echt (ɛçt) adj 1 genuine, real, authentic. 2 pure.
Eck (ɛk) n neu **-e** also **Eck/e** ('ɛkə) nf **-n** 1 corner. 2 angle. **—ig** adj angular. **—stein** nm 1 corner stone. 2 game diamonds.
edel ('e:dəl) adj noble, aristocratic. **—frau** nf noblewoman. **—mann** nm, pl **-leute** nobleman. **—mütig** ('e:dəlmy:tiç) adj magnanimous, generous. **—stein** nm precious stone, gem.
Edikt (e'dikt) n neu **-e** edict.
Edinburg ('e:dinburk) n neu Edinburgh.
Efeu ('e:fɔy) nm **-s** ivy.
Effekt/en (ɛ'fɛktən) n pl 1 comm securities, bonds. 2 personal effects, belongings. **—iv** (ɛfɛk'ti:v) adj 1 actual. 2 effective.
egal (e'ga:l) adv 1 even. 2 equal, the same.
Egoismus (ego'ismus) nm egoism.
ehe (e:) conj before. **—dem** (e:ə'de:m) adv also **—mals** formerly. **—malig** ('e:əma:liç) adj former. **—r** adv 1 sooner, before. 2 rather.
Ehe ('e:ə) nf **-n** marriage. **—brecher** nm **—** adulterer. **—brecherin** nf **-nen** adulteress.

—bruch nm adultery. **—frau** nf wife. **—lich** adj 1 matrimonial. 2 (of a child) legitimate. **—mann** nm husband. **—paar** n neu married couple. **—stand** nm matrimony, married state. **—scheidung** nf divorce.
Ehr/e ('e:rə) nf **-n** honour. **—en** vt honour. **—enwort** n neu word of honour. **—erbietig** adj respectful, deferential. **—furcht** nf reverence, awe, respect. **—geiz** nm ambition. **—geizig** adj ambitious. **—lich** adj 1 honest. 2 sincere. 3 fair. **—lichkeit** nf honesty. **—würdig** adj venerable.
Ei (ai) n neu **-er** egg.
Eich/e ('aiçə) nf **-n** oak. **—el** nf **-n** 1 acorn. 2 game clubs. **—hörnchen** ('aiçhœrnçən) n neu **—** squirrel.
Eid (ait) nm **-e** oath. **einen Eid abnehmen** administer an oath. **unter Eid** on oath. **—bruch** nm perjury. **—genosse** nm **—** 1 confederate. 2 Swiss. **—genossenschaft** nf **-en** 1 confederation. 2 Swiss Confederation, Switzerland. **—genössisch** ('aitgənœsiʃ) adj 1 federal. 2 Swiss.
Eidechse ('aidɛksə) nf **-n** lizard.
Eier/becher ('aiərbɛçər) nm eggcup. **—kuchen** nm 1 (sweet) omelette. 2 pancake. **—schale** nf eggshell.
Eif/er ('aifər) nm zeal, fervour. **—ersucht** nf jealousy. **—ersüchtig** adj jealous. **—rig** adj zealous, eager.
Eigelb ('aigɛlp) n neu **-e** (egg) yolk.
eigen ('aigən) adj 1 own, proper. 2 characteristic. 3 strange. 4 particular, exact.
Eigenart ('aigəna:rt) nf **-en** 1 peculiarity. 2 character. **—ig** adj peculiar.
eigenhändig ('aigənhɛndiç) adj in or by one's own hand, by oneself.
eigenmächtig ('aigənmɛçtiç) adj arbitrary.
Eigenname ('aigənna:mə) nm proper name.
Eigennutz ('aigənnuts) nm self-interest, selfishness. **—ig** adj selfish.
Eigenschaft ('aigənʃaft) nf **-en** characteristic, trait, quality. **—swort** n neu adjective.
Eigensinn ('aigənzin) nm obstinacy. **—ig** adj obstinate.
eigentlich ('aigəntliç) adj 1 real. 2 proper. 3 true. adv 1 actually. 2 just. 3 indeed.
Eigentum ('aigəntu:m) n neu **-er** property. **-̈er** nm **—** owner. **—lich** adj 1 peculiar, characteristic. 2 peculiar, strange.
sich eignen ('aignən) vr suit, be qualified.
Eil/bote ('ailbo:tə) nm express messenger. **—brief** nm express letter. **—e** nf haste,

hurry, speed. **—en** vi also **sich —en** vr hurry, hasten. **—ig** adj hurried, hasty. **—zug** nm fast train.

Eimer (ˈaimər) nm — bucket, pail.

ein, eine, ein (ain, ˈainə) indef art m,f,neu a, an. adj one. **einer, eine, eins** (ˈainər, ˈainə, ains) pron one.

einander (aiˈnandər) pron each other, one another.

einatmen (ˈaina:tmən) vt,vi inhale, breathe in.

Einbahnstraße (ˈainba:nʃtra:sə) nf one-way street.

einbalsamieren (ainbalzaˈmi:rən) vt embalm.

Einband (ˈainbant) nm ⁼e binding, cover (of a book).

einbegreifen* (ˈainbəɡraifən) vt comprise, include.

einbiegen* (ˈainbi:ɡən) vt bend in(wards). vi turn in(to).

sich einbild/en (ˈainbildən) vr imagine. **—ung** nf imagination. **—ungskraft** nf (power of) imagination.

Einblick (ˈainblik) nm 1 insight. 2 glimpse.

einbrech/en* (ˈainbrɛçən) vt,vi 1 break open, down or into. 2 burgle. **—er** nm — burglar.

einbürgern (ˈainbyrɡərn) vt naturalize. **sich einbürgern** vr 1 settle. 2 (of a word, etc.) come into use.

einbüßen (ˈainby:sən) vt 1 lose. 2 forfeit.

eindeutig (ˈaindɔytiç) adj unequivocal, clear.

eindring/en* (ˈaindriŋən) vi 1 enter by force, invade. 2 penetrate.

Eindruck (ˈaindruk) nm ⁼e impression. **—svoll** adj impressive.

einerlei (ˈainərlai) adj of one sort or kind.

einerseits (ˈainərzaits) adv on the one hand.

einfach (ˈainfax) adj 1 simple, plain. 2 single.

einfahr/en* (ˈainfa:rən) vi drive in. vt 1 bring in. 2 break in (horses). **—t** nf -en entrance, drive.

Einfall (ˈainfal) nm ⁼e 1 collapse, fall. 2 invasion. 3 brainwave, sudden idea. **—en*** vi collapse, fall. v imp occur (to someone). **es fiel mir ein** it (suddenly) occurred to me.

einfältig (ˈainfɛltiç) adj simple, stupid.

Einfassung (ˈainfasuŋ) nf -en 1 border (of a dress). 2 enclosure.

sich einfinden* (ˈainfindən) vr turn up, appear.

einflechten* (ˈainflɛçtən) vt 1 plait, interlace. 2 put in (a word, etc.).

Einfluß (ˈainflus) nm -flüsse 1 influx. 2 influence. **—reich** adj influential.

einförmig (ˈainfœrmiç) adj 1 uniform. 2 monotonous.

einfügen (ˈainfy:ɡən) vt 1 insert. 2 join. **sich einfügen** vr adapt, fit in.

Einfuhr (ˈainfu:r) nf -en import(ation). **⁼en** (ˈainfy:rən) vt 1 bring in, introduce. 2 import. 3 install. **—er** (ˈainfy:rər) nm — importer. **—ung** (ˈainfy:ruŋ) nf -en introduction. **—zoll** nm import duty.

Eingang (ˈaingaŋ) nm ⁼e 1 entrance. 2 arrival, receipt (of a letter, etc.). 3 introduction, beginning.

eingebildet (ˈainɡəbildət) adj 1 imaginary. 2 conceited.

eingeboren (ˈainɡəbo:rən) adj 1 native. 2 innate. **—e(r)** nm native.

Eingebung (ˈainɡəbuŋ) nf -en inspiration.

eingehen* (ˈainɡe:ən) vi 1 go or walk in(to), enter. 2 cease. 3 shrink, wither. 4 die. vt conclude (agreement, etc.). **ein Risiko eingehen** run a risk.

eingenommen (ˈainɡənɔmən) adj biased, prejudiced.

Eingeweide (ˈainɡəvaidə) n neu pl intestines, bowels.

eingießen* (ˈainɡi:sən) vt pour in or out.

eingreifen* (ˈainɡraifən) vi 1 intervene, interfere. 2 catch.

einhalten* (ˈainhaltən) vt 1 observe, respect (conditions). 2 restrain. vi stop.

einhändigen (ˈainhɛndiɡən) vt deliver, hand over.

einheimisch (ˈainhaimiʃ) adj native.

Einheit (ˈainhait) nf -en 1 unit. 2 unity. **—lich** adj uniform.

einholen (ˈainho:lən) vt 1 gather (in). 2 shop. 3 catch up.

einig (ˈainiç) adj united, agreed. **—e** (ˈainiɡə) pron,adj a few, some. **—en** vt unite. **sich —en** vr agree. **—ermaßen** (ainiɡərˈma:sən) adv to a certain extent, somewhat. **—keit** (ˈainiçkait) nf unity, concord. **—ung** (ˈainiɡuŋ) nf -en 1 unification. 2 agreement.

einkassieren (ainkasi:rən) vt cash.

Einkauf (ˈainkauf) nm ⁼e purchase. **—en** vt buy. **einkaufen gehen** go shopping. **—er** (ˈainkɔyfər) nm — purchaser. **—spreis** nm wholesale or trade price.

einkehren (ˈainke:rən) vi stop or stay overnight.

Einklang (ˈainklaŋ) nm unison, harmony.

einkommen* (ˈainkɔmən) vi 1 come in. 2 apply. n neu — income, revenue. **—steuer** nf income tax.

einkreisen (ˈainkraizən) vt encircle.

Einkünfte (ˈainkynftə) nf pl revenue, income.

einlad/en* (ˈainlaːdən) vt 1 invite. 2 load. **—ung** nf -**en** 1 invitation. 2 loading.

Einlage (ˈainlaːgə) nf -**n** 1 insert, enclosure. 2 deposit, investment. 3 med arch-support. 4 cul meat or vegetables, etc., added to soup. **—rn** vt store up.

Ein/laß (ˈainlas) nm -**lässe** entrance, admission. **—lassen*** vt admit, put or let in. **sich —lassen*** vr engage in.

einlaufen* (ˈainlaufən) vi 1 enter, arrive. 2 shrink.

einleg/en (ˈainleːgən) vt 1 lay or put in, inlay. 2 insert, enclose. 3 deposit. 4 preserve, pickle. **—er** nm — depositor.

einleit/en (ˈainlaitən) vt 1 introduce. 2 begin. **—ung** nf -**en** introduction.

einlösen (ˈainløːzən) vt comm redeem.

einmachen (ˈainmaxən) vt preserve, pickle (food).

einmal (ˈainmaːl) adv 1 once, one time. 2 formerly, sometime. **noch einmal** once again. **—eins** n neu multiplication table. **—ig** adj unique.

Einmarsch (ˈainmarʃ) nm ⁻e marching in, entry. **—ieren** (ainmarˈʃiːrən) vi march in.

sich einmischen (ˈainmiʃən) vr interfere.

einmünden (ˈainmyndən) vi 1 flow into. 2 join, run into.

Ein/nahme (ˈainnaːmə) nf -**n** 1 income. 2 takings. **—nehmen*** (ˈainneːmən) vt 1 take in (food etc.). 2 receive. 3 influence.

Einöde (ˈainøːdə) nf -**n** 1 desert. 2 isolated place.

einordnen (ˈainɔrdnən) vt 1 arrange, order. 2 file. 3 mot get in lane.

einpacken (ˈainpakən) vt pack or wrap up. vi pack or give up.

einprägen (ˈainprɛːgən) vt impress, imprint.

einrahmen (ˈainraːmən) vt frame.

einräumen (ˈainrɔymən) vt 1 give up, vacate. 2 clear away. 3 concede, admit.

einreden (ˈainreːdən) vt persuade. vi interrupt.

einreichen (ˈainraiçən) vt hand in, submit.

einreihen (ˈainraiən) vt 1 arrange, order. 2 insert. 3 enrol.

Einreise (ˈainraizə) nf -**n** entry (into a country). **—n** vi enter (a country).

einricht/en (ˈainriçtən) vt 1 arrange. 2 establish, set up. 3 fit out, furnish. **—ung** nf -**en** 1 arrangement. 2 institution. 3 furnishing, fittings.

einrücken (ˈainrykən) vi enter. vt insert.

eins (ains) nf -**en** 1 one. 2 ace. pron see **ein.**

einsam (ˈainzaːm) adj lonely. **—keit** nf loneliness, solitude.

Einsatz (ˈainzats) nm 1 insertion, putting in. 2 stake, deposit. 3 employment, engagement.

einschalten (ˈainʃaltən) vt 1 insert. 2 switch on. 3 tune in.

einschiffen (ˈainʃifən) vt load onto a ship.

einschlafen* (ˈainʃlaːfən) vi fall asleep.

Einschlag (ˈainʃlaːk) nm 1 impact. 2 jacket (of a book). 3 touch, hint. 4 woof, weft. **—en*** (ˈainʃlaːgən) vt 1 drive in. 2 strike. 3 wrap. vi shake hands (on a deal).

einschließ/en* (ˈainʃliːsən) vt 1 lock up or in, confine. 2 include. **—lich** adj inclusive of.

einschränk/en (ˈainʃrɛŋkən) vt 1 restrict, confine. 2 curb. **—ung** nf -**en** 1 restriction. 2 reduction.

Einschreib/ebrief (ˈainʃraibəbriːf) nm registered letter. **—en*** vt 1 write in. 2 take down. 3 register. **—ung** nf -**en** registration.

einschüchtern (ˈainʃyçtərn) vt intimidate.

einsehen* (ˈainzeːən) vt 1 understand. 2 look into.

einseitig (ˈainzaitiç) adj one-sided. **—keit** nf bias, one-sidedness.

einsetz/en (ˈainzɛtsən) vt 1 set or put in. 2 insert. 3 institute. 4 employ. vi begin. **—ung** nf -**en** 1 putting in. 2 institution. 3 appointment.

Einsicht (ˈainziçt) nf -**en** 1 insight, understanding. 2 judgment. 3 inspection.

Einsiedler (ˈainziːdlər) nm — hermit, recluse.

einspannen (ˈainʃpanən) vt 1 harness. 2 stretch. 3 clamp.

einsperren (ˈainʃpɛrən) vt lock up, imprison.

einspritzen (ˈainʃpritsən) vt inject.

Einspruch (ˈainʃprux) nm objection, protest. **—srecht** n neu veto.

einst (ainst) adv 1 once. 2 some day.

einsteigen* (ˈainʃtaigən) vi get or climb in.

einstell/en (ˈainʃtɛlən) vt 1 put in. 2 stop, cease, shut down. 3 employ. 4 strike. 5 adjust, tune in. **—ung** nf -**en** 1 attitude. 2 adjustment. 3 stoppage, suspension. 4 appointment, taking on.

einstig (ˈainstiç) adj former.

einstimm/en (ˈainʃtimən) vi 1 agree. 2 join in. **—ig** adj unanimous, in unison. **—igkeit** nf unanimity, unison.

einstmalig (ˈainstmaːliç) adj former.

einstoßen* (ˈainʃtoːsən) vt 1 push in. 2 knock down.

einströmen (ˈainʃtrœːmən) vi stream or flock in, pour in.

einstufen (ˈainʃtuːfən) vt grade, classify.

einstürmen (ˈainʃtyrmən) vi 1 rush in. 2 assault.

Einsturz (ˈainʃturts) · nm 1 collapse. 2 fall. **–en** (ˈainʃtyrtsən) vi fall in. vt demolish.

einstweil/en (ˈainstvailən) adv 1 meanwhile. 2 for now. **–ig** adj temporary.

eintägig (ˈaintɛːɡiç) adj one-day.

Eintausch (ˈaintauʃ) nm **-e** exchange. **–en** vt barter, exchange.

Einteilung (ˈaintailuŋ) nf **-en** 1 division. 2 classification.

eintönig (ˈaintœːniç) adj monotonous. **–keit** nf monotony.

Eintopf (ˈaintɔpf) nm stew, casserole.

Eintracht (ˈaintraxt) nf harmony, unity.

Eintrag (ˈaintraːk) nm **-e** 1 comm registration, entry. 2 damage, detriment. **–en*** (ˈaintraːɡən) vt 1 bring in, yield. 2 register, enter.

eintreten* (ˈaintreːtən) vi 1 step or come in. 2 happen. 3 intercede. vt kick in.

Eintritt (ˈaintrit) nm 1 entry. 2 beginning. **–skarte** nf admission ticket.

einüben (ˈainyːbən) vt 1 practise. 2 train.

einverleiben (ˈainfɛrlaibən) vt 1 incorporate. 2 annex.

einverstanden (ˈainfɛrʃtandən) adj 1 agreed. 2 agreeable.

Einwand (ˈainvant) nm ¨e 1 objection. 2 pretext. **–frei** adj faultless.

Einwander/er (ˈainvandərər) nm — immigrant. **–n** vi immigrate. **–ung** nf **-en** immigration.

einwärts (ˈainvɛrts) adv inward(s).

einwechseln (ˈainvɛksəln) vt (ex)change.

einweichen* (ˈainvaiçən) vt soak, steep.

einweih/en (ˈainvaiən) vt 1 inaugurate. 2 consecrate. 3 initiate. **–ung** nf **-en** 1 inauguration. 2 consecration. 3 initiation.

Einwendung (ˈainvɛnduŋ) nf **-en** objection.

einwickel/n (ˈainvikəln) vt 1 wrap (up). 2 entangle, implicate (someone). **–papier** n neu wrapping paper.

einwillig/en (ˈainviliɡən) vi agree, consent. **–ung** nf **-en** consent.

Einwirkung (ˈainvirkuŋ) nf **-en** 1 influence. 2 effect.

Einwohner (ˈainvoːnər) nm — inhabitant.

Einzahl (ˈaintsaːl) nf gram singular. **–en** vt pay in. **–ung** nf **-en** 1 payment. 2 deposit.

Einzel/fall (ˈaintsəlfal) nm individual case. **–gänger** nm — outsider, loner. **–heit** nf **-en** detail, item. **–person** nf individual.

einziehen* (ˈaintsiːən) vt 1 draw in. 2 collect. 3 call up. 4 seize. vi 1 move in. 2 enter.

einzig (ˈaintsiç) adj single, sole, unique. **–artig** adj unique, singular.

Einzug (ˈaintsuːk) nm entry.

Eis (ais) n neu **-e** 1 ice. 2 ice cream. **–bahn** nf skating rink. **–bär** nm polar bear. **–bein** n neu knuckle of pork. **–berg** nm iceberg. **–ig** adj icy. **–kalt** adj ice-cold. **–schrank** nm refrigerator. **–zapfen** nm icicle. **–zeit** nf ice age.

Eisen (ˈaizən) n neu iron. **–bahn** nf 1 railway. 2 train. **–bahnwagen** nm railway carriage. **–beton** nm reinforced concrete. **–warenhändler** nm ironmonger.

eisern (ˈaizərn) adj 1 iron. 2 hard, inflexible. **Eiserner Vorhang** nm Iron Curtain.

eitel (ˈaitəl) adj 1 vain, conceited. 2 frivolous. 3 idle. **–keit** nf vanity.

Eiter (ˈaitər) nm pus. **–n** vi suppurate.

Eiweiß (ˈaivais) n neu **-e** egg white, albumen.

Ekel (ˈeːkəl) nm aversion, disgust. **–haft** adj loathsome, repulsive. **sich –n** vr feel disgust or loathing.

elastisch (eˈlastiʃ) adj elastic.

Elefant (eleˈfant) nm elephant.

elegant (eleˈɡant) adj elegant.

elektr/ifizieren (elɛktrifiˈtsiːrən) vt electrify (railway). **–iker** (eˈlɛktrikər) nm — electrician. **–isch** (eˈlɛktriʃ) adj electric(al). **–isieren** (elɛktriˈziːrən) vt electrify. **–izität** (elɛktritsiˈtɛːt) nf electricity. **–ode** (elɛkˈtroːdə) nf **-n** electrode. **–on** (eˈlɛktrɔn) n neu **-en** electron.

Element (eleˈmɛnt) n neu **-e** 1 element. 2 battery, cell. **–ar** (elemɛnˈtaːr) adj elementary, elemental.

elend (ˈeːlɛnt) adj miserable. n neu 1 misery. 2 poverty. **–sviertel** n neu slum(s).

elf (ɛlf) adj,nf eleven. **–te** adj eleventh.

Elf (ɛlf) nm **-en** also **Elfe** nf **-n** elf, fairy.

Elfenbein (ˈɛlfənbain) n neu ivory.

Elite (eˈliːtə) nf **-n** elite.

Ellbogen (ˈɛlboːɡən) nm — elbow.

Ellipse (ɛˈlipsə) nf **-n** ellipse.

El/saß (ˈɛlzas) n neu Alsace. **–sässich** adj Alsatian. **–sässer** nm — Alsatian.

Elster (ˈɛlstər) nf **-n** magpie.

elter/lich (ˈɛltərliç) adj parental. **–n** n pl parents.

Email (e'ma:j) *n neu* **-s** enamel.

Emigr/ant (emi'grant) *nm* **-en 1** emigrant. **2** refugee. **—ieren** (emi'gri:rən) *vi* emigrate.

empfahl (ɛm'pfa:l) *v* see **empfehlen.**

Empfang (ɛm'pfaŋ) *nm* **-̈e** reception, welcome. **in Empfang nehmen** receive. **—en*** *vt* receive. *vi* conceive. **-̈er** ('ɛm'pfɛŋər) *nm* — receiver. **-̈lich** (ɛm'pfɛŋliç) *adj* susceptible, impressionable.

empfehl/en* (ɛm'pfɛ:lən) *vt* recommend. **sich empfehlen** *vr* take one's leave. **—ung** *nf* **-en** recommendation.

empfind/en* (ɛm'pfindən) *vt* feel, sense. **—lich** (ɛm'pfintliç) *adj* **1** sensitive. **2** grievous, severe. **—lichkeit** *nf* sensitivity, touchiness. **—ung** *nf* **-en 1** perception. **2** feeling. **3** sentiment.

empfohlen (ɛm'pfo:lən) *v* see **empfehlen.** *adj* recommended.

empor (ɛm'po:r) *adv* up(wards). **-̈en** (ɛm-'pœ:rən) *vt* **1** rouse. **2** shock. **sich -̈en** *vr* revolt. **-̈end** (ɛm'pœ:rənt) *adj* revolting. **—kommen*** *vi* rise. **—kömmling** (ɛm'po:r-kœmliŋ) *nm* **-e** upstart. **-̈ung** (ɛm'pœ:ruŋ) *nf* **-en 1** indignation. **2** rebellion.

emsig ('ɛmziç) *adj* busy, industrious.

End/e ('ɛndə) *n neu* **-n** end. **am Ende** in the end. **zu dem Ende** to that purpose. **zu Ende** over. **—en** *vi,vt also* **—igen** end, stop, finish. **—gültig** ('ɛntgy:ltiç) *adj* final, definitive. **—lich** ('ɛntliç) *adj* **1** final. **2** finite. *adv* at last. **—los** ('ɛntlo:s) *adj* endless. **—punkt** ('ɛntpuŋkt) *nm* end point, extremity. **—spiel** ('ɛntʃpi:l) *n neu sport* final. **—station** ('ɛntstatsio:n) *nf* **-en** terminus. **—ung** *nf* **-en** ending.

Energi/e (enɛr'gi:) *nf* **-n** energy. **—sch** (e'nɛrgiʃ) *adj* energetic.

eng (ɛŋ) *adj* **1** narrow. **2** tight. **3** close. **—e** *nf* **-n 1** narrowness. **2** defile, straits. **—herzig** *adj* petty. **—paß** *nm* **1** narrow pass. **2** bottle-neck. **—stirnig** *adj* narrow-minded.

Engel ('ɛŋəl) *nm* — angel. **—gleich** *adj also* **—haft** angelic.

Eng/land ('ɛŋlant) *n neu* England. **—länder** ('ɛŋlɛndər) *nm* — Englishman. **—länderin** *nf* **-nen** Englishwoman. **—lisch** *adj, n neu* English (language).

en gros (ã'gro:) *adv* wholesale.

Enkel ('ɛŋkəl) *nm* — grandson, grandchild. **—in** *nf* **-nen** granddaughter. **—kind** *n neu* grandchild.

enorm (e'nɔrm) *adj* enormous.

entart/en (ɛnt'artən) *vi* degenerate. **—ung** *nf* degeneration, degeneracy.

entbehrlich (ɛnt'be:rliç) *adj* superfluous.

entbinden* (ɛnt'bindən) *vt* **1** untie, release. **2** *med* deliver.

entblößen (ɛnt'blœ:sən) *vt* **1** uncover, bare. **2** denude, deprive.

entdeck/en (ɛnt'dɛkən) *vt* discover, disclose, invent. **—er** *nm* — discoverer, explorer. **—ung** *nf* **-en 1** discovery. **2** disclosure. **3** invention.

Ente ('ɛntə) *nf* **-n 1** duck. **2** hoax.

entehren (ɛnt'e:rən) *vt* dishonour.

enteign/en (ɛnt'aignən) *vt* expropriate. **—ung** *nf* **-en** expropriation.

enterben (ɛnt'ɛrbən) *vt* disinherit.

entfallen* (ɛnt'falən) *vi* **1** escape the memory of. **2** fall out of. **entfällt** not applicable.

entfalt/en (ɛnt'faltən) *vt* **1** unfold. **2** exhibit, display. **—ung** *nf* **-en 1** unfolding. **2** display.

entfern/en (ɛnt'fɛrnən) *vt* remove. **sich entfernen** *vr* go away, withdraw. **—t** *adj* distant. **—ung** *nf* **-en 1** distance. **2** removal, departure.

entfliehen* (ɛnt'fli:ən) *vi* escape, flee.

entfremd/en (ɛnt'frɛmdən) *vt* alienate, antagonize. **—ung** *nf* alienation.

entführ/en (ɛnt'fy:rən) *vt* carry off, abduct, kidnap. **—ung** *nf* **-en** abduction, kidnapping.

entgegen (ɛnt'ge:gən) *prep,adv* **1** contrary (to), against. **2** towards. **—gehen*** *vi* go to meet. **—gesetzt** *adj* opposite, opposed. **—halten*** *vt* **1** hold out (towards). **2** point out. **3** contrast. **—kommen*** *vi* (come to) meet. *n neu* **1** cooperation. **2** kindness. **—laufen*** *vi* **1** run to meet. **2** oppose. **—setzen** *vt* oppose. **—stellen** *vt* set against, contrast.

entgeg/nen (ɛnt'ge:gnən) *vi* answer. **—nung** *nf* **-en** answer.

entgehen* (ɛnt'ge:ən) *vi* **1** escape. **2** avoid.

Entgelt (ɛnt'gɛlt) *n neu* **1** compensation. **2** remuneration. **—en*** *vt* **1** pay for. **2** compensate.

entgleisen (ɛnt'glaizən) *vi* run off the rails.

entgräten (ɛnt'grɛ:tən) *vt* bone (fish).

enthaaren (ɛnt'ha:rən) *vt* remove hair from, depilate.

enthalt/en* (ɛnt'haltən) *vt* contain, include. **sich enthalten** *vr* abstain. **—sam** *adj* abstemious. **—samkeit** *nf* moderation, abstemiousness.

enthaupten (ɛnt'hauptən) *vt* behead.

enthüllen (ɛnt'hylən) *vt* reveal, disclose, unveil.

Enthusiasmus (ɛntuzi'asmus) nm enthusiasm.
entkernen (ɛnt'kɛrnən) vt stone (fruit, etc.).
entkommen* (ɛnt'kɔmən) vi escape.
entkuppeln (ɛnt'kupəln) vt 1 disconnect. 2 declutch.
entladen* (ɛnt'laːdən) vt 1 unload. 2 (of guns) fire. **sich entladen** vr get rid (of).
entlang (ɛnt'laŋ) adv,prep along.
entlarven (ɛnt'larfən) vt unmask.
entlass/en* (ɛnt'lasən) vt dismiss. **—ung** nf -en dismissal.
entlast/en (ɛnt'lastən) vt 1 unload. 2 relieve. 3 clear, exonerate. **—ung** nf 1 relief. 2 exoneration. **—sstraße** nf bypass.
sich entledigen (ɛnt'leːdɪgən) vr rid oneself of.
entlegen (ɛnt'leːgən) adj remote, distant.
entmilitarisieren (ɛntmilitari'ziːrən) vt demilitarize.
entmutig/en (ɛnt'muːtɪgən) vt discourage. **—ung** nf discouragement.
entnehmen* (ɛnt'neːmən) vt 1 take out or away, remove. 2 infer. 3 learn.
entrahmen (ɛn'traːmən) vt skim.
entrüst/en (ɛnt'rystən) vt anger, provoke. **sich entrüsten** vr grow angry. **—et** adj indignant, angry. **—ung** nf indignation, anger.
entsagen (ɛnt'zaːgən) vi give up, renounce.
entschädig/en (ɛnt'ʃɛːdɪgən) vt 1 compensate. 2 indemnify. **—ung** nf -en 1 compensation. 2 indemnity.
Entscheid (ɛnt'ʃait) nm -en also **Entscheid/ung** (ɛnt'ʃaiduŋ) nf -en decision, verdict. **—en*** vt,vi decide, resolve. **sich —en** vr make up one's mind, decide (on). **—end** adj decisive.
entschieden (ɛnt'ʃiːdən) adj 1 decided. 2 determined. **—heit** nf determination.
sich entschließ/en* (ɛnt'ʃliːsən) vr decide. **—ung** nf -en resolution.
entschlossen (ɛnt'ʃlɔsən) adj determined. **—heit** nf resoluteness, determination.
Entschluß (ɛnt'ʃlus) nm -schlüsse decision.
entschlüsseln (ɛnt'ʃlysəln) vt decode, decipher.
entschuldig/en (ɛnt'ʃuldɪgən) vt 1 pardon. 2 justify. **sich entschuldigen** vr apologize. **—ung** nf -en excuse, apology. **Entschuldigung!** sorry! excuse me!
entsetz/en (ɛnt'zɛtsən) vt 1 frighten. 2 relieve. n neu terror. **—lich** adj terrible, dreadful.
entspann/en (ɛnt'ʃpanən) vt 1 release. 2 relax. **sich entspannen** vr relax, rest. **—ung** nf 1 relaxation. 2 recreation. 3 détente.

entsprechen* (ɛnt'ʃprɛçən) vi correspond (to), answer (to).
entspringen* (ɛnt'ʃprɪŋən) vi 1 rise or spring from. 2 escape.
entstammen (ɛnt'ʃtamən) vi descend (from), spring (from).
entsteh/en* (ɛnt'ʃteːən) vi arise. **—ung** nf -en origin.
enttäusch/en (ɛnt'tɔyʃən) vt disappoint, disillusion. **—ung** nf -en disappointment.
entvölkern (ɛnt'fœlkərn) vt depopulate.
entwaffnen (ɛnt'vafnən) vt disarm.
entwässer/n (ɛnt'vɛsərn) vt 1 drain. 2 dehydrate. **—ung** nf 1 drainage. 2 dehydration.
entweder (ɛnt've:dər) conj **entweder...oder** either...or.
entweichen* (ɛnt'vaiçən) vi 1 flee. 2 escape.
entweihen (ɛnt'vaiən) vt desecrate.
entwerf/en (ɛnt'vɛrfən) vt 1 design, plan. 2 sketch, draw up. **—er** nm — designer, planner.
entwert/en (ɛnt'vɛrtən) vt 1 devalue. 2 cancel (postage stamps, etc.). **—ung** nf -en 1 devaluation. 2 cancellation.
entwick/eln (ɛnt'vikəln) vt 1 develop. 2 explain. 3 unfold. **—ler** nm — developer. **—lung** nf -en 1 development. 2 exposition. **—lungsländer** n neu pl developing countries.
entwirren (ɛnt'virən) vt unravel.
entwischen (ɛnt'viʃən) vi escape, slip away.
entwürdigen (ɛnt'vyrdɪgən) vt degrade.
Entwurf (ɛnt'vurf) nm -̈e plan, draft, outline.
entwurzeln (ɛnt'vurtsəln) vt uproot.
entziehen* (ɛnt'tsiːən) vt withdraw, take away. **sich entziehen** vr evade, shun.
entziffern (ɛnt'tsifərn) vt decipher.
entzück/en (ɛnt'tsykən) vt charm, delight. n neu — delight. **—end** adj charming, delightful.
entzünd/bar (ɛnt'tsyntbaːr) adj inflammable. **—en** (ɛnt'tsyndən) vt 1 inflame. 2 ignite. **—ung** (ɛnt'tsynduŋ) nf -en 1 inflammation. 2 ignition.
entzwei (ɛnt'tsvai) adj in two, broken.
Enzyklopäd/ie (ɛntsyklopɛ'diː) nf -n encyclopedia. **-isch** (ɛntsyklo'pɛ:diʃ) adj encyclopedic.
Enzym (ɛn'tsym) n neu -e enzyme.
Epidem/ie (epide'miː) nf -n epidemic. **—isch** (epi'deːmiʃ) adj epidemic.
Epik (ˈeːpik) nf epic poetry.
Epilepsie (epilɛp'si:) nf epilepsy.
Episode (epi'zoːdə) nf -n episode.

Epos ('e:pɔs) n neu **Epen** epic.

er (e:r, er) pron 3rd pers s he.

erachten (ɛr'axtən) vt think, deem. n neu — opinion. **meines Erachtens** in my opinion.

Erbarm/en (ɛr'barmən) n neu pity, mercy. **sich erbarmen** vr have pity. **⁻lich** (ɛr'bɛrmliç) adj pitiful. **—ungslos** adj merciless.

erbauen (ɛr'bauən) vt construct, build.

Erb/e ('ɛrbə) n neu **-n** inheritance. nm **-n** heir. **—en** ('ɛrbən) vt inherit. **—feind** ('ɛrpfaint) nm traditional enemy, sworn enemy. **—folge** ('ɛrpfɔlgə) nf hereditary succession. **—in** ('ɛrbin) nf **-nen** heiress. **—sünde** nf original sin. **—lich** ('ɛrpliç) adj hereditary. **—schaft** ('ɛrpʃaft) nf **-en** inheritance. **—stück** ('ɛrpʃtyk) n neu heirloom.

erbittern (ɛr'bitərn) vt embitter.

erblassen (ɛr'blasən) vi also **erbleichen*** 1 grow pale. 2 die.

erblinden (ɛr'blindən) vi grow or go blind.

Erbse ('ɛrpsə) nf **-n** pea.

Erd/beben ('e:rtbe:bən) n neu — earthquake. **—beere** nf strawberry. **—boden** nm soil, ground. **—e** ('e:rdə) nf **-n** 1 earth, world. 2 ground. 3 soil. **auf der Erde** on earth **zu ebener Erde** at ground level. **—en** ('e:rdən) vt sci, tech earth. **—geschoß** n neu ground floor. **—kreis** nm globe. **—kunde** nf geography. **—nuß** nf peanut. **—öl** n neu petroleum. **—teil** nm continent.

erdenk/en* (ɛr'dɛŋkən) vt 1 invent, think up. 2 imagine. **—lich** adj conceivable.

Erdichtung (ɛr'dictuŋ) nf **-en** figment, fiction.

erdrosseln (ɛr'drɔsəln) vt strangle, throttle.

sich ereignen (ɛr'aignən) vr happen. **—is** n neu **-se** event.

erfahr/en* (ɛr'fa:rən) vt 1 experience. 2 learn. adj experienced. **—ung** nf **-en** experience.

erfassen (ɛr'fasən) vt 1 grasp. 2 include. 3 understand.

erfind/en* (ɛr'findən) vt 1 invent. 2 find out. **—er** nm — inventor. **—erisch** adj inventive. **—ung** nf **-en** invention, discovery.

Erfolg (ɛr'fɔlk) nm **-e** 1 success. 2 result. **—en** (ɛr'fɔlgən) vi follow, ensue. **—los** adj unsuccessful. **—reich** adj successful.

erforder/lich (ɛr'fɔrdərliç) adj necessary, required. **—n** vt call for, necessitate, require. **—nis** n neu **-se** requisite, requirement.

erforsch/en (ɛr'fɔrʃən) vt 1 investigate. 2 explore. **—er** nm — 1 investigator. 2 explorer. **—ung** nf **-en** 1 investigation. 2 exploration.

erfreu/en (ɛr'frɔyən) vt delight. **sich erfreuen** vr 1 enjoy. 2 be pleased. **—lich** adj delightful, pleasing.

erfrieren (ɛr'fri:rən) vi freeze to death.

erfrisch/en (ɛr'friʃən) vt refresh. **—ung** nf **-en** refreshment. **—ungsraum** nm snack bar.

erfüllen (ɛr'fylən) vt 1 fill (up). 2 fulfil.

ergänz/en (ɛr'gɛntsən) vt 1 complete. 2 supplement. 3 replenish. **—ung** nf **-en** completion.

ergeb/en* (ɛr'ge:bən) vt 1 yield, produce. 2 show, prove. **sich ergeben** vr surrender, yield. **sich ergeben aus** follow from. adj 1 devoted. 2 addicted. **—enheit** nf **-en** 1 devotion. 2 submission. 3 resignation. **—nis** (ɛr'ge:pnis) n neu **-se** result. **—nislos** adj without result, vain. **—ung** nf **-en** 1 surrender. 2 resignation.

ergehen* (ɛr'ge:ən) vi be published or issued. **sich ergehen** vr 1 (take a) walk. 2 indulge.

ergiebig (ɛr'gi:biç) adj productive, fertile.

ergreifen* (ɛr'graifən) vt 1 seize. 2 take up.

erhaben (ɛr'ha:bən) adj 1 raised. 2 sublime. 3 noble.

erhalt/en* (ɛr'haltən) vt 1 receive. 2 maintain, support. **—ung** nf 1 maintenance. 2 preservation.

erheb/en* (ɛr'he:bən) vt 1 raise (up). 2 demand. 3 levy. 4 praise. **sich erheben** vr 1 rise up. 2 rebel. **—lich** (ɛr'he:pliç) adj considerable.

erheitern (ɛr'haitərn) vt cheer (up).

erhöh/en (ɛr'hø:ən) vt raise, increase. **—ung** nf **-en** 1 rise, increase. 2 elevation.

sich erhol/en (ɛr'ho:lən) vr 1 recover. 2 recuperate. **—ung** nf **-en** 1 recovery. 2 recreation.

erinner/n (ɛr'inərn) vt remind. **sich erinnern** vr remember. **—ung** nf **-en** 1 memory. 2 reminder.

erkält/en (ɛr'kɛltən) vt cool, chill. **sich erkälten** vr catch cold. **—ung** nf **-en** cold.

erkämpfen (ɛr'kɛmpfən) vt win or gain by fighting.

erkenn/bar (ɛr'kɛnba:r) adj recognizable. **—en*** vt 1 recognize. 2 perceive. 3 realize. **—ung** nf **-en** recognition. **—ungswort** n neu password.

Erkenntnis[1] (ɛr'kɛntnis) n neu **-se** judgment.

Erkenntnis[2] (ɛr'kɛntnis) nf **-se** recognition, realization.

erklär/en (ɛr'klɛ:rən) vt 1 explain. 2 declare. **—ung** nf **-en** 1 explanation. 2 declaration.

39

erkranken

erkrank/en (ɛr'kraŋkən) vi fall ill. **—ung** nf **-en** illness.

sich erkund/igen (ɛr'kundigən) vr inquire. **—igung** nf **-en** enquiry.

erlahmen (ɛr'laːmən) vi become tired or lame.

erlangen (ɛr'laŋən) vt attain, obtain.

Erlaß (ɛr'las) nm **-lasse** 1 decree, ordinance. 2 remission. **erlassen*** (ɛr'lasən) vt 1 proclaim. 2 issue. 3 remit, pardon.

erlaub/en (ɛr'laubən) vt permit, allow. **—nis** (ɛr'laupnis) nf **-se** permission.

erläutern (ɛr'lɔytərn) vt explain, illustrate.

erleb/en (ɛr'leːbən) vt experience, live to see. **—nis** (ɛr'leːpnis) n neu **-se** experience. 2 adventure.

erledig/en (ɛr'leːdigən) vt 1 settle. 2 finish (off). 3 deal with. **—ung** nf **-en** 1 completion. 2 execution.

erlegen (ɛr'leːgən) vt kill, shoot.

erleichter/n (ɛr'laiçtərn) vt lighten, relieve, ease. **—ung** nf relief.

erlernen (ɛr'lɛrnən) vt learn.

erleucht/en (ɛr'lɔyçtən) vt 1 illuminate. 2 enlighten. **—ung** nf **-en** 1 illumination. 2 enlightenment.

erliegen* (ɛr'liːgən) vi be defeated, succumb.

Erlös (ɛr'løːs) nm **-e** proceeds. **-en** (ɛr'løːzən) vt 1 release. 2 save. **—er** (ɛr'løːzər) nm **—** 1 liberator, deliverer. 2 saviour. **—ung** (ɛr'løː- zuŋ) nf 1 deliverance. 2 salvation.

ermächtig/en (ɛr'mɛçtigən) vt empower. **—ung** nf **-en** authorization.

ermäßig/en (ɛr'mɛːsigən) vt reduce, moderate. **—ung** nf **-en** reduction, moderation.

ermitteln (ɛr'mitəln) vt find out, ascertain.

ermöglichen (ɛr'møːgliçən) vt render possible, enable.

ermorden (ɛr'mɔrdən) vt murder, assassinate.

ermüden (ɛr'myːdən) vi,vt tire.

ermuntern (ɛr'muntərn) vt rouse, cheer (up).

ermutig/en (ɛr'muːtigən) vt encourage, hearten. **—ung** nf **-en** encouragement.

ernähr/en (ɛr'nɛːrən) vt 1 feed. 2 maintain, support. **—er** nm **—** breadwinner. **—ung** nf 1 nourishment. 2 nutrition. 3 maintenance.

ernenn/en* (ɛr'nɛnən) vt 1 appoint. 2 nominate. **—ung** nf **-en**. 1 appointment. 2 nomination.

erneuer/n (ɛr'nɔyərn) vt 1 renew. 2 restore. **—ung** nf **-en** 1 renewal. 2 restoration.

erniedrigen (ɛr'niːdrigən) vt 1 lower. 2 degrade, humiliate.

ernst (ɛrnst) adj serious, earnest. nm 1 serious-

ness. 2 severity. **—haft** adj earnest. **—lich** adj serious, earnest.

Ernte ('ɛrntə) nf **-n** harvest, crop. **—dankfest** n neu harvest festival. **—n** vt,vi harvest, gather in.

ernüchtern (ɛr'nyçtərn) vt 1 sober (up). 2 disillusion.

Erober/er (ɛr'oːbərər) nm **—** conqueror. **—n** vt conquer. **—ung** nf **-en** conquest.

eröffn/en (ɛr'œfnən) vt 1 open. 2 inaugurate, begin. **—ung** nf **-en** 1 opening. 2 inauguration, beginning.

erörter/n (ɛr'œrtərn) vt discuss. **—ung** nf **-en** discussion.

Eroti/k (e'roːtik) nf eroticism. **—sch** adj erotic.

erpress/en (ɛr'prɛsən) vt blackmail. **—er** **—** blackmailer. **—ung** nf **-en** blackmail.

erproben (ɛr'proːbən) vt try, test.

erraten* (ɛr'raːtən) vt 1 guess. 2 solve.

erreg/bar (ɛr're:kbaːr) adj excitable. **—en** (ɛr're:gən) vt 1 excite. 2 irritate. **—ung** (ɛr're:guŋ) nf **-en** excitement.

erreich/bar (ɛr'raiçbaːr) adj attainable. **—en** vt reach, obtain.

errricht/en (ɛr'riçtən) vt 1 erect. 2 establish. **—ung** nf **-en** 1 erection. 2 establishment.

erröten (ɛr'røːtən) vi blush.

Errungenschaft (ɛr'ruŋənʃaft) nf **-en** 1 acquisition. 2 achievement.

Ersatz (ɛr'zats) nm 1 substitute, replacement. 2 reserve. 3 compensation. **—reifen** nm spare tyre. **—teil** n neu spare (part).

erschaff/en* (ɛr'ʃafən) vt create.

erschein/en* (ɛr'ʃainən) vi appear. **—ung** nf **-en** 1 appearance. 2 vision. 3 phenomenon.

erschlagen* (ɛr'ʃlaːgən) vt kill.

erschließen* (ɛr'ʃliːsən) vt 1 open (up). 2 infer.

erschöpf/en (ɛr'ʃœpfən) vt exhaust. **—ung** nf exhaustion.

erschrak (ɛr'ʃraːk) v see **erschrecken.**

erschrecken* (ɛr'ʃrɛkən) vt frighten. vi be frightened.

erschrocken (ɛr'ʃrɔkən) v see **erschrecken.** adj frightened.

erschüttern (ɛr'ʃytərn) vt shake, upset.

ersehen* (ɛr'zeːən) vt 1 see, perceive. 2 observe.

ersetzen (ɛr'zɛtsən) vt replace, make good.

ersichtlich (ɛr'ziçtliç) adj evident.

erspar/en (ɛr'ʃpaːrən) vt spare, save. **—nis** **-se** 1 saving. 2 savings.

erst (ɛrst) adj first. adv 1 at first. 2 only, not

40

till. **der erste beste** the first that comes, anyone or anything. **erste Hilfe** first aid.

erstarren (εr'ʃtarən) vi grow stiff or rigid.

erstatten (εr'ʃtatən) vt 1 compensate, repay. 2 return. 3 give.

Erstaufführung ('εrstauffy:ruŋ) nf -en premiere, first night.

erstaun/en (εr'ʃtaunən) vt astonish. vi be astonished. n neu amazement. -lich adj astonishing.

erstens ('ε:rstəns) adv first(ly).

ersticken (εr'ʃtikən) vt,vi suffocate, choke.

erstklassig ('e:rstklasiç) adj first-class, prime.

ersuchen (εr'zu:xən) vt request.

ertappen (εr'tapən) vt 1 surprise. 2 catch. **auf frischer Tat ertappt** caught red-handed.

Ertrag (εr'tra:k) nm -̈e yield, return, profit. **—en** (εr'tra:gən) vt bear, endure. **—̈lich** (εr'trε:kliç) adj bearable, tolerable.

ertränken (εr'trεŋkən) vt drown.

ertrinken (εr'triŋkən) vt,vi drown.

erwachen (εr'vaxən) vi awake.

erwachsen (εr'vaksən) vi 1 grow up. 2 arise (from). adj adult. **—e(r)** nm adult.

erwäg/en (εr'vε:gən) vt 1 consider. 2 weigh. **—ung** **—en** consideration.

erwähnen (εr'vε:nən) vt mention.

erwärmen (εr'vεrmən) vt warm.

erwart/en (εr'vartən) vt 1 await. 2 expect. **—ung** nf -en expectation.

erwecken (εr'vεkən) vt awaken, (a)rouse.

erweisen (εr'vaizən) vt 1 render. 2 prove.

erweiter/n (εr'vaitərn) vt enlarge. **—ung** nf -en extension.

Erwerb (εr'vεrp) nm -e 1 acquisition. 2 gain, profit. 3 livelihood. **—en** (εr'vεrbən) vt 1 acquire. 2 earn. **—stätig** adj (gainfully) employed.

erwider/n (εr'vi:dərn) vt respond (to), reply (to). **—ung** nf -en reply, response.

erwischen (εr'viʃən) vt 1 catch. 2 surprise.

erwünscht (εr'vynʃt) adj desired.

erwürgen (εr'vyrgən) vt strangle.

Erz (e:rts) n neu -e ore.

erzähl/en (εr'tsε:lən) vt tell, report, relate. **—er** nm — 1 narrator, story-teller. 2 reporter. **—ung** nf -en 1 narrative, story. 2 report.

Erz/bischof ('εrtsbiʃɔf) nm archbishop. **—engel** nm archangel. **—feind** nm archenemy.

erzeug/en (εr'tsɔygən) vt 1 beget, breed. 2 produce, manufacture. **—nis** (εr'tsɔyknis) n

neu **-se** 1 product. 2 produce. **—ung** nf 1 procreation. 2 production.

erzieh/en (εr'tsi:ən) vt 1 bring up. 2 educate. **—ung** nf education.

erzwingen (εr'tsviŋən) vt obtain by force.

es (εs) pron neu s it.

Esche ('εʃə) nf -n ash (tree).

Esel ('e:zəl) nm — ass, donkey.

esoterisch (ezo'te:riʃ) adj esoteric.

essen ('εsən) vt,vi eat. n neu — 1 food. 2 meal.

eß/bar ('εsbar) adj edible. **—löffel** nm tablespoon. **—tisch** nm dining table. **—zimmer** n neu dining room.

Essenz (ε'sεnts) nf -en essence.

Essig ('εsiç) nm -e vinegar.

etablieren (eta'bli:rən) vt establish.

Etage (e'ta:ʒə) nf -n floor, storey.

Etat (e'ta:) nm -s 1 budget. 2 balance-sheet.

Eth/ik ('e:tik) nf ethics. **—isch** adj ethical.

ethnisch ('e:tniʃ) adj ethnic.

Etikett (eti'kεt) n neu -e (price) label, tag.

Etikette (eti'kεtə) nf -en etiquette.

etliche ('εtliçə) pron,adj pl some, a few.

Etui (εt'vi:) n neu -s small case or box.

etwa ('εtva) adv 1 about, nearly 2 perhaps. **—ig** adj possible.

etwas ('εtvas) pron invar some(thing), anything. adj some. adv somewhat. n neu a something.

Etymologie (etymolo'gi:) nf -n etymology.

euch (ɔyç) pron 2nd pers pl fam you, to you.

euer ('ɔyər) poss adj 2nd pers pl fam your. poss pron 2nd pers pl also **eure, der —e,** or **der —ige** yours. **—ethalben** adv also **—etwegen** or **—etwillen** for your sake, on your account.

Eukalyptus (ɔyka'lyptus) nm -ten eucalyptus.

Eule ('ɔylə) nf -n owl.

Eunuch (ɔy'nu:x) nm -en eunuch.

Europa (ɔy'ro:pa) n neu Europe. **—er** (ɔyro-pε:ər) nm — European. **—isch** (ɔyro'pε:iʃ) adj European.

evakuieren (evaku'i:rən) vt 1 empty. 2 evacuate.

evangel/isch (evan'ge:liʃ) adj 1 Protestant. 2 evangelical. **—ist** (evange'list) nm -en evangelist. **—ium** (evan'ge:lium) n neu -ien gospel.

eventuell (evεntu'εl) adj possible.

ewig ('e:viç) adj eternal. **—keit** nf eternity.

exakt (ε'ksakt) adj exact, accurate.

Examen (ε'ksa:mən) n neu — examination.

Exekutionskomm:ando (ɛksekutsi'o:nskɔman-do) n neu **—s** firing squad.

Exempel (ɛ'ksɛmpəl) n neu — example.

Exemplar (ɛksɛm'pla:r) n neu **-e** 1 specimen. 2 copy. **—isch** adj model, exemplary.

Exil (e'ksi:l) n neu **-e** exile.

Exist/enz (ɛksis'tɛnts) nf **-en** 1 existence. 2 livelihood. **—ieren** (ɛksis'ti:rən) vi exist.

exklusiv (ɛksklu'zi:f) adj exclusive.

exotisch (ɛ'kso:tiʃ) adj exotic.

Expedition (ɛkspeditsi'o:n) nf **-en** 1 expedition. 2 dispatching.

Experiment (ɛksperi'mɛnt) n neu **-e** experiment. **—ell** (ɛksperimɛn'tɛl) adj experimental. **—ieren** (ɛksperimɛn'ti:rən) vi experiment.

explodieren (ɛksplo'di:rən) vi explode.

explosiv (ɛksplo'zi:f) adj explosive.

Export (ɛks'pɔrt) nm **-e** export. **—ieren** (ɛkspɔr'ti:rən) vt export.

extrem (ɛks'tre:m) adj extreme.

exzentrisch (ɛks'tsɛntriʃ) adj eccentric.

F

Fabel ('fa:bəl) nf **-n** 1 fable. 2 plot, story. **—haft** adj fabulous.

Fabrik (fa'bri:k) nf **-en** factory. **—at** (fabri'ka:t) n neu **-e** manufacture, product.

fabrizieren (fabri'tsi:rən) vt manufacture.

Fach (fax) n neu **ːer** 1 compartment, pigeon-hole. 2 drawer. 3 subject, field. 4 department. 5 speciality. **—arbeiter** nm skilled worker. **—arzt** nm med specialist. **—berater** nm technical consultant. **—bildung** nf technical education. **—lehrer** nm specialist teacher. **—lich** adj 1 professional. 2 technical. **—mann** nm **ːer** or **-leute** specialist, expert. **—schule** nf technical school. **—werk** n neu 1 half-timbered work. 2 framework.

fächeln ('fɛçəln) vt fan.

Fackel ('fakəl) nf **-n** torch.

fade ('fa:də) adj 1 dull. 2 insipid. 3 stale.

Faden ('fa:dən) nm **ː** thread, string.

Fagott (fa'gɔt) n neu **-e** bassoon.

fähig ('fɛ:iç) adj 1 able, capable. 2 competent. **—keit** nf **—en** ability, capacity, capability.

fahl (fa:l) adj pale, faded.

fahnd/en ('fa:ndən) vi **nach jemandem fahnden** search for someone. **—ung** nf **-en** search.

Fahne ('fa:nə) nf **-n** flag, standard.

fahr/en' ('fa:rən) vt, vi 1 go. 2 drive. 3 travel. 4

sail. **—bahn** nf roadway, carriageway. **—bar** adj 1 passable, negotiable, navigable. 2 mobile. **—er** nm — driver. **—gast** nm passenger. **—geld** n neu fare. **—karte** nf ticket. **—lässig** adj negligent. **—plan** nm timetable. **—rad** n neu bicycle. **—schein** nm ticket. **—schule** nf driving school. **—stuhl** nm lift, elevator. **—zeug** n neu 1 vehicle. 2 vessel.

Fähre ('fɛ:rə) nf **-n** ferry.

Fahrt (fa:rt) nf **-en** 1 drive. 2 ride. 3 journey. 4 voyage.

Fährte ('fɛ:rtə) nf **-n** 1 track, trail. 2 scent.

Faktur (fak'tu:r) nf **-en** invoice. **—ieren** (faktu'ri:rən) vt invoice.

Fakultät (fakul'tɛ:t) nf **-en** (university) faculty.

Falke ('falkə) nm **-n** falcon.

Fall (fal) nm **ːe** 1 fall, downfall. 2 case. **auf jeden Fall** in any case. **für diesen Fall, in diesem Fall** in this case. **—s** conj in case, if.

Fall/e ('falə) nf **-n** 1 trap, snare. 2 catch, latch. **—en'** vi fall. **es fällt mir leicht/schwer** I find it easy/hard. **fallen lassen** drop, let fall. **—schirm** nm **-e** parachute. **—schirmjäger** nm paratrooper. **—schirmspringer** nm parachutist. **—sucht** nf epilepsy.

fäll/en ('fɛlən) vt 1 fell (a tree, etc.). 2 pass (judgment).

fällig ('fɛliç) adj payable, due.

falsch (falʃ) adj 1 false. 2 wrong. **—en** ('fɛlʃən) vt 1 falsify, forge. 2 adulterate. **—er** ('fɛlʃər) nm — falsifier, forger. **—heit** nf **-en** 1 falsehood. 2 deceitfulness.

Falt/e ('faltə) nf **-n** fold, crease, wrinkle. **—en** vt fold, crease, wrinkle.

familiär (famil'jɛ:r) adj familiar.

Familie (fa'mi:liə) nf **-n** family. **—nname** nm surname.

Fanati/ker (fa'na:tikər) nm — fanatic. **—sch** adj fanatic(al).

Fanfare (fan'fa:rə) nf **-n** fanfare.

fand (fant) v see **finden.**

Fang (faŋ) nm **ːe** 1 catching, capture. 2 catch, prey. 3 pl fangs. 4 pl claws. **—en'** vt catch, capture. **sich —en** vr become entangled or ensnared.

Farb/e ('farbə) nf **-n** 1 colour. 2 paint, dye. 3 game suit. **Farbe bekennen** show one's true colours. **—en** ('fɛrbən) vt dye, colour. **—enblind** ('farbənblint) adj colour-blind. **—er** ('fɛrbər) nm — dyer. **—film** nm colour film. **—ig** ('farbiç) adj coloured. **—ige(r)**

('farbigə) nm -n coloured man. **—los** adj colourless. **—stoff** nm pigment, dye.

Fasan (fa'za:n) nm -e pheasant.

Fasching ('faʃiŋ) nm -e (Shrovetide) carnival.

Faschis/mus (fa'ʃismus) nm fascism. **—t** nm -en fascist.

Faser ('fa:zər) nf -n fibre, strand.

Faß (fas) n neu **Fässer** barrel, cask, drum.

fass/en ('fasən) vt 1 take hold of, seize, catch. 2 contain, hold. 3 comprehend, grasp. **sich fassen** vr 1 pull oneself together. 2 control oneself. **sich kurz fassen** express oneself briefly, be brief. **—ung** nf -en 1 composure, self control. 2 setting (of gems). 3 wording, version.

fast (fast) adv almost, nearly.

fast/en ('fastən) vi fast. **—nacht** nf 1 the night of Shrove Tuesday. 2 carnival.

fatal (fa'ta:l) adj 1 unfortunate. 2 disastrous. **—ist** (fata'list) nm -en fatalist.

faul (faul) adj 1 lazy. 2 rotten. **—enzen** vi idle, loaf about. **—heit** nf laziness. **—nis** ('fɔylnis) nf decay, rottenness.

Faust (faust) nf -e fist.

Februar ('fe:brua:r) nm February.

fechten ('fɛçtən) vi fence, fight.

Feder ('fe:dər) nf -n 1 feather. 2 pen(-nib). 3 spring. **—ball** nm shuttlecock. **—n** vi 1 moult. 2 spring, be elastic. **—ung** nf 1 (spring) suspension. 2 elasticity.

Fee (fe:) nf -n fairy.

fegen ('fe:gən) vt,vi sweep.

fehl/bar ('fe:lba:r) adj fallible. **—betrag** nm deficit. **—druck** nm misprint. **—en** vi 1 be absent. 2 be wanting. 3 fail. 4 err. **—er** nm — 1 fault, failing. 2 mistake. **—geburt** nf miscarriage. **—schlag** nm 1 failure. 2 miss. **—schlagen** vi 1 fail. 2 miss. **—schuß** nm bad shot, miss. **—zünden** vi misfire.

Feier ('faiər) nf -n celebration, festival. **—abend** nm 1 evening leisure. 2 (at work) finishing-time, knocking-off time. **—lich** adj 1 ceremonial. 2 festive. 3 solemn, dignified. **—lichkeit** nf 1 ceremony, pomp. 2 solemnity. **—n** vt,vi celebrate. vi rest (from work). **—tag** nm holiday.

feig/e ('faigə) adj cowardly. **—heit** ('faikhait) nf cowardice. **—ling** ('faikliŋ) nm -e coward.

Feige ('faigə) nf -n fig.

feil (fail) adj 1 for sale. 2 venal.

Feil/e ('failə) nf -n file. **—en** vt,vi 1 file. 2 polish.

feilschen ('failʃən) vi barter, haggle.

fein (fain) adj 1 fine. 2 delicate. 3 elegant. 4 distinguished. 5 acute. 6 sensitive. **—fühlig** adj sensitive, delicate. **—schmecker** nm — gourmet. **—sinnig** adj subtle, sensitive.

Feind (faint) nm -e enemy. **—schaft** nf enmity. **—selig** adj hostile.

Feld (fɛlt) n neu -er field. **—bett** n neu camp bed. **—herr** nm commander, general. **—messer** nm surveyor. **—stecher** nm field-glasses. **—wache** nf mil picket. **—webel** nm — sergeant. **—zug** nm 1 campaign. 2 expedition.

Fell (fɛl) n neu -e 1 hide, skin. 2 fur.

Fels (fɛls) nm -en also **Felsen** ('fɛlzən) nm — 1 cliff. 2 rock.

Fenster ('fɛnstər) n neu — window. **—brett** n neu window-sill. **—laden** nm shutter. **—scheibe** nf window-pane.

Ferien ('fe:riən) n pl holidays.

Ferkel ('fɛrkəl) n neu — piglet.

fern (fɛrn) adj distant, far. **Ferne(r) Osten** nm Far East. **—e** nf -n distance, remoteness. **—er** adj farther. adv moreover. **—erhin** adv 1 in the future. 2 moreover. **—gespräch** n neu trunk call, long-distance call. **—meldung** nf 1 telecommunication. 2 remote signalling. **—rohr** n neu telescope. **—sehapparat** nm television set. **—sehen** vi watch television. n neu television. **—sprecher** nm telephone. **—sprechzelle** nf call-box.

Ferse ('fɛrzə) nf -n heel.

fertig ('fɛrtiç) adj 1 ready. 2 finished. **—en** ('fɛrtigən) vt manufacture, produce. **—keit** nf dexterity, proficiency. **—machen** vt finish.

Fessel ('fɛsəl) nf -n fetter, bond. **—n** vt 1 fetter. 2 captivate.

fest (fɛst) adj 1 solid, hard. 2 stable, fixed. **—halten** vt 1 seize. 2 hold tight. 3 record. 4 portray. vi hold fast, stick to (something). **—igen** vt make firm or stable. **—land** n neu mainland. **—machen** vt make fast, fasten. **—stehen** vi stand firm. **—stellen** vt establish, ascertain. **—ung** nf -en fortress.

Fest (fɛst) n neu -e festival, feast. **—lich** adj festive. **—lichkeit** nf -en festivity.

fett (fɛt) adj 1 fat. 2 fertile. 3 greasy. n neu -e fat, grease. **—arm** adj low in fat. **—en** vt oil. **—ig** adj 1 fatty. 2 oily.

Fetzen ('fɛtsən) nm — 1 scrap, piece. 2 rag.

feucht (fɔyçt) adj damp, moist. **—igkeit** nf damp, moisture, humidity.

Feuer ('fɔyər) n neu — fire. **—fest** adj fireproof. **—löscher** nm fire-extinguisher.

—melder nm fire-alarm. **—n** vi 1 fire (on). 2 make a fire. **—wehr** nf fire brigade. **—werk** n neu fireworks. **—zeug** n neu cigarette-lighter.

Feuilleton ('fœjətɔ̃) n neu **-s** cultural section of a newspaper.

feurig ('fɔyriç) adj fiery.

Fibel ('fiːbəl) nf **-n** 1 primer, spelling-book. 2 brooch.

Fichte ('fiçtə) nf **-n** pine, spruce.

ficken ('fikən) vi move to and fro. vt rub. vi,vt tab copulate.

Fieber ('fiːbər) n neu — fever. **—haft** adj feverish.

Fied/el ('fiːdəl) nf **-n** fiddle, violin. **—eln** vt fiddle. **—ler** nm — fiddler.

fiel (fiːl) v see **fallen**.

Figur (fi'guːr) nf **-en** 1 figure. 2 chessman.

Filiale (fili'aːlə) nf **-n** comm branch.

Film (film) nm **-e** film. **—star** nm **-s** film star.

Filt/er ('filtər) nm,neu — filter. **—ern** vt also **—rieren** (fil'triːrən) filter, strain.

Filz (filts) nm **-e** 1 felt. 2 miser, skin-flint. **—en** vt 1 line with felt. 2 sl search, frisk. **—ig** adj 1 felt. 2 miserly.

Finanz (fi'nants) nf **-en** finance. **—iell** (finan-'tsjɛl) adj financial. **—ieren** (finan'tsiːrən) vt finance. **—mann** nm financier.

find/en' ('findən) vt 1 find. 2 think, consider. **—igkeit** nf ingenuity.

fing (fiŋ) v see **fangen**.

Finger ('fiŋər) nm — finger. **—abdruck** nm fingerprint. **—hut** nm thimble. **—nagel** nm fingernail. **—spitze** nf fingertip.

Fink (fiŋk) nm — finch.

Finn/e ('finə) nm **-n** also **Finn/länder** nm — Finn. **—isch** adj Finnish. n neu Finnish (language). **—land** n neu Finland.

finster ('finstər) adj 1 dark, gloomy. 2 ominous, sinister. **—nis** nf **-se** 1 darkness, gloom. 2 sci eclipse.

Firma ('firmə) nf **Firmen** firm.

Firnis ('firnis) nm **-e** varnish. **—sen** vt varnish.

Fisch (fiʃ) nm **-e** 1 fish. 2 pl Pisces. **—en** vt fish (for), catch. **—er** nm — fisherman. **—erei** (fiʃə'rai) nf **-en** fishery, fishing. **—heber** nm fish-slice.

fix (fiks) adj 1 fixed. 2 quick, agile. **—ieren** (fi'ksiːrən) vt 1 fix. 2 stare at.

flach (flax) adj 1 flat. 2 shallow. **—e** ('flɛçə) nf **-n** 1 surface. 2 plain. 3 expanse. 4 (surface) area. **—enmaß** ('flɛçənmaːs) n neu square measure. **—land** n neu plain, lowland.

Flachs (flaks) nm flax.

flackern ('flakərn) vi (of light, flame) flicker.

Flagge ('flagə) nf **-n** flag, standard.

Flamme ('flamə) nf **-n** flame. **—n** vi flame, blaze.

Flanell (fla'nɛl) n neu **-e** flannel.

Flank/e ('flaŋkə) nf **-n** flank. **—ieren** (flaŋ-'kiːrən) vt (out)flank.

Flasche ('flaʃə) nf **-n** bottle, flask. **—nöffner** nm bottle opener.

flattern ('flatərn) vi flutter.

flau (flau) adj 1 weak. 2 slack. 3 dull. 4 stale.

Flaute ('flautə) nf **-n** lull, calm.

Flechte ('flɛçtə) nf **-n** 1 plait, braid. 2 lichen. **—n*** vt braid, plait.

Fleck (flɛk) nm **-e** 1 spot. 2 blemish. 3 patch. **—en** vt,vi spot, stain. nm — 1 spot. 2 blemish. 3 market town. **—ig** adj spotted, stained.

Fledermaus ('fleːdərmaus) nf **¨e** bat.

flehen ('fleːən) vi implore.

Fleisch (flaiʃ) n neu **-e** meat, flesh. **—er** nm — also **—hauer** butcher. **—erei** (flaiʃə'rai) nf **-en** butcher's shop. **—fressend** adj carnivorous. **—ig** adj fleshy, meaty. **—lich** adj 1 carnal, of the flesh. 2 sensual.

Fleiß (flais) nm industry, diligence. **—ig** adj industrious, diligent, hard-working.

flicken ('flikən) vt mend, patch. nm — patch.

Fliege ('fliːgə) nf **-n** fly. **—nklappe** nf fly-swatter.

flieg/en' ('fliːgən) vi fly. **—er** nm — flier, aviator.

fliehen* ('fliːən) vi,vt flee (from).

Fließ/band ('fliːsbant) n neu 1 conveyor belt. 2 production line. **—en'** vi flow. **—end** adj 1 flowing. 2 fluent.

flimmern ('flimərn) vi glimmer, twinkle.

flink (fliŋk) adj nimble, quick. **—heit** nf nimbleness, quickness.

Flinte ('flintə) nf **-n** 1 rifle. 2 shotgun.

Flitterwochen ('flitərvɔxən) nf pl honeymoon.

Flocke ('flɔkə) nf **-n** 1 flake. 2 flock, tuft.

flog (floːk) v see **fliegen**.

Floh (floː) nm **¨e** flea.

Florenz (flo'rɛnts) n neu Florence.

floß (flɔs) v see **fließen**.

Floß (floːs) n neu **¨e** 1 raft. 2 (fishing) float.

Flosse ('flɔsə) nf **-n** fin, flipper.

Flöt/e ('flœːtə) nf **-n** flute. **—ist** nm **-en** flautist.

flott (flɔt) adj 1 afloat. 2 brisk. 3 stylish, gay. **—e** ('flɔtə) nf **-n** fleet, navy.

Fluch (flu:x) *nm* ̈-e curse, swear word. **—en** *vi* curse, swear.

Flucht (fluxt) *nf* **-en 1** flight, escape. **2** row, line. **—ig** ('flyçtiç) *adj* **1** fleeing. **2** fugitive. **3** brief, fleeting. **4** superficial. **—ling** ('flyçtliŋ) *nm* **-e 1** refugee. **2** fugitive.

Flug (flu:k) *nm* ̈-e **1** flight, flying. **2** flock, flight. **—abwehr** *nf* anti-aircraft defence. **—blatt** *n neu* leaflet, pamphlet. **—deck** *n neu* flight deck. **—hafen** *nm* airport. **—post** *nf* airmail. **—zeug** *n neu* aeroplane, aircraft.

Flügel ('fly:gəl) *nm* — wing.

Fluor ('flu:ɔr) *n neu* fluorine.

Flur (flu:r) *nm* **-e** (entrance) hall. *nf* **-en** field, meadow-land.

Fluß (flus) *nm* **Flüsse 1** river, stream. **2** flow.

flüssig ('flysiç) *adj* liquid, fluid. **—keit** *nf* **-en 1** liquid, fluid. **2** liquidity.

flüstern ('flystərn) *vi,vt* whisper.

Flut (flu:t) *nf* **-en 1** flood. **2** (high) tide.

Fohlen ('fo:lən) *n neu* — foal.

Föhn (fœ:n) *nm* **-e** warm south wind.

Folg/e ('fɔlgə) *nf* **-n 1** succession, series. **2** consequence, result. **—en** *vi* **1** follow. **2** ensue. **3** obey. **—endermaßen** *adv* in the following manner. **—ern** *vt* infer, conclude. **—erung** *nf* **-en** inference, conclusion. **—lich** ('fɔlkliç) *conj* consequently.

Folter ('fɔltər) *nf* **-n** torture. **—n** *vt* torture.

Fön (fœ:n) *nm Tdmk* **-e** hair-dryer.

Fonds (fɔ) *nm comm* fund(s), stock.

forcieren (fɔr'si:rən) *vt* **1** force, take by force. **2** overdo.

forder/n ('fɔrdərn) *vt* **1** demand, claim. **2** challenge, summon. **—ung** *nf* **-en 1** demand. **2** challenge.

förder/n ('fœ:rdərn) *vt* **1** further, promote. **2** transport, convey. **—lich** *adj* **1** conducive. **2** advantageous. **—ung** *nf* **-en** advancement.

Forelle (fo'rɛlə) *nf* **-n** trout.

Form (fɔrm) *nf* **-en 1** form, shape. **2** mould. **—el** *nf* **-n** formula. **—ell** (for'mɛl) *adj* also **—lich** ('fœrmliç) formal. **—en** *vt* form, mould. **—ieren** (fɔr'mi:rən) *vt* **1** form. **2** arrange. **sich —ieren** *vr mil* fall in. **—ular** (fɔrmu'la:r) *n neu* **-e 1** form. **2** schedule. **—ulieren** (fɔrmu'li:rən) *vt* formulate.

forsch/en ('fɔrʃən) *vi* **1** search. **2** investigate. **3** research. **—er** *nm* — **1** researcher. **2** investigator. **3** explorer. **—ung** *nf* **-en 1** research. **2** investigation.

Forst (fɔrst) *nm* **-e** forest, wood. **—er** ('fœrstər) *nm* — forester.

fort (fɔrt) *adv* **1** away. **2** off. **3** on. **4** forward.

fortan (fɔrt'an) *adv* henceforth.

fortbestehen * ('fɔrtbəʃte:ən) *vi* **1** continue (to exist). **2** persist.

Fortbildung ('fɔrtbilduŋ) *nf* further education or training.

fortdauern ('fɔrtdauərn) *vi* continue, last.

fortfahren * ('fɔrtfa:rən) *vi* **1** keep or go on. **2** depart. *vt* **1** remove. **2** drive away.

fortgehen * ('fɔrtge:ən) *vi* go away or on.

fortkommen * ('fɔrtkɔmən) *vi* **1** get away. **2** make progress.

fortlaufend ('fɔrtlaufənt) *adj* continuous.

fortpflanzen ('fɔrtpflantsən) *vt* propagate. **sich fortpflanzen** *vr* multiply, propagate.

fortschreiten * ('fɔrtʃraitən) *vi* **1** proceed. **2** progress. **—d** *adj* **1** advancing. **2** progressive.

Fortschritt ('fɔrtʃrit) *nm* **-e** progress. **—lich** *adj* progressive.

fortsetz/en * ('fɔrtzɛtsən) *vt* continue. **—ung** *nf* **-en** continuation.

fortwährend ('fɔrtvɛ:rənt) *adj* perpetual, continual.

Fossil (fɔ'si:l) *n neu* **-ien** fossil.

Fötus ('fœtus) *nm* **-usse** foetus.

Fracht (fraxt) *nf* **-en** freight, cargo. **—en** *vt* ship, freight. **—er** *nm* — freighter. **—gut** *n neu* freight, goods.

Frack (frak) *nm* ̈-e dress coat, tails.

Frag/e ('fra:gə) *nf* **-n** question. **—ebogen** *nm* questionnaire. **—en** *vt* ask, question, inquire. **—ezeichen** *n neu* question mark. **—lich** ('fra:kliç) *adj* questionable. **—los** ('fra:klo:s) *adv* unquestionably. **—würdig** ('fra:kvyrdiç) *adj* doubtful.

Fragment (frag'mɛnt) *n neu* **-e** fragment.

Fraktion (fraktsi'o:n) *nf* **-en 1** fraction. **2** parliamentary party.

Fraktur (frak'tu:r) *nf* **-en 1** fracture. **2** Gothic type or script.

Franken ('fraŋkən) *nm* — (Swiss) franc.

frankieren (fraŋ'ki:rən) *vt* frank, stamp.

Frankreich ('fraŋkraiç) *n neu* France.

Franse ('franzə) *nf* **-n** fringe.

Franz/ose (fran'tso:zə) *nm* **-n** Frenchman. **—ösin** (fran'tsø:zin) *nf* **-nen** Frenchwoman. **—ösisch** (fran'tsœ:ziʃ) *adj* French. *n neu* French (language).

Fratze ('fratsə) *nf* **-n** grimace. **Fratzen schneiden** pull faces.

Frau (frau) *nf* **-en** woman, wife. **—enarzt** *nm* gynaecologist. **—enzimmer** *n neu* **1** woman, female. **2** slut.

Fräulein ('frɔylain) n neu — **1** young or unmarried woman. **2** Miss.

frech (frɛç) adj impudent, cheeky. **—heit** nf impudence, cheek.

frei (frai) adj **1** free, at liberty, unconstrained. **2** free (of charge). **3** vacant. **freier Grundbesitz** freehold.

Freibad ('fraibat) n neu open-air swimming pool.

Freibrief ('fraibri:f) nm charter.

Freie ('fraiə) n neu open air. **im Freien** out of doors.

freigebig ('fraigə:biç) adj generous.

Freiheit ('fraihait) nf freedom. **—sstrafe** nf imprisonment.

Frei/herr ('fraihɛr) nm baron. **—herrin** nf baroness.

freilassen* ('frailasən) vt release.

freilich ('frailiç) adv certainly, of course.

freimütig ('fraimy:tiç) adj frank, candid.

freisprechen* ('fraiʃprɛçən) vt acquit.

Freitag ('fraita:k) nm Friday.

frei/willig ('fraiviliç) adj willing, voluntary. **—willige(r)** ('fraiviligə) nm volunteer.

Freizeit ('fraitsait) nf leisure, spare time.

fremd (frɛmt) adj **1** foreign. **2** strange. **—artig** adj strange, odd. **—e** ('frɛmdə) nf **1** foreign country. **—e(r)** ('frɛmdə) nm **1** foreigner. **2** stranger. **—enführer** ('frɛmdənfy:rər) nm guide. **—enverkehr** ('frɛmdənfɛrkɛ:r) nm tourism. **—enzimmer** ('frɛmdəntsimər) n neu **1** guest-room. **2** room to let. **—sprache** nf foreign language. **—wort** n neu foreign word.

Frequenz (fre'kvɛnts) nf **-en** frequency.

fressen* ('frɛsən) vt (of animals) eat.

Freud/e ('frɔydə) nf **-n** joy, pleasure. **—ig** adj joyful. **—igkeit** nf joyfulness.

freuen ('frɔyən) vt please. **sich freuen** vr be glad. **sich freuen auf** look forward to.

Freund (frɔynt) nm **-e** friend, boyfriend. **—in** ('frɔyndin) nf **-nen** friend, girlfriend. **—lich** adj friendly. **2** kind, pleasant. **—schaft** nf **-en** friendship.

Frevel ('fre:fəl) nm — crime, outrage.

Fried/e(n) ('fri:də) nm peace. **—ensstifter** nm peace-maker. **—ensvertrag** nm peace treaty. **—fertig** ('fri:tfɛrtiç) adj peaceable. **—hof** ('fri:tho:f) nm cemetery. **—lich** ('fri:tliç) adj peaceful, peaceable.

frieren* ('fri:rən) vi,vt freeze.

Fries (fri:s) nm **-e** frieze.

frigid (fri'gi:t) adj frigid. **—ität** (frigidi'tɛ:t) nf frigidity.

frisch (friʃ) adj **1** fresh. **2** cool. **3** new. **—e** nf freshness.

Fris/eur (fri'zœ:r) nm **-e** hairdresser, barber. **—iersalon** (fri'zi:rzalɔ) nm hairdresser's salon. **—ur** (fri'zu:r) nf **-en** hair style, hairdo.

Frist (frist) nf **-en** (period of) time, time-limit. **—los** adj without notice.

froh (fro:) adj happy, glad, merry. **—lich** ('frœ:liç) adj happy, merry. **—lichkeit** nf joyfulness, mirth. **—sinn** nm cheerfulness.

fromm (frɔm) adj **1** devout, pious. **2** docile. **—eln** ('frœməln) vi feign piety. **—igkeit** ('frœmiçkait) nf piety. **—ler** ('frœmlər) nm — bigot.

Fronleichnam (fro:n'laiçna:m) nm rel Corpus Christi Day.

Front (frɔnt) nf **-en** front, facade.

fror (fro:r) v see **frieren.**

Frosch (frɔʃ) nm **-e** frog.

Frost (frɔst) nm **-e** frost, chill. **—ig** adj frosty, chilly.

Frucht (fruxt) nf **-e** fruit. **—bar** adj fruitful, fertile. **—barkeit** nf fertility. **—los** adj fruitless.

früh (fry:) adj early. adv **1** early. **2** in the morning. **—e** nf early hour, morning. **—er** adj earlier, former, sooner. **—jahr** n neu also **—ling** nm **-e** spring. **—reif** adj precocious, premature, forward. **—stück** n neu breakfast. **—stücken** vi breakfast. **—zeitig** adj early, premature.

Fuchs (fuks) nm **-e** fox.

Fug/e ('fu:gə) nf **-n 1** joint. **2** fugue. **—en** ('fy:gən) vt **1** add. **2** join. **sich —en** vr submit, acquiesce.

fühl/en ('fy:lən) vt **1** feel, touch. **2** sense. **sich fühlen** vr feel. **sich traurig fühlen** feel sad. **—er** nm — feeler.

führ/en ('fy:rən) vt **1** lead. **2** direct. **3** manage, control, carry on. **4** keep (books). **—er** nm — **1** leader. **2** manager. **3** guide(book). **4** driver. **5** pilot. **—erschein** nm driving licence. **—ung** nf **1** direction, control. **2** leadership. **3** administration.

Füll/e ('fylə) nf **1** fullness. **2** abundance. **—en** vt fill. **—feder** nf also **—er** nm — fountain pen.

Fundament (funda'mɛnt) n neu **-e** foundation.

fünf (fynf) adj,nf five. **—te** adj fifth. **—zehn** adj,nf fifteen. **—zehnte** adj fifteenth. **—zig** adj,nf fifty. **—zigste** adj fiftieth.

fungieren (fuŋ'gi:rən) vi **fungieren als** act as.

Funk (fuŋk) nm radio, wireless. **—eln** vi sparkle, twinkle. **—en** nm — spark. vi spark. vt 1 radio. 2 broadcast. **—er** nm — radio operator. **—gerät** n neu radio (set).

Funktion (fuŋktsi'o:n) nf **-en** function. **—är** (fuŋktsio'nɛ:r) nm **-e** functionary, official. **—ieren** (fuŋktsio'ni:rən) vi function.

für (fy:r) prep 1 for. 2 in place of. 3 in favour of. 4 on behalf of. **für sich** 1 for oneself. 2 exceptional. **was für** what sort of. **—sorge** nf 1 care. 2 welfare. **—sorger** nm — social or welfare worker. **—wahr** adv truly, indeed. **—wort** n neu pronoun.

Furch/e ('furçə) nf **-n** 1 furrow. 2 wrinkle. **—en** vt furrow.

Furcht (furçt) nf fear. **—bar** adj frightful, horrible. **—en** ('fyrçtən) vt fear. **sich —en** vr be afraid. **—los** adj fearless.

Furnier (fur'ni:r) nm **-e** veneer.

Fürst (fyrst) nm **-en** prince. **—entum** ('fyrstəntu:m) n neu **-er** principality. **—in** nf **-nen** princess. **—lich** adj princely.

Fuß (fu:s) nm **-̈e** foot. **zu Fuß gehen** walk, go on foot. **—ball** nm football. **—boden** nm floor. **—bremse** nf foot-brake. **—gänger** ('fu:sgɛŋər) nm — pedestrian. **—tritt** nm 1 kick. 2 footstep.

Futter ('futər) n neu 1 feed, fodder. 2 lining. **—̈n** ('fytərn) vt 1 feed. 2 line.

G

gab (ga:p) v see **geben.**

Gabe ('ga:bə) nf **-n** gift.

Gabel ('ga:bəl) nf **-n** fork.

gackern ('gakərn) vi cackle.

gähnen ('gɛ:nən) vi yawn.

galant (ga'lant) adj gallant.

Galeere (ga'le:rə) nf **-n** galley.

Galerie (galə'ri:) nf **-n** gallery.

Galgen ('galgən) nm — gallows.

Galione (gali'o:nə) nf **-n** galleon.

Galopp (ga'lɔp) nm **-e** gallop. **—ieren** (galə'pi:rən) vi gallop.

galvanisieren (galvani'zi:rən) vt galvanize.

Gang (gaŋ) nm **-̈e** 1 gait. 2 walking, progress. 3 functioning, operation. 4 corridor, aisle. 5 (of a meal) course. 6 mot gear. **im Gang** 1 going on. 2 working. **—art** nf walk, gait.

Gans (gans) nf **-̈e** goose. **—ebraten** ('gɛnzəbratən) nm roast goose. **—efüßchen** ('gɛnzə-

fy:sçən) n neu pl inf quotation marks. **—emarsch** ('gɛnzəmarʃ) nm single file. **—erich** ('gɛnzəriç) nm **-e** gander.

ganz (gants) adj whole, all. adv 1 quite. 2 wholly, very. **im ganzen** on the whole. **—e(s)** n neu whole. **—lich** ('gɛntsliç) adj whole, entire.

gar (ga:r) adj 1 ready, finished. 2 cul tender, done. adv 1 quite. 2 about. 3 very. **gar nicht** not at all.

Garantie (garan'ti:) nf **-n** guarantee. **—ren** vt guarantee.

Garde ('gardə) nf **-n** guard(s).

Garderobe (gardə'ro:bə) nf **-n** 1 cloakroom. 2 wardrobe.

Gardine (gar'di:nə) nf **-n** curtain.

gär/en ('gɛ:rən) vi ferment. **—ung** nf fermentation.

garnieren (gar'ni:rən) vt 1 garnish. 2 trim.

Garnison (garni'zo:n) nf **-en** garrison.

Gart/en ('gartən) nm — garden. **—ner** ('gɛrtnər) nm — gardener.

Gas (ga:s) n neu **-e** gas. **—herd** nm gas cooker or stove. **—ofen** nm gas stove or oven, gas fire.

Gasse ('gasə) nf **-n** alley, lane.

Gast (gast) nm **-̈e** 1 guest, visitor. 2 stranger. 3 customer. **—arbeiter** nm immigrant worker. **—ebuch** n neu visitors' book. **—freundlich** adj hospitable. **—freundschaft** nf hospitality. **—geber** nm — host. **—geberin** nf **-nen** hostess. **—haus** n neu 1 inn. 2 restaurant. **—hof** nm 1 hotel. 2 restaurant. **—stätte** nf restaurant, cafe

Gatt/e ('gatə) nm — husband, spouse. **—in** nf **-nen** wife, spouse.

Gattung ('gatuŋ) nf **-en** 1 kind, sort. 2 species.

gaukeln ('gaukəln) vi 1 juggle. 2 conjure.

Gaul (gaul) nm **-e** horse, nag.

Gaumen ('gaumən) nm — palate.

Gauner ('gaunər) nm — swindler, rogue.

Gaze ('ga:zə) nf — gauze.

Gazelle (ga'tsɛlə) nf **-n** gazelle.

Gebäck (gə'bɛk) n neu **-e** cakes, pastries.

Gebärde (gə'bɛ:rdə) nf **-n** gesture.

gebär/en (gə'bɛ:rən) vt give birth to, bear. **—mutter** nf womb, uterus.

Gebäude (gə'bɔydə) n neu — building.

geben* ('ge:bən) vt give, present. **sich geben** vr 1 act, behave. 2 pass, abate. **es gibt** there is or are. **von sich geben** utter.

Gebet (gə'be:t) n neu **-e** prayer.

gebeten (gə'be:tən) v see **bitten.**

Gebiet (gə'bi:t) *n neu* **-e** territory, district, area. **—en°** *vt,vi* command. **—er** *nm* — commander, master. **—erisch** *adj* masterful, imperious.

Gebilde (gə'bildə) *n neu* — **1** creation, work. **2** form.

gebildet (gə'bildət) *adj* educated.

Gebirg/e (gə'birgə) *n neu* — mountains, mountain range. **—ig** *adj* mountainous.

Gebiß (gə'bis) *n neu* **-bisse 1** teeth. **2** denture. **3** bit.

gebissen (gə'bisən) *v see* **beißen.**

Gebläse (gə'blɛ:zə) *n neu* — bellows.

geblieben (gə'bli:bən) *v see* **bleiben.**

Gebot (gə'bo:t) *n neu* **-e** command(ment).

gebracht (gə'braxt) *v see* **bringen.**

Gebrauch (gə'braux) *nm* **-e 1** use. **2** custom. **—en** *vt* use. **—lich** (gə'brɔʏçliç) *adj* customary, usual. **—sanweisung** *nf* directions for use. **—t** *adj* used, second-hand.

gebrechlich (gə'brɛçliç) *adj* fragile, weak.

gebrochen (gə'brɔxən) *v see* **brechen.**

Gebrüder (gə'brydər) *nm pl comm* brothers, bros.

Gebühr (gə'by:r) *nf* **-en 1** fee, charge. **2** tax, duty. **—lich** *adj* proper, appropriate.

gebunden (gə'bundən) *adj* **1** bound. **2** connected.

Geburt (gə'burt) *nf* **-en** birth. **—enbeschränkung** *nf also* **—enkontrolle** birth control. **—sort** *nm* birthplace. **—sschein** *nm also* **—surkunde** *nf* birth certificate. **—stag** *nm* birthday.

Gebüsch (gə'byʃ) *n neu* **-e** undergrowth, (clump of) bushes.

gedacht (gə'daxt) *v see* **denken.**

Gedächtnis (gə'dɛçtnis) *n neu* **-se** memory, remembrance.

Gedanke (gə'daŋkə) *nm* **-n** thought, idea.

Gedärm (gə'dɛrm) *n neu* **-e** bowels, intestines.

Gedeck (gə'dɛk) *n neu* **-e 1** cover. **2** menu.

gedeih/en° (gə'daiən) *vi* prosper, flourish.

gedenk/en° (gə'dɛŋkən) *vi* **1** remember. **2** mention. **3** intend. **—stätte** *nf* memorial.

Gedicht (gə'diçt) *n neu* **-e** poem.

gediegen (gə'di:gən) *adj* **1** pure. **2** solid, reliable, good-quality.

Gedräng/e (gə'drɛŋə) *n neu* crowd, press.

Geduld (gə'dult) *nf* patience. **—ig** (gə'duldiç) *adj* patient.

ɕeeignet (gə'aignət) *adj* suitable, appropriate.

Gefahr (gə'fa:r) *nf* **-en** danger. **—den** (gə-

'fɛ:rdən) *vt* endanger. **—lich** (gə'fɛ:rliç) *adj* dangerous.

Gefährte (gə'fɛ:rtə) *nm* **-n** companion.

gefall/en° (gə'falən) *vi* please. **dieses Bild gefällt mir** I like this picture, this picture pleases me. **—n** *neu* — pleasure. **nm** — favour. **—ig** (gə'fɛliç) *adj* pleasing, agreeable. **—igkeit** (gə'fɛliçkait) *nf* **-en 1** kindness. **2** favour. **—igst** (gə'fɛliçst) *adv* please.

gefangen (gə'faŋən) *adj* captive. **gefangen nehmen** take prisoner. **—e(r)** *nm* prisoner, captive. **—schaft** *nf* imprisonment, captivity.

Gefängnis (gə'fɛŋnis) *n neu* **-se 1** prison. **2** imprisonment. **—wärter** *nm* warder, jailer.

Gefäß (gə'fɛ:s) *n neu* **-e** vessel, container.

Gefecht (gə'fɛçt) *n neu* **-e 1** fight. **2** action.

geflogen (gə'flo:gən) *v see* **fliegen.**

geflossen (gə'flɔsən) *v see* **fließen.**

Geflügel (gə'fly:gəl) *n neu* poultry.

Gefolge (gə'fɔlgə) *n neu* retinue, followers.

gefräßig (gə'frɛ:siç) *adj* gluttonous, greedy.

Gefreite(r) (gə'fraitə) *nm* **1** lance corporal. **2** able seaman.

Gefrierpunkt (gə'fri:rpuŋkt) *nm* freezing point.

gefroren (gə'fro:rən) *v see* **frieren.**

gefügig (gə'fy:giç) *adj* pliant, compliant.

Gefühl (gə'fy:l) *n neu* **-e 1** sense, touch. **2** feeling, emotion.

gefunden (gə'fundən) *v see* **finden.**

gegangen (gə'gaŋən) *v see* **gehen.**

gegebenenfalls (gə'ge:bənənfals) *adv* should the occasion or need arise.

gegen ('ge:gən) *prep* **1** against. **2** towards. **3** about. **—angriff** *nm* counter-attack. **—einander** (ge:gənain'andər) *adv* against one another. **—gewicht** *n neu* counterweight. **—gift** *n neu* antidote. **—satz** *nm* **1** contrast. **2** opposition. **im Gegensatz zu 1** contrary to. **2** as opposed to. **—seitig** *adj* **1** mutual. **2** reciprocal. **—stand** *nm* object. **—teil** *n neu* **1** contrary. **2** reverse. **im Gegenteil** on the contrary. **—über** (ge:gən'y:bər) *prep,adv* opposite. *n neu* — person or object opposite. **—wart** *nf* **-en 1** the present (time). **2** presence. **—wärtig** *adj* present, current. **—wehr** *nf* defence.

Gegend ('ge:gənt) *nf* **-en** district, area, neighbourhood.

gegessen (gə'gɛsən) *v see* **essen.**

Gegner ('ge:gnər) *nm* — opponent, enemy.

gegossen (gə'gɔsən) *v see* **gießen.**

gegriffen (gə'grifən) *v see* **greifen.**

gehabt (gə'ha:pt) *v see* **haben.**

Gehalt (gə'halt) *n neu* ¨-er salary. *nm* -e content, contents, capacity.

gehässig (gə'hɛsiç) *adj* 1 hateful. 2 spiteful.

geheim (gə'haim) *adj* secret. —**dienst** *nm* secret service. —**nis** *n neu* -se secret. —**nisvoll** *adj* mysterious.

gehen* ('ge:ən) *vi* 1 go, walk. 2 function, work. **es geht** it's all right. **wie geht es Ihnen?** how are you?

Gehilfe (gə'hilfə) *nm* -n assistant.

Gehirn (gə'hirn) *n neu* -e brain. —**erschütterung** *nf* concussion.

geholfen (gə'hɔlfən) *v see* **helfen.**

Gehör (gə'hœ:r) *n neu* hearing.

gehorchen (gə'hɔrçən) *vi* obey.

gehör/en (gə'hœ:rən) belong. **es gehört sich** it is proper. —**ig** *adj* 1 belonging. 2 suitable, proper.

gehorsam (gə'ho:rza:m) *adj* obedient. *nm* obedience.

Gehrock ('ge:rɔk) *nm* frock coat.

Gehsteig ('ge:ʃtaik) *nm* -e pavement.

Gohwerk ('ge:vɛrk) *n neu* clockwork

Geier ('gaiər) *nm* — vulture.

Geifer ('gaifər) *nm* 1 spittle. 2 foam.

Geige ('gaigə) *nf* -n violin, fiddle. —**nspieler** *nm* violinist, fiddler.

Geisel ('gaizəl) *nm* —, *nf* -n hostage.

Geist (gaist) *nm* -er 1 spirit. 2 mind, intellect. 3 ghost. —**esabwesend** *adj* absent-minded —**esgestört** *adj also* —**eskrank** insane, mentally ill. —**eswissenschaften** *nf pl* humanities, the Arts. —**ig** *adj* 1 spiritual. 2 intellectual, mental. 3 alcoholic (beverage, etc.). —**lich** *adj* 1 spiritual. 2 clerical. —**liche(r)** *nm* -n cleric. —**reich** *adj also* —**voll** 1 witty. 2 ingenious.

Geiz (gaits) *nm* 1 avarice. 2 miserliness. —**hals** *nm* miser. —**ig** *adj* miserly.

gekannt (gə'kant) *v see* **kennen.**

gekünstelt (gə'kynstəlt) *adj* 1 artificial. 2 affected. 3 feigned.

Gelächter (gə'lɛçtər) *n neu* laughter.

geladen (gə'la:dən) *adj* loaded.

Gelage (gə'la:gə) *n neu* — feast, drinking-bout.

Gelände (gə'lɛndə) *n neu* — ground, land.

Geländer (gə'lɛndər) *n neu* — railing, banisters.

gelang *v see* **gelingen.**

gelangen (gə'laŋən) *vi* arrive at, reach.

gelassen (gə'lasən) *adj* calm. —**heit** *nf* calmness, composure.

Gelatine (ʒɛla'ti:nə) *nf* gelatine. —**dynamit** *n neu* gelignite.

geläufig (gə'lɔyfiç) *adj* 1 common. 2 current. 3 familiar. 4 fluent.

gelb (gɛlp) *adj,n neu* yellow. —**sucht** *nf* jaundice.

Geld (gɛlt) *n neu* -er money. —**anweisung** *nf* money order. —**mittel** *n neu pl* funds, means. —**schrank** *nm* safe, strong-box. —**strafe** *nf* fine.

Gelee (ʒe'le:) *n neu* -s jelly.

gelegen (gə'le:gən) *adj* 1 situated. 2 convenient. —**heit** *nf* -en 1 opportunity. 2 occasion. —**tlich** *adj* 1 occasional. 2 incidental.

gelehr/t (gə'le:rt) *adj* learned. —**te(r)** *nm* scholar.

Geleit (gə'lait) *n neu* -e retinue, escort. —**en** *vt* escort.

Gelenk (gə'lɛŋk) *n neu* -e joint.

gelernt (gə'lɛrnt) *adj* trained, skilled

Geliebte(r) (gə'li:ptə) *nm* sweetheart, lover.

gelinde (gə'lində) *adj* mild, soft.

gelingen* (gə'liŋən) *vi imp* succeed. **es gelingt mir, etwas zu tun** I am successful or I succeed in doing something.

gelitten (gə'litən) *v see* **leiden.**

geloben (gə'lo:bən) *vt* vow. **Gelübde** (gə'lypta) *n neu* — vow.

gelogen (gə'lo:gən) *v see* **lügen.**

gelt/en* ('gɛltən) *vi* 1 be valid. 2 be worth. 3 pass for. 4 apply to. —**ung** *nf* -en 1 value. 2 validity.

gelungen (gə'luŋən) *v see* **gelingen.**

Gemach (gə'max) *n neu* ¨-er room, apartment. —**lich** (gə'mɛçliç) *adj* 1 comfortable. 2 leisurely.

Gemahl (gə'ma:l) *nm* -e husband, consort. —**in** *nf* -nen wife, consort.

Gemälde (gə'mɛ:ldə) *n neu* — picture, painting.

gemäß (gə'mɛ:s) *prep* according to. *adj* conformable, appropriate. —**igt** *adj* moderate.

gemein (gə'main) *adj* 1 common, general. 2 vulgar. 3 mean. 4 nasty. —**e(r)** *nm* mil private. —**gut** *n neu* public property. —**heit** *nf* -en 1 vulgarity. 2 mean trick. —**hin** *adv* ordinarily, commonly. —**sam** *adj* common, joint. —**schaft** *nf* -en 1 community. 2 association, union.

Gemeinde (gə'maində) *nf* -n 1 community 2 municipality. 3 parish. 4 congregation, communion. —**steuer** *nf* rates.

Gemenge (gə'mɛŋə) n neu — **1** mixture. **2** scuffle.

gemessen (gə'mɛsən) adj **1** measured, precise. **2** dignified, deliberate.

Gemisch (gə'miʃ) n neu -e mixture.

gemocht (gə'mɔxt) v see **mögen.**

Gemse ('gɛmzə) nf -n chamois.

Gemurmel (gə'murməl) n neu murmuring.

Gemüse (gə'my:zə) n neu — vegetable(s). **—händler** nm greengrocer.

Gemüt (gə'my:t) n neu -er **1** mind, soul. **2** temperament, disposition. **—lich** adj **1** good-natured, genial. **2** comfortable, cosy, agreeable. **—lichkeit** nf **1** geniality, kindliness. **2** comfort, cosiness.

Gen (gɛn) n neu -e gene.

genannt (gə'nant) v see **nennen.**

genau (gə'nau) adj exact, precise.

genehmig/en (gə'ne:migən) vt **1** approve. **2** ratify. **—ung** nf -en **1** approval. **2** permit. **3** ratification.

geneigt (gə'naikt) adj inclined or prone (to).

General (gene'ra:l) nm -e general. **—bevollmächtigte(r)** nm **1** chief representative. **2** commissioner. **—direktor** nm **1** general manager. **2** managing director. **—probe** nf dress rehearsal.

Generation (generatsi'o:n) nf -en generation.

genesen** (gə'ne:zən) vi recover, convalesce.

Genetik (ge'ne:tik) nf genetics.

Genf (gɛnf) n neu Geneva.

genial (geni'a:l) adj brilliant, inspired. **—ität** (geniali'tɛ:t) nf genius, brilliance.

Genick (gə'nik) n neu -e nape of the neck.

Genie (ʒe'ni:) n neu -s genius.

genieren (ʒe'ni:rən) vt **1** embarrass. **2** inconvenience. **sich genieren** vr feel embarrassed.

genieß/bar (gə'ni:sba:r) adj **1** enjoyable. **2** edible. **3** drinkable. **—en**** vt **1** enjoy. **2** eat. **3** drink.

Genitalien (geni'ta:liən) n pl genitals.

genommen (gə'nɔmən) v see **nehmen.**

genoß (gə'nɔs) v see **genießen.**

Genosse (gə'nɔsə) nm -n comrade, colleague. **—nschaft** nf -en **1** association. **2** company. **3** cooperative.

genossen (gə'nɔsən) v see **genießen.**

genug (gə'nu:k) adj enough, sufficient. **—e** (gə'ny:gə) nf sufficiency. **—en** (gə'ny:gən) vi suffice. **—end** (gə'ny:gənt) adj sufficient. **—sam** (gə'ny:kza:m) adj **1** easily satisfied. **2**

unassuming. **3** frugal. **—tuung** (gə'nu:ktu:uŋ) nf -en satisfaction.

Genuß (gə'nus) nm -nüsse **1** enjoyment, pleasure. **2** use. **3** consumption (of food, etc.).

Geograph (geo'gra:f) nm -en geographer. **—ie** (geogra'fi:) nf geography. **—isch** adj geographic(al).

Geolog/e (geo'lo:gə) nm -n geologist. **—ie** (geolo'gi:) nf geology. **—isch** adj geological.

Geometrie (geome'tri:) nf -n geometry.

Gepäck (gə'pɛk) n neu luggage. **—aufbewahrung** nf left-luggage office. **—netz** n neu luggage rack. **—träger** nm porter.

gepfiffen (gə'pfifən) v see **pfeifen.**

Gepflogenheit (gə'pflo:gənhait) nf -en habit, custom.

Geplapper (gə'plapər) n neu babble, prattle.

Geplauder (gə'plaudər) n neu chatter, talk.

Gepräge (gə'prɛ:gə) n neu — **1** impression, stamp. **2** character.

gerade (gə'ra:də) adj **1** straight. **2** even. **3** upright. **4** exact. adv **1** precisely. **2** just (now). **3** directly. **—aus** (gərada'aus) adv straight ahead or on. **—zu** (gəra:də'tsu:) adv directly, frankly.

Geradheit (gə'ra:thait) nf **1** straightness, evenness. **2** honesty.

Geranie (gɛ'ra:niə) nf -n bot geranium.

gerannt (gə'rant) v see **rennen.**

Gerät (gə'rɛ:t) n neu -e tool, implement, appliance.

geraten** (gə'ra:tən) vi **1** come or get into. **2** turn out. adj advisable.

geräumig (gə'rɔymiç) adj spacious, roomy.

Geräusch (gə'rɔyʃ) n neu -e noise.

gerben ('gɛrbən) vt tan (hides).

gerecht (gə'rɛçt) adj **1** straight. **2** just, fair. **3** suitable. **4** righteous. **—igkeit** nf **1** justice, fairness. **2** righteousness.

Gerede (gə're:də) n neu talk, gossip, rumour.

Gericht (gə'riçt) n neu -e **1** (law) court. **2** judgment. **—lich** adj judicial, legal. **—sbarkeit** nf jurisdiction. **—sdiener** nm bailiff. **—shof** nm (law) court.

gerieben (gə'ri:bən) v see **reiben.**

gering (gə'riŋ) adj **1** small, insignificant. **2** poor, inferior. **—fügig** adj insignificant, trivial. **—schätzung** nf disdain.

gerinnen** (gə'rinən) vi coagulate, congeal.

Gerippe (gə'ripə) n neu — skeleton.

gerissen (gə'risən) v see **reißen.** adj **1** torn. **2** clever, wily.

geritten (gə'ritən) v see **reiten.**

German/e (gɛrˈmaːnə) nm -n Teuton. —**isch** adj Germanic, Teutonic.

gern(e) (gɛrn) adv gladly, readily. **etwas gern haben** like something.

gerochen (gəˈrɔxən) v see **riechen.**

Gerste (ˈgɛrstə) nf barley.

Geruch (gəˈruːx) nm ¨e smell, odour. —**sinn** nm sense of smell.

Gerücht (gəˈryçt) n neu -e rumour.

Gerüst (gəˈryst) n neu -e scaffold(ing), frame.

gesamt (gəˈzamt) adj total, whole, entire. —**ausgabe** nf complete edition. —**schule** nf comprehensive school.

gesandt (gəˈzant) v see **senden.**

Gesand/te(r) (gəˈzantə) nm envoy, diplomatic representative. —**schaft** nf -en legation, embassy.

Gesang (gəˈzaŋ) nm ¨e 1 singing. 2 song.

Gesäß (gəˈzɛːs) n neu -e buttocks, seat.

Geschäft (gəˈʃɛft) n neu -e 1 business. 2 shop. —**lich** adj commercial. —**sführer** nm manager. —**smann** nm -**leute** businessman. —**sträger** nm 1 representative. 2 chargé d'affaires.

geschah (gəˈʃaː) v see **geschehen.**

gescheh/en¹ (gəˈʃeːən) vi happen, occur. n neu events, occurrences. —**nis** n neu -se event.

gescheit (gəˈʃait) adj intelligent, clever.

Geschenk (gəˈʃɛŋk) n neu -e present.

Geschicht/e (gəˈʃiçtə) nf -n 1 history. 2 story. 3 affair. —**lich** adj historical. —**sschreiber** nm historian.

Geschick (gəˈʃik) n neu -e 1 skill, aptitude. 2 fate. —**lichkeit** nf -en skill, dexterity. —**t** adj skilful, dexterous.

geschieden (gəˈʃiːdən) v see **scheiden.** adj divorced.

geschienen (gəˈʃiːnən) v see **scheinen.**

Geschirr (gəˈʃir) n neu -e 1 dishes, crockery. 2 harness. —**tuch** n neu tea-towel.

Geschlecht (gəˈʃlɛçt) n neu -er 1 sex. 2 race. 3 species, kind. 4 family, blood. 5 gender. —**lich** adj sexual. —**skrankheit** nf venereal disease. —**sreife** nf puberty, sexual maturity. —**steile** nm pl genitals. —**sverkehr** nm sexual intercourse.

geschlossen (gəˈʃlɔsən) v see **schließen.**

Geschmack (gəˈʃmak) nm ¨e 1 taste. 2 flavour. 3 liking, fancy. —**los** adj tasteless. —**ssinn** nm sense of taste. —**voll** adj tasteful.

Geschnatter (gəˈʃnatər) n neu cackling.

geschnitten (gəˈʃnitən) v see **schneiden.**

geschoben (gəˈʃoːbən) v see **schieben.**

Geschöpf (gəˈʃœpf) n neu -e 1 creature. 2 creation.

Geschoß (gəˈʃɔs) n neu -**schosse** 1 missile. 2 bullet. 3 storey, floor.

geschossen (gəˈʃɔsən) v see **schießen.**

Geschrei (gəˈʃrai) n neu 1 shouting, clamour. 2 fuss.

geschrieben (gəˈʃriːbən) v see **schreiben.**

geschrie(e)n (gəˈʃriː(ə)n) v see **schreien.**

geschritten (gəˈʃritən) v see **schreiten.**

Geschütz (gəˈʃyts) n neu -e gun, cannon.

geschwätzig (gəˈʃvɛtsiç) adj talkative.

geschweige (gəˈʃvaigə) adv,conj also **geschweige denn** not to mention, let alone.

geschwiegen (gəˈʃviːgən) v see **schweigen.**

geschwind (gəˈʃvint) adj swift, quick. —**igkeit** (gəˈʃvindiçkait) nf -en speed. —**igkeitsmesser** nm speedometer. —**igkeitsbegrenzung** nf speed limit.

Geschwister (gəˈʃvistər) n pl brothers and sisters.

Geschworene(r) (gəˈʃvoːrənə) nm juror, juryman.

Geschwür (gəˈʃvyːr) n neu -e 1 ulcer. 2 abscess.

Gesell/e (gəˈzɛlə) nm -n 1 companion, fellow. 2 assistant. 3 journeyman. —**ig** adj sociable, companionable, gregarious. —**igkeit** nf sociability. —**schaft** nf -en 1 society. 2 company. 3 firm. 4 party, social gathering. —**schaftlich** adj 1 social. 2 sociable.

Gesetz (gəˈzɛts) n neu -e 1 law. 2 statute. —**gebend** adj legislative. —**geber** nm legislator. —**gebung** nf -en legislation —**lich** adj lawful, legal. —**los** adj lawless. —**mäßig** adj 1 legal. 2 legitimate. 3 regular. —**widrig** adj illegal.

gesetzt (gəˈzɛtst) adj 1 calm. 2 grave.

Gesicht (gəˈziçt) n neu -er face. —**skreis** nm horizon. —**spunkt** nm point of view.

Gesims (gəˈzims) n neu -e 1 moulding, cornice. 2 ledge.

gesinn/t (gəˈzint) adj minded, disposed. —**ung** nf -en 1 convictions, beliefs. 2 attitude.

Gespann (gəˈʃpan) n neu -e team (of horses, oxen, etc.). —**t** adj 1 tense, strained. 2 curious. 3 anxious, agog.

Gespenst (gəˈʃpɛnst) n neu -er ghost, spectre.

Gespräch (gəˈʃprɛːç) n neu -e conversation, talk.

gesprochen (gəˈʃprɔxən) v see **sprechen.**

gesprungen (gəˈʃpruŋən) v see **springen.**

Gestalt (gə'ʃtalt) *nf* **-en** 1 form, shape. 2 aspect. 3 figure. 4 stature. **—en** *vt* form. **sich —en** *vr* take shape.

gestanden (gə'ʃtandən) *v* see **stehen.**

Geständnis (gə'ʃtɛntnis) *n neu* **-nisse** confession.

Gestank (gə'ʃtaŋk) *nm* stench.

gestatten (gə'ʃtatən) *vt* permit, allow. **sich gestatten** *vr* 1 venture. 2 presume.

Geste ('gɛstə) *nf* **-n** gesture.

gestehen* (gə'ʃte:ən) *vt* confess.

Gestein (gə'ʃtain) *n neu* **-e** 1 stone. 2 mineral.

Gestell (gə'ʃtɛl) *n neu* **-e** 1 stand. 2 frame. 3 trestle.

gest/ern ('gɛstərn) *adv* yesterday. **—rig** ('gɛstriç) *adj* yesterday's.

gestiegen (gə'ʃti:gən) *v* see **steigen.**

gestohlen (gə'ʃto:lən) *v* see **stehlen.**

Gesträuch (gə'ʃtrɔyç) *n neu* **-e** bush(es), shrubbery.

Gesuch (gə'zu:x) *n neu* **-e** petition, request.

gesund (gə'zunt) *adj* healthy, wholesome. **—heit** *nf* health, fitness.

gesungen (gə'zuŋən) *v* see **singen.**

gesunken (gə'zuŋkən) *v* see **sinken.**

getan (gə'ta:n) *v* see **tun.**

Getränk (gə'trɛŋk) *n neu* **-e** drink.

Getreide (gə'traidə) *n neu* cereals, grain, corn.

getreu (gə'trɔy) *adj* faithful, true, loyal.

getrieben (gə'tri:bən) *v* see **treiben.**

getroffen (gə'trɔfən) *v* see **treffen.**

getrost (gə'tro:st) *adj* confident.

getrunken (gə'truŋkən) *v* see **trinken.**

Getto ('gɛto:) *n neu* **-s** ghetto.

gewagt (gə'va:kt) *adj* risky, bold.

gewählt (gə've:lt) *adj* 1 selected. 2 refined.

Gewähr (gə've:r) *nf* guarantee, surety. **—en** *vt* allow, grant. **—leisten** *vt* guarantee.

Gewalt (gə'valt) *nf* **-en** 1 violence, force. 2 power, might. **—ig** *adj* powerful, mighty. **—sam** *adj* violent, forcible.

Gewand (gə'vant) *n neu* **"er** gown, robe.

gewandt (gə'vant) *v* see **wenden.** *adj* agile, skilful.

gewann (gə'van) *v* see **gewinnen.**

Gewässer (gə'vɛsər) *n neu* **—** waters, stretch of water.

Gewebe (gə've:bə) *n neu* **—** 1 tissue. 2 textile, fabric.

geweckt (gə'vɛkt) *adj* alert, bright.

Gewehr (gə've:r) *n neu* **-e** gun, rifle.

Gewerb/e (gə'vɛrbə) *n neu* **—** trade, business, industry. **—lich** (gə'vɛrpliç) *adj* commercial.

Gewerkschaft (gə'vɛrkʃaft) *nf* **-en** trade union. **—ler** *nm* **—** trade-unionist.

gewesen (gə've:zən) *v* see **sein.**

Gewicht (gə'viçt) *n neu* **-e** 1 weight. 2 importance. **—ig** *adj* important, weighty.

gewiesen (gə'vi:zən) *v* see **weisen.**

Gewimmel (gə'viməl) *n neu* swarms, throngs.

Gewinn (gə'vin) *nm* **-e** 1 winning. 2 profit, gain. 3 winnings. **—en*** *vt* 1 win. 2 earn.

Gewirr (gə'vir) *n neu* **-e** confusion, tangle.

gewiß (gə'vis) *adj* sure, certain. **ein gewisser Herr** a certain gentleman. **~adv** indeed, certainly. **—ermaßen** *adv* to a certain extent. **—heit** *nf* **-en** certainty.

Gewissen (gə'visən) *n neu* conscience. **—los** *adj* unscrupulous.

Gewitter (gə'vitər) *n neu* **—** (thunder)storm. **—n** *vi* thunder.

gewogen (gə'vo:gən) *v* see **wiegen.** *adj* 1 affectionate. 2 well-disposed.

gewöhnen (gə'vø:nən) *vt* accustom. **sich gewöhnen** *vr* become accustomed or used (to).

Gewohnheit (gə'vo:nhait) *nf* **-en** habit. **—srecht** *n neu* common law.

gewöhnlich (gə'vø:nliç) *adj* usual, ordinary.

gewohnt (gə'vo:nt) *adj* accustomed.

Gewölbe (gə'vœlbə) *n neu* **—** arch, vault.

gewonnen (gə'vɔnən) *v* see **gewinnen.**

geworden (gə'vɔrdən) *v* see **werden.**

geworfen (gə'vɔrfən) *v* see **werfen.**

Gewürz (gə'vyrts) *n neu* **-e** seasoning, spice. **—ig** *adj* spicy.

gewußt (gə'vust) *v* see **wissen.**

gezogen (gə'tso:gən) *v* see **ziehen.**

gezwungen (gə'tsvuŋən) *v* see **zwingen.** *adj* 1 forced. 2 unnatural.

gibt (gi:bt) *v* see **geben.**

Gicht (giçt) *nf* **-en** gout.

Giebel ('gi:bəl) *nm* **—** gable.

Gier (gi:r) *nf* greed(iness). **—ig** *adj* greedy.

gießen* ('gi:sən) *vt* 1 pour. 2 water. 3 mould, found.

Gift (gift) *n neu* **-e** poison. **—ig** *adj* poisonous.

Gigue (ʒi:g) *nf* **-n** jig.

ging (giŋ) *v* see **gehen.**

Gipfel ('gipfəl) *nm* **—** peak, summit. **—höhe** *nf aviat* ceiling. **—n** *vi* culminate.

Gips (gips) *nm* **-e** plaster (of Paris), gypsum.

Giraffe (gi'rafə) *nf* **-n** giraffe.

Giro ('dʒi:ro:) *n neu* **-s** 1 giro transfer. 2 endorsement.

Gischt (giʃt) *nm* **-e** spray, foam.

Gitarre (gi'tarə) *nf* **-n** guitar.

Gitter ('gitər) *n neu* — **1** grating, lattice. **2** railings, fence.

Glanz (glants) *nm* **1** brilliance, shine, lustre. **2** splendour. **—en** ('glɛntsən) *vi* shine, gleam.

Glas (glaːs) *n neu* **"er 1** glass. **2** drinking-glass. **"ern** (glɛːzərn) *adj* glass(y). **—ur** (glaˈzuːr) *nf* **-en 1** glaze. **2** enamel. **3** *cul* icing.

glatt (glat) *adj* **1** smooth, even. **2** slippery. **3** plain, downright. *adv* smoothly, easily. **"en** ('glɛtən) *vt* smooth, plane, polish.

Glaub/e ('glaubə) *nm* belief, faith. **—en** *vi* believe (in), trust. *vt* think. **—ig** ('glɔybiç) *adj* believing, faithful. **"ige(r)** ('glɔybigə) *nm* believer. **—iger** ('glɔybigər) *nm* — creditor. **—würdig** ('glaupvyrdiç) *adj* credible, trustworthy.

gleich (glaiç) *adj* **1** same, like. **2** equal. **3** level, even. *adv* **1** equally, alike. **2** just. **3** at once, immediately.

gleichbedeutend ('glaiçbədɔytənt) *adj* **1** synonymous. **2** equivalent.

gleichberechtigt ('glaiçbərɛçtikt) *adj* having equal rights.

gleichen* ('glaiçən) *vi* be like or equal.

gleichermaßen ('glaiçərmasən) *adv* in like manner, equally.

gleichfalls ('glaiçfals) *adv* likewise, equally.

Gleichgewicht ('glaiçgəviçt) *n neu* balance, equilibrium.

gleichgültig ('glaiçgyltiç) *adj* **1** indifferent. **2** unimportant.

Gleichheit (glaiçhait) *nf* **-en 1** equality. **2** uniformity. **gleichmäßig** ('glaiçmɛsiç) *adj* **1** equal. **2** uniform. **3** symmetrical.

Gleichnis ('glaiçnis) *n neu* **-se 1** parable. **2** simile. **3** image.

gleichschalten ('glaiçʃaltən) *vt* coordinate, synchronize.

Gleichschritt ('glaiçʃrit) *nm* marching in step.

Gleichstrom ('glaiçʃtroːm) *nm* direct current.

Gleichung ('glaiçuŋ) *nf* **-en** equation.

gleichviel ('glaiçviːl) *adv* **1** no matter. **2** just as much.

gleichwohl ('glaiçvoːl) *adv* nevertheless.

gleichzeitig ('glaiçtsaitiç) *adj* simultaneous.

Gleis (glais) *n neu* **-e 1** track. **2** rails.

gleiten* ('glaitən) *vi* **1** glide. **2** slide.

Gletscher ('glɛtʃər) *nm* — glacier.

Glied (gliːt) *n neu* **-er 1** member, limb. **2** row, rank. **—erung** ('gliːdəruŋ) *nf* **-en 1** arrangement. **2** structure. **3** division. **—maßen** *n pl anat* extremities.

glimpflich ('glimpfliç) *adj* **1** gentle. **2** lenient.

Glocke ('glɔkə) *nf* **-n** bell. **—nblume** *nf* **1** bluebell. **2** harebell. **—nstuhl** *nm* belfry.

glor-/ifizieren (gloriˈfiˈtsiːrən) *vt* glorify. **—reich** ('gloːraiç) *adj* glorious.

glotzen ('glɔtsən) *vi* stare, gape.

Glück (glyk) *n neu* **1** (good) luck. **2** fortune. **3** happiness. **—en** *vi* succeed, prosper. **—lich** *adj* **1** lucky. **2** happy. **—licherweise** *adv* fortunately. **—wunsch** *nm* congratulation(s).

glüh/en ('glyːən) *vi* glow, burn. **—birne** *nf* (light) bulb.

Glut (gluːt) *nf* **-en 1** blaze, glow. **2** live coals, embers. **3** passion.

Gnad/e ('gnaːdə) *nf* **-n 1** grace. **2** mercy. **3** favour. **—enfrist** *nf* reprieve, respite. **—ig** ('gnɛːdiç) *adj* **1** gracious. **2** merciful. **gnädige Frau** Madam.

Gold (gɔlt) *n neu* gold. **—en** ('gɔldən) *adj* gold(en). **—ig** ('gɔldiç) *adj* sweet, lovely, cute.

Golf[1] (gɔlf) *nm* **-e** gulf. **—strom** *nm* Gulf Stream

Golf[2] (gɔlf) *n neu* golf.

gönn/en ('gœnən) *vt* grant, allow. **—er** *nm* — patron, benefactor.

goß (gɔs) *v* see **gießen.**

Gosse ('gɔsə) *nf* **-n** gutter.

Gott (gɔt) *nm* **"er** god. **—esdienst** ('gɔtəsdiːnst) *nm* **1** church service. **2** worship. **—eslästerung** ('gɔtəslɛstəruŋ) *nf* blasphemy. **"in** ('gœtin) *nf* **-nen** goddess. **"lich** *adj* divine.

Götze ('gœtsə) *nm* **-n** idol.

Grab (graːp) *n neu* **"er** grave. **—en*** ('graːbən) *vt* dig. **—mal** *n neu* **1** tomb. **2** tombstone. **—schrift** *nf* epitaph. **—stätte** *nf* tomb, grave. **—stein** *nm* tombstone.

Grad (graːt) *nm* **-e 1** degree. **2** grade, rank.

Graf (graːf) *nm* **-en** count, earl. **"in** ('grɛːfin) *nf* **-nen** countess. **—schaft** *nf* **-en** county.

Gram (graːm) *nm* grief, sorrow.

Gramm (gram) *n neu* **-e** gramme.

Grammat/ik (graˈmatik) *nf* **-en** grammar. **—isch** *adj* grammatical.

Granatapfel (graˈnaːtapfəl) *nm* pomegranate.

Granat/e (graˈnaːtə) *nf* **-n** grenade, shell.

Granit (graˈniːt) *nm* **-e** granite.

graphisch ('graːfiʃ) *adj* graphic.

Gras (graːs) *n neu* **"er** grass. **—en** ('graːzən) *vi* graze.

gräßlich ('grɛsliç) *adj* terrible, horrible.

Grat (graːt) *nm* **-e 1** edge. **2** ridge. **3** crest.

Gräte ('grɛːtə) *nf* **-n** fishbone.

gratis

gratis ('gra:tis) *adj,adv* free (of charge).

gratulieren (gratu'li:rən) *vi* congratulate.

grau (grau) *adj* grey.

grauen[1] ('grauən) *vi* **1** become grey. **2** dawn.

grauen[2] ('grauən) *n neu* — horror, dread. **sich grauen** *vr* be afraid or horrified. **grauenhaft** *adj* horrible, dreadful.

grausam ('grauza:m) *adj* cruel, ferocious.

grausig ('grauzic) *adj* horrible, fearful.

gravieren (gra'vi:rən) *vt* engrave.

greifen* ('graifən) *vt* grasp, seize. *vi* **1** touch. **2** reach. **3** grope.

Greis (grais) *nm* **-e** old man. **—in** ('graisin) *nf* **-nen** old woman.

grell (grɛl) *adj* **1** harsh, sharp. **2** glaring.

Grenz/e ('grɛntsə) *nf* **-n 1** frontier. **2** boundary, limit. **— en** *vi* border (on). **—enlos** *adj* limitless, boundless.

Greuel ('grɔyəl) *nm* — horror, abomination.

Griech/e ('gri:çə) *nm* **-n** Greek. **—enland** *n neu* Greece. **—isch** *adj* Greek. *n neu* Greek (language).

Grieß (gri:s) *nm* **-e 1** gravel, grit. **2** semolina.

griff (grif) *v* see **greifen**.

Griff (grif) *nm* **-e 1** grip, hold. **2** handle.

Grille ('grilə) *nf* **-n 1** *zool* cricket. **2** whim.

grinsen ('grinzən) *vi* grin.

Grippe ('gripə) *nf* **-n** influenza, flu.

grob (gro:p) *adj* **1** coarse, crude. **2** gross.

Groll (grɔl) *nm* **1** grudge. **2** resentment.

Grönland ('grœ:nlant) *n neu* Greenland.

Gros (grɔs) *n neu* **1** gross. **2** main body. **en gros** wholesale.

Groschen ('grɔʃən) *nm* — ten-pfennig (piece).

groß (gro:s) *adj* **1** large, big. **2** tall. **3** great. **im großen 1** in bulk. **2** wholesale. **im großen und ganzen** on the whole.

großartig ('gro:sɑ:rtiç) *adj* **1** grand, splendid. **2** lofty.

Großbritannien (gro:sbri'taniən) *n neu* Great Britain.

Größe ('grœ:sə) *nf* **1** size. **2** height. **3** greatness. **4** importance.

Großeltern ('gro:seltern) *n pl* grandparents.

großenteils ('gro:sentails) *adv* in large part, mostly.

Großhandel ('gro:shandəl) *nm* wholesale trade.

großherzig ('gro:she:rtsik) *adj* magnanimous.

Großindustrie ('gro:sindustri:) *nf* heavy industry.

Großmacht ('gro:smaxt) *nf* great power.

Großmaul ('gro:smaul) *n neu* braggart, boaster.

Großmutter ('gro:smutər) *nf* grandmother.

Großstadt ('gro:sʃtat) *nf* (big) city.

größtenteils ('grœ:stəntails) *adv* for the most part, largely.

Großteil ('gro:stail) *nm* bulk.

Großvater ('gro:sfatə) *nm* grandfather.

großzügig ('gro:stsy:giç) *adj* **1** on a large scale. **2** generous.

grotesk (gro'tɛsk) *adj* grotesque.

Grube ('gru:bə) *nf* **-n 1** hole, pit. **2** mine, quarry.

grübeln ('gry:bəln) *vi* brood, ponder.

grün (gry:n) *adj,n* neu green. **—kohl** *nm* kale.

Grund (grunt) *nm* **-̈e 1** ground. **2** (plot of) land. **3** soil. **4** bottom, depth. **5** reason. **6** basis.

Grundbau ('gruntbau) *nm* foundation.

Grundbesitz ('gruntbəzits) *nm* landed property.

gründ/en ('gryndən) *vt* **1** found. **2** ground. **-̈er** *nm* — founder.

Grundgesetz ('gruntgəzets) *n neu* **1** basic law. **2** constitution.

Grundlage ('gruntla:gə) *nf* foundation.

gründlich ('gryntliç) *adj* **1** thorough. **2** complete.

grundlos ('gruntlo:s) *adj* baseless, groundless.

Grundriß ('gruntris) *nm* **1** outline. **2** plan.

Grundsatz ('gruntzats) *nm* **1** basic or fundamental principle. **2** axiom. **-̈lich** *adj* fundamental.

Grundstück ('gruntʃtyk) *n neu* piece of land.

Gründung ('gryndun) *nf* **-en** foundation, establishment.

grunzen ('gruntsən) *vi* grunt.

Grupp/e ('grupə) *nf* **-n** group. **—ieren** (gru'pi:rən) *vt* group, arrange.

gruselig ('gru:zəliç) *adj* uncanny, creepy.

Gruß (gru:s) *nm* **-̈e** greeting. **-̈en** ('gry:sən) *vt* greet. **grüß Gott!** good day!

gucken ('gukən) *vi* look, peep.

Gulasch ('gu:laʃ) *nm,neu* **-e** goulash.

gültig ('gyltiç) *adj* **1** valid, good. **2** current. **—keit** *nf* **1** validity. **2** currency.

Gummi ('gumi) *nm,neu* **-s 1** rubber. **2** gum. **3** eraser. **—band** *n neu* rubber band, elastic. **—schuh** *nm* overshoe, galosh.

Gunst (gunst) *nf* **-̈e** goodwill, favour. **-̈ig** ('gynstiç) *adj* favourable. **-̈ling** ('gynstlin) *nm* **-e** favourite.

gurgel/n ('gurgəln) *vi* **1** gargle. **2** gurgle. **—wasser** *n neu* gargle.

Gurke ('gurkə) *nf* **-n** cucumber.

Gürtel ('gyrtəl) *nm* — **1** belt. **2** zone.

Guß (gus) *nm* **-üsse 1** pouring out, gush. **2** downpour. **3** casting. **4** *cul* icing.

gut (gu:t) *adj* good. *adv* well. **—achten** *n neu* — (expert) opinion. **—e** ('gy:tə) *nf* 1 goodness. 2 kindness. 3 excellence. **—heißen** *vt* approve (of). **—ig** ('gy:tiç) *adj* 1 kind. 2 good. 3 good-natured. **—willig** *adj* voluntary, willing.

Gut (gu:t) *n neu* **er** 1 possession. 2 landed estate. 3 goods, wares. **—erbahnhof** ('gy:tərba:nhɔf) *nm* goods yard. **—erzug** ('gy:tərtsu:k) *nm* goods train. **—sherr** *nm* 1 lord of the manor. 2 landlord.

Gymnasium (gym'na:zium) *n neu* **-sien** grammar school.

H

Haag, Den (ha:k) *nm* The Hague.

Haar (ha:r) *n neu* **-e** hair. **—bürste** *nf* hairbrush. **—ig** *adj* hairy. **—schnitt** *nm* haircut. **—sträubend** *adj* hair-raising.

Hab/e ('ha:bə) *nf* **-n** property, possessions. **—en'** *vt* have, possess. *n neu* credit. **—enichts** *nm* **-e** pauper. **—gier** ('ha:pgi:r) *nf* avarice, greed. **—seligkeiten** ('ha:pze:liçkaitən) *nf pl* belongings, possessions.

Habicht ('ha:biçt) *nm* **-e** hawk.

hack/en ('hakən) *vt* 1 hash. 2 hack. 3 chop. **—fleisch** *n neu* minced meat, mince.

Hafen ('ha:fən) *nm* **-** harbour, port. **—arbeiter** *nm* docker. **—damm** *nm* jetty. **—stadt** *nf* port.

Hafer ('ha:fər) *nm* **—** oat(s). **—brei** *nm* porridge. **—flocken** *nf pl* oat-flakes, rolled oats.

Haft (haft) *nf* 1 arrest. 2 imprisonment. **—befehl** *nm* warrant of arrest. **—en** *vi* 1 adhere, cling (to). 2 guarantee, answer (for). **—pflichtversicherung** *nf* **-en** third-party insurance. **—ung** *nf* **-en** liability.

Hagedorn ('ha:gədɔrn) *nm* **-e** hawthorn.

Hagel ('ha:gəl) *nm* **—** hail. **—n** *vi* hail.

hager ('ha:gər) *adj* gaunt.

Hahn (ha:n) *nm* **-e** 1 cock. 2 tap. **—chen** ('hɛ:nçən) *n neu* **—** 1 cockerel. 2 *cul* chicken.

Hai (hai) *nm* **-e** *also* **Haifisch** shark.

häkeln ('hɛ:kəln) *vt* crochet.

haken ('ha:kən) *vi* hook (on). *nm* **—** 1 hook. 2 difficulty, snag. **—kreuz** *n neu* swastika.

halb (halp) *adj* half. **—e(r)** ('halbə) *nm* half litre (of beer, wine, etc.). **—insel** *nf* peninsula. **—jährlich** *adj* half-yearly. **—kreis** *nm* semicircle. **—kugel** *nf* hemisphere. **—laut**

adj (of a voice) low. *adv* in a low voice. **—messer** *nm* radius. **—mond** *nm* halfmoon, crescent. **—wegs** ('halpve:ks) *adv* 1 halfway. 2 to some or any extent.

half (half) *v see* **helfen.**

Hälfte ('hɛlftə) *nf* **-n** 1 half. 2 middle.

Halfter ('halftər) *nm,neu* **—**, *nf* **-n** halter.

Hall (hal) *nm* **-e** 1 clang. 2 peal. **—en** *vi* 1 resound. 2 clang.

Halle ('halə) *nf* **-n** 1 hall. 2 porch, lobby. 3 hangar. **—nbad** *n neu* indoor swimming pool.

Halm (halm) *nm* **-e** 1 blade (of grass). 2 stalk.

Hals (hals) *nm* **-e** 1 neck. 2 throat. **—starrig** ('halsʃtariç) *adj* obstinate, stubborn. **—tuch** *n neu* scarf. **—weh** *n neu* sore throat.

Halt (halt) *nm* **-e** 1 stop, halt. 2 support. **—bar** *adj* 1 tenable. 2 firm, lasting. **haltbar sein** (of foodstuffs) keep. **—los** *adj* 1 untenable. 2 unsteady.

halt/en' ('haltən) *vt* 1 hold. 2 keep. *vi* 1 stop, halt. 2 hold out. **halten fur** consider, deem. **sich halten** *vr* maintain oneself. **—estelle** *nf* (bus) stop.

hämisch ('hɛ:miʃ) *adj* malicious.

Hammelfleisch ('haməlflaiʃ) *n neu* mutton.

Hammer ('hamər) *nm* **-** hammer. **—n** ('hɛmərn) *vi,vt* hammer.

Hamster ('hamstər) *nm* **—** hamster.

Hand (hant) *nf* **-e** hand. **an Hand von** with the aid of. **die Hand geben** shake hands. **in der Hand haben** have under one's control.

Handarbeit ('hanta:rbait) *nf* 1 manual work. 2 handwork, craft. 3 needlework.

Handbremse ('hantbremzə) *nf* handbrake.

Handbuch ('hantbux) *n neu* handbook.

Händedruck ('hɛndədruk) *nm* handshake.

Handel ('handəl) *nm* 1 trade, commerce. 2 transaction, deal. **—n** *vi* 1 act, do. 2 deal with. 3 haggle. 4 trade. **es handelt sich um** it is a question of. **—skammer** *nf* chamber of commerce. **—smarke** *nf* trademark, brand name. **—ssperre** *nf* embargo.

handfest ('hantfest) *adj* sturdy, strong.

Handfläche ('hantflɛçə) *nf* palm.

Handgelenk ('hantgələnk) *n neu* wrist.

Handgepäck ('hantgəpɛk) *n neu* hand luggage.

handhaben' ('hantha:bən) *vt* 1 handle. 2 manage.

Handschelle ('hantʃelə) *nf* **-n** handcuff.

Handschrift ('hantʃrift) *nf* 1 handwriting. 2 manuscript.

Handschuh ('hantʃu:) *nm* glove.

Handstreich ('hantʃtraiç) nm **1** raid. **2** surprise.
Handtasche ('hanttaʃə) nf handbag.
Handtuch ('hanttux) n neu towel.
Handwerk ('hantvɛrk) n neu craft, trade. **—er** nm artisan, craftsman.
Händler ('hɛndlər) nm — merchant, trader.
Handlung ('handluŋ) nf **-en 1** act, action. **2** trade. **3** business, shop.
Hang (haŋ) nm **-̈e 1** slope. **2** tendency. **-̈ebrücke** ('hɛŋəbrykə) nf suspension bridge. **-̈ematte** ('hɛŋəmatə) nf hammock. **-̈en*** ('hɛŋən) vi **1** hang. **2** be attached. **3** depend (on). vt **1** hang. **2** attach.
Hannover (ha'noːfər) n neu Hanover.
Harfe ('harfə) nf **-n** harp.
harmlos ('harmloːs) adj harmless.
Harmon/ie (harmo'niː) nf **-n** harmony. **—ika** (har'moːnika) nf **-s 1** concertina. **2** harmonica. **—isch** (har'moːniʃ) adj harmonious, harmonic.
Harnisch ('harniʃ) nm **-e** armour.
Harpune (har'puːnə) nf **-n** harpoon.
harren ('harən) vi **1** wait for. **2** await. **3** hope for.
hart (hart) adj **1** hard. **2** rough. **3** severe. **-̈e** ('hɛrtə) nf **1** hardness. **2** roughness. **3** severity. **—en** ('hɛrtən) vt harden, temper. **—näckig** ('hartnɛkiç) adj obstinate.
Harz (harts) n neu **-e** resin.
Haschisch ('haʃiʃ) n neu hashish.
Hase ('haːzə) nm **-n** hare.
Haselnuß ('haːzəlnus) nf hazelnut.
Haspe ('haspə) nf **-n** hasp, hinge.
Haß (has) nm hate, hatred. **-̈lich** ('hɛsliç) adj **1** ugly. **2** nasty, horrid.
hassen ('hasən) vt hate.
hast (hast) v see **haben.**
hasten ('hastən) vi hasten, hurry.
hat (hat) v see **haben.**
hätscheln ('hɛːtʃəln) vt **1** caress. **2** pamper, spoil.
hatte ('hatə) v see **haben.**
hätte ('hɛtə) v see **haben.**
Haube ('haubə) nf **-n 1** cap, hood. **2** mot bonnet. **3** dome.
Hauch (haux) nm **-e** breath.
Haue ('hauə) nf **-n 1** hoe. **2** thrashing, beating. **—n*** vt **1** chop. **2** fell. **3** thrash, spank.
Haufen ('haufən) nm — **1** heap, pile. **2** mass, large amount. **—en** ('hɔyfən) vt heap up, accumulate. **—enweise** ('haufənvaizə) adv in great quantities, in heaps.

häufig ('hɔyfiç) adj frequent. **—keit** nf **-en** frequency.
Haupt (haupt) n neu **-̈er 1** head. **2** leader. **—bahnhof** nm main or central railway station. **—buch** n neu ledger. **—fach** n neu main subject. **—mann** nm captain. **—quartier** n neu headquarters. **—sache** nf main point or thing. **—sächlich** adj main, principal. **—stadt** nf capital. **—wort** n neu noun.
Haus (haus) n neu **-̈er 1** house. **2** building. **3** home. **nach Hause gehen** go home. **zu Hause** at home. **—arbeit** nf **1** housework. **2** homework. **—en** ('hauzən) vi **1** live (economically). **2** play havoc. **—frau** nf housewife. **—halt** nm **1** housekeeping. **2** household. **3** budget. **—halten*** vi **1** keep house. **2** economize. **—herr** nm **1** head of the family. **2** landlord. **—ieren** (hau'ziːrən) vi peddle. **—meister** nm caretaker. **—tier** n neu domestic animal, pet.
Haut (haut) nf **-̈e 1** skin, hide. **2** membrane, film. **-̈en** ('hɔytən) vt skin.
Hebamme ('heːpamə) nf **-n** midwife.
Heb/el ('heːbəl) nm — lever. **—en*** ('heːbən) vt lift. raise. **sich —en** vr **1** rise. **2** cancel. **—er** ('heːbər) nm — syphon. **—estange** ('heːbəʃtaŋə) nf crowbar. **—ung** ('heːbuŋ) nf **-en 1** elevation. **2** removal.
Hecht (hɛçt) nm **-e** pike.
Heck (hɛk) n neu stern, rear.
Hecke ('hɛkə) nf **-n** hedge. **—nschütze** nm sniper.
Heer (heːr) n neu **-e** army.
Hefe ('heːfə) nf **-n 1** yeast. **2** dregs.
Heft (hɛft) n neu **-e 1** handle. **2** exercise book. **3** (journal) volume, number. **—en** vt **1** fasten. **2** fix. **3** sew. **—klammer** nf paper clip. **—zwecke** nf drawing-pin.
heftig ('hɛftiç) adj **1** violent. **2** strong. **3** vehement. **4** fierce.
hegen ('heːgən) vt cherish, harbour.
Hehl (heːl) n neu **1** secret. **2** secrecy. **—en** vt **1** conceal. **2** receive (stolen property).
hehr (heːr) adj lofty, sublime.
Heide[1] ('haidə) nf **-n** heath. **—kraut** n neu heather. **—lbeere** nf bilberry.
Heid/e[2] ('haidə) nm **-n** heathen, pagan. **—nisch** adj heathen, pagan.
heikel ('haikəl) adj **1** critical. **2** delicate. **3** awkward.
heil (hail) adj **1** well. **2** unhurt. **3** whole. **4** sound, undamaged. n neu **1** welfare. **2**

salvation. **—butt** ('hailbʌt) *nm* halibut. **—en** *vt,vi* heal. **—kraft** *nf* healing power. **—mittel** *n neu* remedy, cure. **—sam** *adj* 1 wholesome. 2 beneficial. **—sarmee** ('hailsarme:) *nf* Salvation Army. **—ung** *nf* -en 1 cure. 2 healing.

Heiland ('hailant) *nm* -e Saviour.

heilig ('hailiç) *adj* holy, sacred. **Heiliger Abend** Christmas Eve. **—e(r)** ('hailigə) *nm* saint. **—en** ('hailigən) *vt* sanctify. **—enschein** *nm* halo. **—keit** *nf* holiness, saintliness.

heim (haim) *adv* home(ward). **—e** *n neu* -e home. **—isch** *adj* domestic. **—kehr** *nf* homecoming. **—lich** *adj* secret. **—suchen** *vt* 1 visit. 2 punish. 3 afflict. **—tückisch** *adj* malicious. **—wärts** ('haimvɛrts) *adv* homeward(s). **—weh** *n neu* homesickness.

Heimat ('haima:t) *nf* 1 home. 2 homeland, native place. **—land** *n neu* homeland. **—los** *adj* homeless.

Heirat ('haira:t) *nf* -en marriage. **—en** *vt* marry. *vi* get married.

heiser ('haizər) *adj* hoarse.

heiß (hais) *adj* hot.

heißen* ('haisən) *vi* 1 be called. 2 mean. *vt* 1 name. 2 command. **das heißt, d.h.** that is, i.e.

heiter ('haitər) *adj* 1 cheerful. 2 serene, calm. 3 (of weather) bright, clear. **—keit** *nf* 1 cheerfulness. 2 brightness. 3 serenity.

Heiz/apparat ('haitsapara:t) *nm* heater. **—en** *vt* heat. **—körper** *nm* radiator. **—stoff** *nm* fuel. **—ung** *nf* -en heating.

Held (hɛlt) *nm* -en men. **—enhaft** ('hɛldənhaft) *adj* heroic. **—in** ('hɛldin) *nf* -nen heroine.

helf/en* ('hɛlfən) *vi* help, assist. **—er** *nm* -- helper, assistant.

hell (hɛl) *adj* 1 bright. 2 light. 3 clear. **—e** *nf* 1 brightness. 2 daylight. 3 clearness.

Helm (hɛlm) *nm* -e helmet.

Hemd (hɛmt) *n neu* -en 1 shirt. 2 vest.

hemm/en ('hɛmən) *vt* 1 restrain, inhibit. 2 block. 3 hinder. 4 stop. **—ung** *nf* -en 1 restriction. 2 restraint. 3 check. 4 inhibition. **—ungslos** *adj* unrestrained, uninhibited.

Hengst (hɛŋst) *nm* -e stallion.

Henker ('hɛŋkər) *nm* -- hangman, executioner.

her (he:r) *adv* 1 here, hither. 2 ago. 3 from.

herab (hɛ'rap) *adv* down(ward). **—lassen*** *vt* lower. **sich —lassen** *vr* condescend. **—setzen** *vt* 1 lower. 2 reduce. 3 degrade. **—setzung** *nf* -en 1 reduction. 2 degradation.

heran (hɛ'ran) *adv* 1 on (here). 2 up to. 3

along. **—kommen*** *vi* draw near. **—treten*** *vi* step up (to), approach. **—ziehen*** *vt* 1 pull or draw up. 2 grow, raise. 3 make use of, call on. *vi* approach.

herauf (hɛ'rauf) *adv* 1 up (here). 2 upwards.

heraus (hɛ'raus) *adv* 1 out. 2 forth. **—finden*** *vt* find out. **—fordern** *vt* 1 challenge. 2 provoke. **—gabe** *nf* 1 publication, publishing. 2 delivering (up). **—geben*** *vt* 1 publish. 2 deliver up. 3 restore, give back. **—geber** *nm* publisher. **—stellen** *vt* put or bring out. **sich —stellen** *vr* turn out, prove to be.

herb (hɛrp) *adj* 1 (of taste, etc.) sharp, tart. 2 (of wine) dry.

herbei (hɛr'bai) *adv* 1 here, hither. 2 on. **—führen** *vt* 1 lead, bring (on). 2 cause, induce.

Herberge ('hɛrbɛrgə) *nf* -n 1 hostel. 2 shelter, lodging. **—n** *vt,vi* lodge, shelter.

Herbst (hɛrpst) *nm* -e autumn.

Herd (he:rt) *nm* -e 1 hearth, fireplace. 2 cooker, stove.

Herde ('he:rdə) *nf* -n herd, flock.

herein (hɛ'rain) *adv* in (here). *interj* come in! **—lassen*** *vt* admit, allow in.

hergeben* ('he:rge:bən) *vt* hand over.

hergebracht ('he:rgəbraxt) *adj* 1 traditional, handed down. 2 established.

Hering ('he:riŋ) *nm* -e herring.

her/kommen* ('he:rkɔmən) *vi* 1 come from. 2 approach. *n neu* -- 1 custom. 2 descent. **—kömmlich** ('he:rkœmliç) *adj* traditional. **—kunft** ('he:rkunft) *nf* descent, origin.

hernach (hɛr'na:x) *adv* after(wards).

Heroin (hero'i:n) *n neu* heroin.

Herr (hɛr) *nm* -en 1 gentleman. 2 master, lord. 3 Mr. **—enhaus** *n neu* manor-house. **—gott** *nm* the Lord God. **—in** *nf* -nen mistress, lady. **—lich** *adj* 1 wonderful. 2 grand. 3 glorious. **—schaft** *nf* -en 1 rule, dominion. 2 power. 3 distinguished people. 4 manor. 5 estate. **—schen** ('hɛrʃən) *vi* 1 rule, govern. 2 dominate. 3 exist. 4 prevail. **—scher** ('hɛrʃər) *nm* -- ruler. **—schsucht** ('hɛrʃzu:xt) *nf* 1 love of power. 2 ambition.

herstell/en ('he:rʃtɛlən) *vt* manufacture, produce. **—ung** *nf* -en manufacture, production.

herüber (hɛ'ry:bər) *adv* 1 over, across. 2 to this side or place.

herum (hɛ'rum) *adv* (a)round, about. **—führen** *vt* show or take (a)round. **—ziehen*** *vi* wander about.

herunter (hɛˈruntər) adv down, downwards. —**kommen** vi 1 come down. 2 decay.

hervor (hɛrˈfoːr) adv 1 forth, out. 2 forward. —**bringen*** vt produce. —**gehen*** vi 1 arise. 2 result. —**heben*** vt 1 stress. 2 highlight. —**ragend** adj 1 eminent. 2 projecting. 3 outstanding, excellent. —**rufen*** vt 1 call forth. 2 cause. —**treten*** vi come forward or out.

Herz (hɛrts) n neu -en heart. —**anfall** nm heart attack. —**lich** adj hearty, cordial. —**los** adj heartless. —**schlag** nm med stroke.

Herzog (ˈhɛrtsoːk) nm -̈e duke. —**in** (ˈhɛrtsoː-gin) nf -nen duchess. —**tum** n neu -tümer duchy, dukedom.

herzu (hɛrˈtsuː) adv 1 (to) here. 2 near. 3 up (to).

Hessen (ˈhɛsən) n neu Hesse.

Hetze (ˈhɛtsə) nf -n 1 hurry. 2 hunt. 3 agitation. —**n** vt 1 hunt. 2 set (dogs) on. 3 incite.

Heu (hɔy) n neu hay. —**gabel** nf pitchfork. —**schnupfen** nm hayfever. —**schrecke** nf -n 1 grasshopper. 2 locust.

Heuchelei (hɔyçəˈlai) nf -en hypocrisy. —**ler** (ˈhɔyçlər) nm — hypocrite.

heulen (ˈhɔylən) vi howl, cry, scream.

heut/e (ˈhɔytə) adv today. —**ig** adj 1 of today. 2 modern, present. —**zutage** (ˈhɔyttsuːtaːgə) adv these days, nowadays.

Hexe (ˈhɛksə) nf -n 1 witch. 2 hag. —**rei** (hɛksəˈrai) nf witchcraft.

Hieb (hiːp) nm -e 1 blow, stroke. 2 cut.

hielt (hiːlt) v see **halten**.

hier (hiːr) adv here. —**auf** (hiːˈrauf) adv hereupon. —**bei** (hiːrˈbai) adv 1 at this. 2 enclosed. —**durch** (hiːrˈdurç) adv hereby. —**her** (hiːrˈheːr) adv 1 this way. 2 here. —**in** (hiːˈrin) adv in this. —**von** (hiːrˈfɔn) adv of this. —**zu** (hiːrˈtsuː) adv in addition, moreover. —**zulande** (hiːrtsuːlandə) adv in this country, in these parts, around here.

hiesig (ˈhiːziç) adj of this place, local.

Hilf/e (ˈhilfə) nf -n help, assistance. **erste Hilfe** first aid. —**eleistung** nf assistance. —**los** adj helpless. —**reich** adj helpful. —**sarbeiter** nm unskilled or temporary worker. —**smittel** n neu 1 remedy. 2 resource.

Himbeere (ˈhimbeːrə) nf -n raspberry.

Himmel (ˈhiməl) nm — 1 sky. 2 heaven. —**fahrt** nf Ascension. —**reich** n neu (kingdom of) heaven.

himmlisch (ˈhimliʃ) adj heavenly.

hin (hin) adv 1 (to) there. 2 gone, lost. 3 ruined. **hin und her** to and fro.

hinab (hiˈnap) adv down(wards).

hinan (hiˈnan) adv up (to), upward(s).

hinauf (hiˈnauf) adv 1 up (to). 2 on high.

hinaus (hiˈnaus) adv out. —**gehen*** vi 1 go out. 2 result (in). —**gehen über** go beyond, exceed. —**wollen*** vi 1 want to go out. 2 aim at.

Hinblick (ˈhinblik) nm **im Hinblick auf** with regard to.

hinder/lich (ˈhindərliç) adj 1 in the way. 2 inconvenient. —**n** vt 1 prevent. 2 hinder. —**nis** n neu -se obstacle.

hindeuten (ˈhindɔytən) vi point (to or at).

hindurch (hinˈdurç) adv 1 through(out). 2 across.

hinein (hiˈnain) adv in(to). —**gehen*** vi 1 go in(to). 2 contain. —**ziehen*** vt draw or pull in.

Hinfahrt (ˈhinfaːrt) nf outward journey.

hinfall/en* (ˈhinfalən) vi fall (down). —**ig** (ˈhinfɛliç) adj 1 obsolete. 2 decaying. 3 weak.

Hin/gabe (ˈhinɡaːbə) nf 1 delivery. 2 devotion. 3 surrender. —**geben*** (ˈhinɡeːbən) vt give away or up.

hingegen (ˈhinɡeːɡən) adv on the other hand.

hingehen* (ˈhinɡeːən) vi 1 go there or to. 2 pass away or over.

hinken (ˈhiŋkən) vi limp.

hinlegen (ˈhinleːɡən) vt lay down. **sich hinlegen** vr lie down.

hinnehmen* (ˈhinneːmən) vt 1 receive, accept. 2 put up with.

hinreichend (ˈhinraiçənt) adj sufficient.

Hinreise (ˈhinraizə) nf outward journey or voyage.

hinricht/en (ˈhinriçtən) vt execute, put to death. —**ung** nf -en execution.

Hinsicht (ˈhinziçt) nf **in dieser Hinsicht** in this respect. —**lich** prep with regard to, as for.

hinten (ˈhintən) adv behind, at the back.

hinter (ˈhintər) prep behind, after. adj posterior, back. —**backe** nf buttock. —**einander** (hintərainˈandər) adv one after another. —**gehen*** vt deceive. —**grund** nm background. —**halt** nm ambush, trap. —**her** (hintərˈheːr) adv after(wards), behind. —**lassen*** vt 1 leave (behind). 2 bequeath. —**list** nf 1 cunning. 2 fraud. —**teil** n neu 1 back part or side. 2 inf bottom, bum, backside. —**tür** nf backdoor.

hinüber (hiˈnyːbər) adv 1 over (there). 2 across. 3 beyond.

hinunter (hi'nuntər) *adv* down (there).

hinweg (hin'vɛk) *adv* 1 away. 2 off. *nm* outward journey.

Hinweis ('hinvais) *nm* -e 1 indication. 2 direction. —en* ('hinvaizən) *vi* 1 point to. 2 allude to. *vt* 1 show. 2 direct (someone).

hinwerfen* ('hinvɛrfən) *vt* 1 throw down. 2 sketch. 3 note.

hinziehen* ('hintsi:ən) *vt* draw out or along. *vi* move (house). **sich hinziehen** *vr* drag or stretch out.

hinzu (hin'tsu:) *adv* 1 in addition. 2 near. —**fügen** *vt* 1 add. 2 enclose.

Hirn (hirn) *n neu* -e brain(s). —**schale** *nf* skull, cranium.

Hirsch (hirʃ) *nm* -e deer, stag.

Hirt (hirt) *nm* -en shepherd, herdsman. —**in** *nf* -nen shepherdess.

hissen ('hisən) *vt* hoist (up).

Histor/iker (hi'sto:rikər) *nm* — historian. —**isch** *adj* historic(al).

Hitz/e ('hitsə) *nf* heat. —**ig** *adj* hot, heated, fiery. —**kopf** *nm* hothead.

hoch (ho:x) *adj* high, tall. *adv* up. *n neu* -s 1 cheer. 2 high (pressure).

Hochachtung ('ho:xaxtuŋ) *nf* respect, esteem. —**svoll** *adj* respectful. *adv* yours respectfully or sincerely.

Hochdruck ('ho:xdruk) *nm* high pressure.

Hochebene ('ho:xe:bənə) *nf* plateau.

hochfahrend ('ho:xfa:rənt) *adj* haughty.

Hochflut ('ho:xflu:t) *nf* high tide.

hochhalten* ('ho:xhaltən) *vt* 1 raise. 2 cherish.

Hochhaus ('ho:xhaus) *n neu* high-rise building.

Hochland ('ho:xlant) *n neu* highland, upland.

Hochmut ('ho:xmut) *nm* pride. —**tig** ('ho:x-my:tiç) *adj* proud.

hochnäsig ('ho:xnɛ:ziç) *adj inf* stuck-up, pretentious.

Hochschätzung ('ho:xʃɛtsuŋ) *nf* esteem.

Hochschule ('ho:xʃulə) *nf* college, university.

höchst (hœ:xst) *adj* 1 highest. 2 extreme. *adv* 1 most. 2 highly. —**ens** ('hœ:xstəns) *adv* at most or best. —**geschwindigkeit** ('hœ:xstgəʃvindiçkait) *nf* maximum speed.

Hochstapler ('ho:xʃta:plər) *nm* — swindler, confidence trickster.

Hochverrat ('ho:xfɛra:t) *nm* high treason.

Hochwasser ('ho:xvasə) *n neu* high water or tide.

Hochzeit ('hɔxtsait) *nf* -en wedding.

hock/en ('hɔkən) *vi* squat, crouch. —**er** *nm* — stool.

Hoden ('ho:dən) *nm* — *also* **Hode** *nf* -n testicle.

Hof (ho:f) *nm* ⁻e 1 court. 2 yard. 3 farm. 4 halo. **jemandem den Hof machen** court or woo someone. —**rat** *nm* privy councillor.

hoff/en ('hɔfən) *vt,vi* hope (for). —**entlich** *adv* 1 hopefully. 2 it is to be hoped that. —**nung** *nf* -en hope. —**nungslos** *adj* hopeless. —**nungsvoll** *adj* hopeful.

höflich ('hœfliç) *adj* polite, courteous. —**keit** *nf* -en courtesy, politeness.

Höhe ('hœ:ə) *nf* -n 1 height, altitude. 2 hill. 3 top. —**punkt** *nm* 1 summit. 2 climax. —**r** *adj* higher, upper.

Hoheit ('ho:hait) *nf* —en grandeur, majesty.

hohl (ho:l) *adj* 1 empty, hollow. 2 concave. ⁻e ('hœ:lə) *nf* -n 1 cave. 2 den. —**maß** *neu* 1 capacity. 2 volume. —**ung** ('hœ:luŋ) *nf* -en 1 excavation. 2 cavity.

Hohn (ho:n) *nm* scorn. ⁻**isch** ('hœ:niʃ) *adj* scornful.

hold (hɔlt) *adj* charming, lovely.

holen ('ho:lən) *vt* 1 fetch. 2 call for.

Hölle ('hœlə) *nf* -n hell.

Holunder (ho'lundər) *nm* — bot elder.

Holz (hɔlts) *n neu* ⁻er wood. —**ern** ('hœltsərn) *adj* wooden. —**kohle** *nf* charcoal. —**schnitt** *nm* woodcut.

Honig ('ho:niç) *nm* honey.

Honorar (hono'ra:r) *n neu* -e 1 honorarium. 2 royalty (payment).

Hopfen ('hɔpfən) *nm* — bot hop(s).

hör/bar ('hœ:rba:r) *adj* audible. —**en** *vt,vi* hear, listen (to). *n neu* hearing. —**er** *nm* — 1 hearer, listener. 2 student. 3 receiver. 4 headset. —**gerät** *n neu* hearing aid. —**saal** *nm* 1 auditorium. 2 lecture room. —**spiel** *n neu* radio play. —**weite** *nf* earshot.

horchen ('hɔrçən) *vi* listen (secretly).

Horde ('hɔrdə) *nf* -n 1 horde. 2 gang.

Horizont (hori'tsɔnt) *nm* -e horizon.

Hormon (hɔr'mo:n) *n neu* -e hormone.

Horn (hɔrn) *n neu* ⁻er horn.

Horoskop (horo'sko:p) *n neu* -e horoscope.

Hose ('ho:zə) *nf* -n trousers. —**nbandorden** *nm* Order of the Garter. —**nträger** *nm pl* braces.

Hotel (ho'tɛl) *n neu* -s hotel.

Hub (hu:p) *nm* ⁻e 1 *tech* stroke. 2 lift(ing). —**schrauber** *nm* — helicopter.

hübsch (hypʃ) *adj* 1 pretty. 2 nice, fine.

Huf (hu:f) *nm* -e hoof.

Hüfte ('hyftə) *nf* -n hip.

59

Hügel ('hy:gǝl) nm — hill, knoll.

Huhn (hu:n) n neu ̈er 1 chicken. 2 hen.
—̈erauge ('hy:nɔraugǝ) n neu med corn.

Huldigung ('huldiguŋ) nf -en homage.

Hülle ('hylǝ) nf -n 1 cover(ing), wrapping. 2
case. —n vt wrap, cover.

Hülse ('hylzǝ) nf -n husk, shell, case.

human (hu'ma:n) adj humane. —itär (humani-
'tɛr) adj humanitarian.

Hummel ('humǝl) nf -n bumblebee.

Hummer ('humǝr) nm — lobster.

Humor (hu'mo:r) nm -e (sense of) humour.

humpeln ('humpǝln) vi hobble.

Hund (hunt) nm -e dog. —in ('hyndin) nf -nen
bitch.

hundert ('hundǝrt) adj,n neu -s hundred.
—jahrfeier (hundǝrt'ja:rfaiǝr) nf centenary.

Hung/er ('huŋǝr) nm hunger. —ersnot nf
famine. —rig adj hungry.

Hupe ('hu:pǝ) nf -n mot horn, hooter. —n vi
sound the horn.

hüpfen ('hypfǝn) vi hop, skip.

Hürde ('hyrdǝ) nf -n 1 hurdle. 2 pen, fold.

Hure ('hu:rǝ) nf -n whore, prostitute.

husten ('hu:stǝn) vi cough. nm — cough.

Hut[1] (hu:t) nm ̈e hat.

Hut[2] (hu:t) nf care, charge, protection.
hüten ('hy:tǝn) vt guard, watch over. **sich
hüten** vr take care, be on one's guard.

Hütte ('hytǝ) nf -n 1 hut, cabin. 2 cottage. 3
forge.

Hyäne (hy'ɛ:nǝ) nf -n hyena.

Hygien/e (hygi'e:nǝ) nf hygiene. —isch adj
hygienic.

Hymne ('hymnǝ) nf -n hymn.

Hypno/se (hyp'no:zǝ) nf -n hypnosis. —tisch
adj hypnotic.

Hypothek (hypo'te:k) nf -en mortgage.

Hypothe/se (hypo'te:zǝ) nf -n hypothesis.
—tisch adj hypothetical.

Hysterie (hyste'ri:) nf -n hysteria.

I

ich (iç) pron 1st pers s I. n neu self, ego.

ideal (ide'a:l) adj ideal. n neu -e ideal. —ismus
(idea'lismus) nm idealism.

Idee (i'de:) nf -n idea.

identisch (i'dɛntiʃ) adj identical.

idiomatisch (idio'ma:tiʃ) adj idiomatic. **idio-
matischer Ausdruck** nm idiom.

Idiot (idi'o:t) nm -en idiot. —isch adj idiotic,
stupid.

Ignorieren (igno'ri:rǝn) vt ignore, disregard.

ihm (i:m) pron 3rd pers s (to) him or it.

ihn (i:n) pron 3rd pers s him, it.

ihnen ('i:nǝn) pron 1 3rd pers pl (to) them. 2
cap 2nd pers s,pl fml (to) you.

ihr (i:r) pron 1 3rd pers s (to) her or it. 2 2nd
pers pl fam you. poss adj 1 3rd pers s her. 2
3rd pers pl their. 3 cap 3rd pers s,pl your.
—er poss pron also **der** —e or **der** —ige 1
3rd pers s hers. 2 cap 3rd pers s,pl fml yours.
3 3rd pers pl theirs. —erseits ('i:rǝrzaits) adv
1 on her or their part. 2 cap on your
part. —ethalben adv also —etwegen or
—etwillen 1 for her or their sake. 2 cap for
your sake.

Illusion (iluzi'o:n) nf -en illusion.

illustrier/en (ilu'stri:rǝn) vt illustrate. —te nf
-n (illustrated or colour) magazine.

im (im) contraction of **in dem.**

Imbiß ('imbis) nm -bisse snack, light meal.
Imbiß-Stube nf snack bar.

Immatrikulation (imatrikulatsi'o:n) nf -en
matriculation.

immer ('imǝr) adv always, ever. —grün adj
evergreen. n neu -e evergreen. —hin adv
nevertheless, yet, still.

Immigrant (imi'grant) nm -en immigrant.

Immobilien (imo'bi:liǝn) nm pl real estate.

Imperfekt ('impɛrfɛkt) n neu -e gram imperfect.

impf/en ('impfǝn) vt vaccinate, inoculate.
—stoff nm vaccine, serum.

imponieren (impo'ni:rǝn) vt impress.

Import ('import) nm -e import(ation). —ieren
(impor'ti:rǝn) vt import.

impotent ('impotɛnt) adj impotent.

improvisieren (improvi'zi:rǝn) vt,vi improvise,
ad-lib.

imstande (im'ʃtandǝ) adv **imstande sein** be
able or capable, be in a position (to).

in (in) prep 1 in(to). 2 at. 3 to. 4 during.

Inbegriff ('inbǝgrif) nm 1 embodiment. 2 contents.

Inbrunst ('inbrunst) nf ardour, fervour.

indem (in'de:m) conj 1 while. 2 as, because.
adv meanwhile.

Inder ('indǝr) nm — (Asian) Indian.

indes (in'dɛs) adv also **indessen** (in'dɛsǝn) 1
meanwhile. 2 however. 3 nevertheless. conj
yet.

Indian/er (indi'a:nǝr) nm — (American) Indian. —isch adj Indian.

Indi/en ('indiən) *n neu* India. **—sch** ('indiʃ) *adj* Indian.

Indikativ ('indikati:f) *nm* **-e** *gram* indicative.

indirekt ('indirɛkt) *adj* indirect.

individu/ell (individu'ɛl) *adj* individual. **—um** (indi'vi:duəm) *nn* **-uen** individual, person.

Indones/ien (indo'ne:ziən) *n neu* Indonesia. **—ier** *nm* — Indonesian. **—isch** *adj* Indonesian.

Industrie (indus'tri:) *nf* **-n** industry. **—ll** (indus-tri'ɛl) *adj* industrial. **—lle(r)** (industri'ɛlə) *nm* industrialist.

ineinander (inain'andər) *adv* into one another.

Infanterie (infantə'ri:) *nf* **-n** infantry, foot.

infizieren (infi'tsi:rən) *vt* infect.

Inflation (inflatsi'o:n) *nf* **-en** inflation.

infolge (in'fɔlgə) *prep* in consequence of, due to. **—dessen** (infɔlgə'desən) *adv* **1** accordingly, then. **2** as a result of this, due to which.

Inform/ation (infɔrmatsi'o:n) *nf* **-en** (item of) information. **—ationsbüro** *n neu* information bureau or centre. **—ieren** (infɔr'mi:rən) *vt* **1** inform. **2** instruct.

Ingenieur (inʒe'njœ:r) *nm* **-e** engineer. **—wesen** *n neu* engineering.

Inhaber ('inha:bər) *nm* — possessor, holder.

Inhalt ('inhalt) *nm* **-e 1** contents. **2** volume. **3** meaning. **—sverzeichnis** *n neu* **1** table of contents. **2** index.

Initiative (initsia'ti:və) *nf* initiative.

Inklusive (inklu'zi:və) *adv* inclusive, including.

Inkrafttreten (in'krafttre:tən) *n neu* coming into force or effect.

Inland ('inlant) *n neu* **1** native country. **2** inland.

inmitten (in'mitən) *prep* amid(st).

inne ('inə) *adv* within. **—halten** *vi* stop. *vt* keep to.

innen ('inən) *adv* within, inside.

inner ('inər) *adj* inner, interior. **—halb** *prep,adv* within, inside. **—lich** *adj* inward, inner. **—st** *adj* inmost.

innig ('iniç) *adj* heartfelt, sincere.

ins (ins) contraction of **in das**. **—besondere** (insbə'zɔndərə) *adv* in particular. **—geheim** (insɡə'haim) *adv* secretly. **—gesamt** (insɡə-'zamt) *adv* altogether.

Insasse ('inzasə) *nm* **-n** inmate, occupant.

Inschrift ('inʃrift) *nf* **-en** inscription.

Insekt (in'zɛkt) *n neu* **-en** insect. **—engift** *n neu* insecticide.

Insel ('inzəl) *nf* **-n** island, isle.

Inserat (inze'ra:t) *n neu* **-e** advertisement, announcement.

insofern (inzo'fɛrn) *adv* also **insoweit** (inzo-'vait) in this respect, to that extent. *conj* in so far as, inasmuch as.

instand halten* (in'ʃtanthaltən) *vt* maintain (in good order).

Instanz (in'stants) *nf* **-en 1** *law* court. **2** authority.

Instinkt (in'stiŋkt) *nm* **-e** instinct.

Institut (insti'tu:t) *n neu* **-e** institute.

Instrument (instru'mɛnt) *n neu* **-e** instrument.

inszenieren (instse'ni:rən) *vt* stage, produce.

intelligen/t (intɛli'ɡɛnt) *adj* intelligent. **—z** (intɛli'ɡɛnts) *nf* **1** intelligence. **2** intelligentsia.

interess/ant (intərɛ'sant) *adj* interesting. **—e** (intə'rɛsə) *n neu* **-n** interest **—ieren** (intərɛ-'si:rən) *vt* interest. **sich —ieren** *vr* be interested.

international (intɛrnatsio'na:l) *adj* international. **—e** *nf pol* International.

intim (in'ti:m) *adj* intimate.

Intrige (in'tri:gə) *nf* **-n** intrigue, plot.

inwendig ('invɛndiç) *adj* interior, inside.

inwiefern (invi:'fɛrn) *adv* also **inwieweit** (invi:-'vait) to what extent, how far.

inzwischen (in'tsviʃən) *adv* meanwhile.

Irak (i'ra:k) *nm* Iraq. **—er** *nm* Iraqi. **—isch** *adj* Iraqi.

irdisch ('irdiʃ) *adj* **1** worldly, earthly. **2** mortal.

irgend ('irɡənt) *pron,adv* some, any. **irgend etwas** something (or other). **irgend jemand** anybody, somebody or other. **—ein** (irɡənt-'ain) *pron,adj* some(one), any(one). **—wann** (irɡənt'van) *adv* at some time. **—was** (irɡənt-'vas) *pron* something (or other). **—wie** (irɡənt'vi:) *adv* somehow. **—wo** (irɡənt'vo:) *adv* somewhere.

Iris ('i:ris) *nf* — *anat* iris.

Ir/land ('irlant) *n neu* Ireland. **—e** ('i:rə) *nm* **-n** also **—länder** — Irishman. **—in** *nf* **-nen** also **—länderin** Irishwoman. **—isch** *adj* Irish.

Ironie (iro'ni:) *nf* **-n** irony. **—isch** (i'ro:niʃ) *adj* ironical.

irr/e ('irə) *adj* **1** stray. **2** mad. **3** unsettled. **4** confused. **—e(r)** *nm* lunatic. **—eführen** *vt* **1** mislead. **2** deceive. **—en** *vi* wander, stray. **sich —en** *vr* **1** err. **2** be mistaken. **—ig** *adj* also **—tümlich** erroneous, false. **—tum** *nm* ⁼er error, fault.

isolieren (izo'li:rən) *vt* **1** isolate. **2** insulate.

ißt (ist) *v* see **essen.**

ist (ist) *v* see **sein²**.

Italien (i'ta:liən) *n neu* Italy. **—er** (itali'e:nər)

ja

nm — Italian. **—isch** (itali'e:niʃ) *adj* Italian. *n neu* Italian (language).

J

ja (ja) *adv* yes, indeed. *n neu* **-s** assent. **mit Ja antworten** reply in the affirmative.
Jacht (jaxt) *nf* **-en** yacht.
Jacke (jakə) *nf* **-n** jacket.
Jagd (ja:kt) *nf* **-en** hunt, hunting.
jag/en (ˈja:gən) *vt* 1 hunt. 2 shoot. 3 drive. *vi* 1 hunt. 2 rush. **—er** (ˈjɛːgər) *nm* — 1 hunter. 2 rifleman. 3 fighter pilot. 4 fighter plane.
jäh (jɛː) *adj* 1 sudden. 2 steep.
Jahr (ja:r) *n neu* **-e** year. **—elang** *adj* lasting for one or several years. *adv* for years. **—eswechsel** *nm* turn of the year, New Year. **—eszeit** *nf* season. **—hundert** (ja:rˈhundərt) *n neu* **-e** century. **—lich** (ˈjɛːrliç) *adj* annual. **—tausend** (ja:rˈtauzənt) *n neu* **-e** millennium. **—zehnt** (ja:rˈtseːnt) *n neu* **-e** decade.
Jammer (ˈjamər) *nm* 1 misery, sorrow. 2 lamentation. **—lich** (ˈjɛːmərliç) *adj* pitiful. **—n** *vi* lament, bewail.
Januar (ˈjanua:r) *nm* January.
Japan (ˈja:pan) *n neu* Japan. **—er** (ja'pa:nər) *nm* — Japanese. **—isch** (ja'pa:niʃ) *adj* Japanese. *n neu* Japanese (language).
jauchzen (ˈjauxtsən) *vi* rejoice, shout with joy.
jawohl (ja'vo:l) *adv* yes indeed, certainly.
Jazz (dʒɛs) *nm* jazz.
je (je:) *adv* 1 ever. 2 each, apiece. **je...desto** the...the. **je nachdem** according as or to.
jedenfalls (ˈje:dənfals) *adv* in any case.
jeder, jede, jedes (ˈje:dər, ˈje:də, ˈje:dəs) *pron,adj m,f,neu* every, each.
jedermann (ˈje:dərman) *pron* everyone.
jederzeit (ˈje:dərtsait) *adv* at any time.
jedesmal (ˈje:dəsma:l) *adv* every time, each time.
jedoch (je'dɔx) *adv* however, yet.
jeglicher (ˈje:kliçər) *pron,adj* every, each.
jemals (ˈje:ma:ls) *adv* at any time, ever.
jemand (ˈje:mant) *pron* someone, anyone.
jener, jene, jenes (ˈje:nər, ˈje:nə, ˈje:nəs) *pron,adj m,f,neu* 1 that. 2 the former.
jenseits (ˈjɛnzaits) *adv* on the other side. *prep* beyond. *n neu* the other world, the life to come.
jetz/ig (ˈjɛtsiç) *adj* present, actual, current. **—t** *adv* at present, now.

Joch (jɔx) *n neu* **-e** yoke.
Jockei (ˈdʒɔki) *nm* **-s** jockey.
Jod (jo:t) *n neu* iodine.
jodeln (ˈjo:dəln) *vi* yodel.
Joghurt (ˈjo:gurt) *n neu* **-s** yoghurt.
Johannisbeere (jo'hanisbe:rə) *nf* redcurrant. **schwarze Johannisbeere** blackcurrant.
Journalist (ʒurna'list) *nm* **-en** journalist.
Jubel (ˈju:bəl) *nm* rejoicing. **—n** *vi* rejoice.
jucken (ˈjukən) *vt,vi* itch.
Jud/e (ˈju:də) *nm* **-n** Jew. **—entum** *n neu* Judaism, Jewry. **—in** (ˈjy:din) *nf* **-nen** Jewess. **—isch** (ˈjy:diʃ) *adj* Jewish.
Judo (ˈju:do) *n neu* judo.
Jugend (ˈju:gənt) *nf* youth. **—lich** *adj* youthful, juvenile. **—herberge** *nf* youth hostel.
Jugoslaw/e (jugo'sla:və) *nm* **-n** Yugoslav. **—ien** *n neu* Yugoslavia. **—isch** *adj* Yugoslav(ian).
Juli (ˈju:li) *nm* July.
jung (juŋ) *adj* young. **—e** *nm* **-n** youth, boy, lad. **—er** (ˈjyŋər) *adj* 1 younger. 2 junior. *nm* — disciple. **—fer** *nf* **-n** maid, virgin. **alte Jungfer** old maid, spinster. **—frau** *nf* 1 virgin, maiden. 2 Virgo. **—geselle** *nm* bachelor. **—ling** (ˈjyŋliŋ) *nm* **-e** youth, young man. **—st** (jyŋst) *adj* 1 youngest. 2 latest. **das Jüngste Gericht** the Last Judgment.
Juni (ˈju:ni) *nm* June.
Junker (ˈjuŋkər) *nm* — (young) nobleman, squire.
Jur/a¹ (ˈju:ra) *n pl* (study of) law. **—ist** (ju'rist) *nm* **-en** lawyer.
Jura² (ˈju:ra) *nm* **-s** the Juras.
just (just) *adv* 1 exactly. 2 just (now). 3 only just.
Justiz (jus'ti:ts) *nf* 1 legal administration. 2 justice.
Juwel (ju've:l) *n neu* **-en** jewel. **—ier** (juvə'li:r) *nm* **-e** jeweller.
Jux (juks) *nm* **-e** joke, prank.

K

Kabarett (kaba'rɛt) *n neu* **-e** cabaret.
Kabel (ˈka:bəl) *n neu* — cable.
Kabine (ka'bi:nə) *nf* **-n** 1 cabin. 2 cubicle.
Kabinett (kabi'nɛt) *n neu* **-e** 1 *pol* cabinet. 2 closet.
Kadett (ka'dɛt) *nm* **-en** cadet.
Käfer (ˈkɛːfər) *nm* — beetle.
Kaffee (ˈkafe) *nm* **-s** coffee.

Käfig ('kɛːfiç) nm -e cage.
kahl (kaːl) adj 1 bald. 2 bare. —**kopf** nm bald head.
Kahn (kaːn) nm ̈e 1 boat, skiff. 2 barge.
Kai (kai) nm -e quay, wharf.
Kaiser ('kaizər) nm — emperor. —**in** nf -nen empress. —**lich** adj imperial. —**reich** n neu empire.
Kakao (ka'kaːo) nm cocoa.
Kaktus ('kaktus) nm -teen cactus.
Kalb (kalp) n neu ̈er calf. —**fleisch** n neu veal. —**sbraten** nm roast veal.
Kalender (ka'lɛndər) nm — calendar.
Kali ('kaːli) n neu potash.
Kalk (kalk) nm -e lime. —**stein** nm limestone.
kalt (kalt) adj 1 cold. 2 frigid. —**blütig** ('kaltblyːtiç) adj cold-blooded. —̈**e** ('kɛltə) nf cold, coldness.
kam (kaːm) v see **kommen.**
Kamel (ka'meːl) n neu -e camel.
Kamera ('kamera) nf -s camera.
Kamerad (kamə'raːt) nm -en, —**in** (kamə'raːdin) nf -nen comrade, companion.
Kamin (ka'miːn) nm -e 1 chimney. 2 fireplace.
Kamm (kam) nm ̈e 1 comb. 2 crest. 3 ridge. —̈**en** ('krman) vt comb.
Kammer ('kamər) nf -n 1 small room, chamber. 2 pol,comm chamber. —**diener** nm valet. —**musik** nf chamber music.
Kampf (kampf) nm ̈e fight, struggle, battle. —**en** ('kɛmpfən) vi fight, struggle. —̈**er** ('kɛmpfər) nm — fighter, combatant.
Kanad/a ('kanada) n neu Canada. —**ier** (ka'naːdiːr) nm — Canadian. —**isch** (ka'naːdiʃ) adj Canadian.
Kanal (ka'naːl) nm ̈e 1 channel. 2 canal. 3 drain. 4 pipe. **Ärmelkanal** English Channel.
Kanarienvogel (ka'naːriənfoːgəl) nm canary.
Kandid/at (kandi'daːt) nm -en candidate. —**ieren** (kandi'diːrən) vi be a candidate, stand.
Känguruh ('kɛŋguruː) n neu -s kangaroo.
Kaninchen ('kaninçən) n neu — rabbit.
kann (kan) v see **können.**
Kannabis ('kanabis) n neu cannabis.
Kanne ('kanə) nf -n 1 can. 2 jug. 3 pot.
kannte ('kantə) v see **kennen.**
Kanon (ka'noːn) nm -s canon.
Kanone (ka'noːnə) nf -n 1 cannon. 2 gun. 3 inf wizard, ace.
Kante ('kantə) nf -n 1 edge. 2 brim, rim.
Kantine (kan'tiːnə) nf -n canteen.
Kanton (kan'toːn) nm -e canton.

Kanzel ('kantsəl) nf -n 1 pulpit. 2 aviat cockpit.
Kanzler ('kantslər) nm — chancellor.
Kap (kap) n neu -s cape, headland.
Kapazität (kapatsi'tɛːt) nf -en 1 capacity. 2 authority.
Kapelle (ka'pɛlə) nf -n 1 chapel. 2 band. 3 choir.
Kapor ('kaːpər) nf -n bot caper.
Kapital (kapi'taːl) n neu -ien capital. —**anlage** nf investment. —**ismus** (kapita'lismus) nm capitalism. —**ist** (kapita'list) nm -en capitalist.
Kapitän (kapi'tɛːn) nm -e captain, skipper.
Kapitel (ka'pitəl) n neu — chapter.
Kaplan (ka'plaːn) nm ̈e chaplain.
Kappe ('kapə) nf -n 1 cap. 2 hood. 3 top. 4 dome.
kaputt (ka'put) adj inf 1 bust, broken. 2 exhausted.
Kapuze (ka'puːtsə) nf -n 1 hood. 2 cowl.
Karat (ka'raːt) n neu -e carat.
Karate (ka'raːtə) n neu karate.
Karawane (kara'vaːnə) nf -n caravan.
Kardinal (kardi'naːl) nm -e cardinal.
Karfreitag (ka:r'fraitaːk) nm Good Friday.
karg (kark) adj 1 thrifty. 2 miserly. 3 poor. 4 meagre. 5 barren. —̈**lich** ('kɛrkliç) adj 1 scanty 2 poor.
kariert (ka'riːrt) adj 1 checked. 2 chequered.
Karies (ka'riɛs) nf med caries.
Karikatur (karika'tuːr) nf -en caricature.
Karneval ('karneval) nm -e carnival.
Karo ('kaːro) n neu -s game diamonds.
Karosserie (karosə'riː) nf -n mot bodywork.
Karotte (ka'rotə) nf -n carrot.
Karpfen ('karpfən) nm — carp.
Karre ('karə) nf -n also **Karren** nm -- 1 cart, (wheel-)barrow.
Karriere (ka'riːrə) nf -n 1 career. 2 gallop.
Karte ('kartə) nf -n 1 card. 2 map. 3 ticket. 4 menu.
Kartell (kar'tɛl) n neu -e cartel.
Kartoffel (kar'tofəl) nf -n potato. —**brei** nm also —**püree** n neu mashed or creamed potatoes.
Karton (kar'tɔn) nm -e, -s cardboard (box), carton.
Kartusche (kar'tuʃə) nf -n cartridge.
Karussell (karu'sɛl) n neu -e merry-go-round.
Kaschmir ('kaʃmir) n neu Cashmere.
Käse ('kɛːzə) nm — cheese.
Kaserne (ka'zɛrnə) nf -n barracks.

Kasino (kaˈziːno) *n neu* -s **1** casino. **2** officers' mess.

Kasse (ˈkasə) *nf* -n **1** till, cash register. **2** cash-desk. **3** booking office. **4** cash. **5** cash-box. **6** strongbox.

Kassette (kaˈsɛtə) *nf* -n **1** casket, box. **2** film spool. **3** cassette (tape). **—nrecorder** *nm* — cassette-recorder.

kassier/en (kaˈsiːrən) *vt* **1** cash. **2** cashier. **3** cancel. **4** annul. **—er** *nm* — **1** cashier. **2** treasurer.

Kastanie (kaˈstaːniə) *nf* -n chestnut.

Kasten (ˈkastən) *nm* ⁝ box, chest.

kastrieren (kaˈstriːrən) *vt* castrate.

Kasus (ˈkaːzus) *nm* — *gram* case.

Katalog (kataˈloːk) *nm* -e catalogue.

Katarrh (kaˈtar) *nm* -e catarrh.

katastroph/al (katastroˈfaːl) *adj* catastrophic. **—e** (kataˈstroːfə) *nf* -n catastrophe.

Kategorie (kategoˈriː) *nf* -n category.

Kater (ˈkaːtər) *nm* — **1** tomcat. **2** *inf* hangover.

Kathedrale (kateˈdraːlə) *nf* -n cathedral.

Kathol/ik (katoˈliːk) *nm* -en, **—ikin** *nf* -nen Catholic. **—isch** (kaˈtoːliʃ) *adj* Catholic.

Katze (ˈkatsə) *nf* -n cat.

Kauderwelsch (ˈkaudərvɛlʃ) *n neu* double-dutch.

kauen (ˈkauən) *vt* chew.

kauern (ˈkauərn) *vi* cower.

Kauf (kauf) *nm* ⁝e **1** purchase, buy(ing). **2** bargain. **in Kauf nehmen 1** accept. **2** put up with. **—en** *vt* buy, purchase. **—er** (ˈkɔyfər) *nm* — buyer, purchaser. **—haus** *n neu* department store. **—kraft** *nf* purchasing power. **—laden** *nm* shop. **—lich** (ˈkɔyfliç) *adj* **1** purchasable, for sale. **2** venal, corrupt. **—mann** *nm* -leute **1** shopkeeper. **2** merchant. **3** businessman.

Kaugummi (ˈkaugumi) *nm* chewing gum.

Kaukasus (ˈkaukazus) *nm* Caucasus.

kaum (kaum) *adv* hardly, scarcely, barely.

Kaution (kauˈtsjoːn) *nf* -en **1** security. **2** bail.

Kauz (kauts) *nm* ⁝e **1** owl. **2** odd fellow.

Kavallerie (kavaləˈriː) *nf* -n cavalry.

Kaviar (ˈkaːviar) *nm* -e caviar.

keck (kkk) *adj* **1** bold, daring. **2** cheeky.

Kegel (ˈkeːgəl) *nm* — **1** skittle(s), ninepin(s). **2** cone. **—bahn** *nf* bowling alley.

Kehl/e (ˈkeːl) *nf* -n throat. **—kopf** *nm* larynx. **—kopfentzündung** *nf* laryngitis.

kehren¹ (ˈkeːrən) *vt* turn.

kehr/en² (ˈkeːrən) *vt* sweep. **—icht** (ˈkeːriçt) *n* **1** sweepings. **2** rubbish.

Keil (kail) *nm* -e wedge. **—en** *vt* **1** (fix or split with a) wedge. **2** thrash. **sich —en** *vr* fight. **—er** *nm* — boar.

Keim (kaim) *nm* -e **1** germ. **2** bud. **3** embryo. **—en** *vi* **1** germinate. **2** sprout.

kein, kein/e, keine (kain, ˈkaine, kain) *adj* no, not any. **es war kein Mensch zu sehen** there was not a soul to be seen. **—er, —e, —es** (ˈkainər, ˈkainə, ˈkainəs) *pron* **1** none. **2** no one. **—erlei** (ˈkainərlai) *adj* of no sort, not any. **—esfalls** (ˈkainəsfals) *adv* on no account. **—eswegs** (ˈkainəsveːks) *adv* not at all, by no means.

Keks (keːks) *nm,neu* -e biscuit.

Keller (ˈkelər) *nm* — cellar.

Kellner (ˈkelnər) *nm* — **1** waiter. **2** barman. **—in** *nf* -nen **1** waitress. **2** barmaid.

kenn/en* (ˈkenən) *vt* know, be acquainted with. **—er** *nm* — expert, connoisseur. **—enlernen** *vt* become acquainted with, get to know. **—tnis** *nf* -se knowledge. **—zeichen** *n neu* characteristic, (distinguishing) feature. **—zeichnen** *vt* **1** mark. **2** distinguish.

Kerbe (ˈkerbə) *nf* -n **1** notch. **2** slot.

Kerker (ˈkerkər) *nm* — prison, jail.

Kerl (kerl) *nm* -e **1** fellow, man. **2** *inf* bloke.

Kern (kern) *nm* -e **1** core. **2** kernel, pip, stone. **3** nucleus. **—energie** *nf* nuclear energy. **—gesund** *adj* thoroughly healthy. **—physik** *nf* nuclear physics. **—waffen** *nf pl* nuclear weapons.

Kerze (ˈkertsə) *nf* -n candle.

Kessel (ˈkesəl) *nm* — **1** kettle. **2** boiler. **3** basin. **4** hollow.

Kette (ˈketə) *nf* -n chain. **—nbrücke** *nf* suspension bridge. **—reaktion** *nf* chain reaction.

Ketzer (ˈketsər) *nm* — heretic. **—ei** (ketsəˈrai) *nf* -en heresy.

keuchen (ˈkɔyçən) *vi* pant, gasp.

Keule (ˈkɔylə) *nf* -n **1** club, cudgel. **2** thigh (of an animal). **3** *cul* leg.

keusch (kɔyʃ) *adj* chaste.

kichern (ˈkiçərn) *vi* giggle.

Kiefer¹ (ˈkiːfər) *nm* — jaw.

Kiefer² (ˈkiːfər) *nf* -n pine, fir.

Kiel (kiːl) *nm* -e **1** keel. **2** quill.

Kieme (ˈkiːmə) *nf* -n *zool* gill.

Kies (kiːs) *nm* -e gravel.

Kieselstein (ˈkiːzəlʃtain) *nm* pebble.

Kilo (ˈkiːlo) *n neu* kilo. **—gramm** (kiːloˈgram) *n neu* kilogram.

Kind (kint) *n neu* -er child. **—erei** (kindəˈrai) *nf* -en childishness. **—erspiel** (ˈkindərʃpiːl) *n* *neu* child's play. **—erstube** ('kɪndərʃtuːbə) *nf* nursery. **—erwagen** ('kɪndərvaːgən) *nm* pram. **—heit** ('kɪnthait) *nf* childhood. **—isch** ('kɪndiʃ) *adj* childish. **—lich** ('kɪntliç) *adj* childlike.

Kinn (kin) *n neu* **-e** chin.

Kino ('kiːno) *n neu* **-s** cinema.

Kiosk (kiˈɔsk) *nm* **-e** 1 kiosk. 2 newsstand.

Kirch/e ('kɪrçə) *nf* **-n** church. **—hof** *nm* 1 churchyard. 2 cemetary. **—lich** *adj* ecclesiastical, church. **-spiel** *n neu* parish. **—turm** *nm* steeple, church tower.

Kirsch (kɪrʃ) *nm also* **Kirschwasser** ('kɪrʃvasər) *n neu* kirsch.

Kirsche ('kɪrʃə) *nf* **-n** cherry.

Kissen ('kisən) *n neu* **—** cushion, pillow.

Kiste ('kistə) *nf* **-n** box, case, crate.

Kitsch (kitʃ) *nm* tasteless rubbish, trash.

kitzeln ('kitsəln) *vt* tickle.

klaffen ('klafən) *vi* gape, yawn.

Klag/e ('klaːgə) *nf* **-n** 1 complaint. 2 *law* action. 3 lament. **—en** *vi* 1 complain. 2 *law* bring an action. 3 lament. **—er** ('klɛːgər) *nm* — plaintiff. **—lich** ('klɛːkliç) *adj* wretched, plaintive.

Klammer ('klamər) *nf* **-n** 1 clip, clamp. 2 peg. 3 bracket. **—n** *vt* fasten.

Klang (klaŋ) *nm* **"e** (ringing) sound. **—farbe** *nf* timbre, tone.

Klapp/e ('klapə) *nf* **-n** 1 flap. 2 lid. 3 stop. 4 valve. 5 *sl* mouth. **—en** *vt* clap. *vi* 1 flap. 2 collapse, fold. **es klappt** it works (well).

Klapper ('klapər) *nf* **-n** rattle. **—n** *vi* rattle.

klar (klaːr) *adj* 1 clear. 2 bright. 3 distinct. 4 evident. 5 pure. **—en** ('klɛːrən) *vt* 1 clarify. 2 purify. **—heit** *nf* clarity, clearness. **—legen** *vt also* **—machen** clear up, explain, point out.

Klarinette (klariˈnɛtə) *nf* **-n** clarinet.

Klasse ('klasə) *nf* **-n** 1 class. 2 category. **—nzimmer** *n neu* classroom.

Klass/iker ('klasikər) *nm* — classic (author). **—isch** *adj* classic(al).

Klatsch (klatʃ) *nm* **-e** 1 clap. 2 gossip. 3 smack. **—en** *vi* 1 clap. 2 gossip. 3 slap, smack.

Klaue ('klauə) *nf* **-n** 1 hoof. 2 claw. 3 *sl* scrawl, handwriting. **—n** *vt* 1 claw. 2 *sl* pinch, steal.

Klausel ('klauzəl) *nf* **-n** clause.

Klavier (klaˈviːr) *n neu* **-e** piano.

kleb/en ('kleːbən) *vt* glue, stick. *vi* 1 stick. 2 cling. **—(e)rig** *adj* sticky. **—estreifen** *nm* adhesive tape. **—stoff** *nm* adhesive, glue.

kleck/ern ('klɛkərn) *vi* dribble, slobber. **—s** (klɛks) *nm* **-e** 1 blot. 2 stain.

Klee (kleː) *nm* clover.

Kleid (klait) *n neu* **-er** 1 dress. 2 garment. 3 *pl* clothes. **—en** ('klaidən) *vt* clothe, dress. **—erschrank** ('klaidərʃraŋk) *nm* wardrobe. **—ung** ('klaiduŋ) *nf* clothing.

klein (klain) *adj* 1 small, little. 2 short. 3 petty, mean. **—asien** (klainˈaːziən) *n neu* Asia Minor. **—geld** *n neu* (small) change. **—handel** *nm* retail trade. **—heit** *nf* smallness. **—igkeit** *nf* **-en** trifle, petty detail. **—laut** *adj* subdued, quiet. **—lich** *adj* petty, mean. **—stadt** *nf* small city or town.

Kleinod ('klainoːt) *n neu* **-ien** gem.

Kleister ('klaistər) *nm* — paste.

Klemme ('klɛmə) *nf* **-n** 1 clamp. 2 (electrical) terminal. 3 dilemma, difficulty.

Klempner ('klɛmpnər) *nm* — plumber.

Klerus ('kleːrus) *nm* clergy.

klettern ('klɛtərn) *vi* climb.

Klima ('kliːma) *n neu* **-te** climate. **—anlage** *nf* 1 air-conditioner. 2 air-conditioning.

Klinge ('kliŋə) *nf* **-n** blade. **—n*** *vi* 1 sound. 2 ring, chink.

Klingel ('kliŋəl) *nf* **-n** 1 bell. 2 door-bell. **—n** *vi* ring, tinkle.

Klinik ('kliːnik) *nf* **-en** clinic, hospital.

Klinke ('kliŋkə) *nf* **-n** 1 latch. 2 handle.

Klippe ('klipə) *nf* **-n** reef, rocks.

klirren ('klirən) *vi* 1 clink. 2 clash, jangle.

Klo (kloː) *n neu* **-s** *inf* toilet, loo.

Kloben ('kloːbən) *nm* — 1 pulley, block. 2 vice. 3 pincers. 4 log.

klopfen ('klɔpfən) *vi,vt* beat, knock.

Klosett (kloˈzɛt) *n neu* **-e** toilet, lavatory. **—papier** *n neu* toilet paper.

Kloster ('kloːstər) *n neu* **"** 1 convent. 2 monastery.

Klotz (klɔts) *nm* **"e** 1 log. 2 block.

Klub (klup) *nm* **-s** club, society.

Kluft (kluft) *nf* **"e** 1 gap. 2 chasm. 3 cleft.

klug (kluːk) *adj* 1 clever, intelligent. 2 prudent. **—heit** *nf* 1 cleverness, intelligence. 2 prudence.

Klumpen ('klumpən) *nm* — 1 lump, clod. 2 heap.

knabbern ('knabərn) *vi,vt* gnaw, nibble.

Knabe ('knaːbə) *nm* **-n** boy, lad.

knacken ('knakən) *vt,vi* crack, snap.

Knall (knal) *nm* **"e** 1 crack. 2 bang, report. **—en** *vi* 1 crack, snap. 2 bang.

knapp

knapp (knap) *adj* 1 tight, close-fitting. 2 scarce, meagre. 3 bare, barely sufficient.

knarren ('knarən) *vi* 1 creak. 2 rattle.

Knecht (knɛçt) *nm* -e 1 servant. 2 farmhand. —schaft *nf* servitude.

kneif/en* ('knaifən) *vt* pinch. *vi* 1 flinch. 2 retreat. —zange *nf* pliers, pincers.

Kneipe ('knaipə) *nf* -n public house, tavern.

kneten ('kne:tən) *vt* knead, massage.

Knicks (kniks) *nm* -e curtsey.

Knie (kni:) *n neu* — knee. —(e)n ('kni:ən) *vi* kneel. —hose *nf* kneebreeches.

Kniff (knif) *nm* -e 1 crease. 2 pinch. 3 trick, knack.

knipsen ('knipsən) *vt* 1 clip. 2 snap (a photograph). *vi* snap one's fingers.

knirschen ('knirʃən) *vi* 1 grate. 2 grind.

Knoblauch ('kno:plaux) *nm* garlic.

Knöchel ('knœçəl) *nm* — 1 ankle. 2 knuckle.

Knoch/en ('knɔxən) *nm* — bone. —ig *adj* bony.

Knödel ('knœ:dəl) *nm* — dumpling.

Knopf (knɔpf) *nm* ⸚e button. —en ('knœpfən) *vt* button.

Knorpel ('knɔrpəl) *nm* — cartilage.

Knospe ('knɔspə) *nf* -n bud. —n *vi* 1 bud. 2 sprout.

Knoten ('kno:tən) *nm* — 1 knot. 2 node. 3 difficulty. —punkt *nm* junction.

knüpfen ('knypfən) *vt* tie, bind.

knusprig ('knuspriç) *adj* crisp.

Koalition (koalitsi'o:n) *nf* -en coalition.

Kobra ('ko:bra) *nf* -s cobra.

Koch (kɔx) *nm* ⸚e, Köchin ('kœçin) *nf* -nen cook. —buch *n neu* cookery book. —en *vt,vi* 1 cook. 2 boil.

Kodex ('ko:dɛks) *nm* -e code.

Koexistenz (koɛksis'tɛnts) *nf* co-existence.

Koffer ('kɔfər) *nm* — 1 suitcase. 2 trunk. —radio *n neu* portable radio. —raum *nm* mot boot.

Kohl (ko:l) *nm* -e cabbage.

Kohle ('ko:lə) *nf* -n 1 coal. 2 charcoal. 3 carbon. —nbergwerk *n neu* coalmine. —nsäure *nf* 1 carbonic acid. 2 carbon dioxide. —nstoff *nm* carbon. —papier *n neu* carbon paper.

Koje ('ko:jə) *nf* -n 1 cabin. 2 bunk.

kokettieren (kokɛ'ti:rən) *vi* flirt.

Kokosnuß ('ko:kɔsnus) *nf* coconut.

Koks (ko:ks) *nm* -e coke.

Kolben ('kɔlbən) *nm* — 1 butt(-end). 2 club. 3 piston. 4 *sci* retort, flask.

Kollege (kɔ'le:gə) *nm* -n, Kollegin *nf* -nen colleague.

kollektiv (kɔlɛk'ti:f) *adj* collective.

Köln (kœln) *n neu* Cologne.

kolon/ial (koloni'a:l) *adj* colonial. —ie (kolo'ni:) *nf* -n colony. —ist (kolo'nist) *nm* -en colonist, settler.

Kolonne (ko'lɔnə) *nf* -n column.

kolossal (kolo'sa:l) *adj* huge, immense.

Kombination (kɔmbinatsi'o:n) *nf* -en 1 combination. 2 conjecture, deduction.

Komet (ko'me:t) *nm* -en comet.

Komfort (kɔm'fo:r) *nm* 1 luxury. 2 comfort.

komisch ('ko:miʃ) *adj* 1 funny. 2 strange.

Komitee (komi'te:) *n neu* -s committee.

Komma ('kɔma) *n neu* -s comma.

Kommand/ant (kɔman'dant) *nm* -e commander. —ieren (kɔman'di:rən) *vi,vt* command.

kommen* ('kɔmən) *vi* 1 come, approach. 2 arrive. 3 happen. auf etwas kommen think of, hit upon something. zu etwas kommen come to, obtain something.

Kommiss/ar (kɔmi'sa:r) *nm* -e 1 commissioner. 2 (police) inspector 3 commissar. —ion (kɔmisi'o:n) *nf* -en commission.

Kommode (kɔ'mo:də) *nf* -n chest of drawers.

kommun (kɔ'mu:n) *adj* common. —al (kɔmu'na:l) *adj* 1 communal. 2 municipal. —e (kɔ'mu:nə) *nf* -n 1 commune. 2 community.

Kommunikation (kɔmu:nikatsi'o:n) *nf* -en communication.

Kommunismus (kɔmu'nismus) *nm* communism. —ist (kɔmu'nist) *nm* -en communist. —istisch (kɔmu'nistiʃ) *adj* communist.

Komödie (ko'mœ:diə) *nf* -n comedy, farce.

Kompaß ('kɔmpas) *nm* -passe compass.

kompetent (kɔmpe'tɛnt) *adj* competent.

Kompliment (kɔmpli'mɛnt) *n neu* -e compliment.

kompliziert (kɔmpli'tsi:rt) *adj* complicated.

kompo/nieren (kɔmpo'ni:rən) *vt* compose. —nist (kɔmpo'nist) *nm* -en composer. —sition (kɔmpozitsi'o:n) *nf* -en composition.

Kompott (kɔm'pɔt) *n neu* -e stewed fruit.

Kompromiß (kɔmpro'mis) *nm* -misse compromise.

Konditorei (kɔndito'rai) *nf* -en coffee-shop, cake-shop.

Kondom (kɔn'do:m) *nm* -e condom.

Konferenz (kɔnfe'rɛnts) *nf* -en conference, meeting.

Konflikt (kɔn'flikt) *nm* -e 1 conflict. 2 dispute.

konfus (kɔn'fu:s) *adj* confused.

66

Kongreß (kɔn'grɛs) nm **-gresse** congress.

König ('køːnɪç) nm **-e** king. **—in** ('køːnɪgɪn) nf **-nen** queen. **—lich** adj royal, regal. **—reich** n neu kingdom.

Konjugation (kɔnjugatsi'oːn) nf **-en** conjugation.

Konjunktiv ('kɔnjunktiːf) nm **-e** subjunctive.

Konjunktur (kɔnjunk'tuːr) nf **-en** economic or commercial situation.

Konkurrenz (kɔnku'rɛnts) nf **-en** competition.

Konkurs (kɔn'kurs) nm **-e** bankruptcy.

können ('kœnən) v mod aux **1** be able. **2** be allowed. vi,vt know (how to do something).

konsequen/t (kɔnze'kvɛnt) adj consistent. **—z** (kɔnze'kvɛnts) nf **-en 1** consistency. **2** consequence. **Konsequenzen ziehen** draw conclusions.

konservativ (kɔnzɛrva'tiːf) adj conservative.

Konserve (kɔn'zɛrvə) nf **-n** tinned food, preserve.

Konsonant (kɔnzo'nant) nm **-en** consonant.

Konstruktion (kɔnstruktsi'oːn) nf **-en 1** construction. **2** design.

Konsul ('kɔnzul) nm **-n** consul. **—at** (kɔnzu'laːt) n neu **-e** consulate.

Konsum (kɔn'zuːm) nm consumption. **—ent** (kɔnzu'mɛnt) nm **-en** consumer. **—verein** nm cooperative society.

Kontakt (kɔn'takt) nm **-e** contact.

Kontinent ('kɔntinɛnt) nm **-e** continent.

kontinuierlich (kɔntinu'iːrlɪç) adj continuous.

Konto ('kɔnto) n neu **-ten** account.

Kontrast (kɔn'trast) nm **-e** contrast.

Kontroll/e (kɔn'trɔlə) nf **-n 1** control. **2** supervision. **—ieren** (kɔntro'liːrən) vt **1** control. **2** supervise. **3** check. **4** audit. **—punkt** nm checkpoint.

konventionell (kɔnvɛntsio'nɛl) adj conventional.

Konversation (kɔnvɛrzatsi'oːn) nf **-en** conversation. **—slexikon** n neu encyclopaedia.

Konzentr/ation (kɔntsɛntratsi'oːn) nf **-en** concentration. **—ieren** (kɔntsɛn'triːrən) vt concentrate.

Konzept (kɔn'tsɛpt) n neu **-e 1** (rough) draft, sketch. **2** design.

Konzert (kɔn'tsɛrt) n neu **-e 1** concert. **2** concerto.

Kopf (kɔpf) nm **ːe** head. **—haut** nf scalp. **—hörer** nm headphone(s). **—kissen** n neu pillow. **—schmerz** nm also **—weh** n neu headache.

Kopie (ko'piː) nf **-n** copy.

Koralle (ko'ralə) nf **-n** coral.

Korb (kɔrp) nm **ːe 1** basket. **2** refusal.

Korinthe (ko'rɪntə) nf **-n** currant.

Kork (kɔrk) nm **-e** cork. **—enzieher** nm corkscrew.

Korn (kɔrn) n neu **ːer 1** grain, corn. **2** seed. **3** whisky. **4** schnaps.

Koronarthrombose (koroːnar'trombozə) nf **-n** coronary thrombosis.

Körper ('kœrpər) nm **— 1** body. **2** substance. **—haltung** nf bearing, deportment. **—lich** adj **1** physical, corporeal. **2** material. **—schaft** nf **-en** corporation, body. **—übung** nf physical exercise.

korrekt (ko'rɛkt) adj correct. **-ur** (kɔrɛk'tuːr) nf **-en 1** correction. **2** (printing) proof.

Korresponden/t (kɔrɛspɔn'dɛnt) nm **-en** correspondent. **—z** (kɔrɛspɔn'dɛnts) nf **-en** correspondence.

Korridor ('kɔridoːr) nm **-e** corridor.

korrigieren (kɔri'giːrən) vt correct.

Kosename ('koːzənaˌmə) nm pet name.

Kosmetik (kɔs'meːtik) nf **-en** cosmetics.

Kost (kɔst) nf **1** food, fare. **2** diet.

kostbar ('kɔstbaːr) adj **1** expensive. **2** precious.

kosten[1] ('kɔstən) vt cost. n pl cost(s). **—los** adj free (of charge).

kosten[2] ('kɔstən) vt taste, sample.

köstlich ('kœstlɪç) adj **1** delightful. **2** delicious.

Kostüm (kɔs'tyːm) n neu **-e 1** costume, dress. **2** suit.

Kot (kɔt) nm **1** mud, dirt. **2** excrement.

Kotelett (kotə'lɛt) n neu **-e** cutlet, chop. **—en** n pl sideburns.

kotzen ('kɔtsən) vi inf spew up, vomit.

Krabbe ('krabə) nf **-n 1** crab. **2** shrimp.

Krach (krax) nm **-e 1** noise. **2** crash. **3** quarrel.

kraft (kraft) prep by virtue of. nf **ːe 1** strength, force, power. **2** efficacy. **3** worker. **außer Kraft setzen** annul. **in Kraft sein** be in force. **in Kraft treten** come into force. **—fahrzeug** n neu motor vehicle. **ːig** ('krɛftɪç) adj strong, powerful. **—igen** ('krɛftigən) vt strengthen. **—wagen** nm **1** motor vehicle. **2** car. **3** lorry. **—werk** n neu power station.

Kragen ('kraːgən) nm **—** collar.

Krähe ('krɛːə) nf **-n** crow.

Kralle ('kralə) nf **-n** claw, talon.

Kram (kraːm) nm **ːe** inf **1** junk, rubbish. **2** things, stuff. **3** affair, business.

Krampf (krampf) nm **ːe 1** cramp. **2** convulsion.

Kran (kraːn) nm **ːe** crane, hoist.

Kranich ('kra:niç) nm -e zool crane.

krank (kraŋk) adj sick, ill. —**e(r)** nm patient. **⸚en** ('krɛŋkən) vt 1 hurt. 2 offend. **sich ⸚en** vr worry. —**enhaus** n neu hospital. —**enkasse** nf health insurance (company). —**enschwester** nf nurse. —**enversicherung** nf health insurance. —**enwagen** nm ambulance. —**haft** adj 1 morbid. 2 diseased. —**heit** nf -en 1 illness. 2 disease.

Kranz (krants) nm ⸚e wreath, garland.

Kratzbürste ('kratsbyrstə) nf -n 1 wire brush. 2 shrew, bad-tempered woman.

kratzen ('kratsən) vt,vi scratch, scrape.

Kraul (kraul) n neu crawl (swimming stroke).

Kraut (kraut) n neu ⸚er 1 plant. 2 herb. 3 cabbage.

Krawall (kra'val) nm -e 1 row. 2 riot. 3 noise.

Krawatte (kra'vatə) nf -n (neck)tie.

Krebs (kre:ps) nm -e 1 crayfish. 2 crab. 3 med cancer. 4 Cancer.

Kredit (kre'di:t) nm -e credit.

Kreide ('kraidə) nf -n chalk.

Kreis (krais) nm -e 1 circle. 2 district. 3 sphere, field. —**en** ('kraizən) vi 1 circle. 2 circulate. —**förmig** ('kraisfœrmiç) adj circular, round. —**lauf** nm 1 circulation. 2 cycle, circuit.

kreischen ('kraiʃən) vi shriek, screech.

Krematorium (krema'to:rjum) n neu -**rien** crematorium.

Kreml ('kre:məl) nm Kremlin.

Krempe ('krɛmpə) nf -n brim.

krepieren (kre'pi:rən) vi 1 (of an animal) die. 2 explode.

Kresse ('krɛsə) nf -n cress.

Kreuz (krɔyts) n neu -e 1 cross. 2 mus sharp (symbol). 3 game club. 4 (small of the) back, rump. **kreuz und quer** crisscross. —**en** vt cross. vi cruise. —**er** nm -e cruiser. —**fahrt** nf 1 cruise. 2 crusade. —**gang** nm cloister(s). —**igen** ('krɔytsigən) vt crucify. —**igung** nf -en crucifixion. —**otter** nf -n adder. —**ung** nf -en crossing. —**zug** nm crusade.

kriech/en* ('kri:çən) vi 1 creep. 2 crawl. 3 cringe. 4 grovel. —**tier** n neu reptile.

Krieg (kri:k) nm -e war. —**er** ('kri:gər) nm — warrior. —**sgefangene(r)** nm prisoner of war. —**sgericht** n neu mil court martial. —**srecht** n neu martial law. —**sverbrechen** n neu war crime.

Krimi ('kri:mi) n neu -s inf detective story.

kriminal (krimi'na:l) adj criminal. —**beamte(r)** nm detective. —**roman** nm detective novel.

Krippe ('kripə) nf -n 1 crib. 2 crèche.

Krise ('kri:zə) nf -n crisis.

Kristall (kri'stal) nm -e crystal.

Krit/ik (kri'ti:k) nf -en 1 criticism. 2 review. —**iker** ('kri:tikər) nm — critic. —**isch** ('kri:-tiʃ) adj critical.

Krokodil (kroko'di:l) n neu -e crocodile.

Kron/e ('kro:nə) nf -n crown. —**leuchter** nm chandelier. **⸚en** ('krœ:nən) vt crown. —**ung** ('krœ:nuŋ) nf -en coronation.

Kröte ('krœ:tə) nf -n toad.

Krücke ('krykə) nf -n crutch.

Krug (kru:k) nm ⸚e 1 jug. 2 mug.

krumm (krum) adj 1 crooked. 2 bent. 3 curved. **⸚en** ('krymən) vt 1 bend. 2 curve.

Krüppel ('krypəl) nm — cripple.

Kruste ('krustə) nf -n crust.

Kruzifix (krutsi'fiks) n neu -e crucifix.

Küche ('kyçə) nf -n 1 kitchen. 2 cookery. —**nschabe** nf -n cockroach.

Kuchen ('ku:xən) nm — cake.

Kuckuck ('kukuk) nm -e cuckoo.

Kugel ('ku:gəl) nf -n 1 ball. 2 sphere, globe. 3 bullet. —**förmig** ('ku:gəlfœrmiç) adj spherical. —**schreiber** nm — ballpoint pen.

Kuh (ku:) nf ⸚e cow.

kühl (ky:l) adj cool, chilly. —**e** nf coolness, cool. —**en** vt,vi 1 cool. 2 refrigerate. —**schrank** nm refrigerator.

kühn (ky:n) adj bold, daring. —**heit** nf -en boldness, daring.

Kulissen (ku'lisən) nf pl Th 1 scenery. 2 wings. **hinter den Kulissen** backstage.

Kult (kult) nm -e 1 cult. 2 worship.

Kultur (kul'tu:r) nf -en 1 culture. 2 cultivation. —**ell** (kultu'rɛl) adj cultural.

Kummer ('kumər) nm 1 grief. 2 distress. 3 worry. **⸚lich** ('kymərliç) adj miserable. **⸚n** ('kymərn) vt worry, be anxious. **sich kümmern um** care about, concern oneself with.

kund (kunt) adj known.

Kund/e¹ ('kundə) nf information, knowledge. —**geben*** ('kuntge:bən) vt make known, declare. —**igen** ('kyndigən) vt,vi 1 give notice. 2 cancel.

Kund/e² ('kundə) nm -n customer, client. —**schaft** ('kuntʃaft) nf customers, clientele.

künftig ('kynftiç) adj future.

Kunst (kunst) nf ⸚e 1 art. 2 skill. —**griff** nm trick, knack. —**ler** ('kynstlər) nm — artist. **⸚lerisch** ('kynstlariʃ) adj artistic. **⸚lich** ('kynstliç) adj artificial, synthetic. —**stück** n neu 1 trick. 2 feat. 3 stunt. —**werk** n neu work of art.

Kupfer ('kupfər) n neu copper. **—stich** nm etching.

Kupp/el ('kupəl) nf **-n** dome, cupola. **—eln** vt 1 couple, pair. 2 join. vi pimp, procure. **—ler** ('kuplər) nm — 1 matchmaker. 2 pimp. **—lung** nf **-en** 1 coupling. 2 clutch.

Kur (kur) nf **-en** cure, treatment. **—ort** nm spa, health resort.

Kurbel ('kurbəl) nf **-n** 1 crank. 2 winch.

Kürbis ('kyrbis) nm **-se** 1 pumpkin. 2 marrow.

Kurs (kurs) nm **-e** 1 course. 2 rate (of exchange). **—buch** n neu timetable.

Kurve ('kurvə) nf **-n** 1 curve. 2 bend. 3 turn.

kurz (kurts) adj 1 short, brief. 2 abrupt, brusque. in kurzem soon, shortly. **kurz gesagt, um es kurz zu sagen** in a word, to cut a long story short. **vor kurzem** a short time ago. in briefly. **—arbeit** nf short-time work. **—e** ('kyrtsə) nf **-n** shortness. **—en** ('kyrtsən) vt 1 shorten. 2 reduce. **—erhand** adv 1 without hesitation. 2 briefly. **—fristig** adj short-term. **—lich** ('kyrtsliç) adv lately, recently. **—schrift** nf shorthand.

Kusine (ku'zi:nə) nf **-n** cousin.

Kuß (kus) nm **Küsse** kiss. **küssen** vt kiss.

Küste ('kystə) nf **-n** coast, shore.

L

Laboratorium (labora'to:rium) n neu **-rien** laboratory.

lächeln ('lɛçəln) vi smile. n neu — smile.

lach/en ('laxən) vi laugh. n neu — laugh, laughter. **—erlich** ('lɛçərliç) adj ridiculous.

Lachs (laks) nm **-e** salmon.

Lack (lak) nm **-e** varnish, lacquer.

lad/en* ('la:dən) vt load. **—eraum** nm hold. **—ung** nf **-en** lo:d(ing), freight.

Laden ('la:dən) nm **—** 1 shop, store. 2 shutter. **—diebstahl** nm shoplifting.

lag (la:k) v see **liegen**.

Lage ('la:gə) nf **-n** 1 situation, position. 2 site, location. 3 layer. 4 mus pitch.

Lager ('la:gər) n neu — 1 camp. 2 warehouse, store. 3 couch, bed. 4 tech bearing. 5 (geological) layer. **—haus** n neu warehouse. **—n** vt store. vi lie down. **sich lagern** vr camp.

Lagune (la'gu:nə) nf **-n** lagoon.

lahm (la:m) adj lame. **lahm legen** paralyse. **—en** ('lɛ:mən) vt 1 paralyse. 2 lame.

Laib (laip) nm **-e** loaf.

Laie ('laiə) nm **-n** layman.

Lakritze (la'kritsə) nf **-n** liquorice.

Lamm (lam) n neu **-er** lamb.

Lampe ('lampə) nf **-n** lamp.

Land (lant) n neu **-er** 1 land. 2 ground, earth. 3 country. 4 state, province. **auf dem Lande** in the country(side).

Landarbeiter ('lanta:rbaitə) nm farm worker.

landen ('landən) vt,vi land.

Landenge ('lantɛŋə) nf isthmus.

Landgut ('lantgut) n neu estate.

Landhaus ('lanthaus) n neu country house.

Landkarte ('lantka:rtə) nf map.

ländlich ('lɛntliç) adj rural, rustic.

Landmann ('lantman) nm **-leute** 1 countryman. 2 farmer.

Landschaft ('lantʃaft) nf **-en** 1 landscape, countryside, scenery. 2 district.

Landsmann ('lantsman) nm **-sleute** fellow countryman.

Landstraße ('lantʃtra:sə) nf highway, main road.

Landstreicher ('lantʃtraiçə) nm — tramp.

Landtag ('lantta:g) nm 1 provincial assembly. 2 state parliament.

Landung ('landuŋ) nf **-en** landing (of ships, aeroplanes, etc.). **—sbrücke** nf jetty.

Landwirtschaft ('lantvirtʃaft) nf agriculture.

lang (laŋ) adj,adv long, tall. **ein Jahr lang** for a year. **lang und breit** at length.

lange ('laŋə) adv long, a long time.

Länge ('lɛŋə) nf **-n** 1 length, tallness. 2 duration. 3 size. 4 longitude. **—ngrad** ('lɛŋəngra:t) nm degree of longitude.

Lang(e)weile ('laŋ(ə)vailə) nf boredom.

langjährig ('laŋjɛːriç) adj of long standing.

längs (lɛŋs) adv lengthways. prep along(side).

langsam ('laŋza:m) adj slow.

längst (lɛŋst) adj longest. adv for a long time, long ago. **längst nicht** not nearly.

längstens ('lɛŋstəns) adv at the latest or most.

langweil/en ('laŋvailən) vt 1 bore. 2 tire. **—ig** adj boring.

Lanze ('lantsə) nf **-n** lance.

Lappen ('lapən) nm — 1 rag, cloth. 2 lobe.

Lärche ('lɛrçə) nf **-n** larch.

Lärm (lɛrm) nm noise, din.

las (la:z) v see **lesen**.

Laser-Strahlen ('la:zərʃtra:lən) nm pl laser beams.

lassen* ('lasən) vt,vi 1 allow, let, permit. 2 cause. 3 have (done). 4 leave.

lässig ('lɛsiç) adj 1 careless. 2 idle.

Last (last) *nf* **-en 1** burden, load. **2** cargo. **3** change. **—auto** *n neu* lorry, van. **—en** *vi* weigh (upon). **—ig** ('lɛstiç) *adj* **1** troublesome, annoying. **2** burdensome. **—kahn** *nm* barge. **—kraftwagen** *nm* lorry, truck, van.

Laster ('lastər) *n neu* — vice. **—lich** ('lɛstərliç) *adj* **1** scandalous. **2** slanderous. **—n** ('lɛstərn) *vt* slander. **—ung** ('lɛstəruŋ) *nf* **-en** defamation, slander.

Latein (la'tain) *n neu* Latin.

Laterne (la'tɛrnə) *nf* **-n 1** lantern. **2** (street) lamp.

Latte ('latə) *nf* **-n 1** slat. **2** board.

lau (lau) *adj* **1** lukewarm. **2** half-hearted.

Laub (laup) *n neu* foliage, leaves. **—baum** *nm* deciduous tree. **—säge** *nf* fretsaw.

Lauch (laux) *nm* **-e** leek.

lauern ('lauərn) *vi* lie in wait, lurk.

Lauf (lauf) *nm* **-e 1** run(ning). **2** course. **3** race. **4** path, passage. **5** (gun) barrel. **—bahn** *nf* **1** career. **2** course. **—en*** *vi* **1** run. **2** walk. **3** go, move. **4** flow. **—end** *adj* **1** running. **2** current. **3** regular, routine. **—er** ('lɔyfər) *nm* — **1** runner. **2** *game* bishop.

Laun/e ('launə) *nf* **-n 1** mood. **2** whim. **—enhaft** *adj* moody, capricious. **—isch** *adj* **1** bad-tempered. **2** moody. **3** capricious.

Laus (laus) *nf* **-e** louse. **—bube** *nm* (young) rascal. **—ig** *adj sl* lousy.

lauschen ('lauʃən) *vi* listen, eavesdrop.

laut (laut) *adj* loud. *adv* loudly, aloud. *prep* according to. *nm* **-e** sound. **—en** *vi* **1** sound. **2** (of a text, letter, etc.) read, run. **—los** *adj* silent, mute. **—sprecher** *nm* (loud)speaker. **—stärke** *nf* loudness, volume.

läuten ('lɔytən) *vi* ring, sound.

lauter ('lautər) *adj invar* **1** only, nothing but. **2** pure. **3** genuine.

lauwarm ('lauvarm) *adj* lukewarm, tepid.

Lawine (la'vi:nə) *nf* **-n** avalanche.

lax (laks) *adj* **1** lax. **2** licentious.

leb/en ('le:bən) *vi* live. *n neu* — life.

lebend ('le:bənt) *adj* living, alive.

lebendig (le'bndiç) *adj* **1** alive. **2** lively.

Lebensart ('le:bənsa:rt) *nf* way of life.

Lebensgefahr ('le:bənsgəfa:r) *nf* danger to (one's) life.

Lebenskraft ('le:bənskraft) *nf* vitality.

Lebenslänglich ('le:bənslɛŋliç) *adj* lifelong.

Lebenslauf ('le:bənslauf) *nm* curriculum vitae.

Lebensmittel ('le:bənsmitəl) *n neu pl* food.

Lebensstandard ('le:bənssta:ndɑ:rt) *nm* standard of living.

Lebensunterhalt ('le:bənsuntərhalt) *nm* livelihood.

Lebensversicherung ('le:bənsversiçəruŋ) *nf* life insurance.

Lebensweise ('le:bənsvaizə) *nf* way of life.

Leber ('le:bər) *nf* **-n** liver. **—wurst** *nf* liver sausage.

Lebewesen ('le:bəve:zən) *n neu* creature.

Lebewohl ('le:bəvo:l) *n neu* farewell.

Lebhaft ('le:phaft) *adj* lively, vivid.

Lebkuchen ('le:pku:xən) *nm* gingerbread.

leblos ('le:blo:s) *adj* **1** lifeless. **2** dull.

leck (lɛk) *adj* leaky, leaking. *n neu* **-e** leak.

lecken ('lɛkən) *vt* lick.

lecker ('lɛkər) *adj* **1** delicious. **2** delicate. **—bissen** *nm* delicacy, titbit.

Leder ('le:dər) *n neu* — leather.

ledig ('le:diç) *adj* **1** unmarried, single. **2** unrestrained, free. **—lich** ('le:dikliç) *adv* merely, only.

Lee (le:) *nf* lee(side).

leer (le:r) *adj* **1** empty. **2** vacant. **—e** *nf* **-en 1** vacuum. **2** emptiness. **—en** *vt* empty.

legal (le'ga:l) *adj* legal.

legen ('le:gən) *vt* lay, place, put. **sich legen** *vr* lie down.

Legende (le'gɛndə) *nf* **-n** legend.

legieren (le'gi:rən) *vt* **1** alloy (metals). **2** thicken (soup).

legitim (legi'ti:m) *adj* legitimate.

Lehm (le:m) *nm* **-e** loam, clay.

Lehn/e ('le:nə) *nf* **-n 1** support. **2** back or arm (of a chair). **—en** *vt,vi* lean. **—sessel** *nm* also **—stuhl** armchair.

lehr/en ('le:rən) *vt* teach, instruct. **—buch** *n neu* textbook. **—e** *nf* **-n 1** teaching, lesson. **2** theory, doctrine. **3** apprenticeship. **4** gauge. **—er** *nm* —, **—erin** *nf* **-nen** teacher, instructor. **—gang** *nm* course, syllabus. **—ling** *nm* **-e** apprentice. **—reich** *adj* instructive. **—stuhl** *nm* professorial chair.

Leib (laip) *nm* **-er** body. **—chen** ('laipçən) *n neu* — bodice. **—esübung** ('laibəsy:buŋ) *nf* physical exercise. **—wache** *nf* bodyguard.

Leich/e ('laiçə) *nf* **-n** corpse. **—enhemd** *n neu* shroud. **—enschau** *nf* **1** inquest. **2** autopsy. **—enschauhaus** *n neu* morgue). **—enwagen** *nm* hearse. **—nam** ('laiçna:m) *nm* **-e** corpse.

leicht (laiçt) *adj* **1** light. **2** easy. **3** slight. **4** unimportant. **5** superficial. **—athletik** *nf* athletics. **—fertig** *adj* **1** frivolous. **2** thoughtless. **—hin** *adv* lightly, casually. **—igkeit** *nf*

1 lightness. 2 ease. **—sinn** nm 1 careless-
ness, thoughtlessness. 2 frivolity.

leid (lait) adv **es tut mir leid** I am sorry, I
regret. n neu 1 sorrow. 2 harm, pain. **—en***
('laidən) vt 1 suffer. 2 permit. 3 tolerate. vi
suffer. n neu — 1 suffering, pain, illness. 2
misfortune.

Leidenschaft ('laidənʃaft) nf **-en** passion.
—lich adj passionate.

leider ('laidər) adv unfortunately.

leihen* ('laiən) vt lend, loan.

Leim (laim) nm **-e** glue, size.

Lein (lain) nm **-e** flax. **—en** adj linen. n neu —
linen. **—wand** nf 1 (cinema) screen. 2 linen.
3 canvas.

Leine ('lainə) nf **-n** 1 rope, line. 2 lead.

leise ('laizə) adj quiet, low, soft.

leist/en ('laistən) vt 1 achieve, do. 2 perform. 3
give. 4 offer. **ich kann es mir nicht leisten** I
can't afford it. **—ung** nf **-en** 1 achievement.
2 work. 3 performance. 4 sci power. **—ungsfähig** adj 1 capable (of work). 2 productive.

leit/en ('laitən) vt 1 lead, guide. 2 manage. 3
direct. 4 conduct (electricity). **—artikel** nm
leader, editorial. **—faden** nm 1 clue. 2
manual. **—gedanke** nm main thought or
idea. **—ung** nf **-en** 1 direction. 2 management 3 lead. 4 circuit.

Leiter[1] ('laitər) nm — 1 leader. 2 head. 3
director. 4 conductor (of electricity, etc.).

Leiter[2] ('laitər) nf **-n** 1 ladder. 2 mus scale.

Lektüre (lɛk'tyːrə) nf **-n** reading (material).

Lende ('lɛndə) nf **-n** 1 loin. 2 haunch, hip.

lenk/en ('lɛŋkən) vt 1 steer. 2 direct. 3 lead.
—rad n neu steering wheel. **—stange** nf
handlebars. **—ung** nf **-en** 1 steering. 2 direction.

Leopard (leo'part) nm **-en** leopard.

Lepra ('leːpra) nf leprosy.

Lerche ('lɛrçə) nf **-n** lark.

lernen (lɛrnən) vt learn.

les/bar ('leːsbaːr) adj legible, readable. **—e**
('leːzə) nf **-n** 1 harvest. 2 vintage. **—en*** vt 1
read. 2 lecture on. 3 gather, pick. 4 select. vi
read. **—er** nm — 1 reader. 2 picker

letzt (lɛtst) adj 1 last. 2 latest. newest. **zum
letzen Mal** for the last time. **—ens** adv
lastly. **—ere** adj latter. **—hin** adv lately,
recently.

Leucht/e ('lɔyçtə) nf **-n** light, lamp, lantern.
—en vi give light, shine. **—er** nm — 1
candlestick. 2 chandelier. **—turm** nm lighthouse.

leugnen ('lɔygnən) vt 1 deny. 2 contradict.

Leukämie (lɔykɛ'miː) nf leukaemia.

Leukoplast (lɔyko'plast) n neu Tdmk (sticking)
plaster.

Leumund ('lɔymunt) nm **-e** reputation.

Leute ('lɔytə) n pl people, persons.

Leutnant ('lɔytnant) nm **-e** lieutenant.

leutselig ('lɔytzeːliç) adj affable.

Lexikon ('lɛksikɔn) n neu **-ka** dictionary.

Liban/on ('liːbanɔn) nm Lebanon. **—ese** (li-
baˈneːzə) nm **-n** Lebanese. **—esisch** adj Lebanese.

Libelle (li'bɛlə) nf **-n** dragon-fly.

liberal (libeˈraːl) adj liberal.

licht (liçt) adj 1 bright. 2 light. n neu **-er** 1 light.
2 candle. 3 lamp. **—bild** n neu photograph.
—en vt 1 clear. 2 thin (out). 3 weigh
(anchor). **sich** —en vi grow thinner. 2
grow brighter. **—ung** nf **-en** clearing, glade.

Lid (liːt) n neu **-er** eyelid.

lieb (liːp) adj 1 dear, beloved. 2 pleasant, nice. 3
kind. 4 sweet.

liebäugeln ('liːpɔygəln) vi 1 ogle. 2 flirt.

Liebchen ('liːpçən) n neu — sweetheart, love.

Liebe ('liːbə) nf **-n** love.

Liebelei (liːbəˈlai) nf **-en** flirtation.

lieben ('liːbən) vt love, like.

liebenswert ('liːbənsveːrt) adj lovely.

liebenswürdig ('liːbənsvyrdiç) adj 1 amiable. 2
kindly.

lieber ('liːbər) adj dearer. adv rather.

Liebesaffäre ('liːbəsafɛːrə) nf **-n** also
Liebschaft nf **-en** affair.

liebhab/en* ('liːphaːbən) vt love (a person).
—er nm — 1 lover. 2 amateur. 3 connoisseur.

liebkosen ('liːpkoːzən) vt cuddle, caress.

lieblich ('liːpliç) adj charming, lovely.

Liebling ('liːpliŋ) nm **-e** darling.

Liebreiz ('liːprais) nm charm, attraction.

Lied (liːt) n neu **-er** 1 song. 2 hymn. 3 tune.

liederlich ('liːdərliç) adj 1 disorderly, slovenly. 2
dissolute.

lief (liːf) v see **laufen.**

Liefer/ant (liːfəˈrant) nm **-en** supplier. **—n** vt
1 deliver. 2 supply. 3 produce. 4 submit.
—ung nf **-en** 1 delivery. 2 supply(ing).

Liege ('liːgə) nf **-n** couch. **—n*** vi 1 lie. 2 be
(situated). **—stuhl** nm deckchair.

ließ (liːs) v see **lassen.**

Liga ('liːga) nf **-gen** league.

Likör (liˈkœːr) nm **-e** liqueur.

lila ('liːla) adj 1 lilac. 2 violet.

Lilie ('li:liə) nf -n lily.

Limonade (limo'na:də) nf -n lemonade.

Linde ('lində) nf -n linden or lime tree.

Lineal (line'a:l) n neu -e rule(r).

Linie ('li:niə) nf -n line.

link (liŋk) adj left. **—e** nf -n 1 left (side). 2 pol Left. **—isch** adj awkward, clumsy. **—s** adv on the left. **—shändig** adj left-handed.

Linse ('linzə) nf -n 1 lentil. 2 lens.

Lippe ('lipə) nf -n lip. **—nstift** nm lipstick.

lispeln ('lispəln) vi 1 lisp. 2 whisper. 3 rustle.

List (list) nf -en 1 trick, ruse. 2 cunning. **—ig** adj cunning, artful.

Liste ('listə) nf -n 1 list. 2 register.

Litanei (lita'nai) nf -en litany.

Liter ('li:tər) n neu or m — litre.

litera/risch (lite'ra:riʃ) adj literary. **—tur** (litəra'tu:r) nf -en literature.

litt (lit) v see **leiden.**

Lizenz (li'tsɛnts) nf -en licence.

Lob (lo:p) n neu -e praise. **—en** ('lo:bən) vt praise. **—enswert** adj praiseworthy. **—rede** nf eulogy.

Loch (lɔx) n neu ⸚er 1 hole. 2 sl prison. **—en** vt puncture, perforate.

Lock/e ('lɔkə) nf -n curl, lock (of hair). **—ig** adj curly.

lock/en ('lɔkən) vt lure, entice. **—mittel** n neu bait.

locker ('lɔkər) adj 1 loose, slack. 2 light. 3 spongy. 4 lax. 5 dissolute. **—n** vt loosen.

lodern ('lo:dərn) vi flame, blaze.

Löffel ('lœfəl) nm — spoon. **—n** vt 1 spoon, ladle. 2 eat with a spoon.

log (lo:g) v see **lügen.**

Loge ('lo:ʒə) nf -n Th box.

Log/ik ('lo:gik) nf logic. **—isch** adj logical.

Lohn (lo:n) nm ⸚e 1 wages, pay. 2 reward, desert. **—arbeiter** nm labourer, workman. **—en** vt pay, reward. **sich —en** vr be worthwhile. **—steuer** nf income tax. **—tag** nm pay day. **—tüte** nf pay-packet.

lokal (lo'ka:l) adj local. n neu -e 1 restaurant. 2 pub.

Lokomotive (lokomo'ti:və) nf -n locomotive.

Lorbeer ('lɔrbe:r) nm -en laurel, bay.

los (lo:s) adj,adv free, loose. adv off, away. **es ist heute nicht viel los** there is not much happening or going on today. **was ist los?** what is the matter? ~**suff** without, free of. **arbeitslos** adj unemployed. **mühelos** adj effortless.

Los (lo:s) n neu -e 1 fate, destiny. 2 lot, share. 3

lottery ticket. **—en** ('lo:zən) vi draw lots. **—ung** ('lo:zuŋ) nf -en password.

lösbar ('lœ:sba:r) adj soluble.

losbinden* (lo:sbindən) vt untie.

lösch/en ('lœʃən) vt 1 extinguish, quench. 2 turn off or out. 3 erase. 4 cancel. **—er** nm — 1 (fire) extinguisher. 2 blotter. **—papier** n neu blotting paper.

lose ('lo:zə) adj free, loose.

Lösegeld ('lœ:zəgɛlt) n neu ransom.

lösen ('lœ:zən) vt 1 loosen, free. 2 solve. 3 dissolve.

losgeben* ('lo:sgebən) vt set free.

loslassen* (lo:slasən) vt let go, release.

losmachen ('lo:smaxən) vt unfasten, free.

losreißen* ('lo:sraisən) vt tear off or away.

lossprechen* ('lo:sʃprɛxən) vt 1 acquit. 2 free.

Lösung ('lœ:zuŋ) nf -en 1 solution. 2 loosening.

losziehen* ('lo:stsi:ən) vi 1 set out. 2 insult, abuse. 3 denounce.

löten ('lœ:tən) vt solder.

Lothringen ('lo:triŋən) n neu Lorraine.

Lotse ('lo:tsə) nm -n pilot. **—n** vt naut pilot.

Lotterie (lɔtə'ri:) nf -n lottery.

Löw/e ('lœ:və) nm -n 1 lion. 2 Leo. **—in** nf -nen lioness.

Luchs (luks) nm -e lynx.

Lücke ('lykə) nf -n 1 gap, chink. 2 omission.

lud (lu:d) v see **laden.**

Luft (luft) nf ⸚e 1 air. 2 draught, breeze. **in der freien Luft** in the open air. **—dicht** adj airtight. **—druck** nm air pressure. **⸚en** ('lyftən) vt 1 air, ventilate. 2 disclose. 3 lift, raise. **—fahrt** nf aviation. **—hafen** nm airport. **—ig** adj airy. **—post** nf airmail. **⸚ung** ('lyftuŋ) nf ventilation. **—verkehrslinie** nf -n also **—gesellschaft** -en airline. **—waffe** nf air force.

Lüg/e ('ly:gə) nf -n lie. **—en*** vi lie, tell a lie. **—ner** nf ('ly:gnər) nm — liar.

Luke ('lu:kə) nf -n 1 skylight. 2 trapdoor.

Lump (lump) nm -en rascal, lout.

Lumpen ('lumpən) nm — rag(s).

Lunge ('luŋə) nf -n lung. **—nentzündung** nf pneumonia.

Lupe ('lu:pə) nf -n magnifying glass.

Lust (lust) nf ⸚e 1 pleasure. 2 joy. 3 desire. **keine Lust haben** have no desire. **Lust auf etwas haben** want or be in the mood for something. **⸚ern** ('lystərn) adj 1 longing. 2 lustful. **—ig** adj 1 funny, amusing. 2 merry, jolly.

Luxus ('luksus) nm luxury.

Luzern (lu'tsɛrn) n *neu* Lucerne.

M

Maat (ma:t) nm **-e** petty officer, mate.

machen ('maxən) vt **1** make. **2** do. **3** produce, manufacture. **4** cause to. **5** amount or come to. **das macht nichts** it doesn't matter.

Macht (maxt) nf **⸚e** power, force, might. **⸚ig** ('mɛçtiç) adj **1** powerful, mighty. **2** thick. **3** immense. **—los** adj powerless.

Mädchen ('mɛ:tçən) n *neu* — girl.

Made ('ma:də) nf **-n** maggot, grub.

mag (ma:k) v see **mögen**.

Magazin (maga'tsi:n) n *neu* **-e 1** storehouse. **2** magazine.

Magen ('ma:gən) nm — stomach.

mager ('ma:gər) adj **1** thin, lean. **2** meagre. **3** poor. **4** scanty.

Magnet (mag'ne:t) nm **-en** magnet. **—isch** adj magnetic.

Mahagoni (maha'go:ni) n *neu* mahogany.

mäh/en ('mɛ:ən) vt mow, reap. **—maschine** nf reaping or mowing machine.

Mahl (ma:l) n *neu* **-e** meal. **—zeit** nf meal.

mahlen* ('ma:lən) vt mill, grind.

Mähne ('mɛ:nə) nf **-n** mane.

mahn/en ('ma:nən) vt **1** warn. **2** remind. **—ung** nf **-en 1** warning. **2** reminder.

Mai (mai) nm **-e** May. **—glöckchen** n *neu* lily of the valley.

Mais (mais) nm maize, corn. **—kolben** nm corn cob.

Majestät (majɛs'tɛ:t) nf **-en** majesty.

Makel ('ma:kəl) nm — **1** blemish. **2** stain.

Makler ('ma:klər) nm — broker, middleman.

Makrele (ma'kre:lə) nf **-n** mackerel.

mal (ma:l) adv **1** just. **2** times, multiplied by.

Mal¹ (ma:l) n *neu* **-e** time. **zum ersten/letzten Mal** for the first/last time.

Mal² (ma:l) n *neu* **-e**, **⸚er 1** sign, mark. **2** spot. **3** boundary. **4** monument.

mal/en ('ma:lən) vt paint. **—er** nm — painter, artist. **—erei** (ma:lə'rai) nf **-en** painting.

Malz (malts) n *neu* malt.

Mama (ma'ma:, 'mama) nf **-s** mummy.

man (man) pron *3rd pers s* **1** one. **2** you. **3** they. **man sagt** it is said, people say.

Manager ('mɛnidʒər) nm — manager.

manch (manç) adj,pron **1** many a. **2** *pl* some, many, several. **—erlei** (mançər'lai) adj

various, different (sorts of). **—mal** adv sometimes.

Mandat (man'da:t) n *neu* **-e 1** mandate. **2** brief.

Mandel ('mandəl) nf **-n 1** almond. **2** tonsil.

Mangel ('maŋəl) nm **⸚ 1** lack, deficiency. **2** defect. **—haft** adj **1** incomplete. **2** faulty. **—n** vi be wanting, lacking.

Mani/e (ma'ni:) nf mania. **—sch** ('ma:niʃ) adj manic.

Manier (ma'ni:r) nf **-en 1** style. **2** *pl* manners.

Manifest (mani'fɛst) n *neu* **-e** manifesto.

Mann (man) nm **⸚er 1** man. **2** husband. **—esalter** n *neu* manhood. **—eskraft** nf virility. **—lich** ('mɛnliç) adj masculine, male. **—schaft** nf **-en 1** team. **2** crew.

Mannequin (manə'kɛ̃) n *neu* **-s** (fashion) model.

mannigfaltig ('maniçfaltiç) adj manifold.

Manöver (ma'nœ:vər) n *neu* — manoeuvre.

Manschette (man'ʃɛtə) nf **-n** cuff.

Mantel ('mantəl) nm **⸚ 1** (over)coat, cloak. **2** case. **3** cover(ing).

Manuskript (manu'skript) n *neu* **-e** manuscript.

Mappe ('mapə) nf **-n 1** briefcase. **2** file, folder.

Märchen ('mɛ:rçən) n *neu* — fairytale.

Margarine (marga'ri:nə) nf **-n** margarine.

Marihuana (mariu'a:na) n *neu* marijuana.

Marine (ma'ri:nə) nf **-n** navy.

marinieren (mari'ni:rən) vt marinate.

Marionette (mario'nɛtə) nf **-n** marionette, puppet.

Mark¹ (mark) nf — mark (coin or currency).

Mark² (mark) n *neu* **1** (bone) marrow. **2** pith.

Marke ('markə) nf **-n 1** mark, sign. **2** trademark, brand. **3** postage stamp. **4** ticket.

Markt (markt) nm **⸚e** market.

Marmelade (marmə'la:də) nf **-n 1** jam. **2** marmalade.

Marmor ('marmɔr) nm **-e** marble.

Marokko (ma'rɔko) n *neu* Morocco.

Marsch¹ (marʃ) nm **⸚e** march. **—ieren** (mar'ʃi:rən) vi march.

Marsch² (marʃ) nf **-en** marsh.

Marschall ('marʃal) nm **⸚e** marshal.

Märtyrer ('mɛrtyrər) nm — martyr.

März (mɛrts) nm **-e** March.

Masche ('maʃə) nf **-n 1** stitch. **2** mesh.

Maschine (ma'ʃi:nə) nf **-n** machine, engine. **—nbau** nm mechanical engineering. **—ngewehr** n *neu* machine gun. **—npistole** nf submachine gun.

Maske ('maskə) nf **-n** mask.

maß (ma:s) v see **messen**.

Maß (maːs) *n neu* **-e 1** measure. **2** size. **3** moderation. **—gebend** *adj* **1** authoritative. **2** standard. **—lg** (ˈmɛːsiç) *adj* moderate. **—igen** (ˈmɛːsigən) *vt* moderate. **—igung** (ˈmɛːsiguŋ) *nf* moderation. **—nahme** *nf* **-n** measure, step. **—stab** *nm* **1** measure. **2** standard.

Masse (ˈmasə) *nf* **-n 1** mass, bulk, substance. **2** quantity, mass. **3** crowd. **4** assets. **—nhaft** *adj* **1** enormous. **2** in great quantities, in a mass. **—nmedien** *n neu pl* mass media.

massiv (maˈsiːf) *adj* **1** massive. **2** solid.

Mast (mast) *nm* **-e(n)** mast, pole.

mästen (ˈmɛstən) *vt* fatten.

Material (materiˈaːl) *n neu* **-ien 1** material, matter. **2** stores. **—ismus** (materiaˈlismus) *nm* materialism.

Materie (maˈteːriə) *nf* **-n** matter, substance. **—ll** (materiˈɛl) *adj* material.

Mathemat/ik (matemaˈtiːk) *nf* mathematics. **—iker** (mateˈmaːtikər) *nm* — mathematician. **—isch** (mateˈmaːtiʃ) *adj* mathematical.

Matratze (maˈtratsə) *nf* **-n** mattress.

Mätresse (mɛˈtrɛsə) *nf* **-n** mistress, lover.

Matrize (maˈtriːtsə) *nf* **-n 1** stencil. **2** mould.

Matrose (maˈtroːzə) *nm* **-n** sailor.

matschig (ˈmatʃiç) *adj* slushy, muddy.

matt (mat) *adj* **1** tired. **2** faint. **3** matt, dull. **4** checkmate. *n neu* **-s** checkmate.

Matte (ˈmatə) *nf* **-n** mat.

Mau/er (ˈmauər) *nf* **-n** wall. **—rer** (ˈmaurər) *nm* — bricklayer, mason.

Maul (maul) *n neu* **⁝er** mouth (of an animal). **—esel** *nm* mule. **—held** *nm* boaster, loudmouth. **—korb** *nm* muzzle. **—tier** *n neu* mule. **—wurf** *nm* ⁝e mole.

Maus (maus) *nf* ⁝e mouse. **—efalle** (ˈmauzəfalə) *nf* mousetrap. **—eloch** (ˈmauzəlɔx) *n neu* mousehole.

maximal (maksiˈmaːl) *adj* maximum.

Mechan/ik (meˈçaːnik) *nf* **-en 1** mechanics. **2** mechanism. **—iker** *nm* — mechanic. **—isch** *adj* mechanical. **—ismus** (meçaˈnismus) *nm* **-men** mechanism.

meckern (ˈmɛkərn) *vi* **1** grumble. **2** bleat.

Medaille (meˈdaljə) *nf* **-n** medal.

Medikament (medikaˈmɛnt) *n neu* **-e** medicine, drug.

Medizin (mediˈtsiːn) *nf* **-en** medicine.

Meer (meːr) *n neu* **-e** sea. **—enge** *nf* **-n** straits. **—rettich** *nm* horseradish.

Mehl (meːl) *n neu* **-e** flour, meal.

mehr (meːr) *adv,adj* more. **immer mehr** more

and more. **—deutig** *adj* ambiguous. **—ere** *adj pl* several. **—fach** *adj* **1** repeated. **2** multiple. **—heit** *nf* **-en** majority. **—mals** *adv* several times, repeatedly. **—wertsteuer** *nf* value added tax. **—zahl** *nf* **1** majority. **2** plural.

meiden* (ˈmaidən) *vt* **1** avoid. **2** shun.

Meile (ˈmailə) *nf* **-n** mile.

mein (main) *poss adj 1st pers* my. **—er** *poss pron 1st pers s also* **der —e** *or* **der —ige** mine. **—erseits** (ˈmainərzaits) *adv* on or for my part. **—esgleichen** (ˈmainəsglaiçən) *pron* people like me. **—ethalben** (ˈmainəthalbən) *adv also* **—etwegen** *or* **—etwillen** for my sake, on my account.

Meineid (ˈmainait) *nm* **-e** perjury. **meineidig werden** commit perjury.

mein/en (ˈmainən) *vt,vi* **1** mean. **2** think. **—ung** *nf* **-en 1** opinion. **2** meaning. **—ungsforschung** *nf* opinion poll.

Meißel (ˈmaisəl) *nm* — chisel.

meist (maist) *adj* most: **am meisten** most (of all). **—ens** *adv* mostly.

Meister (ˈmaistər) *nm* — **1** master. **2** champion. **—haft** *adj* masterly. **—n** *vt* master. **—schaft** *nf* **-en 1** mastery. **2** championship. **—stück** *n neu* masterpiece.

meld/en (ˈmɛldən) *vt* **1** inform of, report. **2** mention. **3** announce. **sich melden** *vr* report, present oneself. **—eamt** *n neu* registration office. **—ung** *nf* **-en 1** announcement. **2** report. **3** application. **4** message.

melken* (ˈmɛlkən) *vt* milk.

Melone (meˈloːnə) *nf* **-n 1** melon. **2** bowler hat.

Membran (memˈbraːn) *nf* **-en** *also* **Membrane -n** membrane, diaphragm.

Menge (ˈmɛŋə) *nf* **-n 1** crowd. **2** quantity.

Mensch (mɛnʃ) *nm* **-en** human being, person. **—enfreundlich** *adj* philanthropic, humanitarian. **—enliebe** *nf* philanthropy. **—enskind!** *interj* good gracious! **—heit** *nf* humanity, mankind. **—lich** *adj* **1** human. **2** humane. **—lichkeit** *nf* humaneness, humanity.

Menstruation (mɛnstruatsiˈoːn) *nf* **-en** menstruation.

merk/bar (ˈmɛrkbaːr) *adj* noticeable. **—en** *vt* **1** observe, notice. **2** note, mark. **sich —en** *vr* remember, make a note of. **—mal** *n neu* **-e 1** characteristic. **2** mark. **—würdig** *adj* remarkable, strange.

Messe (ˈmɛsə) *nf* **-n 1** *rel* mass. **2** fair, market. **3** *mil* mess.

messen ('mɛsən) vt **1** measure. **2** survey (land). **sich messen** vr compete (with).

Messer ('mɛsər) n neu — knife.

Meßgewand ('mɛsgəvant) n neu ¨er vestment.

Messing ('mɛsɪŋ) n neu brass.

Metall (me'tal) n neu -e metal. **—isch** adj metallic, metal.

Metaphysik (metafy'ziːk) nf metaphysics.

Meteor (mete'oːr) nm,neu -e meteor.

Meter ('meːtər) nm,neu - metre.

Method/e (me'toːdə) nf -n method. **—isch** adj methodical.

metrisch ('meːtrɪʃ) adj metric(al).

Mettwurst ('mɛtvurst) nf type of lean pork sausage.

metz/eln ('mɛtsəln) vt **1** slaughter. **2** massacre. **—ger** ('mɛtsgər) nm — butcher.

Meuchelmord ('mɔyçəlmɔrt) nm assassination.

Meuter/ei (mɔytə'rai) nf -en mutiny. **—er** ('mɔytərər) nm — mutineer. **—n** ('mɔytərn) vi mutiny, rebel.

mich (mɪç) pron 1st pers s me, myself.

Mieder ('miːdər) n neu — bodice.

Miene ('miːnə) nf -n **1** air. **2** expression.

mies (miːs) adj miserable, wretched.

Miet/auto ('miːtauto) n neu -s **1** hire car. **2** taxi. **—e** nf -n **1** rent. **2** lease. **—en** vt **1** rent. **2** hire. **3** lease. **—er** nm — tenant.

Mikrophon (mikro'foːn) n neu -e microphone.

Mikroskop (mikro'skoːp) n neu -e microscope.

Milbe ('mɪlbə) nf -n mite.

Milch (mɪlç) nf milk. **—straße** nf Milky Way.

mild (mɪlt) adj **1** mild, gentle. **2** charitable. **—e** ('mɪldə) nf mildness, gentleness. **—ern** ('mɪldərn) vt mitigate, soften.

Militär (mili'tɛːr) n neu army, military. nm -s soldier. **—isch** adj military.

Milliarde (mil'jardə) nf -n **1** thousand million. **2** US billion.

Million (mil'joːn) nf -en million. **—är** (miljo-'nɛːr) nm -e millionaire. **—ste** adj millionth.

Mimik ('miːmik) nf -en **1** mimicry. **2** mime.

minder ('mɪndər) adj **1** less. **2** lower. **3** inferior. **—heit** nf -en minority. **—jährig** adj under age, minor. **—n** vt diminish, reduce. **—wertig** adj inferior.

mindest ('mɪndəst) adj least. **—ens** adv at least.

Mine ('miːnə) nf -n mine.

Mineral (mine'raːl) n neu -ien mineral. **—wasser** n neu mineral water.

Miniatur (minia'tuːr) nf -en miniature.

Minimum ('miːnimum) n neu -ima minimum.

Minister (mi'nɪstər) nm — pol minister. **—iell** (ministeri'ɛl) adj ministerial. **—ium** (mini-'steːrium) n neu -ien ministry. **—präsident** nm prime minister.

minus ('miːnus) adv minus, less.

Minute (mi'nuːtə) nf -n minute.

mir (miːr) pron 1st pers s to or for me, myself.

misch/en ('mɪʃən) vt **1** mix, blend. **2** shuffle (cards). **—ehe** nf mixed marriage. **—masch** ('mɪʃmaʃ) nm -e medley, hotchpotch. **—ung** nf -en mixture, blend.

mißachten (mis'axtən) vt **1** despise. **2** disregard.

Mißbilligung ('misbiligʊŋ) nf disapproval.

Mißbrauch (mis'braux) nm misuse, abuse. **—en** (mis'brauxən) vt misuse, abuse.

mißdeuten (mis'dɔytən) vt misinterpret.

Mißerfolg ('misɛrfɔlk) nm failure.

Missetat (misə'taːt) nf misdeed, crime.

mißfallen* (mis'falən) vi displease.

Mißgeschick ('misgəʃik) n neu misfortune.

mißglücken (mis'glykən) vi fail.

Mißgriff ('misgrif) nm mistake.

mißhandeln (mis'handəln) vt maltreat, abuse.

Mission (misi'oːn) nf -en mission. **—ar** (misio'naːr) nm -e missionary.

mißlich ('mislɪç) adj awkward, difficult.

mißlingen* (v mis'liŋən, n 'misliŋən) vi fail. n neu — failure.

mißtrau/en (mis'trauən) vi distrust. n neu distrust. **—ensvotum** n neu vote of no confidence. **—isch** ('mistrauiʃ) adj distrustful, suspicious.

Mißverständnis ('misfɛrʃtɛntnis) n neu misunderstanding.

Mist (mist) nm -e **1** manure, dung. **2** trash. **—haufen** nm dung heap.

mit (mit) prep **1** with. **2** by. **3** at. **4** upon. adv also, as well.

Mitarbeiter ('mitaːrbaitər) nm fellow worker.

miteinander (mitain'andər) adv together, with one another, jointly.

Mitgefühl ('mitgəfyːl) n neu sympathy.

Mitglied ('mitgliːt) n neu member. **—schaft** nf membership

mithin (mit'hin) adv consequently, therefore.

Mitlaut ('mitlaut) nm consonant.

Mitleid ('mitlait) n neu compassion, sympathy.

mitmachen ('mitmaxən) vt,vi join in, be involved in, be in on.

mitnehmen* ('mitneːmən) vt **1** take with one, take away. **2** wear out, tire.

mitnichten (mit'niçtən) adv by no means, on no account.

Mittag ('mita:k) nm -e midday, noon. **—essen** n neu lunch, dinner. **—s** adv (at) noon or midday.

Mitte ('mitə) nf -n **1** middle. **2** centre. **3** mean.

mitteil/en ('mittailən) vt inform of, communicate. **—ung** nf -en communication, information.

Mittel ('mitəl) n neu — **1** means. **2** average, mean. **3** remedy. **—alter** n neu Middle Ages. **—alterlich** adj medieval. **—bar** adj indirect. **—mäßig** adj mediocre. **—meer** n neu Mediterranean (Sea). **—punkt** nm centre, focus. **—s** prep by means of, with the help of. **—schule** nf middle school. **—stand** nm middle classes.

mitten ('mitən) adv in the middle. **—drin** (mitən'drin) adv in the middle (of it).

Mitternacht ('mitərnaxt) nf midnight.

mittler ('mitlər) adj **1** middle. **2** central. **im mittleren Alter** middle-aged. **Mittlere(r) Osten** Middle East. **~nm** — mediator.

Mittwoch ('mitvɔx) nm Wednesday. **—s** adv on Wednesdays.

mitwirken ('mitvirkən) vi **1** cooperate. **2** contribute.

Möbel ('mœːbəl) n neu — (piece of) furniture.

mobil (mo'biːl) adj movable, mobile. **—isieren** (mobili'ziːrən) vt mobilize. **—machung** nf mobilization.

möblieren (mœ'bliːrən) vt furnish.

mochte ('mɔxtə) v see **mögen.**

Mod/e ('moːdə) nf -n fashion, vogue. **—isch** ('moːdiʃ) adj fashionable, stylish.

Modell (mo'dɛl) n neu -e model, pattern.

Moder ('moːdər) nm mould, decay.

modern (mo'dɛrn) adj modern, up-to-date. **—isieren** (modɛrni'ziːrən) vt modernize.

modifizieren (modifi'tsiːrən) vt modify, alter.

mogeln ('moːgəln) vi cheat.

mögen* ('mœːgən) vt,vi like, wish. v mod aux may, might. **er mag kommen** he may or might come. **das mag sein** that may be, that's as may be. **ich möchte etwas** I would like or I desire something. **ich möchte etwas tun** I would like to do something.

möglich ('mœːgliç) adj possible, feasible. **—erweise** adv possibly. **—keit** nf -en possibility. **—st** adv **möglichst bald/schnell** as soon/quickly as possible.

Mohammedaner (mohame'daːnər) nm — Muslim.

Mohn (moːn) nm -e poppy.

Mohrrübe ('moːrryːbə) nf -n carrot.

Molekül (mole'kyːl) n neu -e molecule.

Molkerei (mɔlkə'rai) nf -en dairy.

Moll (mɔl) n neu mus minor.

Moment (mo'mɛnt) nm -e moment, instant. n neu -e **1** momentum. **2** motive. **3** impulse. **4** element. **—an** (momɛn'taːn) adj momentary, passing.

Monarch (mo'narç) nm -en monarch.

Monat ('moːnat) nm -e month. **—lich** adj monthly.

Mönch (mœnç) nm -e monk.

Mond (moːnt) nm -e moon. **—schein** nm moonlight.

Monopol (mono'poːl) n neu -e monopoly. **—isieren** (monopoli'ziːrən) vt monopolize.

Montag ('moːntaːk) nm Monday. **—s** adv on Mondays.

Moor (moːr) n neu -e **1** moor. **2** fen. **3** swamp.

Moos (moːs) n neu -e **1** moss. **2** sl money.

Moral (mo'raːl) nf -en **1** moral. **2** morality, morals. **3** morale. **—isch** adj moral. **—isieren** (morali'ziːrən) vi moralize. **—ität** (morali'tɛːt) nf morality.

Mord (mɔrt) nm -e murder. **—anschlag** nm **1** murderous attack. **2** attempted murder. **—er** ('mœrdər) nm — murderer.

morgen ('mɔrgən) adv **1** tomorrow. **2** in the morning. nm — tomorrow. **2** in the morning. nm — following day. **(guten) Morgen** interj (good) morning! **morgen früh** (early) tomorrow morning. **—dämmerung** nf also **—grauen** n neu daybreak, dawn. **—land** n neu East, Orient. **—ländisch** adj oriental. **—rot** n neu dawn, (red) morning sky. **—s** adv in the morning.

Morphium ('mɔrfium) n neu morphine.

morsch (mɔrʃ) adj decayed, rotten.

Mosaik (moza'iːk) n neu -en mosaic.

Moschee (mɔ'ʃeː) nf -n mosque.

Mosel ('moːzəl) nf Moselle.

Moskau ('mɔskau) n neu Moscow.

Most (mɔst) nm -e **1** fruit juice or wine. **2** must, new wine. **3** cider.

Motiv (mo'tiːf) n neu -e **1** motive. **2** theme.

Motor ('moːtɔr) nm -en motor, engine. **—boot** n neu motor boat. **—isieren** (motori'ziːrən) vt motorize. **—rad** n neu motorcycle.

Motte ('mɔtə) nf -n moth.

Möwe ('mœːvə) nf -n seagull.

Mücke ('mykə) nf -n gnat, mosquito.

müde ('myːdə) adj tired, exhausted, weary.

Muff (muf) *nm* ̈-e 1 muff. 2 musty smell. **—ig** *adj* 1 surly. 2 musty.

Muff/el ('mufəl) *nm* — grumbler, surly person. **—elig** *adj* surly, grumpy.

Müh/e ('my:ə) *nf* -n trouble, effort. **sich Mühe geben** 1 take pains. 2 make great efforts.

Mühle ('my:lə) *nf* -n 1 mill. 2 grinder.

Mulde ('muldə) *nf* -n 1 trough. 2 valley.

Mull (mul) *nm* muslin.

Müll (myl) *nm* rubbish, refuse. **—eimer** *nm* dustbin. **—wagen** *nm* dust cart.

Müller ('mylər) *nm* — miller.

multiplizieren (multipli'tsi:rən) *vt* multiply.

Mummenschanz ('mumənʃants) *nm* masquerade.

München ('mynçən) *n neu* Munich.

Mund (munt) *nm* ̈-er mouth. **—art** *nf* -en dialect. **—en** ('myndən) *vi* flow (into). **—harmonika** *nf* -s mouth organ. **—lich** ('myntliç) *adj* oral, verbal. **—ung** ('mynduŋ) *nf* -en 1 mouth. 2 estuary. 3 (gun) muzzle.

mündig ('myndiç) *adj* of age, major.

Munition (muni'tsi:o:n) *nf* -en ammunition.

munter ('muntər) *adj* 1 lively, cheerful, merry. 2 awake.

Münze ('myntsə) *nf* -n 1 coin. 2 mint.

mürbe ('myrbə) *adj* 1 (of wood, stone, etc.) brittle, fragile. 2 (of food) soft, tender. 3 unnerved. 4 worn out.

murmeln ('murməln) 1 murmur. 2 mutter.

mürrisch ('myriʃ) *adj* surly, morose.

Muschel ('muʃəl) *nf* -n 1 mussel. 2 shell. 3 earpiece (of a telephone).

Museum (mu'ze:um) *n neu* -**seen** museum.

Musik (mu'zi:k) *nf* 1 music. 2 (military) band. **—alisch** (muzi'ka:liʃ) *adj* of music, musical. **—antenknochen** (muzi'kantənknɔxən) *nm* funny bone. **—er** ('mu:zikər) *nm* — musician.

Muskat (mus'ka:t) *nm* -e nutmeg.

Muskel ('muskəl) *nm* -n muscle.

Muß/e ('mu:sə) *nf* leisure (time), spare time. **—ig** ('my:siç) *adj* 1 idle, lazy. 2 useless, superfluous.

müssen* ('mysən) *v mod aux* have to, be obliged to, must.

Muster ('mustər) *n neu* — 1 model, pattern. 2 paragon. 3 sample. **—n** *vt* 1 inspect, examine. 2 decorate with a pattern.

Mut (mu:t) *nm* courage. **—ig** *adj* brave, courageous. **—maßen** ('mu:tma:sən) *vt* guess, suppose.

Mutter ('mutər) *nf* ̈ mother. **—leib** *nm* womb. **—lich** ('my:tərliç) *adj* maternal, motherly. **—schaf** *n neu* ewe. **—schaft** *nf* maternity, motherhood. **—sprache** *nf* mother tongue.

Mütze ('mytsə) *nf* -n cap.

mysteriös (mysteri'œ:s) *adj* mysterious.

mystifizieren (mystifi'tsi:rən) *vt* mystify.

Mystik ('mystik) *nf* mysticism. **—er** *nm* — mystic.

Mythos ('my:tos) *nm* -then *also* **Mythus** ('my:tus) myth.

N

Nabe ('na:bə) *nf* -n (wheel) hub.

Nabel ('na:bəl) *nm* — navel.

nach (na:x) *prep* 1 after, behind. 2 according to. 3 by. 4 to(wards). **nach London, nach Frankreich** to London, to France. ~*adv* after, behind. **nach und nach** gradually. **nach wie vor** as usual.

nachahmen ('na:xa:mən) *vt* imitate.

Nachbar ('na:xba:r) *nm* -n neighbour. **—schaft** *nf* -en neighbourhood.

nachdem (na:x'de:m) *conj* after. *adv* afterwards.

nachdenk/en* ('na:xdɛŋkən) *vi* reflect, consider, ponder. *n neu* — reflection, consideration. **—lich** *adj* thoughtful, pensive.

Nachdruck ('na:xdruk) *nm* -e 1 reproduction, reprint. 2 emphasis. 3 energy. **—lich** ('na:xdrykliç) *adj* 1 emphatic. 2 energetic. **—srecht** *n neu* copyright.

nacheifern ('na:xaifərn) *vi* emulate.

nacheinander (na:xain'andər) *adv* one after the other.

Nachfolge ('na:xfɔlgə) *nf* succession. **—n** *vi* succeed, follow. **—r** *nm* — successor.

Nachfrage ('na:xfra:gə) *nf* 1 demand. 2 enquiry. **Angebot und Nachfrage** supply and demand.

nachgeben* ('na:xge:bən) *vi* give in, yield, give way.

nachgehen* ('na:xge:ən) *vi* 1 follow. 2 investigate. 3 (of a clock) be slow.

Nachgeschmack ('na:xgəʃmak) *nm* aftertaste.

nachgiebig ('na:xgi:biç) *adj* indulgent.

nachher (na:x'he:r) *adv* afterwards. **bis nachher!** see you later!

Nachhilfe ('na:xhilfə) *nf* assistance.

nachholen ('na:xho:lən) *vi* catch up, make up.

Nachhut ('na:xhu:t) *nf* -en rearguard.

Nachklang ('naːxklaŋ) *nm* resonance, echo.

Nachkomm/e ('naːxkɔmə) *nm* **-n** descendant. **—en*** *vi* **1** follow. **2** comply (with), fulfil. **—enschaft** *nf* posterity, descendants.

Nachkriegszeit ('naːxkriːkstsait) *nf* post-war period.

Nachlaß ('naːxlas) *nm* **-lässe 1** inheritance. **2** estate. **3** reduction.

nachlassen* ('naːxlasən) *vt* **1** leave behind. **2** reduce. **3** temper. *vi* **1** slacken. **2** stop. **3** subside. **4** diminish.

nachmachen ('naːxmaxən) *vt* **1** imitate, copy. **2** counterfeit.

Nachmittag ('naːxmitaːk) *nm* **-e** afternoon. **—s** *adv* in the afternoon.

Nachnahme ('naːxnaːmə) *nf* **-n** cash on delivery, C.O.D.

nachprüfen ('naːxpryːfən) *vt* **1** check. **2** control. **3** verify.

Nachricht ('naːxriçt) *nf* **-en 1** report, information. **2** *pl* news.

Nachruf ('naːxruːf) *nm* **-e** obituary.

nachschlag/en* ('naːxʃlaːgən) *vt* **1** look up, consult· (books). **2** take after (a person)· **—ewerk** *n neu* reference book.

Nachschrift ('naːxʃrift) *nf* **1** transcript. **2** notes. **3** postscript.

Nachschub ('naːxʃuːp) *nm* **1** reinforcement. **2** supplies.

nachsehen* ('naːxzeːən) *vt* **1** examine, inspect. **2** consult, follow (with one's gaze). **3** excuse, overlook. *vi* watch, follow (with one's gaze).

nachsenden* ('naːxzɛndən) *vt* forward, send on.

Nachspeise ('naːxʃpaizə) *nf* **-n** dessert, sweet.

nachsprechen* ('naːxʃprɛçən) *vt* repeat.

nächst (nɛːçst) *adj* nearest, next. *prep* next to. **—e(r)** *nm* fellow, man, neighbour. **—enliebe** *nf* love for one's fellow men or one's neighbour. **—ens** *adv* shortly.

nachstellen ('naːxʃtɛlən) *vt* **1** place behind. **2** adjust. *vi* **1** pursue. **2** persecute.

nachstreben ('naːxʃtreːbən) *vi* **1** strive (for). **2** emulate.

Nacht (naxt) *nf* **-e** night. **—essen** *n neu* supper. **—hemd** *n neu* nightdress, nightshirt. **—lich** ('nɛçtliç) *adj* nocturnal, nightly. **—s** *adv* at night. **—wächter** *nm* night watchman. **—wandeln** *vi* sleepwalk.

Nachteil ('naːxtail) *nm* **-e 1** disadvantage. **2** loss. **—ig** *adj* detrimental, disadvantageous.

Nachtigall ('naxtigal) *nf* **-en** nightingale.

Nachtisch ('naːxtiʃ) *nm* **-e** dessert, sweet.

Nachtrag ('naːxtraːk) *nm* **-e** supplement. **—lich** ('naːxtrɛːkliç) *adj* supplementary.

Nachwahl ('naːxvaːl) *nf* by-election.

Nachweis ('naːxvais) *nm* **-e 1** proof. **2** information. **—en*** ('naːxvaizən) *vt* **1** prove. **2** point out.

Nachwelt ('naːxvɛlt) *nf* posterity.

Nachwirkung ('naːxvirkuŋ) *nf* after-effect.

Nachwuchs ('naːxvuks) *nm* new or rising generation.

nachziehen* ('naːxtsiːən) *vt* **1** draw along or after, drag. **2** trace. *vi* follow.

Nachzügler ('naːxtsyːklər) *nm* **—** straggler.

Nacken ('nakən) *nm* **—** (nape of the) neck.

nackt (nakt) *adj* naked. **—kultur** *nf* nudism.

Nadel ('naːdəl) *nf* **-n** needle, pin. **—baum** *nm,pl* **Nadelhölzer** conifer.

Nagel ('naːgəl) *nm* **— 1** nail, pin. **2** (finger)nail. **—feile** *nf* nail file. **—lack** *nm* nail polish or varnish. **—n** *vt* nail. **—neu** *adj* brand-new.

nag/en ('naːgən) *vi,vt* **1** gnaw. **2** erode. **—etier** *n neu* rodent.

nah/(e) ('naːə) *adj* near, close. **Nahe(r) Osten** *nm* Middle or Near East. **—e** ('nɛːə) *nf* **1** proximity, vicinity. **2** neighbourhood. **in der Nähe** nearby, in the vicinity. **—elegen** *vt* suggest. **—eliegen*** *vi* **1** lie near. **2** be obvious. **—er** ('nɛːər) *adj* **1** nearer. **2** more detailed. **—eres** ('nɛːərəs) *n neu* details. **—ern** ('nɛːərn) *vt* bring near. **sich —ern** *vr* approach. **—estehen*** *vi* **1** be connected (with). **2** be friendly or sympathize (with). **—ezu** ('naːətsuː) *adv* nearly, almost.

näh/en ('nɛːən) *vt,vi* sew. **—maschine** *nf* sewing machine.

nahm (naːm) *v* see **nehmen.**

nähren ('nɛːrən) *vt* feed, nourish. *vi* be nourishing. **sich nähren** *vr* live (on).

nahr/haft ('naːrhaft) *adj* **1** nutritious. **2** productive. **—ung** *nf* nourishment, food, sustenance. **—ungsmittel** *n neu pl* food(stuffs).

Naht (naːt) *nf* **-e 1** seam. **2** *med* stitch(es).

naiv (naˈiːf) *adj* naive, simple.

Nam/e ('naːmə) *nm* **-n** name. **—enlos** *adj* nameless. **—ens** *prep* **1** named. **2** in the name of. **—entlich** *adj* by name. *adv* especially. **—lich** ('nɛːmliç) *adv* that is to say, namely. *adj* same.

nannte ('nantə) *v* see **nennen.**

Napf (napf) *nm* **-e** bowl, basin.

Narbe ('narbə) *nf* **-n** scar.

Narko/se (narˈkoːzə) nf -n anaesthesia. **—tisch** (narˈkoːtiʃ) adj narcotic.

Narr (nar) nm -en fool. **—enhaus** n neu madhouse. **—heit** nf -en folly, madness.

Nase (ˈnaːzə) nf -n nose. **die Nase voll haben von** be fed up with. **—weis** adj cheeky.

naß (nas) adj wet, moist.

Nässe (ˈnɛsə) nf -n 1 moisture. 2 humidity. **—n** vt wet, moisten.

Nation (natsiˈoːn) nf -en nation. **—al** (natsioˈnaːl) adj national. **—alhymne** nf national anthem. **—alismus** (natsionaˈlismus) nm nationalism. **—alität** (natsionaliˈtɛːt) nf -en nationality. **—alsozialismus** nm national socialism, Nazism. **—alsozialist** nm Nazi.

Natter (ˈnatər) nf -n adder.

Natur (naˈtuːr) nf -en 1 nature. 2 disposition, temper. **—alien** (natuˈraːliən) n pl natural produce. **—erscheinung** nf natural phenomenon. **—gemäß** adj natural. **—geschichte** nf natural history. **—gesetz** n neu law of nature, natural law. **—lich** (naˈtyːrlic) adj natural. adv of course, naturally. **—wissenschaft** nf (natural) science.

Navigation (navigatsiˈoːn) nf -en navigation.

Nazi (ˈnaːtsi) nm -s Nazi.

Nebel (ˈneːbəl) nm — fog, mist.

neben (ˈneːbən) prep 1 beside, near, next to. 2 in addition to. **—an** (neːbanˈan) adv 1 close or near by. 2 next door. **—bei** (neːbanˈbai) adv 1 incidentally. 2 besides, moreover. **—einander** (neːbanainˈandər) adv side by side, next to one another. **—fach** n neu subsidiary subject. **—fluß** nm tributary. **—gebäude** n neu annexe. **—her** (neːbanˈheːr) adv 1 incidentally. 2 alongside. **—kosten** n pl incidental costs, extras. **—sächlich** adj incidental.

nebst (neːpst) prep together with.

neck/en (ˈnɛkən) vt tease. **—isch** adj 1 teasing. 2 comical.

Neffe (ˈnɛfə) nm -n nephew.

negativ (negaˈtiːf) adj negative. n neu -e negative.

Neger (ˈneːgər) nm — Negro. **—in** nf -nen Negress.

nehmen* (ˈneːmən) vt 1 take. 2 receive.

Neid (nait) nm envy. **—en** (ˈnaidən) vi envy. **—isch** (ˈnaidiʃ) adj envious.

Neig/e (ˈnaigə) nf -n 1 slope, decline. 2 remnant, dregs. **—en** vt 1 lean. 2 lower. vi incline (to), tend (to). **sich —en** vr 1 incline (to), tend (to). 2 dip. 3 bow. **—ung** nf -en 1 inclination, tendency, preference. 2 slope, incline.

nein (nain) adv no. **mit Nein antworten** reply in the negative.

Nelke (ˈnɛlkə) nf -n 1 carnation. 2 clove.

nenn/en* (ˈnɛnən) vt name, call. **—enswert** adj worth mentioning. **—ung** nf -en 1 naming. 2 sport entry.

Neon (ˈneːɔn) n neu neon.

Nerv (nɛrf) nm -en nerve. **—enzusammenbruch** nm nervous breakdown. **—ös** (nɛrˈvøːs) adj nervous.

Nessel (ˈnɛsəl) nf -n nettle.

Nest (nɛst) n neu -er nest.

nett (nɛt) adj 1 nice. 2 neat. 3 pretty.

netto (ˈnɛto) adv net, clear.

Netz (nɛts) n neu -e 1 net, netting. 2 mains. 3 network, grid. **—haut** nf retina.

neu (nɔy) adj 1 new. 2 modern, recent. 3 fresh.

Neubau (ˈnɔybau) nm 1 new building. 2 building under construction.

neuerdings (ˈnɔyərdiŋs) adv lately, recently.

Neuerung (ˈnɔyərʊŋ) nf -en innovation.

neu(e)stens (ˈnɔystəns) adv lately, of late.

Neugier (ˈnɔygiːr) nf also **Neugier/de** (ˈnɔygiːrdə) curiosity. **—ig** adj curious.

Neuheit (ˈnɔyhait) nf -en 1 novelty. 2 newness.

Neuigkeit (ˈnɔyiçkait) nf -en news.

Neujahr (ˈnɔyjaːr) n neu New Year.

neulich (ˈnɔyliç) adj recently.

Neuphilologie (ˈnɔyfiloloˈgiː) nf (study of) modern languages.

Neureiche(r) (ˈnɔyraiçə) nm new rich, nouveau riche.

Neuzeit (ˈnɔytsait) nf modern age or times. **—lich** adj modern.

neun (nɔyn) adj,nf nine. **—te** adj ninth. **—zehn** adj,nf nineteen. **—zehnte** adj nineteenth. **—zig** (ˈnɔyntsiç) adj,nf ninety. **—zigste** adj ninetieth.

Neurose (nɔyˈroːzə) nf -n neurosis.

Neuseeland (nɔyˈzeːlant) n neu New Zealand.

neutr/al (nɔyˈtraːl) adj neutral, impartial. **—alität** (nɔytraliˈtɛːt) nf neutrality. **—um** (ˈnɔytrum) n neu neuter.

nicht (niçt) adv not. pref non-. **nicht wahr?** is that not so? isn't it? **—raucher** nm nonsmoker. **—wissen** n neu ignorance. **—zutreffend** adj not applicable.

Nichte (ˈniçtə) nf -n niece.

Nichtigkeit (ˈniçtiçkait) nf -en 1 invalidity. 2 worthlessness.

nichts (niçts) pron nothing. n neu nothing-

Nickel

(ness). **—destoweniger** (niçtsdɛsto've:nigər) *adv* nevertheless. **—sagend** *adj* meaningless. **—tuer** ('niçtstu:ər) *nm* — idler, slacker.

Nickel ('nikəl) *n neu* nickel.

nick/en ('nikən) *vi* 1 nod. 2 doze. **—erchen** ('nikərçən) *n neu* — doze, nap.

nie (ni:) *adv* never.

nieder ('ni:dər) *adv* down. *adj* 1 low. 2 inferior.

niederdrücken ('ni:dər'drykən) *vt* 1 press down, weigh down. 2 depress.

Niedergang ('ni:dərgaŋ) *nm* 1 decline. 2 descent.

niedergehen* ('ni:dərge:ən) *vi* 1 go down. 2 alight, land.

niedergeschlagen ('ni:dərgəʃla:gən) *adj* downcast, depressed.

Niederlage ('ni:dərla:gə) *nf* 1 defeat. 2 warehouse. 3 *comm* branch.

Niederland/e ('ni:dərlandə) *n pl* Netherlands. **—er** *nm* — Dutchman. **—isch** *adj* Dutch.

Niederlassung ('ni:dərlasuŋ) *nf* -en settlement.

niederlegen ('ni:dərle:gən) *vt* 1 lay down. 2 demolish. 3 resign, stop. **sich niederlegen** *vr* lie down.

Niedersachsen ('ni:dəzaksən) *n neu* Lower Saxony.

Niederschlag ('ni:dərʃla:k) *nm* 1 precipitation. 2 knock-out. 3 sediment. **—en*** *vt* 1 knock down. 2 defeat. 3 kill. 4 press or move down(wards). 5 calm down. 6 depress. 7 precipitate.

niederträchtig ('ni:dətreçtiç) *adj* base, mean.

niedlich ('ni:dliç) *adj* nice, dainty, pretty.

niedrig ('ni:driç) *adj* 1 low. 2 humble.

niemals ('ni:ma:ls) *adv* never.

niemand ('ni:mant) *pron* nobody, no one.

Niere ('ni:rə) *nf* -n kidney.

nieseln ('ni:zəln) *vi* drizzle.

niesen ('ni:zən) *vi* sneeze.

Niet (ni:t) *nm* -e rivet. **—en** *vt* rivet.

Nikotin (niko'ti:n) *n neu* nicotine.

Nil (ni:l) *nm* Nile. **—pferd** *n neu* hippopotamus.

nimmer ('nimər) *adv* never. **—mehr** *adv* never again.

nimmt (nimt) *v* see **nehmen.**

nippen ('nipən) *vi* sip.

nirgends ('nirgənts) *adv* also **nirgendwo** ('nirgəntvo:) nowhere.

Nische ('ni:ʃə) *nf* -n niche.

nisten ('nistən) *vi* (build a) nest.

Niveau (ni'vo:) *n neu* -s 1 standard. 2 level.

noch (nɔx) *adv* 1 still. 2 yet. 3 besides. **noch**

nicht not yet. **weder...noch** neither...nor. **—mal** *adv* also **—mals** once more, again.

Nomade (no'ma:də) *nm* -n nomad.

Nominativ ('no:minati:f) *nm* -e nominative.

nominell (nomi'nɛl) *adj* nominal.

Nonne ('nɔnə) *nf* -n nun.

Nord (nɔrt) *nm* also **Norden** ('nɔrdən) north.

Nordamerika ('nɔrdame:rika) *n neu* North America.

nordisch ('nɔrdiʃ) *adj* 1 Norse, Nordic. 2 northern.

nördlich ('nœrtliç) *adj* northern.

Nordost (nɔrd'ɔst) *nm* also **Nordosten** (nɔrd'ɔst'ən) north-east. **—lich** *adj* north-eastern.

Nordpol ('nɔrdpo:l) *nm* North Pole.

Nordrhein-Westfalen (nɔrtrainvɛst'fa:lən) *n neu* North Rhine-Westphalia.

Nordsee ('nɔrdze:) *nf* North Sea.

nordwärts ('nɔrtvɛrts) *adv* northward(s), north.

Nordwest (nɔrd'vɛst) *nm* also **Nordwesten** (nɔrd'vɛstən) north-west. **—lich** *adj* north-western.

normal (nɔr'ma:l) *adj* normal.

Normann/e (nɔr'manə) *nm* -n Norman. **—isch** *adj* Norman.

Norweg/en ('nɔrve:gən) *n neu* Norway. **—er** *nm* — Norwegian. **—isch** *adj* Norwegian. *n neu* Norwegian (language).

Not (no:t) *nf* -e 1 need, necessity. 2 emergency. 3 danger. 4 trouble. 5 poverty, misery, distress.

Notar (no'ta:r) *nm* -e notary.

Notbremse ('no:tbrɛmzə) *nf* emergency brake.

Notfall ('no:tfal) *nm* case of emergency or need. **—s** *adv* if necessary, in an emergency.

Nothilfe ('no:thilfə) *nf* emergency or relief service.

notieren (no'ti:rən) *vt* make a note of, take down.

nötig ('nœ:tiç) *adj* necessary. **—en** ('nœ:tigən) *vt* compel, urge.

Notiz (no'ti:ts) *nf* -en 1 notice. 2 note. **—buch** *n neu* notebook.

Notlage ('no:tla:gə) *nf* 1 crisis, emergency. 2 distress.

Notruf ('no:tru:f) *nm* emergency (telephone) call.

Notstand ('no:tʃtand) *nm* (state of) emergency.

notwendig ('no:tvɛndiç) *adj* necessary, requisite. **—keit** *nf* -en necessity.

Notzucht ('no:ttsuxt) *nf* rape.

Novelle (no'vɛlə) *nf* -n short novel or story.

November (no'vɛmbər) *nm* November.

80

Novize (no'vi:tsə) nm,f **-n** novice.
nüchtern ('nʏçtərn) adj **1** sober. **2** prosaic, dull.
Nudeln ('nu:dəln) nf pl noodles.
null (nul) adj **1** nil. **2** null. nf **-en** nought, zero.
numerieren (nume'ri:rən) vt number.
Nummer ('numər) nf **-n 1** number. **2** issue, edition of a magazine, etc.) **3** number, piece, song —**nschild** n neu mot number plate
nun (nu:n) adv now. interj well, well now. —**mehr** adv **1** (by) now. **2** from now on.
nur (nu:r) adv **1** only, solely. **2** merely. conj but.
Nürnberg ('nyrnbɛrk) n neu Nuremberg.
Nuß (nus) n **Nüsse** nut. —**baum** nm walnut tree.
nutz/bar ('nutsba:r) adj useful. —**en** ('nutsən) n neu **1** use. **2** advantage. **3** gain. vt also **̈-en** ('nʏtsən) make use of. vi be useful, help —**lich** ('nʏtsliç) adj useful. —**los** adj useless.
Nylon ('nailɔn) n neu nylon. —**strümpfe** nm pl nylon stockings, nylons.
Nymphe ('nʏmfə) nf **-n** nymph.

O

Oase (o'a:zə) nf **-n** oasis.
ob (ɔp) conj whether. prep **1** above. **2** beyond. **3** on account of. **als ob** conj as if, as though.
Obdach ('ɔpdax) n neu shelter. —**los** adj homeless.
oben ('o:bən) adv **1** above. **2** (high) up. **3** upstairs. **nach oben gehen** go upstairs. —**an** (o:bən'an) adv **1** at the top. **2** at the beginning. **3** at the head. —**drein** (o:bən'drain) adv in addition, into the bargain.
ober ('o:bər) adj **1** upper, higher. **2** superior. **3** senior. nm — (head) waiter.
Oberarm ('o:bərarm) nm upper arm.
Oberbefehlshaber (o:bərbə'fe:lshabər) nm commander-in-chief.
Oberfläch/e ('o:bərflɛçə) nf **1** surface. **2** area. —**lich** ('o:bərflɛçliç) adj superficial.
oberhalb ('o:bərhalp) adv,prep above.
Oberhand ('o:bərhant) nf upper hand.
Oberhaupt ('o:bərhaupt) nm leader, head.
Oberhemd ('o:bərhɛmt) n neu shirt.
Oberin ('o:bərin) nf **-nen** matron.
oberirdisch (o:bər'irdiʃ) adj **1** above ground. **2** overhead.
Oberkellner ('o:bərkɛlnər) nm head waiter.
Oberlicht ('o:bərliçt) n neu skylight.

Oberschicht ('o:bərʃiçt) nf **1** top layer. **2** upper classes, elite.
Oberschule (o:bər'ʃu:lə) nf secondary school.
Oberst ('o:bərst) nm **-en** colonel. —**leutnant** nm mil lieutenant colonel.
obgleich (ɔp'glaiç) conj although.
Obhut ('ɔphu:t) nf protection, care.
obig ('o:biç) adj above(-mentioned).
Objekt (ɔp'jɛkt) n neu **-e** object. —**iv** (ɔpjɛk'ti:f) adj objective.
obliegen* ('ɔpli:gən) vi **einem obliegen** be one's duty.
obligat (obli'ga:t) adj **1** obligatory. **2** necessary. —**orisch** (obliga'to:riʃ) adj compulsory.
Obmann ('ɔpman) nm **1** leader. **2** chairman. **3** spokesman.
Obo/e (o'bo:ə) nf **-n** oboe. —**ist** (obo'ist) nm **-en** oboe player.
Obrigkeit ('o:briçkait) nf **-en 1** authorities. **2** pl government.
obschon (ɔp'ʃo:n) conj although.
Obst (o:pst) n neu fruit. —**garten** nm orchard.
obszön (ɔps'tsœ:n) adj obscene, indecent. —**ität** (ɔpstsœ:ni'tɛ:t) nf **-en** obscenity.
obwohl (ɔp'vo:l) conj although.
Ochse ('ɔksə) nm **-n** ox.
Ode ('o:də) nf **-n** ode.
öde ('œ:də) adj **1** bleak, barren. **2** deserted. **3** dull. nf **-n 1** desert. **2** dullness.
oder ('o:dər) conj or. **entweder...oder** either ... or.
Ofen ('o:fən) nm **̈- 1** stove, oven. **2** heater. **3** furnace.
offen ('ɔfən) adj **1** open. **2** public. **3** frank, candid. **4** vacant. —**bar** (ɔfən'ba:r) adj obvious. —**baren** (ɔfən'ba:rən) vt disclose, reveal. —**barung** (ɔfən'ba:ruŋ) nf **-en** revelation, disclosure. —**heit** nf openness, frankness. —**sichtlich** adj obvious. —**tlichkeit** ('ɔfəntliçkait) nf **1** public. **2** publicity.
offensiv (ɔfɛn'zi:f) adj offensive. —**e** (ɔfɛn'zi:və) nf **-n** offensive
offiziell (ɔfi'tsjɛl) adj official.
Offizier (ɔfi'tsi:r) nm **-e** officer.
öffn/en ('œfnən) vt **1** open. **2** unlock. —**er** nm — opener. —**ung** nf **-en** opening, hole.
oft (ɔft) adv also **öfters** ('œftərs) or **oftmals** ('ɔftma:ls) often, frequently. —**er** ('œftər) adv (more) often. —**malig** ('ɔftma:liç) adj frequent.
Oheim ('o:haim) nm **-e** uncle.
ohn/e ('o:nə) prep without. —**edies** (o:nə'di:s) adv also —**ehin** (o:nə'hin) **1** in any case. **2**

besides. **—macht** nf **1** unconsciousness. **2** powerlessness, impotence. **—mächtig** adj **1** unconscious. **2** powerless.

Ohr (oːr) n neu **-en** ear. **—feige** nf box on the ear. **—ring** nm **-e** earring.

Öhr (œːr) n neu **-e** eye (of a needle).

Ökonom (œkoˈnoːm) nm **-en 1** farmer. **2** steward. **3** economist. **—ie** (œkonoˈmiː) nf **-n 1** economics. **2** economy. **3** agriculture. **—isch** (œkoˈnoːmiʃ) adj economical.

Oktave (ɔkˈtaːvə) nf **-n** octave.

Oktober (ɔkˈtoːbər) nm October.

Okzident (ˈɔktsidɛnt) nm Occident.

Öl (øːl) n neu **-e** oil. **—bild** n neu oil painting. **—en** vt **1** oil. **2** anoint. **—feld** n neu oil field. **—ig** adj oily. **—ung** nf **-en 1** lubrication. **2** anointment.

Olive (oˈliːvə) nf **-n** olive.

Oma (ˈoːma) nf **-s** inf grandma.

Omelett (ɔməˈlɛt) n neu **-s** also **Omelette** nf **-n** omelette.

Omnibus (ˈɔmnibus) nm **-busse** bus, coach.

ondulieren (ɔnduˈliːrən) vt wave (hair).

Onkel (ˈɔŋkəl) nm — uncle.

Opa (ˈoːpa) nm **-s** inf grandpa.

Opal (oˈpaːl) nm **-e** opal.

Oper (ˈoːpər) nf **-n** opera. **—ette** (opəˈrɛtə) nf **-n** operetta. **—nhaus** n neu opera house.

Oper/ation (operatsiˈoːn) nf **-en** operation. **—ationssaal** nm operating theatre. **—ieren** (opeˈriːrən) vt,vi operate (on).

Opfer (ˈɔpfər) n neu **—1** victim. **2** sacrifice. **—n** vt sacrifice.

Opium (ˈoːpium) n neu opium.

opportun (ɔpɔrˈtuːn) adj opportune.

Opposition (ɔpozitsiˈoːn) nf **-en** opposition.

Opt/ik (ˈɔptik) nf optics. **—iker** nm — optician. **—isch** (ˈɔptiʃ) adj optical.

Optimist (optiˈmist) nm **-en** optimist. **—isch** adj optimistic.

Orange (oˈrãːʒə) nf **-n** orange. **—nmarmelade** nf marmelade.

Orchester (ɔrˈkɛstər) n neu **—1** orchestra. **2** band.

Orchidee (ɔrçiˈdeːə) nf **-n** orchid.

Orden (ˈɔrdən) nm **—1** order. **2** decoration. **—sbruder** nm member of an order, monk. **—sschwester** nf sister, nun.

ordentlich (ˈɔrdəntliç) adj **1** orderly, tidy. **2** decent, proper. **3** regular. **—keit** nf **1** orderliness. **2** respectability. **3** regularity.

Order (ˈɔrdər) nf **-n** command, order.

ordinär (ɔrdiˈnɛːr) adj ordinary, vulgar.

Ordinarius (ɔrdiˈnaːrius) nm **-rien 1** professor. **2** class teacher.

ordn/en (ˈɔrdnən) vt **1** (put in) order. **2** sort. **3** regulate. **—er** nm **— 1** organizer. **2** steward. **3** file, folder. **—ung** nf **-en 1** order. **2** regulation. **3** arrangement.

Organ (ɔrˈgaːn) n neu **-e** organ. **—isation** (ɔrganizatsiˈoːn) nf **-en** organization. **—isieren** (ɔrganiˈziːrən) vt organize. **—isch** (ɔrˈgaːniʃ) adj organic. **—ismus** (ɔrgaˈnismus) nm **-ismen** organism.

Orgel (ˈɔrgəl) nf **-n** mus organ.

Orgie (ˈɔrgiə) nf **-n** orgy.

Orient (ˈoːriɛnt) nm Orient. **—alisch** (oriɛnˈtaːliʃ) adj oriental.

orientieren (oriɛnˈtiːrən) vt **1** orientate. **2** inform. **sich orientieren** vr take one's bearings.

origin/al (origiˈnaːl) adj original, first. n neu **-e** original. **—ell** (origiˈnɛl) adj **1** original. **2** unusual. **3** clever.

Orkan (ɔrˈkaːn) nm **-e** hurricane.

Ornat (ɔrˈnaːt) nm **-e** (official) robes.

Ornithologie (ɔrnitoloˈgiː) nf ornithology.

Ort (ɔrt) nm **-e 1** place, spot. **2** point. **3** town. **—lich** (ˈœrtliç) adj local. **—schaft** nf **-en 1** (small) town, village. **2** place.

Orthopädie (ɔrtopɛˈdiː) nf orthopaedics.

Ost (ɔst) nm also **Ost/en** east. **—deutschland** n neu East Germany. **—lich** (ˈœstliç) adj eastern. **—see** nf Baltic Sea. **—wärts** (ˈɔstvɛrts) adv eastward(s), east.

Oster/n (ˈoːstərn) n neu pl Easter. **—ei** n neu Easter egg.

Österreich (ˈœstərraiç) n neu Austria. **—er** nm — Austrian. **—isch** adj Austrian.

Otter[1] (ˈɔtər) nm — otter.

Otter[2] (ˈɔtər) nf **-n** adder.

Ouvertüre (uvɛrˈtyːrə) nf **-n** overture.

oval (oˈvaːl) adj oval.

Oxyd (ɔˈksyːt) n neu **-e** oxide.

Ozean (ˈoːtseaːn) nm **-e** ocean. **—isch** (oːtseˈaːniʃ) adj oceanic.

Ozon (oˈtsoːn) n neu **-e** ozone.

P

Paar (paːr) n neu **-e** pair, couple. **ein paar** a few. **—en** vt pair, couple. **sich —en** vr mate.

Pacht (paxt) nf **-en 1** lease, tenure. **2** rent.

—en vt lease, rent. **—er** ('pɛçtər) nm — tenant, leaseholder. **—vertrag** nm lease.

Pack (pak) nm **-e 1** packet, parcel. **2** pack. n neu mob, rabble. **—chen** ('pɛkçən) n neu — small parcel, packet. **—en** vt **1** grasp, seize. **2** pack. **3** thrill. **—papier** n neu wrapping paper. **—ung** nf **-en** packing.

Pädagog/ik (pɛda'goːgik) nf (theory of) education. **—isch** adj educational. **pädagogische Hochschule** nf teacher training college.

Paddel ('padəl) n neu — paddle. **—boot** n neu canoe. **—n** vi paddle.

Page ('paːʒə) nm **-n** page (boy).

Paket (pa'keːt) n neu **-e** packet, package.

Pakt (pakt) nm **-e** pact, agreement.

Palast (pa'last) nm **-e** palace.

Palästin/a (palɛ'stiːna) n neu Palestine. **—ense(r)** nm: Palestinian. **—isch** adj Palestinian.

Palm/e ('palmə) nf **-n** palm. **—sonntag** nm Palm Sunday.

Pampelmuse ('pampəlmuːzə) nf **-n** grapefruit.

panieren (pa'niːrən) vt coat with breadcrumbs.

Panik ('paːnik) nf **-en** panic.

Panne ('panə) nf **-n** mot breakdown.

Panther ('pantər) nm — panther.

Pantoffel (pan'tɔfəl) nm **-n** slipper.

Pantomime (panto'miːmə) nf **-n** pantomime.

Panzer ('pantsər) nm armour. **—(kampf)wagen** nm mil tank. **—n** vt **1** armour. **2** arm.

Papa (pa'paː, 'papa) nm **-s** dad, daddy.

Papagei (papa'gai) nm **-n** parrot.

Papier (pa'piːr) n neu **-e** paper. **—en** adj paper. **—geld** n neu paper money. **—korb** nm wastepaper basket.

Papp/e ('papə) nf **-n** cardboard. **—schachtel** nf cardboard box, carton.

Pappel ('papəl) nf **-n** poplar.

Paprika (pa'priːka) nm paprika, capsicum.

Papst (paːpst) nm **-e** pope. **—lich** ('pɛːpstlɪç) adj papal.

Parabel (pa'raːbəl) nf **-n 1** parable. **2** parabola.

Parad/e (pa'raːdə) nf **-n 1** parade. **2** parry. **—ieren** (para'diːrən) vi parade.

Paradies (para'diːs) n neu **-e** paradise.

paradox (para'dɔks) adj paradoxical. **—on** (para'dɔksɔn) n neu **-oxa** paradox.

Paragraph (para'graːf) nm **-en** paragraph, article, section.

parallel (para'leːl) adj parallel. **—e** nf **-n** parallel.

Paralyse (para'lyːzə) nf **-n** paralysis.

Parasit (para'ziːt) nm **-en** parasite.

Parenthese (parɛn'teːzə) nf **-n** parenthesis.

Parfüm (par'fyːm) n neu **-e** or **-s** perfume.

parieren (pa'riːrən) vt **1** parry. **2** rein in (a horse). vi obey.

Parität (pari'tɛːt) nf **-en** parity.

Park (park) nm **-s** park. **—anlage** nf park, grounds. **—en** vt park. **—platz** nm car park. **—uhr** nf parking meter.

Parkett (par'kɛt) n neu **-s 1** parquet (floor). **2** Th stalls.

Parlament (parla'mɛnt) n neu **-e** parliament. **—arisch** (parlamɛn'taːriʃ) adj parliamentary.

Parodie (paro'diː) nf **-n** parody.

Parole (pa'roːlə) nf **-n 1** password. **2** pol slogan.

Partei (par'tai) nf **-en** pol party. **—gänger** (par'taigɛŋər) nm party man, partisan. **—isch** adj also **—lich** partial, partisan, biased. **—los** adj impartial, independent.

Parterre (par'tɛr) n neu **-s 1** ground floor. **2** Th pit.

Partie (par'tiː) nf **-n 1** part. **2** party, excursion. **3** match. **4** comm lot.

Partikel (par'tiːkəl) nf **-n** particle.

Partisan (parti'zaːn) nm **-e** partisan, guerrilla.

Partitur (parti'tuːr) nf **-en** mus score.

Partizip (parti'tsiːp) n neu **-ien** participle.

Party ('paːrti) nf **-ties** party.

Parzell/e (par'tsɛlə) nf **-n** allotment. **—ieren** (partsɛ'liːrən) vt divide into lots.

Paß (pas) nm **Pässe 1** passport. **2** pass. **3** passage. **—kontrolle** nf passport control.

Passag/e (pa'saːʒə) nf **-n** passage. **—ier** (pasa'ʒiːr) nm **-e** passenger.

Passant (pa'sant) nm **-en** passer-by.

passen ('pasən) vi **1** fit, suit. **2** sport,game pass. **sich passen** vr be proper or fitting. **—d** adj suitable, fit(ting).

passier/en (pa'siːrən) vt **1** pass (through), cross. **2** sieve, strain. vi happen, occur. **—schein** nm pass, permit.

Passion (pasi'oːn) nf **-en** passion. **—sspiel** n neu Passion Play.

passiv ('pasiːf) adj passive. n neu **-e** gram passive. **—ität** (pasiviˈtɛːt) nf passivity.

Pastete (pa'steːtə) nf **-n** (meat) pie, pasty.

pasteurisieren (pastœriˈziːrən) vt pasteurize.

Pastor ('pastɔr) nm **-en** pastor, vicar. **—al** (pastoˈraːl) adj pastoral.

Pate ('paːtə) nm **-n** godfather. **—nkind** n neu godchild.

patent (pa'tɛnt) adj splendid. n neu **-e 1** patent.

2 commission. **—ieren** (patɛn'tiːrən) vt
patent. **—inhaber** nm patent-holder.
pathetisch (pa'teːtiʃ) adj pathetic.
Pathologie (patolo'giː) nf **-n** pathology.
Patient (patsi'ɛnt) nm **-en** patient.
Patin ('paːtin) nf **-nen** godmother.
Patriot (patri'oːt) nm **-en** patriot. **—isch** adj
patriotic. **—ismus** (patrio'tismus) nm patriot-
ism.
Patrizier (pa'triːtsiər) nm — patrician.
Patron (pa'troːn) nm **-e** patron. **—in** nf **-nen**
patroness.
Patrone (pa'troːnə) nf **-n** 1 cartridge. 2 pattern.
Patrouille (pa'truljə) nf **-n** patrol.
Patt (pat) n neu **-s** stalemate.
Pauke ('paukə) nf **-n** 1 kettledrum. **—n** vi 1 play
the kettledrum 2 inf study, swot.
pauschal (pau'ʃaːl) adj inclusive. **—e** nf **-n** 1
lump sum. 2 all-in price. **—reise** nf package
tour.
Pause ('pauzə) nf **-n** pause, interval.
Pavian ('paːviaːn) nm **-e** baboon.
Pazifik (pa'tsiːfik) nm Pacific (Ocean).
Pazifismus (patsi'fismus) nm pacifism.
Pech (pɛç) n neu **-e** 1 pitch. 2 inf hard luck.
Pedal (pe'daːl) n neu **-e** pedal.
Pedant (pe'dant) nm **-en** pedant.
Pegel ('peːgəl) nm — water-gauge.
peilen ('pailən) vt naut 1 sound. 2 take the
bearings of.
Pein (pain) nf pain, torture. **—lich** adj 1
embarrassing. 2 painful. 3 meticulous.
Peitsche ('paitʃə) nf **-n** whip. **—n** vt whip.
Pelikan ('peːlikaːn) nm **-e** pelican.
Pell/e ('pɛlə) nf **-n** 1 skin. 2 peel. **—en** vt 1
skin. 2 peel. **—kartoffeln** nf pl potatoes
boiled in their skins.
Pelz (pɛlts) nm **-e** pelt, fur. **—ig** adj furry.
—mantel nm fur coat.
Pend/el ('pɛndəl) n neu — pendulum.
—elverkehr nm 1 commuter traffic. 2 shuttle
service. **—ler** nm — commuter.
penibel (pe'niːbəl) adj meticulous.
Pension (pãˈsjoːn) nf **-en** 1 guest house. 2
pension. **—är** (pãsjoˈnɛːr) nm **-e** 1 paying
guest. 2 pensioner. **—ieren** (pãsjoˈniːrən) vt
pension (off).
per (pɛr) prep by, per.
perfekt (pɛrˈfɛkt) adj perfect. **—** n neu **-e** gram
perfect.
Pergament (pɛrgaˈmɛnt) n neu **-e** parchment.
Period/e (periˈoːdə) nf **-n** period, cycle. **—isch**
adj periodic(al).

Perl/e ('pɛrlə) nf **-n** pearl. **—mutter** nf mother-
of-pearl.
Pers/ien ('pɛrziən) n neu Persia. **—er** nm
Persian. **—isch** adj Persian. n neu Persian
(language).
Person (pɛrˈzoːn) nf **-en** 1 person. 2 Th
character. **—al** (pɛrzoˈnaːl) n neu **-e** personnel, staff. adj personal. **—alien** (pɛrzo-
ˈnaːliən) n pl personal particulars. **—ell**
(pɛrzoˈnɛl) adj personal. **—lich** (pɛrˈzœːnliç)
adj personal, private. **—lichkeit** nf **-en** personality.
Perspektive (pɛrspɛkˈtiːvə) nf **-n** perspective.
Perücke (peˈrykə) nf **-n** wig.
pervers (pɛrˈvɛrs) adj perverse.
Pessimis/mus (pɛsiˈmismus) nm pessimism.
—t (pɛsiˈmist) nm **-en** pessimist. **—tisch** adj
pessimistic.
Pest (pɛst) nf **-en** pestilence, plague.
Petersilie (petərˈziːliə) nf **-n** parsley.
Petroleum (peˈtroːleum) n neu 1 petroleum. 2
paraffin.
Pfad (pfaːt) nm **-e** path. **—finder** nm Boy
Scout. **—finderin** nf Girl Guide.
Pfahl (pfaːl) nm **⁻e** stake, post.
Pfalz (pfalts) nf **-en** the Palatinate.
Pfand (pfant) n neu **⁻er** 1 pledge, security. 2
deposit. 3 mortgage. **—brief** nm mortgage
deed. **⁻en** (ˈpfɛndən) vt law seize, take pos-
session of. **—haus** n neu pawnshop. **—leiher**
nm pawnbroker.
Pfann/e ('pfanə) nf **-n** pan. **—kuchen** nm
pancake.
Pfarr/er ('pfarər) nm — parson, rector, min-
ister. **—haus** n neu parsonage, rectory.
—kirche nf parish church.
Pfau (pfau) nm **-en** peacock.
Pfeffer ('pfɛfər) nm pepper. **—dose** nf pepperpot. **—korn** n neu **-er** peppercorn. **—minze**
nf **-n** peppermint. **—n** vt pepper.
Pfeife ('pfaifə) nf **-n** 1 pipe. 2 whistle. **—n*** vt
whistle.
Pfeil (pfail) nm **-e** arrow.
Pfeiler ('pfailər) nm — 1 pillar. 2 pier.
Pfennig ('pfɛniç) nm **-e** 1 a coin, one hundredth
of a mark. 2 penny.
Pferch (pfɛrç) nm **-e** fold, pen.
Pferd (pfeːrt) n neu **-e** horse. **—ebremse**
('pfeːrdəbrɛmzə) nf horsefly. **—erennen**
('pfeːrdərɛnən) n neu 1 horse-race. 2 horseracing. **—estall** ('pfeːrdəʃtal) nm stable.
—estärke ('pfeːrdəʃtɛrkə) nf horse-power.
pfiff (pfif) v see **pfeifen.**

Pfiff (pfif) nm -e whistle. **—ig** adj cunning.

Pfifferling ('pfifərliŋ) nm -e type of mushroom.

Pfingst/en ('pfiŋstən) n neu or nf pl Whitsun(tide). **—rose** nf peony.

Pfirsich ('pfirziç) nm -e peach.

Pflanze ('pflantsə) nf -n plant. **—en** vt plant. **—ung** nf -en plantation.

Pflaster ('pflastər) n neu — 1 pavement, road-surface. 2 (sticking-)plaster. **—n** vt pave. **—stein** nm paving stone.

Pflaume ('pflaumə) nf -n plum.

Pflege ('pfle:gə) nf -n 1 care. 2 cultivation. **—eltern** n pl foster-parents. **—kind** n neu 1 foster-child. 2 nurseling. **—mutter** nf foster-mother **—vater** nf foster-father. **—n** vt 1 care for, tend, foster. 2 cultivate. vi be accustomed to, be in the habit of. **—er** nm —, **—erin** nf -nen 1 nurse. 2 guardian.

Pflicht (pfliçt) nf -en duty, obligation. **—gefühl** n neu sense of duty. **—gemäß** adv according to duty, dutifully. **—treu** adj dutiful. **—vergessen** adj disloyal.

Pflock (pflɔk) nm -e 1 peg. 2 plug.

pflücken ('pflykən) vt pluck, gather.

Pflug (pflu:k) nm -e plough. **—en** ('pfly:gən) vt plough.

Pfort/e ('pfɔrtə) nf -n 1 door, gate. 2 porthole. **—ner** ('pfœrtnər) nm — porter, gate-keeper.

Pfosten ('pfɔstən) nm — 1 post. 2 door-post.

Pfote ('pfo:tə) nf -n paw.

Pfropf (pfrɔpf) nm -e plug, wad. **—en** vt 1 stop, plug. 2 fill, cram. 3 bot graft. nm — stopper, cork.

pfui (pfui) interj 1 shame! 2 ugh! pooh!

Pfund (Pfunt) n neu -e 1 pound, half-kilogram. 2 pound (sterling).

pfusch/en ('pfuʃən) vi,vt bungle, blunder. **—erei** (pfuʃə'rai) nf -en 1 bungling. 2 mess.

Pfütze ('pfytsə) nf -n puddle.

Phänomen (fɛno'me:n) n neu -e phenomenon.

Phantas/ie (fanta'zi:) nf -n 1 imagination, fancy. 2 fantasy. **—ieren** (fanta'zi:rən) vi 1 daydream. 2 mus improvise. 3 talk feverishly. **—tisch** (fan'tastiʃ) adj fantastic, fanciful.

Phantom (fan'to:m) n neu -e phantom, vision.

Phase ('fa:zə) nf -n phase.

Philist/er (fi'listər) nm — Philistine. **—erhaft** adj also **—rös** philistine.

Philosoph (filo'zo:f) nm -en philosopher. **—ie** (filozo'fi:) nf philosophy. **—isch** adj philosophical.

Phonet/ik (fo'ne:tik) nf phonetics. **—isch** adj phonetic.

Phosphor ('fɔsfɔr) nm phosphorus.

Photo ('fo:to) n neu -s photo(graph). **—apparat** nm camera. **—graph** (foto'gra:f) nm -en photographer. **—graphie** (fotogra'fi:) nf photography. **—graphieren** (fotogra'fi:rən) vt photograph. **—graphisch** (foto'gra:fiʃ) adj photographic. **—kopie** (fotoko'pi:) nf photocopy.

Phrase ('fra:zə) nf -n 1 phrase. 2 empty words, cliché. 3 mus phrase, theme.

Physik (fy'zi:k) nf physics. **—alisch** (fyzi'ka:liʃ) adj physical. **—er** ('fy:zikər) nm — physicist.

Physiologie (fyziolo'gi:) nf physiology.

physisch ('fy:ziʃ) adj physical, material, corporeal.

Pianist (pia'nist) nm -en pianist.

Picke ('pikə) nf -n pickaxe. **—l** nm — 1 pimple. 2 pickaxe. 3 ice-axe. **—n** vi pick, peck.

Piep (pi:p) nm -e chirp. **—en** vi chirp.

Pietät (pie'tɛ:t) nf piety.

pikant (pi'kant) adj spicy.

Pikkoloflöte ('pikulufllœ:tə) nf n piccolo.

Pilger ('pilgər) nm — pilgrim. **—n** vi go on a pilgrimage.

Pille ('pilə) nf -n pill.

Pilot (pi'lo:t) nm -en pilot.

Pilz (pilts) nm -e 1 fungus. 2 mushroom.

Pinguin (piŋgu'i:n) nm -e penguin.

Pinne ('pinə) nf -n 1 pin, peg. 2 tiller.

Pinsel ('pinzəl) nm — 1 brush. 2 simpleton.

Pionier (pio'ni:r) nm -e 1 pioneer. 2 mil engineer.

Pistole (pi'sto:lə) nf -n pistol.

Plackerei (plakə'rai) nf drudgery.

plädieren (plɛ'di:rən) vt plead (a case).

Plage ('pla:gə) nf -n 1 nuisance. 2 irony. **—n** vt plague, worry. **sich —n** vr toil.

Plakat (pla'ka:t) n neu -e poster.

Plan (pla:n) nm -e 1 plan. 2 design, draft. 3 project. 4 schedule. **—en** vt,vi 1 plan. 2 design, draft. **—gemäß** adj also **—mäßig** according to plan. **—ung** nf planning.

Plane ('pla:nə) nf -n 1 awning. 2 tarpaulin.

Planet (pla'ne:t) nm -en planet.

planieren (pla'ni:rən) vt plane, level.

Planke ('plaŋkə) nf -n plank.

Plänkelei (plɛŋkə'lai) nf -en skirmish(ing).

Plantage (plan'ta:ʒə) nf -n plantation.

plappern ('plapərn) vi,vt babble, chatter.

Plasti/k ('plastik) nf -en sculpture, plastic art. **—sch** adj plastic.

Plastilin

Plastilin (plasti'li:n) *n neu* **-s** *Tdmk* Plasticine *Tdmk*.

Platin (pla'ti:n) *n neu* platinum.

platt (plat) *adj* **1** flat, even. **2** insipid. **3** silly. **—deutsch** *n neu* Low German.

Platte ('platə) *nf* **-n 1** record, disc. **2** plate. **3** tray. **—nspieler** *nm* record-player.

Platz (plats) *nm* **-e 1** place. **2** square. **3** seat. **4** space. **5** locality. **—karte** *nf* (seat) reservation ticket.

platz/en ('platsən) *vi* burst, explode. **—regen** *nm* **1** heavy shower. **2** downpour.

plaudern ('plaudərn) *vi* chat, talk.

plausibel (plau'zi:bəl) *adj* plausible.

plombieren (plɔm'bi:rən) *vt* fill (a tooth).

plötzlich ('plœtsliç) *adj* sudden.

plump (plump) *adj* **1** coarse, crude. **2** awkward, clumsy.

plündern ('plyndərn) *vt,vi* plunder, pillage.

Plural ('plu:ra:l) *nm* **-e** plural.

Plusquamperfekt ('pluskvampɛrfɛkt) *n neu* **-e** pluperfect.

pneumatisch (pnɔy'ma:tiʃ) *adj* pneumatic.

Pöbel ('pœ:bəl) *nm* rabble, mob.

pochen ('pɔxən) *vi* knock, beat.

Pocken ('pɔkən) *nf pl* smallpox.

Poesie (poe'zi:) *nf* **-en** poetry.

Pokal (po'ka:l) *nm* **-e 1** goblet. **2** *sport* cup.

Pökel ('pœ:kəl) *nm* **—** brine. **—n** *vt* pickle, salt.

Pol (po:l) *nm* **-e** pole (of the earth or of a magnet). **—ar** (po'la:r) *adj* polar. **—arisieren** (polari'zi:rən) *vt* polarize. **—arkreis** (po'la:rkrais) *nm* Arctic Circle.

Polem/ik (po'le:mik) *nf* **-en** polemic. **—isch** *adj* polemic.

Pol/en ('po:lən) *n neu* Poland. **—e** *nm* Pole.

Police (po'li:s, po'li:sə) *nf* **-n** (insurance) policy.

polieren (po'li:rən) *vt* polish.

Polit/ik (poli'ti:k) *nf* **1** politics. **2** policy. **—iker** (po'li:tikər) *nm* **—** politician. **—isch** (po'li:tiʃ) *adj* political. **—isieren** (politi'zi:rən) *vt* politicize. *vi* talk politics.

Poliz/ei (poli'tsai) *nf*-en police. **—eibeamte(r)** *nm* police officer. **—eilich** *adj* (of, by or with the) police. **—eiwache** *nf* police station. **—ist** (poli'tsist) *nm* **-en** policeman.

polnisch ('pɔlniʃ) *adj* Polish. *n neu* Polish (language).

Polster ('pɔlstər) *n neu* **1** cushion. **2** stuffing. **—n** *vt* **1** stuff, pad. **2** upholster.

Poltergeist ('pɔltərgaist) *nm* **-er** poltergeist.

Polypen (po'ly:pən) *nm pl* med adenoids.

Polytechnikum (poly'tɛçnikum) *n neu* **—ken** technical college.

Pommern ('pɔmərn) *n neu* Pommerania.

Pommes frites (pɔm'frit) *n pl* chips, chipped potatoes.

populär (popu'lɛ:r) *adj* popular.

Pore ('po:rə) *nf* **-n** pore.

Pornographie (pɔrnogra'fi:) *nf* pornography. **—isch** (pɔrno'gra:fiʃ) *adj* pornographic.

Portion (pɔrtsi'o:n) *nf*-en portion, helping.

Porto ('pɔrto) *n neu* **-s** postage, carriage. **—frei** *adj* postage paid, post-free.

Porträt (pɔr'trɛ:, pɔr'trɛ:t) *n neu* **-s** portrait, picture.

Porzellan (pɔrtsɛ'la:n) *n neu* **-e** porcelain, china.

Posaune (po'zaunə) *nf* **-n** trombone.

Pose ('po:zə) *nf* **-n** pose.

Position (pozitsi'o:n) *nf* **-en** position.

positiv ('po:ziti:f) *adj* positive.

Poss/e ('pɔsə) *nf* **-n 1** *Th* farce. **2** trick. **—ierlich** (pɔ'si:rliç) *adj* comic, funny.

possessiv ('pɔsɛsi:f) *adj* possessive.

Post (pɔst) *nf* **1** post, mail. **2** (the) Post Office.

Postamt ('pɔstamt) *n neu* post office.

Postanweisung ('pɔstanvaizuŋ) *nf* postal order.

Postbote ('pɔstbo:tə) *nm* postman.

Posten ('pɔstən) *nm* **— 1** post, station. **2** *comm* entry, item. **3** lot. **4** picket. **5** guard.

Postfach ('pɔstfax) *n neu also* **Postschließfach** post-office box, P.O. box.

Postkarte ('pɔstkartə) *nf* postcard.

postlagernd ('pɔstla:gərnt) *adj* poste restante.

Postleitzahl ('pɔstlaitsa:l) *nf* postal code.

Poststempel ('pɔststɛmpəl) *nm* postmark.

Postulat (pɔstu'la:t) *n neu* **-e** postulate.

postwendend ('pɔstvɛndənt) *adv* by return of post.

Postwertzeichen ('pɔstvɛrtsaiçən) *n neu* postage stamp.

potent (po'tɛnt) *adj* potent, capable.

poten/tial (potɛntsi'a:l) *adj also* **poten/tiell** (potɛntsi'ɛl) *adj* potential. *n neu* **-e** potential. **—z** (po'tɛnts) *nf* **-en 1** potency. **2** *math* power.

Pottasche ('pɔtaʃə) *nf* potash.

Pracht (praxt) *nf* **1** splendour, pomp. **2** luxury. **—ig** ('prɛçtiç) *adj* **1** splendid, magnificent. **2** pompous. **—voll** *adj* splendid, magnificent.

Prädikat (prɛdi'ka:t) *n neu* **-e 1** predicate. **2** title.

Präfix (prɛ'fiks) *n neu* **-e** prefix.

Prag (pra:k) *n neu* Prague.

prägen ('prɛːgən) vt **1** stamp. **2** coin.

pragmatisch (prag'maːtiʃ) adj pragmatic.

prägnant (prɛg'nant) adj **1** precise. **2** meaningful.

prahl/en ('praːlən) vi boast. **—erei** (praːləˈrai) nf boasting. **—erisch** ('praːlariʃ) adj boastful.

Prakt/iker ('praktikər) nm — practical or experienced man. **—isch** adj **1** practical. **2** experienced. **3** handy.

Praline (praˈliːnə) nf **-n** chocolate cream.

prall (pral) adj **1** taut, tight. **2** stuffed, full. **3** plump. **4** (of the sun) blazing. nm **-e** collision, impact. **—en** vi **1** bump (into), crash. **2** (of the sun) glare.

Prämie ('prɛmiə) nf **-n 1** premium. **2** prize, bonus.

Präparat (prɛpaˈraːt) n neu **-e** preparation (of medicine, etc.).

Präposition (prɛpozitsiˈoːn) nf **-en** preposition.

Präsens ('prɛːzɛns) n neu gram present.

präsentieren (prɛzɛnˈtiːrən) vt present.

Präsid/ent (prɛziˈdɛnt) nm **-en 1** president. **2** chairman. **—ieren** (prɛziˈdiːrən) vi act as president. vt preside over. **—ium** (prɛˈziːdium) n neu **-len** presidium. **2** presidency. **3** chair.

prasseln ('prasəln) vi patter, drum, crackle.

Präteritum (prɛˈteːritum) n neu **-ita** past tense.

Praxis ('praksis) nf **-xen 1** practice. **2** (doctor's) surgery. **3** (lawyer's) office.

Präzedenzfall (prɛtseˈdɛntsfal) nm precedent.

präzis (prɛˈtsiːs) adj **1** precise. **2** punctual.

predig/en ('preːdigən) vi,vt preach. **—er** nm — preacher. **—t** ('preːdiçt) nf **-en** sermon.

Preis (prais) nm **-e 1** price. **2** prize. **3** praise. **—beaufsichtigung** nf **-en** price control. **—en*** ('praizən) vt praise. **—geben*** vt **1** give up, sacrifice. **2** expose. **—richter** nm umpire, judge. **—stopp** nm **-s** price freeze. **—wert** adj cheap, good value.

Preiselbeere ('praizəlbeːrə) nf **-n** cranberry.

prellen ('prɛlən) vt **1** deceive. **2** bang.

Premiere (premˈjɛːrə) nf **-n** premiere, first night.

Premierminister (premˈjɛːrministər) nm prime minister.

Presse ('prɛsə) nf **-n 1** press, journalism. **2** tech press. **—ausweis** nm press card. **—freiheit** nf freedom of the press. **—n** vt **1** (com)press. **2** urge.

Preßkohle ('prɛskoːlə) nf briquette.

Preßluftbohrer ('prɛsluftboːrər) nm pneumatic drill.

Preuß/en ('prɔysən) n neu Prussia. **-e** nm **-n** Prussian. **—isch** adj Prussian.

prickeln ('prikəln) vi prickle, itch.

Priester ('priːstər) nm — priest. **—in** nf priestess.

prima ('priːma) adj,interj first class. nf **-men** sixth form.

primär (priˈmɛːr) adj primary.

Primel ('priːməl) nf **-n** primrose.

primitiv (primiˈtiːf) adj primitive.

Prinz (prints) nm **-en** prince. **—essin** (prinˈtsɛsin) nf **-nen** princess.

Prinzip (prinˈtsiːp) n neu **-ien** principle. **—iell** (printsipiˈɛl) adj principle. adv on or in principle.

Prise ('priːzə) nf **-n 1** pinch (of salt, etc.). **2** naut prize, spoils.

Prisma ('prisma) n neu **-men** prism.

privat (priˈvaːt) adj private. **—eigentum** n neu private property. **—recht** n neu civil law.

Privileg (priviˈleːk) n neu **-ien** privilege. **—iert** (priviliˈgiːrt) adj privileged.

Prob/e ('proːbə) nf **-n 1** experiment. **2** test. **3** rehearsal. **4** sample. **—en** vt,vi **1** test. **2** rehearse. **—ezeit** nf probation, trial period. **—ieren** (proˈbiːrən) vt **1** try (out), attempt. **2** sample.

Problem (proˈbleːm) n neu **-e** problem. **—atisch** (probleˈmaːtiʃ) adj problematic.

Produkt (proˈdukt) n neu **-e 1** product. **2** result. **—ion** (produktsiˈoːn) nf production. **—ionsmittel** n neu pl means of production. **—iv** (produkˈtiːf) adj productive. **—ivität** (produktiviˈtɛːt) nf productivity.

Produz/ent (produˈtsɛnt) nm **-en** producer. **—ieren** (produˈtsiːrən) vt produce.

Profess/or (proˈfɛsɔr) nm **-en** professor. **—ur** (profɛˈsuːr) nf **-en** professorship.

Profil (proˈfiːl) n neu **-e** profile.

Profit (proˈfiːt) nm **-e** profit. **—ieren** (profiˈtiːrən) vi profit.

Prognose (proˈgnoːzə) nf **-n** forecast, prognosis.

Programm (proˈgram) n neu **-e** programme. **—ieren** vt program.

Projekt (proˈjɛkt) n neu **-e** project. **—ion** (projɛktsiˈoːn) nf **-en** projection.

projizieren (projiˈtsiːrən) vt project.

Prolet (proˈleːt) nm **-en** also **Prolet/arier** (proleˈtaːriər) proletarian. **—ariat** (proletariˈaːt) n neu proletariat.

Prolog (proˈloːk) nm **-e** prologue.

Promenade (proməˈnaːdə) nf **-n** promenade.

Promotion [1] (promotsiˈoːn) nf comm promotion.

Promo/tion[2] (promotsi'o:n) *nf* **-en** award of a doctorate. **—vieren** (promo'vi:rən) *vt, vi* award or be awarded a doctorate.

Pronomen (pro'no:mɛn) *n neu* **-mina** pronoun.

Propaganda (propa'ganda) *nf* propaganda.

Propeller (pro'pɛlər) *nm* — propeller.

Proph/et (pro'fe:t) *nm* **-en** prophet. **—ezeien** (profe'tsaiən) *vt, vi* prophesy.

Proportion (propɔrtsi'o:n) *nf* **-en** proportion.

Prosa ('pro:za) *nf* **-sen** prose. **—isch** (pro'za:iʃ) *adj* prosaic.

prosit ('pro:zit) *interj* cheers! good health!

Prospekt (pro'spɛkt) *nm* **-e** 1 prospect, view. 2 prospectus.

prostituier/en (prostitu'i:rən) *vt* prostitute. **—te** *nf* **-n** prostitute.

Protektorat (protɛkto'ra:t) *n neu* **-e** 1 protectorate. 2 patronage.

Protest (pro'tɛst) *nm* **-e** protest. **—ant** (protɛ'stant) *nm* **-en** Protestant. **—antisch** (protɛ'stantiʃ) *adj* Protestant. **—ieren** (protɛ'sti:rən) *vi* protest.

Protokoll (proto'kɔl) *n neu* **-e** 1 minutes, record. 2 protocol.

Proton ('pro:tɔn) *neu* **-en** proton.

Protz (prɔts) *nm* **-en** snob. **—en** *vi* show off (one's wealth), be ostentatious. **—ig** *adj* 1 snobbish, ostentatious. 2 gaudy.

Proviant (provi'ant) *nm* **-e** provisions, food.

Provinz (pro'vints) *nf* **-en** province. **—ial** (provintsi'a:l) *adj* provincial. **—iell** (provintsi'ɛl) *adj* provincial, narrow-minded, petty.

provisorisch (provi'zo:riʃ) *adj* provisional.

provozieren (provo'tsi:rən) *vt* provoke.

Prozedur (protse'du:r) *nf* **-en** 1 procedure. 2 *law* proceedings.

Prozent (pro'tsɛnt) *n neu* **-e** percent. **—satz** *nm* percentage.

Prozeß (pro'tsɛs) *nm* **-zesse** 1 lawsuit, case, trial. 2 process.

prüde ('pry:də) *adj* prudish.

prüf/en ('pry:fən) *vt* 1 examine. 2 test. 3 inspect. **—er** *nm* — examiner, auditor. **—stein** *nm* yardstick. **—ung** *nf* **-en** 1 examination. 2 test, inspection.

Prügel ('pry:gəl) *nm* 1 stick. 2 beating. **—ei** (pry:gə'lai) *nf* **-en** brawl. **—n** *vt* beat.

Prunk (pruŋk) *nm* splendour, pomp. **—en** *vi* make a show. **—voll** *adj* showy, ornate.

Psalm (psalm) *nm* **-en** psalm.

Psych/iatrie (psyçia'tri:) *nf* psychiatry. **—isch** ('psy:çiʃ) *adj* psychic. **—oanalyse** (psyçoana'ly:zə) *nf* psychoanalysis. **—ologie** (psyçolo-

'gi:) *nf* psychology. **—osomatisch** (psyçoso-'ma:tiʃ) *adj* psychosomatic.

Pubertät (pubɛr'tɛ:t) *nf* puberty.

Publikum ('pu:blikum) *n neu* public.

publizieren (publi'tsi:rən) *vt* publish.

Pudding ('pudiŋ) *nm* **-e** pudding.

Pudel ('pu:dəl) *nm* — poodle.

Puder ('pu:dər) *nm* powder. **—n** *vt* powder.

Puff (puf) *nm* **-̈e** 1 push. 2 thump. 3 bang, crash. 4 *inf* brothel. **—er** *nm* — buffer. **—spiel** *n neu* backgammon.

Puls (puls) *nm* **-e** pulse. **—ieren** (pul'zi:rən) *vi* pulsate, throb.

Pult (pult) *n neu* **-e** desk.

Pulver ('pulvər) *n neu* powder. **—isieren** (pulvəri'zi:rən) *vt* pulverize.

Pumpe ('pumpə) *nf* **-n** pump. **—n** *vt* 1 pump. 2 *inf* borrow or lend.

Punkt (puŋkt) *nm* **-e** 1 point. 2 dot, spot. 3 full stop. 4 item. **—ieren** (puŋk'ti:rən) *vt* 1 punctuate. 2 *med* puncture. **—̈lich** ('pyŋktliç) *adj* 1 punctual. 2 exact. **—̈lichkeit** *nf* punctuality.

Pupille (pu'pilə) *nf* **-n** *anat* pupil.

Puppe ('pupə) *nf* **-n** 1 doll, puppet. 2 chrysalis, pupa. **—nspiel** *n neu* puppet show.

pur (pu:r) *adj* pure.

Purpur ('purpur) *nm* purple.

Purzel/baum ('purtsəlbaum) *nm* somersault. **—n** *vi* fall over, tumble down.

Pustel ('pustəl) *nf* **-n** pimple.

Pute ('pu:tə) *nf* **-n** turkey-hen. **—r** *nm* — turkey-cock.

Putsch (putʃ) *nm* **-e** 1 putsch, coup. 2 uprising.

putz/en ('putsən) *vt* 1 clean(se). 2 polish. 3 wipe. 4 sweep. 5 adorn. **sich putzen** *vr* dress up. **—frau** *nf* charwoman, cleaner. **—lappen** *nm* cleaning rag, duster.

Pyjama (pi'dʒa:ma) *nm, neu* **-s** pyjamas.

Pyramide (pyra'mi:də) *nf* **-n** pyramid.

Pyrenäen (pyre'nɛ:ən) *n pl* Pyrenees.

Q

quabbelig ('kvabəliç) *adj* flabby, wobbly.

Quadrat (kva'dra:t) *n neu* **-e** square. **—meter** *nm, neu* square metre.

quadrieren (kva'dri:rən) *vt math* square.

quäken ('kvɛ:kən) *vi* (of a child, etc.) whine, squeal.

Qual (kva:l) *nf* **-en** pain, torment. **—̈en** ('kvɛ:-

lən) vt torment, torture. **—erei** (kvɛːlǝˈrai) nf torment, torture.

qualifizieren (kvalifiˈtsiːrǝn) vt qualify.

Qualität (kvaliˈtɛːt) nf -en quality.

Qualle (ˈkvalǝ) nf -n jelly-fish.

Quantität (kvantiˈtɛːt) nf -en quantity.

Quarantäne (kvaranˈtɛːnǝ) nf -n quarantine.

Quark (kvark) nm -e 1 curds. 2 sl rubbish, trash. **—käse** nm 1 curd cheese. 2 cream cheese.

Quart (kvart) n neu -e 1 quarto. 2 quart. **—al** (kvarˈtaːl) n neu -e quarter (of a year).

Quartett (kvarˈtɛt) n neu -e quartet.

Quarz (kvarts) nm -e quartz.

Quatsch (kvatʃ) nm nonsense. **—en** vi talk nonsense.

Quecksilber (ˈkvɛkzilbǝr) n neu mercury.

Quelle (ˈkvɛlǝ) nf -n 1 source. 2 spring, fountain. **—n*** vi 1 well, flow. 2 swell. vt soak.

quer (kveːr) adj cross, diagonal. adv crosswise, obliquely. **—en** vt traverse, cross. **—schiff** n neu transept. **—schnitt** nm cross-section **—straße** nf crossroad.

quetschen (ˈkvɛtʃǝn) vt 1 press, crush. 2 squeeze, pinch.

quietschen (ˈkviːtʃǝn) vi squeak.

Quintett (kvinˈtɛt) n neu -e quintet.

Quirl (kvirl) nm -e whisk. **—en** vt whisk.

quitt (kvit) adj even, quits.

Quitte (ˈkvitǝ) nf -n quince.

Quittung (ˈkvituŋ) nf -en receipt.

R

Rabatt (raˈbat) nm -e discount.

Rabbiner (raˈbiːnǝr) nm — rabbi.

Rabe (ˈraːbǝ) nm -n raven.

rabiat (rabiˈaːt) adj rabid, raging, furious.

Rach/e (ˈraxǝ) nf revenge, vengeance. **—durstig** adj vengeful. **—en** (ˈrɛçǝn) vt avenge, revenge. sich **—en** vr take revenge (on).

Rachen (ˈraxǝn) nm — 1 throat. 2 jaws.

Rad (raːt) n neu -̈er 1 wheel. 2 (bi)cycle. **—fahren*** vi cycle. **—fahrer** nm cyclist.

Radar (raˈdaːr) n neu radar.

Rädelsführer (ˈrɛːdǝlsfyːrǝr) nm ringleader.

radier/en (raˈdiːrǝn) vt 1 erase. 2 etch. **—gummi** nm rubber, eraser. **—ung** nf -en 1 etching. 2 erasure.

Radieschen (raˈdiːsçǝn) n neu — radish.

radikal (radiˈkaːl) adj radical.

Radio (ˈraːdio) n neu -s radio.

radioaktiv (radioakˈtiːf) adj radioactive.

Radium (ˈraːdium) n neu radium.

raffen (ˈrafǝn) vt 1 snatch (up), grab. 2 gather up (cloth).

raffinier/en (rafiˈniːrǝn) vt refine. **—t** adj cunning, clever, artful.

ragen (ˈraːgǝn) vi tower (up), project.

Rahm (raːm) nm cream. **—käse** nm cream cheese.

Rahmen (ˈraːmǝn) nm — 1 frame, framework. 2 setting. vt frame.

Rakete (raˈkeːtǝ) nf -n rocket.

Rakett (raˈkɛt) n neu -s sport racket.

Ramme (ˈramǝ) nf -n pile-driver. **—n** vt ram (in).

Rampe (ˈrampǝ) nf -n ramp.

'ran (ran) contraction of **heran.**

Rand (rant) nm -̈er 1 edge. 2 brink. 3 border. **—ern** (ˈrɛndǝrn) vt 1 border. 2 mill (coins).

Rang (raŋ) nm -̈e 1 rank, order. 2 row. **—erhöhung** nf promotion.

rangieren (rãˈʒiːrǝn) vt 1 arrange, classify. 2 shunt. vi 1 be classified. 2 rank.

Ranke (ˈraŋkǝ) nf -n 1 shoot. 2 branch.

rannte (ˈrantǝ) v see **rennen.**

ranzig (ˈrantsiç) adj rancid.

Rapier (raˈpiːr) n neu -e rapier.

rar (raːr) adj 1 rare. 2 exquisite. **sich rar machen** make oneself scarce.

rasch (raʃ) adj hasty, swift.

rascheln (ˈraʃǝln) vi rustle.

rasen (ˈraːzǝn) vi 1 rage. 2 rush. **—d** adj mad, raving.

Rasen (ˈraːzǝn) nm — grass, lawn, turf.

rasier/en (raˈziːrǝn) vt,vi shave. **—apparat** nm shaver, safety razor. **—klinge** nf razor blade. **—krem** nm shaving cream. **—messer** n neu razor. **—wasser** n neu after-shave lotion.

Raspel (ˈraspǝl) nf -n 1 rasp, file. 2 grater. **—n** vt 1 file. 2 grate.

Rass/e (ˈrasǝ) nf -n 1 race. 2 breed. **—enhaß** nm racialism. **—entrennung** nf racial segregation. **—ig** adj 1 thoroughbred. 2 fiery.

rasseln (ˈrasǝln) vi rattle.

Rast (rast) nf -en rest(ing). **—en** vi rest. **—los** adj restless. **—platz** nm layby.

Rasur (raˈzuːr) nf -en shave.

Rat (raːt) nm -̈e 1 advice, counsel. 2 council. 3 councillor. **mit Rat und Tat** by word and deed. **—en*** vt 1 advise. 2 guess. **—geber** nm adviser. **—haus** n neu town hall. **—los**

adj at a loss. **—sam** *adj* advisable. **—schlag** *nm* (piece of) advice, recommendation.
Rate ('ra:tə) *nf* **-n 1** instalment. **2** rate.
Ratif/ ** ation** (ratifikatsi'o:n) *nf* **-en 1** ratification. **2** confirmation. **—izieren** (ratifi'tsi:rən) *vt* ratify.
Ration (ratsi'o:n) *nf* **-en** ration. **—al** (ratsio'na:l) *adj* rational, sensible. **—alisieren** (ratsionali'zi:rən) *vt* rationalize. **—ell** (ratsio'nɛl) *adj* **1** rational, logical. **2** economical. **—ieren** (ratsio'ni:rən) *vt* ration.
Rätsel ('rɛ:tsəl) *n neu* **— 1** puzzle, riddle. **2** mystery. **3** enigma. **—haft** *adj* mysterious, puzzling.
Ratte ('ratə) *nf* **-n** rat.
raub/en ('raubən) *vt* rob. **—er** ('rɔybər) *nm* **—** robber. **—tier** ('raupti:r) *n neu* beast of prey. **—überfall** ('raupy:barfal) *nm* armed robbery, robbery with violence.
Rauch (raux) *nm* smoke. **—en** *vt,vi* smoke. *n neu* smoking. **—er** *nm* **—** smoker. **—ern** ('rɔyçərn) *vt* smoke, cure (meat, etc.). **—fang** *nm* -e chimney, flue. **—ig** *adj* smoky.
'rauf (rauf) contraction of **herauf.**
Raufbold ('raufbɔlt) *nm* -e bully, rowdy.
rauh (rau) *adj* **1** rough. **2** coarse. **3** hoarse. **—eit** ('rauhait) *nf* roughness, coarseness.
Raum (raum) *nm* "-e **1** space. **2** room. **3** area. **—en** ('rɔymən) *vt* **1** remove. **2** clear away. **3** clear, evacuate. **—fahrt** *nf* space travel. **—lich** ('rɔymliç) *adj* spatial. **—schiff** *n neu* space ship.
Raupe ('raupə) *nf* -n **1** caterpillar. **2** caterpillar track.
Rausch (rauʃ) *nm* "-e intoxication. **—en** *vi* **1** rustle. **2** rush. **—gift** *n neu* narcotic, drug. **—giftsüchtige(r)** *nm* (drug) addict. **—mittel** *n neu* drug, intoxicant.
Reagenzglas (re'a:gɛntsgla:s) *n neu* test tube.
reagieren (rea'gi:rən) *vi* react.
Reakt/ion (reaktsi'o:n) *nf* **-en** reaction. **—ionär** (reaktsio'nɛ:r) *nm* -e reactionary. **—or** (re'aktor) *nm* -en reactor.
real (re'a:l) *adj* real. **—isieren** (reali'zi:rən) *vt* **1** realize. **2** perform. **3** convert into money. **—ismus** (rea'lismus) *nm* realism. **—ität** (reali'tɛ:t) *nf* -en reality. **—schule** *nf* (technical) secondary school.
Reb/e ('re:bə) *nf* -n vine. **—stock** ('rɛpstɔk) *nm* vine.
Rebell (re'bɛl) *nm* -en rebel. **—ion** (rɛbɛli'o:n) *nf* -en rebellion.
Rebhuhn ('rɛphu:n) *n neu* "-er partridge.

rechen ('rɛçən) *vt* rake. *nm* **—** rake.
Rechen/maschine ('rɛçənmaʃi:nə) *nf* calculating machine, calculator. **—schaft** *nf* account. **Rechenschaft ablegen** account for.
rechn/en ('rɛçnən) *vt,vi* calculate, reckon, count. **—er** *nm* **—** calculator. **—ung** *nf* -en **1** bill. **2** calculation.
recht (rɛçt) *adj* **1** right, correct. **2** right, right-hand. **3** correct, suitable. **4** real. **5** just. **recht haben** be right or correct. *adv* **1** correctly. **2** very. **3** really. **4** justly. *n neu* -e **1** right, privilege. **2** law.
Rechteck ('rɛçtɛk) *n neu* -e rectangle.
rechtfertigen ('rɛçtfɛrtigən) *vt* justify, vindicate.
rechtgläubig ('rɛçtglɔybiç) *adj* orthodox.
rechthaberisch ('rɛçtha:bəriʃ) *adj* dogmatic, obstinate.
rechtmäßig ('rɛçtmɛsiç) *adj* legal, lawful.
rechts (rɛçts) *adv* on or to the right.
Rechtsanwalt ('rɛçtsanvalt) *nm* lawyer, solicitor, barrister.
rechtschaffen ('rɛçtʃafən) *adj* upright, just.
Rechtschreibung ('rɛçtʃraibuŋ) *nf* -en spelling.
Rechtsfall ('rɛçtsfal) *nm* lawsuit.
Rechtsprechung ('rɛçtʃprexuŋ) *nf* -en **1** administration of justice. **2** jurisdiction.
Rechtsstaat ('rɛçtsʃta:t) *nm* constitutional state.
rechtzeitig ('rɛçttsaitiç) *adj* timely.
recken ('rɛkən) *vt* stretch (one's arms, legs, etc.). **sich recken** *vr* stretch oneself.
Redakt/eur (redak'tœ:r) *nm* -e editor. **—ion** (redaktsi'o:n) *nf* -en **1** editorial staff. **2** editing.
Red/e ('re:də) *nf* -n **1** talk. **2** speech. **nicht der Rede wert** not worth mentioning. **—efreiheit** *nf* freedom of speech. **—egewandt** *adj* eloquent. **—en** *vi* speak, talk. **—ensart** *nf* **1** phrase, expression. **2** empty phrase, cliché. **—ewendung** *nf* -en idiom, expression.
redigieren (redi'gi:rən) *vt* edit, revise.
redlich ('re:tliç) *adj* honest, fair.
Redner ('re:dnər) *nm* **—** speaker, orator.
redselig ('re:tze:liç) *adj* talkative.
reduzieren (redu'tsi:rən) *vt* reduce, decrease.
Reeder ('re:dər) *nm* **—** shipowner.
reell (re'ɛl) *adj* **1** honest. **2** (of business, etc.) fair. **3** respectable.
Referat (refe'ra:t) *n neu* -e **1** report. **2** lecture.
Referent (refe'rɛnt) *nm* -en **1** expert adviser. **2** lecturer, speaker.
reflektieren (reflɛk'ti:rən) *vt,vi* reflect.
reflexiv (reflɛk'si:f) *adj* reflexive.

Reform (re'fɔrm) nf -en reform. —**ieren** (refɔr-'miːrən) vt reform.

Refrain (rə'frɛː) nm -s refrain.

Regal (re'gaːl) n neu -e shelf, book-shelf.

rege ('reːgə) adj lively, active. —**n** vt move, stir.

Regel ('reːgəl) nf -n 1 rule. 2 regulation. 3 menstruation, menses, period. —**n** vt regulate. —**mäßig** adj regular, periodic. —**recht** adj regular, proper. —**ung** nf -en regulation, rule.

Regen ('reːgən) nm -en rain. —**bogen** nm rainbow. —**mantel** nm raincoat. —**schirm** nm umbrella.

Regent (re'gɛnt) nm -en regent.

Regie (re'ʒiː) nf -n 1 Th production, direction. 2 administration. 3 state monopoly.

regier/en (re'giːrən) vt,vi govern, reign (over). —**ung** nf -en government, administration.

Regiment (regi'mɛnt) n neu -er 1 regiment. 2 rule, authority.

Regisseur (reʒi'sœːr) nm -e Th producer, director.

Regist/er (re'gistər) n neu — 1 register. 2 table of contents. 3 index. —**rieren** (regi-'striːrən) vt 1 register. 2 index.

regn/en ('reːgnən) vi rain. —**erisch** ('reː-gnəriʃ) adj rainy.

regulär (regu'lɛːr) adj regular.

regulieren (regu'liːrən) vt regulate, adjust.

Regung ('reːguŋ) nf -en 1 movement. 2 emotion. 3 impulse. —**slos** adj motionless.

Reh (reː) n neu -e roe (deer). —**bock** nm -e roebuck. —**kalb** n neu fawn.

reib/en ('raibən) vt 1 rub. 2 grate. —**erei** (raibə'rai) nf -en 1 friction. 2 conflict. —**ung** nf -en 1 rubbing, friction. 2 clash, conflict. —**ungslos** adj frictionless, smooth.

reich (raiç) adj wealthy, rich. —**haltig** adj copious, ample. —**lich** adj plentiful, abundant. —**tum** nm -̈er wealth, abundance.

Reich (raiç) n neu -e empire, realm.

reich/en ('raiçən) vt hand, offer, pass. vi 1 suffice. 2 reach. —**weite** nf 1 reach. 2 range.

roif (raif) adj mature, ripe. —**e** nf maturity, ripeness. —**ezeugnis** n neu school-leaving certificate.

Reif[1] (raif) nm hoarfrost.

Reif[2] (raif) nm -e 1 band. 2 ring.

Reifen ('raifən) nm — 1 tyre. 2 hoop. 3 collar. —**panne** nf mot puncture.

Reihe ('raiə) nf -n 1 file, row, rank. 2 series. 3

queue. —**n** vt 1 place in a row. 2 arrange. —**nfolge** nf sequence, order. —**nhäuser** n neu pl terraced houses.

Reiher ('raiər) nm — heron.

Reim (raim) nm -e rhyme. —**en** vt,vi rhyme.

rein[1] (rain) adj 1 clean. 2 pure. 3 absolute. —**machefrau** nf cleaner, charwoman. —**heit** nf cleanliness, purity. —**igen** vt 1 clean(se). 2 purify, refine. —**igung** nf -en 1 cleaning. 2 cleansing, purification. —**lich** adj 1 clean. 2 neat.

'rein[2] (rain) contraction of **herein.**

Reis (rais) nm rice.

Reise ('raizə) nf -n journey, trip, tour. —**büro** n neu 1 tourist office. 2 travel agency. —**führer** nm guide(book). —**n** vi travel. —**nde(r)** nm 1 traveller. 2 passenger. —**scheck** nm traveller's cheque.

reiß/en ('raisən) vt 1 tear. 2 drag. vi tear, split. **sich reißen um** fight for or over, scramble for. ~**n** neu inf rheumatism. —**er** nm 1 thriller. 2 (box-office) success. —**verschluß** nm zip(-fastener).

reit/en ('raitən) vt,vi ride. —**er** nm — rider. —**erei** (raitə'rai) nf -en cavalry.

Reiz (raits) nm -e 1 attraction, charm. 2 irritation, annoyance. —**bar** adj 1 sensitive. 2 irritable. —**en** vt 1 attract, charm. 2 irritate. 3 excite. vi game bid. —**end** adj charming, enchanting. —**mittel** n neu stimulant. —**ung** nf -en 1 irritation. 2 provocation. 3 enticement, charm.

Reklame (re'klaːmə) nf -n 1 advertising, publicity. 2 advertisement.

Rekord (re'kɔrt) nm -e record.

Rekrut (re'kruːt) nm -en recruit. —**ieren** (re-kruˈtiːrən) vt recruit. **sich** —**ieren** vr pick or take on recruits.

Rektor ('rɛktɔr) nm -en rector, vice-chancellor, principal.

relativ (rela'tiːf) adj relative.

Relief (reli'ɛf) n neu -s Art,geog relief.

Religi/on (religi'oːn) nf -en religion. —**ös** (religi'œːs) adj religious, pious.

Ren (rɛn) n neu -e reindeer.

Renn/bahn ('rɛnbaːn) nf -en racecourse or racetrack. —**en**[*] vt 1 run. 2 race. vt run. n neu — 1 running. 2 race. 3 racing. —**pferd** n neu racehorse. —**wagen** nm racing car.

Renomm/ee (reno'meː) n neu -s reputation. —**iert** (reno'miːrt) adj widely respected.

renovieren (reno'viːrən) vt renovate.

rentabel (rɛn'taːbəl) adj profitable.

Rent/e ('rɛntə) nf -n 1 pension. 2 annuity. (unearned) income. 3 interest. **—ner** nm — pensioner.

Repar/ation (reparatsi'o:n) nf -en reparation. **—atur** (repara'tu:r) nf -en repair. **—ieren** (repa'ri:rən) vt repair.

Report/age (repɔr'ta:ʒə) nf -n 1 news report. 2 commentary. **—er** (re'pɔrtər) nm — reporter.

Repressalien (reprɛ'sa:liən) n pl reprisals.

Reproduktion (reproduktsi'o:n) nf -en reproduction.

Reptil (rɛp'ti:l) n neu -ien reptile.

Republik (repu'bli:k) nf -en republic.

Reserv/e (re'zɛrvə) nf -n reserve. **—ereifen** n neu mot spare tyre. **—ieren** vt reserve.

Residenz (rezi'dɛnts) nf -en 1 residence (of a government, court, prince, etc.). 2 capital.

Resonanz (rezo'nants) nf -en resonance, echo.

Respekt (re'spɛkt) nm respect. **—abel** (re'spɛk'ta:bəl) adj respectable. **—ieren** (respɛk'ti:rən) vt respect. **—ive** (respɛk'ti:və) adv respectively. **—voll** adj respectful.

Rest (rɛst) nm -e rest, remainder. **—lich** adj remaining.

Restaurant (rɛsto'rã:) n neu -s restaurant.

Restauration (rɛstauratsi'o:n) nf -en 1 restoration. 2 restaurant.

Resultat (rezul'ta:t) n neu -e result, outcome.

Retorte (re'tɔrtə) nf -n sci retort.

rett/en ('rɛtən) vt save, rescue. **—ung** nf -en 1 rescue. 2 escape. **—ungsboot** n neu lifeboat.

Reue ('rɔyə) nf 1 remorse, regret. 2 repentance. **—n** v imp **es reut mich** I regret.

Revanche (re'vã:ʃə) nf -n revenge.

Revers[1] (re'vɛrs) nm -e bond.

Revers[2] (re'vɛrs) nm -e back, reverse (side).

Revers[3] (re'vɛ:r) nm,neu — lapel.

revidieren (revi'di:rən) vt 1 revise. 2 audit.

Revier (re'vi:r) n neu -e 1 district. 2 (policeman's) beat. 3 (delivery) round.

Revision (revizi'o:n) nf -en 1 revision. 2 audit, auditing. 3 law appeal.

Revolte (re'vɔltə) nf -n revolt.

Revolution (revolutsi'o:n) nf -en revolution. **—är** (revolutsio'nɛ:r) nm -e revolutionary. adj revolutionary.

Revolver (re'vɔlvər) nm — revolver.

rezens/ieren (retsɛn'zi:rən) vt Th,lit review. **—ion** (retsɛnzi'o:n) nf -en review.

Rezept (re'tsɛpt) n neu -e 1 prescription. 2 recipe.

Rhabarber (ra'barbər) nm — rhubarb.

Rhein (rain) nm Rhine. **—land** n neu Rhineland. **—land-Pfalz** nf Rhineland-Palatinate.

Rhetor/ik (re'to:rik) nf rhetoric. **—isch** adj rhetorical.

Rheumatismus (rɔyma'tismus) nm rheumatism.

Rhythmus ('rytmus) nm **-men** rhythm.

richt/en ('riçtən) vt 1 set. 2 direct, aim. 3 prepare. 4 arrange. 5 adjust. 6 judge. vi judge. **sich richten** vr 1 prepare. 2 comply. **—er** nm — 1 judge. 2 umpire. **—maß** nf neu gauge. **—ung** nf -en direction.

richtig ('riçtiç) adj 1 correct, right. 2 real. 3 just. **—keit** nf 1 correctness. 2 accuracy.

rieb (ri:p) v see **reiben.**

riechen[*] ('ri:çən) vt,vi smell.

rief (ri:f) v see **rufen.**

Riegel ('ri:gəl) nm — bolt, bar. **—n** vt bolt, bar.

Riemen ('ri:mən) nm — 1 strap, band. 2 belt.

Ries/e ('ri:zə) nm -n giant. **—enhaft** adj gigantic, huge. **—ig** adj giant, enormous.

riet (ri:t) v see **raten.**

Riff (rif) n neu -e reef.

Rille ('rilə) nf -n groove, furrow.

Rind (rint) n neu -er 1 ox, cow. 2 pl cattle. **—fleisch** n neu beef. **—vieh** n neu cattle.

Rinde ('rində) nf -n 1 rind. 2 crust. 3 bark.

Ring (riŋ) nm -e 1 ring. 2 comm combine, syndicate. **—förmig** ('riŋfœrmiç) adj ring-shaped. **—straße** nf ring-road.

ring/en ('riŋən) vi 1 wrestle, struggle. 2 fight (for), strive (after). vt wring (one's hands, etc.). **—kampf** nm wrestling match.

rings (riŋs) adv (a)round. **—um** (riŋs'um) adv also **—umher** or **—herum** all about or around.

Rinn/e ('rinə) nf -n 1 gutter, drain. 2 groove, channel. **—stein** nm gutter, drain.

Ripp/e ('ripə) nf -n 1 rib. 2 cul cutlet, chop. **—chen** n neu — cutlet.

Ris/iko ('ri:ziko) n neu -s, -ken risk. **—kant** (ris'kant) adj risky. **—kieren** (ris'ki:rən) vt risk.

riß (ris) v see **reißen.**

Riß (ris) nm **Risse** 1 tear. 2 crack, crevice. 3 tech drawing, design. 4 fracture.

ritt (rit) v see **reiten.**

Ritt (rit) nm -e ride.

Ritter ('ritər) nm — knight. **—gut** n neu manor, estate. **—lich** adj chivalrous.

rittlings ('ritliŋs) adv astride.

Ritus ('ri:tus) *nm* **-ten** rite.

Ritz (rits) *nm* **-e** *also* **Ritze** ('ritsə) *nf* **-n 1** cleft, fissure. **2** scratch.

Rizinusöl ('ri:tsinusœ:l) *n neu* castor oil.

roch (rɔx) *v see* **riechen.**

Rock (rɔk) *nm* ̈**e 1** skirt. **2** jacket, coat.

rod/en ('ro:dən) *vt* clear (woodland for cultivation). **—ung** *nf* **-en** cleared woodland.

Roggen ('rɔgən) *nm* rye. **—brot** *n neu* ryebread.

roh (ro:) *adj* **1** raw. **2** crude. **3** rough, brutal. **—eit** ('ro:hait) *nf* **-en 1** rawness. **2** roughness, brutality. **—stoff** *nm* raw material.

Rohr (ro:r) *n neu* **-e 1** tube, pipe. **2** reed, cane. **3** barrel (of a gun). ̈**-e** ('roeːrə) *nf* **-n 1** tube, pipe. **2** (radio) valve. **3** oven. **—geflecht** *n neu* wickerwork. **—weite** *nf tech* bore.

Roll/aden ('rɔlladən) *nm* roller blind. **—bahn** *nf aviat* runway. **—en** ('rɔlən) *vt,vi* roll. **—er** *nm* **— 1** (motor) scooter. **2** roller, breaker. **—holz** *n neu* rolling pin. **—schuh** *nm* roller skate. **—stuhl** *nm* wheelchair. **—treppe** *nf* escalator.

Rolle ('rɔlə) *nf* **-n 1** roll. **2** *Th* role. **3** pulley. **4** castor. **5** mangle. **das spielt keine Rolle** that doesn't matter.

Rom (ro:m) *n neu* Rome.

Roman (ro'ma:n) *nm* **-e** novel.

Roman/tik (ro'mantik) *nf* romantic poetry, romanticism. **—tiker** *nm* **—** romanticist. **—tisch** *adj* romantic.

röntgen ('rœntgən) *vt* X-ray. **—aufnahme** *nf also* **—bild** *n neu* X-ray (photograph). **—strahlen** *nm pl* X-rays.

rosa ('ro:za) *adj* pink.

Ros/e ('ro:zə) *nf* **-n** rose. **—enkohl** *nm* Brussels sprout. **—enkranz** *nm* rosary.

Rosine (ro'zi:nə) *nf* **-n** raisin.

Rosmarin (rɔsma'ri:n) *nm* **-e** rosemary.

Roß (rɔs) *n neu* **Rosse** horse, steed.

Rost[1] (rɔst) *nm* **—e 1** grating. **2** *cul* grill. **—braten** *nm* roast (meat). ̈**-n** ('rœ:stən) *vt* **1** roast. **2** toast. **3** grill.

Rost[2] (rɔst) *nm* rust. **—en** *vi* rust.

rot (ro:t) *adj,n neu* red. ̈**-e** ('rœ:tə) *nf* red, redness.

Röteln ('rœtəln) *n pl* German measles.

Rotor ('ro:tɔr) *nm* **-en** rotor, armature.

Rübe ('ry:bə) *nf* **gelbe Rübe** carrot. **weiße Rübe** turnip. **—nzucker** *nm* beet sugar.

Rubin (ru'bi:n) *nm* **-e** ruby.

Rubrik (ru'bri:k) *nf* **-en 1** rubric. **2** heading.

ruch/bar ('ru:xba:r) *adj* notorious. **—los** *adj* wicked, impious.

rückbezüglich ('rykbətsy:kliç) *adj* reflexive.

Rückblende ('rykblɛndə) *nf* flashback.

Rückblick ('rykblik) *nm* **1** retrospect. **2** backward glance.

rücken ('rykən) *vt,vi* move, shift.

Rücken ('rykən) *nm* **—** back.

Rückfahrkarte ('rykfa:rkartə) *nf* return ticket.

Rückfahrt ('rykfa:rt) *nf* return voyage or trip.

Rückfall ('rykfal) *nm* **1** relapse. **2** reversion.

Rückgang ('rykgaŋ) *nm* decline, decrease.

rückgängig ('rykgɛŋiç) *adj* retrograde. **rückgängig machen** cancel, revoke.

Rückgrat ('rykgra:t) *n neu* **-e** backbone, spine.

Rückhalt ('rykhalt) *nm* support.

Rückkehr ('rykke:r) *nf* return.

Rucksack ('rukzak) *nm* **-e** rucksack. **2** sack.

Rückschlag ('rykʃlak) *nm* **1** setback. **2** recoil.

Rücksicht ('rykziçt) *nf* respect, consideration. **—slos** *adj* inconsiderate.

Rückspiegel ('rykʃpi:gəl) *nm* rear-view mirror.

rückständig ('rykʃtɛndiç) *adj* **1** backward. **2** in arrears.

Rückstoß ('rykʃtos) *nm* recoil.

Rücktritt ('ryktrit) *nm* **1** resignation **2** withdrawal.

rückwärts ('rykvɛrts) *adv* backwards.

Rückzug ('ryktsu:k) *nm* retreat.

Rudel ('ru:dəl) *n neu* **—** pack, herd, band.

Ruder ('ru:dər) *n neu* **— 1** oar. **2** rudder. **—boot** *n neu* rowing boat. **—n** *vi,vt* row.

Ruf (ru:f) *nm* **-e 1** cry, call. **2** reputation. **3** summons. **—en**[*] *vt* **1** cry, call. **2** summon. *vi* cry, call. **—nummer** *nf* telephone number.

Rüge ('ry:gə) *nf* **-n** reprimand, reproach. **—n** *vt* **1** reproach, admonish. **2** blame.

Ruh/e ('ru:ə) *nf* **1** quiet. **2** stillness, calm. **3** rest, relaxation. **—elos** *adj* restless. **—en** *vi* **1** rest, sleep. **2** be still. **3** be based (on). **—estand** *nm* retirement. **—ig** ('ru:iç) *adj* **1** quiet, still. **2** calm, peaceful.

Ruhm (ru:m) *nm* fame, glory. ̈**-en** ('ry:mən) *vt* praise. **sich** ̈**-en** *vr* boast. ̈**-lich** ('ry:mliç) *adj* glorious.

Ruhr (ru:r) *nf* dysentery.

rühr/en ('ry:rən) *vt,vi* **1** move. **2** stir. **3** touch. **—ei** *n neu* scrambled eggs. **—selig** *adj* sentimental, emotional. **—ung** *nf* emotion.

Ruhrgebiet ('ru:rgəbi:t) *n neu* Ruhr region.

Ruin/e (ru'i:nə) *nf* **-n** ruin(s). **—ieren** (rui-'ni:rən) *vt* ruin.

Rülps (rylps) *nm* **-e** belch. **—en** *vi* belch.

Rum (rum) nm **-s** rum.
Rumän/ien (ru'mɛːnɪən) n neu Rumania. **—e** nm Rumanian. **—isch** adj Rumanian. n neu Rumanian (language).
Rummel ('ruməl) nm **1** uproar, din. **2** bustle. **—platz** nm fairground, fun-fair.
Rumpf (rumpf) nm **ːe 1** trunk, torso. **2** hull. **3** fuselage.
rümpfen ('rympfən) vt turn up (one's nose).
rund (runt) adj **1** round. **2** plump. adv about, approximately. **—e** ('rundə) nf **-n 1** round. **2** lap. **3** circuit. **4** circle. **—fahrt** nf round trip. **—funk** nm **1** radio, wireless. **2** broadcasting. **—gang** nm **1** round. **2** circuit. **—heraus** (runthɛ'raus) adv in plain terms. **—herum** (runthɛ'rum) adv round about. **—schau** nf panorama, review. **—schreiben** n neu circular.
Runzel ('runtsəl) nf **-n** wrinkle. **—n** vt wrinkle, fold.
rupfen ('rupfən) vt **1** pluck. **2** inf fleece.
Ruß (ruːs) nm soot. **—ig** adj sooty.
Russ/e ('rusə) nm **-n** Russian. **—isch** adj Russian. n neu Russian (language). **—land** n neu Russia.
rüst/en ('rystən) vt **1** prepare. **2** equip. **3** arm. **—ig** adj vigorous. **—ung** nf **-en 1** preparation(s). **2** equipment. **3** armament. **4** armour.
Rute ('ruːtə) nf **-n** rod.
Rutsch (rutʃ) nm **-e** slide, slip. **—bahn** nf **1** slide. **2** chute. **—en** vi slide, slip, skid. **—ig** adj slippery.
rütteln ('rytəln) vt,vi shake (up), jolt.

S

Saal (zaːl) nm **Säle** large room, hall.
Saat (zaːt) nf **-en 1** seed(s). **2** sowing.
Sabbat ('zabat) nm **-e** sabbath.
sabbern ('zabərn) vi inf **1** slobber. **2** drivel.
Säbel ('zɛːbəl) nm **—** sabre.
Saccharin (zaxa'riːn) n neu saccharin.
Sach/e ('zaxə) nf **-n 1** matter. **2** thing. **3** affair, business. **4** law case, issue. **—bearbeiter** nm official or expert (with responsibility for a particular case or field). **—lage** nf state of affairs, situation. **—lich** adj **1** to the point. **2** real. **3** factual. **4** objective, impartial. **ːlich** ('zɛçlɪç) adj neuter.
Sachs/e ('zaksə) nm Saxon. **—en** n neu Saxony. **ːisch** ('zɛksɪʃ) adj Saxon.

sacht (zaxt) adj gentle, soft. adv **1** gradually. **2** cautiously.
Sack (zak) nm **ːe 1** sack, bag. **2** pocket, pouch. **—en** vi **1** sink. **2** sag. **—gasse** nf **1** blind alley, cul-de-sac. **2** deadlock.
Sadismus (za'dismus) nm sadism.
säen ('zɛːən) vt sow.
Saft (zaft) nm **ːe 1** juice. **2** sap. **3** gravy. **—ig** adj juicy.
Sage ('zaːgə) nf **-n** legend, myth. **—nhaft** adj **1** legendary. **2** inf fabulous.
Säge ('zɛːgə) nf **-n** saw. **—n** vt,vi saw.
sagen ('zaːgən) vt,vi **1** say, tell. **2** express, declare. **3** mean.
sah (zaː) v see **sehen.**
Sahn/e ('zaːnə) nf cream. **—ig** adj creamy.
Saison (zɛ'zõː) nf **-s** (high) season.
Saite ('zaitə) nf **-n** string, chord. **—ninstrument** n neu stringed instrument.
Sakrament (zakra'mɛnt) n neu **-e** sacrament.
Salat (za'laːt) nm **-e 1** salad. **2** lettuce. **—soße** nf salad dressing.
Salbe ('zalbə) nf **-n** ointment, salve.
Salbei (zal'bai) nm,f cul sage.
Salut (za'luːt) nm **-e** salute. **—ieren** (zalu-'tiːrən) vt,vi salute.
Salve ('zalvə) nf **-n** mil volley.
Salz (zalts) n neu **-e** salt. **—en** vt salt. **—faß** n neu saltcellar. **—ig** adj salty.
Sam/en ('zaːmən) nm **— 1** seed. **2** sperm, semen. **ːling** ('zɛmlɪŋ) nm **-e** seedling.
Sämischleder ('zɛmiʃleːdər) n neu chamois (leather).
samm/eln ('zaməln) vt,vi collect, gather. **sich sammeln** vr **1** assemble. **2** compose oneself. **—ler** nm **— 1** collector, gatherer. **2** tech accumulator. **—lung** nf **-en 1** collection. **2** concentration.
Samstag ('zamstaːk) nm **-e** Saturday. **—s** adv on Saturdays.
samt (zamt) prep together with. **ːlich** ('zɛmt-lɪç) adj **1** all. **2** complete, entire.
Sand (zant) nm **-e** sand. **—uhr** nf hourglass.
Sandale (zan'daːlə) nf **-n** sandal.
sandte ('zantə) v see **senden.**
sanft (zanft) adj **1** gentle, mild. **2** smooth, soft. **—mut** nf gentleness, sweetness.
sang (zaŋ) v see **singen.**
Sang (zaŋ) nm **ːe** song. **—er** ('zɛŋər) nm **—, ːerin** ('zɛŋərin) nf **-nen** singer.
sanier/en (za'niːrən) vt **1** comm restore, reorganize. **2** heal. **—ung** nf **-en 1** restoration, reconstruction. **2** sanitation.

sanit/är (zani'tɛːr) adj sanitary. **—äter** (zani-'tɛːtər) nm — 1 ambulance man. 2 med orderly.

sank (zaŋk) v see **sinken.**

Sankt (zaŋkt) adj Saint, St.

Sanktion (zaŋktsi'oːn) nf **-en** sanction.

Saphir ('zaːfir) nm **-e** sapphire.

Sardine (zar'diːnə) nf **-n** sardine.

Sarg (zark) nm **ˉe** coffin.

sarkastisch (zar'kasti∫) adj 1 sarcastic. 2 ironic.

saß (zaːs) v see **sitzen.**

Satan ('zaːtan) nm Satan.

Satellit (zatɛ'liːt) nm **-en** satellite. **—enstaat** nm satellite state.

Satin (sa'tɛ̃ː) nm satin.

Satir/e (za'tiːrə) nf **-n** satire. **—isch** adj satirical.

satt (zat) adj 1 satisfied. 2 full. 3 tired (of), sick (of). 4 (of colour) deep. **—igen** ('zɛtigən) vt 1 satisfy, satiate. 2 saturate.

Sattel ('zatəl) nm **ˉ** saddle.

Satz (zats) nm **ˉe** 1 sentence, clause. 2 leap, bound. 3 theorem, thesis. 4 mus movement. 5 dregs. **—lehre** nf syntax.

Satzung ('zatsuŋ) nf **-en** statute, regulation.

Sau (zau) nf **ˉe** sow. **—arbeit** nf sl drudgery. **—erei** (zauə'rai) nf **-en** dirty business.

sauber ('zaubər) adj 1 clean. 2 neat, tidy. 3 inf pretty, fine. **—n** ('zoybərn) vt 1 clean. 2 purge. **—ung** ('zoybəruŋ) nf **-en** 1 cleaning, clearing. 2 purge.

Saudi-Arabien ('zaudiaraːbiən) n neu Saudi-Arabia.

sauer ('zauər) adj 1 sour, acid. 2 (of work, etc.) hard. 3 sulky. **—stoff** nm oxygen.

sauf/en ('zaufən) vt,vi 1 inf booze, drink (excessively). 2 (of animals) drink. **—er** ('zoyfər) nm — drunkard.

saug/en ('zaugən) vt,vi suck. **—er** nm — 1 sucker. 2 teat (of a baby's bottle). **—etier** n neu mammal. **—heber** nm siphon.

säug/en ('zoygən) vt suckle. **—etier** n neu mammal. **—ling** ('zoykliŋ) nm **-e** baby, suckling.

Säule ('zoylə) nf **-n** column, pillar.

Saum (zaum) nm **ˉe** 1 seam. 2 hem. 3 border.

säumen[1] ('zoymən) vt 1 hem. 2 border.

säumen[2] ('zoymən) vi 1 delay. 2 hesitate.

Saumtier ('zaumtiːr) n neu **-e** beast of burden.

Sauna ('zauna) nf **-s** sauna (bath).

Säure ('zoyrə) nf **-n** 1 acid. 2 sourness.

Saxophon (zaksoˈfoːn) n neu **-e** saxophone.

schab/en ('∫aːbən) vt 1 scrape. 2 grate. **—er** nm — scraper.

schäbig ('∫ɛːbiç) adj 1 shabby. 2 mean.

Schablone (∫a'bloːnə) nf **-n** stencil, pattern.

Schach (∫ax) n neu chess. **—matt** adj checkmate.

Schacher ('∫axər) nm bargaining, haggling. **—n** vi haggle, barter.

Schacht (∫axt) nm **ˉe** 1 pit, shaft. 2 tunnel. 3 mine.

Schachtel ('∫axtəl) nf **-n** box.

schad/e ('∫aːdə) interj what a pity or shame! adj **es/das ist schade** it's/that's a pity or shame. **—en** vi 1 harm. 2 damage. nm — 1 damage. 2 harm. 3 loss, damages. **—enersatz** nm compensation. **—enfreude** nf malicious pleasure (in the misfortunes of others). **—igen** ('∫ɛːdigən) vt 1 harm. 2 damage. **—lich** ('∫ɛːtliç) adj harmful, injurious.

Schädel ('∫ɛːdəl) nm — skull.

Schaf/e (∫aːf) n neu **-e** sheep. **—er** ('∫ɛːfər) nm — shepherd. **—erhund** ('∫ɛːfərhunt) nm sheep dog. **deutscher —erhund** Alsatian.

schaffen[1] ('∫afən) vt 1 remove, shift. 2 accomplish, manage. vi work.

schaffen[2] ('∫afən) vt create, make.

Schaffner ('∫afnər) nm — 1 conductor. 2 ticket-collector. 3 guard. 4 steward.

Schaft (∫aft) nm **ˉe** 1 shaft. 2 stalk. 3 gunstock. 4 handle.

Schale (∫aːlə) nf **-n** 1 peel. 2 shell. 3 skin. 4 bowl, dish. **—n** ('∫ɛːlən) vt 1 peel. 2 skin. 3 shell.

Schalk (∫alk) nm **-e** rogue, joker.

Schall (∫al) nm **-e** 1 sound. 2 noise. 3 ring. **—dämpfer** nm silencer. **—dicht** adj soundproof. **—en** vi (re)sound. **—(geschwindigkeits)grenze** nf sound barrier. **—platte** nf (gramophone) record.

Schalt/brett ('∫altbrɛt) n neu **-er** 1 switchboard. 2 dashboard. **—en** vi 1 switch. 2 mot change gear. 3 rule. vt switch. **—er** nm — 1 switch. 2 ticket office. 3 counter. **—hebel** nm mot gear lever. **—jahr** n neu leap year. **—ung** nf **-en** 1 mot gear change. 2 (electric) circuit.

Scham (∫aːm) nf shame, embarrassment. **sich —en** ('∫ɛːmən) vr be ashamed.

Schampun (∫am'puːn) n neu shampoo.

Schand/e ('∫andə) nf shame, disgrace. **—en** ('∫ɛndən) vt 1 dishonour, disgrace. 2 rape. 3 desecrate. 4 disfigure. 5 soil. **—lich** ('∫ɛntliç) adj shameful, base, dishonourable. **—tat**

(ˈʃantsaːt) nf shameful deed, crime. **—ung** (ˈʃɛnduŋ) nf -en 1 shaming, dishonouring. 2 disfigurement. 3 violation, rape.

Schanze (ˈʃantsə) nf -n 1 fortification, earthwork. 2 naut quarterdeck.

Schar (ʃaːr) nf -en troop, host. **sich scharen** vr assemble, crowd together.

scharf (ʃarf) adj 1 sharp. 2 caustic. 3 pungent. 4 severe. 5 shrewd. 6 strong. 7 (of explosives, etc.) live. **—e** (ˈʃɛrfə) nf -n 1 sharpness. 2 shrewdness. 3 severity. **—en** (ˈʃɛrfən) vt 1 sharpen. 2 intensify. **—richter** nm executioner. **—schütze** nm sniper.

Scharlachfieber (ˈʃarlaxfiːbər) n neu scarlet fever.

scharmant (ʃarˈmant) adj charming.

Scharmützel (ʃarˈmytsəl) n neu — skirmish. **—n** vi skirmish.

Scharnier (ʃarˈniːr) n neu -e hinge.

Schatten (ˈʃatən) nm — shadow, shade. **—bild** n neu silhouette. **—haft** adj shadowy. **—seite** nf 1 dark side. 2 drawback, snag.

Schatz (ʃats) nm ⁻e 1 treasure. 2 darling, sweetheart. **—amt** n neu treasury. **—en** (ˈʃɛtsən) vt 1 estimate, assess. 2 esteem, regard (highly). **—meister** nm treasurer. **—ung** (ˈʃɛtsuŋ) nf -en 1 estimate. 2 approximation. 3 esteem. **—ungsweise** (ˈʃɛtsuŋsvaizə) adv approximately.

Schau (ʃau) nf -en 1 show. 2 exhibition. 3 view. **—bühne** nf stage, theatre. **—en** vt,vi 1 see. 2 look (at). **—fenster** n neu shop window. **—spiel** n neu play, drama. **—spieler** nm actor. **—spielerin** nf actress.

schauder/haft (ˈʃaudərhaft) adj horrible. **—n** vi shudder.

Schauer (ˈʃauər) nm — 1 shower. 2 shiver, shudder. 3 terror, awe.

Schaufel (ˈʃaufəl) nf -n 1 shovel. 2 paddle, blade.

Schaukel (ˈʃaukəl) nf -n swing. **—n** vt,vi swing, rock.

Schaum (ʃaum) nm ⁻e foam, froth. **—en** (ˈʃɔymən) vi foam, effervesce.

Scheck (ʃɛk) nm -s cheque.

Scheibe (ˈʃaibə) nf -n 1 slice. 2 disc. 3 pane. 4 target. **—nwischer** nm windscreen-wiper.

Scheid/e (ˈʃaidə) nf -n 1 border. 2 sheath. 3 vagina. **—en** vt 1 separate, divide. 2 divorce. **sich scheiden lassen** get divorced. vi depart, retire. **—ung** nf -en 1 separation. 2 divorce.

Schein (ʃain) nm -e 1 appearance, semblance.

2 shine. 3 light. 4 banknote. 5 certificate. 6 licence. 7 receipt. **—bar** adj apparent. **—en*** vi 1 seem. 2 shine. **—heilig** adj hypocritical. **—werfer** nm 1 searchlight, spotlight. 2 mot headlight. 3 reflector.

Scheiße (ˈʃaisə) nf tab excrement.

Scheitel (ˈʃaitəl) nm — 1 crown (of the head). 2 apex. 3 parting (of the hair). **—punkt** nm zenith, highest point.

scheitern (ˈʃaitərn) vi 1 fail. 2 be wrecked.

Schellfisch (ˈʃɛlfiʃ) nm -e haddock.

Schelm (ʃɛlm) nm -e 1 rogue, rascal. 2 joker.

Schemel (ˈʃeːməl) nm — (foot)stool.

schenk/en (ˈʃɛŋkən) vt 1 give (as a present). 2 endow. 3 pour (out). **—ung** nf -en donation.

Scherbe (ˈʃɛrbə) nf -n 1 fragment. 2 chip. 3 splinter (of glass, pottery, etc.).

Scher/e (ˈʃeːrə) nf -n 1 scissors, shears. 2 zool pincer, claw.

Scherz (ʃɛrts) nm -e 1 joke, jest. 2 prank, lark. **—en** vi 1 joke. 2 lark about. **—haft** adj playful, joking.

scheu (ʃɔy) adj shy, bashful. nf shyness. **—en** vt avoid. **sich —en** vr 1 be afraid (to). 2 be shy (of).

Scheuche (ˈʃɔyçə) nf -n scarecrow.

Scheune (ˈʃɔynə) nf -n barn.

Scheusal (ˈʃɔyzaːl) n neu -e monster.

scheußlich (ˈʃɔysliç) adj hideous.

Schi (ʃiː) nm -er ski. **Schi laufen** ski.

Schicht (ʃiçt) nf -en 1 layer. 2 coat(ing). 3 (social) class. 4 shift. **—arbeit** nf shift work. **—en** vt pile, stack.

schick (ʃik) adj chic, elegant. nm elegance.

schicken (ˈʃikən) vt send. **sich schicken** vr 1 happen. 2 be proper, fitting, or decent.

schicklich (ˈʃikliç) adj proper, decent.

Schicksal (ˈʃikzaːl) n neu -e fate, destiny.

schieb/en* (ˈʃiːbən) vt push, shove. vi profiteer. **—er** nm — 1 slide. 2 bolt (of a door, etc.). 3 profiteer. **—ung** nf -en 1 pushing. 2 profiteering. 3 underhand dealings, corrupt practice.

schied (ʃiːt) v see **scheiden**.

Schieds/gericht (ˈʃiːtsɡəriçt) n neu -e arbitration court. **—richter** nm 1 sport referee. 2 arbitrator.

schief (ʃiːf) adj 1 slanting, oblique. 2 sloping, inclined. 3 wrong, false.

schielen (ˈʃiːlən) vi squint.

schien (ʃiːn) v see **scheinen**.

Schien/e (ˈʃiːnə) nf -n 1 rail (of a railway

track). **2** *med* splint. **—bein** *n neu* **-e** shinbone.

schieß/en* (ˈʃiːsən) *vt* shoot. *vi* **1** shoot. **2** rush. **—pulver** *n neu* gunpowder.

Schiff (ʃif) *n neu* **-e 1** ship, vessel. **2** nave. **—ahrt** (ˈʃifaːrt) *nf* shipping, navigation. **—bruch** *nm* shipwreck.

Schikan/e (ʃiˈkaːnə) *nf* **-n 1** annoyance. **2** chicanery. **—ieren** (ʃikaˈniːrən) *vt* annoy.

Schild (ʃilt) *n neu* **-er 1** name plate. **2** signboard. **3** badge. **4** label. *n neu* **-e 1** shield. **2** coat-of-arms. **3** shell (of a tortoise or crab). **—ern** (ˈʃildərn) *vt* describe, portray. **—kröte** (ˈʃiltkrøːtə) *nf* **1** turtle. **2** tortoise.

Schilf (ʃilf) *n neu* **-e** reed, rush.

Schilling (ˈʃiliŋ) *nm* **-e 1** Austrian unit of currency. **2** shilling.

Schimmel (ˈʃiməl) *nm* **1** mould, mildew. **2** *pl* — white horse. **—ig** *adj* mouldy.

Schimmer (ˈʃimər) *nm* gleam, glimmer. **—n** *vi* gleam, glimmer.

Schimpanse (ʃimˈpanzə) *nm* **-n** chimpanzee.

Schimpf (ʃimpf) *nm* **-e 1** insult. **2** disgrace. **—en** *vt* abuse, insult. *vi* grumble, scold. **—wort** *n neu* **1** insult. **2** swear word.

schind/en* (ˈʃindən) *vt* **1** torment. **2** exploit. **3** skin (an animal). **sich schinden** *vr* toil, slave. **—er** *nm* **1** exploiter. **2** tormentor.

Schinken (ˈʃiŋkən) *nm* ham.

Schirm (ʃirm) *nm* **-e 1** umbrella. **2** shade. **3** screen. **4** protection, shelter. **—en** *vt* shelter, protect. **—herr** *nm* patron.

Schlacht (ʃlaxt) *nf* **-en** battle. **—en** *vt* slaughter, butcher. **—erei** (ʃlɛçtəˈrai) *nf* **-en 1** butcher's shop. **2** massacre. **—feld** *n neu* battlefield. **—haus** *n neu* slaughterhouse abattoir. **—schiff** *n neu* battleship.

Schlaf (ʃlaːf) *nm* sleep. **—anzug** *nm* pyjamas. **—en*** *vi* sleep. **—tablette** *nf* sleeping pill. **—rig** (ˈʃlɛːfriç) *adj* **1** sleepy. **2** dozy. **—sack** *nm* sleeping bag. **—wagen** *nm* sleeping car. **—zimmer** *n neu* bedroom.

schlaff (ʃlaf) *adj* **1** slack. **2** soft. **3** lax. **4** weak.

Schlag (ʃlaːk) *nm* **-e 1** blow, stroke. **2** punch, slap. **3** (electric) shock. **4** peal, clap. **5** kind, sort. **—ader** *nf* artery. **—anfall** *nm med* stroke, fit. **—en*** (ˈʃlaːgən) *vt* **1** strike, beat. **2** defeat. **3** fell. *vi* **1** beat, strike. **2** ring. **sich —en** *vr* **1** fight (with). **2** side (with). **—fertig** *adj* quick-witted, ready. **—sahne** *nf* whipped cream. **—wort** *n neu* slogan. **—zeile** *nf* headline.

Schlager (ˈʃlaːgər) *nm* **— 1** pop song, dance tune. **2** (smash) hit, great success.

Schläger (ˈʃlɛːgər) *nm* **— 1** thug. **2** *cul* beater. **3** rapier. **4** *sport* racket, club, stick.

Schlamm (ʃlam) *nm* **-e** mud, sludge.

Schlamp/e (ˈʃlampə) *nf* **-n** slut. **—erei** (ʃlampaˈrai) *nf* **-en** slovenliness. **—ig** *adj* slovenly, sluttish.

Schlange (ˈʃlaŋə) *nf* **-n 1** snake, serpent. **2** queue.

schlank (ʃlaŋk) *adj* slender, slim.

schlapp (ʃlap) *adj* **1** slack. **2** flabby.

schlau (ʃlau) *adj* **1** sly, cunning. **2** shrewd.

Schlauch (ʃlaux) *nm* **-e 1** tube. **2** hose. **3** *mot* inner tube.

schlecht (ʃlɛçt) *adj* **1** bad, wicked. **2** inferior. **—hin** *adv* simply, perfectly.

Schlegel (ˈʃleːgəl) *nm* **— 1** mallet. **2** club. **3** drumstick.

schleichen* (ˈʃlaiçən) *vi* sneak, creep.

Schleier (ˈʃlaiər) *nm* **—** veil. **—n** *vt* veil.

Schleif/e (ˈʃlaifə) *nf* **-n 1** bow, slipknot. **2** slide, chute. **3** curve, loop. **—en*** *vt, vi* drag. *vt* **1** polish. **2** sharpen.

Schleim (ʃlaim) *nm* **-e** mucus, phlegm.

schleißen* (ˈʃlaisən) *vt* **1** wear out. **2** slit, split.

schlendern (ˈʃlɛndərn) *vi* stroll, dawdle.

schlepp/en (ˈʃlɛpən) *vt* **1** drag, haul. **2** carry. **—er** *nm* — *also* **—dampfer** tug(boat).

Schlesien (ˈʃleːziən) *n neu* Silesia.

Schleuder (ˈʃlɔydər) *nf* **-n 1** sling, catapult. **2** spin-drier. **—n** *vt* **1** hurl, sling. **2** spin-dry. *vi mot* skid.

schleunig (ˈʃlɔyniç) *adj* quick, prompt. **—st** *adv* in all haste, as quickly as possible.

Schleuse (ˈʃlɔyzə) *nf* **-n 1** sluice. **2** lock (of a canal).

schlicht (ʃliçt) *adj* **1** plain, simple. **2** smooth. **—en** *vt* **1** settle (a quarrel). **2** smooth.

schlief (ʃliːf) *v see* **schlafen.**

schließ/en* (ˈʃliːsən) *vi, vt* close, shut. *vt* **1** lock. **2** end, finish. **3** infer, conclude. **—fach** *n neu* **1** locker. **2** safe-deposit box. **—lich** (ˈʃliːsliç) *adj* final. *adv* **1** finally. **2** after all.

schlimm (ʃlim) *adj* **1** bad, serious. **2** sick, ill. **—stenfalls** (ˈʃlimstənfals) *adv* at (the) worst.

Schlinge (ˈʃliŋə) *nf* **-n 1** loop, noose. **2** *med* sling. **3** snare.

schlingen* [1] (ˈʃliŋən) *vt* **1** wind, coil. **2** weave, plait. **3** tie, knot. **4** fling.

schlingen* [2] (ˈʃliŋən) *vi* gulp, eat greedily.

Schlitt/en ('ʃlitən) *nm* — sledge, sleigh. **—schuh** *nm* skate. **—schuhlaufen** *vi* skate.

Schlitz (ʃlits) *nm* -e slit, slot.

schloß (ʃlɔs) *v* see **schließen.**

Schloß (ʃlɔs) *n neu* **Schlösser 1** castle, palace. **2** lock, clasp.

Schlosser ('ʃlɔsər) *nm* — **1** locksmith. **2** metal worker, fitter.

schlotterig ('ʃlɔtəriç) *adj* shaky, tottery.

Schluck (ʃluk) *nm* -e **1** gulp, swig. **2** sip. **—en** *vt* gulp (down), swallow. *nm* hiccup(s).

schlug (ʃlu:k) *v* see **schlagen.**

Schlund (ʃlunt) *nm* ̈e **1** throat, gullet. **2** gulf, chasm.

schlüpf/en ('ʃlypfən) *vi* slip. **—er** *nm* (ladies') knickers, panties. **—rig** *adj* **1** slippery. **2** (of a joke, remark, etc.) obscene.

Schlupfloch ('ʃlupflɔx) *n neu* **1** loophole. **2** hiding place.

Schluß (ʃlus) *nm* **Schlüsse 1** end, close. **2** conclusion, deduction. **—folgerung** *nf* conclusion. **—licht** *n neu* tail-light. **—stein** *nm* keystone.

Schlüssel ('ʃlysəl) *nm* — **1** key. **2** spanner. **3** *mus* clef. **—bein** *n neu* collarbone.

schmächtig ('ʃmɛçtiç) *adj* slender, slim.

schmackhaft ('ʃmakhaft) *adj* appetizing, tasty.

schmal (ʃma:l) *adj* **1** narrow, thin. **2** meagre.

Schmalz (ʃmalts) *n neu* **1** dripping, fat. **2** (exaggerated) sentimentality.

schmarotz/en (ʃma'rɔtsən) *vi* scrounge, sponge. **—er** *nm* sponger, parasite.

Schmarren ('ʃmarən) *nm* — **1** pancake. **2** trash.

schmatzen ('ʃmatsən) *vi* smack (one's lips).

schmecken ('ʃmɛkən) *vt* **1** taste. **2** sample. *vi* taste (good).

Schmeich/elei (ʃmaiçə'lai) *nf* -en flattery. **—eln** ('ʃmaiçəln) *vi* flatter. **—ler** ('ʃmaiçlər) *nm* — flatterer.

schmeißen* ('ʃmaisən) *vt inf* throw, chuck.

schmelzen* ('ʃmɛltsən) *vt,vi* melt.

Schmerz ('ʃmɛrts) *nm* -en **1** pain. **2** grief. **—haft** *adj* also **—lich** painful.

Schmetterling ('ʃmɛtərliŋ) *nm* -e butterfly.

Schmied (ʃmi:t) *nm* -e blacksmith. **—e** ('ʃmi:də) *nf* -n (blacksmith's) forge. **—en** ('ʃmi:dən) *vt* **1** forge. **2** construct.

Schmier/e ('ʃmi:rə) *nf* -n **1** grease. **2** ointment. **—en** *vt* **1** grease, lubricate. **2** smear. **3** spread (butter, etc.). **—ig** *adj* **1** greasy. **2** dirty. **3** sordid.

Schmink/e ('ʃmiŋkə) *nf* -n make-up. **—en** *vt* make up.

Schmor/en ('ʃmo:rən) *vt* **1** stew. **2** braise. **—braten** *nm* — stewed or braised meat.

Schmuck (ʃmuk) *nm* -e **1** ornament(s), jewellery. **2** decoration. **—̈en** ('ʃmykən) *vt* decorate, adorn.

schmugg/eln ('ʃmugəln) *vt,vi* smuggle. **—ler** ('ʃmuglər) *nm* — smuggler.

Schmutz (ʃmuts) *nm* dirt. **—ig** *adj* dirty.

Schnabel ('ʃna:bəl) *nm* ̈ — **1** beak. **2** nozzle.

Schnall/e ('ʃnalə) *nf* -n buckle, fastener. **—en** *vt* buckle, fasten.

Schnaps (ʃnaps) *nm* ̈e spirit, liquor.

schnarchen ('ʃnarçən) *vi* snore.

schnattern ('ʃnatərn) *vi* cackle.

schnaufen ('ʃnaufən) *vi* wheeze, gasp, pant.

Schnauz/e ('ʃnautsə) *nf* -n **1** muzzle. **2** snout. **—en** *vi* bawl, bellow.

Schneck/e ('ʃnɛkə) *nf* -n snail. **—engang** *nm* snail's pace.

Schnee (ʃne:) *nm* snow. **—ball** *nm* snowball. **—flocke** *nf* snowflake. **—glöckchen** *n neu* snowdrop.

Schneid/e ('ʃnaidə) *nf* -n edge, blade. **—en*** *vt* **1** cut, carve. **2** reap, mow. **—er** *nm* — tailor.

schneien ('ʃnaiən) *vi* snow.

schnell (ʃnɛl) *adj* fast, quick, rapid. **—en** *vt* **1** jerk. **2** flick. *vi* spring. **—igkeit** *nf* speed, rapidity. **—zug** *nm* express train.

schnippisch ('ʃnipiʃ) *adj* saucy, cheeky.

schnitt (ʃnit) *v* see **schneiden.**

Schnitt (ʃnit) *nm* -e **1** cut. **2** slice. **3** pattern. **4** cut, fashion. **5** woodcut. **6** crop. **—lauch** *nm* chive(s).

Schnitz/el ('ʃnitsəl) *nm* — **1** cutlet. **2** chip. **—eln** *vt,vi* chip, shred.

Schnitzer ('ʃnitsər) *nm* — **1** carver, cutter. **2** blunder, (bad) mistake.

Schnörkel ('ʃnœrkəl) *nm* — **1** flourish, scroll. **2** squiggle.

schnüffeln ('ʃnyfəln) *vi* **1** sniff. **2** snoop.

Schnupfen ('ʃnupfən) *nm* — cold, chill.

Schnur (ʃnu:r) *nf* ̈e **1** string, cord. **2** flex, (electrical) lead. **—gerade** *adv* straight as a die.

Schnür/band ('ʃny:rbant) *n neu* ̈er lace. **—en** *vt* lace or tie (up). **—senkel** *nm* shoelace.

Schnurrbart ('ʃnurba:rt) *nm* moustache.

schob (ʃo:p) *v* see **schieben.**

Schock (ʃɔk) nm -s shock. —**ieren** (ʃɔˈkiːrən) vt shock.

Schokolade (ʃokoˈlaːdə) nf -n chocolate.

Scholle (ˈʃɔlə) nf -n 1 clod, lump. 2 plaice.

schon (ʃoːn) adv 1 already. 2 yet.

schön (ʃœːn) adj 1 beautiful, handsome. 2 nice, fine. —**heit** nf beauty. —**heitskönigin** nf beauty queen.

schon/en (ˈʃoːnən) vt spare, preserve. —**ung** nf -en 1 clemency, mercy. 2 consideration, care.

Schopf (ʃɔpf) nm ⸚e 1 tuft, lock (of hair). 2 crest (of birds).

schöpf/en (ˈʃœpfən) vt 1 scoop, ladle. 2 get, obtain. —**kelle** nf -n scoop, ladle.

Schöpf/er nm — creator. —**erisch** adj creative. —**ung** nf -en creation.

Schornstein (ˈʃɔrnʃtain) nm -e chimney, funnel. —**feger** nm chimney-sweep.

schoß (ʃɔs) v see **schießen.**

Schoß[1] (ʃoːs) nm -e 1 lap. 2 womb.

Schoß[2] (ʃɔs) nm **Schosse** bot shoot, sprout.

Schote (ˈʃoːtə) nf -n pod, shell.

Schott/e (ˈʃɔtə) nm -n Scot, Scotsman. —**isch** adj Scottish. —**land** n neu Scotland.

schräg (ʃrɛːk) adj oblique, slanting.

Schrank (ʃraŋk) nm ⸚e cupboard, wardrobe.

Schranke (ˈʃraŋkə) nf -n 1 barrier. 2 enclosure, arena. —**nlos** adj boundless.

Schraub/e (ˈʃraubə) nf -n screw. —**en** vt screw, twist. —**enschlüssel** nm spanner, wrench. —**enzieher** nm screwdriver.

Schrebergarten (ˈʃreːbərgartən) nm allotment.

Schreck (ʃrɛk) nm -e also **Schrecken** — 1 fright. 2 terror, horror. —**en** vt frighten. —**lich** adj terrible, dreadful, horrible.

Schrei (ʃrai) nm -e cry, scream. —**en**[*] vi cry, scream.

schreib/en[*] (ˈʃraibən) vt,vi 1 write. 2 spell. n neu — letter. —**maschine** (ˈʃraipmaʃiːnə) nf typewriter. —**papier** (ˈʃraippapiːr) n neu notepaper. —**tisch** (ˈʃraiptiʃ) nm desk.

Schrein (ʃrain) nm -e chest, cabinet. —**er** nm — cabinet-maker, carpenter.

schreiten[*] (ˈʃraitən) vi step, stride.

schrie (ʃriː) v see **schreien.**

schrieb (ʃriːp) v see **schreiben.**

Schrift (ʃrift) nf -en 1 writing, work. 2 handwriting. 3 type, script. 4 scripture(s). —**lich** adj written, in writing. —**sprache** nf written language. —**steller** nm — writer, author.

schritt (ʃrit) v see **schreiten.**

Schritt (ʃrit) nm -e 1 step. 2 pace. —**macher** nm pacemaker.

schroff (ʃrɔf) adj 1 brusque, abrupt. 2 steep, rugged.

Schrot (ʃroːt) nm,neu -e (lead) shot. —**flinte** nf shotgun.

Schrott (ʃrɔt) nm -e scrap metal. —**haufen** nm scrap heap.

schrubben (ˈʃrubən) vt scrub.

schrumpfen (ˈʃrumpfən) vi 1 shrink. 2 become wrinkled.

Schub (ʃuːp) nm ⸚e 1 push, thrust. 2 batch. —**karren** nm wheelbarrow. —**fach** n neu also —**lade** nf drawer.

schüchtern (ˈʃʏçtərn) adj shy, bashful, timid. —**heit** nf shyness.

Schuft (ʃuft) nm -e scoundrel.

Schuh (ʃuː) nm -e shoe, boot. —**löffel** nm shoehorn. —**macher** nm shoemaker.

Schul/e (ˈʃuːlə) nf -n school, college. —**arbeit** nf 1 homework. 2 lesson. —**en** vt school, train. —**er** (ˈʃyːlər) nm — schoolboy. ⸚**erin** (ˈʃyːlərin) nf -nen schoolgirl. —**rat** nm school inspector. —**ung** nf schooling.

Schuld (ʃult) nf -en 1 debt. 2 guilt. 3 offence. —**en** (ˈʃuldən) vt owe. —**ig** (ˈʃuldiç) adj 1 guilty. 2 indebted. —**los** (ˈʃultloːs) adj innocent.

Schulter (ˈʃultər) nf -n shoulder.

Schund (ʃunt) nm trash, rubbish.

Schuppe (ˈʃupə) nf -en 1 zool scale. 2 pl dandruff.

schüren (ˈʃyːrən) vt stir up.

Schurke (ˈʃurkə) nm -n villain, scoundrel.

Schürze (ˈʃyrtsə) nf -n apron, pinafore.

Schuß (ʃus) nm **Schüsse** shot. —**waffe** nf firearm.

Schüssel (ˈʃysəl) nf -n 1 bowl, dish. 2 dish, course.

Schuster (ˈʃuːstər) nm — shoemaker, cobbler.

Schutt (ʃut) nm 1 rubbish. 2 rubble. —**haufen** nm rubbish or rubble heap.

schütteln (ˈʃytəln) vt shake.

schütten (ˈʃytən) vt,vi pour.

Schutz (ʃuts) nm 1 protection, defence. 2 shelter. —**brille** nf goggles. —**e** (ˈʃytsə) nm -n 1 marksman, rifleman. 2 Sagittarius. —**en** (ˈʃytsən) vt 1 protect, defend. 2 shelter. ⸚**er** (ˈʃytsər) nm — protector, patron. —**heilige(r)** nm patron saint. ⸚**ling** (ˈʃytsliŋ) nm —e protégé. —**mann** nm policeman. —**mittel** n neu preservative. —**polizei** nf police.

Schwabe (ˈʃvaːbə) nm -n Swabian. —n n neu Swabia.

schwach (ʃvax) adj weak. -̈e (ˈʃvɛçə) nf -n also -heit weakness. -̈lich (ˈʃvɛçlɪç) adj sickly, feeble. —sinn nm imbecility.

Schwadron (ʃvaˈdroːn) nf -en squadron.

Schwager (ˈʃvaːgər) nm — brother-in-law. -̈in (ˈʃvɛːgərin) nf -nen sister-in-law.

Schwalbe (ˈʃvalbə) nf -n swallow.

Schwall (ʃval) nm -e swell, torrent.

Schwamm (ʃvam) nm -̈e 1 sponge. 2 fungus.

Schwan (ʃvaːn) nm -̈e swan. —engesang nm swan song.

schwanger (ˈʃvaŋər) adj pregnant. —schaft nf -en pregnancy. —sverhütung nf contraception.

schwanken (ˈʃvaŋkən) vi 1 rock, sway. 2 hesitate, waver.

Schwanz (ʃvants) nm -̈e 1 tail. 2 trail, train.

schwärm/en (ˈʃvɛrmən) vi 1 swarm. 2 be enthusiastic, rave (about). —erisch adj wildly enthusiastic.

schwarz (ʃvarts) adj,n neu black. —brot n neu black bread. —e(r) nm Black, Negro. -̈e (ˈʃvɛrtsə) nf black(ness). -̈en (ˈʃvɛrtsən) vt 1 blacken. 2 slander, defame. 3 inf smuggle. —markt nm black market. —wald nm Black Forest. —weiß adj black and white.

schwatzen (ˈʃvatsən) vi prattle, chatter.

Schweb/ebahn (ˈʃveːbəbaːn) nf -en cable railway. —en vi 1 hover, soar. 2 hang. 3 waver.

Schwed/en (ˈʃveːdən) n neu Sweden. —e nm -n Swede. —isch adj Swedish. n neu Swedish (language).

Schwefel (ˈʃveːfəl) nm sulphur.

schweig/en* (ˈʃvaigən) vi fall or be silent. —sam (ˈʃvaikzaːm) adj silent, taciturn.

Schwein (ʃvain) n neu -e pig, swine. **Schwein haben** inf be in luck. —efleisch n neu pork. —ehund nm inf swine. —erei (ˈʃvainəˈrai) nf -en mean trick. —estall nm pigsty.

Schweiß (ʃvais) nm sweat. —en vt weld.

Schweiz (ʃvaits) nf Switzerland. —er nm — Swiss. —erisch adj Swiss.

Schwelle (ˈʃvɛlə) nf -n 1 threshold. 2 sill. 3 beam. 4 (railway) sleeper.

schwellen* (ˈʃvɛlən) vi,vt swell. vi expand, increase.

schwemmen (ˈʃvɛmən) vt 1 water. 2 rinse. 3 float, drift.

Schwengel (ˈʃvɛŋəl) nm — 1 clapper (of a bell). 2 handle (of a pump).

schwenk/en (ˈʃvɛŋkən) vi 1 swivel, swing. 2 tilt. vt 1 swing. 2 shake, flourish. 3 cul toss. 4 rinse.

schwer (ʃveːr) adj 1 heavy. 2 difficult. 3 serious, grave. 4 clumsy. 5 (of food) stodgy. —e nf -n 1 weight. 2 sci gravity. 3 seriousness. 4 difficulty. 5 severity. —beschädigt adj 1 disabled, crippled. 2 badly damaged. —fällig adj clumsy, ponderous. —hörig adj hard of hearing. —industrie nf heavy industry. —lich adv with difficulty, scarcely. —punkt nm 1 centre of gravity. 2 main point. —verletzt adj 1 disabled. 2 badly wounded, seriously injured. —wiegend adj grave, weighty.

Schwert (ʃveːrt) n neu -er 1 sword. 2 naut centre-board, keel. —lilie nf bot iris.

Schwester (ˈʃvɛstər) nf -n sister.

schwieg (ʃviːk) v see **schweigen**.

Schwieger/mutter (ˈʃviːgərmutər) nf -̈ mother-in-law. —sohn nm son-in-law. —tochter nf daughter-in-law. —vater nm father-in-law.

schwierig (ˈʃviːrɪç) adj difficult, hard. —keit nf -en difficulty, trouble.

Schwimm/bad (ˈʃvimbaːt) n neu also **Schwimm/becken** swimming pool. —en* vi 1 swim. 2 float. —er nm — 1 swimmer. 2 float. —weste nf life jacket.

Schwind/el (ˈʃvindəl) nm — 1 dizziness, vertigo. 2 swindle. 3 lie, fib. —(e)lig adj dizzy. —eln vi 1 swindle, cheat. 2 lie. 3 be dizzy. **mir schwindelt** I feel dizzy. —ler (ˈʃvindlər) nm — swindler, fraud.

Schwindsucht (ˈʃvintzuxt) nf med consumption, tuberculosis.

schwingen* (ˈʃviŋən) vt,vi 1 swing. 2 vibrate.

schwitzen (ˈʃvitsən) vi sweat, perspire.

schwören* (ˈʃvœːrən) vi,vt swear, take (an oath).

schwul (ʃvuːl) adj sl queer, homosexual.

schwül (ʃvyːl) adj sultry, humid. —e nf sultriness, oppressive heat.

Schwulst (ʃvulst) nm -̈e bombast.

Schwung (ʃvuŋ) nm -̈e 1 swing. 2 impetus. 3 enthusiasm, verve. 4 flair.

Schwur (ʃvuːr) nm -̈e oath. —gericht n neu assize court.

sechs (zɛks) adj,nf six. —te adj sixth.

sechzehn (ˈzɛçtseːn) adj,nf sixteen. —te adj sixteenth.

sechzig ('zɛçtsiç) *adj,nf* sixty. **—ste** *adj* sixtieth.

See (se:) *nm* **-n** lake. *nf* **-n** sea. **—bad** *n neu* seaside resort. **—fahrt** *nf* **1** voyage. **2** navigation. **—krank** *adj* seasick. **—mann** *nm* **-leute** sailor, marine. **—meile** *nf* nautical mile, knot. **—räuber** *nm* — pirate. **—zunge** *nf* *zool* sole.

Seel/e ('ze:lə) *nf* **-n** soul, mind. **—sorger** *nm* — clergyman.

Segel ('ze:gəl) *n neu* — sail. **—boot** *n neu* sailing boat. **—fliegen** *n neu* gliding. **—n** *vi* **1** sail. **2** soar, glide. **—tuch** *n neu* canvas.

Seg/en ('ze:gən) *nm* — **1** blessing. **2** prayer(s). **3** grace. **—nen** ('ze:gnən) *vt* bless. **—nung** ('ze:gnuŋ) *nf* **-en** blessing.

seh/en* ('ze:ən) *vt,vi* see, look. **—enswert** *adj* worth seeing. **—enswürdigkeit** *nf* **-en** object of interest, sight. **—er** *nm* — prophet.

Sehn/e ('ze:nə) *nf* **-n 1** tendon, sinew. **2** *math* chord. **3** (bow) string. **sich —en** *vr* long (for). **—sucht** *nf* longing.

sehr (ze:r) *adv* very, much.

sei (zai) *v* see **sein²**.

seicht (zaiçt) *adj* **1** shallow. **2** insipid. **3** superficial.

seid (zait) *v* see **sein²**.

Seide ('zaidə) *nf* **-n** silk.

Seidel ('zaidəl) *n neu* — (beer) mug.

Seif/e ('zaifə) *nf* **-n** soap. **—en** *vt* soap.

Seil (zail) *n neu* **-e** rope, cable. **—bahn** *nf* cable railway.

sein¹ (zain) *poss adj* 3rd pers s his, its. **—er** *poss pron* 3rd pers s also **der —e** or **der —ige** his. **—erseits** ('zainərzaits) *adv* for his part. **—esgleichen** ('zainəsglaiçən) *pron* people like him. **—ethalben** ('zainəthalbən) *also* **—etwegen** ('zainətve:gən) *or* **—etwillen** ('zainətvilən) for his sake.

sein² (zain) *vi* be, exist. *n neu* being, existence.

seit (zait) *prep,conj* since. **—dem** (zait'de:m) *conj* since. *adv* since then. **—her** (zait'he:r) *adv* **1** since then. **2** till now.

Seit/e ('zaitə) *nf* **-n 1** side. **2** page. **—engasse** *nf* (small) side street. **—ens** *adv* on the part or side of. **—lich** *adj* lateral, side. **—wärts** ('zaitvɛrts) *adv* sideways.

Sekretär (zekre'tɛ:r) *nm* **-e**, **Sekretärin** *nf* **-nen** secretary.

Sekt (zɛkt) *nm* **-e** champagne.

Sekte ('zɛktə) *nf* **-n** sect.

Sekunde (ze'kundə) *nf* **-n** second.

selber ('zɛlbər) *pron* self.

selbst (zɛlpst) *pron* **1** self. **2** unaided, alone. **ich selbst** I myself. **~n** *neu* self. *adv* even.

Selbstachtung ('zɛlpstaxtuŋ) *nf* self-respect.

selbständig ('zɛlpstɛndiç) *adj* independent, autonomous. **—keit** *nf* independence.

Selbstbedienung ('zɛlpstbədi:nuŋ) *nf* self-service. **—srestaurant** *n neu* cafeteria.

Selbstbeherrschung ('zɛlpstbəhɛrʃuŋ) *nf* self-control.

selbstbewußt ('zɛlpstbəvust) *adj* self confident.

Selbstgefühl ('zɛlpstgəfy:l) *n neu* self-respect, self-reliance, self-confidence.

selbstlos ('zɛlpstlo:s) *adj* selfless.

Selbstmord ('zɛlpstmɔrt) *nm* suicide. **—er** *nm* (person) suicide.

selbstsicher ('zɛlpstziçər) *adj* self-confident.

Selbstsucht ('zɛlpstzuxt) *nf* selfishness. **—ig** ('zɛlpstzyçtiç) *adj* selfish.

selbstverständlich ('zɛlpstfɛrʃtɛntliç) *adj* obvious. *adv* naturally, of course, obviously.

Selbstvertrauen ('zɛlpstfɛrtrauən) *n neu* self-confidence.

selig ('ze:liç) *adj* **1** blessed. **2** happy. **3** deceased, late. **—keit** *nf* **-en** bliss.

Sellerie ('zɛləri:) *nm,f* celery.

selten ('zɛltən) *adj* rare. *adv* seldom, rarely. **—heit** ('zɛltənhait) *nf* **-en 1** rarity. **2** scarcity.

seltsam ('zɛltza:m) *adj* strange, singular.

Semester (ze'mɛstər) *n neu* — semester.

Seminar (zemi'na:r) *n neu* **-e 1** seminar. **2** teacher-training college. **3** (academic) department.

Semmel ('zɛməl) *nf* **-n** roll, bun.

Senat (ze'na:t) *nm* **-e** senate.

send/en* ('zɛndən) *vt* **1** send. **2** broadcast. **—er** *nm* — **1** sender. **2** transmitter. **—ung** *nf* **-en 1** shipment. **2** transmission. **3** mission.

Senf (zɛnf) *nm* **-e** mustard.

Senkel ('zɛŋkəl) *nm* — (shoe)lace.

senk/en ('zɛŋkən) *vt* sink, lower. **sich senken** *vr* **1** sink. **2** slope. **—recht** *adj* vertical, perpendicular.

Sensation (zɛnzatsi'o:n) *nf* **-en 1** sensation. **2** thrill. **—ell** (zɛnzatsio'nɛl) *adj* sensational.

Sense ('zɛnzə) *nf* **-n** scythe.

sensuell (zɛnzu'ɛl) *adj* sensual.

sentimental (zɛntimɛn'ta:l) *adj* sentimental.

September (zɛp'tɛmbər) *nm* September.

Serie ('ze:riə) *nf* **-n** series. **—nbau** *nm* also **—nherstellung** *nf* mass production.

seriös (zeri'œ:s) *adj* **1** serious. **2** reliable.

Serv/ice (zɛr'vi:s) *n neu* — **1** (dinner) service.

101

Serviette

2 service. **—ieren** (zɛrˈviːrən) *vt, vi* serve (food).

Serviette (zɛrviˈɛtə) *nf* **-n** napkin, serviette.

Sessel (ˈzɛsəl) *nm* — armchair. **—lift** *nm* chair-lift.

seßhaft (ˈzɛshaft) *adj* **1** resident. **2** settled.

setzen (ˈzɛtsən) *vt* **1** set, put, place, lay. **2** erect. **3** wager. **4** compose. *vi* leap. **sich setzen** *vr* **1** sit down. **2** subside.

Seuche (ˈzɔyçə) *nf* **-n** epidemic.

seufz/en (ˈzɔyftsən) *vi* **1** sigh. **2** groan. **—er** *nm* — **1** sigh. **2** groan.

Sex (zɛks) *nm* **1** sex, sexual intercourse. **2** sexuality. **—uell** (zɛksuˈɛl) *adj* sexual.

sezieren (zeˈtsiːrən) *vt* dissect.

Sibir/ien (ziˈbiːriən) *n neu* Siberia. **—ier** *nm* — Siberian. **—isch** *adj* Siberian.

sich (ziç) *pron* **1** himself, herself, itself. **2** oneself. **3** themselves. **4** one another, each other.

Sichel (ˈziçəl) *nf* **-n 1** sickle. **2** crescent.

sicher (ˈziçər) *adj* **1** safe, secure. **2** certain. **3** reliable. **—heit** *n* **-en 1** certainty. **2** security. **3** safety. **—heitsdienst** *nm* security service. **—lich** *adv* certainly, surely. **—n** *vt* **1** protect. **2** secure. **3** fasten. **4** guarantee. **sich** *vt* safeguard, secure. **—ung** *nf* **-en 1** safety mechanism. **2** protection. **3** *comm* security, guarantee. **4** fuse.

Sicht (ziçt) *nf* **1** sight. **2** visibility. **auf lange** or **weite Sicht** on a long-term basis. **—bar** *adj* visible. **—lich** *adj* obvious.

sie (ziː) *pron 3rd pers* **1** *s* she, her, it. **2** *pl* they, them. **Sie** *pron 2nd pers fml* *s, pl* you.

Sieb (ziːp) *n neu* **-e** sieve.

sieben[1] (ˈziːbən) *vt* **1** sieve, sift. **2** select.

sieb/en[2] (ˈziːbən) *adj, nf* seven. **—ente** (ˈziːbəntə) *adj* also. **—te** (ˈziːptə) seventh.

siebzehn (ˈziːptseːn) *adj, nf* seventeen. **—te** *adj* seventeenth.

siebzig (ˈziːptsiç) *adj, nf* seventy. **—ste** *adj* seventieth.

sied/eln (ˈziːdəln) *vi* settle, colonize. **—ler** (ˈziːdlər) *nm* — settler. **—ung** (ˈziːdluŋ) *nf* **-en 1** settlement. **2** housing estate.

Siedepunkt (ˈziːdəpuŋkt) *nm* boiling point.

Sieg (ziːk) *nm* **-e 1** victory. **2** conquest. **—en** (ˈziːɡən) *vi* be victorious, win. **—er** (ˈziːɡər) *nm* — victor. **—reich** *adj* victorious.

Siegel (ˈziːɡəl) *n neu* — seal. **—n** *vt* seal.

sieht (ziːt) *v see* **sehen.**

Signal (zigˈnaːl) *n neu* **-e** signal. **—wärter** *nm* signalman.

Signatur (zignaˈtuːr) *nf* **-en 1** sign. **2** mark, stamp. **3** signature.

Silbe (ˈzilbə) *nf* **-n** syllable.

Silber (ˈzilbər) *n neu* silver.

Silvester (zilˈvɛstər) *nm* New Year's Eve.

simpel (ˈzimpəl) *adj* **1** simple. **2** foolish.

Sims (zims) *nm, neu* **-e 1** ledge, sill. **2** shelf.

simulieren (zimuˈliːrən) *vt* simulate, feign. *vi* **1** malinger. **2** feign.

sind (zint) *v see* **sein**[2].

Sinfonie (zinfoˈniː) *nf* **-n** symphony.

singen* (ˈziŋən) *vt, vi* sing.

sinken* (ˈziŋkən) *vi* **1** sink. **2** drop, slump.

Sinn (zin) *nm* **-e 1** sense. **2** faculty. **3** meaning. **4** mind, consciousness. **—bild** *n neu* symbol. **—en*** *vt, vi* **1** think, reflect. **2** plan, scheme. **—lich** *adj* sensual, sensuous. **—los** *adj* senseless. **—voll** *adj* meaningful.

Sintflut (ˈzintfluːt) *nf* **-en** deluge.

Sipp/e (ˈzipə) *nf* **-n 1** clan, tribe. **2** kin.

Sirup (ˈziːrup) *nm* **-e** syrup.

Sitt/e (ˈzitə) *nf* **-n 1** custom. **2** *pl* manners. **3** *pl* morals. **—lich** *adj* **1** moral. **2** decent, respectable. **—lichkeit** *nf* morality, morals.

Situation (zituatsiˈoːn) *nf* **-en** situation.

Sitz (zits) *nm* **-e 1** seat. **2** residence. **3** fit. **—en*** (ˈzitsən) *vi* **1** sit. **2** fit. **—ung** *nf* **—en 1** sitting, session. **2** meeting.

Sizil/ien (ziˈtsiːliən) *n neu* Sicily. **—ianer** (zitsiliˈaːnər) *nm* — Sicilian. **—ianisch** (zitsiliˈaːniʃ) *adj* Sicilian.

Skala (ˈskaːla) *nf* **Skalen** scale.

Skandal (skanˈdaːl) *nm* **-e 1** scandal. **2** row, noise. **—ös** (skandaˈlœːs) *adj* scandalous.

Skandinav/ien (skandiˈnaːviən) *n neu* Scandinavia. **—ier** *nm* — Scandinavian. **—isch** *adj* Scandinavian.

Skelett (skeˈlɛt) *n neu* **-e** skeleton.

skeptisch (ˈskɛptiʃ) *adj* sceptical.

Ski (ʃiː) *nm see* **Schi.**

Skizz/e (ˈskitsə) *nf* **-n** sketch. **—ieren** (skitsiːrən) *vt* sketch.

Sklav/e (ˈsklaːvə) *nm* **-n** slave. **—erei** (sklaːvəˈrai) *nf* slavery. **—isch** (ˈsklaːviʃ) *adj* **1** slavish. **2** servile.

Skorpion (skɔrpiˈoːn) *nm* **-e 1** scorpion. **2** Scorpio.

Skrupel (ˈskruːpəl) *nm* — scruple. **—los** *adj* unscrupulous.

Smaragd (smaˈrakt) *nm* **-e** emerald.

Smoking (ˈsmoːkiŋ) *nm* **-s** dinner-jacket.

so (zoː) *adv* so, thus. **so daß** *conj* so that. **—bald** (zoˈbalt) *conj* as soon as.

Socke (ˈzɔkə) nf -n sock. —**nhalter** nm garter.

Sockel (ˈzɔkəl) nm — pedestal, base.

sodann (zoˈdan) conj then.

Sodawasser (ˈzoːdavasər) n neu soda water.

Sodbrennen (ˈzoːtbrɛnən) n neu heartburn.

soeben (zoˈeːbən) adv just (now).

Sofa (ˈzoːfa) n neu -s sofa, couch.

sofern (zoˈfɛrn) conj 1 as far as, so far as. 2 provided that.

sofort (zoˈfɔrt) adv immediately, at once.

Sog (zoːk) nm -e 1 suction. 2 wake.

sogar (zoˈɡaːr) adv even.

sogenannt (ˈzoːɡənant) adj so-called.

Sohle (ˈzoːlə) nf -n sole (of a shoe). —**n** vt sole.

Sohn (zoːn) nm ⁻e son.

solang (zoˈlaŋ) conj while, so long as.

solch (zɔlç) adj,pron such.

Soldat (zɔlˈdaːt) nm -en soldier.

Söldner (ˈzœldnər) nm — mercenary.

solid (zoˈliːt) adj 1 solid. 2 reliable.

Solist (zoˈlist) nm -en soloist.

sollen* (ˈzɔlən) v mod aux 1 should, ought (to). 2 be said, be supposed (to).

Solo (ˈzoːlo) n neu -s solo.

Sommer (ˈzɔmər) nm — summer. —**sprosse** nf freckle.

Sonate (zoˈnaːtə) nf -n sonata.

Sonde (ˈzɔndə) nf -n probe.

Sonder/angebot (ˈzɔndərangəboːt) n neu -e special offer. —**ausgabe** nf special edition. —**bar** (ˈzɔndərbaːr) adj strange, singular.

sondern[1] (ˈzɔndərn) vt separate.

sondern[2] (ˈzɔndərn) conj but. **nicht nur ...sondern auch** not only...but also.

Sonett (zoˈnɛt) n neu -e sonnet.

Sonnabend (ˈzɔnaːbənt) nm -e Saturday. —**s** adv on Saturdays.

Sonn/e (ˈzɔnə) nf -n sun. —**enaufgang** nm sunrise. —**enbrand** nm sunburn. —**enfinsternis** nf solar eclipse. —**enschein** nm sunshine. —**enstich** nm sunstroke. —**enuhr** nf sundial. —**enuntergang** nm sunset. —**ig** adj sunny.

Sonntag (ˈzɔntaːk) nm -e Sunday. —**s** adv on Sundays.

sonst (zɔnst) adv 1 otherwise. 2 else. 3 besides. —**ig** adj 1 other. 2 former. —**wo** (ˈzɔnstvoː) adv elsewhere.

Sopran (zoˈpraːn) nm -e soprano, treble. —**istin** (zopraˈnistin) nf -nen soprano (singer).

Sorg/e (ˈzɔrɡə) nf -n 1 care. 2 trouble, worry. 3 grief. —**en** vi care, take care. —**en für** care or provide for, take care of, look after. **sich —en** vr worry. —**falt** (ˈzɔrkfalt) nf care, carefulness.

Sort/e (ˈzɔrtə) nf -n sort, type. —**ieren** (zɔrˈtiːrən) vt sort, arrange.

soso (zoˈzoː) adv inf passably, so-so.

Soße (ˈzoːsə) nf -n 1 sauce. 2 gravy.

soweit (zoˈvait) conj so far as.

sowie (zoˈviː) conj 1 as soon as. 2 just as.

sowieso (zoviˈzoː) adv anyhow, anyway.

Sowjet (zɔˈvjɛt) nm -s Soviet. —**isch** adj Soviet. —**union** nf Soviet Union.

sowohl (zoˈvoːl) conj **sowohl...als auch** both...and.

sozial (zotsiˈaːl) adj social. —**demokrat** nm social democrat. —**ismus** (zotsiaˈlismus) nm socialism. —**ist** (zotsiaˈlist) nm -en socialist. —**produkt** n neu pol national product.

Soziolog/e (zotsioˈloːɡə) nm -n sociologist. —**ie** (zotsioloˈɡiː) nf sociology. —**isch** (zotsioˈloːɡiʃ) adj sociological.

sozusagen (zotsuˈzaːɡən) adv so to speak.

Spachtel (ˈʃpaxtəl) nm,f -n 1 scraper. 2 spatula.

spähen (ˈʃpɛːən) vi look out, watch.

Spalt (ʃpalt) nm -e crack, split. —**e** nf -n 1 crack, split. 2 column (of print, etc.). 3 rift. —**en** vt split, divide. —**pilz** nm bacteria.

Span (ʃpaːn) nm ⁻e chip, splinter.

Span/ien (ˈʃpaːniən) n Spain. —**ier** (ˈʃpaːniər) nm — Spaniard. —**isch** (ˈʃpaːniʃ) adj Spanish. n neu Spanish (language).

Spann (ʃpan) nm -e instep.

Spann/e (ˈʃpanə) nf -n span. —**en** vt 1 stretch. 2 tighten. 3 harness. 4 excite. —**ung** nf -en 1 tension. 2 suspense. 3 voltage.

spar/en (ˈʃpaːrən) vt,vi save. vt spare. —**kasse** nf savings bank. ⁻**lich** (ˈʃpɛːrliç) adj meagre, scanty. —**sam** adj thrifty.

Spargel (ˈʃparɡəl) nm asparagus.

Spaß (ʃpaːs) nm ⁻e 1 fun, amusement. 2 joke.

spät (ʃpɛːt) adj late. —**estens** adv at the latest.

Spaten (ˈʃpaːtən) nm — spade.

Spatz (ʃpats) nm -en sparrow.

spazier/en (ʃpaˈtsiːrən) vi (take a) walk, stroll. —**engehen*** vi go for a walk. —**gang** nm walk.

Speck (ʃpɛk) nm 1 bacon. 2 fat.

spedieren (ʃpeˈdiːrən) vt dispatch, forward.

Speer (ʃpeːr) nm -e spear, lance.

Speichel (ˈʃpaiçəl) nm saliva, spittle.

103

Speicher (´ʃpaiçər) *nm* **-e** 1 storeroom. 2 loft. 3 granary. 4 reservoir. **—n** *vt* store (up).

Speise (´ʃpaizə) *nf* **-n** 1 food. 2 meal. 3 dish. **—eis** *n neu* ice cream. **—kammer** *nf* pantry, larder. **—karte** *nf* menu. **—n** *vi* eat, dine. **—saal** *nm* dining room or hall. **—wagen** *nm* dining car.

Spektakel (ʃpɛk´taːkəl) *nm* — uproar, row.

spekulieren (ʃpeku´liːrən) *vi* speculate.

Sperr/e (´ʃpɛrə) *nf* **-n** 1 closing. 2 barrier. 3 block. 4 blockade, embargo. **—en** *vt* 1 close, block (off). 2 shut (out). 3 cut off, stop.

Spesen (´ʃpeːzən) *n pl* expenses, charges.

spez/ialisieren (ʃpetsiali´ziːrən) *vt* specialize. **sich spezialisieren auf** specialize in. **—ialität** (ʃpetsiali´tɛːt) *nf.* **-en** speciality. **—iell** (ʃpetsi´ɛl) *adj* special.

spezifisch (ʃpe´tsiːfiʃ) *adj* specific.

Sphäre (´sfɛːrə) *nf* **-n** sphere.

Spiegel (´ʃpiːgəl) *nm* — mirror. **—ei** *n neu* fried egg. **—n** *vt* reflect. *vi* shine. **—ung** *nf* **-en** reflection.

Spiel (ʃpiːl) *n neu* **-e** 1 game. 2 play. 3 pack (of cards). **—en** *vt,vi* 1 play. 2 perform. 3 gamble. **—karte** *nf* playing card. **—platz** *nm* playground. **—zeug** *n neu* toy.

Spieß (ʃpiːs) *nm* **-e** 1 spear. 2 *cul* spit. **—bürger** *nm* Philistine, (petit) bourgeois. **—ig** *adj* narrow-minded, Philistine.

Spinat (ʃpi´naːt) *nm* spinach.

Spinne (´ʃpinə) *nf* **-n** spider. **—n*** (´ʃpinən) *vt* 1 spin. 2 plot, think. *vi inf* 1 spin yarns, fib. 2 be crazy. **—r** *nm* — *inf* idiot.

Spion (ʃpi´oːn) *nm* **-e** spy.

Spirale (ʃpi´raːlə) *nf* **-n** spiral.

Spital (ʃpi´taːl) *n neu* **ᵈer** hospital.

spitz (ʃpits) *adj* pointed, sharp. **—bube** *nm* rogue, rascal. **—e** *nf* **-n** 1 point. 2 peak, top. 3 lace. **—en** *vt* point, sharpen. **—findig** *adj* subtle. **—ig** *adj* pointed, sharp. **—name** *nm* nickname.

Splitter (´ʃplitər) *nm* — splinter. **—nackt** *adj* stark naked.

spontan (ʃpɔn´taːn) *adj* spontaneous.

Sporn (ʃpɔrn) *nm* **Sporen** spur.

Sport (ʃpɔrt) *nm* **-e** sport, games. **—ler** (´spɔrtlər) *nm* — sportsman, athlete. **—platz** *nm* sports field. **—wagen** *nm* sports car.

Spott (ʃpɔt) *nm* mockery, ridicule. **—en** *vi* mock, ridicule.

sprach (ʃpraːx) *v see* **sprechen.**

Sprach/e (´ʃpraːxə) *nf* **-n** 1 speech. 2 language.

—lehre *nf* grammar. **—lich** *adj* linguistic. **—los** *adj* speechless.

sprang (ʃpraŋ) *v see* **springen.**

sprech/en* (´ʃprɛçən) *vi,vt* speak, talk. **—stunde** *nf* consulting hours, surgery.

spreng/en (´ʃprɛŋən) *vt* 1 explode, blast. 2 sprinkle. *vi* gallop. **—körper** *nm* explosive (charge). **—stoff** *nm* explosive.

spricht (ʃpriçt) *v see* **sprechen.**

Sprichwort (´ʃpriçvɔrt) *n neu* **ᵈer** proverb, saying.

sprießen* (´ʃpriːsən) *vi* sprout, bud.

spring/en* (´ʃpriŋən) *vi* 1 leap, jump. 2 dive.

Sprit (ʃprit) *nm* **-e** 1 spirit, alcohol. 2 *inf* petrol.

Spritze (´ʃpritsə) *nf* **-n** 1 syringe. 2 spray. 3 injection. 4 fire engine. **—n** *vt* 1 spray, squirt. 2 inject. *vi* spurt.

Sproß (ʃprɔs) *nm* **-e** *also* **Sprößling** (´ʃprœslin) shoot, sprout.

Spruch (ʃprux) *nm* **ᵈe** 1 saying. 2 judgment, sentence.

Sprudel (´ʃpruːdəl) *nm* **-e** 1 mineral water. 2 spring.

Sprung (ʃpruŋ) *nm* **ᵈe** 1 leap, spring. 2 dive. 3 short distance, stone's throw. 4 crack. **—brett** *n neu* 1 diving board. 2 stepping stone. **—feder** *nf* spring.

spucken (´ʃpukən) *vi,vt* spit.

Spuk (ʃpuːk) *nm* **-e** ghost. **—en** *vi* haunt.

Spule (´ʃpuːlə) *nf* **-n** spool, reel. 2 coil.

spül/en (´ʃpyːlən) *vt* 1 rinse, wash (up). 2 flush. **—mittel** *n neu* washing-up liquid.

Spur (ʃpuːr) *nf* **-en** 1 track, trail. 2 trace, vestige, mark. 3 footprint.

Staat (ʃtaːt) *nm* **-en** 1 state. 2 pomp. **—lich** *adj* state. **—sangehörigkeit** *nf* nationality. **—sanwalt** *nm* public prosecutor. **—smann** *nm* statesman. **—sstreich** *nm* coup d'état.

Stab (ʃtaːp) *nm* **ᵈe** staff. **—springen*** *vi* pole-vault.

stabil (ʃta´biːl) *adj* stable.

Stachel (´ʃtaxəl) *nm* **-n** 1 prickle. 2 sting. 3 quill, spine. 4 spike. **—beere** *nf* gooseberry. **—draht** *nm* barbed wire. **—schwein** *nm* porcupine.

Stadt (ʃtat) *nf* **ᵈe** city, town. **—isch** (´ʃtɛːtiʃ) *adj* municipal, town. **—viertel** *n neu* quarter, district.

Staffel (´ʃtafəl) *nf* **-n** 1 step, rung. 2 stage, degree. 3 *aviat* squadron. 4 *sport* relay. **—ei** (ʃtafə´lai) *nf* **-en** easel.

stahl (ʃtaːl) *v see* **stehlen.**

Stahl (ʃtaːl) nm -e steel. **̈–ern** (ʃtɛːlərn) adj steel.

Stall (ʃtal) nm ̈e 1 stable. 2 cowshed. 3 pigsty. 4 (dog-)kennel.

Stamm (ʃtam) nm ̈e 1 trunk. 2 stem. 3 family. 4 race. **—baum** nm 1 family tree. 2 pedigree. **—en** vi originate, be descended. **—tisch** nm (table for) regular customers.

stampfen (ʃtampfən) vt,vi 1 stamp. 2 pound.

stand (ʃtant) v see **stehen.**

Stand (ʃtant) nm ̈e 1 stand. 2 situation. 3 location. 4 class, rank. 5 position. **—bild** n neu statue. **—esamt** (ʃtandəsamt) n neu registry office. **—haft** adj steadfast, constant. **—halten'** vi stand firm. **—ort** nm 1 location. 2 garrison. **—punkt** nm point of view, standpoint.

ständig (ʃtɛndiç) adj permanent, continuous. adv constantly, continually.

Stange (ʃtaŋə) nf -n pole, stick. **—nbohne** nf runner bean.

Stänker (ʃtɛŋkər) nm — inf trouble-maker. **—n** vi inf cause trouble, stir things up.

Stanniol (ʃtaniˈoːl) n neu -e tinfoil.

Stapel (ʃtaːpəl) nm — 1 pile. 2 stocks. **—lauf** nm launch(ing). **—n** vt pile up.

stark (ʃtark) adj 1 strong. 2 stout. 3 large. adv 1 strongly. 2 very, greatly. **̈–e** (ʃtɛrkə) nf -n 1 strength. 2 starch. **—en** (ʃtɛrkən) vt 1 strengthen. 2 starch.

starr (ʃtar) adj stiff, rigid. **—köpfig** (ʃtarkœpfiç) adj stubborn.

Start (ʃtart) nm -e 1 start. 2 aviat take-off. **—en** vi 1 start. 2 aviat take off. **—erklappe** nf mot choke.

Station (ʃtatsiˈoːn) nf -en 1 station, stop. 2 (hospital) ward.

Statist/ik (ʃtaˈtistik) nf -en statistics. **—isch** adj statistical.

statt (ʃtat) prep instead of. nf place, stead. **—finden'** vi take place, occur. **—haft** adj 1 permissible. 2 legal.

Stätte (ʃtɛtə) nf -n 1 place, spot. 2 abode. 3 scene (of an accident, etc.).

Statut (ʃtaˈtuːt) n neu -e statute.

Staub (ʃtaup) nm 1 dust. 2 pollen. **—ig** (ʃtaubiç) adj dusty. **—sauger** nm — vacuum cleaner.

Stau/damm (ʃtaudam) nm ̈e dam. **—en** vt dam up.

staunen (ʃtaunən) vi be amazed, wonder. n neu — amazement.

Steak (steːk) n neu steak.

stechen' (ʃtɛçən) vt 1 stab, pierce. 2 cut. 3 game trump. vi 1 sting. 2 burn. **—d** adj stinging.

steck/en (ʃtɛkən) vt 1 put, stick. 2 insert. vi be (found). nm — stick. **—brief** nm (arrest) warrant. **—dose** nf (electric) socket. **—enpferd** (ʃtɛkənpfɛrt) n neu -e hobby-horse. **—er** nm — (electric) plug.

Steg (ʃteːk) nm -e 1 footpath. 2 footbridge. 3 mus bridge.

stehen' (ʃteːən) vi 1 stand. 2 be. **—bleiben'** vi stand still, stop.

stehlen' (ʃteːlən) vt steal.

steif (ʃtaif) adj stiff.

steig/en' (ʃtaigən) vi 1 climb. 2 rise. 3 mount. **—bügel** nm stirrup.

steiger/n (ʃtaigərn) vt 1 increase. 2 raise. **—ung** nf -en 1 rise. 2 increase. 3 intensification.

steil (ʃtail) adj steep.

Stein (ʃtain) nm -e stone, rock. **—alt** adj ancient, as old as the hills. **—bock** nm 1 ibex. 2 Capricorn. **—bruch** nm quarry. **—ern** (ʃtainərn) adj stone. **—ig** adj stony. **—schlag** nm rockfall, avalanche.

Stell/e (ʃtɛlə) nf -n 1 place, site, spot. 2 job, position. 3 office, authority. **—en** vt 1 place, put. 2 arrange. 3 adjust, set. 4 provide, supply. **sich —en** vr 1 present oneself. 2 sham, pretend to be. **—enlos** adj unemployed. **—envermittlung** nf employment agency. **—envertreter** nm deputy, representative.

Stellung (ʃtɛluŋ) nf -en 1 situation. 2 post, job. **—nahme** nf 1 attitude. 2 opinion.

Stelze (ʃtɛltsə) nf -n stilt.

Stempel (ʃtɛmpəl) nm — stamp. **—n** vt stamp, frank.

Stengel (ʃtɛŋəl) nm — stalk, stem.

Stenographie (ʃtenograˈfiː) nf -n shorthand.

Steppe (ʃtɛpə) nf -n steppe.

sterb/en' (ʃtɛrbən) vi die. **—lich** (ʃtɛrpliç) adj mortal.

steril (ʃteˈriːl) adj sterile.

Stern (ʃtɛrn) nm -e star. **—bild** n neu constellation. **—chen** (ʃtɛrnçən) n neu — asterisk. **—deuterei** nf astrology. **—kunde** nf astronomy. **—warte** nf -n observatory.

stet (ʃteːt) adj also **stet/ig** constant, steady. **—s** adv always, constantly.

Steuer¹ (ʃtɔyər) n neu — helm, rudder. **—bord** nm,neu starboard. **—mann** nm helmsman. **—n** vt,vi steer.

Steuer[2] (ˈʃtɔyər) nf -n tax.

Stich (ʃtiç) nm -e 1 prick, sting. 2 stitch. 3 *game* trick. 4 engraving. 5 taunt. **—wort** n neu 1 key-word. 2 cue.

sticken (ˈʃtikən) vt, vi embroider.

Stickstoff (ˈʃtikʃtɔf) nm nitrogen.

Stief/bruder (ˈʃtiːfbruːdər) nm stepbrother. **—mutter** nf stepmother. **—mütterchen** n neu — pansy. **—schwester** nf stepsister. **—sohn** nm stepson. **—tochter** nf stepdaughter. **—vater** nm stepfather.

Stiefel (ˈʃtiːfəl) nm —e boot.

stieg (ʃtiːk) v see **steigen**.

Stiel (ʃtiːl) nm -e 1 handle. 2 stalk.

Stier (ʃtiːr) nm -e 1 bull. 2 Taurus.

stieß (ʃtiːs) v see **stoßen**.

Stift[1] (ʃtift) n neu -e (charitable) institution.

Stift[2] (ʃtift) nm -e 1 peg, pin. 2 pencil.

stift/en (ˈʃtiftən) vt 1 give, donate. 2 found. 3 cause. **—ung** nf -en 1 institution. 2 donation.

Stil (ʃtiːl) nm -e style.

still (ʃtil) adj 1 still, calm. 2 quiet. 3 silent. **Stiller Ozean** Pacific Ocean. **—e** nf -n 1 peace, stillness. 2 quiet, silence. **—egen** (ˈʃtiləgən) vt shut down, stop. **—en** vt 1 still. 2 appease. 3 suckle (a child). 4 quench. 5 quieten. **—schweigend** (ˈʃtilʃvaigənt) adj 1 silent, taciturn. 2 tacit. **—stand** nm standstill.

Stimm/e (ˈʃtimə) nf -n 1 voice. 2 vote. **—en** vi 1 be correct. 2 agree. 3 vote. vt tune. **—ung** nf -en 1 mood, feeling. 2 tuning.

stinken* (ˈʃtiŋkən) vi stink.

Stipendium (ʃtiˈpɛndium) n neu -ien scholarship, grant.

Stirn (ʃtirn) nf -en forehead, brow.

stöbern (ˈʃtœːbərn) vi rummage (around).

Stock (ʃtɔk) nm —e 1 stick, cane. 2 storey, floor. **—en** vi 1 stop, pause. 2 rot. 3 curdle. 4 thicken. **—werk** n neu storey, floor.

Stoff (ʃtɔf) nm -e 1 matter, substance. 2 material, fabric, cloth. 3 topic.

stöhnen (ˈʃtœːnən) vi groan.

Stoi/ker (ˈʃtoːikər) nm — Stoic. **—sch** (ˈʃtoːiʃ) adj stoical.

stolpern (ˈʃtɔlpərn) vi stumble.

stolz (ʃtɔlts) adj 1 proud. 2 noble. 3 vain. nm pride.

stopfen (ˈʃtɔpfən) vt 1 stuff, fill. 2 darn. 3 constipate.

Stoppel (ˈʃtɔpəl) nf -n stubble.

stoppen (ˈʃtɔpən) vt, vi stop, halt.

Stör (ʃtœːr) nm -e sturgeon.

Storch (ʃtɔrç) nm —e stork.

stör/en (ˈʃtœːrən) vt bother, trouble, disturb. **—ung** nf -en 1 disturbance. 2 inconvenience. 3 interference (on a radio, etc.).

Stoß (ʃtoːs) nm —e 1 push, thrust. 2 punch, kick, blow. 3 impact. 4 pile (of books, etc.). **—dämpfer** nm shock-absorber. **—en*** vt 1 push. 2 hit. 3 stab. 4 thrust. vi 1 bump, hit. 2 run (into). **sich —en** vr 1 bump. 2 take offence. **—stange** nf mot bumper.

stottern (ˈʃtɔtərn) vi, vt stammer, stutter.

Straf/anstalt (ˈʃtraːfanʃtalt) nf -en prison, penal institution. **—bar** adj punishable. **—e** nf -n 1 punishment, penalty. 2 fine. **—en** vt punish. **—ling** (ˈʃtrɛːfliŋ) nm -e convict. **—recht** n neu criminal law.

Strahl (ʃtraːl) nm -en 1 ray, beam. 2 jet. 3 flash. **—en** vt, vi 1 radiate. 2 beam. **—ung** nf -en radiation.

stramm (ʃtram) adj 1 taut. 2 robust.

Strand (ʃtrant) nm —e shore, coast, beach. **—gutjäger** nm beachcomber.

strapazieren (ʃtrapaˈtsiːrən) vt 1 tire, exhaust. 2 wear out.

Straße (ˈʃtraːsə) nf -n 1 street, road. 2 straits. **—nbahn** nf tram.

sträuben (ˈʃtrɔybən) vt ruffle (up). **sich sträuben** vr oppose, refuse.

Strauch (ʃtraux) nm —er bush, shrub.

Strauß[1] (ʃtraus) nm —e bouquet, bunch.

Strauß[2] (ʃtraus) nm -e ostrich.

streb/en (ˈʃtreːbən) vi strive (for). **—epfeiler** nm buttress. **—er** nm — climber, pusher.

Strecke (ˈʃtrɛkə) nf -n 1 stretch, section. 2 distance.

Streich (ʃtraiç) nm -e 1 stroke, blow. 2 trick. **—eln** vt stroke, caress. **—en*** vt 1 stroke. 2 strike (out). 3 spread. vi rush, run. **—holz** n neu match. **—instrument** n neu stringed instrument.

Streif (ʃtraif) nm -e also **Streifen** nm — stripe, streak.

Streife (ˈʃtraifə) nf -n 1 patrol. 2 raid.

streifen (ˈʃtraifən) vt 1 streak, stripe. 2 graze. 3 touch on. 4 strip off. vi rove, ramble.

Streik (ʃtraik) nm -e (industrial) strike. **—brecher** nm strikebreaker, blackleg. **—en** vi strike. **—posten** nm picket.

Streit (ʃtrait) nm -e 1 dispute, quarrel. 2 brawl, struggle. **—en*** vi 1 quarrel, argue. 2 fight. **—frage** nf matter in dispute. **—ig** adj in dispute. **—kräfte** nf pl armed forces.

streng (ʃtrɛŋ) *adj* 1 harsh. 2 rigorous. **—e** *nf* 1 harshness. 2 rigour. **—gläubig** *adj* orthodox.

streuen (ʃtrɔyən) *vt* 1 scatter, sprinkle. 2 sow.

Strich (ʃtriç) *nm* **-e** 1 stroke. 2 line. 3 district. 4 touch. 5 (compass) point. 6 (wood) grain. **—punkt** *nm* semicolon.

Strick (ʃtrik) *nm* **-e** cord, rope. **—en** *vt,vi* knit.

strittig (ʃtritiç) *adj* in dispute.

Stroh (ʃtro:) *n neu* straw. **—halm** *nm* (blade of) straw.

Strolch (ʃtrɔlç) *nm* **-e** tramp.

Strom (ʃtro:m) *nm* **-e** 1 (large) river. 2 current. 3 electricity, electric current. 4 flood, torrent. **—abwärts** (ʃtro:m'apvɛrts) *adv* downstream. **—aufwärts** (ʃtro:m'aufvɛrts) *adv* upstream. **—en** (ʃtroe:mən) *vi* 1 stream, flow. 2 flock. **—ung** (ʃtroe:muŋ) *nf* **-en** 1 current. 2 trend. 3 flow.

Struktur (ʃtruk'tu:r) *nf* **-en** structure.

Strumpf (ʃtrumpf) *nm* **-e** stocking. **—band** *n neu* garter. **—halter** *nm* — suspender. **—hose** *nf* tights.

Stube (ʃtu:bə) *nf* **-n** room, chamber. **—nrein** *adj* house-trained.

Stück (ʃtyk) *n neu* **-e** 1 piece. 2 head, item. 3 play. **—arbeit** *nf* piecework. **—chen** (ʃtykçən) *n neu* — scrap, bit.

Student (ʃtu'dɛnt) *nm* **-en**. **—in** *nf* **-nen** student.

Stud/ie (ʃtu'diə) *nf* **-n** 1 study. 2 sketch. **—ienrat** *nm* secondary-school teacher. **—ieren** (ʃtu'di:rən) *vt,vi* study. **—ium** (ʃtu:dium) *n neu* **-ien** 1 studies. 2 university education or course.

Stufe (ʃtu:fə) *nf* **-n** 1 step, stair. 2 rung. 3 stage. 4 *mus* interval. **—nweise** *adv* gradually, in stages.

Stuhl (ʃtu:l) *nm* **-e** chair, seat.

stumm (ʃtum) *adj* 1 dumb, mute. 2 silent.

stumpf (ʃtumpf) *adj* 1 blunt. 2 dull. *nm* **-e** stump. **—sinn** *nm* dullness, stupidity.

Stund/e (ʃtundə) *nf* **-n** 1 hour. 2 lesson. **—enplan** *nm* (school) timetable. **—lich** (ʃtyntliç) *adj* hourly.

stur (ʃtu:r) *adj inf* obstinate.

Sturm (ʃturm) *nm* **-e** 1 storm, gale. 2 attack. **—isch** (ʃtyrmiʃ) *adj* stormy.

Sturz (ʃturts) *nm* **-e** 1 fall. 2 downfall. 3 overthrow. 4 collapse. **—en** (ʃtyrtsən) *vt* 1 overthrow. 2 throw down. *vi* 1 fall. 2 rush. 3 crash. **sich —en** *vr* rush, plunge.

Stute (ʃtu:tə) *nf* **-n** mare. **—nfüllen** *n neu* filly.

Stütze (ʃtytsə) *nf* **-n** 1 support, prop. 2 buttress. 3 help. **—n** *vt* prop (up), support.

Subjekt (zup'jɛkt) *n neu* **-e** subject.

Substantiv (zupstan'ti:f) *n neu* **-e** noun, substantive.

subtil (zup'ti:l) *adj* subtle.

Such/e ('zu:xə) *nf* **-n** search. **—en** *vt,vi* seek, search (for).

süchtig (zyçtiç) *adj* 1 addicted (to). 2 sickly.

Süd (zy:t) *nm also* **Süden** ('zy:dən) south.

Südafrika (zy:t'afrika) *n neu* South Africa.

Südamerika (zyda'mɛrika) *n neu* South America.

südlich ('zy:tliç) *adj* south(ern).

Südost (zyd'ɔst) *nm also* **Sudost/en** (zyd'ɔstən) south-east. **—lich** *adj* south-eastern.

Südpol ('zy:tpo:l) *nm* South Pole.

südwärts ('zy:tvɛrts) *adv* southward(s), south.

Südwest (zyd'vest) *nm also* **Südwest/en** (zyd-'vestən) south-west. **—lich** *adj* south-western.

Sultanine (zulta'ninə) *nf* **-n** *cul* sultana.

Sülze ('zyltsə) *nf* **-n** 1 jellied meat. 2 brine.

Summe ('zumə) *nf* **-n** sum, total.

summen ('zumən) *vt,vi* hum, buzz.

Sumpf (zumpf) *nm* **-e** 1 swamp, marsh, bog. 2 *tech* sump. **—ig** *adj* swampy.

Sund (zunt) *nm* **-e** *naut* straits.

Sünd/e ('zyndə) *nf* **-n** sin. **—enbock** *nm* scapegoat. **—er** *nm* — sinner.

Suppe ('zupə) *nf* **-n** soup.

süß (zy:s) *adj* sweet. **—e** *nf* sweetness. **—igkeit** *nf* **-en** 1 sweetness. 2 *pl* sweets.

Sylvester (zyl'vestər) *nm see* **Silvester.**

Symbol (zym'bo:l) *n neu* **-e** symbol. **—isch** *adj* symbolic.

Synagoge (zyna'go:gə) *nf* **-n** synagogue.

Synonym (zyno'ny:m) *n neu* **-e** synonym.

Syphilis ('zy:filis) *nf* syphilis.

Syr/ien ('zy:riən) *n neu* Syria. **—ier** *nm* — Syrian. **—isch** *adj* Syrian.

System (zys'te:m) *n neu* **-e** 1 system. 2 method. 3 doctrine. **—atisch** (zyste'ma:tiʃ) *adj* systematic.

Szene ('stse:nə) *nf* **-n** 1 scene. 2 stage, set. 3 row, argument.

T

Tabak ('ta:bak) *nm* **-e** tobacco. **—händler** *nm* tobacconist.

Tabelle (ta'bɛlə) *nf* **-n** 1 table. 2 index.

Tadel ('ta:dəl) *nm* — 1 blame. 2 reprimand,

reproach. **3** fault. **—los** adj blameless, flawless. **—n** vt 1 blame. 2 scold, reproach.

Tafel ('taːfəl) nf **-n** 1 board, panel. 2 blackboard. 3 tablet, bar. 4 index. 5 table. **—n** ('teːfəln) vt panel.

Taffet ('tafət) nm **-e** also **Taft** (taft) taffeta.

Tag (taːk) nm **-e** 1 day. 2 daylight. **—ebuch** ('taːgəbuːx) n neu diary. **—en** ('taːgən) vi 1 dawn. 2 meet. **—esordnung** ('taːgəsɔrdnuŋ) nf agenda. **—esanbruch** ('taːgəsanbrux) nm daybreak. **—lich** ('teːkliç) adj daily. **—undnachtgleiche** nf -n equinox. **—ung** ('taːguŋ) nf **-en** 1 meeting. 2 conference.

Taille ('taljə) nf **-n** waist.

Takelwerk ('taːkəlvɛrk) n neu rigging.

Takt (takt) nm **-e** 1 mus time, beat. 2 tact. **—gefühl** n neu tact. **—los** adj tactless. **—stock** nm mus baton. **—voll** adj tactful.

Taktik ('taktik) nf **-en** tactics.

Tal (taːl) n neu **-er** valley.

Talent (ta'lɛnt) n neu **-e** talent, gift.

Talg (talk) nm **-e** 1 suet. 2 tallow.

Talk (talk) nm **-e** talc, talcum powder.

tändeln ('tɛndəln) vi 1 dawdle. 2 flirt.

Tang (taŋ) nm **-e** seaweed.

Tanger ('taŋər) n neu Tangier(s).

Tank (taŋk) nm **-s** 1 (fuel) tank. 2 mil tank. **—en** vi fill up, refuel. **—stelle** nf petrol or filling station.

Tanne ('tanə) nf **-n** fir, pine. **—nbaum** nm fir, pine tree.

Tante ('tantə) nf **-n** aunt.

Tanz (tants) nm **-e** dance. **—en** vt,vi dance. **—er** ('tɛntsər) nm **—**, **—erin** ('tɛntsərin) nf **—nen** dancer. **—gesellschaft** nf dance, ball.

Tap/ete (ta'peːtə) nf **-n** wallpaper. **—ezieren** (tapeˈtsiːrən) vt paper.

tapfer ('tapfər) adj brave, bold. **—keit** nf courage.

tappen ('tapən) vi grope, fumble.

Tarif (taˈriːf) nm **-e** 1 price list, tariff. 2 list of fares. 3 wage scale.

tarn/en ('tarnən) vt camouflage. **—ung** nf **-en** camouflage.

Tasch/e ('taʃə) nf **-n** 1 pocket. 2 wallet. 3 handbag. **—enbuch** n neu pocketbook. **—endieb** nm pickpocket. **—engeld** n neu pocket money. **—enmesser** n neu pocket knife. **—entuch** n neu handkerchief.

Tasse ('tasə) nf **-n** cup.

Tast/e ('tastə) nf **-n** key. **—atur** (tastaˈtuːr) nf

-en keyboard. **—en** ('tastən) vi feel, grope. vt touch. **sich —en** vr feel one's way.

tat (taːt) v see **tun.**

Tat (taːt) nf **-en** deed, action, act. **in der Tat** in fact. **—bestand** nm 1 facts. 2 state of affairs. **—er** ('tɛːtər) nm **—** perpetrator, doer. **—ig** ('tɛːtiç) adj 1 active. 2 working, at work. **—igen** ('tɛːtigən) vt 1 carry out. 2 comm conclude, execute. **—kraft** nf energy. **—sache** nf fact. **—sächlich** ('taːtzɛçliç) adj 1 real. 2 factual. 3 effective. adv really, indeed.

tätowieren (tɛtoˈviːrən) vt tattoo.

Tatze ('tatsə) nf **-n** 1 paw. 2 claw.

Tau[1] (tau) n neu **-e** cable, rope. **—en** ('tauən) vt tow.

Tau[2] (tau) nm dew. **—en** ('tauən) vi melt. **es taut** dew is falling.

taub (taup) adj 1 deaf. 2 empty. 3 numb.

Taube ('taubə) nf **-n** pigeon, dove.

tauch/en ('tauxən) vi dive, plunge. vt plunge, dip. **—sieder** nm **—** immersion heater.

Tauf/becken ('taufbɛkən) n neu also **Tauf/stein** nm (baptismal) font. **—e** nf **-n** baptism. **—en** vt baptize.

taug/en ('taugən) vi be worth, be of use. **—enichts** nm **-e** good-for-nothing. **—lich** ('taukliç) adj 1 useful. 2 suitable. 3 fit, capable.

Taumel ('tauməl) nm **—** 1 staggering. 2 dizziness. 3 frenzy. **—n** vi 1 stagger. 2 be giddy or dizzy.

Tausch (tauʃ) nm **-e** exchange, swap. **—en** exchange, swap. **—handel** nm barter.

täusch/en ('tɔyʃən) vt 1 deceive. 2 cheat. **—ung** nf **-en** 1 deception. 2 cheating.

tausend ('tauzənt) adj,nf thousand. **—ste** adj thousandth.

Tauwerk ('tauvɛrk) n neu rigging, ropes.

Tax/e ('taksə) nf **-n** 1 estimate. 2 rate, fee. 3 duty, tax. **—ieren** (taˈksiːrən) vt evaluate, assess.

Taxi ('taksi) n neu **-s** taxi.

Techn/ik ('tɛçnik) nf **-en** 1 skill, technique. 2 technical sciences. **—iker** nm **—** technician, engineer. **—isch** adj technical. **—ologie** (tɛçnoloˈgiː) nf technology.

Tee (teː) nm **-s** tea. **—beutel** nm teabag. **—kanne** nf teapot. **—löffel** nm teaspoon.

Teer (teːr) nm **-e** tar.

Teich (taiç) nm **-e** pond, pool.

Teig (taik) nm **-e** 1 dough, batter. 2 paste. **—waren** nf pl pasta.

Teil (tail) nm,neu **-e** 1 part. 2 share, portion. **3**

piece. **—bar** adj divisible. **—chen** ('tailçən) n neu — particle. **—en** vt divide. **—haber** nm — partner, associate. **—nahme** nf 1 participation. 2 interest. 3 sympathy. **—nehmen*** vi take part (in). **—nehmer** nm — participant, member. **—s** adv also **—weise** partly, in part. **—ung** nf **-en** 1 division. 2 scale.

Tele/gramm (tele'gram) n neu **-e** telegram. **—fon** see **phon. —graph** (tele'gra:f) nm **-en** telegraph. **—graphieren** (telegra'fi:rən) vi,vt wire, telegraph. **—phon** (tele'fo:n) n neu **-e** telephone. **—phonanruf** nm telephone call. **—phonieren** (telefo'ni:rən) vi,vt telephone. **—phonisch** adj by telephone. **—phonzelle** nf callbox. **—skop** (tele'sko:p) n neu **-e** telescope.

Teller ('tɛlər) nm — plate.

Tempel ('tɛmpəl) nm — temple.

Temperament (tɛmpera'mɛnt) n neu **-e** 1 temperament. 2 liveliness, vivacity. **—voll** adj temperamental.

Temperatur (tɛmpera'tu:r) nf **-en** temperature.

Tempo ('tɛmpo) n neu **-pi** tempo, pace.

Tendenz (tɛn'dɛnts) nf **-en** tendency.

Tender ('tɛndər) nm — (railway) tender.

Tennis ('tɛnis) n neu tennis. **—platz** nm tennis court.

Teppich ('tɛpiç) nm **-e** carpet, rug. **—kehrmaschine** nf carpet sweeper.

Termin (tɛr'mi:n) nm **-e** 1 deadline. 2 term. 3 (fixed) date.

Terminologie (tɛrmino'lo:gi:) nf **-n** terminology.

Terpentin (tɛrpɛn'ti:n) n neu turpentine.

Terrasse (tɛ'rasə) nf **-n** terrace.

Terror ('tɛror) nm terror. **—isieren** (terori'zi:rən) vt terrorize. **—ismus** (tero'rismus) nm terrorism. **—ist** (tero'rist) nm **-en** terrorist.

Terz (tɛrts) nf **-en** mus third. **—ett** (tɛr'tsɛt) n neu **-e** trio.

Testament (tɛsta'mɛnt) n neu **-e** 1 (last) will. 2 rel Testament.

testieren (tɛs'ti:rən) vt 1 bequeath. 2 testify.

teuer ('tɔyər) adj 1 expensive. 2 cherished, dear.

Teuf/el ('tɔyfəl) nm — devil. **—elei** (tɔyfə'lai) nf **-en** devilry. **—lisch** ('tɔyfliʃ) adj devilish, fiendish.

Text (tɛkst) nm **-e** text.

Textil/ien (tɛks'ti:liən) n pl textiles.

Theater (te'a:tər) n neu — theatre. **—stück** n neu play.

Thema ('te:ma) n neu **-men** theme, topic.

Themse ('tɛmzə) nf Thames.

Theolog/e (teo'lo:gə) nm **-n** theologian. **—ie** (teolo'gi:) nf theology. **—isch** (teo'lo:giʃ) adj theological.

Theor/etiker (teo're:tikər) nm — theorist, theoretician. **—etisch** (teo're:tiʃ) adj theoretical. **—etisieren** (teoreti'zi:rən) vi theorize. **—ie** (teo'ri:) nf **-n** theory.

Therapie (tera'pi:) nf **-n** therapy.

therm/isch ('tɛrmiʃ) adj thermal, thermic. **—odynamik** (tɛrmody'na:mik) nf thermodynamics. **—ometer** (tɛrmo'me:tər) n neu thermometer. **—osflasche** (tɛrmosflaʃə) nf Tdmk Thermos flask.

Thron (tro:n) nm **-e** throne. **—erbe** nm heir to the throne. **—folge** nf succession to the throne.

Thunfisch ('tu:nfiʃ) nm tunny (fish).

Thüringen ('ty:riŋən) n neu Thuringia.

Thymian ('ty:mia:n) nm **-e** thyme.

ticken ('tikən) vi 1 tick, click.

tief (ti:f) adj 1 deep. 2 low. 3 profound. n neu **-s** (barometric) depression. **—druck** nm low pressure. **—e** nf **-n** depth. **—kühlen** vt deep-freeze. **—kühlkost** nf frozen food. **—kühltruhe** nf freezer.

Tiegel ('ti:gəl) nm **-e** 1 saucepan. 2 crucible.

Tier (ti:r) n neu **-e** animal, beast. **—arzt** nm veterinary surgeon, vet. **—isch** adj 1 animal. 2 brutish. 3 brutal. **—kreis** nm zodiac.

Tiger ('ti:gər) nm — tiger.

tilg/en ('tilgən) vt 1 erase. 2 eradicate. 3 cancel. 4 repay. **—ung** nf **-en** 1 eradiction. 2 cancellation. 3 repayment.

Tint/e ('tintə) nf **-n** ink. **in der Tinte sitzen** be in a nice mess. **—enfaß** n neu inkwell.

tippen ('tipən) vt,vi 1 type. 2 tap.

Tirol (ti'ro:l) n neu Tyrol.

Tisch (tiʃ) nm **-e** 1 table. 2 board. **—decke** nf also **—tuch** n neu tablecloth. **—ler** ('tiʃlər) nm — 1 joiner, cabinetmaker. 2 carpenter. **—tennis** nm neu table tennis.

Titel ('ti:təl) nm — title.

titulieren (titu'li:rən) vt give a title to, entitle.

Toast (to:st) nm — toast. **—brot** n neu toasting bread. **—er** nm — toaster.

tob/en ('to:bən) vi 1 rage. 2 roar.

Tochter ('tɔxtər) nf — daughter.

Tod (to:t) nm **-e** death. **—esanzeige** ('to:dəsantsaigə) nf obituary. **—esfall** ('to:dəsfal) nm death, casualty. **—eskampf** ('to:dəskampf) nm death agony. **—esstrafe** ('to:dəsʃtra:fə) nf death penalty. **—feind** ('to:tfaint) nm mortal enemy. **—lich** ('tœ:tliç) adj deadly, fatal. **—müde** ('to:tmy:də) *adj* dead tired.

Toilette (toa'lɛtə) *nf* **-n 1** toilet. **2** dressing table. **3** toilette. **—npapier** *n neu* toilet paper.

toleran/t (tole'rant) *adj* tolerant. **—z** (tole'rants) *nf* **1** toleration. **2** tolerance.

toll (tɔl) *adj* **1** mad. **2** raving. **3** wild. **4** *inf* terrific. **—heit** *nf* **-en 1** madness. **2** mad trick. **—kühn** *adj* foolhardy. **—wut** *nf* rabies.

Tölpel ('tœlpəl) *nm* — clumsy person, fool.

Tomate (to'ma:tə) *nf* **-n** tomato.

Ton[1] (ton) *nm* **-e** clay.

Ton[2] (to:n) *nm* **-e 1** sound. **2** *mus* tone, note. **3** fashion. **4** stress, accent. **—art** *nf mus* key. **—band** *n neu* (magnetic) tape. **—bandgerät** *n neu* tape-recorder. **—en** ('tœ:nən) *vi* resound. *vt* shade, tint. **—fall** *nm* intonation. **—leiter** *nf mus* scale.

Tonne ('tɔnə) *nf* **-n 1** ton. **2** barrel.

Topf (tɔpf) *nm* ⁼e pot. ⁼er ('tœpfər) *nm* — potter. **—erwaren** ('tœpfərva:rən) *nf pl* pottery, earthenware.

Tor[1] (to:r) *n neu* **-e 1** gate, door. **2** *sport* goal.

Tor[2] (to:r) *nm* **-en** fool. **—heit** *nf* **-en** folly. **—icht** ('tœ:riçt) *adj* foolish.

Torf (tɔrf) *nm* peat.

torkeln ('tɔrkəln) *vi* stagger.

Torpedo (tɔr'pe:do) *nm* **-s** torpedo.

Torte ('tɔrtə) *nf* **-n** tart, flan.

tot (to:t) *adj* dead. **Totes Meer** *n neu* Dead Sea.

total (to'ta:l) *adj* total, complete. **—itär** (totali-'tɛ:r) *adj* totalitarian.

Tote(r) ('to:tə) *nm* **1** dead man. **2** corpse.

töten ('tœ:tən) *vt* kill.

Totenbett ('to:tənbɛt) *n neu* deathbed.

Totengräber ('to:təngrɛ:bər) *nm* — gravedigger.

Totenhemd ('to:tənhɛmt) *n neu* shroud.

totgeboren ('to:tgəbo:rən) *adj* still-born.

sich totlachen ('to:tlaxən) *vr* roar with laughter, kill oneself laughing.

totschießen* ('to:tʃi:sən) *vt* shoot dead.

Totschlag ('to:tʃlak) *nm* manslaughter.

totschweigen* ('to:tʃvaigən) *vt* hush up.

totsicher ('to:tziçər) *adj* dead certain.

Tour (tu:r) *nf* **-en 1** tour, trip. **2** turn. **—ist** (tu'rist) *nm* **-en** tourist.

Trab (tra:p) *nm* trot. **—en** ('tra:bən) *vi* trot.

Tracht (traxt) *nf* **-en 1** (national) costume. **2** dress. **3** load.

Tradition (traditsi'o:n) *nf* **-en** tradition. **—ell** (traditsio'nɛl) *adj* traditional.

traf (tra:f) *v* see **treffen.**

träg/e ('trɛ:gə) *adj* lazy, sluggish. **—heit** ('trɛ:-khait) *nf* laziness, sluggishness.

trag/en* ('tra:gən) *vt* **1** carry. **2** wear. **3** bear, endure. **4** support. **—bahre** ('tra:kba:rə) *nf* **-n** stretcher. ⁼er ('trɛ:gər) *nm* — **1** porter. **2** carrier. **3** support. **4** pillar, beam. **—weite** ('tra:kvaitə) *nf* **1** range. **2** importance.

trag/isch ('tra:giʃ) *adj* tragic. **—ödie** (tra-'gœ:diə) *nf* **-n** tragedy.

Train/er ('trɛ:nər) *nm* — *sport* trainer, coach. **—ing** *n neu* training.

Traktor ('traktɔr) *nm* **-en** tractor.

trampeln ('trampəln) *vi* trample, stamp.

Tran (tra:n) *nm* **-e** blubber, whale oil.

tranchieren (trã:'ʃi:rən) *vt* carve (up).

Träne ('trɛ:nə) *nf* **-n** tear. **—ngas** *n neu* teargas.

trank (traŋk) *v* see **trinken.**

transatlantisch (transat'lantiʃ) *adj* transatlantic.

transitiv ('tranziti:f) *adj* transitive.

Transmission (transmisi'o:n) *nf* **-en** transmission.

Transport (trans'pɔrt) *nm* **-e** transport. **—ieren** (transpɔr'ti:rən) *vt* transport.

trat (tra:t) *v* see **treten.**

Traube ('traubə) *nf* **-n 1** grape. **2** bunch of grapes.

trau/en ('trauən) *vi* trust. *vt* (of a priest, etc.) marry (a man and a woman). **sich trauen** *vr* dare, venture. **—ring** *nm* wedding-ring. **—ung** *nf* **-en** wedding.

Trau/er ('trauər) *nf* **1** sorrow. **2** mourning. **—ern** *vi* mourn. **—erspiel** *n neu* tragedy. **—rig** ('trauriç) *adj* sad.

Trauf/e ('traufə) *nf* **-n 1** eaves. **2** gutter. ⁼eln ('trɔyfəln) *vi* drip, sprinkle. **—rinne** *nf* **-n** gutter (of a house).

traulich ('trauliç) *adj* cosy, familiar.

Traum (traum) *nm* ⁼e dream. ⁼en ('trɔymən) *vt,vi* dream (of). ⁼er ('trɔymər) *nm* — dreamer. **—haft** *adj* dreamlike.

treff/en* ('trɛfən) *vt,vi* hit, strike. **2** befall. **3** meet, encounter. **sich treffen** *vr* **1** meet. **2** happen. **eine Entscheidung treffen** come to a decision **—en** *n neu* — meeting. **—er** *nm* — (direct or lucky) hit. **—lich** *adj* excellent. **—punkt** *nm* meeting place.

treib/en* ('traibən) *vt* **1** drive. **2** urge. **3** force. **4** carry on, do. **5** work (metal). *vi* drift. *n neu*

activity. **—haus** ('traiphaus) n neu hothouse.
—stoff ('traipʃtɔf) nm fuel.
trenn/bar ('trɛnbaːr) adj divisible. **—en** vt 1
divide, separate. 2 cut off (a telephone
call). **—ung** nf -en separation.
Trepp/e ('trɛpə) nf -n stairs, staircase.
—enhaus n neu stairwell.
tret/en' ('treːtən) vi 1 step, walk. 2 pedal. vt 1
kick. 2 tread on. **—mühle** nf treadmill.
treu (trɔy) adj 1 faithful, loyal. 2 accurate.
—bruch nm breach of faith. **—e** nf loyalty.
—händer ('trɔyhɛndər) nm — trustee. **—lich**
adv faithfully. **—los** adj disloyal.
Tribut (tri'buːt) nm -e tribute.
Trichter ('trɪçtər) nm -1 funnel. 2 crater.
Trick (trɪk) nm -s trick, dodge. **—film** nm
animated cartoon.
trieb (triːp) v see **treiben.**
Trieb (triːp) nm -e 1 drive, force. 2 impulse. 3
bot shoot, sprout. 4 instinct. **—feder** nf
(main)spring. **—haft** adj 1 instinctive. 2
unbridled. **—kraft** nf momentum. **—sand**
nm quicksand.
triefen' ('triːfən) vi drip.
trifft (trɪft) v see **treffen.**
triftig ('trɪftɪç) adj 1 conclusive. 2 valid.
Trigonometrie (trigonome'triː) nf trigonometry.
Triller ('trɪlər) nm — mus trill.
trimmen ('trɪmən) vt trim.
trink/bar ('trɪŋkbaːr) adj drinkable. **—en'** vt, vi
drink. **—geld** n neu tip.
Tripper ('trɪpər) nm gonorrhoea.
tritt (trɪt) v see **treten.**
Tritt (trɪt) nm -e 1 step. 2 kick.
Triumph (tri'umf) nm -e triumph. **—ieren**
(trium'fiːrən) vi triumph.
trock/en ('trɔkən) adj dry. **—nen** vt, vi dry.
Trog (troːk) nm -e trough.
Tromm/el ('trɔməl) nf -n drum. **—eln** vi
drum. **—ler** ('trɔmlər) nm — drummer.
Trompete (trɔm'peːtə) nf -n trumpet.
Trop/en ('troːpən) n pl tropics. **—enhelm** nm
sun-helmet. **—isch** adj tropical.
Tropf (trɔpf) nm -e simpleton. **—eln** ('trœpfəln)
vt, vi drip, trickle. **—en** ('trɔpfən) nm —
drop. vt, vi drip, trickle.
Trost (troːst) nm consolation. **—en** ('trœːstən)
vt console, comfort. **—los** adj 1 inconsolable.
2 bleak, desolate.
Trott (trɔt) nm -e trot.
Trottel ('trɔtəl) nm — idiot.
trotz (trɔts) prep in spite of, despite. nm 1
defiance. 2 obstinacy. **jemandem zum Trotz**

in defiance of someone. **—dem** ('trɔtsdeːm)
adv nevertheless. conj notwithstanding. **—ig**
adj defiant, obstinate.
trüb (tryːp) adj 1 gloomy, dismal. 2 cloudy,
muddy. **—en** ('tryːbən) vt 1 make gloomy. 2
dull, tarnish. **—sal** nf -e distress, affliction.
—sinn nm melancholy, depression.
Trug (truːk) nm 1 deceit, deception. 2 fraud.
—bild n neu phantom, mirage. **—en'** ('tryː-
gən) vt deceive. vi be deceptive. **—erisch**
('tryːgərɪʃ) adj 1 deceptive. 2 deceitful.
Trümmer ('trymər) n neu pl 1 ruins. 2 rubble.
Trumpf (trumpf) nm -e trump. **—en** vt, vi
trump.
Trunk (truŋk) nm -e drink. **—en** adj drunk,
drunken. **—sucht** nf alcoholism.
Trupp (trup) nm -s band, party. **—e** nf -n 1
troop. 2 company, unit. 3 pl troops.
Truthahn ('truːthaːn) nm turkey(-cock).
Tschech/e ('tʃɛçə) nm -n Czech. **—isch** adj
Czech. n neu Czech (language). **—oslowakei**
(tʃɛçoslova'kai) nf Czechoslovakia. **—oslo-
wakisch** adj Czechoslovakian.
Tuberkulose (tuberku'loːzə) nf tuberculosis.
Tuch (tuːx) n neu -e 1 cloth. 2 rag, duster. 3
scarf.
tüchtig ('tyçtɪç) adj 1 able. 2 efficient.
Tück/e ('tykə) nf -n malice, spite. **—isch** adj 1
malicious. 2 insidious.
Tugend ('tuːgənt) nf -en virtue. **—haft** adj
virtuous.
Tulpe ('tulpə) nf -n tulip.
tun' (tuːn) vt, vi 1 do. 2 make. 3 act. 4 put. 5
pretend. n neu doings. **—lich** adj practicable.
Tünche ('tynçə) nf -n whitewash, distemper.
—n vt whitewash, distemper.
Tunke ('tuŋkə) nf -n sauce, gravy. **—n** vt 1
dip. 2 steep.
Tunnel ('tunəl) nm — tunnel.
Tür (tyːr) nf -en door, doorway.
Türk/e ('tyrkə) nm Turk. **—ei** (tyr'kai) nf
Turkey. **—isch** adj Turkish. n neu Turkish
(language).
Türkis (tyr'kiːs) nm -e turquoise.
Turm (turm) nm -e 1 tower, steeple. 2 game
rook, castle. **—chen** ('tyrmçən) n neu —
turret.
turn/en ('turnən) vi do gymnastics. n neu
gymnastics. **—halle** nf gymnasium.
Turnier (tur'niːr) n neu -e tournament.
Tusch/e ('tuʃə) nf -n Indian ink. **—farbe** nf
water-colour.
tuscheln ('tuʃəln) vi whisper.

Tüte ('ty:tə) nf **-n 1** paper bag. **2** carrier bag.

Twen (tvɛn) nm **-s** man or woman in his or her twenties.

Typ (ty:p) nm **-en 1** type. **2** model. **—isch** adj typical.

Typhus ('ty:fus) nm typhoid (fever).

Tyrann (ty'ran) nm **-en** tyrant. **—ei** (tyra'nai) nf tyranny.

U

U-Bahn ('u:ba:n) nf underground (railway).

übel ('y:bəl) adj **1** evil, wrong. **2** bad, nasty. **3** sick. n neu **— 1** evil. **2** nuisance. **3** disease. **—keit** nf **-en** nausea, sickness. **—nehmen*** vt take amiss, take badly.

üben ('y:bən) vt,vi practise, exercise.

über ('y:bər) prep **1** over. **2** above. **3** (up)on. **4** beyond, across. **5** about.

überall (y:bər'al) adv everywhere.

überanstrengen (y:bər'anʃtrɛŋən) vt overexert.

überaus ('y:braus) adv exceedingly.

überbelichten ('y:bərbəliçtən) vt overexpose (a photograph).

überbieten (y:bər'bi:tən) vt outbid.

Überbleibsel ('y:bərblaipsəl) n neu **—** remainder, remnant.

Überblick ('y:bərblik) nm **1** survey. **2** summary. **—en** (y:bər'blikən) vt survey.

überbringen* (y:bər'briŋən) vt deliver, hand over.

überdies (y:bər'di:s) adv besides, moreover.

Überdruß ('y:bərdrus) nm **1** disgust. **2** boredom, weariness.

übereilen (y:bər'ailən) vt rush, hurry.

überein/ander (y:bərain'andər) adv one on top of another. **—kommen*** (y:bər'ainkɔmən) vi come to an agreement. n neu **—** agreement. **—kunft** (y:bər'ainkunft) nf **-̈e** agreement, compromise. **—stimmen** (y:bər'ainʃtimən) vi agree.

überfahr/en* ('y:bərfa:rən) vt **1** drive or pass over. **2** run over. **—t** nf passage, crossing.

Überfall ('y:bərfal) nm surprise attack, raid. **—en*** (y:bər'falən) vt attack suddenly. **—ig** ('y:bərfɛliç) adj overdue.

Über/fluß ('y:bərflus) nm abundance, excess. **—flüssig** ('y:bərflysiç) adj superfluous, excess.

überfordern (y:bər'fɔrdərn) vt overcharge.

überführ/en (y:bərfy:rən) vt **1** transport. **2**

convict. **3** convince. **—ung** (y:bər'fy:ruŋ) nf **1** transportation. **2** fly-over.

Übergabe ('y:bərga:bə) nf **1** surrender. **2** delivery.

Übergang ('y:bərgaŋ) nm **1** passage, crossing. **2** transition.

übergeben* ('y:bərge:bən) vt hand over, deliver. **sich übergeben** vr vomit.

übergehen* (vi 'y:bərge:ən; vt y:bər'ge:ən) vi **1** pass or cross over. **2** change. vt **1** omit. **2** pass or run over. **3** revise.

Übergewicht ('y:bərgeviçt) n neu **-e 1** overweight. **2** preponderance.

überhandnehmen* (y:bər'hantne:mən) vi increase or spread rapidly.

überhäufen (y:bər'hɔyfən) vt overwhelm.

überhaupt (y:bər'haupt) adv **1** in general. **2** altogether. **3** at all.

überheblich (y:bər'he:pliç) adj presumptuous.

überholen ('y:bərho:lən) vt fetch or bring over. (y:bər'ho:lən) vt **1** overtake. **2** recondition.

überkochen ('y:bərkɔxən) vi boil over.

überkommen* (y:bər'kɔmən) vt **1** obtain, receive. **2** befall.

überlassen* (y:bər'lasən) vt **jemandem etwas überlassen** leave something to someone.

überlaufen* (y:bər'laufən) vi run or go over.

überleben (y:bər'le:bən) vt survive, outlive.

überleg/en (y:bər'le:gən) vt consider. adj superior. **—ung** nf **-en** consideration.

überliefer/n (y:bər'li:fərn) vt **1** hand down. **2** deliver. **3** surrender. **—ung** nf **-en 1** tradition. **2** delivery. **3** surrender.

überlisten (y:bər'listən) vt outwit.

Übermacht ('y:bərmaxt) nf superiority, superior strength.

übermäßig ('y:bərmɛsiç) adj excessive.

Übermensch ('y:bərmɛnʃ) nm superman.

übermitteln (y:bər'mitəln) vt **1** transmit. **2** convey.

übermorgen ('y:bərmɔrgən) adv the day after tomorrow.

Übermut ('y:bərmu:t) nm **1** high spirits. **2** insolence. **3** arrogance. **—ig** ('y:bərmy:tiç) adj **1** high-spirited. **2** insolent. **3** arrogant.

übernachten (y:bər'naxtən) vi spend the night.

übernehmen* (y:bər'ne:mən) vt **1** take over. **2** undertake.

überprüfen (y:bər'pry:fən) vt examine, check.

überqueren (y:bər'kve:rən) vt traverse, cross.

überragen (y:bər'ra:gən) vt surpass.

überrasch/en (y:bər'raʃən) vt surprise. **—ung** nf **-en** surprise.

Umgang

überreden (y:bər're:dən) *vt* persuade.

überreichen (y:bər'raiçən) *vt* **1** hand over, present. **2** submit.

Überrest ('y:bərrɛst) *nm* remains, remnant.

überrumpeln (y:bər'rumpəln) *vt* take unawares.

übers ('y:bərs) contraction of **über das.**

überschätzen (y:bər'ʃɛtsən) *vt* overrate, overestimate.

überschauen (y:bər'ʃauən) *vt* survey.

überschreiten* (y:bər'ʃraitən) *vt* **1** step over. **2** exceed, transgress.

Überschrift ('y:bərʃrift) *nf* title, heading.

Überschuh ('y:bərʃu:) *nm* overshoe.

Überschuß ('y:bərʃus) *nm* surplus.

überschwemm/en (y:bər'ʃvɛmən) *vt* flood, swamp. **—ung** *nf* **-en** flood, inundation.

überschwenglich ('y:bərʃvɛnliç) *adj* effusive, rapturous.

Übersee ('y:bərze:) *nf* overseas.

übersehen* (y:bər'ze:ən) *vt* **1** overlook. **2** survey.

übersenden (y:bər'zɛndən) *vt* send, forward.

übersetz/en* (*vt* y:bər'zɛtsən) *vi* ferry over. *vi* pass. (y:bər'zɛtsən) *vt* translate. **—ung** (y:bər'zɛtsuŋ) *nf* **-en 1** translation. **2** *tech* gear.

Übersicht ('y:bərziçt) *nf* **-en** survey, summary. **—lich** *adj* easily understood, clear.

übersiedeln ('y:bərzi:dəln) *vi* **1** (re)move. **2** emigrate.

übersinnlich ('y:bərzinliç) *adj* psychic, supernatural.

überspannen (y:bər'ʃpanən) *vt* **1** stretch over, cover. **2** overstrain. **3** exaggerate.

überspringen* (*vi* y:bər'ʃpriŋən; *vt* y:bər'ʃpriŋən) *vi* leap or jump over. *vt* **1** leap over, jump. **2** omit.

überstehen* (y:bər'ʃte:ən) *vt* survive, overcome.

Überstunden ('y:bərʃtundən) *nf pl* overtime.

überstürzen (y:bər'ʃtyrtsən) *vt* hurry, rush.

übertrag/en* (y:bər'tra:gən) *vt* **1** carry over. **2** transport. **3** transmit, broadcast. **4** translate. **—ung** *nf* **-en 1** transfer. **2** transportation. **3** transmission.

übertreffen* (y:bər'trɛfən) *vt* surpass, excel, outdo.

übertreiben* (y:bər'traibən) *vt* **1** overdo. **2** exaggerate.

übertreten* (*vi* 'y:bərtre:tən; *vt* y:bər'tre:tən) *vi* go or change over. *vt* violate, infringe.

übertrieben (y:bər'tri:bən) *adj* overdone, exaggerated.

überwachen (y:bər'vaxən) *vt* supervise, control.

überwältigen (y:bər'vɛltigən) *vt* overpower.

überweis/en* (y:bər'vaizən) *vt* **1** transfer. **2** remit. **—ung** *nf* **-en 1** remittance. **2** transfer.

überwiegen* (y:bər'vi:gən) *vt* outweigh, prevail.

überwinden (y:bər'vindən) *vt* overcome.

überzeug/en (y:bər'tsɔygən) *vt* convince. **—ung** *nf* **-en** conviction.

überzieh/en* (y:bərtsi:ən) *vt* put on. (y:bər'tsi:ən) *vt* **1** cover. **2** overdraw (an account).

Überzug ('y:bərtsu:k) *nm* coating, cover.

üblich ('y:pliç) *adj* customary, usual.

U-Boot* ('u:bo:t) *n neu* submarine.

übrig ('y:briç) *adj* left over, remaining. **—ens** ('y:brigəns) *adv* **1** by the way. **2** besides. **3** after all.

Übung ('y:buŋ) *nf* **-en 1** exercise. **2** practice. **3** use.

Ufer ('u:fər) *n neu* — **1** bank. **2** shore.

Uhr (u:r) *nf* **-en 1** clock, watch. **2** time, hour. **wieviel Uhr ist es?** what time is it? **—feder** *nf* watch spring.

ulkig ('ulkiç) *adj* funny, comical.

Ulme ('ulmə) *nf* **-n** elm.

um (um) *prep* **1** (a)round, about. **2** at, by, for. **3** on account of. *adv* **1** around, about. **2** over, up, finished. **um...zu** *conj* in order to.

umändern ('umɛndərn) *vt* alter, modify.

umarm/en (um'armən) *vt* embrace, hug. **—ung** *nf* **-en** embrace, hug.

umbauen ('umbauən) *vt* rebuild, remodel.

umbilden ('umbildən) *vt* **1** transform. **2** reform. **3** reconstruct.

umbinden* ('umbindən) *vt* **1** put on. **2** tie round.

sich umblicken ('umblikən) *vr* look round or about.

umbringen* ('umbriŋən) *vt* kill.

umdrehen ('umdre:ən) *vt* turn or twist round. **sich umdrehen** *vr* turn round.

umeinander (umain'andər) *adv* (a)round each other.

umfahren* ('umfa:rən) *vt* knock down, run over. (um'fa:rən) *vt* drive round.

umfallen* ('umfalən) *vi* **1** fall down or over. **2** collapse.

Umfang ('umfaŋ) *nm* **1** circumference. **2** girth. **3** extent, range.

umfassen (um'fasən) *vt* **1** include. **2** enclose. **3** embrace.

Umfrage ('umfra:gə) *nf* inquiry, poll.

Umgang ('umgaŋ) *nm* **1** relations, (social)

113

intercourse. 2 rotation, circuit. **—ssprache** *nf* colloquial or everyday speech.

umgeb/en' (um'ge:bən) *vt* surround. **—ung** *nf* **-en** surroundings, environment.

umgeh/en' (*vi* 'umge:ən; *vt* um'ge:ən) *vi* 1 go round. 2 associate (with). *vt* 1 go round. 2 avoid. **—ungsstraße** (um'ge:-uŋsʃtra:sə) *nf* by-pass.

umgekehrt ('umgəke:rt) *adj* 1 reversed. 2 contrary. *adv* vice versa.

umgraben' ('umgra:bən) *vt* dig up.

umher (um'he:r) *adv* about, around. **—gehen'** *vi* walk about. **—schweifen** *vi* wander, roam.

umhüllen (um'hylən) *vt* wrap (up), cover.

Umkehr ('umke:r) *nf* return. **—en** *vi,vt* turn round.

umkippen ('umkipən) *vt,vi* turn or tip over.

umklammern (um'klamərn) *vt* clasp, cling (to).

sich umkleiden ('umklaidən) *vr* change (one's clothes).

umkommen' ('umkɔmən) *vi* 1 die, perish. 2 (of food) spoil.

Umkreis ('umkrais) *nm* 1 circumference. 2 surroundings.

Umlauf ('umlauf) *nm* 1 circulation. 2 rotation. **—en'** (*vt* um'laufən; *vi* 'umlaufən) *vt* move or run round. *vi* 1 circulate. 2 rotate.

Umlaut ('umlaut) *nm* **-e** vowel modification, umlaut.

umleit/en ('umlaitən) *vt* divert. **—ung** *nf* **-en** diversion.

umlernen ('umlɛrnən) *vt* relearn.

umrahmen (um'ra:mən) *vt* frame.

umrechn/en ('umrɛçnən) *vt* convert, exchange. **—ung** *nf* conversion, exchange.

umreißen' (um'raisən) *vt* outline, sketch. ('umraisən) *vt* pull down.

umringen (um'riŋən) *vt* surround.

Umriß ('umris) *nm* outline, sketch.

umrühren ('umry:rən) *vt* stir up or around.

ums (ums) contraction of **um das.**

Umsatz ('umzats) *nm comm* 1 turnover. 2 sale.

umschalten ('umʃaltən) *vt* 1 switch over. 2 change over.

umschauen ('umʃauən) *vi* look round.

Umschlag ('umʃla:k) *nm* 1 envelope. 2 cover, wrapper. 3 hem, cuff, turn-up. 4 (sudden) change, transformation. 5 poultice. 6 *comm* turnover. **—en'** (um'ʃla:gən) *vi* 1 turn or tip over. 2 change. ('umʃla:gən) *vt* 1 knock down or over. 2 turn over.

umschließen' (um'ʃli:sən) *vt* enclose, embrace.

umschulen ('umʃu:lən) *vt* 1 retrain, re-educate. 2 change (a child's) school.

Umschwung ('umʃvuŋ) *nm* 1 change. 2 *tech* revolution.

sich umsehen' ('umze:ən) *vr* 1 look round or back. 2 look out (for).

umsetzen ('umzɛtsən) *vt* 1 transpose. 2 transform. 3 sell, turn over.

umsichtig ('umziçtiç) *adj* cautious, prudent.

umsiedeln ('umzi:dəln) *vt,vi* resettle.

umsonst (um'zɔnst) *adv* 1 in vain. 2 free, for nothing.

Umstand ('umʃtant) *nm* 1 circumstance, condition. 2 *pl* ceremonies, fuss. **in anderen Umständen** *inf* pregnant, expecting. **—lich** ('umʃtɛntliç) *adj* 1 complicated, involved. 2 ceremonious.

umsteigen' ('umʃtaigən) *vi* change (trains or buses).

umstoßen' ('umʃto:sən) *vt* 1 overturn, overthrow. 2 invalidate. 3 reverse (a judgment).

Umsturz ('umʃturts) *nm* 1 overthrow, downfall. 2 revolution. **—en** ('umʃtyrtsən) *vt* overthrow. *vi* fall down.

umtauschen ('umtauʃən) *vt* exchange.

umwälzen ('umvɛltsən) *vt* 1 revolutionize. 2 roll round. **sich umwälzen** *vr* whirl round.

Umweg ('umve:k) *nm* roundabout way, detour.

Umwelt ('umvɛlt) *nf* environment.

umwenden' ('umvɛndən) *vt* turn over. **sich umwenden** *vr* turn back or round.

umwerben' (um'vɛrbən) *vt* seek the favour of, court.

umwerfen' ('umvɛrfən) *vt* 1 overturn. 2 put on.

umziehen' ('umtsi:ən) *vt* change (one's clothing). *vi* remove, move (house).

umzingeln (um'tsiŋəln) *vt* encircle, surround.

Umzug ('umtsu:k) *nm* 1 removal. 2 procession.

unabänderlich (unap'ɛndərliç) *adj* 1 unchangeable. 2 irrevocable.

unabhängig ('unaphɛŋiç) *adj* independent. **—keit** *nf* independence.

unachtsam ('unaxtza:m) *adj* inattentive.

unanfechtbar (unan'fɛçtba:r) *adj* incontestable.

unangemessen ('unangəmɛsən) *adj* 1 inadequate. 2 improper. 3 unsuitable.

unangenehm ('unangəne:m) *adj* unpleasant.

Unannehmlichkeit ('unanne:mliçkait) *nf* **-en** inconvenience, unpleasantness.

unanständig ('unanʃtɛndiç) *adj* indecent.

unartig ('una:rtiç) *adj* naughty, badly behaved.

unauffällig ('unauffɛliç) *adj* 1 inconspicuous. 2 unassuming.

unausstehlich (unaus'ʃteːliç) *adj* insufferable.

unbändig ('unbɛndiç) *adj* 1 unruly. 2 *inf* tremendous, excessive.

unbeachtet ('unbəaxtət) *adj* unnoticed.

unbedeutend ('unbədɔytənt) *adj* insignificant.

unbedingt (unbə'dɪŋt) *adj* 1 unconditional, absolute. 2 definite. *adv* definitely.

Unbehag/en ('unbəhaːgən) *n neu* 1 uneasiness. 2 discomfort. **—lich** (unbə'haːkliç) *adj* uneasy, uncomfortable.

unbeholfen ('unbəhɔlfən) *adj* clumsy, awkward.

unbekümmert ('unbəkymərt) *adj* 1 carefree, unconcerned. 2 careless.

unbemittelt ('unbəmɪtəlt) *adj* without means.

unbequem ('unbəkveːm) *adj* 1 uncomfortable. 2 inconvenient. **—lichkeit** *nf* 1 discomfort. 2 inconvenience.

unberufen (unbə'ruːfən) *adj* uncalled for. *interj* touch wood!

unbeschreiblich (unbə'ʃraipliç) *adj* indescribable.

unbesonnen ('unbəzɔnən) *adj* thoughtless, rash.

unbestimmt ('unbəʃtimt) *adj* indefinite.

unbestreitbar (unbə'ʃtraitbaːr) *adj* indisputable.

unbestritten ('unbəʃtritən) *adj* undisputed.

unbeweglich ('unbəveːkliç) *adj* 1 immovable. 2 motionless.

unbewußt ('unbəvust) *adj* 1 unconscious, unknowing. 2 instinctive, involuntary.

unbotmäßig ('unboːtmeːsiç) *adj* unruly.

unbrauchbar ('unbrauxbaːr) *adj* useless, unserviceable.

und (unt) *conj* and. **na und?** so what?

undankbar ('undaŋkbaːr) *adj* ungrateful.

undenkbar (un'dɛŋkbaːr) *adj* unthinkable.

undeutlich ('undɔytliç) *adj* indistinct, blurred.

undurchdringlich ('undurçdriŋliç) *adj* impenetrable.

uneben ('uneːbən) *adj* 1 uneven. 2 rough.

unecht ('unɛçt) *adj* artificial, counterfeit.

unehelich ('uneːəliç) *adj* (of a child) illegitimate.

unehrlich ('uneːrliç) *adj* dishonest.

unendlich (un'ɛntliç) *adj* endless, infinite.

unentbehrlich (unɛnt'beːrliç) *adj* indispensable.

unerbittlich (unɛr'bitliç) *adj* relentless, unrelenting, unyielding.

unerfahren ('unɛrfaːrən) *adj* inexperienced.

unerhört (unɛr'hœːrt) *adj* 1 unheard of. 2 outrageous.

unerläßlich (unɛr'lɛsliç) *adj* indispensable.

unerlaubt ('unɛrlaupt) *adj* 1 unauthorized. 2 illegal.

unermeßlich (unɛr'mɛsliç) *adj* immeasurable.

unermüdlich (unɛr'myːtliç) *adj* untiring.

unerreicht (unɛr'raiçt) *adj* unequalled.

unerschrocken ('unɛrʃrɔkən) *adj* undaunted.

unerwünscht ('unɛrvynʃt) *adj* undesirable, unwelcome.

unfähig ('unfɛːiç) *adj* 1 incapable. 2 incompetent. **—keit** *nf* 1 incapacity. 2 incompetence.

Unfall ('unfal) *nm* 1 accident. 2 disaster.

unfaßbar ('unfasbaːr) *adj* inconceivable.

unfehlbar (un'feːlbaːr) *adj* 1 unfailing. 2 infallible.

unfreundlich ('unfrɔyntliç) *adj* unfriendly.

Unfug ('unfuːk) *nm* 1 mischief. 2 offence. 3 disturbance. 4 (public) nuisance. **—sam** ('unfyːkzaːm) *adj* unruly, unmanageable.

Ungar ('uŋgar) *nm* **-n** Hungarian. **—isch** *adj* Hungarian. *n neu* Hungarian (language). **—n** *n neu* Hungary.

ungeachtet ('ungəaxtət) *prep* regardless of.

ungebührlich (ungəbyːrliç) *adj* improper.

Ungeduld ('ungədult) *nf* impatience. **—ig** ('ungəduldiç) *adj* impatient.

ungefähr ('ungəfɛːr) *adv* about, approximately.

ungeheuer ('ungəhɔyər) *adj* huge, monstrous. *n neu* — monster. **—lich** (ungə'hɔyərliç) *adj* monstrous.

ungekürzt ('ungəkyrtst) *adj* unabridged.

ungelegen ('ungəleːgən) *adj* inconvenient.

Ungemach ('ungəmaːx) *n neu* **-e** 1 adversity. 2 discomfort.

ungemein ('ungəmain) *adj* uncommon, extraordinary.

ungemütlich ('ungəmyːtliç) *adj* unpleasant, uncomfortable.

ungeniert ('unʒəniːrt) *adj* unceremonious.

ungeraten ('ungəraːtən) *adj* 1 (of children) spoilt. 2 degenerate.

ungerecht ('ungərɛçt) *adj* unjust.

ungereimt ('ungəraimt) *adj* absurd.

ungern ('ungɛrn) *adv* reluctantly, unwillingly.

ungestüm ('ungəʃtyːm) *adj* 1 impetuous. 2 violent. *n neu* 1 impetuosity. 2 violence.

unge/wöhnlich ('ungəvœːnliç) *adj* unusual, uncommon, strange. **—wohnt** ('ungəvoːnt) *adj* unaccustomed.

Ungeziefer ('ungətsiːfər) *n neu* — vermin.

ungezogen ('ungətsoːgən) *adj* 1 ill-mannered, uncivil, rude. 2 naughty, disobedient.

ungezwungen ('ʊngətsvʊŋən) adj natural, unconstrained, easy(-going).

ungläubig ('ʊnglɔybiç) adj incredulous, unbelieving.

unglaublich ('ʊnglaupliç) adj unbelievable, incredible.

ungleich ('ʊnglaiç) adj unequal, unlike.

Unglimpf ('ʊnglimpf) nm 1 insult. 2 harshness.

Unglück ('ʊnglyk) n neu misfortune. **—lich** adj 1 unhappy. 2 unfortunate. **—licherweise** adv unfortunately. **—sfall** nm accident.

Ungnade ('ʊngnaːdə) nf 1 disgrace. 2 displeasure.

ungünstig ('ʊngynstiç) adj unfavourable.

unhaltbar ('ʊnhaltbaːr) adj untenable.

Unheil ('ʊnhail) n neu 1 harm. 2 disaster, misfortune. **—bar** adj incurable.

unheimlich ('ʊnhaimliç) adj 1 weird, sinister, uncanny. 2 inf tremendous, terrific.

universal (ʊnivɛr'zaːl) adj universal.

Universität (ʊnivɛrzi'tɛːt) nf **-en** university.

Universum (uni'vɛrzum) n neu universe.

unkennt/lich ('ʊnkɛntliç) adj unrecognizable. **—nis** nf ignorance.

unklug ('ʊnkluːk) adj unwise, imprudent.

Unkosten ('ʊnkɔstən) nf pl expenses, costs.

Unkraut ('ʊnkraut) n neu weed(s).

unlängst ('ʊnlɛŋst) adv lately, recently.

unlauter ('ʊnlautər) adj impure, unfair.

unlösbar ('ʊnlœːsbaːr) adj insoluble.

unmäßig ('ʊnmɛːsiç) adj immoderate.

Unmenge ('ʊnmɛŋə) nf enormous number.

Unmensch ('ʊnmɛnʃ) nm brute, barbarian. **—lich** adj brutal, inhuman, barbarous.

unmittelbar ('ʊnmitəlbaːr) adj direct.

unmöglich ('ʊnmœːkliç) adj impossible.

unmoralisch ('ʊnmoraliʃ) adj immoral.

unnötig ('ʊnnœːtiç) adj unnecessary.

unnütz ('ʊnnyts) adj useless, vain, idle.

unord/entlich ('ʊnɔrdəntliç) adj untidy, disorderly. **—nung** nf disorder, confusion.

unparteiisch ('ʊnpartaiiʃ) adj impartial.

unpassend ('ʊnpasənt) adj unsuitable.

Unrat ('ʊnraːt) nm 1 dirt, filth. 2 rubbish.

unratsam ('ʊnra:tzaːm) adj inadvisable.

unrecht ('ʊnrɛçt) adj 1 incorrect. 2 unjust. n neu injustice, wrong. **—mäßig** adj illegal.

unrein ('ʊnrain) adj unclean, dirty.

Unruh/e ('ʊnruːə) nf 1 uneasiness, anxiety. 2 disturbance, riot. 3 unrest. **—ig** adj 1 restless, uneasy. 2 turbulent. **—stifter** nm agitator, troublemaker.

uns (ʊns) pron 1st pers pl 1 us. 2 ourselves.

unsagbar (ʊn'zaːkbaːr) adj unspeakable.

unsauber ('ʊnzaubər) adj dirty, untidy.

unscheinbar ('ʊnʃainbaːr) adj 1 insignificant. 2 unpretentious, plain.

unschlüssig ('ʊnʃlysiç) adj irresolute, undecided.

Unschuld ('ʊnʃult) nf innocence. **—ig** ('ʊnʃuldiç) adj innocent.

unselig ('ʊnzeːliç) adj 1 unfortunate. 2 fatal.

unser ('ʊnzər) poss adj 1st pers pl our. **—er** poss pron 1st pers pl also **der uns(e)re** or **der uns(e)rige** ours. **—(e)seits** ('ʊnzər(ə)zaits) adv for our part. **—(e)sgleichen** ('ʊnzər(ə)sglaiçən) pron people like us. **—thalben** ('ʊnzərthalbən) adv also **—twegen** ('ʊnzərtveːgən) or **—twillen** ('ʊnzərtvilən) for our sake(s), on our account.

unsicher ('ʊnziçər) adj 1 unsafe, insecure. 2 uncertain.

unsichtbar ('ʊnziçtbaːr) adj invisible.

Unsinn ('ʊnzin) nm nonsense. **—ig** adj foolish, stupid.

Unsitt/e ('ʊnzitə) nf bad habit. **—lich** adj immoral, indecent.

unsterblich ('ʊnʃtɛrpliç) adj immortal. **—keit** nf immortality.

unstet ('ʊnʃteːt) adj unsteady, inconstant.

Untat ('ʊnta:t) nf crime, outrage.

untätig ('ʊntɛːtiç) adj inactive.

untauglich ('ʊntaukliç) adj unfit, useless.

unten ('ʊntən) adv 1 below. 2 downstairs.

unter ('ʊntər) prep 1 below, under. 2 among. 3 between. 4 of. 5 during. adj lower, inferior.

Unterarm ('ʊntərarm) nm forearm.

Unterbau ('ʊntərbau) nm **-ten** substructure, foundation.

unterbewußt ('ʊntərbəvust) adj subconscious. **—sein** n neu subconscious.

unterbleiben* (ʊntər'blaibən) vi not take place, be cancelled.

unterbrechen* (ʊntər'brɛçən) vt interrupt.

unterbringen* (ʊntər'briŋən) vt 1 lodge, shelter. 2 place.

unterdes (ʊntər'dɛs) adv also **unterdessen** meanwhile.

unterdrücken (ʊntər'drykən) vt 1 suppress, repress. 2 oppress.

untereinander (ʊntərain'andər) adv 1 among one another, mutually. 2 one beneath the other.

Unterführung (ʊntər'fyːrʊŋ) nf underpass.

Untergang ('untərgaŋ) nm 1 (of the sun) setting. 2 decline, (down)fall.

Untergebene(r) (untər'ge:bənə) nm subordinate.

untergehen* ('untərge:ən) vi 1 perish, die. 2 set, sink.

untergeordnet ('untərgəɔrdnət) adj subordinate.

Untergestell ('untərgəʃtɛl) n neu -e undercarriage, base.

untergraben* (untər'gra:bən) vt 1 undermine. 2 corrupt.

Untergrund ('untərgrunt) nm subsoil. **—bahn** nf underground (railway).

unterhalb ('untərhalp) prep below, under.

Unterhalt ('untərhalt) nm livelihood, subsistence. **—en*** (untər'haltən) vt 1 entertain. 2 maintain. 3 support. **sich —en** vr talk, converse. **—ung** nf -en 1 entertainment. 2 conversation.

unterhand/eln (untər'handəln) vi negotiate. **—lung** (untər'handluŋ) nf negotiation.

Unterhemd ('untərhɛmt) n neu vest.

Unterhosen ('untərho:zən) nf pl underpants.

unterirdisch ('untərirdiʃ) adj underground, subterranean.

unterkommen* ('untərkɔmən) vi 1 find work. 2 find accommodation or shelter. n neu also **Unterkunft** ('untərkunft) nf -e 1 lodging(s), accommodation. 2 mil quarters.

Unterlage ('untərla:gə) nf 1 basis, foundation. 2 (documentary) proof, documents.

unterlassen* (untər'lasən) vt 1 omit. 2 abstain from.

unterlegen (v 'untərle:gən; adj untər'le:gən) vt put under. adj inferior.

Unterleib ('untərlaip) nm abdomen.

unterliegen* (untər'li:gən) vi be defeated.

unternehm/en* (untər'ne:mən) vt undertake, attempt. n neu — undertaking, enterprise. **—er** nm — 1 contractor. 2 entrepreneur. 3 employer.

Unteroffizier ('untərɔfitsi:r) nm non-commissioned or petty officer.

Unterredung (untər're:duŋ) nf -en 1 conversation. 2 conference. 3 talk, interview.

Unterricht ('untərriçt) nm instruction, lessons. **—en** (untər'riçtən) vt instruct, teach, inform.

Unterrock ('untərrɔk) nm petticoat.

unters ('untərs) contraction of **unter das.**

untersagen (untər'za:gən) vt forbid, prohibit.

Untersatz ('untərzats) nm 1 support. 2 saucer.

unterscheid/en* (untər'ʃaidən) vt distinguish, discriminate. **sich unterscheiden** vr differ. **—ung** nf -en distinction, difference.

unterschieben* (untər'ʃi:bən) vt attribute, impute.

Unterschied ('untərʃi:t) nm -e difference. **—lich** adj different.

unterschlagen* (untər'ʃla:gən) vt 1 embezzle. 2 suppress.

Unterschlupf (untər'ʃlupf) nm -e refuge.

unterschreiben* (untər'ʃraibən) vt 1 sign. 2 subscribe to.

Unterschrift ('untərʃrift) nf signature.

Untersee/boot ('untərze:bo:t) n neu submarine. **—isch** ('untərze:iʃ) adj submarine.

untersetzt (untər'zɛtst) adj thick-set, stocky.

unterst ('untərst) adj lowest, last, bottom.

Unterstand ('untərʃtant) nm dugout, shelter.

unterstütz/en (untər'ʃtytsən) vt support, back. **—ung** nf -en support.

untersuch/en (untər'zu:xən) vt examine, inspect. **—ung** nf -en 1 examination. 2 inquiry.

Untertan ('untərta:n) nm -en subject. **—ig** ('untərtɛ:niç) adj 1 subject. 2 submissive.

Untertasse ('untərtasə) nf saucer.

Untertitel ('untərti:təl) nm subtitle, caption.

unterwärts ('untərvɛrts) adv downwards.

Unterwäsche ('untərvɛʃə) nf underwear.

unterwegs (untər've:ks) adv 1 on the way, en route. 2 bound (for).

unterweisen* (untər'vaizən) vt teach, instruct.

Unterwelt ('untərvɛlt) nf underworld.

unterwerfen* (untər'vɛrfən) vt subdue, subject. **sich unterwerfen** vr submit.

unterwürfig (untər'vyrfiç) adj submissive, servile.

unterzeichn/en (untər'tsaiçnən) vt sign. **—ung** nf signature.

unterziehen* (untər'tsi:ən) vt subject to. **sich unterziehen** vr undergo.

untreu ('untrɔy) adj 1 unfaithful. 2 disloyal.

untrüglich (un'try:kliç) adj infallible, unerring.

Untugend ('untu:gənt) nf vice, bad habit.

unumgänglich (un'umgɛŋliç) adj 1 indispensable. 2 unavoidable.

unumwunden ('unumvundən) adj 1 plain, blunt. 2 candid.

ununterbrochen ('ununtərbrɔxən) adj uninterrupted, continuous.

unverantwortlich (unfɛr'antvɔrtliç) adj 1 irresponsible. 2 inexcusable.

unverbesserlich (unfɛr'bɛsərliç) adj incorrigible.

117

unverbindlich ('unfɛrbintliç) adj **1** not binding, without obligation. **2** unkind.

unverdient ('unfɛrdi:nt) adj undeserved.

unverdorben ('unfɛrdɔrbən) adj unspoilt.

unverdrossen ('unfɛrdrɔsən) adj indefatigable.

unvereinbar (unfɛr'ainba:r) adj incompatible.

unvergeßlich (unfɛr'gɛsliç) adj unforgettable.

unvermeidlich (unfɛr'maitliç) adj unavoidable, inevitable.

unvermittelt ('unfɛrmitəlt) adj abrupt.

Unvermögen ('unfɛrmœ:gən) n neu impotence, inability.

unvermutet ('unfɛrmu:tət) adj unexpected.

unvernünftig ('unfɛrnynftiç) adj unreasonable.

unverschämt ('unfɛrʃɛ:mt) adj **1** insolent, cheeky. **2** shameless.

unversehens ('unfɛrze:əns) adv unawares.

unversehrt ('unfɛrze:rt) adj uninjured.

unverständlich ('unfɛrʃtɛntliç) adj unintelligible.

unverträglich ('unfɛrtrɛ:kliç) adj **1** quarrelsome. **2** incompatible.

unverzüglich (unfɛr'tsy:kliç) adj immediate.

unwahr ('unva:r) adj untrue, false, wrong. **—scheinlich** (unva'ainliç) adj **1** improbable. **2** inf incredible.

unweigerlich (un'vaigərliç) adj definite, certain. adv without fail.

unweit ('unvait) adv not far (off). prep near.

Unwetter ('unvɛtər) n neu storm, stormy weather.

unwichtig ('unviçtiç) adj unimportant.

unwiderruflich (unvi:dər'ru:fliç) adj irrevocable.

unwiderstehlich (unvi:dər'ʃte:liç) adj irresistible.

unwillig ('unviliç) adj indignant.

unwillkürlich ('unvilky:rliç) adj involuntary, instinctive.

unwirksam ('unvi:rkza:m) adj ineffective.

unwissen/d ('unvisənt) adj ignorant. **—heit** nf ignorance.

unwürdig ('unvyrdiç) adj unworthy.

Unzahl ('untsa:l) nf great or countless number. **—bar** (un'tsɛ:lba:r) adj also **—ig** (un'tsɛ:liç) innumerable, countless.

Unze ('untsə) nf **-n** ounce.

unzeitgemäß ('untsaitgəmɛ:s) adj inopportune.

unzerbrechlich (untsɛr'brɛçliç) adj unbreakable.

unzertrennlich (untsɛr'trɛnliç) adj inseparable.

unziemlich ('untsi:mliç) adj unseemly.

Unzucht ('untsuxt) nf indecent act, sexual offence.

unzufrieden ('untsufri:dən) adj dissatisfied.

unzugänglich ('untsu:gɛŋliç) adj inaccessible.

unzulänglich ('untsu:lɛŋliç) adj inadequate.

unzulässig ('untsu:lɛsiç) adj inadmissible.

üppig ('ypiç) adj **1** abundant, plentiful. **2** well-developed. **3** voluptuous. **4** presumptuous, cocky. **—keit** nf **1** abundance. **2** voluptuousness. **3** presumption.

uralt ('u:ralt) adj **1** very old, ancient. **2** prehistoric. **3** primeval.

Uran (u'ra:n) n neu uranium.

Uraufführung ('u:rauffy:ruŋ) nf first night or performance, premiere.

urbar ('u:rba:r) adj arable.

Ureinwohner ('u:rainvo:nər) nm pl original inhabitants, aborigines.

Ureltern ('u:rɛltərn) n pl ancestors.

Urgeschichte ('u:rgəʃiçtə) nf earliest history, earliest times.

Urheber ('u:rhe:bər) nm — author, originator.

Urin (u'ri:n) nm urine.

Urkund/e ('u:rkundə) nf **-n** document, deed. **—lich** ('u:rkuntliç) adj documentary.

Urlaub ('u:rlaup) nm **-e** holidays, leave.

Urmensch ('u:rmɛnʃ) nm primitive man.

Urne ('urnə) nf **-n** urn.

urplötzlich ('u:rplœtsliç) adj sudden, abrupt.

Ursache ('u:rzaxə) nf cause, reason.

Ursprung ('u:rʃpruŋ) nm origin, source, beginning. **—lich** ('u:rʃpryŋliç) adj original, primary.

Urteil ('urtail) n neu **1** judgment. **2** opinion. **—en** vi judge.

Urwald ('u:rvalt) nm primeval or virgin forest, jungle.

Urzeit ('u:rtsait) nf remotest antiquity, primitive times.

Utop/ie (uto'pi:) nf **-n** Utopia. **—isch** (u'to:piʃ) adj Utopian.

V

vag (va:k) adj also **vage** ('va:gə) vague.

Vagabund (vaga'bunt) nm **-en** vagabond, tramp.

vakant (va'kant) adj vacant.

Vakuum ('va:kuum) n neu **-kua** vacuum.

Valuta (va'lu:tə) nf **-ten 1** rate of exchange. **2** currency. **3** value.

Vanille (va'niljə) nf vanilla.

Variation (variatsi'o:n) *nf* **-en** variation.
Vase ('va:zə) *nf* **-n** vase.
Vater ('fa:tər) *nm* — father. **—land** *n neu* native country. **—ländisch** ('fa:tərlɛndiʃ) *adj* national, patriotic. **—lich** ('fɛ:tərliç) *adj* fatherly. **—unser** (fa:tər'unzər) *n neu* Lord's Prayer.
Vegetar/ier (vege'ta:riər) *nm* — vegetarian. **—isch** *adj* vegetarian.
Veilchen ('failçən) *n neu* — violet.
Vene ('ve:nə) *nf* **-n** vein.
Venedig (ve'ne:diç) *n neu* Venice.
Ventil (vɛn'ti:l) *n neu* **-e** valve.
verabred/en (fɛr'apre:dən) *vt* agree (upon), fix. **sich verabreden** *vr* make an appointment. **—ung** *nf* **-en 1** agreement. **2** appointment.
verabschieden (fɛr'apʃi:dən) *vt* **1** dismiss. **2** pass (laws). **sich verabschieden** *vr* take one's leave.
veracht/en (fɛr'axtən) *vt* despise. **—lich** (fɛr'ɛçtliç) *adj* **1** contemptuous, scornful. **2** contemptible, despicable.
verallgemeiner/n (fɛralgə'mainərn) *vt* generalize. **—ung** *nf* **-en** generalization.
veralten (fɛr'altən) *vi* become obsolete or out-of-date.
veränder/lich (fɛr'ɛndərliç) *adj* changeable, variable. **—n** *vt* change, alter.
veranlag/t (fɛr'anla:kt) *adj* talented. **—ung** (fɛr'anla:guŋ) *nf* **-en 1** aptitude, talent. **2** assessment.
veranlassen (fɛr'anlasən) *vt* give rise to.
veranschaulichen (fɛr'anʃauliçən) *vt* **1** make clear. **2** illustrate.
veranstalt/en (fɛr'anʃtaltən) *vt* arrange, organize. **—ung** *nf* **-en 1** arrangement. **2** entertainment, show. **3** *sport* event.
verantwort/en (fɛr'antvɔrtən) *vt* answer for. **—lich** *adj* responsible. **—ung** *nf* **-en** responsibility.
verarbeiten (fɛr'arbaitən) *vt* work, process.
verargen (fɛr'argən) *vt* blame. **jemandem etwas verargen** blame someone for something.
verärgern (fɛr'ɛrgərn) *vt* annoy, vex.
veräußer/n (fɛr'ɔysərn) *vt* sell, dispose of. **—ung** *nf* **-en 1** sale. **2** transfer.
Verb (vɛrp) *n neu* **-en** verb.
Verband (fɛr'bant) *nm* **-̈e 1** bandage, dressing. **2** association, union.
verbannen (fɛr'banən) *vt* banish.
verbergen (fɛr'bɛrgən) *vt* hide, conceal.
verbessern (fɛr'bɛsərn) *vt* **1** improve. **2** correct.

sich verbeugen (fɛr'bɔygən) *vr* bow.
verbieten (fɛr'bi:tən) *vt* forbid, prohibit.
verbilligen (fɛr'biligən) *vt* **1** cheapen. **2** reduce (the price of).
verbind/en (fɛr'bindən) *vt* **1** bandage. **2** bind, join. **—lich** (fɛr'bintliç) *adj* **1** obligatory, binding. **2** obliging. **—ung** (fɛr'binduŋ) *nf* **-en 1** union. **2** bond. **3** connection. **4** relation.
verbissen (fɛr'bisən) *adj* grim, dogged.
verbittern (fɛr'bitərn) *vt* embitter.
verblassen (fɛr'blasən) *vi* grow pale, fade.
Verbleib (fɛr'blaip) *nm* whereabouts. **—en** (fɛr'blaibən) *vi* **1** remain. **2** persist, stick (to).
verblenden (fɛr'blɛndən) *vt* **1** delude. **2** dazzle. **3** screen. **4** *arch* face.
verblüffen (fɛr'blyfən) *vt* **1** amaze, astonish. **2** confuse, bewilder.
verbluten (fɛr'blu:tən) *vi* bleed to death.
verbohrt (fɛr'bo:rt) *adj* stubborn.
verborgen (fɛr'bɔrgən) *adj* hidden, secret.
Verbot (fɛr'bo:t) *n neu* **-e** prohibition. **—en** *adj* forbidden.
Verbrauch (fɛr'braux) *nm* consumption, use. **—en** *vt* **1** consume. **2** wear out. **—er** *nm* — consumer, user.
verbrech/en (fɛr'brɛçən) *vt* commit (a crime). *n neu* — crime. **—er** *nm* — criminal. **—erisch** *adj* criminal.
verbreiten (fɛr'braitən) *vt* spread.
verbrennen (fɛr'brɛnən) *vt* **1** burn (up). **2** cremate. *vi* burn to death.
verbringen (fɛr'briŋən) *vt* spend (time).
sich verbrüdern (fɛr'bry:dərn) *vr* fraternize.
Verbum ('vɛrbum) *n neu* **-ben** verb.
verbünd/en (fɛr'byndən) *vt* ally. **sich verbünden** *vr* ally oneself. **—ete(r)** *nm* ally, confederate.
Verdacht (fɛr'daxt) *nm* **-e** suspicion, distrust. **—ig** (fɛr'dɛçtiç) *adj* **1** suspicious. **2** suspect. **—igen** (fɛr'dɛçtigən) *vt* suspect.
verdamm/en (fɛr'damən) *vt* condemn, damn. **—nis** *nf* damnation.
verdampfen (fɛr'dampfən) *vi* evaporate.
verdanken (fɛr'daŋkən) *vt* be indebted for, owe.
verdauen (fɛr'dauən) *vt* digest.
Verdeck (fɛr'dɛk) *n neu* **-e 1** *naut* deck. **2** *mot* hood, top. **3** covering. **—en** *vt* cover (up).
Verderb (fɛr'dɛrp) *nm* ruin, destruction. **—en** (fɛr'dɛrbən) *vt* spoil, corrupt. *vi* spoil, decay. **—lich** (fɛr'dɛrpliç) *adj* **1** perishable. **2** contaminating. **—nis** (fɛr'dɛrpnis) *nf* corruption.
verdeutlichen (fɛr'dɔytliçən) *vt* make clear, explain.

119

verdichten (fɛr'dɪçtən) *vt* condense, compress.

verdicken (fɛr'dɪkən) *vt* thicken.

verdien/en (fɛr'diːnən) *vt* **1** deserve. **2** earn. **—st** *n neu* **-e** merit. *nm* **-e** earnings, gain.

verdingen (fɛr'dɪŋən) *vt* hire out.

verdoppeln (fɛr'dɔpəln) *vt* double.

verdorben (fɛr'dɔrbən) *adj* spoilt, damaged.

verdrängen (fɛr'drɛŋən) *vt* **1** thrust aside. **2** displace. **3** supplant. **4** suppress, repress.

verdrehen (fɛr'dreːən) *vt* **1** distort. **2** twist.

verdrieß/en (fɛr'driːsən) *vt* annoy, vex. **—lich** *adj* **1** annoyed. **2** sulky. **3** annoying.

verdrossen (fɛr'drɔsən) *adj* **1** sulky. **2** annoyed.

verdummen (fɛr'dumən) *vt* make stupid, stupefy. *vi* become stupid.

verdunkeln (fɛr'dʊŋkəln) *vt* **1** darken, black out. **2** overshadow.

veredeln (fɛr'eːdəln) *vt* **1** ennoble. **2** improve. **3** *bot* graft.

verehr/en (fɛr'eːrən) *vt* honour, venerate, worship. **—ung** *nf* worship, veneration.

Verein (fɛr'aɪn) *nm* **-e** **1** association, union. **2** society, club. **—bar** *adj* consistent, compatible. **—baren** *vt* agree upon, arrange. **—barung** *nf* **-en** agreement. **—fachen** *vt* simplify. **—igen** *vt* also **—** unite, join, combine. **die Vereinigten Staaten** the United States. **die Vereinten Nationen** the United Nations. **—igung** *nf* **-en** union, alliance.

vereiteln (fɛr'aɪtəln) *vt* frustrate, thwart.

vererben (fɛr'ɛrbən) *vt* **1** bequeath. **2** transmit. **sich vererben** *vr* be hereditary.

verewigen (fɛr'eːvɪgən) *vt* immortalize.

verfahren (fɛr'faːrən) *vi* act, deal. *vt* muddle. **sich verfahren** *vr* lose one's way. ~*adj* bungled. *n neu* **—** **1** method. **2** process. **3** *law* proceedings.

Verfall (fɛr'fal) *nm* **1** decay, decline. **2** *comm* maturity. **3** *law* forfeiture. **—en** *vi* **1** decay, decline. **2** *comm* mature. **3** be forfeited.

verfälschen (fɛr'fɛlʃən) *vt* **1** falsify. **2** adulterate.

verfass/en (fɛr'fasən) *vt* compose, write. **—er** *nm* **—** author. **—ung** *nf* **-en** **1** *pol* constitution. **2** disposition, frame of mind. **—ungsgemäß** *adj also* **—ungsmäßig** constitutional. **—ungswidrig** *adj* unconstitutional.

verfechten (fɛr'fɛçtən) *vt* **1** defend. **2** advocate.

verfehl/en (fɛr'feːlən) *vt* **1** miss. **2** fail (to do). **—t** *adj* unsuccessful.

verfeinern (fɛr'faɪnərn) *vt* **1** refine. **2** improve.

verfluchen (fɛr'fluːxən) *vt* curse.

verfolg/en (fɛr'fɔlgən) *vt* **1** pursue. **2** follow up.

3 persecute. **4** *law* prosecute. **—er** *nm* **—** **1** pursuer. **2** persecutor. **—ung** *nf* **-en** **1** pursuit. **2** persecution. **3** *law* prosecution.

verfüg/en (fɛr'fyːgən) *vi* **1** have at one's disposal. **2** dispose (of). *vt* order. **—ung** *nf* **-en** **1** disposal. **2** order, instruction.

verführ/en (fɛr'fyːrən) *vt* **1** lead astray. **2** seduce. **3** tempt, lure. **—er** *nf* **—** **1** seducer. **2** tempter. **—erisch** *adj* seductive, alluring. **—ung** *nf* **1** seduction. **2** temptation.

vergang/en (fɛr'gaŋən) *adj* past, gone. **—enheit** *nf* past. **—lich** (fɛr'gɛŋlɪç) *adj* transitory, transient.

Vergaser (fɛr'gaːzər) *nm* — carburettor.

vergaß (fɛr'gaːs) *v see* **vergessen.**

vergeb/en (fɛr'geːbən) *vt* **1** forgive. **2** give away. **—ens** *adv* in vain. **—lich** (fɛr'geːplɪç) *adj* **1** fruitless. **2** futile.

vergegenwärtigen (fɛrgeːgən'vɛrtɪgən) *vt* **1** bring to mind. **2** represent. **sich vergegenwärtigen** *vr* imagine, picture.

vergehen (fɛr'geːən) *vi* **1** pass or fade (away). **2** cease. **3** perish. **sich vergehen** *vr* commit an offence. *n neu* — offence.

vergelten (fɛr'gɛltən) *vt* repay, pay back.

vergessen (fɛr'gɛsən) *vt* forget.

vergeuden (fɛr'gɔydən) *vt* squander.

vergewaltig/en (fɛrgə'valtɪgən) *vt* **1** rape. **2** violate. **—ung** *nf* **-en** **1** rape. **2** violence.

sich vergewissern (fɛrgə'vɪsərn) *vr* ascertain.

vergießen (fɛr'giːsən) *vt* **1** shed (blood or tears). **2** spill.

vergiften (fɛr'gɪftən) *vt* poison.

Vergißmeinnicht (fɛr'gɪsmaɪnnɪçt) *n neu* — forget-me-not.

vergißt (fɛr'gɪst) *v see* **vergessen.**

verglasen (fɛr'glaːzən) *vt* glaze.

Vergleich (fɛr'glaɪç) *nm* **-e** **1** comparison. **2** *law* arrangement, compromise. **—en** *vt* **1** compare. **2** settle.

vergnüg/en (fɛr'gnyːgən) *vt* entertain, amuse. **sich vergnügen** *vr* enjoy or amuse oneself. ~*n neu* — pleasure, enjoyment.

vergöttern (fɛr'gœtərn) *vt* **1** deify. **2** idolize.

vergraben (fɛr'graːbən) *vt* bury.

vergriffen (fɛr'grɪfən) *adj* **1** sold out. **2** out of print.

vergrößern (fɛr'grøːsərn) *vt* enlarge, magnify.

Vergünstigung (fɛr'gynstɪgʊŋ) *nf* **-en** concession, privilege.

vergüten (fɛr'gyːtən) *vt* compensate for, reimburse, make good.

verhaften (fɛr'haftən) *vt* arrest.

verhalt/en* (fɛr'haltən) vt keep back, suppress. **sich verhalten** vr behave. **~n** neu behaviour. **÷nis** (fɛr'hɛltnɪs) n neu **-se 1** relation(ship). **2** proportion. **÷nismäßig** (fɛr'hɛltnɪsmɛːsɪç) adj proportional. adv relatively.

verhand/eln (fɛr'handəln) vi **1** negotiate. **2** deal (with). vt **1** dispose of, sell. **2** discuss. **3** law plead. **—lung** (fɛr'handluŋ) nf **1** negotiation. **2** discussion.

verhäng/en (fɛr'hɛŋən) vt **1** impose, inflict. **2** drape. **3** cover. **—nis** n neu **-se** destiny, fate.

verhaßt (fɛr'hast) adj **1** hated, despised. **2** hateful, despicable.

Verhau (fɛr'hau) nm,neu **-e** entanglement. **—en** vt inf thrash.

verheimlichen (fɛr'haimliçən) vt conceal, keep secret.

verheiraten (fɛr'hairaːtən) vt marry. **sich verheiraten** vr marry, get married.

verheißen* (fɛr'haisən) vt promise.

verhelfen* (fɛr'hɛlfən) vi **jemandem zu etwas verhelfen** help someone in (doing) something.

verherrlichen (fɛr'hɛrliçən) vt glorify.

verhindern (fɛr'hindərn) vt **1** prevent. **2** hamper.

Verhör (fɛr'hœːr) n neu **-e 1** examination. **2** interrogation. **—en** vt **1** examine. **2** question.

verhungern (fɛr'huŋərn) vi die of hunger, starve.

verhüten (fɛr'hyːtən) vt avert, prevent.

sich verirren (fɛr'irən) vr lose one's way.

verjüngen (fɛr'jyŋən) vt rejuvenate.

Verkauf (fɛr'kauf) nm **-e** sale. **—en** vt sell. **÷er** (fɛr'kɔyfər) nm **— 1** retailer. **2** salesman, shop assistant. **÷erin** nf **-nen** saleswoman, shop assistant.

Verkehr (fɛr'keːr) nm **1** traffic. **2** communication, intercourse. **—en** vt **1** reverse. **2** pervert. vi **1** associate (with). **2** (of a vehicle or transport service) run, operate. **—sampel** nf traffic light. **—t** adj **1** wrong. **2** inverted, reversed.

verkennen* (fɛr'kɛnən) vt **1** misjudge. **2** fail to recognize.

verklagen (fɛr'klaːgən) vt **1** accuse. **2** sue.

verklären (fɛr'klɛːrən) vt transfigure.

verkleiden (fɛr'klaidən) vt **1** disguise. **2** coat, face.

verkleinern (fɛr'klainərn) vt **1** diminish, reduce. **2** belittle.

verknüpfen (fɛr'knypfən) vt connect.

verkommen* (fɛr'kɔmən) vi **1** decay. **2** decline. adj **1** decayed. **2** depraved.

verkörpern (fɛr'kœrpərn) vt **1** embody. **2** represent.

verkrüppeln (fɛr'krypəln) vt cripple.

verkündig/en (fɛr'kyndigən) vt proclaim, announce. **—ung** nf **-en** proclamation or announcement.

verkürz/en (fɛr'kyrtsən) vt shorten. **—ung** nf **-en 1** reduction. **2** abbreviation.

verladen* (fɛr'laːdən) vt load, ship.

Verlag (fɛr'laːk) nm **-e** publishing house.

verlangen (fɛr'laŋən) vt **1** demand. **2** require. **verlangen nach** long for. **~n** neu **— 1** desire. **2** demand.

verlängern (fɛr'lɛŋərn) vt **1** lengthen. **2** prolong.

verlangsamen (fɛr'laŋzaːmən) vt slow down.

Verlaß (fɛr'las) nm **1** reliance. **2** dependability. **÷lich** (fɛr'lɛsliç) adj reliable.

verlassen* (fɛr'lasən) vt **1** desert. **2** relinquish. **sich verlassen** vr rely.

Verlauf (fɛr'lauf) nm **1** course. **2** development. **—en*** vi **1** elapse. **2** develop. adj lost. **sich —en** vr lose one's way.

verlautbaren (fɛr'lautbaːrən) vt divulge.

verleg/en (fɛr'leːgən) vt **1** misplace. **2** publish. **3** shift. **4** bar. adj embarrassed, confused. **—enheit** nf **—en** embarrassment, confusion. **—er** nm **—** publisher.

verleihen* (fɛr'laiən) vt **1** lend. **2** bestow.

verleiten (fɛr'laitən) vt **1** mislead. **2** seduce. **3** induce.

verlernen (fɛr'lɛrnən) vt forget.

verletzen (fɛr'lɛtsən) vt **1** wound. **2** violate.

verleugnen (fɛr'lɔygnən) vt **1** deny. **2** disavow. **3** renounce.

verleumd/en (fɛr'lɔymdən) vt slander. **—ung** nf **-en** slander, libel.

sich verlieben (fɛr'liːbən) vr fall in love.

verlieren* (fɛr'liːrən) vt,vi lose. **sich verlieren** vr **1** lose oneself or one's way. **2** disappear.

Verlob/te (fɛr'loːptə) nf fiancée. **—te(r)** nm fiancé. **—ung** (fɛr'loːbuŋ) nf **-en** engagement.

verlocken (fɛr'lɔkən) vt entice, tempt.

verlogen (fɛr'loːgən) adj untruthful.

verlor (fɛr'loːr) v see **verlieren.**

verloren (fɛr'loːrən) v see **verlieren.** adj lost.

Verlust (fɛr'lust) nm **-e 1** loss. **2** damage. **3** waste.

vermach/en (fɛr'maxən) vt bequeath. **÷tnis** (fɛr'mɛçtnɪs) n neu **-se 1** legacy. **2** bequest.

vermähl/en (fɛr'mɛːlən) vt marry. **sich ver-**

mählen vr get married. **—ung** nf -en marriage.

vermehren (fɛrˈmeːrən) vt increase, multiply.

vermeid/en (fɛrˈmaidən) avoid, elude. **—lich** (fɛrˈmaitliç) adj avoidable.

vermeintlich (fɛrˈmaintliç) adj supposed.

Vermerk (fɛrˈmɛrk) nm -e note, notice. **—en** vt note (down).

vermess/en (fɛrˈmɛsən) vt 1 measure. 2 survey. **sich vermessen** vr dare. ~adj bold, insolent. **—ung** nf -en 1 measuring. 2 survey.

vermiet/en (fɛrˈmiːtən) vt let, lease. **—er** nm — landlord.

vermindern (fɛrˈmindərn) vt diminish, decrease.

vermischen (fɛrˈmiʃən) vt mix, blend.

vermissen (fɛrˈmisən) vt miss.

vermitt/eln (fɛrˈmitəln) vi, vt 1 mediate. 2 negotiate. vt obtain. **—lung** (fɛrˈmitluŋ) nf -en 1 mediation. 2 intervention.

vermög/e (fɛrˈmœːgə) prep by virtue of. **—en** vt be able. n neu 1 wealth, assets. 2 ability, power.

vermut/en (fɛrˈmuːtən) vt suppose, presume. **—lich** adj likely, presumable. **—ung** nf -en 1 conjecture. 2 suspicion.

vernachlässigen (fɛrˈnaːxlɛsigən) vt neglect.

vernehmen (fɛrˈneːmən) vt 1 perceive, hear. 2 learn. 3 interrogate.

verneinen (fɛrˈnainən) vt deny.

vernicht/en (fɛrˈniçtən) vt annihilate, destroy. **—ung** nf annihilation, destruction.

vernieten (fɛrˈniːtən) vt rivet.

Vernunft (fɛrˈnunft) nf reason, (common) sense. **jemandem zur Vernunft bringen** bring someone to his senses. **—ig** (fɛrˈnynftiç) adj 1 sensible, reasonable. 2 rational.

veröden (fɛrˈœːdən) vt lay waste. vi become desolate.

veröffentlichen (fɛrˈœfəntliçən) vt publish.

verpachten (fɛrˈpaxtən) vt 1 farm (out). 2 lease.

verpacken (fɛrˈpakən) vt 1 pack (up or away). 2 wrap up.

verpassen (fɛrˈpasən) vt 1 miss (a train, etc.). 2 fit (clothes).

verpfänden (fɛrˈpfɛndən) vt pawn, pledge.

verpfleg/en (fɛrˈpfleːgən) vt cater for, feed. **—ung** nf 1 catering. 2 board.

verpflicht/en (fɛrˈpfliçtən) vt 1 oblige. 2 engage. **—ung** nf -en commitment, obligation.

verplempern (fɛrˈplɛmpərn) vt inf fritter away.

verpönt (fɛrˈpøːnt) adj taboo.

verputzen (fɛrˈputsən) vt 1 plaster. 2 inf squander.

verquicken (fɛrˈkvikən) vt 1 amalgamate. 2 mix up.

Verrat (fɛrˈraːt) nm 1 treason. 2 betrayal. **—en** vt betray. **—er** (fɛrˈrɛːtər) nm — traitor. **—erisch** (fɛrˈrɛːtəriʃ) adj treacherous.

verrechnen (fɛrˈrɛçnən) vt reckon up. **sich verrechnen** vr miscalculate.

verrenk/en (fɛrˈrɛŋkən) vt med 1 sprain. 2 dislocate. **—ung** nf -en 1 sprain. 2 dislocation.

verrichten (fɛrˈriçtən) vt perform, execute.

verringern (fɛrˈriŋərn) vt diminish, lessen.

verrück/en (fɛrˈrykən) vt shift, move. **—t** adj mad, crazy.

Verruf (fɛrˈruːf) nm ill repute, disrepute.

Vers (fɛrs) nm -e verse, stanza.

versag/en (fɛrˈzaːgən) vi fail. vt refuse. **—er** nm — failure.

versamm/eln (fɛrˈzaməln) vt assemble, collect. **—lung** (fɛrˈzamluŋ) nf assembly, meeting.

Versand (fɛrˈzant) nm dispatch.

versäum/en (fɛrˈzɔymən) vt 1 neglect, fail (to). 2 miss (a train, etc.). **—nis** nf,neu -se 1 neglect, omission. 2 delay.

verschaffen (fɛrˈʃafən) vt procure, provide.

verschämt (fɛrˈʃɛːmt) adj 1 bashful, shy. 2 ashamed.

verschanzen (fɛrˈʃantsən) vt entrench.

verschärfen (fɛrˈʃɛrfən) vt 1 sharpen. 2 intensify.

verschieb/en (fɛrˈʃiːbən) vt 1 postpone. 2 displace. 3 sell illegally. **—ung** nf -en 1 postponement. 2 displacement.

verschieden (fɛrˈʃiːdən) adj 1 different. 2 pl several, various. **—es** n neu miscellany, variety (of things). **—heit** nf -en 1 difference. 2 variety.

verschiffen (fɛrˈʃifən) vt ship.

verschimmeln (fɛrˈʃiməln) vi grow mouldy.

verschlafen (fɛrˈʃlaːfən) vt sleep through. vi oversleep.

Verschlag (fɛrˈʃlaːk) nm 1 partition. 2 crate, box. 3 compartment. **—en** (fɛrˈʃlaːgən) vt 1 partition. 2 board up. adj cunning.

verschlechtern (fɛrˈʃlɛçtərn) vt make worse. **sich verschlechtern** vr deteriorate.

verschleiern (fɛrˈʃlaiərn) vt veil.

Verschleiß (fɛrˈʃlais) nm wear (and tear).

verschleudern (fɛrˈʃlɔydərn) vt 1 squander. 2 sell extremely cheaply or at a loss.

verschließen (fɛrˈʃliːsən) vt 1 shut, close. 2 lock. 3 seal (a letter).

verschlimmern (fɛrˈʃlimərn) vt make worse. vi get worse.

verschlingen (fɛrˈʃliŋən) vt 1 devour. 2 twist.

verschlucken (fɛrˈʃlukən) vt swallow.

Verschluß (fɛrˈʃlus) nm 1 fastening. 2 seal. 3 stopper.

verschmähen (fɛrˈʃmɛːən) vt disdain, despise.

verschmitzt (fɛrˈʃmitst) adj crafty, sly.

verschollen (fɛrˈʃɔlən) adj (of a person) missing.

verschönern (fɛrˈʃœːnərn) vt 1 adorn, embellish. 2 improve.

verschränken (fɛrˈʃrɛŋkən) vt cross, fold.

verschreiben (fɛrˈʃraibən) vt 1 prescribe. 2 order.

verschulden (fɛrˈʃuldən) vt be guilty of. n neu — 1 wrong. 2 fault.

verschweigen (fɛrˈʃvaigən) vt keep secret.

verschwend/en (fɛrˈʃvɛndən) vt squander, waste. —**erisch** adj wasteful, extravagant.

verschwiegen (fɛrˈʃviːgən) adj 1 discreet. 2 reserved, reticent. —**heit** nf 1 discretion. 2 reticence.

verschwinden (fɛrˈʃvindən) vi disappear. n neu — disappearance.

verschwommen (fɛrˈʃvɔmən) adj vague, blurred.

verschwör/en (fɛrˈʃvøːrən) vt renounce. sich **verschwören** vr conspire, plot. —**er** nm — conspirator. —**ung** nf -en conspiracy, plot.

versehen (fɛrˈzeːən) vt 1 furnish, provide, equip. 2 overlook. 3 fulfil, perform. sich **versehen** vr err, make a mistake. ~n neu — mistake, error. —**tlich** (fɛrˈzeːəntliç) adv by mistake, mistakenly.

versenden (fɛrˈzɛndən) vt 1 send. 2 ship.

versengen (fɛrˈzɛŋən) vt singe, scorch.

versenk/en (fɛrˈzɛŋkən) vt 1 submerge, sink, immerse. 2 countersink. —**ung** nf -en sinking, submersion, immersion.

versessen (fɛrˈzɛsən) adj **auf etwas versessen sein** 1 be bent on something. 2 be crazy about something.

versetzen (fɛrˈzɛtsən) vt 1 (re)move, transfer. 2 displace. 3 pawn.

verseuchen (fɛrˈzɔyçən) vt infect, contaminate.

versicher/n (fɛrˈziçərn) vt 1 insure. 2 affirm. sich **versichern** vr make sure of. —**ung** nf -en 1 insurance. 2 assurance. 3 confirmation. —**ungsstatistiker** nm actuary.

versiegeln (fɛrˈziːgəln) vt seal (up).

versöhnen (fɛrˈzœːnən) vt reconcile.

versorg/en (fɛrˈzɔrgən) vt 1 provide, supply. 2 look after. —**ung** nf -en 1 maintenance. 2 supply.

verspät/en (fɛrˈʃpɛːtən) vt delay. sich **verspäten** vr be late. —**ung** nf -en delay.

verspielen (fɛrˈʃpiːlən) vt gamble away.

verspotten (fɛrˈʃpɔtən) vt mock, deride.

versprech/en (fɛrˈʃprɛçən) vt promise. n neu — promise. —**ung** nf -en promise.

versprengen (fɛrˈʃprɛŋən) vt disperse.

verstaatlichen (fɛrˈʃtaːtliçən) vt nationalize.

Verstand (fɛrˈʃtant) nm 1 reason. 2 understanding. 3 intellect. —**igen** (fɛrˈʃtɛndigən) vt inform. sich —**igen** vr 1 come to an understanding. 2 make oneself understood. —**igung** (fɛrˈʃtɛndiguŋ) nf -en 1 agreement. 2 information. —**lich** (fɛrˈʃtɛntliç) adj intelligible, clear. —**nis** (fɛrˈʃtɛntnis) n neu 1 comprehension. 2 appreciation.

verstärk/en (fɛrˈʃtɛrkən) vt strengthen. —**er** nm — amplifier. —**ung** nf -en 1 reinforcement(s). 2 strengthening 3 amplification.

verstauchen (fɛrˈʃtauxən) vt sprain.

Versteck (fɛrˈʃtɛk) n neu -e hiding-place. —**en** vt hide.

verstehen (fɛrˈʃteːən) vt understand. sich **verstehen** vr 1 agree. 2 get on (with someone).

versteiger/n (fɛrˈʃtaigərn) vt auction, sell by auction. —**ung** nf on auction.

versteinern (fɛrˈʃtainərn) vt petrify.

verstell/bar (fɛrˈʃtɛlbaːr) adj adjustable. —**en** vt 1 adjust. 2 shift. 3 disguise. 4 pretend, feign. 5 misplace. —**ung** nf 1 pretence. 2 disguise. 3 displacement. 4 adjustment.

verstimmt (fɛrˈʃtimt) adj 1 bad-tempered, annoyed. 2 out of tune.

verstockt (fɛrˈʃtɔkt) adj 1 stubborn. 2 callous.

verstohlen (fɛrˈʃtoːlən) adj furtive, stealthy.

Verstoß (fɛrˈʃtɔs) nm 1 offence. 2 error. —**en** vt 1 repudiate. 2 reject. vi 1 offend. 2 violate.

verstricken (fɛrˈʃtrikən) vt entangle.

verstümmeln (fɛrˈʃtyməln) vt mutilate.

Versuch (fɛrˈzuːx) nm -e 1 attempt, trial. 2 experiment. —**en** vt 1 try, test. 2 tempt. —**ung** nf -en temptation.

vertagen (fɛrˈtaːgən) vt adjourn, postpone.

vertauschen (fɛrˈtauʃən) vt 1 exchange. 2 mistake for.

verteidig/en (fɛrˈtaidigən) vt defend. —**er** nm — defender, advocate. —**ung** nf -en defence.

verteil/en (fɛrˈtailən) vt 1 distribute. 2 divide. **—ung** nf distribution, allocation.

vertiefen (fɛrˈtiːfən) vt deepen. **sich vertiefen** vr be absorbed (in).

vertikal (vɛrtiˈkaːl) adj vertical.

vertilgen (fɛrˈtilgən) vt exterminate, destroy.

Vertrag (fɛrˈtraːk) nm -̈e 1 treaty. 2 agreement, contract. **—lich** adj stipulated, agreed.

vertrag/en* (fɛrˈtraːgən) vt 1 endure, stand, bear. 2 carry away. **sich vertragen** vr 1 get on (with someone). 2 agree. **—lich** (fɛrˈtrɛːkliç) adj 1 compatible. 2 sociable, good-natured.

vertrau/en (fɛrˈtrauən) vi trust, have confidence in. n neu confidence, trust. **—ensvoll** adj trustful. **—ensvotum** n neu vote of confidence. **—enswürdig** adj trustworthy. **—lich** adj 1 confidential. 2 intimate. **—t** adj intimate, familiar.

vertreiben* (fɛrˈtraibən) vt 1 expel, banish. 2 sell.

vertret/en* (fɛrˈtreːtən) vt represent. **—er** nm — 1 representative. 2 advocate.

vertrösten (fɛrˈtrœːstən) vt 1 console. 2 put off.

vertun* (fɛrˈtuːn) vt spend, squander.

vertuschen (fɛrˈtuʃən) vt hush up.

verunglimpfen (fɛrˈunglimpfən) vt disparage, slander.

verunglücken (fɛrˈunglykən) vi 1 meet with or have an accident. 2 perish.

verursachen (fɛrˈuːrzaxən) vt cause.

verurteilen (fɛrˈuːrtailən) vt condemn, sentence.

vervielfältigen (fɛrˈfiːlfɛltigən) vt 1 reproduce. 2 multiply.

vervollkommnen (fɛrˈfɔlkɔmnən) vt perfect.

vervollständigen (fɛrˈfɔlʃtɛndigən) vt complete.

verwachsen* (fɛrˈvaksən) vi 1 grow out of (clothes). 2 grow deformed. 3 heal, close up. 4 become involved, be closely connected (with). adj 1 deformed, stunted. 2 healed. 3 overgrown.

verwahren (fɛrˈvaːrən) vt keep (safe).

verwahrlost (fɛrˈvaːrloːst) adj 1 depraved. 2 neglected, unkempt.

verwalt/en (fɛrˈvaltən) vt 1 administer, administrate. 2 supervise, control. **—er** nm — 1 administrator, controller. 2 steward. **—ung** nf **—en** administration. **—ungsbeamte(r)** nm Civil Servant.

verwandt (fɛrˈvant) adj related. **—e(r)** nm

relative, relation. **—schaft** nf -en 1 relations. 2 relationship.

verwaschen (fɛrˈvaʃən) adj faded.

verwechseln (fɛrˈvɛksəln) vt mistake (for), confuse.

verwegen (fɛrˈveːgən) adj bold.

verweichlicht (fɛrˈvaiçliçt) adj effeminate.

verweigern (fɛrˈvaigərn) vt refuse, deny.

verweilen (fɛrˈvailən) vi linger, stay.

Verweis (fɛrˈvais) nm -e reprimand, reproach. **—en*** (fɛrˈvaizən) vt 1 banish, expel. 2 reprimand.

verwenden (fɛrˈvɛndən) vt use, apply.

verwerf/en* (fɛrˈvɛrfən) vt refuse, reject. **—lich** adj objectionable.

verwesen (fɛrˈveːsən) vi decay, rot. vt administer.

verwickeln (fɛrˈvikəln) vt entangle, involve.

verwirken (fɛrˈvirkən) vt 1 forfeit. 2 incur.

verwirklichen (fɛrˈvirkliçən) vt realize. vi be realized, materialize.

verwirren (fɛrˈvirən) vt 1 confuse. 2 entangle.

verwischen (fɛrˈviʃən) vt 1 wipe or blot out. 2 blur.

verwöhnen (fɛrˈvœːnən) vt spoil, pamper.

verworfen (fɛrˈvɔrfən) adj depraved.

verworren (fɛrˈvɔrən) adj 1 confused. 2 tangled.

verwund/en¹ (fɛrˈvundən) vt wound, hurt. **—ete(r)** nm injured person, casualty.

verwunden² (fɛrˈvundən) adj twisted.

verwundern (fɛrˈvundərn) vt astonish. **sich verwundern** vr wonder.

verwünschen (fɛrˈvynʃən) vt curse.

verwüsten (fɛrˈvyːstən) vt lay waste.

verzagt (fɛrˈtsaːkt) adj despondent, depressed.

verzaubern (fɛrˈtsaubərn) vt enchant, bewitch.

verzehren (fɛrˈtseːrən) vt consume.

verzeichn/en (fɛrˈtsaiçnən) vt catalogue, enter. **—is** n neu -se 1 list, register. 2 index.

verzeih/en* (fɛrˈtsaiən) vt forgive, pardon. **—ung** nf pardon. interj excuse me! sorry!

verzerren (fɛrˈtsɛrən) vt distort.

Verzicht (fɛrˈtsiçt) nm -e renunciation. **—en** vi renounce.

verzögern (fɛrˈtsøːgərn) vt delay.

verzollen (fɛrˈtsɔlən) vt pay duty on.

verzuckern (fɛrˈtsukərn) vt sweeten, sugar.

verzückt (fɛrˈtsykt) adj enraptured.

verzweif/eln (fɛrˈtsvaifəln) vi despair. **—lung** nf despair, desperation.

sich verzweigen (fɛrˈtsvaigən) vr branch out or off.

verzwickt (fɛr'tsvikt) adj complicated, involved, awkward.

Veterinär (veteri'nɛ:r) nm -e veterinary surgeon.

Vetter ('fɛtər) nm -n (male) cousin.

Vieh (fi:) n neu 1 cattle. 2 beast. —**isch** adj 1 bestial. 2 brutal.

viel (fi:l) adj,adv much. adj pl many. —**erlei** ('fi:lərlai) adj of many kinds. —**fach** ('fi:lfax) adj also —**fältig** (fi:lfɛltiç) manifold, multiple. —**leicht** (fi:'laiçt) adv perhaps, maybe, possibly. —**mal(s)** adv many times, frequently, often. —**mehr** (fi:l'me:r) adv rather. —**seitig** ('fi:lzaitiç) adj many-sided.

vier (fi:r) adj,nf four. —**eck** ('fi:rɛk) n neu square. —**eckig** adj square. —**te** adj fourth. —**tel** n neu — quarter. —**teljährlich** ('fi:rtəljɛːrliç) adj quarterly. —**telstunde** (fi:rtəl'ʃtundə) nf quarter of an hour.

vierzehn ('fi:rtseːn) adj,nf fourteen. —**te** adj fourteenth.

vierzig ('fi:rtsiç) adj,nf forty. —**ste** adj fortieth.

Villa ('vila) nf Villen villa.

Vio/la (vi'o:la) nf -len viola. —**line** (vio'li:nə) nf -n violin.

Visum ('vi:zum) n neu -sa visa.

Vlies (fli:s) n neu -e fleece.

Vogel ('fo:gəl) nm ⁼ bird. —**scheuche** nf -en scarecrow.

Vogesen (vo'ge:zən) n pl Vosges.

Vokabel (vo'ka:bəl) nf -n word.

Vokal (vo'ka:l) nm -e vowel.

Volk (fɔlk) n neu ⁼er 1 people, folk. 2 nation, race.

Völkerbund ('fœlkərbunt) nm League of Nations.

Völkerkunde ('fœlkərkundə) nf ethnology.

Völkerrecht ('fœlkərrɛçt) n neu international law.

volkreich ('fɔlkraiç) adj populous.

Volksabstimmung ('fɔlksapʃtimuŋ) nf plebiscite, referendum.

volkseigen ('fɔlksaigən) adj nationalized.

Volkskunde ('fɔlkskundə) nf folklore.

Volkslied ('fɔlksli:t) n neu folksong.

Volksschule ('fɔlksʃuːlə) nf primary school.

volkstümlich ('fɔlksty:mliç) adj 1 popular. 2 national.

Volkswirtschaft ('fɔlksvirtʃaft) nf economics.

voll (fɔl) adj 1 full. 2 complete. —**bringen** (fɔl'briŋən) vt accomplish. —**enden** (fɔl'ɛndən) vt 1 finish, end. 2 complete. —**ig** ('fœliç) adv fully, completely, totally. —**jährig** ('fɔljɛ:riç) adj of age. —**kommen** (fɔl'kɔmən)

adj perfect. —**macht** nf 1 power of attorney. 2 proxy. —**ständig** adj complete. —**strekken** vt carry out, execute. —**ziehen**° (fɔl'tsi:ən) vt carry out, accomplish.

Volontär (volɔn'tɛ:r) nm -e volunteer, trainee.

vom (fɔm) contraction of **von dem.**

von (fɔn) prep 1 of. 2 from. 3 by. **von...an** from, since. —**nöten** (fɔn'nœ:tən) adj necessary.

vor (fo:r) prep before, in front of. —**ab** (fo:r'ap) adv 1 first (of all). 2 in advance.

Vorabend ('fo:ra:bənt) nm eve.

Vorahnung ('fo:ra:nuŋ) nf premonition.

voran (fo'ran) adv before, ahead. —**gehen**° vi go at the head, precede.

voraus (fo'raus) adv in advance, in front, ahead. **im voraus** in advance, beforehand. —**sage** nf prediction. —**sagen** vt predict, forecast. —**setzung** nf -en 1 (pre)condition, prerequisite. 2 assumption. —**sichtlich** adj probable.

Vorbau ('fo:rbau) nm -ten 1 front structure. 2 porch.

Vorbedacht ('fo:rbədaxt) nm forethought, premeditation.

Vorbedingung ('fo:rbədiŋuŋ) nf condition, prerequisite.

Vorbehalt ('fo:rbəhalt) nm -e 1 reservation. 2 proviso. —**en**° vt reserve.

vorbei (fɔr'bai) adv 1 by, along, past. 2 past, done, over. —**gehen**° vi go past, pass (by).

vorbereit/en ('fo:rbəraitən) vt prepare. —**ung** nf -en preparation.

vorbeug/en ('fo:rbɔygən) vi prevent. —**ung** nf prevention.

Vorbild ('fo:rbilt) n neu 1 model. 2 original. —**lich** adj 1 model. 2 typical.

vorbringen° ('fo:rbriŋən) vt 1 bring forward or up. 2 propose. 3 argue.

vordem (fɔr'de:m) adv formerly.

vorder ('fɔrdər) adj front, fore. —**asien** (fɔrdər-'a:ziən) n neu Near East. —**grund** nm foreground. —**hand** adv for the present.

vordring/en° ('fo:rdriŋən) vi advance, press on or forward. —**lich** adj 1 urgent. 2 intrusive.

voreilig ('fo:railiç) adj hasty, premature.

voreingenommen ('fo:raingənɔmən) adj biased, prejudiced.

vorenthalten° ('fo:rɛnthaltən) vt withhold.

vorerst ('fo:re:rst) adv 1 first of all. 2 for the present.

vorerwähnt ('fo:rɛrvɛ:nt) adj above-mentioned, aforesaid.

Vorfahr ('fo:rfa:r) *nm* **-en** ancestor.
Vorfahrt ('fo:rfa:rt) *nf also* **Vorfahrt(s)recht** *n neu* mot right-of-way, priority.
Vorfall ('fo:rfal) *nm* incident, occurrence.
vorführen ('fo:rfy:rən) *vt* 1 present, perform, display. 2 project (films).
Vorgang ('fo:rgaŋ) *nm* 1 proceedings. 2 event. 3 precedent. **—er** ('fo:rgɛŋər) *nm* — predecessor.
vorgeb/en ('fo:rge:bən) *vt* pretend, feign. **—lich** ('fo:rgepliç) *adj* alleged, pretended.
vorgefaßt ('fo:rgəfast) *adj* preconceived.
vorgehen ('fo:rge:ən) *vi* 1 go forward, first, or before. 2 (of a clock) be fast. 3 occur. *n neu* — 1 procedure. 2 *law* action.
vorgenannt ('fo:rgənant) *adj* aforementioned.
Vorgeschichte ('fo:rgəʃiçtə) *nf* prehistory.
Vorgeschmack ('fo:rgəʃmak) *nm* foretaste.
Vorgesetzte(r) ('fo:rgəzɛtstə) *nm* superior, senior.
vorgestern ('fo:rgɛstərn) *adv* the day before yesterday.
vorhaben ('fo:rha:bən) *vt* intend. *n neu* — plan, purpose.
Vorhalle ('fo:rhalə) *nf* entrance-hall, porch.
vorhanden ('fo:rhandən) *adj* 1 available. 2 existing.
Vorhang ('fo:rhaŋ) *nm* curtain.
vorher (fo:r'he:r) *adv* previously, before(hand). **—ig** *adj* previous.
vorhin (fo:r'hin) *adv* a little while ago.
Vorhut ('fo:rhu:t) *nf* **-en** vanguard.
vorig ('fo:riç) *adj* former, preceding, previous.
vorjährig ('fo:rjɛ:riç) *adj* last year's.
Vorkehrung ('fo:rke:ruŋ) *nf* **-en** 1 precaution. 2 provision.
Vorkenntnis ('fo:rkɛntnis) *nf* **-se** previous experience or knowledge.
vorkommen ('fo:rkɔmən) *vi* 1 happen, occur. 2 be found.
vorlad/en ('fo:rla:dən) *vt law* summon. **—ung** *nf* **-en** summons.
vorläufig ('fo:rlɔyfiç) *adj* provisional, preliminary, tentative.
vorlaut ('fo:rlaut) *adj* presumptuous, impudent.
vorlegen ('fo:rle:gən) *vt* 1 propose. 2 display. 3 submit.
vorles/en ('fo:rle:zən) *vt* read aloud. **—ung** *nf* **-en** 1 lecture. 2 reading.
vorletzt ('fo:rlɛtst) *adj* penultimate.
Vorliebe ('fo:rli:bə) *nf* preference, fondness.
vorliegen (fo:r'li:gən) *vi* be present or at hand.
vormals ('fo:rma:ls) *adv* formerly.

vormerken ('fo:rmɛrkən) *vt* note (down).
Vormittag ('fo:rmita:k) *nm* morning. **—s** *adv* in the morning.
Vormund ('fo:rmunt) *nm* **:er** guardian.
vorn (fɔrn) *adv* in front, before, ahead. **von vornherein** from the first or start.
Vorname ('fo:rna:mə) *nm* first or Christian name.
vornehm ('fo:rne:m) *adj* 1 distinguished, noble. 2 elegant. **—en** *vt* 1 put on (an apron). 2 undertake. **sich —en** *vr* resolve (to do something). **—lich** *adj* chiefly, especially.
Vorort ('fo:rɔrt) *nm* suburb.
Vorposten ('fo:rpɔstən) *nm* outpost.
Vorrang ('fo:rraŋ) *nm* precedence, priority.
Vorrat ('fo:rra:t) *nm* stock, store, supply.
Vorrede ('fo:rre:də) *nf* 1 preface. 2 introduction.
vorrücken ('fo:rrykən) *vt,vi* move forward.
Vorsatz ('fo:rzats) *nm* 1 purpose. 2 intention.
Vorschau ('fo:rʃau) *nf* 1 preview. 2 trailer (for a film).
Vorschein ('fo:rʃain) *nm* appearance.
vorschieben ('fo:rʃi:bən) *vt* 1 push forward. 2 pretend. 3 plead.
Vorschlag ('fo:rʃla:k) *nm* suggestion, proposal. **—en** *vt* propose, suggest.
vorschreiben ('fo:rʃraibən) *vt* prescribe, order.
Vorschrift ('fo:rʃrift) *nf* 1 decree. 2 regulation. 3 instructions. 4 prescription.
Vorschub ('fo:rʃu:p) *nm* aid, help, assistance.
Vorschuß ('fo:rʃus) *nm* advance (of money).
Vorsehung ('fo:rse:uŋ) *nf* **-en** providence.
vorsetzen ('fo:rzɛtsən) *vt* 1 set over. 2 put forward. 3 appoint. 4 prefix. 5 offer.
Vorsicht ('fo:rziçt) *nf* caution. **—ig** *adj* cautious.
Vorsilbe ('fo:rzilbə) *nf* prefix.
Vorsitz ('fo:rzits) *nm* chair(manship). **—ende(r)** *nm* chairman, president.
Vorsorg/e ('fo:rzɔrgə) *nf* 1 care. 2 provision. **—en** *vi* provide (for). **—lich** ('fo:rzɔrkliç) *adj* provident.
Vorspeise ('fo:rʃpaizə) *nf* hors d'oeuvre.
vorspiegeln ('fo:rʃpi:gəln) *vt* simulate, pretend.
Vorspiel ('fo:rʃpi:l) *n neu* prelude.
vorspringen ('fo:rʃpriŋən) *vi* 1 project. 2 leap forward.
Vorsprung ('fo:rʃpruŋ) *nm* 1 projection. 2 advantage, start.
Vorstadt ('fo:rʃtat) *nf* suburb.
Vorstand ('fo:rʃtant) *nm* 1 board of directors. 2 executive, management.

vorsteh/en° ('fo:rʃteːən) *vi* 1 protrude. 2 head, manage. **—er** *nm* — superintendent, chief.

vorstell/en ('fo:rʃtɛlən) *vt* 1 introduce, present, put forward. 2 represent. **sich vorstellen** *vr* imagine. **—ung** *nf* 1 (re)presentation. 2 idea. 3 introduction. 4 performance.

Vorstoß ('fo:rʃtɔs) *nm* advance, attack. **—en°** *vi,vt* advance (suddenly).

vorstrecken ('fo:rʃtrɛkən) *vt* 1 stretch forward or out. 2 advance (money).

Vorstufe ('fo:rʃtuːfə) *nf* first step(s), preliminary or primary stage.

Vorteil ('fɔrtail) *nm* 1 advantage. 2 profit. **—haft** *adj* advantageous, profitable.

Vortrag ('fo:rtraːk) *nm* **ː̈e** 1 lecture. 2 report. 3 delivery, performance. 4 *comm* balance carried forward. **—en°** ('fo:rtraːgən) *vt* 1 lecture (on). 2 *comm* carry forward. 3 perform.

vortrefflich (fo:r'trɛfliç) *adj* excellent, admirable.

Vortritt ('fo:rtrit) *nm* precedence.

vorüber (fo'ry:bər) *adv* past, gone (by). **—gehen°** *vi* pass (by or over). **—gehend** *adj* passing, transitory.

Vorurteil ('fo:rurtail) *n neu* prejudice.

Vorwand ('fo:rvant) *nm* pretext.

vorwärts ('fo:rvɛrts) *adv* forward, onward.

vorweg (for'vɛk) *adv* before, beforehand. **—nehmen°** *vt* anticipate.

vorwerfen° ('fo:rvɛrfən) *vt* 1 reproach with. 2 throw forward.

vorwiegend ('fo:rviːgənt) *adj* predominant.

Vorwissen ('fo:rvisən) *n neu* previous knowledge.

Vorwort ('fo:rvɔrt) *n neu* **-e** 1 preface, foreword. 2 *gram* preposition.

Vorwurf ('fo:rvurf) *nm* 1 reproach. 2 subject, theme. **—svoll** *adj* reproachful.

Vorzeichen ('fo:rtsaiçən) *n neu* omen.

vorzeigen ('fo:rtsaigən) *vt* exhibit, show.

vorzeitig ('fo:rtsaitiç) *adj* premature.

vorziehen° ('fo:rtsiːən) *vt* 1 prefer. 2 draw (forward).

Vorzug ('fo:rtsuːk) *nm* 1 preference. 2 advantage. 3 priority. 4 good quality, merit. **ː̈lich** (for'tsy:kliç) *adj* excellent, superior.

vulgär (vul'gɛːr) *adj* vulgar.

Vulkan (vul'kaːn) *nm* **-e** volcano.

W

Waag/e ('vaːgə) *nf* **-n** 1 balance, scale. 2 Libra. **—recht** ('vaːkrɛçt) *adj* horizontal, level.

wabbelig ('vabəliç) *adj* flabby, wobbly.

Wabe ('vaːbə) *nf* **-n** honeycomb.

wach (vax) *adj* 1 awake. 2 alert, alive. **—e** *nf* **-n** guard, watch. **—en** *vi* 1 watch (over). 2 be awake. **—sam** *adj* watchful, alert.

Wachs (vaks) *n neu* **-e** wax.

wachs/en° ('vaksən) *vi* grow. **—tum** *n neu* growth.

Wacht (vaxt) *nf* **-en** guard. **ː̈er** ('vɛçtər) *nm* — guard, keeper, warder. **—meister** *nm* 1 policeman. 2 cavalry sergeant.

Wachtel ('vaxtəl) *nf* **-n** quail.

wackel/ig ('vakəliç) *adj* shaky, wobbly. **—n** *vi* shake, totter.

wacker ('vakər) *adj* 1 valiant. 2 decent.

Wade ('vaːdə) *nf* **-n** anat calf.

Waff/e ('vafə) *nf* **-n** weapon. **—enstillstand** *nm* armistice, truce, cease-fire.

Waffel ('vafəl) *nf* **-n** 1 waffle. 2 wafer.

wag/en ('vaːgən) *vt* risk, dare. **—emut** ('vaːgəmu:t) *nm* daring. **—halsig** ('vaːkhalsiç) *adj* reckless. **—nis** ('vaːknis) *n neu* **-se** risk.

Wagen ('vaːgən) *nm* — 1 car. 2 van, lorry. 3 carriage. 4 wagon, cart.

wägen° ('vɛːgən) *vt* weigh. **erst wägen, dann wagen** look before you leap.

Wahl (vaːl) *nf* **-en** 1 choice, selection. 2 election, vote. **ː̈en** ('vɛːlən) *vt* 1 choose, select. 2 elect, vote. 3 dial. **—er** ('vɛːlər) *nm* — voter. **ː̈erisch** ('vɛːləriʃ) *adj* fastidious. **ː̈erschaft** ('vɛːlərʃaft) *nf* **-en** voters. **—recht** *n neu* franchise, vote. **ː̈erscheibe** ('vɛːlərʃaibə) *nf* dial. **—stimme** *nf* vote. **—zettel** *nm* ballot paper.

Wahn (vaːn) *nm* 1 delusion, illusion. 2 madness, folly. **—bild** *n neu* 1 phantom. 2 hallucination. **—sinn** *nm* 1 madness, insanity. 2 frenzy. **—sinnig** *adj* mad, insane.

wahr (vaːr) *adj* true, real. **—haft** *adj* also **—haftig** 1 truthful, true. 2 genuine. **—haftigkeit** *nf* truthfulness. **—heit** *nf* **-en** truth. **—nehmen°** *vt* 1 perceive, notice. 2 protect (interests). **—sagen** *vt* prophesy. **—scheinlich** (vaːr'ʃainliç) *adj* probable, likely. **—scheinlichkeit** (vaːr'ʃainliçkait) *nf*

-en probability. **—zeichen** *n neu* **1** token. **2** emblem.

wahren ('va:rən) *vt* **1** defend. **2** maintain.

während ('vɛ:rənt) *prep* during. *conj* while. **—dem** (vɛ:rənt'de:m) *adv also* **—des** or **—dessen** meanwhile.

Währung ('vɛ:ruŋ) *nf* **-en** currency, standard.

Waise ('vaizə) *nf* **-n** *also* **Waisenkind** *n neu* orphan. **—nhaus** *n neu* orphanage.

Wal (va:l) *nm* **-e** *also* **Walfisch** ('va:lfiʃ) whale. **—fischspeck** *nm* blubber.

Wald (valt) *nm* **̈-er** wood, forest.

Wall (val) *nm* **̈-e 1** rampart. **2** dam, dike.

wall/en¹ ('valən) *vi see* **wallfahren.**

wall/en² ('valən) *vi* **1** boil (up). **2** flutter. **—ung** *nf* **-en 1** agitation. **2** boiling.

wallfahr/en* ('valfa:rən) *vi* go on a pilgrimage. **—er** *nm* pilgrim. **—t** *nf* pilgrimage.

Walnuß ('valnus) *nf* walnut.

Walroß ('valrɔs) *n neu* **-rosse** walrus.

Walz/e ('valtsə) *nf* **-n** *tech* roller, drum. **—en** *vi* waltz. *vt* roll, crush. **—er** ('valtsər) *nm* — waltz.

Wand (vant) *nf* **̈-e** wall. **—karte** *nf* wall map.

Wand/el ('vandəl) *nm* **1** change, transformation. **2** conduct. **—eln** *vt* change. *vi* wander. **—lung** *nf* **-en** change, transformation.

Wander/er ('vandərər) *nm* — wanderer, rambler. **—lust** *nf* love of rambling or travelling. **—n** *vi* **1** walk, hike. **2** migrate. **—ung** *nf* **-en 1** hike, excursion. **2** migration.

wandte ('vantə) *v see* **wenden.**

Wange ('vaŋə) *nf* **-n** cheek.

wanken ('vaŋkən) *vi* **1** sway, shake. **2** waver.

wann (van) *conj,adv* when.

Wanne ('vanə) *nf* **-n** tub, bath.

Wanze ('vantsə) *nf* **-n** bug, bedbug.

Wappen ('vapən) *n neu* — (coat of) arms.

war (va:r) *v see* **sein².**

wäre ('vɛ:rə) *v see* **sein².**

Ware ('va:rə) *nf* **-n 1** article, ware. **2** *pl* merchandise, goods. **—nhaus** *n neu* department store. **—nzeichen** *n neu* trademark.

warf (va:rf) *v see* **werfen.**

warm (varm) *adj* warm, hot. **-e 1** ('vɛrmə) *nf* warmth. **̈-en** ('vɛrmən) *vt* warm. **̈-flasche** ('vɛrmflaʃə) *nf* hot-water bottle.

warn/en* ('varnən) *vt* warn. **—ung** *nf* **-en** warning.

Warschau ('varʃau) *n neu* Warsaw.

wart/en ('vartən) *vi* wait. *vt* look after. **̈-er** ('vɛrtər) *nm* — attendant, keeper. **—esaal** *nm* waiting room.

warum (va'rum) *adv* why.

Warze ('va:rtsə) *nf* **-n** wart.

was (vas) *pron* what, (that) which.

wasch/en* ('vaʃən) *vt,vi* wash. **—automat** ('vaʃautoma:t) *nm* automatic washing machine. **—becken** *n neu* hand-basin, wash-basin. **̈-e** ('vɛʃə) *nf* **1** wash(ing). **2** underwear. **—echt** *adj* **1** (of colour) fast. **2** genuine. **̈-erei** (vɛʃə'rai) *nf* laundry. **—lappen** *nm* face cloth. **—maschine** *nf* washing machine. **—mittel** *n neu* soap powder, detergent.

Wasser ('vasər) *n neu* **̈-** water. **—dicht** *adj* watertight, waterproof. **—fall** *nm* waterfall. **—hahn** *nm* tap. **—ig** ('vɛsəriç) *adj* watery. **—leitung** *nf* water supply. **—mann** *nm* Aquarius. **̈-n** ('vɛsərn) *vt* **1** water, irrigate. **2** soak. **—stoff** *nm* hydrogen.

Watte ('vatə) *nf* **-n 1** wadding. **2** cotton wool.

weben* ('ve:bən) *vt* weave. **—er** *nm* — weaver.

Wechsel ('vɛksəl) *nm* — **1** (ex)change. **2** bill of exchange. **—geld** *n neu* (small) change. **—n** *vt,vi* **1** change. **2** exchange. **3** vary.

weck/en* ('vɛkən) *vt* wake, rouse. **—er** *nm* — alarm clock.

wedeln ('ve:dəln) *vi* **1** fan. **2** wag.

weder ('ve:dər) *conj* **weder...noch** neither ...nor.

weg (vɛk) *adv* **1** away. **2** gone. **3** off.

Weg (ve:k) *nm* **-e 1** way, route. **2** path. **3** road. **—weiser** ('ve:kvaizər) *nm* — **1** signpost. **2** guide.

wegbleiben* ('vɛkblaibən) *vi* **1** stay away. **2** be omitted.

wegblicken ('vɛkblikən) *vi* look away.

wegen ('ve:gən) *prep* **1** because of. **2** for.

weggehen* ('vɛkge:ən) *vi* depart, leave.

weglassen* ('vɛklasən) *vt* **1** omit. **2** let go.

wegmüssen* ('vɛkmysən) *vi* have to go, be obliged to leave.

wegräumen ('vɛkrɔymən) *vt* clear away.

wegreißen* ('vɛkraisən) *vt* tear or snatch away.

wegschaffen* ('vɛkʃafən) *vt* get rid of.

wegtun* ('vɛktu:n) *vt* put away.

wegwerfen* ('vɛkvɛrfən) *vt* throw away or out.

weh (ve:) *adj* **1** sore, painful. **2** sad. *interj* woe! **weh tun** hurt, be painful. ~*n neu* **-e 1** pain. **2** grief. **—en** *n pl* labour pains. **—mut** *nf* melancholy.

Weh/e ('ve:ə) *nf* **-n** (snow)drift. **—en** *vi* blow.

Wehr¹ (ve:r) *nf* **-en 1** defence. **2** weapon. **3** bulwark. **—dienst** *nm* military service. **—en**

vt **1** restrain. **2** forbid. **sich —en** *vr* resist. **—macht** *nf* armed forces. **—pflicht** *nf* compulsory service, conscription.

Wehr² (ve:r) *n neu* **-e** weir.

Weib (vaip) *n neu* **-er** *inf* **1** woman, female. **2** wife. **—isch** ('vaibiʃ) *adj* effeminate, womanish. **—lich** *adj* feminine, female.

weich (vaiç) *adj* **1** soft. **2** smooth. **—lich** *adj* soft, effeminate. **—ling** *nm* **-e** weakling.

Weiche ('vaiçə) *nf* **-n 1** (railway) points. **2** *anat* flank.

weichen* (vaiçən) *vi* **1** yield. **2** flinch.

Weichsel ('vaiksəl) *nf* Vistula.

Weide ('vaidə) *nf* **-n 1** pasture. **2** willow. **—n** *vi* graze. **sich —n** *vr* gloat.

sich weigern ('vaigərn) *vr* refuse.

Weih/e ('vaiə) *nf* **-n 1** consecration, dedication. **2** initiation. **—en** *vt* **1** consecrate, dedicate. **2** initiate. **—rauch** *nm* incense.

Weihnacht/en ('vainaxtən) *n pl* Christmas. **—slied** *n neu* carol.

weil (vail) *conj* because, since.

Weile ('vailə) *nf* **-n 1** while. **2** time.

Wein (vain) *nm* **-e 1** wine. **2** *also* **Weinstock** ('vainʃtɔk) *nm* vine. **—bau** *nm* vine-growing. **—lese** *nf* vintage, gathering, grape-harvest.

weinen ('vainən) *vi* cry, weep.

weis/e ('vaizə) *adj* wise, prudent. *nm* **-n** wise man, sage. **—heit** ('vaishait) *nf* wisdom. **—lich** (vaisliç) *adv* wisely.

Weise ('vaizə) *nf* **n 1** manner, way, method. **2** tune, melody.

weis/en* ('vaizən) *vt* indicate, show. **—ung** *nf* **-en** direction, instruction.

weiß¹ (vais) *adj,n neu* white. **—e(r)** *nm* white man. **—kohl** *nm* (white) cabbage.

weiß² (vais) *v* see **wissen**.

weit (vait) *adj* **1** distant. **2** wide. **—aus** (vait-'aus) *adv* by far. **—e** *nf* **-n 1** distance. **2** width. **3** scope, size. **—läufig** ('vaitlɔyfiç) *adj* **1** distant. **2** extensive. **3** diffuse. **—reichend** ('vaitraiçənt) *adj* far-reaching. **—sichtig** *adj* **1** long-sighted. **2** far-sighted.

weiter ('vaitər) *adj* **1** further. **2** farther. **3** wider. *adv* **1** further on. **2** else.

Weizen ('vaitsən) *nm* wheat.

welch (vɛlç) *pron* who, which, what, that. *pron,adj* some, any.

welk (vɛlk) *adj* withered, limp.

Welle ('vɛlə) *nf* **-n 1** wave. **2** axle. **3** shaft. **—nlänge** *nf* wavelength.

Welt (vɛlt) *nf* **-en** world. **—all** *n neu* universe. **—anschauung** *nf* philosophy of life, ideology.

—klug *adj* worldly-wise. **—lich** *adj* secular, worldly. **—macht** *nf* world power. **—männisch** ('vɛltmɛniʃ) *adj* sophisticated.

wem (ve:m) *pron* to whom.

wen (ve:n) *pron* whom.

Wend/e ('vɛndə) *nf* **-n** turn, turning point. **—en*** *vt* turn. **—epunkt** *nm* turning point, crisis. **—ung** *nf* **-en 1** turn(ing). **2** figure of speech.

wenig ('ve:niç) *adj,pron* **1** little. **2** *pl* few. **—st** *adj* least. **—stens** *adv* at least.

wer (ve:r) *pron* who, which.

werb/en* ('vɛrbən) *vi* **1** court. **2** advertise (for). *vt* recruit. **—ung** *nf* **-en 1** advertising. **2** recruiting. **3** courting.

Werdegang ('vɛrdəgaŋ) *nm* **1** career. **2** development.

werden* ('vɛrdən) *v mod aux* shall, will. *vi* **1** become. **2** happen. *n neu* **1** growth. **2** origin.

werfen* ('vɛrfən) *vt* throw. *vi* bring forth young.

Werft (vɛrft) *nf* **-en 1** shipyard. **2** wharf.

Werk (vɛrk) *n neu* **-e 1** work(s). **2** deed. **3** mechanism. **—statt** *nf* workshop. **—stoff** *nm* (raw) material. **—zeug** *n neu* tool.

Wermut ('ve:rmu:t) *nm* vermouth.

wert (vɛrt) *adj* **1** worth. **2** worthy. *nm* **-e** worth, value. **—brief** *nm* registered money letter. **—en** *vt* value. **—sache** *nf* valuable. **—voll** *adj* valuable.

Wesen ('ve:zən) *n neu* **— 1** being, creature. **2** essence, character. **3** way, manners. **4** fuss. **—tlich** *adj* **1** substantial. **2** essential.

weshalb (vɛs'halp) *adv,conj also* **weswegen** (vɛs've:gən) *why*, wherefore.

Wespe ('vɛspə) *nf* **-n** wasp.

wessen ('vɛsən) *pron* **1** of whom, whose. **2** of which, of what.

West (vɛst) *nm also* **West/en** ('vɛstən) west. **—deutschland** *n neu* West Germany. **—lich** *adj* west(ern), westerly. **—wärts** ('vɛstvɛrts) *adv* westward(s), west.

Westfalen (vɛst'fa:lən) *n neu* Westphalia.

Westindien (vɛst'indiən) *n neu* West Indies.

wett (vɛt) *adj* even, quits.

Wett/e ('vɛtə) *nf* **-n** bet, wager. **—büro** *n neu* betting shop or office. **—en** *vt,vi* bet, wager. **—kampf** *nm* competition, contest, match. **—laufen*** *vi* (run a) race.

Wetter ('vɛtər) *n neu* **— 1** weather. **2** storm. **—bericht** *nm* weather report or forecast.

wetzen ('vɛtsən) *vt* sharpen, whet.

wichtig ('viçtiç) *adj* important.

Widder ('vidər) *nm* **— 1** ram. **2** Aries.

wider ('vi:dər) *prep* against.

widerfahren* (vi:dər'fa:rən) *vi* happen (to).

Widerhaken ('vi:dərha:kən) *nm* barb, hook.

Widerhall ('vi:dərhal) *nm* **-e 1** echo. **2** response.

widerleg/en (vi:dər'le:gən) *vt* refute. **—ung** *nf* **-en** refutation.

widerlich ('vi:dərliç) *adj* repulsive.

widerrechtlich ('vi:dərrɛçtliç) *adj* illegal.

Widerruf ('vi:dərru:f) *nm* countermand, disavowal. **—en*** (vi:dər'ru:fən) *vt* revoke.

sich widersetz/en (vi:dər'zɛtsən) *vr* oppose. **—lich** *adj* insubordinate. **—lichkeit** *nf* insubordination.

widerspenstig ('vi:dərʃpɛnstiç) *adj* obstinate.

widersprechen* (vi:dər'ʃprɛçən) *vi* contradict.

Widerspruch ('vi:dərsprux) *nm* **1** opposition. **2** contradiction.

Widerstand ('vi:dərʃtant) *nm* **1** resistance. **2** opposition.

widerstehen* (vi:dər'ʃte:ən) *vi* withstand.

widerwärtig ('vi:dərvɛrtiç) *adj* disagreeable, offensive.

widerwillig ('vi:dərviliç) *adj* unwilling.

widmen ('vitmən) *vt* dedicate, devote.

widrig ('vi:driç) *adj* adverse, contrary. **—enfalls** ('vi:driɡənfals) *adv* failing which.

wie (vi:) *adv* how. *conj* **1** how. **2** as. **3** like.

wieder ('vi:dər) *adv* **1** again. **2** back.

Wiederaufnahme (vi:dər'aufna:mə) *nf* **-n** resumption.

wiederbringen* ('vi:dərbriŋən) *vt* bring back, restore.

wiedererkennen* ('vi:dərɛrkɛnən) *vt* recognize.

Wiedergabe ('vi:dərga:bə) *nf* **1** restitution. **2** reproduction.

wiedergeben* ('vi:dərge:bən) *vt* **1** return. **2** reproduce.

Wiedergeburt ('vi:dərgəbu:rt) *nf* **1** rebirth, regeneration. **2** reincarnation.

wiedergutmachen (vi:dər'gu:tmaxən) *vt* compensate for.

wiederhol/en (vi:dər'ho:lən) *vt* repeat. **—ung** *nf* repetition.

wiederhören ('vi:dərhœ:rən) *vt* hear again. **auf Wiederhören** (in a telephone conversation) goodbye.

wiederkäuen ('vi:dərkɔyən) *vt* ruminate.

wiederkehren ('vi:dərke:rən) *vi* return.

wiederkommen* ('vi:dərkɔmən) *vi* come back.

wiedersehen* ('vi:dərze:ən) *vt* see again. **auf Wiedersehen** goodbye.

wiederum ('vi:dərum) *adv* again, anew.

Wieg/e ('vi:gə) *nf* **-n** cradle. **—enlied** *n* neu lullaby.

wiegen* ('vi:gən) *vt,vi* weigh.

Wien (vi:n) *n* neu Vienna.

wies (vi:s) *v* see **weisen.**

Wiese ('vi:zə) *nf* **-n** meadow.

Wiesel ('vi:zəl) *n* neu **—** weasel.

wieso ('vi:zo:) *adv* why.

wieviel (vi:'fi:l) *adv* how much.

wild (vilt) *adj* **1** wild, savage. **2** fierce. **3** angry. *n* neu game. **—dieb** *nm* poacher. **—ern** ('vildərn) *vi* poach. **—hüter** *nm* gamekeeper. **—nis** *nf* **-se** wilderness.

will (vil) *v* see **wollen.**

Will/e ('vilə) *nm* **-n** will. **—enlos** *adj* irresolute, half-hearted. **—enskraft** *nf* will-power. **—kommen** (vil'kɔmən) *adj,n* neu,interj welcome. **—kür** ('vilky:r) *nf* discretion, choice. **—kürlich** ('vilky:rliç) *adj* arbitrary.

wimmeln ('viməln) *vi* swarm (with).

Wimper ('vimpər) *nf* **-n** eyelash. **ohne mit der Wimper zu zucken** without batting an eyelid.

Wind (vint) *nm* **-e** wind. **—beutel** *nm* **1** eclair. **2** *sl* windbag. **—hund** *nm* greyhound. **—ig** ('vindiç) *adj* windy. **—schutzscheibe** *nf* windscreen. **—stille** *nf* calm, lull.

Winde ('vində) *nf* **-n** winch, reel.

Windel ('vindəl) *nf* **-n** nappy.

winden* ('vindən) *vt* wind.

Wink (viŋk) *nm* **-e 1** sign. **2** nod. **3** wave. **—en** *vi* **1** make a sign. **2** wink. **3** wave. **4** nod.

Wink/el ('viŋkəl) *nm* **— 1** angle. **2** corner. **3** nook. **—elmesser** *nm* protractor. **—lig** ('viŋkliç) *adj* angular.

winseln ('vinzəln) *vi* whimper, whine.

Winter ('vintər) *nm* **—** winter. **—lich** *adj* wintry.

Winzer ('vintsər) *nm* **—** vine-grower.

winzig ('vintsiç) *adj* tiny, minute.

Wipfel ('vipfəl) *nm* **—** treetop.

Wippe ('vipə) *nf* **-n** seesaw.

wir (vi:r) *pron* 1st pers pl we.

Wirbel ('virbəl) *nm* **— 1** whirl, eddy. **2** vertebra. **3** peg. **—n** *vi* whirl, swirl. **—säule** *nf* spine, vertebral column.

wird (virt) *v* see **werden.**

wirk/en ('virkən) *vi* work. *vt* **1** work. **2** effect. **3** weave. **—sam** *adj* effective. **—ung** *nf* **-en 1** effect, result. **2** action.

wirklich ('virkliç) *adj* real, actual. **—keit** *nf* **-en** reality.

wirr (vir) *adj* confused, chaotic. **—warr** ('virvar) *nm* muddle, disorder.

wirst (virst) *v see* **werden.**

Wirt (virt) *nm* **-e 1** host. **2** innkeeper, landlord. **—in** *nf* **-nen 1** hostess. **2** landlady. **—schaft** *nf* **-en 1** economy. **2** housekeeping, household. **3** inn, pub. **—schaften** *vi* **1** keep house. **2** manage (well). **—schaft(l)er** *nm* — manager. **—schaftlich** *adj* **1** economic. **2** economical. **—schaftsprüfer** *nm* — chartered accountant. **—shaus** *n neu* inn, pub.

wisch/en ('viʃən) *vt* wipe, rub. **—lappen** *nm* — duster.

wispern ('vispərn) *vi,vt* whisper.

Wißbegier ('visbəgi:r) *nf also* **Wißbegierde** *nf* craving for knowledge, curiosity. **—ig** *adj* eager to learn, inquisitive.

wissen* ('visən) *vt,vi* know. *n neu* knowledge, learning.

Wissenschaft ('visənʃaft) *nf* **-en 1** science. **2** learning. **—ler** *nm* — **1** scientist. **2** scholar. **—lich** *adj* **1** scientific. **2** learned, scholarly.

wittern ('vitərn) *vt* scent, smell.

Witwe ('vitvə) *nf* **-n** widow. **—r** ('vitvər) *nm* — widower.

Witz (vits) *nm* **-e 1** joke. **2** wit. **—eln** *vi* joke. **—ig** *adj* witty.

wo (vo:) *adv,conj* where.

woanders (vo:'andərs) *adv* elsewhere.

wobei (vo:'bai) *adv* whereby. *pron* **1** in or at which. **2** in doing which.

Woche ('vɔxə) *nf* **-n** week. **—nblatt** *n neu* weekly (newspaper). **—nende** *n neu* week end. **—ntlich** ('vœçəntliç) *adj* weekly.

wodurch (vo:'durç) *adv* whereby. *pron* **1** by or through which. **2** in doing which.

wofür (vo:'fy:r) *adv,pron* for which.

wog (vo:k) *v see* **wiegen.**

wogegen (vo:'ge:gən) *adv* in return for which. *conj* whereas.

woher (vo:'he:r) *adv* whence, wherefrom.

wohin (vo:'hin) *adv* whither, (to) where.

wohl (vo:l) *adv* **1** well. **2** probably, presumably. *n neu* welfare, wellbeing.

wohlan (vo:l'an) *interj* come on! well!

wohlauf (vo:l'auf) *adv* well. *interj* well then!

Wohlbehagen ('vo:lbəha:gən) *n neu* comfort.

Wohlfahrt ('vo:lfa:rt) *nf* welfare. **—sstaat** *nm* welfare state. **—sgesellschaft** *nf* affluent society.

wohlfeil ('vo:lfail) *adj* cheap.

wohlhabend ('vo:lha:bənt) *adj* well-off, prosperous.

Wohlklang ('vo:lklaŋ) *nm* harmony.

Wohlstand ('vo:lʃtant) *nm* prosperity.

Wohltat ('vo:lta:t) *nf* benefit. **—er** ('vo:ltɛ:tər) *nm* benefactor.

wohltun* ('vo:ltu:n) *vi* do good, benefit.

Wohlwollen ('vo:lvɔlən) *n neu* goodwill, favour.

wohn/en ('vo:nən) *vi* live, dwell. **—haft** *adj* resident. **—ung** *nf* **-en 1** dwelling, residence. **2** flat, apartment. **—wagen** *nm* caravan. **—zimmer** *n neu* sitting room.

Wölbung ('vœlbuŋ) *nf* **-en 1** vault. **2** dome. **3** arch.

Wolf (vɔlf) *nm* **-e** wolf.

Wolk/e ('vɔlkə) *nf* **-n** cloud. **—enkratzer** *nm* — skyscraper. **—ig** *adj* cloudy, clouded.

Woll/e ('vɔlə) *nf* **-n** wool. **—en** *adj* woollen. **—ig** *adj* woolly, fleecy. **—jacke** *nf* cardigan.

wollen* ('vɔlən) *vi,vt* want, desire. *v mod aux* **1** want or desire (to). **2** intend (to). **3** be about (to).

Wollust ('vɔlust) *nf* **-e** sensual pleasure, lust.

womit (vo:'mit) *adv* with or by which.

womöglich (vo:'mœ:kliç) *adv* where or if possible.

wonach (vo:'na:x) *adv* **1** according to which. **2** after which.

Wonne ('vɔnə) *nf* **-n** delight, joy, bliss.

woran (vo:'ran) *adv,pron* at or about which or what.

worauf (vo:'rauf) *adv,pron* (up)on which or what.

woraus (vo:'raus) *adv,pron* of or from which or what.

worden ('vɔrdən) *v see* **werden.**

worin (vo:'rin) *adv* in(to) which or what.

Wort (vɔrt) *n neu* **-er** (written) word. *n neu* **-e 1** (spoken) word, expression. **2** word, pledge. **—bruch** *nm* breach of one's word. **—erbuch** ('vœrtərbu:x) *n neu* dictionary. **—führer** *nm* **1** spokesman. **2** speaker. **—karg** *adj* taciturn. **—laut** *nm* wording, text. **—lich** ('vœrtliç) *adj* **1** literal. **2** verbal. **3** word-for-word. **—reich** *adj* verbose. **—schatz** *nm* vocabulary.

wovon (vo:'fɔn) *adv,pron* of or from which or what.

wozu (vo:'tsu:) *adv,pron* **1** to or for what, why. **2** in addition to which.

Wrack (vrak) *n neu* **-s** naut wreck.

wringen* ('vriŋən) *vt* wring.

Wucher ('vu:xər) *nm* **1** usury. **2** profiteering. **—er** *nm* — **1** usurer. **2** profiteer. **—isch** *adj* **1** usurious. **2** profiteering. **—n** *vi* grow luxuriantly or abundantly. **2** profiteer.

Wuchs (vu:ks) *nm* 1 growth. 2 figure, size.
Wucht (vuxt) *nf* -en force, weight.
wühl/en ('vy:lən) *vt* stir up, agitate. *vi* burrow.
— **er** *nm* — agitator.
Wulst (vulst) *nm* ⸚e 1 roll, pad. 2 swelling.
wund (vunt) *adj* 1 sore. 2 wounded. — **e**
('vundə) *nf* -en wound.
Wunder ('vundər) *n neu* — 1 miracle. 2
wonder. — **bar** *adj* wonderful, marvellous.
— **kind** *n neu* child prodigy. — **lich** *adj*
strange, odd. — **n** *vt* astound, surprise. **sich**
— **n** *vr* wonder (at). — **schön** *adj* beautiful,
exquisite.
Wunsch (vunʃ) *nm* ⸚e wish, desire. — **en**
('vynʃən) *vt* wish, desire. — **enswert** ('vyn-
ʃənsveːrt) *adj* desirable.
wurde ('vuːrdə) *v* see **werden.**
würde ('vyrdə) *v* see **werden.**
Würd/e ('vyrdə) *nf* -n 1 dignity, honour. 2
rank. — **enträger** *nm* dignitary. — **ig** *adj*
worthy.
Wurf (vurf) *nm* ⸚e 1 throw, cast. 2 litter,
brood. — **scheibe** *nf* discus.
Würfel ('vyrfəl) *nm* — 1 *game* die, dice. 2
cube. — **zucker** *nm* lump sugar.
würgen ('vyrgən) *vi,vt* choke.
Wurm (vurm) *nm* ⸚er worm.
Wurst (vurst) *nf* ⸚e sausage.
Württemberg ('vyrtəmbɛrk) *n neu* Wurtem-
berg.
Würz/e ('vyrtsə) *nf* -n 1 seasoning, spice. 2
flavour. — **en** *vt* season, spice. — **ig** *adj*
spicy, seasoned.
Wurzel ('vurtsəl) *nf* -n root. — **n** *vi* take root.
wußte ('vustə) *v* see **wissen.**
wüst (vy:st) *adj* 1 desert, waste. 2 disorderly. 3
depraved. — **e** *nf* -n desert, wilderness.
— **ling** *nm* -e libertine, depraved person.
Wut (vu:t) *nf* rage, fury. — **end** ('vy:tənt) *adj*
furious.

X

Xenophobie (ksɛnofo'bi:) *nf* xenophobia.
x-mal ('iksma:l) *adv inf* umpteen times.
Xylophon (ksylo'fo:n) *n neu* -e xylophone.

Z

Zack/e ('tsakə) *nf* -n *also* **Zack/en** *nm* — 1
prong. 2 tooth. 3 peak. — **en** *vt* 1 notch. 2
indent. — **ig** *adj* 1 jagged. 2 spirited.
zaghaft ('tsa:khaft) *adj* timid.
zäh (tsɛ:) *adj* 1 tough. 2 resistant. — **igkeit** *nf* 1
toughness. 2 pertinacity.
Zahl (tsa:l) *nf* -en number, numeral. — **bar** *adj*
payable. — **en** *vt,vi* pay. — **los** *adj* countless.
— **reich** *adj* numerous. — **tag** *nm* payday.
— **ung** *nf* -en payment. — **ungsfähig** *adj*
solvent. — **wort** *n neu* numeral.
zähl/en ('tsɛ:lən) *vt,vi* count, number. — **ung**
nf -en counting.
zahm (tsa:m) *adj* tame. — **en** ('tsɛ:mən) *vt* 1
tame. 2 break in (a horse).
Zahn (tsa:n) *nm* ⸚e tooth. — **arzt** *nm* dentist.
— **bürste** *nf* toothbrush. — **pasta** *nf* toothpaste. — **rad** *n neu* cog wheel. — **schmerz**
nm also — **weh** *n neu* toothache. — **stocher**
nm toothpick.
Zange ('tsaŋə) *nf* -n 1 pincers, tweezers. 2
tongs.
Zank (tsaŋk) *nm* ⸚e quarrel. — **en** *vi* quarrel.
— **isch** ('tsɛŋkiʃ) *adj* quarrelsome.
zapfen ('tsapfən) *vt* tap. *nm* — 1 bung, plug. 2
pin. 3 pivot.
zappeln ('tsapəln) *vi* 1 wriggle. 2 fidget.
Zar (tsa:r) *nm* -en tsar.
zart (tsa:rt) *adj* 1 tender. 2 delicate. — **lich**
('tsɛ:rtliç) *adj* tender, affectionate.
Zauber ('tsaubər) *nm* — 1 magic. 2 spell,
charm. — **ei** (tsaubə'rai) *nf* magic. — **er** *nm*
— magician, sorcerer. — **haft** *adj* 1 magical.
2 enchanting. — **n** *vi,vt* conjure (up).
zaudern ('tsaudərn) *vi* hesitate, delay. *n neu*
hesitation.
Zaum (tsaum) *nm* ⸚e bridle, rein. — **en**
('tsɔymən) *vt* bridle.
Zaun (tsaun) *nm* ⸚e fence.
Zeche ('tsɛçə) *nf* -n 1 bill. 2 mine.
Zehe ('tse:ə) *nf* -n toe.
zehn (tse:n) *adj,nf* ten. — **te** *adj* tenth.
zehren ('tse:rən) *vi* 1 feed. 2 waste (away).
Zeichen ('tsaiçən) *n neu* — 1 sign. 2 signal.
zeichn/en ('tsaiçnən) *vt* 1 draw. 2 mark. 3
design. 4 subscribe. — **er** *nm* — 1 designer.
2 draughtsman. 3 subscriber. — **ung** *nf* -en 1
drawing. 2 sketch. 3 design. 4 subscription.
Zeig/efinger ('tsaigəfiŋər) *nm* index finger.

—en vt show. **sich —en** vr appear. **—er** nm — hand, pointer.

Zeile (´tsailə) nf **-n** line.

Zeit (tsait) nf **-en** time. **zur Zeit** at present.

Zeitalter (´tsaitaltər) n neu age, era.

Zeitfolge (´tsaitfolgə) nf chronological order.

Zeitgenoss/e (´tsaitgənœsə) nm contemporary. **—isch** (´tsaitgənœsiʃ) adj contemporary.

zeitig (´tsaitiç) adj **1** early. **2** timely. **—en** vt **1** ripen, mature. **2** cause, produce.

Zeitkarte (´tsaitkartə) nf season ticket.

Zeitlang (´tsaitlaŋ) nf **eine Zeitlang** for some time.

zeitlich (´tsaitliç) adj temporal.

Zeitpunkt (´tsaitpuŋkt) nm **1** moment. **2** point.

Zeitraum (´tsaitraum) nm interval, period.

Zeitschrift (´tsaitʃrift) nf periodical, magazine.

Zeitung (´tsaituŋ) nf **-en** newspaper, journal. **—swesen** n neu journalism.

zeitweilig (´tsaitvailiç) adj **1** temporary. **2** intermittent.

zeitweise (´tsaitvaizə) adv **1** for a time. **2** at times.

Zeitwort (´tsaitvɔrt) n neu **—er** verb.

Zelle (´tsɛlə) nf **-n 1** cell. **2** call-box.

Zelt (tsɛlt) n neu **-e** tent. **—en** vi camp. n neu camping.

Zement (tse´mɛnt) nm **-e** cement.

Zensur (tsɛn´zu:r) nf **-en 1** censorship. **2** educ marks, report.

Zentimeter (tsɛnti´me.tər) nm,neu — centimetre.

Zentner (´tsɛntnər) nm — hundredweight, fifty kilograms.

zentral (tsɛn´tra:l) adj central. **-e** nf **-n 1** head office, headquarters. **2** power station. **—heizung** nf central heating. **—isieren** (tsɛntrali´zi:rən) vt centralize.

zerbrech/en* (tsɛr´brɛçən) vt,vi break into pieces, shatter. **—lich** adj fragile.

zerdrücken (tsɛr´drykən) vt crush, grind.

Zeremonie (tseremo´ni:) nf **-n** ceremony.

Zerfall (tsɛr´fal) nm decay, ruin. **—en*** vi fall into ruin, decay.

zerfetzen (tsɛr´fɛtsən) vt shred.

zergliedern (tsɛr´gli:dərn) vt **1** dismember. **2** analyse. **3** anat dissect.

zerhauen (tsɛr´hauən) vt cut up, mince.

zerlegen (tsɛr´le:gən) vt **1** take apart, divide, dissect. **2** analyse. **3** carve. **4** dispense.

zerlumpt (tsɛr´lumpt) adj ragged, tattered.

zermürben (tsɛr´myrbən) vt wear down.

zerplatzen (tsɛr´platsən) vi burst.

zerquetschen (tsɛr´kvɛtʃən) vt squash, crush.

Zerr/bild (´tsɛrbilt) n neu caricature. **—en** vt **1** tug, pull. **2** strain.

zerreiben* (tsɛr´raibən) vt grind, pulverize.

zerreißen* (tsɛr´raisən) vt,vi tear or rip up.

zerrinnen* (tsɛr´rinən) vi melt away, vanish.

zerschellen (tsɛr´ʃɛlən) vt,vi shatter, smash.

zerschlagen* (tsɛr´ʃla:gən) vt break into pieces. vi come to nothing.

zerschneiden* (tsɛr´ʃnaidən) vt cut up.

zersetz/en (tsɛr´zɛtsən) vt **1** decompose, disintegrate. **2** undermine. **—ung** nf decomposition.

zersplittern (tsɛr´ʃplitərn) vt split up, splinter.

zersprengen (tsɛr´ʃprɛŋən) vt blow up, burst.

zerstäub/en (tsɛr´ʃtɔybən) vt **1** spray. **2** disperse, scatter. **—er** nm — spray.

zerstör/en (tsɛr´ʃtœ:rən) vt destroy. **—er** nm — destroyer. **—ung** nf destruction.

zerstreu/en (tsɛr´ʃtrɔyən) vt **1** disperse, scatter. **2** diffuse. **3** divert, entertain, amuse. **—t** adj **1** absent-minded. **2** dispersed. **—theit** nf absent-mindedness. **—ung** nf **-en 1** dispersion. **2** amusement.

zerteilen (tsɛr´tailən) vt cut up, divide.

zertreten* (tsɛr´tre:tən) vt trample underfoot, stamp out.

zertrümmern (tsɛr´trymərn) vt lay waste, demolish, destroy, ruin.

zetern (´tse:tərn) vi **1** cry out (for help). **2** scold, nag.

Zettel (´tsɛtəl) nm — **1** sheet or slip of paper, note. **2** ticket. **3** label.

Zeug (tsɔyk) n neu **-e 1** thing. **2** stuff. **3** material, cloth. **—haus** n neu arsenal.

Zeug/e (´tsɔygə) nm **-n** witness. **—nis** (´tsɔyknis) n neu **-se 1** evidence, testimony. **2** certificate. **3** reference.

zeug/en[1] (´tsɔygən) vt produce, beget. **—ung** nf **-en** procreation.

zeugen[2] (´tsɔygən) vi give testimony, testify.

Zickzack (´tsiktsak) nm **-e** zigzag.

Ziege (´tsi:gə) nf **-n** (she-)goat.

Ziegel (´tsi:gəl) nm — **1** brick. **2** tile. **—ofen** nm brickkiln.

zieh/en* (´tsi:ən) vt **1** pull, draw (out). **2** cultivate, raise. **3** dig. vi **1** draw, pull. **2** move, go. **es zieht** there is a draught, it is draughty. **sich ziehen** vr **1** extend. **2** move. **3** withdraw. **—harmonika** nf accordion.

Ziel (tsi:l) n neu **-e 1** aim, end. **2** goal. **3** target. **—en** vi aim (at).

ziem/en (´tsi:mən) vi also **sich ziemen** vr **1**

suit. **2** become. **—lich** adv quite, rather, moderately, fairly. adj suitable, fitting.

Zier (tsi:r) nf **-en** also **Zierat** nm **-e** ornament. **—en** vt decorate, adorn. **—lich** adj graceful, pretty, elegant.

Ziffer ('tsifər) nf **-n** figure, cipher.

Zigarette (tsiga'rɛtə) nf **-n** cigarette.

Zigarre (tsi'garə) nf **-n** cigar.

Zigeuner (tsi'gɔynər) nm — gipsy.

Zimmer ('tsimər) n neu — room. **—mann** nm carpenter.

zimperlich ('tsimpərliç) adj **1** prim, prudish. **2** affected.

Zimt (tsimt) nm **-e** cinnamon.

Zink (tsiŋk) n neu zinc.

Zinke ('tsiŋkə) nf **-n 1** prong. **2** dovetail.

Zinn (tsin) n neu tin.

Zins (tsins) nm **-en 1** interest. **2** rent. **—eszins** ('tsinzɔstsins) nm compound interest. **—fuß** nm also **—satz** interest rate.

Zipfel ('tsipfəl) nm — tip, corner, edge.

Zirkus ('tsirkus) nm **-se** circus.

zirpen ('tsirpən) vi chirp.

Zitrone (tsi'tro:nə) nf **-n** lemon.

zittern ('tsitərn) vi tremble, quiver.

Zitze ('tsitsə) nf **-n** teat, nipple.

zivil (tsi'vi:l) adj **1** civil. **2** civilian. **—ist** (tsivi'list) nm civilian.

Zivil/isation (tsivilizatsi'o:n) nf **-en** civilization, culture. **—isieren** (tsivili'zi:rən) vt civilize.

Zofe ('tso:fə) nf **-n** lady's maid.

zog (tso:k) v see **ziehen.**

zöger/n ('tsœ:gərn) vi hesitate, linger. **—ung** nf **-en** delay, hesitation.

Zögling ('tsœ:kliŋ) nm **-e** pupil.

Zoll[1] (tsɔl) nm — inch.

Zoll[2] (tsɔl) nm **-e** custom, duty, toll. **—amt** n neu customs office. **—beamte(r)** nm also **—ner** ('tsœlnər) nm — customs officer. **—en** vt pay. **—frei** adj duty-free. **—pflichtig** adj dutiable, liable to (customs) duty.

Zone ('tso:nə) nf **-n** zone.

Zoo (tso:) nm **-s** zoo. **—loge** (tso:o'lo:gə) nm **-n** zoologist. **—logie** (tso:olo'gi:) nf zoology. **—logisch** (tso:o'lo:giʃ) adj zoological.

Zopf (tsɔpf) nm **-e** plait, pigtail.

Zorn (tsɔrn) nm anger. **—ig** adj angry.

zu (tsu:) prep **1** in, into. **2** to. **3** at. **4** by, with. **5** along with, in addition to. adv **1** too. **2** to(wards). **3** closed, shut.

Zubehör ('tsu:bəhœ:r) n neu **-e 1** accessories. **2** fittings.

zubereiten ('tsu:bəraitən) vt prepare.

zubringen* ('tsu:briŋən) vt **1** bring to. **2** pass (the time).

Zucht (tsuxt) nf **1** discipline. **2** breed(ing). **3** decency. **4** culture. **5** training. **—en** ('tsuçtən) vt **1** breed, rear. **2** grow, cultivate. **—er** ('tsyçtər) nm — **1** breeder. **2** grower. **—ig** ('tsyçtiç) adj chaste, modest. **—igen** ('tsyçtigən) vt **1** punish, discipline. **2** flog, thrash.

zucken ('tsukən) vi **1** twitch. **2** flash. vt **1** shrug (one's shoulders). **2** bat (an eyelid).

Zucker ('tsukər) nm sugar. **—n** vt sugar. **—rohr** n neu sugar cane. **—rübe** nf sugar beet.

zudecken ('tsu:dɛkən) vt cover (up).

zudem (tsu'de:m) adv besides.

Zudrang ('tsu:draŋ) nm rush (towards).

zudrehen ('tsu:dre:ən) vt turn or switch off.

zudringlich ('tsu:driŋliç) adj importunate.

zueinander (tsuain'andər) adv to each other.

zuerst (tsu'e:rst) adv (at) first, above all.

Zufahrt ('tsu:fa:rt) nf **1** approach, drive. **2** access (by road).

Zufall ('tsu:fal) nm chance, accident. **—en*** vi **1** fall to or on. **2** close. **—ig** ('tsu:fɛliç) adj accidental.

zufließen* ('tsu:fli:sən) vi flow (in)to.

Zuflucht ('tsu:fluxt) nf refuge, shelter.

zufolge (tsu'fɔlgə) prep **1** according to. **2** owing to.

zufrieden (tsu'fri:dən) adj satisfied, content(ed). **—heit** nf satisfaction, contentment. **—stellen** vt satisfy.

zufügen ('tsu:fy:gən) vt **1** add (to). **2** cause, do.

Zufuhr ('tsu:fu:r) nf **-en** supply. **—en** ('tsu:-fy:rən) vt **1** lead or bring to. **2** supply.

Zug (tsu:k) nm **-e 1** train. **2** pull(ing), drawing. **3** draught. **4** procession. **5** trait, feature. **6** platoon, section. **—brücke** nf drawbridge.

Zugabe ('tsu:ga:bə) nf **-n 1** addition. **2** supplement.

Zugang ('tsu:gaŋ) nm **1** access, entry. **2** increase. **—lich** ('tsu:gɛŋliç) adj accessible.

zugeben* ('tsu:ge:bən) vt **1** admit, confess. **2** permit. **3** add.

zugegen (tsu'ge:gən) adj present.

zugehen* ('tsu:ge:ən) vi **1** go on or to. **2** shut, close. **3** happen.

zugehör/en ('tsu:gəhœ:rən) vi belong to. **—ig** adj belonging to.

Zügel ('tsy:gəl) nm — **1** rein, bridle. **2** restraint. **—los** adj unbridled. **—n** vt rein in, curb.

Zugeständnis ('tsu:gəʃtɛntnis) n neu **-se 1** concession. **2** admission.

zugestehen* ('tsu:gəʃte:ən) vt **1** admit. **2** concede.

Zugführer ('tsu:kfy:rər) nm (railway) guard.

zugig ('tsu:ɡiç) adj draughty.

zugreifen* ('tsu:ɡraifən) vi **1** grasp. **2** help oneself (at table).

zugrunde (tsu'ɡrundə) adv **zugrunde gehen 1** perish, die. **2** be ruined.

zugunsten (tsu'ɡunstən) adv in favour of.

zugute (tsu'ɡu:tə) adv for the benefit of. **jemandem etwas zugute halten** give someone credit for something. **jemandem zugute kommen** stand someone in good stead.

zuhalt/en* ('tsu:haltən) vt keep shut. vi make for, go towards. **—er** ('tsu:hɛltər) nm — procurer, pimp.

zuhanden (tsu'handən) adv at or to hand.

zuhör/en ('tsu:hœ:rən) vi listen, attend (to). **—er** nm **1** listener. **2** pl audience.

zukommen* ('tsu:kɔmən) vi **1** come to, fall to. **2** be due to.

Zukunft ('tsu:kunft) nf future. **—ig** ('tsu:kynftiç) adj future.

Zulage ('tsu:la:ɡə) nf **1** increase. **2** extra pay or allowance.

zulänglich ('tsu:lɛŋliç) adj sufficient.

zulass/en* ('tsu:lasən) vt **1** leave shut. **2** admit (a person). **3** allow. **4** license (a car, etc.). **—ig** ('tsu:lɛsiç) adj admissible, allowable. **—ung** nf -en **1** admission. **2** permission. **3** (car) licence, registration.

Zulauf ('tsu:lauf) nm **1** rush. **2** crowd. **3** supply.

zuleide ('tsu:laidə) adv **jemandem etwas zuleide tun** hurt or harm someone.

zuleiten ('tsu:laitən) vt lead in or to.

zuletzt ('tsu:lɛtst) adv (at) last, finally.

zuliebe (tsu'li:bə) adv **jemandem zuliebe 1** to please someone. **2** for someone's sake.

zum (tsum) contraction of **zu dem.**

zumachen ('tsu:maxən) vt shut, fasten.

zumal (tsu'ma:l) adv especially.

zumeist (tsu'maist) adv mostly.

zumindest (tsu'mindəst) adv at least.

zumute (tsu'mu:tə) adv **mir ist gut zumute** I feel well, I am in good spirits.

zumut/en ('tsu:mu:tən) vt expect or ask of (a person). **—ung** nf -en (unreasonable) demand, presumption.

zunächst (tsu'nɛ:çst) adv first (of all). prep next to.

Zunahme ('tsu:na:mə) nf -n increase, growth.

Zuname ('tsu:na:mə) nm surname.

zünd/en ('tsyndən) vi,vt ignite. **—er** nm — **1** fuse. **2** detonator. **—kerze** ('tsyntkɛrtsə) nf sparking plug. **—stoff** ('tsyntʃtɔf) nm **1** combustible matter. **2** fuel. **—ung** nf -en **1** mot ignition. **2** priming.

Zunder ('tsundər) nm — tinder.

zunehmen* ('tsu:ne:mən) vi grow, increase, put on (weight).

zuneig/en ('tsu:naigən) vi **1** lean. **2** incline. **—ung** nf -en **1** inclination. **2** sympathy.

Zunft (tsunft) nf -̈e **1** guild. **2** clique.

Zunge ('tsuŋə) nf -n **1** tongue. **2** zool sole.

zunichte (tsu'niçtə) adv ruined. **zunichte machen** ruin. **zunichte werden** come to nothing.

zunicken ('tsu:nikən) vi,vt nod (to).

zuoberst (tsu'o:bərst) adv at the top.

zupfen ('tsupfən) vt **1** pull. **2** pick.

zur (tsu:r) contraction of **zu der.**

zurechn/en ('tsu:rɛçnən) vt **1** add. **2** include. **3** ascribe. **—ung** nf **1** attribution. **2** addition.

zurecht (tsu'rɛçt) adv in order. **—legen** vt arrange. **—machen** vt prepare. **—setzen** vt set right. **—weisen** vt **1** direct. **2** reprimand.

zureden ('tsu:re:dən) vi **1** urge, advise. **2** persuade.

zureichen ('tsu:raiçən) vt hand (over or to). vi suffice.

Zürich ('tsy:riç) n neu Zurich.

zurichten ('tsu:riçtən) vt **1** prepare. **2** tech dress.

zürnen ('tsyrnən) vi be angry.

zurück (tsu'ryk) adv back(wards), behind.

zurückbezahlen (tsu'rykbətsa:lən) vt repay.

zurückbleiben* (tsu'rykblaibən) vi remain or fall behind, be left behind.

zurückbringen* (tsu'rykbriŋən) vt bring back.

zurückkeilen (tsu'rykailən) vi hurry back.

zurückfahren* (tsu'rykfa:rən) vi **1** drive or go back. **2** recoil. vt drive back.

sich zurückfinden* (tsu'rykfindən) vr find one's way back.

zurückführen (tsu'rykfy:rən) vt lead or trace back.

zurückgehen* (tsu'rykge:ən) vi **1** go or fall back. **2** decrease.

zurückgezogen (tsu'rykɡətso:ɡən) adj retired, secluded.

zurückhalt/en* (tsu'rykhaltən) vt **1** hold back or in **2** restrain **3** detain **4** repress vi keep back. **—end** adj reserved. **—ung** nf reserve.

zurückkehren (tsu'rykke:rən) vi return.

zurückkommen* (tsuˈrykkɔmən) vi 1 return. 2 recur.

zurücklegen (tsuˈrykleːgən) vt 1 lay aside. 2 put by. 3 complete. 4 cover (distance). **sich zurücklegen** vr lie back.

zurücknehmen* (tsuˈrykneːmən) vt take back.

zurückrufen* (tsuˈrykruːfən) vt 1 call back. 2 recall.

zurückschlagen* (tsuˈrykʃlaːgən) vt 1 repel. 2 throw off or open. 3 return. vi strike back.

zurücksetzen (tsuˈrykzɛtsən) vt 1 put back. 2 neglect (a person).

zurücktreten* (tsuˈryktreːtən) vi 1 step back. 2 resign. 3 retire.

zurückweichen* (tsuˈrykvaiçən) vi 1 fall back. 2 recede. 3 yield.

zurückweisen* (tsuˈrykvaizən) vt 1 send away or back. 2 decline, reject.

zurückziehen* (tsuˈryktsiːən) vt withdraw.

Zuruf (ˈtsuːruːf) nm shout, call.

Zusage (ˈtsuːzaːgə) nf 1 consent. 2 promise, word. **—n** vt promise. vi agree.

zusammen (tsuˈzamən) adv together.

Zusammenarbeit (tsuˈzamənarbait) nf cooperation, teamwork. **—en** vi cooperate, work together.

zusammenballen (tsuˈzamənbalən) vt 1 roll into a ball. 2 clench (one's fists).

zusammenbrechen* (tsuˈzamənbrɛçən) vi break down, collapse.

Zusammenbruch (tsuˈzamənbrux) nm breakdown, collapse.

zusammenfahren* (tsuˈzamənfaːrən) vi 1 collide. 2 wince, start.

zusammenfass/en (tsuˈzamənfasən) vt 1 comprise. 2 condense. 3 sum up. **—ung** nf summary.

zusammenfügen (tsuˈzamənfyːgən) vt combine.

zusammengesetzt (tsuˈzaməngəzɛtst) adj composed, assembled.

Zusammenhang (tsuˈzamənhaŋ) nm 1 connection. 2 context. 3 continuity.

Zusammenkunft (tsuˈzamənkunft) nf assembly.

zusammenlegen (tsuˈzamənleːgən) vt 1 put together, combine. 2 fold (up). 3 pool.

zusammennehmen* (tsuˈzamənneːmən) vt gather up. **sich zusammennehmen** vr pull oneself together.

zusammenpassen (tsuˈzamənpasən) vi go well together. vt adjust.

zusammenrücken (tsuˈzamənrykən) vt, vi move closer together.

sich zusammenschließen* (tsuˈzamənʃliːsən) vr unite.

Zusammenschluß (tsuˈzamənʃlus) nm 1 union. 2 comm merger.

zusammensetz/en (tsuˈzamənzɛtsən) vt put together. **sich zusammensetzen** vr sit down together. **—ung** nf 1 composition. 2 construction.

zusammenstellen (tsuˈzamənʃtɛlən) vt 1 put together. 2 make up.

zusammenstimmen (tsuˈzamənʃtimən) vi agree, harmonize.

Zusammenstoß (tsuˈzamənʃtɔs) nm 1 collision. 2 conflict. **—en*** vt knock together. vi collide.

zusammentreffen* (tsuˈzaməntrɛfən) vi 1 meet. 2 coincide. n neu 1 meeting. 2 coincidence.

zusammentreten* (tsuˈzaməntreːtən) vi come together.

zusammenzieh/en* (tsuˈzaməntsiːən) vt draw together. **—ung** nf contraction.

Zusatz (ˈtsuːzats) nm 1 addition. 2 appendix.

zuschau/en (ˈtsuːʃauən) vi look on. **—er** nm — spectator.

zuschicken (ˈtsuːʃikən) vt send on, forward.

zuschieben* (ˈtsuːʃiːbən) vt 1 push on. 2 shut.

zuschießen* (ˈtsuːʃiːsən) vt, vi 1 rush (at). 2 contribute (money). vt shoot (a glance, etc.) at.

Zuschlag (ˈtsuːʃlaːk) nm 1 surcharge. 2 increase. **—en*** (ˈtsuːʃlaːgən) vt slam. vi hit out. **—spflichtig** adj liable to surcharge.

zuschließen* (ˈtsuːʃliːsən) vt lock.

zuschneiden* (ˈtsuːʃnaidən) vt 1 cut out. 2 cut to size.

zuschreiben* (ˈtsuːʃraibən) vt ascribe to.

Zuschuß (ˈtsuːʃus) nm 1 extra allowance. 2 subsidy, grant.

zuschütten (ˈtsuːʃytən) vt 1 fill up with. 2 pour in or on.

zusehen* (ˈtsuːzeːən) vi 1 look on. 2 wait. **—ds** adv visibly.

zusenden* (ˈtsuːzɛndən) vt send on, forward.

zusetzen (ˈtsuːzɛtsən) vt 1 add. 2 lose (money). vi importune, pester.

Zuspruch (ˈtsuːʃprux) nm 1 encouragement. 2 consolation. 3 custom(ers).

Zustand (ˈtsuːʃtant) nm 1 condition. 2 situation. **—ig** (ˈtsuːʃtɛndiç) adj 1 appropriate. 2 competent, responsible.

zustatten (tsuˈʃtatən) adv **jemandem gut zu-**

statten kommen stand a person in good stead.

zustellen ('tsuːʃtɛlən) *vt* deliver (letters, mail).

zustimm/en ('tsuːʃtimən) *vi* agree, consent. **—ung** *nf* consent.

zustoßen* ('tsuːʃtoːsən) *vt* slam (shut). *vi* befall.

zustreben ('tsuːʃtreːbrən) *vi* strive (for).

zutage (tsuːˈtaːgə) *adv* **zutage bringen** bring to light.

Zutat ('tsuːtaːt) *nf* **1** *cul* ingredient. **2** seasoning. **3** trimming.

zuteil (tsuːˈtail) *adv* **einem zuteil werden** fall to one's share.

zuteilen ('tsuːtailən) *vt* assign, allocate.

zutiefst (tsuːˈtiːfst) *adv* deeply, intensely.

zutrag/en* ('tsuːtraːgən) *vt* carry (to). **sich zutragen** *vr* happen. **—er** ('tsuːtreːgər) *nm* — informer, gossipmonger. **—lich** ('tsuːtreːkliç) *adj* **1** wholesome. **2** advantageous.

zutrau/en ('tsuːtrauən) *vt* credit. *n neu* confidence. **—lich** *adj* trusting.

zutreffen* ('tsuːtrɛfən) *vi* prove true.

Zutritt ('tsuːtrit) *nm* access, admission.

zuverlässig ('tsuːfɛrlɛsiç) *adj* **1** reliable. **2** certain.

Zuversicht ('tsuːfɛrziçt) *nf* confidence. **—lich** *adj* confident.

zuviel (tsuːˈfiːl) *adv* too much.

zuvörderst (tsuːˈfœrdərst) *adv* first of all.

zuvorkommen* (tsuːˈfoːrkɔmən) *vi* anticipate

zuvortun* (tsuːˈfoːrtuːn) *vi* outdo.

Zuwachs ('tsuːvaks) *nm* increase, growth.

zuweilen (tsuːˈvailən) *adv* at times, sometimes.

zuweisen* ('tsuːvaizən) *vt* allot.

zuwenden* ('tsuːvɛndən) *vt* **1** turn towards. **2** give. **3** procure.

zuwider (tsuːˈviːdər) *prep* **1** contrary to. **2** distasteful to. **—handlung** *nf* violation, infringement. **—laufen*** *vi* run counter (to).

zuzeiten (tsuːˈtsaitən) *adv* at times.

zuziehen* ('tsuːtsiːən) *vt* **1** draw (together), tighten, shut. **2** invite. **3** move in. **2** immigrate. **sich eine Krankheit zuziehen** catch or contract a disease. **sich Schwierigkeiten zuziehen** get into difficulties.

zwang (tsvaŋ) *v see* **zwingen**.

Zwang (tsvaŋ) *nm* **-e 1** compulsion. **2** force. **—los** *adj* unconstrained. **—släufig** ('tsvaŋsløyfiç) *adj* inevitable.

zwängen ('tsvɛŋən) *vt* press, squeeze.

zwanzig ('tsvantsiç) *adj,nf* twenty. **—ste** *adj* twentieth.

zwar (tsvaːr) *adv* indeed. **und zwar** that is, namely, in fact.

Zweck (tsvɛk) *nm* **-e 1** purpose. **2** design. **—los** *adj* useless, purposeless. **—mäßig** *adj* **1** suitable. **2** expedient. **3** practical.

Zwecke ('tsvɛkə) *nf* **-n 1** drawing-pin. **2** tack. **3** peg.

zwei (tsvai) *adj,nf* two.

zweideutig ('tsvaidɔytiç) *adj* ambiguous.

zweierlei (tsvaiərˈlai) *adj* of two kinds.

Zweifel ('tsvaifəl) *nm* — doubt. **—haft** *adj* doubtful. **—los** *adj* doubtless. **—n** *vi* doubt.

Zweig (tsvaik) *nm* **-e** branch, twig. **—stelle** *nf* branch office.

zweijährlich ('tsvaijɛːrliç) *adj* every two years.

Zweikampf ('tsvaikampf) *nm* duel.

zweimal ('tsvaimal) *adv* twice.

zweisprachig ('tsvaiʃpraːxiç) *adj* bilingual.

zweistimmig ('tsvaiʃtimiç) *adj mus* for two voices.

zwei/te ('tsvaitə) *adj* second. **zu Zweit** in twos, two by two. **—tens** ('tsvaitəns) *adv* secondly. **—tklassig** *adj* second-rate.

Zwerchfell ('tsvɛrçfɛl) *n neu* diaphragm.

Zwerg (tsvɛrk) *nm* **-e** dwarf.

zwicken ('tsvikən) *vt* pinch, tweak.

Zwieback ('tsviːbak) *nm* **-e** biscuit, rusk.

Zwiebel ('tsviːbəl) *nf* **-n 1** onion. **2** *bot* bulb.

Zwiegespräch ('tsviːgəʃprɛːx) *n neu* dialogue.

Zwiespalt ('tsviːʃpalt) *nm* **-e** dissension.

Zwietracht ('tsviːtraxt) *nf* discord.

Zwilling ('tsviliŋ) *nm* **-e 1** twin. **2** *pl* Gemini.

Zwinge ('tsviŋə) *nf* **-n 1** clamp. **2** ferrule.

zwingen* ('tsviŋən) *vt* **1** force. **2** overcome.

zwischen ('tsviʃən) *prep* between, among. **—durch** *adv* **1** through. **2** in the midst. **3** between. **—fall** *nm* incident. **—raum** *nm* interval, gap, space. **—spiel** *n neu* interlude. **—wand** *nf* partition. **—zeit** *nf* interim, interval.

Zwist (tsvist) *nm* **-e 1** discord. **2** quarrel. **—ig** *adj* **1** at variance. **2** in dispute.

zwitschern ('tsvitʃərn) *vi* chirp, twitter.

zwo (tsvoː) *adj,nf see* **zwei**.

zwölf (tsvœlf) *adj,nf* twelve. **—te** *adj* twelfth.

Zyklon (tsyˈkloːn) *nm* **-e** cyclone.

Zyklus ('tsyːklus) *nm* **-len 1** cycle. **2** series.

Zylinder (tsiˈlindər) *nm* — **1** cylinder. **2** top-hat.

Zyn/iker ('tsyːnikər) *nm* — cynic. **—isch** ('tsyːniʃ) *adj* cynical.

Zyp/ern ('tsyːpərn) *n neu* Cyprus. **—riot** (tsyˈpriːoːt) *nm* **-en** Cypriot. **—riotisch** (tsypriˈoːtiʃ) *adj* Cypriot.

A

a, an (ə, ən; *stressed* ei, æn) *indef art* **1** ein, eine, ein *m,f,neu.* **2** pro, je.

aback (ə'bæk) *adv* nach hinten, zurück. **taken aback** bestürzt, verblüfft.

abandon (ə'bændən) *n* Ungezwungenheit, Hingabe *f.* *vt* **1** aufgeben, verlassen. **2** verzichten auf. **3** im Stich lassen.

abashed (ə'bæʃt) *adj* verlegen, sich schämend.

abate (ə'beit) *vi* (of wind) abnehmen, sich legen.

abattoir ('æbətwɑː) *n* Schlachthaus *neu.*

abbess ('æbis) *n* Abtissin *f.*

abbey ('æbi) *n* Abtei *f.*

abbot ('æbət) *n* Abt *m.*

abbreviate (ə'briːvieit) *vt* abkürzen. **abbreviation** *n* Abkürzung *f.*

abdicate ('æbdikeit) *vi* abdanken. *vt* niederlegen. **abdication** *n* Abdankung *f.*

abdomen ('æbdəmən) *n* Unterleib, Bauch *m.*

abduct (æb'dʌkt) *vt* entführen. **abduction** *n* Entführung *f.*

abet (ə'bet) *vt* **1** begünstigen. **2** anstiften. **aid and abet** *law* Vorschub leisten.

abhor (əb'hɔː) *vt* verabscheuen. **abhorrence** *n* Abscheu *m.* **abhorrent** *adj* zuwider, verhaßt.

abide (ə'baid) *vi* bleiben, fortdauern. *vt* vertragen, ausstehen. **abide by** treu bleiben, sich halten an.

ability (ə'biliti) *n* **1** Fähigkeit *f.* **2** geistige Anlagen *f pl.*

abject ('æbdʒekt) *adj* gemein, verächtlich.

ablaze (ə'bleiz) *adj,adv* **1** in Flammen. **2** glänzend. **3** erregt.

able ('eibəl) *adj* **1** fähig. **2** geschickt, tüchtig, begabt. **be able to** können.

abnormal (æb'nɔːməl) *adj* **1** ungewöhnlich. **2** anormal, abnorm. **abnormality** *n* **1** Abnormität *f.* **2** Mißbildung *f.*

aboard (ə'bɔːd) *adv* an Bord.

abode (ə'boud) *n* Wohnort *m.* Stätte *f.*

abolish (ə'bɔliʃ) *vt* abschaffen, aufheben. **abolition** *n* Abschaffung, Aufhebung *f.*

abominable (ə'bɔminəbəl) *adj* abscheulich.

Aborigine (æbə'ridʒini) *n* **1** Ureinwohner *m.* **2** *pl* Urbevölkerung *f.* **aboriginal** *adj* eingeboren.

abort (ə'bɔːt) *vi* **1** fehlgebären. **2** fehlschlagen. **abortion** *n* **1** Abtreibung *f.* **2** Fehlgeburt *f.* **abortive** *adj* **1** vorzeitig. **2** fehlgeschlagen, mißlungen.

abound (ə'baund) *vi* reichlich vorhanden sein.

about (ə'baut) *prep* **1** wegen, über. **2** gegen. *adv* **1** herum, umher. **2** ungefähr, etwa. **be about to do something** eben etwas tun wollen.

above (ə'bʌv) *prep* über, oberhalb. *adv* oben, darüber. *adj* obig, oben erwähnt. **aboveboard** *adj* offen, ehrlich.

abrasion (ə'breiʒən) *n* Abschleifen, Abreiben *neu.* **abrasive** *adj* abreibend, abschleifend.

abreast (ə'brest) *adv* **1** nebeneinander. **2** auf dem laufenden. **keep abreast of** Schritt halten mit.

abridge (ə'bridʒ) *vt* (ab-, ver-)kürzen.

abroad (ə'brɔːd) *adv* **1** ins *or* im Ausland. **2** draußen. **3** auswärts.

abrupt (ə'brʌpt) *adj* **1** abrupt, plötzlich. **2** schroff.

abscess ('æbses) *n* Abszeß *m.* Geschwür *neu.*

abscond (əb'skɔnd) *vi* sich heimlich davonmachen, flüchten.

absent (*adj* 'æbsənt; *v* əb'sent) *adj* **1** abwesend. **2** zerstreut. *v* **absent oneself from** sich entfernen von. **absence** *n* **1** Abwesenheit *f.* **2** Mangel *m.* **in the absence of** in Ermangelung von. **absentee** *n* Abwesende(r) *m.* **absenteeism** *n* (unerlaubtes) Fernbleiben *neu.* **absent-minded** *adj* zerstreut, geistesabwesend.

absinthe ('æbsinθ) *n* Absinth *m.*

absolute ('æbsəluːt) *adj* **1** absolut. **2** vollkommen. **absolutely** *adv* völlig, durchaus.

absolve (əb'zɔlv) *vt* freisprechen. **absolution** *n* *rel* Absolution *f.*

absorb (əb'zɔːb) vt **1** absorbieren, aufsaugen. **2** aufnehmen. **be absorbed in** vertieft sein in. **absorbent** adj aufsaugend. **absorption** n Absorption, Aufsaugung f.

abstain (əb'stein) vi sich enthalten. **abstainer** n Abstinenzler m. **abstention** n Enthaltung f. **abstinence** n Enthaltsamkeit, Abstinenz f.

abstract (adj,n 'æbstrækt; v əb'strækt) adj abstrakt, theoretisch. n **1** Abstrakte neu. **2** Auszug m. vt ablenken, absondern. **abstraction** n **1** sci Absonderung f. **2** Abstraktion f. **3** Zerstreutheit f.

absurd (əb'səːd) adj absurd, sinnwidrig, albern. **absurdity** n Albernheit f. Unsinn m.

abundance (ə'bʌndəns) n Überfluß m. Fülle f. **abundant** adj reichlich.

abuse (v ə'bjuːz; n ə'bjuːs) vt **1** mißbrauchen. **2** beschimpfen. n **1** Mißbrauch m. **2** Beschimpfung f. **abusive** adj beleidigend.

abyss (ə'bis) n Abgrund m. **abysmal** adj abgrundtief.

Abyssinia (æbi'siniə) n Abessinien neu. **Abyssinian** adj abessinisch. n Abessinier m.

academy (ə'kædəmi) n (Kunst)Akademie f. **academic** adj **1** akademisch. **2** rein theoretisch. n Akademiker m.

accelerate (ək'seləreit) vt **1** beschleunigen. **2** mot Gas geben. **acceleration** n Beschleunigung f. **accelerator** n Gaspedal neu.

accent (n 'æksənt; v æk'sent) n **1** Akzent m. **2** Betonung f. vt betonen. **accentuate** vt **1** betonen. **2** hervorheben.

accept (ək'sept) vt **1** (an-, entgegen-)nehmen, akzeptieren. **2** anerkennen, gelten lassen. vi annehmen, zusagen. **acceptable** adj **1** annehmbar. **2** angenehm. **acceptance** n **1** Annahme f. **2** Aufnahme f.

access ('ækses) n **1** Zugang, Zutritt m. **2** Zufahrt f. **accessible** adj zugänglich. **accession** n **1** Antritt m. **2** Thronbesteigung f. **accessory** n Zubehörteil m.

accident ('æksidnt) n **1** Zufall m. **2** Unfall m. Unglück neu. **accidental** adj zufällig.

acclaim (ə'kleim) vt **1** (mit Beifall) begrüßen, zujubeln. **2** anerkennen, begrüßen. **acclamation** n **1** Beifall m. **2** Zuruf m.

acclimatize (ə'klaimətaiz) (vi),vt (sich) akklimatisieren, (sich) eingewöhnen. **acclimatization** n Akklimatisierung, Eingewöhnung f.

accommodate (ə'kɔmədeit) vt **1** unterbringen. **2** anpassen. **3** aushelfen. **acommodating** adj

1 gefällig. **2** anpassungsfähig. **accommodation** n **1** Unterkunft f. **2** Anpassung f.

accompany (ə'kʌmpəni) vt begleiten. **accompaniment** n Begleitung f. **accompanist** n mus Begleiter m.

accomplice (ə'kʌmplis) n Mittäter m.

accomplish (ə'kʌmpliʃ) vt vollenden, zustande bringen. **accomplishment** n **1** Vollendung f. **2** Leistung f. **3** pl Talente neu pl.

accord (ə'kɔːd) vt gewähren. vi übereinstimmen. n Übereinstimmung f. **of one's own accord** aus eigenem Antrieb. **accordance** n Übereinstimmung f. **in accordance with** in Übereinstimmung mit, gemäß. **according to** prep **1** gemäß. **2** laut, zufolge.

accordion (ə'kɔːdiən) n Ziehharmonika f.

accost (ə'kɔst) vt ansprechen.

account (ə'kaunt) vi Rechenschaft ablegen. vt ansehen als. n **1** Rechnung f. **2** Bericht m. **3** comm Konto neu. **on no account** auf keinen Fall. **accountable** adj verantwortlich. **accountancy** n Rechnungswesen neu. **accountant** n **1** Rechnungsführer m. **2** Bücherrevisor m.

accumulate (ə'kjuːmjuleit) (vi),vt (sich) anhäufen. **accumulation** n Anhäufung f. **accumulative** adj (sich) anhäufend.

accurate ('ækjurət) adj **1** genau. **2** richtig. **accuracy** n Genauigkeit f.

accusative (ə'kjuːzətiv) n Akkusativ m.

accuse (ə'kjuːz) vt anklagen, beschuldigen. **accused** n Angeklagte(r) m. **accuser** n Kläger m.

accustom (ə'kʌstəm) vt gewöhnen. **become accustomed to** sich gewöhnen an.

ace (eis) n As neu.

ache (eik) vi schmerzen, weh tun. n Schmerz m. **aching** adj schmerzhaft.

achieve (ə'tʃiːv) vt **1** ausführen. **2** zustande bringen. **3** erreichen, erzielen. **achievement** n **1** Ausführung, Vollendung f. **2** Leistung f. Werk neu.

acid ('æsid) adj sauer. n Säure f.

acknowledge (ək'nɔlidʒ) vt **1** anerkennen, zugeben. **2** comm bestätigen. **acknowledgment** n **1** Anerkennung f. **2** Dank m. **3** comm Empfangsbestätigung f.

acne ('ækni) n Akne f. Hautausschlag m.

acorn ('eikɔːn) n Eichel f.

acoustic (ə'kuːstik) adj akustisch. **acoustics** n Akustik f.

acquaint (ə'kweint) vt bekannt machen. **be acquainted with** kennen. **acquaintance** n **1**

Bekanntschaft f. 2 Bekannte(r) m. **make someone's acquaintance** jemanden kennenlernen.

acquiesce ('ækwi'es) vi einwilligen, sich fügen. **acquiescent** adj ergeben, fügsam.

acquire (ə'kwaiə) vt erwerben, erlangen. **acquisition** n Erwerbung f. **acquisitive** adj gewinnsüchtig.

acquit (ə'kwit) vt freisprechen. **acquittal** n Freispruch m.

acre ('eikə) n Morgen m.

acrimony ('ækriməni) n Schärfe, Bitterkeit f. **acrimonious** adj scharf, beißend.

acrobat ('ækrəbæt) n Akrobat m. **acrobatic** adj akrobatisch. **acrobatics** n pl Akrobatik f.

across (ə'krɔs) adv 1 hinüber, herüber, (quer)durch. 2 kreuzweise. prep 1 über. 2 jenseits. **come across** stoßen auf.

acrylic (ə'krilik) n Polyacryl Tdmk neu.

act (ækt) vt darstellen, spielen. **act a part** eine Rolle spielen. vi handeln. **act as** fungieren als. **act on** wirken auf. n 1 Handlung, Tat f. 2 Th Aufzug m 3 Gesetz neu. **acting** adj 1 handelnd. 2 amtierend. n Th Spielen neu.

action ('ækʃən) n 1 Handlung f. 2 Tat f. 3 Wirkung f. 4 law Klage f. 5 mil Gefecht neu.

active ('æktiv) adj tätig, wirksam, aktiv. n gram Aktiv neu. **activate** vt 1 in Tätigkeit setzen. 2 wirksam machen. **activity** n 1 Tätigkeit f. 2 Treiben neu. 3 pl Unternehmungen f pl.

actor ('æktə) n Schauspieler m.

actress ('æktris) n Schauspielerin f.

actual ('æktʃuəl) adj wirklich, tatsächlich, eigentlich.

acupuncture ('ækjupʌŋktʃə) n Akupunktur f.

acute (ə'kju:t) adj 1 akut, heftig. 2 scharf. **acute angle** spitzer Winkel m.

adamant ('ædəmənt) adj unerbittlich.

adapt (ə'dæpt) vt 1 anpassen, zurechtmachen. 2 bearbeiten. **adaptable** adj anpassungsfähig. **adaptation** n 1 Anpassung f 2 Bearbeitung f. **adaptor** n Zwischenstecker m.

add (æd) vt 1 addieren. 2 hinzufügen. vi hinzukommen. **add up** zusammenzählen, addieren. **adding machine** n Addiermaschine f. **addition** n 1 Hinzufügung f. 2 Zusatz m. Zutat f. 3 Addition f. **in addition** außerdem, noch dazu. **in addition to which** wozu (kommt noch). **additional** adj zusätzlich. **additive** n Zusatz m.

addendum (ə'dendəm) n, pl **addenda** 1 Zusatz m. 2 Nachtrag m.

adder ('ædə) n Natter f.

addict ('ædikt) n Süchtige(r) m. **addicted** adj süchtig. **addiction** n Neigung, Sucht f.

addled ('ædld) adj 1 faul. 2 verwirrt.

address (ə'dres) vt 1 anreden, sprechen zu. 2 (a letter) adressieren. n 1 Adresse, Anschrift f. 2 Ansprache, Anrede f. **address book** n Adreßbuch neu.

adenoids ('ædinɔidz) n pl Polypen m pl.

adept ('ædept) adj geschickt.

adequate ('ædikwət) adj 1 ausreichend. 2 angemessen. **adequacy** n Angemessenheit f.

adhere (əd'hiə) vi 1 kleben, haften. 2 festhalten. **adherence** n Festhalten neu. **adherent** n Anhänger m. adj anhaftend. **adhesion** n 1 Anhaften neu. 2 Anhänglichkeit f. **adhesive** adj klebrig, gummiert. n Klebstoff m. **adhesive tape** n Klebestreifen m.

ad hoc (æd 'hɔk) adj,adv für diesen Fall bestimmt.

adjacent (ə'dʒeisənt) adj angrenzend.

adjective ('ædʒiktiv) n Adjektiv, Eigenschaftswort neu.

adjoin (ə'dʒɔin) vt angrenzen.

adjourn (ə'dʒə:n) vt aufschieben, vertagen. vi sich vertagen. **adjournment** n Vertagung f. Verschiebung f.

adjudicate (ə'dʒu:dikeit) vt gerichtlich entscheiden. vi als Schiedsrichter handeln. **adjudication** n 1 richterliche Entscheidung f. 2 Zusprechung f. **adjudicator** n Schiedsrichter m.

adjust (ə'dʒʌst) vt 1 anpassen. 2 einstellen. vi sich anpassen. **adjustable** adj verstellbar. **adjustment** n 1 Anpassung f. 2 Einstellung f.

ad-lib (æd'lib) vt,vi imf improvisieren.

administer (əd'ministə) vt verwalten. vi als Verwalter fungieren. **administrate** vt verwalten. **administration** n 1 Verwaltung f. Verwaltungswesen neu. 2 Regierung f. **administration of justice** Rechtsprechung f. **administrative** adj Verwaltungs—, verwaltend. **administrator** n Verwalter m.

admiral ('ædmərəl) n Admiral m. **admiralty** n Admiralität f.

admire (əd'maiə) vt 1 bewundern. 2 hochschätzen. **admirable** adj bewundernswert, großartig. **admiration** n Bewunderung f. **admirer** n 1 Bewunderer m. 2 Verehrer m.

admit (əd'mit) vt 1 einlassen. 2 zugeben. 3 gelten lassen. **admission** n 1 Zulassung f. 2 Eintritt m. 3 Zugeständnis neu. **admittance** n Einlaß m. Zutritt m. **no admittance** Zutritt verboten.

ado (ə'du:) n Getue, Aufheben neu. **without further ado** ohne weitere Umstände.

adolescence (ædə'lesns) n Jünglingsalter neu. **adolescent** n Jugendliche(r) m. adj jugendlich.

adopt (ə'dɔpt) vt 1 adoptieren. 2 annehmen, sich aneignen. **adoption** n Adoption, Annahme f. **adoptive** adj angenommen, Adoptiv—.

adore (ə'dɔ:) vt 1 anbeten, verehren. 2 lieben, sehr gern haben. **adorable** adj 1 verehrungswürdig. 2 entzückend. **adoration** n Anbetung, Verehrung f.

adorn (ə'dɔ:n) vt schmücken. **adornment** n Schmuck m.

adrenaline (ə'drenəlin) n Adrenalin neu.

Adriatic (eidri'ætik) adj adriatisch. **Adriatic (Sea)** n Adriatisches Meer neu.

adrift (ə'drift) adj,adv 1 (umher)treibend. 2 hilflos.

adroit (ə'drɔit) adj gewandt.

adulation (ædju'leiʃən) n Schmeichelei f.

adult ('ædʌlt) adj erwachsen. n Erwachsene(r) m.

adulterate (ə'dʌltəreit) vt 1 verfälschen. 2 verderben. **adulteration** n Verfälschung f.

adultery (ə'dʌltəri) n Ehebruch m. **adulterer** n Ehebrecher m. **adulteress** n Ehebrecherin f. **adulterous** adj ehebrecherisch.

advance (əd'vɑ:ns) vt 1 vorrücken, vorwärtsbringen. 2 (money) vorschießen. 3 befördern. vi 1 vorrücken, vordringen. 2 Fortschritte machen. n 1 Vorrücken neu. 2 (money) Vorschuß m. 3 mil Vormarsch m. **in advance** im voraus. **advanced** adj fortgeschritten. **advancement** n 1 Beförderung f. 2 Fortschritt m.

advantage (əd'vɑ:ntidʒ) n Vorteil m. **take advantage of** ausnutzen. **advantageous** adj vorteilhaft, günstig.

advent ('ædvent) n 1 Kommen n. Ankunft f. 2 cap rel Advent m.

adventure (əd'ventʃə) n Abenteuer neu. **adventurer** n Abenteurer m. **adventurous** adj 1 abenteuerlich. 2 abenteuerlustig.

adverb ('ædvə:b) n Adverb, Umstandswort neu. **adverbial** adj adverbial.

adverse ('ædvə:s) adj 1 widrig. 2 feindlich. 3 ungünstig. **adversary** n Gegner m. **adversity** n Unglück neu. Not f.

advertise ('ædvətaiz) vt anzeigen. vi Reklame machen. **advertisement** n 1 Anzeige f. 2 Reklame f. **advertising** n Reklame, Werbung f.

advise (əd'vaiz) vt 1 raten, empfehlen. 2 beraten. 3 benachrichtigen, mitteilen. **advice** n 1 Rat m. 2 Ratschlag m. 3 comm Avis m. **advisable** adj ratsam. **adviser** n 1 Ratgeber m. 2 Berater m. **advisory** adj beratend, Beratungs—.

advocate (v 'ædvəkeit; n 'ædvəkət) vt 1 verteidigen. 2 befürworten. n 1 Advokat m. 2 Fürsprecher m. **advocacy** n Verteidigung f. Befürwortung f.

Aegean (i'dʒi:ən) adj ägäisch. **Aegean (Sea)** n Ägäisches Meer neu.

aerial ('eəriəl) adj 1 Luft—. 2 leicht, gasförmig. n tech Antenne f.

aerodynamics (ɛəroudai'næmiks) n pl Aerodynamik f. **aerodynamic** adj aerodynamisch.

aeronautics (ɛərə'nɔ:tiks) n pl Aeronautik f. Flugwesen neu. **aeronautical** adj aeronautisch.

aeroplane ('ɛərəplein) n Flugzeug neu.

aerosol ('ɛərəsɔl) n 1 Sprühdose f. Spray neu. 2 Aerosol neu.

aesthetic (is'θetik) adj ästhetisch, geschmackvoll.

afar (ə'fu:) adv fern. **from afar** aus weiter Ferne.

affable ('æfəbəl) adj leutselig.

affair (ə'fɛə) n 1 Angelegenheit, Sache, Affäre f. 2 (Liebes)Affäre, Liebschaft f

affect¹ (ə'fekt) vt 1 berühren, angehen. 2 beeinflussen, einwirken auf. 3 beeinträchtigen.

affect² (ə'fekt) vt vortäuschen, vorgeben.

affection (ə'fekʃən) n Zuneigung, Liebe f. **affectionate** adj liebevoll, zärtlich.

affiliate (ə'filieit) vt 1 (als Mitglied) aufnehmen. 2 angliedern. **affiliated company** n Tochtergesellschaft f.

affinity (ə'finiti) n enge Beziehungen f pl.

affirm (ə'fə:m) vt behaupten, versichern. vi bestätigen, zustimmen. **affirmation** n Behauptung f. **affirmative** adj bejahend, bestimmt. **answer in the affirmative** bejahen, mit Ja antworten.

affix (ə'fiks) vt 1 aufkleben. 2 aufdrücken.

afflict (ə'flikt) vt 1 betrüben. 2 quälen. **afflicted** adj leidend. **affliction** n 1 Kummer m. 2 Leiden neu.

affluent ('æfluənt) adj 1 reich. 2 wohlhabend. **affluent society** n Wohlstandsgesellschaft f.

afford (ə'fɔ:d) vt 1 sich leisten (können). 2 gewähren.

affront (ə'frʌnt) vt beleidigen. n Beleidigung f.

Afghanistan (æf'gænistɑ:n, -'stæn) n Afghanistan neu. **Afghanistani** adj afghanistanisch. n Afghanistaner m.

afield (ə'fi:ld) adv **far afield** weit weg.

afloat (ə'flout) adv **1** schwimmend. **2** auf dem Meere. **keep afloat** sich über Wasser halten.

afoot (ə'fut) adv **1** im Gang(e). **2** zu Fuß.

aforesaid (ə'fɔ:sed) adj vorerwähnt.

afraid (ə'freid) adj ängstlich, bange, erschrocken. **be afraid 1** Angst haben. **2** bedauern. **be afraid of** sich fürchten vor, Angst haben vor. **be afraid to do something** sich scheuen, etwas zu tun.

afresh (ə'freʃ) adv von neuem.

Africa ('æfrikə) Afrika neu. **African** adj afrikanisch. n Afrikaner m.

aft (ɑ:ft) adv naut achtern, hinten.

after ('ɑ:ftə) prep nach. conj nachdem. adv nachher. **shortly after** kurz darauf. **after-care** n Nachbehandlung f. **after-effect** n Nachwirkung f. **afterlife** n Leben nach dem Tode neu. **aftermath** n Nachwirkungen f pl. **afternoon** n Nachmittag m. **afterthought** nachträglicher Einfall m. **afterwards** adv später, nachher.

again (ə'gen) adv **1** wieder, nochmals. **2** ferner, außerdem. **once again** noch einmal.

against (ə'genst) prep **1** gegen, wider. **2** gegenüber.

age (eidʒ) n **1** Alter neu. **2** Zeitalter neu. **age-group** n Altersklasse f. **be of age** mündig sein. **old age** Alter neu. vi alt werden, altern. vt alt machen. **aged** adj **1** alt. **2** bejahrt, betagt.

agency ('eidʒənsi) n Agentur f.

agenda (ə'dʒendə) n Tagesordnung f.

agent ('eidʒənt) n **1** Agent, Vertreter m. **2** wirkende Kraft f. Mittel neu.

aggravate ('ægrəveit) vt **1** erschweren, verschlimmern. **2** inf ärgern. **aggravating** adj **1** erschwerend. **2** inf ärgerlich. **aggravation** n **1** Erschwerung f. **2** inf Verärgerung f.

aggregate (adj,n 'ægrigit; v 'ægrigeit) adj angehäuft, gesamt. n Anhäufung f. vt anhäufen.

aggression (ə'greʃən) n **1** Angriff m. **2** Aggression f. **aggressive** adj **1** angreifend. **2** streitsüchtig, aggressiv.

aggrieved (ə'gri:vd) adj betrübt, gekränkt.

aghast (ə'gɑ:st) adj entsetzt.

agile ('ædʒail) adj beweglich, behende, agil. **agility** n Beweglichkeit, Behendigkeit f.

agitate ('ædʒiteit) vt **1** bewegen, aufrühren. **2** erregen. vi agitieren. **agitation** n **1** Bewegung f. **2** Unruhe f. Aufruhr m. **agitator** n Agitator, Aufwiegler m.

aglow (ə'glou) adj glühend.

agnostic (æg'nɒstik) n Agnostiker m. adj agnostisch. **agnosticism** n Agnostizismus m.

ago (ə'gou) adv vor, her. **long ago** vor langer Zeit.

agog (ə'gɒg) adv gespannt.

agony ('ægəni) n Qual, Agonie f. **agonize** vt quälen. **agonizing** adj quälend.

agrarian (ə'grɛəriən) adj agrarisch.

agree (ə'gri:) vi übereinstimmen, einwilligen, einverstanden sein. **agree (on)** einig werden (über). **agreeable** adj **1** angenehm. **2** einverstanden. **agreed** adj **1** einig. **2** vereinbart. interj einverstanden! **agreement** n **1** Übereinstimmung f. **2** Abkommen neu. Vertrag m. **make an agreement** ein Abkommen treffen.

agriculture ('ægrikʌltʃə) n **1** Landwirtschaft f. **agricultural** adj landwirtschaftlich.

aground (ə'graund) adv **run aground** stranden. **go aground** stranden.

ahead (ə'hed) adv vorwärts, voran. **go ahead** fangen Sie an! **straight ahead** gerade aus.

aid (eid) vt helfen. n Hilfe f.

aide (eid) n mil Adjutant m.

ailment ('eilmənt) n Leiden neu. **ailing** adj kränklich, leidend.

aim (eim) vt (a gun, etc.) richten. vi **1** zielen. **2** streben. n **1** Ziel neu. **2** Absicht f. Zweck m. **take aim** zielen. **aimless** adj ziellos.

air (ɛə) n **1** Luft f. **2** Miene f. Anschein m. **3** Melodie f. Lied neu. **go by air** fliegen. **put on the air** senden. vt **1** (aus)lüften, trocknen. **2** bekanntmachen.

airborne ('ɛəbɔ:n) adj im Flugzeug befördert. **be airborne** fliegen.

air-conditioning n Klimaanlage f.

aircraft ('ɛəkrɑ:ft) n Flugzeug neu.

airfield ('ɛəfi:ld) n Flugplatz m.

airforce ('ɛəfɔ:s) n Luftwaffe f.

air-hostess ('ɛəhoustis) n Stewardeß f.

air lift n Luftbrücke f.

airline ('ɛəlain) n Luftverkehrslinie, Luftgesellschaft f. **airline passenger** n Fluggast m.

airmail ('ɛəmeil) n Luftpost f.

airman ('ɛəmən) n Flieger m.

airport ('ɛəpɔ:t) n Flughafen m.

air-raid n Luftangriff m.

airtight ('ɛətait) adj luftdicht.

airy ('ɛəri) adj **1** luftig. **2** unbekümmert.

aisle (ail) n Seitenschiff neu.

ajar (ə'dʒɑ:) adj halb offen, angelehnt.

akin (ə'kin) adj 1 verwandt. 2 (sehr) ähnlich.

alabaster ('æləbɑ:stə) n Alabaster m.

alarm (ə'lɑ:m) vt 1 alarmieren. 2 beunruhigen. n 1 Alarm m. 2 Angst f. **alarm clock** n Wecker m. **alarming** adj beunruhigend.

alas (ə'læs) interj ach! o weh! leider!

Albania (æl'beiniə) n Albanien neu. **Albanian** adj albanisch. n Albanier m.

albatross ('ælbətrɔs) n Albatros m.

albeit (ɔ:l'bi:it) conj obgleich, wenn auch.

album ('ælbəm) n Album neu.

alchemy ('ælkəmi) n Alchimie f. **alchemist** n Alchimist m.

alcohol ('ælkəhɔl) n Alkohol m. **alcoholic** adj alkoholistisch. n Alkoholiker m. **alcoholism** n Alkoholismus m.

alderman ('ɔ:ldəmən) n Ratsherr, Stadtrat m.

ale (eil) n Bier neu.

alert (ə'lə:t) adj 1 wachsam. 2 flink, munter. vt warnen. n Warnung f. **be on the alert** auf der Hut sein.

algebra ('ældʒibrə) n Algebra f

Algeria (æl'dʒiəriə) n Algerien neu. **Algerian** adj algerisch. n Algerier m.

alias ('eiliəs) adv alias, sonst...genannt.

alibi ('ælibai) n 1 law Alibi neu. 2 inf Ausrede f.

alien ('eiliən) n Fremde(r) m. Ausländer m. adj fremd, ausländisch. **alienate** vt entfremden. **alienation** n Entfremdung f.

alight[1] (ə'lait) vi 1 absteigen. 2 landen.

alight[2] (ə'lait) adj 1 brennend, in Flammen. 2 erleuchtet.

align (ə'lain) (vi),vt 1 (sich) in gerader Linie aufstellen. 2 (sich) ausrichten. **align oneself** sich anschließen.

alike (ə'laik) adj gleich, ähnlich. adv gleich, in gleicher Weise.

alimentary (æli'mentəri) adj Nahrungs—, nahrhaft. **alimentary canal** n Verdauungskanal m.

alimony ('æliməni) n Alimente neu pl.

alive (ə'laiv) adj 1 lebend, am Leben. 2 lebhaft. **alive to** empfänglich für.

alkali ('ælkəlai) n Alkali neu. **alkaline** adj alkalisch.

all (ɔ:l) adj 1 all, ganz. 2 jeder, jede, jedes m,f,neu. 3 all alle, sämtliche. n Ganze neu. adv ganz. pron alles. **above all** vor allem. **at all** überhaupt. **not at all** durchaus nicht.

allay (ə'lei) vt 1 beruhigen. 2 stillen.

allege (ə'ledʒ) vt 1 behaupten. 2 angeben. **allegation** n Behauptung f. Aussage f.

allegiance (ə'li:dʒəns) n 1 Untertanenpflicht f. 2 Treue f.

allegory ('æligəri) n Allegorie f.

allergy ('ælədʒi) n Allergie f. **allergic** adj allergisch.

alleviate (ə'li:vieit) vt erleichtern, mildern. **alleviation** n Erleichterung, Milderung f.

alley ('æli) n 1 Allee f. 2 Gasse f. 3 Durchgang m. **bowling alley** n Kegelbahn f.

alliance (ə'laiəns) n 1 Verbindung f. 2 Bund m. Bündnis neu. 3 Verwandtschaft f.

allied (ə'laid, 'ælaid) adj verbündet, alliiert.

alligator ('æligeitə) n Alligator m.

allocate ('æləkeit) vt zuteilen, zuweisen. **allocation** n Zuteilung, Zuweisung f.

allot (ə'lɔt) vt 1 verteilen. 2 bestimmen (für). **allotment** n 1 Verteilung f. 2 Parzelle f. 3 Schrebergarten m.

allow (ə'lau) vt 1 erlauben, zulassen. 2 bewilligen. 3 zugeben. **allow for** berücksichtigen. **be allowed to** dürfen. **allowable** adj zulässig. **allowance** n 1 Erlaubnis f. 2 Zuschuß m. 3 Nachsicht f. 4 comm Nachlaß m. **make allowances for** berücksichtigen.

alloy ('æloi) n Legierung f. vt legieren.

allude (ə'lu:d) vi **allude to** anspielen auf, andeuten. **allusion** n Andeutung, Anspielung f.

allure (ə'luə) vt (an-, ver-)locken.

ally (v ə'lai; n 'ælai) (vi),vt (sich) verbünden. n Verbündete(r) m.

almanac ('ɔ:lmənæk) n Almanach m.

almighty (ɔ:l'maiti) adj allmächtig. n Allmächtige(r) m.

almond ('ɑ:mənd) n Mandel f.

almost ('ɔ:lmoust) adv fast, beinahe.

alms (ɑ:mz) n pl Almosen neu.

aloft (ə'lɔft) adv 1 (hoch) oben. 2 nach oben.

alone (ə'loun) adj allein. adv allein, nur. **leave alone** in Ruhe lassen.

along (ə'lɔŋ) prep entlang. adv 1 entlang. 2 vorwärts, weiter. **get along with someone** mit jemandem auskommen, sich mit jemandem verstehen. **alongside** prep neben. adv naut längsseits.

aloof (ə'lu:f) adv fern, abseits. **keep aloof** sich fernhalten. **aloofness** n Zurückhaltung f.

aloud (ə'laud) adv laut, mit lauter Stimme.

alphabet ('ælfəbet) n Alphabet neu. **alphabetical** adj alphabetisch.

alpine ('ælpain) adj Alpen—. **alpinist** n Alpinist m.

Alps (ælps) n pl Alpen f pl.

143

already (ɔːˈredi) *adv* schon, bereits.
Alsace (ˈælsæs) *n* Elsaß *neu.* **Alsatian** *adj* elsässisch. *n* Elsässer *m.* **Alsatian (dog)** deutscher Schäferhund *m.*
also (ˈɔːlsou) *adv* auch, ferner.
altar (ˈɔːltə) *n* Altar *m.* **altarpiece** *n* Altarblatt *neu.* **altar-rail** *n* Altarschranke *f.*
alter (ˈɔːltə) *vt* (um-, ver-)ändern. *vi* sich ändern. **alterable** *adj* veränderlich. **alteration** *n* Veränderung, (Um)Änderung.
alternate (*v* ˈɔːltəneit; *adj* ɔlˈtəːnit) *vi* (*vt*) abwechseln (lassen). *adj* abwechselnd. **alternating** *adj* abwechselnd. **alternating current** *n* Wechselstrom *m.* **alternation** *n* 1 Abwechslung *f.* 2 Wechsel *m.* **alternative** *adj* 1 alternativ. 2 ander-. *n* Alternative, Wahl *f.*
although (ɔːlˈðou) *conj* obgleich, obwohl.
altitude (ˈæljuˈminiəm) *n* Höhe *f.*
alto (ˈæltou) *n* Alt *m.* Altstimme *f.*
altogether (ɔːltəˈgeðə) *adv* 1 gänzlich, ganz und gar. 2 im ganzen (genommen).
aluminium (æljuˈminiəm) *n* Aluminium *neu.*
always (ˈɔːlweiz) *adv* immer, stets.
am (əm; *stressed* æm) *v* see **be.**
amalgamate (əˈmælgəmeit) (*vi*),*vt* 1 (sich) amalgamieren. 2 (sich) vereinigen. 3 *comm* fusionieren.
amass (əˈmæs) *vt* anhäufen.
amateur (ˈæmətə) *n* Amateur, Liebhaber *m.*
amaze (əˈmeiz) *vt* erstaunen, verblüffen. **amazement** *n* (Er)Staunen *neu.* **amazing** *adj* 1 erstaunlich. 2 verblüffend.
ambassador (æmˈbæsədə) *n* Botschafter, Gesandte(r) *m.*
amber (ˈæmbə) *adj* 1 Bernstein—. 2 bernsteinfarben. *n* 1 Bernstein *m.* 2 *mot* Gelb, gelbes Licht *neu.*
ambidextrous (æmbiˈdekstrəs) *adj* 1 beidhändig. 2 ungewöhnlich geschickt.
ambiguous (æmˈbigjuəs) *adj* 1 zweideutig. 2 unklar. **ambiguity** *n* Zweideutigkeit *f.* Doppelsinn *m.*
ambition (æmˈbiʃən) *n* 1 Ehrgeiz *m.* 2 Ziel *neu.* **ambitious** *adj* ehrgeizig.
ambivalent (æmˈbivələnt) *adj* 1 ambivalent. 2 zwiespältig.
amble (ˈæmbəl) *vi* schlendern.
ambulance (ˈæmbjuləns) *n* Krankenwagen *m.*
ambush (ˈæmbuʃ) *n* Hinterhalt *m.* *vt* aus dem Hinterhalt überfallen.
amenable (əˈmiːnəbəl) *adj* 1 zugänglich. 2 gefügig.
amend (əˈmend) *vt* 1 verbessern. 2 abändern. 3

berichtigen. **amendment** *n* 1 Verbesserung *f.* 2 Abänderung *f.* **make amends for** wiedergutmachen.
amenity (əˈmiːniti) *n* 1 Annehmlichkeit *f.* 2 *pl* Vorzüge *m pl.*
America (əˈmerikə) *n* Amerika *neu.* **American** *adj* amerikanisch. *n* Amerikaner *m.*
amethyst (ˈæmiθist) *n* Amethyst *m.*
amiable (ˈeimiəbl) *adj* freundlich.
amicable (ˈæmikəbl) *adj* freundschaftlich.
amid (əˈmid) *prep* mitten in or unter.
amiss (əˈmis) *adj,adv* verkehrt, falsch. **take amiss** übel nehmen.
ammonia (əˈmouniə) *n* Ammoniak *neu.*
ammunition (æmjuˈniʃən) *n* Munition *f.*
amnesty (ˈæmnəsti) *n* Amnestie *f.* Straferlaß *m.*
amoeba (əˈmiːbə) *n* Amöbe *f.*
among (əˈmʌŋ) *prep also* **amongst** 1 unter. 2 inmitten, zwischen. 3 bei.
amoral (eiˈmɔrəl) *adj* amoralisch.
amorous (ˈæmərəs) *adj* 1 verliebt. 2 Liebes—.
amorphous (əˈmɔːfəs) *adj* 1 amorph. 2 formlos.
amount (əˈmaunt) *n* 1 Betrag *m.* Summe *f.* 2 Menge *f.* *vi* sich belaufen, betragen.
ampere (ˈæmpɛə) *n* Ampere *neu.*
amphetamine (æmˈfetəmiːn) *n* Benzedrin *neu.*
amphibian (æmˈfibiən) *n* Amphibie *f.* *adj* amphibisch. **amphibious** *adj* 1 *zool* amphibisch. 2 *tech* Amphibien—.
amphitheatre (ˈæmfiθiətə) *n* Amphitheater *neu.*
ample (ˈæmpəl) *adj* 1 reichlich. 2 weit, groß.
amplify (ˈæmplifai) *vt* 1 *tech* verstärken. 2 erweitern, ausdehnen. **amplifier** *n* Verstärker *m.*
amputate (ˈæmpjuteit) *vt* amputieren, abnehmen. **amputation** *n* Amputation *f.*
amuse (əˈmjuːz) *vt* amüsieren, unterhalten. **be amused** sich amüsieren *or* freuen. **amusement** *n* 1 Unterhaltung *f.* 2 Vergnügen *neu.* **amusing** *adj* amüsant, unterhaltend.
an (ən; *stressed* æn) *indef art* see **a.**
anachronism (əˈnækrənizəm) *n* Anachronismus *m.*
anaemia (əˈniːmiə) *n* Anämie, Blutarmut *f.* **anaemic** *adj* anämisch, bleichsüchtig.
anaesthetic (ænisˈθetik) *n* Betäubungsmittel *neu.* *adj* betäubend, narkotisch. **anaesthetist** *n* Narkotiseur *m.* **anaesthetize** *vt* betäuben, narkotisieren.
anal (ˈein|) *adj* anal, After—.
analogy (əˈnælədʒi) *n* Analogie, Ähnlichkeit *f.* **analogous** *adj* analog, ähnlich.

analysis (ə'næləsis) n, pl **analyses 1** Analyse f. **2** Zergliederung f. **3** Untersuchung f. **analyse** vt **1** analysieren. **2** zergliedern, auswerten. **3** genau untersuchen. **analyst** n Analytiker m. **analytical** adj analytisch.

anarchy ('ænəki) n Anarchie, Gesetzlosigkeit f. **anarchist** n Anarchist m.

anatomy (ə'nætəmi) n Anatomie f. **anatomical** adj anatomisch.

ancestor ('ænsəstə) n Vorfahr, Ahn m.

anchor ('æŋkə) n Anker m. vt verankern. vi ankern.

anchovy ('æntʃəvi) n Anschovis f.

ancient ('einʃənt) adj alt, aus alter Zeit.

ancillary (æn'siləri) adj **1** Hilfs—, Neben— **2** untergeordnet.

and (ən, ənd; stressed ænd) conj und.

anecdote ('ænikdout) n Anekdote f.

anemone (ə'neməni) n Anemone f.

anew (ə'njuː) adv von neuem.

angel ('eindʒəl) n Engel m. **angelic** adj engelhaft.

anger ('æŋgə) n Zorn, Ärger m. vt ärgern.

angle [1] ('æŋgəl) n **1** math Winkel m. **2** Ecke f. **3** Standpunkt m. **4** Seite f.

angle [2] ('æŋgəl) vi angeln. **angler** n Angler m. **angling** n Angeln neu.

Anglican ('æŋglikən) adj anglikanisch. n Anglikaner m.

angry ('æŋgri) adj zornig, ärgerlich, böse.

anguish ('æŋgwiʃ) n Qual, Angst f. Schmerz m.

angular ('æŋgjulə) adj winklig, eckig.

animal ('æniməl) n Tier neu. adj tierisch.

animate ('ænimeit) vt **1** beleben. **2** aufmuntern. **animated** adj lebhaft, munter. **animation** n Lebhaftigkeit, Munterkeit f.

animosity (æni'mɔsiti) n Feindseligkeit f.

aniseed ('ænisiːd) n Anis m.

ankle ('æŋkəl) n (Fuß)Knöchel m.

annals ('ænlz) n pl Annalen f pl.

annex (ə'neks) vt **1** annektieren. **2** anhängen. **3** beifügen. **annexation** n Annexion f. **annexe** n **1** Anbau m. **2** Nebengebäude neu.

annihilate (ə'naiəleit) vt vernichten. **annihilation** n Vernichtung f.

anniversary (æni'vəːsəri) n Jahrestag m. Jahresfeier f.

annotate ('ænəteit) vt mit Anmerkungen versehen.

announce (ə'nauns) vt **1** ankündigen, bekanntmachen. **2** anzeigen. **announcement** n **1** Ankündigung f. **2** Anzeige f. **announcer** n Ansager m.

annoy (ə'nɔi) vt ärgern, belästigen. **be annoyed** sich ärgern. **annoyance** n Belästigung f. Ärgernis neu. **annoying** adj ärgerlich.

annual ('ænjuəl) adj **1** jährlich, Jahres— **2** bot einjährig. n **1** Jahrbuch neu. **2** einjährige Pflanze f.

annul (ə'nʌl) vt für ungültig erklären.

anode ('ænoud) n Anode f.

anoint (ə'nɔint) vt salben.

anomaly (ə'nɔməli) n Anomalie, Unregelmäßigkeit f.

anonymous (ə'nɔniməs) adj anonym, namenlos. **anonymity** n Anonymität f.

another (ə'nʌðə) adj,pron **1** ein anderer. **2** ein zweiter or weiterer. **3** noch einer.

answer ('ɑːnsə) n Antwort f. vt **1** (a question) beantworten. **2** (a person) antworten. **answer for** verantwortlich sein für. **answerable** adj verantwortlich.

ant (ænt) n Ameise f.

antagonize (æn'tægənaiz) vt zum Gegner or Feind machen. **antagonism** n **1** Feindseligkeit f. **2** Widerstand m. **antagonist** n Gegner m. **antagonistic** adj feindlich, gegnerisch.

Antarctic (æn'tɑːktik) n Antarktis f. adj antarktisch, Südpol—. **Antarctic Ocean** n südliches Polarmeer neu.

antelope ('æntiloup) n Antelope f.

antenatal (ænti'neitl) adj vor der Geburt. **antenatal care** n Schwangerschaftsfürsorge f.

antenna (æn'tenə) n **1** pl **antennae** zool Fühler m. **2** pl **antennas** tech Antenne f.

anthem ('ænθəm) n **1** Hymne f. **2** Choral m. **national anthem** n Nationalhymne f.

anthology (æn'θɔlədʒi) n Anthologie f.

anthropology (ænθrə'pɔlədʒi) n Anthropologie f. **anthropological** adj anthropologisch. **anthropologist** n Anthropologe m.

antibiotic (æntibai'ɔtik) n Antibiotikum neu. adj antibiotisch.

antibody ('æntibɔdi) n Antikörper m.

anticipate (æn'tisipeit) vt **1** voraussehen. **2** vorwegnehmen. **3** erwarten, erhoffen. **anticipation** n **1** Vorahnung f. **2** Vorwegnahme f. **3** Hoffnung, Erwartung f.

anticlimax (ænti'klaimæks) n Abfallen neu. Antiklimax m.

anticlockwise (ænti'klɔkwaiz) adv gegen den Uhrzeigersinn.

antics ('æntiks) n pl Posse, Fratze f.

anticyclone (ænti'saikloun) n Hochdruckgebiet neu.

antidote ('æntidout) n Gegengift neu.

antifreeze

antifreeze ('æntifri:z) n Frostschutzmittel neu.

antique (æn'ti:k) n Antike f. alter Kunstgegenstand m. adj **1** antik. **2** alt. **antique dealer** n Antiquitätenhändler m. **antique shop** n Antiquitätengeschäft neu. **antiquated** adj **1** altmodisch. **2** veraltet, überholt. **antiquity** n **1** Altertum neu. **2** pl Antiquitäten f pl.

anti-Semitic adj antisemitisch. **anti-Semitism** n Antisemitismus m.

antiseptic (ænti'septik) adj antiseptisch. n Antiseptikum neu.

antisocial (ænti'souʃəl) adj gesellschaftsfeindlich.

antithesis (æn'tiθəsis) n, pl **-ses** Antithese f. Gegensatz m.

antler ('æntlə) n **1** Geweihsprosse f. **2** pl Geweih neu.

antonym ('æntənim) n Antonym neu.

anus ('einəs) n After m.

anvil ('ænvil) n Amboß m.

anxious ('æŋkʃəs) adj **1** ängstlich, besorgt. **2** begierig. **anxiety** n Angst, Sorge f.

any ('eni) adj **1** (irgend)einer, (irgend)welcher. **2** jeder. **in any case** auf jeden Fall. **not any** kein. ~pron irgendeiner, irgendwelcher. adv **1** etwas. **2** irgendwie. **anybody** pron (irgend)jemand, irgendeiner. **anyhow** adv **1** irgendwie. **2** jedenfalls. **anyone** pron (irgend)jemand, irgendeiner. **anything** pron **1** (irgend)etwas. **2** alles. **anything but** alles andere als. **if anything** wenn überhaupt. **anyway** adv **1** irgendwie. **2** jedenfalls, sowieso. **anywhere** adv **1** irgendwo(hin). **2** überall.

apart (ə'pa:t) adv **1** beiseite. **2** getrennt, abgesondert. **apart from** abgesehen von.

apartheid (ə'pa:tait) n Rassentrennung f.

apartment (ə'pa:tmənt) n **1** Zimmer neu. **2** US Wohnung f. **3** pl Wohnung f.

apathy ('æpəθi) n Apathie, Gleichgültigkeit f. **apathetic** adj apathisch.

ape (eip) n Affe m. vt (nach)äffen.

aperitive (ə'peritiv) n Aperitif m.

aperture ('æpətʃə) n **1** Öffnung f. **2** tech Blende f.

apex ('eipeks) n, pl **apexes** or **apices** Höhepunkt, Gipfel m. Spitze f.

apiece (ə'pi:s) adv **1** je, für jedes Stück. **2** pro Person.

apology (ə'pɔlədʒi) n **1** Entschuldigung f. **2** Rechtfertigung f. **apologetic** adj entschuldigend. **apologize** vi sich entschuldigen.

apostle (ə'pɔsəl) n Apostel m.

apostrophe (ə'pɔstrəfi) n Apostroph m.

146

appal (ə'pɔ:l) vt erschrecken, entsetzen. **appalling** adj entsetzlich, schrecklich.

apparatus (æpə'reitəs) n, pl **-tus** or **-tuses** Apparat m. Gerät neu.

apparent (ə'pærənt) adj **1** augenscheinlich, offenbar. **2** sichtbar. **3** scheinbar. **apparently** adv anscheinend.

appeal (ə'pi:l) vi **1** appellieren, sich wenden. **2** bitten. **3** gefallen, zusagen. **4** sich berufen auf. n **1** (dringende) Bitte f. **2** Appell m. **3** Anziehungskraft f.

appear (ə'piə) vi **1** erscheinen, sich zeigen. **2** scheinen, aussehen. **3** auftauchen. **appearance** n **1** Erscheinen neu. **2** Äußere neu. Erscheinung f. **3** Anschein m. **to all appearances** allem Anschein nach.

appease (ə'pi:z) vt **1** beruhigen. **2** befriedigen.

appendix (ə'pendiks) n, pl **-dixes** or **-dices 1** Anhang m. **2** anat Blinddarm m. **appendicitis** n Blinddarmentzündung f.

appetite ('æpətait) n **1** Appetit m. **2** Verlangen neu.

applaud (ə'plɔ:d) vt **1** beklatschen, Beifall spenden. **2** billigen. vi applaudieren. **applause** n Beifall m.

apple ('æpəl) n Apfel m.

apply (ə'plai) vt **1** anwenden, verwenden. **2** auflegen. vi **1** sich bewerben. **2** sich wenden an. **3** sich anwenden lassen. **apply oneself** sich widmen. **appliance** n Gerät neu. Apparat m. **applicable** adj **1** anwendbar. **2** geeignet. **not applicable** nicht zutreffend. **applicant** n Bewerber, Antragsteller m. **application** n **1** Anwendung f. **2** Antrag m. Bewerbung f. **3** Eifer m. **4** Auflegen neu.

appoint (ə'pɔint) vt **1** ernennen, anstellen. **2** verabreden. **3** ausstatten. **appointment** n **1** Ernennung, Anstellung f. **2** Verabredung f.

appraise (ə'preiz) vt abschätzen, bewerten. **appraisal** n Abschätzung f.

appreciate (ə'pri:ʃieit) vt **1** (richtig) schätzen. **2** Gefallen finden. **3** dankbar sein (für). **4** wahrnehmen, erkennen. vi im Wert steigen. **appreciable** adj merklich, nennenswert. **appreciation** n **1** Schätzung f. **2** Verständnis neu. **appreciative** adj **1** anerkennend. **2** verständnisvoll.

apprehend (æpri'hend) vt **1** verhaften. **2** begreifen. **3** befürchten. **apprehension** n **1** Besorgnis, Befürchtung f. **2** Verstand m. **3** Verhaftung f. **apprehensive** adj besorgt, bedenklich, ängstlich.

apprentice (ə'prentis) n Lehrling m. **apprenticeship** n Lehrzeit f.

approach (ə'prəʊtʃ) vt,vi 1 sich nähern. 2 nahekommen. vt 1 sich wenden an. 2 herantreten an. n 1 (Heran)Nahen neu. Annäherung f. 2 Zugang m. Auffahrt, Zufahrt f. 3 Behandlung f. **approachable** adj zugänglich.

appropriate (adj ə'proupriət; v ə'prouprieit) adj 1 angemessen, geeignet. 2 entsprechend. vt sich aneignen.

approve (ə'pruːv) vt,vi billigen, anerkennen, genehmigen. vt annehmen, akzeptieren. **approval** n Billigung, Genehmigung, Anerkennung f. **on approval** zur Ansicht.

approximate (adj ə'prɔksimət; v ə'prɔksimeit) adj ungefähr. vt nahekommen. vi sich nähern.

apricot ('eiprikɔt) n Aprikose f.

April ('eiprəl) n April m.

apron ('eiprən) n Schürze f.

apt (æpt) adj 1 geeignet. 2 geschickt.

aptitude ('æptitjuːd) n Begabung f. Geschick neu.

aquarium (ə'kwɛəriəm) n, pl **-riums** or **-ria** Aquarium neu.

Aquarius (ə'kwɛəriəs) n Wassermann m.

aquatic (ə'kwætik) adj Wasser—.

aqueduct ('ækwədʌkt) n Aquädukt m.

Arabia (ə'reibiə) n Arabien neu. **Arab** adj arabisch. n Araber m. **Arabian** adj arabisch. n Araber m. **Arabic** adj arabisch. n (language) Arabisch neu.

arable ('ærəbəl) adj Acker—.

arbitrary ('ɑːbitrəri) adj willkürlich, eigenmächtig.

arbitrate ('ɑːbitreit) vt entscheiden, schlichten. vi Schiedsrichter sein. **arbitration** n Schiedsspruch m. **arbitrator** n Schiedsrichter m.

arc (ɑːk) n Bogen m.

arcade (ɑː'keid) n 1 Arkade f. 2 Durchgang m.

arch (ɑːtʃ) n 1 arch Bogen m. 2 Wölbung f. vi sich wölben.

archaeology (ɑːki'ɔlədʒi) n Archäologie f. **archaeological** adj archäologisch. **archaeologist** n Archäologe m.

archaic (ɑː'keiik) adj 1 veraltet. 2 altertümlich. **archaism** n veralteter Ausdruck m.

archbishop (ɑːtʃ'biʃəp) n Erzbischof m.

archduke (ɑːtʃ'djuːk) n Erzherzog m.

archery ('ɑːtʃəri) n Bogenschießen m. **archer** n Bogenschütze m.

archetype ('ɑːkitaip) n Archetyp m.

archipelago (ɑːki'peləgou) n Archipel m.

architect ('ɑːkitekt) n 1 Architekt m. 2 Schöp-

fer, Urheber m. **architecture** n 1 Architektur f. 2 Konstruktion f.

archives ('ɑːkaivz) n pl Archiv neu.

archway ('ɑːtʃwei) n Bogengang m.

Arctic ('ɑːktik) n Arktis f. Nordpolargebiet neu. adj arktisch. **Arctic Ocean** n Nördliches Polarmeer neu.

ardent ('ɑːdnt) adj 1 heiß, glühend. 2 eifrig, begeistert.

ardour ('ɑːdə) n 1 Hitze f. 2 Eifer m. Begeisterung f.

arduous ('ɑːdjuəs) adj schwierig, anstrengend.

are (ə; stressed ɑː) v see **be.**

area ('ɛəriə) n 1 Fläche f. Flächeninhalt m. 2 Gebiet neu. Gegend f. 3 Bereich m. Zone f.

arena (ə'riːnə) n Arena f.

Argentina (ɑːdʒən'tiːnə) n Argentinien neu. **Argentine** adj also **Argentinian** argentinisch. n Argentinier m.

argue ('ɑːgjuː) vt 1 erörtern, diskutieren. 2 behaupten. vi 1 streiten, argumentieren. 2 Einwände machen. **argument** n 1 Beweis m. Beweisführung f. 2 Streit m. 3 Argument neu. **argumentative** adj streitlustig.

arid ('ærid) adj trocken, dürr.

Aries ('ɛəriːz) n Widder m.

arise* (ə'raiz) vi 1 entstehen. 2 aufstehen.

aristocracy (æri'stɔkrəsi) n Aristokratie f. Adel m. **aristocrat** n Aristokrat, Adlige(r) m. **aristocratic** adj aristokratisch.

arithmetic (ə'riθmətik) n Arithmetik f. Rechnen neu. **arithmetical** adj arithmetisch.

arm¹ (ɑːm) n 1 Arm m. 2 (of a chair) Armlehne f. **with open arms** mit offenen Armen. **armchair** n Lehnstuhl, Sessel m. **armful** n Armvoll m. **armhole** n Ärmelloch neu. **armpit** n Achselhöhle f.

arm² (ɑːm) n Waffe f. **arms race** Wettrüsten neu. **coat of arms** Wappen neu. **up in arms** in Aufruhr. ~(vi), vt (sich) bewaffnen, (sich) ausrüsten. **armed forces** n Streitkräfte f pl. **armament** n 1 Bewaffnung f. 2 (Kriegsaus)-Rüstung f.

armour ('ɑːmə) n Panzer m. **armour-plated** adj also **armoured** gepanzert, Panzer—.

army ('ɑːmi) n 1 Armee f. Heer neu. 2 Menge f.

aroma (ə'roumə) n Aroma neu. Duft m. **aromatic** (ærə'mætik) adj aromatisch, würzig.

arose (ə'rouz) v see **arise.**

around (ə'raund) prep 1 um, um...herum. 2 ungefähr. adv 1 rundherum. 2 in der Nähe.

arouse (ə'rauz) vt 1 aufwecken. 2 erregen.

arrange (ə'reindʒ) vt 1 anordnen. 2 einrichten.

3 erledigen. 4 vereinbaren. 5 *mus* bearbeiten. *vi* 1 sich verständigen. 2 Vorkehrungen treffen. 3 sich einigen. **arrangement** *n* 1 Anordnung f. 2 Einrichtung f. 3 Vereinbarung f. Abkommen neu. 4 *mus* Bearbeitung f.

array (ə'rei) *vt* 1 ordnen. 2 kleiden, putzen. *n* 1 Ordnung f. 2 Kleidung, Aufmachung f.

arrears (ə'riəz) *n pl* Rückstände *m pl.* Schulden f *pl.* **in arrears** im Rückstand m.

arrest (ə'rest) *vt* 1 verhaften. 2 aufhalten, hindern. *n* Haft, Verhaftung f. **under arrest** verhaftet. **arresting** *adj* interessant, fesselnd.

arrive (ə'raiv) *vi* 1 ankommen. 2 erreichen, gelangen. 3 erscheinen. **arrival** *n* 1 Ankunft f. 2 Erscheinen neu.

arrogant ('ærəgənt) *adj* arrogant, anmaßend, überheblich. **arrogance** *n* Arroganz, Anmaßung f.

arrow ('ærou) *n* 1 Pfeil m. 2 Pfeilzeichen neu.

arsenic ('a:snik) *n* Arsenik neu.

arson ('a:sən) *n* Brandstiftung f.

art (a:t) *n* 1 Kunst f. 2 Geschick neu. 3 List f. 4 *pl educ* Geisteswissenschaften f *pl.* **work of art** Kunstwerk n. ~*adj* Kunst—. **art gallery** *n* Kunstgalerie, Bildergalerie f. **art school** *n* Kunstschule f. **artful** *adj* 1 listig, schlau. 2 geschickt.

artery ('a:təri) *n* Arterie, Pulsader f. **arterial** *adj* arteriell.

arthritis (a:'θraitis) *n* Arthritis f.

artichoke ('a:tiʃouk) *n* Artischocke f.

article ('a:tikəl) *n* 1 Artikel m. 2 Ware f. Gegenstand m.

articulate (v a:'tikjuleit: *adj* a:'tikjulət) *vt* 1 aussprechen, artikulieren. 2 gliedern. *vi* deutlich sprechen. *adj* 1 deutlich. 2 sich gut ausdrückend.

artificial (a:ti'fiʃəl) *adj* 1 künstlich, Kunst—. 2 gekünstelt.

artillery (a:'tiləri) *n* Artillerie f.

artist ('a:tist) *n* 1 Künstler m. 2 Könner m. **artiste** *n* Artist m. **artistic** *adj* künstlerisch, Kunst—.

as (æz; *stressed* æz) *conj* 1 da, weil. 2 wie, sowie. 3 als, während. *adv* 1 so, wie, ebenso wie. 2 als. **as...as** (eben)so...wie. **as far as** soviel, sofern, soweit. **as if** als ob, als wenn. **as long as** solange. **as well** ebenfalls, auch.

asbestos (æs'bestəs) *n* Asbest m.

ascend (ə'send) *vi* (auf-, hinauf-)steigen. *vt* besteigen. **ascendant** *adj* 1 aufsteigend. 2 vorherrschend. **in the ascendant** im Auf-

steigen. **Ascension** *n rel* Himmelfahrt f. **ascent** *n* Aufstieg m.

ascertain (æsə'tein) *vt* feststellen.

ash[1] (æʃ) *n* Asche f. **ashtray** *n* Aschenbecher m.

ash[2] (æʃ) *n bot* Esche f.

ashamed (ə'ʃeimd) *adj* beschämt. **be ashamed** sich schämen.

ashore (ə'ʃɔ:) *adv* am *or* ans Ufer. **go ashore** an Land gehen.

Ash Wednesday *n* Aschermittwoch m.

Asia ('eiʃə) *n* Asien neu. **Asia Minor** Kleinasien neu. **Asian** *adj* asiatisch. *n* Asiat m. **Asiatic** *adj* asiatisch.

aside (ə'said) *adv* beiseite.

ask (a:sk) *vt* 1 fragen. 2 fragen nach. 3 bitten. 4 fordern, verlangen. **ask about** *or* **after** sich erkundigen nach *or* wegen.

askew (ə'skju:) *adv* schief, schräg.

asleep (ə'sli:p) *adv* schlafend. **be asleep** schlafen. **fall asleep** einschlafen.

asparagus (ə'spærəgəs) *n* Spargel m.

aspect ('æspekt) *n* 1 Aussehen neu. 2 Aspekt m. Hinsicht f. 3 Aussicht f.

asphalt ('æsfælt) *n* Asphalt m.

aspire (ə'spaiə) *vi* 1 streben. 2 sich erheben. **aspiring** *adj* hochstrebend.

aspirin ('æsprin) *n* Aspirin neu.

ass (æs) *n* Esel m.

assassinate (ə'sæsineit) *vt* ermorden. **assassin** *n* (politischer) Mörder m. **assassination** *n* Ermordung f.

assault (ə'sɔ:lt) *vt* angreifen, überfallen. *n* Angriff, Überfall m.

assemble (ə'sembəl) *vt* 1 versammeln. 2 zusammensetzen, montieren. *vi* sich versammeln. **assembly** *n* 1 Versammlung f. 2 Montage f. **assembly hall** *n educ* Aula f. **assembly line** *n* Fließband neu.

assent (ə'sent) *vi* 1 zustimmen. 2 genehmigen. *n* 1 Zustimmung f. 2 Genehmigung f.

assert (ə'sə:t) *vt* 1 behaupten, erklären. 2 bestehen auf. **assert oneself** sich durchsetzen. **assertion** *n* Behauptung f. **assertive** *adj* anmaßend.

assess (ə'ses) *vt* 1 zur Steuer einschätzen. 2 einschätzen. **assessment** *n* Einschätzung f.

asset ('æset) *n* 1 Vorteil m. 2 *pl comm* Vermögen neu.

assign (ə'sain) *vt* 1 anweisen. 2 bestimmen. **assignment** *n* 1 Anweisung f. 2 Aufgabe f.

assimilate (ə'simileit) *vt* 1 absorbieren, aufnehmen. **2** anpassen. **assimilation** n Aufnahme f.

assist (ə'sist) vt **1** helfen. **2** unterstützen. **3** fördern. vi **1** mithelfen. **2** teilnehmen. **3** beiwohnen. **assistance** n **1** Hilfe f. **2** Unterstützung f. **assistant** n **1** Assistent m. **2** Verkäufer m.

assizes (ə'saiziz) n pl Gerichtssitzungen f pl.

associate (v ə'souʃieit; adj,n ə'souʃiit) vt **1** vereinigen, anschließen. **2** verbinden, verknüpfen. vi verkehren. adj verbündet. n Kollege, Mitarbeiter m. **association** n **1** Vereinigung f. **2** Verein, Verband m. **3** Verkehr m. **4** Verbindung f.

assort (ə'sɔːt) vt assortieren. **assorted** adj gemischt. **assortment** n Sortiment neu.

assume (ə'sjuːm) vt **1** annehmen. **2** übernehmen. **3** sich aneignen. **assuming** adj anmaßend. **assumption** n **1** Annahme f. **2** Aneignung f.

assure (ə'ʃuə) vt **1** sichern, sicherstellen. **2** versichern. **assurance** n **1** Versicherung f. **2** Selbstsicherheit f.

asthma ('æsmə) n Asthma neu.

astonish (ə'stɔniʃ) vt erstaunen, überraschen. **be astonished** erstaunt sein. **astonishing** adj erstaunlich. **astonishment** n Erstaunen neu.

astound (ə'staund) vt verblüffen.

astray (ə'strei) adv **go astray** sich verlaufen. **lead astray** irreführen.

astride (ə'straid) prep,adj,adv rittlings.

astrology (ə'strɔlədʒi) n Astrologie, Sterndeuterei f. **astrologer** n Astrologe m. **astrological** adj astrologisch.

astronaut ('æstrənɔːt) n Astronaut m.

astronomy (ə'strɔnəmi) n Astronomie, Sternkunde f. **astronomer** n Astronom m. **astronomical** adj **1** astronomisch, Stern—. **2** riesengroß.

astute (ə'stjuːt) adj scharfsinnig.

asunder (ə'sʌndə) adv auseinander.

asylum (ə'sailəm) n **1** pol Asyl neu. Freistätte f. **2** Heim neu. **lunatic asylum** Irrenanstalt f.

at (ət; stressed æt) prep **1** an, auf. **2** in, zu. **3** bei. **4** für. **5** um. **6** über. **at two o'clock** um zwei Uhr.

ate (eit, et) v see **eat.**

atheism ('eiθiizəm) n Atheismus m. **atheist** n Atheist m.

Athens ('æθinz) n Athen neu.

athlete ('æθliːt) n (Leicht)Athlet, Sportler m. **athletic** adj athletisch, Sport—. **athletics** n pl Athletik f.

Atlantic (ət'læntik) adj atlantisch. **Atlantic (Ocean)** n Atlantik, Atlantischer Ozean m.

atlas ('ætləs) n Atlas m.

atmosphere ('ætməsfiə) n **1** Atmosphäre f. **2** Luft f. **3** Stimmung f.

atom ('ætəm) n Atom neu. **atom bomb** n Atombombe f. **atomic** adj atomisch, Atom—.

atone (ə'toun) vi **1** büßen. **2** wiedergutmachen. **atonement** n Buße f.

atrocious (ə'trouʃəs) adj scheußlich, gräßlich. **atrocity** n Scheußlichkeit, Greueltat f.

attach (ə'tætʃ) vt **1** befestigen. **2** anheften. **3** verbinden. **attachment** n **1** Befestigung f. **2** Zusatzgerät neu. **3** Anhänglichkeit f.

attaché (ə'tæʃei) n Attaché m. **attaché case** n Aktentasche f.

attack (ə'tæk) vt **1** angreifen, überfallen. **2** in Angriff nehmen. **3** kritisieren. vi **1** Angriff, Überfall m. **2** Kritik f. **3** med Anfall m. **attacker** n Angreifer m.

attain (ə'tein) vt erreichen, erlangen. **attain to** gelangen zu. **attainable** adj erreichbar. **attainment** n Erreichung f.

attempt (ə'tempt) vt **1** versuchen. **2** sich wagen (an). n **1** Versuch m. **2** Attentat neu.

attend (ə'tend) vt **1** beiwohnen. **2** (a school) besuchen. **3** pflegen. vi **1** achten. **2** sich besorgen. **3** erledigen. **4** erscheinen. **5** bedienen. **attendance** n **1** Anwesenheit f. **2** Beteiligung f. **3** Pflege, Bedienung f. **4** Besuch m. **attendant** n **1** Diener m. **2** Begleiter m. **3** Bedienungsmann, Wärter m. **attention** n **1** Aufmerksamkeit, Beachtung f. **2** Erledigung f. **3** pl Aufmerksamkeiten f pl. **4** Bedienung f. **pay attention** achtgeben. interj Achtung! **attentive** adj aufmerksam.

attic ('ætik) n Dachstube f.

attire (ə'taiə) vt ankleiden, schmücken. n Kleidung f. Schmuck m.

attitude ('ætitjuːd) n **1** Stellung, Haltung f. **2** Einstellung, Stellungnahme f.

attract (ə'trækt) vt **1** anziehen. **2** reizen, fesseln. **attract attention** Aufmerksamkeit erregen. **attraction** n **1** Anziehung, Attraktion f. **2** Anziehungskraft f. **attractive** adj **1** anziehend, reizvoll. **2** hübsch. **attractiveness** n Reiz m.

attribute (v ə'tribjuːt; n 'ætribjuːt) vt **1** zuschreiben. **2** zurückführen. n Eigenschaft f.

aubergine ('oubəʒiːn) n Aubergine f.

auburn ('ɔːbən) adj kastanienbraun.

auction ('ɔːkʃən) n Auktion, Versteigerung f. v **auction off** versteigern.

149

audacious

audacious (ɔ:'deiʃəs) adj **1** kühn. **2** frech. **audacity** n **1** Kühnheit f. **2** Frechheit f.

audible ('ɔ:dibəl) adj hörbar.

audience ('ɔ:diəns) n **1** Publikum neu. Zuhörer m pl. **2** Audienz f.

audit ('ɔ:dit) vt prüfen, revidieren. n Bücherrevision f. **auditing** n Bücherrevision f. **auditor** n Bücherrevisor m.

audition (ɔ:'diʃən) n Hörprobe f. vt einer Hörprobe unterziehen.

August ('ɔ:gəst) n August m.

aunt (ɑ:nt) n Tante f.

au pair (ou 'pɛə) n also **au pair girl** Aupair-Mädchen neu.

aura ('ɔ:rə) n, pl **auras** or **aurae 1** Aura, Atmosphäre f. **2** Hauch, Duft m.

austere (ɔ:'stiə) adj **1** streng. **2** enthaltsam.

Australia (ɔ'streiliə) n Australien neu. **Australian** adj australisch. n Australier m.

Austria ('ɔ:striə) n Österreich neu. **Austrian** adj österreichisch. n Österreicher m.

authentic (ɔ:'θentik) adj authentisch, echt.

author ('ɔ:θə) n **1** Verfasser m. **2** Autor, Schriftsteller m. **3** Urheber m.

authority (ɔ:'θɔriti) n **1** Autorität f. **2** Gewalt f. **3** Vollmacht f. **4** Quelle f. **5** Fachmann m. **6** pl Behörde f. **authoritarian** adj autoritär. **authoritative** adj **1** maßgebend. **2** herrisch.

authorize ('ɔ:θəraiz) vt **1** ermächtigen. **2** billigen, genehmigen. **authorization** n Genehmigung f.

autobiography (ɔ:təbai'ɔgrəfi) n Autobiographie f. **autobiographical** adj autobiographisch.

autograph ('ɔ:təgrɑ:f) n eigenhändige Unterschrift f. Autogramm neu. vt (eigenhändig) unterschreiben.

automatic (ɔ:tə'mætik) adj **1** automatisch, selbsttätig. **2** unwillkürlich. **automation** n Automation f.

autonomous (ɔ:'tɔnəməs) adj autonom. **autonomy** n Autonomie, Selbständigkeit f.

autumn ('ɔ:təm) n Herbst m.

auxiliary (ɔ:g'ziliəri) adj helfend, Hilfs—. n **1** Helfer m. **2** pl Hilfspersonal neu.

available (ə'veiləbəl) adj verfügbar, vorhanden. **availability** n Verfügbarkeit f. Vorhandensein neu.

avalanche ('ævəlɑ:nʃ) n Lawine f.

avenge (ə'vendʒ) vt rächen.

avenue ('ævənju:) n **1** Allee f. **2** Weg m.

average ('ævridʒ) adj durchschnittlich. n Durchschnitt m. **on average** im Durchschnitt.

aversion (ə'və:ʃən) n Abneigung f.

aviary ('eiviəri) n Vogelhaus neu.

aviation (eivi'eiʃən) n Flugwesen neu.

avid ('ævid) adj gierig.

avocado (ævə'kɑ:dou) n Avocadobirne f.

avoid (ə'vɔid) vt **1** vermeiden. **2** ausweichen. **3** aus dem Wege gehen.

await (ə'weit) vt erwarten, warten auf.

awake* (ə'weik) vt **1** wecken. **2** erwecken. vi **1** aufwachen, erwachen. **2** bewußt werden. adj wach. **wide awake** munter. **awaken** vt **1** wecken. **2** erwecken. vi aufwachen, erwachen. **awakening** n Erwachen neu.

award (ə'wɔ:d) vt **1** zusprechen, verleihen. **2** gewähren. n Belohnung f. Preis m.

aware (ə'wɛə) adj bewußt. **awareness** n Bewußtsein neu. Kenntnis f.

away (ə'wei) adv **1** weg, fort, hinweg. **2** entfernt. **3** fort, verreist.

awe (ɔ:) n Ehrfurcht f. **awe-inspiring** adj ehrfurchtgebietend. **awe-struck** adj von Ehrfurcht ergriffen. **awful** adj **1** schrecklich, furchtbar. **2** inf furchtbar, scheußlich. **awfully** adv inf furchtbar, sehr.

awkward ('ɔ:kwəd) adj **1** ungeschickt, linkisch. **2** peinlich, unangenehm. **3** lästig, schwierig.

awoke (ə'wouk) v see **awake.**

axe (æks) n Axt f. Beil neu.

axis ('æksis) n pl **axes** Achse, Mittellinie f.

axle ('æksəl) n (Rad)Achse f.

B

babble ('bæbəl) vt **1** schwatzen, plappern. **2** plätschern, murmeln. n Geschwätz neu.

baboon (bə'bu:n) n Pavian m.

baby ('beibi) n Baby neu. Säugling m. Kleinkind neu. **baby-sit** vi Kinder beaufsichtigen, babysitten. **babyish** adj babyhaft.

bachelor ('bætʃələ) n Junggeselle m.

back (bæk) n **1** Rücken m. Kreuz neu. **2** Rückseite f. Hinterseite f. adj Nach—, Hinter—. adv **1** zurück. **2** rückwärts. vt **1** wetten auf. **2** unterstützen. **3** rückwärts fahren.

backache ('bækeik) n Rückenschmerz m.

backbone ('bækboun) n Wirbelsäule f. Rückgrat neu.

backdate ('bækdeit) vt zurückdatieren.

backfire ('bækfaiə) vi **1** fehlzünden, frühzünden. **2** fehlschlagen. n Fehlzündung f.

backgammon ('bækgæmən) n Puffspiel neu.

background ('bækgraund) n Hintergrund m.

backhand ('bækhænd) *n* Rückhand *f.* **backhander** *n* **1** Rückhandschlag *m.* **2** geheime Belohnung *f.*

backlash ('bæklæʃ) *n* **1** *tech* Spielraum *m.* **2** (politische) Reaktion *f.* **3** Rückschlag *m.*

backlog ('bæklɔg) *n* Rückstand *m.* Rücklage *f.*

backside (bæk'said) *n inf* Hinterteil *neu.*

backstage (bæk'steidʒ) *adj,adv* hinter den Kulissen.

backstroke ('bækstrouk) *n* Gegenschlag *m.* Rückenschwimmen *neu.*

backward ('bækwəd) *adj* **1** (geistig) zurückgeblieben. **2** rückständig. **3** widerwillig.

backwards ('bækwədz) *adv* zurück, rückwärts.

backwater ('bækwɔtə) *n* Stauwasser *neu.*

bacon ('beikən) *n* Speck *m.*

bacteria (bæk'tiəriə) *n pl* Bakterie *f.*

bad (bæd) *adj* **1** schlecht, schlimm. **2** böse. **bad-tempered** *adj* mißgelaunt.

bade (beid) *v see* **bid.**

badge (bædʒ) *n* Abzeichen *neu.* Medaille *f.*

badger ('bædʒə) *n* Dachs *m.* *vt* belästigen.

badminton ('bædmintən) *n* Federballspiel *neu.*

baffle ('bæfəl) *vt* verwirren, täuschen.

bag (bæg) *n* **1** Beutel *m.* Tüte *f.* **2** Tasche *f.* **3** Sack *m.* *vt* **1** abschießen. **2** erlegen. **baggage** *n* Gepäck *neu.* **baggy** *adj* bauschig, sackartig, schlotterig. **bagpipes** *n* Dudelsack *m.*

bail¹ (beil) *n law* Bürgschaft, Kaution *f.*

bailiff ('beilif) *n* **1** Gerichtsdiener *m.* **2** Gutsverwalter *m.*

bait (beit) *n* **1** Köder *m.* Lockspeise *f.* **2** Lockung *f.* Reiz *m.* *vt* **1** ködern. **2** hetzen, quälen.

bake (beik) *vt* backen. **baker** *n* Bäcker *m.* **bakery** *n* Bäckerei *f.*

balance ('bæləns) *vt* **1** balancieren. **2** erwägen. **3** saldieren. *n* **1** Waage *f.* **2** Gleichgewicht *neu.* **3** Saldo *m.* Guthaben *neu.* **balance sheet** *n* Bilanz *f.* Bilanzbogen *m.*

balcony ('bælkəni) *n* Balkon *m.*

bald (bɔ:ld) *adj* **1** kahl, haarlos. **2** nackt.

bale¹ (beil) *n* Ballen *m.*

bale² (beil) *vt,vi* ausschöpfen. **bale out** mit dem Fallschirm abspringen.

ball¹ (bɔ:l) *n* **1** Ball *m.* **2** Kugel *f.* **ballpoint pen** *n* Kugelschreiber *m.*

ball² (bɔ:l) *n* Ball *m.* Tanzgesellschaft *f.* **ballroom** *n* Tanzsaal, Ballsaal *m.*

ballad ('bæləd) *n* Ballade *f.* Lied *neu.*

ballast ('bæləst) *n* Ballast *m.*

ballet ('bælei) *n* Ballett *neu.* **ballet dancer** *n* Balletttänzer *m.* Balletttänzerin *f.*

ballistic (bə'listik) *adj* ballistisch.

balloon (bə'lu:n) *n* Ballon *m.* Luftballon *m.*

ballot ('bælət) *n* Wahl *f.* Abstimmung *f.* **ballot paper** *n* Stimmzettel *m.*

Baltic ('bɔ:ltik) *adj* baltisch. **Baltic (Sea)** *n* Ostsee *f.*

bamboo (bæm'bu:) *n* Bambus *m.*

ban (bæn) *vt* verbannen, ächten. *n* Bann *m.* Verbannung, Ächtung *f.*

banal (bə'nɑ:l) *adj* banal, alltäglich.

banana (bə'nɑ:nə) *n* Banane *f.*

band¹ (bænd) *n* **1** *mus* Kapelle *f.* Orchester *neu.* **2** Gruppe, Bande *f.*

band² (bænd) *n* **1** Band *neu.* Binde, Schnur *f.* **2** Riemen *m.* **bandage** *n* Bandage, Binde *f.* Verband *m.* *vt* verbinden.

bandit ('bændit) *n* Bandit *m.*

bandy ('bændi) *adj* krummbeinig. *v* **bandy words** hin und herstreiten.

bang (bæŋ) *n* **1** Knall, schallender Schlag *m.* *vi,(vt)* knallen (lassen). **banger** *n inf* **1** Feuerwerkskörper *m.* **2** Wurst *f.*

bangle ('bæŋgəl) *n* Spange *f.* Armband *neu.*

banish ('bæniʃ) *vt* verbannen, vertreiben.

banister ('bænistə) *n* Treppengeländer *neu.*

banjo ('bændʒou) *n* Banjo *neu.*

bank¹ (bæŋk) *n* **1** Ufer *neu.* **2** Damm *m.*

bank² (bæŋk) *n* Bank, Sparkasse *f.* **bank account** *n* Bankkonto *neu.* **bankbook** *n* Bankbuch, Sparbuch *neu.* **bank holiday** *n* (amtlicher) Feiertag *m.* **banknote** *n* Banknote *f.* **banker** *n* Bankier *m.* **banker's card** *n* Scheckkarte, Bankkarte *f.*

bankrupt ('bæŋkrʌpt) *adj* bankrott, zahlungsunfähig. *n* Bankerotteur *m.*

banner ('bænə) *n* Banner *m.* Fahne *f.*

banquet ('bæŋkwit) *n* Bankett, Festessen *neu.*

baptize (bæp'taiz) *vt* taufen. **baptism** *n* Taufe *f.*

bar (bɑ:) *n* **1** Stange *f.* Riegel, Stab *m.* **2** Bar, Schank *f.* *vt* **1** verriegeln, vergittern. **2** ausschließen, verbieten. **barmaid** *n* Kellnerin, Barmädchen *f.* **barman** *n* Kellner *m.*

barbarian (bɑ:'bɛəriən) *n* Barbar *m.* **barbaric** *adj* barbarisch, roh, grausam. **barbarism** *n* Barbarismus *m.* **barbarity** *n* Barbarei, Roheit, Grausamkeit *f.*

barbecue ('bɑ:bikju:) *n* Bratrost *m.* Barbecue *neu.*

barbed wire (bɑ:bd) *n* Stacheldraht *m.*

barber ('bɑ:bə) *n* Barbier, (Herren)Friseur *m.*

barbiturate (bɑ:'bitjurət) *n* Barbiturat *neu.*

bare (bɛə) *adj* **1** nackt, unbekleidet. **2** bloß, unbedeckt, kahl. **3** leer. *vt* **1** entblößen, enthüllen. **2** (one's teeth) blecken. **barefoot** *adj,adv* barfuß. **barely** *adv* kaum.

bargain ('bɑːgin) *n* (vorteilhaftes) Geschäft *neu.* Gelegenheitskauf *m.* **into the bargain** obendrein. ~*vt,vi* feilschen, handeln. **bargain for** erwarten.

barge (bɑːdʒ) *n* Lastkahn *m.* *v* **barge into** *inf* stürzen in.

baritone ('bæritoun) *n* Bariton *m.*

bark[1] (bɑːk) *vi* bellen. *n* Gebell *neu.*

bark[2] (bɑːk) *n* (Baum)rinde, Borke *f.*

barley ('bɑːli) *n* Gerste *f.*

barn (bɑːn) *n* Scheune *f.*

barometer (bə'rɔmitə) *n* Barometer *neu.*

baron ('bærən) *n* Baron, Freiherr *m.* **baroness** *n* Baronin *f.*

baronet ('bærənit) *n* Baronet *m.*

barracks ('bærəks) *n pl* Kaserne *f.*

barrel ('bærəl) *n* **1** Faß *neu.* Tonne *f.* **2** (of a gun) Lauf *m.*

barren ('bærən) *adj* unfruchtbar, öde.

barricade ('bærikeid) *n* Barrikade, Sperre *f.* *vt* versperren.

barrier ('bæriə) *n* Barriere, Schranke *f.*

barrister ('bæristə) *n* Rechtsanwalt *m.*

barrow ('bærou) *n* Karren *m.*

barter ('bɑːtə) *vt* (ein)tauschen. *vi* Tauschhandel treiben. *n* Tauschhandel *m.*

base[1] (beis) *n* **1** Grundfläche, Basis *f.* **2** Fuß, Stützpunkt *m.* *vi* **1** basieren. **2** stützen. **be based on** sich beruhen auf. **baseball** *n* Baseballspiel *neu.* **basement** *n* Kellergeschoß *neu.*

base[2] (beis) *adj* niedrig, gemein, verächtlich.

bash (bæʃ) *vt* heftig schlagen. **have a bash** versuchen.

bashful ('bæʃfəl) *adj* scheu, schüchtern.

basic ('beisik) *adj* **1** einfach. **2** grundlegend. **basically** *adv* im Grunde, grundsätzlich.

basil ('bæzəl) *n* Basilienkraut *neu.*

basin ('beisən) *n* Becken *neu.* Schüssel *f.*

basis ('beisis) *n pl* **-ses** Basis, Grundlage *f.*

bask (bɑːsk) *vi* sich sonnen.

basket ('bɑːskit) *n* Korb *m.* **basketball** *n* Basketballspiel *neu.*

Basle (bɑːl) *n* Basel *neu.*

bass (beis) *mus adj* Baß—. *n* Baß *m.*

bassoon (bə'suːn) *n* Fagott *neu.*

bastard ('bɑːstəd) *n* Bastard *m.*

baste (beist) *vt cul* (mit Fett) begießen.

bat[1] (bæt) *n* Schläger *m.* Schlagholz *neu.* *vt* **1** schlagen. **2** (eyelids, etc.) zucken, zwinkern. **batsman** *n* Schläger *m.*

bat[2] (bæt) *n zool* Fledermaus *f.*

batch (bætʃ) *n* Schub, Stoß *m.*

bath (bɑːθ) *n* **1** Bad *neu.* **2** Badewanne *f.* **bathroom** *n* Badezimmer *neu.* **bathtub** *n* Badewanne *f.*

bathe (beið) (*vi*),*vt* (sich) baden. **bathing costume** *n* Badeanzug *m.* **bathing trunks** *n* Badehose *f.*

baton ('bætən) *mus* Taktstock *m.*

battalion (bə'tæliən) *n* Bataillon *neu.*

batter[1] ('bætə) *vt* schlagen, prügeln.

batter[2] ('bætə) *n cul* Eierteig *m.*

battery ('bætəri) *n* Batterie *f.*

battle ('bætl) *n* Schlacht *f.* Gefecht *neu.* *vi* kämpfen. **battlefield** *n* Schlachtfeld *neu.* **battleship** *n* Schlachtschiff *neu.*

Bavaria (bə'vɛəriə) *n* Bayern *neu.* **Bavarian** *adj* bayrisch. *n* Bayer *m.*

bawl (bɔːl) *vi* schreien, brüllen.

bay[1] (bei) *n* **1** *geog* Bai, Bucht *f.* **2** Lücke, Nische *f.*

bay[2] (bei) *n* **1** Fach. *neu.* Abteilung *f.* **2** Fensternische *f.*

bay[3] (bei) *vi* (dumpf) bellen, kläffen. **keep at bay** in Schach halten.

bay[4] (bei) *n bot* Lorbeer *m.*

bayonet ('beiənit) *n* Bajonett *neu.*

be* (biː) *vi* **1** sein. **2** existieren. **3** sich befinden. *v aux* sein, werden. **there is, there are** es gibt.

beach (biːtʃ) *n* Strand *m.* *vt* stranden. **beachcomber** *n* Strandgutjäger *m.*

beacon ('biːkən) *n* **1** Signalfeuer *neu.* **2** Blinklicht *neu.*

bead (biːd) *n* Perle, Glasperle *f.*

beak (biːk) *n* Schnabel *m.*

beaker ('biːkə) *n* **1** Becher *m.* **2** *sci* Becherglas *neu.*

beam (biːm) *n* **1** Balken *m.* **2** Strahl *m.* *vt,vi* strahlen. *vi* strahlend lächeln.

bean (biːn) *n* Bohne *f.* **full of beans** lebhaft.

bear*[1] (bɛə) *vt* **1** tragen, stützen. **2** erleiden, aushalten. **3** gebären. **bearing** *n* **1** Haltung *f.* **2** Verhalten, Betragen *neu.* **3** Beziehung *f.* **4** Richtung *f.* **5** *tech* Lager *neu.*

bear[2] (bɛə) *n* Bär *m.*

beard (biəd) *n* Bart *m.*

beast (biːst) *n* **1** Tier, Vieh *neu.* **2** Bestie *f.*

beat* (biːt) *vt* **1** schlagen, prügeln, klopfen. **2** besiegen, schlagen. *n* **1** *mus* Rhythmus, Takt *m.* **2** Schlag *m.* **3** (of a policeman) Revier *neu.*

beauty ('bjuːti) *n* Schönheit *f.* **beauty queen** *n*

Schönheitskönigin f. **beautiful** adj schön, hübsch.

beaver ('bi:və) n Biber m.

became (bi'keim) v see **become**.

because (bi'kɔ:z) conj weil. **because of** wegen.

beckon ('bekən) vt,vi heranwinken.

become* (bi'kʌm) vi werden. vt passen, geziemen. **becoming** adj passend, geziemend

bed (bed) n Bett neu. **bed bug** n Wanze f. **bedclothes** n pl Bettwäsche f. **bedding** n 1 Bettzeug neu. 2 Streu f. **bedridden** adj bettlägerig. **bedroom** n Schlafzimmer, Schlafgemach neu. **bed-sitter** n Wohnschlafzimmer neu. **bedspread** n Bettdecke f.

bedraggled (bi'drægəld) adj beschmutzt, naß.

bee (bi:) n Biene f. **beehive** n Bienenstock m.

beech (bi:tʃ) n Buche f.

beef (bi:f) n Rindfleisch neu.

beer (biə) n Bier neu.

beet (bi:t) n Bete, Rübe f. **beetroot** n rote Rübe f.

beetle ('bi:tl) n Käfer m. Schabe f.

befall* (bi'fɔ:l) vi sich ereignen. vt (jemandem) zustoßen

before (bi'fɔ:) conj bevor, ehe, bis. adv 1 voraus, vorn, vorne. 2 vorher, früher, ehe. prep vor. **beforehand** adv zuvor, davor.

befriend (bi'frend) vt befreunden.

beg (beg) vt,vi 1 betteln. 2 bitten. vi erbitten. **beggar** n Bettler m.

begin* (bi'gin) vt,vi anfangen, beginnen. **beginner** n Anfänger m. **beginning** n Anfang, Beginn m.

begrudge (bi'grʌdʒ) vt mißgönnen.

behalf (bi'ha:f) n **on behalf of 1** im Namen or im Auftrag von. 2 zugunsten. **on my behalf** um meinetwillen.

behave (bi'heiv) vi sich verhalten, sich betragen, sich benehmen. **behave oneself** sich gut betragen. **behaviour** n Betragen, Verhalten, Benehmen neu.

behind (bi'haind) adv 1 hinten. 2 zurück prep hinter. n Hinterteil neu. **behindhand** adv verspätet, im Rückstand.

behold* (bi'hould) vt erblicken, sehen.

beige (beiʒ) adj n Beige neu.

being (bi:iŋ) n 1 (Da)Sein neu. Existenz f. 2 Geschöpf, Wesen neu.

belch (beltʃ) vi rülpsen. n Rülpsen neu.

belfry ('belfri) n Glockenturm m.

Belgium ('beldʒəm) n Belgien neu. **Belgian** adj belgisch. n Belgier m.

believe (bi'li:v) vt glauben. **belief** n 1 Glaube

m. 2 Überzeugung f. **believer** n Gläubige(r) m.

bell (bel) n 1 Glocke f. 2 Klingel f. **bellringer** n Glöckner m.

belligerent (bə'lidʒərənt) adj kriegführend.

bellow ('belou) vi brüllen, schreien. n Gebrüll, Geschrei neu.

bellows ('belouz) n pl Gebläse neu

belly ('beli) n Bauch m.

belong (bi'lɔŋ) vi 1 gehören. 2 (to a club, etc.) angehören. **belongings** n pl Eigentum neu.

below (bi'lou) adv unter. prep unter(halb).

belt (belt) n 1 Gürtel, Riemen m. Binde f. 2 Bereich m. Gebiet neu.

bench (bentʃ) n 1 Bank f. 2 Arbeitstisch m.

bend* (bend) n Kurve, Krümmung f. vt biegen, krümmen. vi (sich) beugen.

beneath (bi'ni:θ) prep unter(halb).

benefactor ('benifæktə) n Wohltäter, Gönner m.

benefit ('benifit) n 1 Nutzen, Vorteil m. 2 Wohltat f. vi nützen, Nutzen ziehen (aus). **beneficial** adj 1 wohltuend. 2 vorteilhaft, nützlich.

benevolent (bi'nevələnt) adj wohlwollend, gütig. **benevolence** n Wohlwollen neu. Güte f.

bent (bent) v see **bend**.

bereave* (bi'ri:v) vt berauben. **bereavement** n Beraubung f. Verlust m

berry ('beri) n Beere f.

berth (bə:θ) n 1 Ankerplatz m. 2 Liegeplatz m. Koje f.

beside (bi'said) prep neben, dicht bei. **besides** adv außerdem, ferner. prep außer.

besiege (bi'si:dʒ) vt belagern.

best (best) adj best. adv am besten. **at best** im besten Fall(e). n Beste(r) m. **best man** n die rechte Hand des Bräutigams bei der Hochzeit. **best-seller** n Verkaufsschlager, Bestseller m.

bestow (bi'stou) vt geben, schenken.

bet* (bet) n Wette f. vt,vi wetten. **betting shop** n Wettbüro neu.

betray (bi'trei) vt verraten. **betrayal** n Verrat m.

better ('betə) adj,adv besser. vt 1 (ver)bessern. 2 übertreffen. **better oneself** sich bessern.

between (bi'twi:n) prep zwischen. adv dazwischen.

beverage ('bevridʒ) n Getränk neu.

beware* (bi'wɛə) vi sich vorsehen, sich hüten.

bewilder (bi'wildə) vt verwirren, bestürzen.

beyond (bi'jɔnd) *prep* jenseits, außer. *adv* darüber hinaus, jenseits.

bias ('baiəs) *n* **1** Neigung *f*. **2** Vorurteil *neu*. **biased** *adj* voreingenommen.

bib (bib) *n* Lätzchen *neu*.

Bible ('baibəl) *n* Bibel *f*. **biblical** *adj* biblisch.

bibliography (bibli'ɔgrəfi) *n* Bibliographie *f*.

biceps ('baiseps) *n* Bizeps *m*.

bicker ('bikə) *vi* zanken, streiten.

bicycle ('baisikəl) *n* Fahrrad *neu*.

bid* (bid) *n* **2** Angebot *neu*. **2** Versuch *m*. *vi* **1** bieten. **2** *game* reizen.

biennial (bai'eniəl) *adj* zweijährig.

big (big) *adj* **1** groß. **2** dick.

bigamy ('bigəmi) *n* Bigamie, Doppelehe *f*.

bigot ('bigət) *n* Fanatiker, Frömmler *m*. **bigoted** *adj* bigott, blind ergeben.

bikini (bi'ki:ni) *n* Bikini *m*.

bilingual (bai'liŋgwəl) *adj* zweisprachig.

bilious ('biliəs) *adj* gallig.

bill[1] (bil) *n* **1** Rechnung *f*. **2** Gesetzesvorlage *f*.

bill[2] (bil) *n* (Vogel)Schnabel *m*.

billiards ('biliədz) *n* Billard(spiel) *neu*.

billion ('biljən) *n* **1** Billion *f*. **2** *US* Milliarde *f*.

bin (bin) *n* Behälter, Kasten *m*.

binary ('bainəri) *adj* binär.

bind* (baind) *vt* **1** binden, befestigen, festmachen. **2** verbinden, verpflichten. **binding** *adj* verbindlich. *n* **1** Bindung *f*. **2** Einband *neu*.

binoculars (bi'nɔkjuləz) *n pl* Feldstecher *m*.

biography (bai'ɔgrəfi) *n* Biographie *f*.

biology (bai'ɔlədʒi) *n* Biologie *f*.

birch (bə:tʃ) *n* Birke *f*. *vt* züchtigen.

bird (bə:d) *n* Vogel *m*.

birth (bə:θ) *n* **1** Geburt *f*. **2** Entstehung *f*. **birth certificate** *n* Geburtsschein *m*. Geburtsurkunde *f*. **birth control** *n* Geburtenkontrolle, Geburtenbeschränkung *f*. **birthday** *n* Geburtstag *m*. **birthmark** *n* Muttermal *neu*. **birth rate** *n* Geburtenziffer *f*.

biscuit ('biskit) *n* Keks, Zwieback *m*.

bishop ('biʃəp) *n* Bischof *m*.

bit[1] (bit) *n* **1** Stück, Stückchen, Bißchen *neu*. **2** Gebiß *neu*.

bit[2] (bit) *v see* **bite**.

bitch (bitʃ) *n* **1** Hündin *f*. **2** *sl* gemeine Frau, Dirne *f*.

bite* (bait) *vt* beißen. *n* Biß, Bissen *m*.

bitter ('bitə) *adj* **1** bitter. **2** verbittert.

bizarre (bi'za:) *adj* bizarr, grotesk.

black (blæk) *adj* **1** schwarz *neu*. **2** Schwarze(r), Farbige(r) *m*. **blacken** *vt* **1** schwärzen. **2** anschwärzen, verleumden. *vi*

schwarz *or* dunkel werden. **blackness** *n* Schwärze *f*.

blackberry ('blækbəri) *n* Brombeere *f*.

blackbird ('blækbə:d) *n* Amsel *f*.

blackboard ('blækbɔ:d) *n* (Wand)Tafel *f*.

blackcurrant (blæk'kʌrənt) *n* schwarze Johannisbeere *f*.

blackleg ('blækleg) *n* Streikbrecher *m*.

blackmail ('blækmeil) *n* Erpressung *f*. *vt* erpressen.

black market *n* Schwarzmarkt *m*.

blackout ('blækaut) *n* **1** Verdunkelung *f*. **2** Gedächtnisstörung *f*.

black pudding *n* Blutwurst *f*.

blacksmith ('blæksmiθ) *n* Schmied *m*.

bladder ('blædə) *n* Blase *f*.

blade (bleid) *n* **1** Klinge, Schneide *f*. **2** (of grass, etc.) Halm *m*.

blame (bleim) *n* Schuld, Verantwortung *f*. *vt* **1** tadeln. **2** beschuldigen.

blank (blæŋk) *adj* weiß, blank(o), leer, unausgefüllt.

blanket ('blæŋkit) *n* Wolldecke *f*. *vt* zudecken.

blare (blɛə) *vi* schmettern. *n* Geschmetter *neu*.

blaspheme (blæs'fi:m) *vi* lästern, fluchen. **blasphemy** *n* Gotteslästerung *f*.

blast (bla:st) *n* **1** Windstoß, Sturm *m*. **2** (of trumpets) Schall *m*. **1** Sprengschuß *m*. Explosion *f*. *vt* sprengen.

blatant ('bleitnt) *adj* **1** lärmend. **2** offenkundig.

blaze (bleiz) *vi* brennen, lodern. *n* Feuer *neu*. Flammen *f*. **blazer** *n* Sportjacke *f*. Blazer *m*.

bleach (bli:tʃ) *n* Bleichmittel *neu*. *vt* bleichen.

bleak (bli:k) *adj* **1** kahl, öde. **2** trüb, freudlos.

bleat (bli:t) *vi* blöken, meckern. *n* Blöken *neu*.

bleed* (bli:d) *vi* bluten. *vt* **1** bluten lassen. **2** *inf* schröpfen. **bleeding** *n* Blutung *f*.

blemish ('blemiʃ) *n* **1** Flecken *m*. **2** Fehler *m*. *vt* verunstalten.

blend (blend) *vt* mischen, vermengen. *vi* sich vermischen. *n* Mischung *f*. Gemisch *neu*.

bless (bles) *vt* **1** segnen. **2** preisen, loben. **blessed** *adj* gesegnet. **blessing** *n* Segen *m*. Segnung *f*.

blew (blu:) *v see* **blow**[1].

blind (blaind) *adj* blind. *adv* blindlings. *vt* (ver)blenden. *n* (of a window) Vorhang *m*. Jalousie *f*. **blind alley** *n* Sackgasse *f*. **blindfold** *adj* blindlings. *vt* die Augen verbinden.

blink (bliŋk) *vi* blinzeln. *n* Blinzeln *neu*.

bliss (blis) *n* Wonne, Seligkeit *f*.

blister ('blistə) *n* (Haut)Blase *f*. *vt* Blasen ziehen. *vi* Blasen bekommen.

blizzard ('blizəd) n (dichter) Schneesturm m.
blob (blɔb) n Tropfen m.
bloc (blɔk) n pol Block m. **en bloc** adv im ganzen, en bloc.
block (blɔk) n Block, Klotz m. vt blockieren, sperren, aufhalten, verhindern. **blockade** n Blockade, Sperre f. vt blockieren, sperren.
blond (blɔnd) adj blond, hell(farbig). **blonde** n Blondine f.
blood (blʌd) n Blut neu. **bloodcurdling** adj schrecklich, furchtbar, Mark und Bein durchdringend. **blood donor** n Blutspender m. **blood pressure** n Blutdruck m. **bloodstream** n Blutkreislauf m. **bloodthirsty** adj blutdürstig, blutrünstig. **blood transfusion** n Blutübertragung f. **bloody** adj 1 blutig. 2 sl verdammt.
bloom (blu:m) n Blüte, Blume f. vi blühen.
blossom ('blɔsəm) n Blüte f. vi blühen, Blüten treiben.
blot (blɔt) n 1 Fleck, Klecks m. 2 Makel m. vt beflecken, beklecksen. **blotting paper** n Löschpapier neu.
blotch (blɔtʃ) n Klecks m.
blouse (blauz) n Bluse f.
blow¹ (blou) n 1 Schlag, Stoß m. 2 Unglück neu. Nachteil m.
blow² (blou) vi 1 blasen. 2 (of wind) wehen. 3 keuchen, schnaufen.
blubber ('blʌbə) n Walfischspeck, Tran m. vi inf heulen, plärren.
blue (blu:) adj 1 blau. 2 inf traurig, deprimiert. n Blau neu. **bluebell** n Glockenblume f. **blueprint** 1 Blaudruck m. 2 Plan m.
bluff (blʌf) vi bluffen, täuschen. n Bluff m. Irreführung f. adj grob, derb.
blunder ('blʌndə) n Fehler, Schnitzer m. vi 1 stolpern. 2 irren, unbesonnen handeln.
blunt (blʌnt) adj 1 stumpf. 2 grob, offen. vt stumpfmachen.
blur (blə:) vt beflecken, verwischen. n Fleck m. Verschwommenheit f.
blush (blʌʃ) vi erröten. n Erröten neu.
boar (bɔ:) n Eber, Keiler m.
board (bɔ:d) n 1 Brett neu. 2 Tafel f. 3 Vorstand, Aufsichtsrat m. 4 Verpflegung f. **boarding house** n Pension f. **boarding school** n Internat neu.
boast (boust) vi prahlen, angeben. n Prahlerei f. **boaster** n Prahler, Angeber m.
boat (bout) n 1 Boot neu. 2 Dampfer m. Schiff neu.
bob (bɔb) vi sich auf und ab bewegen, baumeln.

bodice ('bɔdis) n Mieder neu.
body ('bɔdi) n 1 Körper m. 2 Leiche f. Leichnam m. 3 Gruppe f. 4 mot Karosserie f. **bodyguard** n Leibwächter m.
bog (bɔg) n Sumpf m. Moor neu.
bohemian (bə'hi:miən) adj leichtlebig, ungebunden, zigeunerhaft.
boil¹ (bɔil) vt kochen, sieden. **boiler** n 1 Kocher, Kessel m. 2 Dampfkessel m. **boiling point** n Siedepunkt m.
boil² (bɔil) n Geschwür neu.
boisterous ('bɔistərəs) adj ungestüm, heftig, laut.
bold (bould) adj 1 kühn, mutig. 2 frech, unverschämt. **boldness** n Kühnheit f. Mut m.
Bolivia (bə'liviə) n Bolivien neu. **Bolivian** adj bolivianisch. n Bolivianer m.
bolster ('boulstə) n Kissen, Polster neu. v **bolster up** unterstützen.
bolt (boult) n 1 Bolzen m. 2 Riegel m. 3 Bund m. Rolle f. vt 1 verriegeln. 2 (food) hinunterschlingen. vi hastig fliehen.
bomb (bɔm) n Bombe f. vt bombardieren. **bombard** vt bombardieren, beschießen. **bombardment** n Beschuß m.
bond (bɔnd) n 1 Verbindung f. 2 Fesseln f pl. 3 Bürgschaft f. vt verbinden, aufschlichten, verkleben.
bone (boun) n 1 Knochen m. Bein neu. 2 (of fish) Gräte f. **bony** adj 1 knochig. 2 grätig.
bonfire ('bɔnfaiə) n (Garten)Feuer neu.
bonnet ('bɔnit) n 1 Haube, Damenmütze f. 2 Motorhaube f.
bonus ('bounəs) n Zulage, Extrazahlung f.
booby trap ('bu:bi) n (Spreng)Falle f.
book (buk) n 1 Buch neu. 2 Heft neu. vt aufschreiben, eintragen. **bookcase** n Bücherschrank m. Bücherregal neu. **booking office** n Fahrkartenschalter m. **bookkeeper** n Buchhalter m. **bookkeeping** n Buchhaltung, Buchführung f. **booklet** n Büchlein neu. Broschüre f. **bookmaker** n Buchmacher m. **bookshop** n Buchladen m. Buchhandlung f. **bookstall** n Bücherstand m.
boom (bu:m) n 1 comm Hochkonjunktur f. Aufschwung m. 2 naut Baum m. 3 Dröhnen neu. vi dröhnen, brummen.
boost (bu:st) vt 1 heben, unterstützen. 2 verstärken, aufladen. n Aufschwung m.
boot (bu:t) n 1 Stiefel m. 2 mot Kofferraum m. v **boot out** sl hinauswerfen.
booth (bu:θ) n 1 Bude f. 2 Zelle f.

booze (bu:z) *n inf* alkoholisches Getränk *neu. vi inf* saufen, trinken.

border ('bɔ:də) *n* 1 Rand, Saum *m.* 2 Grenze *f. vt* grenzen, begrenzen. **borderline** *adj* unsicher, zweifelhaft. *n* Grenze *f.*

bore[1] (bɔ:) *vi,vt* bohren, durchdringen. *n* 1 Bohrrung, Höhlung *f.* 2 Kaliber *neu.*

bore[2] (bɔ:) *vt* langweilen. *n* langweiliger *or* lästiger Mensch *m.* **boredom** *n* Langeweile *f.* **boring** *adj* langweilig.

bore[3] (bɔ:) *v see* **bear**[1].

born (bɔ:n) *adj* geboren.

borne (bɔ:n) *v see* **bear**[1].

borough ('bʌrə) *n* Verwaltungsbezirk *m.*

borrow ('bɔrou) *vt* borgen, entleihen.

bosom ('buzəm) *n* Busen *m.* Brust *f.*

boss (bɔs) *n* 1 Chef, Boß *m.* 2 Arbeitgeber *m.* **bossy** *adj* herrisch, rechthaberisch.

botany ('bɔtəni) *n* Botanik, Pflanzenkunde *f.* **Botanist** *n* Botaniker, Pflanzenkenner *m.*

both (bouθ) *pron,adj* beide(s). **both...and** sowohl...als(auch).

bother ('bɔðə) *n* Belästigung, Störung *f. vt* belästigen, stören.

bottle ('bɔtl) *n* Flasche *f. vt* in Flaschen füllen. **bottleneck** Engpaß *m.*

bottom ('bɔtəm) *n* 1 Boden, Unterteil *m.* 2 Grund *m.* 3 *inf* Hintern *m. adj* 1 Grund—. 2 letzt.

bough (bau) *n* Ast, Hauptzweig *m.*

bought (bɔ:t) *v see* **buy.**

boulder ('bouldə) *n* Felsbrocken *m.*

bounce (bauns) *vi* springen, aufprallen. *n* Sprung, Aufprall *m.*

bound[1] (baund) *v see* **bind.** *adj* 1 verpflichtet. 2 bestimmt.

bound[2] (baund) *n* Sprung, Satz *m. vi* springen, hüpfen.

bound[3] (baund) *n* Grenze, Schranke *f.* **boundary** *n* Grenze *f.* **boundless** *adj* grenzenlos.

bound[4] (baund) *adv* bestimmt, unterwegs nach.

bouquet (bu'kei) *n* 1 Bukett *neu.* Blumenstrauß *m.* 2 (of wine) Blume *f.*

bourgeois ('buəʒwɑ:) *n* Bürger, Bourgeois *m. adj* bürgerlich, bourgeois. **bourgeoisie** *n* Bürgertum *neu.* Bourgeoisie *f.*

bout (baut) *n* 1 Reihe, Tour *f.* 2 Kampf *m.* 3 *med* Anfall *m.*

bow[1] (bau) *n* Verbeugung, Verneigung *f. vi* sich verbeugen, sich verneigen.

bow[2] (bou) *n* 1 *mil* (Schieß)Bogen *m.* 2 *mus* Bogen *m.* 3 Schleife *f.* 4 Kurve *f.*

bow[3] (bau) *n naut* Bug *m.*

bowels ('bauəlz) *n pl* 1 Darm *m.* Eingeweide *neu pl.* 2 Innere *neu.*

bowl[1] (boul) *n* 1 Schüssel, Schale *f.* 2 Becken *neu.* 3 Pfeifenkopf *m.*

bowl[2] (boul) *n* Kugel *f. vt* werfen, kugeln, schieben, rollen.

box[1] (bɔks) *n* 1 Kasten *m.* Büchse, Schachtel *f.* 2 *Th* Loge *f. vt* einpacken, in Schachteln packen. **box number** *n* Postfachnummer *f.* **box office** *n* Theaterkasse *f.*

box[2] (bɔks) *(vi),vt* (sich) boxen. *n* **box on the ear** Ohrfeige *f.* **boxer** Boxer *m.* **boxing match** *n* Boxkampf *m.*

Boxing Day *n* zweite Weihnachtsfeiertag *m.*

boy (bɔi) *n* Junge, Knabe, Bube *m.* **boyfriend** Freund *m.* **boyhood** *n* Jugend *f.* Knabenalter *neu.*

boycott ('bɔikɔt) *vt* boykottieren. *n* Boykott *m.*

brace (breis) *n* 1 Stütze *f.* 2 Bohrwinde *f.* 3 Paar *neu.* 4 *pl* Hosenträger *m pl. vt* spannen, stützen, festziehen. **brace oneself** sich zusammennehmen.

bracelet ('breislət) *n* Armband *neu.*

bracket ('brækit) *n* 1 Träger *m.* 2 Klammer *f.* 3 Klasse, Kategorie *f.*

brag (bræg) *vi* angeben, prahlen.

braille (breil) *n* Blindenschrift *f.*

brain (brein) *n* 1 (Ge)Hirn *neu.* 2 *pl* Verstand *m.* Intelligenz *f.* **brainwash** *vt* gehirnwaschen. **brainwashing** *n* Gehirnwäsche *f.* **brainwave** *n* Idee, Eingebung *f.* Einfall *m.*

braise (breiz) *vt* schmoren.

brake (breik) *n* Bremse *f. vt,vi* bremsen. *vt* aufhalten.

branch (brɑ:ntʃ) *n* 1 Ast, Zweig *m.* 2 *comm* Zweigstelle, Filiale *f. vi* (ab)zweigen.

brand (brænd) *n* 1 *comm* Marke *f.* Fabrikat *neu.* 2 (Feuer)Brand *m. vt* einbrennen, brandmarken. **brand-new** *adj* nagelneu.

brandy ('brændi) *n* Branntwein, Weinbrand *m.*

brass (brɑ:s) *n* 1 Messing *neu.* 2 Blasinstrumente *neu pl.* 3 *sl* Geld *neu.* **brass band** *n* Blasorchester *neu.* Blaskapelle *f.*

brassiere ('bræziə) *n* Büstenhalter *m.*

brave (breiv) *adj* mutig, tapfer.

brawl (brɔ:l) *n* Streit *m.* Schlägerei *f. vi* streiten, zanken, raufen.

bray (brei) *vi* schreien. *n* Eselsgeschrei *neu.*

brazen ('breizən) *adj* 1 ehern. 2 unverschämt.

Brazil (brə'zil) *n* Brasilien *neu.* **Brazilian** *adj* brasilianisch. *n* Brasilianer *m.*

breach (bri:tʃ) *n* 1 Bruch *m.* Lücke *f.* 2

Vergehen neu. Verstoß m. vt **1** durchbrechen. **2** verstoßen gegen.

bread (bred) n **1** Brot neu. **2** Nahrung f. **breadcrumb** n Brotkrume f. **coated with breadcrumbs** paniert. **breadwinner** n Brotverdiener, Ernährer m.

breadth (bredθ) n Breite f.

break* (breik) vt brechen, zerbrechen, kaputtmachen. n **1** Riß, Bruch m. **2** Pause f. **breakdown** n **1** med Zusammenbruch m. **2** mot (Auto)Panne f. **breakthrough** n Durchbruch m.

breakfast ('brekfəst) n Frühstück neu. vi frühstücken.

breast (brest) n Brust f. Busen m. **breaststroke** n Brustschwimmen neu.

breath (breθ) n **1** Atem, Hauch m. **2** Atemzug m. **breathtaking** adj atemraubend.

breathe (bri:ð) vi,vt atmen.

breed* (bri:d) vt **1** erzeugen, hervorbringen. **2** aufziehen, züchten. vi sich fortpflanzen. n Rasse, Zucht f.

breeze (bri:z) n Brise f. Wind m.

brew (bru:) n Gebräu, Getränk neu. vt brauen. vi (of a storm) sich zusammenziehen. **brewery** n Brauerei f.

bribe (braib) n Bestechung f. vt bestechen.

brick (brik) n Ziegelstein, Mauerstein m.

bride (braid) n Braut f. **bridegroom** n Bräutigam m. **bridesmaid** n Brautjungfer f.

bridge¹ (bridʒ) n **1** Brücke f. **2** mus Steg m. vt überbrücken.

bridge² (bridʒ) n Bridgespiel neu.

bridle ('braidl) n Zaum, Zügel m. vt zügeln, bändigen. **bridlepath** n Reitweg m.

brief (bri:f) adj kurz, flüchtig. **in brief** adv kurz gesagt, kurz gefaßt. ~n law Schriftsatz m. **briefcase** n Aktentasche, Mappe f. **briefing** n Anweisung, Instruktion f. **briefs** n pl (Herren)Unterhose f.

brigade (bri'geid) n Brigade f. **brigadier** n Brigadekommandeur m.

bright (brait) adj **1** hell, glänzend, leuchtend. **2** intelligent, klug. **brighten** vt,vi erhellen, aufleuchten, aufmuntern.

brilliant ('briliənt) adj **1** brillant, strahlend, glänzend. **2** hochbegabt.

brim (brim) n **1** Rand m. **2** (of a hat) Krempe f.

bring* (briŋ) vt (her-, mit-)bringen. **bring about** zustande bringen. **bring up 1** (a child) erziehen, aufziehen. **2** (a question, etc.) aufwerfen.

brink (briŋk) n **1** Rand m. **2** Ufer neu.

brisk (brisk) adj frisch, lebhaft, munter.

bristle ('brisəl) n Borste f.

Britain ('britn) n Großbritannien. **British** adj britisch. **Briton** n Brite m.

brittle ('britl) adj brüchig, zerbrechlich.

broad (brɔ:d) adj breit, ausgedehnt. **broad bean** n Saubohne f. **broadcast** n Radiosendung f. vt **1** senden, funken. **2** verbreiten adj weit verstreut. **broadcasting** n Rundfunk m. **broaden** vt verbreitern, ausdehnen. **broadminded** adj tolerant.

broccoli ('brɔkəli) n Brokkoli pl. Spargelkohl m.

brochure ('brouʃə) n Broschüre f.

broke (brouk) v see **break**. adj inf pleite.

broken ('broukən) v see **break**. adj kaputt.

broker ('broukə) n Vermittler, Makler m.

bronchitis (brɔŋ'kaitis) n Bronchitis f.

bronze (brɔnz) n **1** Bronze f. **2** Bronzefigur f.

brooch (broutʃ) n Spange, Brosche f.

brood (bru:d) vi brüten. n Brut f.

brook (bruk) n Bach m.

broom (bru:m) n Besen m.

brothel ('brɔθəl) n Bordell neu.

brother ('brʌðə) n Bruder m. **brotherhood** n Bruderschaft f. **brother-in-law** n Schwager m. **brotherly** adj brüderlich

brought (brɔ:t) v see **bring.**

brow (brau) n **1** Augenbraue f. **2** Stirn f. **3** (of a hill) Rand m.

brown (braun) adj braun. n Braun neu. vt braunen.

browse (brauz) vi **1** grasen, (ab)weiden. **2** flüchtig lesen, durchblättern, schmökern.

bruise (bru:z) n Quetschung f. vt quetschen.

brunette (bru:'net) n Brünette f. adj brünett

brush (brʌʃ) n **1** Bürste f. **2** Pinsel m. **3** Unterholz m. vt **1** bürsten, fegen. **2** berühren, streifen.

brusque (bru:sk) adj schroff, angebunden.

Brussels ('brʌsəlz) n Brüssel neu. **Brussels sprout** n Rosenkohl m.

brute (bru:t) n Unmensch m. adj roh. **brutal** adj brutal.

bubble ('bʌbəl) n Blase f. vi brodeln, aufwallen, sprudeln.

buck¹ (bʌk) n **1** (Reh)Bock m. **2** (of a rabbit) Männchen neu.

buck² (bʌk) vi bocken. **buck up** sich zusammenreißen, sich beeilen.

bucket ('bʌkit) n Eimer m.

buckle ('bʌkəl) n Schnalle, Spange f. vt anschnallen, (zu)schnallen.

bud (bʌd) n **1** Knospe f. **2** Keim m. **nip in the**

bud im Keime ersticken. ~vi knospen, keimen.

Buddhism ('budizəm) n Buddhismus m.

budget ('bʌdʒit) n Budget neu. Staatshaushalt, Etat m. vi sparen, Geld einteilen.

buffalo ('bʌfələu) n Büffel m.

buffer ('bʌfə) n Puffer, Prellbock m.

buffet[1] ('bʌfit) n Stoß, Schlag m. vt schlagen, stoßen.

buffet[2] ('bufei) n Büfett neu.

bug (bʌg) n 1 Wanze f. 2 inf Bazillus m. 3 inf (microphone) Wanze f. vt stören.

bugger ('bʌgə) n 1 Sodomit m. 2 sl Kerl, Schuft m.

bugle ('bju:gəl) n (Jagd)Horn neu.

build[*] (bild) vt 1 bauen, errichten. 2 zusammenstellen. **building** n Gebäude neu. **building society** n Bausparkasse f.

bulb (bʌlb) n 1 Glühbirne f. 2 bot Knolle, Zwiebel f.

Bulgaria (bʌl'gɛəriə) n Bulgarien neu. **Bulgarian** adj bulgarisch. n Bulgare m.

bulge (bʌldʒ) n (Aus)Bauchung, Ausbuchtung f. vi sich (aus)bauchen, vorstehen.

bulk (bʌlk) n 1 Maße, Größe f. 2 Großteil m.

bull (bul) n Bulle, Stier m. **bulldog** n Bulldogge f. **bulldozer** Bulldozer m. **bullfight** n Stierkampf m.

bullet ('bulit) n Kugel f. Geschoß neu. **bulletproof** adj kugelsicher, gepanzert.

bulletin ('bulətin) n Bulletin neu.

bully ('buli) n Raufbold, Tyrann m. vt einschüchtern, tyrannisieren.

bum (bʌm) n inf Hintern m. Hinterteil neu.

bump (bʌmp) n 1 Stoß, Schlag m. 2 Beule f. vt stoßen, schlagen. **bumper** n mot Stoßstange f. adj ungewöhnlich gut or groß.

bun (bʌn) n 1 Semmel f. Brötchen neu. 2 (of hair) Kauz m.

bunch (bʌntʃ) n 1 Bund neu. 2 Strauß m. 2 Traube f. 4 Büschel m. 5 Gruppe f. vt,vi zusammenfügen, bündeln.

bundle ('bʌndl) n Bündel neu. vt einbündeln, (schnell) zusammenpacken.

bungalow ('bʌngəlou) n Bungalow, Landhaus neu.

bungle ('bʌngəl) vt pfuschen. vi verpfuschen.

bunk (bʌŋk) n Schlafkoje f.

bunker ('bʌŋkə) n 1 Bunker m. 2 Sandloch neu.

buoy (bɔi) n Boje f. **buoyant** adj 1 schwimmfähig. 2 tragfähig.

burden ('bə:dn) n Last, Bürde f. vt beladen, belasten.

bureau ('bjuərou) n 1 Schreibtisch m. 2 Büro neu.

bureaucracy (bju'rɔkrəsi) n Bürokratie f. **bureaucrat** n Bürokrat, Beamte(r) m.

burgle ('bə:gəl) vt einbrechen. **burglar** n Einbrecher m. **burglary** n Einbruch m.

burn[*] (bə:n) vt (ver)brennen, in Brand stecken. vi brennen. n Brandwunde f.

burrow ('bʌrou) n Höhle f. Bau m. vi sich eingraben, wühlen. vt aufwühlen, graben.

burst[*] (bə:st) vi platzen, zerspringen. vt sprengen. **burst into tears/out laughing** in Tränen/Lachen ausbrechen. ~n Bruch m.

bury[*] ('beri) vt begraben. **burial** n Beerdigung f. Begräbnis neu. **burial ground** n Begräbnisplatz m.

bus (bʌs) n (Auto)Bus m. **bus-stop** n Bushaltestelle f.

bush (buʃ) n Busch, Strauch m. Gebüsch neu.

bushy ('buʃi) adj buschig, dicht.

business ('biznis) n 1 Geschäft neu. 2 Gewerbe neu. 3 Angelegenheit f. 4 Beruf m. **businessman** n Geschäftsmann m.

bust[1] (bʌst) n 1 Büste f. 2 (Frauen)Brust f. Busen m.

bust[2] (bʌst) vt brechen, zerbrechen. adj sl 1 kaputt. 2 bankrott, pleite.

bustle ('bʌsəl) n Gewühl, Gedränge neu. vi herumrennen.

busy ('bizi) adj (viel)beschäftigt, fleißig.

but (bət; stressed bʌt) conj 1 aber, jedoch, sondern. 2 außer, als. adv nur, bloß. **all but** fast, beinahe. **not only...but also** nicht nur...sondern auch.

butcher ('butʃə) n Fleischer m. vt schlachten. **butcher's shop** n Fleischerei f.

butler ('bʌtlə) n Butler, Diener m.

butt[1] (bʌt) n 1 dickes Ende neu. 2 Stummel m. 3 Gegenstand m.

butt[2] (bʌt) vt stoßen, schlagen. **butt in** sich einmischen. ~n Stoß m.

butt[3] (bʌt) n Faß neu. Tonne f.

butter ('bʌtə) n Butter f. **buttercup** n Butterblume f. **butterfly** n Schmetterling m.

buttocks ('bʌtəks) n pl Gesäß neu.

button ('bʌtn) n Knopf m. **buttonhole** n Knopfloch neu. vt anhalten.

buttress ('bʌtrəs) n Strebepfeiler m. Stütze f.

buy[*] (bai) vt kaufen, erwerben, einkaufen. n Kauf m.

buzz (bʌz) n Summen neu. vi summen.

by (bai) prep bei, neben, an, nahe bei, von, durch. adv vorbei, dabei. **by** (**the time that**) bis. **by the way** übrigens. **by and by** bald. **by bus** per Bus, mit dem Bus. **by-election** n Nachwahl f. **bylaw** n Ortsstatut neu. **bypass** n Umgehungsstraße f. vt umgehen, meiden.

C

cab (kæb) n **1** Droschke f. Taxi neu. **2** Fahrerhaus neu.

cabaret ('kæbərei) n Kabarett neu.

cabbage ('kæbidʒ) n **1** Kohl m. **2** Kohlkopf m.

cabin ('kæbin) n **1** Hütte f. Häuschen neu. **2** Kabine f. **cabin cruiser** n Kabinenboot neu.

cabinet ('kæbinət) n **1** Schrank m. **2** pol Kabinett neu. **cabinet maker** n Tischler m.

cable ('keibəl) n Kabel neu. Draht m. vt,vi telegraphieren, kabeln.

cackle ('kækəl) vi gackern, schnattern. n Geschnatter neu.

cactus ('kæktəs) n Kaktus m.

cadence ('keidns) n mus Tonfall m.

cadet (kə'det) n Kadett m.

cafe ('kæfei) n Café, Kaffeehaus neu.

cafeteria (kæfi'tiəriə) n Selbstbedienungsrestaurant neu.

caffeine ('kæfi:n) n Koffein neu.

cage (keidʒ) n **1** Käfig m. **2** Fahrkorb m. vt einsperren.

cake (keik) n **1** Kuchen m. **2** (of soap, etc.) Stück neu. vt überziehen, bedecken.

calamity (kə'læməti) n **1** Unheil neu. **2** Katastrophe f.

calcium ('kælsiəm) n Kalzium neu.

calculate ('kælkjuleit) vt kalkulieren, ausrechnen, berechnen. **calculator** n Rechenmaschine f.

calendar ('kælində) n Kalender m.

calf[1] (kɑ:f) n, pl **calves** Kalb neu.

calf[2] (kɑ:f) n, pl **calves** anat Wade f.

calibre ('kælibə) n **1** Kaliber neu. **2** Wert m.

call (kɔ:l) n **1** Ruf m. **2** Anruf m. **3** Besuch m. **4** comm Einforderung, Nachfrage f. vt **1** rufen. **2** anrufen. **3** benennen. vi **1** rufen. **2** besuchen. **be called** heißen. **call for** fordern. **callbox** n Telefonzelle f.

callous ('kæləs) adj gefühllos, hart.

calm (kɑ:m) adj ruhig, gelassen. n Ruhe, Stille f.

calorie ('kæləri) n Kalorie f.

Cambodia (kæm'boudiə) n Kambodscha neu. **Cambodian** n Kambodschaner m. adj kambodschanisch.

came (keim) v see **come.**

camel ('kæməl) n Kamel neu. **camelhair** n Kamelhaar neu.

camera ('kæmrə) n Kamera f. Photoapparat m. **cameraman** n Kameramann m.

camouflage ('kæməflɑ:ʒ) n Tarnung f. vt tarnen.

camp[1] (kæmp) n Lager neu. Lagerplatz m. vi lagern, zelten. **camp bed** n Feldbett neu. **camp fire** n Lagerfeuer neu. **camping** n Zelten, Camping neu. **camping site** n Zeltlager neu. Campingplatz m.

camp[2] (kæmp) adj **1** weibisch. **2** homosexuell.

campaign (kæm'pein) n **1** Feldzug m. **2** Kampagne f. vi kämpfen, Wahlpropaganda machen.

campus ('kæmpəs) n Universitätsgelände neu.

can[1] (kæn) v mod aux **1** können. **2** dürfen. **3** fähig sein.

can[2] (kæn) n Dose, Kanne, Büchse f.

Canada ('kænədə) n Kanada neu. **Canadian** adj kanadisch. n Kanadier m.

canal (kə'næl) n Kanal m.

canary (kə'nɛəri) n Kanarienvogel m.

cancel ('kænsəl) vt **1** stornieren, abbestellen. **2** streichen, entwerten. **3** absagen.

cancer ('kænsə) n **1** med Krebs m. **2** cap Krebs m.

candid ('kændid) adj offen, ehrlich.

candidate ('kændidət) n Kandidat, Bewerber m.

candle ('kændl) n Kerze f. **candlelight** n Kerzenlicht neu. **candlestick** n Kerzenhalter m.

candour ('kændə) n Offenheit f.

cane (kein) n **1** Zuckerrohr neu. **2** Spazierstock m. Rute f. vt mit der Rute schlagen.

canine ('keinain) adj Hunds—. **canine teeth** n Reißzähne m pl.

cannabis ('kænəbis) n Kannabis neu.

cannibal ('kænibəl) n Kannibale m.

cannon ('kænən) n Kanone f. Geschütz neu. vi stoßen gegen. **cannonball** n Kanonenkugel f.

cannot ('kænət) contraction of **can not.**

canoe (kə'nu:) n Kanu neu. vi paddeln.

canon[1] ('kænən) n Kanon m. **canonize** vt kanonisieren, heiligsprechen.

canon[2] ('kænən) n Domherr m.

canopy ('kænəpi) n Dach neu. Traghimmel m.

cant (kænt) n **1** Jargon m. **2** Heuchelei f.

canteen (kæn'ti:n) n Kantine f.

canter ('kæntə) n leichter Galopp m.

canton ('kæntən) n **1** Kanton m. **2** Bezirk m.

canvas ('kænvəs) n **1** Segeltuch neu. **2** Zeltleinwand f.

canvass ('kænvəs) vi 1 untersuchen, prüfen. 2 um Stimmen werben.

canyon ('kænjən) n Schlucht f.

cap (kæp) n 1 Mütze f. 2 Kappe f. vt 1 bedecken. 2 übertreffen.

capable ('keipəbəl) adj fähig. capability n Fähigkeit f.

capacity (kə'pæsiti) n 1 Fassungsvermögen neu. 2 Leistungsfähigkeit f.

cape¹ (keip) n Cape neu. Umhang m.

cape² (keip) n Kap, Vorgebirge neu.

caper ('keipə) n Kapriole f. vi hüpfen.

capital ('kæpitl) n 1 Hauptstadt f. 2 Kapital neu. adj 1 hauptsächlich. 2 todeswürdig, Todes—. 3 großartig. capitalism n Kapitalismus m. capitalist n Kapitalist m. capitalize vt kapitalisieren.

capricious (kə'priʃəs) adj launisch.

Capricorn ('kæprikɔːn) n Steinbock m.

capsicum ('kæpsikəm) n spanischer Pfeffer m.

capsize ('kæpsaiz) vi kentern, umschlagen.

capsule ('kæpsjuːl) n Kapsel, Hülle f.

captain ('kæptin) n 1 Kapitän m. 2 Hauptmann m. 3 Führer m. vt anführen, leiten.

caption ('kæpʃən) n Überschrift f. Titel m.

captive ('kæptiv) n Gefangene(r) m. adj gefangen, eingesperrt. captivate vt fesseln, bezaubern. captivity n Gefangenschaft f.

capture ('kæptʃə) n 1 Gefangennahme f. 2 Fang m. 3 Eroberung f. vt 1 fangen, gefangennehmen. 2 erobern. 3 gewinnen.

car (kɑː) n 1 Wagen m. Auto(mobil) neu. car park n Parkplatz m.

caramel ('kærəməl) n Karamel m.

carat ('kærət) n Karat neu.

caravan ('kærəvæn) n 1 Karawane f. 2 Wohnwagen m.

caraway ('kærəwei) n Kümmel m.

carbohydrate (kɑːbou'haidreit) n Kohlenhydrat neu.

carbon ('kɑːbən) n Kohlenstoff m. carbon dioxide n Kohlensäure f. carbon paper n Kohlepapier neu.

carburettor (kɑːbju'retə) n Vergaser m.

carcass ('kɑːkəs) n Kadaver m.

card (kɑːd) n 1 Karte f. 2 Spielkarte f. 3 Postkarte f. cardboard n Pappe f. cardboard box n Pappschachtel f.

cardigan ('kɑːdigən) n Wolljacke f.

cardinal ('kɑːdinl) n Kardinal m. adj hauptsächlich.

care (kɛə) n 1 Sorge f. 2 Pflege f. 3 Sorgfalt, Vorsicht. f. 4 Kummer m. take care of 1

aufpassen auf. 2 erledigen. ~vi sich sorgen. care for 1 sorgen für. 2 sich kümmern um. 3 gern haben. carefree adj sorgenlos. careful adj 1 sorgfältig. 2 vorsichtig. careless adj 1 sorglos. 2 unordentlich, nachlässig. 3 unüberlegt. caretaker n Hausmeister, Hauswart m.

career (kə'riə) n Karriere, Laufbahn f. vi rasen, jagen.

caress (kə'res) n Liebkosung f. vt liebkosen, streicheln.

cargo ('kɑːgou) n Fracht f. Frachtgut neu.

Caribbean (kæri'biən) adj karibisch. Caribbean (Sea) n Karibisches Meer neu.

caricature ('kærikətjuə) n Karikatur f.

carnal ('kɑːnl) adj fleischlich, geschlectlich.

carnation (kɑː'neiʃən) n Nelke f.

carnival ('kɑːnivəl) n Karneval, Fasching m.

carnivorous (kɑː'nivərəs) adj fleischfressend.

carol ('kærəl) n Weihnachtslied neu.

carpenter ('kɑːpintə) n Zimmermann, Tischler m.

carpet ('kɑːpit) n Teppich m. carpet-sweeper n Teppichkehrmaschine f.

carriage ('kæridʒ) n 1 Wagen m. Kutsche f. 2 (Körper)Haltung f. carriageway n Fahrbahn f.

carrier ('kæriə) n 1 Träger m. 2 Spediteur m. carrier bag n Tragtasche f.

carrot ('kærət) n Karotte f. Mohrrübe f.

carry ('kæri) vt 1 tragen. 2 befördern. carrycot n tragbares Babybett neu.

cart (kɑːt) n Wagen, Karren m. Fuhrwerk neu. vt tragen, schleppen. carthorse n Zugpferd neu.

cartilage (kɑː'tlidʒ) n Knorpel m.

carton ('kɑːtn) n Pappschachtel f. Karton m.

cartoon (kɑː'tuːn) n 1 Karikatur f. 2 Zeichentrickfilm m. 3 Musterzeichnung f.

cartridge ('kɑːtridʒ) n Patrone f.

carve (kɑːv) vt 1 schnitzen. 2 zerlegen, tranchieren. carving-knife n Vorlegemesser neu.

cascade (kæ'skeid) n 1 Kaskade f. Wasserfall m. vi herabregnen.

case¹ (keis) n 1 Fall m. 2 law (Rechts)Fall m. 3 Sache f. in case falls. in case of im Falle von.

case² (keis) n 1 Gehäuse neu. 2 Tasche, Mappe f. 3 Etui neu.

cash (kæʃ) n Bargeld neu. cash desk n Kasse f. cash register n Registrierkasse f. ~vt einlösen.

cashier¹ (kæ'ʃiə) n Kassierer m.

cashier² (kæ'ʃiə) vt kassieren, entlassen.

cashmere (kæʃˈmiə) n Kaschmir m.

casino (kəˈsiːnou) n Spiellokal, Kasino neu.

casket (ˈkɑːskit) n Kästchen neu.

casserole (ˈkæsəroul) n Schmorpfanne f.

cassette (kəˈset) n Kassette f.

cassock (ˈkæsək) n Soutane f.

cast (kɑːst) n 1 Wurf m. 2 tech Guß m. Gußform f. 3 Th Besetzung f. 4 Typ m. Art f. vt 1 werfen. 2 tech gießen. 3 Th Rollen verteilen.

castanets (kæstəˈnets) n Kastagnetten f pl.

caste (kɑːst) n Kaste, Gesellschaftsklasse f.

castle (ˈkɑːsəl) n 1 Schloß neu. Burg, Festung f. 2 game Turm m.

castrate (kæˈstreit) vt kastrieren.

casual (ˈkæʒuəl) adj 1 zufällig, beiläufig. 2 gleichgültig, nachlässig. 3 salopp. 4 lässig. **casualty** n 1 Verunglückte(r) m. 2 pl Verluste m pl.

cat (kæt) n Katze f. **cat's eye** n mot Katzenauge neu. **tom cat** Kater m.

catalogue (ˈkætəlɔg) n Katalog m.

catamaran (kætəməˈræn) n Katamaran, Auslegerboot neu.

catapult (ˈkætəpʌlt) n Katapult m. Wurfmaschine f. vt katapultieren, schleudern.

cataract (ˈkætərækt) n 1 Katarakt, Wasserfall m. 2 med Star m.

catarrh (kəˈtɑː) n Katarrh, Schnupfen m.

catastrophe (kəˈtæstrəfi) n Katastrophe f.

catch (kætʃ) n Fang m. vt 1 fangen. 2 fassen. 3 (rechtzeitig) erreichen.

category (ˈkætigəri) n Kategorie, Klasse, Ordnung f. **categorical** adj kategorisch, unbedingt. **categorize** vt kategorisieren.

cater (ˈkeitə) vi Lebensmittel anschaffen or liefern. **cater for** sorgen für. **catering** (Lebensmittel)Versorgung f. Verpflegungswesen neu.

caterpillar (ˈkætəpilə) n Raupe f. **caterpillar track** n Raupe, Gleiskette f.

cathedral (kəˈθiːdrəl) n Dom m. Kathedrale f.

cathode (ˈkæθoud) n Kathode f.

catholic (ˈkæθlik) adj 1 allgemein, allumfassend. 2 katholisch.

catkin (ˈkætkin) n Kätzchen neu.

cattle (ˈkætl) n Vieh, Rindvieh neu.

caught (kɔːt) v see **catch.**

cauliflower (ˈkɔliflauə) n Blumenkohl m.

cause (kɔːz) n 1 Ursache f. Anlaß, Grund m. 2 Sache f. vt verursachen, bewirken, veranlassen.

causeway (ˈkɔːzwei) n Damm, Fußweg m.

caustic (ˈkɔːstik) adj 1 ätzend, brennend. 2 scharf, beißend, sarkastisch.

caution (ˈkɔːʃən) n 1 Vorsicht f. 2 (Ver)-Warnung f. vt verwarnen.

cavalry (ˈkævəlri) n Kavallerie, Reiterei f.

cave (keiv) n Höhle f.

caviar (ˈkæviɑː) n Kaviar m.

cavity (ˈkæviti) n Höhle n. Höhlung f.

cayenne (keiˈen) n Cayennepfeffer m.

cease (siːs) vi aufhören, unterlassen, einstellen. **cease-fire** n Waffenstillstand m. Feuereinstellung f.

cedar (ˈsiːdə) n Zeder f.

ceiling (ˈsiːliŋ) n Decke f.

celebrate (ˈseləbreit) vt feiern. **celebration** n Feier f. Fest neu. **celebrity** n Berühmtheit, prominente Person f.

celery (ˈseləri) n Sellerie m.

celestial (siˈlestiəl) adj himmlisch.

celibate (ˈselibət) adj unverheiratet.

cell (sel) n Zelle f.

cellar (ˈselə) n Keller(raum) m.

cello (ˈtʃelou) n Cello neu.

Cellophane (ˈseləfein) n Tdmk Cellophan neu.

cement (siˈment) n Zement m. vt zementieren.

cemetery (ˈsemətri) n Friedhof m.

censor (ˈsensə) n Zensor m. vt zensieren. **censorship** n Zensur f.

censure (ˈsenʃə) vt tadeln, verurteilen. n Tadel m. Rüge f. **vote of censure** Mißtrauensvotum neu.

census (ˈsensəs) n Zensus m. Volkszählung f.

cent (sent) n Cent m.

centenary (senˈtiːnəri) adj hundertjährig. n Hundertjahrfeier f.

centigrade (ˈsentigreid) adj Celsius.

centimetre (ˈsentimiːtə) n Zentimeter m.

centre (ˈsentə) n 1 Mittelpunkt m. Zentrum neu. Mitte f. 2 Zentrale, Zentralstelle f. vi sich konzentrieren auf. **central** adj zentral. **central heating** n Zentralheizung f. **centralize** vt zentralisieren. **centre-forward** n Mittelstürmer m. **centre-half** n Mittelläufer m.

centrifugal (senˈtrifjugəl) adj zentrifugal.

century (ˈsentʃəri) n Jahrhundert neu.

ceramic (siˈræmik) adj keramisch. **ceramics** n pl Keramik f.

cereal (ˈsiəriəl) n Getreidepflanze f. adj Getreide—.

ceremony (ˈserəməni) n 1 Zeremonie, Feier f. 2 Feierlichkeit f. **ceremonial** adj zeremoniell, feierlich. **ceremonious** adj steif, förmlich.

certain ('sə:tn) *adj* **1** sicher, überzeugt. **2** gewiß, bestimmt, sicher. **3** gewiß.

certificate (sə'tifikət) *n* Schein *m*. Urkunde, Bescheinigung *f*. **certify** *vi,vt* bescheinigen, bestätigen.

chaffinch ('tʃæfintʃ) *n* Buchfink *m*.

chain (tʃein) *n* **1** Kette *f*. **2** Reihe *f*. *vt* (an)-ketten. **chain-smoke** *vi* kettenrauchen. **chain-store** *n* Filialgeschäft *neu*.

chair (tʃɛə) *n* **1** Stuhl *m*. **2** Lehrstuhl *m*. Professur *f*. *vt* den Vorsitz führen. **chair-lift** *n* Sessellift *m*. **chairman** *n* Vorsitzende(r) *m*.

chalet ('ʃælei) *n* Chalet, Landhaus *neu*.

chalk (tʃɔ:k) *n* **1** Kreide *f*. **2** Kreidestift *m*. *vt* ankreiden.

challenge ('tʃæləndʒ) *n* **1** Herausforderung *f*. **2** Aufforderung *f*. **3** Anfechtung *f*. *vt* **1** herausfordern. **2** auffordern. **3** anzweifeln.

chamber ('tʃeimbə) *n* Kammer *f*. Zimmer *neu*. **chambermaid** *n* Zimmermädchen *neu*. **chamber music** *n* Kammermusik *f*.

chameleon (kə'mi:liən) *n* Chamäleon *neu*.

chamois *n* **1** ('ʃæmwɑ:) Gemse *f*. **2** ('ʃæmi) Sämischleder *neu*.

champagne (ʃæm'pein) *n* Champagner, Sekt *m*.

champion ('tʃæmpiən) *n* **1** Sieger, Meister *m*. **2** Verfechter *m*. *vt* unterstützen, verfechten, eintreten für. **championship** *n* Meisterschaft *f*.

chance (tʃɑ:ns) *n* **1** Zufall *m*. **2** Schicksal, Geschick *neu*. **3** Risiko *neu*. **4** Chance, Aussicht *f*. **5** Gelegenheit, Chance *f*. **by chance** zufällig. **take a chance** sein Glück versuchen. ~*vt* riskieren.

chancellor ('tʃɑ:nsələ) *n* Kanzler *m*.

chandelier (ʃændə'liə) *n* Kronleuchter *m*.

change (tʃeindʒ) *vi,vt* **1** (ab-, ver-)ändern. **2** (ver)wandeln. **3** (ab)wechseln. **4** (um-, aus-)tauschen. **change one's clothes** sich umziehen. **change trains** umsteigen. ~*n* **1** (Ab-, Ver-)Änderung *f*. **2** Wechsel *m*. Abwechselung *f*. **3** Wendung *f*. **4** Wandlung *f*. **5** (Aus)Tausch *m*. **6** Kleingeld, Wechselgeld *neu*.

channel ('tʃænl) *n* **1** Kanal *m*. **2** Fahrrinne *f*. **3** (radio, etc.) Station *f*. Sender *m*. *vt* leiten, lenken.

Channel Islands *n pl* Kanalinseln *f pl*.

chant (tʃɑ:nt) *n* (Kirchen)Gesang *m*. *vt* intonieren, singen.

chaos ('keiɔs) *n* Chaos, Durcheinander *neu*.

chap[1] (tʃæp) *vt* spalten, aufreißen. **chapped skin** aufgesprungene Haut.

chap[2] (tʃæp) *n* Junge, Kerl, Bursche *m*.

chapel ('tʃæpəl) *n* Kapelle *f*.

chaperon ('ʃæpərəun) *n* Anstandsdame *f*. *vt* (als Anstandsdame) begleiten.

chaplain ('tʃæplin) *n* **1** Kaplan, Geistliche(r) *m*. **2** *mil* Feldgeistliche(r) *m*.

chapter ('tʃæptə) *n* Kapitel *neu*.

char[1] (tʃɑ:) *vt* verkohlen, versengen.

char[2] (tʃɑ:) *vi* scheuern, putzen. *n* **1** Putzfrau *f*. **2** *inf* Tee *m*. **charwoman** *n* Scheuerfrau, Putzfrau *f*.

character ('kæriktə) *n* **1** Charakter *m*. Persönlichkeit *f*. Natur *f*. **2** (Schrift)Zeichen *neu*. **3** Figur, Gestalt *f*. **characteristic** *adj* **1** charakteristisch, bezeichnend. **2** typisch. **characterization** *n* Charakterisierung, Kennzeichnung *f*. **characterize** *vt* charakterisieren, kennzeichnen.

charcoal ('tʃɑ:koul) *n* (Holz)Kohle *f*.

charge (tʃɑ:dʒ) *vt* **1** anstürmen, angreifen. **2** (be)laden, belasten. **3** beauftragen. **4** berechnen. **5** *law* anklagen. **6** befehlen. *n* **1** Ladung *f*. **2** Preis *m*. **3** Sorge, Verantwortung *f*. **4** Anklage *f*. **5** *comm* Belastung *f*. **6** Befehl *m*. **charge hand** *n* Vorarbeiter *m*.

chariot ('tʃæriət) *n* Streitwagen *m*.

charisma (kə'rizmə) *n* Charisma *f*.

charity ('tʃæriti) *n* **1** Wohltätigkeit, Nächstenliebe, Güte *f*. **2** Stiftung *f*. Wohltätigkeitsverein *m*. **charitable** *adj* mild, wohltätig.

charm (tʃɑ:m) *n* **1** Zauber *m*. **2** Reiz, Charme *m*. **3** Amulett *neu*. *vt* entzücken, bezaubern.

chart (tʃɑ:t) *n* **1** Seekarte *f*. **2** Übersichtstafel, Tabelle *f*. *vt* entwerfen, verzeichnen.

charter ('tʃɑ:tə) *n* (Verfassungs)Urkunde *f*. Gnadenbrief *m*. *vt* chartern, mieten. **charter flight** *n* Charterflug *m*.

chase (tʃeis) *vt* jagen, verfolgen. *n* Jagd, Verfolgung *f*.

chasm ('kæzəm) *n* Spalte, Kluft *f*.

chassis ('ʃæsi) *n* Fahrgestell *neu*.

chaste (tʃeist) *adj* rein, anständig, keusch.

chastise (tʃæ'staiz) *vt* strafen, züchtigen.

chastity ('tʃæstiti) *n* Keuschheit, Reinheit *f*.

chat (tʃæt) *vi* schwatzen, plaudern. *n* Plauderei, Unterhaltung *f*.

chatter ('tʃætə) *vi* **1** plaudern, schwatzen, plappern. **2** (of teeth) klappern.

chauffeur ('ʃoufə) *n* Chauffeur, Fahrer *m*.

chauvinism ('ʃouvinizəm) *n* Chauvinismus *m*.

cheap (tʃi:p) *adj* **1** billig. **2** gemein, minderwertig.

cheat (tʃi:t) *n* Betrüger, Schwindler *m*. *vi,vt* betrügen, schwindeln.

check (tʃek) *n* **1** Prüfung, Untersuchung, Kontrolle *f*. **2** *game* Schach *neu*. **3** *US* Scheck *m*. *vt* **1** prüfen, untersuchen, kontrollieren. **2** hindern, aufhalten. **checkmate** *n* Schachmatt *neu*. *vt* in Schachmatt stellen *neu*. **checkpoint** *n* Grenzübergang *m*. **checkup** *n* Untersuchung *f*.

cheek (tʃi:k) *n* **1** Wange, Backe *f*. **2** Frechheit *f*. *vt* frech sein gegen. **cheekbone** *n* Backenknochen *m*. **cheeky** *adj* frech, dreist, keck.

cheer (tʃiə) *n* **1** Laune, Stimmung *f*. **2** Hoch, Hurra *neu*. *vt* aufheitern, erfreuen. *vi* hurra rufen. **cheer up** *vt* aufmuntern, aufheitern. **cheerful** *adj* fröhlich, heiter.

cheese (tʃi:z) *n* Käse *m*.

cheetah ('tʃi:tə) *n* Gepard *m*.

chef (ʃef) *n* Küchenchef *m*.

chemistry ('kemistri) *n* Chemie *f*. **chemical** *n* **1** chemisches Präparat *neu*. **2** *pl* Chemikalien *f pl. adj* chemisch. **chemist** *n* **1** *sci* Chemiker *m*. **2** *med* Apotheker *m*. **chemist's shop** *n* Apotheke *f*.

cheque (tʃek) *n* Scheck *m*. **chequebook** *n* Scheckbuch *neu*. **cheque card** *n* Scheckkarte *f*.

cherish ('tʃeriʃ) *vt* **1** (wert)schätzen. **2** (feelings) hegen. **3** (an idea) festhalten an.

cherry ('tʃeri) *n* Kirsche *f*.

cherub ('tʃerəb) *n* Cherub *m*.

chess (tʃes) *n* Schachspiel *neu*. **chessboard** *n* Schachbrett *neu*. **chessman** *n* Schachfigur *f*. **chess set** *n* Schachspiel *neu*.

chest (tʃest) *n* **1** Brust *f*. **2** Truhe, Kiste *f*. **chest of drawers** *n* Kommode *f*.

chestnut ('tʃesnʌt) *n* Kastanie *f*.

chew (tʃu:) *vt* kauen. **chewing gum** *n* Kaugummi *m*.

chicken ('tʃikən) *n* Huhnchen, Hähnchen *neu*. *adj sl* feig. **chick** *n* Küchlein, Kuken *neu*. **chickenpox** *n* Windpocken *f pl*.

chicory ('tʃikəri) *n* Zichorie *f*.

chief (tʃi:f) *n* Hauptling, Anführer *m*. Chef *m*. *adj* haupt, Haupt—, hauptsächlich.

chilblain ('tʃilblein) *n* Frostbeule *f*.

child (tʃaild) *n, pl* **children** Kind *neu*. **childbirth** *n* Geburt, Entbindung *f*. **childhood** *n* Kindheit *f*. **childish** *adj* kindisch. **childlike** *adj* kindlich.

Chile ('tʃili) *n* Chile *neu*. **Chilean** *adj* chilenisch. *n* Chilene *m*.

chill (tʃil) *n* **1** Kälte *f*. **2** Erkältung *f*. **3** Schauer *m*. *adj* kalt. *vt* kühlen. **chilly** *adj* kalt, kühl, frostig.

chilli ('tʃili) *n* spanischer Pfeffer *m*.

chime (tʃaim) *n* **1** Geläut *neu*. **2** Glockensatz *m*. *vi* klingen, tönen. **chime in** einstimmen.

chimney ('tʃimni) *n* Schornstein, Rauchfang, Schlot *m*. **chimneypot** *n* Schornsteinaufsatz *m*. **chimneysweep** *n* Schornsteinfeger *m*.

chimpanzee (tʃimpæn'zi:) *n* Schimpanse *m*.

chin (tʃin) *n* Kinn *neu*.

china ('tʃainə) *n* Porzellan *neu*.

China ('tʃainə) *n* China *neu*. **Chinese** *adj* chinesisch. *n* Chinese *m*.

chink[1] (tʃiŋk) *n* Spalt *m*. Lücke *f*.

chink[2] (tʃiŋk) *n* Geklimper, Klingen *neu*. *vi* klingen, klimpern.

chip (tʃip) *n* **1** Span, Splitter *m*. Holzstückchen *neu*. **2** *pl cul* Pommes frites *pl*. *vt* behauen, beschneiden.

chiropody (ki'rɔpədi) *n* Fußpflege *f*. **chiropodist** *n* Fußpfleger *m*.

chirp (tʃə:p) *vi* zwitschern, zirpen.

chisel ('tʃizəl) *n* Meißel *m*. Stemmeisen *neu*.

chivalry ('ʃivəlri) *n* Ritterlichkeit *f*.

chives (tʃaivz) *n* Schnittlauch *m*.

chlorine ('klɔ:ri:n) *n* Chlor *neu*.

chlorophyll ('klɔrəfil) *n* Blattgrün, Chlorophyll *neu*.

chocolate ('tʃɔklit) *n* Schokolade *f*.

choice (tʃɔis) *n* **1** Wahl *f*. **2** Auswahl *f*. *adj* auserlesen.

choir (kwaiə) *n* Chor *m*. **choirboy** *n* Chorknabe *m*. **choirmaster** *n* Chormeister *m*.

choke (tʃouk) *vt* würgen. *vt,vi* ersticken. *n mot* Starterklappe *f*.

cholera ('kɔlərə) *n* Cholera *f*.

choose* (tʃu:z) *vt* wählen, aussuchen, auslesen.

chop (tʃɔp) *vt* hacken, zerhacken. *n* Kotelett *neu*. **chopper** *n* Beil *neu*.

chopstick ('tʃɔpstik) *n* Eßstäbchen *neu*.

chord (kɔ:d) *n* Akkord *m*.

chore (tʃɔ:) *n* Hausarbeit *f*.

choreography (kɔri'ɔgrəfi) *n* Choreographie *f*.

chorus ('kɔ:rəs) *n* **1** (Sänger)Chor *m*. **2** Refrain *m*. **choral** *n* Choral *m*. *adj* Chor —.

chose (tʃouz) *v* see **choose**.

chosen ('tʃouzən) *v* see **choose**. *adj* auserwählt.

Christ (kraist) *n* Christus *m*.

christen ('krɪsən) vt taufen. **christening** n Taufe f.

Christian ('krɪstʃən) n Christ m. **Christian name** n Vorname m. **Christianity** n Christentum neu.

Christmas ('krɪsməs) n Weihnachten f pl. **Christmas card** n Weihnachtskarte f. **Christmas tree** n Weihnachtsbaum m.

chromatic (krə'mætɪk) adj chromatisch.

chrome (kroum) adj 1 chromgelb. 2 aus Chrom.

chromium ('kroumiəm) n Chrom neu.

chronic ('krɒnɪk) adj 1 chronisch, (an)dauernd. 2 inf schlecht.

chronicle ('krɒnɪkəl) n Chronik, Zeitgeschichte f.

chronological (krɒnə'lɒdʒɪkəl) adj chronologisch.

chrysalis ('krɪsəlɪs) n Puppe f.

chrysanthemum (kri'zænθiməm) n Goldblume, Chrysantheme f.

chubby ('tʃʌbi) adj plump, pausbäckig.

chuck (tʃʌk) vt inf 1 werfen, schleudern. 2 aufgeben.

chuckle ('tʃʌkəl) n Kichern, Gekicher neu. vi kichern, vergnügt lachen.

chunk (tʃʌŋk) n Stück neu. Klotz m.

church (tʃəːtʃ) n Kirche f. **churchgoer** n Kirchengänger m. **churchyard** n Kirchhof m.

churn (tʃəːn) n Butterfaß neu. vt aufwühlen.

chute (ʃuːt) n Gleitbahn, Rinne f.

chutney ('tʃʌtni) n Chutney neu.

cider ('saɪdə) n Apfelwein m.

cigar (si'gaː) n Zigarre f. **cigarette** n Zigarette f. **cigarette lighter** n Feuerzeug m.

cinder ('sɪndə) n 1 ausgeglühte Kohle f. 2 pl Asche pl.

cinecamera ('sɪnikæmrə) n Filmkamera f.

cinema ('sɪnəmə) n Kino neu.

cinnamon ('sɪnəmən) n Zimt m.

circle ('səːkəl) n 1 Kreis m. Ring m. 2 Th Rang m. vt umkreisen, umringen. **circular** adj kreisförmig, rund. **circulate** vi kreisen. vt in Umlauf setzen. **circulation** n 1 Kreislauf m. 2 Umlauf m. Verkehr m. 3 Auflage f.

circuit ('səːkit) n 1 Kreisbewegung f. 2 Runde f. 3 Stromkreis m.

circumcise ('səːkəmsaiz) vt beschneiden.

circumference (sə'kʌmfərəns) n Kreisumfang, Umkreis m.

circumscribe ('səːkəmskraib) vt umschreiben.

circumstance ('səːkəmstæns) n 1 Umstand m. 2 Tatsache f. 3 Formalität f. **circumstantial** adj zufällig, indirekt, nebensächlich.

circus ('səːkəs) n Zirkus m.

cistern ('sɪstən) n Zisterne f.

cite (sait) vt 1 zitieren, anführen. 2 vorladen. **citation** n 1 Zitat neu. 2 Vorladung f.

citizen ('sitizən) n (Staats)Bürger m.

citrus ('sitrəs) n Zitrusfrucht f.

city ('siti) n Stadt, Großstadt f.

civic ('sivik) adj bürgerlich, städtisch.

civil ('sivəl) adj 1 bürgerlich, städtisch. 2 höflich. 3 Staats—. **civil engineering** n Ingenieurbau m. **civil servant** n Staatsbeamte(r) m. **civil service** n Staatsverwaltung f. **civil war** n Bürgerkrieg m.

civilian (si'viliən) n Zivilist m. adj Zivil—.

civilization (sivilai'zeiʃən) n Zivilisation f. **civilize** vt zivilisieren.

clad (klæd) adj bekleidet, bedeckt.

claim (kleim) n 1 Anspruch m. (An)Recht neu. 2 Forderung f. 3 Behauptung f. vt beanspruchen, fordern.

clam (klæm) n Venusmuschel f.

clamber ('klæmbə) vi klettern.

clammy ('klæmi) adj feuchtkalt, klebrig.

clamour ('klæmə) n Lärm m. Geschrei neu. vi schreien, lärmen.

clamp (klæmp) n Klammer, Schelle f. vt festklemmen, befestigen.

clan (klæn) n Stamm m. Sippe f.

clandestine (klæn'destin) adj heimlich.

clang (klæŋ) vi,(vt) klingen or schallen (lassen). n Klang, Schall m.

clank (klæŋk) vi,(vt) rasseln or klirren (mit). n Gerassel neu.

clap (klæp) vi,(vt) klatschen (mit). n 1 Donnerschlag m. 2 Knall m. **clapper** n Klöppel m.

claret ('klærət) n Klarett m.

clarify ('klærifai) vt klarmachen, erläutern, klären. **clarification** n (Er)Klärung f. **clarity** n Klarheit, Reinheit f.

clarinet (klæri'net) n Klarinette f.

clash (klæʃ) n 1 Geklirr neu. 2 Zusammenstoß m. 3 Konflikt m. vi 1 klirren, rasseln. 2 zusammenstoßen.

clasp (klaːsp) n Schnalle, Spange f. vt 1 schnallen. 2 festhalten, umklammern.

class (klaːs) n 1 Klasse, Kategorie f. 2 (Schul-)Klasse f. vt einstufen, einreihen. **classify** vt klassifizieren, einordnen, einteilen. **classification** n Klassifizierung, Einteilung f. **classroom** n Klassenzimmer neu.

classic ('klæsik) adj klassisch. n Klassiker m. **classical** adj klassisch.

clatter ('klætə) vi rasseln, klappern. n Geklapper neu.

clause (klɔ:z) n **1** Satz m. **2** Klausel f.

claustrophobia (klɔstrə'foubiə) n Klaustrophobie f. **claustrophobic** adj eng, überfüllt.

claw (klɔ:) n Klaue f. Kralle f.

clay (klei) n Ton m.

clean (kli:n) adj sauber, rein, gewaschen. vt **1** reinigen, säubern. vi,vt putzen.

cleanse (klenz) vt säubern, heilen.

clear (kliə) adj **1** klar, durchsichtig. **2** verständlich. **3** rein. **4** offen, frei. vt **1** leeren, räumen. **2** freisprechen. **3** (a cheque) einlösen. **4** verzollen. **5** springen über. vi sich (auf)klären. **clear away, out,** or **up** vi,vt ausräumen, aufräumen. **clear off** vi inf abhauen. **clearance** n **1** Aufräumen m. **2** Verzollung f. **3** tech Spielraum m. **4** Räumungsausverkauf m. **clear-headed** adj besonnen, klardenkend. **clearing** n Lichtung f.

clef (klef) n Notenschlüssel m.

clench (klentʃ) vt zusammenpressen, ballen.

clergy ('klə:dʒi) n Klerus m. **clergyman** n Geistliche(r) m.

clerical ('klerikəl) adj **1** geistlich. **2** Büro—. **clerical work** n Büroarbeit f.

clerk (kla:k) n Büroangestellte(r) m.

clever ('klevə) adj geschickt, klug, intelligent.

cliché ('kli:ʃei) n Klischee neu.

click (klik) vi,vt knipsen, knacken, (zu)schnappen. n Schnappen neu. Schlag m.

client ('klaiənt) n Kunde m. **clientèle** n Kundschaft f.

cliff (klif) n Klippe f. Felsen m.

climate ('klaimit) n Klima neu.

climax ('klaimæks) n Höhepunkt m.

climb (klaim) n Aufstieg m. vt,vi klettern, steigen. **climber** n Kletterer, Bergsteiger m.

cling* (kliŋ) vi sich klammern, sich halten, haften.

clinic ('klinik) n Klinik f.

clip[1] (klip) vt schneiden, stutzen, knipsen. n Schlag m. **clipping** n (Zeitungs)Ausschnitt m.

clip[2] (klip) n Klammer f. vt befestigen, zusammenheften.

cloak (klouk) n Gewand neu. Mantel m. vt ummanteln, umhüllen. **cloakroom** n Garderobe f.

clock (klɔk) n Uhr f. **three o'clock** drei Uhr. **clocktower** n Uhrturm m. **clockwise** adj,adv im Uhrzeigersinn. **clockwork** n Uhrwerk neu.

clog (klɔg) n Holzschuh m. (vi),vt (sich) verstopfen.

cloister ('klɔistə) n Kloster neu.

close vt,vi (klouz) zumachen, schließen. adj

(klous) **1** dicht, nahe. **2** intim, vertraut. **3** knapp. n **1** (klous) Sackgasse f. **2** (klouz) Schluß m.

closet ('klɔzit) n Schrank m.

clot (klɔt) n Klumpen m. vi gerinnen.

cloth (klɔθ) n **1** Stoff m. Gewebe, Tuch neu. **2** Lappen m.

clothe (klouð) vt bekleiden. **clothes** n pl Kleider neu pl. Kleidung f. **clothes brush** n Kleiderbürste f. **clothes line** n Wäscheleine f. **clothes peg** n Wäscheklammer f. **clothing** n Kleidung f.

cloud (klaud) n Wolke f. vi,vt bewölken, umnebeln. **cloudburst** n Wolkenbruch m. **cloudy** adj **1** wolkig, bewölkt. **2** trübe.

clove[1] (klouv) n Gewürznelke f.

clove[2] (klouv) n (Knoblauch)Zehe f.

clover ('klouvə) n Klee m.

clown (klaun) n Clown m.

club (klʌb) n **1** Klub m. Verein m. **2** sport Schläger m. **3** Keule f.

clue (klu:) n Hinweis, Anhaltspunkt m.

clump (klʌmp) n **1** Haufen m. **2** Gruppe f.

clumsy ('klʌmzi) adj ungeschickt, schwerfällig.

clung (klʌŋ) v see **cling**.

cluster ('klʌstə) n **1** Gruppe f. **2** bot Traube f. vi sich (ver)sammeln, sich gruppieren.

clutch (klʌtʃ) n **1** Kupplung f. **2** pl Klauen f pl. vt packen, greifen, fassen.

clutter ('klʌtə) n Unordnung f. Durcheinander neu. vt vollstopfen.

coach (koutʃ) n **1** Kutsche f. **2** Bus m. **3** sport Trainer m. vt **1** sport trainieren. **2** educ Nachhilfeunterricht geben.

coal (koul) n (Stein)Kohle f. **coalmine** n Kohlenbergwerk neu.

coalition (kouə'liʃən) n Koalition f.

coarse (kɔ:s) adj **1** grob. **2** rauh, unhöflich.

coast (koust) n Küste f. **coastguard** n Küstenwacht f. **coastline** n Küstenlinie f.

coat (kout) n **1** Mantel m. **2** Pelz m. Fell neu. **3** Belag m. **4** (of paint) Anstrich m. vt bedecken, beschichten. **coat-hanger** n Kleiderbügel m. **coating** n Schicht f. Belag m.

coax (kouks) vt (geduldig) überreden.

cobbler ('kɔblə) n Schuster m.

cobra ('koubrə) n Kobra f.

cobweb ('kɔbweb) n Spinngewebe neu.

cock[1] (kɔk) n **1** Hahn m. **2** (Vogel)Männchen neu. **3** tab Penis m. **cockpit** n Kanzel, Kabine f. **cockroach** n Küchenschabe f. **cocktail** n Cocktail neu. **cocky** adj inf eingebildet, frech.

cock² (kɔk) vt **1** (one's ears) spitzen. **2** (a hat, etc.) schiefmachen, schief aufsetzen.

cockle ('kɔkəl) n Herzmuschel f.

cocoa ('koukou) n Kakao m.

coconut ('koukənʌt) n Kokosnuß f.

cocoon (kə'kuːn) n Puppe f.

cod (kɔd) n Dorsch m.

code (koud) n **1** Kodex m. **2** Schlüssel m. Geheimschrift f. vt verschlüsseln.

codeine ('koudiːn) n Kodein neu.

coeducation (kouedjuˈkeiʃən) n Gemeinschaftserziehung f.

coerce (kouˈəːs) vt zwingen.

coexist (kouigˈzist) vi koexistieren, zusammenleben. **coexistence** n Koexistenz f.

coffee ('kɔfi) n Kaffee m. **coffee bar** n Kaffeehaus, Café neu. **coffee bean** n Kaffeebohne f.

coffin ('kɔfin) n Sarg m.

cog (kɔg) n Radzahn m.

cognac ('kɔnjæk) n Kognak m.

cohabit (kouˈhæbit) vi zusammenleben.

cohere (kouˈhiə) vi zusammenhängen, zusammenkleben. **coherence** n Zusammenhang m. **coherent** adj zusammenhängend, verständlich.

coil (kɔil) n Windung, Spule f. vt aufrollen, aufwinden. vi sich zusammenrollen.

coin (kɔin) n Münze f. vt prägen.

coincide (kouinˈsaid) vi **1** zusammentreffen. **2** übereinstimmen. **coincidence** n Zufall m. Zusammentreffen neu.

colander ('kʌləndə) n Sieb neu.

cold (kould) adj kalt. n **1** Kälte f. **2** Erkältung f. Schnupfen m. **catch a cold** sich erkälten. **cold-blooded** adj kaltblütig.

collaborate (kəˈlæbəreit) vi **1** zusammenarbeiten, mitarbeiten. **2** mit dem Feind arbeiten, kollaborieren. **collaboration** n **1** Zusammenarbeit f. **2** Kollaboration f.

collapse (kəˈlæps) n Zusammenbruch, Einsturz m. vi zusammenbrechen, einstürzen.

collar ('kɔlə) n Kragen m. **collarbone** n Schlüsselbein m.

colleague ('kɔliːg) n Kollege, Mitarbeiter m.

collect (kəˈlekt) vt sammeln, auflesen. **collection** n **1** Sammlung f. **2** Ansammlung f. Anhäufung f. **3** (of mail) Abholung f. **collective** adj vereint, zusammengefaßt, gesamt, kollektiv—. n Kollektiv neu.

college ('kɔlidʒ) n Kollegium neu. Hochschule f.

collide (kəˈlaid) vi zusammenstoßen. **collision** n Zusammenstoß m.

colloquial (kəˈloukwiəl) adj familiär, umgangssprachlich.

Cologne (kəˈloun) n Köln neu.

colon ('koulən) n **1** Doppelpunkt m. Kolon neu. **2** anat Dickdarm m.

colonel ('kəːnl) n Oberst m.

colony ('kɔləni) n Kolonie, Siedlung f. **colonial** adj kolonial.

colossal (kəˈlɔsəl) adj kolossal, riesig.

colour ('kʌlə) n Farbe f. **colour-bar** n Farbschranke f. **colour-blind** adj farbenblind. **coloured** adj farbig, bunt. **coloured (man)** Farbige(r) m.

colt (koult) n Füllen, Fohlen neu.

column ('kɔləm) n **1** Säule f. Pfeiler m. **2** Kolonne f. **3** Rubrik f. **4** (Zeitungs)Spalte f. **columnist** n Kolumnist m.

coma ('koumə) n Koma, anhaltende Bewußtlosigkeit f.

comb (koum) n Kamm m. vt **1** kämmen. **2** durchsuchen.

combat ('kɔmbæt) n Kampf m. vt bekämpfen.

combine (v kəmˈbain: n 'kɔmbain) vt vereinigen, verbinden. n **1** Verband f. **2** Kartell neu. **combine harvester** n Mähdrescher m.

combustion (kəmˈbʌstʃən) n Verbrennung f.

come* (kʌm) vi kommen. **come about** geschehen. **come across** stoßen auf. **comeback** n Rückkehr f. Comeback neu.

comedy ('kɔmədi) n Lustspiel neu. Komödie f. **comedian** n Komiker m. **comic** n **1** Komiker m. **2** Witzblatt neu. adj witzig, komisch. **comical** adj witzig, spaßig.

comet ('kɔmit) n Komet m.

comfort ('kʌmfət) n **1** Trost m. **2** Komfort m. **3** Gemütlichkeit f. vt trösten. **comfortable** adj bequem, behaglich.

comma ('kɔmə) n Komma neu. Beistrich m.

command (kəˈmaːnd) n **1** Befehl m. **2** Führung. vt **1** befehlen. **2** kommandieren. **commander** n Kommandant, Befehlshaber, Führer m. **commandment** n Gebot neu.

commemorate (kəˈmeməreit) vt feiern, gedenken.

commence (kəˈmens) vt,vi anfangen, beginnen. **commencement** n Anfang, Beginn m.

commend (kəˈmend) vt empfehlen, loben.

comment ('kɔment) n **1** Bemerkung f. **2** Stellungnahme f. vi bemerken, kommentieren. **commentary** n Kommentar m. **commentator** n Kommentator, Berichterstatter m.

commerce ('kɔməːs) n Handel(sverkehr) m. **commercial** adj kommerziell, kaufmännisch, geschäftlich. *n* Fernsehreklame *f*. **commercialize** *vt* marktfähig machen. **commercial vehicle** *n* Nutzfahrzeug *neu*.

commission (kə'miʃən) *n* 1 Auftrag *m*. 2 *mil* Offizierspatent *neu*. 3 Kommission *f*. Ausschuß *m*. *vt* 1 bestellen, beauftragen. 2 eine Bestellung geben. **commissioner** *n* Kommissionär *m*.

commit (kə'mit) *vt* 1 begehen. 2 übergeben. **commit oneself** sich verpflichten.

committee (kə'miti) *n* Ausschuß *m*. Komitee *neu*.

commodity (kə'mɔditi) *n* Handelsgut *neu*. Ware *f*.

common ('kɔmən) *adj* 1 allgemein, gemeinsam. 2 gewöhnlich, häufig. 3 alltäglich. *n* Allmende *f*. **Common Market** *n* Gemeinsamer Markt *m*. Europäische Wirtschaftsgemeinschaft *f*. **commonplace** *n* Gewöhnliche(s), Alltägliche(s) *neu*. Gemeinplatz *m*. *adj* gewöhnlich, alltäglich. **common sense** *n* gesunder Menschenverstand *m*. Vernunft *f*. **commonwealth** *n* 1 Staat *m*. Gemeinwesen *neu*. 2 Commonwealth *neu*.

commotion (kə'mouʃən) *n* Aufruhr *m*. Getue *neu*.

commune[1] (kə'mju:n) *vi* 1 sich unterhalten. 2 *rel* Kommunion empfangen. **communion** *n* Kommunion *f*.

commune[2] ('kɔmju:n) *n* Kommune, Gemeinde *f*. **communal** *adj* Kommunal—, Gemeinschafts—.

communicant (kəmju:nikənt) *n* Kommunikant *m*.

communicate (kə'mju:nikeit) *vt* 1 mitteilen. 2 übertragen. *vi* 1 in Verbindung stehen. 2 *rel* Kommunizieren. **communication** *n* 1 Mitteilung *f*. 2 Verbindung, Kommunikation *f*. Verkehr *m*.

communism ('kɔmjunizəm) *n* Kommunismus *m*. **communist** *n* Kommunist *m*. *adj* kommunistisch.

community (kə'mju:niti) *n* 1 Gemeinschaft, Gemeinde *f*. 2 Gemeinsamkeit *f*.

commute (kə'mju:t) *vt* umwandeln, austauschen. *vi* zur Arbeit reisen, pendeln. **commuter** *n* Pendler *m*.

compact[1] (kəm'pækt) *adj* dicht, fest, kompakt. *vt* verdichten, verbinden.

compact[2] ('kɔmpækt) *n* Vertrag, Pakt. *m*. Übereinkommen *neu*.

companion (kəm'pæniən) *n* Begleiter, Kamerad

m. **companionship** *n* Gesellschaft, Kameradschaft *f*.

company ('kʌmpəni) *n* 1 *comm* Firma, Gesellschaft *f*. 2 Gesellschaft *f*.

compare (kəm'pɛə) (*vi*),*vt* (sich) vergleichen. **comparable** *adj* vergleichbar. **comparative** *adj* 1 vergleichend. 2 verhältnismäßig. **comparison** *n* Vergleich *m*.

compartment (kəm'pɑ:tmənt) *n* 1 Abteilung *f*. 2 Fach *neu*. 3 Abteil *neu*.

compass ('kʌmpəs) *n* Kompaß *m*.

compassion (kəm'pæʃən) *n* Mitleid, Erbarmen *neu*. **compassionate** *adj* mitleidsvoll.

compatible (kəm'pætibəl) *adj* vereinbar.

compel (kəm'pel) *vt* zwingen, nötigen.

compensate ('kɔmpənseit) *vi* 1 ausgleichen. 2 wiedergutmachen, entschädigen. **compensation** *n* Entschädigung *f*. Schadenersatz *m*.

compete (kəm'pi:t) *vi* 1 teilnehmen. 2 konkurrieren. **competition** *n* 1 Wettbewerb *m*. 2 Konkurrenz *f*. **competitive** *adj* 1 konkurrenzfähig. 2 wetteifernd, konkurrierend. **competitor** *n* Konkurrent *m*.

competent ('kɔmpitənt) *adj* kompetent, fähig. **competence** *n* Kompetenz, Befähigung *f*.

compile (kəm'pail) *vt* aufstellen, zusammenstellen.

complacent (kəm'pleisənt) *adj* gleichgültig. **complacency** *n* Selbstgefälligkeit.

complain (kəm'plein) *vi* sich beklagen *or* beschweren. **complaint** *n* Klage, Beschwerde *f*.

complement ('kɔmplimənt) *n* 1 Ergänzung. 2 *math* Komplement *neu*. *vt* ergänzen.

complete (kəm'pli:t) *vt* vervollständigen, beenden, fertigstellen. *adj* ganz, vollständig.

complex ('kɔmpleks) *adj* komplex, kompliziert. *n* Komplex *m*. **complexity** *n* Kompliziertheit, Schwierigkeit *f*.

complexion (kəm'plekʃən) *n* Gesichtsfarbe *f*. Teint *m*.

complicate ('kɔmplikeit) *vt* komplizieren, erschweren. **complicated** *adj* kompliziert.

compliment ('kɔmplimənt) *n* Kompliment *neu*. *vt* loben, ein Kompliment machen. **complimentary** *adj* 1 höflich, schmeichelhaft. 2 Gratis—, Frei—.

comply (kəm'plai) *vi* einwilligen, nachgeben, sich fügen. **comply with** erfüllen, befolgen.

component (kəm'pounənt) *n* (Bestand)Teil *m*. *adj* teilbildend.

compose (kəm'pouz) *vt* 1 zusammensetzen. 2 dichten, verfassen. 3 *mus* komponieren. **com-**

composure

pose oneself sich beruhigen, sich fassen. **composed** *adj* ruhig, gelassen. **composition** *n* 1 Zusammensetzung *f.* 2 Aufsatz *m.* 3 *mus* Komposition *f.*

composure (kəmˈpouʒə) *n* Gelassenheit *f.*

compound[1] (*v* kəmˈpaund; *n* ˈkɔmpaund) *vt* 1 zusammensetzen, mischen. 2 verbinden. *n* 1 *sci* Verbindung *f.* 2 Gemisch *neu.* Mischung *f.*

compound[2] (ˈkɔmpaund) *n* eingezäuntes Gelände *neu.*

comprehend (kɔmpriˈhend) *vt* 1 verstehen, begreifen. 2 umfassen, einschließen. **comprehensive** *adj* umfassend, allgemein. **comprehensive school** *n* Gesamtschule *f.*

compress (*v* kəmˈpres; *n* ˈkɔmpres) *vt* komprimieren, zusammendrücken. *n* Kompressionsbinde *f.* **compression** *n tech* Verdichtung *f.*

comprise (kəmˈpraiz) *vt* einschließen, umfassen.

compromise (ˈkɔmprəmaiz) *n* Kompromiß *m. vi* übereinkommen, einen Kompromiß schließen. *vt* kompromittieren, gefährden.

compulsion (kəmˈpʌlʃən) *n* Zwang *m.* **compulsive** *adj* zwingend, Zwangs—. **compulsory** *adj* zwangsläufig, obligatorisch.

compunction (kəmˈpʌŋkʃən) *n* Gewissensbisse *m pl.*

computer (kəmˈpjuːtə) *n* Rechenautomat *neu.* Computer, Datenverarbeiter *m.*

comrade (ˈkɔmrəd, -reid) *n* 1 Kamerad, Gefährte *m.* 2 *pol* Genosse *m.*

concave (ˈkɔŋkeiv) *adj* konkav, hohl.

conceal (kənˈsiːl) *vt* 1 verstecken, verbergen. 2 verschweigen.

concede (kənˈsiːd) *vt* zugestehen, zugeben.

conceit (kənˈsiːt) *n* Eingebildetheit, Eitelkeit *f.*

conceive (kənˈsiːv) *vt* 1 (a child) empfangen. 2 begreifen, sich vorstellen, ersinnen.

concentrate (ˈkɔnsəntreit) *(vi),vt* (sich) konzentrieren. *vt* richten. **concentration** *n* Konzentration *f.*

concentric (kənˈsentrik) *adj* konzentrisch.

concept (ˈkɔnsept) *n* Konzept *neu.* Begriff *m.* **conception** *n* 1 Empfängnis *f.* 2 Auffassungsvermögen *neu.* 3 Vorstellung *f.*

concern (kənˈsəːn) *n* 1 Teilnahme *f.* Belang *m.* 2 Interesse *neu.* 3 Sorge *f.* 4 *comm* Unternehmen *neu. vt* angehen. **concern oneself** sich beschäftigen.

concert (ˈkɔnsət) *n* Konzert *neu.*

concertina (kɔnsəˈtiːnə) *n* Ziehharmonika *f.*

concerto (kənˈtʃɛətou) *n* (Solo)Konzert *neu.*

concession (kənˈseʃən) *n* 1 Konzession *f.* 2 Zugeständnis *neu.*

conciliate (kənˈsilieit) *vt* aussöhnen.

concise (kənˈsais) *adj* knapp, kurz.

conclude (kənˈkluːd) *vt,vi* beenden, schließen. **conclusion** *n* Schluß *m.* **draw conclusions (from)** Schlüsse ziehen (aus).

concoct (kənˈkɔkt) *vt* zusammenbrauen.

concrete (ˈkɔŋkriːt) *n* Beton *m. adj* 1 fest, dicht. 2 konkret, greifbar.

concussion (kənˈkʌʃən) *n* Gehirnerschütterung *f.*

condemn (kənˈdem) *vt* verurteilen. **condemnation** *n* Verurteilung *f.*

condense (kənˈdens) *vt* 1 kondensieren. 2 abkürzen, zusammenfassen. **condensation** *n* 1 Kondensation *f.* 2 Abkürzung *f.*

condescend (kɔndiˈsend) *vi* sich herablassen.

condition (kənˈdiʃən) *n* 1 Zustand *m.* 2 Bedingung, Voraussetzung *f.* **conditional** *adj* bedingt, abhängig.

condolence (kənˈdoulans) *n* Beileid *neu.*

condom (ˈkɔndəm) *n* Kondom *neu.*

condone (kənˈdoun) *vt* billigen.

conduct (*n* ˈkɔndʌkt; *v* kənˈdʌkt) *n* 1 Betragen, Verhalten *neu.* 2 Führung *f. vt* 1 durchführen. 2 leiten, dirigieren. **conduct oneself** sich verhalten.

conductor (kənˈdʌktə) *n* 1 Schaffner *m.* 2 *mus* Dirigent *m.*

cone (koun) *n* Kegel *m.*

confectioner (kənˈfekʃənə) *n* Konditor *m.* **confectionery** *n* Konditorwaren *f pl.*

confederate (*n,adj* kənˈfedərət; *v* kənˈfedəreit) *n* 1 Verbündete(r) *m. adj* 2 Mitschuldige(r) *m. adj* verbündet, Bundes—. *(vi),vt* (sich) verbünden.

confer (kənˈfəː) *vt* verleihen, erteilen. **conference** *n* Konferenz, Tagung *f.*

confess (kənˈfes) *vt,vi* 1 zugeben, bekennen, gestehen. 2 *rel* beichten. **confession** *n* 1 Zugeständnis *neu.* 2 *rel* Beichte *f.* 3 *law* Geständnis *neu.*

confide (kənˈfaid) *vi* vertrauen. *vt* anvertrauen. **confidence** *n* Vertrauen *neu.* Zuversicht *f.* **confidence trick** *n* Schwindel *m.* **confident** *adj* 1 zuversichtlich. 2 selbstsicher. **confidential** *adj* geheim, vertraulich.

confine (kənˈfain) *vt* begrenzen, einschränken.

confirm (kənˈfəːm) *vt* 1 bestätigen, bekräftigen. **confirmation** *n* 1 Bestätigung *f.* 2 *rel* Konfirmation *f.*

confiscate (ˈkɔnfiskeit) *vt* konfiszieren, einziehen.

168

conflict (*v* kən'flikt; *n* 'kɔnflikt) *vi* **1** streiten. **2** widersprechen. *n* Konflikt, Kampf *m*.

conform (kən'fɔ:m) (*vi*),*vt* (sich) anpassen.

confound (kən'faund) *vt* verwirren, verblüffen.

confront (kən'frʌnt) *vt* **1** gegenüberstehen, konfrontieren. **2** entgegenhalten. **confrontation** *n* Konfrontation *f*.

confuse (kən'fju:z) *vt* **1** verwirren, durcheinanderbringen. **2** verwechseln. **confusion** *n* Verwirrung *f*. Durcheinander *neu*.

congeal (kən'dʒi:l) *vi* gerinnen, erstarren.

congenial (kən'dʒi:niəl) *adj* kongenial, gleichartig, übereinstimmend.

congested (kən'dʒestid) *adj* verstopft, überfüllt.

congratulate (kən'grætjuleit) *vt* beglückwünschen, gratulieren. **congratulation** *n* Glückwunsch *m*.

congregate ('kɔŋgrigeit) *vi* sich versammeln. **congregation** *n* **1** Versammlung *f*. **2** Kirchengemeinde *f*.

congress ('kɔŋgres) *n* Kongreß *m*.

conical ('kɔnikəl) *adj* kegelförmig.

conifer ('kɔnifə) *n* **1** Nadelbaum *m*. **2** ~ *pl* Nadelhölzer *neu pl*.

conjugal ('kɔndʒugəl) *adj* ehelich.

conjugate ('kɔndʒugeit) *vt gram* konjugieren.

conjunction (kən'dʒʌŋkʃən) *n* **1** *gramm* Konjunktion *f*. **2** Verbindung *f*.

conjure ('kʌndʒə) *vi* zaubern. **conjure up** *vt* **1** heraufbeschwören. **2** hervorrufen. **conjurer** *n* Zauberer *m*.

connect (kə'nekt) *vt* verbinden, verknüpfen, anschließen. **connection** *n* **1** Verbindung, Verknüpfung *f*. **2** Anschluß *m*. **3** Zusammenhang *m*.

connoisseur (kɔnə'sə:) *n* Kenner *m*.

connotation (kɔnə'teiʃən) *n* Nebenbedeutung *f*.

conquer ('kɔŋkə) *vt* besiegen, erobern. **conqueror** *n* Sieger, Eroberer *m*. **conquest** *n* Eroberung *f*.

conscience ('kɔnʃəns) *n* Gewissen *neu*.

conscientious (kɔnʃi'enʃəs) *adj* gewissenhaft.

conscious ('kɔnʃəs) *adj* **1** bei Bewußtsein. **2** bewußt. **3** wissentlich. **consciousness** *n* Bewußtsein *neu*.

conscript (*n* 'kɔnskript; *v* kən'skript) *n* Wehrdienstpflichtige(r) *m*. *vt* (zwangsweise) einziehen. **conscription** *n* Wehrpflicht *f*.

consecrate ('kɔnsikreit) *vt* weihen. **consecration** *n* Weihung *f*.

consecutive (kən'sekjutiv) *adj* aufeinanderfolgend.

consent (kən'sent) *vi* zustimmen, einwilligen. *n* Zustimmung *f*.

consequence ('kɔnsikwəns) *n* Folge *f*. Ergebnis *neu*. **consequent** *adj* folgend. **consequently** *adv* folglich, deshalb.

conserve (kən'sə:v) *vt* **1** erhalten, bewahren. **2** einmachen. **conservation** *n* **1** Erhaltung *f*. **2** Schutz *m*. **conservative** *adj* konservativ. *n* Konservative(r) *m*. **conservatory** *n* Treibhaus *neu*.

consider (kən'sidə) *vt* betrachten (als). **2** bedenken, überlegen. **3** berücksichtigen. **considerable** *adj* beträchtlich, erheblich. **considerate** *adj* überlegt, rücksichtsvoll. **consideration** *n* **1** Betracht(ung), Überlegung, Berücksichtigung *f*. **2** Rücksicht *f*.

consign (kən'sain) *vt* übergeben, überliefern. **consignment** *n* Lieferung *f*.

consist (kən'sist) *vi* bestehen. **consistency** *n* **1** Dichtigkeit *f*. **2** Übereinstimmung *f*. **3** Konsequenz, Folgerichtigkeit *f*. **consistent** *adj* **1** konsequent, folgerichtig. **2** übereinstimmend.

console (kən'soul) *vt* trösten. **consolation** *n* Trost *m*.

consolidate (kən'sɔlideit) *vt* stärken, festigen, konsolidieren.

consonant ('kɔnsənənt) *n* Konsonant, Mitlaut *m*.

conspicuous (kən'spikjuəs) *adj* auffallend.

conspire (kən'spaiə) *vi* sich verschwören.

constable ('kɔnstəbəl) *n* Polizist *m*.

Constance, Lake ('kɔnstəns) *n* Bodensee *m*.

constant ('kɔnstənt) *adj* **1** dauernd, beständig. **2** treu. **3** unveränderlich. **constantly** *adv* stets, ständig.

constellation (kɔnstə'leiʃən) *n* Konstellation *f*.

constipation (kɔnsti'peiʃən) *n* (Darm)Verstopfung *f*.

constitute ('kɔnstitju:t) *vt* **1** ausmachen, bilden. **2** gründen. **constituency** *n* Wahlkreis, Wahlbezirk *m*. **constituent** *adj* teilbildend. *n* **1** Bestandteil *m*. **2** Wähler *m*. **constitution** *n* **1** *pol* (Staats)Verfassung *f*. **2** Struktur, Konstitution *f*. **constitutional** *adj* verfassungsmäßig.

constraint (kən'streint) *n* **1** Zwang *m*. **2** Zurückhaltung *f*.

constrict (kən'strikt) *vt* **1** zusammenziehen. **2** hemmen, einengen.

construct (kən'strʌkt) *vt* bauen, errichten, konstruieren. **construction** *n* **1** Bau *m*. Errichtung *f*. **2** Bau *m*. Gebäude *neu*. **3** Konstruktion *f*. **constructive** *adj* konstruktiv.

consul ('kɔnsəl) n Konsul m. **consulate** n Konsulat neu.

consult (kən'sʌlt) vi,vt konsultieren, um Rat fragen. **consult a book** in einem Buch nachschlagen. **consultant** n 1 Berater m. 2 med Konsilarius m. **consultation** n 1 Beratung f. 2 Konsultation f.

consume (kən'sju:m) vt 1 konsumieren, essen. 2 verbrauchen. 3 vernichten. **consumer** n Verbraucher m. **consumption** n 1 Verbrauch m. 2 Genuß m.

contact ('kɔntækt) n 1 Kontakt m. Berührung f. 2 Anschluß m. vt sich in Verbindung setzen mit. **contact lenses** n Kontaktlinsen f pl.

contagious (kən'teidʒəs) adj ansteckend.

contain (kən'tein) vt 1 enthalten. 2 zurückhalten. **container** n Behälter m.

contaminate (kən'tæmineit) vt verseuchen, vergiften. **contamination** n Verseuchung f.

contemplate ('kɔntəmpleit) vt 1 betrachten, nachdenken, erwägen. 2 vorhaben. **contemplation** n 1 Betrachtung f. Nachdenken neu. 2 Meditation f.

contemporary (kən'tempərəri) adj zeitgenössisch. n Zeitgenosse m.

contempt (kən'tempt) n 1 Verachtung f. 2 law Mißachtung (des Gerichts) f. **contemptible** adj verächtlich. **contemptuous** adj verachtungsvoll.

content[1] ('kɔntent) n 1 Inhalt m. 2 Gehalt m.

content[2] (kən'tent) adj zufrieden, genügsam. vt zufriedenstellen. **contentment** n Zufriedenheit f.

contest (n 'kɔntest; v kən'test) n 1 Streit m. 2 Wettkampf m. vt bestreiten, anfechten. **contestant** n Teilnehmer, Bewerber m.

context ('kɔntekst) n Zusammenhang m.

continent ('kɔntinənt) n Kontinent m. adj mäßig, keusch. **continental** adj kontinental.

contingency (kən'tindʒənsi) n 1 Möglichkeit f. 2 Zufälligkeit f. **contingent** adj zufällig, nicht notwendig.

continue (kən'tinju:) vt fortsetzen, weitermachen. **continual** adj fortgesetzt. **continually** adv immer wieder, dauernd. **continuation** n Fortsetzung, Weiterführung f. **continuity** n Kontinuität, Stetigkeit f. **continuous** adj ununterbrochen, (fort)dauernd.

contour ('kɔntuə) n 1 Umriß m. Kontur f. 2 geog Höhenlinie f.

contraband ('kɔntrəbænd) n Schmuggelware f.

contraception (kɔntrə'sepʃən) n Empfängnis-

verhütung f. **contraceptive** n Empfängnisverhütungsmittel neu.

contract (n 'kɔntrækt; v kən'trækt) n Vertrag, Kontrakt m. vt 1 verkürzen, zusammenziehen. 2 (an illness) sich zuziehen. vi sich zusammenziehen, kleiner werden.

contradict (kɔntrə'dikt) vt widersprechen. **contradiction** n Widerspruch m.

contralto (kən'træltou) n Alt m. Altstimme f.

contraption (kən'træpʃən) n inf (neuartiges) Gerät neu. Kniff m.

contrary ('kɔntrəri) adj 1 entgegengesetzt, widrig. 2 widerspenstig.

contrast (v kən'tra:st; n 'kɔntra:st) vt kontrastieren, entgegensetzen, gegenüberstellen. vi sich unterscheiden. n Kontrast, Gegensatz m.

contravene (kɔntrə'vi:n) vt 1 übertreten. 2 zuwiderhandeln.

contribute (kən'tribju:t) vt,vi beitragen, beisteuern. **contribution** n Beitrag m.

contrive (kən'traiv) vt 1 erdenken, erfinden. 2 zustande bringen.

control (kən'troul) vt 1 lenken, steuern. 2 beaufsichtigen. 3 beherrschen. 4 kontrollieren. n 1 Macht, Gewalt f. 2 Aufsicht, Kontrolle f. **controller** n 1 Aufseher. 2 (Strom)Regler m.

controversy ('kɔntrəvə:si, kən'trɔvəsi) n Kontroverse f. Streit m. **controversial** adj umstritten.

convalesce (kɔnvə'les) vi genesen, gesund werden.

convenience (kən'vi:niəns) n 1 Bequemlichkeit, Annehmlichkeit f. 2 Gelegenheit f. **convenient** adj passend, geeignet, gelegen.

convent ('kɔnvənt) n Kloster neu.

convention (kən'venʃən) n 1 Tagung, Versammlung f. 2 Brauch m. Sitte, Regel f. **conventional** adj konventionell.

converge (kən'və:dʒ) vi zusammenlaufen, sich nähern.

converse (v kən'və:s; n 'kɔnvə:s) vi sich unterhalten, sprechen. n Umkehrung f. Gegenteil neu. **conversation** n Unterhaltung f. Gespräch neu. **conversational** adj Unterhaltungs—.

convert (v kən'və:t; n 'kɔnvə:t) vt 1 umwandeln, verwandeln. 2 umwechseln. 3 rel bekehren. n Bekehrte(r) m.

convex ('kɔnveks) adj konvex, gewölbt.

convey (kən'vei) vt 1 befördern, transportieren. 2 mitteilen, vermitteln. **conveyor belt** n Fließband neu.

convict (*v* kən'vikt; *n* 'kɔnvikt) *vt law* überführen. *n* Sträfling *m.*

conviction (kən'vikʃən) *n* **1** *law* Überführung, Verurteilung *f.* **2** Überzeugung *f.*

convince (kən'vins) *vt* überzeugen, überreden.

convoy ('kɔnvɔi) *n* **1** Geleitzug *m.* **2** *mil* Kolonne *f.*

cook (kuk) *n* Koch *m.* Köchin *f. vt* kochen. **cookery** *n* Kochen *neu.*

cool (ku:l) *adj* kühl. *vt* kühlen. *vi* sich abkühlen.

coop (ku:p) *n* Brutkorb *m. vt* einsperren.

cooperate (kou'ɔpəreit) *vi* zusammenarbeiten, kooperieren. **cooperation** *n* **1** Zusammenarbeit *f.* **2** Hilfe *f.* **cooperative** *adj* **1** zusammenarbeitend. **2** hilfsbereit. **3** *pol* genossenschaftlich. *n* Arbeitsgenossenschaft *f.* **cooperative society** *n* Konsumverein *m.*

coordinate (*adj, n* kou'ɔ:dnət; *v* kou'ɔ:dineit) *adj* koordiniert. *n* Koordinate *f. vt* koordinieren, gleichstellen. **coordination** *n* Koordinierung, Gleichstellung *f.*

cope (koup) *vi* sich messen mit, meistern.

Copenhagen (koupən'heigən) *n* Kopenhagen *neu.*

copious ('koupiəs) *adj* reichlich.

copper[1] ('kɔpə) *n* Kupfer *neu. adj* Kupfer—.

copper[2] ('kɔpə) *n inf* Polyp, Polizist *m.*

copulate ('kɔpjuleit) *vi* sich paaren.

copy ('kɔpi) *vt* kopieren, nachmachen. *n* **1** Kopie, Abschrift *f.* **2** Exemplar *neu.* **copyright** *n* Verlagsrecht, Copyright *neu.*

coral ('kɔrəl) *n* Koralle *f.*

cord (kɔ:d) *n* Schnur *f.* Strick *m.*

cordial ('kɔ:diəl) *adj* freundlich, herzlich.

cordon ('kɔ:dn) *n* Kette *f.* Gürtel *m.* **cordon off** absperren.

corduroy ('kɔ:dərɔi) *n* Kord(samt) *m.*

core (kɔ:) *n* Kern *m.*

cork (kɔ:k) *n* Korken, Pfropfen *m.* **corkscrew** *n* Korkenzieher *m.*

corn[1] (kɔ:n) *n* Getreide, Korn *neu.* **cornflour** *n* Maismehl *neu.* **cornflower** *n* Kornblume *f.*

corn[2] (kɔ:n) *n med* Hühnerauge *neu.*

corner ('kɔ:nə) *n* Ecke *f.*

cornet ('kɔ:nit) *n* **1** *mus* (Ventil)kornett *neu.* **2** Eiswaffeltüte *f.*

coronary ('kɔrənəri) *adj* koronar. **coronary thrombosis** *n* Koronarthrombose *f.*

coronation (kɔrə'neiʃən) *n* Krönung *f.*

corporal[1] ('kɔ:prəl) *adj* körperlich, physisch.

corporal[2] ('kɔ:prəl) *n* Korporal, Gefreite(r) *m.*

corporation (kɔ:pə'reiʃən) *n* Körperschaft, Korporation *f.*

corps (kɔ:) *n* Armeekorps *neu.*

corpse (kɔ:ps) *n* Leiche *f.* Leichnam *m.*

correct (kə'rekt) *adj* **1** richtig. **2** korrekt. *vt* **1** berichtigen, richtigstellen. **2** korrigieren. **correction** *n* **1** Berichtigung, Verbesserung *f.* **2** Korrektur *f.*

correlate ('kɔrəleit) *vi* entsprechen. *vt* aufeinander beziehen.

correspond (kɔri'spɔnd) *vi* **1** übereinstimmen, entsprechen. **2** einen Briefwechsel führen, korrespondieren. **correspondence** *n* **1** Übereinstimmung *f.* **2** Briefwechsel *m.* **3** Briefe *m pl.* **correspondent** *n* Korrespondent *m.*

corridor ('kɔridɔ:) *n* Korridor, Gang *m.*

corrode (kə'roud) *vt* zerfressen. *vi* rosten.

corrupt (kə'rʌpt) *vt* **1** verderben. **2** verführen. *adj* **1** verdorben, verfault. **2** korrupt.

corset ('kɔ:sit) *n* Korsett *neu.*

cosmetic (kɔz'metik) *adj* kosmetisch. *n* Schönheitsmittel *neu.*

cosmopolitan (kɔzmə'pɔlitən) *adj* weltbürgerlich.

cost[*] (kɔst) *n* **1** Preis *m.* Kosten *pl.* **2** Schaden *m. vi* kosten. *vt* die Kosten berechnen von. **costly** *adj* teuer.

costume ('kɔstju:m) *n* Kostüm *neu.* Tracht *f.*

cosy ('kouzi) *adj* bequem, gemütlich.

cot (kɔt) *n* Kinderbett *neu.*

cottage ('kɔtidʒ) *n* Hütte *f.* Häuschen *n.*

cotton ('kɔtn) *n* Baumwolle *f.* **cotton-wool** *n* Watte *f.*

couch (kautʃ) *n* Couch *f.* Liegesofa *neu.*

cough (kɔf) *n* Husten *m. vi* husten.

could (kud; *unstressed* kəd) *v see* **can.**

council ('kaunsəl) *n* Rat *m.* **councillor** Ratsherr *m.*

counsel ('kaunsəl) *n* Rat(schlag) *m. vt* beraten.

count[1] (kaunt) *vt* **1** zählen. **2** halten für. *vi* **1** zählen. **2** gelten. *n* Zählen *neu.* **countdown** Startzählung *f.*

count[2] (kaunt) *n* Graf *m.*

counter[1] ('kauntə) *n* **1** Ladentisch *m.* **2** Spielmarke *f.* **3** Zähler *m.*

counter[2] ('kauntə) *pref* gegen, entgegen.

counterattack ('kauntərətæk) *n* Gegenangriff *m.*

counterfeit ('kauntəfit) *adj* falsch, unecht, verfälscht. *vt* fälschen.

counterfoil ('kauntəfɔil) *n* Quittung *f.* Kontrollabschnitt *m.*

counterpart ('kauntəpa:t) *n* Gegenstück *neu.*

countess ('kauntis) *n* Gräfin *f.*

country ('kʌntri) *n* **1** Land *neu.* **2** Staat

m. **country house** *n* Landhaus *neu.* **countryside** *n* Landschaft *f.*

county (ˈkaunti) *n* Grafschaft *f.*

coup (ku:) *n* Coup, Putsch *m.* **coup d'état** *n* Staatsstreich *m.*

couple (ˈkʌpəl) *n* Paar *neu.* **a couple of** ein Paar. *vt* **1** paaren, verbinden. **2** koppeln.

coupon (ˈku:pɔn) *n* Gutschein, Kupon *m.*

courage (ˈkʌridʒ) *n* Mut *m.* Tapferkeit *f.*

courgette (kuəˈʒet) *n* Courgette *f.*

courier (ˈkuriə) *n* **1** Kurier, Eilbote *m.* **2** Reiseleiter *m.*

course (kɔ:s) *n* **1** Lauf, Gang *m.* **2** Kurs *m.* Richtung *f.* **3** Rennbahn *f.* **4** *educ* Kursus, Lehrgang *m.* **of course** natürlich, selbstverständlich.

court (kɔ:t) *n* **1** Hof *m.* **2** Spielplatz *m.* *vt* werben um. **court martial** *n* Militärgericht, Kriegsgericht *neu.* **courtship** *n* Werbezeit, Werbung *f.* **courtyard** *n* Hof *m.*

courteous (ˈkə:tiəs) *adj* höflich, verbindlich. **courtesy** *n* Höflichkeit *f.*

cousin (ˈkʌzən) *n* Vetter, Cousin *m.* Kusine *f.*

cove (kouv) *n* Bucht *f.*

cover (ˈkʌvə) *n* **1** Decke *f.* **2** (Be)Deckung *f.* **3** Hülle *f.* *vt* decken, bedecken.

cow (kau) *n* Kuh *f.* **cowboy** *n* Cowboy *m.*

coward (ˈkauəd) *n* Feigling *m.*

cower (ˈkauə) *vi* sich ducken, kauern.

coy (kɔi) *adj* scheu, bescheiden.

crab (kræb) *n* Krebs *m.*

crack (kræk) *vi,vt* **1** knallen. **2** spalten, zerbrechen. *n* **1** Spalt, Riß *m.* **2** Knall *m.*

cracker (ˈkrækə) *n* Keks *m.*

crackle (ˈkrækəl) *vi* knistern. *n* Geknister *neu.*

cradle (ˈkreidl) *n* Wiege *f.* *vt* wiegen.

craft (krɑ:ft) *n* **1** Kunst, Fertigkeit *f.* **2** List, Schlauheit *f.* **craftsman** *n* Künstler, Handwerker *m.* **craftsmanship** *n* Kunstfertigkeit *f.* **crafty** *adj* listig, gerissen.

cram (kræm) *vt* vollstopfen, überladen.

cramp[1] (kræmp) *n* Krampf *m.* **cramped** *adj* beengt, zusammengepfercht.

cramp[2] (kræmp) *n* Klammer, Krampe *f.* *vt* mit Klammern befestigen.

crane (krein) *n* **1** *zool* Kranich *m.* **2** Kran *m.*

crash (kræʃ) *n* **1** Zusammenstoß, Aufprall *m.* **2** Absturz *m.* **3** Krachen *neu.* *vi* **1** zusammenstoßen. **2** abstürzen. **crash-helmet** *n* Sturzhelm *m.*

crate (kreit) *n* Kiste *f.* *vt* verpacken.

crater (ˈkreitə) *n* Krater, Trichter *m.*

crave (kreiv) *vt* sich sehnen nach, flehen um.

crawl (krɔ:l) *vi* kriechen, sich schleppen. *n* **1** Kriechen *neu.* **2** *sport* Kraulschwimmen *neu.*

crayfish (ˈkreifiʃ) *n* (Fluß)Krebs *m.*

crayon (ˈkreiən) *n* Buntstift *m.*

craze (kreiz) *n* Fimmel *m.* Manie, Mode *f.* **crazy** *adj* verrückt, toll.

creak (kri:k) *vi* knarren. *n* Knarren *neu.*

cream (kri:m) *n* **1** Sahne *f.* Rahm *m.* **2** Creme *f.*

crease (kri:s) *n* **1** Falte *f.* **2** Bügelfalte *f.* *vt* **1** falten. **2** bügeln. **crease-resistant** *adj* knitterfrei.

create (kriˈeit) *vt* **1** (er)schaffen, kreieren. **2** verursachen. **3** erheben (zu). **creation** *n* Erschaffung, Schöpfung *f.* **creative** *adj* kreativ, schöpferisch. **creator** *n* Schöpfer *m.* **creature** *n* Geschöpf, Wesen *neu.*

credentials (kriˈdenʃəlz) *n pl* **1** Ausweispapiere *neu pl.* **2** Beglaubigungsschreiben *neu.*

credible (ˈkredibəl) *adj* glaubwürdig.

credit (ˈkredit) *n* **1** Kredit *m.* Guthaben *neu.* **2** Anerkennung *f.* **3** Glaube *m.* *vt* **1** kreditieren, gutschreiben. **2** zutrauen. **credit card** *n* Kreditkarte *f.*

credulous (ˈkredjuləs) *adj* leichtgläubig.

creep* (kri:p) *vi* **1** kriechen, schleichen. **2** sich heimlich nähern. *n sl* Kriecher *m.*

cremate (kriˈmeit) *vt* einäschern, verbrennen. **crematorium** *n* Krematorium *neu.*

crept (krept) *v* see **creep.**

crescent (ˈkresənt) *n* Halbmond *m.*

cress (kres) *n* Kresse *f.*

crest (krest) *n* **1** Familienwappen *neu.* **2** Kamm *m.* **3** Gipfel *m.*

crevice (ˈkrevis) *n* Spalte *f.* Riß *m.*

crew[1] (kru:) *n* Mannschaft, Besatzung *f.*

crew[2] (kru:) *v* see **crow**[1].

crib (krib) *n* Krippe *f.* *vi inf* abschreiben.

cricket[1] (ˈkrikit) *n* Grille *f.*

cricket[2] (ˈkrikit) *n* Kricketspiel *neu.*

crime (kraim) *n* Verbrechen *neu.* **criminal** *n* Verbrecher *m.* *adj* kriminell, verbrecherisch.

crimson (ˈkrimzən) *adj* karmesinrot.

cringe (krindʒ) *vi* sich krümmen, kauern.

crinkle (ˈkriŋkəl) *vi* sich kräuseln. **crinkly** *adj* kraus.

cripple (ˈkripəl) *n* Krüppel *m.* *vt* lahmlegen, schwer schädigen.

crisis (ˈkraisis) *n, pl* **crises** Krise *f.*

crisp (krisp) *adj* **1** knusprig. **2** frisch. **crisps** *n pl* Kartoffelscheiben *f pl.*

criterion (kraiˈtiəriən) *n* Kriterium *neu.*

criticize (ˈkritisaiz) *vt* kritisieren, tadeln. **critic**

n Kritiker *m*. **critical** *adj* **1** kritisch. **2** entscheidend. **criticism** *n* Kritik *f*.

croak (krouk) *n* Quaken *neu*. *vi* quaken, krächzen

crochet ('krouʃei) *vt* hakeln. *n* Häkelarbeit *f*.

crockery ('krɔkəri) Geschirr *neu*.

crocodile ('krɔkədail) *n* Krokodil *neu*.

crocus ('kroukəs) *n* Krokus *m*.

crook (kruk) *n* **1** Haken *m*. **2** Krummstab *m*. **3** Schwindler, Gauner *m*. *vt* krümmen. **crooked** ('krukid) *adj* schief, gebogen, krumm.

crop (krɔp) *n* **1** Feldfrucht *f*. Getreide *neu*. **2** Ernte *f*. **3** Reitpeitsche *f*. *vi* **1** abgrasen, abweiden. **2** stutzen. **crop up** auftauchen.

croquet ('kroukei) *n* Krocketspiel *neu*.

cross (krɔs) *vt* **1** überqueren, hinübergehen. **2** kreuzen. *vi* sich kreuzen. *n* **1** Kreuz *neu*. **2** Querstrich *m*. *adj* **1** böse, verärgert. **2** Quer—, Kreuz—. **cross-examination** *n* Kreuzverhör *m*. **cross-eyed** *adj* schielend. **cross-fire** *n* Kreuzfeuer *neu*. **crossing** *n* **1** Übergang *m*. **2** Kreuzung *f*. **cross-reference** *vt* kreuzverweisen. *n* Kreuzverweis *m*. **crossroads** *n* **1** (Straßen)Kreuzung *f*. **2** Scheideweg *m*. **crossword** *n* Kreuzworträtsel *neu*

crotchet ('krɔtʃit) *n mus* Viertelnote *f*.

crouch (krautʃ) *vi* sich bücken, hocken.

crow[1] (krou) *n* Krähe *f*.

crow[2] (krou) *vi* krähen.

crowd (kraud) *n* **1** (Menschen)Menge *f*. **2** *inf* Clique *f*. *vi* sich drängen. *vt* überfüllen.

crown (kraun) *n* Krone *f*. *vt* krönen. **crowning** *adj* krönend, höchst. **crown prince** *n* Kronprinz *m*.

crucial ('kru:ʃəl) *adj* kritisch, entscheidend.

crucify ('kru:sifai) *vt* kreuzigen. **crucifix** *n* Kruzifix *neu*.

crude (kru:d) *adj* **1** roh, unreif. **2** grob, ungehobelt. **crude oil** *n* Rohöl *neu*.

cruel ('kruəl) *adj* grausam, unbarmherzig. **cruelty** *n* **1** Grausamkeit *f*. **2** Quälerei *f*.

cruise (kru:z) *n* Kreuzfahrt *f*. *vi* kreuzen.

crumb (krʌm) *n* Krume *f*. Brösel *m*.

crumble ('krʌmbl) *vt* zerkrümeln, zerbröckeln. *vi* zerfallen.

crumple ('krʌmpəl) *vt* zerknittern, zusammenbrechen. *vi* faltig werden.

crunch (krʌntʃ) *vt* zerknirschen. *vi* knirschen. **crunchy** *adj* knusprig.

crusade (kru:'seid) *n* Kreuzzug *m*. **crusader** *n* Kreuzfahrer *m*.

crush (krʌʃ) *vt* zerdrücken, zerquetschen.

crust (krʌst) *n* Kruste, Rinde *f*.

crustacean (krʌs'teiʃən) *n* Krustentier *neu*.

crutch (krʌtʃ) *n* Krücke *f*.

cry (krai) *vi* **1** schreien, rufen. **2** weinen. *n* Schrei, Ruf *m*.

crypt (kript) *n* Gruft *f*. **cryptic** *adj* geheim.

crystal ('kristl) *n* Kristall *m*. **crystallize** *vt,vi* kristallisieren.

cub (kʌb) *n* Welpe *m*.

cube (kju:b) *n* Würfel, Kubus *m*. **cubic** *adj* **1** würfelförmig. **2** Kubik—. **cubicle** *n* Kabine *f*.

cuckoo ('kuku:) *n* Kuckuck *m*.

cucumber ('kju:kʌmbə) *n* (Salat)Gurke *f*.

cuddle ('kʌdl) *vt* umarmen, hätscheln. *vi* sich (zusammen)kuscheln. *n* Umarmung *f*.

cue[1] (kju:) *n* **1** Th Stichwort *neu*. **2** Wink *m*.

cue[2] (kju:) *n* Billardstock *m*.

cuff[1] (kʌf) *n* Manschette *f*. Ärmelaufschlag *m*. **cufflink** *n* Manschettenknopf *m*.

cuff[2] (kʌf) *vt* schlagen, knuffen. *n* Ohrfeige *f*.

culinary ('kʌlinri) *adj* kulinarisch, Koch—.

culminate ('kʌlmineit) *vi* kulminieren, gipfeln.

culprit ('kʌlprit) *n* Schuldige(r), Täter *m*.

cult (kʌlt) *n* Kult *m*.

cultivate ('kʌltiveit) *vt* **1** bebauen, kultivieren. **2** pflegen, hegen. **cultivation** *n* **1** Ackerbau *m*. **2** Bebauung. Kultivierung *f*.

culture ('kʌltʃə) *n* **1** Kultur *f*. **2** Zucht *f*. **cultural** *adj* kulturell.

cumbersome ('kʌmbəsəm) *adj* schwerfällig.

cunning ('kʌniŋ) *adj* listig, schlau.

cup (kʌp) *n* **1** Tasse *f*. **2** *sport* Pokal *m*. **cupful** *n* Tasse(voll) *f*.

cupboard ('kʌbəd) *n* Schrank *m*.

curate ('kjuəreit) *n* Unterpfarrer *m*.

curator (kju'reitə) *n* **1** Verwalter *m*. **2** Museumsdirektor *m*.

curb (kə:b) *vt* bändigen, zügeln. *n* **1** Kinnkette *f*. **2** Zügel *m*.

curdle ('kə:dl) *vi,(vt)* gerinnen (lassen).

cure (kjuə) *vt* **1** heilen. **2** *cul* räuchern. *n* **1** Heilung *f*. **2** Heilmittel *neu*. **3** Kur *f*.

curfew ('kə:fju:) *n* Ausgehverbot *m*.

curious ('kjuəriəs) *adj* **1** neugierig. **2** merkwürdig, seltsam. **curiosity** *n* Neugier *f*.

curl (kə:l) *(vi),vt* **1** (sich) locken, (sich) kräuseln. **2** (sich) zusammenrollen. *n* **1** Locke *f*. **2** Windung *f*.

currant ('kʌrənt) *n* Korinthe *f*.

current ('kʌrənt) *n* Strom *m*. *adj* **1** laufend. **2** gegenwärtig. **current account** *n* Kontokorrent *neu*. **currency** *n* **1** *comm* Währung *f*. **2** Umlauf *m*.

curry ('kʌri) *n cul* Curry *m*.

curse (kə:s) vi fluchen, schimpfen. vt (ver)-
fluchen. n Fluch m.

curt (kə:t) adj knapp, barsch.

curtail (kə:'teil) vt **1** verkürzen. **2** beschneiden. **3**
vermindern.

curtain ('kə:tn) n Gardine f. Vorhang m.

curtsy ('kə:tsi) vi einen Knicks machen. n
Knicks m.

curve (kə:v) (vi,)vt (sich) biegen, (sich) krümmen. n Kurve, Krümmung f.

cushion ('kuʃən) n Kissen, Polster neu. vt
dämpfen.

custard ('kʌstəd) n Eierkrem f.

custody ('kʌstədi) n **1** Bewachung f. Schutz m.
2 law Haft f.

custom ('kʌstəm) n Brauch m. Gewohnheit,
Sitte f. **customary** adj gebräuchlich, Ge-
wohnheits— **customer** n Kunde, Klient m.

cut* (kʌt) vt **1** schneiden. **2** vermindern, verkürzen. n Schnitt m. **2** Schlag m. **3** Anteil m.
4 Abzug m. **5** Kürzung f. **cut down 1** fällen.
2 verringern. **cut off** abschneiden. **cut up**
zerschneiden. **cut-price** adj herabgesetzt.
cutting n Ausschnitt m. adj beißend, scharf.

cute (kju:t) adj süß, niedlich.

cuticle ('kju:tikəl) n Oberhaut f.

cutlery ('kʌtləri) n Besteck neu.

cutlet ('kʌtlit) n Kotelett neu.

cycle ('saikəl) n **1** Fahrrad neu. **2** Zyklus m.
Kreislauf m. vi radfahren.

cyclone ('saikloun) n Wirbelsturm m.

cygnet ('signit) n junger Schwan m.

cylinder ('silində) n Zylinder m.

cymbal ('simbəl) n Zimbel f. Becken neu.

cynic ('sinik) n Zyniker m. **cynical** adj zynisch.

cypress ('saiprəs) n Zypresse f.

Cyprus ('saiprəs) n Zypern neu. **Cypriot** n
Zypriot m. adj zypriotisch.

Czech (tʃek) n Tscheche m. adj tschechisch.

Czechoslovakia (tʃekəslə'vækiə) n Tschecho-
slowakei f. **Czechoslovakian** adj tschecho-
slowakisch. n Tschechoslowake m.

D

dab (dæb) vt (be)tupfen.

dabble ('dæbəl) vi **1** benetzen. **2** hineinpfu-
schen. **dabbler** n Dilettant m.

dad (dæd) n inf also **daddy** Vati m.

daffodil ('dæfədil) n Narzisse f.

daft (dɑ:ft) adj blöd, dumm.

dagger ('dægə) n Dolch m.

daily ('deili) adj täglich.

dainty ('deinti) adj zierlich.

dairy ('dɛəri) n Molkerei f. **dairy farm** n Meierei
f.

daisy ('deizi) n Gänseblümchen neu.

dam (dæm) n Damm, Deich m. vt eindämmen.

damage ('dæmidʒ) n Schaden m. Beschädigung
f. vt beschädigen.

damn (dæm) vt **1** verdammen. **2** verfluchen. **3**
verurteilen. interj verflucht! **damnable** adj
verdammt, verflucht. **damnation** n Verdam-
mung f.

damp (dæmp) adj feucht. **dampen** vt **1** an-
feuchten. **2** inf niederschlagen.

damson ('dæmzən) n Zwetschge f.

dance (dɑ:ns) n Tanz m. vi tanzen. **dancer** n
Tänzer m. Tänzerin f.

dandelion ('dændilaiən) n Löwenzahn m.

dandruff ('dændrʌf) n Schuppen f pl.

Dane (dein) n Däne m. **Danish** adj dänisch. n
(language) Dänisch neu.

danger ('deindʒə) n Gefahr f. **dangerous** adj
gefährlich.

dangle ('dæŋgəl) vi,(vt) baumeln, schwenken
(lassen).

Danube ('dænju:b) n Donau f.

dare (dɛə) vt **1** wagen, sich getrauen. **2**
mutig, waghalsig.

dark (dɑ:k) adj dunkel, finster. **darken** vt
verdunkeln. vi sich verdunkeln, trüben. **darkness** n Dunkelheit, Finsternis f.

darling ('dɑ:liŋ) n Liebling m.

darn (dɑ:n) vt stopfen.

dart (dɑ:t) n Wurfpfeil m. vi hervorschießen.

dash (dæʃ) vt **1** zerschlagen. **2** zerstören. vi
eilen, stürzen. n Zusatz, Schuß m. **dashboard**
n Armaturenbrett neu.

data ('deitə) n pl Daten neu pl. **data pro-
cessing** n Datenverarbeitung f.

date¹ (deit) n **1** Datum neu. **2** Termin m. **3**
Periode f. vt **1** datieren. **2** inf sich verabreden
mit. **date line** n Datumsgrenze f.

date² (deit) n Dattel f.

dative ('deitiv) adj dativ. n Dativ m.

daughter ('dɔ:tə) n Tochter f. **daughter-in-law**
n Schwiegertochter f.

dawdle ('dɔ:dl) vi bummeln, trödeln.

dawn (dɔ:n) n Morgendämmerung f. Tagesanbruch m.

day (dei) n Tag m. **daybreak** n Tagesanbruch
m. **daydream** n Träumerei f. **daylight** n
Tageslicht neu.

daze (deiz) n Verwirrung f. vt verwirren, betäuben.

dazzle ('dæzəl) vt blenden.

dead (ded) adj tot, leblos. **deaden** vt abtöten, dämpfen. **deadline** n Frist f. Termin m. **deadlock** n Stillstand m.

deaf (def) adj taub, schwerhörig. **deaf-aid** n Hörgerät neu. **deafen** vt taub machen. **deafmute** n Taubstumme(r) m. adj taubstumm.

deal* (di:l) vi 1 handeln. 2 sich beschäftigen. vt game austeilen. n 1 Geschäft neu. 2 Abkommen neu. 3 Menge f. **a great** or **good deal** sehr viel, eine ganze Menge. **dealer** n 1 Händler m. 2 Verteiler m.

dean (di:n) n Dekan m.

dear (diə) adj 1 lieb, geschätzt. 2 teuer. 3 (in letters) Liebe(r), Sehr geehrte(r). n Liebling neu. **oh dear!** ach je! **dearly** adv 1 herzlich. 2 teuer.

death (deθ) n Tod m. **death certificate** n Sterbeurkunde f.

debase (di'beis) vt verderben, in Wert mindern.

debate (di'beit) vt debattieren, besprechen.

debit ('debit) vt belasten. n Belastung f. Soll neu.

debris ('deibri) n Trümmer pl. Schutt m.

debt (det) n Schuld, Verpflichtung f. **debtor** n Schuldner m.

decade ('dekeid) n Jahrzehnt neu.

decadent ('dekədənt) adj dekadent. **decadence** n Dekadenz f.

decant (di'kænt) vt umfüllen. **decanter** n Karaffe f.

decay (di'kei) n Verfall m. vi verfallen, verfaulen.

decease (di'si:s) vi sterben. **deceased** n Verstorbene(r) m.

deceit (di'si:t) n Täuschung f. Betrug m.

deceive (di'si:v) vt irreführen, betrügen, täuschen.

December (di'sembə) n Dezember m.

decent ('di:sənt) adj dezent, anständig.

deceptive (di'septiv) adj täuschend, trügerisch.

decide (di'said) vi sich entscheiden, sich entschließen. vt bestimmen, entscheiden.

deciduous (di'sidjuəs) adj Laub—.

decimal ('desiməl) adj dezimal.

decipher (di'saifə) vt entziffern.

decision (di'siʒən) n Entscheidung f. Entschluß m. **decisive** (di'saisiv) adj entscheidend.

deck (dek) n 1 Deck neu. 2 game Spielkarten f pl. Pack neu. **deckchair** n Liegestuhl m.

declare (di'klɛə) vt erklären, bekanntgeben. vi

erklären. **declaration** n Erklärung, Anmeldung f.

decline (di'klain) vi 1 verfallen, sich neigen. 2 ablehnen. 3 abnehmen. vt 1 ablehnen. 2 gram deklinieren. n Verfall m. **declension** n Deklination f.

decompose (di:kəm'pouz) vt 1 spalten. 2 scheiden. vi sich auflösen. 2 verfaulen.

decorate ('dekəreit) vt 1 schmücken, dekorieren. 2 tapezieren, streichen. 3 auszeichnen. **decoration** n 1 Schmuck m. Verzierung f. 2 Ausstattung f. 3 Auszeichnung f. Orden m.

decoy (n 'di:koi; v di'koi) n Lockvogel, Köder m. vt locken, verleiten.

decrease (di'kri:s) n Abnahme f. Verminderung f. vt verringern, vermindern. vi abnehmen, sich vermindern.

decree (di'kri:) n Erlaß, Bescheid m.

decrepit (di'krepit) adj 1 hinfällig. 2 verfallen.

dedicate ('dedikeit) vt 1 (ein)weihen. 2 widmen. **dedicated** adj pflichtgetreu. **dedication** n Widmung, Hingabe f.

deduce (di'dju:s) vt folgern, schließen, ableiten.

deduct (di'dʌkt) vt abziehen, abrechnen. **deduction** n 1 Abzug m. 2 Schlußfolgerung f.

deed (di:d) n 1 Tat. Handlung f. 2 Urkunde f.

deep (di:p) adj tief. n Tiefe f. **deep-freeze** n Tiefkühltruhe f. vt tiefkühlen.

deer (diə) n invar Reh neu.

deface (di'feis) vt entstellen, verunstalten.

default (di'fɔ:lt) n Nichterfüllung, Unterlassung f. Versäumnis neu. vi in Verzug geraten.

defeat (di'fi:t) n Niederlage f. vt schlagen, überwinden, besiegen.

defect (n 'di:fekt; v di'fekt) n Mangel, Fehler m. vi übertreten. **defection** n Treubruch m. **defective** adj fehlerhaft, mangelhaft.

defend (di'fend) vt verteidigen. **defence** n Verteidigung f. **defender** n Verteidiger m.

defer (di'fə:) vt verschieben. vi nachgieben, sich beugen. **deference** n 1 Nachgiebigkeit f. 2 (Hoch)Achtung f. **deferential** adj rücksichtsvoll.

defiant (di'faiənt) adj trotzig, herausfordernd. **defiance** n Trotz, Widerstand m. Widerspenstigkeit f.

deficient (di'fiʃənt) adj mangelhaft, unzulänglich. **deficiency** n Mangel m. Unzulänglichkeit f.

deficit ('defisit) n Fehlbetrag, Ausfall m.

define (di'fain) vt 1 definieren, festlegen, bestimmen. 2 abgrenzen. **definition** n 1 Definition f. 2 Deutlichkeit f.

definite ('defənit) adj bestimmt, unbedingt.
deflate (di'fleit) vt entleeren, Luft ablassen aus.
deform (di'fɔːm) vt deformieren, verunstalten.
defraud (di'frɔːd) vt betrügen.
defrost (di'frɔst) vt entfrosten.
deft (deft) adj gewandt, geschickt.
defunct (di'fʌŋkt) adj 1 verstorben. 2 nicht mehr bestehend.
defy (di'fai) vt 1 trotzen. 2 herausfordern.
degenerate (di'dʒenəreit) vi entarten, degenerieren. **degeneration** n Entartung, Degeneration f.
degrade (di'greid) vt degradieren, erniedrigen.
degree (di'griː) n 1 Grad m. 2 Stufe f. 3 educ Grad m.
dehydrate (diː'haidreit) vt trocknen, das Wasser entziehen.
deity ('deiiti) n Gott m. Gottheit f.
dejected (di'dʒektid) adj niedergeschlagen, traurig.
delay (di'lei) n Verzögerung, Verspätung f. vt verzögern, verschieben. vi zögern.
delegate (n 'deligət; v 'deligeit) n Delegierte(r), Abgeordnete(r) m. vt 1 bevollmächtigen, delegieren. 2 übertragen.
delete (di'liːt) vt (aus)streichen.
deliberate (adj di'librət; v di'libreit) adj absichtlich. vi nachdenken, überlegen. **deliberation** n Überlegung.
delicate ('delikət) adj 1 zart, fein. 2 empfindlich. **delicacy** n 1 Delikatesse f. 2 Feinheit f. **delicatessen** n Feinkostgeschäft neu.
delicious (di'liʃəs) adj köstlich, herrlich.
delight (di'lait) n Freude, Wonne f. vt erfreuen, entzücken. vi Freude haben, entzückt sein.
delinquency (di'liŋkwənsi) n Kriminalität f. **delinquent** adj kriminell. n Verbrecher m.
deliver (di'livə) vt 1 (ab-, aus-)liefern, austragen. 2 med entbinden. 3 befreien. **deliverance** n Befreiung f. **delivery** n 1 (Aus)Lieferung f. 2 med Entbindung f. 3 sport Wurf m.
delta ('deltə) n Delta neu.
delude (di'luːd) vt täuschen, irreführen. **delusion** n Wahn m. Täuschung f.
delve (delv) vi sich vertiefen.
demand (di'maːnd) n Forderung f. Verlangen neu. vt fordern, verlangen.
democracy (di'mɔkrəsi) n Demokratie f. **democratic** adj demokratisch.
demolish (di'mɔliʃ) vt abreißen, zerstören. **demolition** n Abreißen neu.
demon ('diːmən) n Dämon m.

demonstrate ('demənstreit) vi,vt demonstrieren, zeigen. **demonstration** n Demonstration f.
demoralize (di'mɔrəlaiz) vt entmutigen.
demure (di'mjuə) adj zurückhaltend, zimperlich.
den (den) n Höhle f. Loch neu.
denial (di'naiəl) n 1 Verweigerung f. 2 (Ab)Leugnung f.
denim (di'nim) n Drillich m.
Denmark ('denmɑːk) n Dänemark neu.
denomination (dinɔmi'neiʃən) n 1 rel Konfession f. 2 Einheit f. 3 Bezeichnung f.
denote (di'nout) vt kennzeichnen, bedeuten.
denounce (di'nauns) vt anzeigen, denunzieren.
dense (dens) adj 1 dicht. 2 beschränkt. **density** n Dichte f.
dent (dent) vt einbeulen. n Beule f.
dental ('dentl) adj zahnärztlich, Zahn—. **dentist** n Zahnarzt m. **denture** n Zahnprothese f.
denunciation (di'nʌnsieiʃən) n Verurteilung, Denunziation f.
deny (di'nai) vt 1 leugnen, verneinen. 2 verweigern.
deodorant (diː'oudərənt) n Desodorans neu.
depart (di'paːt) vi 1 weggehen, abfahren. 2 abweichen. **departure** n Abfahrt f. Abflug m.
department (di'paːtmənt) n Abteilung f. **department store** n Warenhaus, Kaufhaus neu.
depend (di'pend) vi 1 abhängen. 2 ankommen. **dependant** n Abhängige(r), Angehörige(r) m. **dependence** n Abhängigkeit f. **dependent** adj abhängig.
depict (di'pikt) vt 1 zeichnen. 2 schildern.
deplete (di'pliːt) vt 1 (ent)leeren. 2 erschöpfen.
deplore (di'plɔː) vt bedauern, mißbilligen.
deport (di'pɔːt) vt deportieren, ausweisen. **deportation** n Deportation, Ausweisung f.
depose (di'pouz) vt absetzen.
deposit (di'pɔzit) n 1 Anzahlung f. 2 Niederschlag m. vt 1 niederlegen. 2 hinterlegen, anzahlen.
depot ('depou) n Depot, Lagerhaus neu.
deprave (di'preiv) vt (moralisch) verderben. **depraved** adj verdorben. **depravity** n Verdorbenheit f.
depreciate (di'priːʃieit) vt entwerten. vi im Wert sinken.
depress (di'pres) vt 1 bedrücken. 2 niederschlagen, deprimieren. **depression** n 1 Depression f. 2 Vertiefung f. 3 Tiefdruckgebiet neu.
deprive (di'praiv) vt berauben, vorenthalten. **deprivation** n Beraubung, Verlust f.

depth (depθ) n Tiefe f. **in depth** ausführlich, gründlich.

deputy ('depjuti) n Stellvertreter m.

derail (di'reil) vt entgleisen.

derelict ('derəlikt) adj verlassen, aufgegeben, verfallen.

deride (di'raid) vt verlachen, verhöhnen.

derive (di'raiv) vt ableiten, herleiten. vi abstammen. **derivation** n Ableitung, Abstammung f.

derogatory (di'rogətri) adj herabsetzend, abfällig.

descend (di'send) vi 1 herunterkommen. 2 absteigen. 3 aussteigen. 4 sinken. 5 herkommen. **descendant** n Nachkomme m. **descent** (di'sent) n 1 Abstieg m. 2 Niedergang m. 3 Herkunft f.

describe (di'skraib) vt beschreiben. **description** n Beschreibung f.

desert[1] ('dezət) n Wüste, Einöde f.

desert[2] (di'zə:t) vt verlassen. vi desertieren. **deserter** n mil Deserteur m.

desert[3] (di'zə:t) n Verdienst m.

deserve (di'zə:v) vt verdienen.

design (di'zain) n 1 Entwurf m. Zeichnung f. 2 Konstruktion f. 3 Muster neu. 4 Absicht f. Plan m. vt entwerfen, planen.

designate ('dezigneit) vt bezeichnen, vorsehen.

desire (di'zaiə) vt 1 wünschen. 2 begehren. n 1 Wunsch, Wille m. 2 Begierde f. Verlangen neu.

desk (dosk) n Pult neu. Schreibtisch m.

desolate ('desələt) adj 1 wüst, öde. 2 traurig.

despair (di'spɛə) vi verzweifeln. n Verzweiflung f.

desperate ('desprət) adj verzweifelt, hoffnungslos.

despise (di'spaiz) vt verachten. **despicable** adj verächtlich.

despite (di'spait) prep trotz, ungeachtet.

despondent (di'spondənt) adj mutlos, verzweifelt.

dessert (di'zə:t) n Nachtisch m. **dessertspoon** n Dessertlöffel m.

destine ('destin) vt bestimmen, ausersehen. **destination** n Ziel neu. Bestimmungsort m. **destiny** n Schicksal neu.

destitute ('destitju:t) adj mittellos, verarmt.

destroy (di'strɔi) vt zerstören. **destroyer** n Zerstörer m. **destruction** n 1 Zerstörung f. 2 Verwüstung f.

detach (di'tætʃ) vt loslösen, abtrennen. **detached** adj 1 abgetrennt. 2 objektiv. **detachment** n 1 Abtrennung f. 2 Objektivität f.

detail ('di:teil) n Detail neu. Einzelheit f. **in detail** ausführlich. vt detaillieren. **detailed** adj ausführlich.

detain (di'tein) vt zurückhalten, festhalten.

detect (di'tekt) vt 1 entdecken, (heraus)finden. 2 spuren, empfinden. **detective** n Detektiv m.

détente (dei'ta:nt) n pol Entspannung f.

detention (di'tenʃən) n Haft f.

deter (di'tə:) vt abschrecken. **deterrent** n Abschreckmittel neu. Abschreckung f. adj abschreckend.

detergent (di'tə:dʒənt) n Waschmittel neu.

deteriorate (di'tiəriəreit) vi sich verschlechtern. **deterioration** n Verschlechterung f.

determine (di'tə:min) vt 1 entschließen, entscheiden. 2 bestimmen, feststellen. **determination** n Entschlossenheit f.

detest (di'test) vt hassen.

detonate ('detəneit) vi,(vt) explodieren (lassen).

detour ('di:tuə) n Umweg m.

detract (di'trækt) vi herabsetzen. vt entziehen.

devalue (di'vælju:) vt entwerten. **devaluation** n Entwertung f.

devastate ('devəsteit) vt verwüsten, verheeren. **devastation** n Verwüstung f.

develop (di'veləp) vt entwickeln. **development** n Entwicklung f.

deviate ('di:vieit) vi abweichen. **deviation** n Abweichung f. **devious** adj unaufrichtig.

device (di'vais) n 1 Plan m. 2 Apparat m. Gerät neu.

devil ('devəl) n Teufel m.

devise (di'vaiz) vt,vi ausdenken, erfinden.

devoid (di'void) adj ohne, frei von.

devote (di'vout) vt widmen. **devote oneself** sich hingeben. **devotee** n 1 Verehrer m. 2 Anhänger m. **devotion** n Hingabe f.

devour (di'vauə) vt 1 fressen, verschlingen. 2 verzehren. 3 vernichten.

devout (di'vaut) adj fromm, andächtig.

dew (dju:) n Tau m.

dexterous ('dekstrəs) adj gewandt. **dexterity** n Gewandtheit f.

diabetes (daiə'bi:tiz) n Zuckerkrankheit f. **diabetic** adj zuckerkrank. n Zuckerkranke(r) m.

diagonal (dai'agənl) adj diagonal.

diagram ('daiəgræm) n Diagramm, Schema neu.

dial (dail) n 1 (telephone) Wählscheibe f. 2 Ziffernscheibe f. vt,vi wählen.

dialect ('daiəlekt) n Mundart f. Dialekt m.

dialogue

dialogue (ˈdaiəlɔg) *n* Dialog *m*. Zwiegespräch *neu*.

diameter (daiˈæmitə) *n* Durchmesser *m*.

diamond (ˈdaiəmənd) *n* Diamant *m*.

diaphragm (ˈdaiəfræm) *n* 1 Membran *f*. 2 *anat* Zwerchfell *neu*. 3 *phot* Blende *f*.

diarrhoea (daiəˈriə) *n* Durchfall *m*.

diary (ˈdaiəri) *n* Tagebuch *neu*. Kalender *m*.

dice (dais) *n pl or s* Würfel *m*. *vi* würfeln. *vt cul* in Würfel schneiden.

dictate (*v* dikˈteit; *n* ˈdikteit) *vt* diktieren. *n* Gebot *neu*. **dictation** *n* 1 Vorschrift *f*. Diktieren *neu*. 2 Diktat *neu*. **dictator** *n* 1 Diktator *m*. **dictatorship** *n* Diktatur *f*.

dictionary (ˈdikʃənri) *n* Wörterbuch *neu*.

did (did) *v see* **do.**

die (dai) *vi* 1 sterben. 2 (of animals) eingehen.

diesel (ˈdiːzəl) *n tech* Diesel *m*. **diesel engine** Dieselmotor *m*.

diet (ˈdaiət) *n* 1 Ernährung, Kost *f*. 2 Diät *f*.

differ (ˈdifə) *vi* 1 (sich) unterscheiden. 2 abweichen. **difference** *n* Unterschied *m*. Verschiedenheit *f*. **different** *adj* verschieden, ander(s).

difficult (ˈdifikəlt) *adj* schwierig, schwer, mühsam. **difficulty** *n* Schwierigkeit, Mühe *f*.

dig* (dig) *vt,vi* graben.

digest (*v* daiˈdʒest; *n* ˈdaidʒest) *vt* verdauen. *n* Auslese *f*. **digestion** *n* Verdauung *f*.

digit (ˈdidʒit) *n* 1 Finger *m*. 2 *math* Stelle *f*.

dignified (ˈdignifaid) *adj* würdevoll.

dignity (ˈdigniti) *n* Würde, Ehre *f*.

dilapidated (diˈlæpideitid) *adj* verfallen, schäbig.

dilemma (diˈlemə) *n* Dilemma *neu*. Verlegenheit *f*.

diligent (ˈdilidʒənt) *adj* 1 sorgfältig. 2 fleißig.

dilute (daiˈluːt) *vt* verdünnen, wässern.

dim (dim) *adj* 1 düster, trübe. 2 schwach. *vt* verdunkeln.

dimension (diˈmenʃən) *n* Dimension *f*. Ausmaß *neu*.

diminish (diˈminiʃ) *vt* vermindern, verringern. *vi* sich vermindern, abnehmen.

diminutive (diˈminjutiv) *adj* klein, winzig.

dimple (ˈdimpəl) *n* Grübchen *neu*.

din (din) *n* Lärm *m*. Getöse *neu*.

dine (dain) *vi* speisen, essen. **dining car** *n* Speisewagen *m*. **dining room** *n* Speisezimmer, Eßzimmer *neu*.

dinghy (ˈdiŋgi) *n* Beiboot *neu*.

dingy (ˈdindʒi) *adj* schmutzig, schäbig.

dinner (ˈdinə) *n* (Haupt)Mahlzeit *f*. Abendessen, Mittagessen *neu*.

diocese (ˈdaiəsis) *n* Diözese *f*.

dip (dip) *vt* 1 eintauchen. 2 (one's headlights) abblenden. *vi* untertauchen. *n* 1 Vertiefung *f*. 2 Eintauchen *neu*.

diphthong (ˈdifθɔŋ) *n* Doppellaut *m*.

diploma (diˈploumə) *n* Diplom *neu*.

diplomacy (diˈplouməsi) *n* Diplomatie *f*. **diplomat** *n* Diplomat *m*. **diplomatic** *adj* diplomatisch.

direct (diˈrekt) *adj* 1 direkt. 2 gerade, unmittelbar. *vt* 1 führen, leiten. 2 richten. 3 anweisen. **direction** *n* 1 Richtung *f*. 2 *pl* Vorschrift, Anweisung *f*. **direct object** *n* direktes Objekt *neu*. **director** *n* Direktor *m*. Leiter *m*. **directory** *n* Telephonbuch *neu*.

dirt (dəːt) *n* Dreck, Schmutz *m*. **dirty** *adj* schmutzig.

disability (disəˈbiliti) *n* Unfähigkeit, Behinderung *f*. **disabled** *adj* (körper)behindert.

disadvantage (disədˈvaːntidʒ) *n* Nachteil *m*. **disadvantageous** *adj* nachteilig.

disagree (disəˈgriː) *vi* 1 nicht übereinstimmen, nicht einig sein. 2 sich widersprechen. 3 (sich) streiten. **disagreement** *n* 1 Uneinigkeit, Unstimmigkeit *f*. 2 (Meinungs)Verschiedenheit *f*. Streit *m*.

disappear (disəˈpiə) *vi* verschwinden. **disappearance** *n* Verschwinden *neu*.

disappoint (disəˈpoint) *vt* enttäuschen. **disappointment** *n* Enttäuschung *f*.

disapprove (disəˈpruːv) *vt* mißbilligen. **disapproval** *n* Mißbilligung *f*.

disarm (disˈaːm) *vt,vi* entwaffnen, abrüsten. **disarmament** *n* Abrüstung *f*.

disaster (diˈzaːstə) *n* Unglück *neu*. Katastrophe *f*. **disastrous** *adj* unglücklich, schrecklich.

disc (disk) *n* 1 Scheibe *f*. 2 Schallplatte *f*. **disc jockey** *n* Schallplattenansager *m*.

discard (disˈkaːd) *vt* ablegen, aufgeben.

discern (diˈsəːn) *vt* 1 unterscheiden. 2 wahrnehmen.

discharge (disˈtʃaːdʒ) *vt* erfüllen. *n* 1 Entlassung *f*. 2 Erfüllung *f*. 3 *med* Absonderung *f*.

disciple (diˈsaipəl) *n* Schüler, Jünger *m*.

discipline (ˈdisəplin) *n* 1 Disziplin *f*. 2 Wissenszweig *m*. *vt* bestrafen, zurechtweisen.

disclaim (disˈkleim) *vt* 1 verzichten auf. 2 nicht anerkennen, abstreiten.

disclose (disˈklouz) *vt* offenbaren, enthüllen.

discomfort (disˈkʌmfət) *n* Unbehagen *neu*.

disconnect (diskə'nekt) *vt* trennen, unterbrechen.

disconsolate (dis'konsələt) *adj* trostlos.

discontinue (diskən'tinju:) *vt* unterbrechen. *vi* aufhören.

discord (disko:d) *n* Uneinigkeit *f*. Mißklang *m*.

discotheque ('diskətek) *n* Diskothek *f*.

discount ('diskaunt) *n* Rabatt *m*.

discourage (dis'kʌridʒ) *vt* **1** abraten. **2** entmutigen.

discover (dis'kʌvə) *vt* **1** entdecken. **2** herausfinden, erkennen. **discovery** *n* Entdeckung *f*.

discredit (dis'kredit) *vt* **1** in Verruf bringen. **2** anzweifeln. *n* **1** schlechter Ruf *m*. **2** Zweifel *m*.

discreet (dis'kri:t) *adj* besonnen, diskret. **discretion** *n* **1** Belieben *neu*. **2** Takt *m*.

discrepancy (dis'krepənsi) *n* Widerspruch *m*. Unstimmigkeit *f*.

discriminate (dis'krimineit) *vi* unterschiedlich behandeln. *vt* unterscheiden, absondern. **discrimination** *n* Diskriminierung, Unterscheidung *f*.

discus ('diskəs) *n sport* Diskus *m*.

discuss (dis'kʌs) *vt* besprechen, diskutieren, erörtern. **discussion** *n* Erörterung, Diskussion *f*.

disease (di'zi:z) *n* Krankheit *f*.

disembark (disim'ba:k) *vi* ausschiffen.

disengage (disin'geidʒ) *vt* **1** (los)lösen, freimachen. **2** loskuppeln. *vi* sich freimachen.

disfigure (dis'figə) *vt* verunstalten.

disgrace (dis'greis) *n* **1** Schande *f*. **2** Ungnade *f*. *vt* schänden, entehren. **disgraceful** *adj* schändlich.

disgruntled (dis'grʌntəld) *adj* mürrisch.

disguise (dis'gaiz) *vt* **1** verkleiden. **2** verhüllen. *n* Verkleidung *f*. **in disguise** verkleidet.

disgust (dis'gʌst) *n* Ekel *m*. *vt* anekeln. **disgusting** *adj* ekelhaft, widerlich.

dish (diʃ) *n* **1** *cul* Gericht *neu*. **2** Schüssel *f*. **dishcloth** *n* Abwaschtuch *neu*.

dishearten (dis'ha:tn) *vt* entmutigen.

dishevelled (di'ʃevəld) *adj* zerzaust.

dishonest (dis'onist) *adj* unehrlich. **dishonesty** *n* Unehrlichkeit *f*.

dishonour (dis'onə) *vt* entehren. *n* Schande, Unehre *f*.

disillusion (disi'lu:ʒən) *n* Enttäuschung, Ernüchterung *f*. *vt* ernüchtern, enttäuschen. **disillusioned** *adj* enttäuscht, verbittert, ernüchtert.

disinfect (disin'fekt) *vt* desinfizieren. **disinfectant** *n* Desinfektionsmittel *neu*.

disinherit (disin'herit) *vt* enterben.

disintegrate (dis'intigreit) *(vi).vt* (sich) auflösen, (sich) zersetzen. *vi* verfallen. **disintegration** *n* Auflösung, Zersetzung *f*.

disinterested (dis'intrəstid) *adj* unbeteiligt.

dislike (dis'laik) *vt* nicht mögen. *n* Abneigung *f*.

dislocate ('disləkeit) *vt med* verrenken. **dislocation** *n* Verrenkung *f*.

dislodge (dis'lodʒ) *vt* **1** entfernen. **2** vertreiben.

disloyal (dis'loiəl) *adj* untreu.

dismal ('dizməl) *adj* traurig, trübe.

dismantle (dis'mæntl) *vt* demontieren, auseinandernehmen.

dismay (dismei) *n* Bestürzung *f*. *vt* bestürzen.

dismiss (dis'mis) *vt* **1** entlassen. **2** gehen lassen. **3** abweisen. **dismissal** *n* Entlassung *f*.

dismount (dis'maunt) *vi* absteigen.

disobey (disə'bei) *vt* ungehorsam sein gegen, nicht gehorchen. **disobedience** *n* Ungehorsam *m*. **disobedient** *adj* ungehorsam.

disorder (dis'o:də) *n* **1** Unordnung *f*. **2** Unruhe *f*. **3** *med* Störung *f*.

disorganized (dis'o:gənaizd) *adj* in Unordnung, aufgelost.

disown (dis'oun) *vt* nicht anerkennen, verleugnen.

disparage (dis'pæridʒ) *vt* verunglimpfen, herabsetzen.

dispassionate (dis'pæʃənət) *adj* **1** leidenschaftslos. **2** sachlich.

dispatch (dis'pætʃ) *n* Absendung, Abfertigung *f*. *vt* (eilig) wegschicken, absenden.

dispel (dis'pel) *vt* zerstreuen, vertreiben.

dispense (dis'pens) *vt* verteilen, ausgeben. **dispense with** entbehren, verzichten auf. **dispensary** *n* Arzneiausgabe, Apotheke *f*.

disperse (dis'pə:s) *(vi).vt* (sich) zerstreuen, (sich) verteilen. **dispersal** *n* Zerstreuung, Vertreibung *f*.

displace (dis'pleis) *vt* **1** verschieben. **2** *naut* verdrängen. **displacement** *n* Verrückung, Verdrängung *f*.

display (dis'plei) *n* **1** Auslage *f*. **2** *mil* Vorführung *f*. *vt* **1** zur Schau stellen. **2** zeigen.

displease (dis'pli:z) *vt* mißfallen. **displeasure** *n* Mißfallen *neu*.

dispose (dis'pouz) *vt* anordnen. **dispose of** beseitigen, abschaffen. **disposal** *n* **1** Verfügung *f*. **2** Erledigung *f*. **disposition** *n* **1** Neigung *f*. **2** Veranlagung *f*.

disproportion (disprə'po:ʃən) *n* Mißverhältnis *neu*. **disproportionate** *adj* **1** unverhältnismäßig. **2** übertrieben.

disprove

disprove (dis'pruːv) vt widerlegen.

dispute (dis'pjuːt) n Streit m. Debatte f. vi (sich) streiten. vt bestreiten.

disqualify (dis'kwɔlifai) vt **1** ausschließen, disqualifizieren. **2** unfähig erklären.

disregard (disriˈgɑːd) vt **1** mißachten. **2** außer Acht lassen.

disreputable (dis'repjutəbəl) adj verrufen.

disrespect (disri'spekt) n Respektlosigkeit f.

disrupt (dis'rʌpt) vt **1** spalten, zerbrechen. **2** unterbrechen, stören.

dissatisfy (di'sætisfai) vt nicht zufriedenstellen, mißfallen.

dissect (di'sekt) vt sezieren, zergliedern.

dissent (di'sent) n abweichende Meinung f. vi anderer Meinung sein.

dissimilar (di'similə) adj verschieden, unähnlich.

dissociate (di'souʃieit) vt trennen. **dissociate oneself** sich lossagen, abrücken.

dissolve (di'zɔlv) vt auflösen. vi sich auflösen, schmelzen.

dissuade (di'sweid) vt abraten.

distance ('distəns) n Entfernung f. Abstand m. **distant** adj weit, entfernt.

distaste (dis'teist) n Abneigung f. **distasteful** adj widerlich, unangenehm.

distil (dis'til) vt destillieren.

distinct (dis'tiŋkt) adj **1** verschieden. **2** deutlich. **3** ausgeprägt. **distinction** n **1** Unterschied m. **2** Auszeichnung f. **3** Würde f. **distinctive** adj deutlich, kennzeichnend.

distinguish (dis'tiŋgwiʃ) vt,vi unterscheiden. **distinguish oneself** sich auszeichnen.

distort (dis'tɔːt) vt verzerren.

distract (dis'trækt) vt **1** ablenken. **2** beunruhigen.

distraught (dis'trɔːt) adj **1** erregt, verwirrt. **2** wahnsinnig.

distress (dis'tres) n **1** Not f. Elend neu. **2** Leid neu. Schmerz m. vt beunruhigen, quälen.

distribute (dis'tribjuːt) vt verteilen, ausgeben. **distribution** n Verteilung, Verbreitung f.

district ('distrikt) n Bezirk m. Gegend f.

distrust (dis'trʌst) n Mißtrauen. vt mißtrauen.

disturb (dis'təːb) vt **1** stören. **2** beunruhigen. **disturbance** n **1** Störung f. **2** Unruhe f.

ditch (ditʃ) n Graben m. vt inf wegwerfen.

ditto ('ditou) adv dito, desgleichen.

divan (di'væn) n Diwan m.

dive (daiv) n **1** Kopfsprung m. **2** aviat Sturzflug m. vi **1** tauchen. **2** sich stürzen. **3** einen

Kopfsprung machen. **4** einen Sturzflug machen. **diving board** n Sprungbrett neu.

diverge (dai'vɔːdʒ) vi **1** auseinanderlaufen, sich trennen. **2** abweichen.

diverse (dai'vɔːs) adj verschieden, vielfältig.

divert (dai'vɔːt) vt **1** ablenken. **2** umleiten. **3** unterhalten. **diversion** n **1** Umleitung f. **2** Zerstreuung f.

divide (di'vaid) vt **1** teilen. **2** verteilen. **3** zerteilen, spalten. **divisible** adj teilbar. **division** n **1** Teilung f. **2** Trennung f. **3** mil,sport Division f.

dividend ('dividend) n Dividende f. (Gewinn)-Anteil m.

divine (di'vain) adj göttlich, Gottes—. **divinity** n **1** Gottheit f. **2** Theologie f.

divorce (di'vɔːs) n Scheidung f. vi scheiden, sich scheiden lassen.

divulge (di'vʌldʒ) vt enthüllen, bekanntmachen.

dizzy ('dizi) adj **1** schwindelig. **2** unbesonnen.

do* (duː) vt **1** tun, machen. **2** ausführen. vi tun, handeln. **do away with** abschaffen, beseitigen.

docile ('dousail) adj gelehrig, fügsam.

dock[1] (dɔk) n **1** Dock neu. **2** Hafenanlage f. **dockyard** n Werft f.

dock[2] (dɔk) vt **1** stutzen. **2** vermindern.

dock[3] (dɔk) n law Anklagebank f.

doctor ('dɔktə) n **1** med Doktor, Arzt m. **2** educ Doktor m.

doctrine ('dɔktrin) n Lehre, Doktrin f.

document ('dɔkjumənt) n Urkunde f. Dokument, Schriftstück neu. vt dokumentieren, beurkunden. **documentary** n Dokumentarfilm m. adj dokumentarisch, schriftlich.

dodge (dɔdʒ) vi ausweichen. vt vermeiden. n **1** Seitensprung m. **2** Trick, Kniff m.

does (dʌz) v see **do**.

dog (dɔg) n Hund m. vt nachspüren. **dogged** adj verbissen.

dogma ('dɔgmə) n Glaubenssatz m. Dogma neu. **dogmatic** adj dogmatisch.

dole (doul) n Arbeitslosenunterstützung f. v **dole out** austeilen, ausgeben.

doll (dɔl) n Puppe f.

dollar ('dɔlə) n Dollar m.

Dolomites ('dɔləmaits) n Dolomiten pl.

dolphin ('dɔlfin) n Delphin m.

domain (də'mein) n Bereich m.

dome (doum) n Kuppel f.

domestic (də'mestik) adj **1** häuslich. **2** inländisch. **domestic animal** n Haustier neu. **domesticate** vt **1** zähmen. **2** häuslich machen.

180

dominate ('dɔmineit) *vt* beherrschen, herrschen über. dominieren. **dominance** *n* (Vor)Herrschaft *f*. **dominant** *adj* (vor)herrschend. **domination** *n* Herrschaft *f*. **domineer** *vi* den Herrn spielen.

dominion (dɔ'miniən) *n* Herrschaft *f*.

donate (dou'neit) *vt* schenken. *vi* eine Schenkung machen.

done (dʌn) *v* see **do**. *adj* fertig. *interj* abgemacht!

donkey ('dɔŋki) *n* Esel *m*.

donor ('dounə) *n* Spender *m*.

doom (du:m) *n* **1** Schicksal, Verhängnis *neu*. **2** Verderben *neu*. *vt* verdammen. **doomed** *adj* verloren, verdammt.

door (dɔ:) *n* Tür *f*. **door to door** von Haus zu Haus. **out of doors** draußen, im Freien. **doorbell** *n* Türklingel *f*. **doorhandle** *n* Türgriff *m*. Türklinke *f*. **doorstep** *n* Türschwelle *f*. **doorway** *n* Türeingang *m*.

dope (doup) *n sl* Rauschgift *neu*.

dormant ('dɔ:mənt) *adj* schlafend, untätig.

dormitory ('dɔ:mitri) *n* Schlafsaal *m*.

dormouse ('dɔ:maus) *n*, *pl* **dormice** *n* Haselmaus *f*.

dose (dous) *n* Dosis *f*. *vt* dosieren. **dosage** *n* Dosierung *f*.

dot (dɔt) *n* Punkt *m*. *vt* **1** punktieren. **2** verstreuen.

dote (dout) *vi* **dote on 1** schwärmen für. **2** (zärtlich) lieben.

double ('dʌbəl) *adj* doppelt, Doppel—. *adv* doppelt, zu zweien. *n* **1** Doppelte *neu*. **2** Doppelgänger *m*. *(vi),vt* (sich) verdoppeln. **double bass** *n* Kontrabaß *m*. **doublecross** *vt inf* hintergehen, betrügen.

doubt (daut) *n* Zweifel *m*. *vi* zweifeln. *vt* bezweifeln. **no doubt** zweifellos, ohne Zweifel, gewiß. **doubtful** *adj* zweifelhaft, ungewiß.

dough (dou) *n* Teig *m*. **doughnut** *n* Berliner Pfannkuchen *m*.

dove (dʌv) *n* Taube *f*.

dowdy ('daudi) *adj* nachlässig, schlampig.

down[1] (daun) *adv* hinunter, herab, abwärts, nieder.

down[2] (daun) *n* Daunen *f pl*.

downcast ('daunka:st) *adj* niedergeschlagen.

downfall ('daunfɔ:l) *n* **1** Fall *m*. **2** Niedergang *m*.

downhearted (daun'ha:tid) *adj* mutlos, niedergeschlagen.

downhill ('daunhil) *adv* bergab. *adj* Abwärts—.

downpour ('daunpɔ:) *n* Regenguß *m*.

downright ('daunrait) *adj* offen, völlig.

downstairs (daun'stɛəz) *adv* **1** nach unten, die Treppe hinunter. **2** unten. *adj* unter, im Erdgeschoß (liegend).

downstream (daun'stri:m) *adv* flußabwärts.

downtrodden ('dauntrɔdn) *adj* getreten, unterdrückt.

downward ('daunwəd) *adj* Abwärts—.

downwards ('daunwədz) *adv* abwärts.

dowry ('dauəri) *n* Mitgift *f*.

doze (douz) *n* Nickerchen *neu*. kurzer Schlaf *m*. *vi* dösen. **dozy** *adj* schläfrig.

dozen ('dʌzən) *n* Dutzend *neu*.

drab (dræb) *adj* **1** gelbgrau. **2** eintönig, farblos.

draft (dra:ft) *n* **1** Skizze *f*. Entwurf *m*. **2** *comm* Abhebung *f*. **3** *mil* Aushebung *f*. *vt* **1** entwerfen. **2** (zur Armee) einziehen.

drag (dræg) *(vi),vt* (sich) schleppen, (sich) ziehen. *n sl* langweilige Sache.

dragon ('drægən) *n* Drachen *m*. **dragonfly** *n* Libelle *f*.

drain (drein) *n* **1** Abfluß *m*. **2** Abflußrohr *neu*. Gosse *f*. *vt* **1** entwässern. **2** ableiten. *vi* abfliessen. **drainage** *n* Abfluß *m*. Entwässerung *f*. **draining-board** *n* Abtropfbrett *neu*. **drainpipe** *n* Abflußrohr *neu*.

drake (dreik) *n* Enterich *m*.

dram (dræm) *n* Schluck *m*. Gläschen *neu*.

drama ('dra:mə) *n* Drama *neu*. **dramatic** *adj* **1** dramatisch. **2** spannend. **dramatist** *n* Dramatiker *m*. **dramatize** *vt* dramatisieren.

drank (dræŋk) *v* see **drink**.

drape (dreip) *vt* behängen, drapieren. *vi* schön fallen. **draper** ('dreipə) *n* Tuchhändler *m*. **drapery** *n* **1** Tuchwaren *f pl*. **2** Tuchhandel *m*.

drastic ('dræstik) *adj* drastisch, gründlich.

draught (dra:ft) *n* **1** Zug *m*. **2** Entwurf *m*. **3** *pl* Damespiel *neu*. **draught beer** Faßbier *neu*. **draughtsman** *n* Zeichner *m*. **draughty** *adj* zugig.

draw* (drɔ:) *vt* **1** ziehen. **2** zeichnen. **3** anziehen. **4** dehnen. **5** (money) abheben. *vi* **1** ziehen. **2** zeichnen. **3** *sport* unentschieden spielen. **draw near** sich nähern. —*n* **1** Ziehen *neu*. **2** Verlosung *f*. **3** *sport* Unentschieden *neu*. **drawback** *n* Nachteil *m*. **drawbridge** *n* Zugbrücke *f*. **drawer** *n* **1** Zeichner *m*. **2** Schublade *f*. **drawing** *n* Zeichnung *f*. **drawing-board** *n* Zeichenbrett *neu*. **drawingpin** *n* Heftzwecke *f*. **drawing room** *n* Salon *m*.

drawl (drɔːl) n gedehnte Sprechweise f. vi gedehnt sprechen.

dread (dred) n Furcht f. Schrecken m. vt fürchten, sich fürchten vor. **dreadful** adj furchtbar, schrecklich.

dream* (driːm) vi,vt träumen. n Traum m. **dreamer** n Träumer m. **dreamlike** adj traumhaft.

dreary ('driəri) adj öde, eintönig.

dredge (dredʒ) vt 1 mit dem Schleppnetz fangen. 2 ausbaggern. **dredger** n Bagger m.

dregs (dregz) n pl Bodensatz m.

drench (drentʃ) vt durchnässen.

dress (dres) n 1 Kleidung f. Anzug m. 2 (Damen)Kleid neu. 3 Gewand neu. vi sich anziehen. vt 1 ankleiden. 2 schmücken. 3 bearbeiten. **dress circle** n Th erster Rang m. **dressing** n 1 Ankleiden neu. 2 med Verband m. 3 cul Zutat, Soße f. **dressing-gown** n Morgenrock m. **dressing-room** n Ankleidezimmer neu. **dressing-table** n Toilettentisch m. **dressmaker** n Damenschneiderin f.

dresser[1] ('dresə) n Anrichter, Dekorateur m.

dresser[2] ('dresə) n Küchenschrank m.

drew (druː) v see **draw**.

dribble ('dribəl) vi 1 tröpfeln. 2 geifern.

drier ('draiə) n Trockner m.

drift (drift) n 1 Treiben neu. 2 (Schnee)Wehe f. 3 Treibenlassen neu. 4 Tendenz f. vi 1 (dahin)treiben. 2 getrieben werden.

drill (dril) n 1 Bohrer m. 2 mil Exerzieren neu. vt,vi 1 bohren. 2 mil exerzieren.

drink* (driŋk) vi,vi trinken. n 1 Getränk neu. 2 Drink m. 3 Alkohol m. **drinking water** n Trinkwasser neu.

drip (drip) vi tröpfeln, triefen, tropfen. n Tröpfeln neu. **drip-dry** adj bügelfrei.

drive* (draiv) n 1 Fahrt f. 2 Auffahrt f. 3 Trieb, Drang m. 4 tech Antrieb m. vt,vi 1 fahren. 2 treiben. **driver** n 1 Fahrer, Chauffeur m. 2 Führer m. 3 Treiber m. **driving licence** n Führerschein m. **driving school** n Fahrschule f. **driving test** n Fahrprüfung f.

drivel ('drivəl) vi sabbern, geifern. n inf Unsinn m.

drizzle ('drizəl) vi nieseln, sprühen. n Sprühregen, Nieselregen m.

drone[1] (droun) n 1 zool Drohne f. 2 Faulenzer m.

drone[2] (droun) n Summen neu. vi summen.

droop (druːp) vi 1 schlaff werden, herabhängen. 2 verwelken.

drop (drɔp) n 1 Tropfen m. 2 Fall, Sturz m. 3 Bonbon m. vi 1 tropfen. 2 fallen. vt fallen lassen, niederlassen. **drop someone a line** jemandem ein paar Zeilen schreiben. **drop out** vi ausscheiden, aufgeben. **dropout** n inf Aussteiger, Drop-out m.

drought (draut) n Trockenheit, Dürre f.

drove (drouv) v see **drive**.

drown (draun) vi ertrinken. vt ertränken, überschwemmen.

drowsy (drauzi) adj schläfrig.

drudge (drʌdʒ) n Kuli, Sklave m. vi schuften. **drudgery** n mühsame Arbeit, Plackerei f.

drug (drʌg) n 1 Droge f. 2 Rauschgift neu. **drug-addict** n Rauschgiftsüchtige(r) m.

drum (drʌm) n 1 Trommel f. 2 Faß neu. vt,(vi) trommeln (auf).

drunk (drʌŋk) v see **drink**. adj betrunken. **get drunk** sich betrinken. ~n Betrunkene(r) m. **drunken** adj betrunken.

dry (drai) adj 1 trocken. 2 (of wine) herb. vt (ab-, aus-)trocknen. vi trocknen. **dry-clean** vt chemisch reinigen. **dry-cleaning** n chemische Reinigung f.

dual ('djuəl) adj doppelt, zweifach. **dual carriageway** n Doppelfahrbahn f.

dubious ('djuːbiəs) adj zweifelhaft.

duchess ('dʌtʃis) n Herzogin f.

duck[1] (dʌk) n Ente f. **duckling** n Entchen neu.

duck[2] (dʌk) vi 1 untertauchen. 2 sich ducken. vt untertauchen.

duct (dʌkt) n Röhre f. Kanal m.

dud (dʌd) n mil Blindgänger m. adj falsch, verfälscht, wertlos.

due (djuː) adj 1 fällig. 2 erwartet. 3 angemessen, gebührend. **due to** infolge, wegen, zuzuschreiben. adv genau, gerade. n 1 Recht neu. Anteil m. 2 pl Gebühren f pl.

duel ('djuəl) n Duell neu.

duet (dju'et) n mus Duett neu.

dug (dʌg) v see **dig**.

duke (djuːk) n Herzog m.

dull (dʌl) adj 1 stumpfsinnig. 2 matt. 3 (of light) schwach. 4 langweilig. 5 stumpf. vi,vt abstumpfen.

dumb (dʌm) adj 1 stumm. 2 inf dumm. **dumbfound** vt sprachlos machen, verblüffen.

dummy ('dʌmi) n 1 Attrappe f. 2 Puppe f. 3 (for a baby) Schnuller m.

dump (dʌmp) n Müllabladeplatz m. vt abladen, auskippen.

dumpling ('dʌmpliŋ) n Kloß, Knödel m.

dunce (dʌns) n Dummkopf m.

dune (dju:n) *n* Düne *f*.

dung (dʌŋ) *n* Dung, Mist *m*.

dungeon ('dʌndʒən) *n* Kerker *m*.

duplicate (*adj,n* 'dju:plikət; *v* 'dju:plikeit) *adj* 1 doppelt. 2 Duplikat—. *n* Duplikat *neu*. Kopie *f*. *vt* 1 duplizieren. 2 verdoppeln.

durable ('djuərəbl) *adj* dauerhaft.

duration (djuə'reiʃən) *n* Dauer *f*.

during ('djuəriŋ) *prep* während.

dusk (dʌsk) *n* (Abend)Dämmerung *f*. **dusky** *adj* 1 dämmerig. 2 dunkel.

dust (dʌst) *n* Staub *m*. *vt* abstauben. **dustbin** *n* Mülleimer *m*. **duster** *n* Staubtuch *neu*. **dustman** *n* Müllmann *m*. **dustpan** *n* Kehrichtschaufel *f*.

Dutch (dʌtʃ) *adj* holländisch. *n* (language) Holländisch *neu*. **Dutchman** *n* Holländer *m*.

dutiful ('dju:tifəl) *adj* pflichtgetreu.

duty ('dju:ti) *n* 1 Pflicht *f*. 2 Aufgabe *f*. 3 Zoll *m*. Abgabe *f*. **dutiful** *adj* pflichtbewußt. **duty-free** *adj* zollfrei, abgabenfrei.

duvet ('dju:vei) *n* Federbett *neu*. Daunendecke *f*.

dwarf (dwɔ:f) *n* Zwerg *m*. *vt* in den Schatten stellen.

dwell* (dwel) *vi* 1 wohnen. 2 verweilen. **dwelling** *n* Wohnung *f*. Wohnsitz *m*.

dwindle ('dwindl) *vi* schwinden, abnehmen.

dye (dai) *n* Färbemittel *neu*. Farbe *f*. *vt* färben.

dyke (daik) *n* Deich, Damm *m*.

dynamic (dai'næmik) *adj* dynamisch.

dynamite ('dainəmait) *n* Dynamit *neu*.

dynasty ('dinəsti) *n* Dynastie *f*.

dysentery ('disəntri) *n med* Ruhr *f*.

dyslexia (dis'leksiə) *n* Dyslexie. Wortblindheit *f*.

E

each (i:tʃ) *pron, adj* jeder, jede, jedes. *adv* je.

eager ('i:gə) *adj* begierig, eifrig.

eagle ('i:gəl) *n* Adler *m*.

ear[1] (iə) *n* 1 Ohr *neu*. 2 Gehör *neu*. **earache** *n* Ohrenschmerzen *m pl*. **eardrum** *n* Trommelfell *neu*. **earmark** *vt* 1 kennzeichnen. 2 bestimmen. **earring** *n* Ohrring *m*.

ear[2] (iə) *n* (of corn) Ähre *f*.

earl (ə:l) *n* Graf *m*.

early (ə:li) *adj,adv* 1 früh. 2 vorzeitig.

earn (ə:n) *vt* verdienen, erwerben.

earnest ('ə:nist) *adj* 1 ernst(haft). 2 aufrichtig. *n* Ernst *m*.

earth (ə:θ) *n* 1 Erde *f*. 2 (Erd)Boden *m*. **earth-**

enware *n* Steingut *neu*. **earthquake** *n* Erdbeben *neu*.

ease (i:z) *n* 1 Leichtigkeit *f*. 2 Behagen *neu*. Ungezwungenheit *f*. *vt* erleichtern. **easy** *adj* 1 leicht, mühelos. 2 bequem. 3 ungezwungen. **easygoing** *adj* lässig, leichtlebig.

easel ('i:zəl) *n* Staffelei *f*.

east (i:st) *n* 1 Osten *m* 2 Orient *m*. Morgenland *neu*. *adj* östlich, Ost—. *adv* nach Osten, ostwärts. **easterly** *adj* östlich. **eastern** *adj* 1 östlich. 2 oriental, morgenländisch. **eastward** *adj* ostwärts. **eastwards** *adv* ostwärts.

Easter ('i:stə) *n* Ostern *neu*.

eat* (i:t) *vt* 1 essen. 2 (of animals) fressen.

eavesdrop ('i:vzdrɔp) *vi* lauschen, heimlich zuhören.

ebb (eb) *n* 1 Ebbe *f*. 2 Abnahme *f*. *vi* 1 verebben. 2 abnehmen.

ebony ('ebəni) *n* Ebenholz *neu*.

eccentric (ik'sentrik) *adj* exzentrisch. *n* Exzentriker, Sonderling *m*.

ecclesiastical (ikli:zi'æstikəl) *adj* kirchlich.

echo ('ekou) *n, pl* **echoes** Echo *neu*. *vi* widerhallen.

eclair (ei'klɛə) *n* Cremekuchen *m*.

eclipse (i'klips) *n* Verfinsterung, Finsternis *f*. *vt* 1 verfinstern. 2 in den Schatten stellen.

ecology (i:'kɔlədʒi) *n* Ökologie *f*.

economy (i'kɔnəmi) *n* 1 Wirtschaft *f*. 2 Sparsamkeit *f*. 3 Sparmaßnahme *f*. **economic** *adj* wirtschaftlich, Wirtschafts—. **economical** *adj* wirtschaftlich, sparsam. **economics** *n pl* Ökonomie, (Volks)Wirtschaft *f*. **economize** *vt* (ein)sparen.

ecstasy ('ekstəsi) *n* Ekstase, Verzückung *f*. **ecstatic** *adj* ekstatisch, verzückt.

edge (edʒ) *n* 1 Rand *m*. 2 Schneide *f*. *vt* 1 schärfen. 2 umsäumen.

edible ('edibəl) *adj* eßbar.

Edinburgh ('edinbərə) *n* Edinburg *neu*.

edit ('edit) *vt* redigieren, druckfertig machen. **editor** *n* Redakteur *m*. **editorial** *n* Leitartikel *m*. *adj* Redaktions—.

edition (i'diʃən) *n* 1 Auflage *f*. 2 Ausgabe *f*.

educate ('edjukeit) *vt* erziehen, (aus)bilden. **education** *n* Erziehung, Bildung *f*. **educational** *adj* Erziehungs—, pädagogisch.

eel (i:l) *n* Aal *m*.

eerie ('iəri) *adj* unheimlich.

effect (i'fekt) *n* 1 Wirkung *f*. 2 Einfluß *m*. 3 Eindruck *m*. 4 Gültigkeit *f*. *vt* 1 bewirken. 2 einwirken auf. 3 ausführen. **effective** *adj* 1 wirksam. 2 eindrucksvoll.

effeminate (i'feminət) *adj* weibisch.

effervesce (efə'ves) *vi* aufbrausen, sprudeln.

efficient (i'fiʃənt) *adj* 1 leistungsfähig. 2 tüchtig. 3 wirksam. **efficiency** *n* 1 Leistungsfähigkeit *f*. 2 Tüchtigkeit *f*. 3 Wirksamkeit *f*.

effigy ('efidʒi) *n* Bildnis *neu*.

effort ('efət) *n* Anstrengung, Bemühung, Mühe *f*. **effortless** *adj* mühelos.

egg[1] (eg) *n* Ei *neu*. **eggcup** *n* Eierbecher *m*. **eggshell** *n* Eierschale *f*. **eggwhisk** *n* Schneebesen *m*.

egg[2] (eg) *vt* **egg on** aufreizen.

ego ('i:gou) *n* Ich *neu*. **egocentric** *adj* egozentrisch. **egoism** *n* Selbstsucht *f*. **egotism** *n* Selbstgefälligkeit *f*.

Egypt ('i:dʒipt) *n* Ägypten *neu*. **Egyptian** *adj* ägyptisch. *n* Ägypter *m*.

eiderdown ('aidədaun) *n* Daunendecke *f*.

eight (eit) *adj* acht. *n* Acht *f*. **eighth** *adj* achte.

eighteen (ei'ti:n) *adj* achtzehn. *n* Achtzehn *f*. **eighteenth** *adj* achtzehnte.

eighty ('eiti) *adj* achtzig. *n* Achtzig *f*. **eightieth** *adj* achtzigste.

either ('aiðə) *pron, adj* 1 einer (von zweien). 2 beide, jeder (von zweien). **either...or** entweder...oder.

ejaculate (i'dʒækjuleit) *vt* ausstoßen.

eject (i'dʒekt) *vt* ausstoßen, vertreiben.

eke (i:k) *vt* **eke out** ergänzen, verlängern.

elaborate (*adj* i'læbrət; *v* i'læbəreit) *adj* ausgearbeitet, kompliziert. *vt* ausarbeiten.

elapse (i'læps) *vi* vergehen, verstreichen.

elastic (i'læstik) *adj* dehnbar, elastisch. **elasticity** *n* Elastizität *f*.

elated (i'leitid) *adj* erfreut, erregt.

elbow ('elbou) *n* Ell(en)bogen *m*.

elder[1] ('eldə) *adj* älter. *n* 1 (Kirchen)Älteste(r) *m*. 2 Respektsperson *f*.

elder[2] ('eldə) *n bot* Holunder *m*. **elderberry** *n* Holunderbeere *f*.

eldest ('eldist) *adj* ältest.

elect (i'lekt) *vt* wählen, auserwählen. *vi* sich entschließen. **election** *n* Wahl *f*.

electorate (i'lektərət) *n* Wählerschaft *f*.

electricity (ilek'trisiti) *n* Elektrizität *f*. **electric** *adj* also **electrical** elektrisch. **electrician** *n* Elekritriker *m*. **electrify** *vt* 1 elektrisieren. 2 elektrifizieren. **electrocute** *vt* durch elektrischen Strom töten. **electrode** *n* Elektrode *f*. **electron** *n* Elektron *neu*. **electronic** *adj* elektronisch.

elegant ('eligənt) *adj* elegant, geschmackvoll.

element ('eləmənt) *n* 1 Element *neu*. 2 Grund-

bestandteil *neu*. **elemental** *adj* wesentlich. **elementary** *adj* elementar, einfach.

elephant ('eləfənt) *n* Elefant *m*.

elevate ('eləveit) *vt* aufrichten, erheben, erhöhen. **elevation** *n* 1 Erhebung *f*. 2 *math* Aufriß *m*. **elevator** *n* Aufzug, Fahrstuhl *m*.

eleven (i'levən) *adj* elf. *n* Elf *f*. **eleventh** *adj* elfte.

elf (elf) *n, pl* **elves** Elf *m*. Elfe *f*.

eligible ('elidʒəbəl) *adj* 1 annehmbar, wünschenswert. 2 berechtigt. 3 heiratsfähig.

eliminate (i'limineit) *vt* eliminieren, ausstoßen. **elimination** *n* Eliminierung, Ausstoßung *f*.

elite (ei'li:t) *n* Elite *f*.

ellipse (i'lips) *n* Ellipse *f*.

elm (elm) *n* Ulme *f*.

elocution (elə'kju:ʃən) *n* Vortragskunst *f*.

elope (i'loup) *vi* (mit ihrem or seiner Geliebten) entlaufen.

eloquent ('eləkwənt) *adj* redegewandt.

else (els) *adv* sonst. **anyone else** 1 sonst noch jemand? 2 irgend ein anderer. **something else** etwas anderes. **elsewhere** *adv* anderswo, anderswohin.

elucidate (i'lu:sideit) *vt* erläutern, aufklären.

elude (i'lu:d) *vt* umgehen, ausweichen.

emaciated (i'meiʃieitəd) *adj* abgemagert.

emanate ('eməneit) *vi* ausströmen, ausfließen.

emancipate (i'mænsipeit) *vt* emanzipieren, befreien. **emancipation** *n* Befreiung *f*.

embalm (im'ba:m) *vt* einbalsamieren.

embankment (im'bæŋkmənt) *n* 1 Deich, Damm *m*. 2 Uferstraße.

embargo (im'ba:gou) *n* Handelssperre *f*. *vt* sperren.

embark (im'ba:k) *(vi),vt* (sich) einschiffen.

embarrass (im'bærəs) *vt* in Verlegenheit bringen. **embarrassed** *adj* verlegen.

embassy ('embəsi) *n* Botschaft *f*.

embellish (im'beliʃ) *vt* schmücken, verschönern.

ember ('embə) *n* glühende Asche *f*.

embezzle (im'bezəl) *vt* veruntreuen.

embitter (im'bitə) *vt* verbittern.

emblem ('embləm) *n* Abzeichen, Sinnbild *neu*.

embody (im'bɔdi) *vt* verkörpern.

emboss (im'bɔs) *vt* prägen, in Relief ausarbeiten.

embrace (im'breis) *vt* 1 umarmen. 2 umfassen. *n* Umarmung *f*.

embroider (im'brɔidə) *vt* besticken. **embroidery** *n* Stickerei *f*.

embryo ('embriou) *n* Embryo *m*.

emerald ('emrəld) n Smaragd m. adj smaragdgrün.

emerge (i'mɜːdʒ) vi 1 auftauchen. 2 hervorkommen. **emergence** n Auftauchen, Hervorkommen neu.

emergency (i'mɜːdʒənsi) n Notfall m.

emigrate ('emigreit) vi auswandern.

eminent ('eminənt) adj hervorragend, berühmt. **eminently** adv ganz besonders.

emit (i'mit) vt 1 ausstrahlen, aussenden. 2 von sich geben.

emotion (i'mouʃən) n Gemütsbewegung f. Gefühl neu. **emotional** adj 1 emotionell, gefühlvoll. 2 rührend.

empathy ('empəθi) n Einfühlung f.

emperor ('empərə) n Kaiser m.

emphasis ('emfəsis) n Betonung f. **emphasize** vt betonen, unterstreichen. **emphatic** adj nachdrücklich, betont.

empire ('empaiə) n Reich neu.

empirical (im'pirikəl) adj empirisch.

employ (im'plɔi) vt 1 verwenden. 2 beschäftigen. **employee** n Arbeitnehmer m. **employer** n Arbeitgeber m. **employment** n 1 Beschäftigung, Arbeit f. 2 Verwendung f.

empower (im'pauə) vt bevollmächtigen, befähigen.

empress ('empris) n Kaiserin f.

empty ('empti) adj 1 leer. 2 unbeladen. 3 eitel. vt entleeren. **empty-handed** adj mit leeren Händen. **empty-headed** adj ohne Verstand.

emu ('iːmjuː) n Emu m.

emulate ('emjuleit) vt nacheifern.

emulsion (i'mʌlʃən) n Emulsion f.

enable (i'neibəl) vt befähigen, ermöglichen.

enact (i'nækt) vt 1 law erlassen. 2 Th aufführen, darstellen.

enamel (i'næməl) n Emaille f. vt glasieren, emaillieren.

encapsulate (in'kæpsjuleit) vt einkapseln.

enchant (in'tʃɑːnt) vt entzücken.

encircle (in'sɜːkəl) vt einkreisen, umkreisen.

enclose (in'klouz) vt 1 einschließen. 2 beifügen. **enclosure** n 1 Umzäunung f. 2 Anlage f.

encore ('ɔŋkɔː) interj noch einmal! n Zugabe f.

encounter (in'kauntə) n Begegnung f. vt begegnen, stoßen auf.

encourage (in'kʌridʒ) vt 1 ermutigen. 2 unterstützen, fördern. **encouragement** n Unterstützung, Ermutigung f.

encroach (in'kroutʃ) vi unbefugt eingreifen.

encumber (in'kʌmbə) vt belasten, beschweren.

encyclopedia (insaiklə'piːdiə) n Enzyklopädie f.

end (end) n 1 Ende neu. 2 Zweck m. Ziel neu. 3 Tod m. **be at an end** am Ende sein. ~vi enden, zu Ende kommen. vt beendigen, zu Ende führen. **endless** vt endlos, unendlich.

endanger (in'deindʒə) vt gefährden.

endeavour (in'devə) n Bestreben neu. vi streben, sich bemühen.

endemic (en'demik) adj endemisch.

endive ('endaiv) n bot Endivie f.

endorse (in'dɔːs) vt 1 vermerken. 2 bestätigen. **endorsement** n 1 Vermerk m. 2 Bestätigung f.

endow (in'dau) vt 1 schenken. 2 vermachen.

endure (in'djuə) vt (fort)dauern. vt ertragen.

enemy ('enəmi) n Feind, Gegner m. adj feindlich, Feind—.

energy ('enədʒi) n 1 Energie f. 2 Tatkraft f.

enfold (in'fould) vt einhüllen, einschlagen.

enforce (in'fɔːs) vt durchsetzen.

engage (in'geidʒ) vt 1 verpflichten. 2 anstellen. 3 tech einschalten. vi 1 sich verpflichten. 2 sich beschäftigen. **get engaged** sich verloben. **engagement** n 1 Verlobung f. 2 Beschäftigung f. 3 Verabredung f.

engine ('endʒin) n 1 Motor m. 2 Lokomotive f. 3 Maschine f.

engineer (endʒi'niə) n Ingenieur, Techniker m. vt konstruieren, bauen. **engineering** n 1 Ingenieurwesen neu. 2 Maschinenbaukunst f.

England ('iŋglənd) n England neu. **English** adj englisch. n (language) Englisch neu. **Englishman** n Engländer m.

English Channel n (Ärmel)Kanal m.

engrave (in'greiv) vt gravieren.

engrossed (in'groust) adj vertieft, versunken.

engulf (in'gʌlf) vt 1 versenken. 2 verschlingen.

enhance (in'hɑːns) vt erhöhen.

enigma (i'nigmə) n Rätsel neu.

enjoy (in'dʒɔi) vt genießen, Freude haben an. **enjoy oneself** sich (gut) unterhalten. **enjoyment** n Genuß m. Freude f.

enlarge (in'lɑːdʒ) (vi), vt (sich) vergrößern, (sich) erweitern.

enlighten (in'laitn) vt erleuchten, aufklären. **enlightenment** n Aufklärung f.

enlist (in'list) mil vt anwerben. vi sich anwerben lassen.

enormous (i'nɔːməs) adj enorm, ungeheuer.

enough (i'nʌf) adj,adv genug.

enquire (in'kwaiə) vi sich erkundigen. **enquiry** n 1 Erkundigung f. 2 Untersuchung f.

enrage (in'reidʒ) vt wütend machen.

enrich (in'ritʃ) vt bereichern, verzieren.

enrol

enrol (in'roul) *vt* **1** einschreiben. **2** anwerben. *vi* sich einschreiben lassen.
ensign ('ensain) *n* Fahne *f.* Abzeichen *neu.*
enslave (in'sleiv) *vt* versklaven.
ensure (in'ʃuə) *vt* **1** sicherstellen, sichern. **2** dafür sorgen.
entail (in'teil) *vt* mit sich bringen.
entangle (in'tæŋgəl) *vt* verwickeln, verwirren.
enter ('entə) *vt* **1** eintreten (in), betreten. **2** eintragen.
enterprise ('entəpraiz) *n* **1** Unternehmen *neu.* **2** Unternehmungslust *f.* **enterprising** *adj* unternehmungslustig.
entertain (entə'tein) *vt* **1** unterhalten. **2** bewirten. **3** eingehen auf. *vi* Gäste haben *or* einladen. **entertainment** *n* Unterhaltung *f.*
enthral (in'θrɔ:l) *vt* fesseln, bezaubern.
enthusiasm (in'θju:ziæzəm) *n* Begeisterung *f.* Enthusiasmus *m.* **enthusiastic** *adj* beigestert, enthusiastisch.
entice (in'tais) *vt* verlocken.
entire (in'taiə) *adj* vollständig, ganz.
entitle (in'taitl) *vt* berechtigen.
entity ('entiti) *n* Wesen, Dasein *neu.*
entrails ('entreilz) *n pl* Eingeweide *neu pl.*
entrance[1] ('entrəns) *n* **1** Eingang, Eintritt *m.* **2** Eintreten *neu.*
entrance[2] (in'trɑ:ns) *vt* entzücken, bezaubern.
entreat (in'tri:t) *vt* bitten, ersuchen.
entrench (in'trentʃ) *vt mil* verschanzen.
entrepreneur (ɔntrəprə'nə:) *n* Unternehmer *m.*
entrust (in'trʌst) *vt* anvertrauen.
entry ('entri) *n* **1** Eintritt *m.* **2** Einreise, Einfahrt *f.* **3** Eintragung *f.*
entwine (in'twain) *vi* verflechten.
enunciate (i'nʌnsieit) *vt* ausdrücken.
envelop (in'veləp) *vt* einwickeln, umhüllen.
envelope ('envəloup) *n* (Brief)Umschlag *m.*
environment (in'vairənmənt) *n* **1** Umwelt *f.* **2** Umgebung. **environmental** *adj* Umwelt—.
envisage (in'vizidʒ) *vt* ins Auge fassen, sich vorstellen.
envoy ('envɔi) *n* Gesandte(r) *m.*
envy ('envi) *n* Neid *m. vt* beneiden. **envious** *adj* neidisch.
enzyme ('enzaim) *n* Enzym *neu.*
epaulet ('epəlet) *n* Epaulette *f.*
ephemeral (i'femərəl) *adj* vergänglich, flüchtig.
epic ('epik) *adj* episch.
epicure ('epikjuə) *n* Genießer, Feinschmecker *m.*
epidemic (epi'demik) *adj* epidemisch. *n* Epidemie, Seuche *f.*

epilepsy ('epilepsi) *n* Epilepsie, Fallsucht *f.*
epilogue ('epilɔg) *n* Nachwort *neu,* Epilog *m.*
Epiphany (i'pifəni) *n* Dreikönigsfest *neu.*
episcopal (i'piskəpəl) *adj* bischöflich.
episode ('episoud) *n* Episode *f.*
epitaph ('epitɑ:f) *n* Grabschrift *f.*
epitome (i'pitəmi) *n* Auszug, Abriß *m.*
epoch ('i:pɔk) *n* Epoche *f.*
equable ('ekwəbəl) *adj* ausgeglichen.
equal ('i:kwəl) *adj* **1** gleich. **2** entsprechend. **3** fähig, gewachsen. *n* **1** Gleiche(r) *m.* **2** Gleichgestellte(r) *m. vt* gleichen. **equality** *n* Gleichberechtigung *f.* **equalize** *vt* gleichstellen, ausgleichen. *vi sport* ausgleichen.
equate (i'kweit) *vt* gleichsetzen. **equation** *n* Gleichung *f.* **equator** *n* Äquator *m.*
equestrian (i'kwestriən) *n* Reiter *m. adj* Reiter—.
equilateral (i:kwi'lætərəl) *adj* gleichseitig.
equilibrium (i:kwi'libriəm) *n* Gleichgewicht *neu.*
equinox ('i:kwinɔks) *n* Tagundnachtgleiche *f.*
equip (i'kwip) *vt* ausstatten, ausrüsten. **equipment** *n* Ausrüstung, Ausstattung *f.*
equity ('ekwiti) *n* **1** Gerechtigkeit *f.* **2** *pl* Wertpapiere *neu pl.*
equivalent (i'kwivələnt) *adj* **1** gleichwertig. **2** entsprechend.
era ('iərə) *n* Ära *f.*
eradicate (i'rædikeit) *vt* ausrotten, vernichten.
erase (i'reiz) *vt* **1** ausradieren. **2** auslöschen.
erect (i'rekt) *adj* aufrecht. *vt* **1** aufrichten. **2** bauen, errichten. **erection** *n* **1** Errichtung *f.* **2** Bau *m.*
ermine ('ə:min) *n zool* Hermelin *neu.*
erode (i'roud) *vt* **1** zerfressen. **2** erodieren. **erosion** *n* **1** Zerfressung *f.* **2** Erosion *f.*
erotic (i'rɔtik) *adj* erotisch.
err (ə:) *vi* **1** sich irren. **2** abweichen.
errand ('erənd) *n* Botengang, Auftrag *m.*
erratic (i'rætik) *adj* **1** unregelmäßig. **2** unberechenbar, nicht konstant.
error ('erə) *n* Irrtum, Fehler *m.*
erupt (i'rʌpt) *vi* ausbrechen. **eruption** *n* Ausbruch *m.*
escalate ('eskəleit) *(vi),vt* eskalieren, (sich) steigern. **escalator** *n* Rolltreppe *f.*
escalope (i'skæləp) *n cul* Schnitzel *neu.*
escape (i'skeip) *n* **1** Flucht *f.* Entkommen *neu.* **2** Befreiung *f. vi* **1** flüchten, entkommen. **2** ausfließen. *vt* **1** entgehen.
escort ('eskɔ:t) *n* **1** Begleitung *f.* **2** Begleiter *m.* **3** *mil* Eskorte *f. vt* **1** geleiten. **2** begleiten.
Eskimo ('eskimou) *n* Eskimo *m.*

esoteric (esə'terik) adj esoterisch.

especial (i'speʃəl) adj besonder, speziell. **especially** adv besonders, hauptsächlich.

espionage ('espiənɑ:ʒ) n Spionage f.

essay ('esei) n Aufsatz m. Abhandlung f.

essence ('esəns) n Essenz f. Kern m. **essential** adj 1 wesentlich. 2 unentbehrlich.

establish (i'stæbliʃ) vt 1 festlegen, aufstellen. 2 begründen, errichten. **establishment** n 1 Gründung, Errichtung f. 2 Firma f. 3 Anstalt m.

estate (i'steit) n 1 Besitz m. 2 Nachlaß m. **estate agent** n Häusermakler m. **estate car** n mot Kombiwagen m.

esteem (i'sti:m) n Achtung f. vt hochschätzen.

estimate (n 'estimət; v 'estimeit) n Schätzung f. vt schätzen. **estimation** n 1 Schätzung f. 2 Urteil neu.

estuary ('estʃuəri) n Flußmündung f.

eternal (i'tə:nl) adj ewig. **eternity** n Ewigkeit f.

ethereal (i'θiəriəl) adj ätherisch.

ethical ('eθikəl) adj ethisch, sittlich. **ethics** n pl 1 Sitten f pl. Moral f. 2 Sittenlehre f.

Ethiopia (i:θi'oupiə) n Äthiopien neu. **Ethiopian** adj äthiopisch. n Äthiopier m.

ethnic ('eθnik) adj ethnisch, Volks—.

etiquette ('etikit) n Etikette f.

etymology (eti'mɔlədʒi) n Etymologie f.

Eucharist ('ju:kərist) n heiliges Abendmahl neu.

eunuch ('ju:nək) n Eunuch m.

euphemism ('ju:fəmizəm) n Euphemismus m.

euphoria (ju:'fɔ:riə) n 1 Euphorie f. 2 (heftige) Begeisterung f.

Europe ('juərəp) n Europe neu. **European** adj europäisch. n Europäer m.

European Economic Community n Europäische Wirtschaftsgemeinschaft, EWG f.

euthanasia (ju:θə'neiziə) n Sterbehilfe, Euthanasie f. Gnadentod m.

evacuate (i'vækjueit) vt 1 entleeren. 2 evakuieren. 3 räumen.

evade (i'veid) vt,vi ausweichen, umgehen, vermeiden. **evasive** adj ausweichend.

evaluate (i'væljueit) vt abschätzen, berechnen.

evangelical (i:væn'dʒelikəl) adj evangelisch. **evangelist** n Evangelist m.

evaporate (i'væpəreit) vi,(vt) verdampfen (lassen).

eve (i:v) n Vorabend m.

even ('i:vən) adj 1 glatt, eben. 2 gleich. 3 math gerade. 4 quitt. adv gerade, sogar. **even better** noch besser. **not even** nicht einmal. **even-tempered** adj gleichmütig, gelassen.

evening ('i:vəniŋ) n Abend m. **evening dress** n 1 Abendkleid neu. 2 Smoking m.

event (i'vent) n 1 Ereignis neu. Vorfall m. 2 Veranstaltung f. **eventual** adj schließlich. **eventually** adv schließlich, endlich.

ever ('evə) adv 1 immer, stets. 2 je, jemals. 3 überhaupt. **ever so** inf besonders, sehr. **for ever** für immer, auf ewig, stets. **evergreen** n Immergrün neu. adj immergrün. **everlasting** adj 1 ewig. 2 dauerhaft. **evermore** adv immerfort.

every ('evri) pron jeder, jede, jedes m,f,neu. all. **everybody** pron also **everyone** jeder, jedermann. **everyday** adj Alltags— alltäglich. **everything** pron alles. **everywhere** adv überall, überallhin.

evict (i'vikt) vt law ausweisen.

evidence ('evidəns) n 1 Zeugnis neu. 2 Nachweis, Beweis m. **evident** adj offenbar, klar.

evil ('i:vəl) adj böse, übel. n Böse, Übel neu.

evoke (i'vouk) vt hervorrufen.

evolve (i'vɔlv) vi sich entwickeln, enstehen. vt entwickeln. **evolution** n Entwicklung, Evolution f.

ewe (ju:) n Mutterschaf neu.

exact (ig'zækt) adj 1 genau, exakt. 2 streng. vt verlangen, fordern.

exaggerate (ig'zædʒəreit) vt,vi übertreiben.

exalt (ig'zɔ:lt) vt verherrlichen. **exaltation** n Verherrlichung f.

examine (ig'zæmin) vt 1 prüfen. 2 untersuchen. 3 verhören. **examination** n 1 Prüfung f. 2 Untersuchung f. 3 Verhör neu.

example (ig'zɑ:mpəl) n 1 Beispiel neu. 2 Vorbild neu. **for example** zum Beispiel.

exasperate (ig'zɑ:spəreit) vt ärgern, reizen.

excavate ('ekskəveit) vt ausgraben, aushöhlen.

exceed (ik'si:d) vt 1 überschreiten. 2 hinausgehen über. **exceedingly** adv äußerst, höchst.

excel (ik'sel) vt übertreffen. **excel oneself** sich auszeichnen. **excellence** n Vorzüglichkeit f. **excellent** adj vorzüglich, ausgezeichnet.

Excellency ('eksələnsi) n Exzellenz f.

except (ik'sept) prep ausgenommen, außer. **except for** abgesehen von. **except that** nur daß, außer daß. vt ausnehmen, ausschließen. **exception** n Ausnahme f.

excerpt ('eksə:pt) n Auszug m. Szene f.

excess (ik'ses) n 1 Übermaß neu. Überfluß m. 2 pl Unmäßigkeiten f pl. **in excess of** mehr als. **excessive** adj übermäßig.

exchange (iks'tʃeindʒ) vt (aus-, um-)tauschen, wechseln. n 1 (Aus)Tausch m. 2 Wechsel m. 3

187

comm Börse *f.* **4** (Telephon)Zentrale *f.* **exchange rate** *n* Wechselkurs *m.*

exchequer (iks'tʃekə) *n* Staatskasse *f.* Finanzministerium *neu.* **chancellor of the exchequer** *n* Finanzminister *m.*

excise ('eksaiz) *n* (indirekte) Steuer *f.*

excite (ik'sait) *vt* erregen, anregen, aufregen. **excitement** *n* Aufregung *f.*

exclaim (ik'skleim) *vt, vi* ausrufen.

exclamation (ekskləˈmeiʃən) *n* Ausruf *m.* **exclamation mark** *n* Ausrufungszeichen *neu.*

exclude (ik'sklu:d) *vt* ausschließen. **exclusive** *adj* **1** exklusiv. **2** ausschließlich.

excommunicate (ekskə'mju:nikeit) *vt* exkommunizieren.

excrete (ik'skri:t) *vi* ausscheiden, absondern. **excreta** *n pl* Auswurf, Kot *m.*

excruciating (ik'skru:ʃieitiŋ) *adj* qualvoll.

excursion (ik'skə:ʒən) *n* Ausflug *m.*

excuse (*n* ik'skju:s; *v* ik'skju:z) *n* Entschuldigung, Ausrede *f. vt* entschuldigen. **excuse me** entschuldigen Sie!

execute ('eksikju:t) *vt* **1** ausführen, vollziehen. **2** (a person) hinrichten. **executive** *n* **1** Verwaltung *f.* **2** (hoher) Angestellte(r), *adj* vollziehend.

exempt (ig'zempt) *adj* befreit, ausgenommen. *vt* ausnehmen, befreien.

exercise ('eksəsaiz) *n* **1** Übung *f.* **2** Ausübung *f.* **3** Schulaufgabe *f. vt* **1** üben, anwenden. **2** ausüben. **exercise book** *n* Schulheft *neu.*

exert (ig'zə:t) *vt* ausüben. **exert oneself** sich anstrengen. **exertion** *n* Anstrengung *f.*

exhale (eks'heil) *vt, vi* ausatmen.

exhaust (ig'zɔ:st) *n* **1** Abgas *neu.* **2** *mot* Auspuff *m. vt* **1** erschöpfen. **2** ermüden. **exhausted** *adj* erschöpft. **exhaust pipe** *n* Auspuffrohr *neu.*

exhibit (ig'zibit) *vt* **1** ausstellen. **2** zeigen, vorführen. *n* Ausstellungsstück *neu.* **exhibition** *n* **1** Ausstellung *f.* **2** Vorführung *f.* **exhibitionism** *n* Exhibitionismus *m.* Öffentlichkeitsdrang *m.*

exhilarate (ig'ziləreit) *vt* erheitern.

exile ('egzail) *n* **1** Verbannung *f.* Exil *neu.* **2** Verbannte(r) *m. vt* verbannen, vertreiben.

exist (ig'zist) *vi* **1** existieren, sein. **2** leben. **existence** *n* Dasein *neu.* Existenz *f.*

exit ('eksit) *n* **1** Ausgang *m.* **2** Abgang *m. vi Th* (geht) ab.

exonerate (eg'zonəreit) *vt* freisprechen.

exorbitant (ig'zɔ:bitənt) *adj* maßlos, übermäßig.

exorcize ('eksɔ:saiz) *vt* beschwören, austreiben.

exotic (ig'zɔtik) *adj* exotisch.

expand (ik'spænd) (*vi,*)*vt* **1** (sich) ausdehnen, (sich) ausbreiten. **2** (sich) erweitern. **expansion** *n* **1** Ausdehnung, Ausbreitung *f.* **2** *pol* Expansion *f.*

expanse (ik'spæns) *n* Weite, weite Fläche *f.*

expatriate (eks'pætriit) *vt* ausbürgern. *adj* im Ausland lebend. *n* Ausgebürgerte(r) *m.*

expect (ik'spekt) *vt* **1** erwarten. **2** annehmen. **expectancy** *n* Erwartung *f.*

expedient (ik'spi:diənt) *adj* ratsam, zweckmäßig. *n* Ausweg *m.* Hilfsmittel *neu.*

expedition (ekspi'diʃən) *n* Expedition *f.*

expel (ik'spel) *vt* (hin)ausstoßen, vertreiben.

expenditure (ik'spenditʃə) *n* **1** (Geld)Ausgabe *f.* **2** Verbrauch *m.*

expense (ik'spens) *n* **1** Kosten *f pl.* Ausgabe *f.* **2** *pl* Unkosten *f pl.* **at the expense of** auf Kosten. **expensive** *adj* teuer.

experience (ik'spiəriəns) *n* **1** Erfahrung *f.* **2** Erlebnis *neu. vt* erleben, erfahren. **experienced** *adj* erfahren.

experiment (ik'sperimənt) *n* Versuch *m.* Experiment *neu. vi* experimentieren. **experimental** *adj* Experimental—.

expert ('ekspə:t) *n* Fachmann, Experte *m. adj* erfahren, fachmännisch. **expertise** (ekspə-'ti:z) *n* Spezialwissen *neu.* Erfahrung *f.*

expire (ik'spaiə) *vi* **1** ablaufen. **2** sterben. **3** ausatmen. **expiry** *n* Ablauf *m.*

explain (ik'splein) *vt* erklären, erläutern. **explain oneself** sich rechtfertigen. **explanation** *n* Erklärung, Erläuterung *f.*

expletive (ik'spli:tiv) *adj* ausfüllend. *n* **1** Füllwort *neu.* **2** Fluchwort *neu.*

explicit (ik'splisit) *adj* verständlich, ausdrücklich, deutlich.

explode (ik'sploud) *vi* explodieren. *vt* sprengen. **explosion** *n* Explosion *f.* **explosive** *adj* explosiv. *n* Sprengstoff *m.*

exploit[1] ('eksplɔit) *n* Heldentat *f.* Abenteuer *neu.*

exploit[2] (ik'splɔit) *vt* **1** ausbeuten, ausnutzen. **2** auswerten. **exploitation** *n* **1** Ausbeutung *f.* **2** Ausnutzung *f.*

explore (ik'splɔ:) *vt* **1** erforschen. **2** untersuchen.

exponent (ik'spounənt) *n* Exponent, Vertreter *m.*

export (*v* ik'spɔ:t; *n* 'ekspɔ:t) *vt* exportieren, ausführen. *n* Ausfuhr *f.* Export(handel) *m.*

expose (ik'spouz) *vt* **1** aussetzen. **2** enthüllen. **3** bloßstellen. **4** *phot* belichten. **exposure** *n* **1**

fail

Enthüllung f. **2** Aussetzung f. **3** med Entkräftung f. **4** phot Belichtung f.
express (ik'spres) vt ausdrücken, äußern. adj **1** ausdrücklich. **2** Expreß—. **expression** n Ausdruck m. **express letter** Eilbrief m. **express (train)** n Schnellzug m.
exquisite (ek'skwizit) adj vorzüglich, vornehm, auserlesen.
extend (ik'stend) vt **1** ausdehnen, erweitern. **2** ausbauen. **3** verlängern. **4** gewähren, erweisen. vi sich ausdehnen, erstrecken. **extension** n **1** Erweiterung, Ausdehnung f. **2** Verlängerung f. **3** Anbau m. **4** (Telephon)Nebenanschluß m. **extensive** adj umfassend, ausgedehnt.
extent (ik'stent) n **1** Ausdehnung f. **2** Größe f. **3** (Aus)Maß neu. **to some extent** gewissermaßen. **to that/what extent** insofern/inwiefern.
exterior (ek'stiəriə) adj außer, Außen—. n **1** Äußere neu. **2** Außenseite f.
exterminate (ik'stə:mineit) vt ausrotten, vertilgen.
external (ek'stə:nl) adj äußer(lich), Außen—.
extinct (ik'stiŋkt) adj **1** ausgestorben. **2** erloschen.
extinguish (ik'stiŋgwiʃ) vt auslöschen.
extra ('ekstrə) adj zusätzlich, Extra—, Sonder—.
extract (ik'strækt) vt (heraus)ziehen. n **1** Auszug m. **2** Extrakt m.
extramural (ekstrə'mjuərəl) adj educ außerhalb der Mauern (einer Universität).
extraordinary (ik'strɔ:dənri) adj außerordentlich, außergewöhnlich.
extravagant (ik'strævəgənt) adj verschwenderisch. **extravagance** n Verschwendung f.
extreme (ik'stri:m) adj **1** äußerst. **2** extrem, radikal. **3** höchst, außerordentlich. n Äußerste neu. **extremist** n Radikale(r), Fanatiker m. **extremity** n **1** Äußerste neu. **2** Spitze f. **3** pl Gliedmaßen pl.
extricate ('ekstrikeit) vt herausziehen, freimachen.
extrovert ('ekstrəvə:t) n Extravertierte(r), Extravert m.
exuberant (ig'zju:bərənt) adj **1** üppig. **2** überschwenglich.
eye (ai) n **1** Auge neu. **2** Blick m. **3** Ansicht f. vt ansehen.
eyeball ('aibɔ:l) n Augapfel m.
eyebrow ('aibrau) n Augenbraue f.
eye-catching adj auffällig.

eyelash ('ailæʃ) n Wimper f.
eyelid ('ailid) n Augenlid neu.
eye-opener n aufschlußreiche or überraschende Entdeckung f.
eye shadow n Lidschatten, Augenschatten m.
eyesight ('aisait) n Sehkraft f.
eyesore ('aisɔ:) n Dorn im Auge m.
eyestrain ('aistrein) n Überanstrengung des Auges f.
eyewitness (ai'witnis) n Augenzeuge m.

F

fable ('feibəl) n Fabel f. Märchen neu.
fabric ('fæbrik) n **1** Stoff m. Gewebe neu. **2** Struktur f. **fabricate** vt erfinden, fabrizieren.
fabulous ('fæbjuləs) adj **1** fabelhaft. **2** inf toll, fantastisch.
facade (fə'sɑ:d) n Fassade f.
face (feis) n **1** Gesicht neu. **2** Oberfläche f. **3** Vorderseite f. **in the face of** angesichts. **pull faces** Fratzen schneiden. ~vt **1** gegenüberstehen. **2** ansehen. **face up to 1** entgegentreten. **2** hinnehmen. **3** gewachsen sein. **face value** n Nennwert m. **take at face value** für bare Münze nehmen.
facet ('fæsit) n Seite f. Aspekt m.
facetious (fə'si:ʃəs) adj witzig, spaßig.
facile ('fæsail) adj **1** leicht. **2** gefällig, nachgiebig. **facilitate** vt erleichtern, fördern. **facility** n **1** Möglichkeit f. **2** Leichtigkeit f. **3** pl Einrichtungen f pl.
facing ('feisiŋ) prep gegenüber.
facsimile (fæk'siməli) n Faksimile neu.
fact (fækt) n **1** Tatsache, Wahrheit f. **2** pl Tatbestand m. **in fact** tatsächlich, in der Tat. **factual** adj tatsächlich.
faction ('fækʃən) n **1** Partei, Splittergruppe f. **2** Zwietracht f.
factor ('fæktə) n Faktor, Umstand m.
factory ('fæktri) n Fabrik f. Betrieb m.
faculty ('fækəlti) n **1** Vermögen neu. Kraft f. **2** educ Fakultät f.
fad (fæd) n inf Liebhaberei, Mode f.
fade (feid) vi **1** verblassen. **2** verklingen. **3** verschwinden.
fag (fæg) n **1** sl Zigarette f. **2** Plackerei f.
fail (feil) vi **1** scheitern, versagen. **2** nachlassen. **3** versäumen. **4** educ durchfallen. vt **1** educ durchfallen lassen. **2** im Stich lassen. **without fail** unbedingt. **failing** prep in Ermangelung. n Schwäche f. **failure** n **1** Scheitern, Ver-

sagen *neu.* **2** Verfall *m.* **3** Versäumnis *neu.* **4** Mißerfolg *m.* **5** *educ* Durchfallen *neu.*

faint (feint) *adj* **1** schwach, matt. **2** leise. **3** ohnmächtig. *vi* ohnmächtig werden. **faint-hearted** *adj* zaghaft, verzagt.

fair¹ (feə) *adj* **1** hübsch, schön. **2** blond, hell. *adj,adv* gerecht, fair. **fairly** *adv* ziemlich, ganz schön. **fair-minded** *adj* gerecht, ehrlich. **fairness** *n* Gerechtigkeit *f.*

fair² (feə) *n* **1** Ausstellung, Messe *f.* **2** Jahrmarkt *m.* **fairground** *n* Rummelplatz *m.*

fairy (ˈfɛəri) *n* Fee *f.* Elf *m.* **fairytale** *n* Märchen *neu.*

faith (feiθ) *n* **1** Vertrauen *neu.* Glaube *m.* **2** Treue *f.* **3** Religion *f.* **faithful** *adj* **1** treu. **2** zuverlässig, genau. **3** gläubig. **yours faithfully** hochachtungsvoll.

fake (feik) *n* Fälschung *f. adj* verfälscht. *vt* fälschen, nachmachen.

falcon (ˈfɔːlkən) *n* Falke *m.*

fall¹ (fɔːl) *n* **1** Fall, Sturz *m.* **2** Niedergang, Verfall *m.* **3** Sinken, Abnehmen *neu.* **3** *US* Herbst *m. vi* **1** fallen, stürzen. **2** sinken, abnehmen. **fall behind** zurückbleiben. **fall down** niederfallen. **fall through** durchfallen, scheitern.

fallacy (ˈfæləsi) *n* Täuschung *f.* Irrtum *m.*

fallible (ˈfæləbəl) *adj* fehlbar.

fallow (ˈfælou) *adj* **lie fallow** brachliegen.

false (fɔːls) *adj* **1** falsch. **2** trügerisch. **3** künstlich. **false alarm** *n* blinder Alarm *m.* **falsehood** *n* Falschheit, Unwahrheit *f.* **false pretences** *pl* Vorspiegelung falscher Tatsachen *f.* Betrug *m.* **false teeth** *n pl* künstliche Zähne *m pl.* **falsify** *vt* verfälschen, unrichtig darstellen.

falter (ˈfɔːltə) *vi* **1** stolpern. **2** zögern.

fame (feim) *n* Ruhm, Ruf *m.*

familiar (fəˈmiliə) *adj* **1** vertraut, bekannt. **2** gewohnt. **familiarity** *n* Vertrautheit *f.* **familiarize** *vt* vertraut machen.

family (ˈfæmili) *n* **1** Familie *f.* **2** Gruppe *f.*

famine (ˈfæmin) *n* Hungersnot *f.*

famous (ˈfeiməs) *adj* berühmt.

fan¹ (fæn) *n* **1** Fächer *m.* **2** *tech* Ventilator *m.* **fanbelt** *n mot* Keilriemen *m.*

fan² (fæn) *n* Anhänger, Liebhaber *m.*

fanatic (fəˈnætik) *n* Fanatiker *m. adj also* **fanatical** fanatisch.

fancy (ˈfænsi) *n* **1** Neigung, Vorliebe *f.* **2** Einbildung, Phantasie *f. adj* verziert, geschmückt. *vt* mögen, Lust haben auf. **fancy oneself** *inf* sich einbilden. **fancy someone**

inf auf jemanden ein Auge haben. **fancy dress** *n* Maskenkostüm *neu.* **fanciful** *adj* phantasievoll.

fanfare (ˈfænfɛə) *n* Fanfare *f.*

fang (fæŋ) *n* Reißzahn *m.*

fantastic (fænˈtæstik) *adj* **1** phantastisch. **2** eingebildet. **3** *inf* wunderbar, toll.

fantasy (ˈfæntəsi) *n* Phantasie *f.*

far (fɑː) *adj* weit, entfernt. *adv* weit, fern. **by far** weitaus, bei weitem. **far and wide** weit und breit. **in so far as** insofern als. **faraway** *adj* **1** weit entfernt. **2** verträumt. **far-fetched** *adj* weit hergeholt, phantastisch. **far-off** *adj* entfernt, weit. **far-reaching** *adj* weitreichend.

farce (fɑːs) *n Th* Posse, Farce *f.*

fare (fɛə) *n* **1** Fahrgeld *neu.* **2** Kost *f. vi* (er)gehen.

Far East *n* Ferne(r) Osten *m.*

farewell (fɛəˈwel) *n* Lebewohl *neu.* Abschied *m. interj* lebe wohl!

farinaceous (færiˈneiʃəs) *adj* mehlig, Mehl— **farinaceous food** *n* Teigwaren *f pl.*

farm (fɑːm) *n* **1** Bauernhof *m.* **2** Farm *f. vt* bewirtschaften. *n* Bauer *m.* **farmhouse** *n* Bauernhaus *neu.* **farming** *n* Landwirtschaft *f.* **farmland** *n* Ackerland *neu.* **farmyard** *n* Hofplatz *m.*

farther (ˈfɑːðə) *adv* weiter, ferner. *adj* entfernter.

farthest (ˈfɑːðist) *adj* weitest, fernst. *adv* am weitesten.

farthing (ˈfɑːðiŋ) *n* **1** Farthing *m.* **2** Kleinigkeit *f.*

fascinate (ˈfæsineit) *vt* faszinieren.

fascism (ˈfæʃizəm) *n* Faschismus *m.* **fascist** *adj* faschistisch. *n* Faschist *m.*

fashion (ˈfæʃən) *n* **1** Mode *f.* **2** Art, Weise *f. vt* bilden, gestalten.

fast¹ (fɑːst) *adj,adv* **1** schnell. **2** fest, befestigt. **3** waschecht.

fast² (fɑːst) *n* Fasten *neu. vi* fasten.

fasten (ˈfɑːsən) *vt* **1** befestigen. **2** anschnallen. *vi* sich klammern an.

fastidious (fəˈstidiəs) *adj* anspruchsvoll, penibel, wählerisch.

fat (fæt) *adj* fett, dick. *n* Fett *neu. vt* **1** fett machen. **2** (animals) mästen. *vi* fett werden.

fatal (ˈfeitl) *adj* **1** tödlich. **2** verhängnisvoll, fatal. **fatality** *n* Todesfall *m.*

fate (feit) *n* Schicksal *neu.*

father (ˈfɑːðə) *n* Vater *m. vt* zeugen. **father-in-law** *n* Schwiegervater *m.* **fatherland** *n* Vaterland *neu.* Heimat *f.*

fathom ('fæðəm) n Faden m. vt 1 ergründen, begreifen. 2 sondieren.

fatigue (fə'tiːg) n Ermüdung f. vi ermüden.

fatuous ('fætjuəs) adj albern, blödsinnig.

fault (fɔːlt) n 1 Fehler m. 2 Schuld f. 3 tech Störung f. Defekt m. **be at fault** sich irren. **find fault** tadeln.

fauna ('fɔːnə) n Fauna, Tierwelt f.

favour ('feivə) n 1 Gefallen m. 2 Begünstigung f. vt 1 begünstigen. 2 vorziehen. **favourable** adj günstig, vorteilhaft, gelegen. **favourite** adj Lieblings—. n Liebling m. Favorit m.

fawn¹ (fɔːn) n Rehkalb neu. adj rehbraun.

fawn² (fɔːn) vi 1 kriechen. 2 schmeicheln.

fear (fiə) n Furcht, Angst f. vt (be)fürchten, sich fürchten vor. **fearless** adj furchtlos.

feasible ('fiːzəbəl) adj möglich, ausführbar.

feast (fiːst) n 1 Fest, Festmahl neu. vi sich ergötzen. **feast-day** n Festtag m.

feat (fiːt) n 1 Kunststück neu. 2 Heldentat f.

feather ('feðə) n Feder f. **featherbed** n Federbett neu. **featherweight** n Federgewicht neu.

feature ('fiːtʃə) n 1 (Gesichts)Zug m. 2 Grundzug m. 3 Merkmal neu. 4 (in a newspaper) Feature neu. spezieller Artikel m. vt 1 charakterisieren. 2 in der Hauptrolle zeigen.

February ('februəri) n Februar m.

feckless ('fekləs) adj 1 hilflos. 2 wirkungslos.

fed (fed) v see **feed.**

federal ('fedərəl) adj 1 Bundes—, bundesstaatlich. 2 (in Switzerland) eidgenössisch. **federate** adj verbündet. **federation** n Vereinigung f. 2 pol Bundesstaat m.

fee (fiː) n Gebühr, Bezahlung f. Honorar neu.

feeble ('fiːbəl) adj 1 schwach, lahm, kraftlos. **feeble-minded** adj geistesschwach. **feeblemindedness** n Schwachsinn m.

feed* (fiːd) vt 1 ernähren. 2 füttern. vi 1 sich (er)nähren. 2 weiden. n 1 Nahrung f. 2 Futter neu. **be fed up with** satt haben. **feedback** n Feedback m.

feel* (fiːl) vt 1 betasten, (be)fühlen. 2 spüren, wahrnehmen. 3 empfinden. vi 1 sich fühlen, sich vorkommen. 2 glauben. **feel like doing something** Lust haben, etwas zu tun. **feeler** n Fühler m. **feeling** n 1 Gefühl neu. 2 Empfindung f. 3 Ahnung f. **with feeling** adv gefühlvoll.

feign (fein) vi,vt vorgeben, simulieren. vt heucheln. **feigned** adj vorgeblich, heuchlerisch.

feint¹ (feint) n 1 Finte f. 2 Verstellung f.

feint² (feint) adj,adv schwach.

feline ('fiːlain) adj Katzen—, katzenartig.

fell¹ (fel) v see **fall.**

fell² (fel) vt 1 niederschlagen. 2 fällen.

fellow ('felou) n 1 Gefährte m. 2 Mitglied neu. 3 Kerl, Bursche m. **fellow passenger** Mitreisende(r) m. **fellowship** n Gemeinschaft f. Gesellschaft f.

felon ('felən) n Verbrecher m. **felonious** adj verbrecherisch. **felony** n schwere Verbrechen neu.

felt¹ (felt) v see **feel.**

felt² (felt) n Filz m.

female ('fiːmeil) n 1 Weib neu. 2 (of animals) Weibchen neu. adj weiblich.

feminine ('feminin) adj weiblich. **femininity** n Weiblichkeit f. weibliches Wesen neu.

feminism ('feminizəm) n Frauenrechtlertum neu. **feminist** n Frauenrechtler m.

fence (fens) n 1 Einzäunung f. Zaun m. vi fechten. **fence in** einzäunen. **fencing** n 1 Fechtkunst f. 2 Einzäunung f.

fend (fend) vt **fend off** abwehren. vi **fend for** sorgen für.

fennel ('fenl) n bot Fenchel m.

ferment (n 'fəːment; v fə'ment) n Gärungsmittel neu. vi gären, fermentieren. vt gären lassen. **fermentation** n Gärung f.

fern (fəːn) n Farn m. Farnkraut neu.

ferocious (fə'rouʃəs) adj 1 wild. 2 grausam. **ferocity** n 1 Wildheit f. 2 Grausamkeit f.

ferret ('ferit) n Frettchen neu. v **ferret out** n herausjagen. 2 ausforschen.

ferry ('feri) n Fähre f. vt übersetzen.

fertile ('fəːtail) adj 1 fruchtbar. 2 ergiebig. **fertility** n Fruchtbarkeit f. **fertilize** vt 1 fruchtbar machen. 2 bot befruchten. 3 düngen. **fertilization** n 1 Befruchtung f. 2 Düngung f. **fertilizer** n Düngemittel neu.

fervent ('fəːvənt) adj glühend, leidenschaftlich. **fervour** n Leidenschaft f. Eifer m.

fester ('festə) vi 1 eitern. 2 verfaulen.

festival ('festivəl) n Fest neu. Feier f. **festive** adj festlich. **festivity** n Festlichkeit f.

festoon (fes'tuːn) n Girlande f. vt schmücken.

fetch (fetʃ) vt 1 holen. 2 (in a sale) bringen. **fetching** adj inf reizend, anziehend.

fête (feit) n Fest neu. vt feiern.

fetid ('fetid) adj stinkend.

fetish ('fetiʃ) n Fetisch m.

fetter ('fetə) n Fessel f. vt fesseln.

feud (fjuːd) n 1 Fehde f. 2 Lehen neu. **feudal** adj feudal. **feudalism** n Feudalismus m.

fever ('fiːvə) n 1 med Fieber neu. 2 fieberhafte

191

Aufregung f. **feverish** adj 1 fiebrig. 2 aufgeregt, fieberhaft.

few (fju:) adj,pron wenige. **a few** ein paar.

fiance (fi'ɔnsei) n Verlobte(r) m. **fiancee** n Verlobte, Braut f.

fiasco (fi'æskou) n Fiasko neu.

fib (fib) n Schwindelei, (kleine) Lüge f.

fibre ('faibə) n Faser, Fiber f. **fibreglass** n Fiberglas neu. **fibrous** adj faserig.

fickle ('fikəl) adj wankelmutig, unbeständig. **fickleness** n Wankelmut m. Unbeständigkeit f.

fiction ('fikʃən) n 1 Romanliteratur f. 2 Erdichtung f. **fictional** adj erdichtet, erfunden. **fictitious** adj unwirklich, erfunden.

fiddle ('fidl) n 1 Geige, Fiedel f. 2 inf Schwindelei f. vi 1 fiedeln. 2 tändeln. 3 beschwindeln.

fidelity (fi'deliti) n Treue f.

fidget ('fidʒit) vi (herum)zappeln. **fidgety** adj zappelig.

field (fi:ld) n 1 Feld neu. 2 Gebiet, Fach neu. Bereich m. 3 sport Platz m. **fieldwork** n praktische (wissenschaftliche) Arbeit f.

fiend (fi:nd) n 1 Teufel m. 2 Unhold m. **fiendish** adj teuflisch, unmenschlich.

fierce (fiəs) adj 1 wild, grimmig. 2 heftig. 3 (of light) grell. **fierceness** n 1 Wildheit f. 2 Heftigkeit f.

fiery ('faiəri) adj feurig, leidenschaftlich.

fifteen (fif'ti:n) adj fünfzehn. n Fünfzehn f. **fifteenth** adj fünfzehnte.

fifth (fifθ) adj fünfte. **fifthly** adv fünftens.

fifty ('fifti) adj fünfzig. n Fünfzig f. **fifty-fifty** adv halb und halb. **fiftieth** adj fünfzigste.

fig (fig) n Feige f.

fight (fait) n 1 Kampf m. 2 Konflikt m. 3 Schlägerei f. vt bekämpfen. vi kämpfen, sich schlagen. **fighter** n Kämpfer m.

figment ('figmənt) n (reine) Einbildung f.

figure ('figə) n 1 Ziffer f. 2 Gestalt, Figur f. 3 Persönlichkeit f. 4 Statue f. vi 1 erscheinen, auftreten. 2 meinen, denken. vt bildlich darstellen. **figure out** ausrechnen. **figurative** adj bildlich, symbolisch. **figurehead** n Repräsentationsfigur f. Strohmann m.

filament ('filəmənt) n 1 Faden m. Faser f. 2 (in an electric appliance) Glühfaden m.

file[1] (fail) n 1 Akte f. 2 Mappe f. Ordner m. 3 Reihe f. **in single file** hintereinander. vt (ein)ordnen, ablegen. **filing cabinet** n Aktenschrank m.

file[2] (fail) n Feile f. vt (zu)feilen, glätten.

filial ('filiəl) adj kindlich, Kindes—.

fill (fil) vt 1 (ab-, er-)füllen. 2 sättigen. 3 besetzen. 4 (a tooth) plombieren. vi sich füllen. **fill up (with petrol)** (auf)tanken. **filling** n 1 Einlage f. 2 Füllung f. 3 med Zahnplombe f. adj sättigend. **filling station** n Tankstelle f.

fillet ('filit) n cul Filet neu.

filly ('fili) n weibliches Füllen or Fohlen neu.

film (film) n 1 Film m. 2 Haut, Membrane f. 3 med Schleier. vt (ver)filmen, drehen. vi drehen. **film star** n Filmstar, Filmschauspieler m.

filter ('filtə) n Filter m. vt filtern, filtrieren.

filth (filθ) n Dreck, Schmutz m. **filthiness** n Schmutzigkeit f. **filthy** adj schmutzig, dreckig.

fin (fin) n Flosse, Finne f.

final ('fainl) adj 1 letzt. 2 End—, Schluß—. 3 endgültig. n sport Endspiel neu. **finale** n Finale neu. **finalize** vt 1 vollenden, abschließen. 2 endgültige Form geben. **finally** adv 1 endlich, schließlich. 2 zum Schluß.

finance ('fainæns) n Finanz f. Finanzwesen neu. vt finanzieren. **financial** adj finanziell, Finanz—. **financier** n Finanzier m.

finch (fintʃ) n Fink m.

find[*] (faind) vt 1 finden, entdecken. 2 halten für, denken. **find out** herausfinden. ~n Fund m.

fine[1] (fain) adj 1 fein. 2 schön. 3 scharf. **finery** n 1 Putz m. 2 Eleganz f.

fine[2] (fain) n 1 Geldstrafe f. vt zu einer Geldstrafe verurteilen.

finesse (fi'nes) n 1 Finesse f. 2 Schlauheit f.

finger ('fingə) n Finger m. vt fingern, betasten. **fingermark** n Fingerabdruck m. **fingernail** n Fingernagel m. **fingerprint** n Fingerabdruck m. **fingertip** n Fingerspitze f.

finish ('finiʃ) vt 1 beenden. 2 vollenden. vi 1 enden, aufhören. vt 1 sport Ziel neu. 2 Ende neu.

finite ('fainait) adj begrenzt, endlich. **finite verb** n gram Verbum finitum neu.

Finland ('finlənd) n Finnland neu.

Finn n Finne m. **Finnish** adj finnisch. n (language) Finnisch neu.

fir (fə:) n Tanne f. **fircone** n Tannenzapfen m.

fire (faiə) n 1 Feuer neu. 2 Brand m. **on fire** in Flammen. ~vt 1 anzünden. 2 anfeuern. vi feuern. **fire away!** schieß los!

fire alarm n Feuermelder, Feueralarm m.

fire brigade n Feuerwehr f.

flee

fire drill n Feueralarmübung f.

fire-engine n Motorspritze f. Feuerwehrauto neu.

fire-escape n Nottreppe f.

fire-extinguisher n Feuerlöscher m.

fireman ('faiəmən) n Feuerwehrmann m.

fireplace ('faiəpleis) n (offener) Kamin m.

fireproof ('faiəpru:f) adj feuerfest.

fireside ('faiəsaid) n Kamin m. adj häuslich.

fire station n Feuerwache f.

firework ('faiəwə:k) n Feuerwerk neu.

firing squad n Exekutionskommando neu.

firm[1] (fə:m) adj 1 fest. 2 standhaft. 3 entschlossen. **firmness** n 1 Festigkeit f. 2 Entschlossenheit f.

firm[2] (fəim) n Firma f.

first (fə:st) adj 1 erste. 2 beste. adv 1 erstens. 2 zuerst. **at first** anfangs, zuerst. **first of all** zuallererst. ~n Erste(r) m. **first aid** n Nothilfe f. adj Unfalls—. **first class** n erste Klasse f. **first-class** adj prima, erstklassig, ausgezeichnet. **first-hand** adv aus erster Hand, direkt. **first name** n Vorname m. **first person** n gram erste Person f. **first-rate** adj ausgezeichnet.

fiscal ('fiskəl) adj fiskalisch. Finanz—.

fish (fiʃ) n, pl **fishes** or **fish** Fisch m. **queer fish** n komischer Kauz m. **a pretty kettle of fish** eine schöne Bescherung f. vi fischen, angeln. **fisherman** n Fischer m. **fish finger** n Fischstäbchen neu. **fishing** n Fischen, Angeln neu. **fishing rod** n Angelrute f. **fishmonger** n Fischhändler m. **fishslice** n Fischheber m. **fishy** adj 1 fischig. 2 verdächtig.

fission ('fiʃən) n Spaltung f.

fist (fist) n Faust f.

fit[1] (fit) adj 1 passend. 2 sport in Form, fit. 3 fähig. **fit as a fiddle** kerngesund. ~vt 1 passen. 2 passend machen, anpassen. vi 1 sich eignen. 2 (of clothes) sitzen. n (of clothes) Sitz m. **fitting** adj passend, schicklich.

fit[2] (fit) n 1 med Anfall m. 2 Ausbruch m. **fitful** adj 1 unbeständig. 2 launenhaft.

five (faiv) adj fünf. n Fünf f.

fix (fiks) vt 1 befestigen, anheften. 2 (one's eyes) richten, heften. 3 bestimmen, festsetzen. vi fest werden. **fix up** arrangieren. **fixation** n Fixierung f. **fixed** adj starr. 2 bestimmt. **fixture** n Zubehör(teil) m.

fizz (fiz) vi zischen, sprudeln. n Zischen neu. **fizzle** vi zischen. **fizzle out** verpuffen.

fjord (fjɔ:d) n Fjord m.

flabbergast ('flæbəga:st) vt verblüffen.

flabby ('flæbi) adj schlaff, schlapp.

flag[1] (flæg) n Fahne, Flagge f. vt beflaggen. **flagpole** n Fahnenstange f.

flag[2] (flæg) vi 1 ermatten. 2 mutlos werden.

flagon ('flægən) n (bauchige) Flasche f.

flagrant ('fleigrənt) adj 1 schamlos. 2 offenkundig.

flair ('flɛə) n Spürsinn, Flair m.

flake (fleik) n 1 Flocke f. 2 Schuppe f. Blatt neu. vi (sich) flocken. vi,vt abblättern. **flaky** adj flockig, schuppig.

flamboyant (flæm'bɔiənt) adj 1 auffallend. 2 überladen. 3 flammend.

flame (fleim) n 1 Flamme f. 2 Leidenschaft f. vi flammen, lodern.

flamingo (flə'miŋgou) n Flamingo m.

flan (flæn) n Torte f.

flank (flæŋk) n 1 mil Flanke f. 2 zool Weiche f. vt flankieren.

flannel ('flænļ) n 1 Flanell m. 2 Waschlappen m.

flap (flæp) n 1 anat Lappen m. 2 Klappe f. 3 (Flügel)Schlag m. vi 1 flattern. 2 lose herabhängen.

flare (flɛə) vi 1 flackern. 2 sich bauschen. n 1 flackerndes Licht neu. 2 Lichtsignal neu. v **flare up** 1 aufflackern. 2 aufbrausen.

flash (flæʃ) n 1 Blitz m. 2 Aufblitzen neu. vi (auf)blitzen. vt werfen. **flashback** n Rückblende f. **flashbulb** n Blitzlichtlampe f. **flashlight** n 1 Blitzlicht neu. Taschenlampe f.

flask (fla:sk) n 1 (Taschen-, Reise-) Flasche f. 2 sci Kolben m.

flat[1] (flæt) adj 1 flach, platt. 2 eben. n 1 Fläche f. 2 Flachland neu. **flatfish** n Plattfisch m. **flat-footed** adj plattfüßig. **flatten** vt platt machen, (ein)ebnen. vi flach werden.

flat[2] (flæt) n Wohnung f.

flatter ('flætə) vt schmeicheln. **flatterer** n Schmeichler m. **flattering** adj schmeichelhaft. **flattery** n Schmeichelei f.

flaunt (flɔ:nt) vt 1 prunken. 2 offen zeigen.

flautist ('flɔ:tist) n Flötist m.

flavour ('fleivə) n Geschmack m. Aroma neu. **flavouring** n Würze f. Geschmacksstoff m.

flaw (flɔ:) n 1 Sprung m. 2 Makel m. **flawless** adj 1 makellos. 2 tadellos.

flax (flæks) n Flachs m.

flea (fli:) n Floh m.

fleck (flek) n Fleck m. vt sprenkeln.

fled (fled) v see **flee.**

flee* (fli:) vi fliehen. vt meiden.

fleece (fliːs) n Fell, Vlies neu. vt schröpfen. **fleecy** adj wollig.

fleet (fliːt) n Flotte f.

fleeting ('fliːtiŋ) adj flüchtig, vergänglich.

Flemish ('flemiʃ) adj flämisch. n (language) Flämisch neu.

flesh (fleʃ) n Fleisch neu. **fleshy** adj 1 fleischig. 2 fett.

flew (fluː) v see **fly**¹.

flex (fleks) n Kabel neu. vt biegen, beugen. **flexible** adj 1 biegsam. 2 flexibel. **flexibility** n Biegsamkeit f.

flick (flik) vt schnellen. n (leichter) Hieb m.

flicker ('flikə) n Flackern neu. vi flackern.

flight¹ (flait) n 1 Flug m. 2 Schwarm m. **flight deck** n Flugdeck neu. **flight of stairs** n Treppe f.

flight² (flait) n Flucht f. **flighty** adj flüchtig.

flimsy ('flimzi) adj 1 dünn. 2 schwach.

flinch (flintʃ) vi zurückschrecken, zucken.

fling* (fliŋ) vt werfen, schleudern. n Hieb m.

flint (flint) n 1 Kiesel m. 2 Flint m.

flip (flip) n Klaps m. vt klapsen, schnellen. **flipper** n 1 zool Flosse f. 2 Schwimmflosse f.

flippant ('flipənt) adj leichtfertig. **flippancy** n Leichtfertigkeit, Frechheit f.

flirt (fləːt) vi flirten. **flirtation** n Liebelei f. Flirt m. **flirtatious** adj kokett.

flit (flit) vi 1 flitzen. 2 wegziehen, sich entfernen.

float (flout) vi 1 (obenauf) schwimmen. 2 schweben. vt 1 bewässern. 2 flottmachen. 3 flößen. n 1 tech Schwimmer m. 2 Floß neu.

flock¹ (flɔk) n 1 Herde f. 2 Schar f. vi 1 sich scharen. 2 zusammenströmen.

flock² (flɔk) n (Woll)Flocke f.

flog (flɔg) vt 1 (aus)peitschen. 2 prügeln, züchtigen. 3 sl verkaufen. **flogging** n 1 Prügelstrafe f. 2 (Aus)Peitschen neu.

flood (flʌd) n 1 Flut f. 2 Überschwemmung f. vt,vi 1 überfluten. 2 überschwemmen. **floodlight** n Scheinwerfer m. Flutlicht neu.

floor (flɔː) n 1 Fußboden m. 2 Stock m. Stockwerk, Geschoß neu. Etage f. vt 1 einen Fußboden legen. 2 inf verblüffen. **floorboard** n Diele f. Fußbodenbrett neu.

flop (flɔp) vi 1 (hin)plumpsen. 2 flattern, schlottern. 3 Th durchfallen. n 1 Plumps m. 2 Versager, Durchfall m. **floppy** adj schlapp.

flora ('flɔːrə) n Flora, Pflanzenwelt f. **floral** adj Blumen—, Blüte—. **florist** n Blumenhändler m.

flounce¹ (flauns) vi stürzen.

flounce² (flauns) n Volant m.

flounder¹ ('flaundə) vi taumeln, stolpern.

flounder² ('flaundə) n Flunder f.

flour ('flauə) n Mehl neu. vt mit Mehl bestreuen.

flourish ('flʌriʃ) n 1 Schnörkel m. 2 Schwingen neu. 3 mus Verzierung f. vi 1 blühen, gedeihen. 2 Schnörkel machen. vt schwingen.

flout (flaut) vt verspotten, verhöhnen.

flow (flou) vi 1 fließen. 2 wallen. n Fluß m.

flower ('flauə) n 1 Blume f. 2 Blüte f. vi blühen. **flowerbed** n Blumenbeet neu. **flowerpot** n Blumentopf m. **flowery** adj blumig.

flown v see **fly**¹.

fluctuate ('flʌktʃueit) vi schwanken, fluktuieren. **fluctuation** n 1 Schwanken neu. Schwankung f. 2 comm Fluktuieren neu.

flue (fluː) n Kaminrohr, Abzugsrohr neu.

fluent ('fluːənt) adj fließend. **fluency** n Fluß m. Geläufigkeit f.

fluff (flʌf) n 1 Flaum m. 2 Staubflocke f. **fluffy** adj 1 flaumig. 2 flockig.

fluid ('fluːid) n 1 Flüssigkeit f. adj 1 flüssig. 2 fließend. 3 veränderlich.

flung (flʌŋ) v see **fling**.

fluorescent (fluəˈresənt) adj fluoreszierend. **fluorescence** n Fluoreszenz f.

fluoride ('fluəraid) n Fluor neu.

flush¹ (flʌʃ) vi erröten. vt (aus)spülen. n 1 Erröten neu. 2 Spülung f.

flush² (flʌʃ) adj eben, glatt. **be flush** inf gut bei Kasse sein.

fluster ('flʌstə) n Verwirrung f. vt verwirren.

flute (fluːt) n mus Flöte f.

flutter ('flʌtə) vi,(vt) flattern (lassen).

flux (flʌks) n 1 Fluß m. 2 beständiger Wechsel m.

fly*¹ (flai) vi 1 fliegen. 2 fliehen. vt fliegen (lassen). **flyover** n (Straßen)Überführung f.

fly² (flai) n Fliege f.

foal (foul) n Fohlen neu. vi fohlen.

foam (foum) n Schaum m. vi schäumen. **foamy** adj schaumig.

focal ('foukəl) adj im Brennpunkt stehend, fokal. **focus** n Fokus, Brennpunkt m. vt fokussieren, einstellen.

fodder ('fɔdə) n Futter neu. vt füttern.

foe (fou) n Feind m.

foetus ('fiːtəs) n Fötus m. Leibesfrucht f.

fog (fɔg) n 1 (dicker) Nebel m. 2 Schleier, Dunst m. vt,vi verschleiern. **foggy** adj 1 nebelig. 2 verschleiert, unklar. **foghorn** n Nebelhorn neu.

foible (ˈfɔibəl) n Schwäche f.

foil[1] (fɔil) vt vereiteln.

foil[2] (fɔil) n Folie f. Blattmetall neu.

foil[3] (fɔil) n sport Florett neu.

foist (fɔist) vt 1 aufhalsen. 2 unterschieben.

fold[1] (fould) vt 1 falten. 2 (one's arms) kreuzen. vi 1 sich falten. 2 sich zusammenklappen (lassen). n Falte f.

fold[2] (fould) n 1 (Schaf)Hürde f. 2 Herde f.

foliage (ˈfouliidʒ) n Laub neu.

folk (fouk) n pl Leute pl. adj Volks—. **folkdance** n Volkstanz m. **folklore** n Volkssagen f pl. **folksong** n Volkslied neu.

follicle (ˈfɔlikəl) n 1 Follikel m. 2 Haarbalg m.

follow (ˈfɔlou) vt,vi folgen, nachgehen. **follower** n 1 Nachfolger m. 2 Anhänger m. **following** n Anhängerschaft f.

folly (ˈfɔli) n Torheit, Narrheit f.

fond (fɔnd) adj 1 liebevoll. 2 (of a hope, etc.) töricht. **be fond of** gern haben.

fondle (ˈfɔndl) vt liebkosen, streicheln.

font (fɔnt) n Taufstein m.

food (fuːd) n 1 Nahrung, Kost f. Essen neu. Lebensmittel neu pl. 2 Futter neu.

fool (fuːl) n Narr, Dumme(r) m. vt zum Narren haben. vi Spaß machen. **foolish** adj 1 närrisch, albern, dumm. 2 unklug. **foolishness** n Dummheit f.

foolscap (ˈfuːlzkæp) n 1 Kanzleipapier neu. 2 Aktenformat neu.

foot (fut) n, pl **feet** 1 Fuß m. 2 Fußende neu. **on foot** zu Fuß. ~vt (bill) bezahlen. **foot it** inf zu Fuß gehen. **football** n 1 Fußball m. 2 Fußballspiel neu. **footbridge** n Steg m. Fußgängerbrücke f. **foothold** n 1 fester Stand m. 2 Halt m. **footing** n 1 Halt m. 2 Grundlage f. 3 Verhältnis neu. **footlights** n pl Th 1 Rampenlichter neu pl. 2 Bühne f. **footnote** n Anmerkung, Fußnote f. **footprint** n Fußspur f. **footstep** n 1 Spur f. 2 Tritt m. **footwear** n Schuhwerk neu.

for (fə; stressed fɔː) prep 1 für. 2 zu, nach. 3 aus, vor. 4 lang. conj denn.

forage (ˈfɔridʒ) n Futter neu. vi 1 Futter holen. 2 durchstöbern, herumsuchen.

forbear* (fəˈbɛə) vi 1 sich enthalten. 2 gedulden. vt sich enthalten, unterlassen. **forbearance** n 1 Geduld f. 2 Unterlassung f.

forbid* (fəˈbid) vt verbieten, untersagen. **forbidding** adj 1 abstoßend. 2 gefährlich.

force (fɔːs) n 1 Kraft, Stärke f. 2 Zwang m. 3 Gewalt f. 4 pl Streitkräfte f pl. vt 1 zwingen. 2 (a door) aufbrechen. **force-feed** vt zwangs-

weise ernähren. **forceful** adj 1 kräftig. 2 eindringlich. **forcible** adj gewaltsam.

forceps (ˈfɔːseps) n s or pl Zange f.

ford (fɔːd) n Furt f. vt durchwaten.

fore (fɔː) adv vorn n. Vorderteil neu. adj vorder, Vorder—.

forearm[1] (ˈfɔːrɑːm) n Vorderarm m.

forearm[2] (fɔːˈrɑːm) vt im voraus bewaffnen.

forebear (faˈbɛə) n Vorfahr m.

forecast (ˈfɔːkɑːst) n Vorhersage, Voraussage f. **weather forecast** n Wetterbericht m. ~vt vorhersagen, voraussagen.

forefather (ˈfɔːfɑːðə) n Vorfahr m.

forefinger (ˈfɔːfiŋgə) n Zeigefinger m.

forefront (ˈfɔːfrʌnt) n 1 Vorderseite f. 2 vorderste Reihe f.

foreground (ˈfɔːgraund) n Vordergrund m.

forehand (fɔːˈhænd) n Vorhand f. adj mit Vorhand gespielt.

forehead (ˈfɔrid) n Stirn f.

foreign (ˈfɔrin) adj 1 fremd. 2 ausländisch. **foreigner** n 1 Ausländer m. 2 Fremde(r) m. **foreign exchange** n Devisen f pl.

foreleg (ˈfɔːleg) n Vorderbein neu.

forelock (ˈfɔːlɔk) n Stirnlocke f.

foreman (ˈfɔːmən) n Aufseher, Vorarbeiter m.

foremost (ˈfɔːmoust) adj vorderst, erst. adv zuerst.

forensic (fəˈrensik) adj gerichtlich, Gerichts—.

forerunner (ˈfɔːrʌnə) n Vorläufer m.

foresee* (fɔːˈsiː) vt voraussehen. **forseeable** adj absehbar.

foresight (ˈfɔːsait) n Voraussicht f.

forest (ˈfɔrist) n Wald, Forst m. adj Wald—, Forst—. vt beforsten. **forester** n Förster m. **forestry** n Forstwirtschaft f.

forestall (fɔːˈstɔːl) vt vereiteln.

foretaste (ˈfɔːteist) n Vorgeschmack m.

foretell* (fɔːˈtel) vt 1 voraussagen. 2 vorbedeuten.

forethought (ˈfɔːθɔːt) n Vorbedacht m.

forfeit (ˈfɔːfit) n 1 Verwirkung f. 2 Buße f. 3 Pfand neu. vt 1 verwirken. 2 einbüßen. 3 verlieren. adj verwirkt.

forge[1] (fɔːdʒ) n Schmiede f. vt 1 schmieden. 2 fälschen.

forge[2] vi (fɔːdʒ) **forge ahead** sich vorwärtsdrängen, an die Spitze kommen.

forgery (ˈfɔːdʒəri) n Fälschung f.

forget* (fəˈget) vt 1 vergessen. 2 vernachlässigen. **forgetful** adj vergeßlich.

forgive* (fəˈgiv) vt verzeihen, vergeben. **for-**

giveness n Verzeihung, Vergebung f. **for-giving** adj versöhnlich.

forgo* (fɔːˈgou) vt verzichten auf.

fork (fɔːk) n **1** Gabel f. **2** (in a road, etc.) Gabelung f. vi sich gabeln. **fork out** Geld herausrücken. **forked** adj gabelförmig.

forlorn (faˈlɔːn) adj **1** verloren. **2** hoffnungslos. **3** hilflos.

form (fɔːm) n **1** Form, Figur, Gestalt f. **2** Art, Weise, Methode f. **3** Förmlichkeit f. **4** Formular neu. **5** (Schul)Klasse f. **6** (Schul)Bank f. vt **1** formen, bilden, gestalten. **2** erdenken. **3** schließen. vi sich formen. **formal** adj **1** formal, förmlich. **2** formell, feierlich. **formality** n Formalität, Förmlichkeit f. **formation** n **1** Bildung, Gestaltung f. **2** Formation f. **formative** adj bildend, gestaltend. **formative years** n pl Entwicklungsjahre neu pl.

former (ˈfɔːmə) adj **1** vorig. **2** ehemalig. **3** jene. **formerly** adv ehemals.

formidable (ˈfɔːmidəbəl) adj **1** furchtbar, erschreckend. **2** ungeheuer, gewaltig.

formula (ˈfɔːmjulə) n Formel f. **formulate** vt formulieren.

forsake* (faˈseik) vt **1** aufgeben. **2** verlassen.

fort (fɔːt) n Fort neu. Festung f.

forte (ˈfɔːtei) n Stärke f. adv mus forte.

forth (fɔːθ) adv hervor. **from this day forth** von heute an. **forthcoming** adj bevorstehend.

fortify (ˈfɔːtifai) vt **1** befestigen. **2** stärken. **fortification** n **1** Befestigung f. **2** Stärkung f.

fortnight (ˈfɔːtnait) n vierzehn Tage m pl.

fortress (ˈfɔːtrəs) n Festung f.

fortune (ˈfɔːtʃən) n **1** Glück neu. **2** Schicksal neu. **3** Vermögen neu. **fortunate** adj glücklich. **fortunately** adv glücklicherweise.

forty (ˈfɔːti) adj vierzig. n Vierzig f. **fortieth** adj vierzigste.

forum (ˈfɔːrəm) n **1** Forum neu. **2** Tribunal neu.

forward (ˈfɔːwəd) adj **1** vorder, vornliegend. **2** fortschrittlich. **3** vorlaut. adv **1** vorwärts. **2** nach vorn. vt **1** befördern. **2** nachsenden. **forwards** adv vorwärts.

fossil (ˈfɔsəl) n Fossil neu. adj versteinert.

foster (ˈfɔstə) vt **1** pflegen, aufziehen. adj Pflege—. **fosterchild** n Pflegekind neu. **fostermother** n Pflegemutter f.

fought (fɔːt) v see **fight.**

foul (faul) adj **1** schmutzig, ekelhaft, übel, widrig. vi schmutzig werden. vt verschmutzen. n sport Regelverstoß m. Foul neu.

found[1] (faund) v see **find.**

found[2] (faund) vt (be)gründen, stiften. **foundation** n Gründung, Stiftung f. adj Grund—.

founder (ˈfaundə) vi **1** naut sinken, untergehen. **2** scheitern. vt zum Scheitern bringen.

foundry (ˈfaundri) n Gießerei, Hütte f.

fountain (ˈfauntin) n **1** Springbrunnen m. **2** Quelle f. **fountain pen** n Füllfeder f.

four (fɔː) adj vier. n Vier f. **four-poster** n Himmelbett neu. **foursome** n **1** sport Viererspiel neu. **2** Quartett neu. **fourth** adj vierte. **fourthly** adv viertens.

fourteen (fɔːˈtiːn) adj vierzehn. n Vierzehn f. **fourteenth** adj vierzehnte.

fowl (faul) n **1** Geflügel neu. **2** Huhn neu.

fox (fɔks) n Fuchs m. vt täuschen, betrügen, verwirren. **foxglove** n bot Fingerhut m. **foxhunting** n Fuchsjagd f.

foyer (ˈfɔiei) n Foyer neu.

fraction (ˈfrækʃən) n **1** math Bruch m. **2** Bruchteil m.

fracture (ˈfræktʃə) n med Knochenbruch m. vt brechen.

fragile (ˈfrædʒail) adj zerbrechlich, zart.

fragment (ˈfrægmənt) n Bruchstück neu. Splitter m. Scherbe f. **fragmentary** adj bruchstückhaft, unvollständig, fragmentarisch.

fragrant (ˈfreigrənt) adj duftend.

frail (freil) adj **1** zerbrechlich. **2** schwach. **frailty** n Schwachheit f.

frame (freim) n **1** Rahmen m. **2** Gestell neu. vt **1** (ein)rahmen. **2** bilden, bauen. **framework** n **1** Gerippe neu. **2** Bau m. **3** Rahmen m.

franc (fræŋk) n **1** (französischer) Franc m. **2** (schweizerischer) Franken m.

France (frɑːns) n Frankreich neu.

franchise (ˈfræntʃaiz) n **1** Wahlrecht neu. **2** Bürgerrecht neu. **3** US Konzession f.

frank (fræŋk) adj offen, freimütig. vt (maschinell) frankieren.

frankfurter (ˈfræŋkfəːtə) n Frankfurter f.

frantic (ˈfræntik) adj **1** wahnsinnig. **2** verzweifelt, außer sich.

fraternal (frəˈtəːnl) adj brüderlich. **fraternity** n **1** Brüderlichkeit f. **2** Bruderschaft f. **fraternize** vi sich verbrüdern. **fraternization** n Verbrüderung f.

fraud (frɔːd) n **1** Betrug m. **2** Schwindel m. **3** Betrüger, Schwindler m. **fraudulence** n Betrügerei f. **fraudulent** adj betrügerisch.

fraught (frɔːt) adj beladen, voll (von).

fray[1] (frei) n Streit m. Schlägerei f.

fray[2] (frei) (vt), vi (sich) ausfransen.

freak (friːk) n **1** Laune f. Einfall m. **2** Abnormität, Mißbildung f. adj 1 launenhaft. 2 abnorm, grotesk.

freckle (ˈfrekəl) n Sommersprosse f.

free (friː) adj 1 frei. 2 ungebunden, unabhängig. 3 kostenlos, umsonst, gratis. 4 freigebig, großzügig. vt befreien. **freedom** n Freiheit f. **freehand** adj freihändig. **freehold** n eigener Grundbesitz m. **freelance** adj freischaffend, selbständig. **freely** adv 1 freiwillig. 2 reichlich. **Freemason** n Freimaurer m. **free will** n freier Wille m.

freeze* (friːz) vi 1 (ge)frieren. 2 erstarren. vt 1 frieren, tiefkühlen. 2 (credit) sperren. 3 (wages, prices) stoppen. n 1 (Ge)frieren neu. 2 Lohnstopp m. 3 Preisstopp m. **freezing** adj eisig. **freezing point** n Gefrierpunkt m.

freight (freit) n 1 Fracht f. 2 Frachtgeld neu. vt 1 beladen. 2 befrachten. **freight train** n Güterzug m.

French (frentʃ) adj französisch. n (language) Französisch neu. **French bean** n grüne Bohne f. **French horn** n Waldhorn neu. **Frenchman** n Franzose m. **French window** n Flügeltür f. **Frenchwoman** n Französin f.

frenzy (ˈfrenzi) n Wahnsinn m. Raserei f. **frenzied** adj wahnsinnig, rasend.

frequency (ˈfriːkwənsi) n 1 Häufigkeit f. 2 sci Frequenz f. **frequent** adj häufig, öfters. vt häufig or öfters besuchen, frequentieren.

fresco (ˈfreskou) n Fresko(gemälde) neu.

fresh (freʃ) adj 1 frisch. 2 unerfahren. 3 neu. 4 sl frech. **freshen up** vt,vi auffrischen. **freshwater** n Süßwasser neu. adj Süßwasser—.

fret[1] (fret) vt zerfressen. vi sich ärgern. **fretful** adj ärgerlich, mürrisch.

fret[2] (fret) n Flechtband neu. **fretsaw** n Laubsäge f.

friar (ˈfraiə) n Mönch m. **friary** n Mönchskloster neu.

friction (ˈfrikʃən) n Reibung f.

Friday (ˈfraidi) n Freitag m.

fridge (fridʒ) n inf Kühlschrank m.

fried (fraid) v see **fry**. adj gebraten, Brat—. **fried egg** n Spiegelei neu.

friend (frend) n 1 Freund m. 2 Bekannte(r) m. **make friends with** sich anfreunden mit. **friendliness** n Freundlichkeit f. **friendly** adj 1 freundlich. 2 befreundet. 3 wohlwollend. **friendship** n Freundschaft f.

frieze (friːz) n Fries m.

fright (frait) n Schreck, Schrecken m. **frighten** vt erschrecken. **be frightened of** Angst haben vor. **frightful** adj schrecklich.

frigid (ˈfridʒid) adj 1 kalt. 2 frigid. **frigidity** n 1 Kälte f. 2 Frigidität f.

frill (fril) n Krause f. vt kräuseln.

fringe (frindʒ) n 1 Franse f. 2 Rand m. vt 1 mit Fransen besetzen. 2 säumen.

frisk (frisk) vi hüpfen. vt sl durchsuchen, filzen. **frisky** adj 1 hüpfend. 2 munter.

fritter[1] (ˈfritə) vt **fritter away** verzetteln, verschwenden, vergeuden.

fritter[2] (ˈfritə) n in Eierteig gebackene Obstscheiben f pl.

frivolity (friˈvɔliti) n Leichtfertigkeit f. **frivolous** adj leichtfertig.

frizz (friz) (vi),vt (sich) kräuseln. **frizzy** adj kraus, gekräuselt.

frizzle[1] (ˈfrizl) (vi),vt (sich) kräuseln.

frizzle[2] (ˈfrizəl) vi zischen.

fro (fro) adv **to and fro** hin und her, auf und ab.

frock (frɔk) n 1 Damenkleid, Kinderkleid neu. 2 rel Kutte f. **frockcoat** n Gehrock m.

frog (frɔg) n Frosch m. **frogman** n Froschmann m.

frolic (ˈfrɔlik) n 1 lustiger Streich, Spaß m. 2 Lustbarkeit f. vi scherzen. **frolicsome** adj lustig, vergnügt.

from (frəm; stressed frɔm) prep 1 von, aus, von...her. 2 seit. 3 nach.

front (frʌnt) n 1 Vorderseite f. Vorderteil m. 2 Front f. adj Vorder—. **in front** adv vorne. **in front of** prep vor.

frontier (ˈfrʌntiə) n Grenze f. adj Grenz—.

frost (frɔst) n Frost m. **frostbite** n Erfrierung f. **frosty** adj frostig.

froth (frɔθ) n Schaum m. vi schäumen. vt zu Schaum schlagen. **frothy** adj schaumig.

frown (fraun) n 1 Stirnrunzeln neu. 2 finsterer Blick m. vi 1 die Stirn runzeln. 2 finster blicken.

froze (frouz) v see **freeze**.

frozen (ˈfrouzn) v see **freeze**. adj 1 gefroren. 2 cul Gefrier—. **frozen food** n tiefgekühlte Lebensmittel f pl.

frugal (ˈfruːgəl) adj 1 frugal, mäßig. 2 sparsam. **frugality** n 1 Mäßigkeit f. 2 Sparsamkeit f.

fruit (fruːt) n 1 Frucht f. 2 Früchte f pl. Obst neu. **fruitful** adj 1 fruchtbar. 2 ergiebig. **fruition** n 1 Genuß m. 2 Erfüllung f. **fruitless** adj 1 unfruchtbar. 2 vergeblich, fruchtlos. **fruit machine** n Spielautomat m. **fruit salad** n Obstsalat m. **fruity** adj fruchtig, saftig.

frustrate (frʌsˈtreit) vt vereiteln, verhindern. **frustration** n Vereitelung, Enttäuschung f.

fry (frai) vt braten, (in der Pfanne) backen.

197

frying pan n Bratpfanne f. **out of the frying pan into the fire** aus dem Regen in die Traufe.

fuchsia ('fju:ʃə) n Fuchsie f.

fuck (fʌk) vi,(vt) tab sich paaren (mit).

fudge (fʌdʒ) n Weichkaramelle f. vt inf (zu-recht)pfuschen.

fuel ('fju:əl) n 1 Brennstoff m. 2 Treibstoff m. vt 1 mit Brennstoff versehen. 2 tanken.

fugitive ('fju:dʒitiv) n Flüchtling m. adj flüchtig.

fulcrum ('fʌlkrəm) n Drehpunkt m.

fulfil (ful'fil) vt erfüllen. **fulfilment** n Erfüllung f.

full (ful) adj 1 voll. 2 besetzt. 3 satt. adv direkt, gerade, völlig. **to the full** adv vollständig. **full-length** adj in Lebensgröße f. **full moon** n Vollmond m. **fullness** n Fülle f. **full stop** n Punkt m. **full-time** adj ganztägig, Vollzeit—. **fully** adv voll, ausführlich.

fumble ('fʌmbəl) vi umhertappen, fummeln. **fumbling** adj 1 tappend. 2 linkisch.

fume (fju:m) n 1 Dunst, Dampf, Rauch m. 2 pl Abgase neu. vi 1 dunsten, rauchen. 2 wütend sein, aufgebracht sein.

fun (fʌn) n Spaß, Scherz m. **make fun of** vi sich lustig machen über. **funfair** n Rummelplatz, Jahrmarkt m.

function ('fʌŋkʃən) n 1 Funktion, Aufgabe f. 2 Veranstaltung f. vi funktionieren. **functional** adj funktionell. **functionary** n Beamte(r) m.

fund (fʌnd) n 1 Kapital neu. Fonds m. 2 Vorrat, Schatz m. 3 pl Geldmittel neu pl.

fundamental (fʌndə'mentl) adj Grund—, wesentlich, grundsätzlich, fundamental.

funeral ('fju:nərəl) n Beerdigung. adj Trauer—.

fungus ('fʌŋgəs) n, pl fungi Schwamm, Pilz m.

funnel ('fʌnl) n 1 Trichter m. 2 Schornstein m.

funny ('fʌni) adj 1 komisch. 2 sonderbar. **funny bone** n inf Musikantenknochen m.

fur (fə:) n 1 Pelz m. 2 med Belag m. 3 pl Pelzwaren f pl. adj Pelz—.

furious ('fjuəriəs) adj wütend, rasend.

furnace ('fə:nis) n Schmelzofen m.

furnish ('fə:niʃ) vt 1 versehen. 2 möblieren. **furnished** adj möbliert. **furnishing** n Einrichtung f.

furniture ('fə:nitʃə) n Möbel neu pl.

furrow ('fʌrou) n Furche, Rinne f. vt (durch)-furchen.

further ('fə:θə) adj weiter, ferner. vt fördern. **furthermore** adv überdies, weiter.

furthest ('fə:ðist) adj weitest. adv am weitesten.

furtive ('fə:tiv) adj verstohlen, heimlich.

fury ('fjuəri) n Wut f. Zorn m.

fuse¹ (fju:z) n 1 (Schmelz)Sicherung f. 2 Zünder m. vi durchbrennen.

fuse² (fju:z) vt schmelzen. vi verschmelzen.

fuselage ('fju:zəla:ʒ) n (Flugzeug)Rumpf m.

fusion ('fju:ʒən) n 1 Schmelzen neu. 2 Verschmelzung f. 3 comm Fusion f.

fuss (fʌs) n Getue neu. Aufregung f. vi sich aufregen über. **fussy** adj penibel.

futile ('fju:tail) adj unnütz, nutzlos, vergeblich. **futility** n Nutzlosigkeit, Sinnlosigkeit f.

future ('fju:tʃə) n 1 Zukunft f. 2 gram Futur neu. adj (zu)künftig.

fuzz (fʌz) n 1 Fussel f. Flaum m. 2 sl Polizei f. **fuzzy** adj 1 fusselig. 2 verschwommen. 3 kraus.

G

gabble ('gæbəl) n Geschnatter, Geplapper neu. vi,vt schnattern, plappern.

gable ('geibəl) n Giebel m.

gadget ('gædʒit) n Apparat m. Dings neu.

gag¹ (gæg) n Knebel m. vt knebeln.

gag² (gæg) n 1 Gag m. Pointe f.

gaiety ('geiəti) n Heiterkeit, Fröhlichkeit f.

gaily ('geili) adv heiter, fröhlich.

gain (gein) n 1 Gewinn m. 2 Profit m. vt 1 gewinnen. 2 erlangen, erreichen. vi (of a clock) vorgehen.

gait (geit) n 1 Gangart f. 2 Haltung f.

gala ('ga:lə) n Fest neu. Festlichkeit f.

galaxy ('gæləksi) n Milchstraße f.

gale (geil) n Sturm m.

gallant ('gælənt) adj 1 tapfer, ritterlich. 2 galant, höflich.

galleon ('gæliən) n Galeone f.

gallery ('gæləri) n Galerie f.

galley ('gæli) n 1 Galeere f. 2 Schiffsküche f.

gallon ('gælən) n Gallone f.

gallop ('gæləp) n Galopp m. vi galoppieren.

gallows ('gælouz) n pl Galgen m.

galore (gə'lɔ:) adv in Hülle und Fülle.

galvanize ('gælvənaiz) vt 1 galvanisieren. 2 beleben, anspornen.

gamble ('gæmbəl) vi (um Geld) spielen. **gamble away** versplielen. ~n Risiko neu. **gambling** n Glücksspiel neu.

game (geim) n 1 Spiel neu. 2 Partie f. 3 (animals) Wild neu. adj inf bereit, aufgelegt (zu). **gamekeeper** n Wildhüter m.

gammon ('gæmən) n (geräucherter) Schinken m.

gander ('gændə) n Gänserich m.

gang (gæŋ) n 1 Arbeitskolonne f. 2 Gruppe, Bande f. v **gang up** sich zusammenrotten. **gangster** n Gangster, Verbrecher m.

gangrene (gæŋ'gri:n) n Gangrän f.

gangway ('gæŋwei) n 1 Durchgang m. 2 naut Fallreep neu.

gap (gæp) n Lücke f.

gape (geip) vi 1 klaffen. 2 starren, glotzen. **gape at** angaffen.

garage ('gæra:ʒ) n 1 Garage f. 2 Reparaturwerkstatt f. vt einstellen, garagieren.

garble ('ga:bəl) vt verstümmeln, entstellen.

garden ('ga:dn) n Garten m. vi im Garten arbeiten. **gardner** n Gärtner m.

gargle ('ga:gəl) vi gurgeln. n Gurgelwasser neu.

garland ('ga:lənd) n Girlande f. Kranz m. vt bekränzen.

garlic ('ga:lik) n Knoblauch m.

garment ('ga:mənt) n Kleidungsstück, Gewand neu.

garnish ('ga:niʃ) vt i cul garnieren. 2 verzieren, schmücken. n 1 Garnierung f. 2 Schmuck m. Verzierung f.

garrison ('gærisən) n Garnison f.

garter ('ga:tə) n Strumpfband neu.

gas (gæs) n Gas neu. vt vergasen. **gas cooker** n Gasherd, Gasofen m. **gas fire** n Gasfeuer neu.

gash (gæʃ) n 1 (klaffende) Wunde f. 2 Riß m. vt tief schneiden in.

gasket ('gæskit) n tech Dichtung f.

gasp (ga:sp) vi keuchen. n Keuchen neu.

gastric ('gæstrik) adj gastrisch, Magen—. **gastronomic** adj gastronomisch. **gastronomy** n Gastronomie, Kochkunst f.

gate (geit) n 1 Tor neu. 2 Pforte f. **gatecrasher** n inf uneingeladener Gast, Eindringling m.

gateau ('gætou) n Torte f.

gather ('gæðə) vt 1 (ein-, ver-)sammeln. 2 ernten, lesen. 3 pflücken. 3 (cloth) raffen. vi sich versammeln. **gathering** n Versammlung f.

gauche (gouʃ) adj linkish, taktlos.

gaudy ('gɔ:di) adj bunt, grell, protzig.

gauge (geidʒ) n 1 Normalmaß neu. 2 Maßstab m. 3 Meßgerät neu. vt 1 eichen. 2 (aus-)messen. 3 abschätzen, beurteilen.

gaunt (gɔ:nt) adj hager, mager.

gauze (gɔ:z) n Gaze f.

gave (geiv) v see **give.**

gay (gei) adj 1 heiter. 2 bunt. 3 ausschweifend. 4 sl homosexuell.

gaze (geiz) vi starren. **gaze at** anstarren. ~n (starrer) Blick m.

gazelle (gə'zel) n Gazelle f.

gear (giə) n 1 Zeug neu. 2 Ausrüstung f. 3 Getriebe neu. 4 mot Gang m. 5 (Be)Kleidung f. **gearbox** n Getriebe neu. **gear lever** n Schalthebel m.

gelatine ('dʒeləti:n) n Gelatine f.

gelignite ('dʒelignait) n Gelatinedynamit neu.

gem (dʒem) n 1 Edelstein m. 2 Gemme f.

Gemini ('dʒeminai) n pl Zwillinge m pl.

gender ('dʒendə) n Geschlecht neu.

genealogy (dʒini'ælədʒi) n Genealogie f.

general ('dʒenərəl) adj 1 allgemein. 2 gewöhnlich. 3 Allgemein—. **in general** im allgemeinen. ~n General m. **general election** n allgemeine Wahlen f pl. **general practitioner** n praktischer Arzt m. **generalize** vi verallgemeinern. **generalization** n Verallgemeinerung f.

generate ('dʒenəreit) vt 1 tech erzeugen, hervorbringen. 2 verursachen. 3 zeugen. **generation** n 1 Erzeugung f. 2 Menschenalter neu. Generation f. **generator** n 1 Erzeuger m. 2 tech Generator m.

generic (dʒi'nerik) adj 1 allgemein, generell. 2 generisch, Gattungs—.

generous ('dʒenərəs) adj 1 großzügig. 2 großmütig. 3 reichlich. **generosity** n 1 Großzügigkeit f. 2 Großmut f.

genetic (dʒi'netik) adj Entstehungs—, genetisch. **genetics** n pl Genetik, Vererbungslehre f.

Geneva (dʒi'ni:və) n Genf neu.

genial ('dʒi:niəl) adj 1 freundlich, herzlich. 2 mild. 3 heiter, jovial. **geniality** n 1 Freundlichkeit f. 2 Herzlichkeit f.

genital ('dʒenitl) adj 1 Zeugungs—. 2 Geschlechts—. **genitals** n pl Genitalien neu pl. Geschlechtsteile m pl.

genitive ('dʒenitiv) n gram Genitiv m.

genius ('dʒi:niəs) n Genie neu. Genius m.

genteel (dʒen'ti:l) adj 1 vornehm. 2 fein.

gentile ('dʒentail) n Heide m. adj heidnisch.

gentle ('dʒentl) adj 1 mild, sanft. 2 vornehm. **gentleman** n 1 Herr m. 2 Gentleman m.

genuflect ('dʒenjuflekt) vi die Knie beugen. **genuflection** n Kniebeugung f.

genuine ('dʒenjuin) adj 1 echt. 2 wirklich.

genus ('dʒi:nəs) n Gattung f.

geography

geography (dʒiˈɔgrəfi) *n* Erdkunde, Geographie *f.*

geology (dʒiˈɔlədʒi) *n* Geologie *f.*

geometry (dʒiˈɔmətri) *n* Geometrie *f.*

geranium (dʒəˈreiniəm) *n* Geranie *f.*

germ (dʒə:m) *n* Keim, Bazillus *m.* Bakterie *f.* **germinate** *vi* keimen.

Germany (ˈdʒə:məni) *n* Deutschland *neu.* **German** *adj* deutsch. *n* **1** Deutsche(r) *m.* **2** (language) Deutsch *neu.* **German measles** *n pl* Röteln *pl.* **Germanic** *adj* germanisch.

gerund (ˈdʒerənd) *n* Gerundium *neu.*

gesticulate (dʒisˈtikjuleit) *vi* gestikulieren, sich lebhaft gebärden.

gesture (ˈdʒestʃə) *n* Gebärde, Geste *f.*

get* (get) *vt* **1** bekommen, erhalten. **2** *inf* kriegen. **3** gewinnen. **4** veranlassen. **5** besorgen. *vi* **1** gelangen, kommen. **2** werden. **get in** einsteigen. **get off** aussteigen. **get over** hinwegkommen über. **get ready** fertig machen. **get up** aufstehen.

geyser (ˈgi:zə) *n* **1** Geiser, Geysir *m.* **2** Durchlauferhitzer *m.*

ghastly (ˈgɑ:stli) *adj* gräßlich, schrecklich.

gherkin (ˈgə:kin) *n* Essiggurke *f.*

ghetto (ˈgetou) *n* Getto *neu.*

ghost (goust) *n* Gespenst *neu.* Geist *m.*

giant (ˈdʒaiənt) *n* Riese *m. adj* riesig.

giddy (ˈgidi) *adj* **1** schwindlig. **2** leichtsinnig.

gift (gift) *n* **1** Geschenk *neu.* **2** Begabung *f.*

gigantic (dʒaiˈgæntik) *adj* riesenhaft, gigantisch.

giggle (ˈgigəl) *vi* kichern. *n* Gekicher *neu.*

gild (gild) *vt* vergolden.

gill (gil) *n zool* Kieme *f.*

gilt (gilt) *adj* vergoldet. *n* Vergoldung *f.*

gimmick (ˈgimik) *n inf* Trick, Kniff *m.*

gin (dʒin) *n* Gin, Wacholderschnaps *m.*

ginger (ˈdʒindʒə) *n* Ingwer *m.* **ginger beer** *n* Ingwerbier *neu.* **gingerbread** *n* Pfefferkuchen *m.*

gipsy (ˈdʒipsi) *n* Zigeuner *m.*

giraffe (dʒiˈrɑ:f) *n* Giraffe *f.*

girder (ˈgə:də) *n* Tragbalken, Träger *m.*

girdle (ˈgə:dl) *n* (Hüft)Gürtel *m.*

girl (gə:l) *n* Mädchen *neu.* **girlfriend** *n* Freundin *f.*

Giro (ˈdʒairou) *n* Giro *neu.*

girth (gə:θ) *n* **1** (Sattel)Gurt *m.* **2** Umfang *m.*

give* (giv) *vt* **1** geben, schenken. **2** erteilen. **give away** verschenken. **give back** zurückgeben. **give in** nachgeben. **give out** **1** verteilen, ausgeben. **2** zu Ende gehen. **give up** aufgeben.

glacier (ˈglæsiə) *n* Gletscher *m.*

glad (glæd) *adj* **1** froh, erfreut. **2** fröhlich.

glamour (ˈglæmə) *n* Glanz, Zauber *m.* **glamorize** *vt* verherrlichen. **glamorous** *adj* bezaubernd, schön.

glance (glɑ:ns) *n* (flüchtiger) Blick, Schimmer *m. vi* flüchtig blicken.

gland (glænd) *n* Drüse *f.*

glare (glɛə) *vi* **1** (wütend) anblicken, starren. **2** hell glänzen. *n* **1** blendender Glanz *m.* **2** (wütender) Blick *m.*

glass (glɑ:s) *n* **1** Glas *neu.* **2** *pl* Brille *f.*

glaze (gleiz) *n* Glasur *f. vt* **1** verglasen. **2** glasieren.

gleam (gli:m) *n* Schimmer, Lichtstrahl *m. vi* strahlen, schimmern.

glean (gli:n) *vt* (auf-, nach-)lesen.

glee (gli:) *n* Fröhlichkeit *f.*

glib (glib) *adj* zungenfertig, glatt.

glide (glaid) *vi* **1** (vorüber)gleiten, fließen. **2** im Gleitflug fliegen. **glider** *n* Segelflugzeug *neu.*

glimmer (ˈglimə) *n* Schimmer *m.*

glimpse (glimps) *n* flüchtiger Blick *m.*

glisten (ˈglisən) *vi* glänzen, schimmern.

glitter (ˈglitə) *vi* glitzern. *n* Glanz *m.*

gloat (glout) *vi* sich weiden, sich hämisch freuen.

globe (gloub) *n* (Erd)Kugel *f.* Globus *m.*

gloom¹ (glu:m) *n* Dunkelheit, Düsternis *f.*

gloom² (glu:m) *n* Schwermut *f.* Trübsinn *m.*

glory (ˈglɔ:ri) *n* Ruhm, Glanz *m.* **glorify** *vt* verherrlichen. **glorious** *adj* glorreich, herrlich, prachtvoll.

gloss¹ (glɔs) *n* Glanz, Schein *m. v* **gloss over** vertuschen.

gloss² (glɔs) *n* Randbemerkung, Glosse *f.*

glossary (ˈglɔsəri) *n* (Spezial)Wörterverzeichnis *neu.*

glove (glʌv) *n* Handschuh *m.*

glow (glou) *vi* glühen. *n* Glühen *neu.* Glut *f.*

glucose (ˈglu:kous) *n* Traubenzucker *m.*

glue (glu:) *n* Klebstoff *m. vt* kleben.

glum (glʌm) *adj* mürrisch, verdrießlich.

glut (glʌt) *n* **1** Sättigung, Stillung *f.* **2** *comm* Überangebot *neu.*

glutton (ˈglʌtn) *n* **1** Vielfraß *m.* **2** unersättliche(r) Mensch *m.*

gnarled (nɑ:ld) *adj* knorrig.

gnash (næʃ) *vt* knirschen.

gnat (næt) *n* Mücke *f.*

gnaw (nɔ:) *vt,vi* nagen.

gnome (noum) n Zwerg, Erdgeist m. Gnom m.

go* (gou) vi **1** gehen, fahren, laufen. **2** funktionieren. **3** reichen. **go abroad** ins Ausland gehen. **go ahead 1** losgehen. **2** vorausgehen. **go away 1** weggehen. **2** verreisen. **go back** zurückkehren. **go down** hinuntergehen, untergehen. **go into** eintreten. **go off 1** weggehen. **2** (of food) schlecht werden. **go on** weitergehen. **go out** (hin)ausgehen. **go through 1** durchgehen. **2** durchmachen. **go up** (hinauf)steigen.

goad (goud) vt anspornen, anstacheln.

goal (goul) n **1** Ziel m. **2** sport Tor neu. **goalkeeper** n Torwart m. **goalpost** n Torpfosten m.

goat (gout) n Ziege f.

gobble ('gobəl) vt (hinunter-, ver-)schlingen.

goblin ('goblin) n Kobold m.

god (god) n Gott m. **godchild** n Patenkind neu. **goddaughter** n Patentochter f. **godfather** n Pate m. **godmother** n Patin f. **godson** n Patensohn m.

goddess ('godis) n Göttin f.

goggles ('gogəlz) n pl Schutzbrille f.

going ('gouiŋ) adj laufend, im Gang. n Gehen neu. Abreise f.

gold (gould) n Gold neu. adj golden. **golden** adj golden. **goldfish** n Goldfisch m.

golf (golf) n Golf(spiel) neu. **golfball** n Golfball m. **golfclub** n Golfschläger m. **golfcourse** n Golfplatz m.

gondola ('gondələ) n Gondel f. **gondolier** n Gondoliere m.

gone (gon) v see **go**. adj **1** vergangen. **2** fort. **3** tot.

gong (gon) n Gong m.

good (gud) adj **1** gut. **2** ordentlich. **3** artig, brav. **4** law gültig. n **1** Gut(e) neu. **2** Wohl neu. **3** pl Waren, Güter pl. **for good** auf immer. **good afternoon** interj guten Tag. **goodbye** interj auf Wiedersehen. n Lebewohl neu. **good evening** interj guten Abend. **good-looking** adj gut aussehen, schön, hübsch. **good morning** interj guten Morgen. **good night** interj gute Nacht. **goods train** n Güterzug m. **goodwill** n **1** Wohlwollen neu. guter Wille m. **2** Kundschaft f.

Good Friday n Karfreitag m.

goose (gu:s) n, pl **geese** Gans f. **gooseberry** n Stachelbeere f.

gore[1] (go:) n (geronnenes) Blut neu.

gore[2] (go:) vt durchbohren, aufspießen.

gorge (go:dʒ) n Schlucht f. vt,vi gierig essen. **gorge oneself** sich vollstopfen.

gorgeous ('go:dʒəs) adj **1** prächtig, großartig. **2** inf phantastisch. **3** inf sehr schmackhaft.

gorilla (gə'rilə) n Gorilla m.

gorse (go:s) n Stechginster m.

gory ('go:ri) adj blutig.

gosh (goʃ) interj Donnerwetter!

gosling ('gozliŋ) n Gänschen neu.

gospel ('gospəl) n Evangelium neu.

gossip ('gosip) n **1** Geschwätz neu. **2** Klatschbase f. vi schwatzen.

got (got) v see **get**.

Gothic ('goθik) adj gotisch.

goulash ('gu:læʃ) n Gulasch neu.

gourd (guəd) n Kürbis m.

gourmet (guə'mei) n Gourmet, Feinschmecker m.

govern ('gʌvən) vt **1** regieren, beherrschen. **2** bestimmen. vi regieren, herrschen. **government** n Regierung f. **governor** n **1** Gouverneur, Statthalter m. **2** Direktor m.

gown (gaun) n **1** (Damen)Kleid neu. **2** Robe f.

grab (græb) vt schnappen, ergreifen. vi gierig greifen.

grace (greis) n **1** Gnade f. **2** Reiz m. **3** Tischgebet neu. **4** Gunst f. **5** Anmut f. **His/Her/Your Grace** Sein/Ihr/Euer Gnaden. ~vt **1** schmücken. **2** ehren. **graceful** adj **1** anmutig. **2** taktvoll. **gracious** adj gütig, gnädig, anmutig.

grade (greid) n **1** Rang, Grad m. **2** Qualität f. vt ordnen, sortieren, einteilen. **gradient** n **1** Neigung f. **2** Hang m. **3** Steigerung f. **4** Gefälle neu. **gradual** adj allmählich, stufenweise, schrittweise. **graduate** n Graduierte(r) m. vi ein Diplom erwerben. vt einteilen.

graffiti (grə'fi:ti) n pl Graffiti neu.

graft[1] (gra:ft) vt **1** bot (auf-, ein-)pfropfen. **2** med verpflanzen. n **1** Propfreis neu. **2** Verpflanzung f.

graft[2] inf n **1** Schiebung, Bestechung f. **2** Gaunerei f. vt **1** schieben. **2** (er)gaunern.

grain (grein) n **1** Getreide neu. **2** Samenkorn neu. **3** (Holz)Faser f.

gram (græm) n Gramm neu.

grammar ('græmə) n Grammatik f. **grammar school** n Gymnasium neu. **grammatical** adj grammatisch, grammatikalisch.

gramophone ('græməfoun) n Plattenspieler m. Gramophon neu.

granary ('grænəri) n Kornspeicher m.

grand (grænd) adj groß, erhaben, stattlich.

201

grand piano n Flügel m. **grandeur** n Erhabenheit, Größe f. **grandiose** adj großartig, grandios.

grandad ('grændæd) n inf also **grandpa** Opa m.

grandchild ('grænt∫aild) n Enkelkind neu.

grand-daughter ('græn,dɔ:tə) n Enkelin f.

grandfather ('grænfɑ:ðə) n Großvater m.

grandma ('grænmɑ:) n inf also **granny** Oma f.

grandmother ('grænmʌðə) n Großmutter f.

grandparents ('grænpɛərənts) n pl Großeltern pl.

grandson ('grænsʌn) n Enkel m.

grandstand ('grændstænd) n Zuschauertribüne f.

granite ('grænit) n Granit m.

grant (grɑ:nt) n 1 Bewilligung f. 2 Verleihung f. 3 Zuschuß m. 4 educ Stipendium. vt 1 bewilligen. 2 verleihen. 3 zugestehen.

grape (greip) n Weintraube f. **grapefruit** n Grapefruit, Pampelmuse f.

graph (græf) n Diagramm neu. Kurve f. **graphic** adj 1 graphisch. 2 anschaulich.

grapple ('græpəl) vi ringen. vt 1 packen. 2 befestigen (an). **grapple with** in Angriff nehmen, sich auseinandersetzen mit.

grasp (grɑ:sp) vt 1 greifen, fassen. 2 begreifen, verstehen. n Griff m.

grass (grɑ:s) n 1 Gras neu. 2 Rasen m. **grassroots** n pl Wurzel f. adj volksnah, volkstümlich.

grate[1] (greit) n (Feuer)Rost m. Gitter neu.

grate[2] (greit) vt 1 cul reiben. 2 krächzen. 3 knirschen mit. vi kratzen, knirschen, knarren.

grateful ('greitfəl) adj dankbar. **gratify** vt erfreuen, befriedigen, zufriedenstellen.

gratitude ('grætitju:d) n Dankbarkeit f.

grave[1] (greiv) n Grab neu. **gravestone** n Grabstein m. **graveyard** n Friedhof m.

grave[2] (greiv) adj ernst(haft).

gravel ('grævəl) n Kies m.

gravity ('græviti) n 1 sci Gravität, Schwerkraft f. 2 Schwere f. Ernst m.

gravy ('greivi) n (Braten)Soße f.

graze[1] (greiz) n 1 flüchtige Berührung f. 2 Abschürfung f. vt 1 streifen. 2 abschürfen.

graze[2] (greiz) vi weiden, grasen.

grease (gri:s) n 1 Fett neu. 2 Schmiere f. vt schmieren, einfetten. **greasepaint** n Bühnenschminke f. **greaseproof** adj fettdicht.

great (greit) adj 1 groß. 2 beträchtlich. 3 bedeutend. 4 berühmt. 5 inf toll, sagenhaft, prima.

Great Britain n Großbritannien neu.

Greece (gri:s) n Griechenland neu. **Greek** adj also **Grecian** griechisch. n 1 Grieche m. 2 (language) Griechisch neu.

greed (gri:d) n (Hab)Gier f. **greedy** adj gierig.

green (gri:n) adj 1 grün. 2 inf unerfahren. n 1 Grün neu. 2 Grünfläche f. 3 pl Grüngemüse neu pl. **greenery** n Laub(werk) neu. **greenfly** n grüne Blattlaus f. **greengage** n Reineclaude f. **greengrocer** n Obst- und Gemüsehändler m. **greenhouse** n Treibhaus neu.

Greenland ('gri:nlənd) n Grönland neu. **Greenlander** n Grönlander m.

greet (gri:t) vt (be)grüßen. **greeting** n Gruß m.

gregarious (gri'gɛəriəs) adj gesellig.

grenade (gri'neid) n Granate f.

grew (gru:) v see **grow**.

grey (grei) adj grau. n Grau neu. **greyhound** n Windhund m.

grid (grid) n 1 Gitter neu. 2 Netz neu.

grief (gri:f) n Kummer, Schmerz m.

grieve (gri:v) vi trauern, sich kränken über. **grievance** n Beschwerde f. Groll m.

grill (gril) n Bratrost m. vt grillen, rosten.

grille (gril) n Gitter neu.

grim (grim) adj 1 grimmig, finster. 2 hart.

grimace (gri'meis) n Grimasse f. vi Grimassen schneiden.

grime (graim) n (fettiger) Schmutz m.

grin (grin) vi grinsen. n Grinsen neu.

grind* (graind) vt (zer)reiben, (zer)mahlen. n inf Plackerei f.

grip (grip) vt packen, (er)greifen. n Griff m.

gristle ('grisəl) n Knorpel m.

grit (grit) n grober Sand, Kies m.

groan (groun) vi stöhnen, seufzen. n Stöhnen neu.

grocer ('grousə) n Lebensmittelhändler m.

groin (grɔin) n Leiste f.

groom (gru:m) n 1 Stallknecht, Reitknecht m. 2 Bräutigam m. vt versorgen, pflegen.

groove (gru:v) n Rinne, Furche, Rille f.

grope (group) vi herumtappen, herumtappen.

gross (grous) adj 1 comm brutto. 2 dick. 3 grob, roh. n Gros neu.

grotesque (grou'tesk) adj grotesk.

grotto ('grotou) n Grotte f.

ground[1] (graund) n 1 Grund, Boden m. 2 pl Gelände n. Anlagen f pl. 3 (Beweg)Grund m. vt 1 begründen. 2 hinlegen. **ground floor** n Erdgeschoß neu. **groundsheet** n Zeltbahn f. **groundsman** n (Sportplatz)Wärter m.

ground[2] (graund) v see **grind**.

group (gru:p) n Gruppe f. vt gruppieren.
grouse[1] (graus) n Rebhuhn neu.
grouse[2] (graus) vi inf murren, meckern.
grove (grouv) n Gehölz neu. Waldung f.
grovel ('grɔvəl) vi (auf dem Bauch) kriechen.
grow[*] (grou) vi **1** wachsen. **2** werden. **3** zunehmen. vt (an)bauen, züchten, wachsen lassen. **growth** n **1** Wachstum neu. Entwicklung f. **2** Zunahme, Vergrößerung f.
growl (graul) vi,vt grollen, knurren, brummen. n Brummen, Knurren, Grollen neu.
grub (grʌb) n **1** Made f. **2** sl Futter neu. Fraß m. vi graben.
grubby ('grʌbi) adj schmutzig, dreckig.
grudge (grʌdʒ) n Groll m. vt beneiden, mißgönnen.
gruelling ('gru:əliŋ) adj erschöpfend.
gruesome ('gru:səm) adj grausig.
gruff (grʌf) adj **1** schroff, barsch. **2** mürrisch.
grumble ('grʌmbəl) vi murren, schimpfen.
grumpy ('grʌmpi) adj verdrießlich, mürrisch.
grunt (grʌnt) vi grunzen. n Grunzen neu.
guarantee (gærən'ti:) n **1** Garantie, Bürgschaft f. vt garantieren, gewährleisten. **guarantor** n Bürge, Garant m.
guard (gɑ:d) vt bewachen, (be)schützen. vi sich hüten. n **1** Wache f. **2** (railway) Schaffner m. **guardian** n **1** law Vormund m. **2** Wächter m. **guard's van** n Gepäckwagen m.
guerrilla (gə'rilə) n Guerillakämpfer m.
guess (ges) vt erraten, vermuten. n Vermutung, Mutmaßung f. **guesswork** n Vermutungen f pl.
guest (gest) n Gast m. **guesthouse** n Pension f.
guide (gaid) n **1** Führer m. **2** Leitfaden m. **3** Ratgeber m. vt führen. **Girl Guide** n Pfadfinderin f. **guidebook** n Reiseführer m. **guidedog** n Blindenhund m. **guidance** n Führung, Anleitung f.
guild (gild) n Zunft f.
guillotine (gilə'ti:n) n Guillotine f.
guilt (gilt) n Schuld f. **guilty** adj schuldig, schuldhaft.
guinea ('gini) n Guinee f. **guinea pig** n **1** zool Meerschweinchen neu. **2** Versuchskaninchen neu.
guitar (gi'tɑ:) n Gitarre f.
gulf (gʌlf) n **1** Golf m. **2** Abgrund m. **3** Kluft f.
gull (gʌl) n Möwe f.
gullet ('gʌlit) n Speiseröhre f. Schlund m.
gulp (gʌlp) n Schluck m. vt hinunterschlingen. vi schlucken.

gum[1] (gʌm) n Gummi neu. vt (an)kleben.
gum[2] (gʌm) n anat Zahnfleisch neu.
gun (gʌn) n **1** Gewehr, Geschütz neu. **2** Flinte f. **3** Revolver m. **gunboat** n Kanonenboot neu. **gunman** n bewaffneter Verbrecher m. **gunpowder** n Schießpulver neu. **gunrunning** n Waffenschmuggel m. **gunshot** n **1** Schuß m. **2** Schußweite f.
gurgle ('gə:gəl) vi glucksen, gurgeln.
gush (gʌʃ) vi **1** sich ergießen. **2** strömen. n **1** Erguß m. **2** Flut f.
gust (gʌst) n Windstoß m.
gut (gʌt) n **1** Darm m. **2** pl Eingeweide pl. **3** pl sl Mut f. vt ausweiden.
gutter ('gʌtə) n **1** Rinnstein m. **2** Dachrinne f. **3** Gosse f.
guy[1] (gai) n sl Kerl, Bursche m.
guy[2] (gai) n Spannschnur f.
gymnasium (dʒim'neiziəm) n Turnhalle f. **gymnast** n Leichtathlet, Turner m. **gymnastic** adj gymnastisch, Turn—. **gymnastics** n pl Turnen neu. Gymnastik f.
gynaecology (gaini'kɔlədʒi) n Gynäkologie f. **gynaecologist** n Frauenarzt, Gynakologe m.
gypsum ('dʒipsəm) n Gips m.
gyrate (dʒai'reit) vi wirbeln, kreisen.

H

haberdasher ('hæbədæʃə) n Kurzwarenhändler m. **haberdashery** n Kurzwarenhandlung f.
habit ('hæbit) n Gewohnheit f. **get into the habit of** sich angewöhnen. **habitual** adj gewohnt, üblich.
habitable ('hæbitəbəl) adj bewohnbar.
hack[1] (hæk) vt (zer)hacken. **hacksaw** n Metallsäge f.
hack[2] (hæk) n **1** Mietpferd neu. **2** Gaul m. **3** Lohnschreiber m.
hackneyed ('hæknid) adj abgedroschen.
had (hæd) v see **have.**
haddock ('hædək) n Schellfisch m.
haemorrhage ('heməridʒ) n Blutung f.
hag (hæg) n häßliches altes Weib neu.
haggard ('hægəd) adj **1** verstört. **2** hager.
haggle ('hægl) vi streiten, feilschen.
Hague, The (heig) n Den Haag m.
hail[1] (heil) n Hagel m. vi hageln. **hailstone** n Hagelkorn neu. **hailstorm** n Hagelschauer m.
hail[2] (heil) vt (be)grüßen, zurufen.
hair (hɛə) n Haar neu. **hairbrush** n Haarbürste

203

f. **haircut** n Haarschnitt m. **hairdresser** n Friseur m. Friseuse f. **hairpin** n Haarnadel f. **hair-raising** adj haarsträubend. **hairstyle** n Haartracht f.

half (hɑːf) n, pl **halves** Hälfte f. adj,adv halb.

half-dozen n halbes Dutzend neu.

half-and-half adj,adv halb und halb.

half-back n sport Läufer m.

half-breed n also **half-caste** Mischling m.

half-brother n Halbbruder m.

half-hearted adj lau, zaghaft.

half-hour n halbe Stunde f.

half-mast n Halbmast m. **at half-mast** halbmast.

half-sister n Halbschwester f.

half-term n Semesterhalbzeit f.

half-time n Halbzeit f.

halfway (hɑːfˈwei) adj,adv auf halbem Wege, halbwegs.

halfwit (ˈhɑːfwit) n Schwachkopf, Idiot m.

halibut (ˈhælibət) n Heilbutt m.

hall (hɔːl) n **1** Halle f. **2** Saal m. **3** Diele f. Flur m.

hallelujah (hæliˈluːjə) interj halleluja!

hallmark (ˈhɔːlmɑːk) n **1** Feingehaltsstempel m. **2** Kennzeichen neu.

hallo (həˈlou) interj **1** guten Tag! grüß Gott! **2** hallo!

hallowed (ˈhæloud) adj geheiligt.

Hallowe'en (hælouˈiːn) n Abend vor Allerheiligen m.

hallucination (həluːsiˈneiʃən) n Halluzination, Sinnestäuschung f.

halo (ˈheilou) n pl **-os** or **-oes** **1** Heiligenschein m. **2** sci Hof m.

halt (hɔːlt) n Halt m. Pause f. vt,vi (an)halten.

halter (ˈhɔːltə) n Halfter neu.

halve (hɑːv) vt halbieren.

ham (hæm) n Schinken m.

hamburger (ˈhæmbɔːgə) n Frikadelle f.

hammer (ˈhæmə) n Hammer m. vt,vi hämmern.

hammock (ˈhæmək) n Hängematte f.

hamper[1] (ˈhæmpə) vt (be)hindern, hemmen.

hamper[2] (ˈhæmpə) n Packkorb m.

hamster (ˈhæmstə) n Hamster m.

hand (hænd) n Hand f. **give** or **lend a hand** behilflich sein. **on the one hand...on the other** einerseits...andererseits. **~vt** übereichen. **hand in** einreichen. **hand on** weitergeben. **hand out** verteilen. **hand over** übergeben.

handbag (ˈhændbæg) n Handtasche f.

handbook (ˈhændbuk) n Handbuch neu.

handbrake (ˈhændbreik) n Handbremse f.

handcart (ˈhændkɑːt) n Handwagen m.

handcuff (ˈhændkʌf) vt Handschellen anlegen. **handcuffs** n pl Handschellen f pl.

handful (ˈhændful) n Handvoll f.

handicap (ˈhændikæp) n **1** Nachteil m. **2** sport Vorgabe f. vt benachteiligen.

handicraft (ˈhændikrɑːft) n Handwerk neu.

handiwork (ˈhændiwɔːk) n **1** Handarbeit f. **2** Werk neu.

handkerchief (ˈhæŋkətʃif) n Taschentuch neu.

handle (ˈhændl) n Griff m. vt **1** anfassen. **2** handhaben. **3** behandeln. **handlebars** n pl Lenkstange f.

handmade (hændˈmeid) adj handgearbeitet, Hand—.

hand-out n **1** Almosen neu. **2** Werbezettel m.

hand-pick vt auslesen, auswählen.

handrail (ˈhændreil) n Geländer neu.

handshake (ˈhændʃeik) n Händedruck m.

handsome (ˈhænsəm) adj **1** hübsch, schön, gut aussehend. **2** beträchtlich.

handstand (ˈhændstænd) n sport Handstand m.

handwriting (ˈhændraitiŋ) n Handschrift f.

handy (ˈhændi) adj **1** handlich, zur Hand. **2** geschickt.

hang* (hæŋ) vt (auf-, ein-)hängen. vi hängen. **hanger** n Kleiderbügel m. **hangman** n Henker m. **hangover** n inf Kater m.

hanker (ˈhæŋkə) vi sich sehnen.

Hanover (ˈhænəvə) n Hannover neu.

haphazard (hæpˈhæzəd) adj zufällig.

happen (ˈhæpən) vi geschehen, sich ereignen, vorkommen, passieren. **happen to do something** etwas zufällig tun.

happy (ˈhæpi) adj **1** glücklich, zufrieden. **2** erfreulich. **happily** adv glücklicherweise. **happiness** n Glück neu.

harass (ˈhærəs) vt belästigen, quälen.

harbour (ˈhɑːbə) n Hafen m. vt beherbergen.

hard (hɑːd) adj **1** hart. **2** schwer. **3** streng. **4** schlecht. adv **1** heftig. **2** mühsam. **3** fleißig. **hardback** n Buch mit steifem Einband or Leineneinband neu. **hardboard** n Hartfaserplatte f. **hard-boiled** adj hartgekocht. **harden** vt (ab)härten, hart machen. vi hart werden. **hard-headed** adj nüchtern, eigensinnig. **hard-hearted** adj hartherzig. **hardship** n Strapaze, Bedrängnis f. **hardware** n Eisenwaren f pl.

hardly (ˈhɑːdli) adv **1** kaum, schwerlich. **2** mit Mühe.

hardy (ˈhɑːdi) adj abgehärtet, zäh.

hare ('hɛə) n Hase m.

haricot ('hærikou) n weiße Bohne f.

hark (ha:k) vi horchen.

harm (ha:m) n Schaden m. vt Leid or Schaden zufügen, schaden. **harmful** adj schädlich.

harmonic (ha:'mɔnik) adj harmonisch. **harmonica** n Mundharmonika f. **harmonize** vt 1 mus harmonisieren. 2 in Einklang bringen. vi in Einklang sein. **harmony** n 1 mus Harmonie f. 2 Einklang m.

harness ('ha:nis) n Geschirr neu. vt anschirren, anspannen.

harp (ha:p) n Harfe f.

harpoon (ha:'pu:n) n Harpune f.

harpsichord ('ha:psikɔ:d) n Spinett neu.

harsh (ha:ʃ) adj 1 rauh, hart. 2 streng.

harvest ('ha:vist) n 1 Ernte f. 2 (Wein)Lese f. vt ernten, einbringen.

has (hæz) v see **have.**

haste (heist) n Eile, Hast f. **hasten** vi eilen, sich beeilen. vt beschleunigen.

hat (hæt) n Hut m.

hatch[1] (hætʃ) vt ausbrüten. vi brüten. n Brut f.

hatch[2] (hætʃ) n Luke, Klapptür f.

hatchet ('hætʃit) n Beil neu.

hate (heit) vt hassen. n Haß m. **hateful** adj verhaßt.

haughty ('hɔ:ti) adj hochmütig.

haul (hɔ:l) vt schleppen, zerren, transportieren. n Fang m.

haunch (hɔ:ntʃ) n Hüfte, Keule f.

haunt (hɔ:nt) vt 1 häufig besuchen. 2 heimsuchen. 3 spuken. n Aufenthalt m.

have* (hæv) vt haben. v aux haben, sein. **have something done** etwas tun lassen. **have to do something** etwas tun müssen.

haven ('heivən) n Hafen, Zufluchtsort m.

haversack ('hævəsæk) n Rucksack m.

havoc ('hævək) n 1 Verwüstung f. 2 Zerstörung f. **cause havoc** große Zerstörungen verursachen.

hawk (hɔ:k) n Habicht, Falke m.

hawthorn ('hɔ:θɔ:n) n Hagedorn m.

hay (hei) n Heu neu. **hayfever** n Heuschnupfen m. **haystack** n Heuschober m. **go haywire** kaputt gehen.

hazard ('hæzəd) n 1 Risiko neu. Gefahr f. 2 Zufall m. vt wagen, riskieren.

haze (heiz) n 1 Dunst m. 2 Unklarheit f.

hazel ('heizəl) n Hasel f. Haselstrauch m. **hazelnut** n Haselnuß f.

he (hi:) pron 3rd pers s er.

head (hed) n 1 Kopf m. Haupt neu. 2 Leiter,

Chef m. 3 Spitze f. vorderes Ende neu. 4 Stück neu. 5 Höhepunkt m. vt führen, vorstehen.

headache ('hedeik) n Kopfweh neu. Kopfschmerzen m pl.

heading ('hediŋ) n Überschrift f.

headlight ('hedlait) n Scheinwerfer m.

headline ('hedlain) n Schlagzeile f.

headlong ('hedlɔŋ) adv kopfüber. adj ungestüm, unbesonnen.

headmaster (hed'ma:stə) n (Schul)Direktor m.

headphones ('hedfouns) n pl Kopfhörer m.

headquarters ('hedkwɔ:təz) n pl 1 Hauptquartier neu. 2 Hauptgeschäftsstelle f.

headscarf ('hedska:f) n Kopftuch neu.

headstrong ('hedstrɔŋ) adj starrköpfig, halsstarrig.

headway ('hedwei) n Fortschritte m pl.

heal (hi:l) vt,vi heilen.

health (helθ) n Gesundheit f. **your health** interj prosit! auf Ihr Wohl! **healthy** adj 1 gesund. 2 kräftig.

heap (hi:p) n 1 Haufen m. 2 inf Menge f. v **heap up** anhäufen.

hear* (hiə) vi,vt hören. **hearing** n 1 Hören neu. 2 Verhör neu. **hearing aid** n Hörgerät neu.

hearse (hə:s) n Leichenwagen m.

heart (ha:t) n 1 Herz neu. 2 Kern m. 3 Mut m. **heart attack** n Herzanfall m. **heartbeat** n Herzschlag, Puls m. **heartbroken** adj untröstlich. **heartless** adj herzlos. **hearty** adj herzhaft, herzlich.

hearth (ha:θ) n Herd m.

heat (hi:t) n 1 Hitze f. 2 Eifer m. 3 sport Runde f. vt heizen. **heater** n Heizapparat m. **heating** n Heizung f. **heatwave** n Hitzewelle f.

heath (hi:θ) n Heide f.

heathen ('hi:ðən) n Heide m. adj heidnisch.

heather ('heðə) n Heidekraut neu. Erika f.

heave (hi:v) vt (hoch)heben. vi sich heben und senken.

heaven ('hevən) n Himmel m. **heavenly** adj himmlisch.

heavy ('hevi) adj 1 schwer, gewichtig. 2 schwerfällig. **heavyweight** n Schwergewicht neu.

Hebrew ('hi:bru:) adj hebräisch. n 1 Hebräer m. 2 (language) Hebräisch neu.

heckle ('hekəl) vt (jemandem) Fangfragen stellen. **heckler** n Zwischenrufer m.

hectare ('hektɛə) n Hektar neu.

hectic ('hektik) adj hektisch, fieberhaft.

hedge (hedʒ) n Hecke f. **hedgehog** n Igel m.

heed (hi:d) vt achten auf.

her (hi:l) *n* **1** Ferse *f.* **2** Absatz *m.*

hefty ('hefti) *adj* kräftig.

height (hait) *n* **1** Höhe *f.* **2** Höhepunkt *m.* **heighten** *vt* **1** erhöhen. **2** verstärken.

heir (εə) *n* Erbe *m.* **heirloom** *n* Erbstück *neu.*

held (held) *v* see **hold.**

helicopter ('helikɔptə) *n* Hubschrauber *m.*

hell (hel) *n* Hölle *f. interj* verdammt!

hello (hə'lou) *interj* **1** guten Tag! grüß Gott! **2** hallo!

helm (helm) *n* Ruder *neu.*

helmet ('helmit) *n* Helm *m.*

help (help) *vt* helfen, unterstützen. *vi* helfen. **help oneself** sich bedienen. ~*n* Hilfe *f.* **helpless** *adj* hilflos.

hem (hem) *n* Saum *m. vt* säumen.

hemisphere ('hemisfiə) *n* Halbkugel, Hemisphäre *f.*

hemp (hemp) *n* Hanf *m.*

hen (hen) *n* **1** Huhn *neu.* **2** Weibchen *neu.*

hence (hens) *adv* **1** hieraus, daher, daraus. **2** von hier.

henna ('henə) *n* Henna *f.*

her (hə:) *pron 3rd pers s* **1** sie. **2** ihr. *poss adj 3rd pers s* ihr.

herald ('herəld) *n* Herold *m. vt* ankündigen.

herb (hə:b) *n* Kraut *neu.*

herd (hə:d) *n* Herde *f. vt* weiden, hüten. **herdsman** *n* Hirt *m.*

here (hiə) *adv* **1** hier. **2** hierher.

hereditary (hi'reditri) *adj* erblich.

heredity (hi'rediti) *n* Vererbung *f.*

heresy ('herəsi) *n* Ketzerei *f.*

heritage ('heritidʒ) *n* **1** Erbschaft *f.* **2** Erbrecht *neu.*

hermit ('hə:mit) *n* Einsiedler *m.*

hero ('hiərou) *n, pl* **heroes** Held *m.* **heroine** *n* Heldin *f.*

heroin ('herouin) *n* Heroin *neu.*

heron ('herən) *n* Reiher *m.*

herring ('heriŋ) *n* Hering *m.*

hers (hə:z) *poss pron 3rd pers s* ihrer, der ihre or ihrige. **herself** *pron 3rd pers s* **1** sich. **2** sich selbst. **3** sie selbst. **by herself** allein, von selbst.

hesitate ('heziteit) *vi* zögern. **hesitation** *n* Zögern, Schwanken *neu.*

hexagon ('heksəgən) *n* Sechseck *neu.*

hibernate ('haibəneit) *vi* überwintern.

hiccup ('hikʌp) *n* Schluckauf *m. vi* den Schluckauf haben.

hide¹ (haid) *vt* **1** verstecken, verbergen. **2** verheimlichen. *vi* sich verbergen.

hide² (haid) *n* Fell *neu.* Haut *f.*

hideous ('hidiəs) *adj* **1** scheußlich, gräßlich. **2** häßlich.

hiding¹ ('haidiŋ) *n* Versteck *neu.* **hiding-place** *n* Schlupfwinkel *m.*

hiding² ('haidiŋ) *n* Prügel *f.*

hierarchy ('haiəra:ki) *n* Hierarchie *f.*

high (hai) *adj* **1** hoch. **2** groß. **3** bedeutend. **4** vornehm. **highly** *adv* **1** in hohem Maße, äußerst, hoch. **2** lobend.

highbrow ('haibrau) *adj inf* intellektuell.

high-fidelity *adj* Hi-Fi.

high frequency *n* Hochfrequenz *f.*

high jump *n* Hochsprung *m.*

highland ('hailnd) *n* Hochland *neu.*

highlight ('hailait) *n* **1** Glänzlicht *neu.* **2** Höhepunkt *m. vt* hervorheben.

highness ('hainis) *n* **His/Her/Your Highness** Seine/Ihre/Eure Hoheit *f.*

highpitched ('haipitʃd) *adj* schrill, hoch.

high-rise *adj* vielstöckig. **high-rise building** *n* Hochhaus *neu.*

high-spirited *adj* übermütig, wagemütig.

highway ('haiwei) *n* Landstraße *f.*

hijack ('haidʒæk) *vt* **1** (be)rauben. **2** (an aeroplane) entführen.

hike (haik) *vi* wandern. *n* Wanderung *f.*

hilarious (hi'lεəriəs) *adj* lustig, fröhlich.

hill (hil) *n* Hügel, Berg *m.* **hillside** *n* Abhang *m.* **hilltop** *n* Bergspitze *f.*

him (him) *pron 3rd pers s* **1** ihn. **2** ihm. **himself** *pron 3rd pers s* **1** sich. **2** sich selbst. **3** er selbst. **by himself** allein, von selbst.

hind (haind) *adj* hinter. **hindleg** *n* Hinterbein *neu.* **hindsight** *n* späte Einsicht, Nachsicht *f.*

hinder ('hində) *vt* (ver)hindern, hemmen.

Hindu ('hindu:) *n* Hindu *m.* **Hinduism** *n* Hinduismus *m.*

hinge (hindʒ) *n* Scharnier *f.* Gelenk *neu. vi* abhängen, ankommen.

hint (hint) *n* Hinweis, Wink *m. vt* andeuten.

hip (hip) *n* Hüfte *f.*

hippopotamus (hipə'potəməs) *n* Nilpferd *neu.*

hire (haiə) *vt* mieten. *n* Miete *f.* **hire car** *n* Mietauto *neu.*

his (hiz) *poss adj 3rd pers s* sein. *poss pron 3rd pers s* seiner, der seine or seinige.

hiss (his) *vi* zischen. *n* Zischen *neu.*

history ('histri) *n* Geschichte *f.* **historian** *n* Historiker *m.* **historical** *adj* geschichtlich, historisch.

hit⁎ (hit) *vt,vi* **1** schlagen. **2** treffen. *n* **1** Treffer *m.* **2** Schlag *m.* **3** *mus* Schlager *m.*

hitch (hitʃ) vt **1** festmachen. **2** rücken. **hitch-hike** vi per Anhalter fahren, trampen.

hive (haiv) n Bienenstock m.

hoard (hɔːd) n Vorrat, Schatz m. vi,vt hamstern, horten.

hoarding ('hɔːdiŋ) n **1** Bauzaun m. **2** Reklamewand f.

hoarse (hɔːs) adj heiser.

hoax (houks) n Täuschung, Fopperei f. vt zum besten haben, anführen.

hobble ('hɔbəl) vi humpeln.

hobby ('hɔbi) n Hobby, Steckenpferd neu.

hock[1] (hɔk) n Sprunggelenk neu.

hock[2] (hɔk) n Rheinwein m.

hockey ('hɔki) n Hockey neu.

hoe (hou) n Haue, Hacke f. vt,vi hacken.

hog (hɔg) n Schwein neu. vt sl an sich reißen.

hoist (hɔist) vt hochziehen. n Aufzug, Kran m. Winde f.

hold[1] (hould) vt **1** (fest)halten. **2** zurückhalten. **3** besitzen. **4** abhalten. **5** fassen, enthalten. **6** vertreten. vi **1** gelten. **2** sich halten. n Griff, Halt m. **holdall** n Reisetasche f. **holder** n **1** Behälter m. **2** Inhaber m.

hold[2] (hould) n Laderaum, Schiffsraum m.

hole (houl) n Loch neu. Höhle f.

holiday ('hɔlidi) n **1** Feiertag m. **2** pl Ferien pl. Urlaub m. **holiday camp** n Ferienlager neu. **holiday-maker** n Urlauber m.

Holland ('hɔlənd) n Holland neu.

hollow ('hɔlou) adj hohl. n Höhle, Aushöhlung f.

holly ('hɔli) n Stechpalme f.

holster ('houlstə) n Pistolenhalfter f.

holy ('houli) adj heilig.

homage ('hɔmidʒ) n Huldigung f.

home (houm) n **1** Heim neu. **2** Heimat f. adv heim, nach Hause. **at home** zu Hause. ~adj **1** einheimisch. **2** häuslich. **homecoming** n Heimkehr f. **homeland** n Heimatland neu. Heimat f. **homesick** adj **be homesick** Heimweh haben. **homework** n Schularbeit f. Schulaufgaben f pl.

homosexual (houmə'sekʃuəl) adj homosexuell. n Homosexuelle(r) m.

honest ('ɔnist) adj ehrlich.

honey ('hʌni) n Honig m. **honeymoon** n Flitterwochen f pl.

honour ('ɔnə) n **1** Ehre, Würde f. **2** Ruf m. **3** Auszeichnung f. **His/Her/Your Honour** Sein/Ihr/Euer Ehrwürden or Gnaden. ~vt **1** (be)ehren, verehren. **honorary** adj Ehren—.

hood (hud) n **1** Kapuze f. **2** mot Verdeck neu.

hoof (huːf) n Huf m.

hook (huk) n Haken m. vt (an-, zu-)haken, fangen.

hooligan ('huːligən) n Rowdy m.

hoop (huːp) n Reifen, Ring m.

hoot (huːt) vi **1** mot hupen. **2** schreien.

Hoover ('huːvə) n Tdmk Staubsauger m. vt (ab)saugen.

hop[1] (hɔp) vi hüpfen, springen. n Hüpfer, Sprung m.

hop[2] (hɔp) n bot Hopfen m.

hope (houp) vt,vi (er)hoffen. n Hoffnung f.

horde (hɔːd) n Horde f.

horizon (hə'raizən) n Horizont m. **horizontal** adj waagerecht, horizontal.

horn (hɔːn) n **1** Horn neu. **2** mot Hupe f.

horoscope ('hɔrəskoup) n Horoskop neu.

horrible ('hɔrəbl) adj **1** schrecklich, entsetzlich. **2** gräßlich.

horrid ('hɔrid) adj gräßlich, scheußlich.

horrify ('hɔrifai) vt entsetzen, erschrecken.

horror ('hɔrə) n **1** Entsetzen neu. **2** Grausen neu. **3** Greuel m.

hors d'oeuvres (ɔː 'dɔːv) n pl Vorspeise f.

horse (hɔːs) n **1** Pferd neu. **2** mil Reiterei f. **on horseback** adv zu Pferde. **horse chestnut** n Roßkastanie f. **horseman** n Reiter m. **horsepower** n Pferdestärke f. **horseracing** n Pferderennen neu. **horseshoe** n Hufeisen neu.

horticulture ('hɔːtikʌltʃə) n Gartenbau m.

hose (houz) n **1** Schlauch m. **2** (lange) Strümpfe f pl.

hosiery ('houziəri) n Strumpfwaren f pl.

hospitable ('hɔspitəbl) adj gastfreundlich.

hospital ('hɔspitl) n Krankenhaus, Spital neu.

hospitality (hɔspi'tæliti) n Gastfreundschaft f.

host[1] (houst) n **1** Gastgeber m. **2** Wirt m.

host[2] (houst) n Menge f.

hostage ('hɔstidʒ) n Geisel m,f.

hostel ('hɔstl) n **1** Herberge f. **2** Wohnheim neu.

hostess ('houstis) n Gastgeberin f.

hostile ('hɔstail) adj feindlich.

hot (hɔt) adj **1** heiß. **2** scharf, pikant. **hotplate** n Kochplatte f. **hot-tempered** adj heißblütig, feurig. **hot-water bottle** n Wärmflasche f.

hotel (hou'tel) n Hotel neu.

hound (haund) n Jagdhund m.

hour (auə) n Stunde f.

house (n haus; v hauz) n Haus neu. vt unterbringen.

houseboat ('hausbout) n Hausboot neu.

housebound ('hausbaund) adj gezwungen, zu Hause zu bleiben.

household ('haushould) *n* Haushalt *m*.
housekeeper ('hauski:pə) *n* Haushälterin *f*.
housemaid ('hausmeid) *n* Hausmädchen *neu*.
House of Commons *n* Abgeordnetenhaus, Unterhaus *neu*.
House of Lords *n* Herrenhaus, Oberhaus *neu*.
houseproud ('hauspraud) *adj* penibel.
housewife ('hauswaif) *n* Hausfrau *f*.
housework ('hauswə:k) *n* Hausarbeit *f*.
housing ('hauziŋ) *n* Unterkunft, Unterbringung *f*.
hover ('hɔvə) *vi* schweben. **hovercraft** *n* Luftkissenfahrzeug *neu*.
how (hau) *adv* wie. **how do you do?** wie geht es (Ihnen)? **how much** wieviel. **however** *adv* wie auch (immer). *conj* dennoch, doch, jedoch, aber.
hub (hʌb) *n* **1** Nabe *f*. **2** Angelpunkt *m*.
huddle ('hʌdl) *vi* sich (zusammen)drängen.
huff (hʌf) *n* üble Laune *f*.
hug (hʌg) *vt* umarmen. *n* Umarmung *f*.
huge (hju:dʒ) *adj* ungeheuer, riesig.
hulk (hʌlk) *n* **1** Schiffsgerippe *f*. **2** unförmige Masse *f*.
hull (hʌl) *n* Schiffsrumpf *m*.
hullo (hə'lou) *interj* **1** guten Tag! grüß Gott! **2** hallo!
hum (hʌm) *vi,vt* summen.
human ('hju:mən) *adj* menschlich. *n* Mensch *m*. **humane** *adj* menschlich, human. **humanism** *n* Humanismus *m*. **human nature** *n* menschliche Natur *f*.
humanity (hju:'mæniti) *n* **1** Menschheit *f*. **2** Menschlichkeit *f*. **humanitarian** *adj* menschenfreundlich. *n* Menschenfreund *m*.
humble ('hʌmbəl) *adj* bescheiden, demütig.
humdrum ('hʌmdrʌm) *adj* eintönig, fad, langweilig. *n* Eintönigkeit *f*.
humid ('hju:mid) *adj* feucht.
humiliate (hju:'milieit) *vt* demütigen.
humility (hju:'militi) *n* Demut, Bescheidenheit *f*.
humour ('hju:mə) *n* **1** Humor *m*. **2** Laune *f*. *vt* willfahren, aufheitern. **humorist** *n* Humorist *m*. **humorous** *adj* komisch, lustig.
hump (hʌmp) *n* Buckel *m*.
hunch (hʌntʃ) *vi* nach vorn rücken. *vt* krümmen. *n inf* Ahnung *f*. Verdacht *m*. **hunchback** *n* Bucklige(r) *m*.
hundred ('hʌndrəd) *adj* hundert. *n* Hundert *neu*. **hundredth** *adj* hundertste. **hundredweight** *n* Zentner *m*.
hung (hʌŋ) *v see* **hang**.
Hungary ('hʌŋgəri) *n* Ungarn *neu*. **Hungarian** *adj* ungarisch. *n* **1** Ungar *m*. **2** (language) Ungarisch *neu*.
hunger ('hʌŋgə) *n* Hunger *m*. *vi* hungern (nach). **hunger-strike** *n* Hungerstreik *m*. **hungry** *adj* hungrig. **be hungry** Hunger haben.
hunt (hʌnt) *vt,vi* jagen. *n* Jagd *f*. **hunting** *n* Jagen *neu*. **huntsman** *n* Jäger, Weidmann *m*.
hurdle ('hə:dl) *n* Hürde *f*.
hurl (hə:l) *vt* schleudern.
hurrah (hu'rɑ:) *interj* hurra!
hurricane ('hʌrikein) *n* Orkan *m*.
hurry ('hʌri) *vi* eilen, sich beeilen. *vt* beschleunigen, antreiben. *n* Eile, Hast *f*. **be in a hurry** Eile *or* es eilig haben.
hurt (hə:t) *vt* **1** verletzen. **2** weh tun. *vi* weh tun. *n* **1** Schmerz *m*. **2** Verletzung *f*.
husband ('hʌzbənd) *n* Ehemann, Mann, Gatte *m*.
hush (hʌʃ) *interj* still! *n* Stille *f*. *v* **hush up** verschweigen.
husk (hʌsk) *n* Hülse, Schale *f*. *vt* schälen.
husky ('hʌski) *adj* heiser.
hussar (hu'zɑ:) *n* Husar *m*.
hustle ('hʌsəl) *vi* eilen. *vt* drängen. *n* Drängen *neu*.
hut (hʌt) *n* Hütte *f*.
hutch (hʌtʃ) *n* **1** Kasten *m*. **2** Verschlag *m*.
hyacinth ('haiəsinθ) *n* Hyazinthe *f*.
hybrid ('haibrid) *n* Mischling *m*. Hybride *f*.
hydraulic (hai'drɔ:lik) *adj* hydraulisch.
hydro-electric *adj* hydroelektrisch.
hydrogen ('haidrədʒən) *n* Wasserstoff *m*.
hyena (hai'i:nə) *n* Hyäne *f*.
hygiene ('haidʒi:n) *n* Hygiene *f*. **hygienic** *adj* hygienisch.
hymn (him) *n* Hymne *f*. Kirchenlied *neu*. **hymnbook** *n* Gesangbuch *neu*.
hyphen ('haifən) *n* Bindestrich *m*.
hypnosis (hip'nousis) *n* Hypnose *f*. **hypnotism** *n* Hypnotismus *m*.
hypochondria (haipə'kɔndriə) *n* Hypochondrie *f*. **hypochondriac** *n* Hypochonder *m*.
hypocrisy (hi'pɔkrəsi) *n* Heuchelei *f*. **hypocrite** *n* Heuchler, Scheinheilige(r) *m*.
hypodermic (haipə'də:mik) *adj* **hypodermic syringe** Spritze *f*.
hypothesis (hai'pɔθəsis) *n pl* **-ses** Hypothese *f*.
hysterectomy (histə'rektəmi) *n* Hysterektomie *f*.
hysteria (his'tiəriə) *n* Hysterie *f*. **hysterical** *adj* hysterisch.

I

I (ai) *pron 1st pers sing* ich.
ice (ais) *n* Eis *neu.* **iceberg** *n* Eisberg *m.* **ice-cream** *n* Eiskrem *f.* (Speise)Eis *neu.* **icerink** *n* Eisbahn *f.* **ice skate** *n* Schlittschuh *m.* **icing** *n* Zuckerguß *m.* **icy** *adj* eisig.
Iceland ('aisland) *n* Island *neu.* **Icelander** *n* Isländer *m.* **Icelandic** (ais'lændik) *adj* isländisch. *n* (language) Isländisch *neu.*
idea (ai'diə) *n* Idee *f.* Begriff, Gedanke *m.*
ideal (ai'diəl) *n* Ideal *neu. adj* ideal, vorbildlich. **idealistic** *adj* idealistisch. **idealize** *vt* idealisieren.
identify (ai'dentifai) *vt* identifizieren. **identification** *n* Identifizierung *f.*
identity (ai'dentiti) *n* **1** Identität, Gleichheit *f.* **2** Persönlichkeit *f.* **identical** *adj* **1** identisch. **2** derselbe. **identical twins** *n pl* eineiige Zwillinge *m pl.* **identity card** *n* (Personal)Ausweis *m.*
ideology (aidi'ɔlədʒi) *n* Ideologie *f.*
idiom ('idiəm) *n* **1** Idiom *neu.* **2** Mundart *f.*
idiosyncrasy (idiə'siŋkrəsi) *n* Eigenart *f.*
idiot ('idiət) *n* Idiot, Schwachsinnige(r) *m.*
idle ('aidl) *adj* **1** müßig. **2** faul. **3** unbenutzt.
idol ('aidl) *n* Idol *neu.* Abgott *m.* **idolatry** *n* Abgötterei *f.*
idyllic (i'dilik) *adj* idyllisch.
if (if) *conj* **1** wenn, falls. **2** ob. **as if** als ob.
igloo ('iglu:) *n* Iglu *m.*
ignite (ig'nait) (vi),vt (sich) entzünden. **ignition** *n* **1** Entzündung *f.* Anzünden *neu.* **2** mot Zündung *f.*
ignorant ('ignərənt) *adj* **1** unwissend, ungebildet. **2** nicht wissend.
ignore (ig'nɔ:) *vt* ignorieren, nicht beachten *or* berücksichtigen.
ill (il) *adj* krank. *adj,adv* übel, schlecht. **ill-bred** *adj* ungezogen, unhöflich, schlecht erzogen. **illness** *n* Krankheit *f.* **ill-treat** *vt* mißhandeln, mißbrauchen. **ill will** *n* Mißgunst *f.*
illegal (i'li:gəl) *adj* ungesetzlich, illegal.
illegible (i'ledʒəbl) *adj* unlesbar.
illegitimate (ili'dʒitimət) *adj* unehelich.
illicit (i'lisit) *adj* gesetzwidrig.
illiterate (i'litərət) *adj* analphabetisch. *n* Analphabet *m.*
illogical (i'lɔdʒikəl) *adj* unlogisch.
illuminate (i'lu:mineit) *vt* beleuchten.
illusion (i'lu:ʒən) *n* Illusion, Täuschung *f.*

illustrate ('iləstreit) *vt* **1** illustrieren. **2** erläutern. **illustration** *n* **1** Illustration *f.* Bild *neu.* **2** Erläuterung *f.* **3** Beispiel *neu.*
illustrious (i'lʌstriəs) *adj* berühmt.
image ('imidʒ) *n* **1** Bild, Abbild *neu.* **2** Sinnbild *neu.* **imagery** *n* Bildersprache *f.*
imagine (i'mædʒin) *vt* sich vorstellen. **imaginary** *adj* imaginär, eingebildet. **imagination** *n* Einbildung(skraft), Phantasie, Vorstellungskraft *f.* **imaginative** *adj* phantasievoll, einfallsreich.
imbalance (im'bæləns) *n* Unausgewogenheit *f.*
imbecile ('imbəsi:l) *n* Schwachsinnige(r) *m.*
imitate ('imiteit) *vt* nachahmen. **imitation** *n* **1** Nachahmung *f.* **2** Nachbildung *f. adj* Kunst—.
immaculate (i'mækjulət) *adj* fleckenlos
immature (imə'tjuə) *adj* unreif.
immediate (i'mi:diət) *adj* unmittelbar, sofortig. **immediately** *adv* sofort, gleich.
immense (i'mens) *adj* gewaltig, ungeheuer.
immerse (i'mə:s) *vt* eintauchen, vertiefen. **immersion** *n* Eintauchen, Vertieftsein *neu.* **immersion heater** *n* Tauchsieder *m.*
immigrate ('imigreit) *vi* einwandern. **immigrant** *n* Einwanderer *m.*
imminent ('iminənt) *adj* bevorstehend.
immobile (i'moubail) *adj* unbeweglich, bewegungslos. **immobilize** *vt* unbeweglich machen.
immoral (i'mɔrəl) *adj* unmoralisch, unsittlich.
immortal (i'mɔ:tl) *adj* unsterblich.
immovable (i'mu:vəbl) *adj* **1** unbeweglich. **2** unerschütterlich.
immune (i'mju:n) *adj* **1** immun. **2** geschützt. **immunize** *vt med* immunisieren, impfen.
imp (imp) *n* **1** Kobold *m.* **2** Spitzbube *m.*
impact ('impækt) *n* **1** Zusammenstoß, Aufprall *m.* **2** Einfluß *m.* Wirkung *f.*
impair (im'pεə) *vt* beeinträchtigen.
impart (im'pa:t) *vt* **1** mitteilen. **2** geben.
impartial (im'pa:ʃəl) *adj* unparteiisch.
impassable (im'pa:səbəl) *adj* unbefahrbar.
impatient (im'peiʃənt) *adj* ungeduldig. **impatience** *n* Ungeduld *f.*
impeach (im'pi:tʃ) *vt* **1** anklagen. **2** zur Rechenschaft ziehen.
impeccable (im'pekəbəl) *adj* **1** sündlos. **2** einwandfrei.
impediment (im'pedimənt) *n* **1** Hindernis *neu.* **2** (of speech) Sprachfehler *m.*
imperative (im'perativ) *adj* **1** erforderlich. **2** befehlend. *n* Befehlsform *f.* Imperativ *m.*

imperfect (im'pə:fikt) adj 1 unvollkommen. 2 mangelhaft. n Imperfekt neu.

imperial (im'piəriəl) adj kaiserlich, Reichs—.

impersonal (im'pə:sənl) adj unpersönlich.

impersonate (im'pə:səneit) vt 1 verkörpern. 2 sich ausgeben als.

impertinent (im'pə:tinənt) adj unverschämt, frech.

impetuous (im'petʃuəs) adj ungestüm.

impetus ('impitəs) n Antrieb, Anstoß m.

impinge (im'pindʒ) vi 1 stoßen. 2 einwirken.

implement ('impləmənt) n Werkzeug, Gerät neu. vt durchführen.

implicate ('impləkeit) vt 1 hineinziehen, verwickeln. 2 implizieren.

implicit (im'plisit) adj implizit, inbegriffen.

implore (im'plɔ:) vt anflehen.

imply (im'plai) vt 1 implizieren, in sich schließen. 2 andeuten, zu verstehen geben. **implication** n 1 Bedeutung f. 2 Folge f.

import (v im'pɔ:t; n 'impɔt) vt einführen, importieren. n 1 Einfuhr f. Import m. 2 pl Einfuhrwaren f pl. 3 Bedeutung f. **importation** n Einfuhr f. Import m.

importance (im'pɔ:tns) n 1 Wichtigkeit f. 2 Bedeutung f. **important** adj 1 wichtig. 2 bedeutend. 3 einflußreich.

impose (im'pouz) vt auferlegen, aufbürden. **impose upon** zu sehr beanspruchen. **imposing** adj imponierend, eindrucksvoll.

impossible (im'posəbl) adj unmöglich.

impostor (im'pɔstə) n Betrüger, Hochstapler m.

impotent ('impətənt) adj 1 unfähig. 2 med impotent.

impound (im'paund) vt beschlagnehmen.

impoverish (im'pɔvəriʃ) vt arm machen.

impress (im'pres) vt 1 beeindrucken, Eindruck machen auf. 2 (ein)drücken, einprägen. **impression** n 1 Eindruck m. 2 Abdruck m. 3 (of a book) Auflage f.

imprint (n 'imprint; v im'print) n 1 Aufdruck m. 2 Eindruck m. vt aufdrücken, einprägen.

imprison (im'prizn) vt einsperren, ins Gefängnis werfen. **imprisonment** n 1 Gefangenschaft f. 2 Gefängnisstrafe f.

improbable (im'prɔbəbl) adj 1 unwahrscheinlich. 2 unglaubhaft.

improper (im'prɔpə) adj 1 unanständig. 2 ungeeignet.

improve (im'pru:v) vt (ver)bessern. vi sich (ver)bessern, besser werden.

improvise ('imprəvaiz) vt improvisieren.

impudent ('impjudənt) adj unverschämt, frech.

impulse ('impʌls) n 1 (An)Trieb, Stoß m. 2 Impuls, Drang m.

impure (im'pjuə) adj unrein, unsauber.

in (in) prep 1 in. 2 an. 3 auf. 4 nach. adv 1 hinein, herein. 2 innen.

inability (inə'biliti) n Unfähigkeit f.

inaccurate (in'ækjurət) adj 1 ungenau, unrichtig. 2 fehlerhaft.

inadequate (in'ædikwit) adj unangemessen, unzulänglich, ungenügend.

inadvertent (inəd'və:tnt) adj 1 unachtsam. 2 unabsichtlich. 3 nachlässig.

inane (i'nein) adj sinnlos, nichtig, geistlos.

inarticulate (inɑ:'tikjulət) adj 1 unartikuliert, undeutlich. 2 sich schlecht ausdrückend.

inasmuch (inəz'mʌtʃ) conj **inasmuch as** (in)sofern (als), da, weil.

inaugurate (i'nɔ:gjureit) vt einweihen.

incapable (in'keipəbəl) adj unfähig.

incendiary (in'sendiəri) n 1 Brandstifter m. 2 Brandbombe f.

incense[1] ('insens) n Weihrauch m.

incense[2] (in'sens) vt in Wut bringen, erzürnen.

incessant (in'sesənt) adj unaufhörlich.

incest ('insest) n Blutschande f. Inzest m.

inch (intʃ) n Zoll m.

incident ('insidənt) n 1 Zwischenfall m. 2 Zufall m. **incidental** adj 1 beiläufig. 2 gelegentlich. 3 zufällig. 4 Neben—.

incite (in'sait) vt aufregen, anstacheln.

incline (in'klain) vi sich neigen, geneigt sein zu. n Hang, Abhang m.

include (in'klu:d) vt einschließen, enthalten.

incoherent (inkou'hiərənt) adj unzusammenhängend.

income ('inkʌm) n Einkommen neu. Einkünfte f pl.

incompatible (inkəm'pætibəl) adj unvereinbar, nicht zusammenpassend.

incompetent (in'kɔmpətənt) adj unfähig.

incomplete (inkəm'pli:t) adj unvollständig.

incomprehensible (inkɔmpri'hensibəl) adj 1 unverständlich. 2 unbegreiflich.

inconceivable (inkən'si:vəbəl) adj unbegreiflich.

incongruous (in'kɔŋgruəs) adj unvereinbar.

inconsiderate (inkən'sidərət) adj rücksichtslos.

inconsistent (inkən'sistənt) adj 1 widersprechend. 2 inkonsequent. 3 unbeständig.

inconvenient (inkən'vi:niənt) adj ungelegen, unbequem, lästig.

incorporate (in'kɔ:pəreit) vt einverleiben, aufnehmen, vereinigen.

incorrect (inkə'rekt) *adj* unrichtig, falsch.
increase (*v* in'kri:s; *n* 'inkri:s) *vt* **1** erhöhen, steigern. **2** vermehren. *vi* **1** sich vermehren. **2** sich vergrößern, zunehmen. *n* **1** Vergrößerung *f*. **2** Zunahme *f*. Wachstum *neu*.
incredible (in'kredəbl) *adj* unglaublich.
incubate ('inkjubeit) *vt* ausbrüten.
incur (in'kə:) *vt* **1** sich zuziehen. **2** herbeiführen. **3** eingehen. **4** (debts) machen.
incurable (in'kjuərəbl) *adj* unheilbar.
indecent (in'di:sənt) *adj* unanständig. **indecency** *n* Unanständigkeit *f*.
indeed (in'di:d) *adv* **1** in der Tat, tatsächlich. **2** zwar. **3** gewiß. *interj* **1** wirklich? **2** so!
indefinite (in'defənit) *adj* unbestimmt.
indemnity (in'demniti) *n* Entschädigung *f*.
indent (in'dent) *vt* **1** auszacken, einschneiden. **2** bestellen. *n* **1** Einschnitt *m*. **2** Bestellung *f*.
independent (indi'pendənt) *adj* unabhängig, selbständig. **independence** *n* Unabhängigkeit, Selbständigkeit *f*.
index ('indeks) *n* **1** Zeiger *m*. **2** Inhaltsverzeichnis *neu*. **index finger** *n* Zeigefinger *m*.
India ('indiə) *n* Indien *neu*. **Indian** *adj* **1** indisch. **2** (of America) indianisch. *n* **1** Inder *m*. **2** (of America) Indianer *m*.
indicate ('indikeit) *vt* (an)zeigen, hinweisen. **indicator** *n* **1** Zeiger *m*. **2** *mot* Winker *m*.
indifferent (in'difrənt) *adj* **1** gleichgültig. **2** mittelmäßig.
indigenous (in'didʒənəs) *adj* eingeboren, einheimisch.
indigestion (indi'dʒestʃən) *n* Verdauungsstörung *f*.
indignant (in'dignənt) *adj* entrüstet, empört.
indirect (indi'rekt) *adj* indirekt.
indiscreet (indi'skri:t) *adj* indiskret.
indispensable (indi'spensəbl) *adj* unentbehrlich.
individual (indi'vidʒuəl) *adj* **1** einzeln. **2** persönlich. **3** individuell. *n* Individuum *neu*.
indoctrinate (in'dɔktrineit) *vt* schulen, belehren. **indoctrination** *n* Schulung, Belehrung *f*.
indolent ('indələnt) *adj* lässig, träge.
Indonesia (ində'ni:ziə) *n* Indonesien *neu*. **Indonesian** *adj* indonesisch. *n* Indonesier *m*.
indoor ('indɔ:) *adj* **1** Innen—, Haus—, häuslich. **2** *sport* Hallen—. **indoors** *adv* innen, im Hause, drinnen.
induce (in'dju:s) *vt* **1** dazu bringen, bewegen. **2** herbeiführen.
indulge (in'dʌldʒ) *vt* **1** sich hingeben, nachgeben. **2** schwelgen. **3** verwöhnen. *vi* sich hingeben.
industry ('indəstri) *n* **1** Industrie *f*. **2** Fleiß *m*. **industrial** *adj* industriell, gewerblich. **industrialisation** *n* Industrialisierung *f*. **industrious** *adj* fleißig, arbeitsam.
inefficient (ini'fiʃənt) *adj* **1** unwirksam. **2** unwirtschaftlich. **3** untüchtig.
inept (i'nept) *adj* **1** unpassend. **2** ungeschickt.
inequality (ini'kwɔliti) *n* Ungleichheit *f*.
inert (i'nə:t) *adj* **1** träge. **2** *sci* wirkungslos. **inertia** *n* Trägheit, Untätigkeit *f*.
inevitable (in'evitəbl) *adj* unvermeidlich.
inexpensive (inik'spensiv) *adj* preiswert, billig.
inexperienced (inik'spiəriənst) *adj* unerfahren.
infallible (in'fæləbl) *adj* unfehlbar.
infamous ('infəməs) *adj* berüchtigt, ehrlos.
infancy ('infənsi) *n* (frühe) Kindheit *f*.
infant ('infənt) *n* (Klein)Kind *neu*.
infantry ('infəntri) *n* Infanterie *f*.
infatuate (in'fætʃueit) *vt* verblenden, betören. **be infatuated with** verliebt *or* vernarrt sein in. **infatuation** *n* Verblendung *f*.
infect (in'fekt) *vt* infizieren, anstecken. **infection** *n* Ansteckung, Infektion *f*. **infectious** *adj* ansteckend.
infer (in'fə:) *vt* folgern, schließen.
inferior (in'fiəriə) *adj* **1** minderwertig. **2** niedriger. **3** untergeordnet. **inferiority** *n* Minderwertigkeit *nf*. **inferiority complex** *n* Minderwertigkeitskomplex *m*.
infernal (in'fə:nl) *adj* teuflisch, höllisch.
infest (in'fest) *vt* **1** (in Schwärmen) überlaufen, überschwemmen. **2** heimsuchen, plagen.
infidelity (infi'deliti) *n* Untreue *f*.
infiltrate ('infiltreit) *vt* durchsickern lassen, infiltrieren. *vi* eindringen.
infinite ('infinit) *adj* unendlich. **infinity** *n* Unendlichkeit *f*.
infinitive (in'finitiv) *n* Infinitiv *m*.
infirm (in'fə:m) *adj* schwach, gebrechlich.
inflame (in'fleim) *vt* **1** *med* entzünden. **2** entflammen, erregen.
inflammable (in'flæməbl) *adj* **1** (leicht) entzündlich. **2** feuergefährlich.
inflate (in'fleit) *vt* aufblasen, aufpumpen. **inflation** *n* Inflation *f*.
inflection (in'flekʃən) *n* **1** *gram* Flexion, Abwandlung *f*. **2** Modulation *f*.
inflict (in'flikt) *vt* **1** zufügen. **2** auferlegen.
influence ('influəns) *n* **1** Einfluß *m*. **2** Wirkung *f*.
influenza (influ'enzə) *n* Grippe *f*.

influx ('inflʌks) n 1 Zustrom m. 2 Einfließen neu.

inform (in'fɔːm) vt informieren, mitteilen.

informal (in'fɔːməl) adj 1 zwanglos, nicht formell. 2 ungezwungen. **informality** n Ungezwungenheit, Zwanglosigkeit f.

information (infə'meiʃən) n 1 Auskunft f. 2 Information, Nachricht f.

infringe (in'frindʒ) vt,vi verletzen, übertreten.

infuriate (in'fjuərieit) vt rasend machen, aufbringen.

ingenious (in'dʒiːniəs) adj geistreich, erfinderisch, originell.

ingredient (in'griːdiənt) n Bestandteil m. Zutat f.

inhabit (in'hæbit) vt bewohnen. **inhabitant** n 1 Einwohner m. 2 Bewohner m.

inhale (in'heil) vt einatmen.

inherent (in'hiərənt) adj 1 innewohnend. 2 angeboren.

inherit (in'herit) vt erben. **inheritance** n Erbschaft f.

inhibit (in'hibit) vt 1 hemmen. 2 hindern. **inhibition** n 1 Hemmung f. 2 (Be)Hinderung f.

inhospitable (in'hɔspitəbəl) adj 1 nicht gastfreundlich. 2 ungastlich.

inhuman (in'hjuːmən) adj unmenschlich.

iniquity (i'nikwiti) n 1 Ungerechtigkeit f. 2 Schlechtigkeit f. 3 Schandtat f.

initial (i'niʃəl) adj ursprünglich, anfänglich. n Anfangsbuchstabe m.

initiate (i'niʃieit) vt einweihen. vt,vi anfangen, beginnen. vi die Initiative ergreifen.

initiative (i'niʃətiv) n Initiative f.

inject (in'dʒekt) vt 1 einspritzen. 2 ausspritzen. **injection** n 1 Einspritzung f. 2 med Injektion, Spritze f.

injure ('indʒə) vt 1 beschädigen. 2 verletzen. 3 schaden. 4 beleidigen. **injury** n 1 Verletzung f. 2 Unrecht neu. 3 Beleidigung f.

injustice (in'dʒʌstis) n Ungerechtigkeit f.

ink (iŋk) n 1 Tinte f. 2 Druckerschwärze f.

inkling ('iŋkliŋ) n Andeutung, Ahnung f.

inland ('inlənd) adj inländisch, Binnen—. n Binnenland neu. adv 1 landeinwärts. 2 im Inland. **Inland Revenue** n 1 Steuereinnahmen f pl. 2 (Einkommens)Steuerbehörde f.

inmate ('inmeit) n 1 Insasse m. 2 Mitbewohner m.

inn (in) n Wirtshaus, Gasthaus neu.

innate (i'neit) adj angeboren.

inner ('inə) adj inner, Innen—, innerlich.

innocent ('inəsənt) adj 1 unschuldig. 2 harmlos.

3 einfältig. **innocence** n 1 Unschuld f. 2 Harmlosigkeit f. 3 Einfalt f.

innocuous (i'nɔkjuəs) adj harmlos, unschädlich.

innovation (inə'veiʃən) n Neuerung f.

innuendo (inju'endou) n Anspielung f.

innumerable (i'njuːmərəbəl) adj unzählbar, zahllos.

inoculate (i'nɔkjuleit) vt (ein)impfen. **inoculation** n (Ein)Impfung f.

inquest ('inkwest) n gerichtliche Untersuchung f.

inquire (in'kwaiə) vi (nach)fragen, sich erkundigen. **inquiry** n 1 Nachfrage, Erkundigung f. 2 Untersuchung f. 3 pl Auskünfte f pl.

inquisition (inkwi'ziʃən) n 1 Untersuchung f. 2 Inquisition f.

inquisitive (in'kwizitiv) adj 1 neugierig. 2 wißbegierig. **inquisitiveness** n 1 Neugier f. 2 Wißbegierde f.

insane (in'sein) adj 1 wahnsinnig. 2 verrückt. **insanity** n 1 Wahnsinn m. 2 Verrücktheit f.

insatiable (in'seiʃəbəl) adj unersättlich.

inscribe (in'skraib) vt 1 einschreiben. 2 beschriften. 3 eintragen. **inscription** n 1 Inschrift f. 2 Eintragung f.

insect ('insekt) n Insekt neu. **insecticide** n Insektengift neu.

insecure (insi'kjuə) adj unsicher. **insecurity** n Unsicherheit f.

inseminate (in'semineit) vt 1 befruchten. 2 einpflanzen. **insemination** n Befruchtung f.

insensitive (in'sensitiv) adj unempfindlich.

inseparable (in'sepərəbəl) adj untrennbar.

insert (in'səːt) vt 1 einsetzen. 2 (a coin, etc.) einwerfen. 3 (an advertisement, etc.) aufgeben. **insertion** n 1 Einsetzung f. 2 Einwurf m. 3 Inserat neu.

inside (in'said) n Innere neu. Innenseite f. adj inner, Innen—. adv 1 drinnen. 2 hinein, herein. prep innerhalb.

insidious (in'sidiəs) adj heimtückisch.

insight (in'sait) n Einsicht f.

insignificant (insig'nifikənt) adj 1 unbedeutend. 2 bedeutungslos.

insincere (insin'siə) adj unaufrichtig. **insincerity** n Unaufrichtigkeit f.

insinuate (in'sinjueit) vt 1 anspielen auf. 2 unbemerkt hineinbringen. 3 zu verstehen geben. 4 sich einschmeicheln. **insinuation** n 1 Andeutung f. 2 Einschmeichelung f.

insist (in'sist) vi bestehen. **insistence** n Bestehen neu.

insolent ('insələnt) *adj* unverschämt, frech. **insolence** *n* Unverschämtheit, Frechheit *f*.

insomnia (in'sɔmniə) *n* Schlaflosigkeit *f*.

inspect (in'spekt) *vt* 1 untersuchen. 2 inspizieren, besichtigen. **inspection** *n* 1 Untersuchung *f*. 2 Inspektion, Besichtigung *f*.

inspire (in'spaiə) *vt,vi* 1 inspirieren, eingeben, begeistern. 2 einatmen. **inspiration** *n* 1 Eingebung, Begeisterung *f*. 2 Einatmung *f*. **inspiring** *adj* begeisternd, belebend.

instability (instə'biliti) *n* Unbeständigkeit *f*.

install (in'stɔ:l) *vt* 1 einsetzen. 2 installieren, einrichten. **installation** *n* 1 Einsetzung *f*. 2 Installierung, Einrichtung *f*. Montage *f*.

instalment (in'stɔ:lmənt) *n* 1 Rate *f*. 2 (Teil)- Lieferung *f*. **by instalments** *adv* ratenweise.

instance ('instəns) *n* 1 Beispiel *neu*. 2 (besonderer) Fall *m*. 3 Bitte *f*. 4 *law* Instanz *f*. **for instance** zum Beispiel. **instant** *adj* 1 sofortig, augenblicklich. 2 dringend. *n* Augenblick *m*. **instantaneous** *adj* sofortig, augenblicklich. **instantly** *adv* sogleich, sofort.

instead (in'sted) *adv* statt dessen. **instead of** (ən)statt.

instep ('instep) *n* Rist, Spann *m*.

instigate ('instigeit) *vt* anstiften. **instigation** *n* Anstiftung *f*. **instigator** *n* Anstifter *m*.

instil (in'stil) *vt* 1 einträufeln. 2 einflößen. **instillation** *n* 1 Einträufeln *neu*. 2 Einflößung *f*.

instinct ('instiŋkt) *n* (Natur)Trieb, Instinkt *m*. **instinctive** *adj* unwillkürlich, instinktiv.

institute ('institju:t) *vt* einsetzen, einführen, gründen. *n* Institut *neu*. **institution** *n* 1 Institut *neu*. Anstalt *f*. 2 Stiftung *f*. 3 Einführung *f*. 4 Institution, Einrichtung *f*.

instruct (in'strʌkt) *vt* 1 unterrichten. 2 unterweisen. 3 anweisen. **instruction** *n* 1 Unterricht *m*. 2 Unterweisung *f*. 3 Vorschrift, Anordnung. 4 Anweisung *f*. **instructive** *adj* instruktiv, lehrreich.

instrument ('instrumənt) *n* 1 Instrument *neu*. 2 Werkzeug *neu*. 3 Mittel *neu*. **instrumental** *adj* 1 behilflich, förderlich. 2 Instrumental—.

insubordinate (insə'bɔ:dinət) *adj* aufsässig, widersetzlich, ungehorsam. **insubordination** *n* Widersetzlichkeit *f*. Ungehorsam *m*.

insular ('insjulə) *adj* 1 insular, Insel—. 2 beschränkt.

insulate ('insjuleit) *vt* isolieren. **insulation** *n* Isolierung *f*.

insulin ('insjulin) *n* Insulin *neu*.

insult (*v* in'sʌlt; *n* 'insʌlt) *vt* beleidigen, beschimpfen. *n* Beleidigung, Beschimpfung *f*.

insure (in'ʃuə) *vt* versichern. **insurance** *n* Versicherung *f*. *adj* Versicherungs—.

intact (in'tækt) *adj* unberührt, intakt.

intake ('inteik) *n* 1 *tech* Einlaß *m*. 2 (Neu)- Aufnahme *f*.

integral ('intigrəl) *adj* 1 integral, ganz, vollständig. 2 *math* Integral—.

integrate ('intigreit) *vt* 1 ergänzen. 2 integrieren. **integration** *n pol* Integration *f*.

integrity (in'tegriti) *n* 1 Vollständigkeit *f*. 2 Redlichkeit, Integrität *f*.

intellect ('intəlekt) *n* Intellekt, Verstand *m*. **intellectual** *adj* 1 Verstandes—, geistig. 2 intellektuell. *n* Intellektuelle(r) *m*.

intelligent (in'telidʒənt) *adj* 1 intelligent. 2 klug. **intelligence** *n* 1 Intelligenz *f*. 2 Verstand *m*. 3 *pol* (geheimer) Nachrichtendienst *m*. **intelligentsia** *n* Intelligenz, Intelligentsia *f*. **intelligible** *adj* verständlich.

intend (in'tend) *vt* 1 vorhaben, die Absicht haben zu. 2 meinen. 3 bestimmen. **intended** *adj* absichtlich.

intense (in'tens) *adj* 1 intensiv. 2 angespannt. 3 heftig. **intensify** (*vi*),*vt* (sich) verstärken. **intensity** *n* 1 Intensität *f*. 2 Anspannung *f*. 3 Heftigkeit *f*. **intensive** *adj* 1 intensiv, heftig. 2 verstärkend.

intent[1] (in'tent) *n* 1 Absicht *f*. 2 Plan *m*.

intent[2] (in'tent) *adj* 1 versessen. 2 gespannt.

intention (in'tenʃən) *n* 1 Absicht *f*. 2 Zweck *m*. **intentional** *adj* absichtlich.

inter (in'tə:) *vt* beerdigen.

interact (intə'rækt) *vt* sich gegenseitig beeinflussen. **interaction** *n* Wechselwirkung *f*.

intercept (intə'sept) *vt* 1 abfangen. 2 unterbrechen. **interception** *n* 1 Abfangen *neu*. 2 Unterbrechung *f*.

interchange (intə'tʃeindʒ) *vt* austauschen. *vi* abwechseln. *n* 1 Austausch *m*. 2 Abwechslung *f*. **interchangeable** *adj* austauschbar.

intercourse ('intəkɔ:s) *n* Verkehr, Umgang *m*.

interest ('intrəst) *n* 1 Interesse *neu*. Anteilnahme *m*. 2 Beteiligung *f*. 3 Nutzen *m*. 4 *comm* Zins *m*. *vt* 1 interessieren. 2 angehen. **take an interest in** sich interessieren für. **interesting** *adj* interessant.

interfere (intə'fiə) *vi* 1 sich einmischen. 2 stören. **interference** *n* 1 Einmischung *f*. 2 Störung *f*. 3 Dazwischentreten *neu*.

interim ('intərim) *n* Interim *neu*. Zwischenzeit *f*. *adj* vorläufig, Interims—.

213

interior (in'tiəriə) *adj* inner, Innen—, innerlich. *n* **1** Innere *neu.* **2** Binnenland *neu.*

interjection (intə'dʒekʃṇ) *n* Ausruf, Einwurf *m.* Interjektion *f.*

interlude ('intəlu:d) *n* Zwischenspiel *neu.*

intermediate (intə'mi:diət) *adj* **1** dazwischenliegend. **2** Mittel—, Zwischen—. **intermediary** *adj* **1** dazwischen befindlich. **2** vermittelnd. *n* Vermittler *m.*

interminable (in'tə:minəbəl) *adj* endlos, unendlich.

intermission (intə'miʃən) *n* **1** Aussetzen *neu.* **2** Unterbrechung *f.* **3** Pause *f.*

intermittent (intə'mitṇt) *adj* aussetzend, mit Unterbrechungen.

intern (in'tə:n) *vt* internieren. **internment** *n* Internierung *f.*

internal (in'tə:nl) *adj* **1** inner(lich). **2** inländisch. **internal-combustion engine** *n* Verbrennungsmotor *m.*

international (intə'næʃṇl) *adj* international. *n sport* internationaler Spieler *m.*

interpose (intə'pouz) *vt* **1** einlegen. **2** einwerfen. *vi* **1** dazwischenstellen. **2** vermitteln.

interpret (in'tə:prit) *vt* **1** interpretieren, auslegen, erklären. **2** dolmetschen. **3** darstellen. **interpretation** *n* **1** Interpretation, Auslegung, Erklärung *f.* **2** Darstellung *f.* **interpreter** *n* Dolmetscher *m.*

interrogate (in'terəgeit) *vt* **1** befragen. **2** verhören. **interrogation** *n* **1** Befragen *neu.* **2** Verhör *neu.*

interrogative (intə'rɔgətiv) *adj* fragend, Frage—.

interrupt (intə'rʌpt) *vt* unterbrechen. **interruption** *n* Unterbrechung *f.*

intersect (intə'sekt) *vt* durchschneiden. *vi* (sich) schneiden. **intersection** *n* **1** Durchschnitt *m.* **2** Schnittpunkt *m.* **3** *mot* Kreuzung *f.*

interval ('intəvəl) *n* **1** Zwischenraum *m.* **2** Pause *f.* **3** *mus* Intervall *neu.*

intervene (intə'vi:n) *vi* **1** dazwischenkommen. **2** dazwischenliegen. **3** intervenieren. **intervention** *n* **1** Dazwischenkommen *neu.* **2** Intervention *f.*

interview ('intəvju:) *n* **1** Unterredung *f.* **2** Interview *neu. vt* interviewen. **interviewer** *n* Interviewer *m.*

intestine (in'testin) *n* **1** Darm *m.* **2** *pl* Eingeweide *neu pl.*

intimate[1] ('intimit) *adj* **1** vertraut, intim. **2** innig. **intimacy** *n* Vertraulichkeit, Intimität *f.*

intimate[2] ('intimit) *vt* **1** andeuten. **2** zu verstehen geben.

intimidate (in'timideit) *vt* einschüchtern. **intimidation** *n* Einschüchterung *f.*

into ('intə; *stressed* 'intu:) *prep* in, in...hinein.

intolerable (in'tɔlərəbəl) *adj* unerträglich. **intolerant** *adj* intolerant, unduldsam. **intolerance** *n* Intoleranz, Unduldsamkeit *f.*

intonation (intə'neiʃən) *n* **1** Anstimmung *f.* **2** Tonfall *m.* **3** *mus* Tongebung *f.*

intoxicate (in'tɔksikeit) *vt* berauschen. **intoxication** *n* **1** Berauschung *f.* **2** Rausch *m.*

intransitive (in'trænsitiv) *adj gram* intransitiv.

intricate ('intrikət) *adj* **1** kompliziert. **2** schwierig. **intricacy** *n* **1** Kompliziertheit *f.* **2** Schwierigkeit *f.*

intrigue (in'tri:g) *n* **1** Intrige *f.* **2** (Liebes-) Verhältnis *neu. vi* intrigieren. *vt* neugierig machen. **intriguing** *adj* interessant, faszinierend.

intrinsic (in'trinsik) *adj* **1** innerlich. **2** wahr, eigentlich, wesentlich.

introduce (intrə'dju:s) *vt* **1** einführen, einleiten. **2** (a person) vorstellen. **introduction** *n* **1** Einführung, Einleitung *f.* **2** Vorstellung *f.* **introductory** *adj* einführend, einleitend.

introspective (intrə'spektiv) *adj* beschaulich, nach innen gekehrt, introspektiv.

introvert ('intrəvə:t) *vt* einwärts kehren. *n* introvertierter Mensch *m.*

intrude (in'tru:d) *vt* einzwängen. *vi* **1** sich eindrängen. **2** stören. **intruder** *n* Eindringling *m.* **intrusion** *n* Eindringen *neu.*

intuition (intju'iʃən) *n* Intuition *f.* **intuitive** *adj* intuitiv.

inundate ('inʌndeit) *vt* überschwemmen. **inundation** *n* Überschwemmung *f.*

invade (in'veid) *vt* **1** einfallen in, eindringen in. **2** befallen. **invasion** *n* Einfall *m.* Invasion *f.*

invalid[1] ('invəli:d) *n* **1** Kranke(r) *m.* **2** Invalide *m.*

invalid[2] (in'vælid) *adj* ungültig. **invalidate** *vt* ungültig machen.

invaluable (in'væljubəl) *adj* unschätzbar.

invariable (in'veəriəbəl) *adj* unveränderlich. **invariably** *adv* immer, stets.

invent (in'vent) *vt* **1** erfinden. **2** erdichten. **invention** *n* **1** Erfindung *f.* **2** Erdichtung *f.* **inventive** *adj* erfinderisch. **inventor** *n* Erfinder *m.*

inventory ('invəntəri) *n* **1** Inventar *neu.* **2** *comm* Inventur *f.*

invert (in'və:t) vt umkehren. **inverted commas** Anführungszeichen neu pl.

invertebrate (in'və:tabreit) adj 1 wirbellos. 2 rückgratlos. n wirbelloses Tier neu.

invest (in'vest) vt 1 comm anlegen, investieren. 2 bekleiden. **invest in** inf kaufen. **investor** n Geldanleger m. **investment** n Kapitalanlage f.

investigate (in'vestigeit) vt erforschen, untersuchen. **investigation** n Untersuchung f.

invincible (in'vinsəbəl) adj unüberwindlich.

invisible (in'vizəbəl) adj unsichtbar.

invite (in'vait) vt 1 einladen. 2 anlocken. **invitation** n Einladung f.

invoice ('invois) n Faktura, Rechnung f.

invoke (in'vouk) vt 1 anrufen. 2 (a spirit) beschwören. **invocation** n Anrufung, Beschwörung f.

involve (in'vɔlv) vt verwickeln, hineinziehen. **involvement** n 1 Verwicklung f. 2 Schwierigkeit f.

inward ('inwəd) adj 1 innerlich. 2 nach innen gehend. **inwards** adv einwärts, nach innen.

iodine ('aiədi:n) n Jod nou.

Iran (i'ra:n) n Iran m. **Iranian** adj iranisch. n Iranier m.

Iraq (i'ra:k) n Irak m. **Iraqi** adj irakisch. n Iraker m.

Ireland ('aiələnd) n Irland neu. **Irish** adj irisch. **Irishman** n Ire, Irländer m. **Irishwoman** n Irin, Irländerin f.

iris ('airis) n 1 anat Iris f. 2 bot Schwertlilie f.

iron ('aiən) n 1 Eisen neu. 2 dom Bügeleisen neu. adj eisern, Eisen—. vt bügeln. **ironing board** n Bügelbrett neu. **ironmonger** n Eisenwarenhändler m.

Iron Curtain n Eiserner Vorhang m.

irony ('aiərəni) n Ironie f. **ironic** adj ironisch, spöttisch.

irrational (i'ræʃənl) adj irrational, unvernünftig. **irrationality** n Unvernunft f.

irregular (i'regjulə) adj unregelmäßig. **irregularity** n Unregelmäßigkeit f.

irrelevant (i'reləvənt) adj 1 irrelevant, nicht zur Sache gehörig. 2 belanglos. **irrelevance** n Belanglosigkeit f.

irresistible (iri'zistəbəl) adj unwiderstehlich.

irrespective (iri'spektiv) adj **irrespective of** ohne Rücksicht auf, unabhängig von.

irresponsible (iri'spɔnsəbəl) adj verantwortungslos. **irresponsibility** n Verantwortungslosigkeit f.

irrevocable (i'revəkəbəl) adj unwiderruflich.

irrigate ('irigeit) vt bewässern. **irrigation** n Bewässerung f.

irritate ('iriteit) vt reizen. **irritable** adj reizbar. **irritating** adj aufreizend, ärgerlich.

is (iz) v see **be.**

Islam ('izla:m) n Islam m. **Islamic** adj islamisch.

island ('ailənd) n Insel f. **islander** n Inselbewohner m.

isle (ail) n Insel f.

isolate ('aisəleit) vt 1 absondern. 2 isolieren. **isolated** adj 1 abgesondert. 2 abgeschieden, isoliert. **isolation** n 1 Absonderung f. 2 Isolierung f.

Israel ('izreiəl) n Israel neu. **Israeli** adj israelisch. n Israeli m.

issue ('iʃu:) n 1 Herauskommen, Herausgeben neu. 2 Ausgabe f. 3 Nummer f. 4 Ergebnis neu. 5 Streitfrage f. vi herauskommen. vt 1 aussenden. 2 emittieren. 3 herausgeben.

isthmus ('isməs) n Landenge f. Isthmus m.

it (it) pron 3rd pers s 1 er m. sie f. es neu. 2 ihn m. sie f. es neu. 3 ihm m,neu. ihr f.

italic (i'tælik) adj kursiv. **italics** n pl Kursivdruck m.

Italy ('itəli) n Italien neu. **Italian** adj italienisch. n 1 Italiener m. 2 (language) Italienisch neu.

itch (itʃ) n Jucken neu. Krätze f. vi jucken. **itchy** adj juckend, krätzig.

item ('aitəm) n 1 Einzelheit f. 2 (Zeitungs)Notiz f. 3 (Rechnungs)Posten m.

itinerary (ai'tinərəri) n 1 Reiseroute f. 2 Reisebericht m. **itinerant** adj 1 (herum)-reisend. 2 Wander—, Reise—.

its (its) poss adj 3rd pers s sein m. neu. ihr f. **itself** pron 3rd pers s 1 selbst. 2 sich. 3 sich selbst. **by itself** allein, von selbst.

ivory ('aivəri) n Elfenbein neu. adj Elfenbein—.

ivy ('aivi) n Efeu m.

J

jab (dʒæb) n 1 Stich m. 2 inf med Spritze f. vt stechen.

jack (dʒæk) n 1 mot Wagenheber m. 2 game Bube m. 3 naut Bugflagge f. vt heben.

jackdaw ('dʒækdɔ:) n Dohle f.

jacket ('dʒækit) n 1 Jacke f. 2 (Schutz)-Umschlag m.

jackpot ('dʒækpɔt) n game Jackpot m.

jade (dʒeid) n Jade, Nephrit m.

jaded ('dʒeidid) adj abgehetzt, ermüdet.

jagged ('dʒægid) adj zackig.

jaguar ('dʒægjuə) n Jaguar m.

jail (dʒeil) n Gefängnis neu. vt ins Gefängnis bringen, einsperren. **jailer** n Gefängniswärter m.

jam¹ (dʒæm) vt **1** (fest)klemmen. **2** versperren. vi sich (ver-, ein-)klemmen. n Gedränge neu.

jam² (dʒæm) n Marmelade f. **jam-jar** n Marmeladenglas neu.

Jamaica (dʒə'meikə) n Jamaika neu. **Jamaican** adj jamaikisch. n Jamaiker m.

January ('dʒænjuəri) n Januar m.

Japan (dʒə'pæn) n Japan neu. **Japanese** (dʒæpə'niːz) adj japanisch. n. **1** Japaner m. **2** (language) Japanisch neu.

jar¹ (dʒɑ:) n **1** Glas neu. **2** Krug m.

jar² (dʒɑ:) n Knarren neu. vi knarren.

jargon ('dʒɑːgən) n Jargon m. Fachsprache f.

jasmine ('dʒæzmin) n Jasmin m.

jaundice ('dʒɔːndis) n med Gelbsucht f. **jaundiced** adj **1** gelbsüchtig. **2** neidisch.

jaunt (dʒɔːnt) n Ausflug m. **jaunty** adj flott, munter.

javelin ('dʒævlin) n **1** Wurfspieß m. **2** sport Speer m.

jaw (dʒɔː) n **1** Kiefer m. **2** pl Rachen m. vi sl schwatzen. **jawbone** n Kieferknochen m.

jazz (dʒæz) n Jazz m. v **jazz up** sl Leben bringen in, aufmöbeln. **jazzy** adj inf grell, schreiend.

jealous ('dʒeləs) adj eifersüchtig, neidisch. **jealousy** n Eifersucht f. Neid m.

jeans (dʒiːnz) n pl Jeans pl.

jeep (dʒiːp) n Jeep m.

jeer (dʒiə) vi höhnen, spotten. vt verhöhnen. n Spott m. **jeering** adj spöttisch, höhnisch.

jelly ('dʒeli) n Gelee neu. **jellyfish** n Qualle f.

jeopardize ('dʒepədaiz) vt gefährden. **jeopardy** n Gefahr f.

jerk (dʒɜːk) vt rucken. vi ziehen, schleudern. n **1** Ruck, plötzlicher Stoß m. **jerky** adj **1** ruckartig. **2** holprig.

jersey ('dʒɜːzi) n (Woll)Pullover m.

Jersey ('dʒɜːzi) n (Insel) Jersey neu.

jest (dʒest) n Scherz, Spaß, Witz m. vi scherzen. **jester** n (Hof)Narr m.

Jesus ('dʒiːzəs) n Jesus m.

jet (dʒet) n **1** (Wasser-, Gas-)Strahl m. **2** Düse f. **jet-plane** n Düsenflugzeug neu.

jetty ('dʒeti) n **1** Hafendamm m. **2** Landungsbrücke f.

Jew (dʒuː) n Jude m. **jewish** adj jüdisch. **Jewry** n Judentum neu.

jewel ('dʒuːəl) n Juwel neu,m. **jeweller** n Juwelier m. **jewellery** n Schmuck m.

jig (dʒig) n Gigue f. vi Gigue tanzen, (herum)hüpfen.

jiggle ('dʒigəl) (vi),vt (umher)wackeln.

jigsaw ('dʒigsɔː) n Zusammensetzspiel neu.

jilt (dʒilt) vt sitzen lassen.

jingle ('dʒingəl) n **1** Geklingel neu. **2** Wortgeklingel neu. vi,vt klingeln, klimpern.

job (dʒɔb) n **1** Arbeit f. **2** Stelle f. Job m. **3** Sache, Aufgabe f.

jockey ('dʒɔki) n Jockei m.

jodhpurs ('dʒɔdpəz) n pl Reithose f.

jog (dʒɔg) vt (an)stoßen, rütteln. vi (dahin)trotten. n **1** Stoß m. **2** Rütteln neu. **3** Trott m.

join (dʒɔin) vt **1** verbinden. **2** fügen. **3** zusammenbringen, vereinigen. **4** eintreten in, Mitglied werden. vi **1** sich verbinden. **2** angrenzen. **join in** mitmachen, teilnehmen. ~n **1** Verbindung(sstelle) f. **2** Fuge f. **3** Naht f. **joiner** n Tischler m. **joinery** n Tischlerarbeit f. **joint** n **1** Verbindung(sstelle) f. **2** anat Gelenk neu. **3** cul Braten m. **4** sl Lokal neu. Bude f. **5** sl Marihuana-Zigarette f. Joint m. adj **1** verbunden. **2** gemeinsam. vt **1** zusammenfügen. **2** verbinden. **3** mit Gelenken versehen.

joist (dʒɔist) n Querbalken m.

joke (dʒouk) n Scherz, Witz, Spaß m. vi scherzen. **joker** n **1** Spaßvogel m. **2** game Joker m. **practical joke** n Streich m.

jolly ('dʒɔli) adj lustig. adv inf ganz schön.

jolt (dʒoult) vt,vi rütteln. vi holpern. n Rütteln neu.

Jordan ('dʒɔːdn) n Jordanien neu. **Jordanian** adj jordanisch. n Jordanier m.

jostle ('dʒɔsəl) vt anstoßen. vi sich drängen. n (Zusammen)Stoß m. Gedränge neu.

journal ('dʒɜːnl) n **1** Journal neu. **2** Tagebuch neu. **3** Zeitschrift f. **journalism** n Zeitungswesen neu. Journalismus m. **journalist** n Journalist m.

journey ('dʒɜːni) n **1** Reise f. **2** Fahrt f. vi reisen, wandern.

jovial ('dʒouviəl) adj heiter, jovial. **joviality** n Heiterkeit, Jovialität f.

joy (dʒɔi) n Freude f. **joyful** adj **1** freudig. **2** froh. **joyfulness** n Fröhlichkeit f.

jubilee ('dʒuːbiliː) n Jubiläum f.

Judaism ('dʒuːdeiizəm) n Judaismus m.

judge (dʒʌdʒ) n **1** law Richter m. **2** Schiedsrichter m. **3** Beurteiler m. vi **1** urteilen. vt **1** beurteilen. **2** ein Urteil fällen über. **judgment**

n 1 Urteil *neu.* 2 Meinung *f.* 3 Urteilvermögen *neu.*

judicial (dʒuːˈdiʃəl) *adj* 1 Gerichts—, gerichtlich. 2 richterlich. 3 kritisch.

judicious (dʒuːˈdiʃəs) *adj* einsichtsvoll.

judo (ˈdʒuːdou) *n* Judo *neu.*

jug (dʒʌg) *n* Krug *m.* Kanne *f.*

juggernaut (ˈdʒʌgənɔːt) *n inf* Fernlaster *m.*

juggle (ˈdʒʌgəl) *vi,vt* jonglieren, Kunststücke machen. **juggler** *n* Jongleur *m.*

juice (dʒuːs) *n* 1 Saft *m.* 2 *mot sl* Sprit *m.* **juicy** *adj* 1 saftig. 2 *inf* pikant.

jukebox (ˈdʒuːkbɔks) *n* Musikautomat *m.*

July (dʒuˈlai) *n* Juli *m.*

jumble (ˈdʒʌmbəl) *n* Mischmasch *m.* Durcheinander *neu. vt* durcheinanderwerfen. *vi* durcheinandergeraten. **jumble sale** *n* Wohltätigkeitsbasar *m.*

jump (dʒʌmp) *vi* 1 springen, hüpfen. 2 auffahren. *vt* hinwegspringen über. **jump the queue** sich vordrängen. ∼*n* Sprung, Satz *m.*

jumper (ˈdʒʌmpə) *n* Pullover *m.*

junction (ˈdʒʌŋkʃən) *n* 1 Verbindung *f.* 2 Kreuzung *f.* 3 Knotenpunkt *m.*

June (dʒuːn) *n* Juni *m.*

jungle (ˈdʒʌŋgəl) *n* Dschungel *m.*

junior (ˈdʒuːniə) *adj* 1 jünger. 2 Unter—. *n* 1 Jüngere(r) *m.* 2 Junior *m.*

juniper (ˈdʒuːnipə) *n* Wacholder *m*

junk[1] (dʒʌŋk) *n* Altwaren *f pl.* alter Kram *m.*

junk[2] (dʒʌŋk) *n* Dschunke *f.*

junta (dʒʌntə) *n* Junta *f.*

Jupiter (ˈdʒuːpitə) *n* Jupiter *m.*

jurisdiction (dʒuərisˈdikʃən) *n* 1 Rechtsprechung *f.* 2 Gerichtsbarkeit, Zuständigkeit *f.*

jury (ˈdʒuəri) *n* 1 die Geschworenen *pl.* Jury *f.* **juror** *n* Geschworene(r) *m.*

just (dʒʌst) *adj* 1 gerecht. 2 richtig. 3 gehörig. *adv* 1 gerade, eben. 2 genau.

justice (ˈdʒʌstis) *n* 1 Gerechtigkeit *f.* 2 Recht *neu.* 3 Richter *m.*

justify (ˈdʒʌstifai) *vt* rechtfertigen.

jut (dʒʌt) *vi* hervorragen, vorspringen. *n* Vorsprung *m.*

jute (dʒuːt) *n bot* Jute *f.*

juvenile (ˈdʒuːvənail) *adj* jung, jugendlich, Jugend—. **juvenile delinquency** *n* Jugendkriminilität *f.* **juvenility** *n* 1 Jugendlichkeit *f.* 2 Kinderei *f.*

juxtapose (dʒʌkstəˈpouz) *vt* nebeneinanderstellen.

K

kaftan (ˈkæftæn) *n* Kaftan *m.*

kaleidoscope (kəˈlaidəskoup) *n* Kaleidoskop *neu.*

kangaroo (kæŋgəˈruː) *n* Känguruh *neu.*

karate (kəˈrɑːti) *n* Karate *neu.*

kebab (kəˈbæb) *n* Kebab *m.*

keel (kiːl) *n* Kiel *m.* **on an even keel** *n* gleichmäßig, ausgeglichen.

keen (kiːn) *adj* 1 scharf. 2 eifrig. 3 heftig. **keen on** *inf* erpicht auf, scharf auf.

keep* (kiːp) *vt* 1 halten. 2 unterhalten. 3 (auf)bewahren. 4 (accounts. etc.) führen. *vi* sich halten. *n* 1 Unterhalt *m.* 2 Bergfried *m.* **keeper** *n* Wärter *m.* **keepsake** *n* Andenken *neu.*

keg (keg) *n* Fäßchen *neu.*

kennel (ˈkenl) *n* 1 Hundehütte *f.* 2 *pl* Hundezwinger *m.*

Kenya (ˈkenjə) *n* Kenya *f.* **Kenyan** *adj* Kenianisch. *n* Kenianer *m.*

kept (kept) *v see* **keep.**

kerb (kəːb) *n* Strassenkante *f.*

kernel (ˈkəːnl) *n* 1 Kern *m.* 2 Korn *neu.*

kettle (ˈketl) *n* Kessel *m.* **kettledrum** *n* (Kessel)Pauke *f.*

key (kiː) *n* 1 Schlüssel *m.* 2 Taste *f.* 3 *mus* Tonart *f.* **keyboard** *n* Tastatur *f.*

khaki (ˈkɑːki) *n* Khaki *neu. adj* khakifarben.

kibbutz (kiˈbuts) *n* Kibbuz *m.*

kick (kik) *vt* mit dem Fuß stoßen *or* treten. *vi* 1 ausschlagen. 2 (zurück)stoßen. **kick off** anstoßen. **kick-off** *n* Anstoß *m.* **kick one's heels** *inf* wartend herumstehen. **kick the bucket** ins Gras beißen. ∼*n* 1 Fußtritt *m.* 2 Rückstoß *m.* 3 *inf* Schwung *m.* Energie *f.* **get a kick out of** Spaß daran haben.

kid[1] (kid) *n* 1 *zool* Zicklein *neu.* 2 Ziegenleder *neu.* 3 *inf* Kind *neu.*

kid[2] (kid) *vt* foppen, aufziehen. *vi* scherzen.

kidnap (ˈkidnæp) *vt* entführen. **kidnapper** *n* Entführer, Kidnapper *m.*

kidney (ˈkidni) *n* Niere *f.* **kidney bean** *n* weiße Bohne *f.*

kill (kil) *vt* 1 töten. 2 umbringen, morden. 3 abschlachten. **kill time** die Zeit totschlagen.

kiln (kiln) *n* Ziegelofen, Brennofen *m.*

kilo (ˈkiːlou) *n* Kilo *neu.*

kilogram (ˈkiləgræm) *n* Kilogramm *neu.*

kilometre (kiˈlɔmitə) *n* Kilometer *m.*

kilt

kilt (kilt) n Schottenrock, Kilt m.

kimono (ki'mounou) n Kimono m.

kin (kin) n 1 Geschlecht neu. Sippe f. 2 (Bluts)Verwandtschaft f. **the next of kin** die nächsten Verwandten.

kind[1] (kaind) adj freundlich, gütig, gut.

kind[2] (kaind) n 1 Art, Sorte f. 2 Geschlecht neu. **all kinds of** allerlei. **what kind of?** was für?

kindergarten ('kində:ga:tn) n Kindergarten m.

kindle ('kindl) vt anzünden. vi (sich) entzünden, aufflammen.

kinetic (ki'netik) adj kinetisch, bewegend. **kinetics** n pl Kinetik f.

king (kiŋ) n König m. **kingdom** n Königreich neu. **kingfisher** n Eisvogel m.

kink (kiŋk) n 1 Schleife f. Knick m. 2 Fimmel m. vt knicken. vi (sich) verfilzen.

kiosk ('kiosk) n Kiosk m.

kipper ('kipə) n Räucherhering m.

kiss (kis) vi,vt küssen. n Kuß m.

kit (kit) n 1 Ausrüstung f. 2 Werkzeug neu. 3 Bausatz m.

kitchen ('kitʃin) n Küche f.

kite (kait) n (Papier)Drachen m.

kitten ('kitn) n Kätzchen neu. junge Katze f.

kitty ('kiti) n (gemeinsame) Kasse f.

kiwi ('ki:wi) n Kiwi m.

kleptomania (kleptə'meiniə) n Kleptomanie f. **kleptomaniac** n Kleptomane m.

knack (næk) n 1 Kniff, Trick m. 2 Geschicklichkeit f.

knapsack ('næpsæk) n Rucksack m.

knead (ni:d) vt kneten.

knee (ni:) n Knie neu. **kneecap** n anat Kniescheibe f.

kneel '(ni:l) vi knien.

knew (nu:) v see **know.**

knickers ('nikəz) n pl (Damen)Schlüpfer m. **knickerbockers** n pl Kniehosen f pl.

knife (naif) n, pl **knives** Messer neu. vt (er)stechen.

knight (nait) n 1 Ritter m. 2 game Springer m. vt zum Ritter schlagen. **knighthood** n Ritterwürde f.

knit (nit) vt 1 stricken. 2 (ver)knüpfen. **knit one's brows** die Stirn runzeln. **knitting** n 1 Stricken neu. 2 Strickzeug neu. **knitting needle** n Stricknadel f. **knitwear** n Strickwaren f pl.

knob (nob) n Knopf m.

knobbly ('nobli) adj knorrig.

knock (nok) vi,vt klopfen, schlagen, pochen.

knock down 1 niederschlagen. **2** überfahren.

knock off 1 abschlagen, abziehen. **2** inf Feierabend machen. **3** sl stehlen. **knock out** k.o. schlagen. **knockout** n knockout m. ~n 1 Klopfen neu 2 Stoß, Schlag m.

knot (not) n 1 Knoten m. **2** Ast m. **3** Schwierigkeit f. vi,vt (ver)knoten, (ver)knüpfen.

know' (nou) vt 1 wissen. 2 kennen. **get to know** kennenlernen. **know the ropes** sich auskennen. **knowing** adj 1 erfahren. 2 verständnisvoll.

knowledge ('nolidʒ) n 1 Wissen neu. 2 Kenntnis f. **to my knowledge** meines Wissens. **knowledgeable** adj 1 kenntnisreich. 2 gut informiert.

knuckle ('nʌkəl) n Knöchel m. v **knuckle under** nachgeben.

Korea (kə'riə) n Korea neu. **Korean** adj koreanisch. n Koreaner m.

kosher ('kouʃə) adj koscher.

Kuwait (ku'weit) n Kuwait neu.

L

label ('leibəl) n 1 Zettel neu. 2 Bezeichnung f. vt beschriften, mit einem Zettel versehen.

laboratory (lə'borətri) n Laboratorium, Labor neu. **laboratory assistant** n Laborant m.

labour ('leibə) vi 1 arbeiten. 2 sich anstrengen. 3 sich schwer bewegen. vt 1 ausarbeiten. 2 ausführlich eingehen. n 1 Arbeit f. 2 Mühe, Anstrengung f. 3 (Geburts)Wehen f pl. 4 Arbeitskräfte f pl. **hard labour** n Zwangsarbeit f. **labour force** n Arbeiterschaft f. **Labour Party** n Labour Party, Arbeiterpartei f. **labour-saving** adj arbeitssparend. **laborious** adj mühsam, anstrengend. **labourer** n Arbeiter m.

laburnum (lə'bə:nəm) n Goldregen m.

labyrinth ('læbərinθ) n Labyrinth neu.

lace (leis) n 1 Spitze f. 2 Schnur f. vt 1 mit Spitze besetzen. 2 (zu)schnüren.

lack (læk) n Mangel m. Fehlen neu. vt ermangeln. vi fehlen, mangeln.

lacquer ('lækə) n Lack m. vt lackieren. **lacquered** adj Lack—.

lad (læd) n Bursche, Junge m.

ladder ('lædə) n 1 Leiter f. 2 (in stockings) Laufmasche f. vi eine Laufmasche bekommen.

laden ('leidn) adj beladen.

ladle ('leidl) n Schöpflöffel m. Kelle f. v **ladle out 1** schöpfen. **2** austeilen.

218

lady ('leidi) n 1 Dame f. 2 Herrin f. **Ladies and Gentleman!** Meine Damen und Herren! **ladybird** n Marienkäfer m.

lag [1] (læg) vi sich verzögern, zurückbleiben. n 1 Rückstand m. 2 Zeitabstand m.

lag [2] (læg) vt verschalen, verkleiden.

lager ('lɑ:gə) n Lagerbier neu.

laid (leid) v see **lay** [1]. **laid up** adj inf bettlägerig.

lain (lein) v see **lie** [1].

laity ('leiəti) n Laien m pl.

lake (leik) n See m.

lamb (læm) n 1 Lamm m. 2 Lammfleisch neu.

lame (leim) adj lahm. vt lähmen. **lameness** n Lahmheit f.

lament (lə'ment) n 1 (Weh)Klage f. 2 Klagelied neu. vt beklagen. vi trauern.

lamp (læmp) n Lampe f. **lamppost** n Laternenpfahl m. **lampshade** n Lampenschirm m.

lance (lɑ:ns) n Lanze f.

land (lænd) n 1 (festes) Land neu. 2 Boden, Grund m. 3 Grundbesitz m. vi,vt landen. **landing** n 1 Landung f. 2 Treppenabsatz m. **landlady** n (Haus)Wirtin f. **landlord** n (Haus)Wirt m. **landmark** n 1 Grenzstein m. 2 Wendepunkt m. **landscape** n Landschaft f.

lane (lein) n 1 Feldweg m. 2 Gasse f. 3 (on motorways, etc.) Fahrbahn f.

language ('læŋgwidʒ) n 1 Sprache f. 2 pl Fremdsprachen pl. **bad language** Schimpfworte m pl. **language laboratory** n Sprachlabor neu.

lanky ('læŋki) adj schlaksig, schlank.

lantern ('læntən) n Laterne f.

lap [1] (læp) n Schoß m.

lap [2] (læp) vt 1 übereinanderlegen, umschlagen 2 sport überrunden. vi (ein)hüllen. n sport Runde f.

lap [3] (læp) vt (auf)lecken. vi plätschern.

lapel (lə'pel) n Aufschlag m.

Lapland ('læplænd) n Lappland neu. **Lapp** adj lappisch. n 1 Lappländer, Lappe m. 2 (language) Lappisch neu.

lapse (læps) n 1 Verlauf m. 2 Verfallen neu. 3 Versehen neu. vi verlaufen. 2 (ver)fallen.

larceny ('lɑ:səni) n Diebstahl m.

larch (lɑ:tʃ) n Lärche f.

lard (lɑ:d) n Schmalz, Schweinefett neu.

larder ('lɑ:də) n Speiseschrank m.

large (lɑ:dʒ) adj 1 groß. 2 reichlich. 3 weitherzig. **largely** adv zum großen Teil.

lark [1] (lɑ:k) n zool Lerche f.

lark [2] (lɑ:k) n Streich m.

larva ('lɑ:və) n Larve, Puppe f.

larynx ('læriŋks) n Kehlkopf m. **laryngitis** n med Kehlkopfentzündung f.

laser ('leizə) n Laser m. **laser beams** n Laserstrahlen m pl.

lash (læʃ) n 1 Peitschenschnur f. 2 (Peitschen)-Hieb m. 3 anat Wimper f. vt peitschen, geißeln. **lash out** ausschlagen.

lass (læs) n inf Mädchen neu.

lasso (læ'su:) n Lasso m,neu. vt mit dem Lasso fangen.

last [1] (lɑ:st) adj 1 letzt. 2 vorig. n 1 Letzte(r) m. 2 Ende neu. **at last** 1 schließlich. 2 zuletzt. **last but not least** nicht zuletzt.

last [2] (lɑ:st) vi 1 dauern. 2 halten. 3 ausreichen.

latch (lætʃ) n 1 Klinke f. 2 Sicherheitsschloß neu. **on the latch** (nur) eingeklinkt. ~vt einklinken.

late (leit) adj 1 spät. 2 verspätet. 3 (jüngst) verstorben, selig. 4 ehemalig. **be late 1** zu spät kommen. 2 Verspätung haben. **lately** adv vor kurzem, neulich, in letzter Zeit.

latent ('leitnt) adj 1 verborgen. 2 latent.

lateral ('lætərəl) adj seitlich, Seiten—. Quer—.

latest ('leitist) adj 1 spätest, neuest, letzt. **at the latest** adv spätestens.

lathe (leið) n Drehbank f.

lather ('lɑ:ðə) n (Seifen)Schaum m. vt einseifen. vi schäumen.

Latin ('lætin) adj lateinisch. n 1 Latiner m. 2 (language) Latein neu. **Latin America** n Lateinamerika neu.

latitude ('lætitju:d) n 1 geog Breite f. 2 Spielraum m. **latitudinal** adj Breiten—.

latter ('lætə) adj 1 letzter. 2 neuer.

lattice ('lætis) n Gitter neu.

laugh (lɑ:f) vi lachen. **laugh at** auslachen. ~n Lachen neu. **laughable** adj lächerlich. **laughter** n Gelächter neu.

launch [1] (lɔ:ntʃ) vt 1 naut vom Stapel lassen. 2 loslassen. 3 (a rocket) abschießen. **launch into** sich stürzen in. **launching pad** n Raketenabschußrampe f.

launch [2] (lɔ:ntʃ) n 1 Barkasse f. 2 Ausflugsdampfer m.

launder ('lɔ:ndə) (vi),vt (sich) waschen. **launderette** n Schnellwäscherei f. **laundry** n 1 Wäscherei f. 2 Wäsche f.

laurel ('lɔrəl) n Lorbeer m.

lava ('lɑ:və) n Lava f.

lavatory ('lævətri) n Toilette f.

lavender ('lævində) n Lavendel m.

lavish ('læviʃ) adj 1 verschwenderisch, freige-

219

big. **2** reichlich. *vt* verschwenden. **lavishness** *n* (verschwenderische) Freigebigkeit *f*.

law (lɔ:) *n* **1** Gesetz, Recht *neu*. **2** Jura *neu pl*. **law-abiding** *adj* gesetzestreu, friedlich. **lawsuit** *n* **1** Verfahren *neu*. **2** Klage *f*. **lawyer** *n* **1** Rechtsanwalt *m*. **2** Jurist *m*.

lawn (lɔ:n) *n* Rasen *m*. **lawn-mower** *n* Rasenmäher *m*.

lax (læks) *adj* lax, locker, nachlässig.

laxative ('læksətiv) *n* Abführmittel *neu*.

lay¹ (lei) *vt* **1** legen. **2** (the table) decken. **3** setzen, (hin)stellen. **layer** *n* Schicht, Lage *f*. *vt* überlagern. *vi* sich lagern.

lay² (lei) *v see* **lie**¹.

lay³ (lei) *adj* **1** Laien—. **2** laienhaft. **layman** *n* Laie *m*.

laze (leiz) *vi* faulenzen. **laze away** vertrödeln. **laziness** *n* Faulheit, Trägheit *f*. **lazy** *adj* faul, träge. **lazy bones** *n inf* Faulenzer *m*.

lead¹ (li:d) *vt,vi* **1** führen, leiten. **2** vorangehen. *n* **1** Führung *f*. **2** *tech* (Zu)Leitung *f*. **3** (Hunde)Leine *f*. **4** *Th* Hauptrolle *f*. **5** Hinweis *m*. Beispiel *neu*. **leading** *adj* Haupt—, herrschend, führend, Leit—. **leader** *n* **1** Führer *m*. **2** Leiter *m*. **3** (in a newspaper) Leitartikel *m*. **leadership** *n* Führerschaft *f*.

lead² (led) *n* **1** Blei *neu*. **2** Bleistiftmine *f*. *adj* bleiern.

leaf (li:f) *n* **1** Blatt *neu*. **2** Flügel *m*. **3** Klappe *f*. *v* **leaf through** durchblättern. **leaflet** *n* **1** Blättchen *neu*. **2** Prospekt *m*.

league (li:g) *n* **1** Bund *m*. **2** *sport* Liga *f*.

leak (li:k) *n* **1** Leck *neu*. **2** *pol* Durchsickern *neu*. *vi* **1** lecken. **2** durchsickern. **leakage** *n* **1** Durchsickern *neu*. **2** Schwund *m*.

lean*¹ (li:n) *vi* sich lehnen, sich neigen. *vt* lehnen, stützen. **lean on** sich stützen auf.

lean² (li:n) *adj* mager.

leap* (li:p) *vi* springen, hüpfen. *vt* überspringen. *n* Sprung, Satz *m*. **look before you leap** erst wägen, dann wagen. **leapfrog** *n* Bockspringen *neu*. **leap year** *n* Schaltjahr *neu*.

learn* (lɜ:n) *vt* **1** lernen. **2** erfahren, erlernen. **learned** *adj* **1** gelehrt. **2** erfahren. **learner** *n* **1** Anfänger *m*. **2** *mot* Fahrschüler *m*.

lease (li:s) *n* **1** Pachtvertrag *m*. **2** Pacht *f*. *vt* (ver)pachten. **leasehold** *n* **1** Pacht *f*. **2** Pachtbesitz *m*. *adj* Pacht—. **leaseholder** *n* Pächter *m*.

leash (li:ʃ) *n* (Koppel)Leine *f*.

least (li:st) *adj* wenigst, mindest. *adv* am wenigsten. *n* Wenigste, Mindeste *neu*. **at least** wenigstens, mindestens, zumindest.

leather ('leðə) *n* Leder *neu*. *adj* ledern, Leder—. **leathery** *adj* zäh.

leave¹ (li:v) *vt* **1** verlassen. **2** lassen. *vi* abfahren, (fort-, weg-)gehen.

leave² (li:v) *n* **1** Erlaubnis *f*. **2** Urlaub *m*. **take one's leave** Abschied nehmen.

Lebanon ('lebənən) *n* Libanon *m*. **Lebanese** *adj* libanesisch. *n* Libanese(r) *m*.

lecherous ('letʃərəs) *adj* wollüstig.

lectern ('lektən) *n* Lesepult *neu*.

lecture ('lektʃə) *n* **1** Vorlesung *f*. Vortrag *m*. **2** Strafpredigt *f*. *vi* eine Vorlesung halten. *vt* abkanzeln. **lecturer** *n* Dozent *m*.

led (led) *v see* **lead**¹.

ledge (ledʒ) *n* **1** Sims *m*. **2** Felsbank *f*.

ledger ('ledʒə) *n comm* Hauptbuch *neu*.

lee (li:) *n* **1** Schutz *m*. **2** *naut* Leeseite *f*.

leech (li:tʃ) *n* Blutegel *m*.

leek (li:k) *n* Lauch *m*.

leer (liə) *vi* schielen. *n* lüsterner Seitenblick *m*.

left¹ (left) *adj* link. *n* linke Seite, Linke *f*. *adv* (nach) links. **left-hand** *adj* link, linksseitig. **left-handed** *adj* linkshändig. **left-wing** *adj pol* Links—, linksradikal.

left² (left) *v see* **leave**¹. *adj* übrig. **left-luggage office** *n* Gepäckaufbewahrung *f*.

leg (leg) *n* **1** Bein *neu*. **2** *cul* Keule *f*. **pull someone's leg** jemanden auf den Arm nehmen.

legacy ('legəsi) *n* Vermächtnis *neu*.

legal ('li:gəl) *adj* **1** gesetzlich. **2** juristisch. **3** Rechts—. **legality** *n* Gesetzlichkeit *f*. **legalize** *vt* rechtskräftig machen, legalisieren.

legend ('ledʒənd) *n* Legende *f*. Sage *f*.

legible ('ledʒibəl) *adj* leserlich, lesbar.

legion ('li:dʒən) *n* Legion *f*. **legionary** *adj* Legions—. *n* Legionär *m*.

legislate ('ledʒisleit) *vi* Gesetze geben. **legislation** *n* Gesetzgebung *f*.

legitimate (li'dʒitimət) *adj* **1** legitim, rechtmäßig. **2** (of a child) ehelich. **legitimize** *vt* legitimieren, für rechtmäßig erklären.

leisure ('leʒə) *n* Muße, freie Zeit *f*. **at your leisure** wenn es Ihnen paßt. **be at leisure** Muße haben. *—adj* müßig, Muße—. **leisurely** *adj,adv* gemächlich, ohne Hast.

lemon ('lemən) *n* Zitrone *f*. **lemonade** *n* (Zitronen)Limonade *f*.

lend* (lend) *vt* **1** (ver-, aus-)leihen. **2** leisten, gewähren.

length (leŋθ) *n* **1** Länge *f*. **2** Strecke *f*. **3** Dauer *f*. **at length** *adv* **1** ausführlich. **2** endlich.

lengthen (vi),vt (sich) verlängern. **lengthy** adj 1 sehr lang. 2 weitschweifig.

lenient ('li:niənt) adj mild, nachsichtig.

lens (lenz) n Linse f.

lent (lent) v see **lend**.

Lent (lent) n Fastenzeit f. Fasten f pl.

lentil ('lentĺ) n Linse f.

Leo ('li:ou) n Löwe m.

leopard ('lepəd) n Leopard m.

leper ('lepə) n Aussätzige(r) m. **leprosy** n Aussatz m. Lepra f. **leprous** adj aussätzig.

lesbian ('lezbiən) n Lesbierin f. adj lesbisch.

less (les) adv weniger. adj kleiner, geringer. **lessen** (vi),vt (sich) vermindern.

lesson ('lesən) n 1 Lektion f. 2 educ Stunde f. 3 rel Lesung f. 4 pl Unterricht m. **teach someone a lesson** jemandem eine Lektion erteilen.

lest (lest) conj damit or daß nicht.

let* (let) vt 1 lassen. 2 vermieten. **let on** inf es verraten. **let someone down** jemanden im Stich lassen. ~n sport Netzball m.

lethal ('li:θəl) adj tödlich.

lethargy ('leθədʒi) n Lethargie f. **lethargic** adj lethargisch.

letter ('letə) n 1 Brief m. 2 Buchstabe m. 3 Type f. **man of letters** Literat m. **to the letter** buchstäblich. **letterbox** n Briefkasten m.

lettuce ('letis) n Kopfsalat m.

leukaemia (lu:'ki:miə) n Leukämie f.

level ('levəl) adj 1 eben. 2 ausgeglichen. **level crossing** n Bahnübergang m. **level-headed** adj vernünftig. ~n 1 ebene Fläche, Ebene f. 2 Niveau neu. Höhe f. vt 1 gleichmachen. 2 nivellieren. 3 ebnen, planieren.

lever ('li:və) n 1 Hebel m. 2 Hebestange f. vt mit einem Hebel bewegen. **leverage** n Hebelkraft f.

levy ('levi) n 1 Erhebung f. Beitrag m. 2 mil Aushebung f. vt 1 erheben. 2 ausheben.

lewd (lu:d) adj unzüchtig. **lewdness** n Unzucht f.

liable ('laiəbəl) adj 1 verantwortlich. 2 haftpflichtig. 3 ausgesetzt. **be liable to** neigen zu. **liability** n 1 Verantwortlichkeit f. 2 Haftpflicht f. 3 Neigung f. 4 pl Verbindlichkeiten f pl.

liaison n 1 Verbindung f. 2 Liebschaft f.

liar ('laiə) n Lügner m.

libel ('laibəl) n 1 Schmähschrift f. 2 Verleumdung f. vt 1 schmähen. 2 (schriftlich) verleumden.

liberal ('libərəl) adj 1 liberal. 2 großzügig, freigebig. 2 reichlich. 3 freisinnig. n Liberale(r) m.

liberate ('libəreit) vt befreien. **liberation** n Befreiung f.

liberty ('libəti) n Freiheit f.

Libra ('li:brə) n Waage f.

library ('laibrəri) n Bücherei, Bibliothek f. **lending library** Leihbücherei f. **librarian** n Bibliothekar m.

libretto (li'bretou) n Libretto neu.

Libya ('libiə) n Libyen neu. **Libyan** adj libysch. n Libyer m.

licence ('laisəns) n 1 Lizenz f. 2 Erlaubnis f. 3 Konzession f. 4 Zügellosigkeit f. 5 Freiheit f. **driving licence** Führerschein m. **license** vt lizenzieren, genehmigen, zulassen. **licensing hours** n pl Ausschankstunden f pl. **licensee** n Lizenzinhaber m.

lick (lik) vt 1 lecken. 2 inf besiegen, übertreffen. vi (of flames) züngeln. n Lecken neu.

lid (lid) n 1 Deckel m. 2 anat Augenlid neu.

lie*[1] (lai) vi liegen. **lie down** sich (hin-, nieder-) legen. ~n Lage f.

lie[2] (lai) n Lüge f. **white lie** Notlüge f. vi lügen.

lieutenant (lef'tenənt) n Leutnant m. **lieutenant colonel** n Oberstleutnant m.

life (laif) n, pl **lives** 1 Leben neu. 2 Menschenleben neu. 3 Lebendigkeit f. **lifebelt** n Rettungsgürtel m. **lifeboat** n Rettungsboot neu. **lifebuoy** n Rettungsboje f. **lifeguard** n Bademeister m. **lifeline** n Rettungsleine f. **lifetime** n Lebenszeit f.

lift (lift) vt 1 (auf-, hoch-)heben. 2 erheben. vi sich heben. n 1 Aufzug, Fahrstuhl m. 2 (Auf)Heben neu. 2 Erhebung f. **give someone a lift** jemanden im Auto mitnehmen.

light*[1] (lait) n 1 Licht. 2 Beleuchtung f. 3 Lampe f. 4 (for tobacco) Feuer neu. 5 Leuchte f. **lighthouse** n Leuchtturm m. ~vt 1 anzünden. 2 beleuchten. adj hell. **lighter** n 1 Anzünder m. 2 Feuerzeug neu. **lighting** n Beleuchtung f.

light[2] (lait) adj 1 leicht. **light-headed** adj leichtsinnig. **light-hearted** adj leichtherzig, fröhlich. **lightweight** adj leicht. n Leichtgewichtler m.

light[3] (lait) vi **light upon** stoßen auf.

lighten[1] ('laitn) vi 1 erleuchten. 2 sich erhellen. 3 blitzen.

lighten[2] ('laitn) (vi),vt (sich) erleichtern.

lightning ('laitniŋ) n Blitz m.

like[1] (laik) adj,adv gleich, ähnlich. prep wie. **like-minded** adj gleichgesinnt. **likeness** n 1

like

Ähnlichkeit f. 2 Abbild neu. **likewise** adv
gleichfalls, auch, ebenso.

like (laik) vt mögen, gern haben, lieben,
gefallen. **like doing something** etwas gern
tun. **I like this picture** dieses Bild gefällt mir.

likely ('laikli) adj,adv wahrscheinlich.

lilac ('lailək) adj lila. n 1 bot (spanischer) Flieder
m. 2 Lila neu.

lily ('lili) n Lilie f. **lily-of-the-valley** n Mai-
glöckchen neu.

limb (lim) n 1 Glied neu. 2 Ast m. **artificial
limb** n Prothese f.

limbo ('limbou) n 1 Vorhölle f. 2 Vergessenheit
f. 3 Gefängnis, Kittchen neu.

lime[1] (laim) n Kalk m. vt mit Kalk düngen.
limelight n 1 Kalklicht neu. 2 Scheinwerfer-
licht neu. 3 Rampenlicht neu. **limestone** n
Kalkstein m.

lime[2] (laim) n 1 Limone f. 2 Linde f.

limerick ('limərik) n Limerick m.

limit ('limit) n Grenze f. Äußerste neu. **that is
the limit!** das ist (doch wirklich) die Höhe!
~vt begrenzen, beschränken. **limitation** n 1
Begrenzung, Beschränkung f. 2 Grenze f.

limp[1] (limp) vi hinken. n Hinken neu.

limp[2] (limp) adj 1 schlaff. 2 kraftlos.

limpet ('limpit) n Napfschnecke f.

linden ('lindən) n Linde f. Lindenbaum m.

line[1] (lain) n 1 Linie f. 2 Reihe f. 3 Zeile f. 4
Fach neu. vt 1 linieren. 2 aufstellen. 3 (um-)
säumen. **lineage** n Abstammung f. **linear** adj
linear, Linien—.

line[2] (lain) vt (a coat, etc.) füttern.

linen ('linin) n 1 Leinen neu. Leinwand f. 2
Wäsche f. **linen basket** n Wäschekorb m.
~adj Leinen, Leinen—.

liner ('lainə) n Passagierdampfer m.

linger ('liŋgə) vi 1 zögern. 2 verweilen. 3 sich
hinziehen. 4 schlendern.

lingerie ('lɔnʒəri) n Damenunterwäsche f.

linguist ('liŋgwist) n Linguist, Sprachwissen-
schaftler m. **linguistic** adj linguistisch, sprach-
lich, Sprach—. **linguistics** n pl Linguistik,
Sprachwissenschaft f.

lining ('lainiŋ) n 1 Futter neu. 2 Verkleidung f.

link (liŋk) n 1 Glied neu. 2 Verbindung f. (vi),vt
(sich) verketten, (sich) verbinden.

linoleum (li'nouliəm) n also **lino** Linoleum neu.

linseed ('linsi:d) n Leinsamen m. **linseed oil** n
Leinöl neu.

lion ('laiən) n Löwe m.

lip (lip) n 1 Lippe f. 2 Rand m. 3 inf Unver-

222

schämtheit f. **lip-read** von den Lippen
ablesen. **lipstick** n Lippenstift m.

liqueur (li'kjuə) n Likör m.

liquid ('likwid) adj flüssig. n Flüssigkeit f.
liquidation n 1 comm Liquidation f. 2 Besei-
tigung f. **go into liquidation** sich auflösen.
liquidize (vi),vt (sich) verflüssigen.

liquor ('likə) n 1 Flüssigkeit f. 2 Alkohol m.

liquorice ('likəris) n Lakritze f.

lira ('liərə) n, pl **lire** or **liras** Lira f.

lisp (lisp) vi lispeln. n Lispeln neu.

list[1] (list) n Liste f. Verzeichnis neu. vt (in eine
Liste) eintragen, verzeichnen.

list[2] (list) vi naut Schlagseite haben. n Schlagseite f.

listen ('lisən) vi 1 (an-, zu-)hören. 2 lauschen.
listener n (Zu)Hörer m.

listless ('listləs) adj lustlos, träg. **listlessness** n
Lustlosigkeit, Trägheit f.

lit (lit) v see **light**[1].

litany ('litəni) n Litanei f.

literal ('litərəl) adj 1 buchstäblich, wörtlich. 2
genau.

literary ('litərəri) adj 1 literarisch. 2 literarisch
gebildet.

literate ('litərət) adj gebildet.

literature ('litərətʃə) n Literatur f.

litre ('li:tə) n Liter m,neu.

litter ('litə) n 1 Tragbahre f. 2 (of animals) Wurf
m. 3 Abfall m. **litter-bin** n Abfallkorb m. ~vt
1 verstreuen. 2 verunreinigen.

little ('litl) adj 1 klein. 2 kurz. 3 wenig. adv
wenig. n Wenige neu. **a little** ein wenig, ein
bißchen.

liturgy ('litədʒi) n Liturgie f.

live[1] (liv) vi 1 leben. 2 wohnen. vt (a life)
führen.

live[2] (laiv) adj 1 lebend, lebendig. 2 Direkt—. 3
stromführend. **livestock** n Vieh neu.

livelihood ('laivlihud) n Lebensunterhalt m.

lively ('laivli) adj lebhaft.

liver ('livə) n Leber f.

livid ('livid) adj 1 bläulich. 2 inf wütend.

living ('liviŋ) adj lebend(ig), Lebens—. n
Lebensunterhalt m. **living room** n Wohnzimmer neu.

lizard ('lizəd) n Eidechse f.

llama ('lɑ:mə) n Lama neu.

load (loud) n 1 Last f. 2 Belastung f. 3 Ladung
f. **loads of** inf sehr viel, eine ganze Menge.
~vt 1 (be-, auf-)laden. 2 überhäufen, überladen.

loaf[1] (louf) n Brotlaib m.

loaf² (louf) *vi* bummeln, gammeln. **loafer** *n* Bummler, Gammler *m*.

loan (loun) *n* 1 Anleihe *f*. 2 Leihgabe *f*. **on loan** leihweise.

loathe (louð) *vt* sich ekeln vor, verabscheuen. **loathsome** *adj* ekelhaft, widerlich.

lob (lɔb) *n sport* Hochschlag *m*. *vt* hochschlagen.

lobby ('lɔbi) *n* 1 Vorhalle *f*. 2 Interessengruppe *f*. 3 Lobby *neu*. *vt* beeinflussen.

lobe (loub) *n* 1 Lappen *m*. 2 (of the ear) (Ohr)Läppchen *neu*.

lobster ('lɔbstə) *n* Hummer *m*.

local ('loukəl) *adj* örtlich, Orts—. Lokal—. *n* Ortsbewohner *m*. **local authority** *n* Ortsbehörden *f pl*. **locality** *n* 1 Örtlichkeit *f*. Ort *m*. 2 Lage *f*. **localize** *vt* lokalisieren. **locate** *vt* 1 ausfindig machen. 2 unterbringen, errichten. **location** *n* 1 Standort *m*. 2 Lage *f*.

loch (lɔx) *n* See *m*. Bucht *f*.

lock¹ (lɔk) *n* 1 Schloß *neu*. 2 (on a canal, etc.) Schleuse *f*. *vt* (ver)schließen. *vi* sich schließen. **locksmith** *n* Schlosser *m*.

lock² (lɔk) *n* (of hair, etc.) Locke *f*.

locker ('lɔkə) *n* Kasten *m*.

locket ('lɔkit) *n* Medaillon *neu*.

locomotive (loukə'moutiv) *n* Lokomotive *f*.

locust ('loukəst) *n* Heuschrecke *f*.

lodge (lɔdʒ) *n* 1 (Jagd)Hütte *f*. 2 Forsthaus, Parkhaus *neu*. *vt* 1 aufnehmen. 2 unterbringen. 3 hinterlegen. 4 (a complaint) einreichen. *vi* 1 wohnen, logieren. 2 steckenbleiben. **lodger** *n* (Unter)Mieter *m*. **lodgings** *pl* (Miets)Wohnung *f*.

loft (lɔft) *n* Dachboden *m*. **lofty** *adj* 1 (sehr) hoch. 2 hochmütig. 3 erhaben.

log (lɔg) *n* (Holz)Klotz *m*. **log-book** *n* 1 Logbuch *neu*. 2 mot Zulassungsbuch *neu*.

logarithm ('lɔgəriðəm) *n* Logarithmus *m*.

logic ('lɔdʒik) *n* Logik *f*. **logical** *adj* logisch.

loins (lɔinz) *n pl* Lenden *f pl*.

loiter ('lɔitə) *vi* bummeln, herumlungern.

lollipop ('lɔlipɔp) *n* Lutscher *m*.

London ('lʌndən) *n* London *neu*.

lonely ('lounli) *adj* einsam. **loneliness** *n* Einsamkeit *f*.

long¹ (lɔŋ) *vi* sich sehnen.

long² (lɔŋ) *adj* lang. **in the long run** auf die Dauer. **long-distance** *adj* Fern—, Weit—. **long jump** *n* Weitsprung *m*. **long-playing record** *n* Langspielplatte *f*. **long-range** *adj* weittragend, auf weite Sicht. **long-sighted** *adj* weitsichtig. **longstanding** *adj* seit langer

Zeit bestehend, alt. **long-term** *adj* langfristig. **long wave** *n* Langwelle *f*. **longwinded** *adj* langatmig.

longevity (lɔn'dʒeviti) *n* Langlebigkeit *f*.

longitude ('lɔndʒitjuːd) *n* Länge *f*.

loo (luː) *n inf* Klo *neu*.

look (luk) *n* 1 Blick *m*. 2 Aussehen *neu*. *vi* 1 (an)blicken, sehen, schauen. 2 zusehen. 3 nachsehen. 4 aussehen. **look for** suchen. **look up** (for reference) nachschlagen.

loom¹ (luːm) *n* Webstuhl *m*.

loom² (luːm) *vi* (drohend) aufragen.

loop (luːp) *n* Schleife *f*. *vt* in Schleifen legen. *vi* eine Schleife machen.

loophole ('luːphoul) *n* Schlupfloch *neu*.

loose (luːs) *adj* 1 locker. 2 schlaff. 3 (of clothes) weit. 4 frei. 5 lose, nicht verpackt. **at a loose end** beschäftigungslos. **loosen** *(vi)*.*vt* (sich) lösen, (sich) lockern.

loot (luːt) *n* Beute *f*. *vi*,*vt* plündern.

lop (lɔp) *vt* beschneiden, stutzen.

lopsided (lɔp'saidid) *adj* 1 schief. 2 einseitig.

lord (lɔːd) *n* 1 Herr *m*. 2 Edelmann *m*. 3 Lord *m*. **lordly** *adj* 1 edel. 2 herrisch. **lordship** *n* Herrlichkeit *f*.

lorry ('lɔri) *n* Lastkraftwagen, Lastwagen *m*.

lose* (luːz) *vt* verlieren. *vi* 1 sich verlieren. 2 (of a clock) nachgehen. **lose weight** abnehmen. **loss** (lɔs) *n* 1 Verlust *m*. 2 Schaden *m*. **at a loss** in Verlegenheit.

lost (lɔst) *adj* verloren.

lot (lɔt) *n* 1 Los *neu*. 2 Schicksal *neu*. 3 Menge *f*. **draw lots** losen.

lotion ('louʃən) *n* Schönheitswasser *neu*.

lottery ('lɔtəri) *n* Lotterie *f*.

lotus ('loutəs) *n* Lotos *m*.

loud (laud) *adj* 1 laut. 2 grell. **loud-mouth** *n inf* Maulheld *m*. **loudness** *n* Lautheit, Lautstärke *f*. **loudspeaker** *n* Lautsprecher *m*.

lounge (laundʒ) *n* 1 Wohnzimmer *neu*. 2 Salon *m*. *vi* faulenzen, herumlungern. **lounge suit** *n* Straßenanzug *m*.

louse (laus) *n* Laus *f*. **lousy** *adj* lausig.

love (lʌv) *n* 1 Liebe *f*. 2 Liebling *m*. 3 liebe Grüße *m pl*. 4 *sport* Null *f*. **be in love with** verliebt sein in. **fall in love with** sich verlieben in. ~*adj* Liebes—. *vt* 1 lieben. 2 gern haben. **love affair** *n* Liebschaft *f*. **lovesick** *adj* liebeskrank. **lovely** *adj* 1 lieblich, reizend. 2 *inf* wunderschön. **lover** *n* Liebhaber, Geliebte(r) *m*. **loving** *adj* liebevoll, liebend.

low¹ (lou) *adj* 1 niedrig. 2 tief. 3 niedergeschlagen. 4 gemein. **lowbrow** *adj* nicht intellektuel, geistig anspruchslos. **low frequency** n Niederfrequenz f. **low-grade** n Unterstufe f. **lowland** n Tiefland neu. **low-necked** adj tief ausgeschnitten. **low-pitched** adj tief.

low[2] (lou) vi muhen. n Muhen neu.

lower ('louə) adj **1** niedriger. **2** niedere, untere, Unter—. **lower class** n untere Klassen f pl. ~vt **1** niederlassen, herunterlassen. **2** senken. **3** (one's eyes) niederschlagen.

Lower Saxony ('sæksəni) n Niedersachsen neu.

loyal ('lɔiəl) adj treu. **loyalty** n Treue f.

lozenge ('lɔzindʒ) n Pastille f.

lubricate ('lu:brikeit) vt schmieren. **lubricant** n Schmiermittel neu. **lubrication** n Schmierung f. Ölen neu.

Lucerne (lu:'sə:n) n Luzerne f.

lucid ('lu:sid) adj **1** hell. **2** klar, deutlich.

luck (lʌk) n **1** Glück neu. **2** Geschick neu. **bad luck** n Unglück, Pech neu. **lucky** adj glücklich. **be lucky** Glück haben. **luckily** adv glücklicherweise.

lucrative ('lu:krətiv) adj lukrativ.

ludicrous ('lu:dikrəs) adj lächerlich.

lug (lʌg) vt schleppen, zerren.

luggage ('lʌgidʒ) n Gepäck neu.

lukewarm (lu:k'wɔ:m) adj lauwarm.

lull (lʌl) vt **1** einlullen. **2** beruhigen. vi sich legen. n Stille f. **lullaby** n Wiegenlied neu.

lumbago (lʌm'beigou) n Hexenschuß m.

lumber[1] ('lʌmbə) n **1** Gerümpel neu. **2** Bauholz neu. **lumberjack** n Holzfäller m. ~vt mit Gerümpel vollpacken.

lumber[2] ('lʌmbə) vi sich schwerfällig schleppen.

luminous ('lu:minəs) adj **1** leuchtend, Leuchter—. **2** hellerleuchtet. **3** klar, einleuchtend.

lump (lʌmp) n **1** Klumpen m. **2** Beule f. **lump sum** Pauschalsumme f. ~vt zusammenwerfen.

lunacy ('lu:nəsi) n Irrsinn, Wahnsinn m.

lunar ('lu:nə) adj Mond—.

lunatic ('lu:nətik) adj wahnsinnig. n Irre(r) m.

lunch (lʌntʃ) n Mittagessen m. **lunch-hour** n Mittagspause f. ~vi zu Mittag essen.

lung (lʌŋ) n Lunge f.

lunge (lʌndʒ) n Ausfall, Stoß m. vi **1** ausfallen. **2** (dahin)stürmen.

lurch[1] (lə:tʃ) vi taumeln. n Taumeln neu.

lurch[2] (lə:tʃ) n **leave someone in the lurch** jemanden im Stich lassen.

lure (luə) n **1** Köder m. **2** Lockung f. vt **1** ködern. **2** (an)locken.

lurid ('luərid) adj unheimlich, düster.

lurk (lə:k) vi lauern.

luscious ('lʌʃəs) adj köstlich.

lush (lʌʃ) adj saftig, üppig.

lust (lʌst) n **1** (Wol)Lust f. **2** Sucht, Gier f. v **lust for** begehren, gelüsten (nach).

lustre ('lʌstə) n **1** Glanz m. **2** Lüster m.

Luxembourg ('lʌksəmbə:g) n Luxemburg neu.

luxury ('lʌkʃəri) n **1** Luxus m. **2** Luxusartikel m. **luxurious** adj luxuriös.

lynx (liŋks) n Luchs m.

lyre ('laiə) n Leier, Lyra f.

lyrical ('lirikəl) adj lyrisch.

lyrics ('liriks) n pl Lyrik f.

M

mac (mæk) n inf Regenmantel m.

macabre (mə'ka:b) adj grausig, makaber.

mace[1] (meis) n **1** Keule f. **2** Amtsstab m.

mace[2] (meis) n bot Muskatblüte f.

machine (mə'ʃi:n) n Maschine f. vt maschinell bearbeiten, herstellen. **machine-gun** n Maschinengewehr neu. **machinery** n **1** Mechanismus m. **2** Maschinerie f.

mackerel ('mækrəl) n Makrele f.

mackintosh ('mækintɔʃ) n Regenmantel m.

mad (mæd) adj **1** wahnsinnig, verrückt. **2** toll, wild. **3** inf wütend. **madness** n Wahnsinn m.

madam ('mædəm) n gnädige Frau f.

made (meid) v see **make.**

Madonna (mə'dɔnə) n Madonna f.

magazine (mægə'zi:n) n **1** Magazin neu. **2** Illustrierte f.

maggot ('mægət) n Made f.

magic ('mædʒik) n **1** Magie f. **2** Zauber m. Zauberei f. adj **1** magisch. **2** zauberhaft, Zauber—. **magician** n Zauberer, Magier m.

magistrate ('mædʒistreit) n Friedensrichter m.

magnanimous (mæg'næniməs) adj großmütig.

magnate ('mægneit) n Magnat m.

magnet ('mægnit) n Magnet m. **magnetic** adj **1** magnetisch. **2** anziehend. **magnetic tape** n (Ton)Band m. **magnetism** n **1** Magnetismus m. **2** Anziehungskraft f. **magnetize** vt **1** magnetisieren. **2** anziehen, fesseln.

magnificent (mæg'nifisənt) adj herrlich, prächtig, großartig. **magnificence** n Herrlichkeit, Pracht f.

magnify ('mægnifai) vt vergrößern. **magnifying glass** n Vergrößerungsglas neu. Lupe f.

magnitude ('mægnitju:d) n **1** Größe f. **2** Bedeutung f.

magnolia (mæg'nouliə) n Magnolie f.

magpie ('mægpai) n Elster f.

mahogany (mə'hɔgəni) n Mahagoni(holz) neu.

maid (meid) n **1** Mädchen neu. Dienstmädchen neu. **old maid** n alte Jungfer f. **maiden** n Jungfrau f. **maiden name** n Mädchenname m.

mail (meil) n Post f. vt (mit der Post) schicken. **mailbag** n Postsack m. **mail order firm** n Postversandhaus neu.

maim (meim) vt verstümmeln, zum Krüppel machen.

main (mein) adj Haupt—, hauptsächlich. n **1** Hauptleitung f. **2** pl Stromnetz neu. **mainland** n Festland neu. **mainsail** n Großsegel neu. **mainspring** n **1** Hauptfeder f. **2** treibende Kraft f. **mainstream** n Hauptstrom m.

maintain (mein'tein) vt **1** erhalten. **2** unterhalten. **3** behaupten. **maintenance** n **1** Erhaltung f. **2** Unterhalt m.

maize (meiz) n Mais m.

majesty ('mædʒisti) n Majestät f. **majestic** adj majestätisch.

major ('meidʒə) adj **1** größer. **2** bedeutend, wichtig. **3** law volljährig, mündig. n **1** law Volljährige(r). **2** mil Major m. **3** mus Dur neu. **major general** n Generalmajor m. **majority** n **1** Mehrheit f. größter Teil m. **2** law Volljährigkeit f.

make* (meik) vt **1** machen. **2** bauen. **3** herstellen. **4** zwingen. **5** sich belaufen auf. **6** inf erreichen. **7** inf schaffen. n Marke f. **make for** sich ergeben nach. **make good** wiedergutmachen. **make off** sich davonmachen. **make out 1** ausmachen. **2** ausstellen. **3** vorgeben. **make up 1** erdichten. **2** sich schminken. **3** sich versöhnen. **4** wiedergutmachen. **5** bilden. **makebelieve** n Verstellung f. Vorwand m. **makeshift** adj Behelfs—. n Notbehelf m. **make-up** n **1** Schminke f. Make-up neu. **2** Veranlagung, Natur f.

maladjusted (mælə'dʒʌstid) adj **1** schlecht angepaßt. **2** milieu gestört.

malaria (mə'lɛəriə) n Malaria f. Sumpffieber m.

male (meil) adj männlich, Männer—. n **1** Mann. **2** zool Männchen.

malfunction (mæl'fʌŋkʃən) vi schlecht funktionieren. n Funktionsstörung f.

malice ('mælis) n **1** Böswilligkeit f. **2** law böse Absicht f. **malicious** adj **1** böswillig. **2** boshaft.

malignant (mə'lignənt) adj **1** med bösartig. **2** boshaft.

malinger (mə'liŋgə) vi simulieren, sich krank stellen. **malingerer** n Simulant m.

mallet ('mælət) n **1** Holzhammer m. **2** sport Schlagholz neu.

malnutrition (mælnju:'triʃən) n Unterernährung f.

malt (mɔ:lt) n Malz neu. vt mälzen.

Malta ('mɔ:ltə) n Malta neu. **Maltese** adj maltesisch. n Malteser m.

maltreat (mæl'tri:t) vt mißhandeln, schlecht behandeln. **maltreatment** n Mißhandlung, schlechte Behandlung f.

mammal ('mæməl) n Säugetier neu.

mammoth ('mæməθ) n Mammut neu. adj riesig.

man (mæn) n **1** Mann m. **2** Mensch m. **3** Menschheit f. vt bemannen. **manhandle** vt **1** durch Menschenkraft bewegen. **2** rauh behandeln, mißhandeln. **manhole** n Einsteigeöffnung, Luke f. **manly** adj männlich. **manmade** adj künstlich, Kunst—. **manpower** n **1** Arbeitskräfte f pl. **2** Menschenkraft f. **manslaughter** n Totschlag m.

Man, Isle of (mæn) n (Insel) Man neu.

manage ('mænidʒ) vt **1** handhaben. **2** leiten, führen. **3** beaufsichtigen. vi **1** es schaffen. **2** auskommen. **management** n **1** Handhabung f. **2** (Geschäfts)Leitung f. Management neu. **manager** n (Betriebs)Leiter, Manager m.

mandarin ('mændərin) n **1** Mandarin m. **2** bot Mandarine f.

mandate ('mændeit) n **1** Mandat neu. Auftrag m. **2** Befehl m. **mandatory** adj **1** verbindlich, obligatorisch. **2** Mandats—.

mane (mein) n Mähne f.

mange (meindʒ) n Räude f.

mangle[1] ('mæŋgəl) vt zerstückeln, zerfleischen.

mangle[2] ('mæŋgəl) n Wäscherolle, Wringmaschine f. vt mangeln, rollen, wringen.

mango ('mæŋgou) n Mangopflaume f.

mania ('meiniə) n **1** Manie f. **2** Wahnsinn m. **3** inf Fimmel m. **maniac** n Wahnsinnige(r), Verrückte(r) m. **manic** adj manisch.

manicure ('mænikjuə) n Maniküre, Nagelpflege f. vt maniküren. **manicurist** n Maniküre f.

manifest ('mænifest) adj offenbar, manifest, klar. vt **1** offenbaren. **2** zeigen. **manifestation** n **1** Offenbarung, Kundgebung f. **2** Erscheinung f.

manifesto (mæni'festou) n Manifest neu.

manifold ('mænifould) adj mannigfaltig.

manipulate (mə'nipjuleit) vt **1** (geschickt) handhaben. **2** manipulieren. **manipulation** n **1** Handhabung f. **2** Manipulation f.

mankind ('mænkaind) n Menschheit f.

manner ('mænə) n **1** Art, Weise f. **2** Manier f. **3** Benehmen neu. **4** pl Manieren pl. Betragen neu. **mannerism** n **1** Manieriertheit f. **2** (of style) Manierismus m.

manoeuvre (mə'nuːvə) n Manöver neu. vi,(vt) manövrieren (lassen).

manor ('mænə) n Gut neu. **lord of the manor** n Gutsherr m. **manor house** n Herrensitz m.

mansion ('mænʃən) n **1** herrschaftliches Wohnhaus neu. **2** pl Mietshaus neu.

mantle ('mæntl) n **1** (Deck)Mantel m. **2** Hülle f. vt verhüllen. **mantlepiece** n Kaminsims m.

manual ('mænjuəl) adj **1** Hand—. **2** handgefertigt. **3** manuell. n **1** Handbuch neu. **2** mus Manual neu.

manufacture (mænju'fæktʃə) n **1** Herstellung, Fabrikation, Erzeugung f. **2** Fabrikat neu. vt **1** herstellen, erzeugen, anfertigen. **2** erfinden, erdichten. **manufactured** adj Fabrik—, Fertig—.

manure (mə'njuə) n Dünger m. vt düngen.

manuscript ('mænjuskript) n **1** Manuskript neu. Handschrift f. **2** Druckvorlage f.

many ('meni) adj viele. **how many** wieviele. **many a** manch (ein). **many times** oft, häufig. **the many** die Masse f. die Vielen pl.

map (mæp) n **1** Landkarte, Seekarte f. **2** Stadtplan m. vt aufzeichnen, eintragen.

maple ('meipəl) n bot Ahorn m.

mar (maː) vt **1** verderben. **2** verunstalten.

marathon ('mærəθən) adj Dauer—. **marathon race** n Langstreckenlauf, Marathonlauf m.

marble ('maːbəl) n **1** Marmor m. **2** Marmorkunstwerk neu. **3** Murmel f. adj marmorn.

march (maːtʃ) n Marsch m. **march past** n Vorbeimarsch m. ~vi,(vt) marschieren (lassen). **marching** adj Marsch—.

March (maːtʃ) n März m.

marchioness ('maːʃənis) n Marquise f.

mare (mɛə) n Stute f.

margarine (maːdʒə'riːn) n Margarine f.

margin ('maːdʒin) n **1** Rand m. **2** Grenze f.

marguerite (maːgə'riːt) n Gänseblümchen neu.

marigold ('mærigould) n Dotterblume f.

marijuana (mæri'waːnə) n Marihuana f.

marinade (n mæri'neid; v 'mærineid) n cul Marinade f. vt marinieren.

marine (mə'riːn) adj **1** See—, Marine—. **2** Schiffs—. n **1** Marine f. **2** Marineinfanterist

m. **maritime** adj **1** See—. **2** Küsten—. **3** Schiffahrts—.

marital ('mæritl) adj ehelich.

marjoram ('maːdʒərəm) n Marjoran m.

mark[1] (maːk) n **1** Marke f. Zeichen neu. **2** Fleck m. **3** Kennzeichen neu. **4** educ Note f. **5** Ziel neu. vt **1** (aus)zeichnen. **2** educ zensieren, korrigieren. **3** beachten. **4** markieren. vi beflecken. **marked** adj auffällig, deutlich, gezeichnet. **marksman** n (guter) Schütze m.

mark[2] (maːk) n Mark f.

market ('maːkit) n Markt m. vt auf den Markt bringen. **market garden** n Handelsgärtnerei f. **market place** n Marktplatz m. **market research** n Marktforschung f.

marmalade ('maːməleid) n Orangenmarmelade f.

maroon[1] (mə'ruːn) adj dunkelrot.

maroon[2] (mə'ruːn) vt **1** (auf einer öden Insel) aussetzen. **2** verlassen, im Stich lassen.

marquee (maː'kiː) n großes Zelt neu.

marquess ('maːkwis) n Marquis m.

marriage ('mæridʒ) n **1** Ehe f. **2** Ehestand m. **3** Hochzeit, Heirat f. **civil marriage** n standesamtliche Trauung f. **marriage certificate** n Trauschein m.

marrow ('mærou) n **1** (Knochen)Mark neu. **2** Kern m. **3** bot Kürbis m. **marrowbone** n Markknochen m.

marry ('mæri) vt **1** (ver)heiraten, trauen. **2** sich verheiraten mit. vi sich verheiraten, heiraten.

Mars (maːz) n Mars m.

marsh (maːʃ) n Sumpfland neu.

marshal ('maːʃəl) n **1** (Feld)Marschall m. **2** Zeremonienmeister, Festordner m. vt **1** ordnen. **2** (feierlich) führen.

martial ('maːʃəl) adj **1** kriegerisch. **2** Kriegs—.

martin ('maːtin) n zool Mauerschwalbe f.

martyr ('maːtə) n Märtyrer m. vt zum Märtyrer machen. **martyrdom** n **1** Märtyrertum neu. **2** Martyrium neu.

marvel ('maːvəl) n Wunder m. vi sich wundern.

marvellous ('maːvələs) adj wunderbar, erstaunlich.

Marxism ('maːksizəm) n Marxismus m. **Marxist** adj marxistisch. n Marxist m.

marzipan ('maːzipæn) n Marzipan neu.

mascara (mæ'skaːrə) n Wimperntusche f.

mascot ('mæskət) n Maskottchen neu.

masculine ('mæskjulin) adj männlich. n gram Maskulinum neu.

mash (mæʃ) n **1** Gemisch neu. **2** Brei m. **3** Mengfutter neu. vt **1** mischen. **2** zerquetschen, zerstampfen. **mashed potatoes** n pl Kartoffelpüree m.

mask (mɑːsk) n Maske f. vt verbergen.

mason ('meisən) n Maurer m. **masonry** n Mauerwerk neu.

masquerade (mæskə'reid) **1** Maskenball m. **2** Maskerade f. vi sich maskieren.

mass[1] (mæs) n **1** Masse f. **2** Menge f. (vi),vt (sich) anhäufen, (sich) ansammeln. **mass media** n pl Massenmedien neu pl. **mass-produce** vt serienmäßig herstellen. **mass production** n Serienbau m. Serienproduktion f.

mass[2] (mæs) n rel Messe f.

massacre ('mæsəkə) n Gemetzel, Massaker neu. vt niedermetzeln.

massage ('mæsɑːʒ) n Massage f. vt massieren.

massive ('mæsiv) adj **1** massiv. **2** schwer. **3** massig. **4** fest.

mast (mɑːst) n Mast m. **masthead** n Mastkorb m.

mastectomy (mæs'tektəmi) n med Brustamputation f.

master ('mɑːstə) n **1** Meister m. **2** Herr m. **3** Lehrer m. vt beherrschen. **masterpiece** n Meisterstück neu. **masterful** adj **1** herrisch. **2** meisterhaft. **mastery** n **1** Herrschaft f. **2** Beherrschung f.

masturbate ('mæstəbeit) vi masturbieren.

mat (mæt) n Matte f.

match[1] (mætʃ) n Streichholz, Zündholz neu. **matchbox** n Streichholzschachtel f.

match[2] (mætʃ) n **1** Passende(r), Gleiche(r) m. **2** Wettspiel neu. (Wett)Kampf m. **3** Partie f. **4** Match neu. vt **1** anpassen. **2** passen zu. vi zusammenpassen, dazupassen.

mate (meit) n **1** Gefährte m. Gefährtin f. **2** Gatte m. Gattin f. **3** zool Männchen, Weibchen neu. **4** naut Maat m. (vi),vt (sich) paaren.

material (mə'tiəriəl) n Material neu. Stoff m. adj materiell, stofflich. **materialism** n Materialismus m. **materialist** n Materialist m. **materialize** vi sich verwirklichen.

maternal (mə'təːnl) adj **1** mütterlich. **2** mütterlicherseits. **maternity** n Mutterschaft f. adj Schwangerschafts—, Umstands—.

mathematics (mæθə'mætiks) n Mathematik f.

matins ('mætinz) n pl Frühmesse f.

matinee ('mætinei) n Nachmittagsvorstellung f.

matriarchal ('meitriɑːkəl) adj matriarchalisch.

matrimony ('mætriməni) n Ehe f. Ehestand m.

matrix ('meitriks) n, pl **-ices** f. **1** Matrix f. **2** tech Matrize f. **3** Nährboden m.

matron ('meitrən) n **1** Matrone f. **2** Vorsteherin f.

matter ('mætə) n **1** Materie f. Stoff m. Substanz f. **2** Sache, Angelegenheit f. vi etwas bedeuten, etwas ausmachen. **it doesn't matter** es macht nichts. **what's the matter?** was ist los?

mattress ('mætrəs) n Matratze f.

mature (mə'tjuə) adj reif, entwickelt. vi reifen. **maturity** n Reife f.

maudlin ('mɔːdlin) adj sentimental.

maul (mɔːl) vt verprügeln, zerreißen.

mausoleum (mɔːsə'liəm) n Mausoleum neu.

mauve (mouv) adj malvenfarbig. n Malvenfarbe f.

maxim ('mæksim) n Grundsatz m. Maxime f.

maximum ('mæksiməm) n Maximum, Höchstmaß neu. **maximize** vt vergrößern, verstärken.

may* (mei) v mod aux **1** mögen, können. **2** dürfen. **maybe** adv vielleicht.

May (mei) n Mai m. **May Day** n erster Mai m. **maypole** n Maibaum m.

mayonnaise (meiə'neiz) n Mayonnaise f.

mayor ('mɛə) n Bürgermeister m.

maze (meiz) n Irrgarten m.

me (miː) pron 1st pers s **1** mich. **2** mir.

meadow ('medou) n Wiese f.

meagre ('miːgə) adj mager, ärmlich.

meal[1] (miːl) n Mahlzeit f. Mahl, Essen neu.

meal[2] (miːl) n (grobes) Mehl neu.

mean*[1] (miːn) vt bedeuten, heißen, meinen. vi,vt beabsichtigen.

mean[2] (miːn) adj **1** gering, niedrig. **2** geizig.

meander (mi'ændə) vi sich winden. n Windung f. Krümmung f.

meaning ('miːniŋ) n Bedeutung f. Sinn m.

means (miːnz) n pl Mittel neu pl. **by means of** mittels, durch.

meanwhile ('miːnwail) adv inzwischen.

measles ('miːzəlz) n Masern f pl.

measure ('meʒə) vt (ab-, aus-)messen. n **1** Maß neu. **2** Maßnahme f. **measurement** n **1** Messung f. **2** Maß neu.

meat (miːt) n Fleisch neu. **2** Kern m.

mechanic (mi'kænik) n Mechaniker, Autoschlosser m. **mechanical** adj mechanisch. **mechanical engineering** n Maschinenbau m. **mechanics** n pl **1** Mechanik f. Konstruktion f. **mechanism** n Mechanismus m. Arbeitsweise f. **mechanize** vt mechanisieren

medal ('medl) n Orden m. Medaille f. **medallion** n Medaille f.

meddle ('medl) vi sich einmischen.

media ('miːdiə) n Nachrichtenmittel, Medien neu pl.

medial ('miːdiəl) adj durchschnittlich, Mittel—.

median ('miːdiən) adj in der Mitte liegend, mittler. n Mittelwert m.

mediate ('miːdieit) vi vermitteln.

medical ('medikəl) adj medizinisch, ärztlich. **medication** n medizinische Behandlung, Verordnung f. **medicine** n 1 Medizin f. 2 Arzneimittel neu.

medieval (medi'iːvəl) adj mittelalterlich.

mediocre (miːdi'oukə) adj mittelmäßig. **mediocrity** n Mittelmäßigkeit f.

meditate ('mediteit) vi 1 meditieren. 2 überlegen. 3 nachdenken.

Mediterranean (meditə'reiniən) adj Mittelmeer—. **Mediterranean (Sea)** n Mittelmeer neu.

medium ('miːdiəm) n, pl **media** 1 Mitte f. 2 Mittel neu. 3 Medium neu. adj mittler.

meek (miːk) adj sanft, demütig, mild.

meet* (miːt) vt 1 begegnen. 2 treffen. 3 erfüllen. **meeting** n 1 Begegnung f. 2 Zusammenkunft f. 3 Versammlung, Sitzung f.

megaphone ('megəfoun) n Megaphon neu.

melancholy ('melənkəli) n Schwermut, Melancholie f. adj schwermütig, melancholisch.

mellow ('melou) adj 1 ausgereift. 2 mild.

melodrama ('melədrɑːmə) n Melodrama neu.

melody ('melədi) n Melodie f. **melodic** adj melodisch.

melon ('melən) n Melone f.

melt* (melt) vt,vi schmelzen. **melting point** n Schmelzpunkt m.

member ('membə) n 1 Mitglied neu. 2 anat Glied neu. **membership** n Mitgliedschaft f.

membrane ('membrein) n Membrane f.

memento (mə'mentou) n Memento neu.

memo ('memou) n inf Notiz, Mitteilung f.

memoirs ('memwɑːz) n pl Memoiren, Lebenserinnerungen f pl.

memorandum (memə'rændəm) n, pl **-da** Notiz, Mitteilung f.

memory ('meməri) n 1 Gedächtnis neu. 2 Erinnerung f. **memorable** adj denkwürdig. **memorial** n Denkmal neu. adj Gedächtnis—. **memorize** vt auswendig lernen, im Gedächtnis behalten.

menace ('menəs) vt (be)drohen. n 1 Drohung f. 2 inf lästiger Mensch m. lästiges Kind neu.

menagerie (mə'nædʒəri) n Menagerie f.

mend (mend) vt reparieren, ausbessern.

menial ('miːniəl) adj niedrig, gemein.

menopause ('menəpɔːz) n Menopause f. Wechseljahre neu pl.

menstrual ('menstruəl) adj 1 monatlich, Monats—. 2 Menstruations—. **menstruate** vi menstruieren, die Regel haben. **menstruation** n Monatsblutung, Menstruation, Regel f.

mental ('mentl) adj 1 geistig, intellektuell, Geistes—. 2 sl verrückt. **mental hospital** n Nervenklinik f. **mental illness** n Geisteskrankheit f. **mentality** n Mentalität, Denkweise f.

menthol ('menθɔl) n Menthol neu.

mention ('menʃən) vt erwähnen. n Erwähnung f. **don't mention it!** bitte! gern geschehen! **not to mention** ganz zu schweigen von.

menu ('menjuː) n Speisekarte f.

mercantile ('məːkəntail) adj kaufmännisch.

mercenary ('məːsənəri) adj 1 käuflich. 2 Gewinn—, Geld—. n Söldner m.

merchant ('məːtʃənt) n 1 (Groß)Händler m. 2 (Groß)Kaufmann m. **merchant bank** n Handelsbank f. **merchant navy** n Handelsflotte f. **merchandise** n Güter neu pl. Waren f pl.

mercury ('məːkjuri) n 1 sci Quecksilber neu. 2 cap Merkur m.

mercy ('məːsi) n Gnade, Barmherzigkeit f.

mere (miə) adj bloß.

merge (məːdʒ) vi aufgehen, sich verschmelzen. vt verschmelzen, aufgehen lassen. vt,vi comm fusionieren. **merger** n comm Fusionierung f.

meridian (mə'ridiən) n Meridian m.

meringue (mə'ræŋ) n Meringe f. Baiser neu.

merit ('merit) n 1 Verdienst neu. 2 Wert m. vt verdienen.

mermaid ('məːmeid) n Meerjungfer, Seenixe f.

merry ('meri) adj 1 lustig, fröhlich. 2 inf beschwipst, leicht betrunken. **merry-go-round** n Karussell neu.

mesh (meʃ) n Masche f. Netz neu. vt verfangen. vi tech ineinandergreifen.

mesmerize ('mezməraiz) vt mesmerisieren.

mess (mes) n 1 Unordnung f. 2 Verwirrung f. Durcheinander neu. 3 Schmutz m. 4 mil Messe f.

message ('mesidʒ) n 1 Botschaft f. 2 Mitteilung f. **messenger** n Bote m.

met (met) v see **meet.**

metabolism (mi'tæbəlizəm) n Stoffwechsel m.

metal ('metl) n Metall neu. **metallurgy** n Metallurgie, Hüttenkünde f.

metamorphosis (metə'mɔːfəsis) n Metamorphose, Verwandlung f.

metaphor ('metəfə) n Metapher f.

metaphysics (metə'fiziks) n Metaphysik f.

meteor ('mi:tiə) n Meteor neu. **meteorology** n Meteorologie, Wetterkunde f.

meter ('mi:tə) n Messer, Zähler m.

methane ('mi:θein) n Methan, Sumpfgas neu.

method ('meθəd) n 1 Methode f. 2 Weise f. tech Verfahren neu. **methodical** adj methodisch. **methodology** n Methodologie f.

Methodist ('meθədist) n Methodist m.

meticulous (mi'tikjuləs) adj peinlich genau, penibel, übergenau.

metre ('mi:tə) n 1 Meter m,neu. 2 lit Versmaß neu. **metric** adj metrisch.

metropolis (mə'trɔpəlis) n Hauptstadt, Metropole f. **metropolitan** adj großstädtisch.

Mexico ('meksikou) n Mexiko neu. **Mexican** adj mexikanisch. n Mexikaner m.

miaow (mi'au) n Miauen neu. vi miauen.

microbe ('maikroub) n Mikrobe f.

microphone ('maikrəfoun) n Mikrophon neu.

microscope ('maikrəskoup) n Mikroskop neu.

mid (mid) adj in der Mitte, mittler. **midday** n Mittag m. **midland** n Mittelland neu. **midnight** n Mitternacht f. **midstream** n Strommitte f. **midsummer** n Hochsommer m. **midway** adj,adv auf halbem Wege. **midweek** n Mitte der Woche f.

middle ('midl) n Mitte f. Zentrum neu. **middle-aged** adj im mittleren Alter. **middle class** n Mittelstand m. Bürgertum neu. **middle-class** adj Mittelstands—.

Middle Ages n Mittelalter neu.

Middle East n Nahe(r) Osten m.

midget ('midʒit) n Zwerg m.

midst (midst) n Mitte f. **in the midst of** mitten unter, inmitten.

midwife ('midwaif) n Hebamme f.

might[1] (mait) v see **may.**

might[2] (mait) n 1 Macht f. 2 Gewalt f. **mighty** adj mächtig.

migraine ('mi:grein) n Migräne f.

migrate (mai'greit) vi (aus)wandern.

mike (maik) n sl Mikrophon neu.

Milan (mi'læn) n Mailand neu.

mild (maild) adj 1 mild. 2 sanft.

mildew ('mildju:) n 1 Meltau m. 2 Moder m.

mile (mail) n Meile f. **mileage** n Meilenzahl f. **mileometer** n Meilenzähler, Kilometerzähler m **milestone** n 1 Meilenstein m. 2 Markstein m.

militant ('militənt) adj militant, kämpferisch. n Kämpfer m. **military** adj militärisch. n Militär neu.

milk (milk) n Milch f. **milkman** n Milchmann m. **Milky Way** n Milchstraße f.

mill (mil) n 1 Mühle f. 2 Fabrik f. vt mahlen. vi herumirren. **millstone** n Mühlstein m.

millennium (mi'leniəm) n Jahrtausend neu.

milligram ('miligræm) n Milligramm neu.

millilitre ('milili:tə) n Milliliter m.

millimetre ('milimi:tə) n Millimeter m,neu.

million ('miljən) n Million f. **millionth** adj millionste. **millionaire** n Millionär m.

mime (maim) n Mime m. vt,vi mimen. **mimic** vt nachahmen. n Mimiker, Nachahmer m.

minaret (minə'ret) n Minarett neu.

mince (mins) vt zerhacken, zerstückeln. n Hackfleisch neu.

mind (maind) n 1 Geist, Verstand m 2 Sinn m 3 Meinung f. 4 Gedächtnis neu. vt 1 achten or aufpassen auf. 2 sorgen für, sehen nach. 3 sich kümmern um. 4 sich hüten vor. vt,vi etwas dagegen haben. **never mind!** macht nichts!

mine[1] (main) poss pron 1st pers s meiner, der meine or meinige.

mine[2] (main) n 1 min Mine f. Bergwerk neu. 2 mil Mine f. vi graben. vt 1 mil verminen. 2 abbauen.

mineral ('minərəl) n Mineral neu. Bodenschatz m. adj mineralisch. **mineral water** n Mineralwasser neu.

mingle ('miŋgəl) (vi),vt (sich) vermischen.

miniature ('miniətʃə) n Miniatur f. adj Klein—. Miniatur—.

minim ('minim) n Halbnote f.

minimum ('miniməm) n, pl -ma Minimum neu. **minimal** adj Mindest—, minimal.

mining ('mainiŋ) n Bergbau m.

minister ('ministə) n Minister m. **ministry** n Ministerium neu.

mink (miŋk) n Nerz m.

minor ('mainə) adj 1 kleiner, geringer. 2 geringfügig. n 1 Minderjährige(r). 2 Moll neu. **minority** n Minderheit, Minorität f.

minstrel ('minstrəl) n 1 Minnesänger m. 2 Sänger m.

mint[1] (mint) n bot Minze f.

mint[2] (mint) n Münzanstalt f.

minuet (minju'et) n Menuett neu.

minus ('mainəs) prep wenigor, minus.

minute[1] ('minit) n Minute f.

minute[2] (mai'nju:t) adj winzig.

miracle ('mirəkəl) n 1 Wunder neu. 2 Wundertat f. **miraculous** adj wunderbar.

mirage ('mira:ʒ) n Täuschung f.

mirror ('mirə) n Spiegel m. vt widerspiegeln.

mirth (mə:θ) n 1 Fröhlichkeit f. 2 Heiterkeit f.

misbehave (misbi'heiv) vi sich schlecht benehmen.

miscarriage (mis'kæridʒ) n Fehlgeburt f. **miscarriage of justice** n Rechtsbeugung f.

miscellaneous (misə'leiniəs) adj verschiedenartig. n (newspaper column) Verschiedenes neu. **miscellany** n Gemisch neu. Sammlung f.

mischance (mis'tʃɑ:ns) n Mißgeschick neu.

mischief ('mistʃif) n 1 Unheil neu. Schaden m. 2 Unfug m. **mischievous** adj 1 schelmisch. 2 verderblich.

misconceive (miskən'si:v) vt mißverstehen, falsch begreifen. **misconception** n Mißverständnis neu.

misconduct (mis'kɔndʌkt) n schlechtes or unangemessenes Verhalten neu.

misdeed (mis'di:d) n Missetat f.

miser ('maizə) n Geizhals m.

miserable ('mizərəbəl) adj 1 elend, erbärmlich. 2 unglücklich.

misery ('mizəri) n Elend neu.

misfire (mis'faiə) vi 1 mot fehlzünden. 2 mil versagen. 3 scheitern.

misfit ('misfit) n 1 schlechtpassendes Stück neu. 2 Mensch, der sich seiner Umwelt nicht anpassen kann m.

misfortune (mis'fɔ:tʃən) n Unglück, Mißgeschick neu.

misgiving (mis'giviŋ) n Befürchtung f. Zweifel m.

misguided (mis'gaidid) adj irregeführt.

mishap ('mishæp) n Unfall m. Unglück neu.

mislay * (mis'lei) vt verlegen.

mislead * (mis'li:d) vt irreführen.

misprint ('misprint) n Druckfehler m.

miss¹ (mis) vt 1 verfehlen. 2 vermissen. 3 versäumen, verpassen. n Fehlschuß m. **missing** adj fehlend, abwesend.

miss² (mis) n 1 Fräulein neu. 2 cap (title of address) Fräulein, Frl.

missile ('misail) n Geschoß neu.

mission ('miʃən) n 1 Mission. f. 2 Auftrag m. **missionary** n Missionar.m.

mist (mist) n Nebel, Dunst m.

mistake * (mis'teik) n Fehler,· Irrtum m. vt verwechseln, falsch verstehen.

mister ('mistə) n Herr m.

mistletoe ('misəltou) n Mistel f.

mistress ('mistrəs) n 1 Lehrerin f. 2 Geliebte f. 3 Herrin f. 4 Frau des Hauses f.

mistrust (mis'trʌst) vt mißtrauen. n Mißtrauen neu.

misunderstand * (misʌndə'stænd) vt mißverstehen. **misunderstanding** n Mißverständnis neu.

misuse (v mis'ju:z; n mis'ju:s) vt mißbrauchen. n Mißbrauch m.

mitre ('maitə) n Bischofsmütze f.

mitten ('mitn) n Fausthandschuh m.

mix (miks) vt (ver)mischen. **mix up** 1 verwechseln. 2 vermischen. ~n Mischung f. **mixture** n Mischung f.

moan (moun) vi 1 stöhnen. 2 jammern, meckern.

moat (mout) n Burggraben m.

mob (mɔb) n 1 Pöbel m. Gesindel neu. 2 Bande f.

mobile ('moubail) adj mobil, beweglich. **mobility** n Beweglichkeit f. **mobilize** vt mobilisieren.

mock (mɔk) vt verspotten, verhöhnen. adj nachgemacht, unecht, Pseudo—.

mode (moud) n 1 Weise, Methode f. 2 Form, Art f.

model ('mɔdl) n 1 Modell neu. 2 Vorbild neu. adj 1 Modell—. 2 vorbildlich.

moderate ('mɔdərət) adj mäßig. **moderation** n Maß neu. Mäßigung f.

modern ('mɔdən) adj modern. **modernize** vt modernisieren.

modest ('mɔdist) adj bescheiden. **modesty** n Bescheidenheit f.

modify ('mɔdifai) vt abändern, modifizieren. **modification** n Abänderung, Modifikation f.

modulate ('mɔdjuleit) vt 1 abstimmen, anpassen. 2 abstufen. 3 dämpfen. 4 modulieren.

module ('mɔdju:l) n Modul, Model m.

mohair ('mouhɛə) n Mohär m.

moist (mɔist) adj feucht. **moisten** vt (be-an-)feuchten, nässen. **moisture** n Feuchtigkeit f. **moisturizing cream** n Feuchtigkeitscreme f.

mole¹ (moul) n Muttermal neu. Leberfleck m.

mole² (moul) n Maulwurf m.

molecule ('mɔlikju:l) n Molekül neu.

molest (mə'lest) vt belästigen.

mollusc ('mɔləsk) n Weichtier neu. Molluske f.

molten ('moultən) adj 1 geschmolzen. 2 (of metal) flüssig.

moment ('moumənt) n Moment, Augenblick m. **momentary** adj momentan, augenblicklich. **momentous** adj bedeutend, gewichtig.

momentum n Triebkraft, Schwungkraft f. Impuls m.

monarch ('monək) n Monarch m.

monastery ('monəstri) n (Mönchs)Kloster neu.

Monday ('mʌndi) n Montag m.

money ('mʌni) n Geld neu. **get one's money's worth** etwas für sein Geld bekommen. **moneybox** n Sparbüchse f. **money order** n Postanweisung f. **monetary** adj 1 Geld—. 2 finanziell.

mongrel ('mʌngrəl) n Mischling m. Kreuzung f.

monitor ('monitə) n Monitor m. vt 1 abhören. 2 kontrollieren, überwachen.

monk (mʌŋk) n Mönch m.

monkey ('mʌŋki) n Affe m.

monogamy (mə'nogəmi) n Monogamie, Einehe f.

monologue ('monəlog) n Monolog m.

monopolize (mə'nopəlaiz) vt monopolisieren. **monopoly** n Monopol neu.

monosyllable ('monəsiləbəl) n einsilbiges Wort neu. **speak in monosyllables** einsilbige Antworten geben.

monotone ('monətoun) n Eintönigkeit, Monotonie f. **monotonous** adj eintönig, monoton.

monsoon (mon'su:n) n Monsun m.

monster ('monstə) n 1 Ungeheuer neu. 2 Scheusal neu. **monstrous** adj 1 ungeheuer, riesig. 2 ungeheuerlich. 3 scheußlich.

month (mʌnθ) n Monat m.

monument ('monjumənt) n Denkmal, Monument neu.

moo (mu:) vi muhen.

mood[1] (mu:d) n Laune, Stimmung f. **be in a good/bad mood** guter/schlechter Laune sein. **moody** adj launisch.

mood[2] (mu:d) n Modus m.

moon (mu:n) n Mond m. **moonlight** n Mondlicht neu. Mondschein m.

moor[1] (muə) n Moor neu. **moorhen** n Teichhuhn neu. **moorland** n Moor(land) neu.

moor[2] (muə) vt festmachen, verankern.

Moor (muə) n Maure m. **Moorish** adj maurisch.

mop (mop) n Mop, Staubbesen m. vt (auf)-wischen.

mope (moup) vi traurig sein.

moped ('mouped) n Moped neu.

moral ('morəl) n 1 Moral, Lehre f. 2 pl Moral f. Sitten f pl. adj moralisch. **morale** n Moral f. **morality** n 1 Moral(ität) f. 2 Sittlichkeit f. **moralize** vi moralisieren.

morbid ('mɔ:bid) adj krankhaft, morbid.

more (mɔ:) adj 1 mehr. 2 mehr, noch (etwas), weiter. adv 1 mehr. 2 noch. **more and more** immer mehr. **more or less** mehr oder weniger. **moreover** adv außerdem, weiter, ferner.

morgue (mɔ:g) n Leichenschauhaus neu.

morning ('mɔ:niŋ) n 1 Morgen m. 2 Vormittag m. **in the mornings** morgens. **this morning** heute früh, heute morgen.

Morocco (mə'rɔkou) n Marokko neu. **Moroccan** adj marokkanisch. n Marokkaner m.

moron ('mɔ:rɔn) n Schwachsinnige(r) m.

morose (mə'rous) adj mürrisch, verdrießlich.

morphine ('mɔ:fi:n) n Morphium neu.

morse code ('mɔ:s) n Morsealphabet neu.

mortal ('mɔ:tl) adj sterblich. **mortality** n Sterblichkeit f.

mortar[1] ('mɔ:tə) n Mörser m.

mortar[2] ('mɔ:tə) n (for building) Mörtel m.

mortgage ('mɔ:gidʒ) n Hypothek f. vt 1 eine Hypothek nehmen auf. 2 verpfänden.

mortify ('mɔ:tifai) vt 1 demütigen. 2 abtöten.

mortuary ('mɔ:tjuəri) n Leichenhalle f.

mosaic (mou'zeiik) n Mosaik neu.

Moselle (mou'zel) n 1 Mosel f. 2 Moselwein m.

mosque (mɔsk) n Moschee f.

mosquito (mə'ski:tou) n pl **-oes** or **-os** Mücke f. Moskito m.

moss (mɔs) n Moos neu.

most (moust) adj 1 die meisten. 2 meist, höchst. adv am meisten, Meist—. n 1 das meiste, das Höchste neu. 2 der größte Teil m. **mostly** adv 1 hauptsächlich. 2 größtenteils.

motel (mou'tel) n Motel neu.

moth (mɔθ) n Motte f.

mother ('mʌðə) n Mutter f. vt bemuttern. **motherhood** n Mutterschaft f. **mother-in-law** n Schwiegermutter f. **mother superior** n Äbtissin f.

motion ('mouʃən) n 1 Bewegung f. 2 Gang m. 3 Antrieb m. vt zuwinken.

motive ('moutiv) n Beweggrund m.

motor ('moutə) n Motor m. **motor car** n Auto(mobil) neu. Personenkraftwagen m. **motorcycle** n Motorrad neu. **motorcyclist** n Motorradfahrer m. **motorist** n Autofahrer m. **motorway** n Autobahn f.

mottled ('motld) adj gefleckt.

motto ('motou) n Motto neu. Sinnspruch m.

mould[1] (mould) n 1 tech (Guß)Form f. 2 Art f. vt 1 tech gießen. 2 formen, bilden.

mould[2] (mould) n Schimmel m. **mouldy** adj schimm(e)lig.

moult (moult) vi **1** (of birds) sich mausern. **2** (of animals) sich häuten.

mound (maund) n Hügel, Erdwall m.

mount[1] (maunt) vt **1** besteigen. **2** hinaufgehen. **3** einbauen. **4** aufkleben. **5** montieren.

mount[2] (maunt) n Berg m.

mountain ('mauntin) n Berg m. **mountaineer** n Alpinist, Bergsteiger m.

mourn (mɔ:n) vt betrauern. vi trauern. **mourning** n Trauer f. **go into mourning** Trauer anlegen.

mouse (maus) n, pl **mice** Maus f. **mousetrap** n Mausefalle f. **mousy** adj **1** mauseartig. **2** grau.

mousse (mu:s) n Kremeis neu.

moustache (məˈstɑːʃ) n Schnurrbart m.

mouth (mauθ) n **1** Mund m. **2** Öffnung f. **3** geog Mündung f. **mouthpiece** n Mundstück neu. **mouth-watering** adj schmackhaft.

move (mu:v) (vi), vt **1** (sich) bewegen. **2** (sich) rühren. **3** umziehen. vi **1** Bewegung f. **2** Umzug m. **3** Schritt m. **4** (taktischer) Zug m. **movable** adj beweglich. **movement** n **1** Bewegung f. **2** mus Satz m. **3** Lauf m. **moving** adj **1** (sich) bewegend. **2** rührend, packend.

mow* (mou) vt mähen.

Mr ('mistə) (title of address) Herr.

Mrs ('misiz) (title of address) Frau.

much (mʌtʃ) adj viel. adv **1** sehr. **2** viel. **3** bei weitem. **how much** wieviel.

muck (mʌk) n **1** Mist m. **2** Dreck, Schmutz m. **mucky** adj dreckig.

mud (mʌd) n Schlamm, Schmutz m. **muddy** adj schlammig. **mudguard** n Kotflügel m.

muddle ('mʌdl) n Durcheinander, Wirrwarr m. vt verwirren. **muddle up** verwechseln. **muddle through** sich durchwursteln.

muff (mʌf) n Muff m. vt inf verpfuschen.

muffle ('mʌfəl) vt dämpfen, unterdrücken.

mug (mʌg) n **1** Becher, Krug m. **2** inf Dumme(r) m.

mulberry ('mʌlbəri) n Maulbeere f.

mule[1] (mju:l) n Maultier neu.

mule[2] (mju:l) n Pantoffel m.

multiple ('mʌltipəl) adj mehrfach, vielfach.

multiply ('mʌltiplai) vt math multiplizieren. (vi), vt (sich) vermehren.

multitude ('mʌltitju:d) n Menge, große Zahl f.

mum (mʌm) n inf Mutti f.

mumble ('mʌmbəl) vi, vt murmeln.

mummy[1] ('mʌmi) n Mumie f.

mummy[2] ('mʌmi) n inf Mutti f.

mumps (mʌmps) n Mumps, Ziegenpeter m.

munch (mʌntʃ) vt, vi hörbar kauen, schmatzen.

mundane ('mʌndein) adj **1** alltäglich, banal. **2** weltlich, irdisch.

Munich ('mju:nik) n München neu.

municipal (mju'nisipəl) adj städtisch, Stadt—. **municipality** n Stadt f. Stadtbezirk m.

mural ('mjuərəl) n Wandgemälde neu.

murder ('mə:də) n Mord m. vt ermorden. **murderer** n Mörder m.

murmur ('mə:mə) n Murmeln neu. vt murmeln.

muscle ('mʌsəl) n Muskel m.

muse (mju:z) n Muse f. vi (nach)sinnen, (nach)-denken.

museum (mju'ziəm) n Museum neu.

mushroom ('mʌʃrum) n Pilz, Champignon m.

music ('mu:zik) n Musik f. **musical** adj musikalisch. **musician** n Musiker m.

musk (mʌsk) n **1** zool Moschus m. **2** bot Moschuspflanze f.

musket ('mʌskit) n Muskete, Flinte f.

Muslim ('muzlim) n Muselmann, Mohammedaner m. adj mohammedanisch.

muslin ('mʌzlin) n Musselin m.

mussel ('mʌsəl) n Muschel f.

must*[1] (mʌst) v mod aux müssen.

must[2] (mʌst) n Most m.

mustard ('mʌstəd) n Senf m. adj senfgelb.

mute (mju:t) adj **1** stumm. **2** still, schweigend. n Stumme(r) m.

mutilate ('mju:tileit) vt verstümmeln, entstellen. **mutilation** n Verstümmelung f.

mutiny ('mju:tini) n Meuterei f.

mutter ('mʌtə) vt, vi murren, murmeln.

mutton ('mʌtn) n Hammelfleisch neu.

mutual ('mju:tjuəl) adj **1** gegenseitig. **2** gemeinsam.

muzzle ('mʌzəl) n **1** Maul neu. Schnauze f. **2** (of a gun) Mündung f. vt knebeln.

my (mai) poss adj 1st pers s mein. **myself** pron 1st pers s **1** mich. **2** mich selbst. **3** ich selbst. **by myself** allein.

myrrh (mə:) n Myrrhe f.

mystery ('mistəri) n **1** Geheimnis neu. **2** Rätsel neu. **mysterious** adj geheimnisvoll, mysteriös, rätselhaft.

mystic ('mistik) n Mystiker m. adj mystisch. **mysticism** n Mystizismus m.

mystify ('mistifai) vt **1** verwirren, irremachen. **2** täuschen. **3** in Dunkel hüllen.

mystique (mi'sti:k) n **1** Atmosphäre des Mysteriösen f. **2** Geheimnis neu.

myth (miθ) n Mythos m. **mythology** n Mythologie f.

N

nag[1] (næg) vt nörgeln.

nag[2] (næg) n inf Gaul m.

nail (neil) n Nagel m. **hit the nail on the head** den Nagel auf den Kopf treffen. **nailbrush** n Nagelbürste f. **nailfile** n Nagelfeile f. **nail varnish** n Nagellack m. ~vt nageln.

naive (naiˈiːv) adj naiv.

naked (ˈneikid) adj 1 nackt. 2 bloß.

name (neim) n Name m. **namesake** n Namensvetter m. vt nennen. **nameless** adj 1 namenlos. 2 unbekannt. 3 unerwähnt. **namely** adv nämlich.

nanny (ˈnæni) n Kinderpflegerin f.

nap (næp) n inf Schläfchen, Nickerchen neu.

napkin (ˈnæpkin) n Serviette f.

Naples (ˈneiplz) n Neapel neu.

nappy (ˈnæpi) n Windel f.

narcotic (naːˈkɔtik) n Betäubungsmittel, Narkotikum neu. adj betäubend, narkotisch.

narrate (nəˈreit) vt erzählen. **narrative** n Erzählung f.

narrow (ˈnærou) adj eng, schmal. **narrow minded** adj beschränkt, kleinlich, engstirnig.

nasal (ˈneizəl) adj nasal, Nasen—.

nasturtium (nəˈstəːʃəm) n Kapuzinerkresse f.

nasty (ˈnaːsti) adj 1 unangenehm, widerlich. 2 gemein. 3 schlimm, ernst.

nation (ˈneiʃən) n Nation f. Volk neu. **nation-wide** adj allgemein, die Nation umfassend, weit verbreitet. **national** adj national. **national anthem** n Nationalhymne f. **national insurance** n Sozialversicherung f. **national service** n Militärdienst m. **nationalism** n Nationalismus m. **nationality** n Nationalität, Staatsangehörigkeit f. **nationalize** vt nationalisieren, verstaatlichen.

native (ˈneitiv) n 1 Eingeborene(r) m. 2 Einheimische(r) m. adj einheimisch.

nativity (nəˈtiviti) n Geburt (Christi) f. **nativity play** Christfestspiel neu.

natural (ˈnætʃərəl) adj natürlich. **natural gas** n Erdgas neu. **natural history** n Naturgeschichte f. **natural science** n Naturwissenschaft f. **naturalize** vt naturalisieren, einbürgern.

nature (ˈneitʃə) n 1 Natur f. 2 Wesen neu. Art f. 3 Charakter m.

naughty (ˈnɔːti) adj unartig, schlimm.

nausea (ˈnɔːsiə, -ziə) n 1 Übelkeit f. 2 Ekel m. **nauseate** vt anekeln.

nautical (ˈnɔːtikəl) adj nautisch, See—.

naval (ˈneivəl) adj Marine—, See—, Flotten—.

nave (neiv) n Kirchenschiff neu.

navel (ˈneivəl) n Nabel m.

navigate (ˈnævigeit) vt steuern, befahren. vi navigieren. **navigation** n Nautik, Navigation f.

navy (ˈneivi) n Kriegsmarine, (Kriegs)Flotte f. **navy blue** adj marineblau. n Marineblau neu.

near (niə) prep nahe, in der Nähe von. adj,adv nahe. **nearby** adj nahe(gelegen). adv in der Nähe. **nearly** adv nahe, fast, beinahe. **nearside** n Fahrerseite f.

neat (niːt) adj sauber, nett, ordentlich.

nebulous (ˈnebjuləs) adj nebelhaft, unbestimmt, verschwommen.

necessary (ˈnesəsəri) adj notwendig, nötig, erforderlich. **necessarily** adv 1 notwendigerweise. 2 unbedingt. **necessity** n 1 Notwendigkeit f. 2 Bedürfnis neu.

neck (nek) n Hals, Nacken m. **neckband** n Halsband m. **necklace** n Halskette f.

nectar (ˈnektə) n Nektar m.

need (niːd) n 1 Notwendigkeit f. 2 Bedarf m. Bedürfnis neu. 3 Not, Armut f. vt 1 benötigen. 2 brauchen. **needless** adj unnötig. **needless to say** selbstverständlich.

needle (ˈniːdl) n Nadel f. **needlework** n Näherei f. ~vt sl sticheln, reizen.

negate (niˈgeit) vt verneinen, leugnen, negieren. **negation** n Verneinung, Negation f. **negative** adj negativ. n 1 (of a photograph) Negativ neu. 2 Negation f. **answer in the negative** mit Nein antworten, verneinen.

neglect (niˈglekt) n 1 Nachlässigkeit f. vt 1 vernachlässigen. 2 unterlassen. **negligent** adj nachlässig. **negligible** adj unbedeutend, geringfügig.

negotiate (niˈgouʃieit) vt 1 verhandeln. 2 überwinden. vi verhandeln. **negotiation** n 1 Verhandlung f. 2 Überwindung f.

Negro (ˈniːgrou) n, pl **-oes** Neger m. **Negress** n Negerin f.

neigh (nei) vi wiehern. n Wiehern neu.

neighbour (ˈneibə) n Nachbar m. **neighbourhood** n Nachbarschaft f. **neighbouring** adj angrenzend, benachbart.

neither (ˈnaiðə) conj auch nicht. **neither...nor** weder...noch. adj,pron keiner (von beiden).

neon (ˈniːɔn) n Neon neu.

nephew (ˈnevjuː) n Neffe m.

nepotism (ˈnepətizəm) n Nepotismus m.

Neptune (ˈneptjuːn) n Neptun m.

nerve (nə:v) n **1** Nerv m. **2** inf Frechheit f. Mut m. **3** pl Nervosität f. **nerve-racking** adj nervenaufreibend. **nervous** adj **1** nervös. **2** Nerven—. **nervous breakdown** n Nervenzusammenbruch m. **nervous system** n Nervensystem neu.

nest (nest) n Nest neu. vi nisten.

nestle ('nesəl) vi sich schmiegen an.

net[1] (net) n Netz neu. vt fangen. **netball** n Korbballspiel neu. **network** n Netz neu.

net[2] (net) adj netto.

Netherlands ('neðələndz) n pl Niederlande f pl. **Netherlander** n Niederländer m.

nettle ('netl) n Nessel f.

neurosis (njuə'rousis) n Neurose f. **neurotic** adj neurotisch.

neuter ('nju:tə) n Neutrum neu. adj **1** sächlich. **2** geschlechtslos. vt kastrieren.

neutral ('nju:trəl) adj **1** neutral. **2** unparteiisch. **neutrality** n Neutralität f. **neutralize** vt neutralisieren.

never ('nevə) adv nie, niemals. **on the never-never** inf auf Abzahlung. **nevertheless** adv dennoch, nichtsdestoweniger.

new (nju:) adj neu. **newcomer** n Neuankömmling m. **newly** adv neulich, kürzlich. **news** n Nachrichten f pl. **a piece of news** Neuigkeit, Nachricht f. **newsagent** n Zeitungshändler m. **newspaper** n Zeitung f. **newsreel** n Wochenschau f.

newt (nju:t) n Wassermolch m.

New Testament n Neues Testament neu.

New Year n Neujahr neu. **New Year's Day** n Neujahrstag m. **New Year's Eve** n Silvester m.

New Zealand ('zi:lənd) n Neuseeland neu. adj neuseeländisch. **New Zealander** n Neuseeländer m.

next (nekst) adj **1** nächst. **2** folgend. **next door** nebenan. ~adv **1** nächstens. **2** das nächste Mal. n Nächste(r) m.

nib (nib) n (of a pen) Spitze f.

nibble ('nibəl) vi,(vt) knabbern or nagen (an).

nice (nais) adj **1** nett. **2** schön. **3** lieb, freundlich.

niche (nitʃ) n **1** Nische f. **2** passende Stelle f.

nick (nik) vt einkerben. n Kerbe f. **in the nick of time** gerade rechtzeitig.

nickel ('nikəl) n Nickel neu.

nickname ('nikneim) n Spitzname m.

nicotine ('nikəti:n) n Nikotin neu.

niece (ni:s) n Nichte f.

Nigeria (nai'dʒiəriə) n Nigeria neu. **Nigerian** adj nigerianisch. n Nigerianer m.

nigger ('nigə) n derog Neger, Schwarze(r) m.

niggle ('nigəl) vi nörgeln, herumtüfteln.

night (nait) n **1** Nacht f. **2** Abend m. **last night** gestern Abend. **spend the night** übernachten. **nightclub** n Nachtklub m. **nightdress** n also **nightgown** Nachthemd neu. **nightmare** n Alptraum m.

nightingale ('naitiŋgeil) n Nachtigall f.

nil (nil) n Null f.

Nile (nail) n Nil m.

nimble ('nimbəl) adj flink, behend.

nine (nain) adj neun. n Neun f. **ninth** adj neunte.

nineteen (nain'ti:n) adj neunzehn. n Neunzehn f. **nineteenth** adj neunzehnte.

ninety ('nainti) adj neunzig. n Neunzig f. **ninetieth** adj neunzigste.

nip[1] (nip) n leichter Biß, Kniff m. vt beißen, kneifen. vi flitzen. **nippy** adj inf spritzig.

nip[2] (nip) n Schlückchen neu.

nipple ('nipəl) n Brustwarze f.

nitrogen ('naitrədʒən) n Stickstoff m. Nitrogen neu.

no[1] (nou) adv nein.

no[2] (nou) adj kein. **in no way** keineswegs.

noble ('noubəl) adj **1** vornehm, edel. **2** adlig. n Edelmann m. **nobleman** n Edelmann, Adlige(r) m. **nobility** n **1** Adel m. **2** Vornehmheit f.

nobody ('noubədi) pron also **no-one** niemand, keiner. n inf Null f. Niemand m.

nocturnal (nɔk'tə:nl) adj nächtlich.

nod (nɔd) vt,vi (mit dem Kopf) nicken. n Kopfnicken neu.

node (noud) n Knoten m.

noise (nɔiz) n **1** Geräusch neu. Lärm m. **2** Krach m. **noisy** adj lärmend.

nomad ('noumæd) n Nomade m. **nomadic** adj nomadisch.

nominal ('nɔminl) adj nominell.

nominate ('nɔmineit) vt (er)nennen, nominieren.

nominative ('nɔminətiv) n Nominativ m.

non- pref nicht—.

nonchalant ('nɔnʃələnt) adj **1** gleichgültig. **2** unbekümmert. **3** nonchalant.

nondescript ('nɔndiskript) adj schwer zu beschreiben.

none (nʌn) pron **1** kein. **2** niemand. adv keineswegs.

nonentity (nɔn'entiti) n 1 inf unbedeutender Mensch, Null f. 2 Nichts neu.

nonsense ('nɔnsəns) n Unsinn m.

noodles ('nuːdlz) n pl Nudeln f pl.

noon (nuːn) n Mittag m.

noose (nuːs) n Schlinge f.

nor (nɔː) conj noch, auch nicht. **neither...nor** weder...noch.

norm (nɔːm) n Norm, Regel, Richtschnur f. **normal** adj normal.

Norman ('nɔːmən) adj normannisch. n Normanne m.

Normandy ('nɔːməndi) n Normandie f

Norse (nɔːs) adj altnorwegisch. n (language) Altnorwegisch neu.

north (nɔːθ) n Nord(en) m. adj nördlich, Nord—. adv nördlich. **northeast** n Nordost(en) m. adj,adv nordöstlich. **northeasterly** adj,adv nordöstlich. **northeastern** adj nordöstlich. **northerly** adj nördlich. **northern** adj nördlich. **northwards** adv nordwärts. **northwest** n Nordwest(en) m. adj,adv nordwestlich. **northwesterly** adj,adv nordwestlich. **northwestern** adj nordwestlich.

North America n Nordamerika neu.

Northern Ireland n Nordirland neu.

North Pole n Nordpol m.

North Rhine-Westphalia (west'feiliə) n Nordrhein-Westfalen neu.

Norway ('nɔːwei) n Norwegen neu. **Norwegian** adj norwegisch. n 1 Norweger m. 2 (language) Norwegisch neu.

nose (nouz) n Nase f. **nosy** adj inf neugierig.

nostalgia (nɔ'stældʒiə) n 1 Nostalgie, Sehnsucht f. 2 Heimweh neu. **nostalgic** adj wehmütig, voll Heimweh.

nostril ('nɔstril) n Nasenloch neu.

not (nɔt) adv nicht. **not a** kein.

notch (nɔtʃ) n Kerbe f. vt einkerben.

note (nout) n 1 Zettel m. 2 Notiz f. 3 Vermerk m. 4 Ton m. 5 Bedeutung f. **notebook** n Notizbuch neu. **notepaper** n Briefpapier neu. **noteworthy** adj bemerkenswert. ~vt 1 merken. 2 vermerken, aufschreiben. **notable** adj bemerkenswert, beträchtlich, hervorragend. **notation** n 1 Aufzeichnung f. 2 Schreibweise f.

nothing ('nʌθiŋ) pron nichts. n Nichts neu. **nothing of the kind** nichts dergleichen.

notice ('noutis) n 1 Notiz f. 2 Meldung f. Hinweis m. 3 Kündigung(sfrist) f. 4 Anschlag m. Plakat neu. **notice board** n Anschlagtafel

f. vt bemerken. **noticeable** adj 1 bemerkenswert. 2 merklich.

notify ('noutifai) vt benachrichtigen, bekanntgeben. **notification** n Benachrichtigung f.

notion ('nouʃən) n 1 Begriff, Gedanke m. 2 Idee f. 3 Vorstellung f.

notorious (nou'tɔːriəs) adj berüchtigt, notorisch, allbekannt.

notwithstanding (nɔtwiθ'stændiŋ) prep ungeachtet, trotz.

nought (nɔːt) n Null f. pron nichts.

noun (naun) n Hauptwort neu. Substantiv m.

nourish ('nʌriʃ) vt (er)nähren. **nourishing** adj nahrhaft.

novel¹ ('nɔvəl) n Roman m. **novelist** n Romanschriftsteller m.

novel² ('nɔvəl) adj neuartig. **novelty** n 1 Neuheit f. 2 Ungewöhnlichkeit f.

November (nou'vembə) n November m.

novice ('nɔvis) n 1 Anfänger m. 2 rel Novize m.

now (nau) adv 1 nun, jetzt. 2 sofort. 3 eben. conj nun. **nowadays** adv heutzutage.

nowhere ('nouwɛə) adv nirgends, nirgendwo.

noxious ('nɔkʃəs) adj schädlich.

nozzle ('nɔzəl) n 1 Schnauze. 2 Ausgußröhre f. 3 Düse f.

nuance ('njuːəns) n 1 Nuance f. 2 Abtönung f. 3 Schattierung f.

nucleus ('njuːkliəs) n 1 sci Kern m. 2 Mittelpunkt m. **nuclear** adj Kern—, Atom—, nuklear.

nude (njuːd) adj nackt. n 1 Nackte(r) m. 2 Art Akt m.

nudge (nʌdʒ) vt leicht anstoßen.

nugget ('nʌgit) n Goldklumpen, Nugget m.

nuisance ('njuːsəns) n 1 Ärgernis neu. Belästigung f. 2 lastiger Mensch m.

null (nʌl) adj nichtig, ungültig, null.

numb (nʌm) adj starr, empfindungslos. vt starr machen, betäuben.

number ('nʌmbə) n 1 Nummer f. 2 Zahl, Ziffer f. 3 (An)Zahl f. **numberplate** n mot Nummernschild neu. **numeral** n 1 Zahlzeichen neu. 2 Zahlwort neu. **numerate** adj rechenkundig. **numerical** adj zahlenmäßig, numerisch. **numerous** adj zahlreich.

nun (nʌn) n Nonne f.

Nuremberg ('njuərəmbəːg) n Nürnberg neu.

nurse (nɔːs) n Krankenschwester f. vt 1 pflegen. 2 aufziehen. **nursing home** n (Privat)Klinik f. Sanatorium neu. **nursery** n 1 Kinderzimmer neu. 2 bot Pflanzschule f. **nursery rhyme**

Kinderreim m. Kinderlied neu. **nursery school** n Kindergarten m.

nurture (ˈnɑːtʃə) vt **1** ernähren. **2** hegen.

nut (nʌt) n **1** Nuß f. **2** tech (Schrauben)Mutter f. **3** inf Kopf m. **in a nutshell** kurz gefaßt. **nutcrackers** n Nußknacker m. **nutmeg** n Muskatnuß f. **nutshell** n Nußschale f.

nutrition (njuːˈtriʃən) n Nahrung, Ernährung f.

nuzzle (ˈnʌzəl) vi **1** schnüffeln. **2** sich anschmiegen.

nylon (ˈnailən) n Nylon neu. **nylon stockings** n pl also **nylons** Nylonstrümpfe m pl.

nymph (nimf) n Nymphe f.

O

oak (ouk) n Eiche f.

oar (ɔː) n Ruder neu. **oarsman** n Ruderer m.

oasis (ouˈeisis) n Oase f.

oath (ouθ) n Eid, Schwur m.

oats (outs) n pl **1** Hafer m pl. **2** Haferflocken f pl. **oatmeal** n Hafermehl m.

obedient (əˈbiːdiənt) adj gehorsam. **obedience** n Gehorsam m.

obese (ouˈbiːs) adj fettleibig.

obey (əˈbei) vt **1** gehorchen. **2** befolgen.

obituary (əˈbitjuəri) n Todesanzeige f.

object (n ˈɔbdʒikt; v əbˈdʒekt) n **1** Gegenstand m. Objekt neu. **2** Ziel neu. Zweck m. vi **1** einwenden. **2** protestieren. **objection** n **1** Einwand m. **2** Abneigung f. **objective** n Ziel neu. Absicht f. adj sachlich, objektiv.

oblige (əˈblaidʒ) vt **1** binden, verpflichten. **2** nötigen. **3** gefällig sein. **be obliged to do something** etwas tun müssen. **be obliged to someone** jemandem dankbar sein. **obligation** n Verpflichtung f. **obligatory** adj verbindlich, verpflichtend.

oblique (əˈbliːk) adj schräg, schief.

obliterate (əˈblitəreit) vt **1** auslöschen, ausradieren. **2** unkenntlich machen.

oblivion (əˈbliviən) n Vergessenheit f. **oblivious** adj **1** vergeßlich. **2** nicht bewußt.

oblong (ˈɔblɔŋ) n Rechteck neu. adj rechteckig, länglich.

obnoxious (əbˈnɔkʃəs) adj anstößig, verhaßt.

oboe (ˈoubou) n Oboe f.

obscene (əbˈsiːn) adj obszön, unzüchtig.

obscure (əbˈskjuə) adj **1** dunkel, finster. **2** unbekannt. vt verdecken, verdunkeln.

observe (əbˈzɑːv) vt **1** beobachten. **2** bemerken. **observance** n **1** Beobachtung f. **2** Befolgung

f. **observant** adj aufmerksam, wachsam. **observation** n **1** Beobachtung f. **2** Bemerkung f. **observatory** n Sternwarte f. Observatorium neu.

obsess (əbˈses) vt verfolgen, quälen. **obsession** n Besessenheit f.

obsolescent (ɔbsəˈlesənt) adj veraltend.

obsolete (ˈɔbsəliːt) adj veraltet, überholt.

obstacle (ˈɔbstəkəl) n Hindernis neu.

obstinate (ˈɔbstinət) adj hartnäckig, eigensinnig. **obstinacy** n Hartnäckigkeit f.

obstruct (əbˈstrʌkt) vt **1** verstopfen, blockieren. **2** (ver)hindern. **obstruction** n **1** Verstopfung f. **2** Hindernis neu.

obtain (əbˈtein) vt erhalten, bekommen.

obtrusive (əbˈtruːsiv) adj aufdringlich.

obtuse (əbˈtjuːs) adj stumpf, stumpfwinkelig.

obverse (ˈɔbvəːs) adj Vorder—. n Kehrseite f.

obvious (ˈɔbviəs) adj offensichtlich, klar.

occasion (əˈkeiʒən) n **1** Gelegenheit f. **2** Anlaß m. **on the occasion of** anläßlich.

Occident (ˈɔksidənt) n Westen m. Abendland neu. **occidental** adj westlich, abendländisch.

occult (ɔˈkʌlt) adj okkult. **occultism** n Okkultismus m.

occupy (ˈɔkjupai) vt **1** besetzen. **2** bewohnen. **3** beschäftigen. **occupy oneself** sich beschäftigen. **occupation** n **1** Beruf m. Beschäftigung f. **2** mil Besetzung, Besatzung f.

occur (əˈkəː) vi **1** vorkommen, sich ereignen. **2** einfallen. **occurrence** n **1** Ereignis neu. **2** Vorfall m.

ocean (ˈouʃən) n Meer neu. Ozean m.

ochre (ˈoukə) n Ocker m. adj ockergelb.

octagon (ˈɔktəgən) n Achteck neu. **octagonal** adj achteckig.

octane (ˈɔktein) n Oktan neu.

octave (ˈɔktiv) n Oktave f.

October (ɔkˈtoubə) n Oktober m.

octopus (ˈɔktəpəs) n, pl **-puses** or **-pi** Krake m. Polyp m.

oculist (ˈɔkjulist) n Augenarzt m.

odd (ɔd) adj **1** ungleich. **2** seltsam, sonderbar. **3** (of numbers) ungerade. **oddity** n Seltsamkeit, seltsame Sache f. **oddment** Überbleibsel neu. Rest m. **odds** n pl Gewinnchancen f pl.

ode (oud) n Ode f.

odious (ˈoudiəs) adj verhaßt.

odour (ˈoudə) n Geruch m.

oesophagus (iˈsɔfəgəs) n, pl **-gi** Speiseröhre f.

of (əv; stressed ɔv) prep **1** von. **2** aus.

off (ɔf) adv **1** davon, fort, weg. **2** nicht frisch. **well/badly off** gut/schlecht daran.

offal (ˈɔfəl) n Fleischabfall m.

offend (əˈfend) vt beleidigen. **offence** n 1 Beleidigung f. Anstoß m. 2 Vergehen neu. **take offence** Anstoß nehmen. **offensive** adj anstößig, beleidigend. n Offensive f. Angriff m.

offer (ˈɔfə) vt anbieten. n Angebot neu.

offhand (ɔfˈhænd) adj 1 kurz (angebunden). 2 improvisiert, spontan, aus dem Stegreif. adv spontan.

office (ˈɔfis) n 1 Büro neu. 2 Dienst m. Amt neu. **officer** n 1 mil Offizier m. 2 Beamte(r) m. **official** adj offiziell. n Beamte(r) m.

officious (əˈfiʃəs) adj offiziös, aufdringlich.

offing (ˈɔfiŋ) n offene See f. **in the offing** in (Aus)Sicht, im Werden.

off-licence n Ausschank über die Straße m.

off-peak adj außerhalb der Hauptverkehrszeit.

off-putting adj abstoßend.

off-season adj außer Saison.

offset (ˈɔfset) vt ausgleichen.

offshore (ɔfˈʃɔː) adj 1 von der Küste entfernt. 2 vom Land kommend, ablandig.

offside (ɔfˈsaid) adj,adv sport abseits. n rechte Seite f.

offspring (ˈɔfspriŋ) n 1 Nachkomme m. 2 Nachkommenschaft f.

offstage (ɔfˈsteidʒ) adj hinter der Bühne f.

often (ˈɔfən) adv oft, häufig.

ogre (ˈougə) n Unhold, Riese m.

oil (ɔil) n 1 Öl neu. 2 Erdöl neu. vt ölen, schmieren. **oilfield** n Ölfeld neu. **oil painting** n Ölgemälde neu. **oil rig** n 1 Ölplattform f. 2 Ölbohrturm m. **oilskin** n 1 Öltuch neu. 2 pl Ölkleidung f.

ointment (ˈɔintmənt) n Salbe f.

old (ould) adj alt. **six years old** sechs Jahre alt. **old age** n Alter neu. **old-fashioned** adj altmodisch, veraltet.

Old Testament n Altes Testament neu.

olive (ˈɔliv) n 1 Olive f. Ölbaum m. 2 Olive f. adj olivgrün. **olive oil** n Olivenöl neu.

omelette (ˈɔmlət) n Omelett neu.

omen (ˈoumen) n Omen neu. Vorzeichen neu.

ominous (ˈɔminəs) adj unheilvoll, drohend.

omit (əˈmit) vt auslassen, weglassen. **omission** n Auslassung f.

omnibus (ˈɔmnibəs) n Omnibus, Bus m.

omnipotent (ɔmˈnipətənt) adj allmächtig.

on (ɔn) prep 1 auf. 2 an. 3 über, zu. adv 1 auf. 2 an. 3 weiter, vorwärts. **be on 1** an(geschaltet) sein. 2 los sein. **from...on** von...an.

once (wʌns) adv 1 einmal. 2 einst. **at once 1**

auf einmal. 2 sofort. **once and for all** ein für allemal.

one (wʌn) adj eins. n Eins f. pron 3rd pers s einer, man. **oneself** pron 3rd pers s sich (selbst). **by oneself** allein. **one-sided** adj einseitig. **one way** adj Einweg—. **one-way street** Einbahnstraße f.

onion (ˈʌniən) n Zwiebel f.

onlooker (ˈɔnlukə) n Zuschauer m.

only (ˈounli) adj einzig. adv 1 nur. 2 erst. **not only...but also** nicht nur...sondern auch. ~conj nur daß, jedoch.

onset (ˈɔnset) n 1 Anfang m. 2 Angriff m.

onslaught (ˈɔnslɔːt) n (plötzlicher) Angriff m.

onus (ˈounəs) n Last f.

onward (ˈɔnwəd) adv vorwärts, weiter. adj weitergehend. **onwards** adv vorwärts, weiter.

ooze (uːz) vi (durch)sickern, triefen.

opal (ˈoupəl) n Opal m.

opaque (ouˈpeik) adj undurchsichtig.

open (ˈoupən) vt 1 (er)öffnen. 2 aufmachen. 3 anfangen. adj offen, offenstehend, auf. **open-air** adj Freiluft—. **in the open air** im Freien. **open-air swimming pool** Freibad neu. **open-ended** adj offenendig. **open-handed** adj großzügig, freigebig. **open-hearted** adj offenherzig. **open-minded** adj aufgeschlossen, unvoreingenommen. **open-mouthed** adj 1 mit offenem Mund. 2 verblüfft, erstaunt. **open-plan** adj Großraum—. **opening 1** Öffnung, Lücke f. 2 Eröffnung f.

opera (ˈɔprə) n Oper f. **opera house** n Opernhaus neu. **operetta** n Operette f.

operate (ˈɔpəreit) vi 1 laufen, funktionieren. 2 handeln, Geschäft betreiben. 3 med operieren. vt betätigen. **operation** n 1 Arbeitslauf, Betrieb m. 2 Betätigung f. 3 med Operation. 4 mil Unternehmung, Operation f. **operative** adj tätig, wirksam. n Arbeiter, Handwerker m.

opinion (əˈpinjən) n Meinung, Ansicht f. **opinion poll** n Meinungsumfrage f.

opium (ˈoupiəm) n Opium neu.

opponent (əˈpounənt) n Gegner m.

opportune (ɔpəˈtjuːn) adj 1 günstig. 2 rechtzeitig.

opportunity (ɔpəˈtjuːniti) n Gelegenheit, Möglichkeit f.

oppose (əˈpouz) vt 1 ablehnend gegenüberstehen, bekämpfen. 2 entgegenstellen. vi Widerstand leisten, opponieren. **opposed** adj 1 entgegengesetzt. 2 feindlich. **as opposed to** im Vergleich zu.

opposite (ˈɔpəzit) adj 1 gegenüberliegend. 2

gegensätzlich. *n* Gegensatz *m*. **opposition** *n* 1 Widerstand *m*. 2 *pol* Opposition *f*.

oppress (ə'pres) *vt* unterdrücken, tyrannisieren. **oppression** *n* Unterdrückung *f*.

opt (ɔpt) *vi* wählen. **opt for** sich entscheiden für.

optical ('ɔptikəl) *adj* optisch. **optician** *n* Optiker *m*.

optimism ('ɔptimizəm) *n* Optimismus *m*. **optimist** *n* Optimist *m*. **optimistic** *adj* optimistisch.

option ('ɔpʃən) *n* 1 Wahl, Alternative *f*. 2 Option *f*. Vorkaufsrecht *neu*.

opulent ('ɔpjulənt) *adj* reich, üppig.

or (ɔ:) *conj* oder.

oral ('ɔːrəl) *adj* mündlich.

orange ('ɔrindʒ) *n* Apfelsine, Orange *f*. *adj* orangenfarbig.

orator ('ɔrətə) *n* Redner *m*.

orbit ('ɔːbit) *n* Umlaufbahn *f*. *vt* umkreisen.

orchard ('ɔːtʃəd) *n* Obstgarten *m*.

orchestra ('ɔːkistrə) *n* Orchester *neu*. **orchestral** *adj* orchestral.

orchid ('ɔːkid) *n* Orchidee *f*.

ordain (ɔː'dein) *vt* 1 bestimmen. 2 *rel* weihen.

ordeal (ɔː'diːl) *n* Qual, Plage, Nervenprobe *f*.

order ('ɔːdə) *n* 1 Befehl *m*. 2 Ordnung *f*. 3 *comm* Bestellung *f*. Auftrag *m*. 4 Stand *m*. **in order that** damit. **in order to** um...zu. *vt* 1 befehlen. 2 bestellen. 3 ordnen. **orderly** *n* Ordner *m*. *adj* ordentlich.

ordinal ('ɔːdin|) *adj* Ordinal—. *n* Ordnungszahl *f*.

ordinary ('ɔːdənri) *adj* 1 gewöhnlich, normal. 2 mittelmäßig, Durchschnitts—.

ore (ɔː) *n* Erz *neu*.

oregano (ɔri'gaːnou) *n* Origanum *neu*.

organ ('ɔːgən) *n* 1 Organ *neu*. 2 *mus* Orgel *f*.

organism ('ɔːganizəm) *n* Organismus *m*. **organic** *adj* 1 organisch. 2 geordnet.

organize ('ɔːgənaiz) *vt* 1 organisieren. 2 einrichten. **organization** *n* Organisation *f*. 2 systematischer Aufbau *m*. 3 Gesellschaft *f*.

orgasm ('ɔːgæzəm) *n* Orgasmus *m*.

orgy ('ɔːdʒi) *n* Orgie *f*.

Orient ('ɔːriənt) *n* Orient, Osten *m*. Morgenland *neu*. **oriental** *adj* orientalisch, morgenländisch. *n* Orientale *m*.

orientate ('ɔːrienteit) *vt* orientieren, richten. **orientation** *n* Orientierung *f*.

origin ('ɔridʒin) *n* 1 Ursprung *m*. 2 Herkunft *f*. **original** *adj* 1 original, ursprünglich. 2 origi-

nell, schöpferisch. **originate** *vi* entspringen, entstehen, ausgehen.

Orlon ('ɔːlɔn) *n Tdmk* Orlon *neu*.

ornament ('ɔːnəmənt) *n* Schmuck *m*. Ornament *neu*. Verzierung *f*. **ornamental** *adj* ornamental. **ornamentation** *n* Verzierung *f*.

ornate (ɔː'neit) *adj* geschmückt, veriert.

ornithology (ɔːni'θɔlədʒi) *n* Ornithologie, Vogelkunde *f*.

orphan ('ɔːfən) *n* Waise *m*.

orthodox ('ɔːθədɔks) *adj* 1 *rel* orthodox, rechtgläubig. 2 konventionell.

orthopaedic (ɔːθə'piːdik) *adj* orthopädisch.

oscillate ('ɔsəleit) *vi* 1 schwingen, oszillieren. 2 schwanken.

ostensible (ɔ'stensəbəl) *adj* 1 scheinbar. 2 angeblich.

ostentatious (ɔsten'teiʃəs) *adj* prahlerisch, prunkhaft.

osteopath ('ɔstiəpæθ) *n* Chiropraktiker *m*.

ostracize ('ɔstrəsaiz) *vt* verbannen, ausstoßen.

ostrich ('ɔstritʃ) *n* Strauß *m*.

other ('ʌðə) *adj* 1 ander. 2 weiter. 3 zweite. *adv* anders, ander. *pron* ander. **each other** einander. **otherwise** *adv* 1 sonst. 2 anders. 3 anderweitig.

otter ('ɔtə) *n* Otter *m*.

ought (ɔːt) *v mod aux* sollen.

ounce (auns) *n* Unze *f*.

our (auə) *poss adj 1st pers pl* unser. **ours** *poss pron 1st pers pl* unser, der uns(e)re or uns(e)rige. **ourselves** *pron 1st pers pl* 1 uns. 2 uns selbst. 3 wir selbst.

oust (aust) *vt* vertreiben, verdrängen.

out (aut) *adv* 1 aus. 2 heraus, hinaus. 3 draußen. 4 fort. **out and out** durch und durch.

outboard ('autbɔːd) *adj* Außenbord—.

outbreak ('autbreik) *n* Ausbruch *m*.

outburst ('autbɔːst) *n* Ausbruch *m*.

outcast ('autkɑːst) *n* Ausgestoßene(r) *m*.

outcome ('autkʌm) *n* Resultat, Ergebnis *neu*.

outcry ('autkrai) *n* Aufschrei *m*.

outdo (aut'duː) *vt* übertreffen.

outdoor ('autdɔː) *adj* Außen—, im Freien. **outdoors** *adv* draußen, im Freien.

outer ('autə) *adj* äußere, Außen—.

outfit ('autfit) *n* 1 Ausstattung, Ausrüstung *f*. 2 Gruppe, Mannschaft *f*.

outgoing ('autgouiŋ) *adj* 1 weggehend, abgehend. 2 gesellig. **outgoings** *n pl* Ausgaben *f pl*.

outgrow (aut'grou) *vt* herauswachsen aus.

outhouse ('authaus) n Nebengebäude neu.

outing ('autiŋ) n Ausflug m.

outlandish (aut'lændiʃ) adj fremdartig.

outlaw ('autlɔ:) n **1** Geächtete(r) m. **2** Bandit m. vt ächten.

outlay ('autlei) n Auslage f.

outlet ('autlet) n **1** Abfluß, Auslauf m. **2** Absatzmarkt m.

outline ('autlain) n **1** Umriß m. **2** Überblick m. **3** Abriß m. vt umreißen.

outlive (aut'liv) vt überleben.

outlook ('autluk) n **1** Aussicht f. **2** Standpunkt m. Weltanschauung f.

outlying ('autlaiiŋ) adj abgelegen, abseits liegend.

outnumber (aut'nʌmbə) vt an Zahl übertreffen.

outpatient ('autpeiʃənt) n ambulanter Patient m.

outpost ('autpoust) n Vorposten m.

output ('autput) n Leistung, Produktion f.

outrage (aut'reidʒ) n Gewalttat, Schandtat f. Exzeß m. vt schockieren, Gewalt antun.

outrageous (aut'reidʒəs) adj unerhört, empörend, schändlich.

outright ('autrait) adj,adv völlig, total.

outside (aut'said) n Außenseite f. adv **1** außen, draußen. **2** hinaus. **outsider** n Außenseiter m.

outsize ('autsaiz) adj übergroß.

outskirts ('autskə:ts) n pl Randgebiet neu. Vororte m pl.

outspoken (aut'spoukən) adj freimütig, offen.

outstanding (aut'stændiŋ) adj hervorragend.

outstrip (aut'strip) vt überholen, übertreffen.

outward ('autwəd) adj **1** äußere. **2** Auswärts—. adv auswärts, nach außen. **outwards** adv auswärts, nach außen.

outweigh (aut'wei) vt überwiegen.

outwit (aut'wit) vt überlisten.

oval ('ouvəl) adj oval. n Oval neu.

ovary ('ouvəri) n Eierstock m.

ovation (ou'veiʃən) n Huldigung, Ovation f.

oven ('ʌvən) n Ofen, Backofen m.

over ('ouvə) prep **1** über. **2** zu Ende, aus. **3** während. adv **1** (hin-, her-)über. **2** drüben. **3** übermäßig. **over again** von neuem nochmals.

overall ('ouvərɔ:l) adj gesamt, Gesamt—. n Arbeitsanzug, Schutzanzug m.

overbalance (ouvə'bæləns) vt,vi umkippen.

overboard ('ouvəbɔ:d) adv über Bord.

overcast ('ouvəkɑ:st) adj bewölkt.

overcharge (ouvə'tʃɑ:dʒ) vt **1** zu viel verlangen von. **2** überladen.

overcoat ('ouvəkout) n Mantel m.

overcome* (ouvə'kʌm) vt überwinden, überwältigen. adj überwältigt.

overdo* (ouvə'du:) vt übertreiben.

overdose ('ouvədous) n Überdosis f.

overdraft ('ouvədrɑ:ft) n Überziehung f.

overdraw* (ouvə'drɔ:) vt,vi überziehen.

overdue (ouvə'dju:) adj **1** überfällig. **2** verspätet.

overestimate (ouvər'estimeit) vt überschätzen.

overfill (ouvə'fil) vt überfüllen, überladen.

overflow (v ouvə'flou; n 'ouvəflou) vi überlaufen, überfließen. n Überlauf m. Überfließen neu.

overgrow* (ouvə'grou) vt überwachsen.

overhang (v ouvə'hæŋ; n 'ouvəhæŋ) vt überhängen über. n Überhang m.

overhaul (ouvə'hɔ:l) vt überholen. n Überholung f.

overhead (adv ouvə'hed; adj,n 'ouvəhed) adv oben, droben. adj obenliegend, Hoch—. **overheads** n pl (allgemeine) Unkosten f pl.

overhear* (ouvə'hiə) vt (zufällig) hören.

overheat (ouvə'hi:t) vi heißlaufen.

overjoyed (ouvə'dʒɔid) adj entzückt, überglücklich.

overland (adv ouvə'lænd; adj 'ouvəlænd) adv über Land. adj Überland—.

overlap (v ouvə'læp; n 'ouvəlæp) vi,(vt) sich überschneiden (mit). n Überschneidung f. Übergreifen neu.

overlay* (ouvə'lei) vt bedecken, überziehen.

overleaf (ouvə'li:f) adv umseitig.

overload (v ouvə'loud; n 'ouvəloud) vt überladen, überbelasten. n Überladung f.

overlook (ouvə'luk) vt übersehen.

overnight (adv ouvə'nait; adj 'ouvənait) adv über Nacht f. adj **1** Nacht—. **2** plötzlich.

overpower (ouvə'pauə) vt überwältigen.

overrate (ouvə'reit) vt überbewerten.

overreach (ouvə'ri:tʃ) vt (zu weit) hinausreichen über. **overreach oneself** sich übernehmen.

overrule (ouvə'ru:l) vt zurückweisen.

overrun* (ouvə'rʌn) vt überrennen.

overseas (ouvə'si:z) adv in Übersee. adj Übersee—.

overshadow (ouvə'ʃædou) vt überschatten.

overshoot* (ouvə'ʃu:t) vt hinausschießen über, zu weit gehen.

oversight ('ouvəsait) n Versehen neu.

oversleep* (ouvə'sli:p) vi verschlafen.

overspill* ('ouvəspil) n Überschuß m.

239

overt ('ouvə:t) *adj* offen(bar), offensichtlich.

overtake* (ouvə'teik) *vt* überholen.

overthrow* (*v* ouvə'θrou; *n* 'ouvəθrou) *vt* umwerfen, umstürzen. *n* Umsturz *m*.

overtime ('ouvətaim) *n* Überstunden *f pl*. **work overtime** Überstunden machen.

overtone ('ouvətoun) *n* **1** Unterton, Beiklang *m*. **2** *pl* Nebenbedeutungen, Assoziationen *f pl*.

overture ('ouvətʃə) *n* **1** Vorspiel *neu*. Einleitung *f*. **2** *mus* Ouvertüre *f*.

overturn (ouvə'tə:n) *vt* umstürzen, umstoßen, umkippen. *vi* umkippen, umschlagen, umfallen. *n* Umsturz *m*.

overweight (*n* 'ouvəweit; *adj* ouvə'weit) *n* Übergewicht *neu*. **be overweight** Übergewicht haben.

overwhelm (ouvə'welm) *vt* **1** überschütten, überhäufen. **2** überwältigen.

overwork (*v* ouvə'wə:k; *n* 'ouvəwə:k) *vt* **1** überanstrengen, mit Arbeit überlasten. *vi* sich überarbeiten. *n* Überarbeitung *f*.

overwrought (ouvə'rɔ:t) *adj* überarbeitet, überreizt.

ovulate ('ɔvjuleit) *vi* ovulieren. **ovulation** *n* Eiausstoßung, Ovulation *f*.

owe (ou) *vt* **1** schulden, schuldig sein. **2** verdanken. *vi* Schulden haben. **owing to** *prep* infolge.

owl (aul) *n* Eule *f*.

own (oun) *adj* eigen. **get one's own back** sich revanchieren. ~*vt* besitzen. *vi* sich bekennen. **own up** *inf* gestehen. **ownership** *n* **1** Eigentumsrecht *neu*. **2** Besitz *m*.

ox (ɔks) *n*, *pl* **oxen** Ochse *m*. Rind *neu*.

oxygen ('ɔksidʒən) *n* Sauerstoff *m*.

oyster ('ɔistə) *n* Auster *f*.

P

pace (peis) *n* **1** Schritt *m*. **2** Tempo *neu*. **3** Gangart *f*. *vt* **1** durchschreiten, überschreiten. **2** *sport* Schritt machen für. *vi* (einher)schreiten.

Pacific (pə'sifik) *adj* pazifisch. **Pacific (Ocean)** *n* Pazifik, Stiller Ozean *m*.

pacify ('pæsifai) *vt* **1** befrieden, den Frieden bringen. **2** besänftigen. **pacifism** *n* Pazifismus *m*. **pacifist** *n* Pazifist *m*. *adj* pazifistisch.

pack (pæk) *n* **1** Paket, Bündel *neu*. **2** Menge *f*. Haufen *m*. **3** Pack *neu*. Bande *f*. **4** Päckchen *neu*. Packung *f*. *vt* **1** (ver)packen. **2** vollstopfen. *vi* **1** packen. **2** sich zusammen-

drängen. **package** *n* **1** Packung *f*. Paket *neu*. **2** Ballen *m*. *vt* (in Pakete) (ver)packen. **packet** *n* Paket, Päckchen *neu*. **packing** *n* **1** Packen *neu*. **2** Packmaterial *neu*.

pact (pækt) *n* Pakt, Vertrag *m*.

pad[1] (pæd) *n* **1** Polster, Kissen *neu*. Bausch *m*. **2** Stempelkissen *neu*. **3** (Brief)Block *m*. **padding** *n* Wattierung, Polsterung *f*.

pad[2] (pæd) *n* (leises) Tappen, Trotten *neu*.

paddle[1] ('pædl) *n* Paddel *neu*. *vi* paddeln.

paddle[2] ('pædl) *vi* (im Wasser) spielen, herumpaddeln.

paddock ('pædək) *n* Pferdekoppel *f*.

paddyfield ('pædifi:ld) *n* Reisfeld *neu*.

padlock ('pædlɔk) *n* Vorhängeschloß *neu*.

paediatric (pi:di'ætrik) *adj med* pädiatrisch. **paediatrician** *n* Kinderarzt *m*.

pagan ('peigən) *n* Heide *m*. *adj* heidnisch.

page[1] (peidʒ) *n* Seite *f*. Blatt *neu*.

page[2] (peidʒ) *n* Page, Boy *m*.

pageant ('pædʒənt) *n* **1** (großartiges) Schauspiel *neu*. **2** Festspiel *neu*. **pageantry** *n* Prunk *m*. Gepränge *neu*.

paid (peid) *v see* **pay.**

pain (pein) *n* **1** Schmerz *m*. Pein *f*. **2** Leid *neu*. **3** Strafe *f*. **be in pain** Schmerzen haben. **take pains** sich Mühe geben. ~*vt* weh tun. **painful** *adj* **1** schmerzhaft. **2** schmerzlich. **3** peinlich. **painstaking** *adj* sorgfältig, gewissenhaft.

paint (peint) *vt* **1** malen. **2** anstreichen. *vi* malen. *n* **1** Farbe *f*. **2** Anstrich *m*. **3** Lack *m*. **wet paint!** frisch gestrichen! **paintbrush** *n* Pinsel *m*. **painter** *n* **1** Maler *m*. **2** Anstreicher *m*. **painting** *n* **1** Malen *neu*. Malerei *f*. **2** Gemälde, Bild *neu*.

pair (pɛə) *n* Paar *neu*. *vi* **1** sich paaren. **2** sich verbinden. *vt* paarweise anordnen, paaren.

Pakistan (pɑ:ki'stɑ:n) *n* Pakistan *neu*. **Pakistani** *adj* pakistanisch. *n* Pakistaner *m*.

pal (pæl) *n inf* Kumpel, Freund, Kamerad *m*.

palace ('pælis) *n* Palast *m*. Schloß *neu*.

palate ('pælət) *n* **1** Gaumen *m*. **2** Geschmack *m*. **palatable** *adj* **1** wohlschmeckend. **2** annehmbar, angenehm.

pale (peil) *adj* **1** blaß, bleich. *vi* blaß werden, erblassen. *vt* bleich machen.

Palestine ('pælistain) *n* Palästina *neu*. **Palestinian** *adj* palästinisch. *n* Palästiner *m*.

palette ('pælit) *n* Palette *f*. Farbenteller *m*.

palm[1] (pɑ:m) *n* Handfläche *f*. Handteller *m*. *vt* **1** berühren. **2** (in der Hand) verbergen. **palm off** abschieben. **palmistry** *n* Handlesekunst *f*.

palm[2] (pɑːm) *n bot* Palme *f.* **palm tree** Palmenbaum *m.*

Palm Sunday *n* Palmsonntag *m.*

pamper ('pæmpə) *vt* verwöhnen, hätscheln.

pamphlet ('pæmflət) *n* 1 Flugschrift *f.* 2 Broschüre *f.* **pamphleteer** *n* Pamphletist *m.*

pan (pæn) *n* Pfanne *f.* **frying pan** Bratpfanne *f.* **pancake** *n* Pfannkuchen *m.* **flat as a pancake** flach wie ein Brett.

Panama ('pænəmɑː) *n* Panama *neu.*

pancreas ('pæŋkriəs) *n* Pankreas *neu.*

panda ('pændə) *n* Panda, Katzenbär *m.*

pander ('pændə) *n* Kuppler *m. vt* verkuppeln. *vi* 1 kuppeln. 2 Vorschub leisten.

pane (pein) *n* 1 (Fenster)Scheibe *f.*

panel ('pænl) 1 (Tür)Füllung, Täfelung *f.* 2 *law* Geschworene *pl.* 3 Diskussionsteilnehmer *m pl.* Ausschuß *m.* **instrument panel** Armaturenbrett *neu.* ~*vt* täfeln, paneelieren. **panelling** *n* Täfelung *f.* Tafelwerk *neu.*

pang (pæŋ) *n* stechender Schmerz, Stich *m.*

panic ('pænik) *adj* panisch *n* Panik *f. vi* Angst bekommen, in eine Panik ausbrechen. **panic-stricken** von panischem Schrecken ergriffen.

pannier ('pæniə) *n* (großer) Korb *m.*

panorama (pænə'rɑːmə) *n* Panorama *neu.*

pansy ('pænzi) *n bot* Stiefmütterchen *neu.*

pant (pænt) *vi* keuchen, schnaufen. *n* Keuchen, Schnaufen *neu.*

panther ('pænθə) *n* Panther *m.*

pantomime ('pæntəmaim) *n* Pantomime *f.*

pantry ('pæntri) *n* Speisekammer *f.*

pants (pænts) *n pl* 1 Herrenunterhose *f.* 2 (lange) Hose *f.*

papal ('peipəl) *adj* päpstlich.

paper ('peipə) *n* 1 Papier *neu.* 2 *pl* (Ausweis)Papiere, Urkunden *f.* 3 Zeitung *f.* 4 *educ* schriftliche Prüfung *f. adj* Papier—. **paper money** Papiergeld *neu.* ~*vt* tapezieren. **paperback** *n* 1 Buch im Pappeinband *neu.* 2 Taschenbuch, Paperback *neu.* **paperclip** *n* Heftklammer, Büroklammer *f.* **paperwork** *n* Schreibarbeit, Büroarbeit *f.*

papier-mâché (pæpiei'mæʃei) *n* Papiermaché *neu.*

paprika ('pæprikə) *n* Paprika *m.*

par (pɑː) *n* 1 Gleichheit *f.* Pari *nou.* 2 Nonnwort *m.* 3 Normalmaß *neu.* **on a par with** auf derselben Ebene wie.

parable ('pærəbəl) *n* Parabel *f.* Gleichnis *neu.*

parachute ('pærəʃuːt) *n* Fallschirm *m.* **parachutist** *n* Fallschirmabspringer *m.*

parade (pə'reid) *vt* 1 *mil* vorführen, paradieren.

2 zur Schau stellen. *vi* 1 promenieren. 2 paradieren. *n* Parade, Vorführung *f.*

paradise ('pærədais) *n* Paradies *f.*

paradox ('pærədɔks) *n* Paradoxon *neu.* widersprüchliche Aussage *f.* **paradoxical** *adj* paradox, widersinnig.

paraffin ('pærəfin) *n* Paraffin *neu.*

paragon ('pærəgon) *n* Muster, Vorbild *neu.*

paragraph ('pærəgrɑːf) *n* Absatz, Paragraph *m.*

parallel ('pærəlel) *adj* 1 gleichlaufend, parallel. 2 entsprechend, Parallel—. *n math* Parallele *f.* 2 Parallelfall *m.* **draw a parallel** einen Vergleich anstellen. ~*vt* 1 gleich sein mit. 2 parallel laufen.

paralyse ('pærəlaiz) *vt* paralysieren, lähmen. **paralysis** *n* Lähmung, Paralyse *f.*

paramilitary (pærə'militəri) *adj* halbmilitärisch.

paramount (pærə'maunt) *adj* höchst, oberst.

paranoia (pærə'nɔiə) *n* Paranoia *f.* **paranoiac** *adj* paranoisch.

parapet ('pærəpit) *n* 1 *mil* Brustwehr *f.* 2 Geländer, Brüstung *f.*

paraphernalia (pærəfə'neiliə) *n pl* 1 *law* Paraphernalgüter *neu.* 2 Ausstattung *f.* Zubehör *neu.* 3 Drum und Dran *neu.*

paraphrase ('pærəfreiz) *n* Paraphrase, Umschreibung *f. vt* umschreiben, paraphrasieren.

parasite ('pærəsait) *n* Schmarotzer, Parasit *m.* **parasitic** *adj* schmarotzend, parasitisch.

paratrooper ('pærətruːpə) *n* Fallschirmjäger *m.*

parcel ('pɑːsəl) *n* 1 Paket, Bündel *neu.* 2 Los *neu.* 3 Parzelle *f.* **v parcel out** austeilen, verteilen.

parch (pɑːtʃ) *vt* (aus)dörren, austrocknen. **be parched** vor Durst verschmachten.

parchment ('pɑːtʃmənt) *n* Pergament *neu.*

pardon ('pɑːdn) *n* Verzeihung, Vergebung *f.* I **beg your pardon** ich bitte um Entschuldigung. ~*vt* verzeihen, entschuldigen. **pardon me** entschuldigen Sie! **pardonable** *adj* verzeihlich.

pare (pεə) *vt* 1 (be)schneiden. 2 schälen.

parent ('pεərənt) *n* 1 Vater *m.* Mutter *f.* 2 *pl* Eltern *pl.* 3 Elternteil *m.* **parental** *adj* 1 elterlich. 2 väterlich. 3 mütterlich. **parenthood** *n* Elternschaft *f.*

parenthesis (pə'rɛnθəsis) *n, pl* **-ses** 1 Parenthese *f.* 2 *pl* Klammern *f pl.*

Paris ('pæris) *n* Paris *neu.*

parish ('pæriʃ) *n* Pfarrbezirk *m.* Kirchspiel *neu adj* Pfarr—, zum Kirchspiel gehörig.

parity ('pæriti) *n* Gleichheit, Parität *f.*

park (pɑːk) *n* Park *m.* Parkanlagen *f pl.* **car**

park Parkplatz *m.* ~*vt* parken, abstellen. *vi* parken. **parking meter** *n* Parkuhr *f.*

parliament ('pɑ:ləmənt) *n* Parlament *neu.* **parliamentary** *adj* parlamentarisch.

parlour ('pɑ:lə) *n* Wohnzimmer *neu.* Salon *m.*

parochial (pə'roukiəl) *adj* 1 Pfarr—, Gemeinde—. 2 beschränkt, begrenzt.

parody ('pærədi) *n* Parodie *f. vt* parodieren.

parole (pə'roul) *n* 1 Ehrenwort *neu.* 2 *mil* Losungswort *neu.* Parole *f.* 3 bedingte Haftentlassung *f.* **on parole** auf Ehrenwort.

paroxysm (pærəksizm) *n* 1 (krankhafter) Anfall, Krampf *m.* 2 Steigerung (einer Krankheit) *f.*

parquet ('pɑ:kei) *n* Parkett *neu.*

parrot ('pærət) *n* Papagei *m.*

parsley ('pɑ:sli) *n* Petersilie *f.*

parsnip ('pɑ:snip) *n* Pastinak *m.* Pastinake *f.*

parson ('pɑ:sən) *n* Pastor, Pfarrer, Geistliche(r) *m.* **parsonage** *n* Pfarrhaus *neu.*

part (pɑ:t) *n* 1 Teil *m.* Stück *neu.* 2 Aufgabe, Pflicht *f.* 3 *Th* Rolle *f.* **play a part** eine Rolle spielen. ~*vi* 1 sich trennen, auseinandergehen. 2 Abschied nehmen. *vt* 1 teilen, trennen. 2 (the hair) scheiteln. *adv* teils, zum Teil. **parting** *n* 1 Scheiden *neu.* Abschied *m.* 2 (of the hair) Scheitel *m. adj* scheidend, Trennungs—. **part-time** *adj* teilzeitbeschäftigt. *adv* halbtags. **part-time job** Nebenbeschäftigung, Teilzeitbeschäftigung *f.*

partake (pɑ:'teik) *vi* 1 teilnehmen, teilhaben. 2 etwas an sich haben. *vt* teilen.

partial ('pɑ:ʃəl) *adj* 1 einseitig, parteiisch. 2 Teil—, partiell. **be partial to** eine Vorliebe haben für.

participate (pɑ:'tisipeit) *vi* teilnehmen, sich beteiligen. **participation** *n* Teilnahme *f.*

participle ('pɑ:tisəpəl) *n* Partizip *neu.*

particle ('pɑ:tikəl) *n* 1 Teilchen, Stückchen *neu.* 2 Partikel *n.*

particular (pə'tikjulə) *adj* 1 individuell, einzeln. 2 ungewöhnlich. 3 ausführlich. 4 peinlich, genau. **nothing particular** nichts Besonderes. ~*n* Einzelheit *f.* **in particular** besonders, insbesondere.

partisan (pɑ:ti'zæn) *n* 1 Anhänger, Parteigänger *m.* 2 *mil* Partisan *m.*

partition (pɑ:'tiʃən) *n* 1 (Auf)Teilung, Trennung *f.* 2 Trennwand *f.* 3 Abteilung *f. vt* (ver-, auf-)teilen. **partition off** abteilen, abtrennen.

partly ('pɑ:tli) *adv* teilweise, zum Teil.

partner ('pɑ:tnə) *n* 1 Teilhaber, Partner *m.* 2 Gatte *m.* Gattin *f. vt* sich zusammentun mit.

zusammenarbeiten mit. **partnership** *n* Teilhaberschaft, Partnerschaft *f.*

partridge ('pɑ:tridʒ) *n* Rebhuhn *neu.*

party ('pɑ:ti) *n* 1 Partei *f.* 2 Gesellschaft, Party *f.* 3 Gruppe *f.* 4 Beteiligte(r) *m. adj* Partei—. **party line** *n* festgelegte Parteipolitik, Parteilinie *f.* **follow the party line** linientreu sein.

pass (pɑ:s) *vt* 1 vorbeigehen, übergehen, überschlagen. 3 bestehen. 4 passieren. 5 verbringen. 6 durchgehen lassen. *vi* 1 vorbeigehen. 2 gehen. **pass away** sterben. **pass off** ausgeben. **pass through** durchfahren. ~*n* 1 Engpaß, enger Weg *m.* 2 Paß *m.* 3 (in an exam) Bestehen *neu.* **password** *n* Losungswort *neu.* Parole *f.*

passage ('pæsidʒ) *n* 1 Durchgang *m.* Passage, Durchfahrt, Durchfahrt *f.* 2 enger Gang, Weg *m.* Gasse *f.* 3 (in a book) Stelle *f.*

passenger ('pæsindʒə) *n* Fahrgast, Passagier *m.*

passion ('pæʃən) *n* 1 Leidenschaft *f.* 2 Zorn *m.* Wut *f.* 3 Liebhaberei *f.* **passionate** *adj* leidenschaftlich.

passive ('pæsiv) *adj* 1 passiv. 2 zurückhaltend, still, widerstandslos. *n* Passiv *neu.*

Passover ('pɑ:souvə) *n* Passahfest *neu.*

passport ('pɑ:spɔ:t) *n* (Reise)Paß, Ausweis *m.*

past (pɑ:st) *adj* 1 vergangen. 2 ehemalig. **past participle** *n* Partizip der Vergangenheit *neu. n* Vergangeheit *f.* Vergangene *neu. adv* vorbei, vorüber. *prep* 1 nach. 2 an...vorbei. 3 über...-hinaus.

pasta ('pæstə) *n* Teigwaren *f pl.*

paste (peist) *n* 1 Kleister, Klebstoff *m.* 2 Teig *m.* Paste *f. vt* (fest)kleben, kleistern.

pastel ('pæstəl) *n* Pastellfarbe *f.*

pasteurize ('pæstəraiz) *vt* pasteurisieren.

pastime ('pɑ:staim) *n* 1 Zeitvertreib *m.* 2 Erholung *f.* Belustigung *f.*

pastoral ('pæstərəl) *adj* Hirten—, Schäfer—.

pastry ('peistri) *n* 1 Gebäck, Backwerk *neu.* 2 Torten *f pl.* 3 Blätterteig *m.*

pasture ('pɑ:stʃə) *n* Weide *f.* Weideland *neu.*

pasty[1] ('peisti) *adj* 1 teigig, teigartig. 2 bläßlich, kränklich.

pasty[2] ('pæsti) *n* (Fleisch)Pastete *f.*

pat[1] (pæt) *n* Klopfen *neu.* Klaps *m. vt,vi* klopfen, klapsen.

pat[2] (pæt) *adj* bereit, glatt. *adv* genau.

patch (pætʃ) *n* 1 Lappen, Flicken *m.* 2 Fleck *m.* 3 (of land) kleines Stück *neu.* *vt* flicken. **patchwork** *n* 1 Flickarbeit *f.* 2 Buntgemustertes *neu.*

pâté ('pætei) n Pastete, Leberwurst f.

patent ('peitnt) adj 1 offen, offenkundig. 2 patentiert. 3 Patent—. n 1 Patent neu. Patentbrief m. vt patentieren. **patent leather** n Lackleder neu.

paternal (pə'tə:nl) adj väterlich, Vater—. **paternity** n 1 Vaterschaft f.

path (pɑ:θ) n 1 Pfad, Weg m. 2 Bahn f.

pathetic (pə'θetik) adj 1 rührend, ergreifend, pathetisch. 2 inf jämmerlich, armselig.

pathology (pə'θɔlədʒi) n med Krankheitslehre, Pathologie f. **pathologist** n Pathologe m.

patience ('peiʃəns) n 1 Geduld f. 2 Ausdauer f. **patient** n Kranke(r), Patient m. adj geduldig.

patio ('pætiou) n Innenhof, Terasse, Veranda f.

patriarchal (peitri'ɑ:kəl) adj patriarchalisch.

patrician (pə'triʃən) n Patrizier m. adj 1 patrizisch. 2 aristokratisch.

patriot ('peitriət) n Patriot m. **patriotic** adj 1 patriotisch. 2 vaterländisch.

patrol (pə'troul) n 1 mil Patrouille f. 2 (Polizei)-Streife f. (vt), vi (ab)patrouillieren.

patron ('peitrən) n 1 Patron, Schutzherr m. 2 Gönner m. 3 Kunde m. **patronage** n 1 Gönnerschaft, Protektion f. 2 law Patronatsrecht neu. 3 Schutz m. 4 Kundschaft f. **patronize** vt 1 gönnerhaft behandeln. 2 in Schutz nehmen, beschützen. 3 Kunde sein bei. **patronizing** adj gönnerhaft, herablassend.

patter[1] ('pætə) vi 1 klatschen, platschen. 2 trappeln. n 1 Platschen, Prasseln. neu. 2 Getrappel neu.

patter[2] ('pætə) n 1 Jargon m. 2 Geplapper neu. vi schwatzen, plappern.

pattern ('pætən) n 1 Muster neu. Schablone f. 2 Plan m. Anlage f.

paunch (pɔ:ntʃ) n 1 Bauch, Wanst m. 2 zool Pansen m.

pauper ('pɔ:pə) n Arme(r) m.

pause (pɔ:z) n 1 Pause, Unterbrechung f. vi innehalten, pausieren, warten.

pave (peiv) vt pflastern. **pave the way** den Weg bahnen. **pavement** n 1 Gehsteig m. 2 Pflaster neu.

pavilion (pə'viliən) n Pavillion m.

paw (pɔ:) n Pfote, Tatze f. vt mit den Pfoten kratzen, scharren, stampfen. vi scharren, kratzen.

pawn[1] (pɔ:n) vt verpfänden, versetzen. n Pfand neu. **pawnbroker** n Pfandleiher m.

pawn[2] (pɔ:n) n game Bauer m.

pay• (pei) vi 1 zahlen, Zahlung leisten. 2 sich lohnen, sich rentieren. vt 1 bezahlen. 2 schenken. 3 abstatten, machen. n 1 Bezahlung f. 2 Lohn m. 3 Belohnung f. **pay-packet** n Lohntüte f. **payroll** n Lohnliste f.

pea (pi:) n Erbse f.

peace (pi:s) n 1 Frieden m. 2 Ruhe f. **peaceful** adj friedlich, ruhig. **peacemaker** n Friedensstifter m.

peach (pi:tʃ) n Pfirsich m.

peacock ('pi:kɔk) n Pfau m.

peak (pi:k) n 1 Spitze, Bergspitze f. 2 Gipfel, Höhepunkt m. adj Hoch—, Spitzen—. **peak hours** n pl Hauptverkehrszeit f.

peal (pi:l) n 1 Geläute neu. 2 Getöse neu. Krach m. vi 1 läuten. 2 erschallen.

peanut ('pi:nʌt) n Erdnuß f.

pear (pɛə) n Birne f.

pearl ('pə:l) n Perle f.

peasant ('pɛzənt) n Bauer, Landmann m. adj bäuerlich, ländlich.

peat (pi:t) n Torf m.

pebble ('pebəl) n Kieselstein m.

peck (pek) n 1 Picken, Hacken neu. 2 Küßchen neu. vt, vi picken, hacken.

peckish ('pekiʃ) adj inf hungrig.

peculiar (pi'kju:liə) adj 1 eigen(tümlich). 2 eigenartig. **peculiarity** n Eigentümlichkeit f.

pedal ('pedl) n Pedal neu. Fußhebel m. vt fahren, treten. vi 1 das Pedal treten. 2 radfahren.

peddle ('pedl) vt, vi hausieren

pedestal ('pedistəl) n Postament neu. Ständer, Sockel m. **put on a pedestal** aufs Podest heben.

pedestrian (pi'destriən) n Fußgänger m. adj 1 Fuß—, zu Fuß (gehend). 2 prosaisch, alltäglich. **pedestrian crossing** n Fußgängerübergang m.

pedigree ('pedigri:) n Stammbaum m.

pedlar ('pedlə) n Hausierer m.

peel (pi:l) n Schale, Rinde, Haut f. vt 1 schälen, entrinden. 2 abstreifen. vi sich abschälen, sich abblättern.

peep (pi:p) n Gucken neu. neugieriger Blick m. vi neugierig gucken.

peer[1] (piə) n 1 Peer, Adlige(r) m. 2 Gleiche(r) m.

peer[2] (piə) vi 1 spähen, scharf blicken. 2 sich zeigen, erscheinen.

peevish ('pi:viʃ) adj verdrießlich, mürrisch.

peg (peg) n 1 Pflock. Stift m. 2 (Wäsche)-Klammer f. vt 1 mit Pflocken befestigen, anpflocken. 2 (an)nageln.

pejorative (pɪˈdʒɔrətɪv) *adj* verschlechternd, herabsetzend, pejorativ.

pelican (ˈpelɪkən) *n* Pelikan *m*.

pellet (ˈpelɪt) *n* 1 Kügelchen *neu*. 2 Schrotkugel *f*. *vt* mit Kugeln bewerfen.

pelmet (ˈpelmɪt) *n* Vorhangsfalbel *f*.

pelt¹ (pelt) *vt* (be)werfen. *vi* 1 niederprasseln. 2 eilen. **pelting rain** *n* Platzregen *m*. ~*n* 1 Wurf, Schlag *m*. 2 Prasseln, Klatschen *neu*. 3 Eile, Geschwindigkeit *f*.

pelt² (pelt) *n* Pelz, Fell *m*.

pelvis (ˈpelvɪs) *n* Becken *neu*.

pen¹ (pen) *n* (Schreib)Feder *f*. *vt* 1 schreiben. 2 verfassen. **penfriend** *n* Brieffreund *m*. **penknife** *n* Taschenmesser *neu*.

pen² (pen) *n* Gehege *neu*. Pferch *m*. Koppel *f*. *vt* einpferchen, einschließen.

penal (ˈpiːnl) *adj* 1 Straf—. 2 strafbar. **penalize** *vt* 1 bestrafen. 2 belasten. **penalty** *n* Strafe, Buße *f*. **penalty (kick)** *sport* Strafstoß, Elfmeter *m*.

penance (ˈpenəns) *n* Buße *f*.

pencil (ˈpensl) *n* 1 Bleistift *m*. 2 Stift *m*. **pencil-sharpener** *n* Bleistiftspitzer *m*.

pendant (ˈpendənt) *n* 1 Anhänger *m*. 2 Hängeleuchter *m*. *adj also* **pendent** 1 herabhängend. 2 schwebend.

pending (ˈpendɪŋ) *adj* 1 hängend. 2 schwebend, unentschieden. 3 bevorstehend. *prep* 1 bis zu. 2 während.

pendulum (ˈpendjuləm) *n* Pendel *neu*.

penetrate (ˈpenɪtreɪt) *vt* 1 eindringen, durchdringen. 2 erforschen, ergründen. *vi* eindringen. **penetration** *n* Eindringen *neu*. Eindringungsvermögen *neu*. 3 Ergründung *f*.

penguin (ˈpeŋgwɪn) *n* Pinguin *m*.

penicillin (penɪˈsɪlɪn) *n* Penicillin *neu*.

peninsula (pəˈnɪnsjulə) *n* Halbinsel *f*.

penis (ˈpiːnɪs) *n* 1 Penis *m*. 2 *zool* Rute *f*.

penitent (ˈpenɪtənt) *adj* reuig, bußfertig. *n* Büßer *m*.

pennant (ˈpenənt) *n* Wimpel *m*. Fähnchen *neu*.

penny (ˈpeni) *n* 1 *pl* **pence** British unit of currency. 2 *pl* **pennies** Pfennig, Penny *neu*. **penniless** *adj* ohne Geld, mittellos. **be penniless** keinen roten Heller haben.

pension (ˈpenʃən) *n* Pension, Rente *f*. *v* **pension off** pensionieren, in den Ruhestand versetzen. **pensioner** *n* Rentner, Pensionist *m*.

pensive (ˈpensɪv) *adj* gedankenvoll, nachdenklich.

pent (pent) *adj* **pent up** 1 eingepfercht. 2 (of feelings) verhalten.

pentagon (ˈpentəgən) *n* *math* Fünfeck *neu*.

Pentecost (ˈpentɪkɔst) *n* Pfingsten *neu*.

penthouse (ˈpenthaus) *n* 1 Schutzdach *neu*. 2 Dachterrassenwohnung *f*.

people (ˈpiːpəl) *n* *pl* 1 Leute *pl*. 2 Volk *neu*. 3 Bevölkerung *f*. *vt* bevölkern, besiedeln. **people say** man sagt.

pepper (ˈpepə) *n* Pfeffer *m*. *vt* 1 pfeffern. 2 bestreuen. **peppercorn** *n* Pfefferkorn *neu*. **peppermill** *n* Pfeffermühle *f*. **peppermint** *n* 1 Pfefferminze *f*. 2 Pfefferminzbonbon *m,neu*. **pepperpot** *n* Pfefferstreuer *m*.

per (pə:) *pre* 1 pro. 2 per, durch, mit. **as per** gemäß, laut.

perambulator (pəˈræmbjuleɪtə) *n* Kinderwagen *m*.

perceive (pəˈsiːv) *vt,vi* 1 wahrnehmen, empfinden. 2 erkennen, begreifen.

per cent (pə ˈsent) *n* Prozent *neu*. *adj* —prozentig.

percentage (pəˈsentɪdʒ) *n* 1 Prozentsatz *m*. 2 Gewinnanteil *m*. Provision *f*.

perception (pəˈsepʃən) *n* 1 (geistige) Wahrnehmung *f*. 2 Empfindungsvermögen *neu*. 3 Vorstellung *f*. **perceptive** *adj* 1 wahrnehmend, empfindend. 2 auffassungsfähig.

perch (pə:tʃ) *n* (Sitz)Stange *f*. *vi* sich setzen.

percolate (ˈpə:kəleɪt) *vt* 1 filtern, perkolieren. 2 klären. *vi* durchsickern, durchlaufen.

percussion (pəˈkʌʃən) *n* 1 Schlag, Stoß *m*. 2 *mus* Schlaginstrumente *neu pl*.

perennial (pəˈreniəl) *n* perennierende Pflanze *f*. *adj* 1 fortdauernd, beständig. 2 perennierend.

perfect (*adj,n* ˈpə:fɪkt; *v* pəˈfekt) *adj* 1 vollkommen. 2 gründlich. 3 geschickt. 4 gänzlich, vollständig. *n* Perfekt *neu*. *vt* 1 vollenden. 2 vervollkommnen.

perforate (ˈpə:fəreɪt) *vt* durchbohren, durchlochen, perforieren.

perform (pəˈfɔ:m) *vi* 1 eine Vorstellung geben. 2 seine Aufgabe erfüllen. 3 arbeiten, leisten. *vt* 1 verrichten, ausführen. 2 vollenden. 3 aufführen, vortragen. **performance** *n* 1 Ausführung, Vollziehung *f*. 2 Aufführung, Darstellung *f*. 3 Leistung *f*. 4 Benehmen *neu*. 5 *inf* Theater, Getue *neu*.

perfume (ˈpə:fjuːm) *n* 1 Parfüm *neu*. 2 Duft *m*. *vt* parfümieren.

perhaps (pəˈhæps) *adv* vielleicht.

peril (ˈperəl) *n* Gefahr *f*. Risiko *neu*. **at one's peril** auf eigene Gefahr.

perimeter (pə'rimitə) n **1** math Umkreis m. **2** Peripherie f.

period ('piəriəd) n **1** Periode f. Zeitabschnitt m. **2** Pause f. Absatz m. **3** Weile f. **4** med Periode, Menstruation f. **5** educ (Unterrichts)-Stunde f. **periodical** n Zeitschrift f. Magazin neu. adj regelmäßig wiederkehrend, periodisch.

peripheral (pə'rifərəl) adj peripherisch, Umfangs—.

periscope ('periskoup) n Periskop neu.

perish ('periʃ) vi **1** umkommen, sterben. **2** verfallen, vergehen. vt zerstören.

perjure ('pə:dʒə) vt **perjure oneself** eidbrüchig or meineidig werden. **perjurer** n Meineidige(r) m. **perjury** n Meineid m.

perk (pə:k) vi **1** sich brüsten, den Kopf hochtragen. **2** sich vorrecken. **perk up** munter werden or machen, in Stimmung kommen. **perky** adj keck, munter.

perm (pə:m) n inf Dauerwelle f.

permanent ('pə:mənənt) adj **1** beständig, (fort)-dauernd, permanent. **2** dauerhaft. **permanence** n Beständigkeit, Permanenz f.

permeate ('pə:mieit) vt durchdringen. vi eindringen.

permit (v pə'mit; n 'pə:mit) vt,vi erlauben, gestatten. n **1** Erlaubnis, Genehmigung f. **2** Passierschein m. **permissible** adj zulässig. **permission** n Erlaubnis, Zulassung, Bewilligung f. **permissive** adj gestattend, zulassend.

permutation (pə:mju'teiʃən) n Permutation f.

pernicious (pə:'niʃəs) adj verderblich, schädlich.

perpendicular (pə:pən'dikjulə) adj senkrecht, lotrecht. n Senkrechte f.

perpetrate ('pə:pitreit) vt verüben, begehen. **perpetrator** n Täter m.

perpetual (pə'petʃuəl) adj **1** unaufhörlich, beständig. **2** lebenslänglich.

perpetuate (pə'petʃueit) vt verewigen, immerwährend fortsetzen.

perplex (pə'pleks) vt verwirren, verblüffen.

persecute ('pə:sikju:t) vt **1** verfolgen. **2** plagen, belästigen.

persevere (pə:si'viə) vi beharren, nicht nachgeben.

Persia ('pə:ʃə) n Persien neu. **Persian** adj persich. n **1** Perser m. **2** (language) Persisch neu.

persist (pə'sist) vi beharren, hartnäckig bestehen.

person ('pə:sən) n **1** Person f. Individuum neu.

2 Persönlichkeit f. **personal** adj persönlich. **personality** n **1** Persönlichkeit f. **2** Ausstrahlung f.

personify (pə'sɔnifai) vt verkörpern, personifizieren.

personnel (pə:sə'nel) n Personal neu. Angestellte(n) pl. **personnel manager** n Personalchef m.

perspective (pə'spektiv) n **1** Perspektive f. **2** Aussicht, Fernsicht f. adj perspektivisch. **in perspective** in richtiger Perspektive.

Perspex ('pə:speks) n Tdmk Plexiglas Tdmk neu.

perspire (pə'spaiə) vi schwitzen, transpirieren. vt ausschwitzen. **perspiration** n Schweiß m.

persuade (pə'sweid) vt **1** überreden, verleiten. **2** überzeugen. **persuasion** n **1** Überredung f. **2** Überzeugung f. **3** Glaube m.

pert (pə:t) adj **1** keck, schnippisch. **2** munter, flink.

pertain (pə'tein) vi **1** (an)gehören. **2** sich ziemen. **pertinent** adj **1** angemessen, passend. **2** gehörig.

perturb (pə'tə:b) vt beunruhigen, ängstigen.

Peru (pə'ru:) n Peru neu. **Peruvian** adj peruanisch. n Peruaner m.

pervade (pə'veid) vt durchdringen, erfüllen.

perverse (pə'və:s) adj **1** schlecht, böse. **2** pervers, widernatürlich. **3** verstockt, störrisch. **4** verkehrt.

pervert (v pə'və:t; n 'pə:və:t) vt **1** verkehren, verdrehen. **2** verführen. n **1** perverser Mensch m. **2** Abtrünnige(r) m.

pessimism ('pesimizəm) n Pessimismus m. **pessimist** n Pessimist m. **pessimistic** adj pessimistisch.

pest (pest) n **1** Pest f. **2** Schädling m. **pesticide** n Schädlingsbekämpfungsmittel neu.

pester ('pestə) vt plagen, belästigen.

pet[1] (pet) n **1** (zahmes) Haustier neu. **2** Liebling m. adj Lieblings—. vt verhätscheln.

pet[2] (pet) n üble Laune f. vi übler Laune or mürrisch sein.

petal ('petl) n Blumenblatt neu.

peter ('pi:tə) vi **peter out** allmählich aufhören, sich totlaufen.

petition (pi'tiʃən) n Bitte, Bittschrift, Petition f. vt bitten, petitionieren. vi ansuchen.

petrify ('petrifai) vt **1** versteinern. **2** bestürzen, erschrecken. vi sich versteinern, zu Stein werden.

petroleum (pi'trouliəm) n Petroleum, Erdöl neu. **petrol** n Benzin neu.

petticoat ('petikout) n (Frauen)Unterrock m.

petty ('peti) adj 1 klein, unbedeutend. 2 engstirnig, kleinlich, beschränkt. **petty cash** n kleine Summen f pl. geringe Beträge m pl. **petty officer** n Maat m.

petulant ('petjulənt) adj 1 reizbar, launisch. 2 mürrisch, eigensinnig.

pew (pju:) n Kirchenstuhl m.

pewter ('pju:tə) n (Hart)Zinn neu.

phallus ('fæləs) n Phallus m.

phantom ('fæntəm) n Phantom neu. Erscheinung f.

pharmacy ('fɑ:məsi) n 1 Pharmazie f. 2 Apotheke f. **pharmacist** n Apotheker m.

pharynx ('færiŋks) n Schlund, Rachen m.

phase (feiz) n 1 Phase f. 2 Entwicklungsstadium neu. 3 Aspekt m. v **phase out** abwickeln.

pheasant ('fezənt) n Fasan m.

phenomenon (fi'nɔminən) n Phänomen neu. Erscheinung f. **phenomenal** adj phänomenal, außerordentlich.

philanthropy (fi'lænθrəpi) n Menschenliebe f. **philanthropist** n Menschenfreund, Philanthrop m.

philately (fi'lætəli) n Philatelie, Briefmarkenkunde f.

Philippines ('filipi:nz) n pl Philippinen pl.

Philistine ('filistain) n 1 Philister m. 2 Spießbürger m. adj spießbürgerlich, beschränkt.

philosophy (fi'lɔsəfi) n Philosophie f. **philosopher** n Philosoph m. **philosophical** adj 1 philosophisch. 2 gleichmütig.

phlegm (flem) n 1 med Phlegma neu. Schleim m. 2 Gleichgültigkeit f.

phlegmatic (fleg'mætik) adj 1 phlegmatisch, schleimhaltig. 2 phlegmatisch, gleichgültig, träge.

phobia ('foubiə) n Phobie, krankhafte Angst f.

phoenix ('fi:niks) n Phoenix m.

phone (foun) inf n 1 Telefon neu. Fernsprecher m. vi,vt anrufen, telefonieren.

phonetic (fə'netik) adj phonetisch.

phoney ('founi) adj unecht, falsch, Schein—.

phosphate ('fɔsfeit) n Phosphat neu.

phosphorescence (fɔsfə'resəns) n Phosphoreszenz f. Nachleuchten neu.

phosphorous ('fɔsfərəs) n Phosphor m.

photo ('foutou) n Photo neu.

photocopy ('foutoukɔpi) n Photokopie f. vt photokopieren.

photogenic (foutə'dʒenik) adj photogen.

photograph ('foutəgrɑ:f) n Photographie f. Lichtbild neu. vt photographieren. **photog-**

rapher n Photograph m. **photography** n Photographie f.

phrase (freiz) n 1 Redensart, (Rede)Wendung f. 2 Phrase f. 3 Satz m. vt formulieren, ausdrücken. **phrasebook** n Konversations-Handbuch neu.

physical ('fizikəl) adj 1 physisch, körperlich. 2 physikalisch. **physical education** n Leibeserziehung f.

physician (fi'ziʃən) n Arzt m.

physics ('fiziks) n Physik f. **physicist** n Physiker m.

physiology (fizi'ɔlədʒi) n Physiologie f.

physiotherapy (fiziou'θerəpi) n Physiotherapie f.

physique (fi'zi:k) n Körperbau m.

piano (pi'ænou) n Klavier, Piano neu. **pianist** n Klavierspieler, Pianist m.

pick¹ (pik) vt 1 hacken, picken. 2 auswählen. 3 pflücken, lesen. vi hacken, picken. **pick out** auswählen. **pick up 1** aufheben. 2 sl auflesen. 3 mot mitnehmen. 4 sich erholen. 5 (sound) abnehmen. ∼n Auswahl, Auslese f. **pickpocket** n Taschendieb m. **pick-up** n sl zufällige Bekanntschaft f. 2 kleiner Lieferwagen m.

pick² (pik) n Spitzhacke, Picke f.

picket ('pikit) n 1 Pfahl, Pflock m. 2 Streikposten m. vt einzäunen. vi (als) Streikposten stehen.

pickle ('pikəl) n 1 Eingepökeltes neu. 2 eingelegtes Gemüse neu. vt einpökeln, einsalzen, marinieren.

picnic ('piknik) n Mahlzeit im Freien f. Picknick neu.

pictorial (pik'tɔ:riəl) adj bildlich, illustriert, Bild—. n Illustrierte f.

picture ('piktʃə) n 1 Bild neu. 2 Gemälde neu. Zeichnung f. 3 pl Kino neu. vt sich vorstellen, darstellen.

picturesque (piktʃə'resk) adj pittoresk, malerisch, anschaulich.

pidgin ('pidʒən) n Verkehrssprache f. **pidgin English** Pidgin-Englisch neu.

pie (pai) n 1 Pastete f. 2 Torte f. **have a finger in the pie** die Hand im Spiel haben.

piece (pi:s) n 1 Stück neu. 2 Teil m. 3 (Geld)Stück neu. 4 game Figur f. **piecemeal** adv stückweise, Stück für Stück. **piecework** n Akkordarbeit f. ∼v **piece together 1** zusammensetzen. 2 zusammenreimen.

pied (paid) adj buntscheckig.

pier (piə) n 1 Pier m. 2 Landungssteg m. 3 Hafendamm m. 4 Pfeiler m.

pierce (piəs) vt 1 durchstechen, durchbohren. 2 durchdringen. vi eindringen.

piety ('paiəti) n Frömmigkeit, Pietät f.

pig (pig) n 1 Schwein, Ferkel neu. **pig-headed** adj dickschädelig, stur. **pig-iron** n Masseleisen, Roheisen neu. **piglet** n Schweinchen, Ferkel neu. **pigskin** n Schweinsleder neu. **pigsty** n Schweinestall m. **pigtail** n Zopf m.

pigeon ('pidʒən) n Taube f. **pigeonhole** n (Brief)Fach neu. vt einordnen.

piggyback ('pigibæk) adj,adv huckepack.

pigment ('pigmənt) n 1 Pigment neu. 2 Farbe f. Farbstoff m. vt pigmentieren, färben.

pike (paik) n Hecht m.

pilchard ('piltʃəd) n Sardine f.

pile[1] (pail) n 1 Haufen, Stapel, Stoß m. vt anhäufen, stapeln. **pile up** sich ansammeln, anhäufen. **pile-up** n mot (Massen)Zusammenstoß m.

pile[2] (pail) n 1 zugespitzter Pfahl m. 2 Pfeiler m. **piledriver** n Ramme f.

pile[3] (pail) n 1 Flaum m. 2 Flor m. 3 Haar, Fell neu.

piles (pailz) n med Hämorrhoiden f pl.

pilfer ('pilfə) vt,vi 1 stehlen. 2 mausen, klauen.

pilgrim ('pilgrim) n Pilger, Wallfahrer m. adj pilgernd, Wallfahrts—. **pilgrimage** n Pilgerfahrt, Wallfahrt f. **go on a pilgrimage** pilgern, wallfahren.

pill (pil) n Pille f. **the pill** inf die Pille.

pillage ('pilidʒ) vt ausplündern, rauben.

pillar ('pilə) n 1 Pfeiler m. 2 Säule f. **pillar-box** n Briefkasten m.

pillion ('piliən) n 1 Damensattel m. 2 Soziussitz m.

pillow ('pilou) n Kopfkissen neu. **pillowcase** n Kissenbezug m.

pilot ('pailət) n Pilot, Flugzeugführer m. vt 1 steuern, lotsen. 2 leiten, führen. **pilot-light** n 1 Zündflamme f. 2 Kontrollampe f.

pimento (pi'mentou) n Piment m.

pimp (pimp) n Zuhälter, Kuppler m.

pimple ('pimpəl) n Pickel, Pustel f.

pin (pin) n 1 Nadel f. 2 Stift, Bolzen m. vt 1 mit einer Nadel festmachen. 2 festnageln, festhalten. **pinball** n Kugelspiel neu. Flipper m. **pincushion** n Nadelkissen neu. **pin-money** n 1 Geldbetrag für kleine Sonderausgaben m. 2 Nadelgeld neu. **pinpoint** vt genau feststellen. **pinstripe** n Nadelstreifen m.

pinafore ('pinəfɔ:) n (Kinder)Schürze f.

pincers ('pinsəz) n pl 1 (Kneif) Zange f. 2 zool Krebsschere f.

pinch (pintʃ) vt 1 kneifen, drücken. 2 inf klauen. 3 beschränken, einschränken. vi drücken, kneifen. n 1 Kneifen, Zwicken neu. 2 Druck m. 3 cul Prise f.

pine[1] (pain) n bot Kiefer, Föhre f.

pine[2] (pain) vi sich sehnen, schmachten.

pineapple ('painæpəl) n Ananas f.

ping-pong ('piŋpoŋ) n Tischtennis, Pingpong neu.

pinion ('piniən) n 1 Flügelspitze f. 2 Flügel m. vt 1 beschneiden, stutzen. 2 binden, fesseln.

pink (piŋk) adj rosa. n bot Nelke f.

pinnacle ('pinəkəl) n 1 Spitzturm m. 2 Gipfel m. Spitze f.

pint (paint) n 1 Pinte f. 2 Schoppen m.

pioneer (paiə'niə) n 1 Pionier m. 2 Wegbereiter m. vt den Weg bahnen für, bahnbrechende Arbeit leisten.

pious ('paiəs) adj fromm.

pip[1] (pip) n Obstkern m.

pip[2] (pip) n Ton m. vi piepsen.

pipe (paip) n 1 Pfeife f. 2 Röhre f. Rohr neu. 3 Rohrleitung f. 4 pl mus Dudelsack m. vt durch ein Rohr leiten. **pipedream** n Luftschloß neu. **pipeline** n Pipeline, Rohrleitung f. **pipette** n Pipette f.

piquant ('pi:kənt) adj pikant, würzig.

pique (pi:k) n Groll, Ärger m. vt ärgern.

pirate ('pairət) n Pirat, Seeräuber m. vi plündern.

pirouette (piru'et) n Pirouette, Kreiseldrehung f. vi pirouettieren.

Pisces ('pisi:z) n Fische m pl.

piss (pis) vi tab urinieren, harnen. **piss off!** interj schleich dich! verzieh dich!

pistol ('pistəl) n Pistole f.

piston ('pistən) n 1 tech Kolben m. 2 mus Ventil neu.

pit (pit) n 1 Grube, Höhle f. 2 Zeche f. 3 Abgrund m. 4 (Pocken)Narbe f. vt 1 mit Narben bedecken. 2 zerfressen. **pitfall** n 1 Falle, Fallgrube f. 2 Gefahr f.

pitch[1] (pitʃ) vt 1 werfen, schleudern. 2 errichten, aufstellen. 3 mus stimmen. 4 festsetzen. 5 gabeln. vi hinstürzen. n 1 Wurf m. 2 mus Tonhöhe. 3 Stufe f. Grad m. **pitchfork** n Heugabel, Mistgabel f.

pitch[2] (pitʃ) n Pech neu. vt (ver)pechen.

pith (piθ) n 1 Mark neu. 2 Innere neu. Kern m. 3 Bedeutung f.

pittance ('pitns) n 1 Hungerlohn m. 2 kleiner Anteil m.

pituitary gland (pi'tjuətri) n Hypophyse f. Hirnanhang m.

pity ('piti) n 1 Mitleid, Erbarmen neu. 2 Jammer m. **what a pity!** wie schade! ~vt bemitleiden.

pivot ('pivət) n 1 Drehpunkt m. 2 (Tür)Angel f. vi sich drehen. vt 1 schwenken. 2 mit Angeln versehen.

pizza ('pi:tsə) n Pizza f.

placard ('plækɑ:d) n Plakat neu.

placate (plə'keit) vt besänftigen, beruhigen.

place (pleis) n 1 Ort m. 2 Stelle f. 3 Platz m. 4 Stand, Rang m. 5 Stadt f. 6 inf Wohnung f. Haus neu. **all over the place** inf überall. ~vt 1 stellen, legen, setzen. 2 unterbringen. 3 identifizieren. **placename** n Ortsname m.

placenta (plə'sentə) n Plazenta f.

placid ('plæsid) adj ruhig, gelassen.

plagiarize ('pleidʒəraiz) vt abschreiben, plagieren, nachahmen. vi ein Plagiat begehen.

plague (pleig) n 1 Plage f. 2 Seuche, Pest f. 3 Quälgeist m. vt quälen, verfolgen, belästigen.

plaice (pleis) n Scholle f.

plaid (plæd) n Plaid m,neu Schottenmuster neu. adj buntkariert.

plain (plein) adj 1 klar. 2 offen. 3 einfach, schlicht. 4 schmucklos, ungemustert. 5 unschön. **plain sailing** n einfache Sache, reibungslose Affäre f. ~adv klar. n Ebene, Fläche f. **plain-clothes** n Zivilkleidung f.

plaintiff ('pleintif) n law Kläger m.

plaintive ('pleintiv) adj 1 klagend, kläglich. 2 traurig.

plait (plæt) n 1 Falte f. 2 Zopf m. vt 1 (zu einem Zopf) flechten. 2 falten.

plan (plæn) n 1 Plan m. 2 Skizze f. Entwurf m. 3 Absicht f. vt 1 entwerfen, skizzieren. 2 planen, beabsichtigen.

plane[1] (plein) adj flach, eben. n 1 Ebene f. 2 Höhe f. Niveau neu. 3 Flugzeug neu. vi gleiten.

plane[2] (plein) Hobel m. vt ebnen, glätten, hobeln.

planet ('plænit) n Planet m.

plank (plæŋk) n Planke, Bohle f.

plankton ('plæŋktən) n Plankton neu.

plant (plɑ:nt) n 1 bot Pflanze f. 2 Fabrik f. Werk neu. vt 1 pflanzen. 2 bepflanzen. **plantation** n (An)Pflanzung f. Plantage f.

plaque (plɑ:k) n 1 (Schmuck)Platte f. 2 Brosche f. 3 Gedenktafel f.

plasma ('plæzmə) n Plasma neu.

plaster ('plɑ:stə) n 1 Pflaster neu. 2 Mörtel m. 3 Gips m. **plaster of Paris** n (gebrannter) Gips m. **sticking plaster** Heftpflaster neu. ~vt 1 (be)pflastern. 2 verputzen.

plastic ('plæstik) n Kunststoff m. adj 1 Plastik—, Kunststoff—. 2 bildend. 3 plastisch.

Plasticine ('plæstisi:n) n Tdmk Plastilin Tdmk neu.

plate (pleit) n 1 Tafel, Platte f. 2 Teller m. 3 Silbergeschirr neu. vt plattieren, überziehen. **platelayer** n Schienenleger, Streckenarbeiter m.

plateau ('plætou) n Plateau neu. Hochebene f.

platform ('plætfɔ:m) n 1 Rednerbühne f. 2 Bahnsteig m. 3 Plattform f.

platinum ('plætnəm) n Platin neu.

platonic (plə'tɔnik) adj platonisch.

plausible ('plɔ:zəbəl) adj 1 plausibel, einleuchtend. 2 überzeugend.

play (plei) n 1 Spiel neu. 2 Schauspiel, Theaterstück neu. 3 Verhalten neu. 4 Spielraum m. vi 1 spielen. 2 tändeln, flirten. 3 mus Musik machen. vt spielen. **playboy** n Playboy m. **playful** adj spielerisch, scherzhaft. **playground** n 1 Spielplatz m. 2 Schulhof m. **playgroup** n Spielgruppe f. **playhouse** n 1 Schauspielhaus neu. 2 Puppenhaus neu. **playing card** n Spielkarte f. **playing field** n Sportplatz m. **playmate** n Spielkamerad m. **playschool** n Kindergarten m. **playwright** n Dramatiker m.

plea (pli:) n 1 Gesuch neu. Bitte f. 2 Vorwand m. 3 law Einspruch m.

plead (pli:d) vi law plädieren, sich verteidigen. vt 1 vertreten. 2 verteidigen. 3 vorbringen, geltend machen. **plead guilty** sich schuldig bekennen.

please (pli:z) vt 1 gefallen, Freude machen. 2 befriedigen. vi gefallen, angenehm sein. adv bitte. **please yourself** tun Sie, was Sie wollen. **pleasant** adj 1 angenehm. 2 freundlich, liebenswürdig. **pleasure** n 1 Vergnügen neu. Freude f. 2 Genuß m.

pleat (pli:t) n Falte f. vt in Falten legen, plissieren.

plectrum ('plektrəm) n Plektron neu.

pledge (pledʒ) n 1 Pfand neu. Bürgschaft f. 2 Versprechen neu. Zusage f. 3 Trinkspruch, Toast m. vt 1 verpfänden, als Pfand geben. 2 versprechen. 3 verpflichten.

plenty ('plenti) n Fülle f. Reichtum m. adj

reichlich. **in plenty** reichlich, im Überfluß. **plenty of** viel, reichlich.

pliable ('plaɪəbəl) adj 1 biegsam. 2 nachgiebig, fügsam.

pliers ('plaɪəz) n (Kneif)Zange f.

plight (plaɪt) n Notlage, Zwangslage f.

plimsoll ('plɪmsəl) n Turnschuh m.

plod (plɔd) vi 1 (mühsam) daherstampfen, sich hinschleppen. 2 sich abmühen, sich mühsam durcharbeiten.

plonk (plɔŋk) vt hinplumpsen.

plot[1] (plɔt) n 1 lit Handlung f. 2 Plan m. 3 Verschwörung f. vi sich verschwören. vt 1 (heimlich) planen. 2 entwerfen. 3 ersinnen. 4 graphisch darstellen, aufzeichnen.

plot[2] (plɔt) n Parzelle f. Grundstück neu.

plough (plau) n Pflug m. vt pflügen.

pluck (plʌk) vt 1 pflücken. 2 rupfen. 3 reißen, zerren. vi reißen, zerren. n 1 Ruck, Zug m. 2 Mut m. Beherztheit f.

plug (plʌg) n Stöpsel, Pfropf m. vt verstopfen.

plum (plʌm) n bot Pflaume f.

plumage ('plu:mɪdʒ) n Gefieder neu.

plumb (plʌm) n Senkblei, Lot neu. adj senkrecht, lotrecht. vt 1 sondieren. 2 erforschen. vi klempnern. **plumber** n Klempner, Installateur m. **plumbing** n 1 Kempnerarbeit f. 2 Ausloten neu.

plume (plu:m) n 1 Feder f. 2 Federbusch m. vt mit Federn schmücken.

plump[1] (plʌmp) adj rundlich, dick.

plump[2] (plʌmp) vi plumpsen. **plump for** sich entscheiden für.

plunder ('plʌndə) n 1 Plünderung f. 2 Beute f.

plunge (plʌndʒ) vt 1 tauchen. 2 stürzen. vi 1 tauchen. 2 sich hineinstürzen. n 1 Tauchen neu. 2 Sturz m.

pluperfect (plu:'pə:fikt) n Plusquamperfekt neu.

plural ('pluərəl) adj mehrfach, Plural—. n Plural m. Mehrzahl f.

plus (plʌs) prep plus, und. n Plus, Mehr neu. adj 1 positiv, Plus—. 2 mehr, Extra—.

plush (plʌʃ) n Plüsch m. adj Plüsch—.

Pluto ('plu:tou) n Pluto m.

ply[1] (plaɪ) vt 1 ausüben 2 handhaben. vi regelmässig fahren, verkehren.

ply[2] (plaɪ) n 1 Schicht f. 2 Strähne f. 3 Neigung f. **plywood** n Sperrholz neu.

pneumatic (nju:'mætɪk) adj pneumatisch, Luft—. **pneumatic drill** n Preßluftbohrer m.

pneumonia (nju:'mouniə) n Lüngenentzündung, Pneumonie f.

poach[1] (poutʃ) vi 1 wildern, unerlaubt jagen. 2 widerrechtlich betreten.

poach[2] (poutʃ) vt cul pochieren. **poached egg** n pochiertes or verlorenes Ei.

pocket ('pɔkit) n Tasche f. vt in die Tasche stecken. **pocket-money** n Taschengeld neu.

pod (pɔd) n Schote, Schale f. vt ausschoten.

poem ('pouim) n Gedicht neu.

poet ('pouit) n Dichter m. **poetic** adj dichterisch, poetisch. **poetry** n 1 Dichtung, Poesie f. 2 Gedichte neu pl.

poignant ('pɔinjənt) adj 1 scharf. 2 pikant. 3 rührend, ergreifend.

point (pɔint) n 1 Punkt m. 2 Spitze f. 3 Frage, Sache f. 4 Zweck m. Absicht f. 5 Stufe f. Zeitpunkt m. 6 Stelle f. **be on the point of doing** eben tun wollen. **beside the point** nicht zur Sache gehörig. **point-blank** adj, adv 1 (schnur)gerade. 2 (auf kurze Entfernung) direkt, offen. 3 mil Kern—, Kernschuß—. ~vt 1 richten. 2 spitzen. 3 deuten auf. **point out** aufmerksam machen auf. **point to** hinweisen auf. **pointed** adj 1 spitz. 2 scharf, treffend.

poise (pɔiz) n 1 Gleichgewicht neu. 2 Haltung f. 3 Ruhe, Gelassenheit f. vt 1 balancieren. 2 im Gleichgewicht halten. vi schweben.

poison ('pɔizən) n Gift neu. vt vergiften. **poisonous** adj giftig.

poke (pouk) n Stoß, Puff m. vi stoßen, stochern, tasten. vt 1 stoßen, knuffen. 2 (a fire) schüren.

poker[1] (poukə) n Feuerhaken m.

poker[2] (poukə) n Poker(spiel) neu.

Poland ('poulənd) n Polen neu.

polar ('poulə) adj polar, Polar—. **polar bear** n Eisbär m. **polarize** vt polarisieren.

pole[1] (poul) n 1 Pfahl m. 2 Stange f. Pfosten m. Stock m. vt staken. **pole-vault** n Stabhochsprung m.

pole[2] (poul) n Pol m. **Pole Star** n Polarstern m.

Pole (poul) n Pole m.

polemic (pə'lemik) adj 1 polemisch. 2 streitsüchtig. n Polemik f.

police (pə'li:s) n Polizei f. vt 1 polizeilich bewachen. 2 schützen. 3 kontrollieren. **policeman** n Polizist, Schutzmann m. **police station** n Polizeiwache f.

policy[1] ('pɔlisi) n 1 Politik, politische Linie f. 2 Taktik, Methode f.

policy[2] ('pɔlisi) n (Versicherungs)Police f.

polish ('pɔliʃ) vt 1 polieren, glätten. 2 bohnern. 3 verfeinern. vi glatt werden, Glanz annehmen. *n* **1** Glanz *m.* Politur *f.* **2** Putzmittel *neu.*

Polish ('pouliʃ) *adj* polnisch *n* (language) Polnisch *neu.*

polite (pə'lait) *adj* **1** höflich, zuvorkommend. **2** fein, schön.

politics ('pɒlitiks) *n* Politik *f.* **political** *adj* politisch. **politician** *n* Politiker *m.*

polka ('pɒlkə) *n* Polka *f.*

poll (poul) *n* **1** Wahl, Abstimmung *f.* **2** Wählerliste *f.* **3** Umfrage. **4** Stimmabgabe *f.* **go to the polls** zur Wahl gehen. ~*vt* **1** (votes) erhalten. **2** stutzen, abschneiden. *vi* wählen, stimmen.

pollen ('pɒlən) *n* Blütenstaub, Pollen *m.*

pollute (pə'lu:t) *vt* **1** verschmutzen, verunreinigen. **2** schänden, entweihen. **pollution** *n* (Umwelts)Verschmutzung *f.*

polygamy (pə'ligəmi) *n* Polygamie *f.*

polygon ('pɒligən) *n* Vieleck *neu.*

polytechnic (pɒli'teknik) *adj* polytechnisch. *n* polytechnische Hochschule *f.*

polythene ('pɒliθi:n) *n* **1** *sci* Polyäthylen *neu.* **2** Plastik—.

pomegranate ('pɒmigrænət) *n* Granatapfel *m.*

pomp (pɒmp) *n* Pomp, Prunk *m.* Pracht *f.* **pompous** *adj* **1** pompös, prunkvoll. **2** hochtrabend, anmaßend.

pond (pɒnd) *n* Teich *m.*

ponder ('pɒndə) *vt* erwägen, nachdenken über. *vi* tief nachdenken, nachsinnen.

pony ('pouni) *n* Pony *neu.* **ponytail** *n* Pferdeschwanz *m.*

poodle ('pu:dl) *n* Pudel *m.*

pool[1] (pu:l) *n* **1** Teich *m.* **2** Pfütze *f.*

pool[2] (pu:l) *n* **1** Pool, Ring *m.* Interessengemeinschaft *f.* **2** gemeinsame Kasse *f.* *vt* zusammenlegen, vereinigen.

poor (puə, pɔ:) *adj* **1** arm, bedürftig. **2** schlecht. **3** jämmerlich.

pop[1] (pɒp) *n* **1** Knall, Puff *m.* **2** *inf* Sprudel *m.* Limonade *f.* *vt* knallen lassen. *vi* puffen, knallen. **pop up** plötzlich auftauchen *or* erscheinen. *interj* paff! **popcorn** *n* Popcorn *neu.* Puffmais *m.*

pop[2] (pɒp) *adj* *inf* populär, beliebt. **pop music** *n* Popmusik *f.* **pop song** *n* Schlager *m.*

pope (poup) *n* Papst *m.*

poplar ('pɒplə) *n* Pappel *f.*

poppy ('pɒpi) *n* Mohn *m.* Mohnpflanze *f.*

popular ('pɒpjulə) *adj* **1** populär. **2** beliebt. **3** volkstümlich.

population (pɒpju'leiʃən) *n* Bevölkerung *f.*

porcelain ('pɔ:slin) *adj* Porzellan—. *n* Porzellan *neu.*

porch (pɔ:tʃ) *n* **1** Portal *neu.* **2** Vorhalle *f.* **3** Veranda *f.*

porcupine ('pɔ:kjupain) *n* Stachelschwein *neu.*

pore[1] (pɔ:) *n anat* Pore *f.*

pore[2] (pɔ:) *vi* **pore over** eifrig studieren, aufmerksam untersuchen.

pork (pɔ:k) *n* Schweinefleisch *neu.*

pornography (pɔ:'nɒgrəfi) *n* Pornographie *f.* **pornographic** *adj* pornographisch.

porous ('pɔ:rəs) *adj* porös, durchlässig.

porpoise ('pɔ:pəs) *n* Tümmler *m.*

porridge ('pɒridʒ) *n* Hafer(flocken)brei *m.*

port[1] (pɔ:t) *n* Hafen *m.*

port[2] (pɔ:t) *adj* Backbord—. *n* Backbord *neu.*

port[3] (pɔ:t) *n* Portwein *m.*

port[4] (pɔ:t) *n* Tor *neu.* Pforte *f.*

portable ('pɔ:təbəl) *adj* tragbar, portabel.

portent (pɔ:'tent) *n* **1** Vorbedeutung *f.* übles Vorzeichen *neu.* **2** Wunder *neu.*

porter[1] ('pɔ:tə) *n* Gepäckträger *m.*

porter[2] ('pɔ:tə) *n* Pförtner, Portier *m.*

portfolio (pɔ:'fouliou) *n* **1** (Brief)Mappe *f.* **2** Geschäftsbereich (eines Ministers) *m.*

porthole ('pɔ:thoul) *n* Pfortluke *f.*

portion ('pɔ:ʃən) *n* **1** Portion *f.* **2** Anteil *m.* *vt* einteilen, zuteilen.

portrait ('pɔ:trit) *n* Porträt, Bildnis *neu.*

portray (pɔ:'trei) *vt* **1** porträtieren, abmalen. **2** beschreiben, schildern.

Portugal ('pɔ:tjugəl) *n* Portugal *neu.* **Portuguese** *adj* portugiesisch. *n* **1** Portugiese *m.* **2** (language) Portugiesisch *neu.*

pose (pouz) *n* Stellung, Pose *f.* *vi* posieren. *vt* **1** (questions) stellen. **2** aufstellen. **pose as** auftreten als.

posh (pɒʃ) *adj* *inf* elegant, schick, prima.

position (pə'ziʃən) *n* **1** Position, Stellung *f.* **2** Rang *m.* **3** Standpunkt *m.* Einstellung *f.* **4** Lage *f.* *vt* (richtig hin)stellen.

positive ('pɒzitiv) *adj* **1** positiv. **2** genau, exakt. **3** konstruktiv. **4** definitiv, eindeutig. *n* **1** Positivum *neu.* **2** *phot* Positiv *neu.*

possess (pə'zes) *vt* **1** besitzen, haben. **2** in Besitz nehmen. **possession** *n* **1** Besitz *m.* **2** *pl* Habe *f.* Reichtum *m.* **be in possession of** besitzen. **possessive** *adj* **1** besitzgierig. **2** anhänglich. **3** *gram* Possessiv.

possible ('pɒsəbəl) *adj* **1** möglich. **2** eventuell.

post[1] (poust) *n* Pfosten, Pfahl *m.* *vt* ankleben, anschlagen.

post[2] (poust) n **1** Stellung f. **2** Posten m. vt postieren, aufstellen.

post[3] (poust) n **1** Post f. **2** Postamt neu. vt (per Post) schicken. **postage** n Porto neu. Postgebühr f. **postal order** n Postanweisung f. **postbox** n Briefkasten m. **postcard** n Postkarte f. **postcode** n Postleitzahl f. **postman** n Briefträger m. **postmark** n Poststempel f. vt abstempeln. **post office** n Postamt neu.

poster ('pousta) n Plakat neu.

posterior (pɔs'tiaria) adj **1** später. **2** folgend, hinter. n Hinterteil neu.

posterity (pɔs'teriti) n **1** Nachkommenschaft f. **2** Nachwelt f.

postgraduate (poust'grædjuat) n Doktorand m. adj **1** vorgeschritten. **2** Forschungs—.

posthumous ('pɔstjumas) adj **1** posthum. **2** nachträglich.

post-mortem (poust'mɔ:təm) adj nach dem Tode. **post mortem (examination)** n Autopsie f.

postpone (pas'poun) vt **1** verschieben. **2** unterordnen.

postscript ('pouskript) n Postskriptum neu. Nachschrift f. Nachtrag m.

postulate (v 'pɔstjuleit; n 'pɔstjulat) vt **1** postulieren. **2** fordern, verlangen. n **1** Postulat neu. **2** Forderung f.

posture ('pɔstʃa) n **1** Stellung, Haltung f. **2** Lage f.

pot (pɔt) n **1** Topf m. **2** Krug m. vt **1** in einen Topf tun. **2** einmachen.

potassium (pa'tæsiəm) n **1** Pottasche f. **2** Kalium neu.

potato (pa'teitou) n Kartoffel f.

potent ('poutnt) adj **1** stark, kräftig **2** potent.

potential (pa'tenʃal) adj möglich, potentiell. n Potential neu.

pothole ('pɔthoul) n Schlagloch neu.

potion ('pouʃan) n Trank m.

potter ('pɔta) n Töpfer m.

pottery ('pɔtari) n **1** Töpferwaren f pl. **2** Töpferei f.

pouch (pautʃ) n Tasche f. Beutel m. (vi),vt (sich) bauschen.

poultice ('poultis) n Umschlag m. Packung f.

poultry ('poultri) n Geflügel neu.

pounce (pauns) vi sich stürzen, herabstoßen. n Sprung, Satz m.

pound[1] (paund) vt **1** zerstoßen, zerstampfen. **2** schlagen, stoßen. vi schlagen, hämmern.

pound[2] (paund) n Pfund neu.

pour (pɔ:) vt gießen, schütten. vi **1** fließen, strömen. **2** stark regnen. n **1** Guß m. **2** (Regen)Guß m.

pout (paut) vi **1** die Lippen spitzen. **2** schmollen. n Schmollen neu.

poverty ('pɔvəti) n **1** Armut f. **2** Elend neu. Not f. **poverty-stricken** adj verarmt, bedürftig.

powder ('pauda) n Pulver neu. Puder m. vt **1** (ein)pudern, bestreuen. **2** pulverisieren. vi zu Pulver werden. **powder room** n Damentoilette f.

power ('paua) n **1** Kraft, Stärke f. **2** Macht, Autorität f. **3** Gewalt f. **4** math Potenz f. **5** Energie. vt antreiben. **powerful** adj mächtig, stark, kräftig.

practicable ('præktikabal) adj ausführbar, möglich.

practical ('præktikal) adj praktisch.

practice ('præktis) n **1** Praxis f. **2** Brauch m. Gewohnheit f. **3** Übung f. **4** Verfahren neu.

practise ('præktis) vt **1** ausüben, betreiben. **2** üben. vi **1** üben. **2** praktisch tätig sein. **3** sport trainieren.

practitioner (præk'tiʃana) n **1** med praktischer Arzt m. **2** law Rechtsanwalt m. **3** Praktiker m.

pragmatic (præg'mætik) adj pragmatisch.

Prague (prɑ:g) n Prag neu.

prairie ('prɛəri) n Prärie, Steppe f.

praise (preiz) vt preisen, loben. n Lob neu. Preis m. Anerkennung f. **praiseworthy** adj lobenswert.

pram (præm) n Kinderwagen m.

prance (prɑ:ns) vi **1** sich bäumen. **2** umherspringen. **3** einherstolzieren.

prank (præŋk) n Streich, Ulk m.

prattle ('prætl) vi schwazen, plappern. n Geschwätz, Geplapper neu.

prawn (prɔ:n) n Garnele f.

pray (prei) vi beten. vt bitten, anflehen. **prayer** n Gebet neu. **prayerbook** n Gebetbuch neu.

preach (pri:tʃ) vi,vt predigen.

precarious (pri'kɛarias) adj **1** prekär, unsicher, riskant. **2** law widerruflich.

precaution (pri'kɔ:ʃan) n **1** Vorsichtsmaßnahme f. **take precautions** Vorsichtsmaßnahmen treffen

precede (pri'si:d) vi,vt vorausgehen, vorangehen. **precedence** n Vorrang m. Priorität f. **precedent** n Präzedenzfall m.

precinct ('pri:siŋkt) n **1** Bezirk m. **2** pl Umgebung f.

precious ('preʃas) adj kostbar, vertvoll. adv inf recht, sehr.

precipice ('presipis) *n* Abgrund *m*.
precipitate (prə'sipiteit) *vt* 1 hinabstürzen. 2 überstürzen, übereilen. *vi* 1 sich übereilen. 2 sich niederschlagen. *adj* voreilig, überstürzt. **precipitation** *n* 1 Niederschlag *m*. 2 Überstürzung *f*.
precis ('preisi) *n* Zusammenfassung *f*. *vt* zusammenfassen.
precise (pri'sais) *adj* 1 präzis, genau. 2 korrekt. **precision** *n* Präzision *f*.
preclude (pri'klu:d) *vt* 1 ausschließen. 2 (ver)-hindern.
precocious (pri'kouʃəs) *adj* frühreif, altklug.
preconceive (pri:kən'si:v) *vt* sich vorher vorstellen, vorher ausdenken. **preconception** *n* Vorurteil *m*. vorgefaßte Meinung *f*.
predatory ('predətəri) *adj* räuberisch, Raub—.
predecessor (pri:disesə) *n* Vorgänger *m*.
predestine (pri:'destin) *vt* vorherbestimmen, vorher festlegen. **predestination** *n* Prädestination, Vorherbestimmung *f*.
predicament (pri'dikəmənt) *n* heikle *or* mißliche Lage *f*.
predicate (*n* 'predikit; *v* 'predikeit) *n* Prädikat *neu*. *vt* 1 aussagen, feststellen. 2 begründen.
predict (pri'dikt) *vt* vorhersagen, prophezeien.
predominate (pri'dɔmineit) *vi* 1 vorherrschen. 2 überlegen sein.
pre-eminent *adj* hervorragend.
preen (pri:n) *vt* (of a bird) putzen.
prefabricate (pri:'fæbrikeit) *vt* vorfabrizieren.
preface ('prefis) *n* Vorrede, Einleitung *f*. *vt* einleiten.
prefect ('pri:fekt) *n* 1 *pol* Präfekt *m*. 2 *educ* Aufsichtsschüler *m*.
prefer (pri'fə:) *vt* 1 vorziehen, lieber tun *or* haben. 2 einreichen. 3 begünstigen. **preference** *n* 1 Bevorzugung *f*. 2 Vorliebe *f*. 3 Vortritt, Vorrecht *neu*.
prefix ('pri:fiks) *n* Präfix *neu*. Vorsilbe *f*.
pregnant ('pregnənt) *adj* 1 schwanger. 2 wichtig, gehaltvoll, bedeutsam. **pregnancy** *n* Schwangerschaft *f*.
prehistoric (pri:his'tɔrik) *adj* vorgeschichtlich, urgeschichtlich, prähistorisch.
prejudice ('predʒədis) *n* 1 Vorurteil *neu*. 2 Beeinträchtigung *f*. Schaden *m*. *vt* ungünstig beeinflussen, beeinträchtigen. **prejudiced** *adj* voreingenommen.
preliminary (pri'liminəri) *adj* vorbereitend, einleitend, vorläufig.
prelude ('prelju:d) *n* 1 Einleitung *f*. 2 *mus* Vorspiel *neu*.

premarital (pri:'mæritl) *adj* vorehelich.
premature ('premətʃə) *adj* 1 frühreif. 2 vorzeitig, frühzeitig.
premeditate (pri:'mediteit) *vt* vorher überlegen. **premeditation** *n* Vorbedacht *m*.
premier ('premiə) *n* Premierminister *m*. *adj* 1 erst. 2 frühest.
premiere ('premiɛə) *n* Erstaufführung, Premiere *f*.
premise ('premis) *n* 1 Prämisse, Voraussetzung *f*. 2 *pl* Grundstück *neu*. 3 *pl* Haus *neu*.
premium ('pri:miəm) *n* Prämie *f*.
preoccupied (pri:'ɔkjupaid) *adj* vertieft, in Gedanken versunken.
prepare (pri'pɛə) *vt* 1 vorbereiten. 2 zubereiten. 3 präparieren. *vi* 1 Vorbereitungen treffen, sich vorbereiten. 2 *mil* sich rüsten. **preparation** *n* 1 Vorbereitung *f*. 2 *pl* Vorkehrungsmaßnahmen *n pl*. **preparatory** *adj* vorbereitend, Vorbereitungs—.
preposition (prepə'ziʃən) *n* Präposition *f*. Verhältniswort *neu*.
preposterous (pri'pɔstərəs) *adj* unnatürlich, unsinnig, grotesk, lächerlich.
prerogative (pri'rɔgətiv) *n* Vorrecht, Privileg *neu*. Prärogative *f*. *adj* bevorrechtet.
prescribe (pri'skraib) *vt* 1 vorschreiben. 2 *med* verordnen. *vi* Vorschriften machen, Anweisungen geben. **prescription** *n* 1 Vorschrift, Verordnung *f*. 2 *med* Rezept *neu*.
presence ('prezəns) *n* 1 Gegenwart *f*. 2 Anwesenheit. 3 Aussehen, Äußere *neu*.
present[1] ('prezənt) *adj* 1 gegenwärtig. 2 anwesend. 3 vorhanden. 4 augenblicklich. **present participle** *n* Partizip des Präsens *neu*. ~*n* Gegenwart *f*. **at present** im Augenblick. **presently** *adv* 1 bald. 2 kurz darauf.
present[2] (*v* pri'zent; *n* 'prezənt) *vt* 1 vorstellen. 2 schenken, überreichen. 3 darbieten, vorführen. *n* Geschenk *neu*.
preserve (pri'zə:v) *vt* 1 bewahren, schützen. 2 *cul* einmachen, konservieren. 3 beibehalten, aufrechterhalten. *n* Konserve *f*.
preside (pri'zaid) *vi* präsidieren, den Vorsitz führen.
president ('prezidənt) *n* 1 Präsident *m*. 2 Vorsitzende(r) *m*.
press (pres) *vt* 1 drücken, pressen. 2 bügeln. *vi* 1 Druck ausüben, drücken. 2 dringend bitten. 3 drängen. *n* 1 Druck *m*. 2 Presse *f*. 3 Gedränge *neu*. **press conference** *n* Pressekonferenz *f*. **press-gang** *n* Anwerbetrupp

m. **press-stud** *n* Druckknopf *m.* **press-up** *n sport* Liegestütz *m.*

pressure ('preʃə) *n* **1** Druck *m.* Druckkraft *f.* **2** Dringlichkeit *f.* **3** Druck, Zwang *m.* **pressure cooker** *n* Schnellkochtopf *m.* **pressurize** *vt* **1** unter Druck setzen. **2** Druck ausüben auf, zwingen.

prestige (pres'tiːʒ) *n* Prestige, Ansehen *neu.*

presume (pri'zjuːm) *vt* vermuten, annehmen. *vi* **1** vermuten. **2** wagen, sich erlauben. **3** mißbrauchen. **presumption** *n* **1** Vermutung *f.* **2** Anmaßung *f.* **presumptuous** *adj* anmaßend.

pretend (pri'tend) *vt* vorgeben, vorspiegeln. *vi* vorgeben. **pretend to 1** tun, als ob. **2** Anspruch machen auf. **pretence** *n* Vorwand *m.* **pretension** *n* Anspruch *m.* **pretentious** *adj* anspruchsvoll, angeberisch.

pretext ('priːtekst) *n* Vorwand *m.* Ausrede *f.*

pretty ('priti) *adj* hübsch, schön. *adv* ziemlich.

prevail (pri'veil) *vi* **1** die Oberhand gewinnen, sich durchsetzen. **2** vorherrschen. **prevalent** *adj* **1** vorherrschend. **2** überlegen.

prevent (pri'vent) *vt* abhalten, zurückhalten, verhindern, verhüten. **prevention** *n* Verhinderung *f.*

preview ('priːvjuː) *n* (private) Vorschau, Vorbesichtigung *f. vt* vorher sehen.

previous ('priːviəs) *adj* vorhergehend, früher. **previously** *adv* vorher, früher.

prey (prei) *n* Raub *m.* Beute *f.* **bird of prey** Raubvogel *m.* **v prey on** Jagd machen auf.

price (prais) *n* **1** Preis *m.* **2** Wert *m. vt* **1** bewerten. **2** den Preis festsetzen von. **price-list** *n* Preisliste *f.*

prick (prik) *n* **1** Dorn *m.* **2** Stich *m. vt* stechen. *vi* stechen, prickeln. **prickle** *n* Stachel, Dorn *m. vt* stechen, prickeln.

pride (praid) *n* **1** Stolz *m.* **2** Hochmut *m. v* **pride oneself on** stolz sein auf.

priest (priːst) *n* **1** Priester, Geistliche(r) *m.* **priesthood** *n* Priesteramt *neu.*

prim (prim) *adj* gekünstelt, (über)korrekt, steif.

primary ('praiməri) *adj* **1** erst, ursprünglich, Grund—. **2** hauptsächlich, Haupt—. **3** elementar. **primary school** *n* Grundschule, Volksschule, Elementarschule *f.*

primate *n* **1** ('praimit) Erzbischof *m.* **2** ('praimeit) *zool* Primat *m.*

prime (praim) *adj* **1** erst, Haupt—, Ober—. **2** höchst. *n* Vollkommenheit, Blute *f. vt* vorbereiten, fertigmachen. **prime minister** *n* Ministerpräsident, Premierminister *m.*

primitive ('primitiv) *adj* **1** ursprünglich, Ur—. **2** primitiv.

primrose ('primrouz) *n* Primel, Schlüsselblume *f. adj* blaßgelb.

prince (prins) *n* Fürst, Prinz *m.* **princess** *n* Fürstin, Prinzeß *f.*

principal ('prinsəpəl) *adj* **1** hauptsächlich, Haupt—. **2** wichtigst. *n* Chef, Vorsitzende(r) *m.* **principality** *n* Fürstentum *neu.*

principle ('prinsəpəl) *n* Prinzip *neu.* Grundsatz *m.* **in/on principle** im/aus Prinzip.

print (print) *vt* **1** drucken. **2** stempeln. **3** herausgeben, veröffentlichen. *n* **1** Druck *m.* **2** Abzug *m.* **3** Spur *f.*

prior ('praiə) *adj* eher, früher, vorausgehend. *n* Prior *m.* **priority** *n* Priorität *f.* Vorrang *m.*

prise (praiz) *vt* **prise open** aufbrechen.

prism ('prizəm) *n* Prisma *neu.*

prison ('prizən) *n* Gefängnis *neu.* **prisoner** *n* Gefangene(r) *m.*

private ('praivit) *adj* **1** privat. **2** persönlich. **3** nicht öffentlich, Privat—. **4** heimlich. *n* gemeiner Soldat *m.* **in private** im Vertrauen, unter vier Augen. **private eye** *n* Privatdetektiv *m.* **privacy** *n* **1** Geheimhaltung *f.* **2** Ruhe, Ungestörtheit *f.* **3** Privatleben *neu.*

privet ('privit) *n* Liguster *m.* Rainweide *f.*

privilege ('privilidʒ) *n* Privileg, Vorrecht *neu. vt* privilegieren, bevorrechten.

privy ('privi) *adj* **1** eingeweiht, mitwissend. **2** Privat—, Geheim—.

prize[1] (praiz) *n* Preis *m.*

prize[2] (praiz) *vt* hoch einschätzen.

probable ('prɔbəbəl) *adj* wahrscheinlich.

probation (prə'beiʃən) *n* **1** Prüfung *f.* **2** Probezeit *f.* **3** *law* Bewährungsfrist *f.* **on probation 1** auf Probe. **2** *law* auf Bewährung. **probation officer** *n* Bewährungshelfer *m.*

probe (proub) *n* **1** *med* Sonde *f.* **2** Untersuchung *f. vt* **1** sondieren. **2** untersuchen.

problem ('prɔbləm) *n* **1** Problem *neu.* **2** Schwierigkeit *f.* **3** *math* Aufgabe *f. adj* Problem—, problematisch. **problematic** *adj* problematisch.

proceed (prə'siːd) *vi* **1** vorwärtsgehen. **2** weitermachen, fortfahren. **3** übergehen. **4** handeln, verfahren. **procedure** *n* **1** Verfahren, Vorgehen *neu.* **2** Prozedur *f.*

process ('prouses) *n* **1** Vorgang *m.* **2** Verfahren *neu.* Prozeß *m.* **in process** im Gang. *~vt* **1** behandeln, verarbeiten. **2** *law* prozessieren, gerichtlich belangen.

procession (prə'seʃən) n Prozession f. Umzug. (Fest)Zug m.

proclaim (prə'kleim) vt proklamieren, verkünden.

procreate ('proukrieit) vt 1 erzeugen. 2 hervorbringen.

procure (prə'kjuə) vt 1 verschaffen, anschaffen, besorgen. 2 zustandebringen, bewirken. vi Kuppelei betreiben. **procurer** n Kuppler m.

prod (prɔd) n 1 Stich m. 2 Stoß m. vt 1 stechen. 2 stoßen.

prodigal ('prɔdigəl) adj verschwenderisch.

prodigy ('prɔdidʒi) n Wunder neu. **child prodigy** Wunderkind neu.

produce (v prə'djuːs; n 'prɔdjuːs) vt 1 herstellen, erzeugen, produzieren. 2 vorzeigen. 3 veranlassen, bewirken. n Ertrag m. Frucht f. Produkt neu. **product** n 1 Erzeugnis, Produkt neu. 2 Ergebnis neu. 3 math Resultat neu. **production** n Erzeugung, Produktion f.

profane (prə'fein) vt entweihen, profanieren. adj 1 weltlich, profan. 2 gottlos.

profess (prə'fes) vt 1 gestehen, bekennen. 2 erklären. vi ein Bekenntnis ablegen. **profession** n 1 Beruf m. 2 Bekenntnis neu.

professor (prə'fesə) n Professor m.

proficient (prə'fiʃənt) adj 1 geübt, erfahren. 2 tüchtig.

profile ('proufail) n Profil neu. Querschnitt m.

profit ('prɔfit) n Gewinn, Profit m. vi profitieren, Nutzen ziehen.

profound (prə'faund) adj 1 (tief)liegend. 2 tiefsinnig, gründlich, profund.

profuse (prə'fjuːs) adj 1 überreichlich. 2 verschwenderisch.

programme ('prougræm) n 1 Programm neu. 2 Sendung f. **program** (computers) n Programm neu. vt programmieren.

progress (n 'prougres; v prə'gres) n Fortgang, Fortschritt m. vi fortschreiten, Fortschritte machen. **progression** n 1 Fortschreiten neu. Fortschritt m. 2 Progression f. **progressive** adj 1 fortschreitend. 2 fortschrittlich.

prohibit (prə'hibit) vt verbieten, verhindern.

project (n 'prɔdʒekt; v prə'dʒekt) n Projekt neu. Plan m. vt 1 schleudern. 2 werfen. 3 projizieren. 4 entwerfen. **projectile** n Projektil, (Wurf)Geschoß neu. **projection** n 1 Wurf m. 2 Entwurf, Plan m. 3 Projektion f. **projector** n Projektionsapparat m.

proletariat (prouli'tɛəriət) n Proletariat neu.

proliferate (prə'lifəreit) vi 1 sprossen. 2 med wuchern.

prolific (prə'lifik) adj 1 fruchtbar. 2 reich.

prologue ('proulɔg) n Prolog m. Einleitung f.

prolong (prə'lɔŋ) vt verlängern.

promenade (prɔmə'nɑːd) n 1 Promenade f. 2 Spaziergang m. vi spazierengehen.

prominent ('prɔminənt) adj 1 hervorragend. 2 berühmt, prominent.

promiscuous (prə'miskjuəs) adj 1 unterschiedslos. 2 gemeinsam. 3 vermischt.

promise ('prɔmis) n Versprechen neu. Zusage f. vt versprechen, zusagen.

promote (prə'mout) vt 1 begünstigen, fördern. 2 erheben, befördern. 3 anpreisen. **promotion** n 1 Förderung f. 2 Beförderung f. 3 Werbung f.

prompt (prɔmpt) adj schnell, rasch, prompt. vt anspornen, veranlassen.

prone (proun) adj 1 geneigt, neigend. 2 auf dem Gesicht liegend.

prong (prɔŋ) n Zinke, Spitze f.

pronoun ('prounaun) n gram Pronomen, Fürwort neu.

pronounce (prə'nauns) vt 1 aussprechen. 2 verkünden. vi sich aussprechen. **pronunciation** n Aussprache f.

proof (pruːf) n 1 Beweis, Nachweis m. 2 Abzug m. 3 Probe f. adj fest, sicher, undurchdringlich. vt imprägnieren. **proofread** vt korrigieren.

prop¹ (prɔp) n Stütze, Strebe f. vt stützen.

prop² (prɔp) n Th (Bühnen)Requisit neu.

propaganda (prɔpə'gændə) n Propaganda f.

propagate ('prɔpəgeit) vt 1 fortpflanzen, übertragen. 2 ausbreiten.

propel (prə'pel) vt vorwärtstreiben. **propeller** n Propeller m.

proper ('prɔpə) adj 1 passend, angebracht. 2 eigen(tlich). 3 richtig, korrekt. 4 ordnungsgemäß. **proper noun** n Eigenname m.

property ('prɔpəti) n 1 Eigentum neu. Besitz m. 2 Eigenschaft, Eigentümlichkeit f. 3 Grundbesitz m. Immobilien pl.

prophecy ('prɔfisi) n Prophezeiung, Weissagung f. **prophesy** vt prophezeien, weissagen.

prophet ('prɔfit) n Prophet m.

proportion (prə'pɔːʃən) n 1 Proportion f. Verhältnis neu. 2 Maß neu. 3 pl Ausmaß neu.

propose (prə'pouz) vt 1 vorschlagen. 2 (a toast) ausbringen. vi 1 beabsichtigen. 2 einen Heiratsantrag machen. **proposal** n 1 Vorschlag m. 2 (Heirats)Antrag m. **proposition** n 1 Vorschlag, Antrag m. 2 Behauptung f.

proprietor (prəˈpraiətə) n Besitzer, Eigentümer m.

propriety (prəˈpraiəti) n Anstand m. Angemessenheit f.

propulsion (prəˈpʌlʃən) n Antrieb m.

prose (prouz) n Prosa f. adj Prosa—, prosaisch. **prosaic** adj prosaisch, alltäglich.

prosecute (ˈprɔsikjuːt) vt 1 law strafrechtlich verfolgen. 2 verfolgen. 3 betreiben. vi law Klage erheben.

prospect (ˈprɔspekt) n 1 Aussicht f. 2 Erwartung, Voraussicht f. **prospective** adj voraussichtlich, künftig. **prospectus** n Prospekt m.

prosper (ˈprɔspə) vi gedeihen. vt begünstigen. **prosperity** n Wohlstand m. **prosperous** adj 1 erfolgreich, gedeihend. 2 wohlhabend.

prostitute (ˈprɔstitjuːt) n Prostituierte, Dirne f. vt 1 prostituieren. 2 entehren. **prostitution** n Prostitution f.

prostrate (v prɔsˈtreit; adj ˈprɔstreit) vt 1 niederwerfen. 2 entkräften. 3 demütigen. adj 1 auf der Erde hingestreckt. 2 unterwürfig. 3 kraftlos.

protagonist (prəˈtægənist) n lit Held m. Hauptperson f. Verfechter m.

protect (prəˈtekt) vt (be)schützen, bewahren. **protection** n Schutz m. Beschützung f.

protégé (ˈprɔtiʒei) n Schützling m.

protein (ˈproutiːn) n Protein, Eiweiß neu.

protest (n ˈproutest; v prəˈtest) n Protest, Einspruch m. vt 1 beteuern. 2 protestieren gegen. vi protestieren, Einspruch erheben.

Protestant (ˈprɔtistənt) adj protestantisch. n Protestant m.

protocol (ˈproutəkɔl) n Protokoll neu.

prototype (ˈproutətaip) n Prototyp, Urtyp m.

protractor (prəˈtræktə) n Winkelmesser m.

protrude (prəˈtruːd) vi (her)vorragen, (her)vorstehen. vt (her)vortreten lassen.

proud (praud) adj 1 stolz. 2 hochmütig. 3 stattlich, prächtig.

prove (pruːv) vt 1 beweisen, erweisen. 2 bestätigen. vi sich herausstellen. **proven** adj 1 bewiesen. 2 bewährt.

proverb (ˈprɔvəːb) n Sprichwort neu.

provide (prəˈvaid) vt 1 beschaffen, versorgen. 2 bereitstellen. vi Vorkehrungen treffen. **provision** n 1 Vorsorge, Vorkehrung f. 2 Bestimmung f. 3 pl Proviant m. vt mit Proviant versorgen. **provisional** adj provisorisch.

province (ˈprɔvins) n 1 Provinz f. 2 (Arbeits)-Gebiet neu. **provincial** adj 1 provinziell. 2 engstirnig, beschränkt. n Provinzbewohner m.

proviso (prəˈvaizou) n law Klausel f. Vorbehalt m.

provoke (prəˈvouk) vt 1 provozieren, reizen. 2 hervorrufen. 3 veranlassen. **provocation** n 1 Provokation f. 2 Aufreizung f. 3 Anlaß m. **provocative** adj provozierend.

prow (prau) n naut Bug m.

prowess (ˈprauis) n 1 Geschicklichkeit f. Können neu. 2 Tapferkeit f.

prowl (praul) vt durchstreifen. vi umherstreifen. n Umherstreifen neu. **be on the prowl** umherstreifen.

proximity (prɔkˈsimiti) n Nähe f.

proxy (ˈprɔksi) n 1 Vollmacht f. 2 Bevollmächtigte(r) m. 3 (Stell)Vertreter m.

prude (pruːd) n Spröde, Prüde f. **prudish** adj prüde, zimperlich.

prudent (ˈpruːdnt) adj 1 klug, weis. 2 vorsichtig. 3 sparsam.

prune[1] (pruːn) n (Dörr)Pflaume f.

prune[2] (pruːn) vt beschneiden, (zu)stutzen.

Prussia (ˈprʌʃə) n Preußen neu. **Prussian** adj preußisch. n Preuße m.

pry (prai) vi neugierig schauen, spähen. **pry into** seine Nase stecken in.

psalm (sɑːm) n Psalm m.

pseudonym (ˈsjuːdənim) n Pseudonym neu.

psychedelic (saikiˈdelik) adj psychedelisch.

psychiatry (saiˈkaiətri) n Psychiatrie f. **psychiatric** adj psychiatrisch. **psychiatrist** n Psychiater m.

psychic (ˈsaikik) adj 1 psychisch, seelisch. 2 übersinnlich.

psychoanalysis (saikouəˈnælisis) n Psychoanalyse f. **psychoanalyst** n Psychoanalytiker m.

psychology (saiˈkɔlədʒi) n Psychologie f. **psychological** adj psychologisch. **psychologist** n Psychologe m.

psychopathic (saikəˈpæθik) adj med psychopathisch.

psychosomatic (saikousəˈmætik) adj psychosomatisch.

pub (pʌb) n inf Kneipe f. Lokal, Wirtshaus neu.

puberty (ˈpjuːbəti) n Pubertät f.

public (ˈpʌblik) adj 1 öffentlich, allgemein. 2 national, Volks—. 3 bekannt. n 1 Publikum neu. 2 Öffentlichkeit f. **in public** öffentlich. **public house** n Wirtshaus neu. Gaststätte f. **public relations** n öffentliche Meinungspflege f. Public Relations pl. **public school** n Internat neu. Privatschule f.

publication (pʌbliˈkeiʃən) n 1 Veröffentlichung f. 2 Publikation, Druckschrift f.

publicity (pʌbˈlisiti) n 1 Öffentlichkeit, Publizität f. 2 Reklame f.

publicize (ˈpʌblisaiz) vt bekanntmachen, publizieren.

publish (ˈpʌbliʃ) vt 1 herausgeben, verlegen, veröffentlichen. 2 bekanntmachen.

pucker (ˈpʌkə) (vi),vt (sich) falten, (sich) runzeln. n Falte, Runzel f.

pudding (ˈpudiŋ) n Pudding m. Süßspeise f. **black pudding** Blutwurst f.

puddle (ˈpʌdl) n Pfütze, Lache f.

puff (pʌf) n 1 Windstoß m. 2 Hauch m. 3 Zug m. Paffen neu. vi 1 puffen, blasen. 2 schnaufen, keuchen. **puff up** or **out** aufblasen, schwellen. **puff pastry** n Blätterteig m.

pull (pul) vt 1 ziehen. 2 zerren. 3 schleppen. vi ziehen, zerren. **pull down** niederreißen, abreißen. **pull oneself together** sich zusammenreißen. **pull through** inf durchkommen. ~n 1 Zug, Ruck m. 2 Anziehungskraft f. **pullover** n Pullover m.

pulley (ˈpuli) n (Riemen)Scheibe, Rolle f.

pulp (pʌlp) n 1 Brei m. 2 Fruchtfleisch neu. 3 Pulpe f. Papierbrei m. vt in Brei verwandeln.

pulpit (ˈpulpit) n Kanzel f. Kathedar neu.

pulsate (pʌlˈseit) vi pulsieren, pochen.

pulse (pʌls) n Puls(schlag) m.

pulverize (ˈpʌlvəraiz) vt pulverisieren, zermahlen. vi zu Staub zerfallen.

pump (pʌmp) n Pumpe f. vt 1 pumpen. 2 ausfragen. vi pumpen.

pumpkin (ˈpʌmpkin) n Kürbis m.

pun (pʌn) n Wortspiel neu. vi ein Wortspiel machen, witzeln.

punch[1] (pʌntʃ) vt (mit der Faust) schlagen. n Faustschlag, Knuff m.

punch[2] (pʌntʃ) vt 1 lochen. 2 stempeln. n 1 Locheisen neu. 2 Locher m. 3 Stempel m.

punch[3] (pʌntʃ) n Punsch m. Bowle f.

punctual (ˈpʌŋktʃuəl) adj pünktlich. **punctuality** n Pünktlichkeit f.

punctuate (ˈpʌŋktʃueit) vt 1 interpunktieren. 2 unterbrechen. **punctuation** n Interpunktion f.

puncture (ˈpʌŋktʃə) n 1 Loch neu. Stich m. 2 mot Reifenpanne f. 3 med Punktur f. vt 1 durchstoßen, perforieren. 2 med punktieren. vi (of a tyre) ein Loch bekommen.

pungent (ˈpʌndʒənt) adj scharf, beißend.

punish (ˈpʌniʃ) vt (be)strafen, züchtigen.

punt[1] (pʌnt) n 1 Punt, Flachboot neu. 2 sport Fallstoß m. vt 1 staken. 2 stoßen.

punt[2] (pʌnt) vi wetten.

pupil[1] (ˈpjuːpl) n Schüler m. Schülerin f.

pupil[2] (ˈpjuːpəl) n anat Pupille f.

puppet (ˈpʌpit) n Puppe f. Marionette f.

puppy (ˈpʌpi) n junger Hund, Welpe m.

purchase (ˈpəːtʃis) vt kaufen. n Kauf m.

pure (pjuə) adj 1 rein, sauber. 2 unberührt. **purify** vt 1 reinigen. 2 klären.

purgatory (ˈpəːgətri) n Fegefeuer neu.

purge (pəːdʒ) vt 1 reinigen. 2 pol säubern. n 1 Reinigung f. 2 pol Säuberung f.

Puritan (ˈpjuəritən) n Puritaner m. adj also **puritanical** puritanisch.

purl (pəːl) vt linksstricken.

purple (ˈpəːpəl) adj purpurn. n Purpur m.

purpose (ˈpəːpəs) n Absicht f. Zweck m. **purposeful** adj 1 entschlossen. 2 zweckmäßig.

purr (pəː) vi schnurren.

purse (pəːs) n Geldbeutel m. Portemonnaie neu.

pursue (pəˈsjuː) vt 1 verfolgen. 2 fortsetzen. 3 betreiben. **pursuit** n Verfolgung f.

pus (pʌs) n Eiter m.

push (puʃ) vt 1 schieben, stoßen. 2 drängen. 3 treiben. **push off** 1 abstoßen. 2 inf abhauen. **push on** vordringen. **push through** durchsetzen. ~n 1 Stoß m. 2 Drang m. Energie f. **pushbike** n inf Fahrrad neu. **pushchair** n (leichter) Kinderwagen m.

pussy (ˈpusi) n inf Kätzchen neu. Mieze f.

put[*] (put) vt 1 setzen, stellen, legen. 2 ausdrücken. 3 richten, tun. 4 sport schleudern, werfen. **put away** 1 weglegen. 2 sparen. **put by** zurücklegen. **put down** 1 niedersetzen. 2 unterdrücken. 3 demütigen. 4 töten. **put forward** 1 vorschlagen. 2 vorbringen. **put off** 1 verschieben. 2 abhalten. **put on** 1 anziehen. 2 herausbringen. 3 zunehmen. 4 vorgeben. **put through** 1 durchführen. 2 verbinden. **put up** 1 errichten, erhöhen. 2 unterbringen.

putrid (ˈpjuːtrid) adj verfault, verwest.

putt (pʌt) vt sport putten. n Putten neu.

putty (ˈpʌti) n (Fenster)Kitt m.

puzzle (ˈpʌzəl) n Rätsel neu. vt verwirren.

PVC n PVC neu.

Pygmy (ˈpigmi) n Pygmäe, Zwerg m.

pyjamas (pəˈdʒɑːməz) n pl Schlafanzug, Pyjama m.

pylon (ˈpailən) n Leitungsmast m.

pyramid (ˈpirəmid) n Pyramide f.

Pyrenees (pirəˈniːz) n pl Pyrenäen pl.

Pyrex (ˈpaireks) *n Tdmk* Jenaer Glas *Tdmk neu.*
python (ˈpaiθən) *n* Pythonschlange *f.*

Q

quack[1] (kwæk) *vi* (of a duck, etc.) quaken.
quack[2] (kwæk) *n* Quacksalber, Kurpfuscher *m.*
quadrangle (ˈkwɔdræŋgəl) *n* **1** Viereck *neu.* **2** Hof *m.*
quadrant (ˈkwɔdrənt) *n* Quadrant *m.*
quadrilateral (kwɔdriˈlætərəl) *adj* vierseitig. *n* Viereck *neu.*
quadruped (ˈkwɔdruped) *n* Vierfüßer *m.*
quadruple (ˈkwɔdrupəl) *adj* vierfach. **quadruplet** *n* Vierling *m.*
quail (kweil) *n* Wachtel *f.*
quaint (kweint) *adj* malerisch, kurios.
quake (kweik) *vi* zittern, beben. *n* **1** Zittern *neu.* **2** Erdbeben *neu.*
Quaker (ˈkweikə) *n* Quäker *m.*
qualify (ˈkwɔlifai) *vt* **1** befähigen, qualifizieren. **2** einschränken. *vi* sich eignen. **qualification** *n* **1** Qualifikation, Befähigung *f.* **2** Voraussetzung *f.* **3** Einschränkung *f.*
quality (ˈkwɔliti) *n* **1** Eigenschaft *f.* **2** Qualität *f.*
qualm (kwɑːm) *n* **1** Skrupel, Zweifel *m.* **2** Übelkeit *f.*
quandary (ˈkwɔndəri) *n* Verlegenheit *f.*
quantify (ˈkwɔntifai) *vt* quantitativ bestimmen, messen.
quantity (ˈkwɔntiti) *n* Menge, Größe, Quantität *f.*
quarantine (ˈkwɔrəntiːn) *n* Quarantäne *f. vt* isolieren.
quarrel (ˈkwɔrəl) *n* Streit, Zank *m. vi* streiten, zanken.
quarry[1] (ˈkwɔri) *n* **1** Steinbruch *m.* **2** Quelle *f. vt* **1** brechen. **2** ausgraben.
quarry[2] (ˈkwɔri) *n* (verfolgtes) Wild *neu.* Beute *f.*
quart (kwɔːt) *n* Quart *neu.*
quarter (ˈkwɔːtə) *n* **1** Viertel *neu.* **2** *pl* Unterkunft *f.* Quartier *neu. vt* **1** vierteln. **2** einquartieren. **quarterdeck** *n* Achterdeck *neu.* **quartermaster** *n* **1** *mil* Quartiermeister *m.* **2** *naut* Steuerer *m.*
quartet (kwɔːˈtet) *n* Quartett *neu.*
quartz (kwɔːts) *n* Quarz *m.*
quash[1] (kwɔʃ) *vt* unterdrücken, vernichten.
quash[2] (kwɔʃ) *vt law* annullieren, abweisen, niederschlagen.

quaver (ˈkweivə) *vi* **1** zittern. **2** trillern. *n mus* Achtelnote *f.*
quay (kiː) *n* Kai *m.*
queasy (ˈkwiːzi) *adj* unwohl.
queen (kwiːn) *n* Königin *f.*
queer (kwiə) *adj* **1** wunderlich, sonderbar. **2** komisch, kurios. **3** *sl* schwul, homosexuell.
quell (kwel) *vt* unterdrücken, bezwingen.
quench (kwentʃ) *vt* löschen.
query (ˈkwiəri) *n* Frage, Erkundigung *f. vt* (be)fragen, sich erkundigen.
quest (kwest) *n* Suche *f.*
question (ˈkwestʃən) *n* **1** Frage *f.* **2** Problem *neu. vt* **1** (be)fragen. **2** bezweifeln. **question mark** *n* Fragezeichen *neu.* **questionnaire** *n* Fragebogen *m.*
queue (kjuː) *n* Schlange, Reihe *f. vi* Schlange stehen.
quibble (ˈkwibəl) *n* Spitzfindigkeit *f. vi* spitzfindig sein, Haarspalterei betreiben.
quick (kwik) *adj* **1** schnell, rasch, geschwind. **2** flink. **3** scharf. **4** lebend. **quicken** *(vi),vt* **1** (sich) beschleunigen. **2** (sich) beleben. **quicksand** *n* Treibsand *m.* **quicksilver** *n* Quecksilber *neu.* **quickstep** *n* Quickstep *m.* **quick-tempered** *adj* jähzornig, reizbar. **quick-witted** *adj* schlagfertig.
quid (kwid) *n sl* Pfund (sterling) *neu.*
quiet[1] (ˈkwaiət) *n* Stille, Ruhe *f.* Frieden *m.* **quioten** *vt* beruhigen.
quiet[2] (ˈkwaiət) *adj* still, ruhig. **quietness** *n* Ruhe, Stille *f.*
quill (kwil) *adj* Feder *f.*
quilt (kwilt) *n* Steppdecke *f. vt* **1** steppen. **2** wattieren.
quinine (kwiˈniːn) *n* Chinin *neu.*
quintessence (kwinˈtesəns) *n* Quintessenz *f.*
quintet (kwinˈtet) *n* Quintett *neu.*
quirk (kwəːk) *n* Eigenart, Verschrobenheit *f.*
quit*(kwit) *vi inf* seine Stelle aufgeben. *vt* **1** aufgeben. **2** verlassen.
quite (kwait) *adv* **1** ziemlich. **2** ganz, durchaus, völlig.
quiver[1] (ˈkwivə) *vi* zittern, beben. *n* Zittern, Beben *neu.*
quiver[2] (ˈkwivə) *n* Köcher *m.*
quiz (kwiz) *n, pl* **quizzes** Quiz *neu.*
quizzical (ˈkwizikəl) *adj* **1** seltsam, komisch. **2** spöttisch.
quota (ˈkwoutə) *n* Anteil *m.* Quote *f.*
quote (kwout) *vt* **1** anführen, zitieren. **2** angeben. *n* Zitat *neu.* **quotation** *n* **1** Zitat *neu.* **2**

comm (Kurs)Notierung *f.* **quotation marks** *n pl* Anführungszeichen *neu pl.*

R

rabbi (ˈræbai) *n* Rabbiner *m.*

rabbit (ˈræbit) *n* Kaninchen *neu.*

rabble (ˈræbəl) *n* Pöbel, Mob *m.*

rabies (ˈreibi:z) *n* Tollwut *f.* **rabid** *adj* 1 tollwütig. 2 wütend, rasend. 3 fanatisch.

race¹ (reis) *vi* rennen. *n* (Wett)Rennen *neu.* **racecourse** *n* Rennbahn *f.* **racehorse** *n* Rennpferd *neu.*

race² (reis) *n* Rasse *f.* **race relations** *n pl* Rassenbeziehungen *f pl.* **racial** *adj* rassisch, Rassen–. **racialism** *n* Rassenvorurteil *neu.*

rack (ræk) *n* 1 Gestell *neu.* 2 Ständer *m.* 3 Gepäcknetz *neu.* 4 Folterbank *f.*

racket¹ (ˈrækit) *n* 1 Lärm *m.* 2 Gaunerei *f.*

racket² (ˈrækit) *n* Schläger *m.* Rakett *neu.*

radar (ˈreidə) *n* Radar *neu.*

radial (ˈreidiəl) *adj* radial.

radiant (ˈreidiənt) *adj* strahlend, glänzend.

radiate (ˈreidieit) *vt,vi* ausstrahlen. **radiation** *n* (Aus)Strahlung *f.* **radiator** *m pl.* **radiator** *n* 1 Heizkörper *m.* 2 *mot* Kühler *m.*

radical (ˈrædikəl) *adj* 1 *pol* radikal. 2 gründlich.

radio (ˈreidiou) *n* Radio *neu.* Rundfunk *m.*

radioactive (reidiouækˈtiv) *adj* radioaktiv. **radioactivity** *n* Radioaktivität *f.*

radish (ˈrædiʃ) *n* Radieschen *neu.* Rettich *m.*

radium (ˈreidiəm) *n* Radium *neu.*

radius (ˈreidiəs) *n, pl* **radii** 1 Halbmesser, Radius *m.* 2 Bereich *m.*

raffia (ˈræfiə) *n* Raffiabast *f.*

raffle (ˈræfəl) *n* Verlosung *f.* *vt* verlosen.

raft (rɑːft) *n* Floß *neu.*

rafter (ˈrɑːftə) *n* Dachbalken *m.*

rag¹ (ræg) *n* 1 Fetzen, Lumpen, Lappen *m.* 2 Schundblatt *neu.* **ragged** *adj* zerlumpt.

rag² (ræg) *vt* 1 anschnauzen. 2 aufziehen. *n* Streich, Ulk, Unfug *m.*

rage (reidʒ) *n* Wut *f.* *vi* wüten.

raid (reid) *n* 1 Überfall, Angriff *m.* 2 (by the police) Razzia *f.*

rail (reil) *n* 1 Riegel *m.* 2 Geländer *neu.* **by rail** mit der Eisenbahn. **railway** *n* Eisenbahn *f.*

rain (rein) *n* Regen *m.* *vi* regnen. **rainbow** *n* Regenbogen *m.* **rainfall** *n* Niederschlagsmenge *f.*

raise (reiz) *vt* 1 (auf-, er-)heben. 2 errichten. 3 erhöhen, steigern. 4 aufbringen.

raisin (ˈreizən) *n* Rosine *f.*

rake (reik) *n* Rechen *m.* *vt* rechen.

rally (ˈræli) *n* 1 Versammlung *f.* 2 *mot* Sternfahrt *f.* 3 *sport* Schlagwechsel *m.* *vt* 1 wieder sammeln. 2 aufmuntern. *vi* 1 sich wieder sammeln. 2 sich erholen. **rally round** sich scharen um.

ram (ræm) *n* 1 *zool* Widder *m.* 2 Ramme *f.* Rammbock *m.* *vt* rammen.

ramble (ˈræmbəl) *vi* 1 wandern. 2 umherschweifen. *n* Wanderung *f.*

ramp (ræmp) *n* Rampe *f.*

rampage (ˈræmpeidʒ) *vi* (herum)toben.

rampant (ˈræmpənt) *adj* 1 zügellos. 2 wuchernd.

rampart (ˈræmpɑːt) *n* (Schutz)Wall *m.*

ramshackle (ˈræmʃækəl) *adj* baufällig.

ran (ræn) *v see* **run.**

ranch (rɑːntʃ) *n* Ranch, Viehfarm *f.*

rancid (ˈrænsid) *adj* ranzig.

rancour (ˈræŋkə) *n* Groll *m.* Erbitterung *f.*

random (ˈrændəm) *adj* zufällig, planlos. **at random** aufs Geratewohl.

rang (ræŋ) *v see* **ring**².

range (reindʒ) *n* 1 Reihe *f.* 2 *geog* Kette *f.* 3 Reichweite *f.* 4 Kollektion *f.* 5 Herd *m.* *vt* 1 einreihen. 2 durchstreichen. *vi* 1 sich erstrecken. 2 reichen. 3 streifen.

rank¹ (ræŋk) *n* 1 Reihe *f.* 2 Rang *m.* 3 Stand *m.* Klasse *f.* *vt* 1 einordnen. 2 rangieren. *vi* gehören. **rank and file** *n* 1 Mannschaftstand *m.* 2 die Masse *f.*

rank² (ræŋk) *adj* 1 üppig, überwuchert. 2 stinkend. 3 unanständig. 4 rein, kraß.

rankle (ˈræŋkəl) *vi* nagen, wühlen.

ransack (ˈrænsæk) *vt* durchwühlen, plündern.

ransom (ˈrænsəm) *n* Lösegeld *neu.* *vt* loskaufen.

rap (ræp) *vi* klopfen. *n* Klopfen *neu.*

rape (reip) *vt* vergewaltigen. *n* Vergewaltigung, Notzucht *f.*

rapid (ˈræpid) *adj* schnell, eilig, rapid.

rapier (ˈreipiə) *n* Rapier *neu.* (Stoß)Degen *m.*

rapture (ˈræptʃə) *n* Entzücken *neu.* Verzückung *f.*

rare¹ (rɛə) *adj* selten, rar.

rare² (rɛə) *adj* nicht durchgebraten.

rascal (ˈrɑːskəl) *n* 1 Schurke *m.* 2 Spitzbube *m.*

rash¹ (ræʃ) *adj* 1 übereilt. 2 tollkühn.

rash² (ræʃ) *n* Hautausschlag *m.*

rasher (ˈræʃə) *n* Speckschnitte *f.*

raspberry (ˈrɑːzbri) *n* Himbeere *f.*

rat (ræt) *n* Ratte *f.*

rate (reit) *n* 1 Grad *m.* 2 Verhältnis *neu.* Maßstab *m.* 3 Geschwindigkeit *f.* 4 *comm*

Kurs *m.* **5** Gebühr *f.* **6** *pl* Gemeindesteuer *f.* **at any rate** auf jeden Fall. *vt* einschätzen.

rather (ˈrɑːðə) *adv* **1** eher, lieber. **2** ziemlich.

ratio (ˈreiʃiou) *n* Verhältnis *neu.*

ration (ˈræʃən) *n* Ration *f.* *vt* rationieren.

rational (ˈræʃənəl) *adj* rational, vernünftig. **rationalize** *vt* **1** rational erklären. **2** rationalisieren.

rattle (ˈrætl) *vt,vi* rasseln, klappern. *n* **1** Gerassel *neu.* **2** Klapper *f.*

raucous (ˈrɔːkəs) *adj* heiser, rauh.

ravage (ˈrævidʒ) *vt* verwüsten, verheeren.

rave (reiv) *vi* rasen, toben, wüten. **rave about** schwärmen für.

raven (ˈreivən) *n* Rabe *m.* **ravenous** *adj* gefräßig, heißhungrig.

ravine (rəˈviːn) *n* (Berg)Schlucht *f.*

ravish (ˈræviʃ) *vt* **1** entzücken, hinreißen. **2** vergewaltigen. **3** fortraffen.

raw (rɔː) *adj* **1** rauh. **2** roh. **3** unreif, unerfahren.

ray (rei) *n* Strahl *m.*

rayon (ˈreiɔn) *n* Kunstseide *f.* Rayon *neu.*

razor (ˈreizə) *n* Rasiermesser *neu.* **electric razor** elektrischer Rasierapparat *m.* **safety razor** Rasierapparat *m.* **razor blade** Rasierklinge *f.*

reach (riːtʃ) *vt* (er)reichen. *vi* reichen. **1** Reichweite *f.* **2** Bereich *m.*

react (riˈækt) *vi* reagieren. **reaction** *n* **1** Reaktion *f.* **2** Rückwirkung *f.* **reactionary** *adj* reaktionär. *n* Reaktionär *m.*

read⁴ (riːd) *vt,vi* lesen.

readjust (riːəˈdʒʌst) *vt* wieder anpassen, einstellen. *vi* sich umorientieren, sich wieder anpassen.

ready (ˈredi) *adj* **1** bereit, fertig. **2** schnell. **readily** *adv* bereitwillig, ohne weiteres.

real (riəl) *adj* **1** wirklich, tatsächlich. **2** echt, wahr. **real estate** *n* Grundbesitz *m.* **really** *adv* wirklich, tatsächlich. **realism** *n* Realismus *m.* **realize** *vt* **1** verwirklichen. **2** sich vorstellen. **3** begreifen. **4** *comm* realisieren.

realm (relm) *n* **1** Reich *neu.* **2** Bereich *m.*

reap (riːp) *vt* **1** ernten. **2** mähen, schneiden.

reappear (riːəˈpiə) *vi* wieder erscheinen.

rear¹ (riə) *n* **1** Rückseite *f.* **2** Hintergrund *m.* *adj* hinterst. **rear admiral** *n* Konteradmiral *m.* **rearguard** *n* Nachhut *f.*

rear² (riə) *vt* **1** züchten, (er)ziehen. **2** erheben. *vi* **1** sich (auf)bäumen. **2** hochfahren.

rearrange (riəˈreindʒ) *vt* neuordnen.

reason (ˈriːzən) *n* **1** Vernunft *f.* **2** Grund, Anlaß

m. *vi* vernünftig denken. **reasonable** *adj* **1** vernünftig. **2** angemessen, annehmbar.

reassure (riːəˈʃuə) *vt* **1** beruhigen. **2** wieder beteuern.

rebate (ˈriːbeit) *n* **1** Rabatt *m.* **2** Zurückzahlung *f.*

rebel (*n,adj* ˈrebəl; *v* riˈbel) *n* Rebell *m.* *adj* aufrührerisch. *vi* sich empören, sich auflehnen.

rebound (*v* riˈbaund; *n* ˈriːbaund) *vi* zurückprallen. *n* **1** Rückprall *m.* **2** Rückschlag *m.*

rebuff (riˈbʌf) *n* Abweisung *f.* *vt* abweisen.

rebuild⁴ (riːˈbild) *vt* wiederaufbauen.

rebuke (riˈbjuːk) *vt* tadeln. *n* Tadel *m.*

recall (riˈkɔːl) *vt* **1** zurückrufen. **2** sich erinnern an. *n* Widerruf *m.*

recede (riˈsiːd) *vi* zurückweichen, zurückgehen.

receipt (riˈsiːt) *n* **1** Quittung *f.* **2** Empfang *m.*

receive (riˈsiːv) *vt* **1** empfangen. **2** erhalten. **3** annehmen. **receiver** *n* **1** Empfänger *m.* **2** *comm* Konkursverwalter *m.* **3** (telephone) Hörer *m.*

recent (ˈriːsənt) *adj* letzt, neu, jung. **recently** *adv* kürzlich, in letzter Zeit, neulich.

receptacle (riˈseptəkəl) *n* Behälter *m.*

reception (riˈsepʃən) *n* **1** Empfang *m.* **2** Aufnahme *f.* **receptive** *adj* empfänglich, aufnahmebereit.

recess (riˈses) *n* **1** Pause *f.* Ferien *pl.* **2** Nische *f.* *vt* einsenken.

recession (riˈseʃən) *n* **1** Rezession *f.* Konjunkturrückgang *m.* **2** Zurücktreten *neu.*

recipe (ˈresipi) *n* Rezept *neu.*

recipient (riˈsipiənt) *n* Empfänger *m.* *adj* empfänglich.

reciprocate (riˈsiprəkeit) *vi* einen Gegendienst leisten. *vt* **1** erwidern. **2** austauschen. **reciprocal** *adj* gegenseitig, wechselseitig.

recite (riˈsait) *vt* **1** vortragen. **2** Aufzählung *f.* **3** Bericht *m.*

reckless (ˈrekləs) *adj* **1** unbekümmert. **2** rücksichtslos. **3** fahrlässig.

reckon (ˈrekən) *vt* **1** zählen, rechnen. **2** *inf* meinen, glauben.

reclaim (riˈkleim) *vt* **1** zurückfordern. **2** urbar machen.

recline (riˈklain) *vi* sich zurücklehnen.

recluse (riˈkluːs) *n* Einsiedler *m.* *adj* **1** abgeschieden. **2** einsiedlerisch.

recognize (ˈrekəgnaiz) *vt* **1** wiedererkennen. **2** (an)erkennen. **3** zugeben. **recognition** **1** Erkenntnis *f.* **2** Anerkennung *f.*

recoil (riˈkɔil) *vi* **1** zurückschrecken, zurückfahren. **2** zurückweichen. *n* Rückstoß *m.*

recollect

recollect (rekə'lekt) *vt* sich erinnern an.

recommence (ri:kə'mens) *vt,vi* wieder beginnen *or* anfangen.

recommend (rekə'mend) *vt* empfehlen. **recommendation** *n* Empfehlung *f.* Vorschlag *m.*

recompense ('rekəmpəns) *vt* **1** entschädigen, belohnen. **2** wiedergutmachen. *n* **1** Entschädigung, Belohnung *f.* **2** Rückerstattung *f.*

reconcile ('rekənsail) *vt* versöhnen.

reconstruct (ri:kən'strʌkt) *vt* **1** wiederaufbauen. **2** rekonstruieren.

record (*v* ri'kɔ:d; *n,adj* 'rekɔ:d) *vt* **1** aufzeichnen. **2** *tech* aufnehmen. **3** eintragen. *n* **1** Niederschrift *f.* Bericht *m.* **2** Schallplatte *f.* **3** *sport* Rekord *m. adj* Rekord—. **recording** *n* Aufnahme *f.* **record-player** *n* Plattenspieler *m.*

recount (ri'kaunt) *vt* erzählen.

recover (ri'kʌvə) *vt* wiederfinden, zurückgewinnen. *vi* sich erholen. **recovery** *n* **1** Rettung *f.* **2** Erholung *f.*

recreation (rekri'eiʃən) *n* Erholung *f.* **recreation ground** Sportplatz, Spielplatz *m.*

recruit (ri'kru:t) *vt* rekrutieren, anwerben. *n* Rekrut *m.* **recruitment** *n* Rekrutierung *f.*

rectangle ('rektæŋgəl) *n* Rechteck *neu.* **rectangular** *adj* rechteckig.

rectify ('rektifai) *vt* berichtigen, korrigieren.

recuperate (ri'kju:pəreit) *vi* sich erholen. **recuperation** *n* Erholung *f.*

recur (ri'kə:) *vi* wiederkehren, zurückkehren.

red (red) *adj* rot. *n* Rot *neu.* **caught red-handed** auf frischer Tat ertappt. **redcurrant** *n* Rote Johannisbeere *f.* **redden** *vi* **1** erröten. **2** rot werden.

redeem (ri'di:m) *vt* **1** zurückkaufen. **2** einlösen. **3** wiedergutmachen. **4** (er)retten. **5** *rel* erlösen. **redemption** *n* **1** Rückkauf *m.* **2** Einlösung *f.* **3** Wiedergutmachung *f.* **4** (Er-)Rettung *f.* **5** *rel* Erlösung *f.*

redevelop (ri:di'veləp) *vt,vi* neu entwickeln.

Red Indian *n* Indianer *m.*

redress (ri'dres) *vt* **1** abhelfen, beseitigen. **2** wiederherstellen. *n* Abhilfe, Behebung *f.*

reduce (ri'dju:s) *vt* **1** vermindern. **2** erniedrigen. **3** verwandeln. **4** zwingen. *vi* abnehmen. **reduction** *n* **1** Verminderung *f.* **2** Abnahme *f.*

redundant (ri'dʌndənt) *adj* **1** überflüssig. **2** übermäßig. **make redundant** entlassen. **redundancy** *n* **1** Entlassung *f.* **2** Überfluß *m.*

reed (ri:d) *n* **1** Rohr *neu.* **2** *mus* (Rohr)Blatt *neu.*

reef (ri:f) *n* (Felsen)Riff *m.*

reek (ri:k) *vi* stinken. *n* Gestank *m.*

reel[1] (ri:l) *n* Spule, Rolle *f. vt* spulen.

reel[2] (ri:l) *vi* **1** taumeln. **2** schwanken.

re-establish (ri:i'stæbliʃ) *vt* wiederherstellen.

refectory (ri'fektəri) *n* **1** Speisesaal *m.* **2** Mensa *f.*

refer (ri'fə:) *vt* verweisen. *vi* **1** sich beziehen. **2** hinweisen. **referee** *n* Schiedsrichter *m.* **reference** *n* **1** Hinweis *m.* **2** Bezugnahme *f.* **3** Quellenangabe *f.* **4** Zeugnis *neu.* **referendum** *n, pl* **-da** Volksabstimmung *f.* Referendum *neu.*

refill (*v* ri:'fil; *n* 'ri:fil) *vt* nachfüllen, auffüllen. *n* Nachfüllung, Ersatzfüllung *f.*

refine (ri'fain) *vt* **1** läutern, raffinieren. **2** verfeinern. **refined** *adj* **1** raffiniert. **2** kultiviert. **refinement** *n* **1** Feinheit, Kultiviertheit *f.* **2** Raffinierung *f.* **refinery** *n* Raffinerie *f.*

reflation (ri'fleiʃən) *n* Wirtschaftsbelebung, Reflation *f.*

reflect (ri'flekt) *vt* wiederspiegeln. *vi* **1** zurückstrahlen, reflektieren. **2** nachdenken. **reflection** *n* **1** Rückstrahlung, Reflexion *f.* **2** Spiegelbild *neu.* **3** Überlegung *f.* **reflector** *n* **1** Reflektor *m.* **2** *mot* Rückstrahler *m.*

reflex (*adj,n* 'ri:fleks) *adj* **1** rückwirkend. **2** Reflex—. *n* Reflex *m.* **reflexive** *adj gram* rückbezüglich, reflexiv.

reform (ri'fɔ:m) *n* Reform, Verbesserung *f. vt* reformieren. *vi* sich bessern. **reformation** *n* **1** Umgestaltung *f.* **2** *cap rel* Reformation *f.*

refract (ri'frækt) *vt* brechen.

refrain[1] (ri'frein) *vi* sich enthalten, unterlassen.

refrain[2] (ri'frein) *n mus* Refrain, Kehrreim *m.*

refresh (ri'freʃ) *vt* **1** erfrischen. **2** erneuern. **refreshment** *n* Erfrischung *f.*

refrigerator (ri'fridʒəreitə) *n* Kühlschrank *m.*

refuel (ri:'fju:əl) *vt,vi* (auf)tanken.

refuge ('refju:dʒ) *n* Zuflucht *f.* Zufluchtsort *m.* **refugee** *n* Flüchtling *m.*

refund (*v* ri'fʌnd; *n* 'ri:fʌnd) *vt* zurückzahlen. *n* Rückzahlung *f.*

refuse[1] (ri'fju:z) *vt* **1** ablehnen. **2** verweigern. *vi* sich weigern.

refuse[2] ('refju:s) *n* Abfall, Müll *m.*

refute (ri'fju:t) *vt* widerlegen.

regain (ri'gein) *vt* wiedergewinnen.

regal ('ri:gəl) *adj* **1** königlich. **2** prunkvoll.

regard (ri'gɑ:d) *vt* **1** ansehen, betrachten. **2** berücksichtigen. *n* **1** Rücksicht *f.* **2** Achtung *f.* **regardless** *adj, adv* ohne Rücksicht.

regatta (ri'gɑ:tə) *n* Regatta *f.*

regent ('ri:dʒənt) *n* Regent *m.*

regime (rei'ʒi:m) *n* Regime *neu.*

regiment (ˈredʒimənt) n Regiment neu. vt reglementieren. **regimental** adj Regiments—.

region (ˈriːdʒən) n Gegend f. Gebiet neu. Bereich m. **in the region of** ungefähr.

register (ˈredʒistə) n 1 Liste f. Verzeichnis neu. 2 mus,lit Register neu. vt 1 eintragen. 2 zeigen. vi sich eintragen, sich (an)melden. **registrar** n Standesbeamte(r) m.

regress (riˈgres) vi zurückgehen. n Rückschritt m.

regret (riˈgret) vt bedauern. n Bedauern neu. **regrettable** adj bedauerlich.

regular (ˈregjulə) adj 1 regelmäßig. 2 ordentlich. 3 gewöhnlich. **regularity** n Regelmäßigkeit f.

regulate (ˈregjuleit) vt regeln, ordnen, regulieren. **regulation** n 1 Vorschrift f. 2 Regelung f.

rehabilitate (riːəˈbiliteit) vt rehabilitieren.

rehearse (riˈhəːs) Th vt,vi proben. **rehearsal** n Probe f.

reign (rein) n Regierung(szeit) f. vi regieren.

reimburse (riːimˈbəːs) vt 1 entschädigen. 2 zurückzahlen.

rein (rein) n Zügel m. vt zügeln.

reincarnation (riːinkaːˈneiʃən) n 1 Wiedergeburt f. 2 (Wieder)Verkörperung f

reindeer (ˈreindiə) n Renntier, Ren neu.

reinforce (riːinˈfɔːs) vt 1 verstärken. 2 bewehren. **reinforced concrete** n Eisenbeton m.

reinstate (riːinˈsteit) vt wiedereinsetzen.

reinvest (riːinˈvest) vt wieder anlegen.

reissue (riːˈiʃuː) vt wieder ausgeben. n Neuausgabe f

reject (v riˈdʒekt; n riːdʒekt) vt 1 zurückweisen, ablehnen. 2 abstoßen. n Ausschußartikel m. **rejection** n Zurückweisung, Ablehnung f.

rejoice (riˈdʒɔis) vi sich freuen.

rejoin (riˈdʒɔin) vi erwidern.

rejuvenate (riˈdʒuːvəneit) vt verjüngen.

relapse (riˈlæps) n Rückfall m. vi wieder verfallen, rückfällig werden.

relate (riˈleit) vt 1 berichten, erzählen. 2 verbinden. vi sich beziehen.

relation (riˈleiʃən) n 1 Verwandte(r) m. 2 Verhältnis neu. Beziehung f. **relationship** n 1 Verwandtschaft f. 2 Verbindung f. Verhältnis neu.

relative (ˈrelətiv) adj 1 bezüglich, relativ. 2 verhältnismäßig. n Verwandte(r) m. **relatively** adv verhältnismäßig. **relativity** n Relativität f.

relax (riˈlæks) vi 1 sich entspannen. 2 sich lockern. 3 nachlassen. vt 1 lockern. 2 entspannen. 3 abschwächen. **relaxation** n 1 Entspannung f. 2 Lockerung f. 3 Nachlassen neu.

relay (n ˈriːlei; v riˈlei) n 1 sport Staffel f. 2 tech Relais neu. vt 1 übertragen. 2 weitergeben. **relay race** Staffellauf m.

release (riˈliːs) vt 1 freilassen, loslassen. 2 aufgeben. 3 freigeben. n 1 Entlassung, Befreiung f. 2 Aufgabe f.

relent (riˈlent) vi sich erweichen lassen. **relentless** adj unbarmherzig.

relevant (ˈreləvənt) adj relevant, belangvoll. **relevance** n Relevanz, Bedeutung f.

reliable (riˈlaiəbəl) adj zuverlässig, verläßlich. **reliability** n Zuverlässigkeit f.

relic (ˈrelik) n 1 rel Reliquie f. 2 Überbleibsel neu.

relief (riˈliːf) n 1 Erleichterung f. 2 Ablösung f. 3 Entlastung f.

relieve (riˈliːv) vt 1 erleichtern. 2 entlasten. 3 entheben. 4 ablösen.

religion (riˈlidʒən) n Religion f. Glaube m. **religious** adj 1 religiös. 2 fromm.

relinquish (riˈliŋkwiʃ) vt aufgeben, loslassen.

relish (ˈreliʃ) vt genießen. n 1 pikante Würze f. 2 Geschmack m.

relive (riːˈliv) vt wieder erleben.

reluctant (riˈlʌktənt) adj widerwillig, ungern. **reluctance** n Abneigung f. Widerwille m.

rely (riˈlai) vi **rely on** sich verlassen auf.

remain (riˈmein) vi 1 bleiben. 2 übrigbleiben. **remains** n pl Reste m pl. **remainder** n Rest m.

remand (riˈmaːnd) vt in die Untersuchungshaft zurückschicken. n Untersuchungshaft f.

remark (riˈmaːk) vt bemerken. n Bemerkung f. **remarkable** adj bemerkenswert.

remarry (riːˈmæri) vi (sich) wieder (ver)heiraten.

remedy (ˈremədi) n 1 Heilmittel neu. 2 Gegenmittel neu. vt 1 abhelfen. 2 in Ordnung bringen.

remember (riˈmembə) vt 1 sich erinnern an. 2 sich merken. 3 grüßen. **remembrance** n 1 Erinnerung f. 2 Gedenken neu.

remind (riˈmaind) vt erinnern, mahnen.

reminiscence (remiˈnisəns) n Erinnerung f. **reminiscent** adj (sich) erinnernd.

remiss (riˈmis) adj nachlässig, säumig. **remission** n Erlaß m. Ermäßigung f.

remit (riˈmit) vt 1 überweisen. 2 erlassen. **remittance** n (Geld)Sendung, Überweisung f.

remnant (ˈremnənt) n 1 Überrest m. 2 Spur f.

remorse (ri'mɔːs) *n* Reue *f*.
remote (ri'mout) *adj* entfernt, abgelegen.
remove (ri'muːv) *vt* 1 entfernen, beseitigen. 2 zurückziehen, wegnehmen. 3 ausziehen. *vi* umziehen. **removal** *n* 1 Entfernung *f*. 2 Abhebung *f*. 3 Umzug *m*.
remunerate (ri'mjuːnəreit) *vt* 1 belohnen. 2 vergüten. **remuneration** *n* 1 Lohn *m*. Honorar *neu*. 2 Belohnung *f*.
renaissance (ri'neisəns) *n* 1 Wiedergeburt *f*. 2 *cap* Renaissance *f*.
rename (riː'neim) *vt* umbenennen.
render ('rendə) *vt* 1 übergeben. 2 leisten, erweisen. 3 machen. 4 interpretieren, darstellen. 5 übertragen.
rendezvous ('rɔndivuː) *n* 1 Treffpunkt *m*. 2 Verabredung *f*. Rendezvous *neu*.
renew (ri'njuː) *vt* 1 erneuern. 2 wieder aufnehmen.
renounce (ri'nauns) *vt* verzichten auf, entsagen, ablehnen.
renovate ('renəveit) *vt* renovieren, erneuern.
renown (ri'naun) *n* Ruhm, Ruf *m*. Ansehen *neu*. **renowned** *adj* berühmt, renommiert.
rent (rent) *n* Miete *f*. *vt* 1 mieten. 2 vermieten. **rental** *n* Mietbetrag *m*.
reopen (riː'oupən) *vt,vi* wieder (er)öffnen.
reorganize (riː'ɔːgənaiz) *vt* reorganisieren.
repair (ri'pɛə) *vt* reparieren, ausbessern. *n* Reparatur, Ausbesserung *f*.
repartee (repɑ'tiː) *n* 1 Schlagfertigkeit *f*. 2 schlagfertige Antwort *f*.
repatriate (ri'pætrieit) *vt* repatriieren.
repay (ri'pei) *vt* 1 zurückzahlen. 2 erwidern.
repeal (ri'piːl) *vt* aufheben. *n* Aufhebung *f*.
repeat (ri'piːt) *vt* 1 wiederholen. 2 nachsagen. *n* Wiederholung *f*.
repel (ri'pel) *vt* 1 zurücktreiben, zurückschlagen. 2 abweisen, abstoßen, zuwider sein.
repent (ri'pent) *vt* bereuen. *vi* Reue empfinden. **repent of** bereuen.
repercussion (riːpə'kʌʃən) *n* Rückwirkung *f*.
repertoire ('repətwɑː) *n* Spielplan *m*. Repertoire *neu*.
repetition (repə'tiʃən) *n* Wiederholung *f*.
replace (ri'pleis) *vt* 1 ersetzen. 2 wieder hinstellen.
replay ('riːplei) *n sport* Wiederholungsspiel *neu*.
replenish (ri'pleniʃ) *vt* (wieder) auffüllen.
replica ('replikə) *n* 1 Kopie *f*. 2 Ebenbild *neu*.
reply (ri'plai) *vi* antworten, erwidern. *n* Antwort, Erwiderung *f*.
report (re'pɔːt) *n* 1 Bericht *m*. 2 Gerücht *neu*. 3 Knall *m*. *vt* 1 berichten. 2 melden. *vi* 1 berichten. 2 sich melden. **reporter** *n* Reporter, Berichterstatter *m*.
repose (ri'pouz) *n* Ruhe *f*. *vi* ruhen.
represent (repri'zent) *vt* 1 vertreten, repräsentieren. 2 darstellen. 3 bedeuten. **representation** *n* 1 Vertretung, Repräsentation *f*. 2 Darstellung *f*. 3 Vorstellung, Aufführung *f*. **representative** *adj* 1 darstellend. 2 (stell)vertretend. 3 typisch. *n* 1 Vertreter, Repräsentant *m*. 2 Beauftragte(r) *m*.
repress (ri'pres) *vt* 1 unterdrücken. 2 verdrängen. **repression** *n* 1 Unterdrückung *f*. 2 Verdrängung *f*.
reprieve (ri'priːv) *vt* begnadigen. *n* Begnadigung, Gnadenfrist *f*.
reprimand ('reprimɑːnd) *n* Verweis *m*. *vt* einen Verweis erteilen.
reprint (*v* riː'print; *n* 'riːprint) *vt* neu auflegen *or* drucken. *n* Neudruck *m*.
reprisal (ri'praizəl) *n* Repressalie *f*.
reproach (ri'proutʃ) *vt* vorwerfen. *n* Vorwurf *m*. **reproachful** *adj* vorwurfsvoll.
reproduce (riːprə'djuːs) *vt* 1 (wieder) hervorbringen. 2 wiedergeben. 3 erzeugen. 4 kopieren. *vi* sich fortpflanzen. **reproduction** *n* 1 Wiedergabe *f*. 2 Kopie, Nachbildung *f*. 3 Fortpflanzung, Vermehrung *f*.
reptile ('reptail) *n* Kriechtier, Reptil *neu*.
republic (ri'pʌblik) *n* Republik *f*.
repudiate (ri'pjuːdieit) *vt* 1 nicht anerkennen. 2 ablehnen, abweisen.
repugnant (ri'pʌgnənt) *adj* zuwider, widerlich.
repulsion (ri'pʌlʃən) *n* 1 Widerwille *m*. Abscheu *f*. 2 Abstoßung *f*. **repulsive** *adj* 1 widerwärtig. 2 abstoßend.
repute (ri'pjuːt) *n* Ruf *m*. *vt* halten für. **reputed** *adj* angeblich. **reputable** *adj* 1 angesehen. 2 geachtet. **reputation** *n* 1 Ruf *m*. 2 Ansehen *neu*.
request (ri'kwest) *n* Bitte *f*. Gesuch, Verlangen *neu*. *vt* 1 bitten. 2 beantragen.
requiem ('rekwiəm) *n* Requiem *neu*.
require (ri'kwaiə) *vt* 1 verlangen. 2 erfordern.
re-route (riː'ruːt) *vt* umleiten.
resale (riː'seil) *n* Weiterverkauf *m*.
rescue ('reskjuː) *vt* 1 retten. 2 befreien. *n* 1 Rettung *f*. 2 Befreiung *f*.
research (ri'səːtʃ) *n* 1 Forschung *f*. 2 Untersuchung *f*.
resell (riː'sel) *vt* weiterverkaufen.
resemble (ri'zembəl) *vt* ähnlich sein, gleichen. **resemblance** *n* Ähnlichkeit *f*.

resent (ri'zent) vt übelnehmen. **resentful** adj ärgerlich, aufgebracht. **resentment** n Ressentiment neu.

reserve (ri'zə:v) vt 1 aufbewahren. 2 reservieren. 3 sich vorbehalten. n 1 Reserve f. 2 Zurückhaltung f. **reservation** n 1 Vorbestellung, Reservierung f. 2 Vorbehalt m. **reserved** adj 1 reserviert, zurückgelegt. 2 zurückhaltend.

reservoir ('rezəvwa:) n 1 Reservoir neu. 2 Staubecken neu.

reside (ri'zaid) vi wohnen, leben. **residence** n 1 Wohnsitz m. 2 Aufenthalt m. **resident** adj wohnhaft, ansässig. n Einwohner m.

residue ('rezidju:) n 1 Rest m.

resign (ri'zain) vi zurücktreten. vt 1 aufgeben. 2 niederlegen. **resign oneself to** sich versöhnen mit. **resignation** n 1 Rücktritt m. 2 Resignation f.

resilient (ri'ziliənt) adj 1 federnd. 2 elastisch. 3 nicht unterzukriegen.

resin ('rezin) n Harz neu.

resist (ri'zist) vt 1 sich widersetzen. 2 widerstehen. vi sich widersetzen. **resistance** n Widerstand m.

resit (ri:'sit) vt (an exam) wiederholen.

resolve (ri'zɔlv) vt 1 auflösen. 2 lösen. 3 beschließen. vi 1 sich auflösen. 2 sich entschließen. **resolute** adj entschlossen. **resolution** n 1 Beschluß f. 2 Resolution f. 3 Lösung f. 3 Entschlossenheit f.

resonant ('rezənənt) adj 1 widerhallend. 2 mitschwingend.

resort (ri'zɔ:t) vi **resort to** 1 sich begeben nach. 2 zurückgreifen auf. ~n 1 Mittel neu. 2 Ferienort m. **last resort** letzter Ausweg m.

resound (ri'zaund) vi widerhallen.

resource (ri'zɔ:s) n 1 Hilfsquelle f. 2 Findigkeit f. 3 pl Rohstoffquellen. 4 pl Bodenschätze m pl. **resourceful** adj findig, einfallsreich.

respect (ri'spekt) n 1 Respekt m. Achtung f. 2 Rücksicht f. 3 Hinsicht f. 4 pl Grüße m pl. vt 1 achten. 2 respektieren. **respectable** adj anständig, respektabel. **respective** adj jeweilig. **respectively** adv beziehungsweise.

respite ('respit) n 1 Frist f. Aufschub m. 2 Ruhepause f.

respond (ri'spɔnd) vi 1 antworten. 2 entgegenkommen. 3 reagieren. **response** n 1 Antwort f. 2 Reaktion f. **responsibility** n 1 Verantwortlichkeit f. 2 Verantwortung f. 3 pl Verpflichtungen f pl. **responsible** adj 1 verantwortlich. 2 verantwortungsbewußt. **respon-**

sive adj 1 empfänglich. 2 zugänglich. 3 entgegenkommend.

rest[1] (rest) n 1 Ruhe f. 2 Rast f. 3 Pause f. 4 Stütze f. vi 1 ruhen. 2 sich verlassen. vt 1 stützen. 2 begründen. **restless** adj 1 unruhig. 2 ruhelos.

rest[2] (rest) n 1 Rest m. 2 das Übrige.

restaurant ('restərɔnt) n Restaurant neu.

restore (ri'stɔ:) vt 1 zurückgeben. 2 wiederherstellen. 3 restaurieren. **restoration** n 1 Wiederherstellung f. 2 Rückerstattung f. 3 cap Restauration f.

restrain (ri'strein) vt 1 zurückhalten. 2 hindern. 3 einschränken. **restraint** n 1 Zurückhaltung f. 2 Zwang m.

restrict (ri'strikt) vt einschränken, beschränken.

result (ri'zʌlt) n Ergebnis neu. Folge f. vi 1 sich ergeben. 2 zur Folge haben.

resume (ri'zju:m) vt 1 wiederaufnehmen. 2 zurücknehmen.

résumé ('rezumei) n Zusammenfassung f. Resümee neu.

resurrect (rezə'rekt) vt 1 ausgraben. 2 wieder aufleben lassen. **resurrection** n Auferstehung f.

retail ('ri:teil) n Kleinhandel m. adj Einzelhandels—. vt im kleinen verkaufen. adv en detail.

retain (ri'tein) vt 1 bewahren. 2 zurückhalten.

retaliate (ri'tælieit) vi sich rächen, Vergeltung üben. **retaliation** n Vergeltung f.

retard (ri'ta:d) vt verzögern, verlangsamen. **retarded** adj med zurückgeblieben.

reticent ('retisənt) adj verschwiegen, zurückhaltend.

retina ('retinə) n Netzhaut, Retina f.

retire (ri'taiə) vi 1 in den Ruhestand treten. 2 sich zurückziehen. vt 1 in den Ruhestand versetzen.

retort[1] (ri'tɔ:t) vi erwidern. n Erwiderung f.

retort[2] (ri'tɔ:t) n sci Retorte f.

retrace (ri'treis) vt zurückverfolgen.

retract (ri'trækt) vt 1 zurücknehmen. 2 widerrufen. 3 einziehen.

retreat (ri'tri:t) n 1 Rückzug m. 2 Zurückweichen neu. 3 Zuflucht f. vi 1 sich zurückziehen. 2 zurückweichen.

retrieve (ri'tri:v) vt 1 wiederbekommen. 2 wiedergewinnen.

retrograde ('retrəgreid) adj 1 rückläufig. 2 rückschrittlich. 3 retrograd.

retrogress (retrə'gres) vi zurückgehen, sich verschlechtern.

retrospect (ˈretrəspekt) n Rückblick m. **in retrospect** rückblickend.

return (riˈtəːn) vi zurückkehren. vt 1 zurückgeben. 2 erwidern. n 1 Rückkehr f. 2 Rückgabe f. 3 comm Umsatz m. 4 Bericht m.

reunite (riːjuːˈnait) vt wiedervereinigen.

reveal (riˈviːl) vt 1 offenbaren, enthüllen. 2 zeigen. **revelation** n Offenbarung, Enthüllung f.

revel (ˈrevəl) vi sich weiden an.

revenge (riˈvendʒ) n Rache f. vt (sich) rächen.

revenue (ˈrevənjuː) n Einkommen neu. Einnahmen f pl.

reverberate (riˈvəːbəreit) vi widerhallen, reflektiert werden.

reverence (ˈrevərəns) n 1 Ehrfurcht f. 2 Verehrung f.

reverse (riˈvəːs) adj umgekehrt. n 1 Gegenteil neu. 2 Rückseite f. 3 Rückschlag m. 4 tech,mot Rückwärtsgang m. vt 1 umkehren, umdrehen. 2 rückwärts fahren. vi rückwärts fahren.

revert (riˈvəːt) vi 1 zurückfallen. 2 sich zurückverwandeln.

review (riˈvjuː) n 1 Überblick m. 2 Nachprüfung f. 3 Rezension, Besprechung f. 4 Rundschau f. vt 1 nachprüfen. 2 überblicken. 3 rezensieren.

revise (riˈvaiz) vt 1 überprüfen. 2 verbessern, bearbeiten. vi studieren.

revive (riˈvaiv) vt wiederbeleben.

revoke (riˈvouk) vt widerrufen, aufheben.

revolt (riˈvoult) vi sich erheben, rebellieren. vt abstoßen. n Revolte f. Aufstand m. **revolting** adj abstoßend.

revolution (revəˈluːʃən) n 1 pol Revolution f. 2 Umdrehung f.

revolve (riˈvolv) vi sich drehen. vt kreisen. **revolver** n Revolver m.

revue (riˈvjuː) n Revue f.

revulsion (riˈvʌlʃən) n Abscheu f. Ekel m.

reward (riˈwoːd) n Belohnung f. vt belohnen.

rhetoric (ˈretərik) n Rhetorik, Redekunst f. **rhetorical** adj rhetorisch.

rheumatism (ˈruːmətizəm) n Rheumatismus m.

Rhine (rain) n Rhein m. **Rhineland-Palatinate** n Rheinland-Pfalz neu.

rhinoceros (raiˈnosərəs) n Nashorn neu.

Rhodesia (rouˈdiːʃə) n Rhodesien neu. **Rhodesian** adj rhodesisch. n Rhodesier m.

rhododendron (roudəˈdendrən) n Rhododendron m,neu.

rhubarb (ˈruːbaːb) n Rhabarber m.

rhyme (raim) n Reim m. vt,vi reimen.

rhythm (ˈriðəm) n Rhythmus m.

rib (rib) n Rippe f.

ribbon (ˈribən) n Band neu. Streifen m.

rice (rais) n Reis m.

rich (ritʃ) adj 1 reich. 2 fett. 3 voll. 4 kräftig.

rickety (ˈrikiti) adj wackelig, baufällig.

rid* (rid) vt befreien. adj los, frei. **get rid of** los werden.

riddance (ˈridns) n Loswerden neu. Befreiung f. **good riddance** den wäre ich glücklich los.

riddle[1] (ˈridl) n Rätsel neu.

riddle[2] (ˈridl) vt 1 durchlöchern. 2 durchsieben.

ride (raid) vt,vi 1 reiten. 2 fahren. n 1 Ritt m. 2 Fahrt f.

ridge (ridʒ) n 1 geog Kamm m. 2 Rücken m.

ridicule (ˈridikjuːl) n Spott m. Verspottung f. vt verspotten, lächerlich machen. **ridiculous** adj lächerlich.

rife (raif) adj 1 weit verbreitet. 2 zahlreich. 3 voll von.

rifle[1] (ˈraifəl) n mil Gewehr neu. Büchse f.

rifle[2] (ˈraifəl) vt plündern, berauben.

rift (rift) n 1 Spalt m. 2 Riß m.

rig (rig) n 1 naut Takelwerk neu. 2 Ausrüstung f. vt 1 einrichten. 2 (auf)takeln.

right (rait) adj 1 richtig. 2 recht. n 1 Recht neu. 2 Rechte f. adv 1 richtig. 2 rechts. 3 sehr, ganz. vt 1 aufrichten. 2 in Ordnung bringen. **right angle** n rechter Winkel m. **right-hand** adj recht. **right-handed** adj rechtshändig. **right of way** n 1 Vorfahrtsrecht neu. 2 Wegerecht neu. **right wing** n rechter Flügel m. adj Rechts—, rechtradikal.

righteous (ˈraitʃəs) adj gerecht, rechtschaffen.

rigid (ˈridʒid) adj 1 steif. 2 unbeugsam.

rigour (ˈrigə) n 1 Strenge f. 2 Härte f.

rim (rim) n Rand m. Kante f.

rind (raind) n Rinde, Schale f.

ring[1] (riŋ) n 1 Ring m. 2 Kreis m. 3 Bande f. vt einkreisen. **ringleader** n Rädelsführer m. **ring-road** n Ringstraße f.

ring*[2] (riŋ) vt 1 läuten. 2 erklingen. 3 anrufen. vi läuten, klingeln, ertönen. **ring up** anrufen. ~n 1 Klingeln, Geklingel neu. 2 Klang m. 3 inf Anruf m.

rink (riŋk) n Eisbahn f.

rinse (rins) vt (aus)spülen.

riot (ˈraiət) n Aufruhr, Tumult m. vi an einem Aufruhr teilnehmen. **run riot** 1 sich austoben. 2 umherschwärmen.

rip (rip) vt (zer)reißen. vi reißen. n Riß m.

ripe (raip) adj reif. **ripen** vi reifen, reif werden. vt reifen lassen.

ripple ('ripəl) n kleine Welle f. (vi),vt (sich) kräuseln.

rise* (raiz) vi 1 aufstehen. 2 sich erheben. 3 sich empören. 4 aufgehen. 5 (an)steigen. n 1 Steigen neu. 2 Erhebung f. 3 Aufstieg m. 4 Erhöhung f.

risk (risk) n Risiko neu. vt riskieren, wagen.

rissole ('risoul) n cul Frikadelle f.

rite (rait) n Ritus m. Zeremonie f.

ritual ('ritjuəl) adj feierlich. n Ritual neu.

rival ('raivəl) n Rivale, Nebenbuhler m. adj rivalisierend, wetteifernd. vt wetteifern mit, rivalisieren mit. **rivalry** n Rivalität, Wetteifer m.

river ('rivə) n Fluß, Strom m. **riverbed** n Flußbett neu. **riverside** n Flußufer neu.

rivet ('rivit) n Niet m. Niete f. vt 1 (ver)nieten. 2 (attention) fesseln.

road (roud) n 1 (Land)Straße f. 2 Weg m. **roadblock** n Straßensperre f. **roadside** n Straßenrand m.

roam (roum) vi umherstreifen. vt durchstreifen.

roar (rɔː) vi brüllen. n Gebrüll neu.

roast (roust) vt braten, rösten. n Braten m. adj gebraten, geröstet.

rob (rɔb) vt (be)rauben. **robber** n Räuber m.

robe (roub) n 1 Gewand, Kleid neu. 2 rel,law Talar m.

robin ('rɔbin) n Rotkehlchen neu.

robot ('roubɔt) n Roboter m.

robust (rou'bʌst) adj stark, kräftig, robust.

rock[1] (rɔk) n 1 Gestein neu. 2 Fels(en) m. **rock-bottom** adj allerniedrigst. **rockery** n Steingarten m.

rock[2] (rɔk) vt,vi schaukeln. **rocker** n 1 Kufe f. 2 tech Wippe f. **rocking-chair** n Schaukelstuhl m. **rocking-horse** n Schaukelpferd neu.

rocket ('rɔkit) n Rakete f. vi hochschießen.

rod (rɔd) n 1 Rute f. 2 Stange f.

rode (roud) v see **ride**.

rodent ('roudṇt) n Nagetier neu.

roe (rou) n Fischlaich, Rogen m.

rogue (roug) n Schurke, Schelm m.

role (roul) n Rolle f.

roll (roul) vi 1 rollen. 2 schwanken. 3 sich wälzen. vt 1 rollen, wälzen. 2 walzen. 3 zusammenrollen. n 1 Rolle f. 2 Verzeichnis neu. 3 Brötchen neu. 4 Rollen neu. **rollcall** n 1 Namensaufruf m. 2 mil Appell m. **roller** n Rolle, Walze f. **roller-skate** n Rollschuh m. vi Rollschuh laufen. **rolling pin** n Teigrolle f.

Roman Catholic adj (römisch-)katholisch. n Römisch-Katholische(r), Katholik m.

romance ('roumæns) n 1 lit Romanze f. 2 Liebschaft f. 3 Übertreibung f. **romantic** adj romantisch. n Romantiker m. **romanticize** vt romantisch darstellen, romantisieren.

Rome (roum) n Rom neu. **Roman** adj römisch. n Römer m.

romp (rɔmp) vi herumspielen, balgen. n Balgerei f. **rompers** n pl Spielanzug m.

roof (ruːf) n Dach neu. vt bedachen.

rook (ruk) n Saatkrähe f. vt sl betrügen.

room (ruːm) n 1 Zimmer neu. Stube f. 2 Raum, Platz m.

roost (ruːst) vi 1 auf der Stange sitzen. 2 schlafen. n 1 Hühnerstange f. 2 Ruheplatz m.

root[1] (ruːt) n 1 Wurzel f. 2 Quelle f. Kern m. vi einwurzeln. **take root** Wurzel schlagen.

root[2] (ruːt) vi wühlen. vt durchwühlen.

rope (roup) n Seil, Tau neu. vt anseilen.

rosary ('rouzəri) n rel Rosenkranz m.

rose[1] (rouz) n 1 Rose f. adj rosa. **rosette** n Rosette f. **rosy** adj rosig.

rose[2] (rouz) v see **rise**.

rosemary ('rouzməri) n Rosmarin m.

rot (rɔt) vi verfaulen. n 1 Fäulnis f. 2 inf Unsinn, Quatsch m. **rotten** adj 1 faul, verfault, zersetzt. 2 verdorben. 3 sl gemein.

rota ('routə) n Dienstturnus m. Dienstliste f. **rotary** adj (sich) drehend. **rotate** vi sich drehen. vt 1 drehen. 2 wechseln. **rotation** n 1 Umdrehung f. 2 Abwechselung f.

rouge (ruːʒ) n (rote) Schminke f. Rouge neu.

rough (rʌf) adj 1 rauh. 2 roh, grob. 3 wild. **roughly** adv ungefähr.

roulette (ruː'let) n Roulett neu.

round (raund) adj rund, kreisförmig. adv herum, rundum. n 1 Runde f. 2 Serie f. vt runden. prep um. **roundabout** adj indirekt, umständlich, weitschweifig. n 1 Kreisverkehr m. 2 Karussell neu.

rouse (rauz) vt (auf)wecken, erregen.

route (ruːt) n Route f. Weg m. vt leiten, senden.

routine (ruː'tiːn) n Routine f. adj üblich, Routine-.

rove (rouv) vi umherschweifen.

row[1] (rou) n Reihe, Zeile f.

row[2] (rou) vi,vt rudern.

row[3] (rau) n inf Krach, Streit m. vi streiten.

rowdy ('raudi) n Raufbold, Rowdy m. adj rauflustig.

royal ('rɔiəl) adj königlich. **royalty** n 1 königlicher Rang m. **2** Mitglieder der königlichen Familie pl. **3** Verfasserhonorar neu.

rub (rʌb) vt,vi reiben.

rubber ('rʌbə) n **1** Gummi neu. **2** Radiergummi neu. **rubber band** n Gummiband neu.

rubbish ('rʌbiʃ) n **1** Müll, Abfall m. **2** inf Quatsch m.

rubble ('rʌbəl) n Bauschutt m.

ruby ('ru:bi) n Rubin m.

rucksack ('rʌksæk) n Rucksack m.

rudder ('rʌdə) n (Steuer)Ruder neu.

rude (ru:d) adj **1** unhöflich. **2** roh. **3** rauh.

rudiment ('ru:dimənt) n **1** Rudiment neu. **2** pl Rudimente neu pl. Grundlagen f pl.

rueful ('ru:fəl) adj kummervoll, reumütig.

ruff (rʌf) n Halskrause f.

ruffian ('rʌfiən) n Raufbold m.

ruffle ('rʌfəl) vt **1** kräuseln. **2** sträuben. **3** verärgern. n **1** Kräuselung f. **2** Kräuseln neu.

rug (rʌg) n **1** Decke f. **2** Vorleger m. kleiner Teppich m.

rugby ('rʌgbi) n Rugby neu.

rugged ('rʌgid) adj uneben, rauh, derb.

ruin ('ru:in) n **1** Ruine f. **2** Verfall m. **3** Trümmer m pl. vt **1** verderben. **2** zugrunde richten, ruinieren.

rule (ru:l) n **1** Regel f. **2** Gewohnheit f. **3** Herrschaft f. **4** Lineal neu. vt **1** regeln, bestimmen. **2** regieren, beherrschen. **3** ziehen. **ruler** n **1** Herrscher m. **2** Lineal neu.

rum (rʌm) n Rum m.

Rumania (ru:'meiniə) n Rumänien neu. **Rumanian** adj rumänisch. n **1** Rumäne m. **2** (language) Rumänisch m.

rumble ('rʌmbəl) vi rumpeln. n Rumpeln neu.

rummage ('rʌmidʒ) vi (herum)stöbern. **rummage through** durchstöbern.

rumour ('ru:mə) n Gerücht neu. **rumour has it** es geht das Gerücht.

rump (rʌmp) n Steiß m. **rump steak** n Rumpsteak neu.

run* (rʌn) vi **1** rennen, laufen. **2** fließen. **3** lauten. **4** im Gang sein. vt **1** betreiben. **2** rennen, laufen. **3** in Gang halten. **4** befördern. **run away** davonlaufen. **run out** **1** hinauslaufen. **2** zu Ende gehen. **run over** überfahren. ∼n **1** Lauf m. Rennen neu. **2** Zustrom neu. **3** comm Zulauf m. **runner** n **1** Läufer m. **2** Bote m. **runner bean** n Stangenbohne f. **runner-up** n Zweitbeste(r) m. **running** n **1** Laufen, Rennen neu. **2** Betrieb m. **runway** n aviat Startbahn, Landebahn f.

rung[1] (rʌŋ) v see **ring**[2].

rung[2] (rʌŋ) n **1** (of a ladder) Sprosse f. **2** Stufe f.

rupture ('rʌptʃə) n Bruch, Riß m. vt sprengen, brechen, (zer)reißen. vi einen Bruch or Riß bekommen.

rural ('ruərəl) adj ländlich, Land—.

rush[1] (rʌʃ) vi (sich) stürzen, stürmen. vt **1** drängen, hetzen. **2** sich stürzen auf. n **1** Hast f. **2** Andrang m. **rush hour** Hauptverkehrszeit f.

rush[2] (rʌʃ) n bot Binse f.

Russia ('rʌʃə) n Rußland neu. **Russian** adj russisch. n **1** Russe m. **2** (language) Russisch neu.

rust (rʌst) n Rost m. vi (ver)rosten. **rusty** adj **1** verrostet. **2** außer Übung.

rustic ('rʌstik) adj **1** bäuerisch. **2** ländlich, rustikal.

rustle ('rʌsəl) vi,(vt) rascheln (mit). n Geraschel neu.

rut (rʌt) n **1** Furche f. **2** (Rad)Spur f. **be in a rut** stagnieren.

ruthless ('ru:θləs) adj **1** erbarmungslos. **2** rücksichtslos.

rye (rai) n Roggen m.

S

Sabbath ('sæbəθ) n Sabbat m.

sable ('seibəl) n Zobel m.

sabotage ('sæbətɑ:ʒ) n Sabotage f. vt sabotieren.

sabre ('seibə) n Säbel m.

saccharin ('sækərin) n Saccharin neu.

sachet ('sæʃei) n **1** Sachet neu. **2** Schampoobeutel m. **3** Duftkissen neu.

sack (sæk) n Sack m. **get the sack** sl entlassen werden. ∼vt sl entlassen.

sacrament ('sækrəmənt) n Sakrament neu.

sacred ('seikrid) adj heilig, geweiht.

sacrifice ('sækrifais) n **1** Opfer neu. **2** Verlust m. vt opfern.

sacrilege ('sækrilidʒ) n Sakrileg neu. Entweihung, Kirchenschändung f.

sad (sæd) adj **1** traurig. **2** ernst, schlimm. **3** düster. **sadden** vt betrüben, traurig machen. vi traurig werden.

saddle ('sædl) n Sattel m. vt satteln.

sadism ('seidizəm) n Sadismus m. **sadist** n Sadist m. **sadistic** adj sadistisch.

safari (sə'fɑ:ri) n Safari f.

safe (seif) adj **1** sicher. **2** heil. **3** vorsichtig. **play**

safe kein Risiko eingehen. ~*n* Geldschrank, Safe *m*. **safeguard** *n* Vorsichtsmaßnahme *f*. Schutz *m*. *vt* 1 schützen. 2 sichern. **safety** *n* Sicherheit *f*. **safety belt** *n* Sicherheitsgürtel *m*. **safety pin** *n* Sicherheitsnadel *f*.

saffron ('sæfrən) *n* Safran *m*. *adj* safrangelb.

sag (sæg) *vi* 1 sacken. 2 nachlassen.

saga ('sɑːgə) *n* Saga *f*.

sage[1] (seidʒ) *n* Weise(r) *m*. *adj* weise.

sage[2] (seidʒ) *n* Salbei *m,f*.

Sagittarius (sædʒi'tɛəriəs) *n* Schütze *m*.

sago ('seigou) *n* Sago *m*.

said (sed) *v* see **say.**

sail (seil) *n* 1 Segel *neu*. 2 Seefahrt *f*. *vi,vt* segeln. fahren. **sailor** *n* Matrose, Seemann *m*.

saint (seint) *n* Heilige(r) *m*.

sake (seik) *n* **for the sake of** um...willen. **for my sake** um meinetwillen.

salad ('sæləd) *n* Salat *m*. **salad dressing** *n* Salatsoße *f*.

salami (sə'lɑːmi) *n* Salami *f*.

salary ('sæləri) *n* Gehalt *neu*. *vt* besolden.

sale (seil) *n* 1 Verkauf *m*. 2 Ausverkauf *m*. 3 Absatz *m*. **salesman** *n* Verkäufer *m*.

saliva (sə'laivə) *n* Speichel *m*. **salivate** *vi* Speichel absondern.

sallow ('sælou) *adj* bläßlich, gelblich.

salmon ('sæmən) *n* Lachs *m*.

salon ('sælɔn) *n* Salon *m*.

saloon (sə'luːn) *n* Salon, Saal *m*. **saloon car** Limousine *f*.

salt (sɔːlt) *n* Salz *neu*. *adj* salzig, Salz—. *vt* (ein)salzen. **salt-cellar** *n* Salzfäßchen *neu*. **salty** *adj* salzig.

salute (sə'luːt) *n* 1 Gruß *m*. 2 *mil* Ehrenbezeichnung *f*. *vi* grüßen. *vt* 1 (be)grüßen. 2 *mil* salutieren vor.

salvage ('sælvidʒ) *n* Bergung *f*. *vt* bergen.

salvation (sæl'veiʃən) *n* 1 *rel* Erlösung *f*. 2 (Er)Rettung *f*.

same (seim) *adj,pron* derselbe, der gleiche. *adv* ebenso. **all the same** trotzdem.

sample ('sɑːmpəl) *n* 1 Probe *f*. 2 Auswahl *f*. 3 Muster *neu*. *vt* (aus)probieren.

sanatorium (sænə'tɔːriəm) *n, pl* **-iums** *or* **-ia** Sanatorium *neu*. Heilanstalt *f*.

sanction ('sæŋkʃən) *n* 1 Sanktion, Billigung *f*. 2 Zwangsmaßnahme *f*. *vt* billigen, gutheißen.

sanctity ('sæŋktiti) *n* Heiligkeit *f*.

sanctuary ('sæŋktʃuəri) *n* 1 Asyl *neu*. 2 *rel* Heiligtum *neu*.

sand (sænd) *n* 1 Sand *m*. 2 *pl* Sandfläche *f*. Strand *m*.

sandal ('sændl) *n* Sandale *f*.

sandwich ('sænwidʒ) *n* Sandwich, belegtes Brot, Butterbrot *neu*.

sane (sein) *adj* 1 geistig gesund. 2 vernünftig.

sang (sæŋ) *v* see **sing.**

sanitary ('sænitri) *adj* gesundheitlich, hygienisch. **sanitary towel** *n* Damenbinde *f*.

sank (sæŋk) *v* see **sink.**

sap (sæp) *n bot* Saft *m*.

sapphire ('sæfaiə) *n* Saphir *m*.

sarcasm ('sɑːkæzm) *n* Sarkasmus, bitterer Hohn *m*. **sarcastic** *adj* sarkastisch.

sardine (sɑː'diːn) *n* Sardine *f*.

Sardinia (sɑː'diniə) *n* Sardinien *neu*.

sardonic (sɑː'dɔnik) *adj* höhnisch, sardonisch.

sash[1] (sæʃ) *n* Schärpe *f*.

sash[2] (sæʃ) *n* Fensterrahmen *m*. **sash-window** *n* Schiebefenster *neu*.

sat (sæt) *v* see **sit.**

Satan ('seitn) *n* Satan *m*.

satchel ('sætʃəl) *n* Schultasche *f*.

satellite ('sætəlait) *n* Satellit *m*.

satin ('sætin) *n* Atlas, Satin *m*.

satire ('sætaiə) *n* 1 Satire *f*. 2 Spott *m*. **satirical** *adj* satirisch.

satisfy ('sætisfai) *vt* 1 zufriedenstellen, befriedigen. 2 genügen. 3 überzeugen. **satisfaction** *n* 1 Zufriedenheit *f*. 2 Genugtuung *f*.

saturate ('sætʃəreit) *vt* sättigen.

Saturday ('sætədi) *n* Sonnabend, Samstag *m*.

Saturn ('sætən) *n* Saturn *m*.

sauce (sɔːs) *n* 1 Soße *f*. 2 *inf* Frechheit *f*. **saucepan** *n* Kochtopf *m*. **saucer** *n* Untertasse *f*. **saucy** *adj* frech.

Saudi Arabia ('saudi) *n* Saudi-Arabien *neu*.

sauna ('sɔːnə) *n* Sauna *f*.

saunter ('sɔːntə) *vi* schlendern. *n* Schlendern *neu*.

sausage ('sɔsidʒ) *n* Wurst *f*.

savage ('sævidʒ) *adj* wild. *n* Wilde(r) *m*.

save[1] (seiv) *vt* 1 (er)retten. 2 bewahren. 3 (money) sparen. **savings** *n pl* Ersparnisse *f pl*.

save[2] (seiv) *prep* außer, ausgenommen.

saviour ('seiviə) *n* 1 *rel* Erlöser, Heiland *m*. 2 Retter *m*.

savoury ('seivəri) *adj* 1 schmackhaft. 2 würzig. *n* pikantes Gericht *neu*.

saw[1] (sɔː) *n* Säge *f*. *vi,vt* sägen. **sawdust** *n* Sägemehl *neu*.

saw[2] (sɔː) *v* see **see**[1].

Saxon

Saxon (ˈsæksən) *adj* **1** sächsisch. **2** angelsächsisch. *n* **1** Sachse *m.* **2** Angelsachse *m.*

saxophone (ˈsæksəfoun) *n* Saxophon *neu.*

say* (sei) *vt,vi* **1** ·sagen. **2** sprechen. **3** äußern. **4** heißen, bedeuten. *n* Wort *neu.* Rede *f.* **saying** *n* **1** Sprichwort *neu.* **2** Redensart *f.*

scab (skæb) *n* Schorf *m.* Krätze *f.*

scaffold (ˈskæfəld) *n* **1** (Bau)Gerüst *neu.* **2** Schafott *neu.* **scaffolding** *n* Gerüst *neu.*

scald (skɔːld) *vt* (ver)brühen. *n* Verbrühung *f.* **scalding** *adj* **1** brühend. **2** brühheiß.

scale[1] (skeil) *n* **1** *zool* Schuppe *f.* **2** Kesselstein *m.* *vt* abschuppen.

scale[2] (skeil) *n* **1** Waagschale *f.* **2** *pl* Waage *f.*

scale[3] (skeil) *n* **1** Maßstab *m.* **2** Skala *f.* **3** Ausmaß *neu.* **4** *mus* Tonleiter *f.* *vt* ersteigen.

scallop (ˈskɔləp) *n* Kammuschel *f.*

scalp (skælp) *n* Kopfhaut *f.*

scalpel (ˈskælpəl) *n* Skalpell *neu.*

scampi (ˈskæmpi) *n* Kaiserhummer *m.*

scan (skæn) *vt* **1** untersuchen, prüfen. **2** abtasten. **3** *lit* skandieren.

scandal (ˈskændl) *n* **1** Skandal *m.* **2** Verleumdung *f.* **scandalous** *adj* skandalös.

Scandinavia (skændiˈneiviə) *n* Skandinavien *neu.* **Scandinavian** *adj* skandinavisch. *n* Skandinavier *m.*

scapegoat (ˈskeipgout) *n* Sündenbock *m.*

scar (skaː) *n* Narbe, Schramme *f.* *vt* **1** schrammen. **2** entstellen. *vi* vernarben.

scarce (skɛəs) *adj* **1** knapp. **2** spärlich. **scarcely** *adv* kaum.

scare (skɛə) *vt* erschrecken. *n* Schreck(en) *m.*

scarf (skaːf) *n* Schal *m.* Halstuch *neu.*

scarlet (ˈskaːlit) *adj* scharlachrot. **scarlet fever** *n* Scharlachfieber *neu.*

scathing (ˈskeiðiŋ) *adj* scharf, beißend, ätzend.

scatter (ˈskætə) *vt* **1** (ver)streuen. **2** zerstreuen. *vi* sich zerstreuen.

scavenge (ˈskævindʒ) *vt* reinigen. *vi* Nährung suchen. **scavenger** *n* **1** Aasgeier *m.* **2** Straßenkehrer *m.*

scene (siːn) *n* **1** Szene *f.* **2** Schauplatz *m.* **3** Bild *neu.* **behind the scenes** hinter den Kulissen.

scenery (ˈsiːnəri) *n* **1** Bühnenbild *neu.* **2** Landschaft *f.*

scent (sent) *n* **1** Geruch, Duft *m.* **2** Parfüm *neu.* **3** Spur *f.* *vt* **1** riechen. **2** parfümieren.

sceptic (ˈskeptik) *n* Skeptiker *m.* **sceptical** *adj* skeptisch. **scepticism** *n* Skeptizismus *m.*

sceptre (ˈseptə) *n* Zepter *neu.*

schedule (ˈʃedjuːl) *n* **1** Arbeitsplan *m.* **2**

Fahrplan *m.* **3** Liste *f.* *vt* **1** aufzeichnen. **2** planen.

scheme (skiːm) *n* **1** Plan *m.* **2** Intrige *f.* **3** Schema *neu.* *vi* Ränke schmieden, intrigieren.

schizophrenia (skitsouˈfriːniə) *n* Schizophrenie *f.* **schizophrenic** *adj* schizophren. *n* Schizophrene(r) *m.*

scholar (ˈskɔlə) *n* **1** Gelehrete(r) *m.* **2** Studierende(r) *m. f.* **3** Stipendiat *m.* **scholarship** *n* **1** Stipendium *neu.* **2** Gelehrsamkeit *f.*

scholastic (skəˈlæstik) *adj* **1** akademisch. **2** Schul—, schulisch.

school[1] (skuːl) *n* Schule *f.* *vt* schulen. **schoolboy** *n* Schüler *m.* **schoolgirl** *n* Schülerin *f.* **schoolmaster** *n* Lehrer, Schulleiter *m.* **schoolmistress** *n* Lehrerin *f.*

school[2] (skuːl) *n* *zool* Schule *f.* Schwarm *m.*

schooner (ˈskuːnə) *n* **1** *naut* Schoner *m.* **2** (hohes) Bierglas *or* Weinglas *neu.*

science (ˈsaiəns) *n* **1** Wissenschaft *f.* **2** Naturwissenschaft *f.* **science fiction** *n* Zukunftsroman *m.* **scientific** *adj* wissenschaftlich. **scientist** *n* (Natur)Wissenschaftler *m.*

scissors (ˈsizəz) *n pl* Schere *f.*

scoff[1] (skɔf) *vi* spotten. *n* Spott *m.*

scoff[2] (skɔf) *vt sl* fressen.

scold (skould) *vt* ausschimpfen. *vi* schimpfen.

scone (skoun) *n* (flaches) Teegebäck *neu.*

scoop (skuːp) *n* **1** Schaufel *f.* **2** Schöpfkelle *f.* **3** Schub *m.* **4** Erstmeldung *f.* *vt* schaufeln, schöpfen.

scooter (ˈskuːtə) *n* (Motor)Roller *m.*

scope (skoup) *n* **1** Spielraum *m.* **2** Gebiet *neu.* Bereich *m.*

scorch (skɔːtʃ) *vt* **1** versengen. **2** verbrennen. *vi* verbrennen.

score (skɔː) *n* **1** *sport* (Punkt)Zahl *f.* **2** Rechnung *f.* **4** *mus* Partitur *f.* **5** Kerbe *f.* *vt* **1** gewinnen. **2** einkerben. **3** (a goal) schießen. *vi* Punkte gewinnen. **scoreboard** *n* Anschreibetafel *f.*

scorn (skɔːn) *n* Hohn *m.* Verachtung *f.* *vt* verachten. **scornful** *adj* verächtlich.

Scorpio (ˈskɔːpiou) *n* Skorpion *m.*

scorpion (ˈskɔːpiən) *n* Skorpion *m.*

Scotland (ˈskɔtlənd) *n* Schottland *neu.* **Scot** *n* Schotte *m.* **Scotch** *adj* schottisch. *n* (schottischer) Whisky *m.* **Scots** *n* schottischer Dialekt. *adj* schottisch. **Scottish** *adj* schottisch.

scoundrel (ˈskaundrəl) *n* Schurke, Schuft *m.*

scour[1] (ˈskauə) *vt* **1** scheuern. **2** wegwischen.

scour[2] (ˈskauə) *vt* durchsuchen, durchstreifen.

scout (skaut) *n* **1** Späher, Kundschafter *m.* **2** Pfadfinder *m.* *vi,vt* kundschaften, spähen.

scowl (skaul) *vi* finster blicken. *n* finsterer Blick *m*.

scramble ('skræmbəl) *vi* 1 krabbeln. 2 sich balgen. *n* 1 Krabbelei *f*. 2 Balgerei *f*.

scrap (skræp) *n* 1 Stückchen *neu*. Brocken *m*. 2 Schrott *m*. *vt* 1 wegwerfen. 2 verzichten auf. 3 verschrotten. *adj* Schrott—. **scrapbook** *n* Einklebebuch *neu*.

scrape (skreip) *vt* 1 kratzen, schaben. *vi* kratzen. *n* 1 Kratzen *neu*. 2 Klemme *f*.

scratch (skrætʃ) *vt* kratzen. *n* 1 Kratzen *neu*. 2 Schramme *f*. Riß *m*.

scrawl (skrɔːl) *vt,vi* kritzeln. *n* Gekritzel *neu*.

scream (skriːm) *vi,vt* schreien. *n* Schrei *m*.

screech (skriːtʃ) *vi,vt* kreischen, schreien. *n* Kreischen *neu*.

screen (skriːn) *n* 1 Schirm *m*. 2 (Lein)Wand *f*. *vt* 1 (ab)schirmen. 2 überprüfen. 3 (a film) vorführen.

screw (skruː) *n* Schraube *f*. *vt* schrauben. **screwdriver** *n* Schraubenzieher *m*.

scribble ('skribəl) *vt,vi* kritzeln. *n* Gekritzel *neu*.

script (skript) *n* 1 *Th* Manuskript *neu*. 2 (of a film) Drehbuch *neu*. 3 Schrift *f*.

Scripture ('skriptʃə) *n* Heilige Schrift *f*.

scroll (skroul) *n* 1 Schriftrolle *f*. 2 Schnörkel *m*.

scrounge (skraundʒ) *vt,vi* schnorren, klauen.

scrub[1] (skrʌb) *vi,vt* schrubben, scheuern. *n* Schrubben *neu*. **scrubbing brush** *n* Scheuerbürste *f*.

scrub[2] (skrʌb) *n* Gestrüpp *neu*. Busch *m*.

scruffy ('skrʌfi) *adj inf* schäbig.

scruple ('skruːpəl) *n* Skrupel *m*. Bedenken *neu*. **have scruples** sich ein Gewissen machen. **scrupulous** *adj* gewissenhaft.

scrutiny ('skruːtini) *n* 1 Untersuchung *f*. 2 prüfender Blick *m*. **scrutinize** *vt* 1 (genau) prüfen, untersuchen. 2 genau ansehen.

scuffle ('skʌfəl) *n* Balgerei, Schlägerei *f*. *vi* sich balgen, raufen.

scullery ('skʌləri) *n* Spülküche *f*.

sculpt (skʌlpt) *vt* (heraus)meißeln, schnitzen. *vi* bildhauern. **sculptor** *n* Bildhauer *m*. **sculpture** *n* Bildhauerei, Skulptur *f*.

scum (skʌm) *n* 1 Schaum *m*. 2 Abschaum *m*.

scurf (skəːf) *n* 1 Schuppen *f pl*. 2 Schorf *m*.

scythe (saið) *n* Sense *f*. *vt* (ab)mähen.

sea (siː) *n* See *f*. Meer *neu*. **by the sea** an der See.

seabed ('siːbed) *n* Meeresgrund *m*.

seafront ('siːfrʌnt) *n* Strandpromenade *f*.

seagull ('siːgʌl) *n* Möwe *f*.

seal[1] (siːl) *n* 1 Siegel *neu*. 2 Stempel *m*. 3 Dichtung *f*. *vt* 1 (ver)siegeln. 2 bestätigen. 3 abdichten.

seal[2] (siːl) *n* Seehund *m*. Robbe *f*. **sealskin** *n* Seehundfell *neu*.

sea-level *n* Meersspiegel *m*. Meereshöhe *f*.

sea-lion *n* Seelöwe *m*.

seam (siːm) *n* 1 Saum *m*. Naht *f*. 2 Spalt *m*. Schicht *f*. *vt* säumen.

seaman ('siːmən) *n* Seemann, Matrose *m*.

search (səːtʃ) *vt* durchsuchen. 2 erforschen. *vi* suchen, forschen. *n* Suche *f*. **searchlight** *n* Scheinwerfer *m*.

seashore ('siːʃɔː) *n* Seeküste *f*.

seasick ('siːsik) *adj* seekrank.

seaside ('siːsaid) *n* Seeküste *f*. **go to the seaside** an die See fahren. ~*adj* See—. **seaside resort** *n* Seebad *neu*.

season ('siːzən) *n* 1 Jahreszeit *f*. 2 Saison *f*. **season ticket** *n* Dauerkarte *f*. *vt* 1 *cul* würzen. 2 ausreifen lassen. **seasoning** *n* Würze *f*.

seat (siːt) *n* 1 Sitz, Platz *m*. 2 Bank *f*. 3 Wohnsitz *m*. 3 Gesäß *nou*. *vt* 1 setzen. 2 Raum haben für. **seat-belt** *n* Sitzgurt *m*.

seaweed ('siːwiːd) *n* Alge *f*.

secluded (si'kluːdid) *adj* abgelegen, abgeschlossen.

second[1] ('sekənd) *adj* 1 zweite. 2 nächst. **second best** *adj* zweitbest. **second-class** *adj,adv* zweiter Klasse. *adj* zweitrangig. **second-hand** *adj* aus zweiter Hand, gebraucht. **secondly** *adv* zweitens. **second-rate** *adj* zweitrangig, minderwertig. **secondary** *adj* 1 untergeordnet. 2 sekundär. 3 Neben—. **secondary school** *n* Oberschule *f*.

second[2] ('sekənd) *n* Sekunde *f*.

secret ('siːkrət) *n* Geheimnis *neu*. *adj* geheim, heimlich. **secrecy** *n* Geheimhaltung, Verschwiegenheit *f*. **secretive** *adj* geheimtuerisch.

secretary ('sekrətri) *n* 1 Sekretär *m*. Sekretärin *f*. 2 Schriftführer *m*. 3 Schreibtisch *m*.

secrete (si'kriːt) *vt* 1 verbergen, verheimlichen. 2 *anat* absondern.

sect (sekt) *n* Sekte *f*. **sectarian** *adj* sektiererisch.

section ('sekʃən) *n* 1 Abschnitt, Teil *m*. 2 Abteilung *f*. 3 Schnitt *m*. 4 Sektion *f*.

sector ('sektə) *n* 1 Abschnitt *m*. 2 *math* Sektor *m*.

secular ('sekjulə) *adj* weltlich, säkular.

secure (si'kjuə) *adj* 1 sicher. 2 fest. *vt* 1 sichern.

2 sicherstellen. **3** festbinden, festmachen. **security** n Sicherheit f.

sedate (si'deit) adj gesetzt, ernst, ruhig. **sedation** n Beruhigung f. **sedative** adj beruhigend, stillend. n Beruhigungsmittel neu.

sediment ('sediment) n **1** Satz m. **2** Sediment neu. **3** Ablagerung f.

seduce (si'dju:s) vt verführen. **seduction** n Verführung f.

see*1 (si:) vt,vi **1** sehen. **2** verstehen. **3** besichtigen, ansehen. **4** besuchen. **see off** fortbegleiten. **see out** hinausbegleiten. **see through 1** durchschauen. **2** durchführen.

see2 (si:) n Bischofssitz m.

seed (si:d) n **1** Same(n) m. Saat f. **2** Keim m. **seedling** n Sämling neu. **seedy** adj schäbig, mies.

seek* (si:k) vt,vi suchen.

seem (si:m) vi **1** (er)scheinen. **2** aussehen. **seeming** adj anscheinend.

seep (si:p) vi sickern.

seesaw ('si:so:) n Wippe f. vi wippen.

seethe (si:ð) vi **1** sieden, kochen. **2** brodeln.

segment ('segment) n Abschnitt m.

segregate ('segrigeit) vt absondern, trennen. vi sich absondern.

seize (si:z) vt **1** ergreifen, packen. **2** an sich reißen. **3** begreifen.

seldom ('seldəm) adv selten.

select (si'lekt) vt aussuchen, auswählen. adj ausgewählt. **selection** n Auswahl f. **selective** adj auswählend, selektiv.

self (self) n, pl **selves** Selbst, Ich neu. pron selbst.

self-assured adj selbstsicher.

self-aware adj selbstbewußt.

self-centred adj egozentrisch, ichbezogen.

self-confident adj selbstsicher.

self-conscious adj **1** befangen. **2** selbstbewußt.

self-contained adj **1** selbständig. **2** zurückhaltend. **3** (in sich) geschlossen.

self-defence n Notwehr, Selbstverteidigung f.

self-discipline n Selbstdisziplin f.

self-employed adj selbständig.

self-expression n Ausdruck der eigenen Persönlichkeit m.

self-indulgent adj schwächlich, genußsüchtig.

self-interest n Eigennutz m.

selfish ('selfiʃ) adj selbstsüchtig, eigennützig. **selfishness** n Selbstsucht f.

self-pity n Selbstbemitleidung f.

self-portrait n Selbstporträt neu.

self-respect n Selbstachtung f.

self-righteous adj selbstgerecht, pharisäisch.

self-sacrifice n Selbstaufopferung f.

selfsame ('selfseim) adj eben derselbe.

self-satisfied adj selbstzufrieden.

self-service n Selbstbedienung f.

self-sufficient adj unabhängig, selbständig.

self-will n Eigensinn m.

sell* (sel) vt verkaufen. vi handeln. **sell out** or **up** ausverkaufen.

Sellotape ('seləteip) n Tdmk Klebestreifen m.

semantic (si'mæntik) adj semantisch. **semantics** n Semantik f.

semaphore ('seməfɔ:) n Semaphor m.

semibreve ('semibri:v) n mus ganze Note f.

semicircle ('semisə:kəl) n Halbkreis m.

semicolon (semi'koulən) n Strichpunkt m.

semidetached (semidi'tætʃt) adj halb freistehend.

semifinal (semi'fainl) n Vorschlußrunde f. Semifinale neu.

seminar ('seminɑ:) n Seminar neu.

semiprecious (semi'preʃəs) adj Halbedel—.

semiquaver (semi'kweivə) n mus Sechzehntelnote f.

semivowel ('semivauəl) n Halbvokal m.

semolina (semə'li:nə) n Grieß m.

senate ('senət) n Senat m. **Senator** n Senator m.

send* (send) vt schicken, (ab)senden. **send for** kommen lassen. **send word** mitteilen. **sender** n (Ab)Sender m.

senile ('si:nail) adj altersschwach.

senior ('si:niə) adj **1** älter. **2** Senior—. n **1** Ältere(r) m. **2** Senior m.

sensation (sen'seiʃən) n **1** Empfindung f. **2** Sensation f. **sensational** adj sensationell.

sense (sens) n **1** Sinn m. **2** Empfindung f. **3** Vernunft f. **4** Bedeutung f. **talk sense** vernünftig reden. ~vt empfinden, spüren, fühlen. **senseless** adj **1** sinnlos. **2** bewußtlos.

sensible ('sensəbəl) adj **1** verständig, vernünftig. **2** fühlbar. **3** empfänglich. **sensibility** n **1** Empfindungsvermögen neu. **2** Empfindlichkeit f.

sensitive ('sensitiv) adj empfindlich, sensibel, feinfühlig. **sensitivity** n **1** Empfindlichkeit f. **2** Empfindungsvermögen neu. **3** Feingefühl neu.

sensual ('senʃuəl) adj sinnlich. **sensuality** n Sinnlichkeit f.

sensuous ('senʃuəs) adj sinnenfreudig, sinnlich.

sentence ('sentəns) n **1** Satz m. **2** Urteil neu. vt verurteilen.

sentiment ('sentimənt) n **1** Gefühl neu. Empfindung f. **2** pl Gesinnung f. **sentimental** adj sentimental. **sentimentality** n Sentimentalität f.

sentry ('sentri) n Wache f.

separate (v 'separeit; adj 'seprit) (vi),vt (sich) trennen, (sich) scheiden. adj getrennt, gesondert. **separation** n Trennung, Scheidung f.

September (sep'tembə) n September m.

septic ('septik) adj septisch, eitrig.

sequel ('si:kwəl) n **1** Folge f. **2** Fortsetzung f.

sequence ('si:kwəns) n **1** (Reihen)Folge f. **2** Szene f.

sequin ('si:kwin) n Zechine f.

serenade (serə'neid) n Ständchen neu. Serenade f. vt ein Ständchen bringen.

serene (si'ri:n) adj **1** heiter. **2** ruhig. **serenity** n **1** Heiterkeit f. **2** Ruhe f.

serf (sə:f) n **1** Leibeigene(r) m. **2** Sklave m.

sergeant ('sɑ:dʒənt) n **1** mil Feldwebel m. **2** (Polizei)Sergeant m. **sergeant-major** n mil Hauptfeldwebel m.

serial ('siəriəl) adj **1** Fortsetzungs—. **2** serienmäßig. n Fortsetzungsroman m. **serialize** vt in Fortsetzungen veröffentlichen.

series ('siəri:z) n **1** Reihe f. **2** Serie f. **3** Folge f.

serious ('siəriəs) adj ernst, ernsthaft. **seriousness** n Ernst m. Ernsthaftigkeit f.

sermon ('sə:mən) n Predigt f.

serpent ('sə:pənt) n Schlange f.

servant ('sə:vənt) n Diener m.

serve (sə:v) vt,vi **1** (be)dienen. **2** erfüllen. **3** nützen. **4** sport aufschlagen. **it serves him right** das geschieht ihm recht. n sport Aufschlag m.

service ('sə:vis) n **1** Dienst m. **2** Bedienung f. **3** sport Aufschlag m. **4** rel Gottesdienst m. **5** Kundendienst m. **6** mot Service neu. **serviceable** adj **1** dienlich. **2** betriebsfähig. **service station** n Tankstelle f.

serviette (sə:vi'et) n Serviette f.

servile ('sə:vail) adj **1** unterwürfig, servil. **2** sklavisch.

session ('seʃən) n Sitzung f. **be in session** tagen.

set* (set) vt **1** setzen. **2** stellen. **3** legen. **4** (ein)richten. vi **1** (of the sun) untergehen. **2** cul gerinnen. **set an example** ein Beispiel geben. **set off** sich auf den Weg machen. ~adj **1** fest. **2** bestimmt. **3** vorgeschrieben. n **1** Satz m. Sammlung f. **2** Serie f. **setback** n Rückschlag m. **setting** n **1** Setzen neu. **2** (of a gem) Fassung f. **3** Bühnenausstattung f.

settee (se'ti:) n Sofa neu.

settle ('setl) vt **1** (fest)setzen. **2** erledigen. **3** entscheiden. **4** beruhigen. vi **1** sich ansiedeln. **2** (of the weather) beständig werden. **settle down** sich niederlassen. **settle with** sich begnügen mit. **settlement** n **1** Regelung f. **2** (Be)Siedlung f. **settler** n Siedler m.

seven ('sevən) adj sieben. n Sieben f. **seventh** adj siebente, siebte.

seventeen (sevən'ti:n) adj siebzehn. n Siebzehn f. **seventeenth** adj siebzehnte.

seventy ('sevənti) adj siebzig. n Siebzig f. **seventieth** adj siebzigste.

several ('sevrəl) adj **1** mehrere. **2** einige. **3** besonder, eigen. **several times** mehrmals.

severe (si'viə) adj **1** streng, hart. **2** schwer. **3** heftig. **severity** n **1** Strenge, Härte f. **2** Schwere f.

sew* (sou) vt,vi nähen. **sew up** zunähen. **sewing** n Nähen neu. **sewing machine** n Nähmaschine f.

sewage ('su:idʒ) n Abwasser neu.

sewer ('su:ə) n Abwasserkanal m. Kloake f.

sex (seks) n Geschlecht neu. adj Geschlechts—. **sexual** adj geschlechtlich, geschlechts, sexuell, Sexual—. **sexual intercourse** n Geschlechtsverkehr neu. **sexy** adj sexy.

sextet (seks'tet) n Sextett neu.

shabby ('ʃæbi) adj schäbig.

shack (ʃæk) n Hütte f.

shade (ʃeid) n **1** Schatten m. **2** Spur f. **3** (of a lamp, etc.) Schirm m. vt **1** beschatten. **2** abschirmen. **3** schattieren. **shady** adj **1** schattig. **2** anrüchig, fragwürdig.

shadow ('ʃædou) n **1** Schatten m. **2** Phantom neu. **3** Spur m. vt **1** beschatten. **2** verfolgen. **shadow cabinet** n Schattenkabinett neu.

shaft (ʃɑ:ft) n **1** Schaft m. **2** tech Welle f. **3** (of light) Strahl m.

shaggy ('ʃægi) adj zottig.

shake* (ʃeik) vt **1** schütteln. **2** erschüttern. vi zittern, wackeln. **shake hands with someone** jemandem die Hand geben. ~n **1** Schütteln neu. **2** Erschütterung f. **3** Beben neu. **shaky** adj **1** wacklig. **2** zitterig.

shall* (ʃəl; stressed ʃæl) v mod aux **1** werden. **2** wollen. **3** sollen.

shallot (ʃə'lɔt) n Schalotte f.

shallow ('ʃælou) adj seicht. n Untiefe f.

sham (ʃæm) adj **1** falsch. **2** Schein—. vt vortäuschen, vorgeben. n Täuschung f.

shame (ʃeim) n **1** Scham f. **2** Schamgefühl neu. **3** Schande f. **what a shame!** wie schade! ~vt beschämen. **shamefaced** adj schamhaft, ver-

shampoo

schämt. **shameful** adj schändlich, schmäch-
lich. **shameless** adj schamlos.

shampoo (ʃæmˈpuː) n Shampoo, Haarwasch-
mittel neu. vt schampunieren.

shamrock (ˈʃæmrɔk) n 1 Feldklee m. 2 (Irish
emblem) Kleeblatt neu.

shanty[1] (ˈʃænti) n Matrosenlied neu.

shanty[2] (ˈʃænti) n Bude f. **shanty town** n
Elendsviertel neu. schäbige Vorstadt f.

shape (ʃeip) n Gestalt, Form f. **in good shape**
in gutem Zustand. ~vt gestalten, formen,
bilden. vi sich entwickeln. **shapely** adj wohl-
gestaltet.

share (ʃɛə) n 1 Anteil m. 2 Beitrag m. 3 comm
Aktie f. **have a share in** teilhaben an.
shareholder n Aktionär m. vt teilen. **share
out** verteilen.

shark (ʃɑːk) n 1 Hai(fisch) m. 2 Gauner m.

sharp (ʃɑːp) adj 1 scharf. 2 spitz. 3 schrill. n
mus Kreuz neu. **sharp-sighted** adj scharf-
sichtig. **sharpen** vt 1 (ver)schärfen. 2 (a
pencil) spitzen. **sharpener** n 1 Schärfer m. 2
Spitzer m. **sharpness** n Schärfe f.

shatter (ˈʃætə) vt zerschmettern, zerbrechen.
shattered adj 1 erschüttert. 2 erschöpft.

shave (ʃeiv) vt 1 rasieren. 2 (wood) (ab)-
schälen. vi sich rasieren. n Rasieren neu.
have a close shave knapp davonkommen.

shawl (ʃɔːl) n Schal m.

she (ʃiː) pron 3rd pers s sie.

sheaf (ʃiːf) n 1 Garbe f. 2 Bündel neu.

shear* (ʃiə) vt scheren. **shears** n pl (große)
Schere f.

sheath (ʃiːθ) n Scheide f. **sheathe** vt 1 in die
Scheide stecken. 2 umhüllen.

shed[1] (ʃed) n Hütte f. Schuppen m.

shed*² (ʃed) vt 1 vergießen. 2 verbreiten. 3
abwerfen.

sheen (ʃiːn) n Glanz m.

sheep (ʃiːp) n, pl **sheep** Schaf m. **sheepdog** n
Schäferhund m. **sheepskin** n 1 Schaffell neu.
2 Schafleder neu. **sheepish** adj blöd.

sheer[1] (ʃiə) adj 1 steil. 2 rein, bloß.

sheer[2] (ʃiə) vi naut abscheren.

sheet (ʃiːt) n 1 Bettuch neu. 2 Platte f. 3 Blatt
neu. 4 (of water) Fläche f.

shelf (ʃelf) n, pl **shelves** 1 Brett neu. 2 Regal
neu. 3 geog Riff m.

shell (ʃel) n 1 Muschel f. 2 Schale f. 3 (of a
building) Gerippe neu. 4 Granate f. vt 1
schälen. 2 beschießen, bombardieren. **shell-
fish** n Schalentier neu.

shelter (ˈʃeltə) n 1 Obdach neu. Schutz m. 2

Schirm m. vt 1 (be)schützen. 2 Zuflucht
gewähren. vi Schutz suchen.

shelve (ʃelv) vt 1 auf ein Brett stellen. 2
beiseite legen. 3 aufschieben.

shepherd (ˈʃepəd) n Hirt, Schäfer m. vt 1
hüten. 2 geleiten, (an)führen.

sheriff (ˈʃerif) n Sheriff m.

sherry (ˈʃeri) n Sherry m.

shield (ʃiːld) n 1 Schild neu. 2 Schutz, Schirm
m. vt (be)schirmen.

shift (ʃift) vt 1 (ver-, weg-)schieben. 2 umlegen.
3 wechseln. 4 verändern. vi sich bewegen. n 1
Wechsel m. 2 Arbeitsschicht f. **shifty** adj
schlau, raffiniert. **shiftwork** n Schichtarbeit f.

shilling (ˈʃiliŋ) n Schilling m.

shimmer (ˈʃimə) vi schimmern. n Schimmer m.

shin (ʃin) n Schienbein m.

shine* (ʃain) vi 1 scheinen, leuchten. 2 glänzen.
vt polieren. n 1 Schein m. 2 Glanz m.

ship (ʃip) n Schiff neu. vt 1 an Bord nehmen. 2
verschiffen. **shipment** n 1 Verschiffung f. 2
Ladung f. **shipshape** adj ordentlich. **shipwreck** n Schiffbruch m. vi scheitern, Schiffbruch leiden. **shipyard** n Schiffswerft f.

shirk (ʃəːk) vt sich drücken, vermeiden. **shirker**
n Drückeberger m.

shirt (ʃəːt) n Hemd neu.

shit (ʃit) n tab Kot m. Exkremente pl.

shiver (ˈʃivə) n Schauer m. vi 1 schauern. 2
frösteln.

shock[1] (ʃɔk) n 1 (An)Stoß m. 2 Erschütterung
f. vt 1 (an)stoßen. 2 erschüttern, schockieren.
shock absorber n Stoßdämpfer m.

shock[2] (ʃɔk) n (Haar)Schopf m.

shoddy (ˈʃɔdi) adj minderwertig, schlecht.

shoe* (ʃuː) n 1 Schuh m. 2 (of a horse)
Hufeisen neu. vt (a horse) beschlagen.
shoelace n Schnürsenkel m.

shone (ʃɔn) v see **shine.**

shook (ʃuk) v see **shake.**

shoot* (ʃuːt) n 1 bot Sproß m. 2 Jagd-
gesellschaft f. vt 1 schießen. 2 erschießen. 3
(a film) drehen. vi schießen.

shop (ʃɔp) n 1 Laden m. Geschäft neu. 2 Fabrik,
Werkstatt f. vi einkaufen gehen. **shop assistant** n Verkäufer m. **shop floor** 1 Werkstatt f.
2 Arbeiter m pl. **shopkeeper** n Ladeninhaber
m. **shoplifter** n Ladendieb m. **shop steward**
n Betriebsrat m. **shopwindow** n Schau-
fenster neu. **shopping** n 1 Einkaufen neu. 2
Einkäufe m pl. adj Einkaufs—.

shore[1] (ʃɔː) n 1 Strand m. 2 Küste f.

shore[2] (ʃɔː) n Stütze f. v **shore up** stützen.

shorn (ʃɔ:n) v see **shear.**

short (ʃɔ:t) adj 1 kurz. 2 klein. 3 knapp. **short cut** n Abkürzung f. **shorts** n pl kurze Hose f. **shorten** vt (ab-, ver-)kürzen. vi kürzer werden.

shortage (ˈʃɔ:tidʒ) n Mangel m. Knappheit f.

shortbread (ˈʃɔ:tbred) n Mürbekuchen m.

shortcoming (ˈʃɔ:tkʌmiŋ) n Unzulänglichkeit f.

shorthand (ˈʃɔ:thænd) n Stenographie f. **shorthand typist** n Stenotypistin f.

shortlived (ˈʃɔ:tlivd) adj kurzlebig.

short-sighted adj kurzsichtig.

short-tempered adj reizbar, leicht aufgebracht.

short-term adj kurzfristig.

short-wave adj Kurzwellen—.

shot[1] (ʃɔt) n 1 Schuß m. 2 Kugel f. 3 Schütze m. 4 sport Stoß m. 5 phot Aufnahme f. 6 Schrotkugel f. **have a shot at** inf versuchen. **like a shot** wie der Blitz. **shotgun** n Schrotflinte f.

shot[2] (ʃɔt) v see **shoot.**

should (ʃəd; stressed ʃud) v see **shall.**

shoulder (ˈʃouldə) n Schulter f. vt auf sich nehmen. **shoulder-blade** n Schulterblatt neu.

shout (ʃaut) vi 1 (laut) schreien. 2 jauchzen n (lauter) Schrei m.

shove (ʃʌv) n Schub m. vt schieben.

shovel (ˈʃʌvəl) n Schaufel f. vt schaufeln.

show[*] (ʃou) vt 1 zeigen. 2 ausstellen. 3 erweisen. vi erscheinen. **show off** angeben, sich aufspielen. ~n 1 Schau f. 2 Ausstellung f. 3 Anschein m. 4 Th Aufführung f. **show business** n Unterhaltungsindustrie f. **showcase** n Schaukasten m. **show-jumping** n Schauspringen neu. **showroom** n Ausstellungsraum m.

shower (ˈʃauə) n 1 (Regen)Schauer m. 2 Dusche f. 3 Fülle f. vt 1 herabschütten. 2 übergießen. vi sich duschen. **showerproof** adj wasserdicht.

shrank (ʃræŋk) v see **shrink.**

shred (ʃred) n 1 Schnitzel m. 2 Fetzen m. vt 1 (zer)schnitzeln. 2 zerfetzen. 3 reißen.

shrew (ʃru:) n 1 zool Spitzmaus f. 2 inf Kratzbürste f.

shrewd (ʃru:d) adj scharfsinnig.

shriek (ʃri:k) vi schreien, kreischen. n (greller) Schrei m.

shrill (ʃril) adj 1 schrill, gellend. 2 grell. vi schrillen, gellen.

shrimp (ʃrimp) n 1 Garnele f. 2 Knirps m.

shrine (ʃrain) n 1 Reliquienschrein m. 2 Altar m.

shrink[*] (ʃriŋk) vi 1 (ein-, zusammen-)schrumpfen. 2 sich zurückziehen. vt einschrumpfen lassen.

shrivel (ˈʃrivəl) vi,(vt) schrumpfen (lassen).

shroud (ʃraud) n 1 Leichentuch neu. 2 Umhüllung f. vt 1 in ein Leichentuch einhüllen. 2 (ein)hüllen.

Shrove Tuesday (ʃrouv) n Fastnachtsdienstag m.

shrub (ʃrʌb) n Strauch, Busch m. **shrubbery** n Strauchpflanzung f. Strauchwerk neu.

shrug (ʃrʌg) (vi),vt (die Achseln) zucken. **shrug off** abtun. n (Achsel)Zucken neu.

shrunk (ʃrʌŋk) v see **shrink.** adj 1 eingeschrumpft. 2 eingefallen.

shudder (ˈʃʌdə) vi 1 schaudern. 2 erbeben. n 1 Schauder m. 2 Erbeben neu.

shuffle (ˈʃʌfəl) vt 1 game mischen. 2 hin und herschieben. vi schlurfen. n 1 Mischen neu. 2 Schlurfen neu. 3 Schiebung f.

shun (ʃʌn) vt (ver)meiden.

shunt (ʃʌnt) vt rangieren. n Rangieren neu.

shut[*] (ʃʌt) vt (ver)schließen, zumachen. vi (sich) schließen, zugehen. **shut out** ausschließen. **shut up!** int halt den Mund! ~adj zu, geschlossen.

shutter (ˈʃʌtə) n 1 Rolladen m. 2 phot Verschluß m.

shuttlecock (ˈʃʌtəlkɔk) n Federball m.

shy (ʃai) adj 1 scheu. 2 schüchtern. vi scheuen.

Sicily (ˈsisəli) n Sizilien neu. **Sicilian** adj sizilianisch n Sizilianer m.

sick (sik) adj 1 krank. 2 übel. 3 überdrüssig. 4 inf (of humour) schwarz. **be sick** sich erbrechen. **be sick of** satt haben. **sicken** vi krank werden. vt anekeln. **sickening** adj ekelhaft. **sickness** n 1 Krankheit f. 2 Übelkeit f.

sickle (ˈsikəl) n Sichel f.

side (said) n 1 Seite f. 2 Flanke f. 3 Partei f. adj Seiten—, Neben—. v **side with** Partei ergreifen für. **sideboard** n Büffett neu. Anrichte f. **side effect** n Nebenwirkung f. **sidelight** n Seitenlampe f. **sideline** n Nebenbeschäftigung, Seitenlinie f. **sideshow** n Nebenvorstellung f. **sidestep** vi beiseite treten. **sidetrack** vt inf 1 ablenken. 2 abschieben. **sideways** adv seitwärts. **siding** n Nebengleis neu.

sidle (ˈsaidl) vi **sidle up to** sich heranschleichen an.

siege (si:dʒ) n Belagerung f. **lay siege to** belagern.

273

sieve (siv) n Sieb neu. vt sieben.

sift (sift) vt 1 sieben. 2 prüfen.

sigh (sai) vi seufzen. n Seufzer m.

sight (sait) n 1 Sehkraft f. 2 Anblick m. 3 Sicht f. 4 pl Sehenswürdigkeiten f pl. **catch sight of** erblicken. **know by sight** vom Sehen kennen. ~vt sichten. **sightread** vt vom Blatt singen or spielen. **sightseeing** n Besichtigung von Sehenswürdigkeiten f.

sign (sain) n 1 Zeichen neu. 2 Schild neu. 3 Wink m. vi winken. vt unterschreiben. **signpost** n Wegweiser m.

signal ('sign̩l) n 1 Signal neu. 2 Zeichen neu. vi,vt signalisieren.

signature ('signɑtʃɑ) n Unterschrift f.

signify ('signifai) vt 1 bedeuten. 2 bezeichnen. **significant** adj 1 bedeutsam. 2 bezeichnend. **significance** n 1 Bedeutsamkeit f. 2 Bedeutung f.

silence ('sailɑns) n 1 Schweigen neu. 2 Ruhe f. vt zum Schweigen bringen. **silencer** n 1 Schalldämpfer m. 2 mot Auspufftopf m.

silent ('sailɑnt) adj 1 still. 2 ruhig. 3 schweigsam. 4 stumm.

Silesia (sai'liːziɑ) n Schlesien neu.

silhouette (silu:'et) n 1 Silhouette f. **be silhouetted against** sich abheben gegen.

silk (silk) n 1 Seide f. adj Seiden—. **silkworm** n Seidenraupe f.

sill (sil) n 1 Fensterbrett neu. 2 Schwelle f.

silly ('sili) adj albern, dumm.

silt (silt) n Schlamm m.

silver ('silvɑ) n Silber neu. adj silbern, Silber—. vt versilbern. vi silberweiß werden.

similar ('similɑ) adj ähnlich. **similarity** n Ähnlichkeit f.

simile ('simili) n Gleichnis, Simile neu.

simmer ('simɑ) vi,(vt) sieden (lassen).

simple ('simpɑl) adj 1 einfach. 2 einfältig. **simply** adv einfach, nur. **simplify** vt vereinfachen.

simultaneous (simɑl'teiniɑs) adj gleichzeitig.

sin (sin) n Sünde f. vi sündigen.

since (sins) prep seit. adv seitdem, seither. conj 1 seitdem. 2 da, weil.

sincere (sin'siɑ) adj aufrichtig, ehrlich. **yours sincerely** Ihr ergebener. **sincerity** n Aufrichtigkeit f.

sinew ('sinjuː) n Sehne f.

sing* (siŋ) vt 1 singen. 2 summen. **singer** n Sänger m. Sängerin f.

singe (sindʒ) vt 1 (ver)sengen.

single ('siŋgɑl) adj 1 einzig. 2 einzeln. 3 ledig. 4 einfach. v **single out** auswählen. **single file** n Gänsemarsch m. **single-handed** adj,adv allein, eigenhändig. **single-minded** adj 1 zielbewußt. 2 aufrichtig.

singular ('siŋgjulɑ) adj 1 einzigartig. 2 sonderbar. n gram Singular m. Einzahl f.

sinister ('sinistɑ) adj unheilvoll, finster.

sink* (siŋk) vi 1 sinken. 2 sich senken. 3 eindringen. vt versenken. n Spülbecken neu.

sinner ('sinɑ) n Sünder m.

sinus ('sainɑs) n (Neben)Höhle f. Sinus m.

sip (sip) n Schlückchen neu. vt nippen.

siphon ('saifɑn) n 1 Siphon m. 2 Siphonflasche f. vt absaugen.

sir (sɑː) n 1 Herr m. 2 cap Sir m.

siren ('sairɑn) n Sirene f.

sirloin ('sɑːlɔin) n cul Lendenstück neu.

sister ('sistɑ) n 1 Schwester f. 2 med Oberschwester f. **sisterhood** n rel Schwesternschaft f. **sister-in-law** n Schwägerin f.

sit* (sit) vi 1 sitzen. 2 tagen. **sit down** sich (hin)setzen. **sit-in** n Sitzstreik m. **sitting** n Sitzung f. **sitting room** n Wohnzimmer neu.

site (sait) n 1 Lage f. 2 Bauplatz m. 3 Gelände neu.

situation (sitju'eiʃɑn) n 1 Lage f. 2 Stellung f. **be situated** liegen, sich befinden.

six (siks) adj sechs. n Sechs f. **sixth** adj sechste.

sixteen (siks'tiːn) adj sechzehn. n Sechzehn f. **sixteenth** adj sechzehnte.

sixty ('siksti) adj sechzig. n Sechzig f. **sixtieth** adj sechzigste.

size (saiz) n 1 Größe f. 2 Maß neu. v **size up** inf einschätzen.

sizzle ('sizɑl) vi zischen. n Zischen neu.

skate[1] (skeit) n Schlittschuh m. vi Schlittschuh laufen.

skate[2] (skeit) n Rochen m.

skeleton ('skelɑtn) n 1 Skelett neu. 2 Gerippe neu.

sketch (sketʃ) n 1 Skizze f. 2 Entwurf m. vt 1 skizzieren. 2 entwerfen.

skewer ('skjuɑ) n Fleischspieß m. vt spießen.

ski (skiː) n 1 Schi or Ski m. vi Schi or Ski laufen. **ski-lift** n Schilift m.

skid (skid) n 1 Rutschen neu. 2 mot Schleudern neu. vi 1 ausrutschen. 2 schleudern.

skill (skil) n Geschicklichkeit f. **skilful** adj geschickt. **skilled** adj gelernt, Fach—.

skim (skim) vt entrahmen. **skim over** dahingleiten über. **skim through** durchblättern.

skimp (skimp) vi knapp halten. **skimpy** adj knapp.

skin (skin) n 1 Haut f. 2 Fell m. 3 Schale f. vt 1 enthäuten. 2 schälen. **skin-diving** n Sporttauchen neu. **skin-tight** adj hauteng. **skinny** adj mager.

skip (skip) vi 1 hüpfen. 2 seilhüpfen. n Sprung m. **skipping-rope** n Springseil neu.

skipper ('skipə) n Schiffsherr, Kapitän m.

skirmish ('skə:miʃ) n Scharmützel neu. vi plänkeln.

skirt (skə:t) n Rock m. vt entlangfahren. **skirting board** n Scheuerleiste f.

skittle ('skitl) n Kegel m.

skull (skʌl) n Schädel m. **skull and crossbones** n Totenkopf m.

skunk (skʌŋk) n Stinktier neu. Skunk m.

sky (skai) n Himmel m. **sky-high** adj himmelhoch. **skylark** n Feldlerche f. **skyline** n Horizont m. **skyscraper** n Wolkenkratzer m.

slab (slæb) n 1 Platte, Tafel f. 2 Holzschwarte f.

slack (slæk) adj 1 schlaff. 2 lose. 3 nachlässig. **slacken** vi 1 schlaff werden. 2 nachlassen. vt 1 schlaff machen. 2 nachlassen.

slacks (slæks) n pl Damenhose f.

slalom ('slɑ:ləm) n Slalom m.

slam (slæm) vt 1 zuschlagen. 2 knallen. vi zuschlagen. n 1 Zuschlagen neu. 2 Knall m.

slander ('slændə) n Verleumdung f. vt verleumden.

slang (slæŋ) n Slang, Jargon m.

slant (slɑ:nt) n Schräge, Neigung f. vi schräg liegen. **slanting** adj schräg, schief.

slap (slæp) n Klaps, Schlag m. vt klapsen, schlagen. **slapdash** adj 1 hastig, übereilt. 2 unbekümmert. **slapstick** n Schwank m.

slash (slæʃ) vt 1 (auf)schlitzen. 2 inf drastisch kürzen. n Schnitt m.

slat (slæt) n Lamelle f. Streifen m.

slate (sleit) n 1 Schiefer m. 2 Schiefertafel f.

slaughter ('slɔ:tə) n 1 Schlachten neu. 2 Blutbad neu. vt 1 schlachten. 2 niedermetzeln. **slaughterhouse** n Schlachthaus m.

slave (sleiv) n Sklave m. vi inf schuften. **slavery** n Sklaverei f.

sledge (sledʒ) n Schlitten m. vi Schlitten fahren.

sledgehammer ('sledʒhæmə) n Schmiedehammer m.

sleek (sli:k) adj geschmeidig, glatt.

sleep (sli:p) vi schlafen. n Schlaf m. **go to sleep** einschlafen. **sleeper** n 1 Schläfer m. 2 (railway) Schwelle f. **sleeping-bag** n Schlaf-

sack m. **sleeping-car** n Schlafwagen m. **sleeping-pill** n Schlafmittel neu. **sleepwalk** vi nachtwandeln. **sleepy** adj schläfrig.

sleet (sli:t) n Graupelregen m. vi graupeln.

sleeve (sli:v) n Ärmel m. **have something up one's sleeve** etwas im Schilde führen.

sleigh (slei) n Schlitten m.

slender ('slendə) adj 1 schlank. 2 gering.

slept (slept) v see **sleep.**

slice (slais) n 1 Scheibe f. Schnitte f. 2 Kelle f. vt in Scheiben schneiden.

slick (slik) adj 1 glatt. 2 raffiniert.

slide (slaid) vi,(vt) gleiten (lassen). n 1 Gleiten neu. 2 phot Dia(positiv) neu. 3 Schlittenbahn f. **slide-rule** n Rechenschieber m.

slight (slait) adj 1 schmächtig. 2 gering. n Geringschätzung f. vt geringschätzig behandeln. **slightly** adv etwas.

slim (slim) adj 1 schlank. 2 dürftig. vi Schlankheitskur machen, abnehmen.

slime (slaim) n Schlamm m. **slimy** adj schlammig.

sling (sliŋ) n 1 Schleuder f. 2 med Schlinge f. vt 1 schleudern. 2 umhängen.

slink (sliŋk) vi schleichen. **slink off** sich wegschleichen.

slip[1] (slip) vi rutschen, schlüpfen. vt schlüpfen lassen. **slip on/off** überstreifen/abstreifen. 1 (Aus)Rutschen neu. 2 Fehltritt m. 3 Fehler m. **slippery** adj schlüpfrig, glitschig.

slip[2] (slip) n Zettel m.

slipper ('slipə) n Pantoffel, Hausschuh m.

slippery ('slipri) adj schlüpfrig, glitschig.

slit (slit) n Schlitz m. Spalte f. vt,vi (zer-, auf-)splittern.

slobber ('slɔbə) vi sabbern. n Sabber m.

sloe (slou) n 1 Schlehe f. 2 Schlehdorn m.

slog (slɔg) vt (heftig) schlagen. n inf schuften. n 1 Hieb m. 2 Plackerei f.

slogan ('slougən) n 1 Schlagwort neu. 2 Werbeslogan m.

slop (slɔp) vt verschütten. **sloppy** adj 1 labberig. 2 schlampig. **slops** n pl Spülicht neu.

slope (sloup) n 1 Abhang m. 2 Neigung f. vi 1 abfallen. 2 sich neigen. vt abschrägen. **sloping** adj schräg.

slot (slɔt) n Schlitz m. **slot-machine** n 1 Warenautomat m. 2 Spielautomat m.

slouch (slautʃ) vi latschig gehen or sitzen.

slovenly ('slʌvənli) adj schlampig.

slow (slou) adj 1 langsam 2 schwerfällig 3 langweilig. vt verlangsamen. vi langsamer werden or gehen.

slug[1] (slʌg) *n.* **1** Schnecke *f.* **2** Kugel *f.* **sluggish** *adj* **1** träge. **2** faul.

slug[2] (slʌg) *vt* (mit dem Faust) heftig schlagen. *n* heftiger Schlag *m.*

sluice (slu:s) *n* Schleuse *f.* *vt* (aus)spülen.

slumber ('slʌmbə) *n* Schlummer *m.* *vi* schlummern.

slump (slʌmp) *n* **1** (Preis)Sturz *m.* **2** Tiefstand, Rückgang *m.* *vi* **1** stürzen. **2** hinplumpsen.

slums (slʌmz) *n pl* Elendsviertel *neu.*

slung (slʌŋ) *v see* **sling.**

slur (slə:) *vt* verschlucken. **2** *mus* binden. *n* **1** Fleck, Tadel *m.* **2** *mus* Bindebogen *neu.*

slush (slʌʃ) *n* **1** Matsch *m.* **2** *inf* Kitsch *m.*

sly (slai) *adj* schlau. **on the sly** heimlich.

smack[1] (smæk) *n* (Bei)Geschmack *m.* *v* **smack of** schmecken nach.

smack[2] (smæk) *n* **1** Klatsch, Klaps *m.* **2** Schmatz *m.* *vt* klatschen, jemandem einen Klaps geben. **smack the lips** mit den Lippen schmatzen.

small (smɔ:l) *adj* **1** klein. **2** gering. **in a small way** bescheiden. **make someone feel small** einen beschämen. **smallholding** *n* Kleinbauernbesitz *m.* **small-minded** *adj* kleinlich, engstirnig. **smallpox** *n* Pocken *f pl.*

smart (sma:t) *adj* **1** heftig. **2** adrett. **3** fein. **4** gescheit. *n* Schmerz *m.* *vi* schmerzen. **smarten up** *vt* herausputzen. *vi* sich schön machen.

smash (smæʃ) *vt* **1** zerbrechen. **2** vernichtend schlagen. *vi* **1** zerbrechen. **2** zusammenstoßen. **3** krachen. *n* **1** Krach *m.* **2** Zusammenbruch *m.* **3** Zusammenstoß *m.*

smear (smiə) *vt* **1** beschmieren. **2** verleumden. *n* **1** Schmiere *f.* **2** Fleck *m.*

smell* (smel) *n* Geruch *m.* *vt* riechen. **smelly** *adj* übelriechend.

smile (smail) *vi* lächeln. *n* Lächeln *neu.*

smirk (smə:k) *vi* grinsen. *n* Grinsen *neu.*

smog (smɔg) *n* Smog, rauchiger Nebel *m.*

smoke (smouk) *n* Rauch *m.* **1** rauchen. **2** *cul* räuchern. *vi* rauchen.

smooth (smu:ð) *adj* **1** glatt. **2** fließend. **3** sanft. **4** gewandt. **smoothen** *vt also* **smooth 1** glätten. **2** ebnen. **smoothly** *adv* reibungslos, glatt.

smother ('smʌðə) *vt,vi* ersticken.

smoulder ('smouldə) *vi* **1** glimmen, schwelen. **2** glühen.

smudge (smʌdʒ) *vt* beschmieren. *n* Klecks *m.*

smug (smʌg) *adj* selbstgefällig, überheblich.

smuggle ('smʌgəl) *vt* schmuggeln. **smuggler** *n* Schmuggler *m.* **smuggling** *n* Schmuggel *m.*

snack (snæk) *n* Imbiß *m.* **snack-bar** *n* Imbißstube *f.*

snag (snæg) *n* **1** Aststumpf *m.* **2** Schwierigkeit *f.* Haken *m.* **3** Nachteil *m.*

snail (sneil) *n* Schnecke *f.*

snake (sneik) *n* Schlange *f.* *vi* sich schlängeln.

snap (snæp) *vt* **1** schnappen. **2** *phot* knipsen. **3** knicken. *vi* **1** (zu)schnappen. **2** knacken. **snap at** anschnauzen. ~*n* **1** Schnappen *neu.* **2** Knacks *m.* **snapshot** *n* Schnappschuß *m.*

snarl (sna:l) *vi,vt* knurren. *n* Knurren *neu.*

snatch (snætʃ) *vt* **1** haschen, packen. **2** ergreifen. *n* **1** Haschen *neu.* Griff *m.* **2** Stückchen *neu.*

sneak (sni:k) *vi* **1** schleichen. **2** *sl* petzen. *n* **1** Schleicher, Kriecher. **2** *sl* Petzer *m.*

sneer (sniə) *vi* **1** hohnlächeln. **2** spotten. *n* **1** Hohnlächeln *neu.* **2** Spott *m.*

sneeze (sni:z) *vi* niesen. *n* Niesen *neu.*

sniff (snif) *vt* riechen. *vi* schnüffeln. **sniff at** die Nase rümpfen über. ~*n* **1** Schnüffeln *neu.* **2** Naserümpfen *neu.*

snip (snip) *vt* schnipseln. *n* Schnipsel *m.*

snipe (snaip) *n* *zool* Schnepfe *f.* *vt,vi* aus dem Hinterhalt schießen. **sniper** *n* Heckenschütze *m.*

snivel ('snivəl) *vi* **1** aus der Nase triefen. **2** wimmern, schnüffeln, heulen.

snob (snɔb) *n* Snob, Vornehmtuer *m.*

snooker ('snu:kə) *n* eine Art Billardspiel *neu.*

snoop (snu:p) *vi* (herum)schnüffeln.

snooty ('snu:ti) *adj* hochnäsig, arrogant.

snooze (snu:z) *vi* ein Schläfchen machen. *n* Schläfchen *neu.*

snore (snɔ:) *vi* schnarchen. *n* Schnarchen *neu.*

snort (snɔ:t) *vi* schnauben. *n* Schnauben *neu.*

snout (snaut) *n* **1** Schnauze *f.* **2** (of a pig) Rüssel *m.*

snow (snou) *n* Schnee *m.* *vi* schneien. **snowball** *n* Schneeball *m.* *vt* mit Schneebällen bewerfen. **snowdrift** *n* Schneewehe *f.* **snowdrop** *n* Schneeglöckchen *neu.* **snowflake** *n* Schneeflocke *f.* **snowman** *n* Schneemann *m.* **snowplough** *n* Schneepflug *m.*

snub (snʌb) *vt* (kurz) abweisen, zurückweisen. *n* Zurückweisung, Abfertigung *f.*

snuff (snʌf) *n* Schnupftabak *m.* **take snuff** schnupfen.

snug (snʌg) *adj* **1** behaglich. **2** eng.

snuggle ('snʌgəl) *vi* **snuggle up to** sich schmiegen an.

so (sou) adv so. conj deshalb, so. **so that** damit ~interj so, also. **and so on** und so weiter. **so-and-so** n so und so. **so-called** adj sogenannt. **so-so** adj,adv so so.

soak (souk) vt **1** durchnässen. **2** durchtränken. vi **1** einweichen. **2** durchsickern. **soak up** aufsaugen.

soap (soup) n Seife f. vt einseifen. **soap-powder** n Seifenpulver neu. **soapy** adj seifig.

soar (sɔ:) vi **1** sich erheben. **2** sich aufschwingen. **3** schweben. **4** (auf)steigen. **5** comm in die Höhe schießen.

sob (sɔb) vi schluchzen. n Schluchzen neu.

sober ('soubə) adj nüchtern. vt ernüchtern. **sober up** nüchtern werden.

social ('souʃəl) adj **1** gesellschaftlich. **2** sozial, Sozial—. **Social Services** n pl soziale Einrichtungen f pl. **sociable** adj gesellig, gemütlich. **socialism** n Sozialismus m. **socialist** n Sozialist m. adj sozialistisch.

society (sə'saiəti) n **1** Gesellschaft f. **2** Verein, Verband m.

sociology (sousi'ɔlədʒi) n Sozialwissenschaft, Soziologie f. **sociological** adj soziologisch. **sociologist** n Soziologe m.

sock¹ (sɔk) n Socke f.

sock² (sɔk) sl vt (ver)hauen. n Schlag m.

socket ('sɔkit) n **1** anat Höhle, Pfanne f. **2** tech Muffe f. **3** (electrical) Steckdose f.

soda ('soudə) n **1** Soda f,neu. **soda-water** n Sodawasser, Mineralwasser neu.

sofa ('soufə) n Sofa neu.

soft (sɔft) adj **1** weich. **2** leise. **3** weichlich. **soft drink** n alkoholfreies Getränk neu. **softhearted** adj weichherzig. **soften** vt weich machen. vi **1** (sich) erweichen. **2** mildern.

soggy ('sɔgi) adj durchnäßt, feucht.

soil¹ (sɔil) n Boden m. Erde f.

soil² (sɔil) vt **1** beschmutzen. **2** beflecken.

solar ('soulə) adj Sonnen—.

sold (sould) v see **sell**.

solder ('sɔldə) vt löten. n Lötmetall neu.

soldier ('souldʒə) n Soldat m.

sole¹ (soul) adj einzig, Allein—. **solely** adv allein, ausschließlich.

sole² (soul) n Sohle f. vt besohlen.

sole³ (soul) n Seezunge f.

solemn ('sɔləm) adj **1** feierlich. **2** ernst. **solemnity** n Feierlichkeit f.

solicitor (sə'lisitə) n Anwalt m.

solid ('sɔlid) adj **1** fest. **2** dauerhaft. **3** kräftig. n Körper m. **solidarity** n Solidarität f. **solidify** (vi),vt (sich) verfestigen.

solitary ('sɔlitri) adj **1** einsam. **2** einzeln, allein. **solitary confinement** n Einzelhaft f.

solitude ('sɔlitju:d) n Einsamkeit f.

solo ('soulou) n mus Solo neu. adj Allein—, Einzel—.

solstice ('sɔlstis) n Sonnenwende f.

soluble ('sɔljubəl) adj löslich, (auf)lösbar.

solution (sə'lu:ʃən) n **1** Lösung f. **2** sci (Auf)-Lösung f.

solve (sɔlv) vt (auf)lösen. **solvent** adj **1** (auf)lösend. **2** comm zahlungsfähig. n Lösungsmittel neu.

sombre ('sɔmbə) adj düster, trübe.

some (sʌm) adj **1** irgendein, irgendwelche. **2** einige. **3** etwas. **4** gewisse. **5** manche. **6** etwa, ungefähr. **somebody** pron also **someone** jemand. **somehow** adv irgendwie. **something** pron **1** etwas. **2** irgendetwas. **sometime** adv irgendwann, eines Tages. **sometimes** adv manchmal. **somewhat** adv etwas, ziemlich. **somewhere** adv irgendwo(hin).

somersault ('sʌməsɔ:lt) n Purzelbaum m. **turn a somersault** einen Purzelbaum schlagen.

son (sʌn) n Sohn m. **son-in-law** n Schwiegersohn m.

sonata (sə'nɑ:tə) n Sonate f.

song (sɔŋ) n **1** Lied neu. **2** Gesang m.

sonic ('sɔnik) adj Schall—.

sonnet ('sɔnit) n Sonett neu.

soon (su:n) adv **1** bald. **2** gern. **as soon as** sobald wie. **sooner** adv **1** eher. **2** lieber. **no sooner than** kaum...als. **no sooner said than done** gesagt, getan.

soot (sut) n Ruß m. vt verrußen.

soothe (su:ð) vt **1** beruhigen. **2** lindern.

sophisticated (sə'fistikeitid) adj **1** verfeinert. **2** hochentwickelt. **3** kultiviert.

soprano (sə'prɑ:nou) n Sopran m.

sordid ('sɔ:did) adj schmutzig, gemein.

sore (sɔ:) adj **1** wund, weh. **2** schlimm. **3** verletzt. n wunde Stelle f.

sorrow ('sɔrou) n **1** Trauer f. **2** Kummer m. Leid neu. vi trauern. **sorrowful** adj **1** traurig, betrübt. **2** elend.

sorry ('sɔri) adj **1** bekümmert. **2** erbärmlich. interj Verzeihung! **I am sorry** es tut mir leid.

sort (sɔ:t) n Sorte, Art f. **what sort of** was für. vt sortieren. **sort out 1** aussortieren. **2** inf erledigen.

soufflé ('su:flei) n Soufflé neu. Auflauf m.

sought (sɔ:t) v see **seek**. **sought-after** adj gesucht, begehrt.

soul (soul) n Seele f. **soul-destroying** adj

seelentötend, bedrückend. **soulful** adj seelenvoll. **soulless** adj seelenlos.

sound[1] (saund) n 1 Ton, Laut m. 2 Klang m. 3 Geräusch neu. vi 1 klingen. 2 tönen, lauten. vt ertönen or erklingen lassen.

sound[2] (saund) adj 1 gesund. 2 ganz. 3 fest. 4 vernünftig. 5 kräftig.

sound[3] (saund) vt 1 naut loten. 2 sondieren.

soup (su:p) n Suppe f.

sour (sauə) adj 1 sauer, scharf. 2 bitter, mürrisch. vi sauer or bitter werden. vt 1 säuern. 2 erbittern.

source (sɔ:s) n 1 Quelle f. 2 Ursprung m.

south (sauθ) n Süd(en) m. adj Süd—, südlich. adv südwärts, nach Süden. **south-east** n Südosten m. **south-eastern** adj südöstlich. **southerly** adj südlich. **southern** adj Süd—, südlich. **southwards** adv südwärts, nach Süden. **south-west** n Südwesten m. **south-western** adj südwestlich.

South Africa n Südafrika neu.

South America n Südamerika neu.

South Pole n Südpol m.

souvenir (su:və'niə) n Andenken neu.

sovereign ('sɔvrin) adj 1 souverän. 2 höchst. n Souverän, Monarch m.

Soviet Union ('souviət) n Sowjetunion f.

sow[*1] (sou) vt 1 (aus)säen. 2 besäen.

sow[2] (sau) n zool Sau f.

soya bean ('sɔiə) n Sojabohne f.

spa (spɑ:) n Kurort m. Bad neu.

space (speis) n 1 Weltraum m. 2 Platz m. 3 Zwischenraum m. 4 Zeitraum m. vt 1 einteilen. 2 sperren. **spaceship** n Raumschiff m. **spacious** adj 1 geräumig. 2 weit.

spade[1] (speid) n Spaten m. vt graben.

spade[2] (speid) n game Pik neu.

Spain (spein) n Spanien neu. **Spaniard** n Spanier m. **Spanish** adj spanisch. n (language) Spanisch neu.

span (spæn) n 1 (Zeit)Spanne f. 2 Spannweite f. vt 1 (um-, über-)spannen. 2 (aus)messen.

spank (spæŋk) vt schlagen. n Schlag m.

spanner ('spænə) n Schraubenschlüssel m.

spare (spɛə) adj 1 spärlich. 2 mager. 3 übrig. 4 Ersatz—. n Ersatzteil neu. vt 1 (ver)schonen. 2 übrig haben or können. **sparing** adj sparsam.

spark (spɑ:k) n Funken m. **spark plug** n Zündkerze f. ~vi Funken sprühen. **spark off** auslösen.

sparkle ('spɑ:kəl) vi 1 funkeln. 2 sprühen. 3 schäumen. n Funkeln neu.

sparrow ('spærou) n Sperling, Spatz m.

sparse (spɑ:s) adj spärlich, dünn.

spasm ('spæzəm) n Krampf m. **spasmodic** adj 1 krampfhaft. 2 unregelmäßig. **spastic** adj spastisch, Krampf—.

spat (spæt) v see **spit**.

spatial ('speiʃəl) adj räumlich, Raum—.

spatula ('spætjulə) n Spatel m. Spachtel f.

spawn (spɔ:n) n Laich m. vi laichen. vt hervorbringen.

speak[*] (spi:k) vi sprechen, reden. vt (aus)-sprechen, äußern. **speaking!** am Apparat!

spear (spiə) n Speer, Spieß m. vt (auf)spießen.

special ('speʃəl) adj 1 besonder. 2 Sonder—, speziell, Spezial—, extra. **specialist** n 1 Spezialist, Fachmann m. 2 med Facharzt m. **speciality** n 1 Besonderheit f. 2 Spezialfach neu. 3 Spezialität f. **specialize** vi sich spezialisieren.

species ('spi:ʃi:z) n, pl **species** Art, Spezies f.

specify ('spesifai) vt spezifizieren. **specific** adj 1 spezifisch. 2 bestimmt. **specification** n Spezifizierung f.

specimen ('spesimən) n Muster, Exemplar neu.

speck (spek) n Fleck m. vt flecken.

spectacle ('spektəkəl) n 1 Schauspiel neu. 2 Schau f. 3 pl Brille f. **spectacular** adj 1 auffallend, spektakulär. 2 eindrücksvoll.

spectator (spek'teitə) n Zuschauer m.

spectrum ('spektrəm) n Spektrum neu.

speculate ('spekjuleit) vi 1 nachsinnen. 2 comm spekulieren. **speculation** n 1 (theoretische) Betrachtung f. 2 comm Spekulation f.

speech (spi:tʃ) n 1 Sprache f. 2 Rede f. **speechless** adj sprachlos.

speed[*] (spi:d) n 1 Geschwindigkeit f. 2 Eile f. 3 phot Lichtempfindlichkeit f. **speed-boat** n Rennboot neu. **speedometer** n Geschwindigkeitsmesser neu. ~vi schnell fahren. **speed up** beschleunigen. **speedy** adj geschwind.

spell[*1] (spel) vt 1 buchstabieren. 2 inf bedeuten. vi richtig schreiben. **spelling** n Rechtschreibung f.

spell[2] (spel) n Zauber(spruch), Bann m. **spellbound** adj gebannt.

spell[3] (spel) n 1 Schicht f. 2 Weilchen neu.

spend[*] (spend) vt 1 (money) ausgeben. 2 (time) verbringen. 3 (energy) verwenden. **spendthrift** n Verschwender m. adj verschwenderisch.

spent (spent) v see **spend**. adj erschöpft, matt.

sperm (spə:m) n Same m. Sperma neu.

sphere (sfiə) n 1 Kugel f. 2 Sphäre f. Bereich m. **spherical** adj kugelförmig.

spice (spais) *n* Gewürz *neu.* Würze *f. vt* würzen.
spicy *adj* pikant, würzig.

spider ('spaidə) *n* Spinne *f.*

spike (spaik) *n* Spitze *f. vt* 1 festnageln. 2 aufspießen. **spiky** *adj* spitzig.

spill* (spil) *vt* 1 verschütten. 2 vergießen. *vi* 1 verschüttet werden. 2 überlaufen.

spin* (spin) *vi,vt* 1 spinnen. 2 wirbeln. 3 (a coin) hochwerfen. 4 (a tale) ausdenken. *vi* Wirbeln *neu.* **spin-dry** *vt* schleudern. **spin-dryer** *n* Wäscheschleuder *f.*

spinach ('spinidʒ) *n* Spinat *m.*

spindle ('spindl) *n* Spindel *f.* **spindly** *adj* spindeldürr.

spine (spain) *n* 1 Rückgrat *neu.* Wirbelsäule *f.* 2 Stachel *m.*

spinster ('spinstə) *n* 1 unverheiratete Frau, Junggesellin *f.* 2 alte Jungfer *f.*

spiral ('spaiərl) *n* 1 Spirale *f.* 2 Wirbel *m. adj* 1 spiralig. 2 schraubenförmig. *vi* sich schrauben.

spire (spaiə) *n* Turmspitze *f.* Kirchturm *m.*

spirit ('spirit) *n* 1 Geist *m.* 2 Temperament *neu.* 3 Mut *m.* 4 Spiritus *m.* 5 *pl* Stimmung *f.* 6 *pl* Spirituosen *pl.* **~ spirit away** wegzaubern. **spirited** *adj* lebhaft. **spiritual** *adj* 1 geistig. 2 geistlich.

spit* ¹ (spit) *vi* 1 spucken. 2 (of rain) sprühen. **spit out** ausspucken. *n* Spucke *f.*

spit ² (spit) *n* 1 Bratspieß *m.* 2 Landzunge *f.*

spite (spait) *n* 1 Bosheit, Gehässigkeit *f.* **in spite of** trotz. **~** *vt* ärgern. **spiteful** *adj* boshaft, gehässig.

splash (splæʃ) *n* 1 Spritzfleck *m.* 2 Patschen *neu. vt* (be)spritzen. *vi* patschen.

splendid ('splendid) *adj* 1 herrlich. 2 großartig. **splendour** *n* Herrlichkeit, Pracht *f.*

splint (splint) *n med* Schiene *f. vt* schienen. **splinter** *n* Splitter *m. vi,vt* (zer)splittern.

split* (split) *vt* 1 (zer)spalten. 2 teilen. *vi* 1 sich spalten. 2 sich entzweien. **split hairs** Haarspalterei treiben. **~** *n* 1 Spalt, Riß *m.* 2 Spaltung *f.*

splutter ('splʌtə) *vi* 1 spritzen. 2 stottern, plappern. *n* 1 Spritzen *neu.* 2 Geplapper *neu.*

spoil* (spɔil) *vt* 1 verderben. 2 (a child) verwöhnen. 3 plündern. *vi* schlecht werden. **spoils** *n pl* Beute *f.* Gewinn *neu.* **spoil-sport** *n* Spielverderber *m.*

spoke ¹ (spouk) *v see* **speak**.

spoke ² (spouk) *n* Speiche *f.*

spoken ('spoukən) *v see* **speak**.

spokesman ('spouksmən) *n* Wortführer *m.*

sponge (spʌndʒ) *n* Schwamm *m. vt* mit einem Schwamm (ab)wischen. *vi* schmarotzen.

sponsor ('spɔnsə) *n* 1 Pate *m.* 2 Bürge *m.* 3 Förderer *m. vt* 1 fördern. 2 finanzieren.

spontaneous (spɔn'teiniəs) *adj* 1 spontan. 2 freiwillig. 3 *tech* Selbst—. **spontaneity** *n* 1 Spontaneität *f.* 2 Freiwilligkeit *f.*

spool (spu:l) *n* Spule *f.*

spoon (spu:n) *n* Löffel *m. vt* löffeln. **spoonfed** *adj* verhätschelt.

sport (spɔ:t) *n* 1 Sport *m.* 2 Scherz *m.* **a good sport** *n* feiner Kerl *m.* **do** *or* **play sport** Sport treiben. **sportsman** *n* Sportler *m.* **~** *vi* scherzen. *vt* zur Schau tragen.

spot (spɔt) *n* 1 Fleck *m.* 2 Stelle *f.* 3 Pickel *m.* **be on the spot** zur Stelle sein. **spotlight** *n* Scheinwerfer *m. vt* 1 beflecken. 2 bemerken. **spotless** *adj* fleckenlos.

spouse (spaus) *n* Gatte *m.* Gattin *f.*

spout (spaut) *n* 1 Schnauze *f.* 2 Ausgußröhre *f.* 3 Wasserstrahl *m. vt* (heraus)spritzen.

sprain (sprein) *vt* verrenken. *n* Verrenkung *f.*

sprang (spræŋ) *v see* **spring**.

sprawl (sprɔ:l) *vi* 1 sich rekeln. 2 wuchern.

spray ¹ (sprei) *n* 1 Gischt *m.* 2 Spray *m. vt* besprühen, spritzen.

spray ² (sprei) *n* 1 Zweig *m.* 2 Blütenzweig *m.*

spread* (spred) *vt* 1 (aus-, ver-)breiten. 2 **aufstreichen** *vi* sich verbreiten. *n* 1 Verbreitung *f.* 2 Spanne *f.* 3 Brotaufstrich *m.*

spree (spri:) *n* 1 Jux *m.* 2 Orgie *f.*

sprig (sprig) *n* 1 Sproß *m.* 2 Sprößling *m.*

sprightly ('spraitli) *adj* lebhaft, munter.

spring* (spriŋ) *vi* 1 springen. 2 entstehen. *vt* sprengen. **spring a leak** leck werden. **~** *n* 1 Sprung *m.* 2 Sprungkraft *f.* 3 Triebfeder *f.* 4 Quelle *f.* Brunnen *m.* 5 Frühling *m.* **springboard** *n* Sprungbrett *neu.* **spring-cleaning** *n* Frühjahrsputz *m.*

sprinkle ('spriŋkəl) *vt* (be)streuen. *vi* sprühen.

sprint (sprint) *vi* sprinten. *n* Sprint *m.*

sprout (spraut) *vi* sprießen. *n* Sproß *m.*

sprung (sprʌŋ) *v see* **spring**.

spun (spʌn) *v see* **spin**.

spur (spɔ:) *n* 1 Reitsporn *m.* 2 Ansporn *m. vt* (an)spornen.

spurt (spɔ:t) *vi* 1 *sport* spurten. 2 herausspritzen. *n* 1 Spurt *m.* 2 Wasserstrahl *m.*

spy (spai) *n* Spion *m. vt* (er)spähen. *vi* spionieren. **spy on someone** jemandem nachspionieren.

squabble ('skwɔbəl) *vi* sich zanken. *n* Zank *m.*

squad (skwɔd) n Gruppe f. Trupp m. Kommando neu.

squadron ('skwɔdrən) n 1 mil Schwadron f. 2 aviat Staffel f. 3 naut Geschwader neu.

squalid ('skwɔlid) adj armselig, verwahrlost. **squalor** n Schmutz m. Verwahrlosung f.

squander ('skwɔndə) vt verschwenden.

square (skwɛə) adj 1 viereckig. 2 quadratisch. 3 ehrlich. 4 quitt. n 1 Viereck neu. 2 Quadrat neu. 3 (in a town) Platz m. vt 1 viereckig machen. 2 quadrieren. 3 (an account) ausgleichen. vi passen.

squash (skwɔʃ) n 1 Gedränge neu. 2 Fruchtgetränk neu. 3 sport Squash neu. vt 1 (zer)quetschen. 2 (er)drücken, zerdrücken.

squat (skwɔt) vi 1 kauern, hocken. 2 unbefugt besetzen. adj 1 kauernd. 2 untersetzt. **squatter** n Siedler ohne Rechtstitel, Squatter m.

squawk (skwɔːk) vi kreischen. n Kreischen neu.

squeak (skwiːk) vi 1 quietschen. 2 knarren. n 1 Gequieke, Quietschen neu. 2 Knarren neu.

squeal (skwiːl) vi 1 quieken, quietschen. 2 inf verpfeifen. n Quieken, Quietschen neu.

squeamish ('skwiːmiʃ) adj 1 überempfindlich. 2 heikel.

squeeze (skwiːz) vt 1 drücken, pressen. 2 bedrängen. vi dringen, drängen. n 1 Druck m. 2 inf Gedränge. **squeezer** n Presse f.

squid (skwid) n Tintenfisch m.

squiggle ('skwigəl) n Kritzelei f. Schnörkel m. vi kritzeln.

squint (skwint) vi schielen. n Schielen neu.

squire ('skwaiə) n Landjunker, Gutsherr m.

squirm (skwəːm) vi sich winden, sich krümmen.

squirrel ('skwirl) n Eichhörnchen neu.

squirt (skwəːt) vt spritzen. n Spritze f.

Sri Lanka (sriːˈlæŋkə) n Sri Lanka neu.

stab (stæb) n Stich m. **stab in the back** hinterlistiger Angriff m. ~vt erstechen. vi stechen.

stabilize ('steibəlaiz) vt stabilisieren. **stability** n 1 Stabilität f. 2 Festigkeit f.

stable[1] ('steibəl) n Stall m. vt einstallen.

stable[2] ('steibəl) adj 1 stabil. 2 beständig.

stack (stæk) n 1 Schober m. 2 Schornstein m. 3 Stapel m. vt (auf)stapeln.

stadium ('steidiəm) n Stadion neu.

staff (stɑːf) n 1 Stab m. 2 Personal neu. Belegschaft f. vt (mit Personal) besetzen.

stag (stæg) n Hirsch m.

stage (steidʒ) n 1 Bühne f. 2 Schauplatz m. 3 Stufe f. 4 Teilstrecke f. **stage manager** n Regisseur m. ~vt inszenieren, vorführen.

stagger ('stægə) vi 1 taumeln, schwanken. vt 1 verblüffen. 2 staffeln. n Schwanken neu.

stagnant ('stægnənt) adj 1 stagnierend 2 träge. **stagnate** vi stocken, stagnieren.

stain (stein) n 1 Flecken m. 2 Makel m. 3 Beize f. vt 1 beflecken. 2 beizen. **stained glass** n buntes Glas neu. **stainless** adj 1 fleckenlos 2 (of steel) rostfrei.

stair (stɛə) n 1 Stufe f. 2 pl Treppe f. **staircase** n Treppenhaus neu.

stake[1] (steik) n Pfahl m.

stake[2] (steik) n game,sport Einsatz m. **be at stake** auf dem Spiele stehen.

stale (steil) adj 1 alt, schal. 2 fad.

stalemate ('steilmeit) n 1 game Patt neu. 2 Stillstand m.

stalk[1] (stɔːk) n 1 Stiel m. 2 (of corn) Halm m.

stalk[2] (stɔːk) vt beschleichen. vi stolzieren.

stall[1] (stɔːl) n 1 Pferdebox f. 2 (Markt)Bude f. 3 pl Th Parkett neu. 4 Chorstuhl m. vt einstallen. vi mot aussetzen, stehenbleiben.

stall[2] (stɔːl) n inf Verwand m. Ausflucht f. vt ausweichen. vi Ausflüchte machen.

stallion ('stæliən) n Hengst m.

stamina ('stæminə) n Ausdauer, Vitalität f.

stammer ('stæmə) vi stammeln. n Stammeln neu.

stamp (stæmp) n 1 Stempel m. 2 (Brief)Marke f. 3 Gepräge neu. vt 1 stempeln. 2 frankieren. 3 prägen. vi stampfen.

stampede (stæmˈpiːd) n Panik, wilde Flucht f. vi flüchten, durchgehen.

stand* (stænd) vi 1 stehen. **stand by 1** treu bleiben. 2 in Bereitschaft halten. **stand-by** n Beistand m. **stand for 1** bedeuten. 2 ertragen. 3 kandidieren für. **stand up** aufstehen. ~n 1 Stand m. 2 Standpunkt m. 3 Bude f. **standing** adj 1 stehend. 2 (be)ständig. n 1 Stellung f. 2 Ruf m. **standstill** n Stillstand m. **come to a standstill** zum Stehen kommen.

standard ('stændəd) n 1 Standarte f. 2 Standard m. Norm f. 3 Stufe f. adj maßgebend, Normal—, Standard—.

stank (stæŋk) v see **stink**.

stanza ('stænzə) n Strophe, Stanze f.

staple[1] ('steipəl) n 1 Krampe f. 2 Heftklammer f. **stapler** n Heftmaschine f.

staple[2] ('steipəl) adj Haupt—, Stapel—. n 1 Haupterzeugnis neu. 2 Hauptgegenstand m.

star (stɑ:) n 1 Stern m. 2 Star m. vi die Hauptrolle spielen. **starfish** n Seestern m.

starboard (ˈstɑːbəd) n Steuerbord neu.

starch (stɑːtʃ) n (Wäsche)Stärke f. vt stärken. **starchy** adj inf steif.

stare (stɛə) vi große Augen machen, starren. **stare at** anstarren. ~n 1 Starren neu. 2 starrer Blick m.

stark (stɑːk) adj 1 steif, starr. 2 völlig. **stark naked** adj splitternackt.

starling (ˈstɑːliŋ) n Star m.

start (stɑːt) vi 1 anfangen. 2 starten. 3 abgehen, abfahren. 4 auffahren. vt 1 in Gang bringen. 2 starten lassen. 3 anfangen. ~n 1 Auffahren neu. 2 Anfang, Beginn m. 3 sport Start m.

startle (ˈstɑːtl) vt erschrecken.

starve (stɑːv) vi,(vt) verhungern (lassen). **starvation** n (Ver)Hungern neu. adj Hunger—.

state (steit) n 1 pol Staat m. 2 Zustand m. **get into a state** inf sich aufregen. ~vt 1 angeben. 2 darlegen. 3 feststellen. 4 aufstellen. adj Staats—. **stately** adj 1 stattlich. 2 prächtig. 3 erhaben. **statement** n 1 Angabe f. 2 Darlegung f. 3 Kontoauszug m. 4 Behauptung f. **statesman** n Staatsmann m.

static (ˈstætik) adj statisch.

station (ˈsteiʃən) n 1 (railway) Bahnhof m. 2 (Polizei)Wache f. 3 Platz m. 4 Station f. vt mil stationieren. **station-master** n Stationsvorsteher m.

stationary (ˈsteiʃənri) adj 1 stillstehend. 2 stationär.

stationer (ˈsteiʃənə) n Schreibwarenhändler m. **stationery** n Schreibwaren f pl.

statistics (stəˈtistiks) n pl Statistik f.

statue (ˈstætjuː) n Statue f. Standbild neu.

stature (ˈstætʃə) n 1 Statur f. Gestalt f. 2 Größe f.

status (ˈsteitəs) n 1 Rang m. 2 Status m.

statute (ˈstætjuːt) n 1 Statut, (Landes)Gesetz neu. 2 Satzung f. **statutory** adj gesetzlich.

stay¹ (stei) vi 1 (sich) aufhalten. 2 bleiben. 3 wohnen. n Aufenthalt m.

stay² (stei) n Stütze f.

steadfast (ˈstedfɑːst) adj 1 fest. 2 (of a look) unverwandt. 3 standhaft.

steady (ˈstedi) adj 1 (be)ständig. 2 sicher. 3 fest. 4 ruhig. vt 1 sicher machen. 2 (sich) festigen. 3 (sich) beruhigen.

steak (steik) n 1 Steak neu. 2 (Fisch)Filet neu.

steal (stiːl) vi,vt stehlen.

steam (stiːm) n 1 Dampf m. 2 Dunst m. vi dampfen. vt cul dünsten. **steam-engine** n

Dampfmaschine f. **steam-roller** n Dampfwalze f. **steamer** n 1 Dampfer m. Dampfschiff neu. 2 Dampfkochtopf m.

steel (stiːl) n Stahl m. adj stählern, Stahl—. vt stählen.

steep¹ (stiːp) adj 1 steil, jäh. 2 inf stark.

steep² (stiːp) vt 1 einweichen. 2 versenken.

steeple (ˈstiːpəl) n Kirchturm m. **steeplechase** n Hindernisrennen neu.

steer (stiə) vt steuern. **steer clear of** vermeiden. **steering-wheel** n Steuerrad neu.

stem¹ (stem) n 1 Stamm m. 2 Stengel m. v **stem from** stammen von.

stem² (stem) vt eindämmen.

stencil (ˈstensəl) n 1 Schablone f. 2 Matrize f. vt schablonieren.

step (step) n 1 Schritt m. 2 (Fuß)Tritt m. 3 Stufe f. 4 Maßnahme f. vi 1 schreiten. 2 treten, gehen. **stepladder** n Trittleiter f.

stepbrother (ˈstepbrʌðə) n Stiefbruder m.

stepdaughter (ˈstepdɔːtə) n Stieftochter f.

stepfather (ˈstepfɑːðə) n Stiefvater m.

stepmother (ˈstepmʌðə) n Stiefmutter f.

stepsister (ˈstepsistə) n Stiefschwester f.

stepson (ˈstepsʌn) n Stiefsohn m.

stereo (ˈsteriou) adj Stereo—. n Stereoanlage f. **stereophonic** adj stereophonisch.

stereotype (ˈsteriətaip) n Stereotype f. vt stereotypieren. **stereotyped** adj stereotyp.

sterile (ˈsterail) adj 1 steril. 2 unfruchtbar. **sterilize** vt 1 sterilisieren. 2 unfruchtbar machen. **sterilization** n Sterilisierung f.

sterling (ˈstɑːliŋ) adj 1 gediegen. 2 Sterling—. n Sterling m.

stern¹ (stɑːn) adj streng, hart.

stern² (stɑːn) n naut Heck neu. Spiegel m.

stethoscope (ˈsteθəskoup) n Stethoskop neu.

stew (stjuː) n Schmorgericht neu. vt schmoren.

steward (ˈstjuːəd) n 1 Steward m. 2 Verwalter m. 3 Ordner m. **stewardess** n Stewardeß f.

stick¹ (stik) n Stock m. **get hold of the wrong end of the stick** die Geschichte in den falschen Hals kriegen.

stick² (stik) vt 1 ankleben. 2 stecken. vi 1 kleben. 2 steckenbleiben. **sticker** n Klebzettel m. **sticky** adj klebrig. **come to a sticky end** ein schlimmes Ende nehmen.

stiff (stif) adj 1 steif. 2 starr. 3 (of a drink) stark. **stiffen** vt steifen. vi 1 sich versteifen. 2 erstarren.

stifle (ˈstaifəl) vt ersticken.

stigma (ˈstigmə) n Stigma neu.

stile (stail) n Zauntritt m. Steige f.

281

still¹ (stil) adj still. adv 1 immer noch. 2 noch, immer. conj doch, dennoch. vt 1 stillen. 2 beruhigen. n Photographie f. **stillborn** adj totgeboren. **still life** n Stilleben neu.

still² (stil) n Destillierapparat m.

stilt (stilt) n Stelze f. **stilted** adj gespreizt, geschraubt.

stimulus ('stimjuləs) n 1 Antrieb m. 2 Reizmittel neu. **stimulate** vt anreizen, stimulieren.

sting* (stiŋ) vi,vt 1 stechen. 2 schmerzen. n 1 (of an insect) Stachel m. 2 Stich m.

stink* (stiŋk) vi stinken. n Gestank m.

stint (stint) vt einschränken. n 1 Einschränkung f. 2 Schicht f.

stipulate ('stipjuleit) vt festsetzen, vereinbaren. **stipulation** n 1 Festsetzung f. 2 Bedingung f.

stir (stə:) vt 1 rühren. 2 aufregen. vi sich rühren. n 1 Rühren neu. 2 (Auf)Regung f.

stirrup ('stirəp) n Steigbügel m.

stitch (stitʃ) n 1 Stich m. 2 Masche f. vt nähen, heften.

stoat (stout) n Hermelin neu.

stock (stɔk) n 1 Vorrat m. 2 Stamm m. 3 Stock m. 4 pl Aktien f pl. 5 cul Brühe f. **take stock of** abschätzen. ~adj 1 Standard—. 2 stereotyp. vt 1 versehen. 2 vorrätig haben. **stockbreeding** n Viehzucht f. **stockbroker** n Börsenmakler m. **stock exchange** n Börse f. **stockpile** n Vorrat m. vt aufstapeln. **stocktaking** n Inventur f.

stocking ('stɔkiŋ) n Strumpf m.

stocky ('stɔki) adj untersetzt.

stodge (stɔdʒ) n schwerverdauliches Essen neu. **stodgy** adj 1 schwer. 2 schwerfällig.

stoical ('stouikļ) adj stoisch.

stoke (stouk) vt (an)schüren.

stole¹ (stoul) v see **steal**.

stole² (stoul) n Pelzkragen m. Stola f.

stolen ('stoulən) v see **steal**.

stomach ('stʌmək) n Magen m. vt 1 verdauen. 2 ertragen. **stomach-ache** n Magenschmerzen m pl.

stone (stoun) n 1 Stein m. 2 Kern m. vt 1 steinigen. 2 (fruit) entsteinen. **stony** adj 1 steinig. 2 steinern.

stood (stud) v see **stand**.

stool (stu:l) n Hocker m.

stoop (stu:p) vi 1 sich bücken. 2 sich erniedrigen. 3 krumm gehen.

stop (stɔp) vt 1 (an)halten. 2 hindern. 3 aufhören. 4 verstopfen. vi 1 anhalten. 2 aufhören. 3 stehenbleiben. n 1 Halt m. 2 Pause f. 3 Hemmung f. 4 (Bus)Haltestelle f. 5

Punkt m. **stopgap** n Notbehelf m. **stopwatch** n Stoppuhr f. **stoppage** n 1 Stockung f. 2 Einstellung f. 3 Sperrung f. **stopper** n Stöpsel m. vt zustöpseln.

store (stɔ:) n 1 Vorrat m. 2 Lagerhaus neu. 3 Fülle f. 4 pl Kaufhaus neu. 5 Schiffsbedarf m. vt lagern, aufbewahren. **set store by** Wert legen auf. **storage** n 1 Aufbewahrung, Lagerung f. 2 (of electricity) Speicherung f.

storey ('stɔ:ri) n Stock m. Stockwerk, Geschoß neu.

stork (stɔ:k) n Storch m.

storm (stɔ:m) n Sturm m. vt stürmen. vi toben. **stormy** adj stürmisch.

story ('stɔ:ri) n 1 Geschichte f. 2 Erzählung f. 3 Handlung f.

stout (staut) adj 1 stark. 2 dick. 3 tapfer. n Starkbier neu.

stove (stouv) n 1 Ofen m. 2 (for cooking) Herd m.

stow (stou) vt verstauen. **stowaway** n blinder Passagier m.

straddle ('strædl) vi breitbeinig gehen or stehen. vt spreizen.

straggle ('strægəl) vi 1 verstreut hegen. 2 umherschweifen. 3 wuchern. **straggling** adj weitläufig, lose.

straight (streit) adj 1 gerade. 2 aufrichtig. 3 glatt. **get straight** klarmachen. **put straight** in Ordnung bringen. **straight ahead** adv geradeaus. **straight away** adv sofort, unmittelbar. **straighten** vt gerademachen. vi gerade werden. **straightforward** adj 1 gerade. 2 redlich.

strain¹ (strein) n 1 Anstrengung f. 2 Druck m. 3 med Zerrung f. vt 1 anstrengen. 2 zerren. 3 (durch)seihen. vi sich anstrengen. **strainer** n Seiher m. Sieb neu.

strain² (strein) n Abstammung f. Rasse f.

strand¹ (strænd) vi,(vt) stranden (lassen).

strand² (strænd) n Strähne f.

strange (streindʒ) adj 1 fremd. 2 seltsam. **stranger** n 1 Fremde(r) m. 2 Neuling m.

strangle ('stræŋgəl) vt 1 erwürgen. 2 unterdrücken.

strap (stræp) n 1 Riemen m. 2 Träger m. vt festschnallen.

strategy ('strætidʒi) n Strategie f. **strategic** adj strategisch.

straw (strɔ:) n 1 Stroh neu. 2 Strohhalm m. adj Stroh—. **strawberry** n Erdbeere f.

stray (strei) vi 1 sich verirren. 2 abirren. adj verirrt. n verirrtes Tier neu.

streak (stri:k) n 1 Streifen m. 2 Spur f. vt streifen. **streaky** adj 1 streifig. 2 (of bacon) durchwachsen.

stream (stri:m) n 1 Bach m. 2 Strom m. vi 1 strömen. 2 flattern. **streamer** n Papierschlange f. **streamline** n Stromlinie f. vt modernisieren.

street (stri:t) n Straße f.

strength (streŋθ) n Kraft, Stärke f. **on the strength of** kraft. **strengthen** vt (be)kräftigen, (be)stärken. vi erstärken.

strenuous ('strenjuəs) adj 1 emsig. 2 eifrig. 3 anstrengend.

stress (stres) n 1 Ton m. Betonung f. 2 Nachdruck m. Gewicht neu. 3 med Streß m. vt 1 betonen. 2 unterstreichen.

stretch (stretʃ) vt 1 strecken. 2 (aus)dehnen. 3 anspannen. vi 1 sich erstrecken. 2 sich dehnen. n 1 Strecke f. 2 Dehnung f. **at a stretch** in einem Zug. **stretcher** n Tragbahre f.

strict (strikt) adj 1 streng. 2 genau. **strictly speaking** streng genommen.

stride* (straid) vi schreiten. n (langer) Schritt m.

strike* (straik) vt 1 schlagen. 2 treffen. 3 auffallen. 4 anzünden. vi 1 schlagen. 2 streiken. n Streik m.

string* (striŋ) n 1 Schnur f. 2 mus Saite f. Reihe f. vt 1 aufreihen. 2 mus besaiten. **stringed instruments** n pl Saiteninstrumente neu pl.

stringent ('strindʒənt) adj 1 streng. 2 fest. 3 knapp. **stringency** n 1 Strenge f. 2 Härte f. 3 Knappheit f.

strip[1] (strip) vi sich ausziehen. vt 1 entkleiden. 2 entblößen. 3 abreißen. **striptease** n Striptease neu.

strip[2] (strip) n (schmaler) Streifen m.

stripe (straip) n Streifen m. **striped** adj gestreift.

strive* (straiv) vi 1 streben. 2 ringen.

stroke[1] (strouk) n 1 Schlag, Hieb m. 2 Streich m. 3 Strich m. **stroke of luck** n glücklicher Zufall m.

stroke[2] (strouk) vt streicheln.

stroll (stroul) vi 1 bummeln, schlendern. 2 spazierengehen. n 1 Bummel m. 2 Spaziergang m.

strong (stroŋ) adj 1 stark. 2 kräftig. 3 fest. **stronghold** n Festung f. **strong-minded** adj willensstark.

struck (strʌk) v see **strike.**

structure ('strʌktʃə) n 1 Bau m. 2 Struktur f. **structural** adj 1 Bau—. 2 strukturell.

struggle ('strʌgəl) vi 1 sich (ab)mühen. 2 kämpfen, ringen. 3 zappeln. n 1 Kampf m. 2 Ringen neu.

strum (strʌm) vi,(vt) klimpern (auf).

strung (strʌŋ) v see **string.**

strut[1] (strʌt) vi stolzieren. n Stolzieren neu.

strut[2] (strʌt) n Strebe, Stütze f.

stub (stʌb) n 1 Stumpf m. 2 Stummel m. vt stoßen. **stub out** ausdrücken.

stubborn ('stʌbən) adj 1 hartnäckig. 2 halsstarrig. **stubbornness** n Hartnäckigkeit f.

stud[1] (stʌd) n 1 Beschlagnagel m. 2 Kragenknopf m. vt 1 beschlagen. 2 bestreuen.

stud[2] (stʌd) n Gestüt neu.

student ('stju:dnt) n Student m. Studentin f.

studio ('stju:diou) n 1 Atelier neu. 2 Senderaum m. 3 Studio neu.

study ('stʌdi) n 1 Studium neu. 2 Studierzimmer neu. 3 Art Studie f. vt 1 studieren. 2 genau beobachten. vi studieren. **studious** adj 1 fleißig. 2 beflissen.

stuff (stʌf) n 1 Stoff m. 2 Zeug neu. vt 1 (voll-, aus-)stopfen. 2 cul füllen. **stuffing** n 1 cul Füllung f. 2 Polsterung f. **stuffy** adj 1 muffig. 2 inf spießig.

stumble ('stʌmbəl) vi stolpern. **stumble upon** stoßen auf. ~n Stolpern neu. **stumbling block** n Stein des Anstoßes m.

stump (stʌmp) n 1 Stumpf m. 2 sport Stab m. vt inf verblüffen. vi stapfen.

stun (stʌn) vt betäuben. **stunning** adj 1 betäubend. 2 inf sagenhaft, toll.

stung (stʌŋ) v see **sting.**

stunk (stʌŋk) v see **stink.**

stunt[1] (stʌnt) vt im Wachstum hindern.

stunt[2] (stʌnt) n 1 Kunststück neu. 2 Trick m.

stupid ('stju:pid) adj 1 dumm. 2 blöd. **stupidity** n Dummheit f.

sturdy ('stə:di) adj 1 derb. 2 stämmig.

stutter ('stʌtə) vi stottern. n Stottern neu.

sty (stai) n 1 Schweinestall m. 2 med Gerstenkorn neu.

style (stail) n Stil m. **in style** adv vornehm. **stylish** adj 1 stilvoll. 2 elegant.

stylus ('stailəs) n 1 Griffel m. 2 Grammophonnadel f.

subconscious (sʌb'kɔnʃəs) adj unterbewußt. n Unterbewußte neu.

subcontract (sʌbkən'trækt) n Nebenvertrag m.

subdue (səb'dju:) vt 1 unterwerfen. 2 dämpfen.

subject (n,adj 'sʌbdʒikt; v səb'dʒekt) n 1 pol

283

Untertan, Staatsangehörige(r) m. **2** Thema neu. **3** Fach neu. **4** Subjekt neu. adj **1** unterworfen. **2** abhängig. **subject to** vorbehaltlich. ~vt **1** unterwerfen. **2** unterziehen. **3** aussetzen. **subjective** adj subjektiv.

subjunctive (sǝb'dʒʌŋktiv) n Konjunktiv m. adj konjunktivisch.

sublime (sǝ'blaim) adj **1** erhaben. **2** inf großartig.

submachine-gun (sǝbmǝ'ʃiːŋgʌn) n Maschinenpistole f.

submarine (sʌbmǝ'riːn) n Unterseeboot neu. adj Untersee—.

submerge (sǝb'mɔːdʒ) vt **1** untertauchen. **2** überschwemmen. vi untertauchen.

submit (sǝb'mit) vt vorlegen. vi **1** sich unterwerfen. **2** sich ergeben. **submission** n **1** Vorlage f. **2** Unterwerfung f. **submissive** adj unterwürfig.

subnormal (sʌb'nɔːmǝl) adj unternormal, subnormal.

subordinate (sǝ'bɔːdinǝt) adj **1** untergeordnet. **2** Neben—. n Untergebene(r) m. vt **1** unterordnen. **2** unterwerfen. **subordination** n Unterordnung f.

subscribe (sǝb'skraib) vt **1** unterschreiben (mit). **2** (money) zeichnen. vi **subscribe to** abonnieren. **2** zustimmen. **subscriber** n Abonnent m. **subscription** n **1** Unterzeichnung f. **2** Abonnement neu. **3** Mitgliedsbeitrag m.

subsequent ('sʌbsikwǝnt) adj folgend. **subsequently** adv **1** hinterher. **2** anschließend.

subservient (sǝb'sǝːviǝnt) adj **1** unterwürfig. **2** dienlich.

subside (sǝb'said) vi **1** sich senken. **2** sich legen. **subside into** verfallen in. **subsidence** n Senkung f.

subsidiary (sǝb'sidiǝri) adj Hilfs—, Neben—.

subsidize ('sʌbsidaiz) vt (mit Geld) unterstützen, subventionieren. **subsidy** n **1** Beihilfe f. **2** Subvention f.

subsist (sǝb'sist) vi **1** leben. **2** bestehen. vt unterhalten. **subsistence** n **1** Lebensunterhalt m. **2** Dasein neu.

substance ('sʌbstǝns) n **1** Substanz f. **2** Wesen neu. **3** Inhalt m. **4** Wirklichkeit f. **substantial** adj **1** wesentlich. **2** wirklich. **3** solid. **substantive** adj **1** gram substantivisch. **2** selbständig. **3** fest. n Substantiv neu.

substitute ('sʌbstitjuːt) vt ersetzen. vi vertreten. n **1** Ersatz m. **2** Stellvertreter m. adj Ersatz—.

subtitle ('sʌbtait]) n Untertitel m.

subtle ('sʌt]) adj **1** fein(sinning). **2** spitzfindig. **subtlety** n **1** Feinheit f. **2** Spitzfindigkeit f.

subtract (sǝb'trækt) vt subtrahieren, abziehen. **subtraction** n Subtraktion f. Abzug m.

suburb ('sʌbǝːb) n Vorstadt f. Vorort m. **suburban** adj vorstädtisch, Vorstadt—.

subvert (sʌb'vǝːt) vt umstürzen. **subversive** adj umstürzlerisch, subversiv.

subway ('sʌbwei) n Fußgängerunterführung f.

succeed (sǝk'siːd) vi **1** Erfolg haben. **2** gelingen. **3** (nach)folgen. vt (nach)folgen. **success** n Erfolg m. **successful** adj erfolgreich. **be successful** Erfolg haben. **succession 1** Nachfolge, Reihenfolge f. **2** Erbfolge f. **3** Thronfolge f. **in succession** adv nacheinander. **successive** adj aufeinanderfolgend.

succulent ('sʌkjulǝnt) adj **1** saftig. **2** fleischig.

succumb (sǝ'kʌm) vi **1** unterliegen. **2** sich ergeben.

such (sʌtʃ) adj **1** solch. **2** derartig. **3** so. pron solch. **suchlike** adj dergleichen.

suck (sʌk) vt **1** saugen. **2** ansaugen. **3** (sweets, etc.) lutschen. **suck up to** sl sich einschmeicheln bei.

sucker ('sʌkǝ) n **1** Sauger m. **2** bot Sprößling m. **suckle** vt säugen, nähren.

suction ('sʌkʃǝn) n **1** Saugen neu. **2** Ansaugung f. adj Saug—.

Sudan (suː'dæn) n Sudan m. **Sudanese** adj sudanesisch. n Sudanese m.

sudden ('sʌdn) adj plötzlich.

suds (sʌdz) n pl (Seifen)Lauge f.

sue (suː) vt verklagen. vi klagen.

suede (sweid) n Wildleder neu. adj Wildleder—.

suet ('suːit) n **1** Nierenfett neu. **2** Talg m.

suffer ('sʌfǝ) vi leiden. vt erdulden, erleiden. **suffering** n Leiden neu.

sufficient (sǝ'fiʃǝnt) adj genug, genügend. **be sufficient** genügen.

suffix ('sʌfiks) n Nachsilbe f. Suffix neu.

suffocate ('sʌfǝkeit) vi,vt ersticken. **suffocation** n Erstickung f.

sugar ('ʃugǝ) n Zucker m. vt **1** zuckern. **2** versüßen. **sugar beet** n Zuckerrübe f. **sugar cane** n Zuckerrohr neu. **sugary** adj **1** zuckerig. **2** zuckersüß.

suggest (sǝ'dʒest) vt **1** vorschlagen. **2** andeuten. **3** eingeben. **suggestion** n **1** Vorschlag m. **2** Andeutung f. **3** Eingebung f. **suggestive** adj **1** andeutend. **2** zweideutig.

suicide ('suːisaid) n **1** Selbstmord m. **2** Selbstmörder m. **suicidal** adj selbstmörderisch.

suit (sju:t) n 1 (Herren)Anzug m. 2 (Damen)-Kostüm neu. 3 Bitte f. 4 game Farbe f. vi,vt passen. **suit oneself** tun, was einem beliebt. **suitcase** n (Hand)Koffer m. **suitable** adj passend, geeignet.

suite (swi:t) n 1 Gefolge neu. 2 Garnitur f. 3 mus Suite f. **suite of rooms** Zimmerflucht f.

sulk (sʌlk) vi schmollen. **sulky** adj schmollend. 2 mürrisch, launisch.

sullen ('sʌlən) adj verdrossen.

sulphur ('sʌlfə) n Schwefel m. **sulphuric** adj Schwefel–.

sultana (sʌl'ta:nə) n cul Sultanine f.

sultry ('sʌltri) adj 1 schwül. 2 stechend heiß.

sum (sʌm) n 1 Summe f. 2 Rechenaufgabe f. **do sums** rechnen. v **sum up** zusammenfassen.

summarize ('sʌməraiz) vt zusammenfassen. **summary** n Zusammenfassung f.

summer ('sʌmə) n Sommer m. **summertime** n Sommerzeit f.

summit ('sʌmit) n Gipfel m. **summit conference** n Gipfelkonferenz f.

summon ('sʌmən) vt 1 auffordern. 2 rufen. 3 vorladen. **summon up** aufbieten. **summons** n 1 Aufforderung f. 2 gerichtliche Vorladung f.

sun (sʌn) n Sonne f. **sunny** adj sonnig. v **sun oneself** sich sonnen.

sunbathe ('sʌnbeið) vi ein Sonnenbad nehmen.

sunburn ('sʌnbə:n) n Sonnenbrand m.

Sunday ('sʌndi) n Sonntag m.

sundial ('sʌndaiəl) n Sonnenuhr f.

sundry ('sʌndri) adj verschieden. n pl Verschiedenes neu.

sunflower ('sʌnflauə) n Sonnenblume f.

sung (sʌŋ) v see **sing**.

sunglasses ('sʌnglɑːsiz) n pl Sonnenbrille f.

sunk (sʌŋk) v see **sink**.

sunlight ('sʌnlait) n Sonnenlicht neu.

sunrise ('sʌnraiz) n Sonnenaufgang m.

sunset ('sʌnset) n Sonnenuntergang m.

sunshine ('sʌnʃain) n Sonnenschein m.

sunstroke ('sʌnstrouk) n Sonnenstich m.

suntan ('sʌntæn) n Sonnenbräune f.

super ('su:pə) adj inf prima, erstklassig.

superannuation (su:pərænju'eiʃən) n 1 Pensionierung f. 2 Ruhegehalt neu. Pension f.

superb (su:'pə:b) adj 1 prächtig. 2 herrlich.

superficial (su:pə'fiʃəl) adj oberflächlich.

superfluous (su:'pə:fluəs) adj überflüssig.

superhuman (su:pə'hju:mən) adj übermenschlich.

superimpose (su:pərim'pouz) vt auflegen.

superintendent (su:pərin'tendənt) n 1 Aufseher m. 2 Inspektor m. adj aufsichtführend.

superior (su'piəriə) adj 1 ober. 2 höher. 3 besser, überlegen. n 1 höherer Offizier m. 2 Vorgesetzte(r) m. 3 rel Superior m. **superiority** n Überlegenheit f.

superlative (su'pə:lətiv) adj 1 höchst. 2 gram superlativisch. n Superlativ m.

supermarket ('su:pəmɑ:kit) n Supermarkt m.

supernatural (su:pə'nætʃrəl) adj übernatürlich.

supersede (su:pə'si:d) vt 1 ersetzen. 2 verdrängen. 3 überholen.

supersonic (su:pə'sɔnik) adj Überschall–.

superstition (su:pə'stiʃən) n Aberglaube m. **superstitious** adj abergläubisch.

supervise ('su:pəvaiz) vt beaufsichtigen. **supervision** n 1 Beaufsichtigung f. 2 Aufsicht f. **supervisor** n Aufseher m.

supper ('sʌpə) n Abendessen, Abendbrot neu.

supple ('sʌpəl) adj biegsam, geschmeidig.

supplement ('sʌplimənt) n 1 Ergänzung f. 2 Nachtrag m. 3 Beilage f. vt ergänzen. **supplementary** adj 1 Ergänzungs–. 2 Nachtrags–.

supply (sə'plai) vt 1 (be)liefern, versorgen, besorgen. 2 decken. n 1 Versorgung f. 2 Vorrat m. 3 Angebot neu. 4 pl Vorräte m pl. **supply and demand** Angebot und Nachfrage. **supplier** n Lieferant m.

support (sə'pɔ:t) vt 1 (unter)stützen. 2 tragen. n 1 Unterstützung f. 2 Stütze f. Träger m.

suppose (sə'pouz) vt 1 annehmen. 2 voraussetzen. vi vermuten, glauben.

suppress (sə'pres) vt 1 unterdrücken. 2 hemmen. **suppression** n Unterdrückung f.

supreme (sə'pri:m) adj höchst, oberst.

surcharge ('sə:tʃɑ:dʒ) n Zuschlag m. vt mit Zuschlag belegen.

sure (ʃuə) adj 1 sicher, gewiß. 2 zuverlässig. **surely** adv 1 gewiß, sicherlich. 2 vermutlich. **surety** n 1 Bürge f. 2 Sicherheit f.

surf (sə:f) n Brandung f.

surface ('sə:fis) n 1 Oberfläche f. 2 Äußere neu. vi auftauchen. adj Oberflächen–.

surfeit ('sə:fit) n Übermaß neu. vt übersättigen.

surge (sə:dʒ) vi 1 branden. 2 aufwallen. 3 vorwärtsdrängen. n 1 Brandung f. 2 Flut f.

surgeon ('sə:dʒən) n Chirurg m. **surgery** n 1 Chirurgie f. 2 Sprechzimmer neu. 3 Sprechstunde f.

surly ('sə:li) adj mürrisch.

surmount (sə'maunt) vt 1 übersteigen. 2 überwinden.

surname ('sɔ:neim) n Zuname, Familienname m.

surpass (sɔ'pɑ:s) vt übertreffen.

surplus ('sɔ:plis) n Überschuß m. adj überschüssig.

surprise (sɔ'praiz) vt 1 überraschen. 2 ertappen. n Überraschung f. **surprised** adj überrascht, verblüfft.

surrealism (sɔ'riəlizəm) n Surrealismus m.

surrender (sɔ'rendə) vt 1 übergeben. 2 aufgeben. vi sich ergeben. n Übergabe f.

surreptitious (sʌrəp'tiʃəs) adj heimlich, verstohlen.

surround (sɔ'raund) vt 1 umgeben. 2 umzingeln, einschließen. **surrounding** adj umgebend. **surroundings** n pl Umgebung f.

survey (sɔ'vei) n 1 Überprüfung f. 2 Überblick m. 3 Landvermessung f. vt 1 (über)prüfen. 2 überblicken. 3 vermessen. **surveyor** (sɔ'veiə) n 1 Feldmesser, Geometer m. 2 Aufseher m.

survive (sɔ'vaiv) vt,vi überleben. **survivor** n Überlebende(r) m.

susceptible (sɔ'septəbəl) adj empfänglich, anfällig.

suspect (v sɔ'spekt; n,adj 'sʌspekt) vt 1 verdächtigen. 2 vermuten. 3 mißtrauen. n Verdächtigte(r) m. adj verdächtig.

suspend (sɔ'spend) vt 1 aufhängen. 2 verschieben. 3 einstellen. 4 unterbrechen. **suspense** n 1 Spannung f. 2 Ungewißheit f. **suspension** n 1 Aufhängung f. 2 mot Federung f. 3 Verschiebung f. 4 Einstellung f.

suspicion (sɔ'spiʃən) n 1 Verdacht m. 2 Vermutung f. 3 Spur f. **suspicious** adj 1 verdächtig. 2 mißtrauisch.

sustain (sɔ'stein) vt 1 aushalten. 2 unterstützen.

swab (swɔb) n 1 Tupfer m. 2 Scheuerlappen m. vt 1 aufwischen, scheuern. 2 betupfen.

Swabia ('sweibiə) n Schwaben neu. **Swabian** adj schwäbisch. n Schwabe m.

swagger ('swægə) vi 1 stolzieren. 2 prahlen. n 1 stolzierender Gang m. 2 Prahlerei f.

swallow¹ ('swɔlou) vt (ver)schlucken, verschlingen. vi schlucken. n Schluck m.

swallow² ('swɔlou) n zool Schwalbe f.

swam (swæm) v see **swim**.

swamp (swɔmp) n Sumpf m. vt überschwemmen.

swan (swɔn) n Schwan m.

swank (swæŋk) n inf Prahlerei, Angeberei f. vi inf aufschneiden, prahlen.

swap (swɔp) vt also **swop** (aus)tauschen. n Tausch m.

swarm (swɔ:m) n Schwarm m. vi 1 schwärmen. 2 wimmeln.

swastika ('swɔstikə) n Hakenkreuz neu.

swat (swɔt) vt zerquetschen, schlagen.

sway (swei) vi schwanken, schaukeln. vt 1 beeinflussen. 2 mitreißen. n 1 Herrschaft f. 2 Einfluß m.

swear* (sweə) vi 1 fluchen. 2 schwören. vt (be)schwören. **swearword** n Fluchwort neu.

sweat (swet) vi,vt schwitzen. n 1 Schweiß m. 2 inf Plackerei f. **sweater** n Pullover m.

swede (swi:d) n Steckrübe f.

Sweden ('swi:dn) n Schweden neu. **Swede** n Schwede m. **Swedish** ('swi:diʃ) adj schwedisch. n (language) Schwedisch neu.

sweep* (swi:p) vt 1 fegen, kehren. 2 durchstreifen. vi vorbeirauschen. n 1 Schornsteinfeger m. 2 Fegen neu.

sweet (swi:t) adj süß. n 1 Bonbon m. Süßigkeit f. 2 Nachtisch m. **sweetbread** n Bries m. **sweet corn** n Zuckermais m. **sweetheart** n Liebchen neu. Liebste(r) m. **sweet pea** n Wicke f. **sweeten** vt 1 süßen. 2 versüßen.

swell* (swel) vi (an)schwellen. adj sl 1 prima. 2 vornehm.

swelter ('sweltə) vi vor Hitze umkommen.

swept (swept) v see **sweep**.

swerve (swɔ:v) vi 1 (plötzlich) abbiegen. 2 ausweichen.

swift (swift) adj schnell, rasch.

swig (swig) inf n Schluck, Zug m. vt saufen, hinunterschlucken.

swill (swil) n 1 Schweinefutter neu. 2 Spülwasser neu. vt spülen.

swim* (swim) vi schwimmen. vt durchschwimmen. n Schwimmen neu. **swimming** n Schwimmen neu. **swimming costume** n Badeanzug m. **swimming pool** n Schwimmbad m. **indoor swimming pool** n Hallenbad neu.

swindle ('swindl) vt betrügen, beschwindeln. n Schwindel, Betrug m.

swine (swain) n Schwein neu.

swing* (swiŋ) vi,vt schwingen, schaukeln. n 1 Schwung m. 2 Schaukel f.

swipe (swaip) vt,vi hauen. n wilder Schlag m.

swirl (swɔ:l) vi,vt (herum)wirbeln. n Wirbel m.

swish (swiʃ) n 1 rascheln. 2 schwirren. vt schwirren lassen. adj schick, elegant.

Swiss (swis) adj schweizerisch. n Schweizer m.

switch (switʃ) n 1 Schalter m. 2 Umstellung f.

Wechsel m. 3 Rute f. vt 1 wechseln, tauschen. 2 umstellen. vi umstellen, übergehen. **switch off** ausschalten. **switch on** anschalten. **switchboard** n Schalttafel f.

Switzerland ('switsələnd) n Schweiz f.

swivel ('swivəl) (vi,)vt (sich) drehen.

swollen ('swoulən) adj geschwollen.

swoop (swu:p) vi sich stürzen, herabschießen. n plötzlicher Angriff, Sturz m.

swop (swɔp) v see **swap.**

sword (sɔ:d) n Schwert neu. **swordfish** n Schwertfisch m. **swordsman** n Fechter m.

swore (swɔ:) v see **swear.**

sworn (swɔ:n) adj 1 eidlich. 2 geschworen.

swot (swɔt) vi inf pauken. n Streber m.

swum (swʌm) v see **swim.**

swung (swʌŋ) v see **swing.**

sycamore ('sikəmɔ:) n bot Bergahorn m.

syllable ('siləbəl) n Silbe f.

syllabus ('siləbəs) n 1 Lehrplan m. 2 Verzeichnis neu.

symbol ('simbəl) n Symbol, Sinnbild neu. **symbolism** n 1 Symbolismus m. 2 Symbolik f. **symbolize** vt symbolisieren.

symmetry ('simitri) n Symmetrie f. Ebenmaß neu. **symmetrical** adj symmetrisch.

sympathy ('simpəθi) n 1 Mitgefühl, Mitleid neu. 2 Sympathie f. **sympathetic** adj 1 mitfühlend. 2 verständnisvoll. 3 wohlwollend. **sympathize** vi 1 mitfühlen, Mitleid haben. 2 übereinstimmen. 3 wohlwollen.

symphony ('simfəni) n Sinfonie, Symphonie f.

symposium (sim'pouziəm) n 1 Konferenz f. Symposion neu. 2 Tagungsbericht m.

symptom ('simptəm) n Symptom, Anzeichen neu. **symptomatic** adj symptomatisch.

synagogue ('sinəgɔg) n Synagoge f.

synchronize ('siŋkrənaiz) vt synchronisieren.

syndicate (n 'sindikət; v 'sindikeit) n Syndikat, Kartell neu. vt zu einem Syndikat vereinigen.

syndrome ('sindroum) n Syndrom neu.

synonym ('sinənim) n Synonym neu.

synopsis (si'nɔpsis) n Übersicht f. Abriß m.

syntax ('sintæks) n Syntax f. Satzbau m.

synthesis ('sinθəsis) n Synthese, Zusammensetzung f. **synthetic** adj synthetisch.

syphilis ('sifəlis) n Syphilis f.

Syria ('siriə) n Syrien neu. **Syrian** adj syrisch. n Syrier m.

syringe (si'rindʒ) n Spritze f.

syrup ('sirəp) n Sirup m.

system ('sistəm) n 1 System neu. 2 Verfahren

neu. Methode f. **systematic** adj systematisch, methodisch.

T

tab (tæb) n Aufhänger m. Etikett neu. **keep tabs on** kontrollieren.

tabby ('tæbi) n getigerte Katze f.

table ('teibəl) n 1 Tisch m. 2 Tafel f. 3 Liste f. **tablecloth** n Tischtuch neu. **tablemat** n Untersatz m. **tablespoon** n Eßlöffel m. **table tennis** n Tischtennis neu.

tablet ('tæblət) n 1 med Tablette f. 2 Tafel f.

taboo (tə'bu:) n Tabu neu. adj tabu, verboten.

tack (tæk) n 1 Zwecke f. 2 Heftstich m. 3 naut Lavieren neu. vi naut lavieren. vt (an)heften, befestigen.

tackle ('tækəl) n 1 Gerät neu. Ausrüstung f. 2 naut Takelwerk. 3 sport Angreifen neu. vt 1 angreifen. 2 angehen.

tact (tækt) n 1 Takt m. 2 Feingefühl neu. **tactful** adj taktvoll.

tactics ('tæktiks) n pl Taktik f. **tactical** adj taktisch.

tadpole ('tædpoul) n Kaulquappe f.

taffeta ('tæfitə) n Taft, Taffet m.

tag (tæg) n 1 Etikett neu. Anhängezettel m. 2 Stift m. vt anheften. **tag along** hinterherlaufen.

tail (teil) n 1 Schwanz m. 2 Ende neu. vt beschatten, verfolgen.

tailor ('teilə) n Schneider m. vt schneidern.

taint (teint) vt 1 beflecken. 2 verderben. n Makel, Fleck m.

take* (teik) vt 1 nehmen. 2 bringen. 3 ergreifen. 4 gewinnen. 5 fangen. 6 halten. **take in** 1 aufnehmen. 2 einschließen. **take off** vi abfliegen. vt ausziehen, abnehmen. **take-off** n aviat Abflug m. **take-over** n Übernahme f. **take place** stattfinden.

talcum powder ('tælkəm) n Talkpuder m.

tale (teil) n 1 Erzählung f. 2 Lüge f.

talent ('tælənt) n Begabung, Talent neu.

talk (tɔ:k) vi reden, sprechen. n 1 Rede f. 2 Gespräch neu. 3 Gerede, Geschwätz neu. **talkative** adj geschwätzig, gesprächig.

tall (tɔ:l) adj 1 groß. 2 hoch. 3 lang. **tall story** n Spinnerei, unglaubliche Geschichte f.

tally ('tæli) n Rechnung f. vi übereinstimmen.

talon ('tælən) n Kralle, Klaue f.

tambourine (tæmbə'ri:n) n Tambourin neu.

tame (teim) adj zahm, gezähmt. vt zähmen.

tamper

tamper (ˈtæmpə) vi **tamper with 1** sich einmischen in. **2** herumbasteln an.

tampon (ˈtæmpɒn) n Wattebausch, Tampon m.

tan (tæn) n **1** Lohe f. **2** Bräune f. adj gelbbraun. vt **1** gerben. **2** bräunen. vi braun werden.

tangent (ˈtændʒənt) n Tangente f.

tangerine (tændʒəˈriːn) n Mandarine f.

tangible (ˈtændʒəbəl) adj **1** greifbar. **2** fühlbar.

Tangier (tænˈdʒiə) n Tanger neu.

tangle (ˈtæŋgəl) n Wirrwarr m. Verwirrung f. vt **1** verwirren, verwickeln. **2** verknoten.

tank (tæŋk) n **1** Zisterne f. **2** Tank m. **3** mil Panzer m. v **tank up** tanken. **tanker** n Tanker m.

tankard (ˈtæŋkəd) n Kanne f. Bierkrug m.

tantalize (ˈtæntəlaiz) vt quälen.

tantrum (ˈtæntrəm) n Wutanfall m.

tap¹ (tæp) vt,vi klopfen. n Klopfen neu.

tap² (tæp) n Hahn, Zapfen m. vt **1** anzapfen. **2** (a telephone) anzapfen.

tape (teip) n **1** Band neu. **2** Tonband m. vt **1** auf Band aufnehmen. **2** mit einem Band befestigen. **tape measure** n Maßband neu. **tape-recorder** n Tonbandgerät neu.

taper (ˈteipə) vi,(vt) spitz zulaufen (lassen). n dünne Kerze f.

tapestry (ˈtæpistri) n Wandteppich m.

tapioca (tæpiˈoukə) n Tapioka f.

tar (tɑː) n Teer m. vt teeren.

tarantula (təˈræntjulə) n Tarantel f.

target (ˈtɑːgit) n **1** Zielscheibe f. **2** Ziel neu.

tariff (ˈtærif) n **1** Zolltarif m. **2** Preisliste f.

Tarmac (ˈtɑːmæk) n Tdmk Asphalt m.

tarnish (ˈtɑːniʃ) vt **1** trüben. **2** beflecken. vi sich trüben.

tarragon (ˈtærəgən) n Estragon m.

tart¹ (tɑːt) adj **1** sauer, herb. **2** beißend.

tart² (tæːt) n **1** (Obst)Torte f. **2** sl Dirne f.

tartan (ˈtɑːtn) n **1** karierter Wollstoff m. **2** kariertes Schottenmuster neu.

task (tɑːsk) n Aufgabe f. **take someone to task** jemanden zur Rede stellen.

Tasmania (tæzˈmeiniə) n Tasmanien neu.

tassel (ˈtæsəl) n Quaste f.

taste (teist) vt **1** schmecken. **2** kosten. vi schmecken. n **1** Geschmack m. **2** Kostprobe f. **tasty** adj schmackhaft.

tattoo¹ (təˈtuː) n mil Zapfenstreich m.

tattoo² (təˈtuː) vt tätowieren. n Tätowierung f.

taught (tɔːt) v see **teach**.

taunt (tɔːnt) vt sticheln. n Stichelei f.

Taurus (ˈtɔːrəs) n Stier m.

taut (tɔːt) adj **1** gespannt, straff. **2** steif.

tautology (tɔːˈtɒlədʒi) n Tautologie f.

tavern (ˈtævən) n Schenke, Kneipe f.

tax (tæks) n Steuer f. vt **1** besteuern. **2** anstrengen. **income tax** Einkommensteuer f. **tax evasion** n Steuerhinterziehung f.

taxi (ˈtæksi) n Taxi neu. vi aviat rollen.

tea (tiː) n **1** Tee m. **2** Teemahlzeit f. **high tea** n Abendbrot neu. **tea-bag** n Teebeutel m. **tea-break** n Teepause f. **tea-cloth** n Geschirrtuch neu. **teacup** n Teetasse f. **tealeaves** n pl Teesatz m. **teapot** n Teekanne f. **teaspoon** n Teelöffel m.

teach° (tiːtʃ) vt lehren, unterrichten. vi unterrichten. **teacher** n Lehrer m. Lehrerin f. **teacher training college** n pädagogische Hochschule f.

teak (tiːk) n **1** Tiekbaum m. **2** Tiekholz neu.

team (tiːm) n **1** sport Mannschaft f. **2** (of horses) Gespann neu. **3** Team neu. v **team up** sich zusammentun.

tear¹ (tiə) n Träne f. **tear-gas** n Tränengas neu.

tear°² (tɛə) vt (zer)reißen. vi **1** (zer)reißen. **2** zerren. **3** inf rasen. n Riß m.

tease (tiːz) vt **1** necken, ärgern, quälen. **2** tech (aus)zupfen, kämmen.

teat (tiːt) n **1** Brustwarze, Zitze f. **2** Lutscher m.

technical (ˈteknikəl) adj **1** technisch. **2** fachlich. **technician** n Techniker m. **technique** n Technik f. Verfahren neu. **technology** n Technologie. **2** Gewerbekunde f.

tedious (ˈtiːdiəs) adj langweilig, ermüdend.

tee¹ (tiː) n tech T-Stück neu.

tee² (tiː) n sport Abschlagestelle f. v **tee off** den Ball abschlagen.

teenage (ˈtiːneidʒ) adj jugendlich, Teenager—. **teenager** n Teenager m.

teetotal (tiːˈtoutl) adj antialkoholisch, abstinent. **teetotaller** n Abstinenzler m.

telegram (ˈteligræm) n Telegramm neu.

telegraph (ˈteligrɑːf) vt telegraphieren. n Telegraph m. **telegraph pole** n Telegraphenstange f.

telepathy (tiˈlepəθi) n Telepathie f.

telephone (ˈtelifoun) n Telephon neu. Fernsprecher m. vt,vi telephonieren, anrufen. **telephone box** Telephonzelle f. **telephone call** Anruf m.

telescope (ˈteliskoup) n Fernrohr, Teleskop neu.

televise (ˈtelivaiz) vt im Fernsehen übertragen. **television** n Fernsehen neu. **television (set)** n Fernsehapparat m.

288

telex ('teleks) n Fernschreibnetz neu.

tell (tel) vt 1 sagen, erzählen. 2 mitteilen. 3 erkennen. 4 unterscheiden. vi 1 erzählen. 2 Wirkung haben. **telltale** adj verräterisch. n Zuträger m.

temper ('tempə) n 1 Laune f. 2 Wut f. 3 tech Härtegrad m. vt 1 mildern. 2 tech härten. **temperament** n Temperament neu. **temperamental** adj temperamentvoll. **temperate** adj 1 mäßig. 2 mild. **temperature** n Temperatur f. **have a temperature** Fieber haben.

tempestuous (tem'pestjuəs) adj stürmisch.

temple[1] ('tempəl) n rel Tempel m.

temple[2] ('tempəl) n anat Schläfe f.

tempo ('tempou) n Tempo neu.

temporal ('tempərəl) adj 1 weltlich. 2 zeitlich. **temporary** adj vorübergehend, vorläufig.

tempt (tempt) vt 1 versuchen. 2 verlocken. **temptation** n 1 Versuchung f. 2 Anreiz m.

ten (ten) adj,n Zehn f. **tenth** adj zehnte.

tenacious (tə'neiʃəs) adj beharrlich, zäh.

tenant ('tenənt) n Mieter, Pächter m. **tenancy** n Mietverhältnis neu.

tend[1] (tend) vi 1 neigen. 2 führen, gehen.

tend[2] (tend) vt 1 pflegen, hüten. 2 bedienen. **tendency** ('tendənsi) n Neigung, Tendenz f.

tender[1] ('tendə) adj 1 weich, zart. 2 empfindlich. **tenderness** n Zartheit f.

tender[2] ('tendə) n anbieten. n Angebot neu.

tendon ('tendən) n Sehne f.

tendril ('tendril) n Ranke f.

tenement ('tenəmənt) n 1 Mietwohnung f. 2 Miethaus neu.

tennis ('tenis) n Tennis neu. **tennis court** n Tennisplatz m.

tenor ('tenə) n 1 mus Tenor m. 2 Sinn m.

tense[1] (tens) adj gespannt, straff. (vi),vt (sich) anspannen. **tension** n Spannung f.

tense[2] (tens) n gram Zeit(form) f.

tent (tent) n Zelt neu.

tentacle ('tentəkəl) n Fühler m.

tentative ('tentətiv) adj 1 Versuchs—. 2 zögernd. **tentatively** adv versuchsweise.

tenuous ('tenjuəs) adj 1 dürftig. 2 dünn.

tepid ('tepid) adj (lau)warm.

term (tə:m) n 1 Termin m. 2 educ Trimester, Semester neu. 3 Ausdruck m. 4 pl Bedingungen f pl. 5 pl (persönliche) Beziehungen f pl. 6 pl Zahlungsforderungen f pl. vt (be)nennen.

terminal ('tə:minl) adj letzt, End—. n 1 Endstation f. 2 (electricity) Pol m. 3 Flughafengebäude neu.

terminate ('tə:mineit) vt 1 (be)endigen. 2 kündigen. vi aufhören, zu Ende kommen.

terminology (tə:mi'nɔlədʒi) n Terminologie f.

terminus ('tə:minəs) n 1 Endpunkt m. 2 Endstation f.

terrace ('terəs) n 1 Terrasse f. 2 Häuserreihe f.

terrestrial (tə'restriəl) adj irdisch, Erd—.

terrible ('teribəl) adj schrecklich, furchtbar.

terrier ('teriə) n Terrier m.

terrify ('terifai) vt erschrecken. **terrific** adj 1 fürchterlich. 2 inf großartig.

territory ('teritri) n Gebiet neu.

terror ('terə) n 1 Entsetzen neu. Schrecken m. 2 pol Terror m. **terrorist** n Terrorist m. **terrorize** vt terrorisieren.

Terylene ('terili:n) n Tdmk Terylene neu.

test (test) vt 1 prüfen, testen. 2 untersuchen. n 1 Prüfung, Probe f. 2 Test m. **test-tube** n Reagenzglas neu.

testament ('testəmənt) n Testament neu.

testicle ('testikəl) n Hoden m.

testify ('testifai) vt bezeugen. vi Zeugnis ablegen.

testimony ('testiməni) n 1 Zeugenaussage f. 2 Beweis m. **testimonial** n 1 Empfehlungsschreiben neu. 2 Gedenkzeichen neu.

tether ('teðə) n Haltestrick m. **be at the end of one's tether** nicht mehr weiter wissen. ~vt anbinden.

Teutonic (tju:'tɔnik) adj teutonisch.

text (tekst) n Text, Wortlaut m. **textbook** n Lehrbuch neu.

textile ('tekstail) n 1 Webstoff m. 2 pl Textilien pl. adj gewebt, Textil—. **Web**—.

texture ('tekstʃə) n 1 Gewebe neu. 2 Struktur f.

Thames (temz) n Themse f.

than (ðən; stressed ðæn) conj,prep als.

thank (θæŋk) vt danken. **thanks** n Dank m. interj also **thank you** danke (schön), vielen Dank. **thankful** adj dankbar.

that (ðæt) adj,pron jener, jene, jenes, der, die, das. pron der, die, das, welch. conj 1 daß. 2 daß, damit. **in that** insofern als. **so that** so daß.

thatch (θætʃ) n Dachstroh neu. vi mit Stroh decken.

thaw (θɔ:) vt,vi (auf)tauen. n Tauwetter neu.

the (ðə; stressed ði:) def art 1 der, die, das. 2 pl die. **the...the** je...desto.

theatre ('θiətə) n 1 Theater, Schauspielhaus neu. 2 med Operationssaal m. **theatrical** adj 1 bühnenmäßig. 2 theatralisch.

theft (θeft) n Diebstahl m.

289

their (ðɛə) poss adj 3rd pers pl ihr.

theirs (ðɛəz) poss pron 3rd pers pl ihrer, der ihre or ihrige.

them (ðəm; stressed ðem) pron 3rd pers pl 1 sie. 2 ihnen. **themselves** pron 3rd pers pl 1 sich. 2 sich selbst. 3 sie selbst.

theme (θi:m) n Thema neu. **thematic** adj thematisch.

then (ðən; stressed ðen) adv 1 dann, da, darauf, damals. 2 dann, demnach, weiter. conj also, dann. **until then** bis dahin.

theology (θi'ɔlədʒi) n Theologie f. **theologian** n Theologe m. **theological** adj theologisch.

theorem ('θɪərəm) n Lehrsatz m. Theorem neu.

theory ('θɪəri) n Theorie f. **theoretical** adj theoretisch. **theorize** vi Theorien aufstellen.

therapy ('θerəpi) n Therapie f. Heilverfahren neu. **therapeutic** adj therapeutisch.

there (ðɛə) adv dort(hin), da(rin). interj na nu! na also! **over there** dort drüben. **there is** es gibt, es ist. **there are** es gibt, es sind. **thereabouts** adv 1 da herum, in der Gegend. 2 so etwa, ungefähr. **thereafter** adv danach. **thereby** adv dadurch. **therefore** adv deshalb, deswegen, infolgedessen. **thereupon** adv darauf, danach. **therewith** adv damit.

thermal ('θə:məl) adj also **thermic** 1 thermisch. 2 warm.

thermodynamics (θə:moudai'næmiks) n Thermodynamik f.

thermometer (θə'mɔmitə) n Thermometer neu. Temperaturmesser m.

thermonuclear (θə:mou'nju:kliə) adj thermonuklear.

Thermos ('θə:məs) n Tdmk also **thermos flask** Thermosflasche f.

thermostat ('θə:məstæt) n Thermostat m.

these (ði:z) adj,pron pl diese, die.

thesis ('θi:sis) n, pl **-ses** 1 These, Behauptung f. 2 Dissertation f.

they (ðei) pron 3rd pers pl sie. **they say** man sagt.

thick (θik) adj 1 dick, dicht. 2 sl dumm. **thick-skinned** adj dickfellig. **thicken** vt 1 dick machen. 2 eindicken. vi 1 dick werden. 2 sich verdichten. **thickness** n 1 Dicke f. 2 Dichtheit f.

thief (θi:f) n, pl **thieves** Dieb m. **stop thief!** haltet den Dieb!

thigh (θai) n (Ober)Schenkel m. **thigh-bone** n Oberschenkelknochen m.

thimble ('θimbəl) n Fingerhut m.

thin (θin) adj 1 dünn, mager. 2 spärlich. vt 1 dünn machen. 2 verdünnen. **thin-skinned** adj empfindlich. **thinness** n 1 Dünnheit f. 2 Dürftigkeit f.

thing (θiŋ) n 1 Ding neu. Sache f. 2 Geschöpf neu. **among other things** unter anderem. **no such thing** nichts dergleichen. **the very thing** genau das.

think* (θiŋk) vt,vi 1 denken. 2 sich vorstellen. 3 überlegen. **think of/about** denken an/über, halten von. **I think so** ich denke schon.

third (θə:d) adj dritte. n Drittel neu. **third party** n Dritte(r) m. **third-party insurance** n Haftpflichtversicherung f. **third person** n dritte Person f. **third-rate** adj drittrangig.

thirst (θə:st) n 1 Durst m. 2 Sehnsucht f. vi also **be thirsty** dürsten, Durst haben. **thirsty** adj 1 durstig. 2 begierig.

thirteen (θə:'ti:n) adj dreizehn. n Dreizehn f. **thirteenth** adj dreizehnte.

thirty ('θə:ti) adj dreißig. n Dreißig f. **thirtieth** adj dreißigste.

this (ðis) adj,pron dieser, diese, dies(es). **this minute** augenblicklich. **this morning** heute morgen.

thistle ('θisəl) n Distel f.

thorn (θɔ:n) n Dorn m. **thorny** adj dornig.

thorough ('θʌrə) adj 1 vollständig. 2 gründlich. **thoroughbred** n Vollblüter m. adj Vollblut—. **throughfare** n 1 Verkehrsader f. 2 Durchfahrt f. **thoroughly** adv 1 gründlich. 2 höchst.

those (ðouz) adj,pron pl jene, diejenigen.

though (ðou) conj 1 obgleich, obschon. 2 zwar. **as though** als ob.

thought[1] (θɔ:t) n 1 Denken neu. 2 Gedanke m. 3 Überlegung f. 4 Rücksicht f. **thoughtful** adj 1 rücksichtsvoll. 2 gedankenvoll. **thoughtless** adj 1 rücksichtslos. 2 gedankenlos. 3 unbesonnen.

thought[2] (θɔ:t) v see **think**.

thousand ('θauzənd) adj tausend. n Tausend neu. **thousandth** adj tausendste.

thrash (θræʃ) vt 1 prügeln. 2 besiegen.

thread (θred) n 1 Faden m. 2 tech Gewinde neu. vt einfädeln. vi sich durchziehen. **threadbare** adj fadenscheinig, abgedroschen.

threat (θret) n Drohung f. **threaten** (vt),vi (be)drohen.

three (θri:) adj drei. n Drei f. **three-cornered** adj dreieckig. **three-dimensional** adj dreidimensional. **threequarters** adj dreiviertel. **threesome** n Dreier neu. Dreiergruppe f.

thresh (θreʃ) vt (aus)dreschen.

threshold ('θreʃhould) n Schwelle f.

threw (θruː) v see **throw**.

thrift (θrift) n Sparsamkeit f. **thrifty** adj sparsam.

thrill (θril) n 1 Schauer m. 2 Sensation f. vt 1 erregen. 2 durchschauern. vi beben. **thriller** n 1 Sensationsfilm m. 2 Sensationsroman.

thrive (θraiv) vi gedeihen.

throat (θrout) n Kehle f. Schlund m.

throb (θrɔb) vi pochen, klopfen. n 1 Klopfen, Pochen neu. 2 Erregung f.

throne (θroun) n Thron m.

throng (θrɔŋ) n 1 Gedränge neu. Andrang m. 2 Menge f. vi (sich) drängen. vt bedrängen.

throttle ('θrɔtl) n Drosselventil neu. vt 1 erdrosseln. 2 ersticken.

through (θruː) prep 1 durch. 2 mit Hilfe (von). adv durch. **throughout** prep 1 überall in. 2 während. adv 1 überall. 2 durchaus.

throw* (θrou) vt werfen, schleudern. n Wurf m. **throw away** wegwerfen. **throw off** abwerfen. **throw out** hinauswerfen. **throw up** inf kotzen.

thrush (θrʌʃ) n zool Drossel f.

thrust* (θrʌst) vt 1 stoßen. 2 stecken. vi stoßen. n Stoß m.

thud (θʌd) n dumpfer Schlag m. vi dumpf aufschlagen.

thumb (θʌm) n Daumen m. vt durchblättern. **well-thumbed** adj (of a book) abgegriffen.

thump (θʌmp) n (dumpfer) Schlag, Puff m. vt schlagen. vi klopfen.

thunder ('θʌndə) n Donner m. vi donnern. **thunderstorm** n Gewitter neu.

Thuringia (θju'rindʒiə) n Thüringen neu.

Thursday ('θəːzdi) n Donnerstag m.

thus (ðʌs) adv so, also, auf diese Weise.

thwart (θwɔːt) vt durchkreuzen, vereiteln.

thyme (taim) n Thymian m.

thyroid ('θairɔid) adj 1 Schilddrüsen—. 2 Schildknorpel—. n 1 Schilddrüse f. 2 Schildknorpel m.

tiara (ti'aːrə) n Tiara f. Stirnreif m.

tick[1] (tik) vi 1 ticken. 2 inf funktionieren. vt abhaken. n 1 Ticken m. 2 Häkchen neu.

tick[2] (tik) n zool Zecke f.

ticket ('tikit) n 1 Karte f. 2 Fahrschein m. Fahrkarte f. 3 Zettel m. **return ticket** Rückfahrkarte f. **season ticket** Zeitkarte f. **single ticket** einfache Fahrkarte f. **ticket collector** n Bahnsteigschaffner m. **ticket-office** n Fahrkartenschalter m.

tickle ('tikəl) vt,vi kitzeln. **ticklish** adj 1 kitz(e)lig. 2 heikel.

tide (taid) n 1 Ebbe und Flut f. 2 Strom m. **high tide** Flut f. **low tide** Ebbe f. **tidemark** n Gezeitenmarke f.

tidy ('taidi) adj ordentlich, sauber. vt also **tidy up** aufräumen.

tie (tai) vt (ver)binden, schnüren. n 1 Schlips m. 2 Band neu. 3 sport Unentschieden neu.

tier (tiə) n Reihe f. Rang m.

tiger ('taigə) n Tiger m.

tight (tait) adj 1 fest. 2 dicht. 3 eng, knapp. 4 straff, gespannt. 5 sl beschwipst. **tight-fisted** adj knauserig. **tightrope** n Drahtseil neu. **tights** n pl Strumpfhose f. **tighten** vt 1 straff spannen. 2 enger machen. 3 zusammenziehen.

tile (tail) n 1 Dachziegel m. 2 Fliese f. vt mit Ziegeln or Fliesen decken.

till[1] (til) prep,conj bis.

till[2] (til) vt bebauen, bearbeiten.

till[3] (til) n Kasse, Geldschublade f.

tiller ('tilə) n Ruderpinne, Steuerstange f.

tilt (tilt) v(i),vt (sich) kippen, (sich) neigen. n Neigung f. Hang m.

timber ('timbə) n 1 Bauholz, Nutzholz neu. 2 Balken m. adj holzern.

time (taim) n 1 Zeit f. 2 Mal neu. 3 mus Takt m. 4 pl Zeitalter neu. vi 1 die Zeit bestimmen. 2 die Zeit messen von. **time bomb** n Zeitbombe f. **timetable** n 1 Stundenplan m. 2 Fahrplan m.

timid ('timid) adj 1 furchtsam. 2 scheu.

tin (tin) n 1 Zinn, (Weiß)Blech neu. 2 Dose, Büchse f. adj zinnern. vt 1 konservieren. 2 verzinnen. **tin-opener** n Büchsenöffner m.

tinge (tindʒ) n 1 Färbung f. 2 Anhauch m. vt 1 färben. 2 einen Anhauch geben.

tingle ('tiŋgəl) vi 1 prickeln. 2 klingen. n 1 Klingen neu. 2 Prickeln neu.

tinker ('tiŋkə) n Kesselflicker m. vi basteln.

tinkle ('tiŋkəl) vi klingeln. n Geklingel neu.

tinsel ('tinsəl) n 1 Flitter m. 2 Lametta neu.

tint (tint) n Tönung f. vt leicht tönen.

tiny ('taini) adj winzig.

tip[1] (tip) n Spitze f. vt mit einer Spitze versehen. **tiptoe** vi auf Zehenspitzen gehen.

tip[2] (tip) vt,vi umkippen. n Abladeplatz m.

tip[3] (tip) n 1 Trinkgeld neu. 2 Wink, Tip m. vt 1 ein Trinkgeld geben. 2 einen Wink geben.

tipsy ('tipsi) adj beschwipst.

tire ('taiə) vt 1 müde machen. 2 erschöpfen. vi müde werden. **tired** adj 1 müde. 2 erschöpft. **be tired of something** etwas satt haben.

tissue ('tiʃu:) n **1** (feines) Gewebe neu. **2** Papiertaschentuch neu.

title ('taitl) n Titel m. vt betiteln.

to (tə; stressed tu:) prep **1** zu. **2** vor. **3** nach. **4** an. **5** gegen. **6** auf. conj um zu. **to and fro** adv hin und her. **to-do** n Getue neu.

toad (toud) n Kröte f. **toadstool** n Giftpilz m.

toast[1] (toust) n Toast m. vt **1** toasten, rösten. **2** wärmen.

toast[2] (toust) n Trinkspruch m. vt trinken auf.

tobacco (tə'bækou) n Tabak m. **tobacconist** n Tabakhändler m.

toboggan (tə'bɔgən) n Rodelschlitten m. vi rodeln.

today (tə'dei) adv heute, heutzutage.

toddler ('tɔdlə) n kleines Kind neu.

toe (tou) n Zehe f. **toenail** n Zehennagel m.

toffee ('tɔfi) n Karamelle f. Toffee neu.

together (tə'geðə) adv **1** zusammen, miteinander. **2** zugleich.

toil (tɔil) vi arbeiten, sich mühen. n Mühe, Plackerei f.

toilet ('tɔilət) n **1** Toilette f. **2** Klo(sett) neu. **toilet paper** n Klosettpapier neu.

token ('toukən) n **1** Zeichen neu. **2** Andenken neu. **3** Gutschein m.

told (tould) v see **tell.**

tolerate ('tɔləreit) vt **1** dulden. **2** aushalten. **3** tolerieren. **tolerance** n Duldsamkeit, Toleranz f. **tolerant** adj tolerant.

toll[1] (toul) vt,vi läuten, schlagen.

toll[2] (toul) n **1** Wegegeld neu. Zoll m. **2** Tribut m. **tollgate** n Schlagbaum m.

tomato (tə'mɑ:tou) n, pl **-oes** Tomate f.

tomb (tu:m) n Grab(mal) neu.

tomorrow (tə'mɔrou) adv morgen. **the day after tomorrow** übermorgen. **tomorrow morning** morgen früh. **tomorrow week** morgen in acht Tagen.

ton (tʌn) n Tonne f.

tone (toun) n **1** Ton m. **2** Tönung f. vt abtönen.

tongs (tɔŋz) n pl Zange f.

tongue (tʌŋ) n **1** anat Zunge f. **2** Sprache f. **hold one's tongue** den Mund halten. **tongue in cheek** ironisch. **tongue-tied** adj stumm. **tongue-twister** n Zungenbrecher m.

tonic ('tɔnik) adj **1** tonisch, stärkend. **2** mus Grundton— . n **1** Stärkungsmittel neu. **2** mus Grundton m. **tonic water** n Sprudel(wasser) m, neu.

tonight (tə'nait) adv heute abend or nacht.

tonsil ('tɔnsəl) n Mandel f. **tonsilitis** n Mandelentzündung f.

too (tu:) adv **1** (all)zu. **2** sehr. **3** auch, dazu. **all too** viel zu, allzu.

took (tuk) v see **take.**

tool (tu:l) n Werkzeug, Gerät neu.

tooth (tu:θ) n, pl **teeth** Zahn m. **toothache** n Zahnweh neu. Zahnschmerzen m pl. **toothbrush** n Zahnbürste f. **toothpaste** n Zahnpasta f. **toothpick** n Zahnstocher m.

top[1] (tɔp) n **1** Spitze f. Wipfel, Gipfel m. **2** Oberfläche f. Oberteil m. **3** Deckel m. adj **1** oberst, höchst. **2** best. vt **1** übertreffen. **2** köpfen. **3** anführen. **top hat** n Zylinder m. **top-heavy** adj kopflastig.

top[2] (tɔp) n Kreisel m.

topaz ('toupæz) n Topaz m.

topic ('tɔpik) n Gegenstand m. Thema neu. **topical** adj **1** aktuell. **2** med örtlich.

topography (tə'pɔgrəfi) n Topographie f.

topple ('tɔpəl) vi kippen, stürzen. **topple down** or **over** umkippen, niederstürzen.

topsoil ('tɔpsɔil) n Ackerkrume f.

topsy-turvy (tɔpsi'tə:vi) adj,adv inf das Oberste zuunterst, drunter und drüber.

torch (tɔ:tʃ) n **1** Taschenlampe f. **2** Fackel f.

tore (tɔ:) v see **tear.**

torment ('tɔ:mənt) n Qual f. vt quälen.

torn (tɔ:n) v see **tear.**

tornado (tɔ:'neidou) n Tornado, Wirbelsturm m.

torpedo (tɔ:'pi:dou) n Torpedo m. vt torpedieren.

torrent ('tɔrənt) n **1** Sturzbach m. **2** Wolkenbruch m. **3** Strom m. **4** Wortschwall m.

torso ('tɔ:sou) n Torso m.

tortoise ('tɔ:təs) n Schildkröte f.

tortuous ('tɔ:tʃuəs) adj gewunden, krumm.

torture ('tɔ:tʃə) n Folter, Marter, Qual f. vt foltern, martern, quälen.

Tory ('tɔ:ri) n britische(r) Konservative(r) m.

toss (tɔs) vt **1** (hoch)werfen. **2** schütteln. vi **1** sich unruhig bewegen. **2** schlingern. n Wurf m.

tot[1] (tɔt) n Schluck m.

tot[2] (tɔt) vt **tot up** zusammenrechnen.

total ('toutl) adj **1** gesamt. **2** ganz, völlig, total. n **1** Ganze neu. **2** Summe f. Gesamtbetrag m. vi sich belaufen auf. **totalitarian** adj totalitär.

totem ('toutəm) n Totem neu. **totem pole** n Totempfahl m.

totter ('tɔtə) vi schwanken, wanken.

touch (tʌtʃ) vt (an-, be-)rühren. vi in Berührung kommen, berühren. **touch down** aviat landen. **touch up** auffrischen. ~n **1** Berührung

f. 2 Tastsinn m. 3 Spur f. Hauch m. 4 Hand f. **touchy** adj reizbar, überempfindlich.

tough (tʌf) adj 1 zäh. 2 hart. **toughen** vt zäh(er) machen, abhärten.

toupee ('tu:pei) n Toupet neu.

tour (tuə) n Tour, Reise, Rundfahrt f. Rundgang m. vi bereisen, besuchen. vi reisen. **tourism** n Fremdenverkehr, Tourismus m. **tourist** n Tourist m.

tournament ('tuənəmənt) n Tournier neu.

tow (tou) vt 1 (ab)schleppen. 2 bugsieren. **towrope** n Schlepptau neu.

towards (tə'wɔ:dz) prep also **toward** 1 gegen. 2 nach (...zu), auf...zu or hin. 3 entgegen.

towel ('tauəl) n Handtuch, Badetuch nou.

tower ('tauə) n Turm m. vi sich erheben, emporragen. **tower-block** n Hochhaus neu.

town (taun) n Stadt f. **town clerk** n Stadtsyndikus m. **town hall** n Rathaus neu. **town-planning** n Städteplanung f.

toxic ('tɔksik) adj giftig, toxisch.

toy (tɔi) n Spielzeug neu. v **toy with** spielen mit.

trace (treis) n Spur f. vt 1 folgen, nachgehen. 2 zurückverfolgen. 3 durchzeichnen.

track (træk) n 1 Weg, Pfad m. 2 (of a railway) Gleis neu. 3 Spur f. 4 Sport Bahn f. vt (ver)folgen, nachspüren. **tracksuit** n Trainingsanzug m.

tract[1] (trækt) n 1 Strecke f. 2 anat System neu. 3 Zeitraum m.

tract[2] (trækt) n rel Traktat m,neu.

tractor ('træktə) n Schlepper, Traktor m.

trade (treid) n 1 Handel m. 2 Gewerbe f. Geschäft neu. vi handeln. vt austauschen. **trademark** n Schutzmarke f. **tradesman** n Ladenbesitzer, Händler m. **trade union** n Gewerkschaft f.

tradition (trə'diʃən) n 1 Tradition, Überlieferung f. 2 Brauch m. **traditional** adj traditionell.

traffic ('træfik) n 1 Verkehr m. 2 comm Handel m. **traffic jam** n Verkehrsstockung f. **traffic lights** n pl Verkehrsampel f. **traffic warden** n Verkehrsaufseher m.

tragedy ('trædʒədi) n Trauerspiel neu. Tragödie f. **tragic** adj tragisch.

trail (treil) n 1 Spur f. 2 Schweif m. vt 1 nachschleppen. 2 verfolgen. vi schleifen. **trailer** n 1 mot Anhänger m. 2 (of a film) Vorschau m.

train (trein) n 1 Zug m. 2 Reihe f. 3 Gefolge neu. vt 1 schulen, ausbilden. 2 sport trainie-

ren. vi sport trainieren. **trainee** n Lehrling, Praktikant m.

traitor ('treitə) n Verräter m.

tram (træm) n Straßenbahn f.

tramp (træmp) vi 1 wandern. 2 trampeln, treten. n 1 Landstreicher m. 2 Wanderung f.

trample ('træmpəl) vt zertrampeln. vi herumtreten.

trampoline ('træmpəli:n) n Trampoline f.

trance (trɑ:ns) n 1 Verzückung f. 2 Trance f.

tranquil ('træŋkwil) adj still, ruhig, gelassen. **tranquillity** n 1 Ruhe f. 2 Gelassenheit f. **tranquillizer** n Beruhigungsmittel neu.

transact (træn'zækt) vt durchführen. **transaction** n Geschäft neu. Verhandlung f.

transatlantic (trænzət'læntik) adj transatlantisch.

transcend (træn'send) vt übersteigen, überschreiten.

transcribe (træn'skraib) vt 1 umschreiben. 2 mus umsetzen.

transfer (v træns'fə:; n 'trænsfə:) vt 1 übertragen. 2 versetzen. 3 (money) überweisen. n 1 Übertragung f. 2 Versetzung f. 3 Überweisung f. 4 Versand m. 5 Abziehbild neu.

transform (træns'fɔ:m) vt verwandeln, umformen. **transformation** n Verwandlung f. **transformer** n tech Transformator m.

transfuse (træns'fju:z) vt 1 med übertragen. 2 durchtränken. **transfusion** n 1 med Blutübertragung f. 2 Durchtränkung f.

transistor (træn'zistə) n Transistor m. **transistor** (**radio**) Transistorradio neu.

transit ('trænsit) n 1 Durchgang m. 2 Durchgangsverkehr m. **in transit** unterwegs.

transition (træn'ziʃən) n Übergang m.

transitive ('trænsitiv) adj transitiv.

translate (trænz'leit) vt übersetzen, übertragen.

translucent (trænz'lu:sənt) adj 1 nicht ganz durchsichtig. 2 lichtdurchlässig.

transmit (trænz'mit) vt 1 (by radio, etc.) (über)senden, übertragen. 2 überliefern. **transmitter** n Sender m. **transmission** n 1 (by radio, etc.) Sendung f. 2 tech Getriebe neu. 3 Übersendung f.

transparent (træns'pærənt) adj durchsichtig.

transplant (v træns'plɑ:nt; n 'trænsplɑ:nt) vt 1 umpflanzen. 2 med transplantieren. n 1 Umpflanzung f. 2 Transplantation f.

transport (v træns'pɔ:t; n,adj 'trænspɔ:t) vt befordern, transportieren. n 1 Beförderung f. Spedition f. Transport m. Versand m. 2 Begeisterung f. adj Transport—.

293

transpose (træns'pouz) vt **1** umsetzen. **2** mus transponieren.

trap (træp) n Falle f. vt (ein)fangen, erwischen. **trapdoor** n Falltür f.

trapeze (trə'pi:z) n Trapez neu.

trash (træʃ) n **1** wertloses Zeug neu. Kitsch m. **2** Unsinn m. **3** Abfall m.

trauma ('trɔ:mə) n Trauma neu.

travel ('trævəl) vi reisen. vt bereisen. n **1** Reise f. Reisen neu. **2** pl Reisen f pl. **travel agency** n Reisebüro neu. **traveller** n Reisende(r) m. **traveller's cheque** n Reisescheck m.

trawl (trɔ:l) n Schleppnetz neu. vi mit dem Schleppnetz fischen. **trawler** n Schleppnetz-fischerboot neu. Trawler m.

tray (trei) n Tablett, Servierbrett neu.

treachery ('tretʃəri) n Verrat m. Untreue f. **treacherous** adj **1** verräterisch. **2** gefährlich.

treacle ('tri:kəl) n Sirup m. Melasse f.

tread (tred) vi treten. vt betreten. n **1** Schritt, Tritt m. **2** mot Reifenprofil neu.

treason ('tri:zən) n Verrat m. **high treason** Hochverrat m.

treasure ('treʒə) n Schatz m. vt **1** (hoch)-schätzen. **2** anhäufen. **treasurer** n Schatz-meister, Kassenwart m. **treasury** n **1** Schatz-kammer f. **2** Finanzministerium neu.

treat (tri:t) vt **1** behandeln. **2** freihalten. n Genuß m. Vergnügen neu. **treatment** n Behandlung f.

treatise ('tri:tiz) n Abhandlung f.

treaty ('tri:ti) n Vertrag m. Abkommen neu.

treble ('trebəl) adj **1** dreifach. **2** mus Sopran—. n mus Sopran, Diskant m.

tree (tri:) n Baum m.

trek (trek) vi trecken. n lange Reise f. Treck m.

trellis ('trelis) n **1** Gitter neu. **2** Spalier neu.

tremble ('trembəl) vi zittern, beben.

tremendous (tri'mendəs) adj **1** furchtbar. **2** inf riesig, gewaltig.

tremor ('tremə) n Zittern, Beben neu.

trench (trentʃ) n Graben m. vt mit Gräben durchziehen.

trend (trend) n **1** Neigung, Tendenz f. Trend m. **2** Mode f.

trespass ('trespəs) n **1** unerlaubtes Betreten neu. **2** Vergehen neu. vi **1** widerrechtlich betreten. **2** verstoßen.

trestle ('tresəl) n Bock m. Gestell neu.

trial ('traiəl) n **1** Gerichtsverfahren neu. Prozeß m. **2** Versuch m. Probe f. **3** Prüfung f.

triangle 'traiæŋgəl) n **1** Dreieck neu. **2** mus Triangel m. **triangular** adj dreieckig.

tribe (traib) n (Volks)Stamm m. **tribesman** n Stammesangehörige(r).

tribunal (trai'bju:nl) n **1** Gericht, Tribunal neu. **2** Gerichtshof m.

tributary ('tribjutəri) adj **1** zinspflichtig. **2** zufließend. n Nebenfluß m.

tribute ('tribju:t) n **1** Tribut m. **2** Lob neu.

trick (trik) n **1** Streich m. **2** Trick, Kniff m. **3** game Stich m. vt überlisten, betrügen. **tricky** adj **1** schlau. **2** verwickelt, heikel.

trickle ('trikəl) vi tröpfeln. n Tröpfeln neu.

tricycle ('traisikəl) n Dreirad neu.

tried (traid) adj erprobt.

trifle ('traifəl) n **1** Kleinigkeit f. **2** cul (süßer) Auflauf m. v **trifle with** spielen, spielen.

trigger ('trigə) n Abzug, Drücker m. vt auslösen.

trill (tril) vi trillern. n Triller m.

trim (trim) adj **1** nett, hübsch. **2** ordentlich, in Ordnung. vt **1** beschneiden. **2** garnieren. **3** naut trimmen. n **1** Schmuck m. **2** Ordnung f.

trio ('triou) n Trio neu.

trip (trip) n **1** Reise f. **2** Ausflug m. vi stolpern. vt ein Bein stellen.

tripe (traip) n **1** cul Kaldaunen f pl. **2** inf Quatsch m.

triple ('tripəl) adj dreifach. (vi),vt (sich) ver-dreifachen. **triplet** n **1** lit Dreireim m. **2** Dreiergruppe f. **3** Drilling m.

tripod ('traipɔd) n Dreifuß m.

trite (trait) adj abgedroschen, platt.

triumph ('traiʌmf) n Triumph m. vi triumphie-ren, siegen. **triumphant** adj triumphierend, jubelnd.

trivial ('triviəl) adj trivial, unbedeutend.

trod (trɔd) v see **tread.**

trodden ('trɔdn) v see **tread.**

trolley ('trɔli) n **1** (Hand)Karren m. **2** Kon-taktrolle f. **trolley bus** n Obus m.

trombone (trɔm'boun) n Posaune f.

troop (tru:p) n **1** Truppe f. **2** Trupp m. Schar f. vi sich sammeln, sich scharen.

trophy ('troufi) n Trophäe f. Siegeszeichen neu. Preis m.

tropic ('trɔpik) n **1** Wendekreis m. **2** pl Tropen pl.

trot (trɔt) vi traben, trotten. n Trab m. **trotter** n **1** Traber m. **2** pl cul Hammelfüße, Schweins-füße m pl.

trouble ('trʌbəl) n **1** Unruhe, Schwierigkeit f. **2** Kummer m. Unglück neu. **3** tech Störung f. **in trouble** in Verlegenheit or Not. ~vt **1**

beunruhigen, stören. **2** belästigen. *vi* sich bemühen. **troublemaker** *n* Unruhestifter, Störenfried *m*. **troublesome** *adj* lästig, störend.

trough (trɔf) *n* Mulde *f*. Trog *m*.

troupe (truːp) *n* (Theater)Truppe *f*.

trousers ('trauzəz) *n pl* Hose *f*. Hosen *f pl*.

trout (traut) *n* Forelle *f*.

trowel ('trauəl) *n* **1** Maurerkelle *f*. **2** Ausheber *m*.

truant ('truənt) *n* **1** Schulschwänzer *m*. **2** Müßiggänger *m*. *adj* **1** schulschwänzend. **2** müßig. **play truant** (die Schule) schwänzen.

truce (truːs) *n* Waffenstillstand *m*.

truck (trʌk) *n* **1** Güterwagen *m*. **2** Lastkraftwagen *m*.

trudge (trʌdʒ) *vi* sich (mühsam) schleppen.

true (truː) *adj* **1** wahr, richtig. **2** echt, wirklich. **3** treu. **truly** *adv* **1** wirklich, tatsächlich. **2** aufrichtig. **yours truly** Hochachtungsvoll.

truffle ('trʌfəl) *n* Trüffel *f*.

trump (trʌmp) *n* Trumpf *m*. *vt* stechen.

trumpet ('trʌmpit) *n* Trompete *f*.

truncheon ('trʌntʃən) *n* Knüttel, Knüppel *m*.

trunk (trʌŋk) *n* **1** *bot* Stamm *m*. **2** *anat* Rumpf *m*. **3** *zool* Rüssel *m*. **4** (Schrank)Koffer *m*. **5** *pl* Badehose *f*.

trust (trʌst) *vt* (ver)trauen, sich verlassen auf. *vi* **1** vertrauen, sich verlassen. **2** (zuversichtlich) hoffen. *n* **1** Vertrauen *neu*. **2** *comm* Kartell *neu*. **3** *law* Pflegschaft *f*. **trustworthy** *adj* zuverlässig, vertrauenswürdig. **trustee** *n* Treuhänder, Vermögensverwalter *m*.

truth (truːθ) *n* Wahrheit *f*. **truthful** *adj* **1** ehrlich, wahrhaftig. **2** wahrheitsgemäß.

try (trai) *vt* **1** versuchen. **2** probieren. **3** *law* verhören. **4** proben. *n* Versuch *m*. **trying** *adj* **1** unangenehm, lästig. **2** anstrengend.

tsar (tsɑː) *n* Zar *m*.

T-shirt *n* Trikot, Sporthemd *neu*.

tub (tʌb) *n* **1** Faß *neu*. **2** (Bade)Wanne *f*. **tubby** *adj inf* rundlich, dickbauchig.

tuba ('tjuːbə) *n* Tuba *f*.

tube (tjuːb) *n* **1** Rohr *neu*. Röhre *f*. **2** Schlauch *m*. **3** Tube *f*. **4** Untergrundbahn, U-Bahn *f*.

tuber ('tjuːbə) *n bot* Knolle *f*.

tuberculosis (tjuːbəːkjuˈlousis) *n* Tuberkulose *f*.

tuck (tʌk) *n* **1** Falte *f*. Umschlag *m*. **2** *sl* Süßigkeiten *f pl*. *vt* **1** falten. **2** einschlagen. **tuck away** wegstecken. **tuck in** *inf* zugreifen, einhauen.

Tuesday ('tjuːzdi) *n* Dienstag *m*.

tuft (tʌft) *n* Büschel *neu*.

tug (tʌg) *vt* **1** zerren, ziehen. **2** *naut* schleppen. *vi* ziehen. *n* **1** Ruck *m*. **2** *naut* Schlepper *m*. **tug of war** *n* Tauziehen *neu*.

tuition (tjuːˈiʃən) *n* Unterricht *m*.

tulip ('tuːlip) *n* Tulpe *f*.

tumble ('tʌmbəl) *vi* **1** (hin)fallen. **2** purzeln. *vt* (um)stürzen. *n* Sturz, Fall *m*. **tumbler** *n* Becher *m*. Trinkglas *neu*.

tummy ('tʌmi) *n inf* Magen, Bauch *m*.

tumour ('tjuːmə) *n* Geschwulst *f*. Tumor *m*.

tumult ('tjuːmʌlt) *n* Tumult *m*. Getümmel *neu*. Aufruhr *m*.

tuna ('tjuːnə) *n* Thunfisch *m*.

tune (tjuːn) *n* **1** Melodie *f*. **2** Stimmung *f*. *vt* stimmen. **in tune** (gut) gestimmt. **out of tune** verstimmt. **tuneful** *adj* melodisch.

tunic ('tjuːnik) *n* **1** Bluse *f*. Überkleid *neu*. **2** Soldatenrock *m*.

Tunisia (tjuːˈniziə) *n* Tunesien *neu*.

tunnel ('tʌnl) *n* Tunnel *m*.

tunny ('tʌni) *n* see **tuna**.

turbine ('təːbain) *n* Turbine *f*.

turbot ('təːbət) *n* Steinbutt *m*.

turbulent ('təːbjulənt) *adj* **1** unruhig. **2** aufgeregt, stürmisch, turbulent.

turf (təːf) *n* **1** Rasen *m*. **2** Torf *m*. **3** Pferderennen *neu*. *vt* mit Rasen belegen. **turf accountant** *n sport* Buchmacher *m*.

Turk (təːk) *n* Türke *m*.

turkey ('təːki) *n* Truthahn *m*. Pute *f*.

Turkey ('təːki) *n* Türkei *f*. **Turkish** *adj* türkisch. *n* (language) Türkisch *neu*. **Turkish bath** *n* Schwitzbad *neu*.

turmeric ('təːmərik) *n* Gelbwurz *f*.

turmoil ('təːmɔil) *n* Aufruhr, Tumult *m*.

turn (təːn) *vt* **1** drehen. **2** machen, verwandeln. **3** (um)wenden. **4** lenken, abbringen. **5** werden. *vi* **1** sich drehen. **2** werden. **3** sich umwenden. **4** gehen. **turn down** ablehnen. **turn off** **1** abbiegen. **2** abstellen, abdrehen. **turn on** anstellen, einschalten. **turn up** auftauchen. ~*n* **1** Drehung *f*. **2** Wendung *f*. **3** Runde *f*. **4** Versuch *m*. **5** Veränderung *f*. **turning** *n* **1** Drehen *neu*. **2** Kurve *f*. **3** Ecke *f*. **4** Querstraße *f*. **turnover** *n* **1** Umschwung *f*. **2** *comm* Umsatz *m*. **3** *cul* (Apfel)Tasche *f*. **turnstile** *n* Drehkreuz *neu*. **turntable** *n* Plattenteller *m*.

turnip ('təːnip) *n* (weiße) Rübe *f*.

turpentine ('təːpəntain) *n* Terpentin *f*.

turquoise ('təːkwɔiz) *n* Türkis *m*.

turret ('tʌrət) *n* Türmchen *neu*. Turm *m*.

turtle ('təːtl) *n* Schildkröte *f*.

tusk (tʌsk) *n* Stoßzahn *m*.

tussle (ˈtʌsəl) *n* Kampf *m*. Balgerei *f*. *vi* kämpfen, sich balgen.

tutor (ˈtjuːtə) *n* **1** *law* Vormund *m*. **2** (at a university) Tutor *m*. **3** Privatlehrer *m*. *vt* Unterricht geben.

tweed (twiːd) *n* Tweed *m*.

tweezers (ˈtwiːzəz) *n pl* Pinzette *f*.

twelve (twelv) *adj* zwölf. *n* Zwölf *f*. **twelfth** *adj* zwölfte.

twenty (ˈtwenti) *adj* zwanzig. *n* Zwanzig *f*. **twentieth** *adj* zwanzigste.

twice (twais) *adv* zweimal.

twiddle (ˈtwidl) *vt* müßig herumdrehen, spielen mit.

twig (twig) *n* Zweig *m*.

twilight (ˈtwailait) *n* Zwielicht *neu*. Dämmerung *f*.

twin (twin) *n* Zwilling *m*. *adj* doppelt, Zwillings—.

twine (twain) *n* Bindfaden *m*. Zwirn *m*. *vt* (ineinander) verflechten, winden. *vi* winden, sich verflechten.

twinge (twindʒ) *n* **1** (stechender) Schmerz *m*. **2** Gewissensbiß *m*.

twinkle (ˈtwiŋkəl) *vi* blinken, funkeln. *n* Blinzeln, Funkeln *neu*.

twirl (twəːl) *vi,vt* zwirbeln, herumwirbeln. *n* Wirbel *m*.

twist (twist) *vt* **1** (zusammen)drehen, winden. **2** verdrehen. **3** biegen. *vi* sich drehen, sich winden. *n* **1** Drehung, Windung *f*. **2** Biegung *f*. **3** Verdrehung *f*.

twitch (twitʃ) *vi* zucken. *vt* zwicken. *n* Ruck *m*. Zucken *neu*.

twitter (ˈtwitə) *vi* zwitschern. *n* Gezwitscher *neu*.

two (tuː) *adj* **1** zwei. **2** beide. *n* Zwei *f*. **in twos** zu zweit. **in two** entzwei. **two-faced** *adj* **1** doppelgesichtig. **2** heuchlerisch. **twosome** *n* Paar, Pärchen *neu*. **two-way** *adj* **1** Doppel—. **2** Gegen—.

tycoon (taiˈkuːn) *n inf* Industriekapitän *m*.

type (taip) *n* **1** Typ *m*. Art, Sorte *f*. **2** Klasse, Kategorie *f*. **3** Muster *neu*. **4** Type *f*. *vi,vt* tippen, mit der Maschine schreiben. **typewriter** *n* Schreibmaschine *f*. **typical** *adj* typisch, kennzeichnend. **typify** *vt* verkörpern, typisch sein für. **typist** *n* Maschinenschreiberin *f*.

typhoid (ˈtaifɔid) *n* Typhus *m*.

typhoon (taiˈfuːn) *n* Taifun *m*.

tyrant (ˈtairənt) *n* Tyrann *m*. **tyranny** *n* Tyrannei *f*.

tyre (ˈtaiə) *n* Reifen *m*.

Tyrol (tiˈroul) *n* Tirol *neu*.

U

ubiquitous (juːˈbikwitəs) *adj* allgegenwärtig.

udder (ˈʌdə) *n* Euter *neu*.

ugly (ˈʌgli) *adj* häßlich. **ugliness** *n* Häßlichkeit *f*.

ukulele (juːkəˈleːli) *n* Ukulele *neu*.

ulcer (ˈʌlsə) *n* Geschwür *neu*.

ulterior (ʌlˈtiəriə) *adj* **1** jenseitig. **2** verborgen.

ultimate (ˈʌltimət) *adj* **1** äußerst. **2** letzt. **ultimatum** *n* Ultimatum *neu*.

ultraviolet (ʌltrəˈvaiələt) *adj* ultraviolett.

umbrella (ʌmˈbrelə) *n* Regenschirm *m*.

umlaut (ˈumlaut) *n* Umlaut *m*.

umpire (ˈʌmpaiə) *n* Schiedsrichter *m*.

umpteen (ʌmpˈtiːn) *adj inf* zahllos. **umpteen times** x-mal.

unable (ʌnˈeibəl) *adj* unfähig.

unacceptable (ʌnəkˈseptəbəl) *adj* unannehmbar, nicht akzeptabel.

unaccompanied (ʌnəˈkʌmpnid) *adj* unbegleitet.

unanimous (juːˈnaniməs) *adj* einstimmig.

unarmed (ʌnˈɑːmd) *adj* unbewaffnet.

unattractive (ʌnəˈtræktiv) *adj* reizlos.

unavoidable (ʌnəˈvɔidəbəl) *adj* unvermeidlich.

unaware (ʌnəˈwɛə) *adj* **1** nicht bewußt. **2** ahnungslos. **unawares** *adv* unversehens, unerwartet. **catch unawares** überraschen.

unbalanced (ʌnˈbælənst) *adj* **1** unausgeglichen, unstet. **2** (of mind) gestört.

unbearable (ʌnˈbɛərəbəl) *adj* unerträglich.

unbelievable (ʌnbiˈliːvəbəl) *adj* unglaublich, unglaubhaft.

unbend (ʌnˈbend) *vi* **1** sich entspannen. **2** gerade werden. *vt* entspannen, losmachen. **unbending** *adj* unnachgiebig.

unbreakable (ʌnˈbreikəbəl) *adj* unzerbrechlich.

unbridled (ʌnˈbraidld) *adj* zügellos.

uncalled-for *adj* unnötig, unangebracht.

uncanny (ʌnˈkæni) *adj* unheimlich.

uncertain (ʌnˈsəːtn) *adj* **1** unbestimmt. **2** ungewiß. **3** unzuverlässig.

uncle (ˈʌŋkəl) *n* Onkel *m*.

uncomfortable (ʌnˈkʌmftəbəl) *adj* **1** unbequem. **2** unbehaglich.

unconscious (ʌnˈkɔnʃəs) *adj* **1** bewußtlos, ohnmächtig. **2** unbewußt. *n* Unbewußte *neu*.

unconventional (ʌnkən'venʃənəl) *adj* unkonventionell, ungezwungen.

uncooked (ʌn'kukt) *adj* ungekocht, roh.

uncouth (ʌn'ku:θ) *adj* grob, roh, ungebildet.

uncover (ʌn'kʌvə) *vt* 1 aufdecken. 2 bloßlegen.

uncut (ʌn'kʌt) *adj* 1 ungeschnitten. 2 (of a gem) ungeschliffen.

undecided (ʌndi'saidid) *adj* unentschlossen.

undeniable (ʌndi'naiəbəl) *adj* unleugbar.

under ('ʌndə) *prep* unter. *adv* (nach) unten.

under age *adj,adv* minderjährig.

undercharge (ʌndə'tʃa:dʒ) *vt,vi* zu wenig berechnen.

undercoat ('ʌndəkout) *n* (of paint) Untergrund, Grundanstrich *m*.

undercover ('ʌndəkʌvə) *adj* Geheim—.

undercut (ʌndə'kʌt) *vt comm* unterbieten.

underdeveloped (ʌndədi'veləpd) *adj* unterentwickelt.

underdone (ʌndə'dʌn) *adj* nicht gargekocht.

underestimate (ʌndər'estimeit) *vt* unterschätzen.

underfoot (ʌndə'fut) *adv* unter den Füßen.

undergo* (ʌndə'gou) *vt* 1 erleben. 2 erdulden. 3 sich unterziehen.

undergraduate (ʌndə'grædjuət) *n* Student *m*. Studentin *f*. Nichtgraduierter *m*.

underground (*adv* ʌndə'graund; *adj,n* 'ʌndəgraund) *adv,adj* 1 unterirdisch. 2 geheim. *n* Untergrund *m*. **underground** (**railway**) *n* Untergrundbahn, U-Bahn *f*.

undergrowth ('ʌndəgrouθ) *n* Unterholz *neu*.

underhand (ʌndə'hænd) *adj* hinterlistig.

underline (ʌndə'lain) *vt* unterstreichen.

undermine (ʌndə'main) *vt* untergraben.

underneath (ʌndə'ni:θ) *adv* unten, darunter. *prep* unter(halb).

underpants ('ʌndəpænts) *n pl* Unterhose *f*.

underpass ('ʌndəpɑ:s) *n* Unterführung *f*.

underprivileged (ʌndə'prividʒd) *adj* benachteiligt, unterprivilegiert.

understand* (ʌndə'stænd) *vt* verstehen, begreifen. **understanding** *n* Verständnis *neu*. Verstand *m*. *adj* verständnisvoll.

understate (ʌndə'steit) *vt* untertreiben.

understudy ('ʌndəstʌdi) *n* 1 Ersatzschauspieler *m*. 2 Ersatzmann *m*.

undertake* (ʌndə'teik) *vt* 1 unternehmen. 2 zusagen. **undertaker** *n* Leichenbestatter *m*. **undertaking** *n* 1 Unternehmen *neu*. 2 Versprechen *neu*.

undertone ('ʌndətoun) *n* 1 gedämpfte Stimme *f*. 2 Unterton *m*.

underwear ('ʌndəwɛə) *n* Unterwäsche *f*.

underworld ('ʌndəwə:ld) *n* Unterwelt *f*.

underwrite* ('ʌndərait) *vt* 1 unterschreiben. 2 *comm* versichern, übernehmen.

undesirable (ʌndi'zaiərəbəl) *adj* unerwünscht.

undo* (ʌn'du:) *vt* 1 aufmachen. 2 aufknöpfen, losbinden. 3 rückgängig machen. 4 ruinieren.

undoubted (ʌn'dautid) *adj* unbezweifelt.

undress (ʌn'dres) *(vi),vt* (sich) ausziehen.

undue (ʌn'dju:) *adj* 1 unangemessen, ungebührlich. 2 unnötig. 3 unzulässig.

undulate ('ʌndʒəleit) *vi* wogen, wellen.

unearth (ʌn'ə:θ) *vt* 1 ausgraben. 2 ans Licht bringen. **unearthly** *adj* 1 unirdisch. 2 unheimlich.

uneasy (ʌn'i:zi) *adj* unruhig, ängstlich.

uneducated (ʌn'edjukeitid) *adj* ungebildet.

unemployed (ʌnim'plɔid) *adj* 1 arbeitslos. 2 unbeschäftigt. **the unemployed** *n* die Arbeitslosen *pl*. **unemployment** *n* Arbeitslosigkeit *f*.

unequal (ʌn'i:kwəl) *adj* ungleich.

uneven (ʌn'i:vən) *adj* 1 uneben. 2 unausgeglichen.

unfair (ʌn'fɛə) *adj* unfair, ungerecht.

unfaithful (ʌn'feiθfəl) *adj* treulos, untreu.

unfamiliar (ʌnfə'miliə) *adj* nicht vertraut.

unfit (ʌn'fit) *adj* 1 untauglich. 2 unfähig.

unfold (ʌn'fould) *(vi),vt* (sich) entfalten.

unfortunate (ʌn'fɔ:tʃunət) *adj* unglücklich.

unfurnished (ʌn'fə:niʃt) *adj* 1 nicht ausgerüstet. 2 unmöbliert.

ungrateful (ʌn'greitfəl) *adj* undankbar.

unhappy (ʌn'hæpi) *adj* unglücklich.

unhealthy (ʌn'helθi) *adj* ungesund.

unicorn ('ju:nikɔ:n) *n* Einhorn *neu*.

uniform ('ju:nifɔ:m) *adj* gleich(förmig), einförmig. *n* Uniform *f*.

unify ('ju:nifai) *vt* vereinheitlichen, vereinigen.

unilateral (ju:ni'lætərəl) *adj* einseitig.

uninhabited (ʌnin'hæbitid) *adj* unbewohnt.

uninterested (ʌn'intrəstid) *adj* uninteressiert.

union ('ju:niən) *n* 1 Vereinigung, Verbindung *f*. 2 Union *f*. 3 Verein *m*. 4 Einheit *f*.

Union Jack *n* britische Nationalflagge *f*.

unique (ju:'ni:k) *adj* 1 einzigartig, einmalig. 2 einzig.

unison ('ju:nizən) *n* 1 Einklang *m*. 2 *mus* Unisono *neu*.

unit ('ju:nit) *n* Einheit *f*.

unite (ju:'nait) *(vi),vt* (sich) vereinigen *or* vereinen. **unity** *n* 1 Einheit *f*. 2 Einigkeit *f*.

United Kingdom n das Vereinigte Königreich neu.

United States of America n die Vereinigten Staaten m pl.

universe ('juːnivəːs) n Weltall, Universum neu. **universal** adj 1 allgemein, universal. 2 allumfassend.

university (juːni'vəːsiti) n Universität, Hochschule f.

unjust (ʌn'dʒʌst) adj ungerecht.

unkempt (ʌn'kempt) adj zerzaust, ungepflegt.

unkind (ʌn'kaind) adj unfreundlich, herzlos.

unknown (ʌn'noun) adj unbekannt.

unlawful (ʌn'lɔːfəl) adj ungesetzlich.

unless (ʌn'les) conj 1 es sei denn, daß. 2 wenn...nicht.

unlike (ʌn'laik) adj unähnlich, ungleich. prep im Gegensatz zu. **unlikely** adj,adv unwahrscheinlich.

unload (ʌn'loud) vt ausladen, entladen.

unlock (ʌn'lɔk) vt aufschließen.

unlucky (ʌn'lʌki) adj unglücklich.

unnatural (ʌn'nætʃərəl) adj unnatürlich.

unnecessary (ʌn'nesəsri) adj unnötig.

unofficial (ʌnə'fiʃəl) adj nicht amtlich, inoffiziell.

unorthodox (ʌn'ɔːθədɔks) adj unorthodox.

unpack (ʌn'pæk) vt,vi auspacken.

unpleasant (ʌn'plezənt) adj 1 unangenehm. 2 unfreundlich.

unpopular (ʌn'pɔpjulə) adj unbeliebt.

unprecedented (ʌn'presidentid) adj einmalig, unerhört, beispiellos.

unravel (ʌnrævəl) vt entwirren.

unreasonable (ʌn'riːzənəbəl) adj unvernünftig, unsinnig.

unrelenting (ʌnri'lentiŋ) adj unerbittlich.

unreliable (ʌnri'laiəbəl) adj unzuverlässig.

unrest (ʌn'rest) n Unruhe f.

unruly (ʌn'ruːli) adj unbändig, ungestüm.

unscrew (ʌn'skruː) vt abschrauben, losschrauben.

unsettle (ʌn'setl) vt verwirren, durcheinanderbringen, ins Wanken bringen.

unsightly (ʌn'saitli) adj unansehnlich.

unsound (ʌn'saund) adj 1 ungesund. 2 unsicher. 3 unsolid(e). 4 falsch.

unsteady (ʌn'stedi) adj 1 wackelig. 2 unstet, unbeständig.

unsuccessful (ʌnsək'sesfəl) adj erfolglos.

untangle (ʌn'tæŋgəl) vt entwirren.

untidy (ʌn'taidi) adj unordentlich.

untie (ʌn'tai) vt aufbinden, auflösen.

until (ʌn'til) prep,conj bis. **not until** nicht vor, erst.

untrue (ʌn'truː) adj falsch, unwahr.

unusual (ʌn'juːʒuəl) adj ungewöhnlich, seltsam.

unwell (ʌn'wel) adj unwohl.

unwind (ʌn'waind) vt abwinden. vi 1 sich abwickeln. 2 inf sich entspannen.

unwrap (ʌn'ræp) vt auswickeln.

up (ʌp) adv 1 auf(wärts). 2 hinauf. 3 empor. 4 nach oben. 5 oben, hoch. prep auf. **be up against** gegenüberstehen. **what's up?** inf was ist los?

upbringing ('ʌpbriŋiŋ) n Erziehung f.

upheaval (ʌp'hiːvəl) n Erhebung f. Umsturz m.

uphill (ʌp'hil) adv bergauf. adj 1 ansteigend. 2 anstrengend.

uphold (ʌp'hould) vt aufrecht(er)halten.

upholster (ʌp'houlstər) vt polstern. **upholstery** n Polsterung f.

upkeep ('ʌpkiːp) n Instandhaltung f.

uplift (v ʌp'lift; n 'ʌplift) vt emporheben. n Hebung f.

upon (ə'pɔn) prep auf.

upper ('ʌpə) adj ober, höher. **upper class** n Oberklasse f. **upper house** n Oberhaus neu. **uppermost** adj oberst, höchst. adv am höchsten.

upright ('ʌprait) adj 1 aufrecht. 2 aufrichtig.

uprising (ʌp'praiziŋ) n Aufstand m. Erhebung f.

uproar ('ʌprɔː) n Aufruhr, Lärm m.

uproot (ʌp'ruːt) vt entwurzeln.

upset* (v, adj ʌp'set; n 'ʌpset) vt 1 umkippen. 2 (um)stürzen. 3 bestürzen. adj 1 umgekippt. 2 außer Fassung. n 1 Umsturz m. 2 Verstimmung f.

upshot ('ʌpʃɔt) n (End)Ergebnis neu. **in the upshot** am Ende.

upside down (ʌpsaid 'daun) adv 1 mit dem Kopf nach unten. 2 drunter und drüber.

upstairs (ʌp'stɛəz) adv 1 (nach) oben. 2 die Treppe hinauf. adj ober.

upstream (ʌp'striːm) adv stromaufwärts.

upward ('ʌpwəd) adj ansteigend. adv aufwärts. **upwards** adv aufwärts.

uranium (ju'reiniəm) n Uran neu.

Uranus (ju'reinəs) n Uranus m.

urban ('əːbən) adj städtisch.

urge (əːdʒ) vt 1 (auf)drängen. 2 dringend bitten. n Drang m.

urgent ('əːdʒənt) adj dringend.

urine ('juərin) n Urin, Harn m. **urinate** vi urinieren.

urn (əːn) n Urne f.

verb

us (ʌs) pron 1st pers pl uns.

usage ('juːsidʒ) n 1 Brauch m. 2 Gebrauch m.

use (vt juːz; vi,n juːs) vt 1 benutzen, gebrauchen. 2 anwenden. 3 ausnutzen. vi pflegen. n 1 Gebrauch m. 2 Anwendung f. 3 Nutzen neu. **useful** adj nützlich, brauchbar. **useless** adj 1 nutzlos. 2 unbrauchbar.

usher ('ʌʃə) n Platzanweiser m. vt (her-, hin)einführen. **usherette** n Platzanweiserin f.

usual ('juːʒuəl) adj gewöhnlich, üblich.

usurp (juːˈzəːp) vt an sich reißen. vi sich widerrechtlich bemächtigen. **usurper** n 1 Usurpator, Thronräuber m. 2 Eindringling m.

utensil (juːˈtensəl) n Gerät neu.

uterus ('juːtərəs) n Gebärmutter f.

utility (juːˈtiliti) n Nützlichkeit f.

utmost ('ʌtmoust) adj also **uttermost** äußerst, höchst. n äußerste neu.

utter[1] ('ʌtə) vt äußern, sagen.

utter[2] ('ʌtə) adj 1 äußerst. 2 endgültig. 3 vollkommen.

V

vacant ('veikənt) adj 1 leer. 2 frei. 3 unbewohnt. 4 ausdruckslos. **vacancy** n 1 freie or offene Stelle f. 2 Leere f. **vacate** vt 1 räumen. 2 niederlegen. **vacation** n Ferien pl.

vaccine ('væksiːn) n Impfstoff neu. **vaccinate** vt impfen.

vacillate ('væsəleit) vi 1 schwanken. 2 zaudern.

vacuum ('vækjuəm) n Vakuum neu. **vacuum cleaner** n Staubsauger m. **vacuum flask** n Thermosflasche f.

vagina (vəˈdʒainə) n anat Scheide f.

vagrant ('veigrənt) n Landstreicher m. adj wandernd.

vague (veig) adj vage, ungenau, undeutlich.

vain (vein) adj 1 eitel. 2 leer. **in vain** umsonst.

valiant ('væliənt) adj tapfer, mutig.

valid ('vælid) adj gültig. **validity** n Gültigkeit f.

valley ('væli) n Tal neu.

value ('væljuː) n Wert m. vt 1 bewerten. 2 (hoch)schätzen. **valuable** adj wertvoll. **valuables** n pl Wertsachen f pl.

valve ('vælv) n 1 Ventil neu. 2 Klappe f.

vampire ('væmpaiə) n Vampir, Blutsauger m.

van (væn) n Lieferwagen, Lastwagen m.

vandal ('vændl) n Vandale m. **vandalism** n Vandalismus m.

vanilla (vəˈnilə) n Vanille f.

vanish ('væniʃ) vi verschwinden.

vanity ('væniti) n Eitelkeit f.

vapour ('veipə) n Dunst, Dampf m.

variety (vəˈraiəti) n 1 Vielfalt, Auswahl f. 2 Art f. **variety show** n Varietévorstellung f.

various ('vɛəriəs) adj verschieden(artig).

varnish ('vaːniʃ) n 1 Firnis m. 2 Politur f. 3 Lack m. vt 1 firnissen. 2 polieren. 3 lackieren.

vary ('vɛəri) vt 1 (ab-, ver-)ändern. 2 wechseln. vi variieren. **variable** adj 1 veränderlich, wechselnd. 2 tech regelbar, variabel. **variant** adj abweichend. **variation** n 1 Veränderung f. Wechsel m. 2 Variation f.

vase (vaːz) n Vase f.

vasectomy (væˈsektəmi) n Vasektomie f.

vast (vaːst) adj 1 riesig. 2 ausgedehnt.

vat (væt) n Faß neu. Bottich m.

Vatican ('vætikən) n Vatikan m.

vault[1] (vɔːlt) n 1 Gewölbe neu. 2 Stahlkammer f. 3 Grabgewölbe neu. Gruft f.

vault[2] (vɔːlt) vi springen. vt überspringen.

veal (viːl) n Kalbfleisch neu.

veer (viə) (vi,)vt 1 drehen, (sich) wenden. vi umschwenken.

vegetable ('vedʒtəbəl) n 1 Gemüse neu. 2 Pflanze f. **vegetarian** n Vegetarier m. adj vegetarisch. **vegetation** n Vegetation f.

vehement ('viːimənt) adj heftig, vehement.

vehicle ('viːikəl) n 1 Fahrzeug neu. 2 Vehikel neu.

veil (veil) n Schleier m. vt verschleiern.

vein (vein) n 1 anat Vene f. 2 Ader f.

velocity (vəˈlɔsiti) n Geschwindigkeit f.

velvet ('velvit) n Samt m. adj 1 samtartig. 2 sanft.

vendetta (venˈdetə) n Blutrache f.

veneer (viˈniə) n 1 Furnier neu. vt furnieren.

venerate ('venəreit) vt (ver)ehren, hochachten.

venereal disease (viˈniəriəl) n Geschlechtskrankheit f.

Venetian (viˈniːʃən) adj venezianisch. **Venetian blind** n Jalousie f.

vengeance ('vendʒəns) n Rache f.

Venice ('venis) n Venedig neu.

venison ('venisən) n Wildbret, Rehfleisch neu.

venom ('venəm) n Gift neu.

vent[1] (vent) n 1 Luftloch neu. 2 Öffnung f.

vent[2] (vent) vt freien Lauf lassen, auslassen.

ventilate ('ventileit) vt (durch)lüften.

venture ('ventʃə) n 1 Wagnis neu. 2 Unternehmen neu. vt wagen.

Venus ('viːnəs) n Venus f.

verb (vəːb) n Zeitwort, Verb(um) neu.

verdict ('vɜ:dikt) n 1 law Urteilsspruch, Wahrspruch m. 2 Urteil neu.

verge (vɜ:dʒ) n Rand m. vi grenzen.

verify ('verifai) vt 1 prüfen. 2 bestätigen. 3 beglaubigen.

vermin ('vɜ:min) n Ungeziefer neu.

vermouth ('vɜ:məθ) n Wermut m.

vernacular (və'nækjulə) n 1 Landessprache f. 2 Umgangssprache f. 3 Jargon m.

versatile ('vɜ:sətail) adj 1 vielseitig, wendig. 2 wandelbar.

verse (vɜ:s) n 1 Vers m. Strophe f. 2 Poesie f.

version ('vɜ:ʃən) n 1 Gestaltung f. 2 Auffassung, Version f.

vertebrate ('vɜ:tibreit) n Wirbeltier neu.

vertical ('vɜ:tikəl) adj senkrecht, vertikal.

verve (vɜ:v) n Begeisterung f. Feuer neu.

very ('veri) adv sehr. adj 1 genau. 2 bloß. 3 derselbe.

vessel ('vesəl) n 1 naut Schiff neu. 2 Gefäß neu.

vest (vest) n Unterhemd neu.

vestment ('vestmənt) n Gewand neu.

vestry ('vestri) n Sakristei f.

vet (vet) inf n Tierarzt m. vt untersuchen.

veteran ('vetərən) n Veteran m.

veterinary surgeon ('vetrinəri) n Tierarzt m.

veto ('vi:tou) n 1 Veto neu. Einspruch m. 2 Einspruchsrecht neu. vt verbieten.

vex (veks) vt ärgern, plagen. **vexation** n 1 Ärger m. 2 Belästigung f.

via (vaiə) prep über, via.

viable ('vaiəbəl) adj 1 lebensfähig. 2 praktisch, ausführbar.

viaduct ('vaiədʌkt) n Viadukt m. Brücke f.

vibrate (vai'breit) vi schwingen, vibrieren. **vibration** n Schwingung, Vibration f.

vicar ('vikə) n Vikar, Pfarrer m.

vicarious (vi'kɛəriəs) adj 1 aus zweiter Hand. 2 stellvertretend.

vice[1] (vais) n 1 Laster neu. 2 Fehler m.

vice[2] (vais) n Schraubstock m.

vice-chancellor n Vizekanzler m.

vice-president n Vizepräsident m.

vice versa ('vɜ:sə) adj umgekehrt.

vicinity (vi'siniti) n Nähe, Nachbarschaft f.

vicious ('viʃəs) adj 1 bösartig. 2 lasterhaft.

victim ('viktim) n Opfer neu. **victimize** vt 1 (auf)opfern. 2 quälen, belästigen.

Victorian (vik'tɔ:riən) adj 1 viktorianisch. 2 prüde. n Viktorianer m.

victory ('viktri) n Sieg m. **victorious** adj siegreich.

video-tape ('vidiouteip) n Magnetbildband neu.

Vienna (vi'enə) n Wien neu. **Viennese** adj wienerisch. n Wiener m.

Vietnam (viet'næm) n Vietnam neu. **Vietnamese** adj vietnamesisch. n Vietnamese m.

view (vju:) n 1 Aussicht f. 2 Ansicht f. 3 Einstellung f. **with a view to** zu dem Zweck. **view-finder** n Sucher m. ~vt 1 anschauen. 2 besichtigen.

vigil ('vidʒil) n Nachtwache f. **vigilant** adj wachsam.

vigour ('vigə) n 1 Kraft, Lebenskraft f. 2 Intensität f. **vigorous** adj 1 kräftig. 2 lebhaft.

vile (vail) adj 1 widerlich. 2 gemein.

villa ('vilə) n 1 Landhaus neu. 2 Villa f.

village ('vilidʒ) n Dorf neu. **villager** n Dorfbewohner m.

villain ('vilən) n Schurke m.

vindictive (vin'diktiv) adj rachsüchtig.

vine (vain) n 1 Rebe f. 2 Weinstock m. **vineyard** n Weinberg m.

vinegar ('vinigə) n Essig m.

vintage ('vintidʒ) n Lese f. adj hervorragend.

vinyl ('vainil) n Vinyl neu.

viola (vi'oulə) n Viola f.

violate ('vaiəleit) vt 1 verletzen, brechen. 2 schänden.

violence ('vaiələns) n 1 Gewalt(tätigkeit) f. 2 Heftigkeit f. **violent** adj 1 gewalttätig, gewaltsam. 2 heftig.

violet ('vaiələt) adj violett. n 1 bot Veilchen neu. 2 Violett neu.

violin (vaiə'lin) n Violine, Geige f. **violinist** n Violinist m.

viper ('vaipə) n Viper, Natter f.

virgin ('vɜ:dʒin) n Jungfrau f. adj also **virginal** jungfräulich.

Virgo ('vɜ:gou) n Jungfrau f.

virile ('virail) adj männlich.

virtue ('vɜ:tju:) n 1 Tugend f. 2 Vorzug m. **by virtue of** kraft. **virtual** adj eigentlich, tatsächlich. **virtuous** adj tugendhaft.

virus ('vairəs) n Virus m,neu.

visa ('vi:zə) n Visum neu. Einreisebewilligung f.

viscount ('vaikaunt) n Vicomte m.

vision ('viʒən) n 1 Sehvermögen neu. 2 Erscheinung f. 3 Anblick m. **visible** adj 1 sichtbar. 2 offensichtlich.

visit ('vizit) vt besuchen. n Besuch m.

visual ('viʒuəl) adj visuell, Seh—. **visualize** vt sich (klar) vorstellen.

vital ('vaitl̩) adj 1 lebenswichtig. 2 Lebens—. 3 vital. **vitality** n Lebenskraft, f.

ward

vitamin ('vitəmin) *n* Vitamin *neu.*
vivacious (vai'veiʃəs) *adj* lebhaft, munter.
vivid ('vivid) *adj* lebhaft, deutlich.
vixen ('viksən) *n* zool Füchsin *f.*
vocabulary (və'kæbjuləri) *n* 1 Wortschatz *m.* Vokabular *neu.* 2 Wörterverzeichnis *neu.*
vocal ('voukəl) *adj* 1 mündlich, stimmlich. 2 stimmhaft. **vocal chords** *n pl* Stimmbänder *neu pl.*
vocation (vou'keiʃən) *n* 1 Berufung *f.* 2 Beruf *m.*
vodka ('vodkə) *n* Wodka *m.*
voice (vois) *n* Stimme *f. vt* äußern.
void (void) *adj* 1 leer. 2 unwirksam. 3 ungültig. *n* 1 Leere *f.* 2 Lücke *f.*
volatile ('volətail) *adj* 1 flüchtig. 2 vorübergehend. 3 unbeständig. 4 lebhaft.
volcano (vol'keinou) *n, pl* **-oes** Vulkan *m.*
volley ('voli) *n* 1 mil Salve *f.* Hagel *m.* 2 sport Flugball *m.*
volt (voult) *n* Volt *neu.*
volume ('volju:m) *n* 1 Umfang *m.* 2 Inhalt *m.* Volumen *neu.* 3 Lautstärke *f.* 4 Band *m.*
volunteer (volən'tiə) *n* Freiwillige(r) *m. vi* sich freiwillig melden. *vt* freiwillig anbieten. **voluntary** *adj* freiwillig.
voluptuous (və'lʌptʃuəs) *adj* 1 wollüstig. 2 sinnlich.
vomit ('vomit) *vi* sich erbrechen *or* übergeben. *vt* auswerfen, ausspeien. *n* Erbrochene *neu.*
voodoo ('vu:du:) *n* Wodu, Wudu *m.*
vote (vout) *n* 1 Stimme *f.* 2 Stimmrecht *neu.* 3 Wahl *f. vi* abstimmen, wählen.
vouch (vautʃ) *vi* **vouch for** bürgen für.
voucher ('vautʃə) *n* 1 Gutschein *m.* 2 Unterlage *f.*
vow (vau) *n* Gelübde *neu. vt* geloben.
vowel ('vauəl) *n* Vokal *m.*
voyage ('voiidʒ) *n* (See)Reise *f. vi* reisen.
vulgar ('vʌlgə) *adj* 1 gemein, vulgär. 2 unanständig. 3 gewöhnlich.
vulnerable ('vʌlnərəbl) *adj* 1 verwundbar. 2 anfällig.
vulture ('vʌltʃə) *n* Geier *m.*

W

wad (wod) *n* 1 Bündel *neu.* Stoß *m.* 2 Bausch *m.* **wadding** *n* Watte, Wattierung *f.*
waddle ('wodl) *vi* watscheln. *n* Watscheln *neu.*
wade (weid) *vi* waten. **wade through** sich durcharbeiten durch.

wafer ('weifə) *n* 1 Waffel *f.* 2 rel Oblate *f.*
waft (woft) *vt,vi* wehen. *n* Wehen *neu.*
wag (wæg) *vt* 1 schütteln. 2 (a tail) wedeln.
wage (weidʒ) *n* Lohn *m.*
waggle ('wægəl) *vt* wackeln.
wagon ('wægən) *n* 1 Lastwagen *m.* 2 Güterwaggon *neu.*
waif (weif) *n* verwahrlostes Kind *neu.*
wail (weil) *vi* wehklagen. *n* Klagen. *neu.*
waist (weist) *n* Taille *f.* **waistband** *n* Bund *m.* **waistcoat** *n* Weste *f.*
wait (weit) *vi* 1 warten. 2 bedienen. **wait for** erwarten, warten auf. **waiting list** *n* Warteliste *f.* **waiting room** *n* 1 Wartezimmer *neu.* 2 (of a station) Wartesaal *m.* **waiter** *n* Kellner *m.* **waitress** *n* Kellnerin *f.*
waive (weiv) *vt* verzichten auf.
wake* (weik) *also* **wake up** *vt* (auf-, er-) wecken. *vi* erwachen, aufwachen. **waken** *vi* erwachen, aufwachen. *vt* (auf-, er-)wecken.
Wales ('weilz) *n* Wales *neu.*
walk (wo:k) *vi* 1 laufen, (zu Fuß) gehen. 2 wandern. *n* 1 Spaziergang *m.* 2 Gang *m.* **go for a walk** spazierengehen. **walking stick** *n* Spazierstock *m.* **walkout** *n* Streik *m.* **walkover** ('wo:kouvə) *n* leichter Sieg *m.*
wall (wo:l) *n* 1 Mauer *f.* 2 Wand *f.* **wallflower** *n* 1 bot Goldlack *m.* 2 inf Mauerblümchen *neu.* **wallpaper** *n* Tapete *f.*
wallet ('wolit) *n* Brieftasche *f.*
wallop ('woləp) *inf vt* prügeln, (heftig) schlagen. *n* (heftiger) Schlag *m.*
wallow ('wolou) *vi* sich wälzen.
walnut ('wo:lnʌt) *n* Walnuß *f.*
walrus ('wo:lrəs) *n* Walroß *neu.*
waltz (wo:ls) *n* Walzer *m. vi* Walzer tanzen.
wand (wond) *n* 1 (Zauber)Stab *m.* 2 mus Taktstock *m.*
wander ('wondə) *vi* 1 wandern. 2 irregehen. 3 abbiegen.
wane (wein) *vi* 1 (of the moon) abnehmen. 2 nachlassen, schwächer werden.
wangle ('wæŋgəl) *vt sl* 1 hinkriegen, organisieren. 2 abluchsen.
want (wont) *vt* 1 wollen. 2 benötigen. *vi* mangeln. *n* 1 Bedürfnis *neu.* 2 Not *f.* 3 Begierde *f.*
wanton ('wontən) *adj* 1 mutwillig. 2 geil.
war (wo:) *n* Krieg *m.* **wage war** Krieg führen. **warfare** *n* Kriegsführung *f.* Krieg *m.*
warble ('wo:bəl) *vi,vt* trillern, singen.
ward (wo:d) *n* 1 Abteilung *f.* 2 med Station *f.* 3 law Mündel *neu.* *v* **ward off** abwehren.

warden n 1 Vorsteher. m. 2 Jugendherbergs-vater m. **warder** n (Gefängnis)Wärter m.

wardrobe ('wɔːdroub) n 1 Kleiderschrank m. 2 Garderobe f.

warehouse ('wɛəhaus) n Lagerhaus neu.

warm (wɔːm) adj warm. vt (er)wärmen. vi sich erwärmen. **warm-blooded** adj warmblütig. **warm-hearted** adj warmherzig.

warn (wɔːn) vt warnen. **warning** n Warnung f. adj warnend.

warp (wɔːp) (vi),vt (sich) werfen, (sich) ver-ziehen. n Verwerfung f. Krümmung f.

warrant ('wɔrənt) n 1 Vollmacht f. 2 Rechtfer-tigung f. 3 Haftbefehl, m. vt 1 rechtfertigen. 2 haften für. **warrant officer** n 1 Stabsfeld-webel m. 2 Stabsbootsmann m.

warren ('wɔrən) n Gehege neu.

warrior ('wɔriə) n Krieger m.

wart (wɔːt) n Warze f.

wary ('wɛəri) adj vorsichtig, behutsam.

was (wəz; stressed wɔz) v see **be**.

wash (wɔʃ) vt 1 waschen. 2 spülen. vi (sich) waschen. **wash up** spülen. ~n 1 Waschen neu. 2 Wäsche f. 3 naut Kielwasser neu. **washbasin** n Waschbecken neu. **washer** n tech Dichtungsring m. **washing** n 1 Wäsche f. 2 Waschen neu. **washing machine** n Waschmaschine f. **wash-out** n sl Fiasko neu. **washroom** n Toilette f.

wasp (wɔsp) n Wespe f.

waste (weist) vt 1 verschwenden. 2 verwüsten. vi also **waste away** abnehmen, schwinden. ~adj 1 wüst. 2 unnütz. 3 Ab—. n 1 Müll, Abfall m. 2 Öde f. 3 Verschwendung f. **wastepaper basket** Papierkorb m.

watch (wɔtʃ) n 1 bewachen. 2 beobachten. 3 zusehen. vi 1 aufpassen. 2 zuschauen. 3 wachen. **watch television** fernsehen. ~n 1 Armbanduhr f. 2 Taschenuhr f. 3 Wache f. **watchdog** n Wachhund m. **watchful** adj aufmerksam, wachsam.

water ('wɔːtə) n Wasser neu. **drinking water** Trinkwasser neu. vt (be)wässern, (be)-gießen. **water down** verwässern. **watering-can** n Gießkanne f.

water-closet n Klosett neu.

watercolour ('wɔːtəkʌlə) n 1 Aquarell neu. 2 Wasserfarbe f.

watercress ('wɔːtəkres) n Brunnenkresse f.

waterfall ('wɔːtəfɔːl) n Wasserfall m.

waterlily ('wɔːtəlili) n Seerose f.

waterlogged ('wɔːtəlɔgd) adj vollgesogen.

watermill ('wɔːtəmil) n Wassermühle f.

waterproof ('wɔːtəpruːf) adj wasserdicht. n Regenmantel m. vt imprägnieren.

water-ski n Wasserschi m. vi Wasserschi fahren.

watertight ('wɔːtətait) adj wasserdicht.

waterway ('wɔːtəwei) n Wasserweg m.

waterworks ('wɔːtəwəːks) n pl Wasserwerk neu.

watery ('wɔːtəri) adj wässerig.

watt (wɔt) n Watt neu.

wave (weiv) n Welle f. vi 1 winken. 2 wehen. vt 1 winken. 2 schwingen. 3 wellen. **waveband** n Frequenzband neu. **wavelength** n Wellen-länge f. **wavy** adj wellig, gewellt.

waver ('weivə) vi schwanken, zittern.

wax[1] (wæks) n Wachs neu. vt bohnern, wachsen. adj also **waxen** or **waxy** wächsern.

wax[2] (wæks) vi 1 wachsen, zunehmen. 2 werden.

way (wei) n 1 Weg m. 2 Mittel neu. 3 Richtung f. 4 Weise f. **by the way** übrigens, nebenbei. **under way** 1 unterwegs. 2 im Gange. **way in** Eingang m. **way out** Ausgang m.

waylay (wei'lei) vt auflauern.

wayward ('weiwəd) adj 1 widerspenstig. 2 launisch.

we (wiː) pron 1st pers pl wir.

weak (wiːk) adj schwach. **weak-minded** adj 1 schwachsinnig. 2 charakterschwach. **weak-willed** adj willensschwach. **weaken** vt 1 schwächen. 2 verdünnen. vi schwächer wer-den. **weakling** n Schwächling m. **weakness** n Schwäche f.

wealth (welθ) n Reichtum m. **wealthy** adj wohlhabend, reich.

weapon ('wepən) n Waffe f.

wear* (wɛə) vt tragen. vi haltbar sein. **wear out** 1 abtragen, abnutzen. 2 ermüden.

weary ('wiəri) adj erschöpft, müde. vt 1 er-müden. 2 langweilen.

weasel ('wiːzəl) n Wiesel neu.

weather ('weðə) n Wetter neu. vt überstehen.

weave* (wiːv) vt 1 weben, wirken. 2 (ver)-flechten. vi 1 weben. 2 sich verflechten.

web (web) n 1 Gewebe neu. 2 Netz neu.

wedding ('wediŋ) n Hochzeit f. **wedding anniversary** n Hochzeitstag m. **wedding ring** n Trauring m.

wedge (wedʒ) n Keil m. vt verkeilen.

Wednesday ('wenzdi) n Mittwoch m.

weed (wiːd) n Unkraut neu. vt jäten. **weed out** aussondern.

week (wiːk) n Woche f. **weekday** n Wochen-tag m. **weekend** n Wochenende neu.

weekly adj,adv wöchentlich. n Wochen-zeitung f.

weep (wi:p) vt,vi weinen.

weigh (wei) vt (ab)wiegen, abwägen. vi wiegen. **weighbridge** n Brückenwaage f. **weight** n 1 Gewicht neu. 2 Last f. **weight-lifting** n Gewichtheben neu.

weird ('wiəd) adj 1 unheimlich. 2 inf ulkig.

welcome ('welkəm) adj,interj willkommen. vt willkommen heißen, begrüßen. n Willkommen neu.

weld (weld) vt schweißen.

welfare ('welfɛə) n Wohlfahrt f.

well[1] (wel) n Brunnen m. vi quellen. **well up** hervorquellen.

well[2] (wel) adv 1 gut. 2 wohl. adj gesund. interj also, na. **as well** auch. **do well** 1 gut tun. 2 wohlauf sein. 3 Erfolg haben. **feel good** wohlauf sein. **just as well** ebenso gut.

well-bred adj wohlerzogen.

well-built adj gut gebaut.

well-known adj (wohl)bekannt.

well-off adj wohlhabend.

well-paid adj wohlbezahlt.

well-spoken adj redegewandt

well-worn adj abgenutzt.

Welsh (welʃ) adj walisisch. n (language) Walisisch neu. **Welshman** n Waliser m.

went (went) v see **go**.

wept (wept) v see **weep**.

were (wə:) v see **be**.

west (west) n 1 West(en) m. 2 cap Westen m. Abendland neu. adj westlich. adv westwärts, nach Westen. **westerly** adj westlich. n Wildwest-film m. **westward** adj nach Westen. **westwards** adv westwärts.

West Indies ('indiz) n pl Westindien neu. **West Indian** adj westindisch. n Westindier m.

Westphalia (west'feiliə) n Westfalen neu.

wet (wet) adj naß, feucht. n Nässe f. vt naßmachen, nässen.

whack (wæk) inf vt schlagen. n 1 heftiger Schlag m. 2 Anteil m.

whale (weil) n Wal(fisch) m.

wharf (wɔ:f) n Kai m. Landungsbrücke f.

what (wɔt) pron,interj was, wie. adj welch, was für ein. **what for?** wozu? **what sort of?** was für? **whatever** pron was auch immer, alles was. adj 1 welch auch immer. 2 überhaupt.

wheat (wi:t) n Weizen m.

wheedle ('wi:dl) vt beschwatzen, überreden. vi schmeicheln.

wheel (wi:l) n Rad neu. vt 1 rollen. 2 drehen. vi rollen. **wheelbarrow** n Schubkarren m. **wheelchair** n Rollstuhl m.

wheeze (wi:z) vi keuchen. n Keuchen neu.

whelk (welk) n Wellhornschnecke f.

when (wen) adv wann, zu welcher Zeit. conj als, wenn. **whenever** adv wann auch immer. conj wenn (immer), so oft als.

where (wɛə) adv,conj wo, wohin, woher. **whereabouts** n pl 1 Aufenthalt(sort) m. 2 Verbleib m. adv wo herum. **whereas** conj während, während. **whereby** adv,conj wodurch, wie. **whereupon** adv,conj worauf. **wherever** adv wo(hin) auch immer.

whether ('weðə) conj ob.

which (witʃ) pron 1 welch. 2 der. 3 was. adj welch. **whichever** pron welcher auch immer.

whiff (wif) n Hauch m. vt,vi paffen.

while (wail) conj also **whilst** während, solange. n Weile f.

whim (wim) n Laune, Grille f.

whimper ('wimpə) vi,vt wimmern.

whimsical ('wimzikəl) adj wunderlich.

whine (wain) vi wimmern, winseln.

whip (wip) n Peitsche f. vt 1 peitschen, schlagen. 2 reißen.

whippet ('wipit) n Whippet m.

whirl (wə:l) vi,vt wirbeln. n 1 Wirbeln neu. 2 Wirbel m. **whirlwind** n Wirbel(wind) m.

whirr (wə:) vi,(vt) schwirren (lassen). n Schwirren neu.

whisk[1] (wisk) vt 1 fegen. 2 rasch wegnehmen.

whisk[2] (wisk) cul vt schlagen. n Schneebesen m.

whiskers ('wiskəz) n pl 1 Backenbart m. 2 zool Schnurrhaare neu pl.

whisky ('wiski) n Whisky m.

whisper ('wispə) vi flüstern. n Geflüster neu.

whistle ('wisəl) vi,vt pfeifen. n 1 Pfeife f. 2 Pfiff m.

white (wait) adj weiß. n 1 Weiß neu. 2 Weiße(r) m. **whitewash** n (weiße) Tünche f. vt 1 tünchen, weißen. 2 reinwaschen. **whiting** n Weißfisch m.

Whitsun ('witsən) n Pfingsten neu.

whiz (wiz) vi sausen. n Sausen neu.

who (hu:) pron 1 wer. 2 der, welch. **whoever** pron 1 wer auch immer. 2 jeder der.

whole (houl) adj 1 ganz, vollständig. n Ganze neu. Gesamtheit f. **wholehearted** adj rückhaltslos. **wholemeal** adj Vollkorn—. **wholesale** n Großhandel m. adj 1 Großhandels—. 2 vollständig. adv 1 im großen. 2 en gros.

wholesome *adj* gesund, heilvoll. **wholly** *adv* ganz, völlig.

whom (hu:m) *pron* **1** wen, wem. **2** den, welchen.

whooping cough ('hu:piŋ) *n* Keuchhusten *m*.

whore (hɔ:) *n* Hure *f*. *vi* huren.

whose (hu:z) *pron* **1** wessen. **2** dessen.

why (wai) *adv, conj* warum, weshalb, wozu. *interj* nun, doch.

wick (wik) *n* Docht *m*.

wicked ('wikid) *adj* böse, boshaft.

wicket ('wikit) *n sport* Tor *neu*. Dreistab *m*.

wide (waid) *adj* breit, weit. **widely** *adv* **1** weit, breit. **2** in hohem Maße. **widen** *vt* erweitern. **widespread** *adj* weit verbreitet.

widow ('widou) *n* Witwe *f*. **widower** *n* Witwer *m*.

width (widθ) *n* Breite, Weite *f*.

wield (wi:ld) *vt* **1** handhaben. **2** ausüben.

wife (waif) *n, pl* **wives** (Ehe)Frau *f*.

wig (wig) *n* Perücke *f*.

wiggle ('wigəl) *vi,(vt)* wackeln mit.

wigwam ('wigwæm) *n* Wigwam *m*.

wild (waild) *adj* wild. **run wild 1** sich austoben. **2** wild wachsen. **wildlife** *n* Wild *neu*.

wilderness ('wildənəs) *n* Wildnis, Wüste *f*.

wilful ('wilfəl) *adj* **1** eigensinnig. **2** absichtlich.

will¹ (wil) *v mod aux* **1** werden. **2** wollen. **3** sollen.

will² (wil) *n* **1** Wille *f*. **2** Testament *neu*. **willpower** *n* Willenskraft *f*.

willing ('wiliŋ) *adj* (bereit)willig.

willow ('wilou) *n* Weide *f*.

wilt (wilt) *vi* (ver)welken.

win* (win) *vt* **1** gewinnen. **2** erlangen. *vi* gewinnen, siegen. *n* Sieg *m*.

wince (wins) *vi* zusammenzucken.

winch (wintʃ) *n* Winde, Kurbel *f*.

wind¹ (wind) *n* Wind *m*. **windbag** *n* Windbeutel *m*. **windfall** *n* **1** Glücksfall *m*. **2** Fallobst *neu*. **wind instrument** *n* Blasinstrument *neu*. **windmill** *n* Windmühle *f*. **windpipe** *n* Luftröhre *f*. **windscreen** *n* Windschutzscheibe *f*. **windscreen wipers** *n pl* Scheibenwischer *m*. **windswept** *adj* sturmgepeitscht. **windy** *adj* windig.

wind*² (waind) *vt* **1** winden, wickeln. **2** drehen. *vi* sich winden.

windlass ('windləs) *n* Winde, Haspel *f*.

window ('windou) *n* Fenster *neu*. **window box** *n* Blumenkasten *m*. **window-shop** *vi* einen Schaufensterbummel machen.

wine (wain) *n* Wein *m*.

wing (wiŋ) *n* **1** Flügel *m*. **2** *aviat* Tragfläche *f*. **3** Gruppe *f*. *vi* fliegen. **wing commander** *n* Oberstleutnant der britischen Luftwaffe *m*.

wink (wiŋk) *vi,vt* blinzeln *n* Blinzeln *neu*.

winkle ('wiŋkəl) *n* Strandschnecke *f*.

winter ('wintə) *n* Winter *m*. *vi,vt* überwintern.

wipe (waip) *vt* (ab)wischen, *n* Wischen *neu*.

wire ('waiə) *n* **1** Draht *m*. **2** Telegramm *neu*. *vt* **1** telegraphieren. **2** mit Draht versehen.

wise (waiz) *adj* weise, klug.

wish (wiʃ) *vt,vi* wünschen. *n* Wunsch *m*.

wisp (wisp) *n* **1** Wisch *m*. **2** Streifen *m*.

wisteria (wis'tiəriə) *n* Glyzine *f*.

wistful ('wistfəl) *adj* sehnsüchtig.

wit (wit) *n* **1** Witz, Esprit *m*. **2** Verstand *m*.

witch (witʃ) *n* Hexe *f*. **witchcraft** *n* Hexerei *f*.

with (wið) *prep* mit, bei.

withdraw (wið'drɔ:) *vi* sich zurückziehen, ausscheiden. *vt* zurückziehen.

wither ('wiðə) *vi* (ver)welken, vertrocknen.

withhold (wið'hould) *vt* **1** zurückhalten. **2** vorenthalten.

within (wið'in) *prep* in, innerhalb, binnen. *adv* drinnen.

without (wið'aut) *prep* ohne. *adv* (dr)außen.

withstand* (wið'stænd) *vt* widerstehen.

witness ('witnəs) *n* Zeuge *m*. *vt* **1** bezeugen. **2** Zeuge sein von.

witty ('witi) *adj* geistreich, witzig.

wizard ('wizəd) *n* Zauberer, Hexenmeister *m*.

wobble ('wɔbəl) *vi* wackeln.

woke (wouk) *v see* **wake**.

woken ('woukən) *v see* **wake**.

wolf (wulf) *n* Wolf *m*.

woman ('wumən) *n* **1** Frau *f*. **2** Weib *neu*.

womb (wu:m) *n* Gebärmutter *f*.

wonder ('wʌndə) *n* **1** Wunder *neu*. **2** Verwunderung *f*. *vi* **1** sich fragen. **2** sich wundern. **wonderful** *adj* wunderbar.

wonky ('wɔŋki) *adj inf* schwankend, wackelig.

wood (wud) *n* **1** Holz *neu*. **2** Wald *m*. **woodcock** *n* Waldschnepfe *f*. **wooden** *adj* **1** hölzern. **2** ausdruckslos, steif. **woodland** *n* Wald *m*. Waldland *neu*. **woodpecker** *n* Specht *m*. **woodpigeon** *n* Ringeltaube *f*. **woodwind** *n* Holzblasinstrument *neu*. **woodwork** *n* Holzwerk *neu*. **woodworm** *n* Holzwurm *m*.

wool (wul) *n* Wolle *f*. **woollen** *adj* wollen, Woll—. **woolly** *adj* **1** wollen. **2** wollig. **3** verschwommen.

word (wə:d) *n* Wort *neu*. *vt* ausdrücken.

wore (wɔ:) *v see* **wear**.

work (wə:k) n 1 Arbeit f. 2 Werk neu. 3 pl Werk neu. Betrieb m. vi 1 arbeiten. 2 funktionieren. vt 1 bearbeiten. 2 betätigen, bedienen. 3 min ausbeuten. **worker** n 1 Arbeiter m. 2 pl Arbeiterschaft f. **working class** n Arbeiterklasse f. **workman** n Arbeiter, Handwerker m. **workmanship** n 1 Kunstfertigkeit f. 2 Arbeit f.

world (wə:ld) n Welt f. adj Welt—. **not for the world** um keinen Preis. **man/woman of the world** n Weltmann, Weltdame m,f. **worldly** adj weltlich. **worldwide** adj weltweit.

worm (wə:m) n Wurm m.

wormwood ('wə:mwud) n Wermut m.

worn (wɔ:n) adj abgenutzt.

worry ('wʌri) vi sich sorgen or beunruhigen. vt 1 beunruhigen. 2 plagen. n 1 Sorge f. Kummer m. 2 Ärger m.

worse (wə:s) adj,adv schlechter, schlimmer. **worsen** (vi),vt (sich) verschlechtern, (sich) verschlimmern.

worship ('wə:ʃip) vt anbeten, verehren. vi beten. n Anbetung, Verehrung f.

worst (wə:st) adj schlechtest, schlimmst. adv am schlimmsten. vt überwältigen.

worth (wə:θ) n Wert m. adj wert. **it is worth doing** es lohnt sich, es zu tun. **worthwhile** adj der Mühe wert. **worthy** adj würdig, wert.

would (wəd; stressed wud) vi see **will** [1].

wound [1] (wu:nd) n Wunde, Verletzung f. vt verwunden, verletzen.

wound [2] (waund) v see **wind** [2].

wove (wouv) v see **weave.**

wrangle ('ræŋgəl) vi zanken. n Zank m.

wrap (ræp) vt (um-, ein-)wickeln. n 1 Hülle f. 2 Schal m. **wrapper** n Hülle f. Umschlag m. **wrapping** n Hülle, Verpackung f. **wrapping paper** n Packpapier neu.

wreath (ri:θ) n 1 Kranz m. 2 Gewinde f.

wreathe (ri:ð) vt 1 winden. 2 bekränzen. vi sich winden or kräuseln.

wreck (rek) n 1 Wrack m. 2 Schiffbruch m. vt 1 zertrümmern. 2 zerstören. **wreckage** n Trümmer.

wren (ren) n Zaunkönig m.

wrench (rentʃ) vt verrenken, verdrehen. n 1 (heftiger) Ruck m. 2 tech Schraubenschlüssel m.

wrestle ('resəl) vi ringen, kämpfen mit. vt ringen n Ringkampf m.

wretch (retʃ) n Elende(r) m. **wretched** adj elend, unglücklich.

wriggle ('rigəl) vi sich winden. n Winden neu.

wring * (riŋ) vt 1 (aus)wringen. 2 (an animal's neck) abdrehen. 3 (one's hands) ringen.

wrinkle ('riŋkəl) n Runzel, Falte. f. (vi),vt (sich) falten, (sich) runzeln.

wrist (rist) n Handgelenk neu. **wristwatch** n Armbanduhr f.

writ (rit) n 1 Erlaß m. 2 law Vorladung f.

write * (rait) vt,vi schreiben. **write down** aufschreiben, niederschreiben. **write off** abschreiben. **write up** (ausführlich) beschreiben. **writer** 1 Verfasser m. 2 Schriftsteller m. **writing paper** n Schreibpapier neu.

writhe (raið) vi sich krümmen, sich winden.

wrong (rɔŋ) adj 1 verkehrt, falsch. 2 unrecht. 3 irrtümlich. adv falsch, verkehrt. **be wrong** unrecht haben. **go wrong** schiefgehen. **something is wrong** etwas stimmt nicht. **what is wrong?** was ist los?

wrote (rout) v see **write.**

wrought iron (rɔ:t) n Schmiedeeisen neu.

wrung (rʌŋ) v see **wring.**

wry (rai) adj schief, verzogen.

X

xenophobia (zenə'foubiə) n Fremdenhaß m.

Xerox ('ziərɔks) Tdmk n Photokopiergerät neu. vt photokopieren.

X-ray n Röntgenstrahl m. vt röntgen.

xylophone ('zailəfoun) n Xylophon neu

Y

yacht (jɔt) n Jacht f. vi segeln. **yachtsman** n 1 Jachtsegler. 2 Jachtbesitzer m.

yank (jæŋk) vi,vi inf heftig ziehen.

yap (jæp) vi kläffen.

yard [1] (ja:d) n Yard neu. **yardstick** n Maßstab m.

yard [2] (ja:d) n Hof m.

yarn (ja:n) n 1 Garn neu. Faden m. 2 Erzählung f. **spin a yarn** ein Seemannsgarn spinnen.

yawn (jɔ:n) vi gähnen. n Gähnen neu.

year (jiə) n Jahr neu. **yearly** adj,adv jährlich.

yearn (jə:n) vi sich sehnen. **yearning** n Sehnsucht f. Sehnen neu.

yeast (ji:st) n Hefe f.

yell (jel) vi,vt (gellend) schreien. n gellende(r) Schrei m

yellow ('jelou) adj gelb. n Gelb neu.

yelp (jelp) vi kläffen.

yes (jes) *adv* ja, jawohl. *n* Ja *neu.*

yesterday ('jestədi) *adv* gestern. *n* der gestrige Tag *m.* **the day before yesterday** vorgestern. **yesterday's** *adj* gestrig.

yet (jet) *adv* **1** (schon) noch. **2** sogar. **3** schon. **4** bis jetzt. *conj* jedoch. **not yet** noch nicht.

yew (ju:) *n* Eibe *f.*

Yiddish ('jidiʃ) *n* Jiddisch *neu.*

yield (ji:ld) *vt* **1** hervorbringen, einbringen. **2** hergeben. **3** tragen. *vi* **1** nachgeben. **2** sich ergeben. **3** tragen. *n* Ertrag *m.*

yodel ('joudl) *vi* jodeln.

yoga ('jougə) *n* Joga *m.*

yoghurt ('jɔgət) *n* Joghurt *m.*

yoke (jouk) *n* Joch *neu. vt* anjochen.

yolk (jouk) *n* Dotter *m.* Eigelb *neu.*

yonder ('jɔndə) *adv* dort drüben. *adj* jener.

you (ju:) *pron 2nd pers* **1** *fam* du, dich, dir. **2** *fml* Sie, Ihnen. **3** *pl fam* ihr, euch. **4** *pl fml* Sie, Ihnen. **5** *imp* man, einen, einem.

young (jʌŋ) *adj* jung. **youngster** *n* Junge *m.*

your (jɔ:, juə) *poss adj 2nd pers* **1** *fam* dein. **2** *fml* Ihr. **3** *pl fam* euer. **4** *pl fml* Ihr. **yours** *poss pron 2nd pers* **1** *fam* deiner, der deine *or* deinige. **2** *fml* Ihrer, der Ihre *or* Ihrige. **3** *pl fam* eurer, der eure *or* eurige. **4** *pl fml* Ihrer, der Ihre *or* Ihrige. **yourself** *pron 2nd pers s* **1** *fam* dich, dich selbst, du selbst. **2** *fml* sich, sich selbst, Sie selbst. **yourselves** *pron 2nd pers pl* **1** *fam* euch, euch selbst, ihr selbst. **2** *fml* sich, sich selbst, Sie selbst.

youth (ju:θ) *n* **1** Jugend *f.* **2** Jüngling *m.* **youth hostel** *n* Jugendherberge *f.*

Yugoslavia (ju:gou'slɑ:viə) *n* Jugoslawien *neu.* **Yugoslav** *n* Jugoslawe *m. adj* jugoslawisch.

Z

Zambia ('zæmbiə) *n* Sambia *neu.*

zeal (zi:l) *n* Eifer *m.*

zebra ('zebrə) *n* Zebra *neu.* **zebra crossing** *n* Zebrastreifen *m pl.*

zero ('ziərou) *n* **1** Null *f.* **2** Gefrierpunkt *m.*

zest (zest) *n* Begeisterung *f.* Reiz *m.*

zigzag ('zigzæg) *n* Zickzack *m. adj, adv* im Zickzack.

zinc (ziŋk) *n* Zink *neu.*

Zionism ('zaiənizəm) *n* Zionismus *m.*

zip (zip) *n* Zischen *neu. vi* sausen. *vt* mit einem Reißverschluß schließen. **zip (fastener)** *n* Reißverschluß *m.*

zodiac ('zoudiæk) *n* Tierkreis *m.*

zone (zoun) *n* **1** Zone *f.* **2** Erdgürtel *m.*

zoo (zu:) *n* Zoo *m.* **zoology** *n* Zoologie *f.* **zoological** *adj* zoologisch. **zoologist** *n* Zoologe *m.*

zoom (zu:m) *vi* **1** summen. **2** *aviat* hochschnellen.

Zurich ('zjuərik) *n* Zürich *neu.*